INTRODUCING THE DIGITAL TOOL!

You are just a click away from the innovative and ground-breaking supplement to *Intermediate Accounting*.

What is the Digital Tool?

The digital tool is an electronic gateway to a comprehensive set of materials that supplement the already comprehensive coverage of accounting topics in *Intermediate Accounting* by Kieso, Weygandt, Warfield, Irvine, Silvester, Young, Wiecek. Included is the "Professional Toolkit", with materials on written communication, working in teams, and ethics. The "Analyst's Toolkit" contains a comprehensive primer on financial statement analysis, and a collection of over 45 real company statements that students can access for financial statement and other research. Also included is the "Student Toolkit", which contains expanded discussions and illustrations for topics such as international accounting, and additional real company disclosures for topics introduced in the text.

Why did we develop the Digital Tool?

Recent developments in the fast-changing business world indicate that accounting professionals must not only have knowledge of accounting facts but must be able to use accounting facts and procedures in various business contexts. That is, accountants must act as well as think and it is important for students to understand the how as well as the why. The content and focus of the Digital Tool respond to this trend by providing an expanded set of materials that can be used to extend and apply the concepts and methods introduced in *Intermediate Accounting*.

How do you use the Digital Tool?

Look for the Digital Tool Icon in *Intermediate Accounting*. Anytime you see it, you are being alerted to expanded materials that are available on the Digital Tool CD. On this CD, you will find ample resources including additional disclosures which supplement financial reporting practices, tips on writing a memo concerning accounting research you have conducted, or real company financial statements for financial statement analysis.

You can access the Digital Tool elements by clicking on the toolkit links or by clicking on a particular chapter; this latter method will provide you with a listing of materials in the Digital Tool related to that chapter.

Intermediate Accounting

SIXTH CANADIAN EDITION

INTERMEDIATE ACCOUNTING

Donald E. Kieso, PhD, CPA
KPMG Peat Marwick Emeritus Professor of Accounting
Northern Illinois University
DeKalb, Illinois

Jerry J. Weygandt, PhD, CPA
Arthur Andersen Alumni Professor of Accounting
University of Wisconsin
Madison, Wisconsin

Terry D. Warfield, PhD
PricewaterhouseCoopers Research Scholar
University of Wisconsin
Madison, Wisconsin

V. Bruce Irvine, PhD, CMA, FCMA
University of Saskatchewan
Saskatoon, Saskatchewan

W. Harold Silvester, PhD, CPA, CA
University of Saskatchewan (Emeritus)
Saskatoon, Saskatchewan

Nicola M. Young, MBA, FCA
Saint Mary's University
Halifax, Nova Scotia

Irene M. Wiecek, CA
University of Toronto
Toronto, Ontario

John Wiley & Sons Canada, Ltd.

National Library of Canada Cataloguing in Publication Data

Kieso, Donald E.
    Intermediate accounting

6th Canadian ed./prepared by V. Bruce Irvine... [et al.]
Includes bibliographical references and index.
ISBN 0-471-64635-0 (v. 1).—ISBN 0-471-64636-9 (v. 2)

1. Accounting. I. Weygandt, Jerry J. II. Irvine, V. Bruce
III. Title

HF5635.I 573 2001   657'.044   C2001-902193-3

Production Credits
Publisher: John Horne
Publishing Services Director: Karen Bryan
Editorial Manager: Karen Staudinger
Sr. Marketing Manager: Janine Daoust
New Media Editor: Elsa Passera
Publishing Services/Permissions Co-ordinator: Michelle Love
Design & Typesetting: Quadratone Graphics Ltd.
Cover Design: Interrobang Graphic Design
Cover Photo: Grant V. Faint/Image Bank
Printing & Binding: Tri-Graphic Printing Limited

Printed and bound in Canada
10 9 8 7 6 5 4 3 2

John Wiley & Sons Canada, Ltd.
22 Worcester Road
Etobicoke, Ontario M9W 1L1
Visit our website at: www.wiley.com/canada

Dedicated to our husbands

   John and George

and to our children

   Hilary

   Tim

   Megan

   Nicholas, and

   Katherine

for their support, encouragement, and tolerance
throughout the writing of this book.

About the Authors

Canadian Edition

Nicola M. Young, MBA, FCA, teaches accounting in the Frank H. Sobey Faculty of Commerce at Saint Mary's University in Halifax, Nova Scotia where her responsibilities have varied from the introductory offering to final year advanced financial courses to the survey course in the Executive MBA program. She is the recipient of the Commerce Professor of the Year and the university-wide Alumni teaching medal, and contributes to the academic and administrative life of the university through membership on the Board of Governors, the Quality of Teaching and other Committees. Professor Young has been associated with the Atlantic School of Chartered Accountancy for over twenty-five years in a variety of roles. These include program and course development, teaching, and most recently, chairing ASCA's Education Reform Impact Study. In addition to contributions to the accounting profession at the provincial level, Professor Young has served on national boards of the CICA dealing with licensure and education. For the last ten years, she has worked with the CICA's Public Sector Accounting Board as an Associate, as a member and chair of the Board, and as a member and chair of the Task Force on the Senior Government Financial Reporting Model.

Irene M. Wiecek, CA is Associate Director of the Master of Management and Professional Accounting Program (MMPA) at the Joseph L. Rotman School of Management, University of Toronto where she is also a Faculty member, lecturing primarily in Financial Reporting. She has taught in the Executive MBA, MBA, MMPA, B Com and Management Major Programs covering material from Introductory Accounting to Advanced Accounting. Currently focusing on the area of integrated learning, she is involved in redesigning the MMPA program and has developed numerous cases, which examine financial reporting, and its link to other functional area such as finance and strategy. A prolific case writer, Irene has won case competitions for writing and presenting cases as well as leading and coaching student teams. She has had several cases published in accounting journals. At the professional level, Irene is involved in an educational capacity with both the Canadian and Ontario Institute of Chartered Accountants, as well as the Society of Management Accountants. Prior to working at the University of Toronto, Irene worked for KPMG as a public accountant and as a consultant in private industry. Irene obtained her Chartered Accountancy designation in 1981.

U.S. Edition

Donald E. Kieso, Ph.D., C.P.A., received his bachelor's degree from Aurora University and his doctorate in accounting from the University of Illinois. He has served as chairman of the Department of Accountancy and is currently the KPMG Peat Marwick Emeritus Professor of Accountancy at Northern Illinois University. He has done postdoctorate work as a Visiting Scholar at the University of California at Berkeley and is a recipient of NIU's Teaching Excellence Award and four Golden Apple Teaching Awards. He has served as a member of the Board of Directors of the Illinois CPA Society, the AACSB's Accounting Accreditation Committees, the State of

Illinois Comptroller's Commission, as Secretary-Treasurer of the Federation of Schools of Accountancy, and as Secretary-Treasurer of the American Accounting Association. From 1989 to 1993 he served as a charter member of the national Accounting Education Change Commission. In 1988, he received the Outstanding Accounting Educator Award from the Illinois CPA Society, in 1992 he received the FSA's Joseph A. Silvoso Award of Merit and the NIU Foundation's Humanitarian Award for Service to Higher Education, and in 1995 he received a Distinguished Service Award from the Illinois CPA Society.

Jerry J. Weygandt, Ph.D., C.P.A., is Arthur Andersen Alumni Professor of Accounting at the University of Wisconsin-Madison. He holds a Ph.D. in accounting from the University of Illinois. Articles by Professor Weygandt have appeared in the Accounting Review, Journal of Accounting Research, Accounting Horizons, Journal of Accountancy, and other academic and professional journals. These articles have examined such financial reporting issues as accounting for price-level adjustments, pensions, convertible securities, stock option contracts, and interim reports. He has served on numerous committees of the American Accounting Association and as a member of the editorial board of the Accounting Review; he also has served as President and Secretary-Treasurer of the American Accounting Association. In addition, he has been actively involved with the American Institute of Certified Public Accountants and has been a member of the Accounting Standards Executive Committee (AcSEC) of that organization. He has served on the FASB task force that examined the reporting issues related to accounting for income taxes and is presently a trustee of the Financial Accounting Foundation. Professor Weygandt has received the Chancellor's Award for Excellence in Teaching and the Beta Gamma Sigma Dean's Teaching Award. He is on the board of directors of M & I Bank of Southern Wisconsin and the Dean Foundation. Recently he received the Wisconsin Institute of CPA's Outstanding Educator's Award and the Lifetime Achievement Award.

Terry D. Warfield, Ph.D., is PricewaterhouseCoopers Research Scholar at the University of Wisconsin-Madison. He received a B.S. and M.B.A. from Indiana University and a Ph.D. in accounting from the University of Iowa. Professor Warfield's area of expertise is financial reporting, and prior to his academic career, he worked for five years in the banking industry. He served as the Academic Accounting Fellow in the Office of the Chief Accountant at the U.S. Securities and Exchange Commission in Washington, D.C., from 1995-1996. While on the staff, he worked on projects related to financial instruments and financial institutions, and he helped coordinate a symposium on intangible asset financial reporting. Professor Warfield's primary research interests concern financial accounting standards and disclosure policies. He has published scholarly articles in The Accounting Review, Journal of Accounting and Economics, Research in Accounting Regulation, and Accounting Horizons, and he has served on the editorial boards of The Accounting Review and Accounting Horizons. He has served on the Financial Accounting Standards Committee of the American Accounting Association (past Chair 1995-1996) and on the Association Council, the Nominations Committee, and the AAA-FASB Research Conference Committee. Professor Warfield has taught accounting courses at the introductory, intermediate, and graduate levels. He has received teaching awards at both the University of Iowa and the University of Wisconsin, and he was named to the Teaching Academy at the University of Wisconsin in 1995.

Preface

This edition of *Intermediate Accounting* represents an important milestone in the evolution of this textbook. As with the prior editions, in planning this edition we conducted extensive market research to help us focus on how the text should evolve.

Two themes emerged from this research. These themes confirmed development decisions made in recent editions of *Intermediate Accounting* and suggested ways that we could further enhance the usefulness of the text to students and instructors. The first theme is the continuing rapid pace of information technology. Support for this information technology trend is reflected in the introduction in this edition of the Digital Tool.

The Digital Tool provides a comprehensive set of materials that supplement the already-comprehensive coverage of accounting topics in the textbook. Included are "professional tools" related to written communication, working in groups, and ethics. A financial analyst's toolkit contains a comprehensive primer on financial statement analysis and a collection of over 45 real-company financial statements that students can access for financial statement and other research. Also included are expanded discussions and illustrations for topics such as international accounting and the accounting for securitizations, and additional real-company disclosures for topics introduced in the text. We believe the Digital Tool will be an invaluable resource to students that will help them get the most out of their Intermediate Accounting investment.

The second theme that emerged from our research is the continuing evolution of the accounting profession and accounting education away from knowledge of accounting facts to the development of skills in how to use accounting facts and procedures in various business contexts. Accountants must act as well as think, and we believe that it is important for students to understand the how as well as the why of accounting. The content and focus of many of the elements of the Digital Tool (writing, working in teams, analyst's toolkit) respond to this trend by providing an expanded set of materials that can be used to extend and apply the concepts and methods introduced within the text.

We continue to strive for a balanced discussion of conceptual and procedural presentation so that these elements are mutually reinforcing. In addition, discussions focus on explaining the rationale behind business transactions before addressing the accounting and reporting for those transactions. As in prior editions, we have thoroughly revised and updated the text to include all the latest developments in the accounting profession and practice. Benefiting from the comments and recommendations of adopters of the fifth edition, we have made significant revisions. Explanations have been expanded where necessary; complicated discussions and illustrations have been simplified; realism has been integrated to heighten interest and relevancy; and new topics and coverage have been added to maintain currency. We have deleted selected fifth edition coverage from the text. To provide the instructor with no loss in material coverage and flexibility in use, discussions of less commonly used methods, more complex, or specialized topics have been moved to the Digital Tool.

NEW FEATURES

Based on extensive reviews, focus groups, and interactions with other intermediate accounting instructors and students, we have developed a number of new pedagogical features and content changes designed both to help students learn more effectively and to answer the changing needs of the course.

Digital Tool

As mentioned earlier, a major new resource developed for this edition is the Digital Tool. This CD-ROM includes a comprehensive set of materials that supplement the already-comprehensive coverage of accounting topics in the textbook. When the Digital Tool icon (shown in the margin) appears in the textbook, the student is directed to expanded materials as described below. Major elements of the Digital Tool are:

Analyst's Toolkit

The Analyst's Toolkit contains the following items.

Database of Real Companies. Over 45 annual reports of well-known companies, including several international companies, are provided on the Digital Tool. These annual reports can be used in a variety of ways. For example, they can be used as illustrations of different presentations of financial information or for comparing note disclosures across companies. In addition, these reports can be used to analyse a company's financial condition and compare its prospects with other companies in the same industry. Assignment material provides some examples of different types of analysis that can be performed.

Company Web Links. Each of the companies in the database of real companies is identified by a Web address to facilitate the gathering of additional information, if desired.

Preformatted Excel Worksheets. Worksheets formatted in Excel are available for some assignments on the Digital Tool. For example, students may be asked to calculate key ratios for a certain company (with a digital calculator provided), and to compare these ratios against those of another company. The other company's ratios are provided on a worksheet to expedite the analysis phase of the assignment.

Additional Enrichment Material. A chapter on Financial Statement Analysis is provided, with related assignment material. This chapter can also be used with the database of annual reports of real companies.

Spreadsheet Tools. Present value templates are provided which can be used to solve time value of money problems.

Additional Internet Links. A number of useful links related to financial analysis are provided to expand expertise in this area.

Professional Toolkit

Consistent with expanding beyond technical accounting knowledge, the Digital Tool emphasizes certain skills necessary to become a successful accountant and financial manager.

Writing Materials. A primer on professional communications is provided that will give students a framework for writing professional materials. This primer discusses issues such as the top ten writing problems, strategies for prewriting, how to do revisions, and tips on clarity. This primer has been class tested and is effective in helping students enhance their writing skills.

Group Work Materials. Recent evaluation of accounting education has identified the need to develop more skills in group problem solving. The Digital Tool provides a second primer dealing with the role that groups play in organizations. Information on what makes a successful group, and how students can participate effectively in the group, is included.

Ethics. Expanded materials on the role of ethics in the profession are part of the Digital Tool, including references to speeches and articles on ethics in accounting and codes of ethics for major professional bodies. It also includes additional case studies on ethics.

Career Professional Spotlights. Every student should have a good understanding of the profession that he or she is entering. Various vignettes in the Digital Tool indicate the types of work that accountants do. These vignettes are interviews with accounting and finance professionals who are at various stages of their careers.

Other aspects of the spotlight on careers are also included. As part of the Digital Tool, the following information is provided to help students make successful career choices:

- A résumé builder, to help students prepare a professional-looking résumé.
- Professional Web links—important links to Web sites that can provide useful career information.

Student Toolkit

Expanded Discussions and Illustrations. This section provides additional topics that are not covered in depth in the textbook. The Digital Tool gives the flexibility to discuss these topics of interest in more detail.

Additional topics for this volume of the text are as follows:

- Presentation of worksheet using the periodic method.
- Specialized journals and methods of processing accounting data.
- Expanded example of transfers of receivables without recourse, with accounting entries.
- Discussion of lesser-used amortization methods, such as the retirement and replacement methods.
- Present-value based measurements.
- Technology Tools for time value problems.

International Accounting. An expanded discussion of international accounting institutions, the evolution of international accounting standards, and a framework for understanding differences in accounting practice is provided. This discussion is designed to complement the international reporting problems in the textbook.

Learning Style Survey. Research on left brain/right brain differences and also on learning and personality differences suggests that each person has preferred ways to receive and communicate information. After completing this survey, students will be able to pinpoint the study aids in the text that will help them learn the material based on their particular learning styles.

In summary, the Digital Tool is a comprehensive complement to the sixth edition of Intermediate Accounting, providing new materials as well as a new way to communicate that material.

New Chapter Openings

We have revised the chapter openings to increase student interest and to draw readers into the chapter more quickly. These openings feature:

Chapter preview and outline. A chapter preview explains the importance of the chapter topic. A graphic outline presents a visual "roadmap" of the important topics covered in the chapter.

Brief Exercises

New exercises that focus students on one study objective or topic have been added to the end-of-chapter material.

New "Using Your Judgement" Features

In the fifth edition, we introduced a new Using Your Judgement section in the end-of-chapter assignment materials. This section contains assignments that help develop students' analytical, critical thinking, and interpersonal communication skills. These materials met with wide acceptance and praise in the market, and in this edition we have added some new features, which will give instructors even more choice of materials with which to develop student abilities. These include the following:

Financial Statement Analysis Case. Each case introduces a real-world company and discusses how financial transactions affect their financial statements. Often, an assessment of the company's liquidity, solvency, or financial profitability is performed.

Comparative Analysis Case. The statements of two well-known companies are compared in relation to the topic(s) discussed in the chapter.

Research Case. Each research case provides an opportunity for the student to conduct independent research into an accounting topic related to the chapter content. In many cases, the student must access a data base (sometimes involving use of the Internet) to find the necessary information.

International Reporting Case. We have extended the international coverage in the text by introducing a number of international reporting cases that are based on real companies and designed to illustrate international accounting differences. These cases illustrate the importance of adjusting international financial statements to make them comparable across countries. This emphasis reinforces the user orientation of the "Using Your Judgement" element.

Integration of Financial Statement Analysis

By understanding the accounting processes that generate statements and the tools required to analyse these statements, students learn to look beyond the numbers. Financial ratios are covered early in the text in an appendix to Chapter 5 to enhance teaching flexibility and enable instructors who want earlier coverage to have access to it when they need it. Ratio analysis is also woven throughout the text to expose students to the significance of economic events. Many financial analysis tools are also provided on the Digital Tool.

International Insights & IAS Notes

International Insight paragraphs that describe or compare the accounting practices in other countries are provided in the margin. We have continued this feature to help students understand that other countries sometimes use different recognition and measurement principles to report financial information.

IAS Notes also appear in the margins and describe how International Accounting Standards are similar to, or differ from, Canadian standards.

ENHANCED FEATURES

We have continued and enhanced many of the features that were included in the fifth edition of Intermediate Accounting, including:

Using Your Judgement

The "Using Your Judgement" elements (Financial Reporting Problems, Financial Statement Analysis, Comparative Analysis, and Research Cases) at the end of each chapter have been revised and updated. In addition, explicit writing and group assignments have been integrated into the exercises, problems, and cases. Exercises, problems, and cases that are especially suited for group or writing assignments are identified with special icons, as shown here in the margin.

Real-World Emphasis

We believe that one of the goals of the intermediate accounting course is to orient students to the application of accounting principles and techniques in practice. Accordingly, we have continued our practice of using numerous examples from real corporations, now highlighted in blue, throughout the text. Illustrations and exhibits marked by the icon shown here are excerpts from actual financial statements of existing firms. In addition, the 2000 annual report of Canadian Tire, is included in Appendix 5B, and many real-company financial reports appear in the database on the Digital Tool.

Streamlined Presentation

We have continued our efforts to keep the topical coverage of Intermediate Accounting in line with the way instructors are currently teaching the course. Accordingly, we have moved some optional topics into appendices and have omitted altogether some topics that formerly were covered in appendices, moving them to the Digital Tool. Details are noted in the list of specific content changes below.

Currency and Accuracy

Accounting continually changes as its environment changes; an up-to-date book is therefore a necessity. As in past editions, we have strived to make this edition the most up-to-date and accurate text available.

CONTENT CHANGES

The following list outlines the revisions and improvements made in chapters of this volume.

Chapter 1

- New material on accounting and capital allocation/markets.
- Updated material on challenges facing the accounting profession.
- Expanded discussions on international accounting and ethics in the chapter and on the Digital Tool.

Chapter 2

- Expanded discussion of present value based measurements (on the Digital Tool) as well as the use of the historical cost principle.

Chapter 3

- Chapter streamlined and restructured by moving the discussion of special journals to the Digital Tool and material on reversing journal entries into an Appendix.
- Accounting equation tracking the incremental impact of transactions on financial statement elements introduced in the margins.

Chapter 4

- New material on quality of earnings added.
- Added disclosures regarding discontinued operations on the Digital Tool.

Chapter 5

- New material on the preparation of the Cash Flow Statement.

- New material on assessing and interpreting cash flow patterns.
- Increased emphasis on financial flexibility.
- New Appendix on ratio analysis.
- Analysis Toolkit included on the Digital Tool.

Chapter 6

- Chapter reorganized to focus on the earnings process and how it is grounded in the nature of the business/industry.
- Examples of revenue recognition policies on the Digital Tool.

Chapter 7

- Introduced calculator and spreadsheet function solutions.
- Cash controls, including petty cash and bank reconciliations now in Chapter Appendix.
- Additional real-company disclosures of cash and receivables.
- Expanded explanation of entries for receivable write-offs and reinstatement.
- Enhanced explanation of accounting for notes receivable.
- Introduction of the "financial asset" terminology.
- Updated discussion of sale of receivables due to CICA Guideline released in 2001.
- Sales of receivables moved out of the Appendix and into the Chapter.
- New section on analysis of receivables.

Chapter 8

- Additional real-company disclosures of inventories.
- Section on variable and absorption costing moved from Appendix into chapter section on costs to be included in inventory.

Chapter 9

- Illustration of effect on financial statements (balance sheet and income statement, for two years) between using NRV and NRV less a normal profit margin.
- Update of CCRA requirements for application of LCM.
- Additional real-company disclosures on the presentation of inventories.
- New section on analysis of inventories.

Chapter 10

- Reference to financial calculator and spreadsheet tool to calculate present values.
- Expanded material on the fair value controversy.

Chapter 11

- Enhanced explanation of entries for deferred payment contracts.
- Reorganized and rewritten explanations of nonmonetary exchanges of assets, exchanges with a significant monetary component, and trade-ins. Introduction of more relevant problem material on this topic.
- Investment tax credit discussion moved to Chapter 11 from Chapter 12 as a topic affecting the cost of an asset.
- Section added on donations (disposals) of capital assets.
- Section on disclosure requirements for tangible capital assets moved to Chapter 12.

Chapter 12

- Terminology changed to amortization and accumulated amortization from depreciation and accumulated depreciation.

- Fuller description of the sum-of-the-years-digits method in a footnote.
- Coverage of the inventory method and retirement and replacement methods transferred to the Digital Tool.
- Increased emphasis on asset impairment.
- Capital cost allowance method covered only in the appendix to the chapter; includes straight-forward investment tax credits and government contributions situations.
- Section added on the analysis of tangible capital assets.

Chapter 13

- Updated to take into account new CICA standards for business combinations and intangible assets released in late July, 2001.
- Description and explanation of new standards re the nonamortization of goodwill and intangibles with indefinite lives and the impairment tests for them.
- Revision to treatment of negative goodwill.
- Explanation of intellectual capital.
- Explicit treatment of pre-operating costs, initial operating losses and advertising costs.
- Revised discussion of the valuation of goodwill.

END-OF-CHAPTER ASSIGNMENT MATERIAL

At the end of each chapter we have provided a comprehensive set of review and homework material consisting of brief exercises, exercises, problems, and short cases. For this edition, many of the exercises and problems have been revised or updated. In addition, the Using Your Judgement sections, which include financial reporting problems, ethics cases, financial statement analysis cases, comparative analysis cases, and research cases have all been updated. A number of international reporting cases that are based on real companies are introduced throughout the textbook. All of the assignment materials have been class tested and/or double checked for accuracy and clarity.

The brief exercises are designed for review, self-testing, and classroom discussion purposes as well as homework assignments. Typically, a brief exercise covers one topic, an exercise one or two topics. Exercises require less time and effort to solve than problems and cases. The problems are designed to develop a professional level of achievement and are more challenging and time-consuming to solve than the exercises. The cases generally require essay as opposed to quantitative solutions; they are intended to confront the student with situations calling for conceptual analysis and the exercise of judgement in identifying problems and evaluating alternatives. The Using Your Judgement assignments are designed to develop students' critical thinking, analytical, interpersonal, and communication skills.

Probably no more than one-fourth of the total exercise, problem, and case material must be used to cover the subject matter adequately; consequently, problem assignments may be varied from year to year.

ACKNOWLEDGMENTS

We thank the users of our fifth edition, including the many students who contributed to this revision through their comments and instructive criticism. Special thanks are extended to the reviewers of and contributors to our sixth edition manuscript and supplements.

Manuscript Reviewers for Volume One were:

Cécile Ashman
Algonquin College

Carolyn J. Davis
Brock University

Mary A. Heisz
University of Western Ontario

Ron Hill
Southern Alberta Institute of Technology

Wayne Irvine
Mount Royal College

G. Selwyn James
Centennial College

Joe Pidutti
Durham College

Wendy Roscoe
Concordia University

Jo-Anne Ryan
Nipissing University

David J. Sale
Kwantlen University College

Stella M. Penner
University of Alberta

Appreciation is also extended to colleagues at the Rotman School of Management, University of Toronto and Saint Mary's University who provided input, suggestions and support, especially Joel Amernic and Dick Chesley—who have provided inspiration through many high-spirited debates on financial reporting theory and practice—and Peter Thomas, who has shared many teaching insights over the years!

Many thanks to the staff at John Wiley and Sons Canada, Ltd. who are superb: President Diane Wood and Publisher John Horne who have been so supportive throughout; Karen Bryan, Publishing Services Director, for her incredible efforts; Elsa Passera, New Media Editor together with Alain Parizeau, Designer who took on the Digital Tool; Michelle Love, Publishing Services/Permissions Coordinator; Carolyn Wells and Darren Lalonde, Sales Managers; Janine Daoust, Sr. Marketing Manager; and of course all the sales representatives who service the front lines. The editorial contributions of Laurel Hyatt and Alan Johnstone were also appreciated. Most of all, however, we are grateful to cool, collected and super-organized Karen Staudinger, Editorial Manager, who conducted the whole show!

Word-processing and other office related services were ably provided to the authors by Megan Young, Sandra Fougere-Mahoney, and Cathy Golden. Special thanks also to Cheryne Lowe, Snezana Beronja, David Schwinghamer, Elizabeth D'Anjou and Fang Mu for their contributions to the Digital Tool and research services.

We appreciate the co-operation of the Accounting Standards Board of the Canadian Institute of Chartered Accountants, especially that of its Director, Ron Salole, as well as that of the CICA itself in allowing us to quote from their materials. We thank Canadian Tire Corporation Limited for permitting us to use its 2000 Annual Report for our specimen financial statements.

Finally, we would like to thank Bruce Irvine and Harold Silvester who, through five editions of this text, provided such a strong foundation. Their enthusiasm for intermediate accounting and their sharing of this with so many students sets a standard for the rest of us to follow.

If this book helps teachers instill in their students an appreciation of the challenges, value, and limitations of accounting, if it encourages students to evaluate critically and understand financial accounting theory and practice, and if it prepares students for advanced study, professional examinations, and the successful and ethical pursuit of their careers in accounting or business, then we will have attained our objective.

Suggestions and comments from users of this book will be appreciated. We have striven to produce an error-free text, but if anything has slipped through the variety of checks undertaken, please let us know so that corrections can be made to subsequent printings.

Irene M. Wiecek
Toronto, Ontario

Nicola M. Young
Halifax, Nova Scotia

July 2001

Brief Contents

Contents

CHAPTER 1

The Canadian Financial Reporting Environment

LEARNING OBJECTIVES

···

After studying this chapter, you should be able to:

1. Describe the essential characteristics of accounting.

2. Identify the major financial statements and other means of financial reporting.

3. Explain how accounting assists in the efficient use of scarce resources.

4. Explain the meaning of stakeholder and identify key stakeholders in financial reporting.

5. Identify the objective of financial reporting.

6. Explain the notion of management bias with respect to financial reporting.

7. Understand the importance of user needs in the financial reporting process.

8. Explain the need for accounting standards.

9. Identify the major entities that influence the standard-setting process and explain how they influence financial reporting.

10. Explain the meaning of generally accepted accounting principles.

11. Explain the significance of professional judgement in applying GAAP.

12. Understand issues related to ethics and financial accounting.

13. Identify some of the challenges facing accounting.

Preview of Chapter 1

North American financial reporting systems are among the best in the world. However, as the business world experiences unprecedented change caused by globalization, deregulation, and computerization, these systems will continue to be challenged. In this changing business world, relevant and reliable information must be provided so that our capital markets work efficiently. The purpose of this chapter is to explain the environment of financial reporting and the many factors affecting it. The content and organization of the chapter are as follows:

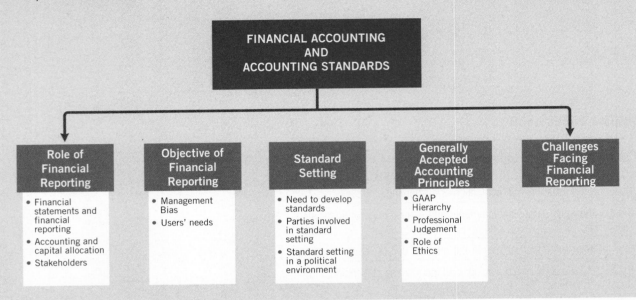

ROLE OF FINANCIAL REPORTING

Like other human activities and disciplines, accounting is largely a product of its environment. The environment of accounting consists of social, economic, political, legal conditions, restraints, and influences that vary from time to time. As a result, accounting objectives and practices are not the same today as they were in the past. **Accounting theory and practice have evolved and will continue to evolve, to meet changing demands and influences.**

Accounting may best be defined by describing the three essential characteristics of accounting: (1) **identification, measurement, and communication of financial information about** (2) **economic entities to** (3) **interested persons**. These characteristics have described accounting for hundreds of years. Yet, in the last 30 years, economic entities have increased so greatly in size and complexity, and the interested persons have increased so greatly in number and diversity, that the responsibility placed on the accounting profession is greater today than ever before.

Financial Statements and Financial Reporting

Financial accounting (financial reporting) is the process that culminates in the preparation of financial reports for the enterprise as a whole for use by both **internal and external** parties. Users of these financial reports include investors, creditors, and others. In contrast, **managerial accounting** is the process of identifying, measuring, analysing, and communicating **financial information** to internal decision-makers. This information may take varied forms, e.g., cost benefit analyses, forecasts, etc. needed by management to plan, evaluate, and control an organization's operations.

Financial statements are the principal means through which financial information is communicated to those outside an enterprise. These statements provide the firm's **history**, quantified in money terms. The financial statements most frequently provided are (1) the **balance sheet**, (2) the **income statement**, (3) the **statement of cash flows**, and (4) the **statement of owners' or shareholders' equity**. In addition, note disclosures are an integral part of each financial statement.

Some financial information is better provided, or can be provided only, through financial reporting other than financial statements. Examples include the president's letter or supplementary schedules in the corporate annual report, prospectuses, reports filed with government agencies, news releases, management's forecasts, and descriptions of an enterprise's social or environmental impact. Such information may be required by authoritative pronouncement, regulatory rule[1] or custom, or because management wishes to disclose it voluntarily. The primary focus of this textbook is the **basic** financial statements.

OBJECTIVE 2

Identify the major financial statements and other means of financial reporting.

Accounting and Capital Allocation

Because resources are limited, people try to conserve them, use them effectively, and identify and encourage those who can make efficient use of them. Through an efficient use of resources, our standard of living increases.

Markets, free enterprise, and competition—not a committee of social engineers—determine whether a business will be successful and thrive. This fact places a substantial burden on the accounting profession to measure performance accurately and fairly on a timely basis, so that managers and companies are able to attract investment capital. For example, accounting enables investors and creditors to compare the income and assets employed by such companies as **IBM**, **Air Canada**, **Microsoft**, and **Barrick Gold Corporation**. As a result, they can assess the relative returns and risks associated with investment opportunities and thereby channel resources (i.e. invest in these companies or lend them money) more effectively. This process of capital allocation works as follows:

OBJECTIVE 3

Explain how accounting assists in the efficient use of scarce resources.

ILLUSTRATION 1-1
Capital Allocation Process

In Canada, the primary exchange mechanisms for allocating resources are **debt and equity markets**[2] as well as **financial institutions** such as banks.

---

[1] All public companies must disclose certain information under provincial securities law. This information is captured by the provincial securities commissions under the Canadian umbrella organization, the Canadian Securities Administrators (CSA), and is available electronically at www.sedar.com.

[2] The largest most senior equity market in Canada is the Toronto Stock Exchange (TSE). The CDNX stock market was created in 2001 to handle startup companies. Smaller, regional markets are undergoing consolidation and these exchanges and markets will likely become part of the TSE or CDNX. The Montreal Exchange is and will remain the prime market for derivatives and futures trading.

An **effective process of capital allocation is critical to a healthy economy**, which promotes productivity, encourages innovation, and provides an efficient and liquid market for buying and selling securities and obtaining and granting credit.[3] Unreliable and irrelevant information leads to **poor capital allocation**, which adversely affects the securities markets. Reported accounting numbers affect the transfer of resources among companies and individuals. Consider the fact that stock prices generally rise when positive news (including financial information) is expected and/or released. Consider also the fact that there are **rating agencies** that rate the financial stability of companies to give investors and creditors additional information.[4] A good rating can mean greater access to capital and at lower costs. In determining these ratings, the bond-rating companies look at financial information.

Stakeholders

OBJECTIVE 4

Explain the meaning of stakeholder and identify key stakeholders in financial reporting.

Stakeholders are parties who have something at stake in the financial reporting environment, e.g., salary, job, investment, reputation etc. Key stakeholders in the financial reporting environment include traditional users of financial information as well as others. In the stakeholder context, **users** may be more broadly defined to include not only parties who are directly relying on the financial information for resource allocation (such as investors and creditors) but also others who facilitate the efficient allocation of resources (financial analysts, regulators).

The broader definition of users and therefore stakeholders includes anyone who **prepares, relies on, reviews, audits, or monitors financial information**. It includes investors, creditors, analysts, managers, employees, customers, suppliers, industry groups, unions, government departments and ministers, the public in general (e.g., consumer groups), regulatory agencies, other companies, standard setters, as well as auditors, lawyers, and others. Illustration 1-2 illustrates the relationships among these stakeholders.

ILLUSTRATION 1-2
Selected Key Stakeholders in the Financial Reporting Environment

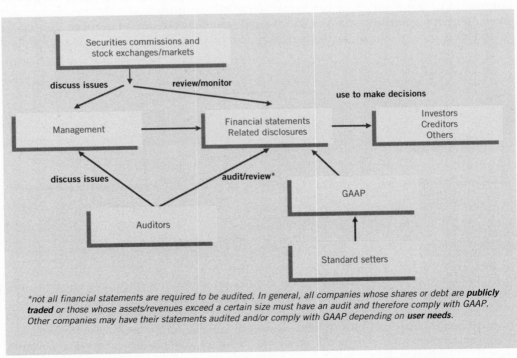

*not all financial statements are required to be audited. In general, all companies whose shares or debt are **publicly traded** or those whose assets/revenues exceed a certain size must have an audit and therefore comply with GAAP. Other companies may have their statements audited and/or comply with GAAP depending on **user needs**.*

---

[3] AICPA Special Committee on Financial Reporting. "Improving Business Reporting—A Customer Focus." *Journal of Accountancy*, Supplement, October 1994.

[4] For example, Dominion Bond Rating Service (DBRS) an independent full-service rating agency, rates issuers of bonds and preferred shares in the Canadian marketplace. Currently, DBRS rates over 700 corporate and government issuers of commercial paper, long-term debt, and preferred shares.

Company management **prepares** the financial statements. The statements are then **audited/reviewed** by auditors who may discuss with management how economic events and transactions have been communicated in the financial statements. Users **use the financial statements to make decisions**. Standard setters **set generally accepted accounting principles**. Securities commissions and stock exchanges **monitor** the financial statements to ensure full and plain disclosure of material information and to ensure that the companies may continue to list their shares on stock exchanges.

Financial statements affect stakeholders, sometimes in a positive manner and sometimes in a negative manner. Consider the case of **The T. Eaton Company (Eaton's)**, historically a major force in the retail industry in Canada and owned by the Eaton family. In 1997 Eaton's underwent a financial restructuring, enabling it to close some of its unprofitable stores. The company hired George Kosich as its new President and CEO to help with the restructuring and to take the company public. Mr. Kosich had significant experience in the retail area. Prior to joining Eaton's, Mr. Kosich spent more than 38 years in the retail sector, primarily in the department store field. He held numerous positions with **Hudson's Bay Company** including President and Chief Operating Officer and then Chief Executive Officer until his "retirement" in 1997.

Net losses for Eaton's for the year ended January 31, 1997 were $170 million and for the year ended January 31, 1998 were $156 million. The company was taken public in June 1998, issuing common shares at $15 per share and raising $175 million in capital.

Several **stockbrokers** were involved in setting the Eaton's share price at $15. The share price was determined in conjunction with Eaton's **management** by carefully analysing the accounting and other information available at the time plus assumptions as to future revenue growth, cost increases, etc. These forecasts/assumptions were reviewed by the company's **auditors** to assess whether they were supported and consistent with company plans. Despite all the care and effort pricing the offer, the share price plummeted a few months later. **Sears** eventually bought out its former rival in the retail business. Many Eaton's **shareholders** lost the majority of their investment. Unfortunately, accounting information does not always allow stakeholders to predict the future.

OBJECTIVE OF FINANCIAL REPORTING

To help establish a foundation for financial accounting and reporting, the accounting profession has articulated an overall objective of financial reporting by business enterprises. This is laid out in the *CICA Handbook* as follows in illustration 1-3.

> "The objective of financial statements is to communicate information that is useful to investors, members, contributors, creditors, and other users in making their resource allocation decisions and/or assessing management stewardship. Consequently, financial statements provide information about:
>
> (a)   an entity's economic resources, obligations, and equity/net assets;
>
> (b)   changes in an entity's economic resources, obligations, and equity/net assets; and
>
> (c)   the economic performance of the entity."
>
> Source – *CICA Handbook*, Section 1000, par. .15

Note the emphasis on **resource (or capital) allocation** decisions and **assessment of management stewardship**.[5] In order to make resource allocation decisions, users look for information about the **ability of an enterprise to earn income and generate future cash flows**, which will be used to meet obligations and generate a return on investment. In order to

OBJECTIVE 5

Identify the objective of financial reporting.

ILLUSTRATION 1-3
Objective of Financial Reporting

---

[5] Management's responsibility to manage assets with care and trust is described as its fiduciary responsibility.

assess management stewardship, users traditionally look at **historical data** to determine (in hindsight) **whether the decisions that management made regarding obtaining and using the company's resources are acceptable and optimize shareholder wealth/value**. Users may also attempt to **predict** the impact of current decisions made by management on the company's future financial health as investors in the Eaton's scenario above did.

Management Bias

Company management is responsible for preparing the financial statements and normally attests to this fact at the beginning of the financial statements. At the **Bank of Montreal**, F. Anthony Comper, Chairman and CEO, as well as Karen Maidment, Executive Vice-President and CFO have both signed the statement for the Bank of Montreal financial statements, which is shown in Illustration 1-4.

INTERNATIONAL INSIGHT

The objectives of financial reporting differ across nations. Traditionally, the primary objective of accounting in many continental European nations and in Japan was conformity with the law. In contrast, Canada, the U.S., the UK, the Netherlands, and many other nations hold the view that the primary objective is to provide information for investors. Insights into international standards and practices will be presented throughout the text.

OBJECTIVE 6

Explain the notion of management bias with respect to financial reporting.

ILLUSTRATION 1-4

Report of Bank of Montreal Management Acknowledging Responsibility for the Financial Statements

Statement of Management's Responsibility for Financial Information

The Bank's management is responsible for presentation and preparation of the annual consolidated financial statements, Management Analysis of Operations ("MAO") and all other information in the Annual Report.

The consolidated financial statements have been prepared in accordance with Canadian generally accepted accounting principles and the requirements of the Securities and Exchange Commission in the United States. The financial statements also comply with the provisions of the Bank Act and related regulations, including the accounting requirements of the Superintendent of Financial Institutions Canada.

The MAO has been prepared in accordance with the requirements of securities regulators including National Policy 47 of the Canadian Securities Administrators as well as Item 303 of Regulation S-K of the Securities Exchange Act, and their related published requirements.

The consolidated financial statements and information in the MAO necessarily include amounts based on informed judgements and estimates of the expected effects of current events and transactions with appropriate consideration to materiality. In addition, in preparing the financial information we must interpret the requirements described above, make determinations as to the relevancy of information to be included, and make estimates and assumptions that affect reported information. The MAO also includes information regarding the estimated impact of current transactions and events, sources of liquidity and capital resources, operating trends, risks and uncertainties. Actual results in the future may differ materially from our present assessment of this information because future events and circumstances may not occur as expected.

The financial information presented elsewhere in the Annual Report is consistent with that in the consolidated financial statements.

In meeting our responsibility for the reliability of financial information, we maintain and rely on a comprehensive system of internal control and internal audit including organizational and procedural controls and internal accounting controls. Our system of internal control includes written communication of our policies and procedures governing corporate conduct and risk management; comprehensive business planning; effective segregation of duties; delegation of authority and personal accountability; careful selection and training of personnel; and sound and conservative accounting policies which we regularly update. This structure ensures appropriate internal control over transactions, assets and records. We also regularly audit internal controls. These controls and audits are designed to provide us with reasonable assurance that the financial records are reliable for preparing financial statements and other financial information, assets are safeguarded against unauthorized use or disposition, liabilities are recognized, and we are in compliance with all regulatory requirements. In order to provide their opinion on our consolidated financial statements, the Shareholders' Auditors review our system of internal control and conduct their work to the extent that they consider appropriate.

The Board of Directors is responsible for reviewing and approving the financial information contained in the Annual Report, including the MAO, and overseeing management's responsibilities for the presentation and preparation of financial information, maintenance of appropriate internal controls, management and control of major risk areas and assessment of significant and related party transactions. The Board delegates these responsibilities to its Audit and Conduct Review Committees, comprised of non-Bank directors, and its Risk Review Committee.

The Shareholders' Auditors and the Bank's Chief Auditor have full and free access to the Board of Directors and its committees to discuss audit, financial reporting and related matters.

(signed)
F. Anthony Comper
Chairman and
Chief Executive Officer

(signed)
Karen E. Maidment
Executive Vice-President
and Chief Financial Officer

Companies have come increasingly under attack for preparing **biased information**, i.e., information that presents the company in its best light. This is sometimes referred to as **aggressive financial reporting** (as compared with **conservative financial reporting**) and might take the form of overstated assets and/or net income, understated liabilities and/or expenses, or carefully selected note disclosures that emphasize only positive events.[6]

There are many reasons why financial statements might be the subject of management bias, including the fact that they give information to users as to **management stewardship**, as previously mentioned. Management compensation is often based on net

---

[6] David Brown, Chairman of the Ontario Securities Commission (OSC), spoke at length on this topic in a speech entitled "Public Accounting at a Crossroads" in 1999. Arthur Levitt, Chair of the Securities and Exchange Commission (SEC) discussed his concerns over this issue in "Numbers Game," a major address to the New York University in 1998. Both the OSC and the SEC review financial statements and financial reporting practices in the course of ensuring that investors have "full and plain disclosure" of all material facts needed to make investment decisions. In their speeches, Mr. Brown and Mr. Levitt both cite specific cases where they feel that the financial reporting practices were problematic.

income or share value. There is also a strong desire to **meet financial analysts' expectations** and thus have continued access to capital markets. Financial analysts monitor earnings announcements carefully and compare them with their prior expectations. They post what they refer to as "**earnings surprises**" daily on their websites.[7] Earnings surprises occur when a company reports net income figures that are different from what the market expects (prior expectations). The focus is on net income or earnings. If net income is lower than expected, this is a negative earnings surprise and the market will generally react in a negative manner, resulting in declining stock prices.

Another reason management might have a financial reporting bias is compliance with contracts entered into by the company. Many lending agreements/contracts require that certain benchmarks be met, often relating to financial stability or liquidity. These requirements, often stipulate that the company maintain certain minimum financial ratios. The lenders then monitor compliance, requesting that the company submit periodic financial statements.

Users' needs

The objective of financial reporting is to provide **useful information to users**. As noted in illustration 1-2, investors and creditors are among the key users of financial information. Providing information that is useful to users is a challenging task given their differing **knowledge levels** and needs. **Institutional investors**[8] hold an increasing percentage of equity share holdings[9] and generally devote significant resources to managing their investment portfolios. Can preparers of financial information assume that the average individual investor has the same needs and knowledge level in terms of business and financial reporting as the institutional investor?

Warren Buffet is the Chairman of **Berkshire Hathaway Inc.**, a holding company whose core business activity is the property and casualty insurance business. The shares of Berkshire Hathaway Inc. have steadily increased in value under Mr. Buffet's guidance and have traded at upwards of $50,000 (U.S.) (per share) for the past several years. Berkshire Hathaway Inc. may be considered to be a very successful **institutional investor**. Its insurance business generates what is known as a "float" (cash), part of which is invested by the company in shares of other companies. The float arises since the premiums taken in by the insurance company are received before any losses are paid out to the insured. Berkshire Hathaway Inc. follows an investment strategy loosely known as "value investing." Value investing involves selecting good, solid investments and holding on to them for a longer time—disregarding swings in the stock price or market.

As a user, Berkshire Hathaway Inc. would be looking at the financial statements of potential investments for long-term earnings potential as opposed to other investors who may be looking to assess short-term liquidity or short-term cash flows.

Meeting all user needs is made more challenging when coupled with the potential for **management bias**. If the financial statements are aggressively prepared, this might be misleading to potential investors who may wish to see the company in the worst light before they invest (as opposed to after). In general, generally accepted accounting principles assume that users have a **reasonable knowledge of business and accounting**.

---

[7] For instance, for the week beginning February 5, 2001, earnings surprises were noted for selected companies. Selected positive earnings surprises noted (i.e., actual results for the 1st quarter ended December 31, 2000 exceeded analyst expectations) included Borg Warner and Jones Apparel Group Inc. Selected negative earnings surprises noted for the same week included PepsiCo and Anheuser Busch.

[8] Institutional investors are corporate investors such as insurance companies, pension plans, mutual funds, and others. They are considered a separate class of investors due to their size, financial expertise, and the large size of the investments that they hold in other companies. In general, institutional investors have greater power than the average investor.

[9] For instance, institutional investors hold more than 50% of the value of all equity shares in the largest capital market in the world, according to the U.S. Federal Reserve Board.

STANDARD SETTING

Need to Develop Standards

The main controversy in financial reporting is, "Whose rules should we play by, and what should they be?" The answer is not immediately clear because the **users of financial statements have both coinciding and conflicting needs for information of various types**. A single set of general-purpose financial statements is prepared with the expectation that the majority of these needs will be met. These statements are expected to **present fairly the enterprise's financial operations**.

As a result, accounting professions in various countries have attempted to develop a set of standards that are **generally accepted and universally practised**. Without these standards, each enterprise would have to develop its own standards, and readers of financial statements would have to familiarize themselves with every company's peculiar accounting and reporting practices. It would be almost impossible to prepare statements that could be compared.

This common set of standards and procedures is called generally accepted accounting principles (GAAP). The term "generally accepted" means either that an **authoritative accounting rule-making body** has established a reporting principle in a given area or that over time a **given practice has been accepted as appropriate because of its universal application**.[10] Although principles and practices have provoked both debate and criticism, most members of the financial community recognize them as the standards that over time have proven to be most useful. A more extensive discussion of what constitutes GAAP is presented later in this chapter.

INTERNATIONAL INSIGHT

Nations also differ in the degree to which they have developed national standards and consistent accounting practices. One indicator of the level of a nation's accounting is the nature of the accounting profession within the country. Professional accounting bodies were established in the Netherlands, the UK, Canada, and the U.S. in the nineteenth century. In contrast, public accountancy bodies were established in Hong Kong, Singapore, and Korea only in the last half century.

Parties Involved in Standard Setting

A number of organizations are instrumental in developing financial reporting standards in Canada. The major organizations are:

1. Canadian Institute of Chartered Accountants (CICA)
2. Provincial Securities Commissions such as the Ontario Securities Commission (OSC)
3. The Financial Accounting Standards Board (FASB) and the Securities and Exchange Commission (SEC)
4. International Accounting Standards Committee (IASC)

Prior to 1900, single ownership was the predominant form of business organization in our economy. Financial reports emphasized **solvency and liquidity** and were limited to internal use and scrutiny by banks and other lending institutions. From 1900 to 1929, the growth of large corporations, with their absentee ownership, led to increasing investment and speculation in corporate stock. The stock market crashed in 1929 and contributed to the Great Depression. These events emphasized the need for **standardized and increased corporate disclosures** that would allow shareholders to make informed decisions.

1. Canadian Institute of Chartered Accountants (CICA)

INTERNATIONAL INSIGHT

The Canadian and U.S. legal systems are based on English common law, whereby the government generally allows professionals to make the rules. These rules (standards) are, therefore, developed in the private sector. Conversely, some countries follow codified law, which leads to government-run accounting systems.

The first official recommendations regarding standards of financial statement disclosure were not published until 1946. Today, the Accounting Standards Board (AcSB) of the Canadian Institute of Chartered Accountants (CICA) has **primary responsibility** for setting GAAP in Canada[11] and produces a variety of authoritative material, includ-

---

[10] The terms "principles" and "standards" are used interchangeably in practice and throughout this textbook.

[11] The Canadian Business Corporations Act and Regulations (CBCA) – Part XIV "Financial Disclosure," as well as provincial corporations acts, require that most companies incorporated under these acts prepare financial statements in accordance with GAAP as prepared by the CICA.

ing the foremost source of GAAP—the **CICA Handbook**. The *CICA Handbook* was originally published in 1968 and now consists of five volumes of accounting and assurance guidance.

The key objective of the CICA AcSB is to ensure that the **framework for measurement and reporting facilitates the** *global* **flow of capital and serves the public interest by enhancing relevance, quality, and credibility of information used for evaluating and improving organizational performance**.[12] Note the emphasis on *global* **capital allocation** and focus on **organizational performance**. Both aspects will be touched upon later in the chapter when emerging trends in the profession are discussed.

Due Process.   Two basic AcSB premises underlying the process of establishing financial accounting standards are: (1) the AcSB should be **responsive to the needs and viewpoints of the entire economic community**, not just the public accounting profession, and (2) it should **operate in full view** of the public through a **"due process"** system that gives interested persons ample opportunity to make their views known. The **Accounting Standards Oversight Council (ASOC)** provides oversight to AcSB activities, setting the agenda, reporting to the public, and raising funds for standard setting, among other things. Membership on the AcSB and the ASOC draws from a wide range of groups interested or involved in the financial reporting process.[13]

The steps shown in Illustration 1-5 show the evolution of a typical addition or amendment to the *CICA Handbook.*

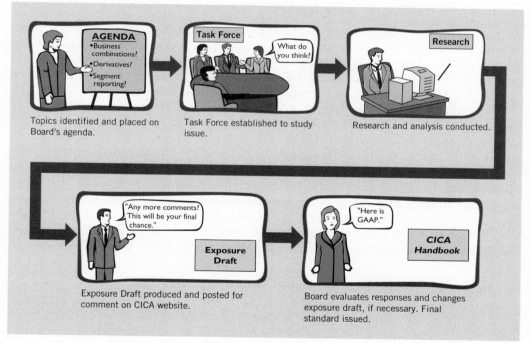

ILLUSTRATION 1-5
Evolution of a New or Revised Standard

---

[12] "Leading change in the CA profession in Canada." Toronto: CICA, 2000. In 1998, partially in response to the CICA's Inter-Institute Vision Task Force, the CICA Task Force on Standard Setting issued its final report. The report reaffirmed, among other things, the fact that standard setting should remain in the private sector, i.e., with the CICA.

[13] Membership includes representatives from professional accounting (Chartered Accountants, CGA Canada, CMA Canada), industry (e.g., Financial Executives Institute Canada), and users of financial statements (including investors and financial analysts such as Canadian Council of Financial Analysts, academics such as the Canadian Academic Accounting Association), regulators, the legal profession, and others. The goal is to achieve full representation across the spectrum of stakeholders.

Due process, by definition, is a **lengthy process**. To react more quickly to current financial reporting issues, the AcSB established the **Emerging Issues Committee (EIC)**. The EIC is a standing committee which meets several times each year. It studies issues presented to it by interested parties such as companies that need a ruling on an accounting issue that may not be dealt with in the *Handbook*. After careful consideration, the EIC produces **EIC Abstracts**, which are then incorporated into the *Handbook*. The AcSB sets standards, while the EIC interprets these standards and provides guidance where the AcSB cannot (due to the lengthy time frame required by due process).

2. Provincial Securities Commissions

Provincial securities commissions oversee and monitor the capital marketplace. They ensure that the participants in the capital markets (e.g. companies, auditors, brokers/dealers, and investors) adhere to securities law/legislation to ensure that the marketplace is fair. For instance, the British Columbia Securities Commission acknowledges responsibility for the following:

- to ensure that investors have access to the information they need to make informed investment decisions;
- to provide rules of fair play for the markets;
- to establish qualifications and standards of conduct for people registered to advise investors and to trade on their behalf; and
- to protect the integrity of the capital market and the confidence of investors.

As part of ensuring that investors have access to the information that they need to make informed decisions, securities law/legislation requires that companies that issue shares to the public and whose shares trade on a Canadian stock exchange or stock market produce GAAP financial statements.[14] The commissions generally rely on the CICA to develop GAAP and professional accountants to use sound judgement in its application.

Ontario is home to the largest stock exchange in Canada, the **Toronto Stock Exchange (TSE)**, and therefore most large public companies are registered with the **Ontario Securities Commission (OSC)**. In the past few years, the OSC has begun to review and monitor the financial statements of companies whose shares are publicly traded with the view to assessing whether the statements present fairly the financial position and results of operations.[15] Further, they have begun to issue disclosure requirements of their own, signalling to companies how the OSC interprets GAAP.[16]

For companies whose shares trade on a stock exchange or market such as the TSE, the stock exchange as well as the securities commissions have the ability to **fine** the company and/or **delist** the company's shares—denying the company access to capital markets.

3. Financial Accounting Standards Board and the SEC

In the U.S., the **Financial Accounting Standards Board (FASB)** is a major standard-setting body. The **American Institute of Certified Public Accountants (AICPA)** is the main professional accounting body for Certified Public Accountants, however unlike Canada, the AICPA does not have primary responsibility for standard setting. The **Securities and Exchange Commission (SEC)** has affirmed its support for the FASB by indicating that financial statements conforming to FASB standards will be presumed to have substantial authoritative support. In short, the SEC requires registrants to adhere

INTERNATIONAL INSIGHT

The International Organization of Securities Commissions (IOSCO) is a group of more than 100 securities regulatory agencies or securities exchanges from all over the world. IOSCO has existed since 1987. Collectively, its members represent a substantial proportion of the world's capital markets.

---

[14] For instance, Ontario Securities Act Sections 75 to 83.

[15] The OSC has a Continuous Disclosure Team that regularly reviews public companies' financial statements. As noted in their last reports, they are becoming increasingly concerned about what they refer to as "selective disclosure" (a form of aggressive financial reporting). In 2000, they also began a specific review of revenue recognition policies.

[16] For instance, in 2000, Rules 51-501 and 52-501 were issued dealing with additional disclosures for interim financial statements. Staff Accounting Notice 52-709 on Income Statement Presentation of Goodwill Charges was also issued.

to GAAP. In addition, it has indicated in its reports to the U.S. government that it continues to believe that the initiative for establishing and improving accounting standards should remain in the private sector, subject to commission oversight. Like the Canadian Securities Commissions, it also signals its position on various financial reporting issues through what it calls "Financial Reporting Releases."

FASB has a **substantial impact** on Canadian financial reporting and Canadian companies. Firstly, since Canadian GAAP is based on principles and is fairly open to interpretation, accounting professionals often look to the more **rule-oriented**, **specific guidance** noted in the FASB pronouncements. Secondly, many Canadian companies also list on U.S. stock markets and exchanges such as NASDAQ (National Association of Securities Dealers Automated Quotation) and the NYSE (New York Stock Exchange). In order to list on a U.S. exchange, these companies must follow U.S. GAAP. Finally, as we move toward international harmonization, the U.S. accounting standards will have a significant impact due to the significant capital pool associated with these markets.[17]

4. International Accounting Standards Committee (IASC)

In Germany, the amortization period for an intangible asset is five years. In Canada, amortization periods are often far in excess of five years. In Mexico, assets are adjusted for price-level changes. In Canada and the United States, assets are not adjusted for the impact of inflation. These are just some of the ways in which reporting practices in Canada differ from those in other countries.

INTERNATIONAL INSIGHT

Many developing and newly industrialized nations, e.g., Nigeria, Singapore, and Malaysia, have adopted IASC standards as their national standards.

Most countries recognize the need for more uniform standards. As a result, the **International Accounting Standards Committee (IASC)** was formed in 1973 to attempt to **narrow the areas of divergence**. The IASC objective in terms of standard setting is "to work generally for the improvement and harmonization of regulations, accounting standards and procedures relating to the presentation of financial statements." **Eliminating differences** is not easy because the financial reporting objectives in each country differ, the institutional structures are often **not comparable**, and strong national tendencies are pervasive. Nevertheless, much headway has been made since IASC's inception, and international standards may gradually supplant national standards. In 2001, a new International Accounting Standards Board (IASB) was created. Its goal according to the new chair, is to increase the transparency of financial reporting by achieving a single, global method of accounting.

See Digital Tool for an expanded discussion of International Accounting.

In 2000, the SEC issued a Concept Release Statement for discussion purposes dealing with whether the SEC would allow foreign companies to use IASC standards in securities offerings in the U.S. The SEC proposed that if the IASC standards were of sufficient high quality and were supported by infrastructure that would ensure that the standards were rigorously interpreted and applied and issues dealt with as they arose, the SEC would consider the issue.

INTERNATIONAL INSIGHT

The IASC recently completed work on a set of core international standards for use in cross-border offerings and listings. The SEC supports the IASC's work and has said that it would consider allowing the use of international standards by foreign issuers when they offer securities in the U.S.

If the SEC did accept IASC standards for foreign companies in securities offerings in the U.S., the possibility exists that U.S.- based companies would petition to use IASC standards instead of U.S.-based standards since comparability and consistency would be important. Canada would likely follow suit.

The AcSB recently re-affirmed its commitment to international harmonization of accounting standards.[18] It is a long-standing member of the IASC and now also has representation on the IASB. The IASC pronouncements are included in the *CICA Handbook* Section 1501, along with a chart that cross references the standards to Canadian standards. Throughout this textbook, international considerations are presented to help you understand the international reporting environment.

---

[17] In the CICA Task Force on Standard Setting, the committee commented that international harmonization was not likely to happen without the SEC's support. It further commented that failure to obtain that support would make FASB the de facto world standard setter.

[18] One of the CICA's long-term goals resulting from its Task Force on Standard Setting was to help create one set of internationally accepted standards in the private sector. The task force committed that Canada would play a significant role in establishing these standards while retaining the authority to set unique Canadian accounting standards where circumstances warrant.

Standard Setting in a Political Environment

Possibly the most powerful force influencing the development of accounting standards is the stakeholders. **Standard-setting stakeholders** are the parties most interested in or affected by accounting standards, rules, and procedures. Like lobbyists in the provincial and national government arena, stakeholders play a significant role. Accounting standards are as much a product of **political action** as they are of careful logic or empirical findings. As part of its mandate, the AcSB includes as its members all stakeholders, allowing them a formal voice in the process. Furthermore, through due process, all interested parties may comment on the proposed changes or new standards.

Stakeholders may want particular **economic events** accounted for or reported in a particular way, and they fight hard to get what they want. They know that the most effective way to influence the standards that dictate accounting practice is to participate in formulating them or to try to **influence or persuade** the formulator.

Should there be **politics** in setting financial accounting and reporting standards? The AcSB does not exist in a vacuum. Standard setting is part of the real world, and it cannot escape politics and political pressures. That is not to say that politics in standard setting is bad. Considering the **economic consequences**[19] of many accounting standards, it is not surprising that special interest groups become vocal and critical (some supporting, some opposing) when standards are being formulated. The AcSB must be **attentive to the economic consequences** of its actions. What the AcSB should not do is issue pronouncements that are **primarily** politically motivated. While paying attention to its constituencies, the AcSB should base its standards on **sound research** and a **conceptual framework** grounded in economic reality.

An illustration of an economic consequence issue is the turmoil caused by the AcSB's standard that certain preferred shares issued in estate freezes[20] be accounted for as debt.[21] For many small companies, the accounting standard relating to these preferred shares would result in the company being in breach of covenants relating to their bank loans.[22] As a result of pressure placed on the AcSB from these stakeholders, the AcSB agreed to **defer the effective dates** for this standard for non-public enterprises-giving the AcSB more time to study the issue.

GENERALLY ACCEPTED ACCOUNTING PRINCIPLES

<table>
<tr><td>

OBJECTIVE 10

Explain the meaning of generally accepted accounting principles.

</td><td>

GAAP as developed by the AcSB has **substantial authoritative support** through the Canadian and provincial business corporations acts and also through securities legislation. All companies whose shares or debt trade on a public market must follow GAAP. Most other incorporated companies also follow GAAP as it provides the most useful information.

</td></tr>
</table>

---

[19] "Economic consequences" in this context means the impact of accounting reports on the wealth positions of issuers and users of financial information and the decision-making behaviour resulting from that impact. The resulting behaviour of these individuals and groups could have detrimental financial effects on the providers (enterprises) of the financial information. For a more detailed discussion of this phenomenon, see Stephen A. Zeff. "The Rise of 'Economic Consequences.'" *Journal of Accountancy*, December 1978, pp. 56-63. Special appreciation is extended to Professor Zeff for his insights on this chapter.

[20] Estate freezes form a common tax planning strategy that facilitates succession planning (passing of family-owned businesses from parents to children) while allowing for tax deferral.

[21] *CICA Handbook*, Section 3860, par. .18.

[22] Often, lenders will require that borrowers meet certain financial tests or **benchmarks** on an ongoing basis in order for the loan to remain in good standing. These benchmarks are incorporated into loan agreements in paragraphs called "**loan covenants.**" Loan covenants often require that a certain debt-to-equity ratio be maintained.

GAAP Hierarchy

The meaning of GAAP is defined in the *CICA Handbook* Section 1000, paragraph .60, as encompassing not only **specific rules, practices, and procedures** relating to particular circumstances but also **broad principles and conventions of general application, including underlying concepts**.

Firstly, accounting **recommendations** in the *CICA Handbook* (those noted in italics) are the **primary source** of GAAP. If the *Handbook* is lacking in guidance, then there are two **secondary sources**: i) **financial statements of other Canadian companies** and ii) **professional judgement**. This is referred to as the GAAP hierarchy. Business is constantly changing and new business transactions/contracts being entered into and therefore the secondary sources are an important source of GAAP.

Primary Source	Accounting *recommendations* covered in the *CICA Handbook* (recommendations are those principles noted in italics in the *CICA Handbook*)
Secondary Sources	Accounting principles that are *generally accepted by a significant number of entities in Canada*
	Accounting principles that are consistent with the recommendations in the *CICA Handbook* and are developed through the exercise of *professional judgement*. Consider other relevant matters dealt with in the *CICA Handbook*, practice in similar situations, accounting guidelines, EIC Abstracts, IASC standards, standards published by standard setting bodies in other jurisdictions, CICA research studies, texts, and journals.

Source—*CICA Handbook*, Section 1000, par. .60

ILLUSTRATION 1-6
The GAAP Hierarchy

Professional Judgement

Professional judgement plays an especially important role in Canada. This is due to the basic philosophy that Canadian accountants hold with respect to standard setting i.e. that there **cannot be a rule for every situation**. Therefore, Canadian standards are based primarily on **general principles** rather than specific rules. The basic premise is that professional accountants with significant education and experience will be able to apply these principles appropriately as they see fit. This is where the professional judgement plays a role. The CICA provides some reference sources in applying professional judgement. These are noted in Illustration 1-6.

OBJECTIVE 11

Explain the significance of professional judgement in applying GAAP.

Role of Ethics

In accounting, as in other areas of business, ethical dilemmas are encountered frequently. Some of these dilemmas are simple and easy to resolve. Many, however, are complex, and solutions are not obvious. Businesses' concentration on maximizing the bottom line, facing the challenges of competition, and stressing short-term results places accountants in an environment of conflict and pressure. Basic questions such as "Is this way of communicating financial information good or bad?", "Is it right or wrong?", "What should I do in the circumstance?" cannot always be answered by simply adhering to GAAP or following the rules of the profession. Technical competence is not enough when ethical decisions are encountered.

Doing the **right thing** and making the right decision is not always easy. Right is not always evident and the pressures to "bend the rules," "play the game," or "just ignore it," can be considerable. For example, "Will my decision affect my job performance negatively?", "Will my superiors be upset?", "Will my colleagues be unhappy with me?" are often questions faced in making a tough ethical decision. The decision is more difficult because a public consensus has not emerged to formulate a comprehensive ethical system to provide guidelines.

This whole process of **ethical sensitivity** and selection among alternatives can be complicated by time pressures, job pressures, client pressures, personal pressures, and

OBJECTIVE 12

Understand issues related to ethics and financial accounting.

Go to the Digital Tool for an expanded discussion of ethical issues in financial reporting.

peer pressures. Throughout this textbook, ethical considerations are presented to sensitize you to the type of situations you may encounter when performing your professional responsibility.

CHALLENGES FACING FINANCIAL REPORTING

OBJECTIVE 13

Identify some of the challenges facing accounting.

In North America, we presently have the most liquid, deep, secure, and efficient public capital markets of any country at any time in history. One reason for this success is that our financial statements and related disclosures have captured and organized financial information in a useful and reliable fashion. However, much still needs to be done.

The financial reporting environment is changing very rapidly characterized by the following:

1. **Globalization of companies and capital markets.** Many companies presently list on foreign stock exchanges. Larger stock exchanges are cultivating these listings. As of July 1999, the largest global equities market, the New York Stock Exchange (NYSE), had 382 non-U.S. company listings[23] from all over the world. This is three times the number five years ago. On-line trading has made these markets (and through the markets, the companies) more accessible in terms of investing. Trading now happens around the clock. The move is toward global markets and global investors. The financial reporting environment is no longer constrained by Canadian borders nor only influenced by Canadian stakeholders.

   The TSE is working closely with the NYSE and six other major exchanges to create the Global Equity Market (GEM). GEM will represent over 60 percent of the world's market capitalization and operate in the three main trading time zones.[24]

2. **Impact of technology.** Accountants are purveyors of information. They identify, measure, and communicate useful information to users. Technology affects this process in many profound ways. The CICA, in its Report of the Inter-Institute Vision Task Force, concluded that we are presently in the third wave of computer technology—the first wave related to mainframes and the second wave related to personal computers. The third wave is driven by use of **networks** and **convergence of computers and telecommunications technologies**. Companies are now connected electronically to their banks, their suppliers, and regulatory agencies. The task force notes that in this third wave, automation focuses on stakeholders, distribution and consumption. This gives stakeholders ready access to a significant amount of very timely company information.

3. **Changing nature of the economy** in North America. Much of North America is transitioning from an economy based or traditional manufacturing and resource extraction to what has become known in the past decade as a **"knowledge-based" economy**.[25] In terms of market value of publicly traded shares, companies, such as Nortel, Microsoft, Cisco, Intel, Lucent AT&T and IBM dominate the top companies in the North American markets. What these companies all have in common is that a significant percentage of the value attributed to their shares is linked to factors such as their relationships with customers and suppliers, knowledge base or intellectual assets, ability to adapt to a changing technological environment, and adept leadership. This is different from the more traditional manufacturing and resource-based economy where value was more closely linked to physical and tangible assets and financing.

   Most of the assets of these "New Economy" companies are not reflected at all in the balance sheet, yet they drive the company value. As noted by the CICA Task Force:

---

[23] This represents greater than 12 percent of the total number of companies listed.

[24] According to a speech by Barbara Stymiest, TSE President and CEO, given to the Canadian Club of Toronto, November 20, 2000.

[25] McLean, R. "The Canadian Performance Reporting Initiative." Toronto: Ontario Premier's Council and the CICA, *ongoing*, Chapter 2.

"In light of these shifts (i.e., in the economy), to maintain its relevancy, the (accounting) profession must move beyond interpreting the past. Increasingly what matters is the ability for organizational decision-makers to be positioned for the future. This ability to look forward is driven by one's ability to measure organizational performance along an increasingly broad spectrum of measures, both financial and non-financial... Chartered Accountants must provide decision-makers with the tools necessary to measure and report on organizational performance in all its aspects, not just the historical and financial."[26]

4. **Increased requirement for accountability of corporations.** There is a growing number of **institutional investors**, partially because more and more is being invested in pension plans and mutual funds. The impact is that investors have become **more sophisticated in terms of knowledge levels**. This also means that these institutional investors are more involved in running the companies and that companies are being prodded toward **increased accountability**.

   Financial performance is rooted in a company's business model of (i.e., the earnings process, how companies finance the process, and what resources companies invest in). This is not always the focus of financial accounting. A company's ability to articulate its strategic vision and carry out that vision affects financial performance.

Impact of these items on financial reporting:

1. **Globalization of companies and capital markets** is already leading to a greater need for **comparability** of financial information across countries. This need is being dealt with head-on by initiatives to standardize/harmonize accounting principles and reporting. The CICA AcSB mandate, as earlier mentioned, focuses on facilitating of **global capital allocation**. Canadian companies will move from a Canadian arena with Canadian stakeholders to a global arena with global stakeholders. This will also bring the study of differing cultural, political, economic, and societal forces into the accounting arena.

2. As **technology** continues to advance at a dramatic pace, giving us greater access to more and more information more and more rapidly, the requirement for more timely information—beyond annual and quarterly financial statements—will rise sharply. Will this lead to **on-line real-time and/or continuous reporting**? Will this **decrease reliance on the annual financial statements** due to their lack of timeliness and therefore relevance? Will this change the role of the public accountant?

   A **continuous reporting model** is already incubating in the capital markets arena. Securities commissions and stock markets already require ongoing disclosures of public companies. These disclosures are already being monitored by the securities commissions and stock markets. Companies can now file required disclosures electronically with securities commissions. Investors can now log on to a website and tap in to conversations including earnings calls, briefings with analysts, and interviews with senior management and market regulators. These conversations were not previously accessible to the average investor. The CICA issued a research study in 1999 to assess the impact of technology on financial reporting.[27]

3. **New economy.** The **knowledge-based companies** that are beginning to dominate capital markets need more **relevant models for measuring and reporting value creating assets** that are currently not recognized on the balance sheet. Not much progress has been made in this area due to the difficulty of objectively valuing these assets and their potential impact on future earnings. Having said this, underwriting firms such as CIBC World Markets are valuing these companies every time one goes public. The market is also valuing these assets and the companies that house these assets through the stock prices. How, if at all, can those values be reflected in the financial statements?

---

[26] "The Report of the Inter-Institute Vision Task Force." Toronto: CICA, 1996, page 9.

[27] "The Impact of Technology on Financial and Business Reporting." Toronto: CICA, 1999.

4. **Accountability** – Will investors move **beyond the financial reporting model** to a more **all-inclusive model of business reporting** that includes not only financial information but other key indicators/measurements that help predict value creation and monitor organizational performance? Once again, the CICA AcSB mandate includes a thrust to develop and support frameworks for measuring and reporting information used for evaluating and improving organizational performance.[28] Changes in these directions would **broaden the focus from financial reporting to business reporting**.

The CICA has also been active in setting up a Criteria for Control Board to deal with designing, assessing, and reporting control systems. The CICA is part of a Committee for Corporate Governance (with the TSE), which has called for public companies to report on internal financial control and regulatory compliance. Although the CICA feels it is premature to issue reporting standards in these areas, the issue is nonetheless on the table and moves financial reporting one step forward toward a broader business-reporting base.

Also related to this theme of "business reporting" is the development and fairly widespread use of a business strategy model called the "Balanced Scorecard".[29] This model notes that financial measures are merely one component of useful information that decision-makers need to make effective decisions about the company. The model views the company from four differing perspectives: financial, customer, internal processes, and learning and growth. These four perspectives are linked to the company's strategic vision and objectives are developed within each of these perspectives. The objectives help the company to achieve its strategic vision. Measures are developed to determine whether the objectives are being met. Illustration 1-7 depicts a "balanced scorecard" model.

ILLUSTRATION 1-7
The Balanced Scorecard Model

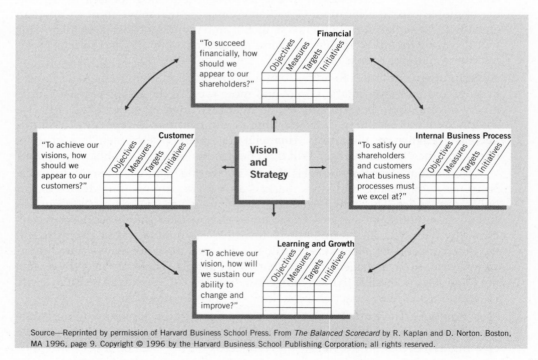

Source—Reprinted by permission of Harvard Business School Press. From *The Balanced Scorecard* by R. Kaplan and D. Norton. Boston, MA 1996, page 9. Copyright © 1996 by the Harvard Business School Publishing Corporation; all rights reserved.

This model is used to help focus a company's internal efforts more effectively to meet its strategic goals. The question is whether external users of financial statements also need to monitor these measures and whether companies should allow access to exter-

---

[28] See the Research Report entitled "Strategic Performance Monitoring and Management: Using Non-Financial Measures to Improve Corporate Governance". This was published by the CICA in 1998.

[29] Kaplan, R. and D. Norton, *The Balanced Scorecard*. Boston: Harvard Business School Press, 1996.

nal parties to this information. If the information is important for company management to make decisions, is it not important for external users as well?

We believe that the challenges presented by these changes must be met in order for the accounting profession to continue to provide the type of information needed for an efficient capital allocation process.

Conclusion

Financial reporting is standing at the threshold of some significant changes. Is the accounting profession up to the challenge to deal with this? At present, we believe that the profession is reacting responsibly and effectively to remedy identified shortcomings and to move forward with a new vision. Because of its substantial resources and expertise, the profession should be able to develop and maintain high standards and meet its mandate. It is and will continue to be a difficult process requiring time, logic, and diplomacy. By a judicious mix of these three ingredients, and a measure of luck, the accounting profession will continue to be a leader on the global business stage.

Summary of Learning Objectives

1. Describe the essential characteristics of accounting. The essential characteristics of accounting are: (1) identification, measurement, and communication of financial information about (2) economic entities to (3) interested persons.

2. Identify the major financial statements and other means of financial reporting. The financial statements most frequently provided are (1) the balance sheet, (2) the income statement, (3) the statement of cash flows, and (4) the statement of owners' or shareholders' equity. Financial reporting other than financial statements may take various forms. Examples include the president's letter or supplementary schedules in the corporate annual report, prospectuses, reports filed with government agencies, news releases, management's forecasts, and descriptions of an enterprise's social or environmental impact.

3. Explain how accounting assists in the efficient use of scarce resources. Accounting provides reliable, relevant, and timely information to managers, investors, and creditors so that resources are allocated to the most efficient enterprises. Accounting also provides measurements of efficiency (profitability) and financial soundness.

4. Explain the meaning of stakeholders and identify the key stakeholders in financial reporting. Stakeholders are parties that have something at stake in the financial reporting environment, e.g., salary, job, investment, reputation. Key stakeholders are investors, creditors, analysts, managers, employees, customers, suppliers, industry groups, unions, government departments and ministers, the public in general (e.g., consumer groups), regulatory agencies, other companies, standard setters, auditors, lawyers, and others.

5. Identify the objective of financial reporting. According to the *CICA Handbook*, the objective of financial statements is to communicate information that is useful to investors, members, contributors, creditors, and other users in making their resource allocation decisions and/or assessing management stewardship. Consequently, financial statements provide information about:

(a) an entity's economic resources, obligations, and equity/net assets;

(b) changes in an entity's economic resources, obligation and equity/net assets; and

(c) the economic performance of the entity.

6. Explain the notion of management bias with respect to financial reporting. Management bias implies that the financial statements are not neutral—that the preparers of the financial information are presenting the information in a manner that may overemphasize the positive and de-emphasize the negative.

7. Understand the importance of user needs in the financial reporting process. The financial reporting process is based on ensuring that users receive decision-relevant information. This is a challenge as different users have different knowledge levels and needs. Management bias may render financial information less useful.

8. Explain the need for accounting standards. The accounting profession has attempted to develop a set of standards that is generally accepted and universally practised. Without this set of standards, each enterprise would have to develop its own standards, and readers of financial statements would have to familiarize themselves with every company's peculiar accounting and reporting practices. As a result, it would be almost impossible to prepare statements that could be compared.

9. Identify the major entities that influence the standard-setting process and explain how they influence financial reporting. The CICA AcSB is the main standard-setting body in Canada. It derives its mandate from the CBCA as well as provincial acts of incorporation. Public companies are required to follow GAAP in order to access capital markets. This is monitored by provincial securities commissions. FASB and the IASC are also important as they influence Canadian standard setting. Canada is committed to international harmonization of GAAP.

10. Explain the meaning of generally accepted accounting principles. Generally accepted accounting principles are either principles that have substantial authoritative support, such as the *CICA Handbook*, or given practices that have been accepted as appropriate over time because of universal application.

11. Explain the significance of professional judgement in applying GAAP. Professional judgement plays an important role in Canadian GAAP since much of GAAP is based on general principles, which need to be interpreted.

12. Understand issues related to ethics and financial accounting. Financial accountants in the performance of their professional duties are called on for moral discernment and ethical decision-making. The decision is more difficult because a public consensus has not emerged to formulate a comprehensive ethical system that provides guidelines in making ethical judgements.

13. Identify some of the challenges facing accounting. Globalization, leading to a requirement for international harmonization of standards; Increased technology, resulting in the need for more timely information; Move to a new economy, resulting in a focus on measuring and reporting non-traditional assets that create value; Increased requirement for accountability, resulting in creation of new measurement and reporting models that look at business reporting as a whole.

CONCEPTUAL CASES

C1-1   Alain Robichaud has recently completed his first year of studying accounting. His instructor for next semester has indicated that the primary focus will be the area of financial accounting.

Instructions
   (a) Differentiate between financial accounting and managerial accounting.
   (b) Financial accounting involves the preparation of financial statements. What are the financial statements most frequently provided?
   (c) What is the difference between financial statements and financial reporting?

C1-2   Celia Cruz, a recent graduate of the local university, works at a large manufacturing company. She has been asked by Angeles Ochoa, controller, to prepare the company's response to a current Exposure Draft published by the Accounting Standards Board (AcSB). Cruz knows that the *CICA Handbook*, Section 1000, deals with basic principles and concepts, and she believes that this material could be used to support the company's response to the Exposure Draft. She has prepared a rough draft of the response, citing the *CICA Handbook*, Section 1000.

Instructions

  (a) Identify the objective of financial reporting as presented in the *CICA Handbook,* Section 1000.

  (b) Describe the level of sophistication expected of the users of financial information.

(CMA adapted)

C1-3

Instructions

Explain how reported accounting numbers might affect an individual's perceptions and actions. Cite two examples.

C1-4   Some argue that having various organizations establish accounting principles is wasteful and inefficient. Rather than mandating accounting standards, each company could voluntarily disclose the type of information it considered important. In addition, if an investor wants additional information, the investor could contact the company and pay to receive the additional information desired.

Instructions

Comment on the appropriateness of this viewpoint.

C1-5

Instructions

  (a) Identify the sponsoring organization of the AcSB and the process by which the AcSB arrives at a decision and issues an accounting standard.

  (b) Identify the EIC's role and indicate the difference between an EIC Abstract and the recommendations in a *CICA Handbook* section.

C1-6   As mentioned in the chapter, The T. Eaton Company (Eaton's) was a private Canadian company that experienced cash flow difficulties and hired new management to turn the company around. The company then went public and the shares sold at $15. Within months, the stock price plummeted and eventually, Sears bought out Eaton's.

Instructions

Who are the stakeholders in this situation? Explain what is at stake and why and how they were affected when the stock price plummeted.

C1- 7   The University of Toronto Bulletin a university newspaper, announced in its January 29, 2001 edition that Moody's Canada Inc. (a financial rating agency) gave the University of Toronto a rating of AA2 after a review of the university's books. This is a strong rating and ranks on a level higher than the university's single largest funder, the Province of Ontario.

Instructions

  (a) Who are the stakeholders in the university financial reporting environment?

  (b) What financial information might Moody's have based its decision on?

  (c) What is the impact (i.e. to the university) of obtaining this strong rating?

  (d) How might this piece of information affect how the stakeholders deal with the university in the future?

C1-8   The following information was drawn from Ontario Securities Commission (OSC) Statement of Allegation dated August 30, 2000 against Philip Services Corp. (Philip). The allegation relates to the information contained in the company prospectus that included audited financial statements for the years ended December 31, 1995 and 1996.

    The prospectus included an unqualified audit opinion, meaning that the auditors had concluded in the audit report that the financial statements presented the company's financial position and results of operations fairly in accordance with GAAP. At the time, the company was a leading integrated service provider of ferrous scrap processing, brokerage, and industrial outsourcing services. The OSC alleged that the company failed to provide full, true, and plain disclosure in the prospectus of material facts in respect of the restructuring and special charges.

Instructions

  (a) Explain the meaning of the term "GAAP" as used in the audit report.

  (b) Explain how you determine whether or not an accounting principle is generally accepted?

(c) Discuss the sources of evidence for determining whether an accounting principle has substantial authoritative support.

(d) Discuss how the auditors might have issued a clean audit opinion when the OSC is alleging that the company did not provide full disclosure of material facts.

C1-9 Some accountants have said that politicization in the development and acceptance of generally accepted accounting principles (i.e., standard setting) is taking place. Some use the term "politicization" in a narrow sense to mean the influence by governmental agencies, particularly the Securities Commissions, on the development of generally accepted accounting principles. Others use it more broadly to mean the compromise that results when the bodies responsible for developing generally accepted accounting principles are pressured by interest groups (securities commissions, stock exchanges, businesses through their various organizations, financial analysts, bankers, lawyers, etc.).

Instructions

(a) What arguments can be raised to support the "politicization" of accounting standard setting?

(b) What arguments can be raised against the "politicization" of accounting standard setting?

(CMA adapted)

C1-10 Presented below are three models for setting accounting standards.

1. The purely political approach, where national legislative action decrees accounting standards.
2. The private, professional approach, where financial accounting standards are set and enforced by private professional actions only.
3. The public/private mixed approach, where standards are set by private sector bodies that behave as though they were public agencies and whose standards to a great extent are enforced through governmental agencies.

Instructions

(a) Which of these three models best describes standard setting in Canada? Comment on your answer.

(b) Why do companies, financial analysts, labour unions, industry trade associations, and others take such an active interest in standard setting?

(c) Cite an example of a group other than the AcSB that attempts to establish accounting standards. Speculate as to why another group might wish to set its own standards.

C1-11 As elsewhere, in the world of accounting and finance, it often helps to be fluent in abbreviations and acronyms.

Instructions

Presented below is a list of common accounting acronyms. Identify the term for which each acronym stands, and provide a brief definition of each term.

(a) AcSB	(f) SEC	(k) CMA
(b) EIC	(g) TSE	(l) CGA
(c) CICA	(h) IASC	(m) CPA
(d) FASB	(i) GAAP	
(e) OSC	(j) CA	

C1-12 The following is a quote taken from the Foreword to "The Impact of Technology on Financial and Business Reporting" a research study published by the CICA in 1999:

"Changes in technology have had, and are continuing to have, a profound effect on how information is captured, summarized and communicated. "

Instructions

Discuss, making reference to the Research Report and current "real life" examples.

C1-13 The following letter was sent to the SEC and the FASB by leaders of the business community.

Dear Sirs:

The FASB has been struggling with accounting for derivatives and hedging for many years. The FASB has now developed, over the last few weeks, a new approach that it proposes to adopt as a final standard. We understand that the Board intends to adopt this new approach as a final standard without exposing it for public comment and debate, despite the evident complexity of the new approach, the speed with which it has been developed, and the significant changes to the exposure draft since it was released more than one year ago. Instead, the Board plans to allow only a brief review by selected parties, limited to issues of operationality and clarity, and would exclude questions as to the merits of the proposed approach.

As the FASB itself has said throughout this process, its mission does not permit it to consider matters that go beyond accounting and reporting considerations. Accordingly, the FASB may not have adequately considered the wide range of concerns that have been expressed about the derivatives and hedging proposal, including concerns related to the potential impact on the capital markets, the weakening of companies' ability to manage risk, and the adverse control implications of implementing costly and complex new rules imposed at the same time as other major initiatives, including the Year 2000 issues and a single European currency. We believe that these crucial issues must be considered, if not by the FASB, then by the Securities and Exchange Commission, other regulatory agencies, or Congress.

We believe it is essential that the FASB solicit all comments in order to identify and address all material issues that may exist before issuing a final standard. We understand the desire to bring this process to a prompt conclusion, but the underlying issues are so important to this nation's businesses, the customers they serve and the economy as a whole that expediency cannot be the dominant consideration. As a result, we urge the FASB to expose its new proposal for public comment, following the established due process procedures that are essential to acceptance of its standards, and providing sufficient time to affected parties to understand and assess the new approach.

We also urge the SEC to study the comments received in order to assess the impact that these proposed rules may have on the capital markets, on companies' risk management practices, and on management and financial controls. These vital public policy matters deserve consideration as part of the Commission's oversight responsibilities.

We believe that these steps are essential if the FASB is to produce the best possible accounting standard while minimizing adverse economic effects and maintaining the competitiveness of U.S. businesses in the international marketplace.

Very truly yours,

(This letter was signed by the chairs of 22 of the largest U.S. companies.)

Instructions

Answer the following questions:

(a) Explain the "due process" procedures followed by the AcSB in developing a financial reporting standard. Based upon the above noted letter, what differences and similarities exist between issuing a standard in the U.S. and Canada.

(b) What is meant by the term "economic consequences" in accounting standard setting?

(c) What economic consequences arguments are used in this letter?

(d) What do you believe is the main point of the letter?

C1-14 The Ontario Securities Commission issued a Discussion Memorandum in 2001 proposing that Canadian companies follow U.S. GAAP.

Instructions

Obtain a copy of the discussion memorandum from the OSC website (www.osc.gov.on.ca) or the library. Discuss.

Using Your Judgement

FINANCIAL REPORTING PROBLEM

Kate Jackson, a new staff accountant, is confused because of the complexities involving accounting standard setting. Specifically, she is confused by the number of bodies issuing financial reporting standards of one kind or another and the level of authoritative support that can be attached to these reporting standards. Kate decides that she must review the environment in which accounting standards are set, if she is to increase her understanding of the accounting profession.

Kate recalls that during her accounting education there was a chapter or two regarding the environment of financial accounting and the development of accounting standards. However, she remembers that little emphasis was placed on these chapters by her instructor.

Instructions

(a) Help Kate by identifying key organizations involved in accounting standard setting.

(b) Kate asks for guidance regarding authoritative support. Please assist her by explaining what is meant by authoritative support.

(c) Give Kate a historical overview of how standard setting has evolved and is continuing to evolve.

(d) What authority for compliance with GAAP has existed throughout the period of standard setting?

RESEARCH CASES

Case 1

As mentioned in the Chapter, the SEC is considering allowing foreign companies who list on U.S. stock exchanges to follow IASC standards. The Ontario Securities Commission (OSC) has also recently suggested that Canadian companies follow U.S. GAAP.

Instructions

Research and prepare an essay considering the following:

(a) Hypothesize why the SEC and OSC have taken these stands.

(b) How might Canadian investors benefit if U.S. standards become Canadian GAAP? How might they be disadvantaged?

(c) How do Canadian and U.S. standards differ (in general)?

(d) Review the financial statements of large Canadian companies whose shares trade on the TSE as well as a U.S. exchange. (Hint: look at www.sedar.com under "Company Profile" then "View this company's documents" then "annual financial statements"). These companies generally include a note to the financial statements reconciling NI under Canadian GAAP to NI under U.S. GAAP. Select five companies and calculate the $ and % difference between the two numbers. Discuss the implications of reporting two separate NI numbers.

Case 2

In 2000, as part of its continuous disclosure review of selected financial accounting practices by Canadian companies, the OSC sent a request to approximately 70 Canadian companies asking for a detailed explanation of how they apply revenue recognition policies in their financial statements. The following specifics were asked for:

(a) for revenue recognition on the sale of goods, an explanation of how the company deals with retained risks or obligations; including a customer's right of return, obligations under maintenance contracts, or obligations to provide complimentary upgrades;

(b) a description of how revenue is accrued for service contracts;

(c) whether any portion of the company's reported revenue represents the "gross" amount of sales transactions in which the company acts essentially as an agent or broker rather than as principal and for which it is compensated on a commission or fee basis;

(d) whether, and if so how, the company compares its revenue recognition accounting practices with those applied generally within the industry in which it operates or by specific companies within that industry.

Instructions

(a) Discuss the implications (of the OSC performing these reviews) for the stakeholders in the financial reporting environment in Canada.

(b) Select 10 companies that list on the TSE (from the same industry) and review their revenue recognition policies. Compare policies between companies considering the information asked for by the OSC. (Hint: look at "listed companies" on the TSE website (www.tse.com), then look up their financial statements as filed with the OSC at www.sedar.com)

INTERNATIONAL REPORTING CASE

Michael Sharpe, Deputy Chairman, International Accounting Standards Committee, made the following comments before the FEI's 63rd Annual Conference: There is an irreversible movement toward the harmonization of financial reporting throughout the world. The international capital markets require an end to:

1. The confusion caused by international companies announcing different results depending on the set of accounting standards applied. Recent announcements by Daimler-Benz (now DaimlerChrysler) highlight the confusion that this causes.

2. Companies in some countries obtaining unfair commercial advantages from the use of particular national accounting standards.

3. The complications in negotiating commercial arrangements for international joint ventures caused by different accounting requirements.

4. The inefficiency of international companies having to understand and use myriad accounting standards depending on the countries in which they operate and the countries in which they raise capital and debt. Executive talent is wasted on keeping up to date with numerous sets of accounting standards and the never-ending changes to them.

5. The inefficiency of investment managers, bankers, and financial analysts as they seek to compare financial reporting drawn up in accordance with different sets of accounting standards.

6. Failure of many stock exchanges and regulators to require companies subject to their jurisdiction to provide comparable, comprehensive, and transparent financial reporting frameworks giving international comparability.

7. Difficulty for developing countries and countries entering the free market economy such as China and Russia, in accessing foreign capital markets because of the complexity of and differences between national standards.

8. The restriction on the mobility of financial service providers across the world as a result of different accounting standards.

Clearly the elimination of these inefficiencies by having comparable high-quality financial reporting used across the world would benefit international businesses.

Instructions

(a) What is the International Accounting Standards Committee?

(b) What stakeholders might benefit from the use of International Accounting Standards?

(c) What do you believe are some of the major obstacles to harmonization?

ETHICS CASE

When the AcSB issues new standards, the implementation date is usually 12 months from date of issuance, with early implementation encouraged. Paula Popovich, controller, discusses with her financial vice-president the need for early implementation of a standard which would result in a fairer presentation of the company's financial condition and earnings. When the financial vice-president determines that early implementation of the standard will adversely affect the reported net income for the year, he discourages Popovich from implementing the standard until it is required.

Instructions

(a) What, if any, is the ethical issue involved in this case?

(b) Is the financial vice-president acting improperly or immorally?

(c) What does Popovich have to gain by advocating early implementation?

(d) Which stakeholders might be affected by the decision against early implementation?

(CMA adapted)

Conceptual Framework Underlying Financial Reporting

LEARNING OBJECTIVES

After studying this chapter, you should be able to:

1. Describe the usefulness of a conceptual framework.

2. Describe the main components of the conceptual framework for financial reporting.

3. Understand the objective of financial reporting.

4. Identify the qualitative characteristics of accounting information.

5. Define the basic elements of financial statements.

6. Describe the basic assumptions of accounting.

7. Explain the application of the basic principles of accounting.

8. Describe the impact that constraints have on reporting accounting information.

Preview of Chapter 2

••

Users of financial statements need relevant and reliable information. To help develop this type of financial information, accountants use a conceptual framework that guides financial accounting and reporting. This chapter discusses the basic concepts underlying this conceptual framework. The content and organization of this chapter are as follows:

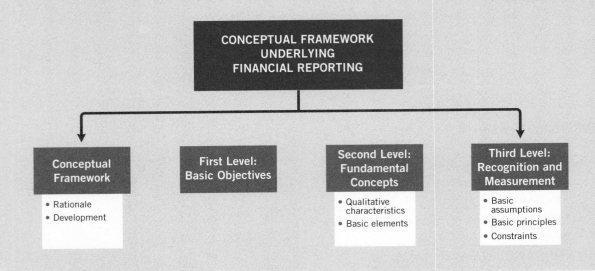

CONCEPTUAL FRAMEWORK

A conceptual framework is like a **constitution**: it is "a coherent system of interrelated objectives and fundamentals that can lead to consistent standards and that prescribes the nature, function, and limits of financial accounting and financial statements."[1] Many have considered the real contribution of American and Canadian standard-setting bodies, and even their continued existence, to depend on the quality and utility of the conceptual framework.

Need for Conceptual Framework

Why is a conceptual framework necessary? First, to be useful, standard setting should **build on and relate to an established body of concepts and objectives**. A soundly developed conceptual framework should enable the AcSB to issue more useful and consistent standards over time. A **coherent set of standards** and rules should result, because they would be built upon the same foundation. The framework should **increase financial statement users' understanding** of and **confidence** in financial reporting, and it should **enhance comparability** among companies' financial statements.

Second, new and emerging practical **problems should be more quickly solved** by referring to an **existing framework of basic theory**. To illustrate an emerging problem: unique debt instruments were issued by companies in the early 1980s as a response to high interest and inflation rates. These included shared appreciation mortgages (debt

---

[1] "Conceptual Framework for Financial Accounting and Reporting: Elements of Financial Statements and Their Measurement," *FASB Discussion Memorandum*, (Stamford, Conn.: FASB, 1976), page 1 of the "Scope and Implications of the Conceptual Framework Project" section.

in which the lender receives equity participation), zero coupon bonds (debt issued at a deep discount with no stated interest rate), and commodity-backed bonds (debt that may be repaid in a commodity). For example, Sunshine Mining (a silver mining company) sold two issues of bonds that it would redeem either with $1,000 in cash or with 50 ounces of silver, whichever was worth more at maturity.

Why did Sunshine Mining issue this type of unique instrument? As a silver miner, Sunshine Mining is exposed to a "price risk" when it sells its silver. Silver prices fluctuate with market supply and demand and therefore, there is a risk that the company might not recover from its sales revenues the costs to extract the metal and make it ready for sale. With issuance of the bonds, Sunshine Mining knew exactly how much it would get for the silver—in fact, when it issued the bond, the amount of cash received was fixed at that point! The silver repayment option allowed Sunshine Mining to offer a lower interest rate and also fix the price on the silver as long as silver did not go below $20 per ounce. Note that if they had made the bond repayable in silver only, this would have completely eliminated the price risk, although this type of bond would not have been as attractive to investors due to its higher risk profile.

Both Sunshine Mining bond issues had a stated interest rate of 8.5%. At what amounts should Sunshine Mining or the bond buyers have measured the bonds given that they might be redeemed in silver? It is difficult, if not impossible, for the AcSB to prescribe the proper accounting treatment quickly for highly complex situations like this. Practising accountants, however, must resolve such problems on a day-to-day basis. Through the exercise of **good judgement** and with the help of a **universally accepted conceptual framework**, it is hoped that practitioners will be able to dismiss certain alternatives quickly and then focus upon a logical and acceptable treatment.

Development of Conceptual Framework

Over the years, numerous organizations, committees, and interested individuals have developed and published their own conceptual frameworks, but no single framework has been universally accepted and relied on in practice. Recognizing the need for a generally accepted framework, the FASB in 1976 issued a three-part discussion memorandum entitled "Conceptual Framework for Financial Accounting and Reporting: Elements of Financial Statements and Their Measurement." It set forth the major issues to be addressed in establishing a conceptual framework for setting accounting standards and resolving financial reporting controversies. From this arose six **Statements of Financial Accounting Concepts**. The AcSB followed suit, issuing **Handbook, Section 1000—Financial Statement Concepts**.

Illustration 2-1 provides an overview of a conceptual framework.[2] At the first level, the objectives identify accounting's **goals and purposes** and are the conceptual framework's building blocks. At the second level are the **qualitative characteristics** that make accounting information useful and the **elements of financial statements** (assets, liabilities, and so on). At the final or third level are the **measurement and recognition concepts** used in establishing and applying accounting standards. These concepts include assumptions, principles, and constraints that describe the present reporting environment.

FIRST LEVEL: BASIC OBJECTIVES

As we discussed in Chapter 1, the objective of financial statements according to the *CICA Handbook*, Section 1000 is to communicate information that is useful to investors, creditors and other users in making their **resource allocation** decisions and/or assessing **management stewardship**. Consequently, financial statements provide information about:

IAS NOTE

The IASC has issued a conceptual framework that is broadly consistent with that of the U.S. and Canada.

OBJECTIVE 2
....
Describe the main components of the conceptual framework for financial reporting.

OBJECTIVE 3
....
Understand the objective of financial reporting.

INTERNATIONAL INSIGHT

In Sweden, the government often provides capital to businesses. Swedish financial reporting is more oriented toward helping government decision-makers manage the economy.

---

[2] Adapted from William C. Norby, *The Financial Analysts Journal*, March–April 1982, p. 22.

ILLUSTRATION 2-1
Conceptual Framework for
Financial Reporting

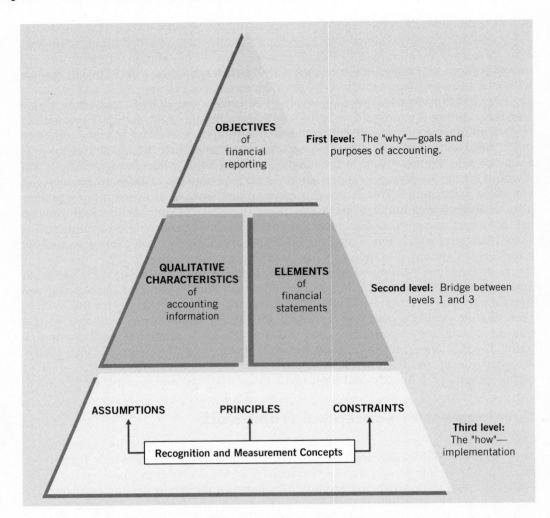

(a) an entity's economic resources, obligations and equity/net assets;

(b) changes in an entity's economic resources, obligations and equity/net assets; and

(c) the economic performance of the entity.[3]

In providing information to users of financial statements, the accounting profession relies on general-purpose financial statements. The intent of such statements is to provide the most useful information possible at minimal cost to various user groups. Underlying these objectives is the notion that users need **reasonable knowledge of business and financial accounting matters** to understand the information contained in financial statements. This point is important: it means that when preparing financial statements, you can assume users have a level of reasonable competence. This impacts the way and extent to which information is reported. As discussed in Chapter 1, there are distinct differences in the knowledge levels of investors.

SECOND LEVEL: FUNDAMENTAL CONCEPTS

The objectives (first level) are concerned with accounting's goals and purposes. Later, we will discuss the ways these goals and purposes are implemented (third level). Between these two levels it is necessary to provide certain **conceptual building blocks** that explain the **qualitative characteristics** of accounting information and define the **elements** of financial statements. These conceptual building blocks form a bridge between the **why** of accounting (the objectives) and the **how** of accounting (recognition and measurement).

INTERNATIONAL INSIGHT

In Switzerland, Germany, Korea, and other nations, capital is provided to business primarily by large banks. Creditors have very close ties to firms and can obtain information directly from them. Creditors do not need to rely on publicly available information, and financial information is focused on creditor protection. This process of capital allocation, however, is starting to change.

---

[3] *CICA Handbook*, Section 1000, par. .15.

Qualitative Characteristics of Accounting Information

How does one decide whether financial reports should provide information on how much a firm's assets cost to acquire (historical cost basis) or how much they are currently worth (current value basis)?

Choosing an acceptable accounting method, the amount and types of information to be disclosed, and the format in which information should be presented involves determining **which alternative provides the most useful information for decision-making purposes** (decision usefulness). The conceptual framework has identified the qualitative characteristics of accounting information that distinguish better (more useful) information from inferior (less useful) information for decision-making purposes.

OBJECTIVE 4

Identify the qualitative characteristics of accounting information.

Decision-Makers (Users) and Understandability

Decision-makers vary widely in the **types of decisions** they make, the **methods of decision-making** they employ, the **information they already possess** or can obtain from other sources, and their **ability to process the information**. For information to be useful, there must be a connection (linkage) between these users and the decisions they make. This link, understandability, is the quality of information that permits reasonably informed users to perceive its significance.[4]

On February 29, 2001, **Torstar Corp.**—a broadly based publishing company that publishes among other things, *The Toronto Star*, issued its audited results for the year ended December 31, 2000. In the announcement, the company noted that **Income from continuing operations** was $83.7 million (up from $80.8 million the previous year). It then went on to note that **Net income** was only $36.1 million (down significantly from $85 million in 1999). Which number is the number that users should focus on—**net income** or **income from continuing operations**? The *CICA Handbook* would presume that users understood that net income is composed of three main components:

(a) net income/loss from continuing operations,

(b) net income/loss from discontinued operations, and

(c) extraordinary items.

Users would further be expected to conclude that **income from continuing operations** was the more **relevant** number for **predictive** purposes as **net income** would be **net of one-time and non-recurring charges**. The income statement will be covered in more detail in Chapter 4.

Relevance and Reliability

Relevance and reliability are qualities that make accounting information useful for decision-making.

Relevance. To be relevant, accounting information must **make a difference in a decision**.[5] If certain information has no bearing on a decision, it is irrelevant to that decision. Relevant information helps users make predictions about the ultimate outcome of past, present, and future events; that is, it has predictive value. Relevant information also helps users confirm or correct prior expectations; it has feedback value.

For example, when **Nortel Networks Corp.** issues an earnings announcement, this information is considered relevant because it provides a basis for forecasting annual

---

[4] Users are presumed to have a reasonable understanding of business and economic activities and accounting as well as a willingness to study the information with reasonable diligence-according to the *CICA Handbook*, Section 1000, par. .19.

[5] "Qualitative Characteristics of Accounting Information," *Statement of Financial Accounting Concepts No. 2* (Stamford, Conn.: FASB, May 1980), par. .47.

earnings. In February 2001, Nortel announced that it would miss earlier projected financial targets for the year by one half—a significant amount. This information provided **feedback value** as to past performance while at the same time providing **predictive value** for the annual earnings. Information has feedback value if it helps users **confirm or correct prior expectations** as in the Nortel case.

For information to be relevant, it must also be available to decision-makers before it loses its capacity to influence their decisions. Thus timeliness is a primary ingredient. If Nortel did not report its interim results until six months after the end of the period, the information would be much less useful for decision-making purposes. In fact, when Nortel made the February announcements, there was some concern over whether the information could have been released even earlier. **For information to be relevant it should have predictive or feedback value, and it must be presented on a timely basis.**

Reliability. Accounting information is reliable to the extent that it is **verifiable, is a faithful representation of the underlying economic reality, and is reasonably free of error and bias (neutral).** Reliability is a necessity for individuals who have neither the time nor the expertise to evaluate the information's factual content.

Verifiability is demonstrated when **independent** measurers, using the **same measurement methods**, obtain similar results. For example, would several independent auditors come to the same conclusion about a set of financial statements? If outside parties using the same measurement methods arrive at different conclusions, then the statements are not verifiable. Auditors could not render an opinion on such statements. Some numbers are more easily verified than others, e.g., cash can be verified by confirming with the bank where the deposit is held. Other numbers, such as accruals for environmental cleanup costs, are more difficult (although not necessarily impossible) to verify as many assumptions are made to arrive at an estimate.

Representational faithfulness means that the numbers and descriptions represent what really existed or happened. The accounting numbers and descriptions agree with the resources or events that these numbers and descriptions purport to represent.

Neutrality means that information cannot be selected to favour one set of stakeholders over another. Factual, truthful, unbiased information must be the overriding consideration. For example, consider the case of **Bre-X Minerals**. Bre-X, a small mining company, announced in the early 1990s that it had discovered a fairly significant gold deposit in Indonesia. The company shares skyrocketed from pennies a share to over $280 per share. Subsequently, it was discovered that the company had been "salting the samples"[6] and that there was little, if any, gold there. This information was not disclosed to the market until long after it was discovered that there was no gold. Many investors lost a significant amount. The company is presently the subject of many lawsuits.

The value of mining companies is often reflected in the underlying mineral reserves that the company has rights to. The company spends a significant amount of money attempting to determine the mineral value through core samples and other exploratory techniques. In the end, however, they are only sampling the minerals and don't really know how much is there until they actually bring it up to the surface and process it. The mineral value is not reflected in the financial statements due to **measurement uncertainty**. Instead, what shows on the balance sheet is often only costs incurred to explore and develop the properties. As a result, additional disclosures are often provided regarding the reserves. Since this information is followed closely by the investment community, **presentation** and **measurement** is a very sensitive issue.

Neutrality in standard setting has come under increasing attack. Some argue that standards should not be issued if they cause undesirable economic effects on an industry or company ("the economic consequences" argument). Standards must be free from bias, however, or we will no longer have credible financial statements. Without credible financial statements, individuals will no longer use this information.

---

[6] The term "salting" refers to the practice of someone tampering with the samples (and adding in some, or more, gold).

Comparability and Consistency

Information about an enterprise is more useful if it can be compared with similar information about another enterprise (comparability) and with similar information about the same enterprise at other points in time (consistency).[7]

Comparability. Information that has been measured and reported in a similar manner for different enterprises is considered comparable. Comparability enables users to **identify the real similarities and differences in economic phenomena** because they have not been obscured by incomparable accounting methods. For example, the accounting for pensions is different in North America and Japan. In Canada and the United States, pension cost is recorded as incurred, whereas in Japan there is little or no charge to income for these costs. As a result, it is difficult to compare and evaluate the financial results of **General Motors** or **Ford** with those of **Nissan** or **Honda**. Also, resource allocation decisions involve **evaluations of alternatives**; a valid evaluation can be made only if comparable information is available.

Consistency. When an entity applies the **same accounting treatment to similar events, from period to period**, the entity is considered to be consistent in its use of accounting standards. It does not mean that companies cannot switch from one accounting method to another. Companies can change methods, but the changes are restricted to situations in which it can be demonstrated that the **newly adopted method is preferable to the old**.[8] Then the accounting change's nature and effect, as well as justification, must be **disclosed in the financial statements** for the period in which the change is made.[9]

When there has been a change in accounting principles, the auditor refers to it in an explanatory paragraph of the audit report. This paragraph identifies the nature of the change and refers the reader to the note in the financial statements that discusses the change in detail.

In summary, accounting reports for any given year are more useful if they can be compared with reports from other companies and with prior reports of the same entity.

Tradeoffs

It is not always possible for financial information to have **all** the qualities of useful information. Sometimes a choice must be made regarding which quality is more important.

For instance, consider that **relevant** information must have **feedback value, predictive value** and be **timely**. **Reliable** information is **verifiable, representative of reality** and **neutral**. Companies must issue annual financial statements. These statements are often released several weeks or months after year end. The reason for this is that management and auditors check the statements to ensure **reliability**. At this point in time however, the information is no longer **timely**. Which is more important—timeliness or reliability? The accounting profession is continually striving to reduce compromises (see Chapter 1—Changes Facing Financial Reporting).

---

[7] As indicated in Chapter 1, the accounting environment is continually changing; comparability and consistency are thereby more difficult to achieve. Tax laws change, new industries (e.g., computer software) grow dramatically, new financial instruments (e.g., financial futures, collateral mortgage obligations, zero-coupon convertible bonds) are created, and mergers and divestitures occur frequently.

[8] The AICPA Special Committee on Financial Reporting noted that users highly value consistency. It notes that a change tends to destroy the comparability of data before and after the change. Some companies take the time to assist users to understand the pre- and post-change data. Generally, however, users say they lose the ability to analyse from period to period.

[9] *CICA Handbook*, Section 1506, par. .16.

Basic Elements

OBJECTIVE 5

Define the basic elements of
financial statements.

An important aspect of developing any theoretical structure is the body of basic elements or definitions to be included in the structure. At present, accounting uses many terms that have peculiar and specific meanings. These terms constitute the language of business or the jargon of accounting.

One such term is **asset**. Is an asset something we own? How do we define "own". Is it based on legal title or possession? If ownership is based on legal title, can we assume that any leased asset would not be shown on the balance sheet? Is an asset something we have the right to use, or is it anything of value used by the enterprise to generate revenues? If the answer is the latter, then why should the enterprise's management not be considered an asset? It seems necessary, therefore, to develop basic definitions for the elements of financial statements. Section 1000 of the *CICA Handbook* defines the seven interrelated elements that are most directly related to measuring an enterprise's performance and financial status. The elements are listed here for your review and information. Each of these elements will be explained and examined in more detail in subsequent chapters.

Elements of Financial Statements[10]

Assets are probable **future economic benefits** obtained or **controlled** by a particular entity as a result of **past transactions or events**.

Liabilities are probable future sacrifices of economic benefits arising from present **duty or responsibility** to others, as a result of **past transactions or events**, where there is **little or no discretion to avoid** the obligation.

Equity/Net Assets is **residual interest** in the assets of an entity that remains after deducting its liabilities. In a business enterprise, the equity is the ownership interest.

Revenues are increases in economic resources, either by inflows or other enhancements of assets of an entity or settlement of its liabilities resulting from **ordinary activities** of an entity.

Expenses are decreases in economic resources, either by outflows or reductions of assets or incurrence of liabilities resulting from an entity's **ordinary revenue-generating activities**.

Gains are increases in equity (net assets) from **peripheral or incidental transactions** of an entity and from **all other transactions** and other events and circumstances affecting the entity during a period, except those that result from revenues or investments by owners.

Losses are decreases in equity (net assets) from **peripheral or incidental transactions** of an entity and from **all other transactions** and other events and circumstances affecting the entity during a period, except those that result from expenses or distributions to owners.

In the U.S., the term comprehensive income represents a relatively new concept. Comprehensive income is more inclusive than the traditional notion of net income. It includes net income and all other changes in equity exclusive of owners' investments and distributions. For example, unrealized holding gains and losses on certain securities, which are currently excluded from net income under U.S. GAAP, are included under comprehensive income. Canada does not at present report comprehensive income.[11]

---

[10] Taken from *CICA Handbook*, Section 1000, pars. .29–.40.

[11] The IASC is working on a project "Reporting Financial Performance," which supports this concept. The AcSB participated in the project as part of the G4+1 group of standard setters, gathering and providing feedback from Canadian stakeholders. The G4+1 group included standard-setting bodies from Australia, Canada, New Zealand, the United Kingdom and the United States. Now that the IASB has been formed, the G4+1 group will disband.

THIRD LEVEL: RECOGNITION AND MEASUREMENT CONCEPTS

The framework's third level consists of concepts that implement the basic objectives of level one. These concepts explain which, when, and how financial elements and events should be **recognized**, **measured**, and **reported** by the accounting system. In general, transactions should be recognized when they are **measurable** and where a liability or asset is concerned, the benefit or obligation is **probable**.[12] For discussion purposes, the concepts are identified as **basic assumptions**, **principles**, and **constraints**. Not everyone uses this classification system, so it is best to focus your attention more on understanding the concepts than on how they are classified and organized. These concepts serve as **guidelines** in developing rational responses to controversial financial reporting issues. They have evolved over time and are fundamental to the specific accounting principles issued by the AcSB.

Basic Assumptions

Four basic assumptions underlie the financial accounting structure: (1) **economic entity**, (2) **going concern**, (3) **monetary unit**, and (4) **periodicity**.

<table>
<tr><td>

OBJECTIVE 6

Describe the basic assumptions of accounting.

</td></tr>
</table>

Economic Entity Assumption

The economic entity assumption means that economic activity can be identified with a **particular unit of accountability**. In other words, a company's business activity can be kept **separate and distinct from its owners** and any other business unit. If there were no meaningful way to separate all the economic events that occur, no basis for accounting would exist.

   The entity concept does not apply solely to segregating activities among given business enterprises. An individual, a department or division, or an entire industry could be considered a separate entity if we chose to define the unit in such a manner. Thus, the entity concept does not necessarily refer to a **legal entity**. A parent and its subsidiaries are separate legal entities, but merging their activities for accounting and reporting purposes does not violate the **economic entity** assumption.[13] In fact, GAAP requires that a company consolidate its subsidiaries' financial statements with the parent company financial statement.

Going Concern Assumption

Most accounting methods are based on the going concern assumption—**that the business enterprise will have a long life**. Experience indicates that, in spite of numerous business failures, companies have a fairly high continuance rate. Although accountants do not believe that business firms will last indefinitely, they do expect them to last long enough to fulfill their objectives and commitments.

   The implications of this assumption are profound. The **historical cost principle would have limited usefulness if eventual liquidation were assumed**. Under a liquidation approach, for example, asset values are better stated at net realizable value (sales price less costs of disposal) than at acquisition cost. **Amortization and amortization policies are justifiable and appropriate only if we assume some permanence to the enterprise**. If a liquidation approach were adopted, the current-noncurrent classification of

---

[12] *CICA Handbook*, Section 1000, par. .44.

[13] The concept of the entity is changing. For example, it is now harder to define the outer edges of companies. There are public companies with multiple public subsidiaries, each with joint ventures, licensing arrangements, and other affiliations and strategic alliances. Increasingly, loose affiliations of enterprises in joint ventures or customer-supplier relationships are formed and dissolved in a matter of months or weeks. These "virtual companies" raise accounting issues about how to account for the entity. See Steven H. Wallman, "The Future of Accounting and Disclosure in an Evolving World: The Need for Dramatic Change," *Accounting Horizons*, September 1995.

assets and liabilities would lose much of its significance. Labelling anything a fixed or long-term asset would be difficult to justify. Indeed, listing liabilities in priority of liquidation would be more reasonable.

The going concern assumption applies in most business situations. Only **where liquidation appears imminent is the assumption inapplicable**. In these cases, a total revaluation of assets and liabilities can provide information that closely approximates the entity's net realizable value. Accounting problems related to an enterprise in liquidation are presented in advanced accounting courses.

INTERNATIONAL INSIGHT

Due to their experiences with persistent inflation, several South American countries produce "constant currency" financial reports. Typically, a general price-level index is used to adjust for the effects of inflation.

Monetary Unit Assumption

The monetary unit assumption means that **money** is the common denominator of economic activity and provides an **appropriate basis for accounting measurement** and analysis. This assumption implies that the monetary unit is the most effective means of expressing to interested parties changes in capital and exchanges of goods and services. The monetary unit is **relevant, simple, universally available, understandable, and useful**. Applying this assumption depends on the even more basic assumption that quantitative data are useful in communicating economic information and in making rational economic decisions.

In Canada and the United States, accountants have chosen generally to ignore the phenomenon of **price-level change** (inflation and deflation) by assuming that the **unit of measure**—the dollar—remains reasonably **stable**. This assumption about the monetary unit has been used to justify adding 1970 dollars to 2001 dollars without any adjustment. Only if circumstances change dramatically (such as if Canada or the U.S. were to experience high inflation similar to that in many South American countries) would the AcSB and FASB consider "inflation accounting."

IAS NOTE

IAS 15 encourages but does not require certain disclosures regarding effects of changing prices.

Periodicity Assumption

The most accurate way to measure enterprise activity results is at the time of the enterprise's eventual liquidation. Business, government, investors, and various other user groups, however, cannot wait that long for such information. Users need to be apprised of **performance and economic status on a timely basis** so that they can evaluate and compare firms. Therefore, information must be reported periodically.

The periodicity (or time period) assumption implies that an enterprise's **economic activities can be divided into artificial time periods**. These time periods vary, but the most common are monthly, quarterly, and yearly.

The shorter the time period, the more difficult it becomes to determine the proper net income for the period. A month's results are usually less reliable than a quarter's results, and a quarter's results are likely less reliable than a year's results. Investors desire and demand that information be quickly processed and disseminated; yet the **more quickly the information is released, the more it is subject to error**. This phenomenon provides an interesting example of the **trade-off between relevance and reliability** in preparing financial data.

IAS NOTE

IAS 29 sets out certain requirements for entities reporting in a hyperinflationary economy.

This problem of defining the time period is becoming more serious because product cycles are shorter and products become obsolete more quickly. Many believe that, given technology advances, more **on-line, real-time financial information** needs to be provided to ensure that relevant information is available.

OBJECTIVE 7

Explain the application of the basic principles of accounting.

Basic Principles of Accounting

Four basic principles of accounting are used to record transactions: (1) **historical cost**, (2) **revenue recognition**, (3) **matching**, and (4) **full disclosure**.

INTERNATIONAL INSIGHT

In the European Community, accounting standards are set by means of directives. The Fourth Directive permits replacement value accounting for some fixed assets. The use of replacement value requires full disclosure of its impact on the financial statements.

Historical Cost Principle

GAAP requires that most assets and liabilities be accounted for and reported on the basis of acquisition price. This is often referred to as the historical cost principle.[14]

---

[14] *CICA Handbook*, Section 1000, par. .53.

How is cost defined? Does it include freight and insurance? Does it include the cost of installation? These questions will be addressed in Chapters 8 and 11. We normally think of cost as relating only to assets. Are liabilities accounted for on a cost basis? The answer is yes if we think of cost as "exchange price."

Sometimes it is not possible to determine cost, e.g., when items are donated. In cases such as that, an attempt is made to estimate the value. This becomes the cost.

Cost has an important advantage over other valuations: it is **reliable**. To illustrate the importance of this advantage, consider the problems that would arise if some other basis were used for keeping records. If **current selling price** were used, for instance, it would be difficult to establish a sales value for a given item without selling it. Every member of the accounting department might have a **different opinion regarding an asset's value**, and management might **desire** still another figure.

How often would it be necessary to establish sales value? All companies close their accounts at least annually, and some calculate their net income every month. These companies would find it necessary to place a sales value on every asset each time they wished to determine income—a laborious task that would result in a figure of **net income materially affected by opinion**. Similar objections have been levelled against current cost (replacement cost, present value of future cash flows) and any other basis of valuation except cost.

What about liabilities? Are they accounted for on a cost basis? Yes. If the term "cost" is changed to "**exchange price**," it applies to liabilities as well. Liabilities, such as bonds, notes, and accounts payable, are issued by a business enterprise in exchange for assets, or perhaps services, upon which an **agreed price** has usually been placed. This price, established by the exchange transaction, is the "cost" of the liability and provides the figure at which it should be recorded in the accounts and reported in financial statements.

Historical cost provides stakeholders with a **reliable**, **stable**, and **consistent benchmark** to **establish historical trends**. Stakeholders are concerned about the **subjectivity** and **potential volatility** in reported results of a model based on some type of current value. This must be balanced by the need for relevant information.

Certain industries use fair value in valuing their assets. Such industries include mutual funds, insurance, and pension fund industries. Companies in these industries tend to hold large amounts of investments—often publicly traded. Thus an objective measure of the value may be easily determined. Illustration 2-2 is an excerpt from the financial statements of a mutual fund company. The accounting policy governing investments is articulated. Note the various methods for determining market value.

Go to the Digital Tool for an Expanded Discussion on Present-Value Based-Measurements.

IAS NOTE

IAS 39 dictates that most financial instruments be carried at fair value.

Basis of determining market value of investments

Short-term instruments are valued at cost with accrued interest or discount earned included in interest receivable, except for the Short Term Canadian Income Fund for which securities are valued at a quotation by major Canadian dealers. Listed securities are valued at the closing sale price reported on that day by the principal securities exchange on which the issue is traded or, if no sale is reported, generally, the average of the bid and ask prices is used. Securities traded over-the-counter are priced at the average of the latest bid and ask prices quoted by major dealers in such securities. Unlisted securities are priced at their fair value as determined by the Manager.

ILLUSTRATION 2-2
Excerpt from the Notes to the Financial Statements for Altamira Mutual Fund

Illustration 2-3 identifies basic assets that are found on many balance sheets along with the basis for valuation. As noted in the illustration, the existing "mixed attribute" system permits the use of **historical cost, fair value** (via **lower of cost and market**), and other valuation bases. Note that the basis for valuation is tied to **management intent** with respect to the asset. Will the company sell it or collect it in the near term? Assets that will be turned over more quickly and that are often more liquid, tend to be valued using **current or market value** (fair value, NRV, net recoverable value). Although the historical cost principle continues to be the primary basis of valuation, recording and reporting of fair value information is increasing.[15]

---

[15] The AcSB and IASC are members of a Joint Working Group (JWG) set up to establish an internationally acceptable standard for accounting for financial instruments. The JWG is proposing using market or fair values for all financial instruments as long as the values are measurable. In the U.S., most financial instruments are presently valued at fair/market value.

ILLUSTRATION 2-3
Valuation of Assets and the
Historical Cost Principle

Asset	Valuation basis	Intent
Accounts receivable	NRV	To collect
Temporary Investments	LCM (a)	To liquidate
Inventories	LCM (b)	To sell and replace
Capital assets	HC or NBV (unless not recoverable from future cash flows)	To use in generating future cash flows
Long-term investments	HC unless decline in value other than temporary—then at market	To retain for longer term

(a) certain industries use full market valuation (i.e. mutual fund, insurance, pension)
(b) market may mean replacement cost or net realizable value

Revenue Recognition Principle

A crucial question for many enterprises is **when revenue should be recognized**. Revenue is generally recognized when **performance** is achieved (**earned**) and **measurability** and **collectibility** are **reasonably assured (realized/realizable)**.[16] This approach has often been referred to as the revenue recognition principle. Revenues are realized when products (goods or services), merchandise, or other assets are **exchanged for cash or claims to cash**. Revenues are realizable when assets received or held are **readily convertible** into cash or claims to cash. Assets are **readily convertible** when they are saleable or interchangeable in an active market at readily determinable prices without significant additional cost.

Revenues are considered earned when the entity has **substantially accomplished what it must do to be entitled to the benefits represented by the revenues—when the earnings process is substantially complete**. Generally, an **objective test**—confirmation by a sale to independent interests—is used to indicate the point at which revenue is recognized. Usually, only at the **date of sale** is there an **objective** and **verifiable** measure of revenue—the sales price. Any basis for revenue recognition short of actual sale opens the door to wide variations in practice. To give accounting reports uniform meaning, a rule of revenue recognition comparable to the cost rule for asset valuation is essential. Recognition at the time of sale provides a uniform and reasonable test.

This rule of thumb is reasonable when the earnings process is a discrete earnings process with one main or critical event. There are, however, exceptions to the rule, as shown in Illustration 2-4.

ILLUSTRATION 2-4
Timing of Revenue Recognition

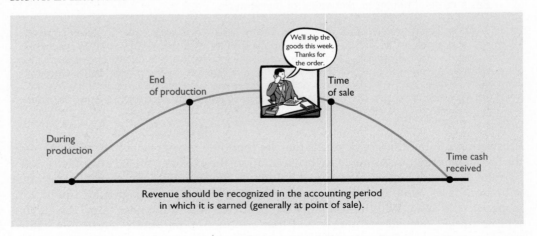

Revenue should be recognized in the accounting period in which it is earned (generally at point of sale).

During Production. **Recognition of revenue is allowed before the contract is completed in certain long-term construction contracts.** In this method, revenue is recognized periodically based on the percentage of the job completed instead of waiting until the entire job is finished. Although technically a transfer of ownership has not occurred, the earning process is considered a continuous earnings process as construction progresses esti-

---

[16] *CICA Handbook*, Section 1000, par. .47.

mates. Naturally, if it is not possible to obtain dependable cost and progress, then revenue recognition is delayed until the job is completed, as the revenues are not measurable.

End of Production. At times, **revenue might be recognized after the production cycle has ended but before the sale takes place**. This is the case where the selling price and amount are certain, as well as the amount. For instance, if products or other assets are saleable in an active market at readily determinable prices without significant additional cost, then revenue can be recognized at the completion of production. An example would be the mining of certain minerals for which, once the mineral is mined, a ready market at a standard price exists. The same holds true for some artificial price supports set by the government in establishing agricultural prices.

Receipt of Cash. **Receipt of cash is another basis for revenue recognition.** The cash basis approach is used only when it is impossible to establish the revenue figure at the time of sale because of collection uncertainty. One form of the cash basis is the instalment sales method where payment is required in periodic instalments over a long period of time. It is most commonly used in retail. Farm and home equipment and furnishings are typically sold by instalment. The instalment method is frequently justified on the basis that the risk of not collecting an account receivable is so great that the sale is not sufficient evidence for recognition to take place. In some instances, this reasoning may be valid. Generally, though, if a sale has been completed, it should be recognized; if bad debts are expected, they should be recorded as separate estimates.

Revenue, then, is recorded in the period when **realized or realizable** and **earned**. Normally, this is the **date of sale**. But circumstances may dictate revenue recognition **during production**, at the **end of production**, or upon the **receipt of cash**.

Matching Principle

In recognizing expenses, the approach followed is "let the expense follow the revenues." Expenses are recognized not when wages are paid, or when the work is performed, or when a product is produced, but when the work (service) or the product actually makes its contribution to revenue. Thus, **expense recognition is tied to revenue recognition**. This practice is referred to as the matching principle because it dictates that **efforts (expenses) be matched with accomplishment (revenues)** whenever reasonable and practicable.

For those costs for which it is difficult to adopt some type of rational association with revenue, some other approach must be developed. Often, a **"rational and systematic"** allocation policy is used that will approximate the matching principle. This type of expense recognition pattern involves **assumptions** about the **benefits** that are being received as well as the **cost associated with those benefits**. The cost of a long-lived asset, for example, must be allocated over all accounting periods during which the asset is used because the asset contributes to revenue generation throughout its useful life.

Some costs are charged to the current period as expenses (or losses) simply because there is no basis for capitalizing or deferring the cost. The transaction occurred in the **period** and benefits the period. Examples of these types of costs are officers' salaries and other administrative expenses.

Summarizing, we might say that costs are analysed to determine whether a relationship exists with revenue. Where this association holds, the costs are expensed and **matched against the revenue** in the period when the revenue is recognized. If no connection appears between costs and revenues, an **allocation of cost** on some systematic and rational basis might be appropriate. Where this method does not seem desirable, the cost may be **expensed immediately**.[17]

---

[17] Costs are generally classified into two groups: product costs and period costs. Product costs such as material, labour, and overhead attach to the product and are carried into future periods if the revenue from the product is recognized in subsequent periods. Period costs such as officers' salaries and other administrative expenses are charged off immediately, even though benefits associated with these costs occur in the future, because no direct relationship between cost and revenue can be determined.

The problem of expense recognition is as complex as that of revenue recognition. Consider the accounting for marketing costs related to **America Online (AOL)**, an interactive on-line consumer service company that provides its subscribers access to many electronic databases. AOL's largest expenditures are the costs of advertising and of free trials to attract subscribers. These promotions are expensive. Not too long ago, subscription acquisition costs totalled $363 million U.S. for AOL, of which only $126 million was charged to expense. The rest was recorded as an asset and amortized over two years. Conversely, **CompuServe**, a major competitor at the time, expensed these costs as incurred. Both companies believed they were matching costs to revenues appropriately. AOL has since changed its accounting and now expenses these costs as incurred.

The matching principle's conceptual validity has been a subject of debate. A major concern is that **matching permits certain costs to be deferred and treated as assets on the balance sheet when in fact these costs may not have future benefits**. If abused, this principle permits the balance sheet to become a "dumping ground" for unmatched costs. In addition, there appears to be **no objective definition** of "**systematic and rational**." For example, Hartwig, Inc. purchased an asset for $100,000 that will last five years. Various amortization methods (all considered systematic and rational) might be used to allocate this cost over the five-year period. However, it is difficult to develop objective criteria to be used in determining what portion of the asset cost should be written off each period.[18]

Full Disclosure Principle

In deciding what information to report, the general practice of providing information important enough to influence the judgement and decisions of an informed user is followed. Often referred to as the full disclosure principle, it recognizes that the nature and amount of information included in financial reports reflects a series of **judgemental trade-offs**. These trade-offs strive for (1) **sufficient detail** to disclose matters that make a difference to users, yet (2) **sufficient condensation** to make the information understandable, keeping in mind costs of preparing and using it. Information about financial position, income, cash flows, and investments can be found in one of three places: (1) within the **main body** of financial statements, (2) in the notes to those statements, or (3) as **supplementary information**.

The **financial statements** are a formalized, structured means of communicating financial information. To be recognized in the **main body** of financial statements, an item should meet the definition of a basic element, be **measurable** with **sufficient certainty**, and be relevant and reliable.

Disclosure is not a substitute for proper accounting.[19] As the SEC's chief accountant recently noted: Good disclosure does not cure bad accounting any more than an adjective or adverb can be used without—or in place of—a noun or verb. Thus, for example, cash basis accounting for cost of goods sold is misleading, even if accrual basis amounts were disclosed in the notes to the financial statements.

The notes to financial statements generally amplify or explain the items presented in the main body of the statements. If the information in the main body of the statements gives an incomplete picture of the enterprise's performance and position, additional information that is needed to complete the picture should be included in the notes. Information in the notes does not have to be quantifiable, nor does it need to qualify as an element. Notes can be partially or totally narrative. Examples of notes are: descriptions of the accounting policies and methods used in measuring the ele-

---

[18] Some would suggest even that procedure is nearly impossible, given that the revenue flow from any given asset is interrelated with the remaining asset structure of the enterprise. For example, see Arthur L. Thomas, "The Allocation Problem in Financial Accounting Theory," *Studies in Accounting Research No. 3*, (Evanston, Ill.: American Accounting Association, 1969), and "The Allocation Problem: Part Two," *Studies in Accounting Research No. 9*, (Sarasota, Fla.: American Accounting Association, 1974).

[19] According to *CICA Handbook*, Section 1000, par. .42, recognition means including of an item within one or more individual statements and does not mean disclosure in the notes to the financial statements.

ments reported in the statements; explanations of uncertainties and contingencies; and statistics and details too voluminous to include in the statements. The notes are not only helpful but essential to understanding the enterprise's performance and position.

Supplementary information may include details or amounts that present a different perspective from that adopted in the financial statements. It may be quantifiable information that is high in relevance but low in reliability, or information that is helpful but not essential. One example of supplementary information is the data and schedules provided by oil and gas companies: typically they provide information on proven reserves as well as the related discounted cash flows.

Supplementary information may also include management's explanation of the financial information and a discussion of its significance. For example, during the past decade many business combinations have produced innumerable conglomerate-type business organizations and financing arrangements that demand new and peculiar accounting and reporting practices and principles. In each of these situations, the same problem must be faced: making sure that enough information is presented to ensure that the **reasonably prudent investor** will not be misled.

A classic illustration of the problem of determining adequate disclosure guidelines is the recent question on what banks should disclose about loans made for highly leveraged transactions such as leveraged buyouts. Investors want to know the percentage of a bank's loans that are of this risky type. The problem is what do we mean by "leveraged"? As one regulator noted: "If it looks leveraged, it probably is leveraged, but most of us would be hard-pressed to come up with a definition." Is a loan to a company with a debt-to-equity ratio of 4 to 1 highly leveraged? Or is 8 to 1 or 10 to 1 high leverage? The problem is complicated because some highly leveraged companies have cash flows that cover interest payments; therefore, they are not as risky as they might appear. In short, providing the appropriate disclosure to help investors and regulators differentiate risky from safe is difficult.

The content, arrangement, and display of financial statements, along with other facets of full disclosure, are discussed in Chapters 4, 5, 24, and throughout the text.

Constraints

In providing information with the qualitative characteristics that make it useful, two overriding constraints must be considered: (1) the **cost-benefit relationship** and (2) **materiality**. Two other less dominant yet important constraints that are part of the reporting environment are **industry practices** and **conservatism**.

OBJECTIVE 8

Describe the impact that constraints have on reporting accounting information.

Cost-Benefit Relationship

Too often, users assume that information is a cost-free commodity. But preparers and providers of accounting information know that it is not. Therefore, the cost-benefit relationship must be considered: the costs of providing the information must be weighed against the benefits that can be derived from using the information. Standard-setting bodies and governmental agencies now use cost-benefit analysis before making their informational requirements final. In order to justify requiring a particular measurement or disclosure, the benefits perceived to be derived from it must exceed the costs perceived to be associated with it.

The difficulty in cost-benefit analysis is that the costs and especially the benefits are **not always evident or measurable**. The costs are of **several kinds**, including costs of collecting and processing, costs of disseminating, costs of auditing, costs of potential litigation, costs of disclosure to competitors, and costs of analysis and interpretation. Benefits accrue to preparers (in terms of greater management control and access to capital) and to users (in terms of allocation of resources, tax assessment, and rate regulation). But benefits are generally more difficult to quantify than costs.

Materiality

The constraint of materiality relates to an item's impact on a firm's overall financial operations. An item is material if its inclusion or omission would influence or change the judgement of a reasonable person.[20] It is immaterial and, therefore, irrelevant if it would have no impact on a decision-maker. In short, **it must make a difference** or it need not be disclosed. The point involved here is one of **relative size and importance**. If the amount involved is significant when compared with the other revenues and expenses, assets and liabilities, or net income of the entity, sound and acceptable standards should be followed. If the amount is so small that it is quite unimportant when compared with other items, applying of a particular standard may be considered of less importance.

It is difficult to provide firm guides in judging when a given item is or is not material because materiality varies both with relative amount and with relative importance. For example, the two sets of numbers presented below illustrate relative size.

ILLUSTRATION 2-5
Materiality Comparison

	Company A	Company B
Sales	$10,000,000	$100,000
Costs and expenses	$9,000,000	$90,000
Income from operations	$1,000,000	$10,000
Unusual gain	$20,000	$5,000

During the period in question, the revenues and expenses and, therefore, the net incomes of Company A and Company B have been proportional. Each has had an unusual gain. In looking at the abbreviated income figures for Company A, it does not appear significant whether the amount of the unusual gain is set out separately or merged with the regular operating income. It is only 2% of the net income and, if merged, would not seriously distort the net income figure. Company B has had an unusual gain of only $5,000, but it is relatively much more significant than the larger gain realized by A. For Company B, an item of $5,000 amounts to 100% of its net income. Obviously, the inclusion of such an item in ordinary operating income would affect the amount of that income materially. Thus we see the importance of an item's relative size in determining its materiality.

Companies and their auditors for the most part have adopted the general rule of thumb that anything above **5-10% of net income** is considered material. This is a fairly **simplistic and one-dimensional view of materiality**, which needs further examination. The **impact** of the items on other factors, for instance **key financial statement ratios** and **management compensation**, should also be considered—in short, any **sensitive number** on the financial statements. Chapter 1 discusses the concept of "earnings surprises" and how the market reacts positively and/or negatively to these surprises. Management is sensitive to this and therefore any items that contribute to or result in earnings surprises might also be considered material.

Both quantitative and qualitative factors must be considered in determining whether an item is material.[21] Qualitative factors might include illegal acts, failure to comply with regulations, or inadequate or inappropriate description of an accounting policy.

Materiality is a factor in a great many **internal** accounting decisions, too. The amount of classification required in a subsidiary expense ledger, the degree of accuracy required in prorating expenses among the departments of a business, and the extent to which adjustments should be made for accrued and deferred items are examples of judgements that should finally be determined on a basis of reasonableness and practicability, which is the materiality constraint sensibly applied. Only by the **exercise of good judgement and professional expertise** can reasonable and appropriate answers be found.

Industry Practices

Another practical consideration is industry practice. **The peculiar nature of some industries and business concerns sometimes requires departure from basic theory.**

INTERNATIONAL INSIGHT

In Japan, capital is also provided by very large banks. Assets are often undervalued and liabilities overvalued. These practices reduce the demand for dividends and protect creditors in event of a default.

[20] FASB Statement of Financial Accounting Concepts No. 2 (par. .132) sets forth the essence of materiality: "The omission or misstatement of an item in a financial report is material if, in the light of surrounding circumstances, the magnitude of the item is such that it is probable that the judgement of a reasonable person relying upon the report would have been changed or influenced by the inclusion or correction of the item." This same concept of materiality has been adopted by the CICA—see *CICA Handbook*, Section 1000, par. .17.

[21] *CICA Handbook*, Section 5130, par. .7.

In the public utility industry, noncurrent assets are reported first on the balance sheet to highlight the industry's capital-intensive nature. Agricultural crops are often reported at market value because it is costly to develop accurate cost figures on individual crops. Such variations from basic theory are not many, yet they do exist. Whenever we find what appears to be a violation of basic accounting theory, we should determine whether it is explained by some peculiar feature of the type of business involved before we criticize the procedures followed.

Conservatism

Few conventions in accounting are as misunderstood as the constraint of conservatism. Conservatism means **when in doubt, choose the solution that will be least likely to overstate assets and income**. Note that there is nothing in the conservatism convention urging that net assets or net income be understated. Unfortunately it has been interpreted by some to mean just that. All that conservatism does, properly applied, is provide a very reasonable guide in difficult situations: refrain from overstatement of net income and net assets. Examples of conservatism in accounting are the use of the lower of cost and market approach in valuing inventories and the rule that accrued net losses should be recognized on firm purchase commitments for goods for inventory. If the issue is in doubt, it is better to understate than overstate net income and net assets. Of course, if there is no doubt, there is no need to apply this constraint.

SUMMARY OF THE STRUCTURE

Illustration 2-6 presents the conceptual framework discussed in this chapter. It is similar to Illustration 2-1, except that it provides additional information for each level. We

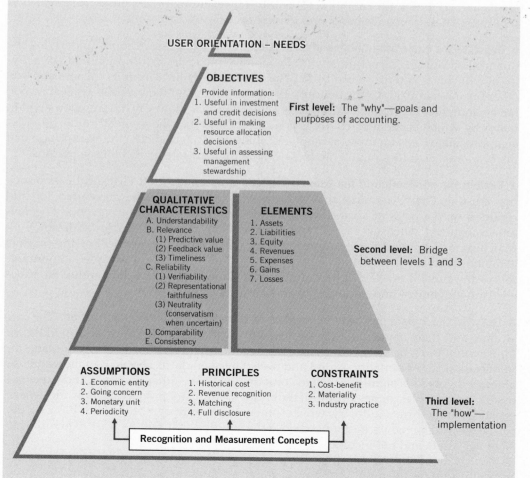

ILLUSTRATION 2-6
Conceptual Framework for Financial Reporting

cannot overemphasize the usefulness of this conceptual framework in helping to understand many of the problem areas that are examined in subsequent chapters.

SUMMARY OF LEARNING OBJECTIVES

1 Describe the usefulness of a conceptual framework. A conceptual framework is needed to (1) build on and relate to an established body of concepts and objectives, (2) provide a framework for solving new and emerging practical problems, (3) increase financial statement users' understanding of and confidence in financial reporting, and (4) enhance comparability among companies' financial statements.

2 Describe the main components of the conceptual framework for financial reporting. The first level deals with the objective of financial reporting. The second level includes the qualitative characteristics of useful information and elements of financial statements. The third level includes assumptions, principles, and constraints.

3 Understand the objective of financial reporting. The objective of financial reporting is to provide information that is useful to those making investment and credit decisions.

4 Identify the qualitative characteristics of accounting information. The overriding criterion by which accounting choices can be judged is decision usefulness; that is, providing information that is most useful for decision-making. Understandability, relevance, reliability, comparability, and consistency are the qualities that make accounting information useful for decision-making.

5 Define the basic elements of financial statements. The basic elements of financial statements are: (1) assets, (2) liabilities, (3) equity, (4) revenues, (5) expenses, (6) gains, and (7) losses. These seven elements are defined on page 32.

6 Describe the basic assumptions of accounting. Four basic assumptions underlying the financial accounting structure are: (1) Economic entity: the assumption that the activity of a business enterprise can be kept separate and distinct from its owners and any other business unit. (2) Going concern: the assumption that the business enterprise will have a long life. (3) Monetary unit: the assumption that money is the common denominator by which economic activity is conducted, and that the monetary unit provides an appropriate basis for measurement and analysis. (4) Periodicity: the assumption that the economic activities of an enterprise can be divided into artificial time periods.

7 Explain the application of the basic principles of accounting. (1) Historical cost principle: existing GAAP requires that most assets and liabilities be accounted for and reported on the basis of acquisition price. (2) Revenue recognition: revenue is generally recognized when (a) earned and (b) measurable and collectible (realizable). (3) Matching principle: expenses are recognized when the work (service) or the product actually makes its contribution to revenue. (4) Full disclosure principle: accountants follow the general practice of providing information that is important enough to influence the judgement and decisions of an informed user.

8 Describe the impact that constraints have on reporting accounting information. The constraints and their impact are: (1) Cost-benefit relationship: the costs of providing the information must be weighed against the benefits that can be derived from using the information. (2) Materiality: sound and acceptable standards should be followed if the amount involved is significant when compared with the other revenues and expenses, assets and liabilities, or net income of the entity. (3) Industry practices: follow the general practices in the firm's industry, which sometimes require departure from basic theory. (4) Conservatism: when in doubt, choose the solution that will be least likely to overstate net assets and net income.

BRIEF EXERCISES

BE2-1 Discuss whether the changes described in each of the cases below require recognition in the audit report as to consistency (assume that the amounts are material).

(a) After three years of calculating amortization under an accelerated method for income tax purposes and under the straight-line method for reporting purposes, the company adopted an accelerated method for reporting purposes.

(b) The company disposed of one of the two subsidiaries that had been included in its consolidated statements for prior years.

(c) The estimated remaining useful life of plant property was reduced because of obsolescence.

(d) The company is using an inventory valuation method that is different from the one used by other companies in its industry.

BE2-2 Identify which qualitative characteristic of accounting information is best described in each item below. (Do not use relevance and reliability.)

(a) The annual reports of Garbo Corp. are audited by public accountants.

(b) Klamoth Corp. and Kutenai, Inc. both use the FIFO cost flow assumption.

(c) Abbado Corp. has used straight-line amortization since it began operations.

(d) Augusta Corp. issues its quarterly reports immediately after each quarter ends.

BE2-3 For each item below, indicate to which category of elements of financial statements it belongs.

(a) Retained earnings	(e) Amortization	(i) Gain on sale of investment
(b) Sales	(f) Loss on sale of equipment	
(c) Goodwill	(g) Interest payable	(j) Issuance of common shares
(d) Inventory	(h) Dividends	

BE2-4 Identify which basic assumption of accounting is best described in each item below.

(a) The economic activities of Kapoor Corp. are divided into 12-month periods for the purpose of issuing annual reports.

(b) Brewer, Inc. does not adjust amounts in its financial statements for the effects of inflation.

(c) Ramsey Ltd. reports current and noncurrent classifications in its balance sheet.

(d) The economic activities of Bateau Corporation and its subsidiaries are merged for accounting and reporting purposes.

BE2-5 Identify which basic principle of accounting is best described in each item below.

(a) Ontario Corporation reports revenue in its income statement when it is earned instead of when the cash is collected.

(b) Nunavut Enterprise recognizes amortization expense for a machine over the five-year period during which that machine helps the company earn revenue.

(c) Lesfleurs, Inc. reports information about pending lawsuits in the notes to its financial statements.

(d) Springdale Farms reports land on its balance sheet at the amount paid to acquire it, even though the estimated fair market value is greater.

BE2-6 Which constraints on accounting information are illustrated by the items below?

(a) Zip's Farms, Inc. reports agricultural crops on its balance sheet at market value.

(b) Crimson Corporation does not accrue a contingent lawsuit gain of $650,000.

(c) Wildcat Ltd. does not disclose any information in the notes to the financial statements unless the value of the information to financial statement users exceeds the expense of gathering it.

(d) Xu Corporation expenses the cost of wastebaskets in the year they are acquired.

BE2-7 Presented below are four concepts discussed in this chapter.

(a) Periodicity assumption.

(b) Historical cost principle.

(c) Conservatism.

(d) Full disclosure principle.

Match these concepts to the following accounting practices. Each letter can be used only once.

1. _____ Preparing financial statements on a quarterly basis.
2. _____ Using the lower of cost or market method for inventory valuation.
3. _____ Recording equipment at its purchase price.
4. _____ Using notes and supplementary schedules in the financial statements.

BE2-8 Presented below are three different transactions related to materiality. Explain whether you would classify these transactions as material.

(a) Marcus Co. has reported a positive trend in earnings over the last three years. In the current year, it reduces its bad debt allowance to ensure another positive earnings year. The impact of this adjustment is equal to 3% of net income.

(b) Sosa Co. has an extraordinary gain of $3.1 million on the sale of plant assets and a $3.3 million loss on the sale of investments. It decides to net the gain and loss because the net effect is considered immaterial. Sosa Co.'s income for the current year was $10 million.

(c) Mohawk Co. expenses all capital equipment under $25,000 on the basis that it is immaterial. The company has followed this practice for a number of years.

BE2-9 If the going concern assumption is not made in accounting, what difference does it make in the amounts shown in the financial statements for the following items?

(a) Land.
(b) Unamortized bond premium.
(c) Amortization expense on equipment.
(d) Merchandise inventory.
(e) Prepaid insurance.

BE2-10 What concept(s) from the conceptual framework does Accra Limited use in each of the following situations?

(a) Accra uses the lower of cost or market basis to value inventories.
(b) Accra was involved in litigation with Kinshasa Ltd. over a product malfunction. This litigation is disclosed in the financial statements.
(c) Accra allocates the cost of its depreciable assets over the life it expects to receive revenue from these assets.
(d) Accra records the purchase of a new IBM PC at its cash equivalent price.

BE2-11 Explain how you would decide whether to record each of the following expenditures as an asset or an expense. Assume all items are material.

(a) Legal fees paid in connection with the purchase of land are $1,500.
(b) Bratt, Inc. paves the driveway leading to the office building at a cost of $21,000.
(c) A meat market purchases a meat-grinding machine at a cost of $345.
(d) On June 30, Alan and Chung, medical doctors, pay six months' office rent to cover the month of June and the next five months.
(e) Taylor's Hardware Company pays $9,000 in wages to labourers for construction on a building to be used in the business.
(f) Kwan's Florists pays wages of $2,100 for November to an employee who serves as driver of its delivery truck.

EXERCISES

E2-1 (Qualitative Characteristics) The conceptual framework identifies the qualitative characteristics that make accounting information useful. Presented below are a number of questions related to these qualitative characteristics and underlying constraints.

1. What is the quality of information that enables users to confirm or correct prior expectations?
2. Identify the two overall or pervasive constraints.
3. The SEC chairman at one time noted, "if it becomes accepted or expected that accounting principles are determined or modified in order to secure purposes other than economic measurement, we assume a grave risk that confidence in the credibility of our financial information system will be undermined." Which qualitative characteristic of accounting information should ensure that such a situation will not occur? (Do not use reliability.)
4. Owens Corp. switches from weighted average cost to FIFO over a two-year period. Which qualitative characteristic of accounting information is not followed?

5. Assume that the profession permits the financial services industry to defer losses on investments it sells, because immediate recognition of the loss may have adverse economic consequences on the industry. Which qualitative characteristic of accounting information is not followed? (Do not use relevance or reliability.)

6. What are the qualities that make accounting information useful for decision-making?

7. Chapman, Inc. does not issue its first-quarter report until after the second quarter's results are reported. Which qualitative characteristic of accounting is not followed? (Do not use relevance.)

8. Predictive value is an ingredient of which of the qualitative characteristics of useful information?

9. Victoria, Inc. is the only company in its industry to depreciate its plant assets on a straight-line basis. Which qualitative characteristic of accounting information may not be followed? (Do not use industry practices.)

10. Joliet Company has attempted to determine the replacement cost of its inventory. Three different appraisers arrive at substantially different amounts for this value. The president, nevertheless, decides to report the middle value for external reporting purposes. Which qualitative characteristic of information is lacking in this data? (Do not use reliability or representational faithfulness.)

E2-2 **(Qualitative Characteristics)**   The qualitative characteristics that make accounting information useful for decision-making purposes are as follows:

Relevance	Timeliness	Representational faithfulness
Reliability	Verifiability	Comparability
Predictive value	Neutrality	Consistency
Feedback value		Conservatism

Instructions

Identify the appropriate qualitative characteristic(s) to be used given the information provided below.

1. Qualitative characteristic being employed when companies in the same industry are using the same accounting principles.
2. Quality of information that confirms users' earlier expectations.
3. Imperative for providing comparisons of a firm from period to period.
4. Ignores the economic consequences of a standard or rule.
5. Requires a high degree of consensus among individuals on a given measurement.
6. Predictive value is an ingredient of this primary quality of information.
7. Neutrality is an ingredient of this primary quality of accounting information.
8. Two primary qualities that make accounting information useful for decision-making purposes.
9. Issuance of interim reports is an example of what primary ingredient of relevance?

E2-3   **(Elements of Financial Statements)**   Seven interrelated elements that are most directly related to measuring the performance and financial status of an enterprise are provided below.

Assets	Expenses	Liabilities
Gains	Equity	Revenues
Losses		

Instructions

Identify the element or elements associated with the 10 items below:

1. Arises from peripheral or incidental transactions.
2. Obligation to transfer resources arising from past transaction.
3. Increases ownership interest.
4. Declares and pays cash dividends to owners.
5. Items characterized by service potential or future economic benefit.
6. Decreases assets during period for the payment of taxes.
7. Arises from income generating activities that constitute the entity's ongoing major or central operations.
8. Residual interest in the enterprise's assets after deducting its liabilities.
9. Increases assets during a period through sale of product.
10. Decreases assets during the period by purchasing the company's own stock.

E2-4   (Assumptions, Principles, and Constraints) Presented below are the assumptions, characteristics, principles, and constraints used in this chapter.

(a) Economic entity assumption	**(e)** Historical cost principle	**(i)** Materiality
(b) Going concern assumption	**(f)** Matching principle	**(j)** Industry practices
(c) Monetary unit assumption	**(g)** Full disclosure principle	**(k)** Revenue Recognition
(d) Periodicity assumption	**(h)** Cost-benefit relationship	

Instructions

Identify by letter the accounting assumption, principle, or constraint that describes each situation below. Do not use a letter more than once.

1. Allocates expenses to revenues in the proper period.
2. Indicates that market value changes subsequent to purchase are not recorded in the accounts. (Do not use revenue recognition principle.)
3. Ensures that all relevant financial information is reported.
4. Rationale why plant assets are not reported at liquidation value. (Do not use historical cost principle.)
5. Anticipates all losses, but reports no gains.
6. Indicates that personal and business record keeping should be separately maintained.
7. Separates financial information into time periods for reporting purposes.
8. Permits the use of market value valuation in certain specific situations.
9. Requires that information significant enough to affect the decision of reasonably informed users should be disclosed. (Do not use full disclosure principle.)
10. Assumes that the dollar is the "measuring stick" used to report on financial performance.

E2-5 (Assumptions, Principles, and Constraints) Presented below are a number of operational guidelines and practices that have developed over time.

1. Price-level changes are not recognized in the accounting records.
2. Lower of cost and market is used to value inventories.
3. Financial information is presented so that reasonably prudent investors will not be misled.
4. Intangibles are capitalized and amortized over periods benefited.
5. Repair tools are expensed when purchased.
6. Brokerage firms use market value for purposes of valuation of all marketable securities.
7. Each enterprise is kept as a unit distinct from its owner or owners.
8. All significant post-balance sheet events are reported.
9. Revenue is recorded at point of sale.
10. All important aspects of bond indentures are presented in financial statements.
11. Rationale for accrual accounting is stated.
12. The use of consolidated statements is justified.
13. Reporting must be done at defined time intervals.
14. An allowance for doubtful accounts is established.
15. Goodwill is recorded only at time of purchase.
16. No profits are anticipated and all possible losses are recognized.
17. A company charges its sales commission costs to expense.

Instructions

Select the assumption, principle, or constraint that most appropriately justifies these procedures and practices. (Do not use qualitative characteristics.)

E2-6 (Assumptions, Principles, and Constraints) A number of operational guidelines used by accountants are described below.

1. The treasurer of Gretzky Co. wishes to prepare financial statements only during downturns in its wine production, which occur periodically when the rhubarb crop fails. He states that it is at such times that the statements could be most easily prepared. In no event would more than 30 months pass without statements being prepared.
2. The Regina Power & Light Company has purchased a large amount of property, plant, and equipment over a number of years. It has decided that because the general price level has changed materially over the years, it will issue only price-level adjusted financial statements.
3. Smith Manufacturing Co. decided to manufacture its own widgets because it would be cheaper than buying them from an outside supplier. In an attempt to make its statements more comparable with those of its competitors, Smith charged its inventory account for what it felt the widgets would have cost if they had been purchased from an outside supplier. (Do not use the revenue recognition principle.)
4. Flanagan's Discount Centres buys its merchandise by the truck and train-carload. Flanagan does not defer any transportation costs in computing the cost of its ending inventory. Such costs, although varying from period to period, are always material in amount.
5. Grab & Run, Inc., a fast-food company, sells franchises for $100,000, accepting a $5,000 down payment and a 50-year note for the remainder. Grab & Run promises for three years to assist in site selection, building, and management training. Grab & Run records the $100,000 franchise fee as revenue in the period in which the contract is signed.

6. Conway Company "faces possible expropriation (i.e., takeover) of foreign facilities and possible losses on sums owed by various customers on the verge of bankruptcy." The company president has decided that these possibilities should not be noted on the financial statements because Conway still hopes that these events will not take place. *Full Disclosure*

7. Singletary, manager of College Bookstore, Inc., bought a computer for his own use. He paid for the computer by writing a cheque on the bookstore chequing account and charged the "Office Equipment" account. *Economic Entity.*

8. Enis, Inc. recently completed a new 60-storey office building that houses its home offices and many other tenants. All the office equipment for the building that had a per item or per unit cost of $1,000 or less was expensed as immaterial, even though the office equipment has an average life of 10 years. The total cost of such office equipment was approximately $26 million. (Do not use the matching principle.)

9. Brokers and other dealers in securities generally value investments at market or fair value for financial reporting purposes. The brokerage firm of James and Williams, Inc. continues to value its trading and investment accounts at cost or market, whichever is lower. *Industry practice*

10. A large lawsuit has been filed against Big Cat Corp. by Perry Co. Big Cat has recorded a loss and related estimated liability equal to the maximum possible amount it feels it might lose. Big Cat is confident, however, that either it will win the suit or it will owe a much smaller amount. *Conservatism Too conservative*

Instructions

For each of the foregoing, list the assumption, principle, or constraint that has been violated. List only one term for each case.

E2-7 (Full Disclosure Principle) Presented below are a number of facts related to Kelly, Inc. Assume that no mention of these facts was made in the financial statements and the related notes.

(a) The company decided that, for the sake of conciseness, only net income should be reported on the income statement. Details as to revenues, cost of goods sold, and expenses were omitted.

(b) Equipment purchases of $170,000 were partly financed during the year through the issuance of a $110,000 notes payable. The company offset the equipment against the notes payable and reported plant assets at $60,000.

(c) During the year, an assistant controller for the company embezzled $15,000. Kelly's net income for the year was $2,300,000. Neither the assistant controller nor the money have been found.

(d) Kelly has reported its ending inventory at $2,100,000 in the financial statements. No other information related to inventories is presented in the financial statements and related notes.

(e) The company changed its method of amortizing equipment from the double-declining balance to the straight-line method. No mention of this change was made in the financial statements.

Instructions

Assume that you are the auditor of Kelly, Inc. and that you have been asked to explain the appropriate accounting and related disclosure necessary for each of these items.

E2-8 (Accounting Principles-Comprehensive) Presented below are a number of business transactions that occurred during the current year for Heffernen Inc.

(a) The president of Heffernen Inc. used his expense account to purchase a new Camaro solely for personal use. The following journal entry was made:

Miscellaneous Expense	29,000	
Cash		29,000

Economic Entity
Withdrawals, Miscellaneous Expense

(b) Merchandise inventory that cost $620,000 is reported on the balance sheet at $690,000, the expected selling price less estimated selling costs. The following entry was made to record this increase in value:

Merchandise Inventory	70,000	
Income		70,000

Historical Cost
Revenue Recognition
Matching Principle

(c) The company is being sued for $500,000 by a customer who claims damages for personal injury apparently caused by a defective product. Company lawyers feel extremely confident that the company will have no liability for damages resulting from the situation. Nevertheless, the company decides to make the following entry:

Loss from Lawsuit	500,000	
Liability for Lawsuit		500,000

Conservatism

(d) Because the general level of prices increased during the current year, Heffernen Inc. determined that there was a $16,000 understatement of amortization expense on its equipment and decided to record it in its accounts. The following entry was made:

Amortization Expense	16,000	
Accumulated Amortization		16,000

(e) Heffernen Inc. has been concerned about whether intangible assets could generate cash in case of liquidation. As a consequence, goodwill arising from a purchase transaction during the current year and recorded at $800,000 was written off as follows:

Matching Principle

Retained Earnings	800,000	
Goodwill		800,000

(f) Because of a "fire sale," equipment obviously worth $200,000 was acquired at a cost of $155,000. The following entry was made:

Historical Cost

Equipment	~~200,000~~ 155,000	
Cash		155,000
~~Income~~		~~45,000~~

Instructions

In each of the situations above, discuss the appropriateness of the journal entries in terms of generally accepted accounting principles.

E2-9 (Accounting Principles-Comprehensive) Presented below is information related to Brooks, Inc.

(a) Amortization expense on the building for the year was $60,000. Because the building was increasing in value during the year, the controller decided to charge the amortization expense to retained earnings instead of to net income. The following entry is recorded.

Matching Principle

Retained Earnings	60,000	
Accumulated Amortization – Buildings		60,000

(b) Materials were purchased on January 1, 2001, for $120,000 and this amount was entered in the Materials account. On December 31, 2001, the materials would have cost $141,000, so the following entry is made:

Historical Cost

Inventory	21,000	
Gain on Inventories		21,000

Revenue Recognition

(c) During the year, the company sold certain equipment for $285,000, recognizing a gain of $69,000. Because the controller believed that new equipment would be needed in the near future, the controller decided to defer the gain and amortize it over the life of any new equipment purchased.

(d) An order for $61,500 has been received from a customer for products on hand. This order was shipped on January 9, 2002. The company made the following entry in 2001.

Accounts Receivable	61,500	
Sales		61,500

Instructions

Comment on the appropriateness of the accounting procedures followed by Brooks, Inc.

CONCEPTUAL CASES

C2-1 Roger Chang has some questions regarding the theoretical framework in which standards are set. He knows that the AcSB has attempted to develop a conceptual framework for accounting theory formulation. Yet, Roger's supervisors have indicated that these theoretical frameworks have little value in the practical sense (i.e., in the real world). Roger did notice that accounting standards seem to be established after the fact rather than before. He thought this indicated a lack of theory structure but never really questioned the process at school because he was too busy doing the homework.

Roger feels that some of his anxiety about accounting theory and accounting semantics could be alleviated by identifying the basic concepts and definitions accepted by the profession and considering them in light of his current work. By doing this, he hopes to develop an appropriate connection between theory and practice.

Instructions

Help Roger recognize the purpose of and benefit of a conceptual framework.

C2-2 Gordon and Medford are discussing various aspects of the CICA Handbook, Section 1000-Financial Statement Concepts. Gordon indicates that this pronouncement provides little, if any, guidance to the practising professional in resolving accounting controversies. He believes that the statement provides such broad guidelines that it would be impossible to apply the objectives to present-day reporting problems. Medford concedes this point but indicates that objectives are still needed to provide a starting point in helping to improve financial reporting.

Instructions

Discuss.

C2-3 Accounting information provides useful information about business transactions and events. Those who provide and use financial reports must often select and evaluate accounting alternatives. The conceptual framework developed in this chapter examines the characteristics of accounting information that make it useful for decision-making. It also points out that various limitations inherent in the measurement and reporting process may necessitate trade-offs or sacrifices among the characteristics of useful information.

Instructions

(a) For each of the following pairs of information characteristics, give an example of a situation in which one of the characteristics may be sacrificed in return for a gain in the other:

    (1) Relevance and reliability.   (3) Comparability and consistency.

    (2) Relevance and consistency.   (4) Relevance and understandability.

(b) What criterion should be used to evaluate trade-offs between information characteristics?

C2-4 You are engaged to review the accounting records of Roenick Corporation prior to the closing of the revenue and expense accounts as of December 31, the end of the current fiscal year. The following information comes to your attention.

1. During the current year, Roenick Corporation changed its policy in regard to expensing purchases of small tools. In the past, these purchases had always been expensed because they amounted to less than 2% of net income, but the president has decided that capitalization and subsequent amortization should now be followed. It is expected that purchases of small tools will not fluctuate greatly from year to year.
2. Roenick Corporation constructed a warehouse at a cost of $1,000,000. The company had been amortizing the asset on a straight-line basis over 10 years. In the current year, the controller doubled amortization expense because the warehouse replacement cost had increased significantly.
3. When the balance sheet was prepared, detailed information as to the amount of cash on deposit in each of several banks was omitted. Only the total amount of cash under a caption "Cash in banks" was presented.
4. On July 15 of the current year, Roenick Corporation purchased an undeveloped tract of land at a cost of $320,000. The company spent $80,000 in subdividing the land and getting it ready for sale. A property appraisal at the end of the year indicated that the land was now worth $500,000. Although none of the lots were sold, the company recognized revenue of $180,000, less related expenses of $80,000, for a net income on the project of $100,000.
5. For a number of years the company used the FIFO method for inventory valuation purposes. During the current year, the president noted that all the other companies in the industry had switched to the LIFO method. The company decided not to switch to LIFO because net income would decrease $830,000.

Instructions

State whether or not you agree with the decisions made by Roenick Corporation. Support your answers with reference, whenever possible, to the generally accepted principles, assumptions, and constraints applicable in the circumstances.

C2-5 After presenting your report on the examination of the financial statements to the board of directors of Bones Publishing Company, one of the new directors expresses surprise that the income statement assumes that an equal proportion of the revenue is earned with the publication of every issue of the company's magazine. She feels that the "critical event" in the process of earning revenue in the magazine business is the cash sale of the subscription. She says that she does not understand why most of the revenue cannot be "recognized" in the period of the sale.

Instructions

Discuss the propriety of timing the recognition of revenue in Bones Publishing Company's account with:
1. The cash sale of the magazine subscription.
2. The publication of the magazine every month.
3. Both events, by recognizing a portion of the revenue with cash sale of the magazine subscription and a portion of the revenue with the publication of the magazine every month.

C2-6 On June 5, 2001, McCoy Corporation signed a contract with Sandov Associates under which Sandov agreed (1) to construct an office building on land owned by McCoy, (2) to accept responsibility for procuring financing for the project and finding tenants, and (3) to manage the property for 35 years. The annual net income from the project, after debt service, was to be divided equally between McCoy Corporation and Sandov Associates. Sandov was to accept its share of future net income as full payment for its services in construction, obtaining finances and tenants, and project management.

By May 31, 2002, the project was nearly completed and tenants had signed leases to occupy 90% of the available space at annual rentals aggregating $4,000,000. It is estimated that, after operating expenses and debt service, the annual net income will amount to $1,500,000. The management of Sandov Associates believed that (a) the economic benefit derived from the contract with McCoy should be reflected on its financial statements for the fiscal year ended May 31, 2002, and directed that revenue be accrued in an amount equal to the commercial value of the services Sandor had rendered during the year, (b) this amount be carried in contracts receivable, and (c) all related expenditures be charged against the revenue.

Instructions

(a) Explain the main difference between the economic concept of business income as reflected by Sandov's management and the measurement of income under generally accepted accounting principles.

(b) Discuss the factors to be considered in determining when revenue should be recognized for the purpose of accounting measurement of periodic income.

(c) Is the belief of Sandov's management in accordance with generally accepted accounting principles for the measurement of revenue and expense for the year ended May 31, 2002? Support your opinion by discussing the application to this case of the factors to be considered for asset measurement and revenue and expense recognition.

(AICPA adapted)

C2-7 An accountant must be familiar with the concepts involved in determining earnings of a business entity. The amount of earnings reported for a business entity depends on the proper recognition, in general, of revenue and expense for a given time period. In some situations, costs are recognized as expenses at the time of product sale; in other situations, guidelines have been developed for recognizing costs as expenses or losses by other criteria.

Instructions

(a) Explain the rationale for recognizing costs as expenses at the time of product sale.

(b) What is the rationale underlying the appropriateness of treating costs as expenses of a period instead of assigning the costs to an asset? Explain.

(c) In what general circumstances would it be appropriate to treat a cost as an asset instead of as an expense? Explain.

(d) Some expenses are assigned to specific accounting periods on the basis of systematic and rational allocation of asset cost. Explain the underlying rationale for recognizing expenses on the basis of systematic and rational allocation of asset cost.

(e) Identify the conditions in which it would be appropriate to treat a cost as a loss.

(AICPA adapted)

C2-8 Accountants try to prepare income statements that are as accurate as possible. A basic requirement in preparing accurate income statements is to match costs against revenues properly. Proper matching of costs against revenues requires that costs resulting from typical business operations be recognized in the period in which they expired.

Instructions

(a) List three criteria that can be used to determine whether such costs should appear as charges in the income statement for the current period.

(b) As generally presented in financial statements, the following items or procedures have been criticized as improperly matching costs with revenues. Briefly discuss each item from the viewpoint of matching costs with revenues and suggest corrective or alternative means of presenting the financial information.

1. Receiving and handling costs.
2. Valuation of inventories at the lower of cost and market.
3. Cash discounts on purchases.

C2-9 Carl Schneider sells and erects shell houses, that is, frame structures that are completely finished on the outside but are unfinished on the inside except for flooring, partition studding, and ceiling joists. Shell houses are sold chiefly to customers who are handy with tools and who have time to do the interior wiring, plumbing, wall completion and finishing, and other work necessary to make the shell houses liveable dwellings.

Schneider buys shell houses from a manufacturer in unassembled packages consisting of all lumber, roofing, doors, windows, and similar materials necessary to complete a shell house. Upon commencing operations in a new area, Schneider buys or leases land as a site for its local warehouse, field office, and display houses. Sample display houses are erected at a total cost of $20,000 to $29,000 including the cost of the unassembled packages. The chief cost of the display houses is the unassembled packages, inasmuch as erection is a short, low-cost operation. Old sample models are torn down or altered into new models every three to seven years. Sample display houses have little salvage value because dismantling and moving costs amount to nearly as much as the cost of an unassembled package.

Instructions

(a) A choice must be made between (1) expensing the costs of sample display houses in the periods in which the expenditure is made and (2) spreading the costs over more than one period. Discuss the advantages of each method.

(b) Would it be preferable to amortize the cost of display houses on the basis of (1) the passage of time or (2) the number of shell houses sold? Explain.

(AICPA adapted)

C2-10 Recently, your Uncle Waldo, who knows that you always have your eye out for a profitable investment, has discussed the possibility of you purchasing some corporate bonds. He suggests that you may wish to get in on the "ground floor" of this deal. The bonds being issued by the Cricket Corp. are 10-year debentures, which promise a 40% rate of return. Cricket manufactures novelty/party items.

You have told Waldo that, unless you can take a look at Cricket's financial statements, you would not feel comfortable about such an investment. Knowing that this is the chance of a lifetime, Uncle Waldo has procured a copy of Cricket's most recent, unaudited financial statements which are a year old. These statements were prepared by Mrs. John Cricket. You peruse these statements, and they are quite impressive. The balance sheet showed a debt-to-equity ratio of .10 and, for the year shown, the company reported net income of $2,424,240.

The financial statements are not shown in comparison with amounts from other years. In addition, no significant note disclosures about inventory valuation, amortization methods, loan agreements, etc. are available.

Instructions

Write a letter to Uncle Waldo explaining why it would be unwise to base an investment decision on the financial statements, which he has provided to you. Be sure to explain why these financial statements are neither relevant nor reliable.

Using Your Judgement

FINANCIAL REPORTING PROBLEM: CANADIAN TIRE CORPORATION LIMITED

The financial statements of **Canadian Tire Corporation Limited** are presented in Appendix 5B.

Refer to these financial statements and the accompanying notes to answer the following questions.

Instructions

(a) Using the notes to the consolidated financial statements, determine **Canadian Tire**'s revenue recognition policies. Comment on whether **Canadian Tire** uses a conservative method for reporting revenue in this area.

(b) Give two examples of where historical cost information is reported on **Canadian Tire**'s financial statements and related notes. Give two examples of the use of fair value information reported in either the financial statements or related notes.

(c) How can we determine that the accounting principles used by **Canadian Tire** are prepared on a basis consistent with those of last year?

FINANCIAL STATEMENT ANALYSIS CASE

Weyerhaeuser Company

Presented below is a statement that appeared about **Weyerhaeuser Company** in a financial magazine.

The land and timber holdings are now carried on the company's books at a mere $422 million U.S. The value of the timber alone is variously estimated at $3 billion to $7 billion and is rising all the time. "The understatement of the company is pretty severe," conceded Charles W. Bingham, a senior vice-president. Adds Robert L. Schuyler, another senior vice-president: "We have a whole stream of profit nobody sees and there is no way to show it on our books."

Instructions

(a) What does Schuyler mean when he says that "we have a whole stream of profit nobody sees and there is no way to show it on our books"?

(b) If the understatement of the company's assets is severe, why does accounting not report this information?

COMPARATIVE ANALYSIS CASE

Abitibi-Consolidated Inc. versus Domtar Inc.

Instructions

Go to the Digital Tool, and use information found there to answer the following questions related to **Abitibi-Consolidated Inc.** and **Domtar Inc.** for the year ended December 31, 1999.

(a) What are the primary lines of business of these two companies as shown in their notes to the financial statements?

(b) Which company has the dominant position in paper product sales? Explain how you used information in the financial statements to conclude this.

(c) What percentage is inventory as compared with total assets? How are inventories for these two companies valued? Which cost allocation method is used to report inventory? How, if at all, does the accounting for inventories affect comparability between the two companies?

(d) Which company had a significant change during 1999, which affected the consistency of the financial results as expressed in the previously issued 1998 financial statements? What was this change?

RESEARCH CASES

Case 1   Retrieval of Information on Public Company

There are several commonly available indexes/reference products that enable individuals to locate articles previously included in numerous business publications and periodicals. Articles can generally be searched by company or by subject matter. Several common indexes/reference sources are *Canadian Business and Current Affairs* (CBCA Fulltext Business), *Investex Plus*, *The Wall Street Journal Index*, *Business Abstracts* (formerly the *Business Periodical Index*), and *ABI/Inform*.

Instructions

Use one of these resources to find an article about a company in which you are interested. Read the article and answer the following questions. (Note: Your library may have hard copy or CD-ROM versions of these sources or they may be available through your library electronic database.)

(a) What is the article about?

(b) What company-specific information is included in the article?

(c) Identify any accounting-related issues discussed in the article.

Case 2   Concepts and Quantitative Guidelines

The textbook indicates that it is "difficult to provide firm guides in judging when a given item is or is not material."

Instructions

FASB Statement of Financial Accounting Concepts No. 2 identifies a number of examples in which specific quantitative guidelines are provided to firms. Identify two of these examples. The CICA also released a Research Study entitled "Materiality: the concept and its application in auditing" (1985) as well as a Draft Guideline entitled "Applying materiality and audit risk concepts in conducting an audit" (2001). Are there any quantitative guidelines provided? Do you think that materiality guidelines should be quantified? Why or why not?

ETHICS CASE

Hinckley Nuclear Power Plant will be "mothballed" at the end of its useful life (approximately 20 years) at great expense. The matching principle requires that expenses be matched to revenue. Accountants Jana Kingston and Pete Henning argue whether it is better to allocate the expense of mothballing over the next 20 years or ignore it until mothballing occurs.

Instructions

Answer the following questions.

(a) What stakeholders should be considered?

(b) What ethical issue, if any, underlies the dispute?

(c) What alternatives should be considered?

(d) Assess the consequences of the alternatives.

(e) What decision would you recommend?

The Accounting Information System

LEARNING OBJECTIVES

....

After studying this chapter, you should be able to:

1. Understand basic accounting terminology.
2. Explain double-entry rules.
3. Identify steps in the accounting cycle.
4. Record transactions in journals, post to ledger accounts, and prepare a trial balance.
5. Explain the reasons for preparing adjusting entries.
6. Prepare closing entries.
7. Explain how inventory accounts are adjusted at year-end.
8. Prepare a 10-column work sheet.

Preview of Chapter 3

A reliable information system is a necessity for all companies. The purpose of this chapter is to explain and illustrate the features of an accounting information system. The content and organization of this chapter are as follows:

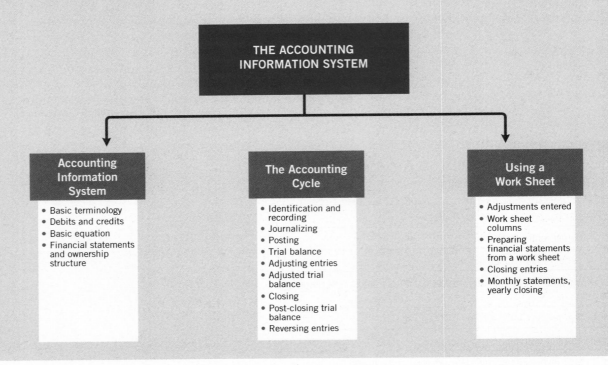

ACCOUNTING INFORMATION SYSTEM

The system of collecting and processing transaction data and disseminating financial information to interested parties is known as the accounting information system. Accounting information systems **vary widely** from one business to another. Factors that shape these systems are the **nature of the business** and the **transactions in which it engages**, the firm's **size**, the **volume of data** to be handled, and the **information demands** that management and others place on the system.

A good accounting information system helps management answer such questions as:

How much and what kind of debt is outstanding?

Were our sales higher this period than last?

What assets do we have?

What were our cash inflows and outflows?

Did we make a profit last period?

Are any of our product lines or divisions operating at a loss?

Can we safely increase our dividends to shareholders?

Is our rate of return on net assets increasing?

Many other questions can be answered when there is an **efficient and effective accounting system** to provide the data. A well-devised accounting information system is beneficial for every business enterprise.

Basic Terminology

Financial accounting rests on a set of concepts (discussed in Chapters 1 and 2) for identifying, recording, classifying, and interpreting transactions and other events relating to enterprises. It is important to understand the **basic terminology** employed in **collecting accounting data**.

OBJECTIVE 1

Understand basic accounting terminology.

BASIC TERMINOLOGY

Event. A happening of consequence. An event generally is the source or cause of changes in assets, liabilities, and equity. Events may be external or internal.

Transaction. An **external event** involving a transfer or exchange between two or more entities or parties.

Account. A systematic arrangement that accumulates transactions and other events. A separate account is kept for each asset, liability, revenue, expense, and for capital (owners' equity).

Permanent and temporary accounts. Permanent (real) accounts are asset, liability, and equity accounts; they appear on the balance sheet. Temporary (nominal) accounts are revenue, expense, and dividend accounts; except for dividends, they appear on the income statement. Temporary accounts are periodically closed; permanent accounts are left open.

Ledger.[1] The book (or electronic database) containing the accounts. Each account usually has a separate page. A **general ledger** is a collection of all the asset, liability, owners' equity, revenue, and expense accounts. A **subsidiary ledger** contains the details related to a given general ledger account.

Journal.[1] The book of original entry where transactions and selected other events are initially recorded. Various amounts are transferred to the ledger from the book of original entry—the journal.

Posting. The process of transferring the essential facts and figures from the book of original entry to the ledger accounts.

Trial balance. A list of all open accounts in the ledger and their balances. A trial balance taken immediately after all adjustments have been posted is called an adjusted trial balance. A trial balance taken immediately after closing entries have been posted is designated as a post-closing or after-closing trial balance. A trial balance may be prepared at any time.

Adjusting entries. Entries made at the end of an accounting period to bring all accounts up to date on an accrual accounting basis so that correct financial statements can be prepared.

Financial statements. Statements that reflect the accounting data's collection, tabulation, and final summarization. Four financial statements are involved: (1) the balance sheet, which shows the enterprise's financial condition at the end of a period, (2) the income statement, which measures the results of operations during the period, (3) the statement of cash flows, which report the cash provided and used by operating, investing, and financing activities during the period, and (4) the statement of retained earnings, which reconciles the balance of the retained earnings account from the beginning to the end of the period.

Closing entries. The formal process by which all temporary accounts are reduced to zero and the net income or net loss is determined and transferred to an owners' equity account, also known as "closing the ledger," "closing the books," or merely "closing."

---

[1] Most companies use accounting software systems instead of manual systems. The software allows the data to be entered into a database and then subsequently, various reports can be generated such as journals, trial balance, ledgers and financial statements.

Debits and Credits

OBJECTIVE 2

Explain double-entry rules.

The terms **debit** and **credit** refer to left and right sides of a general ledger account, respectively. They are commonly abbreviated as Dr. for debit and Cr. for credit. These terms do not mean increase or decrease. The terms debit and credit are used repeatedly in the recording process to describe where entries are made. For example, the act of entering an amount on the left side of an account is called **debiting** the account, and making an entry on the right side is **crediting** the account. When the totals of the two sides are compared, an account will have a **debit balance if the total of the debit amounts exceeds the credits**. Conversely, an account will have a **credit balance if the credit amounts exceed the debits**. The procedure of having debits on the left and credits on the right is an **accounting custom**. We could function just as well if debits and credits were reversed. However, the custom of having debits on the left side of an account and credits on the right side (like the custom of driving on the right-hand side of the road) has been adopted in Canada. This rule applies to all accounts.

The equality of debits and credits provides the basis for the double-entry system of recording transactions (sometimes referred to as double-entry bookkeeping). Under the universally used **double-entry accounting** system, the dual (two-sided) effect of each transaction is recorded in appropriate accounts. This system provides a logical method for recording transactions. It also offers a means of proving the accuracy of the recorded amounts. If every transaction is recorded with equal debits and credits, then the sum of all the debits to the accounts must equal the sum of all the credits.

All **asset and expense** accounts are increased on the left (or debit side) and decreased on the right (or credit side). Conversely, all **liability and revenue** accounts are increased on the right (or credit side) and decreased on the left (or debit side). **Shareholders' equity** accounts, such as Common Shares and Retained Earnings, are increased on the credit side, whereas Dividends is increased on the debit side. The basic guidelines for an accounting system are presented in Illustration 3-1.

ILLUSTRATION 3-1
Double-entry (Debit and Credit)
Accounting System

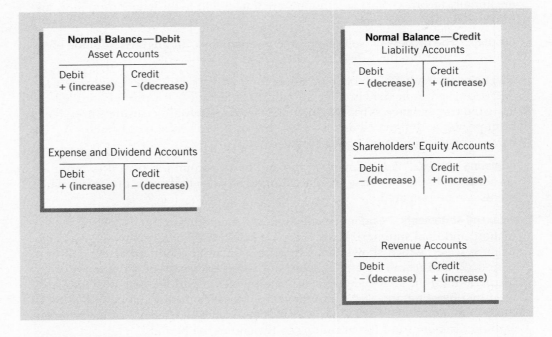

Basic Equation

In a double-entry system, for every debit there must be a credit and vice versa. This leads us to the basic accounting equation (Illustration 3-2).

ILLUSTRATION 3-2
The Basic Accounting Equation

Assets	=	Liabilities	+	Shareholders' Equity

Illustration 3-3 expands this equation to show the accounts that compose shareholders' equity. In addition, the debit/credit rules and effects on each type of account are illustrated. Study this diagram carefully. It will help you understand the fundamentals of the double-entry system. Like the basic equation, the expanded basic equation must balance (total debits equal total credits).

ILLUSTRATION 3-3
Expanded Basic Equation and
Debit/Credit Rules and Effects

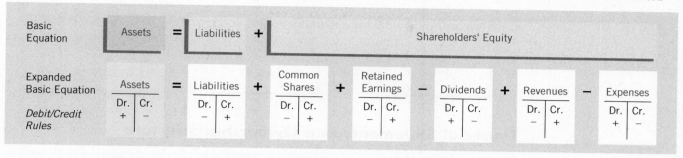

Every time a transaction occurs, the equation elements change, but the basic equality remains. To illustrate, here are eight different transactions for Perez Inc.

1 Owners invest $40,000 in exchange for common shares:

Assets + 40,000	=	Liabilities	+	Shareholders' Equity + 40,000

2 Disburse $600 cash for secretarial wages:

Assets − 600	=	Liabilities	+	Shareholders' Equity − 600 (expense)

3 Purchase office equipment priced at $5,200, giving a 10% promissory note in exchange:

Assets + 5,200	=	Liabilities +5,200	+	Shareholders' Equity

4 Receive $4,000 cash for services rendered:

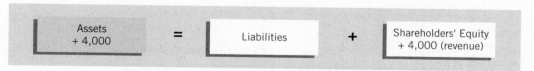

Assets + 4,000	=	Liabilities	+	Shareholders' Equity + 4,000 (revenue)

5 Pay off a short-term liability of $7,000:

Assets − 7,000	=	Liabilities − 7,000	+	Shareholders' Equity

6 Declare a cash dividend of $5,000:

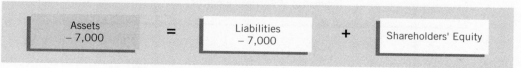

Assets	=	Liabilities + 5,000	+	Shareholders' Equity − 5,000

7 Convert a long-term liability of $80,000 into common shares:

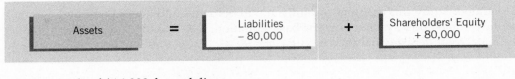

8 Pay cash of $16,000 for a delivery van:

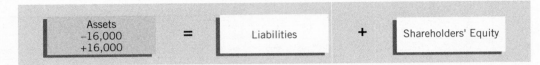

Financial Statements and Ownership Structure

Common shares and retained earnings are reported in the shareholders' equity section of the balance sheet. Dividends are reported on the statement of retained earnings. Revenues and expenses are reported on the income statement. Dividends, revenues, and expenses are eventually transferred to retained earnings at the end of the period. As a result, a change in any one of these three items affects shareholders' equity. The relationships related to shareholders' equity are shown in Illustration 3-4.

The type of ownership structure employed by a business enterprise dictates the types of accounts that are part of or affect the equity section. In a corporation,[2] **Common Shares**, **Contributed Surplus**, **Dividends**, **and Retained Earnings** are accounts commonly used. In a proprietorship or partnership, a **Capital account** is used to indicate the owner's or owners' investment in the company. A **Drawing or withdrawal account** may be used to indicate withdrawals by the owner(s). These two accounts are grouped or netted under Owner's Equity.

ILLUSTRATION 3-4
Financial Statements and Ownership Structure

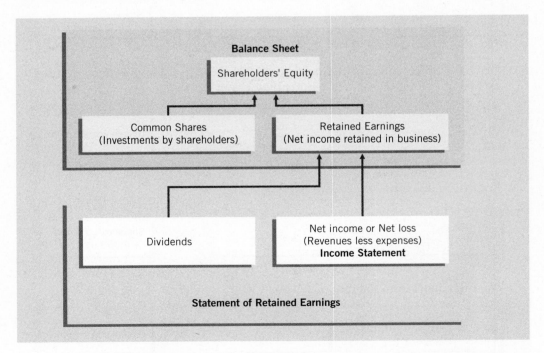

Illustration 3-5 summarizes and relates the transactions affecting shareholders' equity to the temporary and permanent classifications and to the types of business ownership.

---

[2] Corporations are incorporated under a government act such as the Canada Business Corporations Act. The main reason for incorporation is to limit the liability for the owners if the corporation gets sued or goes bankrupt. When companies are incorporated, shares are issued to owners and the company becomes a separate legal entity (separate and distinct from its owners).

ILLUSTRATION 3-5
Effects of Transactions on
Owners' Equity Accounts

Transactions Affecting Owners' Equity	Impact on Owners' Equity	Ownership Structure			
		Proprietorships and Partnerships		Corporations	
		Temporary Accounts	Permanent Accounts	Temporary Accounts	Permanent Accounts
Investment by owner(s)	Increase		Owner's Equity		Common Shares and related accounts
Revenues earned	Increase	Revenue		Revenue	
Expenses incurred	Decrease	Expense	Owner's Equity	Expense	Retained Earnings
Withdrawal by owner(s)	Decrease	Drawing		Dividends	

THE ACCOUNTING CYCLE

Illustration 3-6 flowcharts the steps in the accounting cycle. These are the accounting procedures normally used by enterprises to record transactions and prepare financial statements.

OBJECTIVE 3

Identify steps in the accounting cycle.

ILLUSTRATION 3-6
The Accounting Cycle

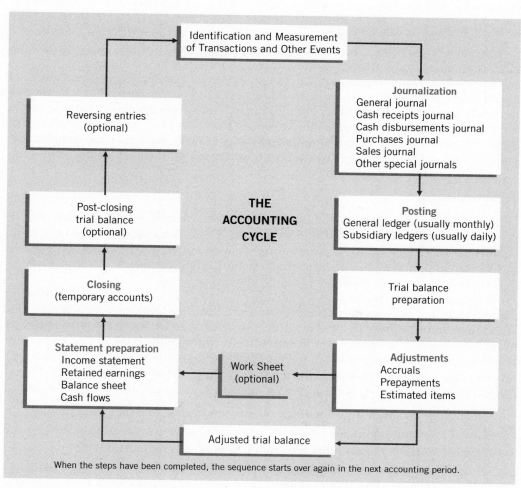

When the steps have been completed, the sequence starts over again in the next accounting period.

Identifying and Recording Transactions and Other Events

The first step in the accounting cycle consists of analysing transactions and selected other events. The problem is determining what to record. No simple rules exist that state whether an event should be recorded. Most agree that changes in personnel, changes in managerial policies, and the value of human resources, though important, should not be recorded in the accounts. On the other hand, when the company makes a cash sale or purchase-no matter how small—it should be recorded. The treatment relates to the accounting concepts presented in Chapter 2. **An item should be recognized in the financial statements if it is an element, is measurable, and for assets and liabilities, is** *probable.*

The phrase "transactions and other events and circumstances that affect a business enterprise" is used to describe the sources or causes of changes in an entity's assets, liabilities, and equity.[3] Events are of two types: (1) **External events** involve interaction between an entity and its environment, such as a transaction with another entity, a change in the price of a good or service that an entity buys or sells, a flood or earthquake, or an improvement in technology by a competitor. (2) **Internal events** occur within an entity, such as using buildings and machinery in its operations or transferring or consuming raw materials in production processes.

Many events have both external and internal elements. For example, acquiring the services of employees or others involves exchange transactions, which are external events; using those services (labour), often simultaneously with their acquisition, is part of production, which is internal. Events may be initiated and controlled by an entity, such as the purchase of merchandise or the use of a machine, or they may be beyond its control, such as an interest rate change, a theft or vandalism, or the imposition of taxes.

Transactions, as particular kinds of external events, may be an **exchange** in which each entity both receives and sacrifices value, such as purchases and sales of goods or services. Alternatively, transactions may be **transfers in one direction** in which an entity incurs a liability or transfers an asset to another entity without directly receiving (or giving) value in exchange. Examples include distributions to owners, payment of taxes, gifts, charitable contributions, casualty losses, and thefts.

In short, as many events as possible that affect the enterprise's financial position are recorded. Some events are omitted because of tradition and others because measuring them is too complex. The accounting profession in recent years has shown signs of breaking with age-old traditions and is more receptive than ever to accepting the challenge of measuring and reporting events and phenomena previously viewed as too complex and immeasurable.[4] These areas will be studied in further depth in the rest of the text.

Journalizing

OBJECTIVE 4

Record transactions in journals, post to ledger accounts, and prepare a trial balance.

Differing effects on the basic business elements (assets, liabilities, and equities) are categorized and collected in **accounts**. The **general ledger** is a collection of all the asset, liability, shareholders' equity, revenue, and expense accounts. A **"T"-account** (as shown in Illustration 3-8) is a convenient method of illustrating the effect of transactions on particular asset, liability, equity, revenue, and expense items.

In practice, transactions and selected other events are not recorded originally in the ledger because a transaction affects two or more accounts, each of which is on a different page in the ledger. To circumvent this deficiency and to have a complete record of each transaction or other event in one place, a **journal** (the book of original entry) is employed. The simplest journal form is a chronological listing of transactions and other events expressed in terms of debits and credits to particular accounts. This is called a **general journal**. It is illustrated on the next page for the following transactions.

Nov. 11 Buys a new delivery truck on account from Auto Sales Inc., $22,400.

Nov. 13 Receives an invoice from the *Evening Graphic* for advertising, $280.

Nov. 14 Returns merchandise to Canuck Supply for credit, $175.

Nov. 16 Receives a $95 debit memo from Confederation Ltd., indicating that freight on a purchase from Confederation Ltd. was prepaid but is our obligation.

---

[3] "Elements of Financial Statements of Business Enterprises," Statement of Financial Accounting Concepts No. 6 (Stamford, Conn.: FASB, 1985), pp. 259–60.

[4] Examples of these include accounting for defined future benefits plans and stock based compensation. These will be covered in chapters 20 and 18 respectively.

Each **general journal entry** consists of four parts: (1) the accounts and amounts to be debited (Dr.), (2) the accounts and amounts to be credited (Cr.), (3) a date, and (4) an explanation. Debits are entered first, followed by the credits, which are slightly indented. The explanation begins below the name of the last account to be credited and may take one or more lines. The "Ref." column is completed when the accounts are posted.

In some cases, businesses use **special journals** in addition to the general journal. Special journals summarize transactions possessing a common characteristic (e.g., cash receipts, sales, purchases, cash payments), thereby reducing the time necessary to accomplish the various bookkeeping tasks.

GENERAL JOURNAL   PAGE 12

Date 2002	Account Title and Explanation	Ref.	Amount Debit	Amount Credit
Nov. 11	Delivery Equipment	8	$22,400	
	Accounts Payable	34		$22,400
	(Purchased delivery truck on account)			
Nov. 13	Advertising Expenses	65	280	
	Accounts Payable	34		280
	(Received invoice for advertising)			
Nov. 14	Accounts Payable	34	175	
	Purchase Returns	53		175
	(Returned merchandise for credit)			
Nov. 16	Transportation-In	55	95	
	Accounts Payable	34		95
	(Received debit memo for freight on merchandise purchased)			

ILLUSTRATION 3-7
General Journal with Sample Entries

Go to the Digital Tool for discussion of special journals.

Posting

The items entered in a general journal must be transferred to the general ledger. This procedure, **posting**, is part of the summarizing and classifying process.

For example, the November 11 entry in the general journal in Illustration 3-7 showed a debit to Delivery Equipment of $22,400 and a credit to Accounts Payable of $22,400. The amount in the debit column is posted from the journal to the debit side of the ledger account (Delivery Equipment). The amount in the credit column is posted from the journal to the credit side of the ledger account (Accounts Payable).

The numbers in the "Ref." column of the general journal refer to the ledger accounts to which the respective items are posted. For example, the "34" placed in the column to the right of "Accounts Payable" indicates that this $22,400 item was posted to Account No. 34 in the ledger.

The general journal posting is completed when all the posting reference numbers have been recorded opposite the account titles in the journal. Thus the number in the posting reference column serves two purposes: (1) to indicate the ledger account number of the account involved, and (2) to indicate that the posting has been completed for the particular item. Each business enterprise selects its own numbering system for its ledger accounts. One practice is to begin numbering with asset accounts and to follow with liabilities, shareholders' equity, revenue, and expense accounts, in that order.

The various ledger accounts in Illustration 3-8 are shown after the posting process is completed. The source of the data transferred to the ledger account is indicated by the reference GJ 12 (General Journal, page 12).

Trial Balance

A **trial balance** is a list of accounts and their balances at a given time. Customarily, a trial balance is prepared at the end of an accounting period. The accounts are listed in the order in which they appear in the ledger, with debit balances listed in the left column and credit balances in the right column. The totals of the two columns must agree.

ILLUSTRATION 3-8
Ledger Accounts, in T-Account Format

Delivery Equipment	No. 8
Nov. 11 GJ 12 $22,400	

Accounts Payable	No. 34
Nov. 14 GJ 12 $175	Nov. 11 GJ 12 $22,400
	13 GJ 12 280
	16 GJ 12 95

Purchase Returns	No. 53
	Nov. 14 GJ 12 $175

Transportation-In	No. 55
Nov. 16 GJ 12 $95	

Advertising Expense	No. 65
Nov. 13 GJ 12 $280	

The primary purpose of a trial balance is to prove the mathematical equality of debits and credits after posting. Under the double-entry system this equality will occur when the sum of the debit account balances equals the sum of the credit account balances. **A trial balance also uncovers errors in journalizing and posting. In addition, it is useful when preparing financial statements.** The procedures for preparing a trial balance consist of:

1. Listing the account titles and their balances.
2. Totalling the debit and credit columns.
3. Proving the equality of the two columns.

The trial balance prepared from the ledger of Pioneer Advertising Agency Inc. is presented below:

ILLUSTRATION 3-9
Trial Balance (Unadjusted)

PIONEER ADVERTISING AGENCY INC.
Trial Balance
October 31, 2002

	Debit	Credit
Cash	$80,000	
Accounts Receivable	72,000	
Advertising Supplies	25,000	
Prepaid Insurance	6,000	
Office Equipment	50,000	
Notes Payable		$50,000
Accounts Payable		25,000
Unearned Service Revenue		12,000
Common Shares		100,000
Dividends	5,000	
Service Revenue		100,000
Salaries Expense	40,000	
Rent Expense	9,000	
	$287,000	$287,000

Note that the total debits $287,000 equal the total credits $287,000. Account numbers to the left of the account titles in the trial balance are also often shown.

A trial balance does not prove that all transactions have been recorded or that the ledger is correct. Numerous errors may exist even though the trial balance columns agree. For example, the trial balance may balance even when (1) a transaction is not journalized, (2) a correct journal entry is not posted, (3) a journal entry is posted twice, (4) incorrect accounts are used in journalizing or posting, or (5) offsetting errors are made in recording a transaction amount. In other words, as long as equal debits and credits are posted, even to the wrong account or in the wrong amount, the total debits will equal the total credits.

Adjusting Entries

In order for revenues to be recorded in the period in which they are earned, and for expenses to be recognized in the period in which they are incurred, adjusting entries are made at the end of the accounting period. In short, **adjustments are needed to ensure that the revenue recognition and matching principles are followed**.

The use of adjusting entries makes it possible to report on the balance sheet the appropriate assets, liabilities, and owners' equity at the statement date and to report on the income statement the proper net income (or loss) for the period. However, the trial balance—the first pulling together of the transaction data—may not contain up-to-date and complete data. This is true for the following reasons:

1. Some events are **not journalized daily because it is not expedient**. Examples are the consumption of supplies and the earning of wages by employees.
2. Some costs are not journalized during the accounting period because these costs **expire with the passage of time** rather than as a result of recurring daily transactions. Examples of such costs are building and equipment deterioration and rent and insurance.
3. Some items may be **unrecorded**. An example is a utility service bill that will not be received until the next accounting period.

Adjusting entries are required every time financial statements are prepared. An essential starting point is an analysis of each trial balance account to determine whether it is complete and up to date for financial statement purposes. The analysis requires a thorough understanding of the company's operations and the interrelationship of accounts. The preparation of adjusting entries is often an involved process that requires the services of a skilled professional. In accumulating the adjustment data, the company may need to make inventory counts of supplies and repair parts. Also it may be desirable to prepare supporting schedules of insurance policies, rental agreements, and other contractual commitments. Adjustments are often prepared after the balance sheet date. However, the entries are dated as of the balance sheet date.

Types of Adjusting Entries

Adjusting entries can be classified as either prepayments or accruals. Each of these classes has two subcategories as shown below:

PREPAYMENTS	ACCRUALS
1. **Prepaid Expenses.** Expenses paid in cash and recorded as assets before they are used or consumed.	3. **Accrued Revenues.** Revenues earned but not yet received in cash or recorded.
2. **Unearned Revenues.** Revenues received in cash and recorded as liabilities before they are earned.	4. **Accrued Expenses.** Expenses incurred but not yet paid in cash or recorded.

Specific examples and explanations of each type of adjustment are given in subsequent sections. Each example is based on the October 31 trial balance of Pioneer Advertising Agency Inc. (Illustration 3-9). We assume that Pioneer Advertising uses an accounting period of one month. Thus, monthly adjusting entries will be made. The entries will be dated October 31.

> **OBJECTIVE 5**
>
> Explain the reasons for preparing adjusting entries.

Adjusting Entries for Prepayments

As indicated earlier, prepayments are either **prepaid expenses** or **unearned revenues**. Adjusting entries for prepayments are required at the statement date to record the portion of the prepayment that represents the **expense incurred or the revenue earned** in the current accounting period. Assuming an adjustment is needed for both types of prepayments, the asset and liability are overstated and the related expense and revenue are understated. For example, in the trial balance, the balance in the asset Supplies shows only supplies purchased. This balance is overstated; the related expense account, Supplies Expense, is understated because the cost of supplies used has not been recognized. Thus the adjusting entry for prepayments will decrease a balance sheet account and increase an income statement account. The effects of adjusting entries for prepayments are depicted in Illustration 3-10.

ILLUSTRATION 3-10
Adjusting Entries for
Prepayments

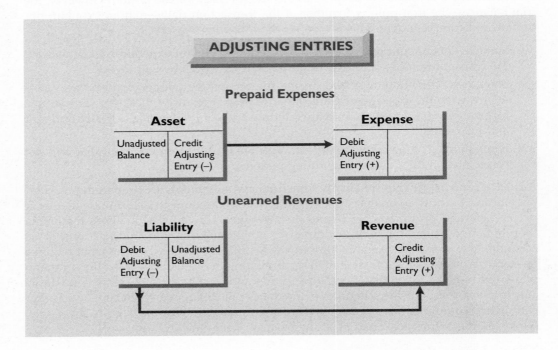

Prepaid Expenses. As stated on page 65, expenses paid in cash and recorded as assets before they are used or consumed are identified as prepaid expenses. When a cost is incurred, an asset account is debited to show the service or benefit that will be received in the future. Prepayments often occur in regard to insurance, supplies, advertising, and rent.

Prepaid expenses expire either with the passage of time (e.g., rent and insurance) or through use and consumption (e.g., supplies). The expiration of these costs does not require daily recurring entries, which would be unnecessary and impractical. Accordingly, it is customary to postpone the recognition of such cost expirations until financial statements are prepared. At each statement date, adjusting entries are made to record the expenses that apply to the current accounting period and to show the unexpired costs in the asset accounts.

Prior to adjustment, assets are overstated and expenses are understated. **Thus, the prepaid expense adjusting entry results in a debit to an expense account and a credit to an asset account.**

SUPPLIES. Several different types of supplies are used in a business enterprise. For example, a CA firm will have office supplies such as stationery, envelopes, and accounting paper. In contrast, an advertising firm will have **advertising supplies** such as graph paper, video film, and poster paper. Supplies are generally debited to an asset account when they are acquired. During the course of operations, supplies are depleted or entirely consumed. However, recognition of supplies used is deferred until the adjustment process when a physical inventory (count) of supplies is taken. The difference between the balance in the Supplies (asset) account and the cost of supplies on hand represents the supplies used (expense) for the period.

Pioneer Advertising Agency purchased advertising supplies costing $25,000 on October 5. The debit was made to the asset Advertising Supplies, and this account shows a balance of $25,000 in the October 31 trial balance. An inventory count at the close of business on October 31 reveals that $10,000 of supplies are still on hand. Thus, the cost of supplies used is $15,000 ($25,000 − $10,000), and the following adjusting entry is made:

Supplies

Oct. 5

Supplies purchased; record asset

Oct. 31

Supplies used; record supplies expense

	Oct. 31		
Advertising Supplies Expense		15,000	
Advertising Supplies			15,000
(To record supplies used)			

After the adjusting entry is posted, the two supplies accounts in T-account form show:

Advertising Supplies					Advertising Supplies Expense			
10/5		$25,000	10/31	Adj. $15,000	10/31	Adj.	$15,000	
10/31	Bal.	$10,000						

A	=	L	+	SE
−15,000				−15,000

ILLUSTRATION 3-11
Supplies Accounts after Adjustment

The asset account Advertising Supplies now shows a balance of $10,000, which is equal to the cost of supplies on hand at the statement date. In addition, Advertising Supplies Expense shows a balance of $15,000, which equals the cost of supplies used in October. **If the adjusting entry is not made, October expenses will be understated and net income overstated by $15,000. Moreover, both assets and shareholders' equity will be overstated by $15,000 on the October 31 balance sheet.**

INSURANCE.   Most companies have fire and theft insurance on merchandise and equipment, personal liability insurance for accidents suffered by customers, and automobile insurance on company cars and trucks. The cost of insurance protection is determined by the payment of insurance premiums. The term and coverage are specified in the insurance policy. The minimum term is usually one year, but three to five-year terms are available and offer lower annual premiums. Insurance premiums normally are charged to the asset account Prepaid Insurance when paid. At the financial statement date, it is necessary to debit Insurance Expense and credit Prepaid Insurance for the cost that has expired during the period.

On October 4, Pioneer Advertising Agency Inc. paid $6,000 for a one-year fire insurance policy. The effective date of coverage was October 1. The premium was charged to Prepaid Insurance when it was paid, and this account shows a balance of $6,000 in the October 31 trial balance. An analysis of the policy reveals that $500 ($6,000/12) of insurance expires each month. Thus, the following adjusting entry is made:

Insurance

Oct. 4

Insurance purchased; record asset

Insurance Policy			
Oct	Nov	Dec	Jan
$500	$500	$500	$500
Feb	March	April	May
$500	$500	$500	$500
June	July	Aug	Sept
$500	$500	$500	$500
1 YEAR $6,000			

Oct. 31

Insurance expired; record insurance expense

	Oct. 31		
Insurance Expense		500	
Prepaid Insurance			500
(To record insurance expired)			

A	=	L	+	SE
−500				−500

After the adjusting entry is posted, the accounts show:

Prepaid Insurance					Insurance Expense			
10/4		$6,000	10/31	Adj. $500	10/31	Adj.	$500	
10/31	Bal.	$5,500						

ILLUSTRATION 3-12
Insurance Accounts after Adjustment

The asset Prepaid Insurance shows a balance of $5,500, which represents the unexpired cost applicable to the remaining 11 months of coverage. At the same time, the balance in Insurance Expense is equal to the insurance cost that has expired in October. **If this adjustment is not made, October expenses will be understated by $500 and net income overstated by $500. Moreover, both assets and owners' equity also will be overstated by $500 on the October 31 balance sheet.**

AMORTIZATION, (known in the U.S. as "depreciation"). A business enterprise typically owns a variety of productive facilities such as buildings, equipment, and motor vehicles. These assets provide a service for a number of years. The term of service is commonly referred to as the asset's useful life. **Because an asset such as a building is expected to provide service for many years, it is recorded as an asset,** rather than an expense, in the year it is acquired. Such assets are recorded at cost, as required by the cost principle.

According to the **matching principle,** a portion of the cost of a long-lived asset should be reported as an expense during each period of the asset's useful life. **Amortization,** is the process of allocating the cost of an asset to expense over its useful life in a rational and systematic manner.

From an accounting standpoint, the acquisition of productive facilities is viewed essentially as a long-term prepayment for services. The need for making periodic adjusting entries for amortization is, therefore, the same as described before for other prepaid expenses; that is, to recognize the cost that has expired (expense) during the period and to report the unexpired cost (asset) at the end of the period.

In determining the useful life of a productive facility, the primary causes of amortization are actual use, deterioration due to the elements, and obsolescence. At the time an asset is acquired, the effects of these factors cannot be known with certainty, so they must be estimated. Thus, you should recognize that **amortization is an estimate rather than a factual measurement of the cost that has expired.** A common procedure in computing amortization expense is to divide the cost of the asset by its useful life. For example, if cost is $10,000 and useful life is expected to be 10 years, annual amortization is $1,000.

For Pioneer Advertising, amortization on the office equipment is estimated at $4,800 a year (cost $50,000 less salvage value $2,000 divided by useful life of 10 years), or $400 per month. Accordingly, amortization for October is recognized by the following adjusting entry:

Oct. 31		
Amortization Expense	400	
Accumulated Amortization—Office Equipment		400
(To record monthly amortization)		

After the adjusting entry is posted, the accounts show:

The balance in the accumulated amortization account will increase $400 each month.

Office Equipment	
10/1 $50,000	

Accumulated Amortization–Office Equipment		Amortization Expense	
	10/31 Adj. $400	10/31 Adj. $400	

Therefore, after journalizing and posting the adjusting entry at November 30, the balance will be $800.

Accumulated Amortization—Office Equipment is a contra asset account. A **contra asset account** is an **account that is offset against an asset account on the balance sheet.** This means that the accumulated amortization account is offset against Office Equipment on the balance sheet and that its normal balance is a credit. This account is used instead

---

Amortization

Oct.1

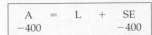

Office equipment purchased; record asset ($50,000)

Office Equipment			
Oct	Nov	Dec	Jan
$400	$400	$400	$400
Feb	March	April	May
$400	$400	$400	$400
June	July	Aug	Sept
$400	$400	$400	$400

Amortization = $4,800/year

Oct. 31
  Amortization recognized; record amortization expense

A	=	L	+	SE
−400				−400

ILLUSTRATION 3-13
Accounts after Adjustment for Amortization

of crediting Office Equipment in order to permit disclosure of **both the original cost of the equipment and the total cost that has expired to date**. In the balance sheet, Accumulated Amortization—Office Equipment is deducted from the related asset account as follows:

Office equipment	$50,000	
Less: Accumulated amortization—office equipment	400	$49,600

ILLUSTRATION 3-14
Balance Sheet Presentation of Accumulated Amortization

The difference between the cost of any depreciable asset and its related accumulated amortization is referred to as the book value of that asset. In Illustration 3-14, the equipment's book or carrying value at the balance sheet date is $49,600. It is important to realize that the asset's **book value and market value are generally two different values**.

Note also that amortization expense identifies that portion of the asset's cost that has expired in October. As in the case of other prepaid adjustments, omitting this adjusting entry would cause total assets, total shareholders' equity, and net income to be overstated and amortization expense to be understated.

If additional equipment is involved, such as delivery or store equipment, or if the company has buildings, amortization expense is recorded on each of these items. Related accumulated amortization accounts also are established. These accumulated amortization accounts would be described in the ledger as follows: Accumulated Amortization—Delivery Equipment; Accumulated Amortization—Store Equipment; and Accumulated Amortization—Buildings.

UNDERLYING CONCEPTS

Historical cost principle requires that depreciable assets be recorded at cost. The matching principle requires the cost be allocated to future periods.

Unearned Revenues. As stated on page 65, revenues received in cash and recorded as liabilities before they are earned are called unearned revenues. Such items as rent, magazine subscriptions, and customer deposits for further service may result in unearned revenues. Airlines such as **Air Canada** and **United** treat receipts from the sale of tickets as unearned revenue until the flight service is provided. Similarly, tuition received prior to the start of a semester is considered to be unearned revenue. Unearned revenues are the opposite of prepaid expenses. Indeed, unearned revenue on the books of one company is likely to be a prepayment on the books of the company that has made the advance payment. For example, if identical accounting periods are assumed, a landlord will have unearned rent revenue when a tenant has prepaid rent.

When the payment is received for services to be provided in a future accounting period, an unearned revenue account (a liability) should be credited to recognize the obligation that exists. **Unearned revenues are subsequently earned through rendering service to a customer.** During the accounting period it may not be practical to make daily recurring entries as the revenue is earned. In such cases, the recognition of earned revenue is delayed until the adjustment process. Then an adjusting entry is made to record the revenue that has been earned and to show the liability that remains. In the typical case, liabilities are overstated and revenues are understated prior to adjustment. Thus, the **adjusting entry for unearned revenues results in a debit (decrease) to a liability account and a credit (increase) to a revenue account**.

Pioneer Advertising Agency received $12,000 on October 2 from R. Knox for advertising services expected to be completed by December 31. The payment was credited to Unearned Service Revenue, and this account shows a balance of $12,000 in the October 31 trial balance. When analysis reveals that $4,000 of these services have been earned in October, the following adjusting entry is made:

Unearned Revenues

Oct. 2

Thank you in advance for your work

I will finish by Dec. 31

~$12,000

Cash is received in advance; liability is recorded

Oct. 31
Service is provided; revenue is recorded

Oct. 31		
Unearned Service Revenue	4,000	
Service Revenue		4,000
(To record revenue for services provided)		

A	=	L	+	SE
		−4,000		+4,000

After the adjusting entry is posted, the accounts show:

ILLUSTRATION 3-15
Service Revenue Accounts after Prepayments Adjustment

Unearned Service Revenue					Service Revenue			
10/31	Adj.	$4,000	10/2	$12,000		10/31	Bal.	$100,000
			10/31 Bal.	$8,000		31	Adj.	4,000
						10/31	Bal.	$104,000

The Unearned Service Revenue now shows a balance of $8,000, which represents the remaining advertising services expected to be performed in the future. At the same time, Service Revenue shows total revenue earned in October of $104,000. **If this adjustment is not made, revenues and net income will be understated by $4,000 in the income statement. Moreover, liabilities will be overstated and shareholders' equity will be understated by $4,000 on the October 31 balance sheet.**

Adjusting Entries for Accruals

The second category of adjusting entries is **accruals**. Adjusting entries for accruals are **required to record revenues earned and expenses incurred** in the current accounting period that have not been recognized through daily entries. If an accrual adjustment is needed, the revenue account (and the related asset account) and/or the expense account (and the related liability account) is understated. Thus, the adjusting entry for accruals will **increase both a balance sheet and an income statement account**. Adjusting entries for accruals are depicted in Illustration 3-16.

ILLUSTRATION 3-16
Adjusting Entries for Accruals

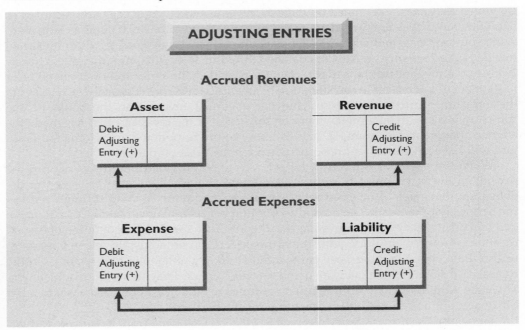

Accrued Revenues. As explained on page 65, revenues **earned but not yet received in cash or recorded** at the statement date are **accrued revenues**. Accrued revenues may **accumulate (accrue) with the passing of time**, as in the case of interest revenue and rent revenue. Or they may result from **services that have been performed but neither billed nor collected**, as in the case of commissions and fees. The former are unrecorded because earning interest and rent does not involve daily transactions; the latter may be unrecorded because only a portion of the total service has been provided.

An adjusting entry is required to show the receivable that exists at the balance sheet date and to record the revenue that has been earned during the period. Prior to adjustment, both assets and revenues are understated. Accordingly, an adjusting entry for accrued revenues results in a debit (increase) to an asset account and a credit (increase) to a revenue account.

In October, Pioneer Advertising Agency earned $2,000 for advertising services that were not billed to clients before October 31. Because these services have not been billed, they have not otherwise been recorded. Thus, the following adjusting entry is made:

Oct. 31		
Accounts Receivable	2,000	
Service Revenue		2,000
(To record revenue for services provided)		

A	=	L	+	E
+2,000				+2,000

After the adjusting entry is posted, the accounts show:

Accounts Receivable				Service Revenue		
10/31		$72,000		10/31		$100,000
31	Adj.	2,000		31		4,000
				31	Adj.	2,000
10/31	Bal.	$74,000		10/31	Bal.	$106,000

ILLUSTRATION 3-17
Receivable and Revenue Accounts after Accrual Adjustment

The asset Accounts Receivable shows that $74,000 is owed by clients at the balance sheet date. The balance of $106,000 in Service Revenue represents the total revenue earned during the month ($100,000 + $4,000 + $2,000). **If the adjusting entry is not made, assets and shareholders' equity on the balance sheet, and revenues and net income on the income statement, will all be understated.**

Accrued Expenses. As indicated on page 65, expenses incurred but not yet paid or recorded at the statement date are called accrued expenses. Interest, rent, taxes, and salaries can be accrued expenses. Accrued expenses result from the same causes as accrued revenues. In fact, an accrued expense on the books of one company is an accrued revenue to another company. For example, the $2,000 accrual of service revenue by Pioneer is an accrued expense to the client that received the service.

Adjustments for accrued expenses are necessary to record the obligations that exist at the balance sheet date and to recognize the expenses that apply to the current accounting period. Prior to adjustment, both liabilities and expenses are understated. Therefore, **the adjusting entry for accrued expenses results in a debit (increase) to an expense account and a credit (increase) to a liability account.**

ACCRUED INTEREST. Pioneer Advertising Agency signed a three-month note payable for $50,000 on October 1. The note requires interest at an annual rate of 12 percent. The interest accumulation amount is determined by three factors: (1) the note's face value, (2) the interest rate, which is always expressed as an annual rate, and (3) the length of time the note is outstanding. In this instance, the total interest due on the $50,000 note at its due date three months hence is $1,500 ($50,000 × 12% × 3/12), or $500 for one month. The formula for calculating interest and its application to Pioneer Advertising Agency for the month of October are shown in Illustration 3-18.

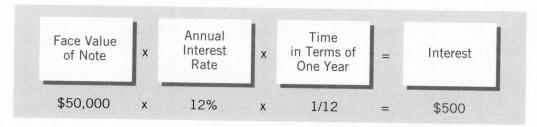

ILLUSTRATION 3-18
Formula for Calculating Interest

Note that the time period is expressed as a fraction of a year. The accrued expense adjusting entry at October 31 is as follows:

Oct. 31		
Interest Expense	500	
Interest Payable		500
(To record interest on notes payable)		

A	=	L	+	E
		+500		−500

After this adjusting entry is posted, the accounts show:

ILLUSTRATION 3-19
Interest Accounts after
Adjustment

Interest Expense		Interest Payable	
10/31 $500		10/31 $500	

Interest Expense shows the interest charges applicable to the month of October. The amount of interest owed at the statement date is shown in Interest Payable. It will not be paid until the note comes due at the end of three months. The Interest Payable account is used instead of crediting Notes Payable to disclose the two types of obligations (interest and principal) in the accounts and statements. **If this adjusting entry is not made, liabilities and interest expense will be understated, and net income and shareholders' equity will be overstated.**

ACCRUED SALARIES.   Some types of expenses, such as employee salaries and commissions, are paid for after the services have been performed. At Pioneer Advertising, salaries were last paid on October 26; the next payment of salaries will not occur until November 9. As shown in the calendar below, three working days remain in October (October 29–31).

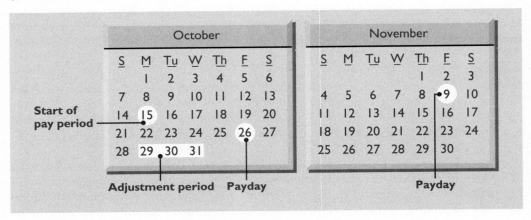

At October 31, the salaries for these days represent an accrued expense and a related liability to Pioneer Advertising. The employees receive total salaries of $10,000 for a five-day workweek, or $2,000 per day. Thus, accrued salaries at October 31 are $6,000 ($2,000 × 3), and the adjusting entry is:

A	=	L	+	E
		+6,000		−6,000

Oct. 31		
Salaries Expense	6,000	
Salaries Payable		6,000
(To record accrued salaries)		

After this adjusting entry is posted, the accounts show:

ILLUSTRATION 3-20
Salary Accounts after Adjustment

Salaries Expense			Salaries Payable		
10/26	$40,000			10/31 Adj	$6,000
31 Adj.	6,000				
10/31 Bal.	$46,000				

After this adjustment, the balance in Salaries Expense of $46,000 (23 days × $2,000) is the actual salary expense for October. The balance in Salaries Payable of $6,000 is the amount of liability for salaries owed as of October 31. **If the $6,000 adjustment for salaries is not recorded, Pioneer's expenses will be understated $6,000, and its liabilities will be understated $6,000.**

At Pioneer Advertising, salaries are payable every two weeks. Consequently, the next payday is November 9, when total salaries of $20,000 will again be paid. The payment consists of $6,000 of salaries payable at October 31 plus $14,000 of salaries expense for November (7 working days as shown in the November calendar × $2,000). Therefore, the following entry is made on November 9:

Nov. 9		
Salaries Payable	6,000	
Salaries Expense	14,000	
Cash		20,000
(To record November 9 payroll)		

A	=	L	+	SE
−20,000		−6,000		−14,000

This entry eliminates the liability for Salaries Payable that was recorded in the October 31 adjusting entry and records the proper amount of Salaries Expense for the period November 1 to November 9.

BAD DEBTS. **Proper matching of revenues and expenses dictates recording bad debts as an expense of the period in which revenue is earned instead of the period in which the accounts or notes are written off.** Properly valuing the receivable balance also requires recognizing uncollectible, worthless receivables. Proper matching and valuation require an adjusting entry.

At the end of each period, an estimate is made of the amount of current period revenue on account that will later prove to be uncollectible. The estimate is based on the amount of bad debts experienced in past years, general economic conditions, how long the receivables are past due, and other factors that indicate the element of uncollectibility. Usually it is expressed as a percent of the revenue on account for the period. Or it may be calculated by adjusting the Allowance for Doubtful Accounts to a certain percent of the trade accounts receivable and trade notes receivable at the end of the period.

To illustrate, assume that experience indicates a reasonable estimate for bad debt expense for the month is $1,600. The adjusting entry for bad debts is:

Oct. 31		
Bad Debt Expense	1,600	
Allowance for Doubtful Accounts		1,600
(To record monthly bad debt expense)		

A	=	L	+	E
−1,600				−1,600

After the adjusting entry is posted, the accounts show:

Accounts Receivable

10/1		$72,000
31	Adj.	2,000
10/31	Bal.	$74,000

Allowance for Doubtful Accounts

| | 10/31 | Adj. | $1,600 |

Bad Debt Expense

| 10/31 | Adj. | $1,600 |

ILLUSTRATION 3-21
Accounts after Adjustment for Bad Debt Expense

Adjusted Trial Balance

After all adjusting entries have been journalized and posted, another trial balance is prepared from the ledger accounts. This trial balance is called an adjusted trial balance. It shows the balance of all accounts, including those that have been adjusted, at the end of the accounting period. The purpose of an adjusted trial balance is to show the effects of all financial events that have occurred during the accounting period.

ILLUSTRATION 3-22
Trial Balance (Adjusted)

PIONEER ADVERTISING AGENCY, INC.
Adjusted Trial Balance
October 31, 2002

	Debit	Credit
Cash	$80,000	
Accounts Receivable	74,000	
Allowance for Doubtful Accounts		$1,600
Advertising Supplies	10,000	
Prepaid Insurance	5,500	
Office Equipment	50,000	
Accumulated Amortization— Office Equipment		400
Notes Payable		50,000
Accounts Payable		25,000
Interest Payable		500
Unearned Service Revenue		8,000
Salaries Payable		6,000
Common Shares		100,000
Dividends	5,000	
Service Revenue		106,000
Salaries Expense	46,000	
Advertising Supplies Expense	15,000	
Rent Expense	9,000	
Insurance Expense	500	
Interest Expense	500	
Amortization Expense	400	
Bad Debt Expense	1,600	
	$297,500	$297,500

Closing

Basic Process

The procedure generally followed to reduce the balance of temporary accounts to zero in order to prepare the accounts for the next period's transactions is known as the **closing process**. In the closing process, all of the revenue and expense account balances (income statement items) are transferred to a clearing or suspense account called Income Summary, which is used only at the end of each accounting period (yearly). Revenues and expenses are matched in the Income Summary account, and the net result of this matching, which represents the net income or net loss for the period, is then transferred to an owners' equity account (retained earnings for a corporation and capital accounts or owner's equity normally for proprietorships and partnerships). All closing entries are posted to the appropriate general ledger accounts.

For example, assume that revenue accounts of Collegiate Apparel Shop Inc. have the following balances, after adjustments, at the end of the year:

Sales Revenue	$280,000
Rental Revenue	27,000
Interest Revenue	5,000

These **revenue accounts** would be closed and the balances transferred by the following closing journal entry:

A	=	L	+	E
				−312,000
				+312,000

Sales Revenue	280,000	
Rental Revenue	27,000	
Interest Revenue	5,000	
Income Summary		312,000
(To close revenue accounts to Income Summary)		

Assume that the expense accounts, including Cost of Goods Sold, have the following balances, after adjustments, at the end of the year:

Cost of Goods Sold	$206,000
Selling Expenses	25,000
General and Adm. Expenses	40,600
Interest Expense	4,400
Income Tax Expense	13,000

These **expense accounts** would be closed and the balances transferred through the following closing journal entry:

Income Summary	289,000	
Cost of Goods Sold		206,000
Selling Expenses		25,000
General and Adm. Expenses		40,600
Interest Expense		4,400
Income Tax Expense		13,000
(To close expense accounts to Income Summary)		

The Income Summary account now has a credit balance of $23,000, which is net income. The **net income is transferred to retained earnings** by closing the Income Summary account to Retained Earnings as follows:

Income Summary	23,000	
Retained Earnings		23,000
(To close Income Summary to Retained Earnings)		

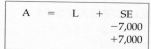

Assuming that dividends of $7,000 were declared and distributed during the year, the Dividends account is closed directly to Retained Earnings as follows:

Retained Earnings	7,000	
Dividends		7,000
(To close Dividends to Retained Earnings)		

After the closing process is completed, each income statement account is balanced out to zero and is ready for use in the next accounting period. Illustration 3-23 shows the closing process in T-account form.

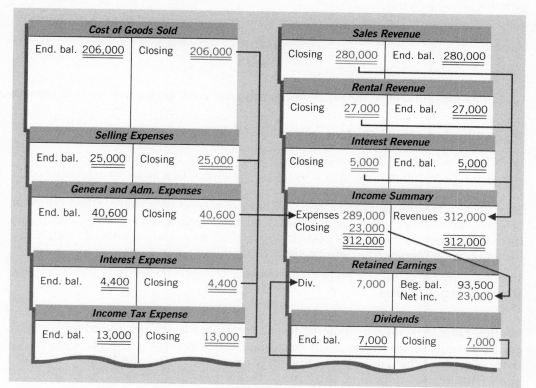

ILLUSTRATION 3-23
The Closing Process

Inventory and Cost of Goods Sold

The closing procedures illustrated above assumed the use of the perpetual inventory system. With a **perpetual inventory system**, purchases and sales are recorded directly in the inventory account as they occur. Therefore, the balance in the Inventory account should represent the ending inventory amount, and no adjusting entries are needed. To ensure this accuracy, a physical count of the items in the inventory is generally made annually. No Purchases account is used because the purchases are debited directly to the Inventory account. However, a Cost of Goods Sold account is used to accumulate the issuances from inventory. That is, when inventory items are sold, the cost of the sold goods is credited to Inventory and debited to Cost of Goods Sold.

With a **periodic inventory system**, a Purchases account is used, and the Inventory account is unchanged during the period. The Inventory account represents the beginning inventory amount throughout the period. At the end of the accounting period, the Inventory account must be adjusted by **closing out the beginning inventory** amount and **recording the ending inventory** amount. The ending inventory is determined by physically counting the items on hand and valuing them at cost or at the lower of cost or market. Under the periodic inventory system, cost of goods sold is, therefore, determined by adding the beginning inventory together with net purchases and deducting the ending inventory.

To illustrate how cost of goods sold is calculated with a periodic inventory system, assume that Collegiate Apparel Shop has a beginning inventory of $30,000; Purchases $200,000; Transportation-In $6,000; Purchase Returns and Allowances $1,000; Purchase Discounts $3,000; and the ending inventory is $26,000. The calculation of cost of goods sold is as follows:

ILLUSTRATION 3-24
Computation of Cost of Goods Sold

Beginning inventory			$30,000
Purchases		$200,000	
Less: Purchase returns and allowances	$1,000		
Less: Purchase discounts	3,000	4,000	
Net purchases		196,000	
Plus: Transportation-in		6,000	
Cost of goods purchased			202,000
Cost of goods available for sale			232,000
Less: Ending inventory			26,000
Cost of goods sold			$206,000

Cost of goods sold will be the same whether the perpetual or periodic method is used.

Post-Closing Trial Balance

We already mentioned that a trial balance is taken after the period's regular transactions have been entered and that a second trial balance (the adjusted trial balance) is taken after the adjusting entries have been posted. A third trial balance may be taken after posting the closing entries. The trial balance after closing, often called the **post-closing trial balance**, shows that equal debits and credits have been posted to the Income Summary account. The post-closing trial balance consists only of asset, liability, and owners' equity (the permanent) accounts.

Reversing Entries

After the financial statements have been prepared and the books have been closed, it is often helpful to reverse some of the adjusting entries before recording the next period's regular transactions. Such entries are called **reversing entries**. **A reversing entry is made at the beginning of the next accounting period and is the exact opposite of the related adjusting entry made in the previous period.** The recording of reversing entries is an **optional** step in the accounting cycle that may be performed at the beginning of the next accounting period. Appendix 3A discusses reversing entries in more detail.

The Accounting Cycle Summarized

The steps in the accounting cycle follow a logical sequence of the accounting procedures used during a fiscal period:

1. Enter the period's transactions in appropriate journals.
2. Post from the journals to the ledger (or ledgers).
3. Take an unadjusted trial balance (trial balance).
4. Prepare adjusting journal entries and post to the ledger(s).
5. Take a trial balance after adjusting (adjusted trial balance).
6. Prepare the financial statements from the second trial balance.
7. Prepare closing journal entries and post to the ledger(s).
8. Take a trial balance after closing (post-closing trial balance).
9. Prepare reversing entries (optional) and post to the ledger(s).

This list of procedures constitutes a complete accounting cycle that is normally performed in every fiscal period.

USING A WORK SHEET

To facilitate the end-of-period (monthly, quarterly, or annually) accounting and reporting process, a work sheet is often used. A **work sheet** is a columnar sheet of paper (or computer spreadsheet) used to adjust the account balances and prepare the financial statements. Using a work sheet helps accountants prepare financial statements on a more timely basis. It is not necessary to delay preparing the financial statements until the adjusting and closing entries are journalized and posted. The **10-column work sheet** illustrated in this chapter (Illustration 3-25) provides columns for the first trial balance, adjustments, adjusted trial balance, income statement, and balance sheet.

> **OBJECTIVE 8**
> ....
> Prepare a 10-column work sheet.

The work sheet does not replace the financial statements. Instead, it is an informal device for accumulating and sorting information needed for the financial statements. Completing the work sheet provides considerable assurance that all of the details related to the end-of-period accounting and statement preparation have been properly brought together.

Adjustments Entered on the Work Sheet

Items (a) through (f) below serve as the basis for the adjusting entries made in the work sheet shown in Illustration 3-25.

(a) Furniture and equipment is amortized at the rate of 10 percent per year based on original cost of $67,000.
(b) Estimated bad debts, one-quarter of 1 percent of sales ($400,000).
(c) Insurance expired during the year, $360.
(d) Interest accrued on notes receivable as of December 31, $800.
(e) The Rent Expense account contains $500 rent paid in advance, which is applicable to next year.
(f) Property taxes accrued December 31, $2,000.

The adjusting entries shown on the December 31, 2002, work sheet are as follows:

(a) Amortization Expense-Furniture and Equipment	6,700	
Accumulated Amortization-Furniture and Equipment		6,700

(b) Bad Debt Expense		1,000	
Allowance for Doubtful Accounts			1,000
(c) Insurance Expense		360	
Prepaid Insurance			360
(d) Interest Receivable		800	
Interest Revenue			800
(e) Prepaid Rent Expense		500	
Rent Expense			500
(f) Property Tax Expense		2,000	
Property Tax Payable			2,000

These adjusting entries are transferred to the work sheet's Adjustments columns and each may be designated by letter. The accounts set up resulting from the adjusting entries that are not already in the trial balance are listed below the totals of the trial balance, as illustrated on the work sheet. The Adjustments columns are then totalled and balanced.

Work Sheet Columns

Trial Balance Columns

Data for the trial balance are obtained from the ledger balances of Uptown Cabinet Corp. at December 31. The amount for Merchandise Inventory, $40,000, is the year-end inventory amount, which results from applying a perpetual inventory system.

Adjustments Columns

After all adjustment data are entered on the work sheet, the equality of the adjustment columns is established. The balances in all accounts are then extended to the adjusted trial balance columns.

Adjusted Trial Balance

The adjusted trial balance shows the balance of all accounts after adjustment at the end of the accounting period. For example, the $2,000 shown opposite the Allowance for Doubtful Accounts in the Trial Balance Cr. column is added to the $1,000 in the Adjustments Cr. column. The $3,000 total is then extended to the Adjusted Trial Balance Cr. column. Similarly, the $900 debit opposite Prepaid Insurance is reduced by the $360 credit in the Adjustments column. The result, $540, is shown in the Adjusted Trial Balance Dr. column.

Income Statement and Balance Sheet Columns

All the debit items in the Adjusted Trial Balance columns are extended into the Income Statement or Balance Sheet columns to the right. All the credit items are similarly extended. The next step is to total the Income Statement columns; the figure necessary to balance the debit and credit columns is the pretax income or loss for the period. The income before income taxes of $15,640 is shown in the Income Statement Dr. column because revenues exceeded expenses by that amount.

Income Taxes and Net Income

The federal and provincial income tax expense and related tax liability are calculated next. The company applies an effective rate of 22 percent to arrive at $3,440. Because the Adjustments columns have been balanced, this adjustment is entered in the Income Statement Dr. column as Income Tax Expense and in the Balance Sheet Cr. column as Income Tax Payable. The following adjusting journal entry is recorded on December 31, 2002, and posted to the general ledger as well as entered on the work sheet.

A	=	L	+	SE
		+3,440		−3,440

(g) Income Tax Expense		3,440	
Income Tax Payable			3,440

Next, the Income Statement columns are balanced with the income taxes included. The $12,200 difference between the debit and credit columns in this illustration represents net income. The net income of $12,200 is entered in the Income Statement Dr. column to achieve equality and in the Balance Sheet Cr. column as the increase in retained earnings.

Go to the Digital Tool for discussion of using a worksheet —periodic inventory method

ILLUSTRATION 3-25 Use of Work Sheet

UPTOWN CABINET CORP.
Ten-Column Work Sheet
For the Year Ended December 31, 2002

Accounts	Trial Balance Dr.	Cr.	Adjustments Dr.	Cr.	Adjusted Trial Balance Dr.	Cr.	Income Statement Dr.	Cr.	Balance Sheet Dr.	Cr.
Cash	1,200				1,200				1,200	
Notes receivable	16,000				16,000				16,000	
Accounts receivable	41,000				41,000				41,000	
Allowance for doubtful accounts		2,000		(b) 1,000		3,000				3,000
Merchandise inventory	40,000				40,000				40,000	
Prepaid insurance	900			(c) 360	540				540	
Furniture and equipment	67,000				67,000				67,000	
Accumulated amortization— furniture and equipment		12,000		(a) 6,700		18,700				18,700
Notes payable		20,000				20,000				20,000
Accounts payable		13,500				13,500				13,500
Bonds payable		30,000				30,000				30,000
Common shares		50,000				50,000				50,000
Retained earnings, Jan. 1, 2002		14,200				14,200				14,200
Sales		400,000				400,000		400,000		
Cost of goods sold	316,000				316,000		316,000			
Sales salaries expense	20,000				20,000		20,000			
Advertising expense	2,200				2,200		2,200			
Travelling expense	8,000				8,000		8,000			
Salaries, office and general	19,000				19,000		19,000			
Telephone and Internet expense	600				600		600			
Rent expense	4,800			(e) 500	4,300		4,300			
Property tax expense	3,300		(f) 2,000		5,300		5,300			
Interest expense	1,700				1,700		1,700			
Totals	541,700	541,700								
Amortization expense— furniture and equipment			(a) 6,700		6,700		6,700			
Bad debt expense			(b) 1,000		1,000		1,000			
Insurance expense			(c) 360		360		360			
Interest receivable			(d) 800		800				800	
Interest revenue				(d) 800		800		800		
Prepaid rent expense			(e) 500		500				500	
Property tax payable				(f) 2,000		2,000				2,000
Totals			11,360	11,360	552,200	552,200	385,160	400,800		
Income before income taxes							15,640			
Totals							400,800	400,800		
Income before income taxes								15,640		
Income tax expense			(g) 3,440				3,440			
Income tax payable				(g) 3,440						3,440
Net income							12,200			12,200
Totals							15,640	15,640	167,040	167,040

Preparing Financial Statements from a Work Sheet

The work sheet provides the information needed to prepare financial statements without referring to the ledger or other records. In addition, the data have been sorted into appropriate columns, which eases the statement preparation.

The financial statements prepared from the 10-column work sheet illustrated are: Income Statement for the Year Ended December 31, 2002 (Illustration 3-26), Statement of Retained Earnings for the Year Ended December 31, 2002 (Illustration 3-27), and Balance Sheet as of December 31, 2002 (Illustration 3-28), as shown below.

ILLUSTRATION 3-26
An Income Statement

UPTOWN CABINET CORP.
Income Statement
For the Year Ended December 31, 2002

Net sales			$400,000
Cost of goods sold			316,000
Gross profit on sales			84,000
Selling expenses			
Sales salaries expense		$20,000	
Advertising expense		2,200	
Travelling expense		8,000	
Total selling expenses		30,200	
Administrative expenses			
Salaries, office and general	$19,000		
Telephone and Internet expense	600		
Rent expense	4,300		
Property tax expense	5,300		
Amortization expense—furniture and equipment	6,700		
Bad debt expense	1,000		
Insurance expense	360		
Total administrative expenses		37,260	
Total selling and administrative expenses			67,460
Income from operations			16,540
Other revenues and gains			
Interest revenue			800
			17,340
Other expenses and losses			
Interest expense			1,700
Income before income taxes			15,640
Income taxes			3,440
Net income			$12,200
Earnings per share			**$1.22**

ILLUSTRATION 3-27
A Statement of Retained Earnings

UPTOWN CABINET CORP.
Statement of Retained Earnings
For the Year Ended December 31, 2002

Retained earnings, Jan. 1, 2002	$14,200
Add net income for 2002	12,200
Retained earnings, Dec. 31, 2002	**$26,400**

Income Statement

The income statement presented is that of a trading or merchandising concern; if a manufacturing concern were illustrated, three inventory accounts would be involved: raw materials, work in process, and finished goods.

ILLUSTRATION 3-28
A Balance Sheet

UPTOWN CABINET CORP.
Balance Sheet
As of December 31, 2002

Assets

Current assets			
Cash			$ 1,200
Notes receivable	$16,000		
Accounts receivable	41,000		
Interest receivable	800	$57,800	
Less: Allowance for doubtful accounts		3,000	54,800
Merchandise inventory			40,000
Prepaid insurance			540
Prepaid rent			500
Total current assets			97,040
Property, plant, and equipment			
Furniture and equipment		67,000	
Less: Accumulated amortization		18,700	
Total property, plant, and equipment			48,300
Total assets			$145,340

Liabilities and Shareholders' Equity

Current liabilities			
Notes payable			$ 20,000
Accounts payable			13,500
Property tax payable			2,000
Income tax payable			3,440
Total current liabilities			38,940
Long-term liabilities			
Bonds payable, due June 30, 2007			30,000
Total liabilities			68,940
Shareholders' equity			
Common shares, issued and outstanding, 10,000 shares		$50,000	
Retained earnings		26,400	
Total shareholders' equity			76,400
Total liabilities and shareholders' equity			$145,340

Statement of Retained Earnings

The net income earned by a corporation may be retained in the business or distributed to shareholders by paying of dividends. In Illustration 3-27, the net income earned during the year was added to the balance of retained earnings on January 1, thereby increasing the balance of retained earnings to $26,400 on December 31. No dividends were declared during the year.

Balance Sheet

The balance sheet prepared from the 10-column work sheet contains new items resulting from year-end adjusting entries. Interest receivable, unexpired insurance, and prepaid rent expense are included as current assets. These assets are considered current because they will be converted into cash or consumed in the ordinary routine of the business within a relatively short period of time. The amount of Allowance for Doubtful Accounts is deducted from the total of accounts, notes, and interest receivable because it is estimated that only $54,800 of $57,800 will be collected in cash.

In the property, plant, and equipment section, the accumulated amortization is deducted from the cost of the furniture and equipment; the difference represents the book or carrying value of the furniture and equipment.

Property tax payable is shown as a current liability because it is an obligation that is payable within a year. Other short-term accrued liabilities would also be shown as current liabilities.

The bonds payable, due in 2007, are long-term liabilities and are shown in a separate section. (Interest on the bonds was paid on December 31.)

Because Uptown Cabinet Corp. is a corporation, the balance sheet's capital section, called the shareholders' equity section in Illustration 3-28, is somewhat different from the capital section for a proprietorship. Total shareholders' equity consists of the common shares, which is the original investment by shareholders, and the earnings retained in the business.

Closing Entries

The entries for the closing process are as follows:

General Journal
December 31, 2002

Interest Revenue	800	
Sales	400,000	
Cost of Goods Sold		316,000
Sales Salaries Expense		20,000
Advertising Expense		2,200
Travelling Expense		8,000
Salaries, Office and General		19,000
Telephone and Internet Expense		600
Rent Expense		4,300
Property Tax Expense		5,300
Amortization Expense—Furniture and Equipment		6,700
Bad Debt Expense		1,000
Insurance Expense		360
Interest Expense		1,700
Income Tax Expense		3,440
Income Summary		12,200
(To close revenues and expenses to Income Summary)		
Income Summary	12,200	
Retained Earnings		12,200
(To close Income Summary to Retained Earnings)		

Monthly Statements, Yearly Closing

The use of a work sheet at the end of each month or quarter permits the preparation of interim financial statements even though the books are closed only at the end of each year. For example, assume that a business closes its books on December 31 but that monthly financial statements are desired. At the end of January, a work sheet similar to the one illustrated in this chapter can be prepared to supply the information needed for statements for January. At the end of February, a work sheet can be used again. Note that because the accounts were not closed at the end of January, the income statement taken from the work sheet on February 28 will present the net income for two months. To obtain an income statement for only the month of February subtract the items in the January income statement from the corresponding items in the income statement for the two months of January and February.

A statement of retained earnings for February only also may be obtained by subtracting the January items. The balance sheet prepared from the February work sheet, however, shows assets, liabilities, and shareholders' equity as of February 28, the specific date for which a balance sheet is desired.

The March work sheet would show the revenues and expenses for three months, and the subtraction of the revenues and expenses for the first two months could be made to supply the amounts needed for an income statement for the month of March only, and so on throughout the year.

SUMMARY OF LEARNING OBJECTIVES

1 Understand basic accounting terminology. It is important to understand the following terms: (1) event, (2) transaction, (3) account, (4) permanent and temporary accounts, (5) ledger, (6) journal, (7) posting, (8) trial balance, (9) adjusting entries, (10) financial statements, (11) closing entries.

2 Explain double-entry rules. The left side of any account is the debit side; the right side is the credit side. All asset and expense accounts are increased on the left or debit side and decreased on the right or credit side. Conversely, all liability and revenue accounts are increased on the right or credit side and decreased on the left or debit side. Shareholders' equity accounts, Common Shares, and Retained Earnings, are increased on the credit side, whereas Dividends is increased on the debit side.

3 Identify steps in the accounting cycle. The basic steps in the accounting cycle are (1) identification and measurement of transactions and other events; (2) journalization; (3) posting; (4) unadjusted trial balance; (5) adjustments; (6) adjusted trial balance; (7) statement preparation; and (8) closing.

4 Record transactions in journals, post to ledger accounts, and prepare a trial balance. The simplest journal form is a chronological listing of transactions and events expressed in terms of debits and credits to particular accounts. The items entered in a general journal must be transferred (posted) to the general ledger. An unadjusted trial balance should be prepared at the end of a given period after the entries have been recorded in the journal and posted to the ledger.

5 Explain the reasons for preparing adjusting entries. Adjustments are necessary to achieve a proper matching of revenues and expenses so as to determine net income for the current period and to achieve an accurate statement of end-of-the-period balances in assets, liabilities, and owners' equity accounts.

6 Prepare closing entries. In the closing process, all of the revenue and expense account balances (income statement items) are transferred to a clearing account called Income Summary, which is used only at the end of the fiscal year. Revenues and expenses are matched in the Income Summary account. The net result of this matching, which represents the net income or net loss for the period, is then transferred to a shareholders' equity account (retained earnings for a corporation and capital accounts for proprietorships and partnerships).

7 Explain how inventory accounts are adjusted at year-end. Under a perpetual inventory system, the balance in the Inventory account should represent the ending inventory amount. When the inventory records are maintained in a periodic inventory system, a Purchases account is used; the Inventory account is unchanged during the period. The Inventory account represents the beginning inventory amount throughout the period. At the end of the accounting period, the inventory account must be adjusted by closing out the beginning inventory amount and recording the ending inventory amount.

8 Prepare a 10-column work sheet. The 10-column work sheet provides columns for the first trial balance, adjustments, adjusted trial balance, income statement, and balance sheet. The work sheet does not replace the financial statements. Instead, it is the accountant's informal device for accumulating and sorting information needed for the financial statements.

KEY TERMS

account, *57*
accounting cycle, *61*
accounting information system, *56*
accrued expenses, *71*
accrued revenues, *70*
adjusted trial balance, *57*
adjusting entry, *65*
amortization, *68*
balance sheet, *57*
book value, *69*
closing entries, *82*
closing process, *74*
contra asset account, *68*
credit, *58*
debit, *58*
double-entry accounting, *58*
event, *57*
financial statements, *57*
general journal, *62*
general ledger, *62*
income statement, *57*
journal, *57*
periodic inventory system, *76*
permanent accounts, *57*
perpetual inventory system, *76*
post-closing trial balance, *57, 76*
posting, *63*
prepaid expenses, *66*
reversing entries, *76*
special journals, *63*
statement of cash flows, *57*
statement of retained earnings, *57*
T-account, *62*
temporary accounts, *57*
transaction, *57*
trial balance, *57, 63*
unearned revenues, *69*
useful life, *68*
work sheet, *77*

APPENDIX 3A

Using Reversing Entries

OBJECTIVE 9

After studying Appendix 3A, you should be able to:
Identify adjusting entries that may be reversed.

The purpose of reversing entries is to simplify recording transactions in the next accounting period. The use of reversing entries does not change the amounts reported in the previous period's financial statements.

ILLUSTRATION OF REVERSING ENTRIES—ACCRUALS

Reversing entries are most often used to reverse two types of adjusting entries: **accrued revenues** and **accrued expenses**. To illustrate the optional use of reversing entries for accrued expenses, we will use the following transaction and adjustment data:

1. October 24 (initial salary entry): $4,000 of salaries incurred between October 1 and October 24 are paid.
2. October 31 (adjusting entry): Salaries incurred between October 25 and October 31 are $1,200. These will be paid in the November 8 payroll.
3. November 8 (subsequent salary entry): Salaries paid are $2,500. Of this amount, $1,200 applied to accrued wages payable at October 31 and $1,300 was incurred between November 1 and November 8.

ILLUSTRATION 3A-1
Comparison of Entries for Accruals, with and without Reversing Entries

The comparative entries are shown in Illustration 3A-1.

Reversing Entries Not Used				Reversing Entries Used			
Initial Salary Entry							
Oct. 24	Salaries Expense	4,000		Oct. 24	Salaries Expense	4,000	
	Cash		4,000		Cash		4,000
Adjusting Entry							
Oct. 31	Salaries Expense	1,200		Oct. 31	Salaries Expense	1,200	
	Salaries Payable		1,200		Salaries Payable		1,200
Closing Entry							
Oct. 31	Income Summary	5,200		Oct. 31	Income Summary	5,200	
	Salaries Expense		5,200		Salaries Expense		5,200
Reversing Entry							
Nov. 1	No entry is made.			Nov. 1	Salaries Payable	1,200	
					Salaries Expense		1,200
Subsequent Salary Entry							
Nov. 8	Salaries Payable	1,200		Nov. 8	Salaries Expense	2,500	
	Salaries Expense	1,300			Cash		2,500
	Cash		2,500				

The comparative entries show that the first three entries are the same whether or not reversing entries are used. The last two entries, however, are different. The November 1 reversing entry eliminates the $1,200 balance in Salaries Payable that was created by the October 31 adjusting entry. The reversing entry also creates a $1,200 credit balance in the Salaries Expense account. As you know, it is unusual for an expense account to have a credit balance; however, the balance is correct in this instance. It is correct because the entire amount of the first salary payment in the new accounting period will be debited to Salaries Expense. This debit will eliminate the credit balance, and the resulting debit balance in the expense account will equal the salaries expense incurred in the new accounting period ($1,300 in this example).

When reversing entries are made, all cash payments of expenses can be debited to the expense account. This means that on November 8 (and every payday), Salaries Expense can be debited for the amount paid without regard to the existence of any accrued salaries payable. Being able to make the same entry each time simplifies the recording process in an accounting system.

ILLUSTRATION OF REVERSING ENTRIES-PREPAYMENTS

Up to this point, we have assumed that all prepayments are recorded as prepaid expense or unearned revenue. In some cases, prepayments are recorded directly in expense or revenue accounts. When this occurs, prepayments may also be reversed. To illustrate the use of reversing entries for prepaid expenses, we will use the following transaction and adjustment data:

1. December 10 (initial entry): $20,000 of office supplies are purchased with cash.
2. December 31 (adjusting entry): $5,000 of office supplies on hand.

The comparative entries are shown in Illustration 3A-2.

ILLUSTRATION 3A-2
Comparison of Entries for Prepayments, with and without Reversing Entries

Reversing Entries Not Used				Reversing Entries Used		
Initial Purchase of Supplies Entry						
Dec. 10	Office Supplies	20,000		Dec. 10	Office Supplies Expense	20,000	
	Cash		20,000		Cash		20,000
Adjusting Entry						
Dec. 31	Office Supplies Expense	15,000		Dec. 31	Office Supplies	5,000	
	Office Supplies		15,000		Office Supplies Expense		5,000
Closing Entry						
Dec. 31	Income Summary	15,000		Dec. 31	Income Summary	15,000	
	Office Supplies Expense		15,000		Office Supplies Expense		15,000
Reversing Entry						
Jan. 1	No entry			Jan. 1	Office Supplies Expense	5,000	
					Office Supplies		5,000

After the adjusting entry on December 31 (regardless of whether reversing entries are used) the asset account Office Supplies shows a balance of $5,000 and Office Supplies Expense a balance of $15,000. If Office Supplies Expense initially was debited when the supplies were purchased, a reversing entry is made to return to the expense account the cost of unconsumed supplies. The company then continues to debit Office Supplies Expense for additional purchases of office supplies during the next period.

With respect to prepaid items, why are all such items not entered originally into real accounts (assets and liabilities), thus making reversing entries unnecessary? Sometimes this practice is followed. It is particularly advantageous for items that need to be apportioned over several periods (e.g., supplies and parts inventories). However, items that do not follow this regular pattern and that may or may not involve two or more periods are ordinarily entered initially in revenue or expense accounts. The revenue and expense accounts may not require adjusting and are systematically closed to Income Summary. Using the temporary accounts adds consistency to the accounting system and makes the recording more efficient, particularly when a large number of such transactions occur during the year. For example, the bookkeeper knows that when an invoice is received for other than a capital asset acquisition, the amount is expensed. The bookkeeper need not worry at the time the invoice is received whether or not the item will result in a prepaid expense at the end of the period, because adjustments will be made at that time.

SUMMARY OF REVERSING ENTRIES

A summary of guidelines for reversing entries is as follows:

1. All accrued items should be reversed.
2. All prepaid items for which the original cash transaction was debited or credited to an expense or revenue account should be reversed.
3. Adjusting entries for amortization and bad debts are not reversed.

Recognize that reversing entries do not have to be used; therefore, some accountants avoid them entirely.

SUMMARY OF LEARNING OBJECTIVE FOR APPENDIX 3A

9 Identify adjusting entries that may be reversed. Reversing entries are most often used to reverse two types of adjusting entries: accrued revenues and accrued expenses. Prepayments may also be reversed if the initial entry to record the transaction is made to an expense or revenue account.

APPENDIX 3B

Cash Basis Accounting versus Accrual Basis Accounting

DIFFERENCES BETWEEN CASH AND ACCRUAL BASES

OBJECTIVE 10

After studying Appendix 3B, you should be able to: Differentiate the cash basis of accounting from the accrual basis of accounting.

Most companies use the **accrual basis** of accounting: they recognize revenue when it is earned and recognize expenses in the period incurred, without regard to the time of receipt or payment of cash. Some small enterprises and the average individual tax-payer, however, use a strict or modified cash basis approach. Under the **strict cash basis**

of accounting, revenue is recorded only when the cash is received and expenses are recorded only when the cash is paid. The determination of income on the cash basis rests upon the collection of revenue and the payment of expenses, and the revenue recognition and the matching principles are ignored. Consequently, cash basis financial statements are not in conformity with generally accepted accounting principles.

To illustrate and contrast accrual basis accounting and cash basis accounting, assume that Quality Contractor signs an agreement to construct a garage for $22,000. In January, Quality Contractor begins construction, incurs costs of $18,000 on credit, and by the end of January delivers a finished garage to the buyer. In February, Quality Contractor collects $22,000 cash from the customer. In March, Quality pays the $18,000 due the creditors. The net incomes for each month under cash basis accounting and accrual basis accounting are as follows:

QUALITY CONTRACTOR
Income Statement — Cash Basis
For the Month of

	January	February	March	Total
Cash receipts	$ – 0 –	$22,000	$ – 0 –	$22,000
Cash payments	– 0 –	– 0 –	18,000	18,000
Net income (loss)	$ – 0 –	$22,000	$(18,000)	$ 4,000

ILLUSTRATION 3B-1
Income Statement—Cash Basis

QUALITY CONTRACTOR
Income Statement — Accrual Basis
For the Month of

	January	February	March	Total
Revenues	$22,000	$ – 0 –	$ – 0 –	$22,000
Expenses	18,000	– 0 –	– 0 –	18,000
Net income (loss)	$ 4,000	$ – 0 –	$ – 0 –	$ 4,000

ILLUSTRATION 3B-2
Income Statement—Accrual Basis

For the three months combined, total net income is the same under both cash basis accounting and accrual basis accounting; the difference is in the **timing** of net income.

The balance sheet is also affected by the basis of accounting. For instance, if cash basis accounting were used, Quality Contractor's balance sheets at each month-end would appear as follows:

QUALITY CONTRACTOR
Balance Sheets — Cash Basis
As of

	January 31	February 28	March 31
Assets			
Cash	$ – 0 –	$22,000	$4,000
Total assets	$ – 0 –	$22,000	$4,000
Liabilities and Owners' Equity			
Owners' equity	$ – 0 –	$22,000	$4,000
Total liabilities and owners' equity	$ – 0 –	$22,000	$4,000

ILLUSTRATION 3B-3
Balance Sheets—Cash Basis

If accrual basis accounting were used, Quality Contractor's balance sheets at each month-end would appear as follows:

ILLUSTRATION 3B-4
Balance Sheets — Accrual Basis

QUALITY CONTRACTOR Balance Sheets — Accrual Basis As of			
	January 31	February 28	March 31
Assets			
Cash	$ – 0 –	$22,000	$4,000
Accounts receivable	22,000	– 0 –	– 0 –
Total assets	$22,000	$22,000	$4,000
Liabilities and Owners' Equity			
Accounts payable	$18,000	$18,000	$ – 0 –
Owners' equity	4,000	4,000	4,000
Total liabilities and owners' equity	$22,000	$22,000	$4,000

An analysis of the preceding income statements and balance sheets shows the ways in which cash basis accounting is inconsistent with basic accounting theory:

1. The cash basis understates revenues and assets from the construction and delivery of the garage in January. It ignores the $22,000 accounts receivable, representing a near-term future cash inflow.

2. The cash basis understates expenses incurred with the construction of the garage and the liability outstanding at the end of January. It ignores the $18,000 accounts payable, representing a near-term future cash outflow.

3. The cash basis understates owners' equity in January by not recognizing the revenues and the asset until February, and it overstates owners' equity in February by not recognizing the expenses and the liability until March.

In short, cash basis accounting violates the theory underlying the elements of financial statements.

The **modified cash basis**, a mixture of cash basis and accrual basis, is the method often followed by professional services firms (doctors, lawyers, accountants, consultants) and by retail, real estate, and agricultural operations. It is the pure cash basis of accounting with modifications that have substantial support, such as capitalizing and amortizing plant assets or recording inventory.[1]

CONVERSION FROM CASH BASIS TO ACCRUAL BASIS

Not infrequently, a cash basis or a modified cash basis set of financial statements is converted to the accrual basis for presentation to investors and creditors. To illustrate this conversion, assume that Dr. Diane Windsor keeps her accounting records on a cash basis. In the year 2002, Dr. Windsor received $300,000 from her patients and paid $170,000 for operating expenses, resulting in an excess of cash receipts over disbursements of $130,000 ($300,000 − $170,000). At January 1 and December 31, 2002, she has accounts receivable, unearned service revenue, accrued liabilities, and prepaid expenses as follows:

ILLUSTRATION 3B-5
Financial Information Related to Dr. Diane Windsor

	January 1, 2002	December 31, 2002
Accounts receivable	$12,000	$9,000
Unearned service revenue	– 0 –	4,000
Accrued liabilities	2,000	5,500
Prepaid expenses	1,800	2,700

---

[1] A cash or modified cash basis might be used in the following situations:

(1) A company that is primarily interested in cash flows (for example, a group of physicians that distributes cash-basis earnings for salaries and bonuses).

(2) A company that has a limited number of financial statement users (small, closely held company with little or no debt).

(3) A company that has operations that are relatively straightforward (small amounts of inventory, long-term assets, or long-term debt).

Service Revenue Calculation

To convert the amount of cash received from patients to service revenue on an accrual basis, changes in accounts receivable and unearned service revenue during the year must be considered. Accounts receivable at the beginning of the year represents revenues earned last year that are collected this year. Ending accounts receivable indicates revenues earned this year that are not yet collected. Therefore, beginning accounts receivable is subtracted and ending accounts receivable is added to arrive at revenue on an accrual basis, as shown in Illustration 3B-6.

Cash receipts from customers	{	− Beginning accounts receivable + Ending accounts receivable	}	Revenue = on an accrual basis

ILLUSTRATION 3B-6
Conversion of Cash Receipts to Revenue—Accounts Receivable

Using similar analysis, beginning unearned service revenue represents cash received last year for revenues earned this year. Ending unearned service revenue results from collections this year that will be recognized as revenue next year. Therefore, beginning unearned service revenue is added and ending unearned service revenue is subtracted to arrive at revenue on an accrual basis, as shown in Illustration 3B-7.

Cash receipts from customers	{	+ Beginning unearned service revenue − Ending unearned service revenue	}	Revenue = on an accrual basis

ILLUSTRATION 3B-7
Conversion of Cash Receipts to Revenue—Unearned Service Revenue

Cash collected from customers, therefore, is converted to service revenue on an accrual basis as follows:

Cash receipts from customers		$300,000
− Beginning accounts receivable	$(12,000)	
+ Ending accounts receivable	9,000	
+ Beginning unearned service revenue	− 0 −	
− Ending unearned service revenue	(4,000)	(7,000)
Service revenue (accrual)		$293,000

ILLUSTRATION 3B-8
Conversion of Cash Receipts to Service Revenue

Operating Expense Calculation

To convert cash paid for operating expenses during the year to operating expenses on an accrual basis, you must consider changes in prepaid expenses and accrued liabilities during the year. Beginning prepaid expenses should be recognized as expenses this year. (The cash payment occurred last year.) Therefore, the beginning prepaid expenses balance is added to cash paid for operating expenses to arrive at operating expense on an accrual basis.

Conversely, ending prepaid expenses result from cash payments made this year for expenses to be reported next year. (The expense recognition is deferred to a future period.) As a result, ending prepaid expenses are deducted from cash paid for expenses, as shown in Illustration 3B-9.

Cash paid for operating expenses	{	+ Beginning prepaid expenses − Ending prepaid expenses	}	Expenses = on an accrual basis

ILLUSTRATION 3B-9
Conversion of Cash Payments to Expenses—Prepaid Expenses

Using similar analysis, beginning accrued liabilities result from expenses recognized last year that require cash payments this year. Ending accrued liabilities relate to expenses recognized this year that have not been paid. Beginning accrued liabilities, therefore, are deducted and ending accrued liabilities added to cash paid for expenses to arrive at expense on an accrual basis, as shown in Illustration 3B-10.

Cash paid for operating expenses	{	− Beginning accrued liabilities + Ending accrued liabilities	}	Expenses = on an accrual basis

ILLUSTRATION 3B-10
Conversion of Cash Payments to Expenses—Accrued Liabilities

Cash paid for operating expenses, therefore, is converted to operating expenses on an accrual basis for Dr. Diane Windsor as follows:

ILLUSTRATION 3B-11
Conversion of Cash Paid to Operating Expenses

Cash paid for operating expenses		$170,000
+ Beginning prepaid expense	$1,800	
− Ending prepaid expense	(2,700)	
− Beginning accrued liabilities	(2,000)	
+ Ending accrued liabilities	5,500	2,600
Operating expenses (accrual)		$172,600

This entire conversion can be shown in work sheet form as follows:

ILLUSTRATION 3B-12
Conversion of Statement of Cash Receipts and Disbursements to Income Statement

DIANE WINDSOR, D.D.S.
Conversion of Income Statement Data from Cash Basis to Accrual Basis
For the Year 2002

	Cash Basis	Adjustments Add	Adjustments Deduct	Accrual Basis
Collections from customers	$300,000			
− Accounts receivable, Jan. 1			$12,000	
+ Accounts receivable, Dec. 31		$9,000		
+ Unearned service revenue, Jan. 1		—	—	
− Unearned service revenue, Dec. 31			4,000	
Service revenue				$293,000
Disbursement for expenses				
+ Prepaid expenses, Jan. 1		1,800		
− Prepaid expenses, Dec. 31			2,700	
− Accrued liabilities, Jan. 1			2,000	
+ Accrued liabilities, Dec. 31	170,000	5,500		
Operating expenses				172,600
Excess of cash collections over disbursements—cash basis	$130,000			
Net income—accrual basis				$120,400

Using this approach, collections and disbursements on a cash basis are adjusted to revenue and expense on an accrual basis to arrive at accrual net income. In any conversion from the cash basis to the accrual basis, depreciation or amortization expense is an expense in arriving at net income on an accrual basis.

THEORETICAL WEAKNESSES OF THE CASH BASIS

The cash basis does report exactly when cash is received and when cash is disbursed. To many people that information represents something solid, something concrete. Isn't cash what it is all about? Does it make sense to invent something, design it, produce it, market and sell it, if you aren't going to get cash for it in the end? If so, then what is the merit of accrual accounting?

Today's economy is based more on credit than cash. And the accrual basis, not the cash basis, recognizes all aspects of the credit phenomenon. Investors, creditors, and other decision makers seek timely information about an enterprise's future cash flows. Accrual basis accounting provides this information by reporting the cash inflows and outflows associated with earnings activities as soon as these cash flows can be estimated with an acceptable degree of certainty. Receivables and payables are forecasters of future cash inflows and outflows. In other words, accrual basis accounting aids in predicting future cash flows by reporting transactions and other events with cash consequences at the time the transactions and events occur, rather than when the cash is received and paid.

Summary of Learning Objective for Appendix 3B

KEY TERMS

accrual basis, *86*
modified cash basis, *88*
strict cash basis, *86*

10 **Differentiate the cash basis of accounting from the accrual basis of accounting.** Accrual basis accounting provides information about cash inflows and outflows associated with earnings activities as soon as these cash flows can be estimated with an acceptable degree of certainty. That is, accrual basis accounting aids in predicting future cash flows by reporting transactions and events with cash consequences at the time the transactions and events occur, rather than when the cash is received and paid.

Note: All asterisked Brief Exercises, Exercises, Problems, and Cases relate to material contained in an appendix to the chapter.

BRIEF EXERCISES

BE3-1 Transactions for Argot Limited for the month of May are presented below. Prepare journal entries for each of these transactions. (You may omit explanations.)

May 1 Invests $3,000 cash in exchange for common shares in a small welding corporation.
      3 Buys equipment on account for $1,100.
     13 Pays $400 to landlord for May rent.
     21 Bills Noble Corp. $500 for welding work done.

BE3-2 Favre Repair Shop Inc. had the following transactions during the first month of business. Journalize the transactions.

August 2 Invested $12,000 cash and $2,500 of equipment in the business.
        7 Purchased supplies on account for $400. (Debit asset account.)
       12 Performed services for clients, for which $1,300 was collected in cash and $670 was billed to the clients.
       15 Paid August rent, $600.
       19 Counted supplies and determined that only $270 of the supplies purchased on August 7 are still on hand.

BE3-3 On July 1, 2002, Blair Ltd. pays $18,000 to Hindi Insurance Ltd. for a three-year insurance contract. Both companies have fiscal years ending December 31. For Blair, journalize the entry on July 1 and the adjusting entry on December 31.

BE3-4 Using the data in BE3-3, journalize the entry on July 1 and the adjusting entry on December 31 for Hindi Insurance Ltd. Hindi uses the accounts Unearned Insurance Revenue and Insurance Revenue.

BE3-5 On August 1, Bell Limited paid $8,400 in advance for two years' insurance coverage. Prepare Bell's August 1 journal entry and the annual adjusting entry on December 31.

BE3-6 Mogilny Corporation owns a warehouse. On November 1, it rented storage space to a lessee (tenant) for three months for a total cash payment of $2,700 received in advance. Prepare Mogilny's November 1 journal entry and the December 31 annual adjusting entry.

BE3-7 Janeway Corp's weekly payroll, paid on Fridays, totals $6,000. Employees work a five-day week. Prepare Janeway's adjusting entry on Wednesday, December 31 and the journal entry to record the $6,000 cash payment on Friday, January 2.

BE3-8 Included in Martinez Corp's December 31 trial balance is a note receivable of $10,000. The note is a four-month, 12 percent note dated October 1. Prepare Martinez's December 31 adjusting entry to record $300 of accrued interest, and the February 1 journal entry to record receipt of $10,400 from the borrower.

BE3-9 Prepare the following adjusting entries at December 31 for DeGads Ltd.
  1. Interest on notes payable of $400 is accrued.
  2. Fees earned but unbilled total $1,400.

3. Salaries earned by employees of $700 have not been recorded.
4. Bad debt expense for year is $900.

Use the following account titles: Service Revenue, Accounts Receivable, Interest Expense, Interest Payable, Salaries Expense, Salaries Payable, Allowance for Doubtful Accounts, and Bad Debt Expense.

BE3-10 At the end of its first year of operations, the trial balance of Rafael Limited shows Equipment $30,000 and zero balances in Accumulated Amortization—Equipment and Amortization Expense. Amortization for the year is estimated to be $3,000. Prepare the adjusting entry for amortization at December 31, and indicate the balance sheet presentation for the equipment at December 31.

BE3-11 Willis Corporation has beginning inventory $81,000; Purchases $540,000; Freight-in $16,200; Purchase Returns $5,800; Purchase Discounts $5,000; and ending inventory $70,200. Calculate cost of goods sold.

BE3-12 Karen Inc. has year-end account balances of Sales $828,900; Interest Revenue $13,500; Cost of Goods Sold $556,200; Operating Expenses $189,000; Income Tax Expense $35,100; and Dividends $18,900. Prepare the year-end closing entries.

*BE3-13 Pelican Inc. made a December 31 adjusting entry to debit Salaries Expense and credit Salaries Payable for $3,600. On January 2, Pelican paid the weekly payroll of $6,000. Prepare Pelican's **(a)** January 1 reversing entry, **(b)** January 2 entry (assuming the reversing entry was prepared), and **(c)** January 2 entry (assuming the reversing entry was not prepared).

*BE3-14 Smith Corp. had cash receipts from customers in 2002 of $152,000. Cash payments for operating expenses were $97,000. Smith has determined that at January 1, accounts receivable was $13,000 and prepaid expenses were $17,500. At December 31, accounts receivable was $18,600, and prepaid expenses were $23,200. Calculate **(a)** service revenue and **(b)** operating expenses.

EXERCISES

E3-1 **(Transaction Analysis-Service Company)** Ben Crusher is a licensed CA. During the first month of operations of his business (a sole proprietorship), the following events and transactions occurred.

April 2	Invested $32,000 cash and equipment valued at $14,000 in the business.
2	Hired a secretary-receptionist at a salary of $290 per week payable monthly.
3	Purchased supplies on account $700 (debit an asset account).
7	Paid office rent of $600 for the month.
11	Completed a tax assignment and billed client $1,100 for services rendered. (Use service revenue account.)
12	Received $3,200 advance on a management consulting engagement.
17	Received cash of $2,300 for services completed for Ferengi Co.
21	Paid insurance expense $110.
30	Paid secretary-receptionist $1,160 for the month.
30	A count of supplies indicated that $120 of supplies had been used.
30	Purchased a new computer for $6,100 with personal funds. (The computer will be used exclusively for business purposes.)

Instructions
Journalize the transactions in the general journal (omit explanations).

E3-2 **(Corrected Trial Balance)** The trial balance of Wanda Landowska Company, a sole proprietorship shown on the next page, does not balance. Your review of the ledger reveals the following: (a) each account had a normal balance, (b) the debit footings in Prepaid Insurance, Accounts Payable, and Property Tax Expense were each understated $100, (c) transposition errors were made in Accounts Receivable and Service Revenue; the correct balances are $2,750 and $6,690, respectively, (d) a debit posting to Advertising Expense of $300 was omitted, and (e) a $1,500 cash drawing by the owner was debited to Wanda Landowska, Capital, and credited to Cash.

WANDA LANDOWSKA COMPANY
Trial Balance
April 30, 2001

	Debit	Credit
Cash	$ 4,800	
Accounts Receivable	2,570	
Prepaid Insurance	700	
Equipment		$8,000
Accounts Payable		4,500
Property Tax Payable	560	
Wanda Landowska, Capital		11,200
Service Revenue	6,960	
Salaries Expense	4,200	
Advertising Expense	1,100	
Property Tax Expense		800
	$20,890	$24,500

Instructions

Prepare a correct trial balance.

E3-3 **(Corrected Trial Balance)** The trial balance of Blues Traveller Corporation does not balance.

BLUES TRAVELLER CORPORATION
Trial Balance
April 30

	Debit	Credit
Cash	$5,912	
Accounts Receivable	5,240	
Supplies on Hand	2,967	
Furniture and Equipment	6,100	
Accounts Payable		$7,044
Common Shares		8,000
Retained Earnings		2,000
Service Revenue		5,200
Office Expense	4,320	
	$24,539	$22,244

An examination of the ledger shows these errors.

1. Cash received from a customer on account was recorded (both debit and credit) as $1,380 instead of $1,830.
2. The purchase on account of a computer costing $3,200 was recorded as a debit to Office Expense and a credit to Accounts Payable.
3. Services were performed on account for a client, $2,250, for which Accounts Receivable was debited $2,250 and Service Revenue was credited $225.
4. A payment of $95 for telephone charges was entered as a debit to Office Expenses and a debit to Cash.
5. The Service Revenue account was totalled at $5,200 instead of $5,280.

Instructions

From this information, prepare a corrected trial balance.

E3-4 **(Corrected Trial Balance)** The trial balance of Antoine Watteau Inc. shown below does not balance.

ANTOINE WATTEAU INC.
Trial Balance
June 30, 2002

	Debit	Credit
Cash		$2,870
Accounts Receivable	$3,231	
Supplies	800	
Equipment	3,800	
Accounts Payable		2,666
Unearned Service Revenue	1,200	
Common Shares		6,000
Retained Earnings		3,000
Service Revenue		2,380
Wages Expense	3,400	
Office Expense	940	
	$13,371	$16,916

Each of the listed accounts has a normal balance per the general ledger. An examination of the ledger and journal reveals the following errors.

1. Cash received from a customer on account was debited for $570 and Accounts Receivable was credited for the same amount. The actual collection was for $750.
2. The purchase of a computer printer on account for $500 was recorded as a debit to Supplies for $500 and a credit to Accounts Payable for $500.
3. Services were performed on account for a client for $890. Accounts Receivable was debited for $890 and Service Revenue was credited for $89.
4. A payment of $65 for telephone charges was recorded as a debit to Office Expense for $65 and a debit to Cash for $65.
5. When the Unearned Service Revenue account was reviewed, it was found that $325 of the balance was earned prior to June 30.
6. A debit posting to Wages Expense of $670 was omitted.
7. A payment on account for $206 was credited to Cash for $206 and credited to Accounts Payable for $260.
8. A dividend of $575 was debited to Wages Expense for $575 and credited to Cash for $575.

Instructions
Prepare a correct trial balance. (Note: It may be necessary to add one or more accounts to the trial balance.)

E3-5 **(Adjusting Entries)** The ledger of Duggan Rental Agency Ltd. on March 31 of the current year includes the following selected accounts before adjusting entries have been prepared.

	Debit	Credit
Prepaid Insurance	$3,600	
Supplies	2,800	
Equipment	25,000	
Accumulated Amortization-Equipment		$8,400
Notes Payable		20,000
Unearned Rent Revenue		9,300
Rent Revenue		60,000
Interest Expense	–0–	
Wage Expense	14,000	

An analysis of the accounts shows the following:

1. The equipment amortization is $250 per month.
2. One-third of the unearned rent was earned during the quarter.
3. Interest of $500 is accrued on the notes payable.
4. Supplies on hand total $850.
5. Insurance expires at the rate of $300 per month.

Instructions

Prepare the adjusting entries at March 31, assuming that adjusting entries are made quarterly. Additional accounts are: Amortization Expense, Insurance Expense, Interest Payable, and Supplies Expense.

E3-6 (Adjusting Entries) Karen Weller, D.D.S., opened a dental practice on January 1, 2002. During the first month of operations the following transactions occurred.

1. Performed services for patients who had dental plan insurance. At January 31, $750 of such services was earned but not yet billed to the insurance companies.
2. Utility expenses incurred but not paid prior to January 31 totalled $520.
3. Purchased dental equipment on January 1 for $80,000, paying $20,000 in cash and signing a $60,000, three-year-note payable. The equipment amortization is $400 per month. Interest is $500 per month.
4. Purchased a one-year malpractice insurance policy on January 1 for $12,000.
5. Purchased $1,600 of dental supplies. On January 31, determined that $500 of supplies were on hand.

Instructions

Prepare the adjusting entries on January 31. Account titles are: Accumulated Amortization-Dental Equipment, Amortization Expense, Service Revenue, Accounts Receivable, Insurance Expense, Interest Expense, Interest Payable, Prepaid Insurance, Supplies, Supplies Expense, Utilities Expense, and Utilities Payable.

E3-7 (Analyse Adjusted Data) A partial adjusted trial balance of Piper Limited at January 31, 2002, shows the following:

PIPER LIMITED
Adjusted Trial Balance
January 31, 2002

	Debit	Credit
Supplies	$ 700	
Prepaid Insurance	2,400	
Salaries Payable		$800
Unearned Revenue		750
Supplies Expense	950	
Insurance Expense	400	
Salaries Expense	1,800	
Service Revenue		2,000

Instructions

Answer the following questions, assuming the year begins January 1:

(a) If the amount in Supplies Expense is the January 31 adjusting entry, and $850 of supplies was purchased in January, what was the balance in Supplies on January 1?

(b) If the amount in Insurance Expense is the January 31 adjusting entry, and the original insurance premium was for one year, what was the total premium and when was the policy purchased?

(c) If $2,500 of salaries was paid in January, what was the balance in Salaries Payable at December 31, 2001?

(d) If $1,600 was received in January for services performed in January, what was the balance in Unearned Revenue at December 31, 2001?

E3-8 (Adjusting Entries) Ben Borg is the new owner of Ace Computer Services Inc. At the end of August 2001, his first month of ownership, Ben is trying to prepare monthly financial statements. Below is some information related to unrecorded expenses that the business incurred during August.

1. At August 31, Mr. Borg owed his employees $1,900 in wages that would be paid on September 1.
2. At the end of the month, he had not yet received the month's utility bill. Based on previous experience, he estimated the bill would be approximately $600.
3. On August 1, Mr. Borg borrowed $30,000 from a local bank on a 15-year mortgage. The annual interest rate is 8 percent.
4. A telephone bill in the amount of $117 covering August charges is unpaid at August 31.

Instructions

Prepare the adjusting journal entries as of August 31, 2001, suggested by the information above.

E3-9 **(Adjusting Entries)** Selected accounts of Urdu Limited are shown below.

Supplies			
Beg. Bal.	800	10/31	470

Accounts Receivable		
10/17	2,400	
10/31	1,650	

Salaries Expense		
10/15	800	
10/31	600	

Salaries Payable		
	10/31	600

Unearned Service Revenue			
10/31	400	10/20	650

Supplies Expense	
10/31	470

Service Revenue		
	10/17	2,400
	10/31	1,650
	10/31	400

Instructions

From an analysis of the T-accounts, reconstruct (a) the October transaction entries, and (b) the adjusting journal entries that were made on October 31, 2001.

E3-10 **(Adjusting Entries)** The trial balance for Greco Resort Limited on August 31 is as follows:

GRECO RESORT LIMITED
Trial Balance
August 31, 2001

	Debit	Credit
Cash	$19,600	
Prepaid Insurance	4,500	
Supplies	2,600	
Land	20,000	
Cottages	120,000	
Furniture	16,000	
Accounts Payable		$ 4,500
Unearned Rent Revenue		4,600
Loan Payable		60,000
Common Shares		91,000
Retained Earnings		9,000
Dividends	5,000	
Rent Revenue		76,200
Salaries Expense	44,800	
Utilities Expense	9,200	
Repair Expense	3,600	
	$245,300	$245,300

Other data:
1. The balance in prepaid insurance is a one-year premium paid on June 1, 2001.
2. An inventory count on August 31 shows $450 of supplies on hand.
3. Annual amortization rates are cottages (4%) and furniture (10%). Salvage value is estimated to be 10 percent of cost.
4. Unearned Rent Revenue of $3,800 was earned prior to August 31.
5. Salaries of $375 were unpaid at August 31.
6. Rentals of $800 were due from tenants at August 31.
7. The loan interest rate is 8 pecent per year.

Instructions

(a) Journalize the adjusting entries on August 31 for the three-month period June 1–August 31.
(b) Prepare an adjusted trial balance on August 31.

E3-11 **(Closing Entries)** The adjusted trial balance of Lopez Limited shows the following data pertaining to sales at the end of its fiscal year October 31, 2001: Sales $800,000, Freight-out $12,000, Sales Returns and Allowances $24,000, and Sales Discounts $15,000.

Instructions

(a) Prepare the sales revenues section of the income statement.

(b) Prepare separate closing entries for (1) sales, and (2) the contra accounts to sales.

E3-12 **(Closing Entries)** Presented is information related to Gonzales Corporation for the month of January 2001.

Cost of goods sold	$208,000	Salary expense	$ 61,000
Freight-out	7,000	Sales discounts	8,000
Insurance expense	12,000	Sales returns and allowances	13,000
Rent expense	20,000	Sales	350,000

Instructions

Prepare the necessary closing entries.

E3-13 **(Work Sheet)** Presented below are selected accounts for Algonquin Inc. as reported in the work sheet at the end of May 2001.

Accounts	Adjusted Trial Balance		Income Statement		Balance Sheet	
	Dr.	Cr.	Dr.	Cr.	Dr.	Cr.
Cash	9,000					
Merchandise Inventory	80,000					
Sales		450,000				
Sales Returns and Allowances	10,000					
Sales Discounts	5,000					
Cost of Goods Sold	250,000					

Instructions

Complete the work sheet by extending amounts reported in the adjusted trial balance to the appropriate columns in the work sheet. Do not total individual columns.

E3-14 **(Missing Amounts)** Presented below is financial information for two different companies:

	Alatorre Ltd.	Eduardo Inc
Sales	$90,000	(d)
Sales returns	(a)	$ 5,000
Net sales	81,000	95,000
Cost of goods sold	56,000	(e)
Gross profit	(b)	38,000
Operating expenses	15,000	23,000
Net income	(c)	15,000

Instructions

Calculate the missing amounts.

E3-15 **(Find Missing Amounts-Periodic Inventory)** Financial information is presented below for four different companies.

	Pamela's Cosmetics Inc.	Dean's Grocery Inc.	Anderson Wholesalers Ltd.	Baywatch Supply Ltd.
Sales	$78,000	(c)	$144,000	$100,000
Sales returns	(a)	$5,000	12,000	9,000
Net sales	74,000	94,000	132,000	(g)
Beginning inventory	16,000	(d)	44,000	24,000
Purchases	88,000	100,000	(e)	85,000
Purchase returns	6,000	10,000	8,000	(h)
Ending inventory	(b)	48,000	30,000	28,000
Cost of goods sold	64,000	72,000	(f)	72,000
Gross profit	10,000	22,000	18,000	(i)

Instructions

Determine the missing amounts (a–i). Show all calculations.

E3-16 (Cost of Goods Sold Section-Periodic Inventory) The trial balance of Mariner Limited at the end of its fiscal year, August 31, 2002, includes the following accounts: Merchandise Inventory $17,500, Purchases $149,400, Sales $200,000, Freight-in $4,000, Sales Returns and Allowances $4,000, Freight-out $1,000, and Purchase Returns and Allowances $2,000. The ending merchandise inventory is $25,000.

Instructions

Prepare a cost of goods sold section for the year ending August 31.

E3-17 (Closing Entries) Presented below are selected account balances for Winslow Inc. as of December 31, 2002.

Merchandise Inventory 12/31/02	$ 60,000	Cost of Goods Sold	$225,700
Common Shares	75,000	Selling Expenses	16,000
Retained Earnings	45,000	Administrative Expenses	38,000
Dividends	18,000	Income Tax Expense	30,000
Sales Returns and Allowances	12,000		
Sales Discounts	15,000		
Sales	410,000		

Instructions

Prepare closing entries for Winslow Inc. on December 31, 2002.

E3-18 (Work Sheet Preparation) The trial balance of Stein Roofing Inc. at March 31, 2002 is as follows:

STEIN ROOFING INC.
Trial Balance
March 31, 2002

	Debit	Credit
Cash	$2,300	
Accounts Receivable	2,600	
Roofing Supplies	1,100	
Equipment	6,000	
Accumulated Amortization-Equipment		$ 1,200
Accounts Payable		1,100
Unearned Service Revenue		300
Common Shares		6,400
Retained Earnings		600
Service Revenue		3,000
Salaries Expense	500	
Miscellaneous Expense	100	
	$12,600	$12,600

Other data:

1. A physical count reveals only $520 of roofing supplies on hand.
2. Equipment is amortized at a rate of $120 per month.
3. Unearned service revenue amounted to $100 on March 31.
4. Accrued salaries are $850.

Instructions

Enter the trial balance on a work sheet and complete the work sheet, assuming that the adjustments relate only to the month of March. (Ignore income taxes.)

E3-19 (Work Sheet and Balance Sheet Presentation) adjusted trial balance of Bradley Company work sheet for the month ended April 30, 2001, contains the following:

BRADLEY COMPANY
Work Sheet (partial)
For the Month Ended April 30, 2001

Account Titles	Adjusted Trial Balance Dr.	Adjusted Trial Balance Cr.	Income Statement Dr.	Income Statement Cr.	Balance Sheet Dr.	Balance Sheet Cr.
Cash	$19,472					
Accounts Receivable	6,920					
Prepaid Rent	2,280					
Equipment	18,050					
Accumulated Amortization		$ 4,895				
Notes Payable		5,700				
Accounts Payable		5,472				
Bradley, Capital		34,960				
Bradley, Drawing	6,650					
Service Revenue		11,590				
Salaries Expense	6,840					
Rent Expense	2,260					
Amortization Expense	145					
Interest Expense	83					
Interest Payable		83				

Instructions

Complete the work sheet and prepare a balance sheet as illustrated in this chapter.

E3-20 **(Partial Work Sheet Preparation)** Jurassic Inc. prepares monthly financial statements from a work sheet. Selected portions of the January work sheet showed the following data:

JURASSIC INC.
Work Sheet (partial)
For Month Ended January 31, 2002

Account Title	Trial Balance Dr.	Trial Balance Cr.	Adjustments Dr.	Adjustments Cr.	Adjusted Trial Balance Dr.	Adjusted Trial Balance Cr.
Supplies	3,256			(a) 1,500	1,756	
Accumulated Amortization		6,682		(b) 257		6,939
Interest Payable		100		(c) 50		150
Supplies Expense			(a) 1,500		1,500	
Amortization Expense			(b) 257		257	
Interest Expense			(c) 50		50	

During February, no events occurred that affected these accounts, but at the end of February, the following information was available:

(a)	Supplies on hand	$715
(b)	Monthly amortization	$257
(c)	Accrued interest	$50

Instructions

Reproduce the data that would appear in the February work sheet and indicate the amounts that would be shown in the February income statement.

E3-21 **(Transactions of a Corporation, Including Investment and Dividend)** Scratch Miniature Golf and Driving Range Inc. was opened on March 1 by Scott Verplank. The following selected events and transactions occurred during March:

Mar. 1 Invested $50,000 cash in the business in exchange for common shares.
3 Purchased Lee Janzen's Golf Land for $38,000 cash. The price consists of land, $10,000; building, $22,000; and equipment, $6,000. (Make one compound entry.)

Mar. 5 Advertised the opening of the driving range and miniature golf course, paying advertising expenses of $1,600.
       6 Paid cash $1,480 for a one-year insurance policy.
      10 Purchased golf equipment for $2,500 from Sluman Ltd. payable in 30 days.
      18 Received golf fees of $1,200 in cash.
      25 Declared and paid a $500 cash dividend.
      30 Paid wages of $900.
      30 Paid Sluman Ltd. in full.
      31 Received $750 of fees in cash.

Scott Verplank uses the following accounts: Cash; Prepaid Insurance; Land; Buildings; Equipment; Accounts Payable; Common Shares; Dividends; Service Revenue; Advertising Expense; and Wages Expense.

Instructions

Journalize the March transactions.

*E3-22 **(Adjusting and Reversing Entries)**   On December 31, adjusting information for Lyman Corporation is as follows:

1. Estimated amortization on equipment $1,100.
2. Personal property taxes amounting to $525 have accrued but are unrecorded and unpaid.
3. Employees' wages earned but unpaid and unrecorded $1,200.
4. Unearned Service Revenue balance includes $1,500 that has been earned.
5. Interest of $250 on a $25,000 note receivable has accrued.

Instructions

(a) Prepare adjusting journal entries.
(b) Prepare reversing journal entries.

*E3-23 **(Closing and Reversing Entries)**   On December 31, the adjusted trial balance of Cree Inc. shows the following selected data:

Accounts Receivable	$4,300	Service Revenue	$96,000
Interest Expense	7,800	Interest Payable	2,400

Analysis shows that adjusting entries were made for **(a)** $4,300 of services performed but not billed, and **(b)** $2,400 of accrued but unpaid interest.

Instructions

(a) Prepare the closing entries for the temporary accounts at December 31.
(b) Prepare the reversing entries on January 1.
(c) Enter the adjusted trial balance data in the four accounts. Post the entries in (a) and (b) and rule and balance the accounts. (Use T-accounts.)
(d) Prepare the entries to record (1) the collection of the accrued commissions on January 10, and (2) the payment of all interest due ($3,000) on January 15.
(e) Post the entries in (d) to the temporary accounts.

*E3-24 **(Adjusting and Reversing Entries)**   When the accounts of Barenboim Inc. are examined, the adjusting data listed below are uncovered on December 31, the end of an annual fiscal period.

1. The prepaid insurance account shows a debit of $5,280, representing the cost of a two-year fire insurance policy dated August 1 of the current year.
2. On November 1, Rental Revenue was credited for $1,800, representing revenue from a subrental for a three-month period beginning on that date.
3. Purchase of advertising materials for $800 during the year was recorded in the Advertising Expense account. On December 31, advertising materials of $290 are on hand.
4. Interest of $770 has accrued on notes payable.

Instructions

Prepare in general journal form: (a) the adjusting entry for each item; (b) the reversing entry for each item where appropriate.

*E3-25 **(Cash and Accrual Basis)**   Rogers Corp. maintains its financial records on the cash basis of accounting. Interested in securing a long-term loan from its regular bank, the company requests you, as an independent CA, to convert its cash basis income statement data to the accrual basis. You are provided with the following summarized data covering 1999, 2000, and 2001.

	1999	2000	2001
Cash receipts from sales:			
On 1999 sales	$295,000	$160,000	$ 30,000
On 2000 sales	–0–	355,000	90,000
On 2001 sales			408,000
Cash payments for expenses:			
On 1999 expenses	185,000	67,000	25,000
On 2000 expenses	40,000a	160,000	55,000
On 20001 expenses		45,000b	218,000

aPrepayments of 2000 expense
bPrepayments of 2001 expense

Instructions

Using the data above, prepare abbreviated income statements for the years 1999 and 2000 on:

(a) cash basis

(b) accrual basis

PROBLEMS

P3-1 Listed below are the transactions of Isao Aoki, D.D.S., for the month of September:

Sept. 1 Isao Aoki begins practice as a dentist and invests $20,000 cash.
2 Purchases furniture and dental equipment on account from Green Jacket Co. for $17,280.
4 Pays rent for office space, $680 for the month.
4 Employs a receptionist, Michael Bradley.
5 Purchases dental supplies for cash, $942.
8 Receives cash of $1,690 from patients for services performed.
10 Pays miscellaneous office expenses, $430.
14 Bills patients $5,120 for services performed.
18 Pays Green Jacket Co. on account, $3,600.
19 Withdraws $3,000 cash from the business for personal use.
20 Receives $980 from patients on account.
25 Bills patients $2,110 for services performed.
30 Pays the following expenses in cash: office salaries, $1,400; miscellaneous office expenses, $85.
30 Dental supplies used during September, $330.

Instructions

(a) Enter the transactions shown above in appropriate general ledger accounts. Use the following ledger accounts: Cash; Accounts Receivable; Supplies on Hand; Furniture and Equipment; Accumulated Amortization; Accounts Payable; Isao Aoki, Capital; Service Revenue; Rent Expense; Miscellaneous Office Expense; Office Salaries Expense; Supplies Expense; Amortization Expense; and Income Summary. Allow 10 lines for the Cash and Income Summary accounts, and five lines for each of the other accounts needed. Record amortization using a 5-year life on the furniture and equipment, the straight-line method, and no salvage value. Do not use a drawing account.

(b) Prepare an adjusted trial balance.

(c) Prepare an income statement, a balance sheet, and a statement of owner's equity.

(d) Close the ledger. Post directly to the general ledger account without writing out the journal entry.

(e) Prepare a post-closing trial balance.

P3-2 Yount Advertising Agency Limited was founded by Thomas Grant in January of 1997. Presented below are both the adjusted and unadjusted trial balances as of December 31, 2001.

YOUNT ADVERTISING AGENCY LIMITED
Trial Balance
December 31, 2001

	Unadjusted		Adjusted	
	Dr.	Cr.	Dr.	Cr.
Cash	$11,000		$11,000	
Accounts Receivable	20,000		21,500	
Art Supplies	8,400		5,000	
Prepaid Insurance	3,350		2,500	
Printing Equipment	60,000		60,000	
Accumulated Amortization		$28,000		$35,000
Accounts Payable		5,000		5,000
Interest Payable		– 0 –		150
Notes Payable		5,000		5,000
Unearned Advertising Revenue		7,000		5,600
Salaries Payable		– 0 –		1,300
Common Shares		10,000		10,000
Retained Earnings		3,500		3,500
Advertising Revenue		58,600		61,500
Salaries Expense	10,000		11,300	
Insurance Expense			850	
Interest Expense	350		500	
Amortization Expense			7,000	
Art Supplies Expense			3,400	
Rent Expense	4,000		4,000	
	$117,100	$117,100	$127,050	$127,050

Instructions

(a) Journalize the annual adjusting entries that were made.

(b) Prepare an income statement and a statement of retained earnings for the year ending December 31, 2001, and a balance sheet at December 31.

(c) Answer the following questions:

    1. If the note has been outstanding three months, what is the annual interest rate on that note?

    2. If the company paid $13,500 in salaries in 2001, what was the balance in Salaries Payable on December 31, 2000?

P3-3 A review of the ledger of Okanagen Inc. Company at December 31, 2001, produces the following data pertaining to the preparation of annual adjusting entries.

1. Salaries Payable $0. There are eight salaried employees. Salaries are paid every Friday for the current week. Five employees receive a salary of $700 each per week, and three employees earn $500 each per week. December 31 is a Tuesday. Employees do not work weekends. All employees worked the last two days of December.

2. Unearned Rent Revenue $369,000. The company began subleasing office space in its new building on November 1. Each tenant is required to make a $5,000 security deposit that is not refundable until occupancy is terminated. At December 31, the company had the following rental contracts that are paid in full for the entire term of the lease.

Date	Term (in months)	Monthly Rent	Number of Leases
Nov. 1	6	$4,000	5
Dec. 1	6	$8,500	4

3. Prepaid Advertising $13,200. This balance consists of payments on two advertising contracts. The contracts provide for monthly advertising in two trade magazines. The terms of the contracts are as follows:

Contract	Date	Amount	Number of Magazine Issues
A650	May 1	$6,000	12
B974	Oct. 1	7,200	24

The first advertisement runs in the month in which the contract is signed.

4. Notes Payable $80,000. This balance consists of a note for one year at an annual interest rate of 12 percent, dated June 1.

Instructions

Prepare the adjusting entries at December 31, 2001. (Show all calculations).

P3-4 The completed financial statement columns of the work sheet for Parsons Limited are shown below.

PARSONS LIMITED
Work Sheet
For the Year Ended December 31, 2002

Account No.	Account Titles	Income Statement Dr.	Income Statement Cr.	Balance Sheet Dr.	Balance Sheet Cr.
101	Cash			8,200	
112	Accounts Receivable			7,500	
130	Prepaid Insurance			1,800	
157	Equipment			28,000	
167	Accumulated Amortization				8,600
201	Accounts Payable				12,000
212	Salaries Payable				3,000
301	Common Shares				20,000
306	Retained Earnings				6,800
400	Service Revenue		42,000		
622	Repair Expense	3,200			
711	Amortization Expense	2,800			
722	Insurance Expense	1,200			
726	Salaries Expense	36,000			
732	Utilities Expense	3,700			
	Totals	46,900	42,000	45,500	50,400
	Net Loss		4,900	4,900	
		46,900	46,900	50,400	50,400

Instructions

(a) Prepare an income statement, retained earnings statement, and a classified balance sheet. Parsons' shareholders made an additional investment in the business of $4,000 during 2002.
(b) Prepare the closing entries.
(c) Post the closing entries and rule and balance the accounts. Use T-accounts. Income Summary is No. 350.
(d) Prepare a post-closing trial balance.

P3-5 Noah's Ark has a fiscal year ending on September 30. Selected data from the September 30 work sheet are presented below:

NOAH'S ARK
Work Sheet
For the Year Ended September 30, 2002

	Trial Balance Dr.	Trial Balance Cr.	Adjusted Trial Balance Dr.	Adjusted Trial Balance Cr.
Cash	37,400		37,400	
Supplies	18,600		1,200	
Prepaid Insurance	31,900		3,900	
Land	80,000		80,000	
Equipment	120,000		120,000	
Accumulated Amortization		36,200		43,000
Accounts Payable		14,600		14,600
Unearned Admissions Revenue		2,700		1,700
Mortgage Payable		50,000		50,000
N. Y. Berge, Capital		109,700		109,700

N. Y. Berge, Drawing	14,000		14,000	
Admissions Revenue		278,500		279,500
Salaries Expense	109,000		109,000	
Repair Expense	30,500		30,500	
Advertising Expense	9,400		9,400	
Utilities Expense	16,900		16,900	
Property Taxes Expense	18,000		21,000	
Interest Expense	6,000		12,000	
Totals	491,700	491,700		
Insurance Expense			28,000	
Supplies Expense			17,400	
Interest Payable				6,000
Amortization Expense			6,800	
Property Taxes Payable				3,000
Totals			507,500	507,500

Instructions

(a) Prepare a complete work sheet.

(b) Prepare a classified balance sheet. (Note: $10,000 of the mortgage payable is due for payment in the next fiscal year.)

(c) Journalize the adjusting entries using the work sheet as a basis.

(d) Journalize the closing entries using the work sheet as a basis.

(e) Prepare a post-closing trial balance.

P3-6 The trial balance of Bishop Fashion Centre Inc. contained the following accounts at November 30, the end of the company's fiscal year.

BISHOP FASHION CENTRE INC.
Trial Balance
November 30, 2002

	Debit	Credit
Cash	$ 26,700	
Accounts Receivable	33,700	
Merchandise Inventory	45,000	
Store Supplies	5,500	
Store Equipment	85,000	
Accumulated Amortization-Store Equipment		$ 18,000
Delivery Equipment	48,000	
Accumulated Amortization-Delivery Equipment		6,000
Notes Payable		51,000
Accounts Payable		48,500
Common Shares		90,000
Retained Earnings		8,000
Sales		757,200
Sales Returns and Allowances	4,200	
Cost of Goods Sold	497,400	
Salaries Expense	140,000	
Advertising Expense	26,400	
Utilities Expense	14,000	
Repair Expense	12,100	
Delivery Expense	16,700	
Rent Expense	24,000	
	$978,700	$978,700

Adjustment data:

1. Store supplies on hand totalled $3,500.

2. Amortization is $9,000 on the store equipment and $7,000 on the delivery equipment.

3. Interest of $11,000 is accrued on notes payable at November 30.

Other data:

1. Salaries expense is 70 percent selling and 30 percent administrative.

2. Rent expense and utilities expense are 80 percent selling and 20 percent administrative.

3. $30,000 of notes payable are due for payment next year.
4. Repair expense is 100 percent administrative.

Instructions

(a) Enter the trial balance on a work sheet and complete the work sheet.
(b) Prepare a multiple-step income statement and retained earnings statement for the year and a classified balance sheet as of November 30, 2002.
(c) Journalize the adjusting entries.
(d) Journalize the closing entries.
(e) Prepare a post-closing trial balance.

P3-7 The Rusch Department Store Incorporated is located near the Village shopping mall. At the end of the company's fiscal year on December 31, 2002, the following accounts appeared in two of its trial balances.

	Unadjusted	Adjusted
Accounts Payable	$79,300	$79,300
Accounts Receivable	50,300	50,300
Accumulated Amortization-Building	42,100	52,500
Accumulated Amortization-Equipment	29,600	42,900
Building	190,000	190,000
Cash	23,000	23,000
Common Shares	160,000	160,000
Retained Earnings	16,600	16,600
Cost of Goods Sold	412,700	412,700
Amortization Expense-Building		10,400
Amortization Expense-Equipment		13,300
Dividends	28,000	28,000
Equipment	110,000	110,000
Insurance Expense		7,200
Interest Expense	3,000	11,000
Interest Payable		8,000
Interest Revenue	4,000	4,000
Merchandise Inventory	75,000	75,000
Mortgage Payable	80,000	80,000
Office Salaries Expense	32,000	32,000
Prepaid Insurance	9,600	2,400
Property Taxes Expense		4,800
Property Taxes Payable		4,800
Sales Salaries Expense	76,000	76,000
Sales	628,000	628,000
Sales Commissions Expense	11,000	14,500
Sales Commissions Payable		3,500
Sales Returns and Allowances	8,000	8,000
Utilities Expense	11,000	11,000

Analysis reveals the following additional data:
1. Insurance expense and utilities expense are 60 percent selling and 40 percent administrative.
2. $20,000 of the mortgage payable is due for payment next year.
3. Amortization on the building and property tax expense are administrative expenses; amortization on the equipment is a selling expense.

Instructions

(a) Prepare a multiple-step income statement, a retained earnings statement, and a classified balance sheet.
(b) Journalize the adjusting entries that were made.
(c) Journalize the closing entries that are necessary.

P3-8 The accounts listed below appeared in the December 31 trial balance of the Alexander Theatre.

	Debit	Credit
Equipment	$192,000	
Accumulated Amortization-Equipment		$60,000
Notes Payable		90,000
Admissions Revenue		380,000

Advertising Expense	13,680
Salaries Expense	57,600
Interest Expense	1,400

Instructions

(a) From the account balances listed above and the information given below, prepare the annual adjusting entries necessary on December 31.

1. The equipment has an estimated life of 16 years and a salvage value of $40,000 at the end of that time. (Use straight-line method.)
2. The note payable is a 90-day note given to the bank October 20 and bearing interest at 10 percent.
3. In December, 2,000 coupon admission books were sold at $25 each; they could be used for admission any time after January 1.
4. Advertising expense paid in advance and included in Advertising Expense, $1,100.
5. Salaries accrued but unpaid, $4,700.

(b) What amounts should be shown for each of the following on the income statement for the year?

1. Interest expense.
2. Admissions revenue.
3. Advertising expense.
4. Salaries expense.

P3-9 Presented below are the trial balance and the other information related to Muhammad Moamar, a consulting engineer.

MUHAMMAD MOAMAR, CONSULTING ENGINEER
Trial Balance
December 31, 2001

	Debit	Credit
Cash	$31,500	
Accounts Receivable	49,600	
Allowance for Doubtful Accounts		$750
Engineering Supplies Inventory	1,960	
Unexpired Insurance	1,100	
Furniture and Equipment	25,000	
Accumulated Amortization-Furniture and Equipment		6,250
Notes Payable		7,200
Muhammad Moamar, Capital		35,010
Service Revenue		100,000
Rent Expense	9,750	
Office Salaries Expense	28,500	
Heat, Light, and Water Expense	1,080	
Miscellaneous Office Expense	720	
	$149,210	$149,210

1. Fees received in advance from clients, $6,900.
2. Services performed for clients that were not recorded by December 31, $4,900.
3. Bad debt expense for the year is $1,430.
4. Insurance expired during the year, $480.
5. Furniture and equipment is being amortized at 12½ percent per year.
6. Muhammad gave the bank a 90-day, 10 percent note for $7,200 on December 1, 2001.
7. Rent of the building is $750 per month. The rent for 2001 has been paid, as has that for January 2002.
8. Office salaries earned but unpaid December 31, 2001, $2,510.

Instructions

(a) From the trial balance and other information given, prepare annual adjusting entries as of December 31, 2001.
(b) Prepare an income statement for 2001, a balance sheet, and a statement of owner's equity. Muhammad Moamar withdrew $17,000 cash for personal use during the year.

P3-10   Alicia Advertising Corporation was founded by Jan Alicia in January 1998. Presented below are both the adjusted and unadjusted trial balances as of December 31, 2002.

ALICIA ADVERTISING CORPORATION
Trial Balance
December 31, 2002

	Unadjusted Dr.	Unadjusted Cr.	Adjusted Dr.	Adjusted Cr.
Cash	$7,000		$ 7,000	
Accounts Receivable	19,000		22,000	
Art Supplies	8,500		5,500	
Prepaid Insurance	3,250		2,500	
Printing Equipment	60,000		60,000	
Accumulated Amortization		$ 27,000		$33,750
Accounts Payable		5,000		5,000
Interest Payable				150
Notes Payable		5,000		5,000
Unearned Service Revenue		7,000		5,600
Salaries Payable				1,500
Common Shares		10,000		10,000
Retained Earnings		4,500		4,500
Service Revenue		58,600		63,000
Salaries Expense	10,000		11,500	
Insurance Expense			750	
Interest Expense	350		500	
Amortization Expense			6,750	
Art Supplies Expense	5,000		8,000	
Rent Expense	4,000		4,000	
	$117,100	$117,100	$128,500	$128,500

Instructions

(a) Journalize the annual adjusting entries that were made.

(b) Prepare an income statement and a statement of retained earnings for the year ending December 31, 2002, and a balance sheet at December 31.

(c) Answer the following questions:

  1. If the useful life of equipment is eight years, what is the expected salvage value?
  2. If the note has been outstanding three months, what is the annual interest rate on that note?
  3. If the company paid $12,500 in salaries in 2002, what was the balance in Salaries Payable on December 31, 2001?

P3-11   Presented below is information related to Joan Anderson, Realtor, at the close of the fiscal year ending December 31.

  1. Joan had paid the local newspaper $335 for an advertisement to be run in January of the next year, charging it to Advertising Expense.
  2. On November 1, Joan borrowed $9,000 from Yorkville Bank issuing a 90-day, 10 percent note.
  3. Salaries and wages due and unpaid December 31: sales, $1,420; office clerks, $1,060.
  4. Interest accrued to date on Grant Muldaur's note, which Joan holds, $500.
  5. Estimated loss on bad debts, $1,210 for the period.
  6. Stamps and stationery on hand, $110, charged to Stationery and Postage Expense account when purchased.
  7. Joan has not yet paid the December rent on the building her business occupies, $1,000.
  8. Insurance paid November 1 for one year, $930, charged to Prepaid Insurance when paid.
  9. Property taxes accrued, $1,670.
  10. On December 1, Joan gave Laura Palmer her (Joan's) 60-day, 12 percent note for $6,000 on account.
  11. On October 31, Joan received $2,580 from Douglas Raines in payment of six months' rent for office space occupied by him in the building and credited Unearned Rent Revenue.
  12. On September 1, she paid six months' rent in advance on a warehouse, $6,600, and debited the asset account Prepaid Rent Expense.
  13. The bill from Light & Power Limited for December has been received but not yet entered or paid, $510.
  14. Estimated amortization on furniture and equipment, $1,400.

Instructions
Prepare annual adjusting entries as of December 31.

P3-12 Following is the trial balance of the Platteville Golf Club, Inc. as of December 31. The books are closed annually on December 31.

PLATTEVILLE GOLF CLUB, INC. Trial Balance December 31		
	Debit	Credit
Cash	$ 15,000	
Accounts Receivable	13,000	
Allowance for Doubtful Accounts		$ 1,100
Land	350,000	
Buildings	120,000	
Accumulated Amortization of Buildings		38,400
Equipment	150,000	
Accumulated Amortization of Equipment		70,000
Unexpired Insurance	9,000	
Common Shares		400,000
Retained Earnings		82,000
Dues Revenue		200,000
Greens Fee Revenue		8,100
Rental Revenue		15,400
Utilities Expense	54,000	
Salaries Expense	80,000	
Maintenance Expense	24,000	
	$815,000	$815,000

Instructions
(a) Enter the balances in ledger accounts. Allow five lines for each account.
(b) From the trial balance and the information given, prepare annual adjusting entries and post to the ledger accounts.
   1. The buildings have an estimated life of 25 years with no salvage value (straight-line method).
   2. The equipment is amortized at 10 percent per year.
   3. Insurance expired during the year, $3,500.
   4. The rental revenue represents the amount received for 11 months for dining facilities. The December rent has not yet been received.
   5. It is estimated that 15 percent of the accounts receivable will be uncollectible.
   6. Salaries earned but not paid by December 31, $3,600.
   7. Dues paid in advance by members, $8,900.
(c) Prepare an adjusted trial balance.
(d) Prepare closing entries and post.

P3-13 Presented below is the December 31 trial balance of Drew Boutique Inc.

DREW BOUTIQUE INC. Trial Balance December 31		
	Debit	Credit
Cash	$18,500	
Accounts Receivable	42,000	
Allowance for Doubtful Accounts		$700
Inventory, December 31	80,000	
Furniture and Equipment	84,000	
Accumulated Amortization of Furniture and Equipment		35,000
Prepaid Insurance	5,100	
Notes Payable		28,000
Common Shares		80,600
Retained Earnings		10,000
Sales		600,000

	Debit	Credit
Cost of Goods Sold	398,000	
Sales Salaries Expense	50,000	
Advertising Expense	6,700	
Administrative Salaries Expense	65,000	
Office Expense	5,000	
	$754,300	$754,300

Instructions

(a) Construct T-accounts and enter the balances shown.

(b) Prepare adjusting journal entries for the following and post to the T-accounts. Open additional T-accounts as necessary. (The books are closed yearly on December 31.)

1. Bad debts are estimated to be $1,400.
2. Furniture and equipment is amortized based on a six-year life (no salvage).
3. Insurance expired during the year, $2,550.
4. Interest accrued on notes payable, $3,360.
5. Sales salaries earned but not paid, $2,400.
6. Advertising paid in advance, $700.
7. Office supplies on hand, $1,500, charged to Office Expense when purchased.

(c) Prepare closing entries and post to the accounts.

*P3-14 (Cash and Accrual Basis) On January 1, 2002, Jill Monroe and Jenni Meno formed a computer sales and service enterprise in Montreal by investing $90,000 cash. The new company, Razorback Sales and Service, has the following transactions during January:

1. Pays $6,000 in advance for 3 months' rent of office, showroom, and repair space.
2. Purchases 40 personal computers at a cost of $1,500 each, 6 graphics computers at a cost of $3,000 each, and 25 printers at a cost of $450 each, paying cash upon delivery.
3. Sales, repair, and office employees earn $12,600 in salaries during January, of which $3,000 was still payable at the end of January.
4. Sells 30 personal computers at $2,550 each, 4 graphics computers for $4,500 each, and 15 printers for $750 each; $75,000 is received in cash in January and $30,750 is sold on a deferred payment plan.
5. Other operating expenses of $8,400 are incurred and paid for during January; $2,000 of incurred expenses are payable at January 31.

Instructions

(a) Using the transaction data above, prepare (1) a cash basis income statement and (2) an accrual basis income statement for the month of January.

(b) Using the transaction data above, prepare (1) a cash basis balance sheet and (2) an accrual basis balance sheet as of January 31, 2002.

(c) Identify the items in the cash basis financial statements that make cash basis accounting inconsistent with the theory underlying the elements of financial statements.

*P3-15 (Cash to Accrual) Dr. John Gleason, M.D., maintains the accounting records of Bones Clinic on a cash basis. During 2001, Dr. Gleason collected $146,000 from his patients and paid $55,470 in expenses.

At January 1, 2001, and December 31, 2001, he had accounts receivable, unearned service revenue, accrued expenses, and prepaid expenses as follows (all long-lived assets are rented):

	January 1, 2001	December 31, 2001
Accounts receivable	$9,250	$16,100
Unearned service revenue	2,840	1,620
Accrued expenses	3,435	2,200
Prepaid expenses	2,000	1,775

Instructions

Last week Dr. Gleason asked you, his CA, to help him determine his income on the accrual basis. Write a letter to him explaining what you did to calculate net income on the accrual basis. Be sure to state net income on the accrual basis and to include a schedule of your calculations.

Using Your Judgement

FINANCIAL REPORTING PROBLEM: CANADIAN TIRE CORPORATION LIMITED

The financial statements of **Canadian Tire** are presented in Appendix 5B.

Refer to these financial statements and the accompanying notes to answer the following questions.

Instructions

(a) What were Canadian Tire's total assets at year-end for both years presented?

(b) How much cash (and cash equivalents) did the company have at year-end?

(c) What were the company's revenues for the current and preceding year?

(d) Using the financial statements and related notes, identify items that may result in adjusting entries for prepayments and accruals.

(e) What were the amounts of Canadian Tire's amortization expense for the past two years?

FINANCIAL STATEMENT ANALYSIS CASE

Kellogg Company

Kellogg Company has its world headquarters in Battle Creek, Michigan. The company manufactures and sells ready-to-eat breakfast cereals and convenience foods including toaster pastries and cereal bars.

Selected data from Kellogg Company's 1998 annual report follows: (dollar amounts and share data in millions)

	1998	1997	1996
Net sales	$6,762.1	$6,830.1	$6,676.6
Cost of goods sold	3,282.6	3,270.1	3,122.9
Selling and administrative expense	2,513.9	2,366.8	2,458.7
Net income	502.6	546.0	531.0

In its 1998 annual report, Kellogg Company outlined its plans for the future, which it described as its five-point "strategy for growth." A brief description of these plans follows.

1. Leading the food industry in innovation—Kellogg Company is rolling out a broader grain-based product portfolio, including great-tasting new cereals, innovative convenience foods, and new grain-based products outside our traditional lines.

2. Investing in our largest cereal markets—During 1999, Kellogg will invest in growth in our seven largest cereal markets.

3. Accelerating the global growth of our convenience foods business—Kellogg is focusing both on an expanded geographic distribution and new distribution channels, particularly single-serve channels.

4. Continuing to reduce cost—From ongoing cost-reduction programs, we anticipate more than $50 million in incremental savings in 1999.

5. Creating a more focused and accountable organization—Kellogg's objective is to develop a talented, diverse global workforce with every person focused on the largest, most important activities.

Instructions

(a) For each of the strategies, describe how gross profit and net income are likely to be affected.

(b) Calculate the percentage change in sales, gross profit, operating costs (cost of goods sold plus selling and administrative expenses), and net income from year to year for each of the three years shown. Evaluate Kellogg Company's performance. Which trend seems to be least favourable? Do you think the global strategies described will improve that trend? Explain.

RESEARCH CASE

The March 1995 issue of Management Review includes an article by Barbara Ettorre, entitled "How Motorola Closes its Books in Two Days."

Instructions
Read the article and answer the following questions.

(a) How often does Motorola close its books? How long did the process used to take?

(b) What was the major change Motorola initiated to shorten the closing process?

(c) What incentive does Motorola offer to ensure accurate and timely information?

(d) In a given year, how many journal entry lines does Motorola process?

(e) Provide an example of an external force that prevents Motorola from closing faster than a day-and-a-half.

(f) According to Motorola's corporate vice-president and controller, how do external financial statement users perceive companies that release information early?

ETHICS CASE

Ernest Banks is the manager and accountant for a small company privately owned by three individuals. Banks always has given the owners cash-based financial statements. The owners are not accountants and do not understand how financial statements are prepared. Recently, the business has experienced strong growth, and inventory, accounts receivable, and capital assets have become more significant company assets. Banks understands generally accepted accounting principles and knows that net income would be lower if he prepared accrual-based financial statements. He is afraid that if he gave the owners financial statements prepared on an accrual basis, they would think he is not managing the business well; they might even decide to fire him.

Instructions
Answer the following questions.

(a) What are the ethical issues involved?

(b) What should Banks do?

Reporting Financial Performance

LEARNING OBJECTIVES

· ·

After studying this chapter, you should be able to:

1.	Identify the uses and limitations of an income statement.
2.	Prepare a single-step income statement.
3.	Prepare a multiple-step income statement.
4.	Explain how irregular items are reported.
5.	Measure and report gains and losses from discontinued operations.
6.	Explain intraperiod tax allocation.
7.	Explain where earnings per share information is reported.
8.	Prepare a retained earnings statement.

PREVIEW OF CHAPTER 4

The way items are reported within the income statement can affect its usefulness. The purpose of this chapter is to examine the many different types of revenues, expenses, gains, and losses that are represented in the income statement and related information. The content and organization of this chapter are as follows:

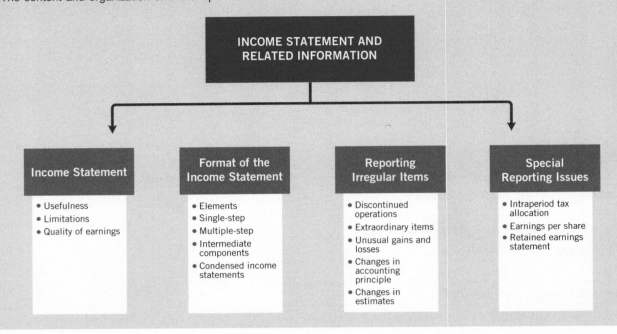

INCOME STATEMENT

OBJECTIVE 1

Identify the uses and limitations of an income statement.

The **income statement**, often called the statement of earnings or statement of income,[1] is the report that **measures the success of enterprise operations** for a given time period. The business and investment community uses this report to determine **profitability**, **investment value**, and **credit worthiness**. It provides investors and creditors with information that helps them allocate resources and assess management stewardship.

Usefulness of the Income Statement

The income statement helps financial statement users allocate resources and assess management stewardship in a number of ways.[2] For example, investors and creditors can use the information in the income statement to:

1. **Evaluate the enterprise's past performance and profitability**. By examining revenues, expenses, gains and losses users can see how the company (and management) performed and compare its performance with its competitors. (Balance sheet information is also useful in assessing profitability, i.e., by calculating return on assets. See Appendix 5A.)

---

[1] *Financial Reporting in Canada, 2000* (Toronto, CICA) indicates that for the 200 companies surveyed, 86 used "earnings", 60 used "income" and 43 used "operations". The use of the latter is increasing while "income" and "earnings" are declining in terms of usage, p. 93.

[2] In support of the usefulness of income information, accounting researchers have documented that the market prices of companies change when income is reported to the market. See W.H. Beaver, "The Information Content of Annual Earnings Announcements," *Empirical Research in Accounting: Selected Studies, Journal of Accounting Research* (Supplement 1968), pp. 67-92.

2. **Provide a basis for predicting future performance**. Information about past performance can be used to determine important trends that, if continued, provide information about future performance. However, success in the past does not necessarily mean the company will have success in the future.

3. **Help assess the risk or uncertainty of achieving future cash flows**. Information on the various components of income—revenues, expenses, gains, and losses—highlights the relationships among them and can be used to assess the risk of not achieving a particular level of cash flows in the future. For example, segregating a company's recurring **operating income** (results from continuing operations) from nonrecurring income sources (discontinued operations, extraordinary items) is useful because operations are usually the primary means by which revenues and cash are generated. Thus, **results from continuing operations** usually have greater significance for predicting future performance than do results from nonrecurring activities.

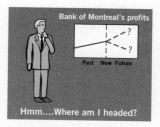

Hmm....Where am I headed?

Recurring items are more certain in the future.

Limitations of the Income Statement

Because net income is an **estimate** and reflects a number of **assumptions**, income statement users must be aware of certain limitations associated with information contained in the income statement. Some of these limitations include:

You left something out!

1. **Items that cannot be measured reliably are not reported in the income statement.** Current practice prohibits recognizing of certain items from the determination of income even though of these items arguably affect an entity's performance from one point in time to another. For example, contingent gains may not be recorded in income, as there is uncertainty regarding whether the gains will ever be realized.

2. **Income numbers are affected by the accounting methods employed.** For example, one company may choose to depreciate its plant assets on an accelerated basis; another chooses straight-line amortization. Assuming all other factors are equal, the first company's income will be lower, even though the companies are essentially the same. In effect, we are comparing apples with oranges.

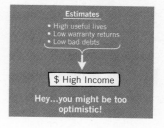

Hmm... Is the income the same?

3. **Income measurement involves the use of estimates.** For example, one company may estimate in good faith that an asset's useful life is 20 years while another company uses a 15-year estimate for the same type of asset. Similarly, some companies may make overly optimistic estimates of future warranty returns and bad debt write-offs, which result in lower expense and higher income.

Hey...you might be too optimistic!

Quality of Earnings

Users need **high quality information** about a company's earnings to make decisions,[3] however, not all income statements provide this. This issue was addressed in part above (limitations of the income statement) and will be examined further here. When analysing information for usefulness, there are two aspects that must be considered— content **and** presentation (i.e. a clear, concise manner that fosters ease of use). The nature of the **content** and the way it is **presented** are referred to as the quality of earnings.

Earnings numbers may be of a **higher quality or conversely, lower quality**. Higher quality earnings are **more reliable**, with a lower margin of potential misstatement. Illustration 4-1 articulates some attributes of high quality earnings.

Looking at Illustration 4-1, there are some factors, which are under management control, such as the **integrity** of the information, i.e., **what information is captured**, how it is **measured** and how it is **presented/disclosed**. Management may also have some control over how quickly cash is generated from operations and how closely this correlates to reported earnings, i.e., through choice of sales and payment terms. (Noted under (2) in the illustration.)

UNDERLYING CONCEPTS

Higher quality earnings have greater predictive value.

---

[3] As noted in Chapter 2, the objective of financial reporting is to provide information useful in "investing and credit decisions and in assessing future cash flows..."

ILLUSTRATION 4-1
Some Attributes of High Quality Earnings

High quality earnings
1. related to the **integrity** of the information itself
   - little, if any **bias** (numbers not subject to manipulation)
   - **objectively determined** (consider need to estimate, accounting choice, application of professional judgement)
   - reflect **economic reality**—all transactions/events captured and appropriately presented
   - **transparency**—no attempt to disguise or mislead
2. related to the **utility** of the information (i.e., its usefulness in specific decision-making such as valuing a company or share price). As a general presumption, **less uncertainty/more stability lends itself to greater usefulness in many decisions.**
   - reflect primarily **earnings generated from ongoing core business** activities (as opposed to one time gains/losses). Earnings that are **sustainable** have greater predictive value.
   - **less volatile** (consider riskiness of business, business strategy, industry, economic and political environments and effects of all these on earnings stability/volatility). Again, less volatile earnings allow creditors and investors to assess future cash flows.
   - more **closely correlated with cash flows from operations** (i.e. when one dollar of earnings is reported, the cash has been received or will be received shortly). Note that this could be a function of accounting choice (i.e. revenue recognition policies) or the nature of the business i.e. a cash based business. Earnings that convert to cash more quickly provide a better measure of real earnings as little or no uncertainty exists as to realizability.

However, factors such as the nature of the business, industry, and economic and political environment are beyond the control of management for the most part although management may certainly devise strategies to identify and minimize risks that lead to volatile earnings.

Companies with higher quality earnings are attributed higher values by the markets, all other things being equal. Earnings that are volatile, subject to significant estimation, choice in accounting policy, bias, etc. are discounted by the markets. Financial analysts assess quality of earnings and factor it into their decisions.

Earnings management may be defined as the process of **targeting certain earnings levels** (whether current or future) or **desired earnings trends** and working backwards to determine what has to be done to ensure that these targets are met (including selection of accounting and other company policies, use of estimates and even execution of transactions). In many cases, earnings management is used to increase income in the current year at the expense of income in future years. For example, companies may prematurely recognize sales before they are complete in order to boost earnings. Some companies may also enter into transactions with the sole objective of making the statements look better, incurring unnecessary transactions costs.

Earnings management can also be used to decrease current earnings in order to increase future income. Reserves are established by using aggressive assumptions to estimate liabilities for such items as sales returns, loan losses, and warranty returns. These reserves can then be reduced in the future to increase income. Such activities have a **negative effect on the quality of earnings** if they distort the information in a way that renders it less useful for predicting future earnings and cash flows.

Although many **users do not believe that management intentionally misrepresents accounting results**, there is concern that much of the information that companies disseminate is **too promotional** and that **troubled companies take great pains to present their results in the best light**. Preparers of financial statements must strive to present information that is of the highest quality. Users of this information must assess the quality of earnings prior to making decisions.

INTERNATIONAL INSIGHT

In many nations, financial reporting is prepared on the same basis as tax returns. In such cases, companies have incentives to minimize reported income.

FORMAT OF THE INCOME STATEMENT

Elements of the Income Statement

Net income results from revenue, expense, gain, and loss transactions. These transactions are summarized in the income statement. This view of the income statement is **transactions based** because it focuses on the income-related **activities** that have occurred during the period.[4] Income can be further classified by customer, product line, or function or by operating and nonoperating, continuing and discontinued, and regular and irregular categories.[5] Income statement presentation/classification will be discussed later in the chapter.

More formal definitions of income-related items, referred to as the major **elements** of the income statement, are as follows:

ELEMENTS OF FINANCIAL STATEMENTS

REVENUES. **Increases in economic resources** either by way of inflows or enhancements of an entity's assets of an entity or settlements of liabilities resulting from its **ordinary activities**.

EXPENSES. **Decreases in economic resources**, either by outflows or reductions of assets or incurrence of liabilities, resulting from an entity's **ordinary revenue-generating activities**.

GAINS. **Increases in equity** (net assets) from **peripheral or incidental transactions** of an entity from all other transactions and other events and circumstances affecting the entity during a period except those that result from revenues or investment by owners.

LOSSES. **Decreases in equity** (net assets) from **peripheral or incidental transactions** of an entity and from **all other transactions** and other events and circumstances affecting the entity during a period except those that result from expenses or distributions to owners.[6]

These are the same **elements** identified in Chapter 2 and the **conceptual framework**. **Revenues** take many forms, such as sales, fees, interest, dividends, and rents. **Expenses** also take many forms, such as cost of goods sold, amortization, interest, rent, salaries and wages, and taxes. **Gains and losses** also are of many types, resulting from the sale of investments, sale of plant assets, settlement of liabilities, write-offs of assets due to obsolescence or casualty, and theft.

The **distinction between** i) revenues and gains and ii) expenses and losses depends to a great extent on how the enterprise's ordinary or **typical business activities** are defined. It is therefore critical to understand the typical business activities of an enterprise. For example, when **McDonald's** sells a hamburger, the selling price is recorded as revenue.

However, when McDonald's sells a french-fryer, any excess of the selling price over the book value would be recorded as a gain. This difference in treatment results because the hamburger sale is part of McDonald's regular operations while the french-fryer sale is not. Similarly, when a manufacturer of french-fryers sells a fryer, the sale proceeds would be recorded as revenue.

The importance of properly presenting these elements should not be underestimated. For most decision-makers, the **parts of a financial statement will often be more useful than the whole**. A company must be able to generate cash flows from **its normal ongoing core business activities** (revenues minus expenses). Having income statement **elements** shown in some detail and in a format which shows prior years' data allows

---

[4] The most common alternative to the transaction approach is the **capital maintenance approach** to income measurement. Under this approach, income for the period is determined based on the **change in equity**, after adjusting for capital contributions (e.g., investments by owners) or distributions (e.g., dividends). The main drawback associated with the capital maintenance approach is that the components of income are not evident in its measurement.

[5] The term "irregular" encompasses transactions and other events that are derived from developments outside the normal business operations.

[6] *CICA Handbook*, Section 1000, pars. .37–.40.

decision-makers to better assess whether a company does indeed generate cash flows from its normal ongoing core business activities and whether it is getting better or worse at it! For instance, in its financial statements for the year ended March 31, 2000, **Molson Inc.** reported a loss from continuing operations of $70 million (compared with a profit from continuing operations in 1999 of $28 million) clearly not a good trend. Net loss was only $44 million (compared with a net profit of $170 million in 1999). In this case, the magnitude of the loss from continuing operations was mitigated by other factors, which reduced the impact of the loss on the bottom line. An investor focusing on **net profit or loss** instead of profit or loss from **continuing operations** might get the wrong picture.

Single-Step Income Statements

OBJECTIVE 2
Prepare a single-step income statement.

In reporting revenues, gains, expenses, and losses, a format known as the single-step income statement is often used. In the **single-step statement**, just two groupings exist: revenues and expenses. Expenses and losses are deducted from revenues and gains to arrive at net income or loss. The expression "single-step" is derived from the single subtraction necessary to arrive at net income. Frequently, income tax is reported separately as the last item before net income to indicate its relationship to income before income tax.

For example, Illustration 4-2 shows the single-step income statement of Dan Deines Corporation.

ILLUSTRATION 4-2
Single-step Income Statement

DAN DEINES CORPORATION Income Statement For the Year Ended December 31, 2002	
Revenues	
Net sales	$2,972,413
Dividend revenue	98,500
Rental revenue	72,910
Total revenues	3,143,823
Expenses	
Cost of goods sold	1,982,541
Selling expenses	453,028
Administrative expenses	350,771
Interest expense	126,060
Income tax expense	66,934
Total expenses	2,979,334
Net income	$ 164,489
Earnings per common share	$1.74

The single-step form of income statement is widely used in financial reporting in smaller, private companies. The multiple-step form described below is used almost exclusively among public companies.[7]

The primary advantage of the single-step format lies in the simplicity of presentation and the absence of any implication that one type of revenue or expense item has priority over another. Potential **classification** problems are thus eliminated.

Multiple-Step Income Statements

OBJECTIVE 3
Prepare a multiple-step income statement.

Some contend that presenting other important revenue and expense data separately makes the income statement more informative and more useful. These further classifications include:

---

[7] *Financial Reporting in Canada, 2000* (Toronto, CICA) Of the 200 companies surveyed, 99% employed the multiple-step form, p. 92.

1. A separation of the company's **operating and nonoperating** activities. For example, enterprises often present an "income from operations" figure and then sections entitled "other revenues and gains" and "other expenses and losses." These other categories include interest revenue and expense, gains or losses from sales of miscellaneous items, and dividends received.

2. A **classification of expenses by functions**, such as merchandising or manufacturing (cost of goods sold), selling, and administration. This permits immediate comparison with costs of previous years and with the cost of other departments during the same year.

A multiple-step income statement is used to recognize these additional relationships. This statement recognizes a separation between **operating transactions** and **nonoperating transactions** and matches costs and expenses with related revenues. It highlights certain intermediate components of income that are used for the computation of ratios used to assess the enterprise's **performance** (i.e. gross profit/margin).

To illustrate, Dan Deines Corporation's multiple-step income statement is presented in Illustration 4-3. Note, for example, that in arriving at net income, at least three main subtotals are presented: net sales revenue, gross profit, and income from operations. The disclosure of **net sales revenue** is useful because regular revenues are reported as a separate item. **Irregular or incidental revenues** are disclosed elsewhere in the income statement. As a result, trends in **revenue from continuing operations** (typical business activities) should be easier to identify, understand, and analyse. Similarly, the reporting of **gross profit** provides a useful number for **evaluating performance and assessing future earnings**. A study of the trend in gross profits may show how successfully a company uses its resources (prices paid for inventory, costs accumulated, wastage); it may also be a basis for understanding how profit margins have changed as a result of competitive pressure (prices the company is able to charge for its products/services). This is a very important ratio in the retail business.

Finally, disclosing **income from operations** highlights the **difference between regular and irregular or incidental activities**. Disclosure of **operating earnings** may assist in **comparing** different companies and assessing operating efficiencies. Note that if this company had **discontinued operations** and **extraordinary items**, these would be added to the bottom of the statement and shown separately. These items are by definition **atypical and/or nonrecurring** and therefore have little **predictive value**. They do, however, give **feedback value** as to prior decisions made by management. Net income that consists primarily of "net income from continuing operations" would be viewed as **higher quality**.

UNDERLYING CONCEPTS

This disclosure helps users recognize that incidental or irregular activities are **unlikely to continue at the same level (predictive value)**.

ILLUSTRATION 4-3
Multiple-step Income Statement

DAN DEINES CORPORATION Income Statement For the Year Ended December 31, 2002			
Sales Revenue			
Sales			$3,053,081
Less: Sales discounts		$24,241	
Less: Sales returns and allowances		56,427	80,668
Net sales revenue			2,972,413
Cost of Goods Sold			
Merchandise inventory, Jan. 1, 2002		461,219	
Purchases	$1,989,693		
Less: Purchase discounts	19,270		
Net purchases	1,970,423		
Freight and transportation-in	40,612	2,011,035	
Total merchandise available for sale		2,472,254	
Less: Merchandise inventory, Dec. 31, 2002		489,713	
Cost of goods sold			1,982,541
Gross profit on sales			989,872
Operating Expenses			

Selling expenses			
Sales salaries and commissions	202,644		
Sales office salaries	59,200		
Travel and entertainment	48,940		
Advertising expense	38,315		
Freight and transportation-out	41,209		
Shipping supplies and expense	24,712		
Postage and stationery	16,788		
Amortization of sales equipment	9,005		
Telephone and Internet expense	12,215	453,028	
Administrative expenses			
Officers' salaries	186,000		
Office salaries	61,200		
Legal and professional services	23,721		
Utilities expense	23,275		
Insurance expense	17,029		
Amortization of building	18,059		
Amortization of office equipment	16,000		
Stationery, supplies, and postage	2,875		
Miscellaneous office expenses	2,612	350,771	803,799
Income from operations			186,073
Other Revenues and Gains			
Dividend revenue		98,500	
Rental revenue		72,910	171,410
			357,483
Other Expenses and Losses			
Interest on bonds and notes			126,060
Income before income tax			231,423
Income tax			66,934
Net income for the year			$164,489
Earnings per common share			$1.74

Intermediate Components of the Income Statement

When a multiple-step income statement is used, some or all of the following sections or subsections may be prepared:

INCOME STATEMENT SECTIONS

1. Continuing Operations

(a) **Operating** Section. A report of the **revenues and expenses** of the company's principal operations.[8]

  i. **Sales or Revenue** Section. A subsection presenting sales, discounts, allowances, returns, and other related information. Its purpose is to arrive at the net amount of sales revenue.

  ii. **Cost of Goods Sold** Section. A subsection that shows the cost of goods that were sold to produce the sales.

  iii. **Selling Expenses.** A subsection that lists expenses resulting from the company's efforts to make sales.

  iv. **Administrative or General Expenses.** A subsection reporting expenses of general administration.

---

[8] Note that the CICA Exposure Draft Business Combinations–Accounting for Goodwill (2001) proposes that goodwill impairment be presented as a separate line item in income before extraordinary items and discontinued operations (par. .46). Whether goodwill is considered part of operating or non-operating would be a matter of professional judgement and depend upon the business situation.

INCOME STATEMENT SECTIONS (cont'd)

(b) **Non-operating** Section. A report of revenues and expenses resulting from the company's secondary or auxiliary activities. In addition, special gains and losses that are infrequent or unusual, but not both, are normally reported in this section. Generally these items break down into two main subsections:

    i. **Other Revenues and Gains.** A list of the revenues earned or gains incurred, generally net of related expenses, from nonoperating transactions.

    ii. **Other Expenses and Losses.** A list of the expenses or losses incurred, generally net of any related incomes, from nonoperating transactions.

(c) **Income Tax.** A short section reporting income taxes levied on income from continuing operations.

2. **Discontinued Operations.** Material gains or losses resulting from the disposition of a **segment of the business** (net of taxes).

3. **Extraordinary Items.** Atypical and infrequent material gains and losses beyond the control of management (net of taxes).

Although the operating section's content is always the same, the organization of the material need not be as described above.

Usually, financial statements that are provided to external users have less detail than internal management reports. The latter tend to have more expense categories— usually grouped along lines of responsibility. This detail allows top management to judge staff performance.

Whether a single-step or multiple-step income statement is used, irregular transactions such as **discontinued operations** and **extraordinary items** are required to be reported separately following income from **continuing operations**.

Condensed Income Statements

In some cases it is impossible to present all the desired expense detail in a single income statement of convenient size. This problem is solved by including only the **totals** of expense groups in the statement of income and preparing **supplementary schedules** of expenses to support the totals. With this format, the income statement itself may be reduced to a few lines on a single sheet. For this reason, readers who wish to study all the reported data on operations must give their attention to the supporting schedules. The income statement shown in Illustration 4-4 for Dan Deines Corporation is a **condensed version** of the more detailed multiple-step statement presented earlier and is more representative of the type found in practice.

UNDERLYING CONCEPTS

This contributes to understandability as it reduces "information overload".

DAN DEINES CORPORATION
Income Statement
For the Year Ended December 31, 2002

Sales		$2,972,413
Cost of goods sold		1,982,541
Gross profit		989,872
Selling expenses (see Note D)	$453,028	
Administrative expenses	350,771	803,799
Income from operations		186,073
Other revenues and gains		171,410
Other expenses and losses		126,060
Income before income tax		231,423
Income tax		66,934
Net income for the year		$164,489
Earnings per share		$1.74

ILLUSTRATION 4-4
Condensed Income Statement

An example of a supporting schedule, cross-referenced as Note D and detailing the selling expenses, is shown in Illustration 4-5.

ILLUSTRATION 4-5
Sample Supporting Schedule

Note D: Selling expenses	
Sales salaries and commissions	$202,644
Sales office salaries	59,200
Travel and entertainment	48,940
Advertising expense	38,315
Freight and transportation-out	41,209
Shipping supplies and expense	24,712
Postage and stationery	16,788
Amortization of sales equipment	9,005
Telephone and Internet expense	12,215
Total selling expenses	$453,028

UNDERLYING CONCEPTS

This is an example of a tradeoff-understandability versus full disclosure

How much detail to include in the income statement is always a problem. On the one hand, a **simple, summarized statement** allows a reader to readily discover important factors. On the other hand, **disclosure of results of all activities** provides users with detailed relevant information. Certain basic elements are always included, but they may be presented in various **formats**.

REPORTING IRREGULAR ITEMS

OBJECTIVE 4

Explain how irregular items are reported.

INTERNATIONAL INSIGHT

In many countries, the "modified all-inclusive" income statement approach does not parallel that required under Canadian GAAP. For example, some gains and losses are not reported on the income statement. Rather, they are taken directly to owners' equity accounts.

Either the **single-step** or the **multiple-step** income statement may be used for financial reporting purposes: flexibility in presenting the income components is thereby permitted. In two important areas, however, specific guidelines have been developed. These two areas relate to what is included in income and how certain **unusual** or **irregular** items are reported.

What should be included in net income has been a controversy for many years. For example, should **irregular gains and losses** and corrections of revenues and prior years' expenses be closed **directly to retained earnings** and therefore not be reported in the income statement? Or should they **first be presented in the income statement and then carried to retained earnings** along with the net income or loss for the period?

In general, income measurement follows a modified all-inclusive approach. This approach indicates that **most items, even irregular ones, are recorded in income.**[9] Three exceptions are i) **errors in prior years' income measurement**, ii) **changes in accounting policies applied retroactively** and iii) **foreign exchange gains or losses on self-sustaining foreign subsidiaries**. Because the first two items relate to earnings already reported in a prior period, they are not included in current income. Rather, these items are recorded as adjustments to **retained earnings**.[10] The latter item is recorded as a separate component of **shareholders' equity**.[11]

Currently there is growing debate concerning how irregular items that are part of current income should be reported within the income statement. This issue is extremely important, because the **reporting of irregular items on the income statement is substantial**. For example, Illustration 4-6 identifies the most common types and number of irregular items reported in a survey of 200 large companies. As indicated, unusual items, which many times contain write-offs and other one-time items, were reported

---

[9] *CICA Handbook*, Section 1000, par. .27. The all-inclusive approach is consistent with a **capital maintenance approach** to measuring income. The capital maintenance approach notes that income is recognized only after capital has been maintained. Therefore, income is equal to the change in capital (net assets) during the year (aside from capital contributions/distributions). *CICA Handbook* Section 1000, par. .55 notes that financial statements are prepared with capital maintenance measured in financial terms.

[10] *CICA Handbook*, Section 1506, par. .31.

[11] This is at present the subject of some debate and there is a question as to whether this item will continue to be excluded from the income statement.

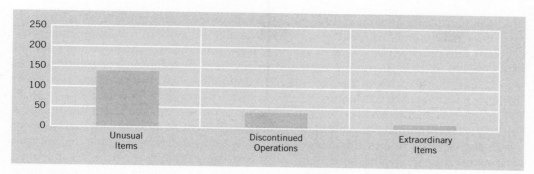

ILLUSTRATION 4-6
Number of Irregular Items
Reported in 1999 by 200
Public Companies

by nearly three quarters of the surveyed firms. About 22% of the surveyed firms reported **discontinued operations**.[12] Thus, developing a framework for reporting irregular items is important to ensure that financial statement users have relevant, high quality income information.[13]

Many users advocate a **current operating performance approach** to income reporting. These analysts argue that the **most useful** income measure will reflect only regular and recurring revenue and expense elements. **Irregular items do not reflect an enterprise's future earning power.** Operating income supporters believe that including one-time items such as write-offs and restructuring charges reduces the income measure's **predictive value**.

In contrast, others warn that a focus on **operating income** potentially misses important information about a firm's performance. Any gain or loss experienced by the firm, whether directly or indirectly related to operations, contributes to its long-run profitability. As one analyst notes, "write-offs matter. . . . They speak to the volatility of (past) earnings."[14] Therefore, they have **feedback value**. As a result, some nonoperating items can be used to assess the riskiness of future earnings—**predictive value**. Furthermore, determining which items are **operating** and which items are **irregular** requires judgement and could lead to differences in the treatment of irregular items and to possible **manipulation of income measures**. In this regard, a recent study reported that users believe that management sometimes reports unusual losses as non-recurring but reports unusual gains as part of regular income.[15]

Discontinued Operations

As indicated in Illustration 4-6, one of the most common types of irregular items relates to **discontinued operations**. Discontinued operations are defined as the operations of an identifiable **business segment** that have been sold, abandoned, shut down, or otherwise disposed of, or that is the subject of a **formal plan** of disposal.[16]

Companies might discontinue operations as part of a downsizing strategy to improve operating results or to focus on core operations or perhaps to generate cash flows. For example, in 1999, **MediSolutions Ltd.** discontinued distribution and support of its dental practice management system in a bid to rationalize its operations. Medi-Solution Ltd. provides a full range of administrative and clinical computer software

OBJECTIVE 5

Measure and report gains and losses from discontinued operations.

---

[12] *Financial Reporting in Canada, 2000* (Toronto, CICA), p. 471.

[13] The IASC has issued a discussion paper, "Reporting Financial Performance: Proposals for Change." A report will be presented to the IASB in late 2001. It generally supports the all-inclusive approach and the income statement would have three categories: business/operating, financing, and other activities.

[14] D. McDermott, "Latest Profit Data Stir Old Debate Between Net and Operating Income," *The Wall Street Journal*, May 3, 1999.

[15] AICPA Special Committee on Financial Reporting, "The Information Needs of Investors and Creditors," November 1993, p. 13.

[16] *CICA Handbook*, Section 3475, par. .02(a).

UNDERLYING CONCEPTS

12% of total losses is **material**

IAS NOTE

IAS 35 allows operating results related to the discontinued operations to be presented either in the notes to the financial statements or in the income statement.

products and professional services to the Canadian healthcare market, including hospital information systems, payroll services, systems integration, consulting, site management, and practice management systems. The dental practice management segment lost $688,448 in 1999 (including expected losses from discontinued operations). This was 12% of the total losses for the year. The following year, the company was profitable—presumably partly due to the spinoff of the discontinued operation.

In order to qualify for separate presentation on the income statement, the business being disposed of must be a **distinguishable component** of an entity, the activities of which represents a **line of business**[17] significant to the entity as a whole and/or that are directed to a significant particular class of customer.[18] A **formal plan** is an **approved** detailed plan for disposing of a business segment.[19] An example will illustrate these concepts below.

Top management of Multiplex Products, Inc., a highly diversified company, **approves a plan** at year end to discontinue its electronics division at year end. The plan among other things identifies steps to find a buyer and includes a time line for disposition, along with a calculation of expected gain/loss on disposition. Given that the company is **highly diversified** (i.e., into many different lines of business) and that the electronics division is a **separate division**, the electronics division may be considered a **separate line of business** and therefore a **business segment**. As top management has approved the disposal and has articulated in reasonable detail which assets are to be disposed of and how, a **formal plan** exists.

The reporting requirements for discontinued operations are complex. In general, a **separate income statement category (separate from Income from continuing operations and Extraordinary items)** for the discontinued operations must be provided. It has the following two components shown **net of tax**:

1. results of operations up to the measurement date
2. net gain/loss (including operating profits/losses from the measurement date to the disposal date)[20]

There are three important points in time when dealing with discontinued operations:

1. measurement date—the date at which the **formal plan** to dispose is approved or the disposal date, whichever is earlier. At this point in time, the company measures whether there will be a gain or loss and generally accrues any expected losses.
2. **year end** for the company. The financial reporting of the discontinued operations must be finalized.
3. disposal date—the actual date that the assets are disposed of. Any expected gains or losses are realized. The period between the measurement date and disposal date may be referred to as the phase-out period.

Assume that the electronics division for Multiplex Products Inc. lost $300,000 (net of tax of $190,000) and that the assets were sold at the year end at a loss of $500,000 (net of tax of $320,000). The information is shown on the current year's income statement as follows:

ILLUSTRATION 4-7
Income Statement Presentation of Discontinued Operations

Income from continuing operations		$20,000,000
Discontinued operations		
Loss from operation of discontinued electronics division (net of tax)	$300,000	
Loss from disposal of electronics division (net of tax)	500,000	800,000
Net income		$19,200,000
Income per share from continuing operations		$2.00
Discontinued operation per share		0.08
Net income per share		$1.92

[17] In making this decision, consider whether two operations are subject to different business risks and rewards, i.e., a wheat farmer faces risks related to crop damage where as a computer manufacturer faces risks related to obsolescence. (*CICA Handbook*, EIC Abstract #45).

[18] *CICA Handbook*, Section 3475, par. .02(b).

[19] *CICA Handbook*, Section 3475, par. .02(c).

[20] *CICA Handbook*, Section 3475, par. .07.

Note that the phrase **"Income from continuing operations"** is used only when gains or losses on discontinued operations or extraordinary items occur.

Examples that **would qualify as a disposal of a business segment** are: (1) sale by a meat-packing company of a 53% interest in a professional football team (meat-packing is a **different line of business** from running a football team), or (2) sale by a communications company of all of its radio stations but none of its television stations or publishing houses (running radio stations is a **different line of business** than running television stations or publishing houses).

Disposal of assets incidental to the evolution of the entity's business is not considered to be disposal of a business segment[21]. Disposals of assets that **would not qualify as disposals of a segment of a business** include the following:

1. disposal of **part of a line** of business
2. **shifting production** or **marketing activities** for a particular line of business from one location to another
3. **phasing out** of a product line or class of service
4. other changes due to a **technological improvement**

When the assets and liabilities of a business segment are being discontinued, they may not be offset against each other on the balance sheet, nor may they be reclassified from noncurrent to current unless the net assets have already been sold.[22]

Discontinued operations are discussed in further detail in Appendix 4A.

Additional Disclosures relating to discontinued operations can be found on the digital tool.

Extraordinary Items

Extraordinary items are **material**, non-recurring items that differ significantly from the entity's typical business activities.[23] They are **presented separately** on the income statement in order to provide sufficient detail for predictive purposes. The criteria for extraordinary items are as follows. All three criteria must be met:

1. infrequent
2. atypical of normal business activities of the company
3. do not depend primarily on decisions or determinations by management or owners[24]

Professional judgement must be applied in considering whether these three criteria are met and because of the third criterion, very few extraordinary items are reported. **How infrequent is infrequent?** Consideration should be given to how often an event has occurred in the past and may recur in the future. For instance, in 2001, a fibre-optics cable supplying 315,000 high-speed Internet customers of **Rogers Cable Inc.** (Rogers) was damaged. This was the second time that it had been damaged in a month. Twice in one month would appear to meet the criteria of frequency for the current year; however, a review of the existence of past damage would confirm whether this was a frequent occurrence for the company over time.

The second criterion involving **whether or not an event is atypical** also involves the use of professional judgement. As a starting point, typical business activities should be identified. What is the company's business and what are typical activities and business risks?

Consider the Rogers example above. Rogers is a subsidiary of Rogers Communications Inc. and is in the business of supplying high-speed cable access to homes and

INTERNATIONAL INSIGHT

Classification of items as extraordinary differs across nations. Even in countries in which the criteria for identifying extraordinary items are similar, they are not interpreted identically; thus, what is extraordinary in North America is not necessarily extraordinary elsewhere.

---

[21] *CICA Handbook*, EIC Abstract #45.

[22] *CICA Handbook*, EIC Abstract #41.

[23] It is often difficult to determine what is extraordinary, because assessing the materiality of individual items requires judgement. However, in making materiality judgements, extraordinary items should be considered individually, and not in the aggregate (*CICA Handbook*, Section 3480, par. .09).

[24] *CICA Handbook*, Section 3480, par. .02

industry for cable television and Internet access. Fixed assets, which include land and distribution cable, account for 51% of the company's total assets—pretty significant. Is damage to high-speed fibre optics cables considered a typical business risk? The cables are normally buried and therefore less likely to be damaged by animals and vandals; however, in this case, they were exposed, being repaired. One factor to consider is if the company insures itself against such losses. If so, this may be an acknowledgement that the company feels that this risk is typical and significant enough to cover with insurance. If completely insured, no loss would occur; however, sometimes companies are not able to obtain insurance for complete coverage and hence if a loss occurs, part of it would be borne by the company itself.

The third criterion looks at **management involvement**. The event must not hinge on or be precipitated by a management/owner decision. This third criterion ensures that items classified as extraordinary items are beyond management control. Thus, decisions to sell assets at losses, downsize, restructure, and other similar expenses are not considered extraordinary.

For further clarification, the CICA specifies that the following gains and losses are not extraordinary items:

1. losses and provisions for losses with respect to bad debt and inventories
2. gains and losses from fluctuations in foreign exchange rates
3. adjustments with respect to contract prices
4. gains and losses from write downs or sale of property, plant and equipment, or other investments
5. income tax reductions on utilization of prior period losses or reversal of previously recorded tax benefits
6. changes in income tax rates or laws[25]

The items listed above are not considered extraordinary because they are usual in nature and may be expected to recur as a consequence of customary and continuing business activities.

In determining whether an item is extraordinary, the **environment in which the entity operates is of primary importance**. The environment includes such factors as industry characteristics, geographic location, and the nature and extent of governmental regulations. Thus, extraordinary item treatment is accorded the loss from hail damages to a tobacco grower's crops only if severe damage from hailstorms in its locality is rare. On the other hand, frost damage to a citrus grower's crop in Florida does not qualify as extraordinary because frost damage is normally experienced every three or four years. In this environment, the criterion of infrequency is not met.

Extraordinary items are to be shown **net of taxes** in a separate section in the income statement, usually just before net income.

Unusual Gains and Losses

Because of the **restrictive criteria** for extraordinary items, financial statement users must carefully examine the financial statements for items that meet only some of the criteria for presentation as an extraordinary item (but not all). As indicated earlier, items such as write-downs of inventories and gains and losses from fluctuation of foreign exchange are not considered extraordinary items. Thus, these items are sometimes shown with the normal, recurring revenues, costs, and expenses. **If they are not material** in amount, they are **combined** with other items in the income statement. If they are material, they are disclosed separately, but are **shown above "income (loss) before extraordinary items."**

---

[25] *CICA Handbook*, Section 3480, par. .04.

For example, **MediSolutions Ltd.**, referred to earlier, presented an unusual charge for restructuring in the following manner in its income statement:

Earnings from continuing operations before restructuring charges	**3,159,844**	1,650,447
Restructuring charges (Note 14)	—	6,634,368
Earnings (loss) from continuing operations	**3,159,844**	(4,983,921)
Earnings (loss) from discontinued operations (Note 15)	**52,601**	(688,448)
NET EARNINGS (LOSS)	**3,212,445**	(5,672,369)
Earnings (loss) per share		
Earnings (loss) from continuing operations	**0.10**	(0.16)
Net earnings (loss)	**0.10**	(0.19)
Weighted average number of common shares outstanding	**31,093,872**	30,577,678

ILLUSTRATION 4-8
Income Statement Presentation of Unusual Charges

As indicated in Illustration 4-6, restructuring charges, like the one reported by Medi-Solutions Ltd., have been common in recent years.[26] There has been a tendency to report unusual items in a separate section just above income from operations before income taxes and extraordinary items, especially when there are multiple unusual items. For example, when **General Electric Company** experienced multiple unusual items in one year, it reported them in a separate "Unusual items" section of the income statement below "Income before unusual items and income taxes."[27]

Changes in Accounting Principle

Changes in accounting occur frequently in practice, because important events or conditions may be in dispute or uncertain at the statement date. One type of accounting change results when an accounting principle is adopted that is different from the one previously used. Changes in accounting principle would include a change in the method of inventory pricing from FIFO to average cost or a change in amortization from the double-declining to the straight-line method.

Changes in accounting principle are recognized through retroactive adjustment, which involves determining the effect of the policy change on the income of prior periods affected. The financial statements for all prior periods that are presented for comparative purposes should be restated except when the effect is not reasonably determinable. If all comparative years are not disclosed, a cumulative amount would be calculated and adjusted through opening retained earnings.

To illustrate, Gaubert Inc. decided in March 2002 to change from the declining balance method of calculating amortization on its plant assets to the straight-line method. The assets originally cost $100,000 in 2000 and have a service life of four years. The data assumed for this illustration and the manner of reporting the change are as shown in Illustration 4-9.

UNDERLYING CONCEPTS
Retroactive application ensures consistency.

IAS NOTE
IAS 8 allows a choice including booking the cumulative impact of the change through the current income statement.

---

[26] Hardly a day goes by that *The Wall Street Journal* does not announce that a well-known company has taken a restructuring charge. A restructuring charge relates to a major reorganization of company affairs, such as costs associated with employee layoffs, plant closing costs, write-offs of assets, and so on. A restructuring charge should not be reported as an extraordinary item, because these write-offs are considered part of a company's ordinary and typical activities.

[27] Many companies report "one-time items." However, some companies have taken restructuring charges practically every year. **Citicorp** (now Citigroup) took restructuring charges six years in a row, between 1988 and 1993, and **Eastman Kodak Co.** did so five out of six years in 1989–1994. Recent research on the market reaction to income containing "one-time" items indicates that the market discounts the earnings of companies that report a series of "nonrecurring" items. Such evidence supports the contention that these elements reduce the quality of earnings. See J. Elliott and D. Hannah, "Repeated Accounting Write-offs and the Information Content of Earnings," *Journal of Accounting Research* (Supplement, 1996).

ILLUSTRATION 4-9
Calculation of a Change in
Accounting Principle

Year	Declining-Balance Amortization	Straight-Line Amortization	Excess of Declining-Balance over Straight-Line Method
2000	$40,000	$25,000	$15,000
2001	30,000	25,000	5,000
Total			$20,000

The information presented in the 2002 financial statements is shown in Illustration 4-10. (The tax rate was 30%.)

ILLUSTRATION 4-10
Statement of Retained Earnings
Presentation of a Change in
Accounting Principle

Retained earnings, January 1, 2002 as previously reported	$120,000
Cumulative effect on prior years of retroactive application of new amortization method (net of $6,000 tax)	14,000
Adjusted balance of retained earnings, January 1, 2002	$134,000

The above assumes no comparatives are shown. A note describing the change and its impact would be required.

Changes in Estimates

Another type of change involves change in estimate. Estimates are inherent in the accounting process. Estimates are made, for example, of useful lives and salvage values of depreciable assets, of uncollectible receivables, of inventory obsolescence, and of the number of periods expected to benefit from a particular expenditure. Not infrequently, as time passes, as circumstances change, or as additional information is obtained, even estimates originally made in good faith must be changed. Such changes in estimates are accounted for in the period of change if they affect only that period, or in the period of change and future periods if the change affects both.

To illustrate a change in estimate that affects only the period of change, assume that DuPage Materials Corp. has consistently estimated its bad debt expense at 1% of credit sales. In 2001, however, DuPage's controller determines that the estimate of bad debts for the current year's credit sales must be revised upward to 2%, or double the prior year's percentage. Using 2% results in a bad debt charge of $240,000 or double the amount using the 1% estimate for prior years. The expense is recorded at December 31, 2001, as follows:

Bad Debt Expense	240,000	
Allowance for Doubtful Accounts		240,000

The entire change in estimate is included in 2001 income because it reflects decisions made and information available in the current year and no future periods are affected by the change. **Changes in estimate are not handled retroactively**, that is, carried back to adjust prior years.

All accounting changes (including correction of errors) will be examined further in Chapter 22.

SPECIAL REPORTING ISSUES

Intraperiod Tax Allocation

OBJECTIVE 6

Explain intraperiod tax
allocation.

As previously noted, **certain irregular items are shown on the income statement net of tax**, thus providing more informative disclosure to statement users. This procedure is called intraperiod tax allocation; that is, allocation of tax balances within a period. Intraperiod tax allocation relates the income tax expense/benefit of the fiscal period to the underlying income statement items/events that give rise to the tax. Intraperiod tax allocation is used for the following items: (1) income from continuing operations, (2) discontinued operations, and (3) extraordinary items.

The income tax expense attributable to "income from continuing operations" is computed by finding the income tax expense related to revenue and to expense transactions used in determining this income. In this tax computation, no effect is given to the tax consequences of the items excluded from the determination of "income from continuing operations." A separate tax effect is then associated with each irregular item.

Extraordinary Gains

In applying the concept of intraperiod tax allocation, assume that Schindler Corp. has income before income tax and extraordinary item of $250,000 and an extraordinary gain from the sale of a single stock investment of $100,000. If the income tax rate is assumed to be 30%, the following information is presented on the income statement:

Income before income tax and extraordinary item		$250,000
Income tax		75,000
Income before extraordinary item		175,000
Extraordinary gain—sale of investment	$100,000	
Less: Applicable income tax	30,000	70,000
Net income		$245,000

ILLUSTRATION 4-11
Intraperiod Tax Allocation, Extraordinary Gain

The income tax of $75,000 ($250,000 × 30%) attributable to "income before income tax and extraordinary item" is determined from revenue and expense transactions related to this income. In this income tax computation, the tax consequences of items excluded from the determination of "income before income tax and extraordinary item" are not considered. The "extraordinary gain—sale of investment" then shows a separate tax effect of $30,000.

Extraordinary Losses

To illustrate the reporting of an extraordinary loss, assume that Schindler has income before income tax and extraordinary item of $250,000 and an extraordinary loss from a major casualty of $100,000. Assuming a 30% tax rate, the presentation of income tax on the income statement would be as follows:

Income before income tax and extraordinary item		$250,000
Income tax		75,000
Income before extraordinary item		175,000
Extraordinary item-loss from casualty	$100,000	
Less: Applicable income tax reduction	30,000	70,000
Net income		$105,000

ILLUSTRATION 4-12
Intraperiod Tax Allocation, Extraordinary Loss

In this case, the loss provides a positive tax benefit of $30,000 and, therefore, is subtracted from the $100,000 loss.

An extraordinary item may be reported "net of tax" with note disclosure as illustrated below:

Income before income tax and extraordinary item	$250,000
Income tax	75,000
Income before extraordinary item	175,000
Extraordinary item, less applicable income tax reduction (Note 1)	70,000
Net income	$105,000

ILLUSTRATION 4-13
Note Disclosure of Intraperiod Tax Allocation

Note 1: During the year, the company suffered a major casualty loss of $70,000, net of applicable income tax reduction of $30,000.

Earnings per Share

OBJECTIVE 7

Explain where earnings
per share information
is reported.

The results of a company's operations are customarily summed up in one important figure: net income. As if this condensation were not enough of a simplification, the financial world has widely accepted an even more distilled and compact figure as its most significant business indicator—**earnings per share**.

The calculation of earnings per share is usually straightforward. **Net income minus preferred dividends (income available to common shareholders) is divided by the weighted average of common shares outstanding to arrive at earnings per share.** To illustrate, assume that Lancer Inc. reports net income of $350,000 and declares and pays preferred dividends of $50,000 for the year. The weighted average number of common shares outstanding during the year is 100,000 shares. Earnings per share is $3.00, as calculated in Illustration 4-14.

ILLUSTRATION 4-14
Equation Illustrating Calculation
of Earnings per Share

$$\frac{\text{Net Income} - \text{Preferred Dividends}}{\text{Weighted Average of Common Shares Outstanding}}$$

$$= \text{Earnings per Share}$$

$$= \frac{\$350,000 - 50,000}{100,000}$$

$$= \$3.00$$

Note that the EPS figure measures the number of dollars **earned** by each common share —but not the dollar amount **paid** to shareholders in the form of dividends.

IAS NOTE

IAS 33 requires presentation of
earnings per share information
for net income only.

"Net income per share" or "earnings per share" is a ratio commonly used in prospectuses, proxy material, and annual reports to shareholders. It is also highlighted in the financial press, by statistical services like Standard & Poor's, and by Bay Street securities analysts. Because of its importance, earnings per share is required to be disclosed on the face of the income statement. A company that reports a discontinued operation or an extraordinary item must report per share amounts for these line items either on the face of the income statement or in the notes to the financial statements.[28] Illustrations 4-7 and 4-8 show how earnings per share may be presented.

Many corporations have **simple** capital structures that include only common shares. For these companies, a presentation such as "earnings per common share" is appropriate on the income statement. In many instances, however, companies' earnings per share are subject to dilution (reduction) in the future because existing contingencies permit the issuance of additional common shares. Presentation for these corporations would include both **basic** EPS and **fully diluted** EPS.[29]

In summary, the simplicity and availability of figures for per share earnings lead inevitably to their widespread use. Because of the undue importance that the public— even the well-informed public—attaches to earnings per share, this figure must be made as meaningful as possible.

Retained Earnings Statement

OBJECTIVE 8

Prepare a retained earnings
statement.

Net income increases retained earnings and a net loss decreases retained earnings. Both cash and share dividends decrease retained earnings. Retroactively applied changes in accounting principles and corrections of errors may either increase or decrease retained earnings. Information related to retained earnings may be shown in different ways. For example, many companies[30] prepare a separate retained earnings statement, as shown in Illustration 4-15.

---

[28] *CICA Handbook*, Section 3500, pars. .60 and .61.

[29] Earnings per share will be covered in significant detail in Chapter 18.

[30] *Financial Reporting in Canada, 2000* (Toronto, CICA) notes that in 1999, 146 out of 200 public companies show the statement of Retained Earnings as a separate statement, p. 53.

ILLUSTRATION 4-15
Retained Earnings Statement

WOODS INC.
Retained Earnings Statement
For the Year Ended December 31, 2002

Balance, January 1, as reported		$1,050,000
Correction for understatement of net income in prior period (inventory error) (net of taxes of $35,000)		50,000
Balance, January 1, as adjusted		1,100,000
Add: Net income		360,000
		1,460,000
Less: Cash dividends	$100,000	
Less: Stock dividends	200,000	300,000
Balance, December 31		$1,160,000

The reconciliation of the beginning to the ending balance in retained earnings provides information about why net assets increased or decreased during the year. The association of dividend distributions with net income for the period indicates what management is doing with earnings: it may be "plowing back" into the business part or all of the earnings, distributing all current income, or distributing current income plus the accumulated earnings of prior years.

Appropriations of Retained Earnings

Retained earnings is often restricted—appropriated—in accordance with contractual requirements, board of directors' policy, or the apparent necessity of the moment. The amounts of retained earnings appropriated are transferred to Appropriated Retained Earnings. The retained earnings section may therefore report two separate amounts: (1) retained earnings free (unrestricted) and (2) retained earnings appropriated (restricted). The total of these two amounts equals the total retained earnings.

Summary of Learning Objectives

1 Identify the uses and limitations of an income statement. The income statement provides investors and creditors with information that helps them predict the amounts, timing, and uncertainty of future cash flows. Also, the income statement helps users determine the risk (level of uncertainty) of not achieving particular cash flows. The limitations of an income statement are: (1) the statement does not include many items that contribute to general growth and well-being of an enterprise; (2) income numbers are often affected by the accounting methods used; and (3) income measures are subject to estimates. The transaction approach focuses on the activities that have occurred during a given period; instead of presenting only a net change, it discloses the components of the change. The transaction approach to income measurement requires the use of revenue, expense, loss, and gain accounts.

2 Prepare a single-step income statement. In a single-step income statement, just two groupings exist: revenues and expenses. Expenses are deducted from revenues to arrive at net income or loss—a single subtraction. Frequently, income tax is reported separately as the last item before net income to indicate its relationship to income before income tax.

3 Prepare a multiple-step income statement. A multiple-step income statement shows two further classifications: (1) a separation of operating results from those obtained through the subordinate or nonoperating activities of the company; and (2) a classification of expenses by functions, such as merchandising or manufacturing, selling, and administration.

4 Explain how irregular items are reported. Irregular gains or losses or nonrecurring items are generally closed to Income Summary and are included in the income statement. These are treated in the income statement as follows: (1) Discontinued operation

KEY TERMS

all-inclusive approach, *122*
appropriated retained earnings, *131*
business segment, *123*
capital maintenance approach, *117*
change in accounting principle, *127*
change in estimate, *128*
current operating performance approach, *123*
discontinued operations, *123*
disposal date, *124*
earnings management, *116*
earnings per share, *130*
extraordinary items, *125*
formal plan, *124*
income statement, *114*
intraperiod tax allocation, *128*
measurement date, *124*
multiple-step income statement, *119*
phase-out period, *124*
quality of earnings, *115*
single-step income statement, *118*
typical business activities, *125*

of a business segment is classified as a separate item, after continuing operations. (2) The unusual, material, nonrecurring items that are significantly different from the customary business activities are shown in a separate section for extraordinary items, below discontinued operations. (3) Other items of a material amount that are of an unusual or nonrecurring nature and are not considered extraordinary are separately disclosed and are included as part of continuing operations.

5 Measure and report gains and losses from discontinued operations. The gain or loss on disposal of a segment involves the sum of: (1) income or loss from operations to the measurement date, and (2) the gain or loss on the disposal of the business segment (operating incomes or losses during the phase-out period and the gain or loss on the sale of the net assets). These two items are reported separately net of tax among the irregular items in the income statement.

6 Explain intraperiod tax allocation. The tax expense for the year should be related, where possible, to specific items on the income statement, to provide a more informative disclosure to statement users. This procedure is called intraperiod tax allocation; that is, allocation within a period. Its main purpose is to relate the income tax expense for the fiscal period to the following items that affect the amount of the tax provisions: (1) income from continuing operations, (2) discontinued operations, and (3) extraordinary items.

7 Explain where earnings per share information is reported. Because of the inherent dangers of focusing attention solely on earnings per share, the profession concluded that earnings per share must be disclosed on the face of the income statement. A company that reports a discontinued operation or an extraordinary item must report per share amounts for these line items either on the face of the income statement or in the notes to the financial statements.

8 Prepare a retained earnings statement. The retained earnings statement should disclose net income (loss), dividends, prior period adjustments, and transfers to and from retained earnings (appropriations).

APPENDIX 4A

Accounting for Discontinued Operations

The chapter discussed how and where gains and losses related to discontinued operations are reported in the income statement. This appendix discusses the more technical aspects of how such a gain or loss is measured, along with the related reporting issues.

First Illustration—No Phase-Out Period

The board of directors of Heartland Inc. decided on October 1, 2000 to sell a division of the company called Concept Cassettes. Concept Cassettes had provided cassette tapes for Heartland's 15 retail stores. Heartland's management could see that the compact disc was revolutionizing the recording industry and would soon render its cassette tape division unprofitable. Fortunately, a buyer was available immediately, and the division was sold on October 1, 2000. Heartland Inc. had income of $2 million for the year 2000, not including a $150,000 loss from operations of Concept Cassettes from January 1 to October 1, 2000. Heartland Inc. was able to sell the division at a gain of $400,000. Its tax rate on all items was 30%.

Since the assets and operations of Concept Cassettes can be easily **identified**, and the **cassette business is distinct from Heartland's other lines of business**, this is a separate **business segment** and this transaction will be accounted for as a discontinued operation.

The **measurement date** is October 1 as this is the date that the board came up with the plan to sell the division. Because the segment was actually sold on October 1, 2000, this is also the **disposal date** and a gain or loss on disposal is computed. The following diagram illustrates Heartland's situation:

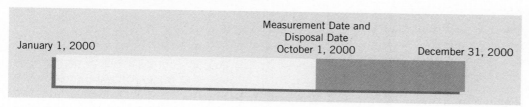

January 1, 2000

Measurement Date and
Disposal Date
October 1, 2000

December 31, 2000

ILLUSTRATION 4A-1
Example of Discontinued
Operations with
No Phase-Out Period

The condensed income statement presentation for Heartland Inc. for 2000 is as follows:

ILLUSTRATION 4A-2
Presentation of Discontinued
Operations, No Phase-Out Period

Income from continuing operations before income taxes		$2,000,000	
Income taxes		600,000	
Income from continuing operations		1,400,000	
Discontinued operations:			
Loss from operation of Concept Cassettes, less applicable income taxes of $45,000	$(105,000)		
Gain on disposal of Concept Cassettes, less applicable income taxes of $120,000	280,000		175,000
Net income			$1,575,000

(Handwritten annotations: (150,000) near the loss line; 400,000 near the gain line.)

Second Illustration—Phase-Out Period

In practice, the **measurement date** and the disposal date are rarely the same. Normally, the disposal date would be later than the measurement date. Thus, the gain or loss on disposal would be the sum of:

1. income (loss) from the measurement date to the disposal date (called the **phase-out period**)
2. gain (loss) on the disposal of the net assets

The reason for aggregating the above two items to calculate the gain (loss) on disposal is that the selling company needs a reasonable period to phase out its discontinued operations. The income (loss) from operations of the discontinued segment is part of the calculation of the gain (loss) on disposal because the phase-out period often enables the seller to obtain a better selling price.

To illustrate the combination of these two components, assume that Heartland's sale of Concept Cassettes does not occur until December 1, 2000, at which time it is sold at a gain of $350,000. During the period October 1, 2000 to December 1, 2000, the Concept Cassettes division suffered a loss of $50,000 from operations. The following diagram illustrates Heartland's situation.

ILLUSTRATION 4A-3
Example of Discontinued
Operations with
Phase-Out Period

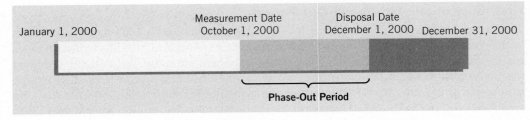

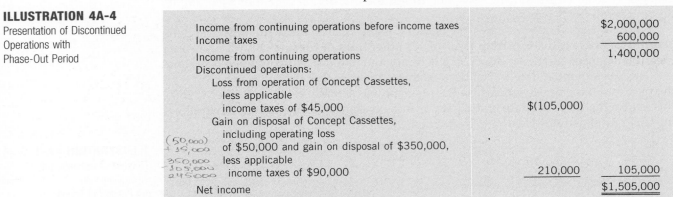

The condensed income statement presentation for Heartland Inc. for 2000 is as follows:

ILLUSTRATION 4A-4
Presentation of Discontinued
Operations with
Phase-Out Period

Income from continuing operations before income taxes		$2,000,000
Income taxes		600,000
Income from continuing operations		1,400,000
Discontinued operations:		
Loss from operation of Concept Cassettes, less applicable income taxes of $45,000	$(105,000)	
Gain on disposal of Concept Cassettes, including operating loss of $50,000 and gain on disposal of $350,000, less applicable income taxes of $90,000	210,000	105,000
Net income		$1,505,000

(handwritten:) (50,000) + 45,000 350,000 −105,000 245,000

Third Illustration—Extended Phase-Out Period

In the preceding illustration, the disposal of the discontinued operation occurred in the **same accounting period as the measurement date**. As a result, determining the proper gain or loss on the disposal of Concept Cassettes at year end was straightforward. However, the phase-out period often extends into another year. If a loss is expected on disposal, the **estimated loss should be reported at the measurement date**. If a gain on disposal is expected, it should be **recognized when realized**, which is ordinarily the disposal date.[31] In other words, the profession has taken a conservative position by recognizing losses immediately but deferring gains until realized.

Implementing these general rules can be troublesome. In order to determine the gain or loss on disposal of the segment, the income (loss) from operations must be estimated and then combined with the estimated gain (loss) on sale. If a net loss results, then it is recognized at the measurement date. If a net gain arises, it generally is recognized at the disposal date. The major exception is when realized gains exceed estimated unrealized and realized net losses. In that special case, realized gains can be recognized in the measurement date period.

Net Loss

To illustrate, assume that Heartland Inc. expects to sell its Concept Cassettes division on May 1, 2001 at a gain of $350,000. In addition, from October 1, 2000 to December 31, 2000, it realized a loss of $400,000 on operations for this segment and expects to lose an additional $200,000 on it from January 1, 2001 to May 1, 2001. The following diagram illustrates Heartland's situation.

ILLUSTRATION 4A-5
Example of Discontinued
Operations with Extended
Phase-Out Period

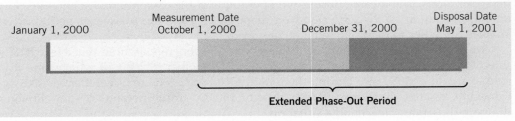

---

[31] *CICA Handbook*, Section 3475, par. .08.

The calculation of the net gain or loss on disposal is shown in Illustration 4A-6.

Actual operating loss October 1–December 31, 2000	$(400,000)
Expected operating loss January 1–May 1, 2001	(200,000)
Expected gain on sale of assets on May 1, 2001	350,000
Net loss on disposal	$(250,000)

ILLUSTRATION 4A-6
Calculation of the Net Loss
on Disposal

Given that a **net loss on disposal is expected**, the loss on disposal is recognized in the period of the measurement date. The condensed income statement presentation for Heartland Inc. for 2000 is therefore reported as shown in Illustration 4A-7.

Income from continuing operations before income taxes		$2,000,000
Income taxes		600,000
Income from continuing operations		1,400,000
Discontinued operations:		

Loss from operation of Concept Cassettes,
    net of applicable
    income taxes of $45,000
	$(105,000)	

Loss on disposal of Concept Cassettes,
    including provision
    for losses during phase-out period,
    $600,000, and estimated
    gain on sale of assets, $350,000,
    net of applicable income
    taxes of $75,000
	(175,000)	(280,000)

Net income		$1,120,000

ILLUSTRATION 4A-7
Presentation of Expected Loss
from Discontinued Operations

If the estimated amount of any item later proves to be incorrect, the correction should be reported in the later period when the estimate is determined to be incorrect. Prior periods should not be restated.

Net Gain

To illustrate recognition of a realized gain and deferral of an unrealized gain in the same discontinued operation, assume that Heartland Inc. expects to sell its Concept Cassettes division on May 1, 2001 at a gain of $350,000. In addition, from October 1, 2000 to December 31, 2000, it realized income of $200,000 on operations for this segment and expects to earn an additional $100,000 of profit on it from January 1, 2001 to May 1, 2001. The calculation of the net gain or loss on disposal is as follows:

Actual operating income October 1–December 31, 2000	$200,000
Expected operating income January 1–May 1, 2001	100,000
Expected gain on sale of assets on May 1, 2001	350,000
Net gain on disposal	$650,000

ILLUSTRATION 4A-8
Calculation of Net Gain
on Disposal

When a **net gain on disposal is expected**, the gain should be analysed and classified into realized (actual) and unrealized (expected) amounts. In this situation, $200,000 of realized income is recognized in 2000 from the October 1–December 31 operations and $450,000 ($100,000 + $350,000) of unrealized gain is deferred to 2001. Assuming that the cassette tape division, as before, suffers a loss of $150,000 from operations between January 1 and October 1, 2000, the discontinued operations section of the income statements for 2000 and 2001 would appear as follows:

ILLUSTRATION 4A-9
Presentation of Gain from
Discontinued Operations

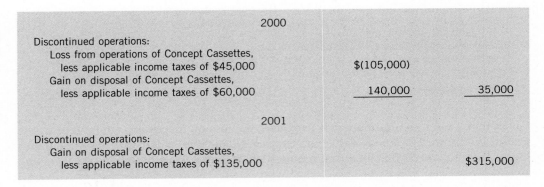

	2000	
Discontinued operations:		
Loss from operations of Concept Cassettes,		
less applicable income taxes of $45,000	$(105,000)	
Gain on disposal of Concept Cassettes,		
less applicable income taxes of $60,000	140,000	35,000
	2001	
Discontinued operations:		
Gain on disposal of Concept Cassettes,		
less applicable income taxes of $135,000		$315,000

If a net unrealized loss of $150,000 had been expected during the 2001 portion of the extended phase-out period, instead of the $450,000 unrealized gain noted above, a net realized gain on disposal of $50,000 ($200,000 − $150,000) before income taxes would be recognized in 2000.

**UNDERLYING
CONCEPTS**

This accounting treatment is the application of conservatism: recognize all losses, but only realized gains.

In summary, **all realized and estimated unrealized gains and losses related to the extended phase-out period are netted as one "event" after the measurement date**. To determine the amount to be reported on the "gain or loss from disposal of a segment" line (the second line of the discontinued operations section), the following simple algorithm may be used: if an overall loss is calculated for the extended phase-out period, the amount reported is the overall loss; if an overall gain is calculated, the amount reported is the lesser of the overall gain or the realized gain.

Extended Phase-Out-Additional Examples

Provided in Illustration 4A-10 are some additional cases to help understand how the gain (loss) on disposal of a segment of a business is reported for an extended phase-out period. The same measurement and disposal dates as in the previous situation will be used. All situations are reported on a pretax basis.

In Case 2, all three components related to the gain (loss) on disposal were losses; therefore a net loss of $1.4 million is reported at the measurement date.

In Case 3, the loss of $600,000 on the sale of the segment assets is greater than the realized $100,000 and expected $400,000 income from operations; therefore a net loss of $100,000 is reported at the measurement date.

In Case 4, the gain of $900,000 on the sale of the segment assets is greater than the realized $500,000 and expected $300,000 losses from operations; therefore a net gain of $100,000 is reported at the disposal date.

In Case 5, both components of operations report income, and a gain is expected on the sale of the segment assets. As a result, the realized income from operations of $400,000 can be reported at the date of measurement because there are no realized or estimated losses. The remaining estimated gain of $550,000 ($300,000 + $250,000) is deferred and recognized at the disposal date.

In Case 6, the realized income from operations of $600,000 exceeds the estimated losses from operations $200,000 and sale $300,000. As a result, a realized gain of $100,000 is reported at the end of 2000, because the net gain is realized.

In Case 7, the net gain on disposal is expected to be $450,000, of which $400,000 is realized and $50,000 is unrealized. The realized $400,000 is recognized in 2000 and the net unrealized gain of $50,000 (the net of a $300,000 expected loss from operations in 2001 and a $350,000 expected gain from disposal in 2001) is recognized in 2001.

In Case 8, the net gain on disposal is expected to be $350,000, all of which is realized and, therefore, recognized in 2000. The $400,000 of realized income from operations is reduced by the net expected unrealized loss of $50,000 from 2001 (the expected loss from operations of $350,000 less the expected gain on sale of $300,000).

Disposals of Segments Involving Extended Phase-Out of Discontinued Operations

Case	Realized Income (Loss) on Operations October 1, 2000 – December 31, 2000	Expected Income (Loss) on Operations January 1, 2001 – May 1, 2001	Expected Gain (Loss) on Sale of Assets		Gain (Loss) on Disposal of Segment
Case 1	$(400,000)	$(200,000)	$350,000	2000	$(250,000)
				2001	0
Case 2	(300,000)	(600,000)	(500,000)	2000	$(1,400,000)
				2001	0
Case 3	100,000	400,000	(600,000)	2000	$(100,000)
				2001	0
Case 4	(500,000)	(300,000)	900,000	2000	0
				2001	$100,000
Case 5	400,000	300,000	250,000	2000	$400,000
				2001	$550,000
Case 6	600,000	(200,000)	(300,000)	2000	$100,000
				2001	0
Case 7	400,000	(300,000)	350,000	2000	$400,000
				2001	$50,000
Case 8	400,000	(350,000)	300,000	2000	$350,000
				2001	0

ILLUSTRATION 4A-10
Gains or Losses Involving Extended Phase-Out of Discontinued Operations

Disclosure Requirements

An example of the note disclosure taken from the annual report of **MediSolutions Ltd.** is shown in Illustration 4A-11. It includes nature of segment, measurement and disposal dates, manner of disposal, description and value of assets, and liabilites and revenues.

15 Discontinued Operations

On February 22, 1999, the Company announced its decision to rationalize its private practice management operations, thereby discontinuing distribution and support of its dental practice management system. A client transfer agreement was signed with Abel Computers Inc. in 1999.

The operating profit to the date of discontinuance, relating entirely to this division, was $11,552. The loss on discontinuance of activities of $700,000 represents the write-down of the inventory, fixed assets, technology and investment at the date of discontinuance of operations together with the expenses related to the discontinuance of activities.

	2000	1999
	$	$
Revenue	—	471,165
Operating earnings	—	11,552
Earnings (loss) on discontinuance	52,601	(700,000)
Earnings (loss) on discontinued operations	52,601	(688,448)

A summary of the assets and liabilities related to discontinued operations is as follows:

	2000	1999
	$	$
Current assets		
—discontinued operations in 1999	—	288,152
	—	288,152
Current liabilities (including estimated costs of disposal)		
—discontinued operations in 1999	23,139	154,716
Current liabilities (including estimated costs of disposal)		
—discontinued operations in 1997	—	13,514
	23,139	168,230
Net assets (liabilities)	(23,139)	119,922

ILLUSTRATION 4A-11
Note on Discontinued Operations-MediSolutions Ltd.

Note: All asterisked Brief Exercises, Exercises, Problems, and Cases relate to material in the appendix to the chapter.

BRIEF EXERCISES

BE4-1 Allen Corp. had sales revenue of $540,000 in 2001. Other items recorded during the year were:

Cost of goods sold	$320,000
Wage expense	120,000
Income tax expense	25,000
Increase in value of company reputation	15,000
Other operating expenses	10,000
Unrealized gain on value of patents	20,000

Prepare a single-step income statement for Allen for 2001. Allen has 100,000 common shares outstanding.

BE4-2 Alley Corporation had net sales of $1,780,000 and investment revenue of $103,000 in 2002. Its 2002 expenses were: cost of goods sold, $1,190,000; selling expenses, $272,000; administrative expenses, $211,000; interest expense, $76,000; and income tax expense, $40,000. Prepare a single-step income statement for Alley Corporation, which has 10,000 common shares outstanding.

BE4-3 Use the information provided in BE4-2 for Alley Corporation to prepare a multiple-step income statement.

BE4-4 Green Corporation had income from continuing operations of $12.6 million in 2002. During 2002, it disposed of its restaurant division at an after-tax loss of $189,000. Prior to disposal, the division operated at a loss of $315,000 (net of tax) in 2002. Green had 10 million common shares outstanding during 2002. Prepare a partial income statement for Green beginning with income from continuing operations.

BE4-5 Boyz Corporation had income before income taxes for 2002 of $7.3 million. In addition, it suffered an unusual and infrequent pretax loss of $770,000 from a volcano eruption. The corporation's tax rate is 30%. Prepare a partial income statement for Boyz beginning with income before income taxes. The corporation had 5 million common shares outstanding during 2002.

BE4-6 Bradley Limited changed from straight-line amortization to double-declining balance amortization at the beginning of 2002. The plant assets originally cost $1.5 million in 2000. Using straight-line amortization, amortization expense is $60,000 per year. Under the double-declining balance method, amortization expense would be $120,000, $110,400, and $101,568 for 2000, 2001, and 2002. If Bradley's tax rate is 30%, by what amount would retained earnings be adjusted?

BE4-7 Kingston Limited has recorded bad debts expense in the past at a rate of 1½% of net sales. In 2002, Kingston decides to increase its estimate to 2%. If the new rate had been used in prior years, cumulative bad debt expense would have been $380,000 instead of $285,000. In 2002, bad debt expense will be $120,000 instead of $90,000. If Kingston's tax rate is 30%, how should this be reflected in the financial statements? Show calculations.

BE4-8 In 2002, Puckett Corporation reported net income of $1.2 million. It declared and paid preferred share dividends of $250,000. During 2002, Puckett had a weighted average of 190,000 common shares outstanding. Calculate Puckett's 2002 earnings per share.

BE4-9 Turgeon Corporation had retained earnings of $529,000 at January 1, 2002. Net income in 2002 was $1,496,000 and cash dividends of $650,000 were declared and paid. Prepare a 2002 retained earnings statement for Turgeon Corporation.

BE4-10 Use the information provided in BE4-9 to prepare a retained earnings statement for Turgeon Corporation, assuming that in 2002 Turgeon discovered that it had overstated 2000 amortization by $125,000 (net of tax).

BE4-11 Garok Inc. decided on Sept. 1, 2002 to dispose of its Cardassian Division. The Cardassian Division operated at a loss of $190,000 during the first eight months of 2002 and a loss of $114,000 during the last four months of the year. Garok estimates the division will incur a loss of $130,000 in 2003 before it is sold at a gain of $85,000. Garok's tax rate is 30%. Prepare the discontinued operations section of Garok's 2002 income statement.

EXERCISES

E4-1 **(Calculation of Net Income)** Presented below are changes in all the account balances of Reiner Furniture Ltd. during the current year, except for retained earnings.

	Increase (Decrease)		Increase (Decrease)
Cash	$ 79,000	Accounts payable	$(51,000)
Accounts receivable (net)	45,000	Bonds payable	82,000
Inventory	127,000	Common shares	125,000
Investments	(47,000)	Contributed surplus	13,000

Instructions

Calculate the net income for the current year, assuming that there were no entries in the Retained Earnings account except for net income and a dividend declaration of $19,000, which was paid in the current year.

E4-2 **(Calculate Net Income—Capital Maintenance Approach)** Presented below is selected information pertaining to the Videohound Video Company during 2002:

Cash balance, January 1, 2002	$ 13,000
Accounts receivable, January 1, 2002	19,000
Collections from customers in 2002	210,000
Capital account balance, January 1, 2002	38,000
Total assets, January 1, 2002	75,000
Cash investment added, July 1, 2002	5,000
Total assets, December 31, 2002	101,000
Cash balance, December 31, 2002	20,000
Accounts receivable, December 31, 2002	36,000
Merchandise taken for personal use	11,000
Total liabilities, December 31, 2002	41,000

Instructions

Calculate the net income for 2002.

E4-3 **(Income Statement Items)** Presented below are certain account balances of Paczki Products Corp.

Rental revenue	$ 6,500	Sales discounts	7,800
Interest expense	12,700	Selling expenses	99,400
Beginning retained earnings	114,400	Sales	390,000
Ending retained earnings	134,000	Income tax	31,000
Dividends earned	71,000	Cost of goods sold	184,400
Sales returns	$ 12,400	Administrative expenses	82,500

Instructions

From the foregoing, calculate the following: (a) total net revenue; (b) net income; (c) dividends declared during the current year.

E4-4 **(Single-step Income Statement)** The financial records of Jones Inc. were destroyed by fire at the end of 2002. Fortunately the controller had kept certain statistical data related to the income statement as presented below.

1. The beginning merchandise inventory was $92,000 and decreased 20% during the current year.
2. Sales discounts amount to $17,000.
3. 20,000 common shares were outstanding for the entire year.
4. Interest expense was $20,000.
5. The income tax rate is 30%.
6. Cost of goods sold amounts to $500,000.
7. Administrative expenses are 20% of cost of goods sold but only 8% of gross sales.
8. Four-fifths of the operating expenses relate to sales activities.

Instructions

From the foregoing information, prepare an income statement for the year 2002 in single-step form.

E4-5 **(Multiple-step and Single-step)** Two accountants for the firm of Elwes and Wright are arguing about the merits of presenting an income statement in a multiple-step versus a single-step format. The discussion involves the following 2002 information related to Singh Company ($000 omitted).

ADMINISTRATIVE EXPENSE	
Officers' salaries	$4,900
Amortization of office furniture and equipment	3,960
Cost of goods sold	60,570
Rental revenue	17,230
SELLING EXPENSE	
Transportation-out	2,690
Sales commissions	7,980
Amortization of sales equipment	6,480
Sales	96,500
Income tax	9,070
Interest expense on bonds payable	1,860

Instructions

(a) Prepare an income statement for the year 2002 using the multiple-step form. Common shares outstanding for 2002 total 40,550 ($000 omitted).

(b) Prepare an income statement for the year 2002 using the single-step form.

(c) Which one do you prefer? Discuss.

E4-6 **(Multiple-step and Extraordinary Items)** The following balances were taken from the books of Voisine Corp. on December 31, 2002.

Interest revenue	$86,000	Accumulated amortization—equipment	$40,000
Cash	51,000	Accumulated amortization—building	28,000
Sales	1,380,000	Notes receivable	155,000
Accounts receivable	150,000	Selling expenses	194,000
Prepaid insurance	20,000	Accounts payable	170,000
Sales returns and allowances	150,000	Bonds payable	100,000
Allowance for doubtful accounts	7,000	Administrative and general expenses	97,000
Sales discounts	45,000	Accrued liabilities	32,000
Land	100,000	Interest expense	60,000
Equipment	200,000	Notes payable	100,000
Building	140,000	Loss from earthquake damage	
Cost of goods sold	621,000	(extraordinary item)	150,000
Common shares	500,000	Retained earnings	21,000

Assume the total effective tax rate on all items is 34%.

Instructions

Prepare a multiple-step income statement; 100,000 common shares were outstanding during the year.

E4-7 **(Multiple-step and Single-step)** The accountant of Whitney Shoe Corp. has compiled the following information from the company's records as a basis for an income statement for the year ended December 31, 2002.

Rental revenue	$29,000
Interest on notes payable	18,000
Market appreciation on land above cost	31,000
Wages and salaries—sales	114,800
Materials and supplies—used	17,600
Income tax	37,400
Wages and salaries—administrative	135,900
Other administrative expense	51,700
Cost of goods sold	496,000
Net sales	980,000
Amortization on plant assets	
(70% selling, 30% administrative)	65,000
Dividends declared	16,000

There were 20,000 common shares outstanding during the year.

Instructions

(a) Prepare a multiple-step income statement.
(b) Prepare a single-step income statement.
(c) Which format do you prefer? Discuss.

E4-8 **(Multiple-step and Single-step-Periodic Inventory Method)** Presented below is income statement information related to Ying-Wai Corporation for the year 2002.

Administrative expenses:		Transportation-in	$14,000
Officers' salaries	$39,000	Purchase discounts	10,000
Amortization expense—building	28,500	Inventory (beginning)	120,000
Office supplies expense	9,500	Sales returns and allowances	15,000
Inventory (ending)	137,000	Selling expenses:	
Flood damage		Sales salaries	71,000
(pretax extraordinary item)	50,000	Amortization expense—store equipment	18,000
Purchases	600,000	Store supplies expense	9,000
Sales	930,000		

In addition, the corporation has other revenue from dividends received of $20,000 and other expense of interest on notes payable of $9,000. There are 20,000 common shares outstanding for the year. The total effective tax rate on all income is 34%.

Instructions

(a) Prepare a multiple-step income statement for 2002.
(b) Prepare a single-step income statement for 2002.
(c) Discuss the relative merits of the two income statements.

E4-9 **(Multiple-step Statement with Retained Earnings)** Presented below is information related to Gottlieb Corp. for the year 2002.

Net sales	$1,300,000	Write-off of inventory due to obsolescence	$ 80,000
Cost of goods sold	780,000	Amortization expense omitted	
Selling expenses	65,000	by accident in 2001	55,000
Administrative expenses	48,000	Casualty loss (extraordinary item) before taxes	50,000
Dividend revenue	20,000	Dividends declared	45,000
Interest revenue	7,000	Retained earnings at December 31, 2001	980,000

Effective tax rate of 34% on all items

Instructions

(a) Prepare a multiple-step income statement for 2002. Assume that 60,000 common shares are outstanding.
(b) Prepare a separate retained earnings statement for 2002.

E4-10 **(Earnings Per Share)** The shareholders' equity section of Tkachuk Corporation appears below as of December 31, 2002:

8% cumulative preferred shares, authorized		
100,000 shares, outstanding 90,000 shares		$4,500,000
Common shares, authorized and issued		
10 million shares		10,000,000
Contributed surplus		20,500,000
Retained earnings	$134,000,000	
Net income	33,000,000	167,000,000
		$202,000,000

Net income for 2002 reflects a total effective tax rate of 34%. Included in the net income figure is a loss of $18 million (before tax) as a result of a major casualty.

Instructions

Calculate earnings per share data as it should appear on the financial statements of Tkachuk Corporation.

E4-11 **(Condensed Income Statement—Periodic Inventory Method)** Presented below are selected ledger accounts of Sooyoun Corporation at December 31, 2002:

Cash	$185,000	Travel and entertainment	$ 69,000
Merchandise inventory	535,000	Accounting and legal services	33,000
Sales	4,275,000	Insurance expense	24,000
Advances from customers	117,000	Advertising	54,000
Purchases	2,786,000	Transportation-out	93,000
Sales discounts	34,000	Amortization of office	48,000
Purchase discounts	27,000	Amortization of sales equipment	36,000
Sales salaries	284,000	Telephone—sales	17,000
Office salaries	346,000	Utilities—office	32,000
Purchase returns	15,000	Miscellaneous office expenses	8,000
Sales returns	79,000	Rental revenue	240,000
Transportation-in	72,000	Extraordinary loss (before tax)	70,000
Accounts receivable	142,500	Interest expense	176,000
Sales commissions	83,000	Common shares	900,000

Spock's effective tax rate on all items is 34%. A physical inventory indicates that the ending inventory is $686,000.

Instructions

Prepare a condensed 2002 income statement for Sooyoun Corporation.

E4-12 **(Retained Earnings Statement)** Zambrano Corporation began operations on January 1, 1999. During its first three years of operations, Zambrano reported net income and declared dividends as follows:

	Net income	Dividends declared
1999	$40,000	$–0–
2000	125,000	$50,000
2001	160,000	$50,000

The following information relates to 2002:

Income before income tax	$240,000
Prior period adjustment: understatement of 2000 amortization expense (before taxes)	$ 25,000
Cumulative decrease in prior year's income from change in inventory methods (before taxes)	$ 35,000
Dividends declared (of this amount, $25,000 will be paid on Jan. 15, 2003	$100,000
Effective tax rate	40%

Instructions

(a) Prepare a 2002 retained earnings statement for Zambrano Corporation.

(b) Assume Zambrano Corporation appropriated retained earnings in the amount of $70,000 on December 31, 2002. After this action, what would Zambrano report as total retained earnings in its December 31, 2002 balance sheet?

E4-13 **(Earnings per Share)** At December 31, 2001, Naoya Corporation had the following shares outstanding:

10% cumulative preferred shares, 107,500 shares outstanding	$10,750,000
Common shares, 4,000,000 shares outstanding	20,000,000

During 2002, Naoya's only share transaction was the issuance of 400,000 common shares on April 1. During 2002, the following also occurred:

Income from continuing operations before taxes	$23,650,000
Discontinued operations (loss before taxes)	$3,225,000
Preferred dividends declared	$1,075,000
Common dividends declared	$2,200,000
Effective tax rate	35%

Instructions

Calculate earnings per share data as it should appear in the 2002 income statement of Naoya Corporation.

*E4-14 (Discontinued Operations) Assume that Alzado Inc. decides to sell CBTV, its television subsidiary, in 2001. This sale qualifies for discontinued operations treatment. Pertinent data regarding the operations of the TV subsidiary are as follows:

Loss from operations from beginning of year to measurement date, $1,000,000 (net of tax).
Realized loss from operations from measurement date to end of 2001, $700,000 (net of tax).
Estimated income from operations from end of year to disposal date of June 1, 2002, $400,000 (net of tax).
Estimated gain on sale of net assets on June 1, 2002, $150,000 (net of tax).

Instructions

(a) What is the gain (loss) on the disposal of the segment reported in 2001? In 2002?
(b) Prepare the discontinued operations section of the income statement for the year ended 2001.
(c) If the amount reported in 2001 as gain or loss from disposal of a segment by Alzado Inc. proves to be materially incorrect, when and how is the correction reported, if at all?
(d) If the TV subsidiary had a realized income of $100,000 (net of tax) instead of a realized loss from the measurement date to the end of 2001, what is the gain or loss on disposal of the segment reported in 2001? In 2002?

*E4-15 (Discontinued Operations) On October 5, 2002, Marzook Inc.'s board of directors decided to dispose of the Song and Elwood Division. Marzook is a real estate firm with approximately 25% of its income from management of apartment complexes. The Song and Elwood Division contracts to clean apartments after tenants move out in the Marzook complexes and several others. The board decided to dispose of the division because of unfavourable operating results.

Net income for Marzook was $91,000 after tax (assume a 30% rate) for the fiscal year ended December 31, 2002. The Song and Elwood Division accounted for only $4,200 (after tax) of this amount and only $1,050 (after tax) in the fourth quarter. Song and Elwood accounted for $50,000 in revenues, of which $8,000 were earned in the last quarter. The average number of common shares outstanding was 20,000 for the year.

Because of the unfavourable results and the extreme competition, the board believes selling the business intact is impossible. Its final decision is to complete all current contracts, the last of which expires on May 3, 2004, and then auction off the cleaning equipment on May 10, 2004. This, the only asset of the division, will have a depreciated value of $25,000 at the disposal date. The board believes the sale proceeds will approximate $5,000 after the auction expenses and estimates Song and Elwood earnings in fiscal year 2003 as $3,800 (before tax), with a loss of $3,000 (before tax) in fiscal year 2004.

Instructions

Prepare the income statement and the appropriate footnotes that relate to the Song and Elwood Division for 2002. The income statement should begin with income from continuing operations before income taxes. Earnings per share calculations are not required.

PROBLEMS

P4-1 Presented below is information related to Zalev Corp. for 2002.

Retained earnings balance, January 1, 2002	$980,000
Sales for the year	25,000,000
Cost of goods sold	17,000,000
Interest revenue	70,000
Selling and administrative expenses	4,700,000
Write-off of goodwill (not tax deductible)	520,000
Income taxes for 2002	905,000
Assessment for additional 1999 income taxes (normal recurring)	300,000
Gain on the sale of investments (normal recurring)	110,000
Loss due to flood damage-extraordinary item (net of tax)	390,000
Loss on the disposition of the wholesale division (net of tax)	440,000
Loss on operations of the wholesale division (net of tax)	90,000
Dividends declared on common shares	250,000
Dividends declared on preferred shares	70,000

Instructions

Prepare a multi-step income statement and a retained earnings statement. Zalev decided to discontinue its entire wholesale operations and to retain its manufacturing operations. On September 15, Zalev sold the wholesale operations to Rogers Ltd. During 2002, there were 300,000 common shares outstanding all year.

P4-2 Presented below is the trial balance of Blige Corporation at December 31, 2002.

BLIGE CORPORATION
Trial Balance
Year Ended December 31, 2002

	Debits	Credits
Purchase discounts		$10,000
Cash	$205,100	
Accounts receivable	105,000	
Rent revenue		18,000
Retained earnings		260,000
Salaries payable		18,000
Sales		1,000,000
Notes receivable	110,000	
Accounts payable		49,000
Accumulated amortization—equipment		28,000
Sales discounts	14,500	
Sales returns	17,500	
Notes payable		70,000
Selling expenses	232,000	
Administrative expenses	99,000	
Common shares		300,000
Income tax expense	38,500	
Cash dividends	45,000	
Allowance for doubtful accounts		5,000
Supplies	14,000	
Freight-in	20,000	
Land	70,000	
Equipment	140,000	
Bonds payable		100,000
Gain on sale of land		30,000
Accumulated amortization—building		19,600
Merchandise inventory	89,000	
Building	98,000	
Purchases	610,000	
Totals	$1,907,600	$1,907,600

A physical count of inventory on December 31 resulted in an inventory amount of $124,000.

Instructions

Prepare a single-step income statement and a retained earnings statement. Assume that the only changes in the retained earnings during the current year were from net income and dividends. Thirty thousand common shares were outstanding the entire year.

P4-3 Charyk Inc. reported income from continuing operations before taxes during 2002 of $790,000. Additional transactions occurring in 2002 but not considered in the $790,000 are as follows:

1. The corporation experienced an uninsured flood loss (extraordinary) in the amount of $80,000 during the year. The tax rate on this item is 46%.
2. At the beginning of 2000, the corporation purchased a machine for $54,000 (salvage value of $9,000) that had a useful life of six years. The bookkeeper used straight-line amortization for 2000, 2001, and 2002 but failed to deduct the salvage value in computing the amortization base.
3. Sale of securities held as a part of its portfolio resulted in a loss of $57,000 (pretax).
4. When its president died, the corporation realized $110,000 from an insurance policy. The cash surrender value of this policy had been carried on the books as an investment in the amount of $46,000 (the gain is nontaxable).
5. The corporation disposed of its recreational division at a loss of $115,000 before taxes. Assume that this transaction meets the criteria for discontinued operations.

6. The corporation decided to change its method of inventory pricing from average cost to the FIFO method. The effect of this change on prior years is to increase 2000 income by $60,000 and decrease 2001 income by $20,000 before taxes. The FIFO method has been used for 2002. The tax rate on these items is 40%.

Instructions

Prepare an income statement for the year 2002 starting with income from continuing operations before taxes. Calculate earnings per share as it should be shown on the face of the income statement. Common shares outstanding for the year are 80,000 shares. (Assume a tax rate of 30% on all items, unless indicated otherwise.)

P4-4 The following account balances were included in the trial balance of Reid Corporation at June 30, 2002.

Sales	$1,678,500	Amortization of office furniture	
Sales discounts	31,150	and equipment	$7,250
Cost of goods sold	896,770	Real estate and other local taxes	7,320
Sales salaries	56,260	Bad debt expense—selling	4,850
Sales commissions	97,600	Building expense—prorated to	
Travel expense—salespersons	28,930	administration	9,130
Freight-out	21,400	Miscellaneous office expenses	6,000
Entertainment expense	14,820	Sales returns	62,300
Telephone and Internet—sales	9,030	Dividends received	38,000
Amortization of sales equipment	4,980	Bond interest expense	18,000
Building expense—prorated to sales	6,200	Income taxes	133,000
Miscellaneous selling expenses	4,715	Amortization understatement due to	
Office supplies used	3,450	error—1999 (net of tax)	17,700
Telephone and Internet—Administration	2,820	Dividends declared on preferred shares	9,000
		Dividends declared on common shares	32,000

The Unappropriated Retained Earnings account had a balance of $287,000 at June 30, 2002, before closing; the only entry in that account during the year was a debit of $50,000 to establish an Appropriation for Bond Retirement. There are 80,000 common shares outstanding.

Instructions

(a) Using the multiple-step form, prepare an income statement and an unappropriated retained earnings statement for the year ended June 30, 2002.
(b) Using the single-step form, prepare an income statement for the year ended June 30, 2002.

P4-5 Presented below is a combined single-step income and retained earnings statement for Pereira Corp. for 2001.

		(000 omitted)
Net sales		$640,000
Cost and expenses:		
Cost of goods sold		500,000
Selling, general, and administrative expenses		66,000
Other, net		17,000
		583,000
Income before income tax		57,000
Income tax		19,400
Net income		37,600
Retained earnings at beginning of period,		
as previously reported	141,000	
Adjustment required for correction of error	(7,000)	
Retained earnings at beginning of period, as restated		134,000
Dividends on common shares		(12,200)
Retained earnings at end of period		$159,400

Additional facts are as follows:

1. "Selling, general, and administrative expenses" for 2001 included a usual but infrequently occurring charge of $10.5 million.
2. "Other, net" for 2001 included an extraordinary item (charge) of $9 million. If the extraordinary item (charge) had not occurred, income taxes for 2001 would have been $22.4 million instead of $19.4 million.

3. "Adjustment required for correction of an error" was a result of a change in estimate (useful life of certain assets reduced to eight years and a catch-up adjustment made).

4. Pereira Company disclosed earnings per common share for net income in the notes to the financial statements.

Instructions

Determine from these additional facts whether the presentation of the facts in the Pereira income and retained earnings statement is appropriate. If the presentation is not appropriate, describe the appropriate presentation and discuss its theoretical rationale. (Do not prepare a revised statement.)

P4-6 Below is the retained earnings account for the year 2002 for LeClair Corp.

Retained earnings, January 1, 2002		$257,600
Add:		
Gain on sale of investments (net of tax)	$41,200	
Net income	84,500	
Refund on litigation with government, (net of tax)	21,600	
Recognition of income earned in 2001, but omitted		
from income statement in that year (net of tax)	25,400	172,700
		430,300
Deduct:		
Loss on discontinued operations (net of tax)	25,000	
Write-off of goodwill (net of tax)	60,000	
Cumulative effect on income in changing from		
straight-line amortization to accelerated		
amortization in 2002	18,200	
Cash dividends declared	32,000	135,200
Retained earnings, December 31, 2002		$295,100

Instructions

(a) Prepare a corrected retained earnings statement. LeClair Corp. normally sells investments of the type mentioned above.

(b) State where the items that do not appear in the corrected retained earnings statement should be shown.

P4-7 The Tamayo Corporation commenced business on January 1, 1999. Recently the corporation has had several unusual accounting problems related to the presentation of its income statement for financial reporting purposes.

You have been the CA for Tamayo for several years and have been asked to examine the following data.

TAMAYO CORPORATION
Income Statement
For the Year Ended December 31, 2002

Sales	$9,500,000
Cost of goods sold	5,900,000
Gross profit	3,600,000
Selling and administrative expense	1,300,000
Income before income tax	2,300,000
Income tax (30%)	690,000
Net income	$1,610,000

In addition, this information was provided:

1. The controller mentioned that the corporation has had difficulty in collecting on several of its receivables. For this reason, the bad debt write-off was increased from 1% to 2% of sales. The controller estimates that if this rate had been used in past periods, an additional $83,000 worth of expense would have been charged. The bad debt expense for the current period was calculated using the new rate and is part of selling and administrative expense.

2. Common shares outstanding at the end of 2002 totaled 400,000. No additional shares were purchased or sold during 2002.

3. The following items were not included in the income statement.
   (a) Inventory in the amount of $72,000 was obsolete.
   (b) The major casualty loss suffered by the corporation was partially uninsured and cost $127,000, net of tax (extraordinary item).

4. Retained earnings as of January 1, 2002 was $2.8 million. Cash dividends of $700,000 were paid in 2002.

5. In January 2002, Tamayo changed its method of accounting for plant assets from the straight-line method to the accelerated method (double-declining balance). The controller has prepared a schedule indicating what amortization expense would have been in previous periods if the double-declining method had been used. (The effective tax rate for 1999, 2000, and 2001 was 30%.)

	Amortization Expense under Straight-Line	Amortization Expense under Double-Declining	Difference
1999	$75,000	$150,000	$75,000
2000	75,000	112,500	37,500
2001	75,000	84,375	9,375
	$225,000	$346,875	$121,875

Instructions

Prepare the income statement for Tamayo Corporation in accordance with professional pronouncements. Do not prepare notes to the financial statements.

P4-8 Rap Corp. has 100,000 common shares outstanding. In 2002, the company reports income from continuing operations before taxes of $1,210,000. Additional transactions not considered in the $1,210,000 are as follows:

1. In 2002, Rap Corp. sold equipment for $40,000. The machine had originally cost $80,000 and had accumulated amortization of $36,000. The gain or loss is considered ordinary.

2. The company discontinued operations of one of its subsidiaries during the current year at a loss of $190,000 before taxes. Assume that this transaction meets the criteria for discontinued operations. The loss on operations of the discontinued subsidiary was $90,000 before taxes; the loss from disposal of the subsidiary was $100,000 before taxes.

3. The sum of $100,000, applicable to a breached 1998 contract, was received as a result of a lawsuit. Prior to the award, legal counsel was uncertain about the outcome of the suit and had not established a receivable.

4. In 2002, the company reviewed its accounts receivable and determined that $26,000 of accounts receivable that had been carried for years appeared unlikely to be collected. No allowance for doubtful accounts was previously set up.

5. An internal audit discovered that amortization of intangible assets was understated by $35,000 (net of tax) in a prior period. The amount was charged against retained earnings.

6. The company sold its only investment in common shares during the year at a gain of $145,000. The gain is taxed at a total effective rate of 40%. Assume that the transaction meets the requirements of an extraordinary item.

Instructions

Analyse the above information and prepare an income statement for the year 2002, starting with income from continuing operations before income taxes. Calculate earnings per share as it should be shown on the face of the income statement. (Assume a total effective tax rate of 38% on all items, unless otherwise indicated.)

*P4-9 Campbell Corporation management formally decided to discontinue operation of its Rocketeer Division on November 1, 2000. Campbell is a successful corporation with earnings in excess of $38.5 million before taxes for each of the past five years. The Rocketeer Division is being discontinued because it has not contributed to this profitable performance.

The principal assets of this division are the land, plant, and equipment used to manufacture engine components. The land, plant, and equipment had a net book value of $56 million on November 1, 2000.

Campbell's management has entered into negotiations for a cash sale of the facility for $39 million. The expected sale date and final disposal of the segment is July 1, 2001.

Campbell Corporation has a fiscal year ending May 31. The results of operations for the Rocketeer Division for the 2000–2001 fiscal year and the estimated results for June 2001 are presented below. The before-tax losses after October 31, 2000 are calculated without amortization on the plant and equipment because the net book value as of November 1, 2000 is being used as a basis for negotiating for the sale.

Period	Before-tax Income (Loss)
June 1, 2000–October 31, 2000	$(4,100,000)
November 1, 2000–May 31, 2001	$(5,900,000)
June 1–30, 2001 (estimated)	$(750,000)

The Rocketeer Division will be accounted for as a discontinued operation on Campbell's 2000–2001 fiscal year financial statements. Campbell is subject to a 30% tax rate on operating income and all gains and losses.

Instructions

    (a) Explain how the Rocketeer Division's assets would be reported on Campbell Corporation's balance sheet as of May 31, 2001.

    (b) Explain how the discontinued operations and pending sale of the Rocketeer Division would be reported on Campbell Corporation's income statement for the year ended May 31, 2001.

    (c) Explain what information ordinarily should be disclosed in the notes to the financial statements regarding discontinued operations.

(CMA adapted)

CONCEPTUAL CASES

C4-1 Amos Corporation was incorporated and began business on January 1, 2001. It has been successful and now requires a bank loan for additional working capital to finance expansion. The bank has requested an audited income statement for the year 2001. The accountant for Amos Corporation provides you with the following income statement, which Amos plans to submit to the bank:

AMOS CORPORATION Income Statement		
Sales		$850,000
Dividends		32,300
Gain on recovery of insurance proceeds from earthquake loss (extraordinary)		38,500
		920,800
Less:		
Selling expenses	$100,100	
Cost of goods sold	510,000	
Advertising expense	13,700	
Loss on obsolescence of inventories	34,000	
Loss on discontinued operations	48,600	
Administrative expense	73,400	780,800
Income before income tax		140,000
Income tax		56,000
Net income		$ 84,000

Instructions

Indicate the deficiencies in the income statement presented above. Assume that the corporation desires a single-step income statement.

C4-2 The following represents a recent income statement for Boeing Corp:

Sales	$21,924,000,000
Costs and expenses	20,773,000,000
Income from operations	1,151,000,000
Other income	122,000,000
Interest and debt expense	(130,000,000)
Earnings before income taxes	1,143,000,000
Income taxes	(287,000,000)
Net income	$ 856,000,000

It includes only five separate numbers (two of which are in billions of dollars), two subtotals, and the net earnings figure.

Instructions

(a) Indicate the deficiencies in the income statement.
(b) What recommendations would you make to Boeing to improve the usefulness of its income statement?

C4-3 Information concerning the operations of a corporation is presented in an income statement or in a combined "income and retained earnings statement." Income statements are prepared on a "current operating performance" basis or an "all-inclusive" basis. Proponents of the two types of income statements do not agree upon the proper treatment of material nonrecurring charges and credits.

Instructions

(a) Define "current operating performance" and "all-inclusive" as used above.
(b) Explain the differences in content and organization of a "current operating performance" income statement and an "all-inclusive" income statement. Include a discussion of the proper treatment of material nonrecurring charges and credits.
(c) Give the principal arguments for the use of each of the three statements, "all-inclusive" income statement, "current operating performance" income statement, and a combined "income and retained earnings statement."

(AICPA adapted)

C4-4 Foxworthy, vice-president of finance for Hand Corp., has recently been asked to discuss with the company's division controllers the proper accounting for extraordinary items. Foxworthy prepared the factual situations presented below as a basis for discussion.

1. An earthquake destroys one of the oil refineries owned by a large multinational oil company. Earthquakes are rare in this geographical location.
2. A publicly held company has incurred a substantial loss in the unsuccessful registration of a bond issue.
3. A large portion of a cigarette manufacturer's tobacco crops are destroyed by a hailstorm. Severe damage from hailstorms is rare in this locality.
4. A large diversified company sells a block of shares from its portfolio of securities acquired for investment purposes.
5. A company sells a block of common shares of a publicly traded company. The block of shares, which represents less than 10% of the publicly held company, is the only security investment the company has ever owned.
6. A company that operates a chain of warehouses sells the excess land surrounding one of its warehouses. When the company buys property to establish a new warehouse, it usually buys more land than it expects to use for the warehouse with the expectation that the land will appreciate in value. Twice during the past five years the company sold excess land.
7. A textile manufacturer with only one plant moves to another location and sustains relocation costs of $725,000.
8. A company experiences a material loss in the repurchase of a large bond issue that has been outstanding for three years. The company regularly repurchases bonds of this nature.
9. A railroad experiences an unusual flood loss to part of its track system. Flood losses normally occur every three or four years.
10. A machine tool company sells the only land it owns. The land was acquired 10 years ago for future expansion, but shortly thereafter the company abandoned all plans for expansion but decided to hold the land for appreciation.

Instructions

Determine whether the foregoing items should be classified as extraordinary items. Present a rationale for your position.

C4-5 Grace Inc. has recently reported steadily increasing income. The company reported income of $20,000 in 1998, $25,000 in 1999, and $30,000 in 2000. A number of market analysts have recommended that investors buy the shares because they expect the steady growth in income to continue. Grace is approaching the end of its fiscal year in 2001, and it again appears to be a good year. However, it has not yet recorded warranty expense.

Based on prior experience, this year's warranty expense should be around $5,000, but some top management has approached the controller to suggest a larger, more conservative warranty expense should be recorded this year. Income before warranty expense is $43,000. Specifically, by recording an $8,000 warranty accrual this year, Grace could report an income increase for this year and still be in a position to cover its warranty costs in future years.

Instructions
(a) What is earnings management?
(b) What is the effect of the proposed accounting in 2001? In 2002?
(c) What is the appropriate accounting in this situation?

C4-6 Allen Corp. is an entertainment firm that derives approximately 30% of its income from the Casino Royale Division, which manages gambling facilities. As auditor for Allen Corp., you have recently overheard the following discussion between the controller and financial vice-president.

VICE-PRESIDENT: If we sell the Casino Royale Division, it seems ridiculous to segregate the results of the sale in the income statement. Separate categories tend to be absurd and confusing to the shareholders. I believe that we should simply report the gain on the sale as other income or expense without detail.

CONTROLLER: Professional pronouncements would require that we disclose this information separately in the income statement. If a sale of this type relates to a separate business segment and there exists a formal plan to dispose of it, it must be reported as a discontinued operation.

VICE-PRESIDENT: What about the walkout we had last month when our employees were upset about their commission income? Would this situation not also be an extraordinary item?

CONTROLLER: I am not sure whether this item would be reported as extraordinary or not.

VICE-PRESIDENT: Oh well, it doesn't make any difference because the net effect of all these items is immaterial, so no disclosure is necessary.

Instructions
Discuss.

C4-7 Anderson Corp. is a major manufacturer of foodstuffs whose products are sold in grocery and convenience stores throughout Canada. The company's name is well known and respected because its products have been marketed nationally for over 50 years.

In April 2001, the company was forced to recall one of its major products. A total of 35 persons in Oshkosh were treated for severe intestinal pain, and eventually three people died from complications. All of the people had consumed Anderson's product.

The product causing the problem was traced to one specific lot. Anderson keeps samples from all lots of foodstuffs. After thorough testing, Anderson and the legal authorities confirmed that the product had been tampered with after it had left the company's plant and was no longer under the company's control.

All of the product was recalled from the market—the only time an Anderson product has been recalled nationally and the only incident of tampering. Persons who still had the product in their homes, even though it was not from the affected lot, were encouraged to return the product for credit or refund. A media campaign was designed and implemented by the company to explain what had happened and what the company was doing to minimize any chance of recurrence. Anderson decided to continue the product with the same trade name and same wholesale price. However, the packaging was redesigned completely to be tamper resistant and safety sealed. This required the purchase and installation of new equipment.

The corporate accounting staff recommended that the costs associated with the tampered product be treated as an extraordinary charge on the 2001 financial statements. Corporate accounting was asked to identify the various costs that could be associated with the tampered product and related recall. These costs ($000 omitted) are as follows.

1.	Credits and refunds to stores and consumers	$30,000
2.	Insurance to cover lost sales and idle plant costs for possible future recalls	5,000
3.	Transportation costs and off-site warehousing of returned product	2,000
4.	Future security measures for other Anderson products	4,000

5. Testing of returned product and inventory	900
6. Destruction of returned product and inventory	2,400
7. Public relations program to reestablish brand credibility	4,200
8. Communication program to inform customers, answer inquiries, prepare press releases, etc.	1,600
9. Higher cost arising from new packaging	800
10. Investigation of possible involvement of employees, former employees, competitors, etc.	500
11. Packaging redesign and testing	2,000
12. Purchase and installation of new packaging equipment	6,000
13. Legal costs for defence against liability suits	750
14. Lost sales revenue due to recall	32,000

Anderson's estimated earnings before income taxes and before consideration of any of the above items for the year ending December 31, 2001 are $225 million.

Instructions

(a) Anderson plans to recognize the costs associated with the product tampering and recall as an extraordinary charge.

1. Explain why Anderson could classify this occurrence as an extraordinary charge.
2. Describe the placement and terminology used to present the extraordinary charge in the 2001 income statement.

(b) Refer to the 14 cost items identified by the corporate accounting staff of Anderson.

1. Identify the cost items by number that should be included in the extraordinary charge for 2001.
2. For any item that is not included in the extraordinary charge, explain why it would not be included in the extraordinary charge.

(CMA adapted)

C4-8 Andy Neville, controller for Tatooed Heart Inc., has recently prepared an income statement for 2002. Mr. Neville admits that he has not examined any recent professional pronouncements, but believes that the following presentation presents fairly the financial progress of this company during the current period.

TATOOED HEART INC.
Income Statement
For the Year Ended December 31, 2002

Sales			$377,852
Less: Sales returns and allowances			16,320
Net sales			361,532
Cost of goods sold:			
Inventory, January 1, 2002		$50,235	
Purchases	$192,143		
Less: Purchase discounts	3,142	189,001	
Cost of goods available for sale		239,236	
Inventory, December 31, 2002		41,124	
Cost of goods sold			198,112
Gross profit			163,420
Selling expenses		41,850	
Administrative expenses		32,142	73,992
Income before income tax			89,428
Other revenues and gains			
Dividends received			40,000
			129,428
Income tax			43,900
Net income			$ 85,528

TATOOED HEART INC.
Retained Earnings Statement
For the Year Ended December 31, 2002

Retained earnings, January 1, 2002			$216,000
Add:			
Net income for 2002	$85,528		
Gain from casualty (net of tax)	10,000		
Gain on sale of plant assets	21,400	$116,928	
Deduct:			
Loss on expropriation (net of tax)	13,000		
Correction of mathematical error in (net of tax)	17,186	(60,186)	56,742
Retained earnings, December 31, 2002			$272,742

Instructions

(a) Determine whether these statements are prepared under the "current operating" or "all-inclusive" concept of income. Cite specific details.

(b) Which method do you favour and why?

(c) Which method must be used, and how should the information be presented? Common shares outstanding for the year are 50,000 shares.

For questionable items, use the classification that ordinarily would be appropriate.

C4-9 The following financial statement was prepared by employees of Klein Corporation.

KLEIN CORPORATION
Income Statement
Year Ended December 31, 2002

Revenues	
Gross sales, including sales taxes	$1,044,300
Less: Returns, allowances, and cash discounts	56,200
Net sales	988,100
Dividends, interest, and purchase discounts	30,250
Recoveries of accounts written off in prior years	13,850
Total revenues	1,032,200
Costs and expenses	
Cost of goods sold	465,900
Salaries and related payroll expenses	60,500
Rent	19,100
Freight-in and freight-out	3,400
Bad debt expense	24,000
Addition to reserve for possible inventory losses	3,800
Total costs and expenses	576,700
Income before extraordinary items	455,500
Extraordinary items	
Loss on discontinued styles (Note 1)	37,000
Loss on sale of marketable securities (Note 2)	39,050
Loss on sale of warehouse (Note 3)	86,350
Tax assessments for 2001 and 2000 (Note 4)	34,500
Total extraordinary items	196,900
Net income	$258,600
Net income per common share	$2.30

Note 1: New styles and rapidly changing consumer preferences resulted in a $37,000 loss on the disposal of discontinued styles and related accessories.

Note 2: The corporation sold an investment in marketable securities at a loss of $39,050. The corporation normally sells securities of this nature.

Note 3: The corporation sold one of its warehouses at an $86,350 loss (net of taxes).

Note 4: The corporation was charged $34,500 for additional income taxes resulting from a settlement in 1999. Of this amount, $17,000 was applicable to 2001, and the balance was applicable to 2000. Litigation of this nature is recurring for this company.

Instructions

Identify and discuss the weaknesses in classification and disclosure in the single-step income statement above. You should explain why these treatments are weaknesses and what the proper presentation of the items would be in accordance with recent professional pronouncements.

C4-10 As audit partner for Noriyuki and Morita, you are in charge of reviewing the classification of unusual items that have occurred during the current year. The following items have come to your attention:

1. A merchandising company incorrectly overstated its ending inventory two years ago by a material amount. Inventory for all other periods is correctly calculated.
2. An automobile dealer sells for $137,000 an extremely rare 1930 S type Invicta, which it purchased for $21,000 10 years ago. The Invicta is the only such display item the dealer owns.
3. A drilling company during the current year extended the estimated useful life of certain drilling equipment from 9 to 15 years. As a result, amortization for the current year was materially lowered.
4. A retail outlet changed its computation for bad debt expense from 1% to ½ of 1% of sales because of changes in its customer clientele.
5. A mining concern sells a foreign subsidiary engaged in uranium mining, although it (the seller) continues to engage in uranium mining in other countries.
6. A steel company changes from straight-line amortization to accelerated amortization in accounting for its plant assets.
7. A construction company, at great expense, prepared a major proposal for a government loan. The loan is not approved.
8. A water pump manufacturer has had large losses resulting from a strike by its employees early in the year.
9. Amortization for a prior period was incorrectly understated by $950,000. The error was discovered in the current year.
10. A large sheep rancher suffered a major loss because the province required that all sheep in the province be killed to halt the spread of a rare disease. Such a situation has not occurred in the province for 20 years.
11. A food distributor that sells wholesale to supermarket chains and to fast-food restaurants (two major classes of customers) decides to discontinue the division that sells to one of the two classes of customers.

Instructions

From the foregoing information, indicate in what section of the income statement or retained earnings statement these items should be classified. Provide a brief rationale for your position.

*C4-11 You are working on the audit team for a multi-divisional, calendar year-end client with annual sales of $90 million. The company primarily sells electronic transistors to small customers and has one division that deals in acoustic transmitters for Navy submarines. The October Division has approximately $18 million in sales.

It's an evening in February 2001, and the audit work is complete. You're working in the client's office on the report, when you overhear a conversation between the financial vice-president, the treasurer, and the controller. They're discussing the sale of the October Division, expected to take place in June of this year, and the related reporting problems.

The vice-president thinks no segregation of the sale is necessary in the income statement because separate categories tend to be abused and confuse the shareholders. The treasurer disagrees. He feels that if an item is unusual or infrequent, it should be classified as an extraordinary item, including the sale of the October Division. The controller says an item should be both infrequent and unusual to be extraordinary. He feels the sale of the October Division should be shown separately, but not as an extraordinary item.

The sale is not new to you because you read about it in the minutes of the December 16, 2000 board of directors meeting. The minutes indicated plans to sell the transmitter plant and equipment by June 30, 2001 to its major competitor, who seems interested. The board estimates that net income and sales will remain constant until the sale, on which the company expects a $700,000 profit.

You also hear the controller disagree with the vice-president that the results of the strike last year and the sale of the old transistor ovens, formerly used in manufacturing, would also be extraordinary items. In addition, the treasurer thinks the government regulation issued last month, which made much of their inventory of raw material useless, would be extraordinary. The regulations set beta emission standards at levels lower than those in the raw materials supply, and there's no alternative use for the materials. Finally, the controller claims the discussion is academic. Since the net effect of all three items is immaterial, no disclosure is required.

Instructions

(a) Does the October Division qualify as a segment of a business in more than one way? If so, why?

(b) Does the October Division qualify as a discontinued operation? Why?

(c) Do the minutes indicate that a formal plan has been established? If not, why?

(d) When should the gain be recognized? What if a loss were anticipated?

(e) Who is correct about reporting the sale? What would the income statement presentation be for the next fiscal year?

(f) Who is right about whether the strike, the sale of fixed assets and the imposition of a new government regulation constitute extraordinary items?

(g) What do you think about the controller's observation on materiality?

(h) What are the earnings per share ramifications of these topics?

C4-12

Roots is a private company started in 1973 by cofounders Michael Budman and Don Green. The company produces sports and leisure wear and is the official outfitter for both the Canadian and U.S. Olympic teams and more recently has articulated that it is in the "lifestyle business." In 2001, Roots announced two strategic moves—one into the airline industry (Roots Air) and the other into the multivitamin area (with Boehringer Ingelheim—a Canadian consumer health care company).

Instructions

In your opinion, is Roots composed of one business segment or more? Argue both sides and give reasoning. More information may be found at www.roots.com.

Using Your Judgement

FINANCIAL REPORTING PROBLEM: CANADIAN TIRE CORPORATION LIMITED

The financial statements of **Canadian Tire Corporation Limited** and accompanying notes, as presented in the Company's Annual Report, are in Appendix 5B.

Instructions

Refer to this information and answer the following questions:

(a) What type of income statement format does the company use? Indicate why this format might be used to present income statement information.

(b) What are the company's primary revenue sources?

(c) Why is it not possible to calculate the company's gross profit for 2000? What other important ratios does this preclude users from calculating? Is this in compliance with GAAP [hint—see *CICA Handbook*, Section 1520)? Speculate why this information might not be provided by the company.

(d) Explain the management actions and strategies that contributed to increased sales and changes in consolidated earnings during 2000.

(e) Explain ongoing strategic initiatives that the company plans to implement in 2001 to boost sales and operating earnings.

(f) Very briefly comment on the company's quality of earnings. Are the earnings of high or low quality and why?

FINANCIAL STATEMENT ANALYSIS CASES

Bank of Montreal

Obtain the 2000 Annual Report for the **Bank of Montreal** from the Digital Tool. Note that financial reporting for Canadian banks is also constrained by the Bank Act and monitored by the Office of the Superintendent of Financial Institutions.

Answer the following questions:

(a) Revenues and expenses are defined as arising from "ordinary activities" of the business. What are the ordinary activities (core business activities) of the Bank of Montreal? What normal expenses must they incur in order to generate core revenues?

(b) Is this reflected in the income statement? (Hint: look at the classification between "revenues" and "other income/gains" and "expenses" and "other costs/losses".)

(c) Calculate the percentage of the various revenues/income streams to total revenues/income. Discuss the trends from year to year; i.e., are these revenue/income streams increasing as a percentage of the total revenue/income or decreasing? What are the primary sources of the revenues/income?

COMPARATIVE ANALYSIS CASE

Abitibi-Consolidated Inc. versus Domtar Inc.

Instructions

Go to the Digital Tool, and use information found there to answer the following questions related to **Abitibi-Consolidated Inc.** and **Domtar Inc.** for the year ended December 31, 1999.

(a) What type of income format(s) do these two companies use? Identify any differences in income statement format between these two companies.

(b) What are the gross profits, operating profit, and net income for these two companies over the three-year period 1997–1999? Which company has had better financial results over this period of time?

(c) Identify the irregular items reported by these two companies in their income statements over the three-year period. Do these irregular items appear to be significant? Explain.

(d) Very briefly comment on the quality of earnings of both companies.

RESEARCH CASES

Case 1

The Canadian Securities Administrators (CSA), an umbrella group of Canadian Provincial Securities Commissions, accumulates all documents required to be filed by public companies under securities law. This electronic database may be accessed from the following website: www.sedar.com. Company financial statements may also be accessed through the company websites.

Instructions

Visit the CSA website (www.sedar.com) and find the company documents for **Bank of Montreal** and **Royal Bank of Canada**. Answer the following questions:

(a) What types of company documents may be found here that provide useful information for investors who are making investment decisions?

(b) Locate the Annual Information Form. Explain the nature of the information that it contains. As a financial statement analyst, is this information useful to you? Why?

(c) Who are the auditors of both banks?

(d) Which stock exchange(s) do the banks trade on?

(e) Go to the company websites directly (www.bmo.com and www.royalbank.com). Look under "Investor relations." What type of information is on these websites and how does it differ from what is on the www.sedar.com website? Should these websites contain the same information as the CSA website?

Case 2

In 1999, the AcSB of the CICA issued an "Invitation to Comment" on the G4+1 "Proposals for Change" regarding "Reporting Financial Performance." The G4+1 was comprised of representatives from various standard setting bodies. Its proposals were the first step in attempting to achieve some standardization internationally with respect to income statement presentation. The G4+1 has since been replaced by the International Accounting Standards Board (IASB).

Instructions

Download the PDF file from the CICA website or obtain from the library. Read the "Invitation to Comment" and answer the following questions:

(a) What are the main problems in reporting financial performance that the "Invitation to Comment" paper identifies?

(b) Provide one real-life example for each of these items (review company income statements).

(c) What are the main proposals that the paper makes? In your opinion, will these proposals result in better information being provided to users of financial statements? Why?

INTERNATIONAL REPORTING CASE

Presented below is the income statement for a British company, Avon Rubber PLC.

	Total £'000
AVON RUBBER PLC **Consolidated Profit and Loss Account** **for the year ended 3 October 1998**	
Turnover	
Continuing activities	251,531
Acquisitions	15,554
Total turnover	**267,085**
Cost of sales	(216,174)
Gross profit	50,911
Net operating expenses	(28,586)
Share of operating profits of joint ventures and associated companies	26
Operating profit	
Continuing activities	19,361
Acquisitions	2,990
Total operating profit	**22,351**
Profit on sale of property	993
Loss on sale of fixed asset investment	(275)
Profit on ordinary activities before interest	**23,069**
Interest payable	(3,014)
Interest receivable	3,850
Profit on ordinary activities before taxation	**23,905**
Taxation	(7,003)
Profit on ordinary activities after taxation	**16,902**
Minority interests	254
Profit for the year	**17,156**
Basic earnings per ordinary share	62.4p

Instructions

(a) Review the Avon Rubber income statements and identify at least three differences between this British income statement and an income statement of a Canadian company as presented in this chapter.

(b) Identify irregular items reported by Avon Rubber. Is the reporting of these items in Avon's income statement similar to reporting of these items in the Canadian companies' income statement? Explain.

ETHICS CASE

Arthur Miller, controller for the Salem Corporation, is preparing the company's income statement at year-end. He notes that the company lost a considerable sum on the sale of some equipment it had decided to replace. Since the company has sold equipment routinely in the past, Miller knows the losses cannot be reported as extraordinary. He also does not want to highlight it as a material loss since he feels that will reflect poorly on him and the company. He reasons that if the company had recorded more amortization during the assets' lives, the losses would not be so great. Since amortization is included among the company's operating expenses, he wants to report the losses along with the company's expenses, where he hopes it will not be noticed.

Instructions

(a) What are the ethical issues involved?

(b) What should Miller do?

Financial Position and Cash Flows

LEARNING OBJECTIVES

....

After studying this chapter, you should be able to:

1. Identify the uses and limitations of a balance sheet.

2. Identify the major classifications of a balance sheet.

3. Prepare a classified balance sheet.

4. Identify balance sheet information requiring supplemental disclosure.

5. Identify major disclosure techniques for the balance sheet.

6. Indicate the purpose of the statement of cash flows.

7. Identify the content of the statement of cash flows.

8. Prepare a statement of cash flows.

9. Understand the usefulness of the statement of cash flows.

Preview of Chapter 5

The **balance sheet** and **statement of cash flows** complement the income statement, offering information about the company's financial position and how the firm generates and uses cash. The purpose of this chapter is to examine the many different types of assets, liabilities, and shareholders'. equity items that affect the balance sheet and the statement of cash flows. The content and organization of this chapter are as follows:

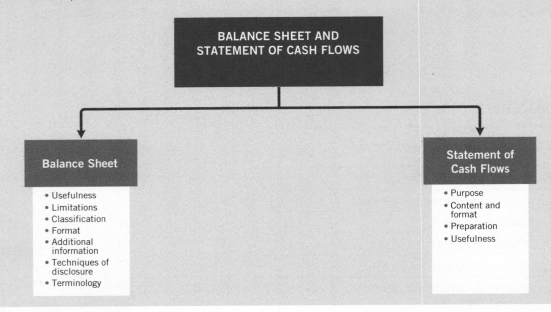

BALANCE SHEET AND STATEMENT OF CASH FLOWS

Balance Sheet

- Usefulness
- Limitations
- Classification
- Format
- Additional information
- Techniques of disclosure
- Terminology

Statement of Cash Flows

- Purpose
- Content and format
- Preparation
- Usefulness

SECTION 1 – Balance Sheet

The balance sheet, sometimes referred to as the statement of financial position, reports a business enterprise's assets, liabilities, and shareholders' equity **at a specific date**. This financial statement provides information about the nature and amounts of investments in enterprise resources, obligations to creditors, and the owners' equity in net resources[1]. It therefore helps in **predicting** the amounts, timing, and uncertainty of future **cash flows**.

USEFULNESS OF THE BALANCE SHEET

OBJECTIVE 1

Identify the uses and limitations of a balance sheet.

By providing information about assets, liabilities, and shareholders' equity, the balance sheet provides a basis for calculating **rates of return** on invested assets and evaluating the enterprise's **capital structure**. Information in the balance sheet is also used to

---

[1] *Financial Reporting in Canada, 2000,* (Toronto, CICA) indicates that approximately 90% of the companies surveyed used the term "balance sheet." The term "statement of financial position" is used infrequently, although it is conceptually appealing, p. 52.

assess business risk[2] and **future cash flows**. In this regard, the balance sheet is useful for analysing a company's **liquidity, solvency, and financial flexibility**, as described below, and helps analyse profitability (even though this is not the main focus of the statement).

Liquidity looks at the **amount of time that is expected to elapse until an asset is realized or otherwise converted into cash or until a liability has to be paid.** Certain ratios help assess overall liquidity, including **current ratio, quick or acid test ratio**, and **current cash debt coverage ratio**. Liquidity of certain assets such as receivables and inventory is assessed through **turnover ratios**. These ratios look at how fast the receivables or inventories are being collected or sold. The formulas for these are noted in Appendix 5A. **Creditors** are interested in short-term liquidity ratios, because they indicate whether the enterprise will have the resources to pay its current and maturing obligations. Similarly, **shareholders** assess liquidity to evaluate the possibility of future cash dividends or the buyback of shares. In general, the greater the liquidity, the lower the risk of enterprise or business failure.[3]

Solvency refers to an **enterprise's ability to pay its debts and related interest**. For example, when a company carries a high level of long-term debt relative to assets, it is at higher risk for insolvency than a similar company with a low level of long-term debt. Companies with **higher debt** are relatively **more risky** because more of their assets will be required to meet these fixed obligations (such as interest and principal payments). Certain ratios assist in assessing solvency. These are often called **"coverage" ratios**, referring to a company's ability to cover its interest and long-term debt payments. The formulas for these ratios are also noted in Appendix 5A.

Liquidity and solvency affect an entity's financial flexibility, which measures the **"ability of an enterprise to take effective actions to alter the amounts and timing of cash flows so it can respond to unexpected needs and opportunities."**[4] For example, a company may become so loaded with debt—so financially inflexible—that its cash sources to finance expansion or to pay off maturing debt are limited or nonexistent. An enterprise with a high degree of financial flexibility is better able to survive bad times, to recover from unexpected setbacks, and to take advantage of profitable and unexpected investment opportunities. Generally, the greater the financial flexibility, the lower the risk of enterprise or business failure.

Planet Hollywood International Inc. (**"Planet"**) filed for **bankruptcy protection** in the U.S. late in 1999 due to an inability to pay its debts. According to court documents filed, debt was almost equal to company assets. Bankruptcy protection gives companies some breathing room in order to reorganize their financial affairs. After a pre-specified time period, the company emerges from the bankruptcy protection period and hopefully carries on business, thus benefiting from the breathing space afforded by the bankruptcy protection. On May 9, 2000, Planet emerged from protection however, in its 2000 Annual Report, the financial statements showed that the company was still losing money and its auditors expressed concern over the company's ability to continue as a going concern. In the December 31, 2000 financial statements, current assets were $25.8 million U.S. with current liabilities being $50.2 million—nearly twice as much. Total debt was $129 million U.S. with total assets $146 million U.S. The following illustration is taken from the notes to the financial statements. Note that the financial statements are prepared on a **going concern** basis.

Obligation Ocean

We are drowning in a sea of debt!

Opportunity Shop

Investments

Can we afford the high payoff investment?

$ IOU

$ IOU

$ IOU

Hmm... I wonder if they will pay me back?

UNDERLYING CONCEPTS

The going concern concept is in question due to the high level of debt and lack of profitability.

---

[2] Risk is an expression of the unpredictability of the enterprise's future events, transactions, circumstances, and results.

[3] Liquidity measures are important inputs to bankruptcy prediction models, such as those developed by Altman and others. See G. White, A. Sondhi, and D. Fried, *The Analysis of Financial Statements* (New York: John Wiley & Sons, 1997), Chapter 18.

[4] "Reporting Income, Cash Flows, and Financial Position of Business Enterprises," Proposed Statement of Financial Accounting Concepts (Stamford, Conn.: FASB, 1981), par. .25.

ILLUSTRATION 5-1

Excerpt from the Notes to
Financial Statements for Planet
Hollywood

Note 2 – Reorganization Results and Management's Plans

The Company's financial statements are presented on the going concern basis, which contemplates the realization of assets and satisfaction of liabilities in the normal course of business. The Company incurred recurring losses from operations in fiscal 1998 and 1999, and on October 12, 1999 (the "Petition Date"), the Company and twenty-five of its domestic operating subsidiaries (the "Debtors") filed voluntary petitions commencing cases under Chapter 11 of the United States Bankruptcy Code with the United States Bankruptcy Court for the District of Delaware (the "Bankruptcy Court"). An Official Committee of Unsecured Creditors (the "Committee"), which represented the interests of all unsecured creditors of the Debtors, was appointed in the Chapter 11 cases. In a Chapter 11 filing, substantially all liabilities as of the Petition Date are subject to compromise or other treatment under a plan of reorganization. Generally, actions to enforce or otherwise effect payment of all pre-Chapter 11 liabilities are stayed while the Company and its subsidiaries continued their business operations as debtors-in-possession. The Company's operating losses were primarily due to declines in comparative restaurant revenues, overall disappointing fiscal operating results, expenses due to the development of the now discontinued Sound Republic concept, and losses from major concepts such as Official All Star Cafe and Cool Planet.

LIMITATIONS OF THE BALANCE SHEET

Timber at   Timber at
Historical Cost   Current Value

**If we sell that land,
we could get more
than we paid.**

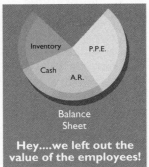

Inventory   P.P.E.

Cash   A.R.

Balance
Sheet

**Hey....we left out the
value of the employees!**

Because the income statement and the balance sheet are interrelated, it is not surprising that the balance sheet has many of the same limitations as the income statement. Here are some of the major limitations of the balance sheet:

1. Most assets and liabilities are stated at **historical cost**. As a result, the information reported in the balance sheet has higher **reliability** but is subject to the criticism that a more **relevant** current fair value is not reported. Use of historical cost and other valuation methods was discussed in Chapter 2.

2. **Judgements and estimates** are used in determining many of the items reported in the balance sheet. This represents the other side of the same issue identified in Chapter 4 when discussing income statement limitations. Estimates for liabilities for post-retirement benefits incorporate significant assumptions and therefore the resulting numbers are often referred to as "soft" numbers (as opposed to "hard" numbers such as cash in the bank)—meaning that they are subject to a significant amount of uncertainty. "Soft" numbers are less **reliable** than "hard" numbers, as well as having less predictive value as they are likely to change.

3. The balance sheet necessarily **omits many items** that are of financial value to the business but cannot be recorded objectively.[5] These may be either assets or liabilities. Again, this represents the other side of the identical issue discussed in Chapter 4. Analysts habitually **capitalize[6] many of the "off balance sheet liabilities"** prior to calculating key **liquidity** and **solvency** ratios. When valuing a company, mergers and acquisition specialists consider **off balance sheet** assets such as goodwill.

CLASSIFICATION IN THE BALANCE SHEET (PRESENTATION)

OBJECTIVE 2

Identify the major classifications
of a balance sheet.

Balance sheet accounts are **classified** (like the income statement) so that similar items are grouped together to arrive at significant subtotals. Furthermore, the material is arranged so that important relationships are shown.

---

[5] Several of these omitted items (such as internally generated goodwill, leases classified as operating leases and through-put arrangements) are discussed in later chapters.

[6] While the term "capitalize" is often used in the context of recording costs as assets, it is sometimes used in the context above. The latter context deals with recognizing the liabilities on the balance sheet.

As with the income statement, **the balance sheet's parts and subsections can be more informative than the whole**. Therefore, as one would expect, the reporting of summary accounts alone (total assets, net assets, total liabilities, etc.) is discouraged. Individual items should be **separately reported** and classified in sufficient detail to permit users to assess the amounts, timing, and uncertainty of future cash flows, as well as the evaluation of liquidity and financial flexibility, profitability, and risk.

Classification in financial statements helps analysts by **grouping items with similar characteristics** and **separating items with different characteristics**:

1. Assets that differ in their **type or expected function** in the central operations or other enterprise activities should be reported as separate items. For example, merchandise inventories should be reported separately from property, plant, and equipment. In this way, investors can see how fast inventory is turning over or being sold.

2. Assets and liabilities with **different implications for the enterprise's financial flexibility** should be reported as separate items. For example, assets used in operations should be reported separately from assets held for investment and assets subject to restrictions, such as leased equipment. Long-term liabilities should be reported separately from current liabilities.

3. Assets and liabilities with **different general liquidity characteristics** should be reported as separate items. For example, cash should be reported separately from inventories.

The three general classes of items included in the balance sheet are assets, liabilities, and equity. The elements related to the balance sheet are defined below:

ELEMENTS OF THE BALANCE SHEET

1. **ASSETS.** Probable **future economic benefits** obtained or **controlled** by a particular entity as a result of **past transactions or events**.
2. **LIABILITIES.** Probable future sacrifices of economic benefits arising from present **duty or responsibility** to others, as a result of **past transactions or events**, where there is **little or no discretion to avoid** the obligation.
3. **EQUITY/NET ASSETS.** **Residual interest** in an entity's assets that remains after deducting its liabilities. In a business enterprise, the equity is the ownership interest.

OBJECTIVE 3

Prepare a classified balance sheet.

These are the same definitions as identified in Chapter 2 and the conceptual framework. Illustration 5-2 indicates the general format of balance sheet presentation.

Assets	Liabilities and Owners' Equity
Current assets	Current liabilities
Long-term investments	Long-term debt
Property, plant, and equipment	Owners' equity
Intangible assets	Capital shares
Other assets	Contributed Surplus
	Retained earnings

ILLUSTRATION 5-2
Balance Sheet Classifications

The balance sheet may be classified in some other manner, but there is very little departure from these major subdivisions in practice. If a proprietorship or partnership is involved, the classifications within the owners' equity section are presented a little differently, as will be shown later in the chapter.

These classifications allow ease of calculation of important ratios such as the **current ratio for assessing liquidity** and **debt-to-equity ratios for assessing solvency**. By showing the breakdown of total assets, users can easily calculate which assets are more significant than others and how these relationships change over time.[7] This gives insight

---

[7] That is by performing a **vertical analysis** and calculating the percentage represented by "specific asset divided by total assets." This number may then be compared with the same percentage from prior years. This latter comparison is generally referred to as a **horizontal or trend analysis**. Horizontal and vertical analyses are discussed further in the Digital Tool under Financial Statement Analysis.

See the Digital Tool for the Analysis Tool kit

into management's strategy and stewardship. Illustration 5-3 illustrates a partial classified balance sheet for **Biovail Corporation**.

ILLUSTRATION 5-3
Partial Classified Balance
Sheet—Excerpt from
Biovail Corporation

BIOVAIL CORPORATION Consolidated Balance Sheets As at December 31, 1999 and 1998		
(All dollar amounts are expressed in thousands of U.S. dollars)		
Liabilities		
Current		
Accounts payable......................................	$ 22,685	$12,244
Accrued liabilities (Note 12)......................	31,107	4,129
Income taxes payable................................	3,585	1,004
Customer prepayments	4,962	4,516
Current portion of long-term debt (Note 13)	12,016	653
	74,355	22,546
Long-Term Debt (Note 13)............................	125,488	126,182
	199,843	148,728
Shareholders' Equity		
Share capital (Note 14)	368,538	19,428
Warrants (Note 14)	8,244	8,244
Retained earnings	57,252	24,748
Cumulative translation adjustment	1,260	(1,229)
	435,294	51,191
	$635,137	$199,919

Note that the long-term debt-to-equity ratio changed significantly from 1998 to 1999. The calculations for the long-term debt-to-equity ratio are as follows:

$$1998 = \$126,182/51,191 = 2.5 \text{ to } 1$$
$$1999 = \$125,488/435,294 = 0.29 \text{ to } 1$$

Note how much the long-term debt-to-equity ratio has improved. The change in ratio was substantially due to a significant issue of shares.

**INTERNATIONAL
INSIGHT**

Basic balance sheet formats differ across nations. For example, in Great Britain and in nations influenced by British financial reporting, the balance sheet is presented with the least liquid asset accounts appearing first and cash appearing last. Canada is influenced more by the U.S.

ILLUSTRATION 5-4
The Business Operating Cycle for
Manufacturing Companies

Current Assets

Current assets are **cash and other assets ordinarily realizable within one year from the date of the balance sheet or within the normal operating cycle where that is longer than a year.**[8] The **operating cycle** is the average time between the acquisition of materials and supplies and the realization of cash through sales of the product for which the materials and supplies were acquired. The cycle operates from cash through inventory, production, and receivables back to cash. When there are several operating cycles within one year, the one-year period is used. If the operating cycle is more than one year, the longer period is used. Illustration 5-4 depicts the operating cycle for manufacturing companies.

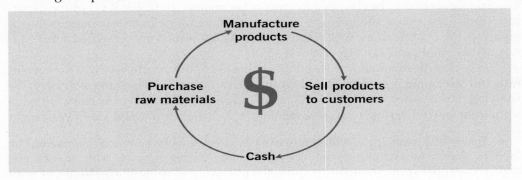

---

[8] *CICA Handbook*, Section 1510, par. .01.

Current assets are generally presented in the balance sheet in order of liquidity for most industries.[9] The five major items found in the current assets section are **cash, short-term investments, receivables, inventories,** and **prepayments. Cash** is included at its stated value; **short-term investments** are generally valued at historical cost or fair value; **accounts receivable** are stated at the estimated amount collectible; **inventories** generally are included at cost or the lower of cost or market; and **prepaid items** are valued at cost.

Cash

Cash is often grouped with other cash-like liquid assets and reported as "cash and cash equivalents."[10] Cash and cash equivalents are defined as **cash, demand deposits, and short-term highly liquid investments that are readily convertible into known amounts of cash and which are subject to insignificant risk of changes in value.**[11]

Any **restrictions** on the general availability of cash or any commitments on its probable disposition must be disclosed. If cash is restricted for purposes other than current obligations, it is excluded from current assets.

Short-term Investments

Short-term or temporary investments are classified as current assets only if they are **capable of reasonably prompt liquidation** and where there is **management intent** to liquidate them within a year.[12] An excerpt from the balance sheet of **Loblaw Companies Limited** illustrates the presentation of "cash and cash equivalents" and "short-term investments." Note the description of the instruments included in these lines as noted in note 5 to the financial statements.

<table>
<tr><td colspan="3" align="center">**LOBLAW COMPANIES LIMITED**
Consolidated Balance Sheets</td></tr>
<tr><td>As at December 30, 2000 ($ millions)</td><td>2000</td><td>1999</td></tr>
<tr><td>**Assets**</td><td></td><td></td></tr>
<tr><td>Current Assets   Cash and cash equivalents (note 5)</td><td>$ 686</td><td>$ 481</td></tr>
<tr><td>Short-term investments (note 5)</td><td>364</td><td>245</td></tr>
<tr><td>Accounts receivable</td><td>381</td><td>325</td></tr>
<tr><td>Inventories</td><td>1,310</td><td>1,222</td></tr>
<tr><td>Prepaid expenses and other assets</td><td>61</td><td>50</td></tr>
<tr><td>Current future income taxes (note 4)</td><td>114</td><td></td></tr>
<tr><td>Taxes recoverable</td><td></td><td>92</td></tr>
<tr><td></td><td>2,916</td><td>2,415</td></tr>
</table>

UNDERLYING CONCEPTS

Grouping these like items together reduces the amount of redundant information on the balance sheet and therefore results in information that is easier to understand.

ILLUSTRATION 5-5

Balance Sheet Presentation of Cash and Cash Equivalents and Short-term Investments—Excerpt from Loblaw Companies Limited Financial Statements

---

[9] The real estate industry is an example of one industry that does not follow this approach. This is due to the fact that the industry feels that a more meaningful presentation results in the most important assets being presented first. In most real estate development companies, the most important and largest asset is "Revenue producing properties." This asset includes hotels, shopping centres, leased buildings etc. that generate revenue or profits for the company. **Brookfield Properties Corporation** records this asset first on the balance sheet. On the liabilities side, the corresponding debt related to the properties is recorded. For Brookfield, this asset represents 73% of total assets. Real estate companies are bound by GAAP and also by specialized industry GAAP (Real Estate GAAP as published by the Canadian Institute of Public and Private Real Estate Companies, CIPREC).

[10] According to a survey of 200 companies, 66 reported "cash and cash equivalents" with most of the others reporting cash grouped with short-term deposits or investments (CICA, *Financial Reporting in Canada, 2000*, p. 224).

[11] *CICA Handbook*, Section 1540, par. .06.

[12] *CICA Handbook*, Section 3010, par. .02.

ILLUSTRATION 5-5
Balance Sheet Presentation
(Continued)

Franchise Investments and Other Receivables	189	160
Fixed Assets (note 6)	4,172	3,549
Future Income Taxes (note 4)	42	—
Goodwill (note 2)	1,641	1,685
Other Assets	63	170
	$9,025	$7,979

Note 5 – Cash, Cash Equivalents and Short-term Investments

Cash, cash equivalents, short-term investments, bank indebtedness, and the Company's commercial paper program form an integral part of the Company's cash management.

The Company had $1,037 (1999 – $714) in cash, cash equivalents, and short-term investments held by its wholly owned non-Canadian subsidiaries. Short-term investments are carried at the lower of cost or quoted market value and consist primarily of U.S. government securities, commercial paper, bank deposits, and repurchase agreements. The income from these investments of $55 (1999 – $35) was included as a reduction of other interest expense. Cash and cash equivalents of $686 (1999 – $481) include short-term investments with a maturity of less than 90 days, and short-term investments of $364 (1999 – $245) have a maturity of greater than 90 days.

Receivables

Accounts should be segregated so as to show **ordinary trade accounts**, amounts owing by **related parties**, and other **unusual items** of a substantial amount.[13] Any anticipated loss due to uncollectibles, the amount and nature of any nontrade receivables, and any receivables designated or pledged as collateral should be clearly identified. **Magnotta Winery Corporation** (Magnotta) reported its receivables as follows:

ILLUSTRATION 5-6
Balance Sheet Presentation of
Receivables—Excerpt from
Magnotta Winery Corporation
Balance Sheet

MAGNOTTA WINERY CORPORATION Consolidated Balance Sheets January 31, 2000 and 1999		
Assets		
Current assets		
Accounts receivable (note 9)	$ 941,921	$ 886,156
Inventories (note 2)	13,843,591	11,198,872
Prepaid expenses and deposits	657,877	649,371
	15,443,389	12,734,399
Capital assets (note 3)	18,713,482	18,371,639
	$34,156,871	$31,106,038

9. **Related party transactions:**
   Included in accounts receivables are amounts due from senior officers in the amount of $391,160 (1999 – $383,465) which are unsecured, non-interest bearing, and due on demand.

UNDERLYING CONCEPTS

The lower of cost and market valuation is an example of the use of conservatism in accounting.

Inventories

For a proper presentation of inventories, the basis of valuation (i.e., lower of cost and market) and the method of pricing (FIFO or LIFO) are disclosed. For a manufacturing concern, the stage of the inventories' completion is also indicated (raw materials, work in progress, and finished goods). Illustration 5-7 shows the breakdown of Magnotta's inventory. Note from Illustration 5-6 that inventory is the most significant current asset on Magnotta's balance sheet (90% of current assets) and that it represents 41% of total assets.

---

13 *CICA Handbook*, Section 3020 par. .01.

MAGNOTTA WINERY CORPORATION

Notes to Consoldiated Financial Statements (Continued)
Years ended January 31, 2000 and 1999

2. Inventories:

	2000	1999
Supplies	$ 2,631,600	$ 2,653,726
Work-in-process	5,953,612	5,265,759
Finished goods	5,258,379	3,279,387
	$13,843,591	$11,198,872

During the year, interest in the amount of $145,606 (1999 – $133,941) was capitalized into
the inventory.

Which types of companies are likely to have significant inventory? Clearly, companies
that retail and manufacture goods will have some inventory (as compared with companies that offer services only). How much inventory is enough or, conversely, how
much inventory is too much? Companies must have at least sufficient inventory to meet
customer demands. On the other hand, inventory ties up significant amounts of cash
flows, incurs storage costs and subjects the company to risk of theft, obsolescence, etc.
Many companies operate on a "just in time" philosophy, meaning that they streamline
their production and supply channels such that they are able to order the raw materials and produce the product in a very short time. Many car manufacturers follow this
philosophy, thus freeing up working capital and reducing need for storing inventory.

Magnotta grows grapes and makes wine, among other products. Why would it
have to carry significant amounts of inventory? It may be due to the fact that the time
between grape harvest and finished bottle of wine (the business cycle) is long. The wine
goes through various production stages, including long periods where the wine sits in
barrels and/or bottles (aging). Another factor is that the company may stock different
vintages for its customers.

Prepaid Expenses

Prepaid expenses included in current assets are **expenditures already made for benefits (usually services) to be received within one year or the operating cycle**, whichever
is longer. These items are current assets because if they had not already been paid, they
would require the use of cash during the next year or the operating cycle. A common
example is the payment in advance for an insurance policy. It is classified as a prepaid
expense at the time of the expenditure because the payment precedes receipt of the
coverage benefit. Prepaid expenses are reported at the amount of the unexpired or
unconsumed cost. Other common prepaid expenses include rent, advertising, taxes,
and office or operating supplies.

Companies often include insurance and other prepayments for two or three years
in current assets even though part of the advance payment applies to periods beyond
one year or the current operating cycle. This is a matter of convention even though it
is inconsistent with the definition of current assets.

Long-term Investments

Long-term investments, often referred to simply as investments, normally consist of
one of four types:

1. Investments in securities, such as bonds, common shares, or long-term notes.
2. Investments in tangible fixed assets not currently used in operations, such as land
   held for speculation.

3. Investments set aside in special funds such as a sinking fund, pension fund, or plant expansion fund. The cash surrender value of life insurance may be included here.

4. Investments in nonconsolidated subsidiaries or affiliated companies.

Long-term investments are to be held for many years. They are not acquired with the **intention** of disposing of them in the near future. They are usually presented on the balance sheet just below **Current Assets** in a separate section called **Investments**. Many securities that are properly shown among long-term investments are, in fact, **readily marketable**. They are not included as current assets unless the **intent** is to convert them to cash in the short-term—within a year or in the operating cycle, whichever is longer. These investments are normally carried at **cost or amortized cost** (in the case of bonds) **unless there is a non-temporary decline in value**. A non-temporary decline in value may exist, for example, when the market value of common shares has been less than carrying value for a number of years. This will be dealt with in greater detail in Chapter 10.

Property, Plant, and Equipment/Capital Assets

Property, plant, and equipment/capital assets are properties of a durable nature used in regular business operations to generate income. These assets consist of physical property such as land, buildings, machinery, furniture, tools, and wasting resources (timberland, minerals). With the exception of land, most assets are either depreciable (such as buildings) or depletable (such as timberlands or oil reserves).

Magnotta has significant capital assets. In fact, in 2000, capital assets represented 55% of total assets. Illustration 5-8 shows the detailed breakdown of these assets as shown in note 3 to the financial statements.

ILLUSTRATION 5-8

Balance Sheet Presentation of Property, Plant, and Equipment—Excerpt from Magnotta Winery Corporation's Notes to Financial Statements

MAGNOTTA WINERY CORPORATION

Notes to Consolidated Financial Statements (continued)
Years ended January 31, 2000 and 1999

3. **Capital assets:**

	Cost	Accumulated amortization	2000 Net book value	1999 Net book value
Land	$ 1,412,337	$ —	$ 1,412,337	$ 1,412,337
Land and vineyards	5,917,378	—	5,917,378	5,576,195
Buildings	4,292,222	476,334	3,815,888	3,974,881
Leaseholds	1,192,100	517,711	674,389	684,707
Equipment	9,936,124	3,322,853	6,613,271	6,428,949
Winery licences	390,316	110,097	280,219	294,570
	$23,140,477	$ 4,426,995	$18,713,482	$18,371,639

During the year, interest in the amount of $148,000 (1999 – $121,000) was capitalized into land and vineyards.

The basis of valuing the property, plant, and equipment, any liens against the properties, and accumulated amortization should be disclosed—usually in notes to the statements.

What type of company has significant amounts of capital assets? Manufacturing, resource-based companies, and pharmaceutical companies are just a few that would need to spend significant amounts of money on capital assets in order to generate revenues. Magnotta's capital assets consist of the land and vineyards needed to grow the grapes. Also significant are the buildings and equipment needed to process and store the grapes. As wine is temperature- and light-sensitive, care must be taken to ensure that it is properly handled and stored, hence the need for larger expenditures on buildings and equipment. As was noted earlier, Magnotta has a significant amount of inventory and therefore needs significant amounts of storage space.

Intangible Assets

Intangible assets **lack physical substance and usually have a higher degree of uncertainty concerning their future benefits.** They include patents, copyrights, franchises, goodwill, trademarks, trade names, and secret processes. Generally, all of these intangibles are written off (amortized) to expense over 5 to 40 years.[14] These accounts typically do not have accumulated amortization contra accounts. Intangibles can represent significant economic resources, yet financial analysts often ignore them, and accountants write them down or off arbitrarily because valuation/measurement is difficult.

A significant portion of the **Biovail Corporation**'s total assets is "Other assets" (39%) as shown in Illustration 5-9. A further look at the detail behind that number shows that this is composed of goodwill, research and development, and property rights, plus other intangible assets.

BIOVAIL CORPORATION
Consolidated Balance Sheets
As at December 31, 1999 and 1998

(All dollar amounts are expressed in thousands of U.S. dollars)	1999	1998
ASSETS		
CURRENT		
Cash and cash equivalents (Note 4)	$178,086	$ 78,279
Short-term investment (Note 5)	65,893	—
Accounts receivable (Note 6)	60,571	42,768
Inventories (Note 7)	12,701	10,542
Assets held for disposal (Note 3)	20,000	—
Executive stock purchase plan loans (Note 8)	—	2,924
Deposits and prepaid expenses	3,172	3,357
	340,423	137,870
LONG-TERM INVESTMENTS (Note 9)	12	10,055
CAPITALS ASSETS, net (Note 10)	45,300	23,677
OTHER ASSETS, net (Note 11)	249,402	28,317
	$635,137	$199,919

ILLUSTRATION 5-9

Balance Sheet Presentation of Intangible Assets—Excerpt from Biovail Corporation's Financial Statements

11. Other assets

The following table summarizes other assets net of accumulated amortization.

	1999	1998
Goodwill	$ 38,514	$ 3,277
Acquired in-process research and development	136,215	—
Core technology and workforce	13,096	—
Product rights and royalty interests	56,945	20,522
Other intangibles	4,632	4,518
	$249,402	$28,317

Amortization amounted to $6,002,000, $1,883,000, and $441,000 in 1999, 1998, and 1997, respectively.

In December 1999, the Company acquired from IPL the product rights to IPL's generic version of Procardia XL for $25,000,000.

In October 1999, the Company acquired from Elan Corporation plc ("Elan") the exclusive marketing rights for the U.S. to Elan's generic version of Adalat CC. The product will be marketed by Teva Pharmaceuticals ("Teva"). The net cost to the Company was $9,000,000, which will be amortized over the life of the product.

In November 1998, the Company completed the issue of U.S. Dollar Senior Notes, due 2005, for gross proceeds of $125,000,000. The expenses associated with this transmission have been deferred and are being amortized on a straight-line basis over the seven-year term of the debt.

---

[14] This is currently under study and will likely be reduced to a 20-year maximum period for amortization. Goodwill will no longer be amortized but will be valued at each reporting date to reflect any declines in value.

ILLUSTRATION 5-9
Balance Sheet Presentation
(Continued)

In March 1998, the Company completed the acquisition of the royalty interest held by Galephar Puerto Rico, Inc. Limited ("Galephar") in certain of the Company's products. The Company paid $15,000,000 to Galephar in full satisfaction of the Company's royalty obligations on the sales of Tiazac® and the Company's generic controlled release version of Cardizem CD in the U.S. and Canada. In September 1998, the Company acquired from Centocor, Inc. the exclusive distribution rights in Canada for Retavase for $4,000,000.

This would appear to make sense since Biovail is in the pharmaceutical industry, where significant amounts of money are spent on research and development. Often this is expensed where there is uncertainty about the research and development being able to generate future cash flows.

Other Assets

The items included in the section Other Assets vary widely in practice. Some of the items commonly included are deferred charges, noncurrent receivables, intangible assets, assets in special funds, future income taxes, property held for sale, and advances to subsidiaries. Care should be taken to disclose these assets in sufficient detail such that users can get a better idea of their nature.

Current Liabilities

Current liabilities are the obligations that are **expected to be liquidated either through the use of current assets or the creation of other current liabilities**.

This concept includes:

1. Payables resulting from the acquisition of goods and services: accounts payable, wages payable, taxes payable, and so on.
2. Collections received in advance for the delivery of goods or performance of services such as unearned rent revenue or unearned subscriptions revenue.
3. Other liabilities whose liquidation will take place within the operating cycle, such as the portion of long-term bonds to be paid in the current period, or short-term obligations arising from purchase of equipment.
4. Short-term financing payable on demand (such as line of credit/overdraft).

At times, a liability payable next year is not included in the current liabilities section. This occurs either when the debt is **expected to be refinanced** through another long-term issue,[15] or when the debt is retired out of noncurrent assets. This approach is used because liquidation does not result from the use of current assets or the creation of other current liabilities.

Current liabilities are not reported in any consistent order. The items most commonly listed first are accounts payable, accrued liabilities or short-term debt; those most commonly listed last are income taxes payable, current maturities of long-term debt, or other current liabilities.

Current liabilities include such items as trade and nontrade notes and accounts payable, advances received from customers, and current maturities of long-term debt. Income taxes and other accrued items are classified separately, if material. Any secured liability—for example, shares held as collateral on notes payable—is fully described in the notes so that the assets providing the security can be identified.

The excess of total current assets over total current liabilities is referred to as working capital (sometimes called **net working capital**). Working capital represents the net amount of a company's relatively **liquid resources**. That is, it is the **liquid buffer available to meet the operating cycle's financial demands**. Working capital as an amount is seldom disclosed on the balance sheet, but it is calculated by bankers and other credi-

---

[15] A more detailed discussion of debt expected to be refinanced and its classification in the balance sheet is noted in Chapter 14

tors as an indicator of a company's short-run liquidity. In order to determine the actual liquidity and availability of working capital to meet current obligations, however, one must analyse the current assets' **composition** and analyse **nearness to cash**.

Long-term Debt/Liabilities

Long-term liabilities are **obligations that are not reasonably expected to be liquidated within the normal operating cycle but instead are payable at some date beyond that time.** Bonds payable, notes payable, some future income tax amounts, lease obligations, and pension obligations are the most common examples. Generally, a great deal of supplementary disclosure is needed for this section, because most long-term debt is subject to various covenants and restrictions to protect lenders.[16] Long-term liabilities that mature within the current operating cycle are classified as current liabilities if their liquidation requires the use of current assets.

Generally, long-term liabilities are of three types:

1. Obligations arising from specific financing situations, such as the issuance of bonds, long-term lease obligations, and long-term notes payable.
2. Obligations arising from the ordinary enterprise operations, such as pension obligations and future income tax liabilities.
3. Obligations that are dependent upon the occurrence or nonoccurrence of one or more future events to confirm the amount payable, or the payee, or the date payable, such as service or product warranties and other contingencies.

It is desirable to report any premium or discount separately as an addition to or subtraction from the bonds payable. The terms of all long-term liability agreements (including maturity date or dates, interest rates, nature of obligation, and any security pledged to support the debt) are frequently described in notes to the financial statements. An example of the financial statement and accompanying note presentation is shown in Illustration 5-10 in the excerpt from **Abitibi-Consolidated Inc.**

ABITIBI-CONSOLIDATED INC.
Consolidated Balance Sheets

As at December 31 (millions of Canadian dollars)	1999	1998
LIABILITIES		
Current Liabilities		
Accounts payable and accrued liabilities	$ 889	$ 768
Dividends payable	19	19
Current portion of long-term debt		
Recourse (note 13(a))	42	44
Non-recourse (note 13(b))	95	18
	1,045	849
Long-term debt		
Recourse (note 13 (a))	2,068	2,087
Non-recourse (note 13(b))	581	310
Deferred income taxes	452	583
	4,146	3,829

ILLUSTRATION 5-10
Balance Sheet Presentation of Long-term Debt—Excerpt from Abitibi-Consolidated Inc.'s Balance Sheet

Note that the debt is split between a current (due within one year) and long-term. It is further split between "recourse" and "non recourse." "Recourse" refers to the terms of the debt. This will be discussed further in Chapter 15.

---

[16] The pertinent rights and privileges of the various securities (both debt and equity) outstanding are usually explained in the notes to the financial statements. Examples of information that should be disclosed are dividend and liquidation preferences, participation rights, call prices and dates, conversion or exercise prices or rates and pertinent dates, sinking fund requirements, unusual voting rights, and significant terms of contracts to issue additional shares, (*CICA Handbook* Sections 3210 and 3240).

Financial Instruments

Financial instruments are defined as cash, an ownership interest, or a contractual right to receive or obligation to deliver cash or another financial instrument.[17] Such contractual rights to receive cash or other financial instruments are **assets**, whereas contractual obligations to pay are **liabilities**. Cash, investments, accounts receivable, and all payables or debt are examples of financial instruments.

Financial instruments are increasing both in use and variety. As a consequence of the increasing use of financial instruments, companies are required to disclose both the carrying value and the estimated fair values of their financial instruments.[18] More extensive discussion of financial instrument accounting and reporting is provided in Chapters 7, 10, 14, 15, and 18. Derivatives will be covered in 18B.

Owners' Equity

The **owners' equity** (shareholders' equity) section is one of the most difficult sections to prepare and understand. This is due to the complexity of capital shares agreements and the various restrictions on residual equity imposed by corporation laws, liability agreements, and boards of directors. The section is usually divided into three parts:

SHAREHOLDERS' EQUITY SECTION

1. *Capital Shares.* The exchange value of shares issued.
2. *Contributed Surplus.* Includes premiums on shares issued, capital donations, and other.
3. *Retained Earnings.* The corporation's undistributed earnings, sometimes referred to as earned surplus.

The major disclosure requirements for capital shares are the authorized, issued, and outstanding amounts. The contributed surplus is usually presented in one amount, although subtotals are informative if the additional capital sources are varied and material. The retained earnings section may be divided between the unappropriated (the amount that is usually available for dividend distribution) and any amounts that are restricted (e.g., by bond indentures or other loan agreements). In addition, any capital shares reacquired (treasury stock) are shown as a reduction of shareholders' equity.[19]

A corporation's ownership or shareholders' equity accounts are considerably different from those in a partnership or proprietorship. Partners' permanent capital accounts and the balance in their temporary accounts (drawing accounts) are shown separately. Proprietorships ordinarily use a single capital account that handles all of the owner's equity transactions.

Presented below is an example of the shareholders' equity section from **Canadian National Railway Company**.

ILLUSTRATION 5-11

Balance Sheet Presentation of Shareholders' Equity—Excerpt from Canadian National Railway Company's Balance Sheet

CANADIAN NATIONAL RAILWAY COMPANY – CANADIAN GAAP
Consolidated Balance Sheet

In millions	December 31	2000	1999
Shareholders' equity:			
Common shares (note 12)		$ 3,124	$ 3,311
Convertible preferred securities (Note 12)		327	327
Contributed surplus		178	190
Currency translation		61	(9)
Retained earnings		2,008	1,687
		5,698	5,506
Total liabilities and shareholders' equity		$15,196	$14,757

---

[17] *CICA Handbook*, Section 3860, par. .05.

[18] As mentioned in Chapter 2, a Joint Working Group of standard-setting bodies has proposed to use market or fair value as long as values are measurable and to recognize all financial instruments on the balance sheet.

[19] In Canada, under the CBCA, shares reacquired must be cancelled. However, some provincial jurisdictions and other countries (e.g., the U.S.) still allow treasury shares to exist.

BALANCE SHEET FORMAT

One method of presentation of a classified balance sheet lists assets by sections on the left side and liabilities and shareholders' equity by sections on the right side. The main disadvantage is the need for two facing pages. To avoid the use of facing pages, another format, shown in Illustration 5-12, lists liabilities and shareholders' equity directly below assets on the same page.

ILLUSTRATION 5-12
Classified Balance Sheet

SCIENTIFIC PRODUCTS, INC.
Balance Sheet
December 31, 2001

Assets

Current assets			
Cash		$ 42,485	
Temporary investments		28,250	
Accounts receivable	$165,824		
Less: Allowance for doubtful accounts	1,850	163,974	
Notes receivable		23,000	
Inventories—at average cost		489,713	
Supplies on hand		9,780	
Prepaid expenses		16,252	
Total current assets			$ 773,454
Long-term investments			
Investments in Warren Co.			87,500
Property, plant, and equipment			
Land—at cost		125,000	
Buildings—at cost	975,800		
Less: Accumulated amortization	341,200	634,600	
Total property, plant, and equipment			759,600
Intangible assets			
Goodwill			100,000
Total assets			$1,720,554

Liabilities and Shareholders' Equity

Current liabilities			
Accounts payable		$247,532	
Accrued interest		500	
Income taxes payable		62,520	
Accrued salaries, wages, and other liabilities		9,500	
Deposits received from customers		420	
Total current liabilities			$ 320,472
Long-term debt *bonds*			
Twenty-year 12% debentures, due January 1, 2011			500,000
Total liabilities			820,472
Shareholders' equity			
Paid in on capital shares			
Preferred, 7%, cumulative			
Authorized, issued, and outstanding, 30,000 shares	$300,000		
Common—			
Authorized, 500,000 shares; issued and outstanding, 400,000 shares	400,000		
Contributed surplus	37,500	737,500	
Retained earnings		162,582	
Total shareholders' equity			900,082
Total liabilities and shareholders' equity			$1,720,554

Most public Canadian companies use this format.[20]

---

[20] In a survey of 200 Canadian companies, the CICA found that 186 out of the 200 used this format (CICA, *Financial Reporting in Canada*, 2000, p. 52).

OBJECTIVE 4
....
Identify balance sheet
information requiring
supplemental disclosure.

IAS NOTE

IAS 30 requires specific
disclosures for financial
institutions such as banks.
The *CICA Handbook* does not
specifically deal with accounting
for banks.

IAS NOTE

IAS 1 specifically requires
disclosure of material
uncertainties that cast doubt on
the company's ability to continue
as a going concern. The *CICA
Handbook* on the other hand,
while not explicitly requiring
disclosure, would expect that the
disclosure be made under the
full disclosure principle.

ADDITIONAL INFORMATION REPORTED

The balance sheet is not complete simply because the assets, liabilities, and owners' equity accounts have been listed. Great importance is given to supplemental information. It may be information not presented elsewhere in the statement, or it may be an elaboration or qualification of items in the balance sheet. There are normally five types of information that are supplemental to account titles and amounts presented in the balance sheet:

SUPPLEMENTAL BALANCE SHEET INFORMATION
1. **Contingencies.** Material events that have an uncertain outcome.
2. **Accounting Policies.** Explanations of the valuation methods used or the basic assumptions made concerning inventory valuations, amortization methods, investments in subsidiaries, etc.
3. **Contractual Situations.** Explanations of certain restrictions or covenants attached to specific assets or, more likely, to liabilities.
4. **Additional Detail.** Expanded details regarding specific balance sheet line items.
5. **Subsequent Events.** Events which happens subsequent to the balance sheet data.

Contingencies

A **contingency** is defined as **an existing situation involving uncertainty as to possible gain (gain contingency) or loss (loss contingency) that will ultimately be resolved when one or more future events occur or fail to occur.**[21] In short, they are material events that have an uncertain future. Examples of gain contingencies are tax operating loss carry-forwards or company litigation against another party. Typical loss contingencies relate to litigation, environmental issues, possible tax assessments, or government investigation. The accounting and reporting requirements involving contingencies are examined fully in Chapter 14, and, therefore, additional discussion is not provided here.

Accounting Policies

CICA Handbook Section 1505 recommends disclosure for all significant accounting principles and methods that involve selection from among alternatives or those that are peculiar to a given industry. For instance, inventories can be calculated under several cost flow assumptions (such as LIFO and FIFO); plant and equipment can be amortized under several accepted methods of cost allocation (such as double-declining balance and straight-line); and investments can be carried at different valuations (such as cost, equity, and fair value). Sophisticated users of financial statements know of these possibilities and examine the statements closely to determine the methods used.

Companies are also required to disclose information about the use of estimates in preparing financial statements, certain significant estimates, and vulnerabilities due to certain concentrations.[22]

Disclosure of significant accounting principles and methods and of risks and uncertainties is particularly useful if given in a separate Summary of Significant Accounting Policies preceding the notes to the financial statements or as the initial note.

---

[21] *CICA Handbook*, Section 3290, par. .02.

[22] *CICA Handbook*, Section 1508 and various other sections.

Contractual Situations

In addition to contingencies and different valuation methods, contractual situations of significance should be disclosed in the notes to the financial statements. It is mandatory, for example, that the essential provisions of lease contracts, pension obligations, and stock option plans be clearly stated in the notes. The analyst who examines a set of financial statements wants to know not only the liability amounts but also how the different contractual provisions affect the company at present and in the future.

Commitments related to obligations to maintain working capital, to limit the payment of dividends, to restrict asset use, and to require the maintenance of certain financial ratios must all be disclosed if material. Considerable judgement is necessary to determine whether omission of such information is misleading. The axiom in this situation is, "When in doubt, disclose." It is better to disclose a little too much information than not enough.

The accountant's judgement should reflect ethical considerations, because the manner of disclosing the accounting principles, methods, and other items that have important effects on the enterprise may subtly represent the interests of a particular stakeholder (at the expense of others). A reader, for example, may benefit by the highlighting of information in comprehensive notes, whereas the company—not wishing to emphasize certain information—may choose to provide limited (rather than comprehensive) note information.

UNDERLYING CONCEPTS

The basis for inclusion of additional information is the full disclosure principle; that is, the information is of sufficient importance to influence the decisions of an informed user.

Additional Detail

For many balance sheet items, further detail is disclosed for clarification. This has already been discussed under the various headings of the balance sheet assets, liabilities and equity.

Subsequent Events

A period of several weeks or months may elapse after the end of the year before the financial statements are issued. This time is used to take and price inventory, reconcile subsidiary ledgers with controlling accounts, prepare necessary adjusting entries, ensure all transactions for the period have been entered and obtain an audit of the financial statements

During this period, important transactions/events may occur that materially affect the company's financial position or operating situation. These events are known as subsequent events. Notes to the financial statements should explain any significant financial events that take place after the formal balance sheet date, but before the issuance of the financial statements.

According to Section 3820 of the *CICA Handbook*, subsequents fall into one of two types or categories:

1. Those which provide further evidence of conditions which **existed at the balance sheet date** (must adjust financial statements for these).
2. Those which are indicative of conditions which **arose subsequent** to the financial statement date (note disclose if the condition causes a significant change to assets, liabilities and/or it will have a significant impact on future operations).

These will be dealt with in further detail in Chapter 24.

TECHNIQUES OF DISCLOSURE

The additional information reported should be disclosed as completely and as intelligently as possible. The following methods of disclosing pertinent information are available: **parenthetical explanations, notes, cross reference and contra items, and supporting schedules**.

OBJECTIVE 5

Identify major disclosure techniques for the balance sheet.

Parenthetical Explanations

Additional information is often provided by **parenthetical explanations** following the item. For example, investments in securities may be shown on the balance sheet under Investments as follows:

Investments in securities (fair value, $330,586)—at cost	$401,500

This device permits disclosure of additional pertinent balance sheet information that adds clarity and completeness. It has an advantage over a note because it brings the additional information into the body of the statement where it is less likely to be overlooked. Of course, lengthy parenthetical explanations that might distract the reader from the balance sheet information must be used with care.

Notes

Notes are used if additional explanations cannot be shown conveniently as parenthetical explanations. For example, inventory-costing methods are reported in **The Quaker Oats Company**'s accompanying notes as follows:

ILLUSTRATION 5-13
Notes Disclosure

THE QUAKER OATS COMPANY

Inventories (Note 1)	
Finished goods	$326,000,000
Grain and raw materials	114,100,000
Packaging materials and supplies	39,000,000
Total inventories	479,100,000

Note 1: Inventories. Inventories are valued at the lower of cost or market, using various cost methods, and include the cost of raw materials, labour, and overhead.
The percentage of year-end inventories valued using each of the methods is as follows:

Average quarterly cost	21%
Last-in, first-out (LIFO)	65%
First-in, first-out (FIFO)	14%

If the LIFO method of valuing certain inventories was not used, total inventories would have been $60,100,000 higher than reported.

The notes must present all essential facts as completely and succinctly as possible. Loose wording may mislead rather than aid readers. Notes should add to the total information made available in the financial statements, not raise unanswered questions or contradict other portions of the statements.

Cross Reference and Contra Items

A direct relationship between an asset and a liability may be "cross referenced" on the balance sheet. For example, on December 31, 2001, among the current assets this might be shown:

Cash on deposit with sinking fund trustee for redemption of bonds payable—see Current liabilities $800,000

Included among the current liabilities is the amount of bonds payable to be redeemed within one year:

Bonds payable to be redeemed in 2002—see Current assets $2,300,000

This cross reference points out that $2.3 million of bonds payable are to be redeemed currently, for which only $800,000 in cash has been set aside. Therefore, the additional cash needed must come from unrestricted cash, from sales of investments, from profits, or from some other source. The same information can be shown parenthetically, if this technique is preferred.

Another common procedure is to establish contra or adjunct accounts. A **contra account** on a balance sheet is an item that reduces either an asset, liability, or owners' equity account. Examples include Accumulated Amortization and Discount on Bonds Payable. Contra accounts provide some flexibility in presenting the financial information. With the use of the Accumulated Amortization account, for example, a reader of the statement can see the asset's original cost as well as the amortization to date.

An **adjunct account**, on the other hand, increases either an asset, liability, or owners' equity account. An example is Premium on Bonds Payable, which, when added to the Bonds Payable account, describes the enterprise's total bond liability.

Supporting Schedules

Often a separate schedule is needed to present more detailed information about certain assets or liabilities, because the balance sheet provides just a single summary item.

Property, plant, and equipment Land, buildings, equipment, and other fixed assets—net (see Schedule 3)	$643,300

ILLUSTRATION 5-14
Disclosure through Use of Supporting Schedules

A separate schedule then might be presented as follows:

SCHEDULE 3
Land, Buildings, Equipment, and Other Fixed Assets

	Total	Land	Buildings	Equipment	Other Fixed Assets
Balance January 1, 2002	$740,000	$46,000	$358,000	$260,000	$76,000
Additions in 2002	161,200		120,000	38,000	3,200
	901,200	46,000	478,000	298,000	79,200
Assets retired or sold in 2002	31,700			27,000	4,700
Balance December 31, 2002	869,500	46,000	478,000	271,000	74,500
Amortization taken to January 1, 2002	196,000		102,000	78,000	16,000
Amortization taken in 2002	56,000		28,000	24,000	4,000
	252,000		130,000	102,000	20,000
Amortization on assets retired in 2002	25,800			22,000	3,800
Amortization accumulated December 31, 2002	226,200		130,000	80,000	16,200
Book value of assets	$643,300	$46,000	$348,000	$191,000	$58,300

TERMINOLOGY

The account titles in the general ledger do not necessarily represent the best terminology for balance sheet purposes. Account titles are often brief and include technical terms that are understood only by accountants. But balance sheets are examined by many persons who are not acquainted with the technical vocabulary of accounting. Thus, they should contain descriptions that will be generally understood and not be subject to misinterpretation.

The profession has recommended that the word "**reserve**" be used only to describe an appropriation of retained earnings. This term had been used in several ways: to describe amounts deducted from assets (contra accounts such as accumulated amortization and allowance for doubtful accounts), and as a part of the title of contingent or estimated liabilities. Because of the different meanings attached to this term, misinterpretation often resulted from its use. The use of "reserve" only to describe appropriated retained earnings has resulted in a better understanding of its significance when it appears in a balance sheet. However, the term "**appropriated**" appears more logical, and its use is encouraged.

INTERNATIONAL INSIGHT

Internationally, accounting terminology is problematic. Confusing differences arise even between nations that share a language. For example, Canadian and U.S. investors normally think of "stock" as "equity" or "ownership," but the British refer to inventory as "stocks." In Canada and the U.S., "fixed assets" generally refers to "property, plant, and equipment," while in Britain, the category includes more items.

Section 2 – Statement of Cash Flows

The balance sheet, the income statement, and the statement of shareholders' equity each present, to a limited extent and in a fragmented manner, information about an enterprise's cash flows during a period. For instance, comparative balance sheets might show what new assets have been acquired or disposed of and what liabilities have been incurred or liquidated. The income statement provides information about resources, but not exactly cash, provided by operations. The statement of retained earnings shows the amount of dividends declared. But none of these statements presents a detailed summary of all the cash inflows and outflows, or the sources and uses of cash during the period. To fill this need, the statement of cash flows (also called the cash flow statement) is required.[23]

PURPOSE OF THE STATEMENT OF CASH FLOWS

OBJECTIVE 6

Indicate the purpose of the statement of cash flows.

The primary purpose of a statement of cash flows is to allow users to assess the enterprise's capacity to generate **cash and cash equivalents** and its needs for cash resources.[24]

Reporting the sources, uses, and net increase or decrease in cash helps investors, creditors, and others know what is happening to a company's most liquid resource. Because most individuals maintain their chequebook and prepare their tax return on a cash basis, they can relate to the statement of cash flows and comprehend the causes and effects of cash inflows and outflows and the net increase or decrease in cash. The statement of cash flows provides answers to the following simple but important questions:

1. Where did the cash come from during the period?
2. What was the cash used for during the period?
3. What was the change in the cash balance during the period?

CONTENT AND FORMAT OF THE STATEMENT OF CASH FLOWS

OBJECTIVE 7

Identify the content of the statement of cash flows.

Cash receipts and cash payments during a period are classified in the statement of cash flows into three different activities: **operating, investing, and financing activities**. These are the main types of activities that companies enter into. These classifications are defined as follows:

1. Operating activities represent the enterprise's principal revenue-producing activities and all other activities not related to investing or financing.
2. Investing activities represent the acquisitions and disposal of long-term assets and other investments not included in "cash equivalents."
3. Financing activities represent activities that result in changes in the size and composition of the enterprise's equity capital and borrowings.[25]

With cash flows classified into those three categories, the statement of cash flows has assumed the following basic format:

---

[23] According to the *CICA Handbook*, Section 1540, par. .03, the cash flow statement should be presented as an integral part of the financial statements.

[24] *CICA Handbook*, Section 1540, par. .01.

[25] *CICA Handbook*, Section 1540, par. .06.

Statement of Cash Flows
Cash flows from operating activities $XXX
Cash flows from investing activities   XXX
Cash flows from financing activities   XXX

Net increase (decrease) in cash   XXX
Cash at beginning of year   XXX

Cash at end of year $XXX

ILLUSTRATION 5-15
Basic Format of Cash Flow Statement

The inflows and outflows of cash classified by activity are shown in Illustration 5-16

The statement's value is that it helps users evaluate liquidity, solvency, and financial flexibility as previously defined. Chapter 23 deals with the preparation and content of the statement of cash flows in detail. Comprehensive coverage of this topic has been deferred to that later chapter so that several elements and complex topics that make up the content of a typical statement of cash flows may be covered in intervening chapters. The presentation in this chapter is introductory, a reminder of the statement of cash flows' existence and usefulness.

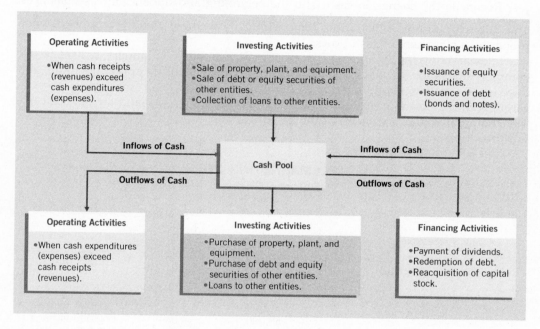

ILLUSTRATION 5-16
Cash Inflows and Outflows

PREPARATION OF THE STATEMENT OF CASH FLOWS

There are two basic ways to prepare a cash flow statement as follows:

1. by analysing the changes in balance sheet accounts (other than the "cash and cash equivalents" accounts) from year to year
2. by analysing the change in the "cash and cash equivalents" accounts (in detail) from year to year

Both ways represent sides of the same coin. The objective of the cash flow statement is to identify and present **material cash transactions. Non-cash transactions are not reported.** Using double entry accounting, all cash transactions and the related journal entries involve a debit or credit to cash and a balancing debit or credit to other balance sheet accounts (including retained earnings, which captures all revenues, gains, expenses, and losses). Therefore, the cash flow statement may be prepared by either analysing changes in non-cash accounts or conversely, by analysing changes in the cash accounts.

If alternative #1 above is used, care must be taken to isolate changes in these accounts that are not represented by cash transactions. For example, if the company purchases a piece of land and the vendor takes back a mortgage, this will cause both the land account and the long-term debt account to change. Although these represent changes in balance sheet accounts, this transaction **would not be reported** in the cash flow statement, as it is not a cash transaction.

If alternative #2 above is used, only the cash transactions will be analysed because the starting point is the **cash** general ledger account. Therefore, there is no need to be concerned about non-cash transactions. Access to the **detailed cash general ledger account** is required. Preparation of the cash flow statement using this method is facilitated if the company **codes** each cash transaction with transactions codes (as operating, investing, or financing) when it is originally posted to the general ledger.

Under alternative #1, the information to prepare the statement of cash flows usually comes from (1) comparative balance sheets, (2) the current income statement, and (3) selected transaction data. Preparing the statement of cash flows from these sources involves the following steps:

1. Determine the cash provided by operations.
2. Determine the cash provided by or used in investing and financing activities.
3. Determine the change (increase or decrease) in cash during the period.
4. Reconcile the change in cash with the beginning and the ending cash balances.

The following simple illustration demonstrates how these steps are applied when preparing a statement of cash flows.

Telemarketing Inc., in its first year of operations, issued on January 1, 2002, 50,000 common shares for $50,000 cash. The company rented its office space, furniture, and telecommunications equipment and performed surveys and marketing services throughout the first year. In June 2002, the company purchased land for $15,000 cash. The comparative balance sheets at the beginning and end of the year 2002 are shown in Illustration 5-17.

ILLUSTRATION 5-17
Comparative Balance Sheets

TELEMARKETING INC.
Balance Sheets

Assets	Dec. 31, 2002	Jan. 1, 2002	Increase/Decrease
Cash	$31,000	$ – 0 –	$31,000 Increase
Accounts receivable	41,000	– 0 –	41,000 Increase
Land	15,000	– 0 –	15,000 Increase
Total	$87,000	$ – 0 –	
Liabilities and Shareholders' Equity			
Accounts payable	$12,000	$ – 0 –	12,000 Increase
Common shares	50,000	– 0 –	50,000 Increase
Retained earnings	25,000	– 0 –	25,000 Increase
Total	$87,000	$ – 0 –	

The income statement and additional information for Telemarketing Inc. are as follows:

ILLUSTRATION 5-18
Income Statement Data

TELEMARKETING INC.
Income Statement
For the Year Ended December 31, 2002

Revenues	$172,000
Operating expenses	120,000
Income before income taxes	52,000
Income tax expense	13,000
Net income	$ 39,000

Additional information:
Dividends of $14,000 were declared and paid during the year.

Cash provided by operations (the excess of cash receipts over cash payments) is determined by converting net income from an **accrual basis to a cash basis**. Two types of adjustments accomplish this:

1. **adding to or deducting from net income** those items in the income statement not affecting cash (add back noncash charges such as accrued expenses, amortization and losses and deduct noncash sales and gains) and

2. **adjusting cash provided by operating activities** for those items that are operating cash flows that do not flow through the income statement (add back cash collected during the year from last year's sales, deduct cash spent on inventory that is still on hand, deduct cash paid to suppliers for expenses accrued last year).

This procedure requires an analysis not only of the current year's income statement but also of the comparative balance sheets and selected transaction data.

Analysis of Telemarketing's comparative balance sheets reveals two items that give rise to noncash credits or charges to the income statement: (1) the increase in accounts receivable reflects a noncash credit of $41,000 to revenues and (2) the increase in accounts payable reflects a noncash charge of $12,000 to expenses. The change in accounts receivables actually has three components:

(a) cash received from sales recorded last year—**add to cash from operations** as this would not be included in the current year's net income

(b) cash received from credit sales made in the current year—already in net income, **no need to adjust**

(c) credit sales made in the current year and not yet collected—**deduct from net income** as these are noncash

These may be netted together. Therefore, to arrive at cash provided by operations, the **increase in accounts receivable** must be deducted from net income and a **decrease must be added back**. This general rule may be applied to all current assets.

Alternatively, the same reasoning can be applied to accounts payable and current liabilities. The change in accounts payable also has three components:

(a) cash paid out during the year for last year's expenses—**deduct from cash from operating activities** as this would not be reflected in the current year's net income

(b) cash paid for current year's accrued expenses that are paid for during the year—already deducted from net income and therefore **no need to adjust**

(c) expenses accrued in the current year that have not yet been paid for—**add back to net income as noncash**

Once again, these may be netted together and increases in accounts payable and other current liabilities are added back to net income while decreases are deducted.

For Telemarketing Inc., cash provided by operations is determined to be $10,000, calculated as follows:

Net income		$39,000
Adjustments to reconcile net income		
to net cash provided by operating activities:		
Increase in accounts receivable	$(41,000)	
Increase in accounts payable	12,000	(29,000)
Net cash provided by operating activities		$10,000

ILLUSTRATION 5-19
Calculation of Net Cash Provided by Operations

The increase of $50,000 in common shares resulting from the issuance of 50,000 shares for cash is classified as a **financing** activity. Likewise, the payment of $14,000 cash in dividends is a **financing** activity. Telemarketing Inc.'s only **investing** activity was the land purchase. The statement of cash flows for Telemarketing Inc. for 2002 is as follows:

ILLUSTRATION 5-20
Statement of Cash Flows

INTERNATIONAL INSIGHT

Statements of cash flows are not required in all countries. Some nations require a statement reporting sources and applications of "funds" (often defined as working capital); others have no requirement for either cash or funds flow statements.

TELEMARKETING INC.
Statement of Cash Flows
For the Year Ended December 31, 2002

Cash flows from operating activities		
Net income		$39,000
Adjustments to reconcile net income to		
net cash provided by operating activities:		
Increase in accounts receivable	$(41,000)	
Increase in accounts payable	12,000	(29,000)
Net cash provided by operating activities		10,000
Cash flows from investing activities		
Purchase of land	(15,000)	
Net cash used by investing activities		(15,000)
Cash flows from financing activities		
Issuance of common shares	50,000	
Payment of cash dividends	(14,000)	
Net cash provided by financing activities		36,000
Net increase in cash		31,000
Cash at beginning of year		– 0 –
Cash at end of year		$31,000

The increase in cash of $31,000 reported in the statement of cash flows agrees with the increase of $31,000 in the Cash account calculated from the comparative balance sheets.

Under alternative #2, the starting point would be the general ledger—Cash account. This is shown in Illustration 5–21.

ILLUSTRATION 5-21
Cash General Ledger Account

GENERAL LEDGER—CASH

	Dr.	Cr.
January	$50,000	
June		$15,000
throughout	131,000 (1)	121,000 (2)
throughout		14,000(3)
subtotal	$181,000	$150,000
net	$ 31,000	

(1) Total sales of $172,000 less credit sales (accounts receivable) of $41,000 = $131,000
(2) Total expenses of $120,000 + 13,000 = $133,000 less accrued expenses (non-cash) of $12,000 (represented by accounts payable) = $121,000
(3) Dividends paid

The next step would be to **classify the debits and credits** (cash inflows and outflows) by **operating, investing, or financing**. This is the same process as in the first alternative and yields exactly the same results:

1. cash provided by operations ($131,000 − 121,000)	$10,000
2. cash used in investing	($15,000)
3. cash provided by financing activities	$36,000
total cash provided during the year	$31,000

The statement's format is not affected by using alternative #1 versus alternative #2 and so the presentation would be the same.

An illustration of a more comprehensive statement of cash flows is presented in Illustration 5-22.

NESTOR CORPORATION Statement of Cash Flows For the Year Ended December 31, 2002		
Cash flows from operating activities		
Net income		$320,750
Adjustments to reconcile net income to net cash provided by operating activities:		
Amortization expense	$88,400	
Amortization of intangibles	16,300	
Gain on sale of plant assets	(8,700)	
Increase in accounts receivable (net)	(11,000)	
Decrease in inventory	15,500	
Decrease in accounts payable	(9,500)	91,000
Net cash provided by operating activities		411,750
Cash flows from investing activities		
Sale of plant assets	90,500	
Purchase of equipment	(182,500)	
Purchase of land	(70,000)	
Net cash used by investing activities		(162,000)
Cash flows from financing activities		
Payment of cash dividend	(19,800)	
Issuance of common shares	100,000	
Redemption of bonds	(50,000)	
Net cash provided by financing activities		30,200
Net increase in cash		279,950
Cash at beginning of year		135,000
Cash at end of year		$414,950

ILLUSTRATION 5-22
Comprehensive Statement of Cash Flows

USEFULNESS OF THE STATEMENT OF CASH FLOWS

Although net income provides a long-term measure of a company's success or failure, **cash is a company's lifeblood**. Without cash, a company will not survive. For small and newly developing companies, cash flow is the single most important element of survival. In a recent survey of over 60,000 companies that failed, over 60% blamed their failure on factors linked to cash flows. Even medium and large companies indicate a major concern in controlling cash flow.

Creditors examine the cash flow statement carefully because they are concerned about being paid. A good starting point in their examination is to find **net cash provided by operating activities**. A high amount of net cash provided by operating activities indicates that a company is able to **generate sufficient cash internally** from operations to pay its bills without further borrowing. Conversely, a low or negative amount of net cash provided by operating activities indicates that a company cannot generate enough cash internally from its operations and, therefore, **must borrow or issue equity securities** to acquire additional cash. Consequently, creditors look for answers to the following questions in the company's cash flow statements:

OBJECTIVE 9

Understand the usefulness of the statement of cash flows.

1. How successful is the company in **generating net cash provided by operating activities**?
2. What are the **trends** in net cash flow provided by operating activities over time?
3. What are the **major reasons** for the positive or negative net cash provided by operating activities?

It is important to recognize that **companies can fail even though they are profitable**. The difference between net income and net cash provided by operating activities can be substantial. The reasons for the difference between a positive net income and a neg-

ILLUSTRATION 5-23
Negative Net Cash Provided by
Operating Activities

ative net cash provided by operating activities are substantial increases in receivables
and/or inventory. To illustrate, Ho Inc., in its first year of operations, reported a net
income of $80,000. Its net cash provided by operating activities, however, was a nega-
tive $95,000, as shown in Illustration 5-23.

HO INC.		
Net Cash Flow from Operating Activities		
Cash Flows from Operating Activities		
Net income		$ 80,000
Adjustments to reconcile net income to net cash provided by		
operating activities:		
Increase in receivables	$(75,000)	
Increase in inventories	(100,000)	(175,000)
Net cash provided by operating activities		$(95,000)

Note that the negative net cash provided by operating activities occurred for Ho even
though it reported a positive net income. Ho could easily experience a "cash crunch"
because it has tied up its cash in receivables and inventory. If problems in collecting
receivables occur or inventory is slow-moving or becomes obsolete, Ho's creditors may
have difficulty collecting on their loans.

Companies that are expanding often experience this type of "cash crunch" as they
must buy increasing inventory amounts to meet increasing sales demands. This means
that the cash outflow to purchase the inventory occurs before the cash inflow from the
customer for sale of that product. This is often referred to as a "lead–lag" factor. The
cash outflow leads (occurs first) and the cash inflow from sales lags (occurs later). The
lead–lag factor requires the company to use up any excess cash that it has on hand or
to borrow more funds. Refer back to Illustration 5-4—the business operating cycle.

As mentioned earlier in the chapter, **financial flexibility** may be assessed by using
information from the financial statements. The cash flow statement is especially suited
for providing this type of information.

Financial Liquidity

One ratio that is often used to assess liquidity is the *current cash debt coverage ratio*.
It indicates whether the company can pay off its current liabilities in a given year from
its operations. The formula for this ratio is:

ILLUSTRATION 5-24
Formula for Current Cash Debt
Coverage Ratio

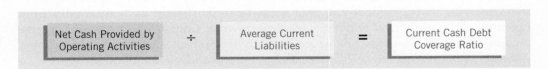

The higher this ratio, the less likely a company will have liquidity problems. For
example, a ratio of at least 1:1 is good because it indicates that the company can meet
all of its current obligations from internally generated cash flow. To benchmark, this
ratio may be compared with similar companies in the industry (or with prior years for
the company itself).

Financial Flexibility

A more long-run measure that provides information on financial flexibility is the **cash
debt coverage ratio**. This ratio indicates a company's ability to repay its liabilities from
net cash provided by operating activities, without having to liquidate the assets
employed in its operations. The formula for this ratio is:

ILLUSTRATION 5-25
Formula for Cash Debt
Coverage Ratio

Net Cash Provided by Operating Activities	÷	Average Total Liabilities	=	Cash Debt Coverage Ratio

The higher this ratio, the less likely the company will experience difficulty in meeting its obligations as they come due. As a result, it signals whether the company can pay its debts and survive if external sources of funds become limited or too expensive.

Cash Flow Patterns

The cash flow statement can yield some interesting results when users look at the various **patterns** between cash inflows and outflows for the following subtotals on the statement: operating, investing, and financing cash flows. For instance, Nestor Company has **cash inflows** ("+") from operating activities, **cash outflows** ("−") from investing activities and **cash inflows** ("+") from financing activities, yielding a "+" "−" "+" pattern.

Interpreting this, Nestor **is getting most of its cash from operations** (which is a very good sign) and also, to a lesser extent, from issuance of common shares. Nestor is using this cash to **expand the business**. The fact that the company is able to raise funds in the capital markets by issuing shares is a positive sign also, indicating that the **capital markets have faith in the company's ability to prosper**. The fact that the bulk of the money being used to finance the assets is generated from operations means that the company is not increasing its solvency risk or diluting its shareholders by issuing more shares. Nestor appears to be a successful company in an expansionary mode.

Companies that generate cash from investing activities may be selling off long-term assets. This generally goes along with a company that is in a downsizing or restructuring mode. Is this good or bad? If the assets being disposed of are excess or redundant assets, then it makes sense to free up the capital that is tied up. Similarly, if the assets being disposed of relate to operations that are not profitable, that reflects a good management decision. However, if the company is in a position where it must sell off core income producing assets, then it may be sacrificing future profitability and revenue producing potential.

Free Cash Flow

A more sophisticated way to examine a company's financial flexibility is to develop a free cash flow analysis. This analysis starts with net cash provided by operating activities and ends with free cash flow, which is calculated as **net cash provided by operating activities less capital expenditures and dividends**.[26] Free cash flow is the amount of **discretionary cash flow** a company has for purchasing additional investments, retiring its debt, purchasing treasury stock, or simply adding to its liquidity. This measure indicates a company's level of financial flexibility. Questions that a free cash flow analysis answers are:

1. Is the company able to pay its dividends without resorting to external financing?
2. If business operations decline, will the company be able to maintain its needed capital investment?
3. What is the free cash flow that can be used for additional investment, retirement of debt, purchase of treasury stock, or addition to liquidity?

Presented below is a free cash flow analysis using the cash flow statement for Nestor shown in Illustration 5-26:

---

[26] In determining free cash flows, some companies do not subtract dividends because they believe these expenditures to be discretionary.

ILLUSTRATION 5-26
Free Cash Flow Calculation

NESTOR CORPORATION Free Cash Flow Analysis	
Net cash provided by operating activities	$411,750
Less: Capital expenditures	(252,500)
Dividends	(19,800)
Free cash flow	$139,450

This analysis shows that Nestor has a positive, and substantial, net cash provided by operating activities of $411,750. Nestor reports on its statement of cash flows that it purchased equipment of $182,500 and land of $70,000 for total capital spending of $252,500. This amount is subtracted from net cash provided by operating activities because without continued efforts to maintain and expand facilities, it is unlikely that Nestor can continue to maintain its competitive position. Capital spending is deducted first on the free cash flow statement to indicate it is the least discretionary expenditure a company generally makes. Dividends are then deducted to arrive at free cash flow. Although a company can cut its dividend, it will usually do so only in a financial emergency. Nestor has more than sufficient cash flow to meet its dividend payment and therefore has satisfactory financial flexibility.

Nestor used its free cash flow to redeem bonds and add to its liquidity. If it finds additional investments that are profitable, it can increase its spending without putting its dividend or basic capital spending in jeopardy. Companies that have strong financial flexibility can take advantage of profitable investments even in tough times. In addition, strong financial flexibility frees companies from worry about survival in poor economic times. In fact, those with strong financial flexibility often fare better in poor economic times because they can take advantage of opportunities that other companies cannot.

Summary of Learning Objectives

1 Identify the uses and limitations of a balance sheet. The balance sheet provides information about the nature and amounts of investments in enterprise resources, obligations to creditors, and the owners' equity in net resources. The balance sheet contributes to financial reporting by providing a basis for (1) calculating rates of return, (2) evaluating the enterprise's capital structure, and (3) assessing the enterprise's liquidity, solvency, and financial flexibility. The limitations of a balance sheet are: (1) The balance sheet does not reflect current value because accountants have adopted a historical cost basis in valuing and reporting assets and liabilities. (2) Judgements and estimates must be used in preparing a balance sheet. The collectibility of receivables, the saleability of inventory, and the useful life of long-term tangible and intangible assets are difficult to determine. (3) The balance sheet omits many items that are of financial value to the business but cannot be recorded objectively, such as human resources, customer base, and reputation.

2 Identify the major classifications of a balance sheet. The balance sheet's general elements are assets, liabilities, and equity. The major classifications within the balance sheet on the asset side are current assets; long-term investments; property, plant, and equipment; intangible assets; and other assets. The major classifications of liabilities are current and long-term liabilities. In a corporation, owners' equity is generally classified as shares, contributed surplus, and retained earnings.

3 Prepare a classified balance sheet. The most common format lists liabilities and shareholders' equity directly below assets on the same page.

4 Identify balance sheet information requiring supplemental disclosure. Five types of information normally are supplemental to account titles and amounts presented in the balance sheet: (1) Contingencies: Material events that have an uncertain outcome, (2) Accounting policies: Explanations of the valuation methods used or the basic assumptions made concerning inventory valuation, amortization methods, investments in subsidiaries, etc., (3) Contractual situations: Explanations of certain restrictions or covenants attached to specific assets or, more likely, to liabilities, (4) Detailed information: Clarifies in more detail the composition of balance sheet items, and (5) Subsequent events: Events that happen after the balance sheet date.

5 Identify major disclosure techniques for the balance sheet. There are four methods of disclosing pertinent information in the balance sheet: (1) Parenthetical explanations: Additional information or description is often provided by parenthetical explanations following the item. (2) Notes: Notes are used if additional explanations or descriptions cannot be shown conveniently as parenthetical explanations. (3) Cross reference and contra items: A direct relationship between an asset and a liability is "cross referenced" on the balance sheet. (4) Supporting schedules: Often a separate schedule is needed to present more detailed information about certain assets or liabilities, because the balance sheet provides just a single summary item.

6 Indicate the purpose of the statement of cash flows. The primary purpose of a statement of cash flows is to provide relevant information about an enterprise's cash receipts and cash payments during a period. Reporting the sources, uses, and net increase or decrease in cash enables investors, creditors, and others to know what is happening to a company's most liquid resource.

7 Identify the content of the statement of cash flows. Cash receipts and cash payments during a period are classified in the statement of cash flows into three different activities: (1) Operating activities: Involve the cash effects of transactions that enter into the determination of net income. (2) Investing activities: Include making and collecting loans and acquiring and disposing of investments (both debt and equity) and property, plant, and equipment. (3) Financing activities: Involve liability and owners' equity items and include (a) obtaining capital from owners and providing them with a return on their investment and (b) borrowing money from creditors and repaying the amounts borrowed.

8 Prepare a statement of cash flows. The information to prepare the statement of cash flows usually comes from (1) comparative balance sheets, (2) the current income statement, and (3) selected transaction data. Preparing the statement of cash flows from these sources involves the following steps: (1) determine the cash provided by operations; (2) determine the cash provided by or used in investing and financing activities; (3) determine the change (increase or decrease) in cash during the period; and (4) reconcile the change in cash with the beginning and the ending cash balances. An alternative method is to analyse in detail the "cash and cash equivalents" general ledger account, grouping cash flows into operating, investing, and financing activities.

9 Understand the usefulness of the statement of cash flows. Creditors examine the cash flow statement carefully because they are concerned about being paid. The amount and trend of net cash flow provided by operating activities in relation to the company's liabilities is helpful in making this assessment. In addition, measures such as a free cash flow analysis provide creditors and shareholders with a better picture of the company's financial flexibility.

APPENDIX **5A**

Ratio Analysis—A Reference

OBJECTIVE 10

After studying Appendix 5A, you should be able to identify the major types of financial ratios and what they measure.

USING RATIOS TO ANALYSE FINANCIAL PERFORMANCE

Qualitative information from financial statements can be gathered by examining relationships between items on the statements and identifying trends in these relationships. A useful starting point in developing this information is the application of ratio analysis.

A ratio expresses the mathematical relationship between one quantity and another. **Ratio analysis** expresses the relationship among selected financial statement data. The relationship is expressed in terms of either a percentage, a rate, or a simple proportion. To illustrate, recently IBM Corporation had current assets of $41,338 million U.S. and current liabilities of $29,226 million U.S. The relationship is determined by dividing current assets by current liabilities. The alternative means of expression are:

> **Percentage:** Current assets are 141% of current liabilities.
>
> **Rate:** Current assets are 1.41 times as great as current liabilities.
>
> **Proportion:** The relationship of current assets to liabilities is 1.41:1.

For analysis of financial statements, ratios can be classified into four types, as follows:

MAJOR TYPES OF RATIOS
Liquidity Ratios.   Measures of the enterprise's short-run ability to pay its maturing obligations.
Activity Ratios.   Measures of how effectively the enterprise is using the assets employed.
Profitability Ratios.   Measures of the degree of success or failure of a given enterprise or division for a given time period.
Coverage Ratios.   Measures of the degree of protection for long-term creditors and investors.

For more coverage of this topic go to the Digital Tool and access the Financial Statement Analysis Primer in the Analyst's Toolkit.

In Chapter 4, profitability ratios were discussed briefly and in this chapter, liquidity, activity, and coverage ratios were touched on. Throughout the remainder of the textbook, ratios are provided to help you understand and interpret the information presented in context of each subject area. The Digital Tool looks at the area of financial statement analysis, of which ratio analysis is one part. Illustration 5A-1 presents some common, basic ratios that will be used throughout the text. In practice, there are many other ratios that are also used that provide useful information.

The key to a refined, information-rich analysis rests with understanding the business and industry first. Specialized industries focus on **different ratios** depending on the **critical success factors** in their business. As discussed throughout the chapter, different companies and businesses would be expected to have different types of assets and capital structures. Furthermore, they would be expected to have differing types of costs and revenue streams. Success in the retail industry for instance, is reflected in the ability to set prices and target customers so that maximum market penetration is effected. Also critical is the ability to minimize inventory shrinkage (there is a high risk of theft) and keep inventory moving so that it does not become obsolete or out of fashion. A company's ability to achieve this or not is reflected in the **gross profit margin** (ratio). This is calculated by taking gross profit divided by revenues. Companies must achieve a sufficiently high gross profit to cover off other costs. A stable gross profit margin is a positive sign that management is dealing with all of the above-mentioned issues.

Summary of Learning Objective for Appendix 5A

10 Identify the major types of financial ratios and what they measure. Ratios express the mathematical relationship between one quantity and another, in terms of either a percentage, a rate, or a proportion. Liquidity ratios measure the short-run ability to pay maturing obligations. Activity ratios measure the effectiveness of asset usage. Profitability ratios measure an enterprise's success or failure of. Coverage ratios measure the degree of protection for long-term creditors and investors.

KEY TERMS

activity ratios, *188*
coverage ratios, *188*
liquidity ratios, *188*
profitability ratios, *188*
ratio analysis, *188*

ILLUSTRATION 5A-1 — A Summary of Financial Ratios

RATIO	FORMULA	PURPOSE OR USE
I. Liquidity		
1. Current ratio	$\dfrac{\text{Current assets}}{\text{Current liabilities}}$	Measures short-term debt-paying ability
2. Quick or acid-test ratio	$\dfrac{\text{Cash, marketable securities, and receivables (net)}}{\text{Current liabilities}}$	Measures immediate short-term liquidity
3. Current cash debt coverage ratio	$\dfrac{\text{Net cash provided by operating activities}}{\text{Average current liabilities}}$	Measures a company's ability to pay off its current liabilities in a given year from its operations
II. Activity		
4. Receivable turnover	$\dfrac{\text{Net sales}}{\text{Average trade receivables (net)}}$	Measures liquidity of receivables
5. Inventory turnover	$\dfrac{\text{Cost of goods sold}}{\text{Average inventory}}$	Measures liquidity of inventory
6. Asset turnover	$\dfrac{\text{Net sales}}{\text{Average total assets}}$	Measures how efficiently assets are used to generate sales
III. Profitability		
7. Profit margin on sales	$\dfrac{\text{Net income}}{\text{Net sales}}$	Measures net income generated by each dollar of sales
8. Rate of return on assets	$\dfrac{\text{Net income}}{\text{Average total assets}}$	Measures overall profitability of assets
9. Rate of return on common share equity	$\dfrac{\text{Net income minus preferred dividends}}{\text{Average common shareholders' equity}}$	Measures profitability of owners' investment
10. Earnings per share	$\dfrac{\text{Net income minus preferred dividends}}{\text{Weighted shares outstanding}}$	Measures net income earned on each common share
11. Price earnings ratio	$\dfrac{\text{Market price of shares}}{\text{Earnings per share}}$	Measures the ratio of the market price per share to earnings per share
12. Payout ratio	$\dfrac{\text{Cash dividends}}{\text{Net income}}$	Measures percentage of earnings distributed in the form of cash dividends
IV. Coverage		
13. Debt to total assets	$\dfrac{\text{Total debt}}{\text{Total assets or equities}}$	Measures the percentage of total assets provided by creditors
14. Times interest earned	$\dfrac{\text{Income before interest charges and taxes}}{\text{Interest charges}}$	Measures ability to meet interest payments as they come due
15. Cash debt coverage ratio	$\dfrac{\text{Net cash provided by operating activities}}{\text{Average total liabilities}}$	Measures a company's ability to repay its total liabilities in a given year from its operations
16. Book value per share	$\dfrac{\text{Common Shareholders' equity}}{\text{Outstanding shares}}$	Measures the amount each share would receive if the company were liquidated at the amounts reported on the balance sheet

APPENDIX **5B**

Specimen Financial Statements

TO THE STUDENT:

The following pages contain the financial statements, accompanying notes, and other information from the 2000 Annual Report of **Canadian Tire Corporation Limited** (Canadian Tire), a significant retailer in Canada. According to Canadian Tire, 9 out of 10 adult Canadians shop at Canadian Tire at least twice a year and 6 out of 10 shop there every month. Eighty-five per cent of the Canadian population lives within a 15-minute drive of a Canadian Tire store.

The Business

Canadian Tire has three distinct businesses:
1. Canadian Tire Retail ("CTR"),
2. Canadian Tire Financial Services ("Financial Services"), and
3. Petroleum.

CTR and its Associate Dealers are together Canada's leading hardgoods retailer. The Associate Dealers own the fixtures, equipment and inventory of the stores they operate and run their individual businesses in accordance with the Corporation's overall strategy.

Financial Services provides credit services to customers. Financial Services also performs third-party transaction processing, operates an emergency roadside assistance service, and markets a variety of insurance products to Canadian Tire customers.

Petroleum is one of the country's largest independent gasoline retailers by volume.

Canadian Tire's accounting and reporting practices are affected by most of the accounting topics covered in this textbook and by nearly every facet of generally accepted accounting principles. We do not expect that you will comprehend Canadian Tire's financial statements and the accompanying notes in their entirety at your first reading. But we expect that by the time you complete the material in this text, your level of understanding and interpretive ability will have grown enormously.

At this point we recommend that you take 20 to 30 minutes to scan the statements and notes to familiarize yourself with the contents and accounting elements. Throughout the following chapters, when you are asked to refer to specific parts of Canadian Tire's financials, do so! Then, when you have completed reading this book, we challenge you to reread Canadian Tire's financials to see how much greater and more sophisticated is your understanding of them.

a new era

OVERVIEW OF THE BUSINESS

Canadian Tire Corporation, Limited ("Canadian Tire" or the "Corporation") comprises three business units: Canadian Tire Retail ("CTR"), Canadian Tire Petroleum ("Petroleum") and Canadian Tire Financial Services ("Financial Services").

The **CTR** business unit is Canada's leading hardgoods retailer, offering consumers more than 100,000 stock-keeping units of automotive parts and accessories, sports and leisure products, and home products, through a network of 441 stores operated by Associate Dealers. CTR, through its Associate Dealers, also operates Canada's largest auto service business and manages the marketing and operations of the Petroleum business through a network of independent agents.

In November 2000, CTR launched Canadian Tire Online. This new service gives customers the added convenience of making purchases via the Internet from an initial offering of 5,500 stock-keeping units, for delivery directly to their homes.

The Corporation also operates *PartSource*, which by the end of 2000 had expanded this business into a chain of 28 specialty automotive parts stores targeted at heavy do-it-yourself enthusiasts and commercial installers.

Canadian Tire Petroleum, one of the largest independent retailers of gasoline in Canada, markets petroleum and related products as well as convenience items through a network of 206 independent agent-operated outlets. It also supports CTR merchandise sales through special promotions and the issuance of *Canadian Tire 'Money'* for cash customers and electronic *Canadian Tire 'Money' on the Card* for Canadian Tire credit card customers. Both are redeemable for goods at Associate Stores across Canada.

The **Financial Services** business unit is engaged in financing and managing customer credit accounts that result from customers' use of their Canadian Tire retail, commercial and MasterCard credit cards. Financial Services also manages the *Canadian Tire 'Money' on the Card* loyalty program, operates an emergency roadside service and markets a variety of insurance and warranty products to Canadian Tire customers.

Canadian Tire Associate Dealers make a major contribution to the success of the combined business. They play an integral part in the continuing development of our customers' shopping experience and have a substantial personal financial investment in their businesses, which they operate in accordance with the Corporation's overall strategy and marketing programs.

The Corporation and Associate Dealers provide employment to over 38,000 Canadians.

CONSOLIDATED RESULTS

The Corporation's consolidated gross operating revenue was a record $5.2 billion for fiscal 2000, a 52-week period ending December 30, 2000. This was an increase of 10.1 percent over consolidated gross operating revenue of $4.7 billion in fiscal 1999, a 52-week period ending January 1, 2000. Pre-tax consolidated earnings rose 6.0 percent to $240.7 million from $227.1 million in the prior year. After-tax consolidated earnings were $148.0 million in 2000 compared with $145.9 million in 1999—a 1.4 percent increase. Consolidated net earnings per share were $1.89, unchanged from 1999.

Major factors affecting 2000 consolidated net earnings include: an expense of $17 million, as part of the $22 million invested in 2000 for the development and launch of Canadian Tire Online; an increase of $13 million in depreciation expense, primarily associated with the Corporation's investment in new-format stores; a reduction of consolidated pre-tax earnings of $10.9 million resulting from weaker industry-wide demand for certain seasonal merchandise; a fourth-quarter expense of $4 million associated with the Corporation's restructuring; a first-quarter $4 million charge for the remainder of a contractual retirement obligation to the former CEO; $2.5 million of expenses to improve the Corporation's distribution capability; and an increase in the effective tax rate to 38.5 percent in 2000, which reduced consolidated net earnings by $6.7 million or approximately $0.09 per share. In 1999, the Corporation's consolidated earnings were reduced by the expensing of $58.5 million of costs in the fourth quarter of the year. These costs were related primarily to improved information technology capabilities, the development of an e-commerce platform and contractual obligations to the former CEO upon his retirement.

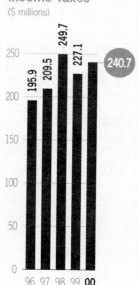

Consolidated Earnings Before Income Taxes
($ millions)

Year	Value
96	195.9
97	209.5
98	249.7
99	227.1
00	240.7

2 1

2000 ANNUAL REPORT

Summary of Key Factors Affecting Consolidated Results

CTR's gross operating revenue rose 5.9 percent to $4.0 billion in 2000 due primarily to a 6.0 percent increase in shipments to Associate Dealers. CTR's operating earnings increased by 10.1 percent to $171.7 million as a result of higher revenues and the absence of 1999 year-end expense adjustments, offset by unseasonable spring and summer weather and increased supply chain costs.

While Petroleum gross operating revenue jumped 37.2 percent to $853.5 million due to higher pump prices and an 11.7 percent increase in gasoline litre sales volume, operating earnings declined 18.6 percent to $12.4 million, due to an escalation of the world cost of crude oil.

Financial Services' gross operating revenue for the year rose 7.7 percent to $329.6 million. Operating earnings increased by 1.2 percent to $56.6 million from the prior year. This earnings performance reflected increased expenses associated with the division's ongoing investment to increase the use of Canadian Tire credit products and the introduction of the *Canadian Tire 'Money' on the Card* loyalty program.

Depreciation and amortization of property and equipment, which is primarily related to expenditures on new-format stores by CTR, totalled $119.7 million in 2000, up 12.6 percent from the $106.3 million recorded in the prior year. The Corporation's effective tax rate was 38.5 percent compared to 35.7 percent in 1999.

Finally, the weighted average number of shares outstanding increased to 78.3 million in 2000 from 77.2 million in 1999. Canadian Tire has a policy of repurchasing over the long term approximately the same number of Class A Non-Voting Shares that are issued under various stock compensation and dividend reinvestment programs. The number of these shares purchased during 2000 under the Corporation's Normal Course Issuer Bid program was 1,400,000. Segmented information of key financial data can be found in Note 14 to the Consolidated Financial Statements.

REVIEW OF OPERATIONS

This discussion of the Corporation's business units reviews their operational and financial performance in 2000 compared to 1999 and provides their outlook for 2001.

Canadian Tire Retail
2000 Operating Highlights

An average first-year sales lift of more than 60 percent from the 45 new-format stores opened in 2000 helped increase total retail sales at Associate Stores by 4.2 percent in 2000. Comparable store sales, however, decreased 1.7 percent due to a combination of unusually cold, wet weather in spring and summer; reduced average contribution from traditional stores in urban areas; the absence of 1999 demand for Y2K-readiness provisions; and weaker sales of seasonal merchandise in the fourth quarter of 2000. The average sales transaction in Associate Stores increased 3.0 percent in 2000 to $30.11.

Higher retail sales resulted in a 6.0 percent increase in net shipments to Associate Dealers. As a result, CTR's gross operating revenue reached $4.0 billion, up 5.9 percent from the $3.8 billion recorded in 1999. All three merchandising divisions of CTR contributed to the growth in shipments. Home Products was the most significant contributor, as customers favourably responded to the introduction of Next Generation merchandising at 44 existing new-format Associate Stores during 2000. Increased retail sales, and a full year of sales from *PartSource* stores opened before 2000, led to increased shipments in Automotive categories. While shipments in Sports & Leisure categories increased, the rate of growth was significantly lower than that of the previous two years for the same reasons that comparable store sales decreased, as mentioned above.

Annual Retail Sales
($ billions)

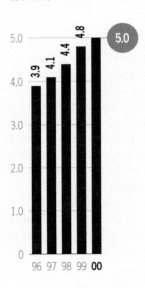

	96	97	98	99	00
	3.9	4.1	4.4	4.8	5.0

CTR operating earnings for the year were $171.7 million, a 10.1 percent increase from the $155.9 million earned in 1999. The improvement was due primarily to the overall increase in shipments to Dealers, a reduction in retail net advertising costs and the absence of year-end 1999 expense adjustments. CTR's earnings performance was impacted by a variety of factors in 2000, including a $22 million investment in Canadian Tire Online, $17 million of which was expensed; comparatively slower growth in shipments in Sports & Leisure categories noted above; and the clearance of excess inventory of seasonal merchandise, which reduced pre-tax earnings by $10.9 million. In addition, supply chain costs as a percentage of net shipments increased 35 basis points due to higher wage costs and capacity constraints at peak periods at CTR distribution centres. The capacity constraints were mitigated by reduced inventory levels. Longer-term growth in shipments will be accommodated in early 2002 with the opening of the new Calgary, Alberta, distribution centre as part of the CustomerLink program, which is discussed in more detail in the 2001 Outlook section for CTR.

Corporate merchandise inventories at the end of 2000 were $60.7 million below 1999 levels, almost equal to those at the end of 1998 despite a 14 percent increase in shipments to Associate Stores over that period. Year-end inventories declined 13 percent in 2000 to $412 million compared to $473 million at the end of the prior year; 1999 year-end inventories had increased by $61 million over 1998 levels due to advance buying in anticipation of customers' needs for Y2K-readiness. Collaborative time phase replenishment processes combined with more efficient merchandise management maintained inventory turns at 8.5 during 2000, even with a 6.0 percent increase in net shipments. This maintains the positive trend of improvement from turns of 5.6 in 1995.

Effective September 1, 2000 the Corporation purchased the shares of Pacific Associate Stores Limited which had operated a chain of Associate Dealer stores in the Greater Vancouver area. The acquisition will allow CTR to further penetrate the Greater Vancouver marketplace, upgrading older traditional stores to the new format and implementing the Associate Dealer framework employed across the rest of the country.

Key Initiatives

During 2000, CTR opened an additional 45 new-format stores at a cost of $292.3 million. Since the rebuilding program was initiated in 1994, 233 new-format stores have been opened representing 53 percent of Canadian Tire's store network. As most of these new stores were replacements or expansions of existing stores, the total store network reached 441 stores at the end of the year as compared with 425 stores prior to the start of this program. These new-format stores have made a major contribution to the $1.8 billion increase in consolidated gross operating revenue since 1993. CTR intends to open approximately 115 additional new-format stores by the end of 2003, which will significantly contribute to revenue growth and continue to enhance the customer experience. The majority of these stores will replace existing traditional stores in the Canadian Tire store network. Next Generation merchandising, which offers customers improved sight lines, easier navigation and expanded assortments in hardware, home improvement, housewares and tires, was incorporated in the 45 stores opened in 2000 and retrofitted in 44 existing new-format stores. As noted above, the 89 stores that have incorporated the Next Generation merchandising innovations to date are beginning to drive even higher sales gains, particularly in highly competitive Home Products categories.

CTR launched the new Canadian Tire Online e-commerce site in November on schedule. The site gives consumers the convenience of a new channel for purchases and home delivery of an initial assortment of 5,500 stock-keeping units. The complex undertaking to develop the appropriate business model, creating the web site, linking with Financial Services' payment systems and establishing third-party distribution necessitated an investment of $22 million in 2000, $17 million of which was expensed. Within two weeks

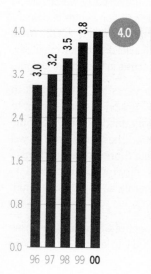

CTR
Gross Operating
Revenue
($ billions)

2 3

2000 ANNUAL REPORT

of its debut, the site was already one of the top five Canadian web sites in terms of customer visits, as measured by Nielsen/Net Ratings, demonstrating the strength of the Canadian Tire brand.

CTR also opened 14 new *PartSource* stores and made an acquisition in 2000, bringing to 28 the total number of these stand-alone specialty auto parts stores in operation at year end. In June, *PartSource* acquired the assets of Auto Village/Drivers, an automotive parts chain in Western Canada. Following the consolidation of some locations, the acquisition added a net six stores in Edmonton, Calgary, Saskatoon and Moose Jaw and will enable *PartSource* to refine its execution in those markets. Complete conversion of the acquired stores to the *PartSource* format is expected by mid-2001. The Corporation has doubled its share of the do-it-yourself automotive hard parts business in markets which include both Canadian Tire stores and a well-established *PartSource* presence.

2001 Outlook

In late 2000, Canadian Tire management initiated a comprehensive strategic review of the Corporation's businesses and their opportunities for long-term growth. The objective of this review is to increase shareholder value over time through consistent and superior growth of key metrics when compared to other North American retailers. Simply stated, Canadian Tire must outperform our market sector to be the preferred choice for investors. While the strategic priorities and timetable for their implementation are being developed, management is committed to improving near-term earnings by continuing to invest in existing programs designed to increase total and comparable store sales and to significantly drive down costs. In addition, the strategic review will result in the development of a long-term strategic plan, which will include the identification of new business opportunities. The review will also ensure that the Corporation has the capital structure and competencies to realize appropriate returns on any such opportunities.

Management is prioritizing its capital investment in 2001 on initiatives to deliver the highest and most immediate returns or that are essential to service existing business more efficiently. New-format stores and CustomerLink are two such initiatives.

In 2001, CTR plans to spend approximately $270 million to open 40 new-format stores. It will also retrofit 40 existing new-format stores with the Next Generation merchandising enhancements. By year end, approximately 170 new-format stores of a total of 273 will incorporate Next Generation features.

CTR will continue to invest in the development of CustomerLink, its multi-year strategy to add flexibility and capacity to Canadian Tire's distribution network. In 2000, work was completed on regional replenishment and storage capacity in a third-party warehouse in Montreal. CTR also broke ground on a 500,000 square foot distribution centre in Calgary that will serve 125 stores in Western Canada when it is operational in early 2002. When completed, CustomerLink will add a much more efficient, multi-channel distribution capability, first in Calgary and subsequently at CTR's current distribution centres in Brampton, Ontario.

The Corporation plans to invest up to $230 million over four years in CustomerLink to develop its multi-channel, supply-chain technology. Some $40 million has been spent to date, with a further $100–110 million committed for 2001 programs. The balance of the expenditure will be invested in the years 2002 through 2004. These investments will enable CTR to accommodate increased shipments to Associate Stores at reduced costs for handling, carrying inventory and transportation. This program is expected to significantly lower these expenses in 2004 and beyond to generate an appropriate return on the capital invested.

Given the focus to prioritize capital investment, the development of Canadian Tire Online will be limited to a further net investment of $10 million in 2001 to enable it to provide

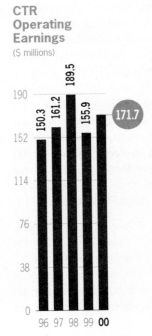

**CTR
Operating
Earnings**
($ millions)

190

152

114

76

38

0

150.3 161.2 189.5 155.9 171.7

96 97 98 99 **00**

Total Cubic Volume Shipped to Associate Dealers

(millions of cubic feet)

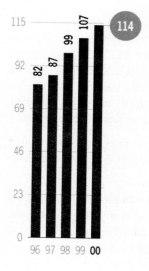

an expanded selection of spring and summer products as well as numerous products from CTR's annual catalogue. Also, additional investment during 2001 in *PartSource* stores will focus on the integration of the Auto Village/Drivers stores acquired in 2000 and on fine-tuning the *PartSource* business model.

During 2001, CTR will roll out several initiatives designed to increase comparable store sales through improved execution of retailing fundamentals. Customer Values, a set of core service principles developed in cooperation with the Associate Dealers, is expected to lead to a significant improvement in customers' in-store experience. The initial focus will be on successful deployment of two of these Values: ensuring that Associate Stores offer improved in-stock positions of regular and promotional merchandise; and providing customers with support from available, friendly and knowledgeable store employees.

CTR, Associate Dealers and vendors have developed a fully operational, on-demand 'e-learning' network to provide employees with the product knowledge they need to serve customers more effectively. The 20- to 30-minute modules covering facets of selected product categories will be delivered to store staff over the Internet beginning in 2001; development of the modules will be accelerated as the number of users grows. The e-learning network will also be a key tool in ensuring alignment between the Corporation, Associate Dealers and their staff on CTR's Customer Values initiatives.

CTR is also gaining even closer alignment with vendors by sharing more detailed and timely point-of-sale information. During 2001, CTR intends to roll out its ExchangePoint program to major vendors, which will enable those vendors to work more closely with CTR to develop, monitor and measure marketing programs and so improve sales. With ExchangePoint, CTR solidifies its position as a leading-edge retailer working closely with its vendors in analyzing retail information.

CTR has established aggressive targets for total and comparable store sales growth even with the possibility of lower economic growth in Canada in 2001 than that achieved in 2000. The combination of a first-year sales lift from 40 new-format stores, and a full year of contribution from the 89 Next Generation stores, 28 *PartSource* stores and the *Canadian Tire 'Money' on the Card* loyalty program will have a beneficial impact on the division's performance.

Canadian Tire Petroleum

2000 Operating Highlights

Petroleum's gross operating revenue was $853.5 million, up 37.2 percent from $622.0 million in 1999. Higher average pump prices resulting from the sharp rise in world oil prices, combined with record volume, drove this revenue increase.

Canada's retail petroleum market grew at 1.5 percent in 2000. By comparison, Petroleum increased gasoline litre sales volume by 11.7 percent over 1999 volumes, indicating a significant gain in national market share during the year. Petroleum pumped a record 1.3 billion litres of gasoline at its 206 gas bars.

Petroleum Gasoline Sales Volume

(millions of litres)

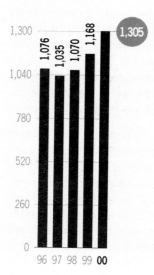

This strong performance resulted from a variety of initiatives designed to build volume. Petroleum benefitted from a full year of its successful marketing campaign, *It Pays to Buy Gas Here*, which gives customers incentives to buy gasoline and use discount coupons for merchandise purchases in Associate Stores. This message was reinforced throughout the year by a very popular campaign that offered consumers limited-time promotions on gasoline during numerous "Gas Relief" events. The multi-year program to upgrade sites to more attractive, high-capacity facilities also helped drive revenue growth. Four new sites and five redevelopments were completed during 2000, which brings the number of upgraded sites to 71 since the program was initiated in 1994. Sixteen Petroleum sites each include a car wash.

Operating earnings decreased 18.6 percent to $12.4 million from the $15.2 million earned in 1999. The decrease was due primarily to lower average margins. While operating costs

Petroleum Gross Operating Revenue*

($ millions)

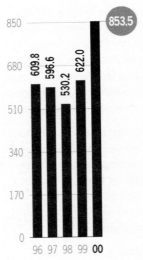

*Gross Operating Revenue includes provincial gasoline taxes

2 6

CANADIAN TIRE

continue to be well controlled, margins were impacted by the increase in crude oil costs during much of 2000. The volatile environment for retail gasoline prices was exacerbated by heightened competition in local markets across the country. By the fourth quarter of the year, relative stability had returned to world oil markets and margins normalized.

2001 Outlook

In the coming year, Petroleum will move towards closer integration with CTR and Financial Services to build on the success of the *Canadian Tire 'Money' on the Card* loyalty program and the *It Pays to Buy Gas Here* campaign. The continuing goal is to drive incremental traffic from Petroleum sites to Associate Stores and from stores to gas bars. As the market share gains in 2000 suggest, the total package of discounts available at Canadian Tire stores and gas bars presents a very competitive value proposition to consumers.

The ongoing redevelopment program in 2001 will focus on sites with the greatest opportunity. Petroleum expects that eight to ten sites will be built or rebuilt, some with car washes, at an investment of approximately $7.5 million.

Overall, Petroleum expects that sales of gasoline, convenience and ancillary products will rise in 2001. Higher revenue and continuing success in expense management, combined with an expected return to more stable gasoline margins, should enable Petroleum to increase its contribution to Canadian Tire's consolidated results in the coming year.

Canadian Tire Financial Services

2000 Operating Highlights

Financial Services' gross operating revenue totalled $329.6 million in 2000, a 7.7 percent increase from the $306.0 million reported in 1999. The growth in revenues stemmed primarily from a 15.5 percent increase in receivables balances attributable to portfolio conversions of Canadian Tire retail cards to the *Options* MasterCard during 1999 and 2000, a higher number of new accounts and the introduction of *Canadian Tire 'Money' on the Card*. Also, an increase in the number of cardholders led to significant growth in revenues from the insurance products marketed to credit customers.

Operating earnings rose 1.2 percent in 2000 to $56.6 million from $56.0 million in the prior year. Earnings were impacted by investments in the relaunch of Canadian Tire branded credit cards under the new *Canadian Tire 'Money' on the Card* loyalty program, new account acquisition expenses, and the changing mix of the portfolio from Canadian Tire retail card receivables to MasterCard receivables. Improved credit scoring and a strong economy led to reduced writeoffs and allowance rates for future credit losses on the Canadian Tire credit cards.

Since the 1950s, *Canadian Tire 'Money'* has been one of the most successful loyalty programs in retailing. In the mid-1990s, Canadian Tire customers were offered the *Options* loyalty program for credit purchases. In 2000, Financial Services relaunched the card loyalty program to capitalize on the popularity and equity of *Canadian Tire 'Money'*. The relaunch included the reissuance of 2.4 million credit cards. The new program gives users of Canadian Tire retail and MasterCard credit cards instant *Canadian Tire 'Money' on the Card* that can be redeemed for additional purchases in Associate Stores, just like *Canadian Tire 'Money'*.

Financial Services was also able to build its credit card portfolio during 2000 in a very competitive marketplace. By year end, the division had boosted its MasterCard accounts to 1.2 million, an increase of 28 percent over 1999; these accounts represented 47 percent of total Canadian Tire credit charge receivables at year end. Aggressive in-store marketing—a very cost-effective means of account acquisition—also added approximately 600,000 Canadian Tire retail cards during 2000, increasing the number of retail card accounts to 3.6 million. This continuing investment in low-cost card acquisition positions Financial Services for strong future revenue and earnings growth.

Petroleum Operating Earnings

($ millions)

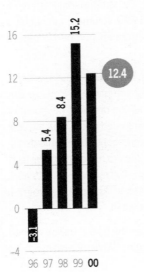

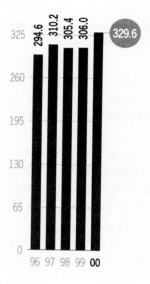

**Financial Services
Gross Operating
Revenue**
($ millions)

325
260
195
130
65
0

294.6 310.2 305.4 306.0 329.6

96 97 98 99 **00**

2001 Outlook

Since 1997, Financial Services has been implementing a strategic change program intended to increase productivity, expand its growth potential and enable it to be more competitive in the Canadian credit card business. A variety of initiatives have been successfully completed, and today Financial Services is a strong, profitable niche player in the very competitive Canadian credit card marketplace.

During 2001, Financial Services will continue to simplify its business structure and processes to reduce operating expenses and focus its resources on building its higher-margin Canadian Tire branded retail and MasterCard portfolio. As a result, Financial Services will be exiting the third-party retail credit card business by winding down a major processing contract and has sold non-securitized third-party portfolios, including the sale of Hamilton Discount, a stand-alone subsidiary dedicated to the third-party credit business. The sale has freed up the capital employed to finance approximately $130 million in unsecuritized receivables while generating a premium on the sale of the receivables. The annualized negative impact of these actions on pre-tax earnings of Financial Services is estimated to be approximately $4 million, which will be offset by the growth of the Canadian Tire credit charge portfolio. In addition, these changes will enable Financial Services to focus all of its financial and human resources on the growth of its own brands.

Financial Services will also continue to make investments in future growth. The business unit intends to acquire a further 700,000 retail and MasterCard cardholders via its successful in-store hostess program and to convert some 150,000 low-risk retail cardmember accounts to the MasterCard portfolio. In addition, Financial Services will test a new in-store warranty service product that is designed to increase customer loyalty while stimulating growth in this profitable segment of the business.

FINANCIAL CONDITION

A primary objective of Canadian Tire is to maintain consistently strong earnings and cash flows, as well as a strong capital structure. This is essential to ensure that the Corporation maintains its ability to fund future growth at competitive rates and to build long-term shareholder value. Management and the Board of Directors review the Corporation's funding requirements at regular intervals.

Capital Structure

One of Canadian Tire's objectives in selecting appropriate funding alternatives is to manage its capital structure in such a way as to diversify its funding sources, minimize its risk and optimize its credit rating. Canadian Tire continues to rank as one of the highest-rated Canadian retailers and has ready access to debt markets at competitive interest rates. At year end, the Corporation's capital structure was as follows:

Capital Structure

	2000	1999
Shareholders' equity	**56.3%**	47.1%
Short-term debt	**—**	8.2
Long-term debt*	**42.9**	43.8
Future taxes	**0.8**	0.9
	100.0%	100.0%

* Includes current portion of long-term debt

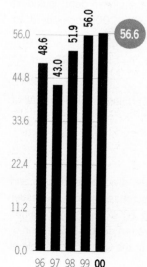

**Financial Services
Operating
Earnings**
($ millions)

56.0
44.8
33.6
22.4
11.2
0.0

48.6 43.0 51.9 56.0 56.6

96 97 98 99 **00**

Shareholders' Equity and Long-term Debt
($ millions)

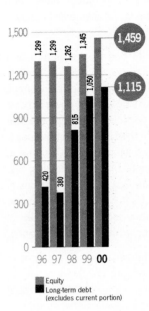

Equity
Long-term debt
(excludes current portion)

96 97 98 99 **00**

Equity   The year-end book value of Common and Class A Non-Voting Shares was $18.58 per share compared to $17.21 at the end of 1999. Total shareholders' equity increased to $1,459 million from $1,345 million in the prior year.

During 2000, the Corporation issued 1.8 million Class A Non-Voting Shares under various corporate and Dealer employee profit-sharing programs as well as under the Corporation's stock purchase, stock option and dividend reinvestment plans. In 1999, 2.5 million shares were issued under these plans.

The issuance of Class A Non-Voting Shares was offset by the purchase during 2000 of 1.4 million of these shares under the Corporation's Normal Course Issuer Bid Program ("Issuer Bid Program") on the Toronto Stock Exchange. During 1999, 2.3 million shares were purchased under that year's Issuer Bid Program.

During 2001, the Corporation intends to purchase up to 2.7 million Class A Non-Voting Shares through its Issuer Bid Program to offset the expected dilutive effect on earnings per share of various programs. A further 3.4 million of these shares may be purchased through the Issuer Bid Program if the purchases can be made on terms that serve the best interests of the Corporation and its shareholders.

Shares Outstanding   At December 30, 2000, there were 75,129,333 Class A Non-Voting Shares and 3,423,366 Common Shares outstanding; this compares to 74,716,081 Class A Non-Voting Shares and 3,423,366 Common Shares outstanding at January 1, 2000.

Dividends   Dividends declared on Common and Class A Non-Voting Shares were $31.3 million in 2000 compared to $30.8 million in 1999. The annual dividend on both classes of shares remained constant at $0.40 per share.

Short-term Debt   The Corporation has a Commercial Paper program with an $800 million authorized limit. At year end, no commercial paper was outstanding compared to $234.0 million at January 1, 2000.

Credit ratings for the Corporation's commercial paper at year end were "A-1" from CBRS Inc. ("CBRS") and "R-1 (low)" from Dominion Bond Rating Service Limited ("DBRS").

The Corporation also has committed lines of credit that are equal to or greater than the maximum projected amount of outstanding commercial paper balances; none of these lines has been drawn upon. Undrawn lines of credit were $755 million at the end of 2000.

Long-term Debt   In order to gain access to debt markets in a timely manner as required, Canadian Tire has filed a shelf prospectus with provincial securities commissions for the issuance of $500 million of Medium Term Notes. This program is evaluated every two years. The last renewal was completed in December 2000. Long-term debt, including the current portion, was $1,115.3 million at December 30, 2000 compared to $1,250.6 million at January 1, 2000.

The Corporation's long-term debt had ratings at year end of "A+" from CBRS and "A" from DBRS.

Like most issuers, Canadian Tire has provided covenants to certain of its lenders. All of the covenants were complied with during 2000 and 1999.

Funding Program
Funding Requirements
The Corporation's capital expenditures, working capital needs, dividend payments and other financing needs, such as debt repayments and share purchases under the Issuer Bid Program, are funded from a combination of sources. In 2000, this pool of funds comprised $65 million of proceeds from the issuance of long-term debt, $502 million of cash generated from operating activities and $115 million from the Corporation's sale of credit charge receivables, described below.

Capital Expenditures

Canadian Tire spent a total of $382.2 million on capital projects in 2000, a 1.3 percent increase over the $377.3 million spent in 1999. Real Estate expenditures totalled $292.3 million, most of which was for construction of new-format Associate Stores; this was a 3.0 percent decrease from the $301.4 million spent in 1999. In addition, CTR spent $50.3 million, with the major portion of the expenditures allocated to information systems development.

Capital expenditures by Financial Services were $13.4 million compared to $18.8 million in 1999; 2000 expenditures were primarily for improved information technology. Capital projects by Petroleum totalled $16.3 million in 2000 compared to $15.8 million in the prior year. The 2000 expenditures represent the third year of a program to upgrade Petroleum sites to the quality and look of CTR's new-format stores. Funds were also used to purchase and install point-of-sale infrastructure that gives customers the option to pay at the pump at 92 Petroleum locations.

2001 Capital Program

Canadian Tire's 2001 capital requirements, which are determined on a consolidated basis, are expected to total just over $422 million. Real Estate projects associated with the roll-out of new-format stores are planned at $270 million. Of the remaining $190 million to be invested in the CustomerLink supply-chain program, up to $110 million is planned for investment in 2001. Petroleum plans to spend $7.5 million for new builds, site upgrades and maintenance. The balance of planned capital expenditures is for CTR, Financial Services and the continuing upgrade of information technology across the Corporation.

Sources of Liquidity

The Corporation has access to funding well in excess of its 2001 requirements.

In 2001 it intends to fund its capital program through a combination of cash flow from operations, improvements in working capital, the use of both commercial paper ($800 million available) and Medium Term Note ($500 million available) programs and additional credit card receivable securitization. The Corporation is also exploring the potential for a real estate based financing transaction.

Working Capital   The Corporation's commitment to better manage working capital in 2000 resulted in a reduction in net working capital of $150.0 million, which increased cash generated from operating activities to $502.3 million. The working capital improvement included a $60.7 million reduction in year-end merchandise inventories from 1999 levels.

Cash and Short-term Investments   At year end, Canadian Tire's cash and short-term investments totalled $131.0 million, a 75.7 percent decrease from the $539.0 million held at January 1, 2000. The cash position at the end of 1999 was purposely high as a Y2K contingency. Significant among the uses of cash in 2000 were the repayment of $200.3 million of long-term debt and the elimination of a $234.0 million commercial paper liability. Short-term investments held at year end 2000 included Canadian and United States' government-guaranteed securities and high-quality commercial paper.

During 2000, cash generated from operations totalled $352.3 million; this was an 8.0 percent increase from $326.1 million in 1999. The 2000 amount represents cash flow from operations of $4.50 per share versus $4.22 in the prior year.

Canadian Tire Financial Services Receivables   The objective of the Corporation's credit charge receivables securitization program is to provide Financial Services, and the Corporation, with a cost-effective, alternative source of funding. The securitization of credit charge receivables is an integral part of the program for funding growth.

In 2000, gross credit charge receivables grew to $1,309 million, up 16 percent from $1,130 million in 1999. Financial Services owned $453 million of net credit charge

MANAGEMENT'S DISCUSSION AND ANALYSIS OF OPERATIONS

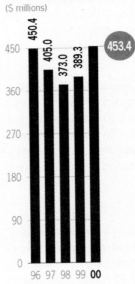

**Financial Services
Net Credit Charge
Receivables***

($ millions)

450.4 405.0 373.0 389.3 453.4

96 97 98 99 **00**

*2000 net credit charge receivables
exclude $856 million of securitized
receivables (1999 – $741 million,
1998 – $604 million,
1997 – $573 million, and
1996 – $470 million)

30

CANADIAN TIRE

receivables at the end of 2000 and $389 million at the end of 1999. The balance of these credit charge receivables is securitized through the sale of co-ownership interests in the credit charge receivables to the *Canadian Tire Receivables Trust®* (the "Trust"). During 2001, the Corporation expects its gross credit charge receivables to grow by approximately $207 million. The majority of this growth will be funded from the sale of additional receivables.

Details of the outstanding asset-backed Notes issued by the Trust are listed in the table below. As the Trust is not controlled by the Corporation, its financial statements have not been consolidated with those of Canadian Tire.

Canadian Tire Receivables Trust Asset-Backed Notes Outstanding

(Dollars in millions)	2000	1999
Series 1997–1 Commercial Paper Notes [1]	$ 222	$ 228
7.48% Series 1995–1 Senior Notes [2]	162	198
7.83% Series 1995–2 Senior Notes [2]	99	99
6.26% Series 1999–1 Senior Notes [2]	200	200
6.665% Series 2000–1 Senior Notes [2]	200	—
7.94% Series 1995–1 Subordinated Notes [3]	2	2
8.46% Series 1995–2 Subordinated Notes [3]	1	1
Floating Rate Series 1999–1 Subordinated Notes [3, 4]	4	4
Floating Rate Series 2000–1 Subordinated Notes [3, 4]	4	—
Total	$ 894	$ 732

[1] The Notes will mature on a business day 364 days or less from the date of issuance.

[2] On December 1, 2000, December 1, 2002, January 5, 2004 and November 20, 2004, respectively, for the Series 1995–1, Series 1995–2, Series 1999–1 and Series 2000–1 Notes, the process for repayment of principal will commence, subject to earlier prepayment in certain events, from allocations to the Trust in the previous month. These final payment dates of June 1, 2001, June 1, 2003, August 5, 2004 and June 20, 2005, respectively, are estimated based upon certain assumptions regarding the performance of the credit charge receivables pool and other factors.

[3] Repayment of the principal amount of the Subordinated Notes will not begin until all principal and interest owing under the related series of Senior Notes have been fully repaid.

[4] Interest on the Series 1999–1 Subordinated Notes and Series 2000–1 Subordinated Notes is payable at Bankers' Acceptance rates plus 1.25%.

The success of these programs is due primarily to the Trust's ability to obtain funds by issuing debt instruments of the highest credit rating. The Trust's asset-backed Commercial Paper program has a rating of "A-1 (high)" from CBRS and "R-1 (high)" from DBRS. The Senior Notes received a rating of "AAA" from CBRS and "AAA" from DBRS. In all cases, these are the rating services' highest categories. The Subordinated Notes have a rating of "AA" from CBRS and "A (high)" from DBRS.

Capital Assets   Capital assets are another source of potential liquidity for Canadian Tire. All of the land and buildings owned by the Corporation are unencumbered.

Financial Ratios

Canadian Tire continues to have a strong balance sheet and financial ratios. These allow the Corporation relatively easy access to funding from financial markets. It is the Corporation's long-standing policy that the ratio of long-term debt to total capitalization not exceed 50 percent. Long-term debt as a percentage of total capital decreased to 42.9 percent from 43.8 percent in 1999.

The current ratio at year end was 1.4:1 compared to 1.3:1 at January 1, 2000. Interest coverage in 2000 on a cash-flow basis, after adjusting earnings from operations for depreciation and amortization, was 4.9 times compared to 4.7 times in 1999.

Funding Costs [1]

The following table summarizes the Corporation's total funding costs (excluding those of the Trust), including the impact of Canadian Tire's risk management program, which is discussed below.

(Dollars in thousands)	2000	1999
Interest expense [1]		
Long-term interest expense	**$74,851**	$ 84,542
Short-term interest expense	**19,836**	12,039
	$94,687	$ 96,581
Effective blended cost of debt	**6.6%**	6.9%

[1] Interest expense is increased or decreased by the interest rate differentials paid on interest rate swap contracts.

The effective average blended cost of debt decreased between 2000 and 1999 as $150 million of Medium Term Notes with a coupon of 6.25 percent issued in September 1999 essentially replaced $150 million of 10.40 percent Series 1 Debentures that matured in January 2000.

RISK MANAGEMENT

Canadian Tire is exposed to a number of risks in the normal course of its business that have the potential to affect the operating performance of the Corporation. These risks, and the actions taken to minimize them, are discussed below.

Retail Competitive Risk   While Canadian Tire competes against national and regional retailers in all major markets across Canada, there is no one organization or type of business that competes directly with all product lines available at Associate Stores. However, several of these retailers, such as department stores, mass merchandisers, home-improvement warehouse operators and specialty marketers are currently in one or more of the business segments in which Associate Stores compete.

CTR actively monitors competitive developments in its markets, particularly its performance relative to competitors. This analysis enables it to determine the competitiveness within a market or business segment and take the necessary steps to both protect and build market share.

Canadian Tire also has core strengths that reduce its competitive risk. Foremost is the network of Associate Dealers whose investment and commitment to their Associate Stores provides a significant competitive advantage. In addition, a primary strength is the convenience of location of their 441 Associate Stores across Canada. Canadian Tire is enhancing this advantage with the ongoing roll-out and refinement of new-format stores. These stores are proving to be very effective at competing with different types of retailers and formats. Since 1994, the Corporation has committed a total of approximately $1.25 billion to this very successful program.

Internal and independent consumer surveys indicate that customers have very high awareness of, and loyalty to, Canadian Tire. In the most recent survey, 59 percent of those interviewed had shopped at an Associate Store within the last 30 days. In addition, Associate Stores hold strong market-share positions in many of the product categories in which they do business. This is particularly evident in automotive and hardware lines and in selected seasonal and sporting goods categories.

These core strengths are reinforced by continuous strategic and operational reviews of core product categories providing a comprehensive and up-to-date awareness of CTR's market position, opportunities and threats. This commitment results in ongoing innovation at Canadian Tire, such as new-format stores, Next Generation merchandising, Canadian Tire Online and *PartSource*, all of which are expected to contribute long-term growth in revenues, market share and profitability.

Specific initiatives designed to enhance CTR's competitive position, and thus reduce the Corporation's retail competitive risk, are described in the CTR section earlier in this Discussion.

Environmental Risk   Canadian Tire's environmental policy affirms management's belief that environmental protection is an essential part of Canadian Tire's corporate mission. Environmental programs are intended to be in the forefront of the retail industry in protecting the environment. In addition, the Corporation's forward-looking procedures for the identification and mitigation of environmental risk, as well as the Corporation's record of accomplishment in this area, have enabled it to purchase environmental insurance coverage at very favourable premiums.

During 2000, the Corporation continued to ensure that management systems were in place to address environmental issues, policies and procedures. The Canadian Tire Board of Directors and its Audit and Social Responsibility Committees receive quarterly and annual reports on environmental and health and safety issues, policies and procedures.

Canadian Tire carries out regular assessments of facilities and procedures to ensure that its operations meet regulatory and corporate requirements. In addition, the Corporation has initiated many proactive programs that set new standards of environmental management. These programs are discussed in more detail under 'Environmental, Health and Safety Stewardship' on page 50.

Concentration Risk   Canadian Tire, by the national nature of its operations, is relatively well diversified across Canada's regional economies. Management believes this makes the Corporation less susceptible to adverse economic conditions in specific regions of the country.

With regard to credit privileges extended to Canadian Tire customers by Financial Services, the card base comprises more than 4.5 million holders across Canada. Approximately half reside in Ontario and Quebec, with the balance distributed in the remaining provinces. In addition, concentration risk is limited with regard to receivables due from Associate Dealers, whose businesses are geographically dispersed. The largest trade receivable balance owed to the Corporation by any one Associate Dealer during 2000 was less than three percent of total Associate Dealer receivables.

Commodity Price Risk   The operating performance of Petroleum is very sensitive to the pricing actions of major competitors in the retail gasoline market, as was experienced during 2000. During the past four years, Petroleum has become as competitive as the 'best in class' gasoline retailers by significantly reducing its operating costs. This gives the division greater flexibility during periods of extreme competition. In addition, Petroleum has a very competitive contract with a major supplier for the acquisition of gasoline that helps offset, to some degree, the impact of commodity price fluctuations.

Seasonality Risk   CTR's offering features many seasonal products and as a result, experiences some seasonal variances in its business. Accordingly, in most years the Corporation records stronger gross operating revenues in the second and fourth quarters and higher consolidated earnings before income taxes in the third quarter. Revenue and earnings in the first quarter are typically the lowest. To improve responsiveness to these seasonal variances, CTR works with its suppliers to plan the timing of their shipments and, where possible, to shorten lead times on product orders. However, it is impossible to entirely remove the risks and uncertainties associated with the seasonal nature of CTR's product offering.

Capital Management Risk

It is important to note that, in implementing financial strategies to reduce risk, Canadian Tire's Treasury department does not operate as a profit centre. Controls are in place to detect and prevent speculative activity.

Financial Products Risk   It is the Corporation's policy to identify and manage currency, interest rate and commodity price risk proactively and conservatively.

There are typically two parties to a financial transaction. The successful completion of the transaction, and thus the mitigation of risk, depends on the ability of both parties to meet their financial commitments under the contract. In the case of Canadian Tire, counterparty credit risk is considered to be negligible as the Corporation restricts the counterparties that it deals with to highly rated financial institutions. A minimum rating of "AA" by CBRS and "AA" by DBRS is required.

Foreign Exchange Risk   The Corporation's guideline is to hedge a minimum of 75 percent of purchases of foreign-denominated goods and services that are expected to be completed within a four- to six-month period.

Credit Charge Receivables Risk   Credit Risk is the risk of loss due to the inability or unwillingness of a counterparty to fulfill its payment obligations. Canadian Tire through its Financial Services business grants credit to its customers on Canadian Tire credit cards with the intention of increasing the loyalty of those customers to shop at Canadian Tire Associate Stores and increasing profitability to the shareholder. With the granting of credit, the Corporation assumes certain credit risks.

Financial Services minimizes those credit risks in three areas of the credit process.

- When granting credit, sophisticated automated credit scoring models are used to determine the creditworthiness of each customer. These credit scoring processes are constantly improved based on new information.

- When monitoring the credit charge portfolio, Financial Services utilizes the latest technology to execute credit decisions by individual customers. These tools allow Financial Services to limit credit risk exposure.

- When collecting credit charge receivables, Financial Services has adopted a collection modeling technology that has significantly improved the effectiveness of the collection process.

Through these methods Canadian Tire has significantly improved the quality of its credit charge portfolio. In addition, with the conversion of over one million qualified credit customer accounts over to the Canadian Tire MasterCard from the retail card, credit risk has been further diminished.

Interest Rate Risk   This risk reflects the sensitivity of Canadian Tire's financial condition to movements in interest rates. The Corporation's exposure is substantially limited to the impact of interest rate fluctuations on cash and short-term investments, commercial paper and Medium Term Notes. As described in Note 13 to the Consolidated Financial Statements, consolidated interest rate sensitivity was minimized at the end of 2000 and 1999. A one percent change in interest rates would not materially affect the Corporation's earnings, cash flow or financial position.

Substantially all of the Corporation's long-term debt has been issued at fixed rates and is thus not sensitive to interest rate movements. Further details are provided in the 'Funding Costs' section on page 31.

Although interest rate sensitivity is primarily managed on a consolidated basis, the Corporation also reviews interest rate sensitivity by business unit. Most of Financial Services' revenue is not interest rate sensitive as it is generated from Canadian Tire's retail cards and the *Options* MasterCard, which each carry a fixed interest rate. Financial Services' funding requirements were reduced during 2000 and 1999 primarily due to the sale of credit charge receivables through the securitization program described on page 29. The balance of Financial Services' funding requirements in 2000 and 1999, however, was met with the issuance of floating rate debt, which makes Financial Services' results somewhat sensitive to changes in interest rates. This impact has been mitigated at a consolidated level to reduce the sensitivity of the interest rate exposure.

Canadian Tire monitors market conditions and the impact of interest rate fluctuations on the Corporation's fixed/floating rate exposure on an ongoing basis.

MANAGEMENT'S RESPONSIBILITY FOR FINANCIAL STATEMENTS

The management of Canadian Tire Corporation, Limited is responsible for the integrity of the accompanying Consolidated Financial Statements and all other information in the annual report. The financial statements have been prepared by management in accordance with generally accepted accounting principles, which recognize the necessity of relying on some best estimates and informed judgements. All financial information in the annual report is consistent with the Consolidated Financial Statements.

To discharge its responsibilities for financial reporting and safeguarding of assets, management depends on the Corporation's systems of internal accounting control. These systems are designed to provide reasonable assurance that the financial records are reliable and form a proper basis for the timely and accurate preparation of financial statements. Management meets the objectives of internal accounting control on a cost-effective basis through: the prudent selection and training of personnel, adoption and communication of appropriate policies, and employment of an internal audit program.

The Board of Directors oversees management's responsibilities for financial statements primarily through the activities of its Audit Committee, which is composed solely of Directors who are neither officers nor employees of the Corporation. This Committee meets with management and the Corporation's independent auditors, Deloitte & Touche LLP, to review the financial statements and recommend approval by the Board of Directors. The Audit Committee is also responsible for making recommendations with respect to the appointment and remuneration of the Corporation's auditors. The Audit Committee also meets with the auditors, without the presence of management, to discuss the results of their audit, their opinion on internal accounting controls, and the quality of financial reporting.

The financial statements have been audited by Deloitte & Touche LLP, whose appointment was ratified by shareholder vote at the annual shareholders' meeting. Their report is presented below.

Wayne C. Sales

Wayne C. Sales   President and Chief Executive Officer

J. Huw Thomas

J. Huw Thomas   Executive Vice-President, Finance and Administration and Chief Financial Officer
March 1, 2001

AUDITORS' REPORT

To the Shareholders, Canadian Tire Corporation, Limited
We have audited the Consolidated Balance Sheets of Canadian Tire Corporation, Limited as at December 30, 2000 and January 1, 2000 and the Consolidated Statements of Earnings and Retained Earnings and Cash Flows for the years then ended. These financial statements are the responsibility of the Corporation's management. Our responsibility is to express an opinion on these financial statements based on our audits.

We conducted our audits in accordance with Canadian generally accepted auditing standards. Those standards require that we plan and perform an audit to obtain reasonable assurance whether the financial statements are free of material misstatement. An audit includes examining, on a test basis, evidence supporting the amounts and disclosures in the financial statements. An audit also includes assessing the accounting principles used and significant estimates made by management, as well as evaluating the overall financial statement presentation.

In our opinion, these Consolidated Financial Statements present fairly, in all material respects, the financial position of the Corporation as at December 30, 2000 and January 1, 2000 and the results of its operations and its cash flows for the years then ended in accordance with Canadian generally accepted accounting principles.

Deloitte & Touche LLP

Chartered Accountants   Toronto, Ontario March 1, 2001

CONSOLIDATED STATEMENTS OF EARNINGS AND RETAINED EARNINGS

(Dollars in thousands except per share amounts)
For the years ended

	December 30, 2000	January 1, 2000
Gross operating revenue	**$ 5,207,574**	$ 4,728,259
Operating expenses		
Cost of merchandise sold and all expenses except for the undernoted items	**4,729,112**	4,254,798
Interest		
Long-term debt	**74,851**	84,542
Short-term debt	**19,836**	12,039
Depreciation and amortization	**127,021**	128,342
Employee profit sharing plans (Note 8)	**16,067**	21,439
Total operating expenses	**4,966,887**	4,501,160
Earnings before income taxes	**240,687**	227,099
Income taxes (Note 9)		
Current	**97,370**	89,314
Future	**(4,705)**	(8,144)
Total income taxes	**92,665**	81,170
Net earnings	**$ 148,022**	$ 145,929
Net earnings per share	**$ 1.89**	$ 1.89
Weighted average number of Common and Class A Non-Voting Shares outstanding	**78,349,097**	77,211,467
Retained earnings, beginning of year	**$ 773,522**	$ 734,042
Adoption of new accounting standard for post retirement benefits (Notes 1, 6)	**(9,234)**	—
Adoption of new accounting standard for future income taxes (Note 1)	**(637)**	—
Retained earnings, beginning of year, as restated	**763,651**	734,042
Net earnings	**148,022**	145,929
Dividends	**(31,328)**	(30,845)
Repurchase of Class A Non-Voting Shares (Note 7)	**(20,216)**	(75,604)
Retained earnings, end of year	**$ 860,129**	$ 773,522

CONSOLIDATED STATEMENTS OF CASH FLOWS

(Dollars in thousands) For the years ended	December 30, 2000	January 1, 2000
Cash generated from (used for):		
Operating activities		
Net earnings	$ **148,022**	$ 145,929
Items not affecting cash		
Depreciation and amortization of property and equipment	**119,726**	106,257
Net provision for credit charge receivables	**73,665**	53,946
Amortization of other assets	**7,295**	22,085
Future tax liability	**1,820**	(8,144)
Post retirement benefits (Note 6)	**1,432**	—
Loss on disposals of property and equipment	**354**	6,068
Cash generated from operations	**352,314**	326,141
Changes in other working capital components (Note 10)	**150,024**	(2,688)
Cash generated from operating activities	**502,338**	323,453
Investing activities		
Additions to property and equipment	**(382,172)**	(377,349)
Investment in credit charge receivables (Note 2)	**(253,043)**	(206,954)
Long-term receivables and other assets	**(24,800)**	(90,913)
Proceeds on disposition of property and equipment	**29,085**	19,457
	(630,930)	(655,759)
Financing activities		
Commercial paper	**(234,025)**	52,257
Repayment of long-term debt	**(200,292)**	(951)
Dividends	**(31,328)**	(30,845)
Securitization of credit charge receivables	**115,217**	136,268
Issuance of long-term debt	**65,000**	435,634
Class A Non-Voting Share transactions (Note 7)	**5,999**	(29,429)
	(279,429)	562,934
Cash (used) generated in the year	**(408,021)**	230,628
Cash position, beginning of year	**539,020**	308,392
Cash position, end of year (Note 10)	$ **130,999**	$ 539,020

CONSOLIDATED BALANCE SHEETS

(Dollars in thousands)
As at

	December 30, 2000	January 1, 2000
ASSETS		
Current assets		
Cash and short-term investments	$ 130,999	$ 539,020
Accounts receivable	515,130	483,559
Credit charge receivables (Note 2)	453,412	389,251
Merchandise inventories	412,381	473,052
Prepaid expenses and deposits	15,777	16,952
Total current assets	1,527,699	1,901,834
Long-term receivables and other assets (Note 3)	122,867	105,362
Property and equipment (Note 4)	2,097,095	1,864,088
Total assets	$ 3,747,661	$ 3,871,284
LIABILITIES		
Current liabilities		
Commercial paper	$ —	$ 234,025
Accounts payable and other	1,038,471	917,071
Income taxes payable	85,965	89,480
Current portion of long-term debt (Note 5)	315	200,292
Total current liabilities	1,124,751	1,440,868
Long-term debt (Note 5)	1,115,027	1,050,342
Long-term liability for post retirement benefits (Note 6)	26,579	8,750
Future tax liability	21,865	26,570
Total liabilities	2,288,222	2,526,530
SHAREHOLDERS' EQUITY		
Share capital (Note 7)	595,116	568,901
Accumulated foreign currency translation adjustment	4,194	2,331
Retained earnings (Note 7)	860,129	773,522
Total shareholders' equity	1,459,439	1,344,754
Total liabilities and shareholders' equity	$ 3,747,661	$ 3,871,284

Gilbert S. Bennett **Director**

Maureen J. Sabia **Director**

1. Significant Accounting Policies

Basis of consolidation

The Consolidated Financial Statements include the accounts of Canadian Tire Corporation, Limited and its subsidiaries.

Fiscal year

The fiscal year of the Corporation consists of a fifty-two or fifty-three week period ending on the Saturday closest to December 31. The results of certain subsidiaries which have different year ends from the Corporation have been included in the financial statements for the twelve months ended December 31.

Revenue recognition

The Corporation's shipments of merchandise to Associate Dealers (retail store owner-operators) are recorded as revenue when delivered. Revenue on the sale of petroleum products is recorded upon sale to the consumer. Merchant fees on credit charge receivables are taken into revenue at the time new receivables are recorded. Service charges are accrued each month on balances outstanding at each account's billing date.

Cash and short-term investments

For purposes of the Consolidated Financial Statements, cash is defined as cash and short-term investments less bank indebtedness. Short-term investments held include Canadian and United States government securities and notes of other creditworthy parties due within three months.

Merchandise inventories

Merchandise inventories are valued at the lower of cost and estimated net realizable value, with cost being determined on a first-in, first-out basis.

Goodwill

Goodwill represents the excess of the cost over the value assigned to net identifiable assets acquired at the date of acquisition and is amortized on a straight-line basis over a maximum period of 10 years. The Company assesses the recoverability of goodwill by determining whether the amortization over the remaining life can be recovered through projected undiscounted future operating results.

Property and equipment

Property and equipment are stated at cost. The cost of real estate includes all direct costs, financing costs on specific and general corporate debt relating to major projects, and certain pre-development costs. Depreciation is provided for using the declining balance method commencing in the month that the equipment or facilities are placed into service. Amortization of leasehold improvements is provided for on a straight-line basis over the terms of the respective leases. Purchased computer software, including direct implementation costs, is amortized on a straight-line basis over a period of up to five years. If property and equipment is subject to permanent impairment, additional depreciation or a writedown is provided.

Debt discount and other issue expenses

Debt discount and other issue expenses are included as other assets on the Consolidated Balance Sheets and are amortized over the term of the respective debt issues.

Deferred expenses

The Corporation capitalizes both direct and indirect costs with respect to ventures which are in the development stage. Capitalization of costs continues until formal operations have commenced, at which time the deferred costs are amortized over a three-year period. Should a venture be abandoned during the development stage, all capitalized costs will be immediately expensed. Canadian Tire Financial Services defers costs pertaining to the acquisition of most new businesses. These acquisition costs are amortized over the terms of the related contracts. All of the above costs are included as other assets on the Consolidated Balance Sheets.

Translation of foreign currencies

The components of the Consolidated Statements of Earnings related to foreign subsidiaries are translated to Canadian dollars using average currency exchange rates in effect during the period and assets and liabilities are translated at the exchange rates in effect at the end of the accounting period. Gains and losses on translation are included in net earnings, except for the exchange gains or losses related to investments in self-sustaining foreign operations. Translation adjustments on self-sustaining foreign operations are included in a separate component of shareholders' equity.

Stock-based compensation plans

The Corporation has five stock-based compensation plans, which are described in Note 8. No compensation expense is recognized when stock options are issued to employees. Any consideration paid by employees on exercise of stock options or purchase of shares is credited to share capital. Compensation expense is recognized for the Corporation's contributions to the Employee Profit Sharing Plans, the Employee Stock Purchase Plan, the Deferred Share Unit Plan and the Restricted Share Unit Plan.

Post retirement benefits other than pensions

Effective January 2, 2000 the Corporation changed its method of accounting for post retirement benefits to conform to the recommendations of The Canadian Institute of Chartered Accountants. The financial statements for the year ended December 30, 2000 have been prepared on this new basis and the comparative figures for the year ended January 1, 2000 have not been restated.

Under the new method, costs for employee future benefits are accrued over the periods in which the employees earn the benefits. The discount rate used for determining the current service cost and the liability for future benefits is the current interest rate at the balance sheet date on high-quality fixed income investments with maturities that match the expected maturity of the obligations.

The cost of employee future benefits earned by employees is actuarially determined using the projected benefit method prorated on services and management's best estimate of salary escalation, retirement ages of employees, employee turnover, and expected health care costs.

The most recent actuarial valuation of the obligation was performed as at January 2, 2000. Past service costs have been recognized retroactively. As a result of the adoption, at January 2, 2000, the accrued benefit liability increased by $16.4 million, and retained earnings decreased by $9.2 million.

Future tax liability

Effective January 2, 2000, the Corporation changed its method of accounting for income taxes to conform with the recommendations of The Canadian Institute of Chartered Accountants. As a result of the adoption, at January 2, 2000, the future tax liability (formerly referred to as deferred income taxes) increased by $637,000 and retained earnings decreased by the same amount. The change in accounting policy was adopted retroactively with no restatement of prior period financial statements.

Financial instruments

Interest rate swap contracts are used to hedge current and anticipated interest rate risks. Interest to be paid or received under such swap contracts is recognized over the life of the contracts as adjustments to interest expense. Unrealized gains or losses resulting from market movements are not recognized.

Foreign currency risks related to certain purchased goods and services are hedged. Any costs associated with these purchases are included in the Canadian dollar cost of these products.

Site-restoration costs

Liabilities have been recorded for site-restoration costs for known obligations as well as when it is probable that obligations will be incurred and the amounts can be reasonably estimated.

Use of estimates

The preparation of the Consolidated Financial Statements in conformity with generally accepted accounting principles requires management to make estimates and assumptions that affect the reported amounts of assets and liabilities, disclosure of contingent assets and liabilities at the date of the Consolidated Financial Statements, and the reported amount of revenue and expenses during the reporting period. Actual results could differ from these estimates.

2. Credit Charge Receivables

The Corporation sells undivided co-ownership interests in a pool of credit charge receivables to an independent trust (the "Trust"). No gain or loss has been recorded on these sales by the Corporation. As at December 30, 2000, the Trust's undivided co-ownership interest in the pool of credit charge receivables was $856 million (1999 – $741 million). Any income generated on the sold co-ownership interest in excess of the Trust's stipulated share of service charges is retained by the Corporation. The Trust's recourse to the Corporation is limited and is based on income earned on the receivables. As the Trust is not controlled by the Corporation, it has not been consolidated in these financial statements.

3. Long-term Receivables and Other Assets

(Dollars in thousands)	2000	1999
Long-term portfolio investment, at cost	$ 75,000	$ 75,000
Other assets	23,791	16,124
Goodwill	10,007	331
Long-term debt issue costs	6,491	7,869
Loans receivable	4,929	5,605
Mortgages receivable	2,649	433
	$ 122,867	$ 105,362

Long-term portfolio investment

Long-term portfolio investment is an investment in preferred shares of a creditworthy third party.

Goodwill

Goodwill of $10.0 million (1999 – $331,000) is stated at cost less accumulated amortization of $2.5 million (1999 – $1.9 million).

Loans receivable

Loans receivable include interest-free loans that have been provided to certain senior executives. These loans have various maturity dates extending to 2010.

4. Property and Equipment

(Dollars in thousands)	2000			1999			
	Cost	Accumulated Depreciation and Amortization	Net Book Value	Cost	Accumulated Depreciation and Amortization	Net Book Value	Depreciation Amortization Rate/Term
Land	$ 545,963	$ —	$ 545,963	$ 472,108	$ —	$ 472,108	
Buildings	1,611,426	479,882	1,131,544	1,451,228	443,492	1,007,736	4%–10%
Fixtures and equipment	346,425	239,901	106,524	322,642	219,012	103,630	10%–33%
Leasehold improvements	167,159	49,041	118,118	155,750	43,120	112,630	Term of lease
Computer software	151,334	70,606	80,728	119,327	41,200	78,127	Up to 5 years
Work in progress	114,218	—	114,218	89,857	—	89,857	
	$ 2,936,525	$ 839,430	$ 2,097,095	$2,610,912	$ 746,824	$1,864,088	

Included in property and equipment is property held for disposal with a cost of $147,014,000 (1999 – $145,690,000) and accumulated depreciation of $55,855,000 (1999 – $53,917,000). The Corporation capitalized interest of $4,926,000 (1999 – $4,474,000) for property and equipment under construction. The interest capitalized related to the Corporation's new-format store program.

5. Long-term Debt

(Dollars in thousands)		2000		1999
Obligation under mortgage payable	$	27	$	342
Unsecured debt				
Medium Term Notes at rates from				
Bankers' Acceptance plus 0.55% to 8.20% maturing at various dates to 2028		965,000		900,000
12.10% Debentures, maturing May 10, 2010 (2010 Debentures)		150,000		150,000
Total – net of current portion		$ 1,115,027		$ 1,050,342

Medium Term Notes

Certain of the Medium Term Notes are redeemable by the Corporation, in whole or in part, at any time, at the greater of par and a formula price based upon interest rates at the time of redemption.

2010 Debentures

The 2010 Debentures are redeemable by the Corporation, in whole or in part, at any time, at the greater of par and a formula price based upon interest rates at the time of redemption. Commencing with the quarter ended October 1, 1994 and for each subsequent quarter, the Corporation may (subject to availability and pricing) be required to purchase up to 1.15 percent of the 2010 Debentures outstanding at the beginning of such quarter. To date, no such purchases have been made.

Debt covenants

The Corporation has provided covenants to certain of its lenders. All of the covenants were complied with during 2000 and 1999.

Repayment requirements

(Dollars in thousands)	2001	2002	2003	2004	2005	Thereafter	Total
Mortgage payable	$ 315	$ 27	$ —	$ —	$ —	$ —	$ 342
Medium Term Notes	—	30,000	200,000	235,000	—	500,000	965,000
2010 Debentures	—	—	—	—	—	150,000	150,000
	$ 315	30,027	200,000	235,000	$ —	$ 650,000	$ 1,115,342

6. Post Retirement Benefits Other than Pensions

The Corporation provides certain health care, life insurance and other benefits, but not pensions, for certain retired employees pursuant to Corporate policy. Information about the Corporation's liability for post retirement benefits is as follows:

(Dollars in thousands)		2000		1999
Accrued post retirement benefit obligation at beginning of year [1, 2]	$	25,147	$	8,750
Total current service cost		761		882
Interest cost		1,839		—
Post retirement benefit expense [3]		2,600		882
Post retirement benefits paid		(1,168)		(882)
Accrued post retirement benefit obligation at end of year [4]	$	26,579	$	8,750

[1] Opening accrued benefit obligation as at January 2, 2000 represents the actuarial present value of post retirement benefits attributed to employee service rendered to date. The accrued benefit obligation increased by $16.4 million as a result of the change in accounting policy (Note 1).

[2] In prior years, the Corporation estimated an obligation to retirees at the time an employee retired using management's estimate of the long-term interest rate.

[3] The effect of the change in accounting policy is to increase fiscal 2000 pre-tax benefit expense by approximately $1.4 million.

[4] There are no plan assets, as funding is provided when benefits are paid. The accrued benefit obligation represents the long-term liability for post retirement benefits recognized on the Corporation's balance sheets.

The significant actuarial assumptions used for the valuation of the Corporation's accrued benefit for the year ended December 30, 2000 and benefit expense for 2000 are as follows: Discount rate – 7.25%, Employee turnover – 8.0%, Salary escalation – 3.0%, Rate of increase in per capita health care costs – 9.0%, Rate of increase in per capita dental care costs – 4.5%. The rate of increase in per capita health care costs was assumed to decrease by 1.0% annually to 5.0% in 2004, and remain constant at 4.5% for 2005 and thereafter.

7. Share Capital

(Dollars in thousands)		**2000**		1999
Authorized				
3,423,366	Common Shares (1999 – 3,423,366)			
100,000,000	Class A Non-Voting Shares			
Issued				
3,423,366	Common Shares (1999 – 3,423,366)	$ 177	$	177
75,129,333	Class A Non-Voting Shares (1999 – 74,716,081)	**594,939**		568,724
		$ 595,116	$	568,901

During 2000 and 1999, the Corporation reissued and repurchased Class A Non-Voting Shares. Reissuances are recorded at the fair value of shares issued. The net excess or shortage of the reissue price over the average cost per share held in treasury was added to or deducted from retained earnings.

During 1999, the Corporation changed its accounting policy whereby repurchases were charged to share capital at the average cost per share outstanding and the excess was charged to retained earnings. Reissuances were recorded at the fair value of shares issued. Prior to 1999, for accounting purposes, shares repurchased were considered to be held in treasury at cost and available for reissue. The net excess of the reissue price over the average cost per share held in treasury was added to retained earnings. The effect of the above noted change in accounting policy on total shareholders' equity was nil.

The following transactions occurred with respect to Class A Non-Voting Shares during 2000 and 1999:

	2000		1999	
(Dollars in thousands)	**Number**	**$**	Number	$
Shares outstanding at the beginning of the year	**74,716,081**	**568,724**	74,469,278	522,549
Issued	**1,813,252**	**37,120**	2,546,803	62,475
Repurchased	**(1,400,000)**	**(31,121)**	(2,300,000)	(91,904)
Excess of repurchase price over average cost	**—**	**20,216**	—	75,604
Shares outstanding at the end of the year	**75,129,333**	**594,939**	74,716,081	568,724

From December 31, 2000 to March 1, 2001, the Corporation issued 161,670 Class A Non-Voting Shares for total proceeds of $3,283,000.

Conditions of Class A Non-Voting Shares and Common Shares

The holders of Class A Non-Voting Shares are entitled to receive a preferential cumulative dividend at the rate of 1¢ per share per annum. After payment of a dividend on each of the Common Shares at the same rate, the holders of the Class A Non-Voting Shares and the Common Shares are entitled to further dividends declared and paid in each year in equal amounts per share. In the event of liquidation, dissolution or winding-up of the Corporation, the Class A Non-Voting Shares and Common Shares rank equally with each other on a share-for-share basis.

The holders of Class A Non-Voting Shares are entitled to receive notice of and to attend all meetings of the shareholders but, except as provided by the *Business Corporations Act* (Ontario) and as hereinafter noted, are not entitled to vote thereat. Holders of Class A Non-Voting Shares, voting separately as a class, are entitled to elect the greater of: i. Three directors or ii. One-fifth of the total number of the Corporation's directors.

Common Shares can be converted, at any time, into Class A Non-Voting Shares on a share-for-share basis. The authorized number of Common Shares cannot be increased without the approval of the holders of Class A Non-Voting Shares. Neither the Class A Non-Voting Shares nor the Common Shares can be changed by way of subdivision, consolidation, reclassification, exchange or otherwise unless at the same time the other class of shares is also changed in the same manner and in the same proportion.

Should an offer to purchase Common Shares be made to all or substantially all of the holders of Common Shares (other than an offer to purchase both Class A Non-Voting Shares and Common Shares at the same price and on the same terms and conditions) and should a majority of the Common Shares then issued and outstanding be tendered and taken up pursuant to such offer, the Class A Non-Voting Shares shall thereupon be entitled to one vote per share at all meetings of the shareholders.

The foregoing is a summary of certain of the conditions attached to the Class A Non-Voting Shares of the Corporation and reference should be made to the Corporation's articles for a full statement of such conditions.

As at December 30, 2000, the Corporation had dividends payable to Class A Non-Voting and Common shareholders of $7.8 million (1999 – $7.8 million).

8. Stock-Based Compensation Plans

The Corporation has five stock-based compensation plans, which are described below.

Employee Profit Sharing Plans

The Corporation offers its employees a Deferred Profit Sharing Plan (DPSP) and an Employee Profit Sharing Plan (EPSP). The amount of the award is contingent on the Corporation's profitability. The amount available is based on 6.75 percent of pre-tax profits, after certain adjustments, and is contributed to a Trustee-managed investment portfolio. The DPSP and the EPSP are required to invest and maintain 10 percent of their holdings in the Corporation's Class A Non-Voting Shares.

In 2000, the Corporation contributed $16.1 million (1999 – $21.4 million) under the terms of the DPSP and the EPSP towards the Trustee-managed investment portfolio. As at December 30, 2000, the DPSP and the EPSP held 419,280 Common Shares (1999 – 419,280) and 3,794,914 Class A Non-Voting Shares (1999 – 3,213,660) of the Corporation.

The participants of the EPSP have elected to terminate the Plan during 2001. Subsequent to year end the assets will be distributed to participants and no further contributions will be made.

Employee Stock Purchase Plan

The Corporation offers an Employee Stock Purchase Plan (ESPP) to its employees, whereby employees can choose to have up to 10 percent of their annual base earnings withheld to purchase Class A Non-Voting Shares of the Corporation. The purchase price of the shares is calculated monthly and is equal to the weighted average share price at which Class A Non-Voting Shares of the Corporation trade on the Toronto Stock Exchange for a given month. The Corporation may elect to match up to 50 percent of employee contributions to the ESPP.

The Corporation contributed $7.9 million in 2000 (1999 – $7.4 million), under the terms of the ESPP, towards the purchase of Class A Non-Voting Shares. These shares were purchased on the Toronto Stock Exchange. Under the Plan, the Corporation issued 817,673 Class A Non-Voting Shares in 2000 (1999 – 404,201) to employees.

Deferred Share Unit Plan

The Corporation offers a Deferred Share Unit Plan (DSUP) for members of the Board of Directors. Under the DSUP each director may elect to receive all or a percentage of his or her annual compensation in the form of notional Class A Non-Voting Shares of the Corporation called deferred share units (DSUs). The issue price of each DSU is equal to the weighted average share price at which Class A Non-Voting Shares of the Corporation trade on the Toronto Stock Exchange during the 10-day period prior to the last day of the quarter in which the DSU is issued. A director must elect to participate or change his or her participation in the DSUP prior to the beginning of a fiscal quarter. The DSU account of each director includes the value of dividends, if any, as if reinvested in additional DSUs. A director is not permitted to convert DSUs into cash until retirement from the Board. The value of the DSUs, when converted to cash, will be equivalent to the market value of the Class A Non-Voting Shares at the time the conversion takes place. The value of the outstanding DSUs as at December 30, 2000 was $331,149 (1999 – $90,594).

Restricted share units

The Corporation has granted restricted share units (RSUs) to certain employees which entitle the participant to receive a cash payment in an amount equal to the weighted average closing price of Class A Non-Voting Shares traded on the Toronto Stock Exchange for the 20-day period prior to and including the last day of the restriction period, multiplied by an applicable multiplier if specific performance-based criteria are met. The restriction period is three years less 30 days from the date of grant. Compensation expense is accrued over the term of the RSU based on the expected total compensation to be paid out at the end of the restriction period, factoring in the probability of any performance-based criteria being met during that period. The compensation expense recorded for the year ended December 30, 2000, in respect of this plan, was $631,249 (1999 – nil).

Stock options

The Corporation has granted options to certain employees for the purchase of Class A Non-Voting Shares, with vesting occurring on a graduated basis over a four-year period. The exercise price of each option equals the weighted average closing price of Class A Non-Voting Shares on the Toronto Stock Exchange for the 10-day period preceding the date of grant. Options may be exercisable over a term of 10 years. The Corporation is authorized to grant options to its employees up to 8.4 million shares of Class A Non-Voting Shares.

The Corporation uses the intrinsic value method of accounting for Stock Option Plans. There is no compensation expense recognized for the options since on the day of the grant the options exercise price is not less than the market price of the underlying stock. When the options are exercised, the proceeds received are credited to Share Capital.

The outstanding options as at December 30, 2000 were granted at prices between $11.06 and $40.82 and expire between March 2001 and November 2010.

Stock option transactions during 2000 and 1999 were as follows:

	2000		1999	
(Dollars in thousands)	Number of Shares	Weighted Average Exercise Price	Number of Shares	Weighted Average Exercise Price
Outstanding at beginning of year	2,068,877	$ 28.70	3,037,999	$ 19.22
Granted	2,213,000	21.53	703,750	39.49
Exercised	(63,834)	14.25	(1,554,922)	15.08
Forfeited and expired	(335,914)	29.35	(117,950)	28.65
Outstanding at end of year	3,882,129	$ 24.79	2,068,877	$ 28.70

The following table summarizes information about stock options outstanding at December 30, 2000:

	Options Outstanding			Options Exercisable	
Range of exercise prices	Number of Outstanding Shares	Weighted Average Remaining Contractual Life	Weighted Average Exercise Price	Number Exercisable at 12/30/2000	Weighted Average Exercise Price
$37.72 to 40.82	534,000	8.14	$ 40.48	138,274	$ 40.44
31.61 to 36.61	476,990	7.54	32.34	192,945	32.07
19.20 to 28.92	1,352,592	8.46	25.87	234,918	25.62
11.06 to 18.41	1,518,547	8.21	15.94	480,047	14.79
$11.06 to 40.82	3,882,129	8.21	$ 24.79	1,046,184	$ 23.80

Since 1988 the Corporation has followed a no dilution policy.

9. Income Taxes

(Dollars in thousands)	2000	1999
Income taxes based on a combined Canadian federal and provincial income tax rate of 42.9% (1999 – 43.6%)	$ 103,182	$ 98,993
Adjustment to income taxes resulting from:		
Large corporations tax	6,118	6,372
Lower income tax rate on earnings of foreign subsidiaries	(17,995)	(23,017)
Non-taxable dividends	482	—
Other	878	(1,178)
	$ 92,665	$ 81,170

10. Notes to the Cash Flow Statement

Working capital components

(Dollars in thousands)	2000	1999
Cash generated from (used for):		
Accounts receivable	$ (31,571)	$ (75,922)
Merchandise inventories	60,671	(61,356)
Prepaid expenses and deposits	1,175	(6,363)
Accounts payable and other	121,400	124,639
Income taxes payable	(3,515)	18,767
Other	1,864	(2,453)
Change in other working capital components	$ 150,024	$ (2,688)

Cash and short-term investments

Cash and short-term investments consist of cash on hand and balances with banks, and investments in money market instruments. Cash and short-term investments included in the cash flow statement comprise the following balance sheet amounts:

(Dollars in thousands)	2000	1999
Cash	$ (91,640)	$ (32,549)
Short-term investments	222,639	571,569
Cash and short-term investments	$ 130,999	$ 539,020

Supplementary information

The Corporation paid during fiscal 2000 income taxes amounting to $98 million (1999 – $83 million) and interest payments of $107 million (1999 – $90 million).

11. Operating Leases

The Corporation is committed to minimum annual rentals (exclusive of taxes, insurance, and other occupancy charges) for equipment and properties under leases with termination dates extending to 2040. Under sublease arrangements with Associate Dealers, the majority of these properties are income-producing. The minimum annual rental payments required in each of the next five years and thereafter are approximately $65 million for each of the years 2001 to 2005 and approximately $379 million cumulatively from 2006 to 2040.

12. Commitments and Contingencies

As at December 30, 2000, the Corporation has committed to letters of credit and guarantees of letters of credit aggregating approximately $182 million. These commitments relate to the financing of its merchandise operations and construction projects.

The Corporation had commitments of approximately $101 million for the acquisition of property and equipment and the expansion of retail store facilities.

The Corporation's Financial Services division has an agreement with a provider of credit card processing services. For the duration of this agreement, the Corporation has committed to pay a minimum of $12 million per year for the credit card processing services.

The Corporation and certain of its subsidiaries are party to a number of legal proceedings. The Corporation believes that each such proceeding constitutes routine litigation incident to the business conducted by the Corporation and that the ultimate disposition of the matters will not have a material adverse effect on its consolidated earnings, cash flow or financial position.

13. Financial Instruments

The purpose of this Note is to disclose the Corporation's exposure related to financial instruments.

Off-balance sheet financial instruments

The Corporation enters into interest rate swap contracts with approved creditworthy counterparties, to manage the Corporation's current and anticipated exposure to interest rate risks. The Corporation also enters into foreign exchange contracts, primarily in U.S. dollars, to hedge future purchases of foreign-denominated goods and services with an emphasis on those that are expected to be completed within a four- to six-month period. The Corporation also enters into equity contracts to hedge future stock-based compensation expenses. The Corporation does not hold or issue derivative financial instruments for trading or speculative purposes, and controls are in place to detect and prevent these activities. Neither the notional principal amounts nor the current replacement value of these outstanding financial instruments is carried on the Consolidated Balance Sheets.

As at December 30, 2000, outstanding off-balance sheet financial instruments of the Corporation are summarized as follows:

(Dollars in thousands)	Notional Amounts Maturing In				**2000** Total	1999 Total
	Less than 1 Year	Over 1 to 5 Years	Over 5 to 10 Years	Over 10 Years		
Interest rate swap contracts	$ —	$ 550,000	$ —	$ 100,000	**$ 650,000**	$ 870,000
Foreign exchange contracts [1]	**$ 762,496**	$ —	$ —	$ —	**$ 762,496**	$ 383,058
Equity contracts	$ —	$ 18,687	$ —	$ —	**$ 18,687**	$ —

[1] May include both forward contracts and options.

For the year ended December 30, 2000, interest expense included approximately $358,000 (1999 – $3,100,000) relating to interest rate swaps. Any unsettled interest differentials outstanding at year end were accrued for and included in accounts payable and other.

The estimated fair values of financial instruments as at December 30, 2000 and January 1, 2000 are based on relevant market prices and information available at that time. The fair value estimates below are not necessarily indicative of the amounts that the Corporation might receive or pay in actual market transactions. For financial instruments which are short-term in nature, carrying value approximates fair value. The fair values of other financial instruments are as follows:

(Dollars in thousands)	**2000**		1999	
	Book Value	Fair Value	Book Value	Fair Value
Financial assets and liabilities				
Loans and mortgages receivable	$ 12,632	$ 12,734	$ 10,606	$ 10,706
Long-term debt	$ (1,115,027)	$ (1,093,587)	$ (1,050,342)	$ (1,050,962)
Off-balance sheet financial instruments				
Interest rate swap contracts	$ —	$ 5,531	$ —	$ 5,884
Foreign exchange contracts	$ —	$ 592	$ —	$ (38)
Equity contracts	$ —	$ (1,506)	$ —	$ —

The fair values of loans and mortgages receivable, long-term debt and interest rate swap contracts were estimated based on quoted market prices (when available) or discounted cash flows, using discount rates based on market interest rates and the Corporation's credit rating. The foreign exchange contracts were valued based on the differential between contract rates and year-end spot rates. The equity contracts were valued based on the differential between contract rates and the year-end closing share price of the Class A Non-Voting Shares of the Corporation on the Toronto Stock Exchange. For the long-term portfolio investment (see Note 3), fair value information is not readily available. For interest rate swap, foreign exchange and equity contracts, the fair values reflect the estimated amounts that the Corporation would receive or pay if it were to unwind the contracts at the reporting date.

Interest rate risk

The following table identifies the Corporation's financial assets and liabilities which are sensitive to interest rate movements and those which are non-interest rate sensitive as they are either non-interest bearing or bear interest at fixed rates.

	2000		1999	
(Dollars in thousands)	Interest Sensitive	Non-Interest Sensitive	Interest Sensitive	Non-Interest Sensitive
Cash and short-term investments	$ 130,999	$ —	$ 539,020	$ —
Credit charge receivables	—	453,412	—	389,251
Loans and mortgages receivable	—	12,632	—	10,606
Commercial paper	—	—	(234,025)	—
Long-term debt (including current portion)	(65,000)	(1,050,342)	—	(1,250,634)
	$ 65,999	$ (584,298)	$ 304,995	$ (850,777)

The Corporation enters into interest rate swap contracts to manage its exposure to interest rate risk. As at December 30, 2000, the Corporation had entered into contracts that exchanged a net notional amount of $50 million from fixed to floating rate debt (1999 – $120 million exchanged from floating to fixed). These contracts hedge the Corporation's net balance sheet interest rate sensitivity position. A one percent change in interest rates would not materially affect the Corporation's earnings, cash flow or financial position.

Credit risk

The Corporation's exposure to concentrations of credit risk is limited. Accounts receivable are primarily from Associate Dealers who individually comprise less than three percent of the total balance outstanding and are spread across Canada. Similarly, credit charge receivables are generated by credit card customers, a large and geographically dispersed group. Current credit exposure is limited to the loss that would be incurred if all of the Corporation's counterparties were to default at the same time. The credit exposure is the current replacement value of only those contracts that are in a gain position. As at December 30, 2000, the credit exposure due to interest rate swap and foreign exchange contracts was $22 million (1999 – $16 million). The Corporation believes that its exposure to credit and market risks for these instruments is negligible.

14. Business Combinations

Effective June 1, 2000, the Corporation purchased the assets of Auto Village/Drivers, an automotive parts chain in Western Canada. The results of operations of Auto Village/Drivers have been included in the Corporation's income statement as of June 1, 2000. Net assets acquired were $4.8 million. Total assets acquired include inventory—$4.5 million and fixed assets—$1.5 million. Current liabilities assumed were $1.2 million. Goodwill arising from the acquisition was $3.5 million and is being amortized over a period of ten years. Total cash consideration given for the assets was $8.3 million.

Effective September 1, 2000, the Corporation purchased the shares of Pacific Associate Stores Limited which had operated a chain of Associate Dealer stores in the Greater Vancouver area. The purchase method was used to account for this business combination and the results of operations of Pacific Associate Stores Limited have been included in the Corporation's income statement as of September 1, 2000. Net assets acquired were $2.2 million. Total assets acquired include inventory—$30.1 million, fixed assets—$7.5 million and other assets—$1.3 million. Total liabilities assumed include current liabilities—$33.7 million and future tax liability—$3.0 million. Goodwill arising from the acquisition was $6.8 million and is being amortized over a period of eight years. Total cash consideration given for the shares was $9.0 million.

15. Segmented Information

The Corporation's reportable operating segments are strategic business units that offer different products and services. The Corporation has three reportable operating segments: Canadian Tire Retail ("CTR"), Canadian Tire Financial Services ("Financial Services") and Canadian Tire Petroleum ("Petroleum"). CTR derives its revenue primarily from shipments of merchandise to the Associate Dealers. Financial Services is primarily engaged in financing and managing customer credit accounts that arise from customers' use of their Canadian Tire retail cards and *Options* MasterCards. Petroleum revenue arises from the sale of petroleum products through its agents.

The accounting policies of the segments are the same as those described in the summary of significant accounting policies in Note 1. The Corporation evaluates performance based on earnings before income taxes. The only significant non-cash item included in segment earnings before income taxes is depreciation and amortization.

(Dollars in thousands)	CTR 2000	1999	Financial Services 2000	1999	Petroleum 2000	1999	Eliminations 2000	1999	Total 2000	1999
Gross operating revenue [1]	$ 4,024,406	$ 3,800,288	$ 329,642	$ 305,997	$ 853,526	$ 621,974	$ —	$ —	$ 5,207,574	$ 4,728,259
Earnings before income taxes	$ 171,680	$ 155,912	$ 56,639	$ 55,989	$ 12,368	$ 15,198	$ —	$ —	$ 240,687	$ 227,099
Income taxes									(92,665)	(81,170)
Net earnings									$ 148,022	$ 145,929
Interest revenue [2]	$ 19,722	$ 24,787	$ 3,931	$ 4,376	$ —	$ —	$ (9,741)	$ (9,272)	$ 13,912	$ 19,891
Interest expense [2]	$ 93,856	$ 94,202	$ 10,572	$ 11,651	$ —	$ —	$ (9,741)	$ (9,272)	$ 94,687	$ 96,581
Depreciation and amortization	$ 100,017	$ 108,306	$ 19,311	$ 14,010	$ 7,693	$ 6,026	$ —	$ —	$ 127,021	$ 128,342
Total assets	$ 3,700,654	$ 3,617,003	$ 557,213	$ 518,767	$ 538,543	$ 303,312	$ (1,048,749)	$ (567,798)	$ 3,747,661	$ 3,871,284
Capital expenditures	$ 352,457	$ 342,747	$ 13,440	$ 18,764	$ 16,275	$ 15,838	$ —	$ —	$ 382,172	$ 377,349

[1] Gross operating revenue includes dividend and interest income.

[2] Interest revenue and expense are not allocated to Petroleum for performance evaluation purposes.

16. Subsequent Event

On March 1, 2001, the Corporation sold a non-securitized third-party portfolio of receivables and its investment in one of its subsidiaries, Hamilton Discount Corporation Limited (HDCL). The Corporation received $135 million in cash proceeds, of which $75 million was used to extinguish HDCL's debt to the Corporation. HDCL operated as part of Financial Services and earned its revenues from the management of third-party credit card portfolios and transaction processing. The sale of these operations will cause an annualized pre-tax reduction in future earnings of approximately $4 million and a reduction in the unsecuritized credit charge receivables balance of approximately $130 million.

17. Comparative Figures

Certain of the prior year's figures have been reclassified to conform to the current year's presentation.

Environment

Canadian Tire has long been a leader among Canadian retailers on issues of proactive waste management, product recycling and environmental stewardship. During 2000, our Supply Chain team improved its management of waste such as corrugated cardboard, scrap metal and stretch film by recycling nearly 20 percent more materials than in 1999—4,700 tonnes in all. As well, efforts at our distribution centres focused on reducing hazardous waste, resulting in a 45 percent decrease in these waste products during 2000. Our corporate office was also an active participant in diverting materials from landfills; nearly half of all building waste was recycled, along with more than 28 metric tonnes of shredded paper.

Canadian Tire's lead-acid battery recycling program marked the completion of its first decade with another successful year. Approximately 20 million pounds of scrap automotive and marine batteries were collected from customers by Associate Stores and recycled in partnership with our battery vendor, Exide Canada. In addition, our Marketing department assisted an additional 48 Stores in Ontario to qualify as test and repair centres for Phase 2 of Drive Clean, the province's mandated vehicle emission testing program. The 58 stores now certified tested the emissions of more than 102,000 vehicles during 2000.

Canadian Tire continues to be a strong industry voice for new recycling programs. We participated actively in regulatory developments involving leftover paint recovery in several jurisdictions, including Quebec and Nova Scotia; used oil and filter recovery in British Columbia, Quebec and Newfoundland; and packaging recycling in Ontario and Quebec.

During 2000, the Corporation sponsored a special Millennium Edition of the Canadian Tire Community Environmental Awards. Under this four-year-old program, employees of Associate Stores can request financial support for non-profit projects that make a significant contribution to the environment in their local community. We funded 14 projects totalling more than $26,000 with awards of up to $2,000 each. Among the projects receiving grants were the creation of an outdoor classroom in Harbour Grace, Newfoundland to teach children how to grow vegetables organically; the restoration of the Cooks Brook salmon habitat near Bridgewater, Nova Scotia; an education and planting project along Quebec shorelines; a cleanup and restoration project along the Mississippi River in Carleton Place, Ontario; and tree planting in Williams Lake, British Columbia designed to attract birds and wildlife that will enhance local Cub Pack and school science activities.

Health and Safety

Canadian Tire's comprehensive health and safety program continued to address employee health and wellness, workplace safety and compliance with both internal and regulatory guidelines for occupational health and safety. As a result of the Corporation's focus on accident prevention, our Distribution Centres achieved record-low workplace accident frequency and accident severity in 2000. This outstanding health and safety performance, one of the best in Canadian retail, allows us to benefit from lower insurance premiums.

Canadian Tire's automated Material Safety Data Sheet Faxback program is a free service that enables employees and customers to request health and safety information on chemical products sold in Associate Stores. Last year, the team added 3,800 new data sheets to our existing database of 8,000. More than 3,000 requests for material safety data sheets were processed in 2000, more than half of them via our automated system.

In 1999, Canadian Tire launched the Foundation for Families as the primary focus of its charitable giving across the country. Bringing hands and hope to families and communities in need, the Foundation's mission is to provide the basic necessities of life to help families back on their feet. It supports local charities that offer assistance to families when they are in need of life's essentials such as a hot meal, warm coat or shelter from the cold. And after a major disaster strikes, the Foundation for Families brings resources and people together to provide the products, goods and services that help communities and whole regions of the country to put their lives back together.

With 38,000 members, the Canadian Tire family and its Foundation are committed to making a difference in the lives of families and their communities. The Foundation matches funds that are donated by our Associate Dealers or raised by employees across Canadian Tire. In its first full year of operation, the Foundation raised approximately $2 million through events such as charity golf tournaments, silent auctions and marketing programs to fund hundreds of charitable projects. To cite just a few examples, $500,000 raised in the 1999 year-end "Family Tree" program went to 200 family assistance charities at the beginning of 2000. There were an additional 200 donations to individual charities through Dealer and Corporate community initiatives. *La Fondation Canadian Tire du Québec* purchased Perce-Neige, a summer camp for physically challenged children; it also donated $800,000 to a variety of charities in the province.

The Foundation's helping hand touched thousands of families in larger efforts during 2000. When Walkerton, Ontario faced an outbreak of deadly *E. coli* bacteria, the Foundation helped the community deal with the crisis by donating bottled water, showerheads and tap aerators. A 10-hour downpour flooded the small town of Vanguard, Saskatchewan; the Foundation worked with Canadian Tire vendors to supply bottled water and support cleanup efforts. When major rainstorms contaminated the water tables of Charlottetown, P.E.I. and Glace Bay, Nova Scotia, the Foundation sent trailer loads of bottled water to help residents cope with the crisis.

DIRECTORS

Wayne C. Sales
President and Chief Executive Officer of the Corporation

Gilbert S. Bennett
Chairman of the Board of the Corporation, Consultant and Corporate Director

Martha G. Billes [1, 4]
Chairman, Governance Committee President of Tire 'N' Me Pty. Ltd., an investment holding company

Adam Bucci [3, 4]
President, Adam Bucci Ltée, which operates a Canadian Tire Associate Store

Gordon F. Cheesbrough [2, 4]
President and Chief Executive Officer, Altamira Investment Services Inc., an investment management company

Lilia C. Clemente [2, 3]
Chairman and Chief Executive Officer, Clemente Capital Inc., a New York-based investment management company

Austin E. Curtin [1, 2, 3]
President, Austin Curtin Sales Ltd., which operates Canadian Tire Associate Stores and Petroleum Outlets

James D. Fisher [2, 3]
Associate Dean, Joseph L. Rotman School of Management, University of Toronto

H. Earl Joudrie [1, 4]
Chairman of the Board, Gulf Canada Resources Limited, a major international, independent oil and gas exploration and production company

Donald C. Lowe [1, 3]
Corporate Director

Rémi Marcoux, FCA [1, 3]
Chairman of the Board, President and Chief Executive Officer, GTC Transcontinental Group Ltd., a company holding interests in printing and publishing companies

Ronald Y. Oberlander [1, 4]
Corporate Director

Frank Potter [2, 3]
Chairman, Emerging Market Advisors Inc., a consulting firm dealing with foreign direct investment

Maureen J. Sabia [1, 2]
President, Maureen Sabia International, a consulting firm, Corporate Director

Graham W. Savage [2, 4]
Managing Director, Savage Walker Capital Inc., a merchant banking company

John M. Stransman [1, 4]
Partner, Stikeman Elliott, a Canadian law firm

BOARD COMMITTEES

[1] **Management Resources and Compensation Committee**
Chairman, H. Earl Joudrie

[2] **Audit Committee**
Chairman, Maureen J. Sabia

[3] **Social Responsibility Committee**
Chairman, Frank Potter

[4] **Governance Committee**
Chairman, Martha G. Billes

OFFICERS

Gilbert S. Bennett
Chairman of the Board

Wayne C. Sales
President and
Chief Executive Officer

J. Huw Thomas
Executive Vice-President,
Finance and Administration
and Chief Financial Officer

A. Mark Foote
President, Canadian Tire Retail

Thomas K. Gauld
President, Canadian Tire
Acceptance, Limited

Alan B. Goddard
Vice-President, Corporate Affairs

Michael B. Medline
Senior Vice-President,
New Business Development

Stanley W. Pasternak
Vice-President and Treasurer

John J. Rankin
Senior Vice-President,
Dealer Relations

Patrick R. Sinnott
Senior Vice-President,
Supply Chain

Cameron D. Stewart
Vice-President, Secretary and
General Counsel

Janice M. Wismer
Vice-President, Human Resources

Andrew T. Wnek
Senior Vice-President,
Information Technology and
Chief Information Officer

Candace A. MacLean
Assistant Treasurer

TEN-YEAR FINANCIAL REVIEW

(Dollars in thousands except per share amounts)	2000	1999	1998
Consolidated Statements of Earnings			
Gross operating revenue	$ 5,207,574	$ 4,728,259	$ 4,347,283
Operating earnings before depreciation and applicable financing charges	455,100	429,937	404,079
Earnings from continuing operations before income taxes	240,687	227,099	249,712
Income taxes	92,665	81,170	82,732
Net earnings from continuing operations	148,022	145,929	166,980
Discontinued operations	—	—	—
Net earnings	148,022	145,929	166,980
Cash generated from operations	352,314	326,141	316,170
Cash generated from operating activities	502,338	323,453	364,381
Earnings retained and reinvested	116,694	115,084	135,681
Capital expenditures	382,172	377,349	303,058
Consolidated Balance Sheets			
Current assets	$ 1,527,699	$ 1,901,834	$ 1,511,338
Long-term receivables and other assets	122,867	105,362	36,021
Property and equipment	2,097,095	1,864,088	1,618,521
Total assets	3,747,661	3,871,284	3,165,880
Current liabilities	1,124,751	1,440,868	1,054,614
Long-term debt (excludes current portion)	1,115,027	1,050,342	815,000
Future tax liability	21,865	26,570	34,714
Shareholders' equity	1,459,439	1,344,754	1,261,552
Consolidated per Share			
Net earnings from continuing operations	$ 1.89	$ 1.89	$ 2.09
Net earnings	1.89	1.89	2.09
Cash generated from operations	4.50	4.22	3.96
Cash generated from operating activities	6.41	4.19	4.69
Dividends paid	0.40	0.40	0.40
Shareholders' equity	18.58	17.21	16.20
Statistics at Year End			
Number of Associate Stores	441	432	430
Number of petroleum outlets	206	202	195
Number of registered Class A Non-Voting shareholders	6,495	6,568	7,354
Number of registered Common shareholders	439	463	494

* 53-week period

1997*	1996	1995	1994	1993	1992*	1991
$ 4,087,802	$ 3,930,400	$ 3,795,641	$ 3,618,530	$ 3,432,024	$ 3,209,477	$ 3,009,566
345,179	320,930	319,174	305,575	281,660	249,835	297,955
209,498	195,914	189,622	185,615	162,980	131,062	219,889
60,927	64,018	67,872	70,846	62,596	44,622	87,832
148,571	131,896	121,750	114,769	100,384	86,440	132,057
—	—	—	(109,277)	(18,979)	(14,147)	(4,981)
148,571	131,896	121,750	5,492	81,405	72,293	127,076
308,686	274,230	254,639	199,566	194,391	213,036	223,894
274,036	302,702	123,895	161,141	285,258	194,546	255,245
115,240	96,978	86,557	(29,946)	45,129	36,417	90,981
253,488	220,728	195,045	90,567	42,362	87,603	177,826
$ 1,438,276	$ 1,339,790	$ 1,558,584	$ 1,655,445	$ 1,388,091	$ 1,308,082	$ 1,225,266
33,351	34,131	30,035	28,669	21,862	28,102	24,169
1,403,413	1,230,135	1,085,887	984,749	990,326	1,009,046	970,680
2,875,040	2,604,056	2,674,506	2,668,863	2,400,279	2,345,230	2,220,115
1,167,330	863,636	911,009	1,044,418	691,610	698,755	653,298
380,401	420,401	509,241	465,027	474,555	449,331	428,447
28,734	20,632	14,914	7,312	25,782	41,404	24,180
1,298,575	1,299,387	1,239,342	1,152,106	1,208,332	1,155,740	1,114,190
$ 1.79	$ 1.51	$ 1.38	$ 1.30	$ 1.11	$ 0.96	$ 1.46
1.79	1.51	1.38	0.06	0.90	0.80	1.41
3.71	3.15	2.89	2.26	2.14	2.36	2.48
3.30	3.48	1.41	1.82	3.15	2.16	2.83
0.40	0.40	0.40	0.40	0.40	0.40	0.40
15.79	15.04	14.00	13.03	13.40	12.87	12.40
430	426	424	423	425	424	420
193	197	199	202	208	213	207
6,999	8,297	8,308	9,294	10,525	10,871	11,012
519	569	571	602	640	674	694

QUARTERLY INFORMATION

Fiscal 2000

(Dollars in thousands except per share amounts)	1st Quarter 2000	1999	2nd Quarter 2000	1999	3rd Quarter 2000	1999	4th Quarter 2000	1999	Year End 2000	1999
Gross operating revenue	$1,104,316	$950,228	$1,398,200	$1,282,269	$1,325,240	$1,209,897	$1,379,818	$1,285,865	$5,207,574	$4,728,259
Operating expenses										
Cost of merchandise sold and all expenses except for the undernoted items	1,005,671	853,116	1,261,555	1,151,383	1,196,619	1,070,698	1,265,267	1,179,601	4,729,112	4,254,798
Interest										
Long-term debt	21,169	19,652	17,263	20,733	17,991	21,063	18,428	23,094	74,851	84,542
Short-term debt	4,504	2,096	4,298	3,517	4,595	4,988	6,439	1,438	19,836	12,039
Depreciation and amortization	31,157	22,413	29,874	24,958	31,242	23,783	34,748	57,188	127,021	128,342
Employee profit sharing plans	2,543	4,648	5,565	6,557	4,828	7,172	3,131	3,062	16,067	21,439
Total operating expenses	1,065,044	901,925	1,318,555	1,207,148	1,255,275	1,127,704	1,328,013	1,264,383	4,966,887	4,501,160
Earnings before income taxes	39,272	48,303	79,645	75,121	69,965	82,193	51,805	21,482	240,687	227,099
Income taxes	15,120	16,477	30,664	26,443	26,936	29,739	19,945	8,511	92,665	81,170
Net earnings	$ 24,152	$ 31,826	$ 48,981	$ 48,678	$ 43,029	$ 52,454	$ 31,860	$ 12,971	$ 148,022	$ 145,929
Net earnings per share	$ 0.31	$ 0.41	$ 0.62	$ 0.63	$ 0.55	$ 0.69	$ 0.41	$ 0.16	$ 1.89	$ 1.89
Weighted average number of Common and Class A Shares outstanding	78,224,021	77,568,406	78,363,940	77,088,791	78,332,443	77,075,014	78,349,097	77,211,467	78,349,097	77,211,467

Stock Trading Activity on the Toronto Stock Exchange

(Share prices in dollars, volume in thousands)

Class A Non-Voting	2000 1st Quarter	2nd Quarter	3rd Quarter	4th Quarter	1999 1st Quarter	2nd Quarter	3rd Quarter	4th Quarter
High	$ 37.00	$ 24.90	$ 23.00	$ 19.30	$ 43.55	$ 46.00	$ 43.40	$ 37.75
Low	18.40	18.70	18.85	15.05	37.50	39.05	33.30	32.50
Close	19.00	22.30	19.10	18.60	40.00	42.30	35.00	34.40
Volume	30,831.0	22,409.8	15,261.1	17,734.3	16,723.7	15,007.9	11,680.3	16,180.1

Common	2000 1st Quarter	2nd Quarter	3rd Quarter	4th Quarter	1999 1st Quarter	2nd Quarter	3rd Quarter	4th Quarter
High	$ 56.00	$ 52.50	$ 50.65	$ 46.50	$ 55.00	$ 53.00	$ 61.00	$ 55.00
Low	48.25	47.00	44.50	37.00	48.05	46.25	47.00	50.00
Close	53.75	49.70	45.00	38.25	53.00	48.50	51.25	52.50
Volume	72.8	39.2	30.8	22.5	14.3	17.7	29.5	19.1

Source: Toronto Stock Exchange

Note: All asterisked Brief Exercises, Exercises, Problems, and Cases relate to material in the appendix to the chapter.

BRIEF EXERCISES

BE5-1 La Bouche Corporation has the following accounts included in its 12/31/02 trial balance: Accounts Receivable $110,000; Inventories $290,000; Allowance for Doubtful Accounts $8,000; Patents $72,000; Prepaid Insurance $9,500; Accounts Payable $77,000; Cash $27,000. Prepare the balance sheet's current assets section balance sheet listing the accounts in proper sequence.

BE5-2 Included in Danton Limited's 12/31/02 trial balance are the following accounts: Prepaid Rent $5,200; long-term Investments in Common Shares $61,000; Unearned Fees $17,000; Land Held for Investment $39,000; Long-term Receivables $42,000. Prepare the balance sheet's long-term investments section.

BE5-3 Adam Corp's 12/31/02 trial balance includes the following accounts: Inventories $120,000; Buildings $207,000; Accumulated Amortization—Equipment $19,000; Equipment $190,000; Land Held for Investment $46,000; Accumulated Amortization—Buildings $45,000; Land $61,000; Capital Leases $70,000. Prepare the balance sheet's property, plant, and equipment section.

BE5-4 Mason Corporation has the following accounts included in its 12/31/02 trial balance: Temporary Investments $21,000; Goodwill $150,000; Prepaid Insurance $12,000; Patents $220,000; Franchises $110,000. Prepare the balance sheet's intangible assets section.

BE5-5 Included in Eicho Limited's 12/31/02 trial balance are the following accounts: Accounts Payable $240,000; Obligations under Long-term Capital Leases $375,000; Discount on Bonds Payable $24,000; Advances from Customers $41,000; Bonds Payable $400,000; Wages Payable $27,000; Interest Payable $12,000; Income Taxes Payable $29,000. Prepare the balance sheet's current liabilities section.

BE5-6 Use the information presented in BE5-5 for Eicho Limited to prepare the balance sheet's long-term liabilities section.

BE5-7 Tang Corp's 12/31/02 trial balance includes the following accounts: Investment in Common Shares $70,000; Retained Earnings $114,000; Trademarks $31,000; Preferred Shares $172,000; Common Shares $55,000; Future Income Taxes $88,000; Contributed Surplus $174,000. Prepare the balance sheet's shareholders' equity section.

BE5-8 Maritime Beverage Limited reported the following items in the most recent year:

Net income	$40,000
Dividends paid	5,000
Increase in accounts receivable	10,000
Increase in accounts payable	5,000
Purchase of equipment (capital expenditure)	8,000
Amortization expense	4,000
Issue of notes payable	20,000

Calculate cash from operations, the net change in cash during the year, and free cash flow for Maritime.

BE5-9 Kes Company reported 2002 net income of $151,000. During 2002, accounts receivable increased by $13,000 and accounts payable increased by $9,500. Amortization expense was $39,000. Prepare the cash flows from the operating activities section of the statement of cash flows.

BE5-10 Perez Corporation engaged in the following cash transactions during 2002:

Sale of land and building	$181,000
Purchase of company's own shares	40,000
Purchase of land	37,000
Payment of cash dividend	85,000
Purchase of equipment	53,000
Issuance of common shares	147,000
Retirement of bonds	100,000

Calculate the net cash provided (used) by investing activities.

BE5-11 Use the information presented in BE5-10 for Perez Corporation to calculate the net cash used (provided) by financing activities.

BE5-12 Using the information in BE5-10, determine Perez's free cash flow, assuming that it reported net cash provided by operating activities of $400,000.

EXERCISES

E5-1 – (Balance Sheet Classifications) Presented below are a number of balance sheet accounts of Something Inc.:

Net loss

1. Investment in Preferred Shares *Current Assets or Long-term investment*
2. Common Shares Distributable *investment*
3. Cash Dividends Payable *Current Liabilities*
4. Accumulated Amortization *Plant, Property and equipment*
5. Warehouse in Process of Construction
6. Petty Cash *Current Assets*
7. Accrued Interest on Notes Payable

8. ~~Deficit~~ *Retained Earnings*
9. Temporary Investments *C/A*
10. Income Taxes Payable *Current Liab*
11. Unearned Subscription Revenue *C/L*
12. Work-in-Process *C/A*
13. Accrued Vacation Pay *C/L*

Share Capital

DR : RE CR: Common Shares Distribution

Other assets

Current Liability

Instructions

For each account above, indicate the proper balance sheet classification. In the case of borderline items, indicate the additional information that would be required to determine the proper classification. (Refer to illustration 5-2 as a guideline.)

E5-2 (Classification of Balance Sheet Accounts) Presented below are the captions of Faulk Limited's balance sheet:

(a) Current Assets
(b) Investments
(c) Property, Plant, and Equipment
(d) Intangible Assets
(e) Other Assets

(f) Current Liabilities
(g) Noncurrent Liabilities
(h) ~~Common~~ *Capital* Shares
(i) Contributed Surplus
(j) Retained Earnings

Instructions

Indicate by letter where each of the following items would be classified:

h 1. Preferred shares
d 2. Goodwill
f 3. Wages payable
f 4. Trade accounts payable
c 5. Buildings
a 6. Temporary Investments
f 7. Current portion of long-term debt
g 8. Premium on bonds payable
a 9. Allowance for doubtful accounts
a 10. Accounts receivable

b 11. Cash surrender value of life insurance
g 12. Notes payable (due next year)
a 13. Office supplies
h 14. Common shares
c 15. Land
b 16. Bond sinking fund
a 17. Merchandise inventory
a 18. Prepaid insurance
g 19. Bonds payable
f 20. Taxes payable

E5-3 (Classification of Balance Sheet Accounts) Assume that Min Inc. uses the following headings on its balance sheet:

(a) Current Assets
(b) Investments
(c) Property, Plant, and Equipment
(d) Intangible Assets
(e) Other Assets

(f) Current Liabilities
(g) Long-term Liabilities
(h) Common Shares
(i) Contributed Surplus
(j) Retained Earnings

Instructions

Indicate by letter how each of the following usually should be classified. If an item should appear in a note to the financial statements, use the letter "N" to indicate this fact. If an item need not be reported at all on the balance sheet, use the letter "X."

1. Unexpired insurance
2. Shares owned in affiliated companies
3. Unearned subscriptions
4. Advances to suppliers
5. Unearned rent
6. Copyrights
7. Petty cash fund
8. Sales tax payable
9. Accrued interest on notes receivable
10. Twenty-year issue of bonds payable which will mature within the next year (no sinking funds exists, and refunding is not planned)
11. Machinery retired from use and held for sale
12. Fully depreciated machine still in use
13. Organization costs
14. Accrued interest on bonds payable
15. Salaries that company budget shows will be paid to employees within the next year
16. Discount on bonds payable (assume related to bonds payable in No. 12.)
17. Accumulated amortization

E5-4 **(Preparation of a Classified Balance Sheet)** Assume that Denis Inc. has the following accounts at the end of the current year:

1. Common Shares
2. Discount on Bonds Payable
3. Raw Materials
4. Preferred Shares Investments—Long-term
5. Unearned Rent
6. Work-in-Process
7. Copyrights
8. Buildings
9. Notes Receivable (short-term)
10. Cash
11. Accrued Salaries Payable
12. Accumulated Amortization—Buildings
13. Cash Restricted for Plant Expansion
14. Land Held for Future Plant Site
15. Allowance for Doubtful Accounts— Accounts Receivable
16. Retained Earnings—Unappropriated
17. Unearned Subscriptions
18. Receivables—Officers (due in one year)
19. Finished Goods
20. Accounts Receivable
21. Bonds Payable (due in 4 years)

Instructions

Prepare a classified balance sheet in good form (no monetary amounts are necessary).

E5-5 **(Preparation of a Corrected Balance Sheet)** Uhura Corp. has decided to expand its operations. The bookkeeper recently completed the balance sheet presented below in order to obtain additional funds for expansion.

UHURA CORP. Balance Sheet For the Year Ended 2002	
Current assets	
Cash (net of bank overdraft of $30,000)	$200,000
Accounts receivable (net)	340,000
Inventories at lower of average cost or market	401,000
Temporary securities—at cost (fair value $120,000)	140,000
Property, plant, and equipment	
Building (net)	570,000
Office equipment (net)	160,000
Land held for future use	175,000
Intangible assets	
Goodwill	80,000
Cash surrender value of life insurance	90,000
Prepaid expense	12,000
Current liabilities	
Accounts payable	105,000
Notes payable (due next year)	125,000
Pension obligation	82,000
Rent payable	49,000
Premium on bonds payable	53,000
Long-term liabilities	
Bonds payable	500,000
Shareholders' equity	
Common shares, authorized 400,000 shares, issued 290,000	290,000
Contributed Surplus	160,000
Retained earnings	?

Instructions

Prepare a revised balance sheet given the available information. Assume that the accumulated amortization balance for the buildings is $160,000 and for the office equipment, $105,000. The allowance for doubtful accounts has a balance of $17,000. The pension obligation is considered a long-term liability.

E5-6 **(Corrections of a Balance Sheet)** The bookkeeper for Nguyen Corp has prepared the following balance sheet as of July 31, 2002:

NGUYEN CORP.
Balance Sheet
As of July 31, 2002

Cash	$ 69,000	Notes and accounts payable	$ 44,000
Accounts receivable (net)	40,500	Long-term liabilities	75,000
Inventories	60,000	Shareholders' equity	155,500
Equipment (net)	84,000		
Patents	21,000		$274,500
	$274,500		

The following additional information is provided:

1. Cash includes $1,200 in a petty cash fund and $15,000 in a bond sinking fund.
2. The net accounts receivable balance is composed of the following three items: (a) accounts receivable—debit balances $52,000; (b) accounts receivable—credit balances $8,000; (c) allowance for doubtful accounts $3,500.
3. Merchandise inventory costing $5,300 was shipped out on consignment on July 31, 2002. The ending inventory balance does not include the consigned goods. Receivables in the amount of $5,300 were recognized on these consigned goods.
4. Equipment had a cost of $112,000 and an accumulated amortization balance of $28,000.
5. Taxes payable of $6,000 were accrued on July 31. Nguyen Corp, however, had set up a cash fund to meet this obligation. This cash fund was not included in the cash balance, but was offset against the taxes payable amount.

Instructions

Prepare a corrected classified balance sheet as of July 31, 2002 from the available information, adjusting the account balances using the additional information.

E5-7 **(Current Assets Section of the Balance Sheet)** Presented below are selected accounts of Kawabata Limited at December 31, 2002:

Cu A	Finished goods	$ 52,000		Cost of goods sold	2,100,000
	Revenue received in advance	90,000	L.T.A	Notes receivable	40,000
Cy L	Bank overdraft	8,000	Cu A	Accounts receivable	161,000
Cap A	Equipment	253,000	Cu A	Raw materials	207,000
Cy A	Work-in-process	34,000		Supplies expense	60,000
Cy A	Cash	37,000	Cu A	Allowance for doubtful accounts	12,000
Cy A	Short-term investments in shares	31,000	Int.a	Licences	18,000
Cy L	Customer advances	36,000		Contributed surplus	88,000
L T I	Cash restricted for plant expansion	50,000		Common shares	22,000

Interest Receivable

The following additional information is available:

1. Inventories are valued at lower of cost and market using FIFO.
2. Equipment is recorded at cost. Accumulated amortization, calculated on a straight-line basis, is $50,600.
3. The short-term investments have a fair value of $29,000.
4. The notes receivable are due April 30, 2004, with interest receivable every April 30. The notes bear interest at 12%. (Hint: Accrue interest due on December 31, 2002).
5. The allowance for doubtful accounts applies to the accounts receivable. Accounts receivable of $50,000 are pledged as collateral on a bank loan.
6. Licences are recorded net of accumulated amortization of $14,000.

Instructions

Prepare the current assets section of Kawabata Limited's December 31, 2002 balance sheet, with appropriate disclosures.

E5-8 **(Current vs. Long-term Liabilities)** Chopin Corporation is preparing its December 31, 2002 balance sheet. The following items may be reported as either a current or long-term liability.

1. On December 15, 2002, Chopin declared a cash dividend of $2.50 per share to shareholders of record on December 31. The dividend is payable on January 15, 2003. Chopin has issued 1 million common shares.
2. Also on December 31, Chopin declared a 10% stock dividend to shareholders of record on January 15, 2003. The dividend will be distributed on January 31, 2003. Chopin's common shares have a market value of $38 per share.
3. At December 31, bonds payable of $100 million are outstanding. The bonds pay 12% interest every September 30 and mature in instalments of $25 million every September 30, beginning September 30, 2003.
4. At December 31, 2001, customer advances were $12 million. During 2002, Chopin collected $30 million of customer advances, and advances of $25 million were earned.
5. At December 31, 2002, retained earnings appropriated for future inventory losses is $15 million.

Instructions

For each item above, indicate the dollar amounts to be reported as a current liability and as a long-term liability, if any.

E5-9 **(Current Assets and Current Liabilities)** The current assets and liabilities sections of the balance sheet of Scarlatti Corp. appear as follows:

SCARLATTI CORP.
Balance Sheet (partial)
December 31, 2002

Cash		$ 40,000	Accounts payable	$ 61,000
Accounts receivable	$89,000		Notes payable	67,000
Allowance for doubtful accounts	7,000	82,000		$128,000
Inventories		171,000		
Prepaid expenses		9,000		
		$302,000		

The following errors in the corporation's accounting have been discovered:

1. January 2003 cash disbursements entered as of December 2002 included payments of accounts payable in the amount of $39,000, on which a cash discount of 2% was taken.
2. The inventory included $27,000 of merchandise that had been received at December 31 but for which no purchase invoices had been received or entered. Of this amount, $12,000 had been received on consignment; the remainder was purchased f.o.b. destination, terms 2/10, n/30.
3. Sales for the first four days in January 2003 in the amount of $30,000 were entered in the sales book as of December 31, 2002. Of these, $21,500 were sales on account and the remainder were cash sales.
4. Cash, not including cash sales, collected in January 2003 and entered as of December 31, 2002 totalled $35,324. Of this amount, $23,324 was received on account after cash discounts of 2% had been deducted; the remainder represented the proceeds of a bank loan.

Instructions

(a) Restate the balance sheet's current assets and liabilities sections. (Assume that both accounts receivable and accounts payable are recorded gross.)

(b) State the net effect of your adjustments on Scarlatti Corp's retained earnings balance.

E5-10 **(Statement of Cash Flows—Classifications)** The major classifications of activities reported in the statement of cash flows are operating, investing, and financing.

Instructions

Classify each of the transactions listed below as:

1. Operating activity—add to net income
2. Operating activity—deduct from net income
3. Investing activity
4. Financing activity
5. Not reported as a cash flow

The transactions are as follows:

(a) Issuance of common shares

(b) Purchase of land and building

(c) Redemption of bonds *payable —*

(d) Sale of equipment *Investing +*

(e) Amortization of machinery *oper +*

(f) Amortization of patent *opex +*

(g) Issuance of bonds for plant assets

(h) Payment of cash dividends *financing —*

(i) Exchange of furniture for office equipment *Nothing*

(j) Loss on sale of equipment *Take out from operating*

(k) Increase in accounts receivable during the year *Oper —*

(l) Decrease in accounts payable during the year *Oper —*

E5-11 **(Preparation of a Statement of Cash Flows)**   The comparative balance sheets of Constantine Cavamanlis Inc. at the beginning and the end of the year 2002 appear below.

CAVAMANLIS INC.

Balance Sheets

Assets	Dec. 31, 2002	Jan. 1, 2002	Inc./Dec.
Cash	$ 45,000	$ 13,000	$32,000 Inc.
Accounts receivable	91,000	88,000	3,000 Inc.
Equipment	39,000	22,000	17,000 Inc.
Less: Accumulated amortization	(17,000)	(11,000)	6,000 Inc.
Total	$158,000	$112,000	

Liabilities and Shareholders' Equity			
Accounts payable	$ 20,000	$ 15,000	5,000 Inc.
Common shares	100,000	80,000	20,000 Inc.
Retained earnings	38,000	17,000	21,000 Inc.
Total	$158,000	$112,000	

Net income of $44,000 was reported and dividends of $23,000 were declared and paid in 2002. New equipment was purchased for cash and none was sold.

Instructions

Prepare a statement of cash flows for the year 2002.

E5-12 **(Preparation of a Statement of Cash Flows)**   Presented below is a condensed version of the comparative balance sheets for Metha Corporation for the last two years at December 31:

	2002	2001
Cash	$177,000	$ 78,000
Accounts receivable	180,000	185,000
Investments	52,000	74,000
Equipment	298,000	240,000
Less: Accumulated amortization	(106,000)	(89,000)
Current liabilities	134,000	151,000
Common shares	160,000	160,000
Retained earnings	307,000	177,000

Additional information:

Investments were sold at a loss (not extraordinary) of $10,000; no equipment was sold; cash dividends declared and paid were $30,000; and net income was $160,000.

Instructions

(a) Prepare a statement of cash flows for 2002 for Metha Corporation.

(b) Determine Metha Corporation's free cash flow.

*E5-13   (Preparation of a Statement of Cash Flows)   A comparative balance sheet for Shabbona Corporation is presented below.

	December 31	
Assets	**2002**	**2001**
Cash	$ 73,000	$ 22,000
Accounts receivable	82,000	66,000
Inventories	180,000	189,000
Land	71,000	110,000
Equipment	260,000	200,000
Accumulated amortization—equipment	(69,000)	(42,000)
Total	$597,000	$545,000
Liabilities and Shareholders' Equity		
Accounts payable	$ 34,000	$ 47,000
Bonds payable	150,000	200,000
Common shares	214,000	164,000
Retained earnings	199,000	134,000
Total	$597,000	$545,000

Additional information:

1. Net income for 2002 was $125,000.
2. Cash dividends of $60,000 were declared and paid.
3. Bonds payable amounting to $50,000 were retired through issuance of common shares.
4. Land was sold for book value

Instructions

(a) Prepare a statement of cash flows for 2002 for Shabbona Corporation.
(b) Determine Shabbona Corporation's current cash debt ratio, cash debt coverage ratio, and free cash flow. Comment on its liquidity and financial flexibility.

E5-14   (Preparation of a Balance Sheet)   Presented below is the trial balance of Kelly Corporation at December 31, 2002.

	Debits	Credits
Cash	$ 197,000	
Sales		$ 8,100,000
Temporary Investment (at market, $145,000)	153,000	
Cost of Goods Sold	4,800,000	
Long-term Investments in Bonds	299,000	
Long-term Investments in Shares	277,000	
Short-term Notes Payable		90,000
Accounts Payable		455,000
Selling Expenses	2,000,000	
Investment Revenue		63,000
Land	260,000	
Buildings	1,040,000	
Dividends Payable		136,000
Accrued Liabilities		96,000
Accounts Receivable	435,000	
Accumulated Amortization—Buildings		152,000
Allowance for Doubtful Accounts		25,000
Administrative Expenses	900,000	
Interest Expense	211,000	
Inventories	597,000	
Extraordinary Gain		80,000
Correction of Prior Year's Error	140,000	
Long-term Notes Payable		900,000
Equipment	600,000	
Bonds Payable		1,000,000
Accumulated Amortization—Equipment		60,000
Franchise	160,000	
Common Shares		809,000
Patent	195,000	
Retained Earnings		218,000
Contributed surplus		80,000
Totals	$12,264,000	$12,264,000

Instructions

Prepare a balance sheet at December 31, 2002 for Kelly Corporation. Ignore income taxes.

E5-15 **(Preparation of a Statement of Cash Flows and a Balance Sheet)** Wood Corporation's balance sheet at the end of 2001 included the following items:

Current assets	$235,000	Current liabilities	$150,000
Land	30,000	Bonds payable	100,000
Building	120,000	Common shares	180,000
Equipment	90,000	Retained earnings	44,000
Accum. amort.—build.	(30,000)	Total	$474,000
Accum. amort.—equip.	(11,000)		
Patents	40,000		
Total	$474,000		

The following information is available for 2002.

1. Net income was $55,000.
2. Equipment (cost $20,000 and accumulated amortization, $8,000) was sold for $10,000.
3. Amortization expense was $4,000 on the building and $9,000 on equipment.
4. Patent amortization expense was $2,500.
5. Current assets other than cash increased by $29,000. Current liabilities increased by $13,000.
6. An addition to the building was completed at a cost of $27,000.
7. A long-term investment in shares was purchased for $16,000.
8. Bonds payable of $50,000 were issued.
9. Cash dividends of $30,000 were declared and paid.

Instructions

(a) Prepare a balance sheet at December 31, 2002.

(b) Prepare a statement of cash flows for 2002.

*E5-16 **(Preparation of a Statement of Cash Flows, Analysis)** The comparative balance sheets of Madrasah Corporation at the beginning and end of the year 2002 appear below.

MADRASAH CORPORATION			
Balance Sheets			
Assets	Dec. 31, 2002	Jan. 1, 2002	Inc./Dec.
Cash	$ 20,000	$ 13,000	$ 7,000 Inc.
Accounts receivable	106,000	88,000	18,000 Inc.
Equipment	39,000	22,000	17,000 Inc.
Less: Accumulated amortization	(17,000)	(11,000)	6,000 Inc.
Total	$148,000	$112,000	
Liabilities and Shareholders' Equity			
Accounts payable	$ 20,000	$ 15,000	5,000 Inc.
Common shares	100,000	80,000	20,000 Inc.
Retained earnings	28,000	17,000	11,000 Inc.
Total	$148,000	$112,000	

Net income of $44,000 was reported and dividends of $33,000 were paid in 2002. New equipment was purchased and none was sold.

Instructions

(a) Prepare a statement of cash flows for the year 2002.

(b) Calculate the current ratio as of January 1, 2002 and December 31, 2002, and calculate free cash flow for the year 2002.

(c) In light of the analysis in (b), comment on Madrasah's liquidity and financial flexibility.

*E5-17 **(Preparation of a Statement of Cash Flows, Analysis)** A comparative balance sheet for Nicholson Industries Inc. is presented on the following page.

NICHOLSON INDUSTRIES INC.
Balance Sheets

Assets	December 31	
	2002	2001
Cash	$ 13,000	$ 22,000
Accounts receivable	112,000	66,000
Inventories	220,000	189,000
Land	71,000	110,000
Equipment	260,000	200,000
Accumulated amortization—equipment	(69,000)	(42,000)
Total	$607,000	$545,000
Liabilities and Shareholders' Equity		
Accounts payable	$ 44,000	$ 47,000
Bonds payable	150,000	200,000
Common shares	214,000	164,000
Retained earnings	199,000	134,000
Total	$607,000	$545,000

Additional information:

1. Net income for 2002 was $125,000.
2. Cash dividends of $60,000 were declared and paid.
3. Bonds payable amounting to $50,000 were retired through issuance of common shares.
4. Land was sold at book value.

Instructions

(a) Prepare a statement of cash flows for the year 2002 for Nicholson.
(b) Calculate the current and acid-test ratios for 2001 and 2002.
(c) Calculate Nicholson's free cash flow and the current cash debt coverage ratio for 2002.
(d) Based on the analyses in (b) and (c), comment on Nicholson's liquidity and financial flexibility.

PROBLEMS

P5-1 Presented below is a list of accounts in alphabetical order.

Accounts Receivable	Inventory—Ending
Accrued Wages	Land
Accumulated Amortization—Buildings	Land for Future Plant Site
Accumulated Amortization—Equipment	Loss from Flood
Advances to Employees	Notes Payable
Advertising Expense	Patent (net of amortization)
Allowance for Doubtful Accounts	Pension Obligations
Bonds Payable	Petty Cash
Buildings	Preferred Shares
Cash in Bank	Premium on Bonds Payable
Cash on Hand	Prepaid Rent
Cash Surrender Value of Life Insurance	Purchase Returns and Allowances
Commission Expense	Purchases
Common Shares	Retained Earnings
Copyright (net of amortization)	Sales
Dividends Payable	Sales Discounts
Equipment	Sales Salaries
Gain on Sale of Equipment	Taxes Payable
Interest Receivable	Temporary Investments
Inventory—Beginning	Transportation-in
	Unearned Subscriptions

Instructions

Prepare a classified balance sheet in good form. (No monetary amounts are to be shown.)

P5-2 Presented below are a number of balance sheet items for Leno, Inc., for the current year, 2002.

Goodwill	$ 125,000	Accumulated amortization—equipment	$ 292,000
Payroll taxes payable	177,591	Inventories	239,800
Bonds payable	300,000	Rent payable—short-term	45,000
Discount on bonds payable	15,000	Taxes payable	98,362
Cash	360,000	Long-term rental obligations	480,000
Land	480,000	Common shares (20,000 shares issued)	200,000
Notes receivable	545,700	Preferred shares (15,000 shares issued)	150,000
Notes payable to banks	265,000	Prepaid expenses	87,920
Accounts payable	590,000	Equipment	1,470,000
Retained earnings	?	Temporary investments	121,000
Income taxes receivable	97,630	Accumulated amortization—building	170,200
Unsecured notes payable (long-term)	1,600,000	Building	1,640,000

Instructions

Prepare a classified balance sheet in good form. 400,000 common shares were authorized, and 20,000 preferred shares were authorized. Assume that notes receivable and notes payable are short-term, unless stated otherwise. Cost and fair value of marketable securities are the same.

P5-3 The trial balance of Kicks Inc. and other related information for the year 2002 is presented below.

KICKS INC.
Trial Balance
December 31, 2002

	Debits	Credits
Cash	$ 41,000	
Accounts Receivable	163,500	
Allowance for Doubtful Accounts		$ 8,700
Prepaid Insurance	5,900	
Inventory	308,500	
Long-term Investments	339,000	
Land	85,000	
Construction Work in Progress	124,000	
Patents	36,000	
Equipment	400,000	
Accumulated Amortization of Equipment		140,000
Unamortized Discount on Bonds Payable	20,000	
Accounts Payable		148,000
Accrued Expenses		49,200
Notes Payable		94,000
Bonds Payable		400,000
Common Shares		500,000
Contributed Surplus		45,000
Retained Earnings		138,000
	$1,522,900	$1,522,900

Additional information:

1. The inventory has a replacement market value of $353,000. The LIFO method of inventory value is used.
2. The cost and fair value of the long-term investments that consist of stocks and bonds is the same.
3. The amount of the Construction Work in Progress account represents the costs expended to date on a building in the process of construction. (The company rents factory space at the present time.) The land on which the building is being constructed cost $85,000, as shown in the trial balance.
4. The patents were purchased by the company at a cost of $40,000 and are being amortized on a straight-line basis.
5. Of the unamortized discount on bonds payable, $2,000 will be amortized in 2003.
6. The notes payable represent bank loans that are secured by long-term investments carried at $120,000. These bank loans are due in 2003.

7. The bonds payable bear interest at 11% payable every December 31, and are due January 1, 2013.
8. Six hundred thousand shares of common shares were authorized, of which 500,000 shares issued are outstanding.

Instructions

Prepare a balance sheet as of December 31, 2002, so that all important information is fully disclosed.

P5-4 Presented below is the balance sheet of Cruise Corporation as of December 31, 2002.

CRUISE CORPORATION
Balance Sheet
December 31, 2002

Assets
Goodwill (Note 2)	$ 120,000
Buildings (Note 1)	1,640,000
Inventories	312,100
Land	750,000
Accounts receivable	170,000
Long-term investments	87,000
Cash on hand	175,900
Assets allocated to trustee for plant expansion	
Cash in bank	70,000
Treasury notes, at cost and fair value	138,000
	$3,463,000

Equities
Notes payable (Note 3)	$ 600,000
Common shares, issued, 1,000,000 shares (authorized unlimited)	1,150,000
Retained earnings	658,000
Appreciation capital (Note 1)	570,000
Income taxes payable	75,000
Reserve for amortization of building	410,000
	$3,463,000

Note 1: Buildings are stated at cost, except for one building that was recorded at appraised value. The excess of appraisal value over cost was $570,000. Amortization has been recorded based on cost.
Note 2: Goodwill in the amount of $120,000 was recognized because the company believed that book value was not an accurate representation of the fair market value of the company. The gain of $120,000 was credited to Retained Earnings.
Note 3: Notes payable are long-term except for the current instalment due of $100,000.

Instructions

Prepare a corrected classified balance sheet in good form. The notes above are for information only.

P5-5 Presented below is the balance sheet of King Corporation for the current year, 2002.

KING CORPORATION
Balance Sheet
December 31, 2002

Current assets	$ 435,000	Current liabilities	$ 330,000
Investments	640,000	Long-term liabilities	1,000,000
Property, plant, and equipment	1,720,000	Shareholders' equity	1,770,000
Intangible assets	305,000		
	$3,100,000		$3,100,000

The following information is presented:

1. The current assets section includes: cash $100,000, accounts receivable $170,000 less $10,000 for allowance for doubtful accounts, inventories $180,000, and unearned revenue $5,000. The cash balance is composed of $114,000, less a bank overdraft of $14,000. Inventories are stated on the lower of FIFO cost or market.

2. The investments section includes the cash surrender value of a life insurance contract $40,000; temporary investments in common shares of another company $80,000 (fair value $80,000) and long-term $140,000; bond sinking fund $250,000; and organization costs $130,000. The cost and fair value of investments in common shares are the same.
3. Property, plant, and equipment includes buildings $1,040,000 less accumulated amortization $360,000; equipment $450,000 less accumulated amortization $180,000; land $500,000; and land held for future use $270,000.
4. Intangible assets include a franchise $165,000, goodwill $100,000, and discount on bonds payable $40,000.
5. Current liabilities include accounts payable $90,000, notes payable—short-term $80,000 and long-term $120,000, and taxes payable $40,000.
6. Long-term liabilities are composed solely of 10% bonds payable due 2010.
7. Shareholders' equity has 70,000 preferred shares (authorized 200,000 shares), which were issued for $450,000, and 100,000 common shares, (authorized 400,000 shares) which were issued at an average price of $10. In addition, the corporation has retained earnings of $320,000.

Instructions

Prepare a balance sheet in good form, adjusting the amounts in each balance sheet classification as affected by the "information" given above.

P5-6 Cooke Inc. had the following balance sheet at the end of operations for 2001:

COOKE INC.
Balance Sheet
December 31, 2001

Cash	$ 20,000	Accounts payable	$ 30,000
Accounts receivable	21,200	Long-term notes payable	41,000
Investments	32,000	Common shares	100,000
Plant assets (net)	81,000	Retained earnings	23,200
Land	40,000		
	$194,200		$194,200

During 2002, the following occurred:

1. Cooke Inc. sold part of its investment portfolio for $17,000. This transaction resulted in a gain of $3,400 for the firm. The company often sells and buys securities of this nature.
2. A tract of land was purchased for $18,000 cash.
3. Long-term notes payable in the amount of $16,000 were retired before maturity by paying $16,000 cash.
4. An additional $24,000 in common shares was issued.
5. Dividends totalling $8,200 were declared and paid to shareholders.
6. Net income for 2002 was $32,000 after allowing for amortization of $12,000.
7. Land was purchased through the issuance of $30,000 in bonds.
8. At December 31, 2002, Cash was $39,000, Accounts Receivable was $41,600, and Accounts Payable remained at $30,000.

Instructions

(a) Prepare a statement of cash flows for 2002.
(b) Prepare the balance sheet as it would appear at December 31, 2002.
(c) How might the statement of cash flows help the user of the financial statements? Calculate two cash flow ratios.
(d) What is the cash flow pattern? Discuss.

P5-7 Anne Spier has prepared baked goods for resale since 1991. She started a baking business in her home and has been operating in a rented building with a storefront since 1996. Spier incorporated the business as MAS Inc. on January 1, 2002, with an initial shares issue of 1,000 shares of common shares for $2,500. Anne Spier is the principal shareholder of MAS Inc.

Sales have increased 30% annually since operations began at the present location, and additional equipment is needed to accommodate expected continued growth. Spier wishes to purchase some additional baking equipment and to finance the equipment through a long-term note from a commercial bank. Kelowna Bank & Trust has asked Spier to submit an income statement for MAS Inc. for the first five months of 2002 and a balance sheet as of May 31, 2002.

Spier assembled the following information from the corporation's cash basis records for use in preparing the financial statements requested by the bank.

1. The bank statement showed the following 2002 deposits through May 31.

Sale of common shares	$ 2,500
Cash sales	22,770
Rebates from purchases	130
Collections on credit sales	5,320
Bank loan proceeds	2,880
	$33,600

2. The following amounts were disbursed through May 31, 2002.

Baking materials	$14,400
Rent	1,800
Salaries and wages	5,500
Maintenance	110
Utilities	4,000
Insurance premium	1,920
Equipment	3,000
Principal and interest payment on bank loan	312
Advertising	424
	$31,466

3. Unpaid invoices at May 31, 2002, were as follows.

Baking materials	$ 256
Utilities	270
	$ 526

4. Customer records showed uncollected sales of $4,226 at May 31, 2002.
5. Baking materials costing $1,840 were on hand at May 31, 2002. There were no materials in process or finished goods on hand at that date. No materials were on hand or in process and no finished goods were on hand at January 1, 2002.
6. The note evidencing the 3-year bank loan is dated January 1, 2002, and states a simple interest rate of 10%. The loan requires quarterly payments on April 1, July 1, October 1, and January 1 consisting of equal principal payments plus accrued interest since the last payment.
7. Anne Spier receives a salary of $750 on the last day of each month. The other employees had been paid through Friday, May 25, 2002, and were due an additional $240 on May 31, 2002.
8. New display cases and equipment costing $3,000 were purchased on January 2, 2002, and have an estimated useful life of five years. These are the only fixed assets currently used in the business. Straight-line amortization is to be used for book purposes.
9. Rent was paid for six months in advance on January 2, 2002.
10. A one-year insurance policy was purchased on January 2, 2002.
11. MAS Inc. is subject to an income tax rate of 20%.
12. Payments and collections pertaining to the unincorporated business through December 31, 2001 were not included in the corporation's records, and no cash was transferred from the unincorporated business to the corporation.

Instructions

Using the accrual basis of accounting, prepare for MAS Inc.:
(a) An income statement for the five months ended May 31, 2002.
(b) A balance sheet as of May 31, 2002.

(CMA adapted)

P5-8 Mansbridge Inc. had the following balance sheet at the end of operations for 2001:

MANSBRIDGE INC.
Balance Sheet
December 31, 2001

Cash	$ 20,000	Accounts payable	$ 30,000
Accounts receivable	21,200	Bonds payable	41,000
Investments	32,000	Common shares	100,000
Plant assets (net)	81,000	Retained earnings	23,200
Land	40,000		
	$194,200		$194,200

During 2002, the following occurred:

1. Mansbridge liquidated its investment portfolio at a loss of $3,000.
2. A tract of land was purchased for $38,000.
3. An additional $26,000 in common shares was issued.
4. Dividends totalling $10,000 were declared and paid to shareholders.
5. Net income for 2002 was $35,000, including $12,000 in amortization expense.
6. Land was purchased through the issuance of $30,000 in additional bonds.
7. At December 31, 2002, Cash was $66,200, Accounts Receivable was $42,000, and Accounts Payable was $40,000.

Instructions

(a) Prepare the balance sheet as it would appear at December 31, 2002.
(b) Prepare a statement of cash flows for the year 2002 for Mansbridge.
(c) Calculate the current and acid-test ratios for 2001 and 2002.
(d) Calculate Mansbridge's free cash flow and the current cash debt coverage ratio for 2002.
(e) What is the cash flow pattern? Discuss where the cash comes from and where it goes.

CONCEPTUAL CASES

C5-1 In an examination of Acevedo Corporation as of December 31, 2002, you have learned that the following situations exist. No entries have been made in the accounting records for these items.

1. The corporation erected its present factory building in 1987. Amortization was calculated by the straight-line method, using an estimated life of 35 years. Early in 2002, the board of directors conducted a careful survey and estimated that the factory building had a remaining useful life of 25 years as of January 1, 2002.
2. An additional assessment of 2001 income taxes was levied and paid in 2002.
3. When calculating the accrual for officers' salaries at December 31, 2002, it was discovered that the accrual for officers' salaries for December 31, 2001 had been overstated.
4. On December 15, 2002, Acevedo Corporation declared a 1% common shares dividend on its common shares outstanding, payable February 1, 2003, to the common shareholders of record December 31, 2002.
5. Acevedo Corporation, which is on a calendar-year basis, changed its inventory method as of January 1, 2002. The inventory for December 31, 2001 was costed by the average method, and the inventory for December 31, 2002 was costed by the FIFO method.

Instructions

Describe fully how each item above should be reported in the financial statements of Acevedo Corporation for the year 2002.

C5-2 Below are the titles of a number of debit and credit accounts as they might appear on the balance sheet of Allen Corporation as of October 31, 2002.

Debits	Credits
Interest accrued on government securities	Preferred shares
Notes receivable	11% first mortgage bonds due in 2009
Petty cash fund	Preferred dividend, payable Nov. 1, 2002
Government securities	Allowance for doubtful accounts receivable
Unamortized bond discount	Income taxes payable
Cash in bank	Customers' advances (on contracts to be
Land	completed next year)
Inventory of operating parts and supplies	Premium on bonds redeemable in 2002
Inventory of raw materials	Officers' 2002 bonus accrued
Patents	Accrued payroll
Cash and government bonds set aside	Notes payable
for property additions	Accrued interest on bonds
Investment in subsidiary	Accumulated amortization
Accounts receivable	Accounts payable
Government contracts	Contributed surplus
Regular	Accrued interest on notes payable
Instalments—due next year	8% first mortgage bonds to be redeemed
Instalments—due after next year	in 2002 out of current assets
Goodwill	
Inventory of finished goods	
Inventory of work in process	
Deficit	

Instructions

Select the current asset and current liability items from among these debits and credits. If there appear to be certain borderline cases that you are unable to classify without further information, mention them and explain your difficulty, or give your reasons for making questionable classifications, if any.

(AICPA adapted)

C5-3 The assets of LaShon Corporation are presented below (000s omitted):

LASHON CORPORATION
Balance Sheet (partial)
December 31, 2002

Assets		
Current assets		
Cash		$ 100,000
Unclaimed payroll cheques		27,500
Marketable securities (cost $30,000) at fair value		37,000
Accounts receivable (less bad debt reserve)		75,000
Inventories—at lower of cost (determined by the		
next-in, first-out method) or market		240,000
Total current assets		479,500
Tangible assets		
Land (less accumulated amortization)		80,000
Buildings and equipment	$800,000	
Less: Accumulated amortization	250,000	550,000
Net tangible assets		630,000
Long-term investments		
Shares and bonds		170,000
Other assets		
Discount on bonds payable		19,400
Sinking fund		975,000
Total other assets		994,400
Total assets		$2,273,900

Instructions

Indicate the deficiencies, if any, in the foregoing presentation of LaShon Corporation's assets. Marketable securities are temporary investments.

C5-4 Presented below is the balance sheet of Bellemy Corporation (000s omitted):

BELLEMY CORPORATION
Balance Sheet
December 31, 2002

Assets

Current assets

Cash	$26,000	
Marketable securities	18,000	
Accounts receivable	25,000	
Merchandise inventory	20,000	
Supplies inventory	4,000	
Investment in subsidiary company	20,000	$113,000
Investments		
Marketable securities		25,000
Property, plant, and equipment		
Buildings and land	91,000	
Less: Reserve for amortization	31,000	60,000
Other assets		
Cash surrender value of life insurance		19,000
		$217,000

Liabilities and Equity

Current liabilities

Accounts payable	$22,000	
Reserve for income taxes	15,000	
Customers' accounts with credit balances	1	$37,001
Deferred credits		
Unamortized premium on bonds payable		2,000
Long-term liabilities		
Bonds payable		60,000
Total liabilities		99,001
Shareholders' Equity		
Common shares issued	85,000	
Earned surplus	24,999	
Cash dividends declared	8,000	117,999
		$217,000

Instructions

Evaluate the balance sheet presented. State briefly the proper treatment of any item criticized.

C5-5 The financial statement below was prepared by employees of your client, Leacock Ltd. The statement is unaccompanied by notes.

LEACOCK LTD.
Balance Sheet
As of November 30, 2002

Current assets		
Cash	$ 100,000	
Accounts receivable (less allowance of $30,000 for doubtful accounts)	419,900	
Inventories	1,954,000	$2,473,900
Less: Current liabilities		
Accounts payable	306,400	
Accrued payroll	28,260	
Accrued interest on mortgage note	12,000	
Estimated taxes payable	66,000	412,660
Net working capital		2,061,240
Property, plant, and equipment (at cost)		

	Cost	Amortization	Value	
Land and buildings	$ 983,300	$410,000	$573,300	
Machinery and equipment	1,135,700	568,699	$567,001	
	$2,119,000	$978,699		1,140,301

Deferred charges		
Prepaid taxes and other expenses	23,700	
Unamortized discount on mortgage note	10,800	34,500
Total net working capital and noncurrent assets		3,236,041
Less: Deferred liabilities		
Mortgage note payable	300,000	
Unearned revenue	1,808,000	2,108,000
Total net assets		$1,128,041
Shareholders' equity		
10% Preferred shares		$ 300,000
Common shares		352,400
Contributed surplus		210,000
Retained earnings		265,641
Total shareholders' equity		$1,128,041

Instructions

Indicate the deficiencies, if any, in the balance sheet above in regard to form, terminology, descriptions, content, and the like.

C5-6 The partner in charge of the Spencer Corporation audit comes by your desk and leaves a letter he has started to the CEO and a copy of the cash flow statement for the year ended December 31, 2001. Because he must leave on an emergency, he asks you to finish the letter by explaining: (1) the disparity between net income and cash flow; (2) the importance of operating cash flow; (3) the sustainable source(s) of cash flow; and (4) possible suggestions to improve the cash position.

SPENCER CORPORATION
Statement of Cash Flows
For the Year Ended December 31, 2001

Cash flows from operating activities		
Net income		$100,000
Adjustments to reconcile net income to net cash provided by operating activities:		
Amortization expense	$ 11,000	
Loss on sale of fixed assets	5,000	
Increase in accounts receivable (net)	(40,000)	
Increase in inventory	(35,000)	
Decrease in accounts payable	(41,000)	(100,000)
Net cash provided by operating activities		– 0 –
Cash flows from investing activities		
Sale of plant assets	$ 25,000	
Purchase of equipment	(100,000)	
Purchase of land	(200,000)	
Net cash used by investing activities		(275,000)
Cash flows from financing activities		
Payment of dividends	$ (10,000)	
Redemption of bonds	(100,000)	
Net cash used by financing activities		(110,000)
Net decrease in cash		(385,000)
Cash balance, January 1, 2001		400,000
Cash balance, December 31, 2001		$ 15,000

Date
James Spencer, III, CEO
James Spencer Corporation
125 Bay Street
Toronto, ON

Dear Mr. Spencer:
I have good news and bad news about the financial statements for the year ended December 31, 2001. The good news is that net income of $100,000 is close to what we predicted in the strategic plan last year, indicating strong performance this year. The bad news is that the cash balance is seriously low. Enclosed is the Statement of Cash Flows, which best illustrates how both of these situations occurred simultaneously . . .

Instructions

Complete the letter to the CEO, including the four components requested by the partner.

Using Your Judgement

FINANCIAL REPORTING PROBLEM: CANADIAN TIRE CORPORATION LIMITED

The 2000 financial statements of **Canadian Tire** appear in Appendix 5B.

Instructions

Refer to those financial statements and the accompanying notes to answer the following questions.

(a) What alternative formats could the company have adopted for its balance sheet? Which format did it adopt?

(b) Identify the various techniques of disclosure the company might have used to disclose additional pertinent financial information. Which techniques does it use in its financials?

(c) What were the company's cash flows from its operating, investing, and financing activities for 2000? What were its trends in net cash provided by operating activities over the period 1999—2000? Why is cash generated from operating activities significantly different from net earnings in 2000? Explain why an increase in accounts payable is added back to net earnings in order to arrive at net cash provided by operating activities.

(d) Calculate the company's (1) current cash debt coverage ratio, (2) cash debt coverage ratio, and (3) free cash flow for 2000. What do these ratios indicate about the company's financial condition?

FINANCIAL STATEMENT ANALYSIS CASES

Case 1

Go to the Digital Tool and use information found there to answer the following questions about **Magna International Inc.**

(a) Calculate the ratios identified in Appendix 5A for both years presented in the financial statements.

(b) Comment on the company's liquidity, solvency, and profitability.

(c) Review the cash flow patterns on the cash flow statements and comment on where the company is getting its cash from and where it is spending it.

(d) Perform a "vertical analysis" of the assets. (Calculate all assets as a percentage of total assets). How has this changed from year to year?

Case 2

Go to the Digital Tool and use information found there to answer the following questions about **Maple Leaf Foods Inc.**

(a) Calculate the ratios identified in Appendix 5A for both years presented in the financial statements.

(b) Comment on the company's liquidity, solvency, and profitability.

(c) Review the cash flow patterns on the cash flow statements and comments on where the company is getting its cash from and where it is spending it.

(d) Perform a "vertical analysis" of the assets. (Calculate all assets as a percentage of total assets). How has this changed from year to year?

COMPARATIVE ANALYSIS CASE

Abitibi-Consolidated Inc. versus Domtar Inc.

Instructions

Go to the Digital Tool and use information found there to answer the following questions related to **Abitibi-Consolidated Inc.** and **Domtar Inc.** for the two years ended December 31, 1999.

(a) What type of balance sheet format do these two companies use?

(b) Calculate the current ratio and debt-to-equity ratios for each company. Based on this very brief analysis, which company is in better shape in terms of liquidity and solvency?

(c) Review the statement of cash flows. Describe the cash flow patterns for each company. Comment on these cash flow patterns, noting changes over the past two to three years.

RESEARCH CASES

Case 1

Obtain the 2000 Annual Report for **Canadian Tire** (see the company's website). Read the material on pages 1 to 33 and answer the following questions:

(a) Explain how Canadian Tire's business has changed in the past year or two. Discuss any strategic initiatives (e.g. expanding into new markets, downsizing, shifting their product focus, etc.)

(b) Looking at the 2000 financial statements, discuss whether (and how) these initiatives are reflected in the balance sheet, income statement, and statement of cash flows.

Case 2

Obtain the 1999 Annual Report for **Abitibi-Consolidated Inc.** (see the company's website). Read the material leading up to the financial statements and answer the following questions:

(a) Explain how the company's business has changed in the past year or two. Discuss any strategic initiatives (e.g. expanding into new markets, downsizing, shifting their product focus, etc.)

(b) Looking at the 1999 financial statements, discuss whether (and how) these initiatives are reflected in the balance sheet, income statement, and statement of cash flows.

INTERNATIONAL REPORTING CASE

Presented on the following page is the balance sheet for **J. Sainsbury PLC**, a British company.

Instructions

(a) Identify at least three differences in balance sheet reporting between British and Canadian firms, as shown in Sainsbury's balance sheet.

(b) Review Sainsbury's balance sheet and identify how the format of this financial statement provides useful information, as illustrated in the chapter.

J. SAINSBURY, PLC
Balance Sheets
3 April 1999

1999	£m
Fixed assets	
Tangible assets	6,409
Investments	41
	6,450
Current assets	
Stocks	843
Debtors	249
Investments	17
Sainsbury's Bank	1,766
Cash at bank and in hand	725
	3,600
Creditors: due within one year	
Sainsbury's Bank	(1,669)
Other	(2,880)
	(4,549)
Net current liabilities	(949)
Total assets less current liabilities	5,501
Creditors: due after one year	(804)
Provisions for liabilities and charges	(8)
Total net assets	4,689
Capital and reserves	
Called up share capital	480
Share premium account	1,359
Revaluation reserve	38
Profit and loss account	2,767
Equity shareholders' funds	4,644
Minority equity interest	45
Total capital employed	4,689

ETHICS CASE

Andrea Pafko, corporate comptroller for Nicholson Industries, is trying to decide how to present "Property, plant, and equipment" in the balance sheet. She realizes that the statement of cash flows will show that the company made a significant investment in purchasing new equipment this year, but overall she knows the company's plant assets are rather old. She feels that she can disclose one figure titled "Property, plant, and equipment, net of amortization," and the result will be a low figure. However, it will not disclose the assets' age. If she chooses to show the cost less accumulated amortization, the assets' age will be apparent. She proposes the following:

Property, plant, and equipment, net of amortization	$10,000,000
rather than	
Property, plant and equipment	$50,000,000
Less: Accumulated amortization	(40,000,000)
Net book value	$10,000,000

Instructions
Answer the following questions:

(a) What are the ethical issues involved?

(b) What should Pafko do?

CHAPTER 6

Revenue Recognition

LEARNING OBJECTIVES

· ·

After studying this chapter, you should be able to:

1. Apply the revenue recognition principle.

2. Describe accounting issues involved with revenue recognition for sale of goods.

3. Explain accounting for consignment sales.

4. Describe accounting issues involved with revenue recognition for services and long-term contracts.

5. Apply the percentage-of-completion method for long-term contracts.

6. Apply the completed-contract method for long-term contracts.

7. Account for losses on long-term contracts.

8. Discuss how to deal with measurement uncertainty.

9. Discuss how to deal with collection uncertainty.

10. Explain and apply the instalment sales method of accounting.

11. Explain and apply the cost recovery method of accounting.

Preview of Chapter 6

"When should revenue be recognized?" This is a complex question. The answer lies with analysing the earnings process. The purpose of this chapter is to provide you with general principles used in recognizing revenues for most business transactions. The content and organization of the chapter are as follows:

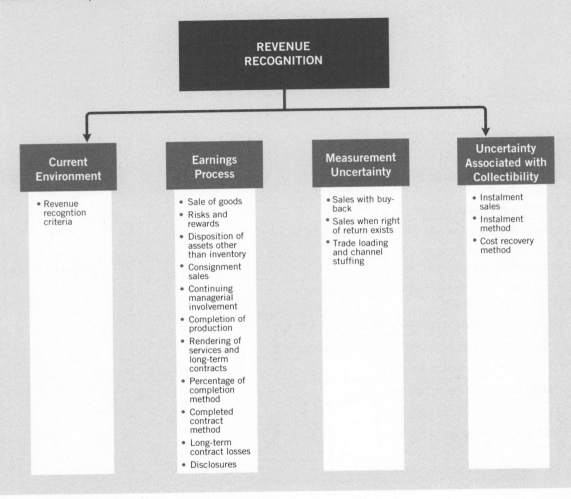

Go to the Digital Tool for examples of revenue recognition policies

THE CURRENT ENVIRONMENT

The issue of the "proper" time to recognize revenue has received considerable attention over the last few years. A series of highly publicized cases of companies recognizing revenue prematurely has caused the OSC and SEC to increase their enforcement actions in this area. In some of these cases, significant adjustments to previously issued financial statements were made.[1]

---

[1] The OSC completed a review of revenue recognition practices in 2001 as it felt that some users were placing undue emphasis on revenue growth as a key indicator of value and performance. The review targeted 75 public companies in the technology and related areas. The survey findings indicated that there was need for improving the nature and extent of disclosure and the OSC identified cases that were later investigated to determine whether financial reporting practices related to revenue recognition reflected appropriate application of relevant GAAP.

Revenue Recognition Criteria

Revenues are **realized** when goods and services are exchanged for cash or claims to cash (receivables). Revenue **recognition**[2] is governed by **general** principles and therefore there is a wide array of **practical applications**. Different companies interpret these principles in different ways.[3] Revenues are **recognized** according to the revenue recognition principle. Under the **revenue recognition principle**, revenue is recognized when **performance** is substantially complete and when **collection** is reasonably assured.[4]

The concept of **performance** has two components: the company has **earned** the revenues and the revenues are **measurable**. Performance occurs when the entity can **measure** the revenue and when it has substantially accomplished what it must do to be entitled to the benefits represented by the revenues; that is, when the **earnings process is complete or virtually complete**.[5] Both these components are important. If a company cannot **measure** the transaction, then either there is too much uncertainty surrounding the transaction or the company has not completed all that it has to do to earn the revenues.

In short, revenues are recognized when the following criteria are met:

1. **Earnings process** is substantially complete
2. **Measurability** is reasonably assured
3. **Collectibility** is reasonably assured[6]

Each of these will be examined in more detail below.

OBJECTIVE 1

Apply the revenue recognition principle.

UNDERLYING CONCEPTS

Revenues are increases in economic resources, either by an entity's inflows or other enhancements of assets of an entity or settlement of its liabilities resulting from its ordinary activities.

IAS NOTE

IAS 18 also requires measurability, both of revenues and related costs.

OBJECTIVE 2

Describe accounting issues involved with revenue recognition for sale of goods.

EARNINGS PROCESS

What does the company do to create valuable products or services that customers will pay for? How does it add value? **Earnings process** is a term that refers to the actions that a company undertakes to add value. It is unique to each company. In identifying and reviewing an entity's earnings process, it is useful to focus on which industry the company operates in, including whether it sells **goods** or **services** (or both). Different industries add value in different ways.

Sale of Goods

A manufacturing company such as **Magnotta Winery Corporation** makes wine (among other products). Its business involves the following steps as shown in Illustration 6-1.

---

[2] Recognition is "the process of including an item in the financial statements of an entity" (*CICA Handbook*, Section 1000). Recognition is not the same as realization, although the two are sometimes used interchangeably in accounting literature and practice. Realization is "the process of converting noncash resources and rights into money and is most precisely used in accounting and financial reporting to refer to sales of assets for cash or claims to cash" (SFAC No. 3, par. 83).

[3] Because of this and partially due to the increased profile of the revenue recognition issues with the securities commissions, companies generally disclose the revenue recognition method in their notes to the financial statements. The number of companies disclosing their policies has increased 25% for the period 1996 to 1999 (*Financial Reporting in Canada, 2000*, CICA, 2000, p. 61.).

[4] *CICA Handbook*, Section 3400, par. .06.

[5] Ibid. par. .07.

[6] It should be noted that the SEC believes that revenue is realized or realizable and earned when all of the following criteria are met: (1) Persuasive evidence of an arrangement exists; (2) delivery has occurred or services have been rendered; (3) the seller's price to the buyer is fixed or determinable; and (4) collectability is reasonably assured. See "Revenue Recognition in Financial Statements," SEC Staff Accounting Bulletin No. 101, December 3, 1999. The SEC has provided more specific guidance because general criteria are often difficult to interpret.

ILLUSTRATION 6-1
Magnotta Winery's Earnings
Process

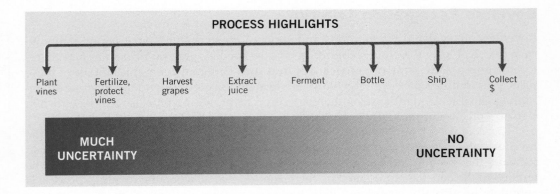

Magnotta must **perform** all of these acts in order to **earn** the revenues from sales of its wine. At the early points in the earnings process, there is significant **uncertainty** as to how much product will be produced and at what quality. What if the vines get diseased? What if temperatures are too low or there is excess rainfall? What if there is no market for the product? Moving along the earnings process timeline (from left to right), the conditions underlying the uncertainty resolve themselves. At the far right-hand side of the earnings process, all uncertainty as to ability to deliver, measurability, and collectibility is eliminated once the product is shipped and paid for.

Often, there is one main act or **critical event** in the earnings process that signals **substantial completion** or **performance**. At this point, although all uncertainty is not eliminated, it is at an **acceptable level** for the revenues to be recognized under accrual accounting. In businesses involving **sale of goods**, this is normally at the **point of delivery**. This is generally when the **risks and rewards of ownership** pass. Where the earnings process has a critical event, it is often referred to as a **discrete earnings process**.

Risks and Rewards of Ownership

The concept of **risks and rewards (benefits) of ownership** is a core concept in financial reporting. It helps establish ownership[7] and when ownership passes from one party to another.

Illustration 6-2 depicts some risks and rewards associated with the sale of wine at Magnotta.

ILLUSTRATION 6-2
Risk and Rewards of Ownership—
Case of Wine

Risks	Rewards
— wine will not age well and thus will decline in value — wine will be stolen/vandalized — improper storage	— wine will age well and appreciate in value — consumption — wine inventory may be used as collateral for bank loan — wine may be sold for cash

In determining who has the risks and rewards of ownership and hence whether a sale has occurred at the point of delivery, it is important to look at who has **possession** of the goods and who has **legal title**. The risks and rewards usually stem from these two factors e.g., Magnotta is not entitled to **sell** or **pledge the inventory as collateral** unless it has **legal title** to it. Likewise **legal title** and **possession** expose the company to risk of loss.

When determining whether **legal title** to the product has passed to the buyer, consider the terms of sale e.g., **FOB shipping point** means that the legal title belongs to the buyer when the goods leave the shipping docks. If the terms are **FOB destination**, then the legal title does not pass until the goods reach the customer's location.

---

[7] That is, in order to recognize an **asset** on the balance sheet, a company must prove that it has the risks and rewards of ownership. If it no longer has the risks and rewards, they have been passed on to another party and a disposition has occurred.

Disposition of Assets other than Inventory

The risks and rewards concept deals not only with sale of inventory as in the case of Magnotta's wine inventory, but also with items disposed of that are not sold as part of the normal earnings process, e.g., income producing or capital assets. In these cases, a **gain**[8] would be generated (as opposed to **revenues**). Care should be taken to establish that in **substance**, a sale has actually occurred. In certain cases, a company may sell a fixed asset and receive a note receivable that is secured by the asset itself. If very little other consideration is received, has the asset really been sold? Have the **risks and rewards** really passed?

UNDERLYING CONCEPTS

The legal form of the transaction is a sale. However, analysis of the economic substance might show that this is not a sale.

If the purchaser does not pay, legal title to the asset may revert back to the vendor **at little or no loss to the purchaser**. This indicates that the risks and rewards may still rest with the vendor. In general, the purchaser must demonstrate **substantial commitment to pay**. This is normally evidenced when the purchaser makes a commitment with a fair value of not less than 15% of the consideration's fair value. An example of this is when the purchaser pays nonrefundable cash equal to at least 15% of the total consideration.[9]

Consignment Sales

Under some distribution arrangements, the point of delivery does not provide evidence of full **performance** because the vendor **retains legal title** to the goods. This specialized method of marketing for certain types of products makes use of a device known as a **consignment**. Under this arrangement, the consignor (e.g., manufacturer) ships merchandise to the consignee (e.g., dealer), who acts as an **agent** for the consignor in selling the merchandise. Both consignor and consignee are interested in selling—the former to make a **profit** or develop a market, the latter to make a **commission** on the sales.

OBJECTIVE 3

Explain accounting for consignment sales.

The consignee accepts the merchandise and agrees to exercise due diligence in caring for and selling it. Cash received from customers is remitted to the consignor by the consignee, after deducting a sales commission and any chargeable expenses. Revenue is recognized only after the consignor receives **notification of sale**. The merchandise is carried throughout the consignment as the consignor's **inventory**, separately classified as Merchandise on Consignment. It is not recorded as an asset on the consignee's books.

Upon sale of the merchandise, the consignee has a liability for the net amount due the consignor. The consignor periodically receives from the consignee a report that shows the merchandise received, merchandise sold, expenses chargeable to the consignment, and the cash remitted.

To illustrate consignment accounting entries, assume that Nelba Manufacturing Corp. ships merchandise costing $36,000 on consignment to Best Value Stores. Nelba pays $3,750 of freight costs and Best Value pays $2,250 for local advertising costs that are reimbursable from Nelba. By the end of the period, two-thirds of the consigned merchandise has been sold for $40,000 cash. Best Value notifies Nelba of the sales, retains a 10% commission, and remits the cash due Nelba. The following journal entries would be made by the consignor (Nelba) and the consignee (Best Value):

Nelba Mfg. Corp. (Consignor)		Best Value Stores (Consignee)	
Shipment of consigned merchandise			
Inventory on Consignment	36,000	No entry (record memo of merchandise received)	
Finished Goods Inventory	36,000		
Payment of freight costs by consignor			
Inventory on Consignment	3,750	No entry.	
Cash	3,750		

ILLUSTRATION 6-3
Entries for Consignment Sales

[8] Gains (as contrasted with revenues) commonly result from transactions and other events that do not involve an "earning process." For gain recognition, being **earned** is generally less significant than being **realized or realizable**.

[9] *CICA Handbook*, EIC Abstract #79

ILLUSTRATION 6-3
Entries for Consignment Sales
(continued)

Nelba Mfg. Corp. (Consignor)		Best Value Stores (Consignee)	
Shipment of consigned merchandise			
Payment of advertising by consignee			
No entry until notified.		Receivable from Consignor	2,250
		Cash		2,250
Sales of consigned merchandise			
No entry until notified.		Cash	40,000
		Payable to Consignor		40,000
Notification of sales and expenses and remittance of amount due			
Cash	33,750	Payable to Consignor	40,000
Advertising Expense	2,250	Receivable from	
Commission Expense	4,000	Consignor		2,250
		Commission Revenue		4,000
Revenue from			
Consignment Sales		40,000	Cash		33,750
Adjustment of inventory on consignment for cost of sales			
Cost of Goods Sold	26,500	No entry.	
Inventory on Consignment		26,500		
[2/3 ($36,000 + $3,750) = $26,500]			

Why would companies use consignment to sell their goods? The company selling the goods will often use this type of distribution mechanism to induce consignees to take their goods and sell them. Under the consignment arrangement, the manufacturer (consignor) retains the **risk** that the merchandise might not sell and relieves the dealer (consignee) of the need to commit part of its working capital to inventory. Presumably, if the products sell very well to third parties, the consignor could push for the consignee to actually purchase the good outright. A variety of different systems and account titles are used to record consignments, but they all share the common goal of postponing the recognition of revenue until it is known that a sale to a third party has occurred.

Continuing Managerial Involvement

UNDERLYING CONCEPTS

The legal form of these transactions is a sale. However, the economic substance may be that the seller still retains the risks and rewards of ownership.

In some cases, the vendor **retains some involvement in the product sold**, such as the responsibility to fix the product if it breaks or to provide ongoing product support to the customer.

For instance, in order to induce a sale, the company might promise that the purchaser will receive a certain amount on resale of the asset (guaranteed minimum resale value). In this case the seller still retains risk of value loss and consideration should be given to whether a sale should be recognized.[10] Alternatively, the vendor may promise, in the case of a sold building, certain cash flows from the building (e.g., rent). Has a real sale occurred? As a general rule, in order to recognize revenues, the seller should "retain no continuing managerial involvement in or effective control of the goods transferred to a degree normally associated with ownership."[11] The determination of whether continuing managerial involvement precludes revenue recognition is a matter of professional judgement.

Completion of Production

Revenue may be recognized at the **completion of production** even though no customer has yet been identified. Examples of such situations involve precious metals or agricultural products with assured prices and ready markets. Revenue is recognized when

---

[10] *CICA Handbook*, EIC Abstract #84, suggests that no sale should be recognized.

[11] *CICA Handbook*, Section 3400, par. .07.

these metals are mined or crops harvested because the sales price is reasonably assured, the units are interchangeable, and no significant costs are involved in distributing the product. Thinking back to Illustration 6-1, the argument is that earlier recognition is acceptable under accrual accounting as there is **little or no uncertainty** with respect to **measurement** (price) or finding a customer. Performance is substantially complete.

Rendering of Services and Long-term Contracts

Unlike earnings processes relating solely to sales of goods, where the **benchmark/critical event** for revenue recognition is normally "delivery," the focus in providing services is on **performance of the service**. Often the earnings process has **numerous significant events** as opposed to one **critical event or discrete act**. The earnings process is said to be an ongoing or continuous earnings process as opposed to a **discrete earnings process**.

OBJECTIVE 4

Describe accounting issues involved with revenue recognition for services and long-term contracts.

Consider a public accounting firm, where an auditor accepts an engagement to provide assurance to a company's shareholders regarding the company's financial position and operations. The earnings process is noted in Illustration 6-4.

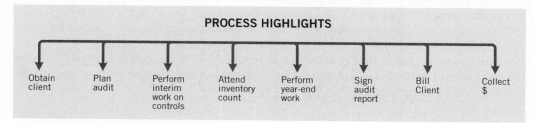

PROCESS HIGHLIGHTS

Obtain client — Plan audit — Perform interim work on controls — Attend inventory count — Perform year-end work — Sign audit report — Bill Client — Collect $

ILLUSTRATION 6-4
Earnings Process of Public Accounting Firm in Providing Assurance to Client on Financial Statements

Businesses that provide **services** are different from businesses that sell **goods** since the **customer/client** is usually identified before the services are performed. (In the case of sale of goods, as noted in Illustration 6-1, the goods are produced and then a customer found). Often a **contract**, establishing the terms of the relationship/engagement, is signed upfront. This contract establishes the nature of the services to be provided and the value of the services, among other things. In the case of the auditor, an **engagement letter** would be signed upfront and serves as the contract.

Consider the **performance "test."** When does performance occur in the earnings process noted in illustration 6-4? Should the company wait until the audit report is signed (engagement **completed**) before recognizing the revenue? There is no easy answer. The issue becomes even more complicated if the process is a **long-term process** (as many service contracts are) as the services are performed over longer periods of time, often **spanning one or more fiscal year ends**. With these types of contracts, there may also be a "**service**" component **and** a "**goods**" component, e.g., a construction company building a road for the government.

Long-term contracts such as construction-type contracts, development of military and commercial aircraft, weapons delivery systems, and space exploration hardware frequently provide that the seller (builder) may **bill the purchaser** at intervals, as various points in the project are reached (referred to as billings). When the project consists of separable units such as a group of buildings or kilometres of roadway, **passage of title** and **billing** may take place at stated stages of completion, such as the completion of each building unit or every 10 km of road. Such contract provisions provide for delivery in instalments, and the accounting records may reflect this by recording sales when instalments are "delivered."

Two distinctly different methods of accounting for long-term construction contracts are recognized.[12] They are:

1. Percentage-of-Completion Method. Revenues and gross profit are recognized each period based upon the construction progress; that is, the percentage of com-

---

[12] *CICA Handbook*, Section 3400, par. .08.

OBJECTIVE 5

Apply the percentage-of-completion method for long-term contracts.

pletion. Construction costs plus gross profit earned to date are accumulated in an inventory account (Construction in Process), and progress billings are accumulated in a contra inventory account (Billings on Construction in Process).

2. **Completed-Contract Method.** Revenues and gross profit are recognized only when the contract is completed. Construction costs are accumulated in an inventory account (Construction in Process), and progress billings are accumulated in a contra inventory account (Billings on Construction in Process).

The method that best relates the revenues to be recognized to the work performed should be used.[13] In other words, if performance requires **numerous ongoing acts (continuous earnings process)** the percentage-of-completion method should be used as long as the company is able to **measure** the transaction. Alternatively, the completed contract method should be used where performance consists of **a single act (discrete earnings process)** or when there is a continuous earnings process but the revenues are not **measurable**.

The rationale for using percentage-of-completion accounting is that under most of these contracts, the buyer and seller have obtained **enforceable rights**. The buyer has the **legal right to require specific performance** on the contract; the seller has the **right to require progress payments** that provide evidence of the buyer's ownership interest. As a result, a continuous sale occurs as the work progresses, and revenue should be recognized accordingly.

The presumption is that percentage of completion is the better method and that the completed-contract method should be used only when the percentage-of-completion method is inappropriate.[14]

Percentage-of-Completion Method

The **percentage-of-completion method** recognizes revenues, costs, and gross profit as progress is made toward completion on a long-term contract. To defer recognition of these items until completion of the entire contract is to misrepresent the efforts (costs) and accomplishments (revenues) of the interim accounting periods. In order to apply the percentage-of-completion method, one must have some **basis or standard for measuring the progress toward completion at particular interim dates**.

Measuring progress toward completion requires significant **judgement**. Costs, labour hours worked, tonnes produced etc., are often used. The various measures are identified and classified as either input or output measures.[15] Input measures (costs incurred, labour hours worked) measure **efforts** devoted to a contract. Output measures (tonnes produced, storeys of a building completed, kilometres of a highway completed) measure **results**. Neither is universally applicable to all long-term projects; their use requires careful tailoring to the circumstances and the exercise of **judgement**.

Use of either input or output measures has certain disadvantages. The input measure is based on an established relationship between a unit of input and productivity. If inefficiencies cause the productivity relationship to change, inaccurate measurements result. Another potential problem, called "front-end loading," produces higher estimates of completion by virtue of incurring significant costs upfront. Some early-stage construction costs should be disregarded if they do not relate to contract performance; for example, costs of uninstalled materials or costs of subcontracts not yet performed.

Output measures can result in inaccurate measures if the units used are not comparable in time, effort, or cost to complete. For example, using storeys completed can be deceiving; completing the first storey of an eight-storey building may require more than one-eighth the total cost because of the substructure and foundation construction.

---

13 *CICA Handbook*, Section 3400, par. .08

14 *Accounting Trends and Techniques—1999* reports that, of the 91 of its 600 sample companies that referred to long-term construction contracts, 88 used the percentage-of-completion method and 1 used the completed-contract method (2 were not determinable).

15 *CICA Handbook*, EIC Abstract #78.

One of the more popular input measures used to determine the progress toward completion is cost, sometimes referred to as the cost-to-cost basis. Under the cost-to-cost basis, the percentage of completion is measured by comparing **costs incurred to date** with the most recent estimate of the **total costs** to complete the contract, as shown in the following formula:

$$\frac{\text{Costs incurred to date}}{\text{Most recent estimate of total costs}} = \text{percent complete}$$

ILLUSTRATION 6-5
Formula for Percentage of Completion, Cost-to-Cost Basis

The percentage that costs incurred bear to total estimated costs is applied to the total revenue or the estimated total gross profit on the contract in arriving at the revenue or the gross profit amounts to be recognized to date.

Percent complete	×	Estimated total revenue (for gross profit)	=	Revenue (or gross profit) to be recognized to date

ILLUSTRATION 6-6
Formula for Total Revenue to Be Recognized to Date

To find the amounts of revenue and gross profit recognized each period, we would need to subtract total revenue or gross profit recognized in prior periods, as shown in the following formula:

Revenue (or gross profit) to be recognized to date	−	Revenue (or gross profit) recognized in prior periods	=	Current period revenue (or gross profit)

ILLUSTRATION 6-7
Formula for Amount of Current Period Revenue, Cost-to-Cost Basis

Illustration of Percentage-of-Completion Method—Cost-to-Cost Basis

To illustrate the percentage-of-completion method, assume that the Hardhat Construction Ltd. (Hardhat) has a contract starting July 2001 to construct a $4.5 million bridge that is expected to be completed in October 2003, at an estimated cost of $4 million. The following data pertain to the construction period (note that by the end of 2002 the estimated total cost has increased from $4 million to $4,050,000):

	2001	2002	2003
Costs to date	$1,000,000	$2,916,000	$4,050,000
Estimated costs to complete	3,000,000	1,134,000	—
Progress billings during the year	900,000	2,400,000	1,200,000
Cash collected during the year	750,000	1,750,000	2,000,000

The percent complete would be calculated as follows:

	2001	2002	2003
Contract price	$4,500,000	$4,500,000	$4,500,000
Less estimated cost:			
Costs to date	1,000,000	2,916,000	4,050,000
Estimated costs to complete	3,000,000	1,134,000	—
Estimated total costs	4,000,000	4,050,000	4,050,000
Estimated total gross profit	$ 500,000	$ 450,000	$ 450,000
Percent complete:	25% $\left(\dfrac{\$1,000,000}{\$4,000,000}\right)$	72% $\left(\dfrac{\$2,916,000}{\$4,050,000}\right)$	100% $\left(\dfrac{\$4,050,000}{\$4,050,000}\right)$

ILLUSTRATION 6-8
Application of Percentage-of-Completion Method, Cost-to-Cost Basis

Based on the data above, the following entries would be prepared to record (1) the costs of construction, (2) progress billings, and (3) collections. These entries appear as summaries of the many transactions that would be entered individually as they occur during the year:

ILLUSTRATION 6-9
Journal Entries—Percentage-of-Completion Method, Cost-to-Cost Basis

	2001		2002		2003	
To record cost of construction:						
Construction in Process	1,000,000		1,916,000		1,134,000	
Materials, Cash, Payables, etc.		1,000,000		1,916,000		1,134,000
To record progress billings:						
Accounts Receivable	900,000		2,400,000		1,200,000	
assets Billings on Construction in Process		900,000		2,400,000		1,200,000
To record collections:						
Cash	750,000		1,750,000		2,000,000	
Accounts Receivable		750,000		1,750,000		2,000,000

In this illustration, the costs incurred to date as a proportion of the estimated total costs to be incurred on the project are a measure of the extent of progress toward completion. The estimated revenue and gross profit to be recognized for each year are calculated as follows:

ILLUSTRATION 6-10
Percentage-of-Completion, Revenue and Gross Profit, by Year

	2001	2002	2003
Revenue recognized in:			
2001 $4,500,000 x 25%	$1,125,000		
2002 $4,500,000 x 72%		$3,240,000	
Less: Revenue recognized in 2001		1,125,000	
Revenue in 2002		$2,115,000	
2003 $4,500,000 x 100%			$4,500,000
Less: Revenue recognized in 2001 and 2002			3,240,000
Revenue in 2003			$1,260,000
Gross profit recognized in:			
2001 $500,000 x 25%	$ 125,000		
2002 $450,000 x 72%		$ 324,000	
Less: Gross profit recognized in 2001		125,000	
Gross profit in 2002		$ 199,000	
2003 $450,000 x 100%			$ 450,000
Less: Gross profit recognized in 2001 and 2002			$ 324,000
Gross profit in 2003			$ 126,000

The entries to recognize revenue and gross profit each year and to record completion and final approval of the contract are shown below.

ILLUSTRATION 6-11
Journal Entries to Recognize Revenue and Gross Profit and to Record Contract Completion-Percentage-of-Completion Method, Cost-to-Cost Basis

	2001		2002		2003	
To recognize revenue and gross profit:						
Construction in Process (gross profit)	125,000		199,000		126,000	
Construction Expenses	1,000,000		1,916,000		1,134,000	
Revenue from Long-Term Contract		1,125,000		2,115,000		1,260,000
To record completion of the contract:						
Billings on Construction in Process					4,500,000	
Construction in Process						4,500,000

Note that gross profit as calculated above is debited to Construction in Process, while Revenue from Long-Term Contract is credited for the amounts as calculated above. The difference between the amounts recognized each year for revenue and gross profit is debited to a nominal account, Construction Expenses (similar to cost of goods sold in a manufacturing enterprise), which is reported in the income statement. That amount is the actual cost of construction incurred in that period. For example, in the Hardhat cost-to-cost illustration, the actual costs of $1 million in 2001 are used to calculate both the gross profit of $125,000 and the percent complete (25%).

Costs must continue to be accumulated in the Construction in Process account to maintain a record of total costs incurred (plus recognized profit) to date. Although theoretically a series of "sales" takes place using the percentage-of-completion method, the inventory cost cannot be removed until the construction is completed and transferred to the new owner. The Construction in Process account would include the following summarized entries over the term of the construction project.

Construction in Process				
2001 construction costs	$1,000,000	12/31/03	to close	
2001 recognized gross profit	125,000		completed	
2002 construction costs	1,916,000		project	$4,500,000
2002 recognized gross profit	199,000			
2003 construction costs	1,134,000			
2003 recognized gross profit	126,000			
Total	$4,500,000		Total	$4,500,000

ILLUSTRATION 6-12
Content of Construction in Process Account—Percentage-of-Completion Method

The Hardhat illustration contained a change in estimate in the second year, 2002, when the estimated total costs increased from $4 million to $4,050,000. By adjusting the percent completed to the new estimate of total costs and then deducting the amount of revenues and gross profit recognized in prior periods from revenues and gross profit calculated for progress to date, the change in estimate is accounted for in a cumulative catch-up manner. That is, the change in estimate is accounted for in the period of change so that the balance sheet at the end of that period and the accounting in subsequent periods are the same as if the revised estimate had been the original estimate.

Financial Statement Presentation—Percentage of Completion

Generally when a receivable from a sale is recorded, the Inventory account is reduced. In this case, however, both the receivable and the inventory continue to be carried. Subtracting the balance in the Billings account from Construction in Process avoids doublecounting the inventory. During the life of the contract, the difference between the Construction in Process and the Billings on Construction in Process accounts is reported in the balance sheet as a **current asset** if a debit, and as a **current liability** if a credit.

When the costs incurred plus the gross profit recognized to date (the balance in Construction in Process) exceed the billings, this excess is reported as a **current asset** entitled "Cost and Recognized Profit in Excess of Billings." The unbilled portion of revenue recognized to date can be calculated at any time by subtracting the billings to date from the revenue recognized to date as illustrated below for 2001 for Hardhat:

Contract revenue recognized to date: $4,500,000 × $\frac{\$1,000,000}{\$4,000,000}$ = $1,125,000

Billings to date 900,000

Unbilled revenue $ 225,000

ILLUSTRATION 6-13
Calculation of Unbilled Contract Price at 12/31/01

When the billings exceed costs incurred and gross profit to date, this excess is reported as a **current liability** entitled "Billings in Excess of Costs and Recognized Profit." Separate disclosures of the dollar volume of billings and costs are preferable to a summary presentation of the net difference. Note that if the contract will extend beyond the year, the net amount may be classified as long-term.

Using data from the previous illustration, Hardhat would report the status and results of its long-term construction activities under the percentage-of-completion method as follows:

ILLUSTRATION 6-14
Financial Statement Presentation—
Percentage-of-Completion Method

HARDHAT CONSTRUCTION LTD.

Income Statement	2001	2002	2003
Revenue from long-term contracts	$1,125,000	$2,115,000	$1,260,000
Costs of construction	1,000,000	1,916,000	1,134,000
Gross profit	$ 125,000	$ 199,000	$ 126,000

Balance Sheet (12/31)	2001	2002
Current assets		
Accounts receivable	$ 150,000	$ 800,000
Inventories		
Construction in process $1,125,000		
Less: Billings 900,000		
Costs and recognized profit in excess of billings	$ 225,000	
Current liabilities		
Billings ($3,300,000) in excess of costs and recognized profit ($3,240,000)		$ 60,000

Note 1. *Summary of significant accounting policies.*
LONG-TERM CONSTRUCTION CONTRACTS. The company recognizes revenues and reports profits from long-term construction contracts, its principal business, under the percentage-of-completion method of accounting. These contracts generally extend for periods in excess of one year. The amounts of revenues and profits recognized each year are based on the ratio of costs incurred to the total estimated costs. Costs included in construction in process include direct materials, direct labour, and project-related overhead. Corporate general and administrative expenses are charged to the periods as incurred and are not allocated to construction contracts.

Completed-Contract Method

OBJECTIVE 6

Apply the completed-contract method for long-term contracts.

UNDERLYING CONCEPTS

The completed-contract method does not violate the matching concept because the costs are also deferred until the contract completion.

Under the **completed-contract method**, revenue and gross profit are recognized when the contract is completed. Costs of long-term contracts in process and current billings are accumulated, but there are no interim charges or credits to income statement accounts for revenues, costs, and gross profit.

The principal advantage of the completed-contract method is that reported revenue is based on final results rather than on estimates of unperformed work. Its major disadvantage is that it **does not reflect current performance when the period of a contract extends into more than one accounting period**. Although operations may be fairly uniform during the contract period, revenue is not reported until the year of completion, creating a **distortion of earnings**.[16]

The annual entries to record costs of construction, progress billings, and collections from customers would be identical to those illustrated under the percentage-of-completion method with the significant exclusion of the recognition of revenue and gross profit. For the bridge project of Hardhat illustrated on the preceding pages, the following entries are made in 2003 under the completed-contract method to recognize revenue and costs and to close out the inventory and billing accounts:

Billings on Construction in Process	4,500,000	
Revenue from Long-Term Contracts		4,500,000
Costs of Construction	4,050,000	
Construction in Process		4,050,000

Comparing the two methods in relation to the same bridge project, Hardhat would have recognized gross profit as follows:

---

[16] In fact, *CICA Handbook* EIC Abstract #65 states that law firms must use the percentage-of-completion method, the completed-contract method being inappropriate.

	Percentage-of-Completion	Completed-Contract
2001	$125,000	$ 0
2002	199,000	0
2003	126,000	450,000

ILLUSTRATION 6-15
Comparison of Gross Profit
Recognized under Different
Methods

Hardhat would report its long-term construction activities as follows:

HARDHAT CONSTRUCTION LTD.

ILLUSTRATION 6-16
Financial Statement
Presentation-Completed-Contract
Method

Income Statement	2001	2002	2003
Revenue from long-term contracts	—	—	$4,500,000
Costs of construction	—	—	4,050,000
Gross profit	—	—	$ 450,000

Balance Sheet (12/31)	2001	2002
Current assets		
Accounts receivable	$150,000	$800,000
Inventories		
Construction in process $1,000,000		
Less: Billings 900,000		
Unbilled contract costs	$100,000	
Current liabilities		
Billings ($3,300,000) in excess of contract costs ($2,916,000)		$384,000

Note 1. *Summary of significant accounting policies.*

LONG-TERM CONSTRUCTION CONTRACTS. The company recognizes revenues and reports profits from long-term construction contracts, its principal business, under the completed-contract method. These contracts generally extend for periods in excess of one year. Contract costs and billings are accumulated during the periods of construction, but no revenues or profits are recognized until contract completion. Costs included in construction in process include direct material, direct labour, and project-related overhead. Corporate general and administrative expenses are charged to the periods as incurred.

Long-Term Contract Losses

Two types of losses can become evident under long-term contracts:

1. *Loss in Current Period on a Profitable Contract.* This condition arises when, during construction, there is a significant increase in the estimated total contract costs but the increase does not eliminate all profit on the contract. Under the percentage-of-completion method only, the estimated cost increase requires a current period adjustment of excess gross profit recognized on the project in prior periods. This adjustment is recorded as a loss in the current period because it is a change in accounting estimate (discussed in Chapter 22).

2. *Loss on an Unprofitable Contract.* Cost estimates at the end of the current period may indicate that a loss will result on completion of the entire contract. Under both the percentage-of-completion and the completed-contract methods, the entire expected contract loss must be recognized in the current period.

The treatment described for unprofitable contracts is consistent with the accounting custom of anticipating foreseeable losses to avoid overstatement of current and future income (conservatism).

OBJECTIVE 7
· ·
Account for losses on long-term contracts.

UNDERLYING CONCEPTS

Conservatism justifies recognizing the losses immediately. Loss recognition does not require realization; it only requires evidence that an impairment of asset value has occurred.

Loss in Current Period

To illustrate a loss in the current period on a contract expected to be profitable upon completion, assume that on December 31, 2002, Hardhat estimates the costs to complete the bridge contract at $1,468,962 instead of $1,134,000. Assuming all other data are the same as before, Hardhat would calculate the percent complete and recognize the loss as shown in Illustration 6-17. Compare these caculations with those for 2002 in Illustration 6-8. The "percent complete" has dropped from 72% to 66½% due to the increase in estimated future costs to complete the contract.

The 2002 loss of $48,500 is a cumulative adjustment of the "excessive" gross profit recognized on the contract in 2001. Instead of restating the prior period, the prior period misstatement is absorbed entirely in the current period. In this illustration, the adjustment was large enough to result in recognition of a loss.

ILLUSTRATION 6-17
Calculation of Recognizable Loss, 2002—Loss in Current Period

Cost to date (12/31/02)	$2,916,000
Estimated costs to complete (revised)	1,468,962
Estimated total costs	$4,384,962
Percent complete ($2,916,000 / $4,384,962)	66½%
Revenue recognized in 2002	
($4,500,000 × 66½%) − $1,125,000	$1,867,500
Costs incurred in 2002	1,916,000
Loss recognized in 2002	$ 48,500

Hardhat would record the loss in 2002 as follows:

Construction Expenses	1,916,000	
Construction in Process (loss)		48,500
Revenue from Long-Term Contract		1,867,500

The loss of $48,500 will be reported on the 2002 income statement as the difference between the reported revenues of $1,867,500 and the costs of $1,916,000.[17] Under the completed-contract method, no loss is recognized in 2002 because the contract is still expected to result in a profit to be recognized in the year of completion.

Loss on an Unprofitable Contract

To illustrate the accounting for an overall loss on a long-term contract, assume that at December 31, 2002, Hardhat estimates the costs to complete the bridge contract at $1,640,250 instead of $1,134,000. Revised estimates relative to the bridge contract appear as follows:

	2001 Original Estimates	2002 Revised Estimates
Contract price	$4,500,000	$4,500,000
Estimated total cost	4,000,000	4,556,250*
Estimated gross profit	$ 500,000	
Estimated loss		$ (56,250)

*($2,916,000 + $1,640,250)

Under the percentage-of-completion method, $125,000 of gross profit was recognized in 2001 (see Illustration 6-10). This $125,000 must be offset in 2002 because it is no longer expected to be realized. In addition, the total estimated loss of $56,250 must be recognized in 2002 since losses must be recognized as soon as estimable. Therefore, a total loss of $181,250 ($125,000 + $56,250) must be recognized in 2002.

---

[17] In 2003, Hardhat will recognize the remaining 33½% of the revenue ($1,507,500) with costs of $1,468,962 as expected, and report a gross profit of $38,538. The total gross profit over the three years of the contract would be $115,038 [$125,000 (2001) − $48,500 (2002) + $38,538 (2003)], which is the difference between the total contract revenue of $4,500,000 and the total contract costs of $4,384,962.

The revenue recognized in 2002 is calculated as follows:

ILLUSTRATION 6-18
Calculation of Revenue
Recognizable, 2002—
Unprofitable Contract

Revenue recognized in 2002:

Contract price	$4,500,000
Percent complete	× 64%*
Revenue recognizable to date	2,880,000
Less: Revenue recognized prior to 2002	1,125,000
Revenue recognized in 2002	$1,755,000

*Cost to date (12/31/02)	$2,916,000
Estimated cost to complete	1,640,250
Estimated total costs	$4,556,250

Percent complete: $2,916,000 / $4,556,250 = 64%

To calculate the construction costs to be expensed in 2002 we add the total loss to be recognized in 2002 ($125,000 + $56,250) to the revenue to be recognized in 2002. This calculation is shown below.

ILLUSTRATION 6-19
Calculation of Construction
Expense, 2002—Unprofitable
Contract

Revenue recognized in 2002 (calculated above)		$1,755,000
Total loss recognized in 2002:		
Reversal of 2001 gross profit	$125,000	
Total estimated loss on the contract	56,250	181,250
Construction cost expensed in 2002		$1,936,250

Hardhat would record the long-term contract revenues, expenses, and loss in 2002 as follows:

Construction Expenses	1,936,250	
Construction in Process (Loss)		181,250
Revenue from Long-Term Contracts		1,755,000

At the end of 2002, Construction in Process has a balance of $2,859,750 as shown below.[18]

ILLUSTRATION 6-20
Content of Construction in
Process Account at End of 2002—
Unprofitable Contract

Construction in Process

2001 Construction costs	1,000,000		
2001 Recognized gross profit	125,000		
2002 Construction costs	1,916,000	2002 Recognized loss	181,250
Balance	2,859,750		

Under the completed-contract method, the contract loss of $56,250 is also recognized in the year in which it first became evident through the following entry in 2002:

Loss from Long-Term Contracts	56,250	
Construction in Process (Loss)		56,250

Just as the Billings account balance cannot exceed the contract price, neither can the balance in Construction in Process exceed the contract price. In circumstances where the Construction in Process balance exceeds the billings, the recognized loss may be deducted on the balance sheet from such accumulated costs. That is, under both the percentage-of-completion and the completed-contract methods, the provision for the loss (the credit) may be combined with Construction in Process, thereby reducing the inven-

---

[18] If the costs in 2003 are $1,640,250 as projected, at the end of 2003 the Construction in Process account will have a balance of $1,640,250 + $2,859,750, or $4,500,000, equal to the contract price. When the revenue remaining to be recognized in 2003 of $1,620,000 [$4,500,000 (total contract price) − $1,125,000 (2001) − $1,755,000 (2002)] is matched with the construction expense to be recognized in 2003 of $1,620,000 [total costs of $4,556,250 less the total costs recognized in prior years of $2,936,250 (2001, $1,000,000; 2002, $1,936,250)], a zero profit results. Thus the total loss has been recognized in 2002, the year in which it first became evident.

tory balance. In those circumstances, (as in the 2002 illustration above) where the billings exceed the accumulated costs, the amount of the estimated loss must be reported separately on the balance sheet as a **current liability**. That is, under **both** the percentage-of-completion and the completed-contract methods, the amount of the loss of $56,250, as estimated in 2002, would be taken from the Construction in Process account and reported separately as a current liability entitled **Estimated Liability from Long-Term Contracts**.

Disclosures in Financial Statements

In addition to making the financial statement disclosures required of all businesses, construction contractors usually make some unique disclosures. Generally these additional disclosures are made in the notes to the financial statements. For example, a construction contractor should disclose the **method of recognizing revenue**, the **basis used to classify assets and liabilities as current** (the nature and length of the operating cycle), the basis for recording inventory, the effects of any **revision of estimates**, the amount of **backlog** on uncompleted contracts, and the details about **receivables** (billed and unbilled, maturity, interest rates, and significant individual or group concentrations of credit risk).

MEASUREMENT UNCERTAINTY

OBJECTIVE 8
....
Discuss how to deal with
measurement uncertainty.

Measurement uncertainty stems from inability to measure the consideration itself (as with the consignment sales) or inability to measure returns. Returns will be dealt with below.

Sales with Buyback Agreements

If a company sells inventory in one period and agrees to buy it back in the next accounting period, has the company sold the product? In essence, this is a 100% return. **Legal title** has transferred in this situation, but the **economic substance** of the transaction is that the seller retains **risks of ownership**. In the U.S., the profession has taken steps to curtail the recognition of revenue from this practice. When a repurchase agreement exists at a set price and this price covers all costs of the inventory plus related holding costs, the inventory and related liability remain on the seller's books.[19] In other words, no sale. In Canada, this type of transaction is not specifically dealt with and the determination of whether a sale exists or not would be made based on whether **risks and rewards of ownership** have passed. Professional judgement must be exercised.[20]

In the case of the inventory, if the buyback cost is fixed, one could argue that the original **vendor retains the price risk**. Furthermore, who is covering the cost of insurance? The party that buys insurance is acknowledging responsibility for risk of loss—although sometimes the insurance cost may be passed on to the original vendor as well-indicating that the original vendor bears the risk.

Sales when Right of Return Exists

Whether cash or credit sales are involved, a special problem arises with claims for returns and allowances. In Chapter 7, the accounting treatment for normal returns and allowances is presented. However, certain companies experience such a high rate of returns—a high ratio of returned merchandise to sales—that they find it necessary to postpone reporting sales until the return privilege has substantially expired.

For example, in the publishing industry, the rate of return approaches 25% for hardcover books and 65% for some magazines. The high rate of return is a function of two

---

[19] "Accounting for Product Financing Arrangements," Statement of Financial Accounting Standards No. 49 (Stamford, Conn.: FASB, 1981).

[20] *CICA Handbook*, EIC Abstract # 93.

factors: (1) the publishers wanting to induce sales and therefore shipping more product and (2) the power resting with the retailers in the industry. **Chapters Inc.**, the largest retailer in Canada, which was formed through the merger between **WH Smith** and **Coles Book Stores**, engaged in very aggressive return activities after the merger. In 2001, Trilogy, the company that owns **Indigo Bookstores**, acquired control over Chapters Inc.

Since this deal created an even greater concentration in the retail book industry in Canada, the deal was reviewed by the Canadian Competition Tribunal. The Tribunal concluded, among other things, that the deal could go through as long as 24 Chapters stores were sold to an unrelated party and that the new company owned by Trilogy adhere to a business code of conduct. The code of conduct stipulated that returns would be limited and payments to publishers would have to be made within a reasonable time frame.

Returns in this and other industries are frequently effected either through a right of contract or as a matter of practice involving "guaranteed sales" agreements or consignments.

Three alternative revenue recognition methods are available when the seller is exposed to continued **risks of ownership** through return of the product. These are: (1) not recording a sale until all return privileges have expired; (2) recording the sale, but reducing sales by an estimate of future returns; and (3) recording the sale and accounting for the returns as they occur. Method #2 is only an option where returns are measurable but is preferrable under accrual accounting.

Trade Loading and Channel Stuffing

The domestic cigarette industry at one time engaged in a distribution practice known as **trade loading**. A magazine article described it as this: "Trade loading is a crazy, uneconomic, insidious practice through which manufacturers—trying to show sales, profits, and market share they don't actually have—induce their wholesale customers, known as the trade, to buy more product than they can promptly resell."[21]

In the computer software industry this same practice is referred to as **channel stuffing**. When a software maker needed to make its financial results look good, it offered deep discounts to its distributors to overbuy and recorded revenue when the software left the loading dock.[22] Of course, the distributors' inventories become bloated and the marketing channel gets stuffed but the software maker's financials are improved-to the detriment of future periods' results, unless the process is repeated.

Trade loading and channel stuffing overstate sales and distort operating results. If used without an appropriate allowance for sales returns, channel stuffing is a classic example of booking tomorrow's revenue today. The practices of trade loading and channel stuffing need to be discouraged. Business managers need to be aware of the ethical dangers of misleading the financial community by engaging in such practices to improve their financial statements.

UNCERTAINTY ASSOCIATED WITH COLLECTIBILITY

At the point of sale, where there is reasonable assurance as to ultimate collection, revenues are recognized.[23] Note that as long as an estimate can be made of uncollectible amounts at point of sale (e.g. perhaps based on historical data) the sale is booked and the potential uncollectible amount accrued. Alternatively, when collectibility cannot be established, revenues may not be recognized. In cases such as this, the presumption is that if collectibility is not established at the time of sale, then **in substance**, no real sale has been made.

> **OBJECTIVE 9**
>
> Discuss how to deal with collection uncertainty.

---

[21] "The $600 Million Cigarette Scam," *Fortune*, December 4, 1989, p. 89.

[22] "Software's Dirty Little Secret," *Forbes*, May 15, 1989, p. 128.

[23] *CICA Handbook*, Section 3400, par. .16.

Certain types of sales transactions such as those that require or allow **payment over longer periods** pose greater collectibility risk. Instalment sales are an example of this type of sale. If collectibility is established but the uncollectible amounts are not estimable, one of two methods is generally employed to defer revenue and/or profit recognition until the cash is received:

1. **instalment sales method** or
2. **cost recovery method**.

In some situations cash is received prior to delivery or transfer of the property and is recorded as a **deposit** because the sale transaction is incomplete.

Instalment Sales

The expression "instalment sales" is generally used to describe any type of sale for which payment is required in periodic instalments over an extended period of time. It is used in retailing where all types of farm and home equipment and furnishings are sold on an instalment basis. It is also sometimes used in the heavy equipment industry in which machine installations are paid for over a long period.

Because of the greater risk of collectibility, various devices are used to **protect the seller**. In merchandising, the two most common are (1) the use of a **conditional sales contract** that provides that **title** to the item sold does not pass to the purchaser until all payments have been made, and (2) use of notes secured by a **chattel** (personal property) **mortgage** on the article sold. Either of these permits the seller to "repossess" the goods sold if the purchaser defaults on one or more payments. The repossessed merchandise is then resold at whatever price it will bring to compensate the seller for the uncollected instalments and the expense of repossession.

Instalment Method

The instalment sales method is one way of dealing with **sales agreements that allow extended payment terms**. It **emphasizes collection** rather than sale, recognizing income in the collection periods rather than the sale period. This method is justified on the basis that when there is no reasonable approach for estimating the degree of collectibility, income should not be recognized until cash is collected.

Under the instalment sales method of accounting, **income recognition is deferred until the period of cash collection. Both revenues and costs of sales are recognized in the period of sale but the related gross profit is deferred** to those periods in which cash is collected. Thus, instead of the sale being deferred to the future periods of anticipated collection and then related costs and expenses being deferred, only the **proportional gross profit is deferred**.

Other expenses, such as selling and administrative expense, are not deferred. Thus, the theory that cost and expenses should be matched against sales is applied in instalment sales transactions through the gross profit figure, but no further. Companies using the instalment sales method of accounting generally record operating expenses without regard to the fact that some portion of the year's gross profit is to be deferred. This practice is often justified on the basis that (1) these expenses do not follow sales as closely as does the cost of goods sold, and (2) accurate apportionment among periods would be so difficult that it could not be justified by the benefits gained.[24]

Procedure for Deferring Revenue and Cost of Sales of Merchandise

By deferring only the gross profit the net effect is the same as deferring both sales and cost of sales but it requires only one deferred account rather than two.

---

[24] Other theoretical deficiencies of the instalment sales method could be cited. For example, see Richard A. Scott and Rita K. Scott, "Installment Accounting: Is it Inconsistent?" *The Journal of Accountancy*, November 1979.

The steps to be used are as follows:

For the sales in any one year:

1. During the year, record **both sales and cost of sales in the regular way**, using the special accounts described later, and **calculate the rate of gross profit** on instalment sales transactions.
2. At year end, **apply the rate of gross profit to the cash collections** of the current year's instalment sales to arrive at the realized gross profit.
3. The **gross profit not realized should be deferred** to future years.

For sales made in prior years:

The gross profit rate of each year's sales must be applied against **cash collections** of accounts receivable resulting from that year's sales to arrive at the **realized gross profit**. From the preceding discussion of the general practice followed in taking up income from instalment sales, it is apparent that special accounts must be used. These accounts provide certain special information required to determine the realized and unrealized gross profit in each year of operations. The requirements for special accounts are as follows:

1. Instalment sales transactions must be **kept separate** in the accounts from all other sales.
2. **Gross profit** on sales sold on instalment must be determinable.
3. The amount of **cash collected** on instalment sales accounts receivable must be known, and the total collected on the current year's and on each preceding year's sales must be determinable.
4. Provision must be made for **carrying forward** each year's deferred gross profit.

In each year, ordinary operating expenses are charged to expense accounts and are closed to the Income Summary account as under customary accounting procedure. Thus, the only peculiarity in calculating net income under the instalment sales method as generally applied is the deferral of gross profit until realized by accounts receivable collection.

To illustrate the instalment sales method in accounting for the sales of merchandise, assume the following data:

	2001	2002	2003
Instalment sales	$200,000	$250,000	$240,000
Cost of instalment sales	150,000	190,000	168,000
Gross profit	$ 50,000	$ 60,000	$ 72,000
Rate of gross profit on sales	25%(a)	24%(b)	30%(c)
Cash receipts			
2001 sales	$ 60,000	$100,000	$ 40,000
2002 sales		100,000	125,000
2003 sales			80,000

(a) $50,000/200,000   (b) $60,000/250,000   (c) $72,000/240,000

To simplify the illustration, interest charges have been excluded. Summary entries in general journal form for year 2001 are shown below.

2001

Instalment Accounts Receivable, 2001	200,000	
Instalment Sales		200,000
(To record sales made on instalment in 2001)		
Cash	60,000	
Instalment Accounts Receivable, 2001		60,000
(To record cash collected on instalment receivables)		

Cost of Instalment Sales	150,000	
Inventory (or Purchases)		150,000
(To record cost of goods sold on instalment in 2001 on either a perpetual		
or a periodic inventory basis)		
portion of		
Deferred (unrealized) Gross Profit—current year		
(income statement)	35,000	
Liability. Deferred Gross Profit (balance sheet)		35,000
(to defer gross profit recognition for unrealized gross profits		
[25% ($200,000 − 60,000)])		

Summary entries in journal form for year 2 (2002) are shown below.

2002

Instalment Accounts Receivable, 2002	250,000	
Instalment Sales		250,000
(To record sales made on instalment in 2002)		
Cash	200,000	
Instalment Accounts Receivable, 2001		100,000
Instalment Accounts Receivable, 2002		100,000
(To record cash collected on instalment receivables)		
Cost of Instalment Sales	190,000	
Inventory (or Purchases)		190,000
(To record cost of goods sold on instalment in 2002)		
Deferred Gross Profit, (balance sheet)	25,000	
Realized Gross Profit-prior year sales		
(income statement)		25,000
(to record 2001 realized gross profits [25% × $100,000])		
portion of		
Deferred (unrealized) Gross Profit—		
current year (income statement)	36,000	
Deferred Gross Profit (balance sheet)		36,000
(to defer gross profit recognition for unrealized gross profits		
[24% ($250,000 − 100,000)])		

The two income statement accounts, i.e., Realized Gross Profit–Prior Year Sales and Deferred (Unrealized) Gross Profit—Current Year, would generally be netted against each other. The entries in 2003 would be similar to those of 2002, and the gross profit realized on prior year's sales would be $40,000, as shown by the following calculations:

From 2001	$40,000 × 25% =	$10,000
From 2002	$125,000 × 24% =	$30,000
		$40,000

Deferred gross profit on 2003 sales would be calculated as follows:

30% ($240,000 − 80,000) = $48,000

Additional Problems of Instalment Sales Accounting

In addition to calculating realized and deferred gross profit currently, other problems are involved in accounting for instalment sales transactions. These problems are related to:

1. interest on instalment contracts,
2. uncollectible accounts, and
3. defaults and repossessions.

Interest on Instalment Contracts. Because the collection of instalment receivables is spread over a long period, it is customary to charge the buyer interest on the unpaid balance. A schedule of equal payments consisting of interest and principal is set up. Each successive payment is attributable to a smaller amount of interest and a correspondingly larger amount attributable to principal, as shown in Illustration 6-21. This illustration assumes that an asset costing $2,400 is sold for $3,000 with interest of 8% included in the three instalments of $1,164.10.

Date	Cash (Debit)	Interest Earned (Credit)	Instalment Receivables (Credit)	Instalment Unpaid Balance	Realized Gross Profit (20%)
1/2/01	—	—		$3,000.00	—
1/2/02	$1,164.10(a)	$240.00(b)	$924.10(c)	2,075.90(d)	$184.82(e)
1/2/03	1,164.10	166.07	998.03	1,077.87	199.61
1/2/04	1,164.10	86.23	1,077.87	– 0 –	215.57
					$600.00

(a) Periodic payment = Original unpaid balance / PV of an annuity of $1.00 for three periods at 8%; $1,164.10 = $3,000 / 2.57710.
(b) $3,000.00 × .08 = $240.
(c) $1,164.10 − $240.00 = $924.10.
(d) $3,000.00 − $924.10 = $2,075.90.
(e) $924.10 × .20 = $184.82.

ILLUSTRATION 6-21
Instalment Payment Schedule

Interest should be accounted for separately from the gross profit recognized on the instalment sales collections during the period. It is recognized as interest revenue at the time of the cash receipt.

Uncollectible Accounts. The problem of bad debts or uncollectible accounts receivable is somewhat different for concerns selling on an instalment basis because of a repossession feature commonly incorporated in the sales agreement. This feature gives the selling company an opportunity to recoup any uncollectible accounts through repossession and resale of repossessed merchandise. If the company's experience indicates that repossessions do not, as a rule, compensate for uncollectible balances, it may be advisable to provide for such losses through charges to a special bad debt expense account just as is done for other credit sales.

Defaults and Repossessions. Depending on the sales contract terms and credit department policy, the seller can repossess merchandise sold under an instalment arrangement if the purchaser fails to meet payment requirements. Repossessed merchandise may be **reconditioned** before being offered for sale. It may be resold for cash or instalment payments.

The accounting for repossessions recognizes that the related instalment receivable account is not collectible and that it should be written off. Along with the account receivable, the applicable deferred gross profit must be removed from the ledger using the following entry:

Repossessed Merchandise (an inventory account)	xx	
Deferred Gross Profit (balance sheet)	xx	
Instalment Accounts Receivable		xx

The entry above assumes that the repossessed merchandise is to be recorded on the books at exactly the amount of the uncollected account less the deferred gross profit applicable. This assumption may or may not be proper. The condition of the merchandise repossessed, the cost of reconditioning, and the market for second-hand merchandise of that particular type must all be considered. The objective should be to put any asset acquired on the books at its fair value or, when fair value is not ascertainable, at the best possible approximation of fair value. If the fair value of the merchandise repossessed is less than the uncollected balance less the deferred gross profit, a "loss on repossession" should be recorded at the repossession date.

To illustrate the required entry, assume that a refrigerator was sold to Marilyn Hunt for $500 on September 1, 2001. Terms require a down payment of $200 and $20 on the first of every month for 15 months, starting October 1, 2001. It is further assumed that the refrigerator cost $300 and that it is sold to provide a 40% rate of gross profit on selling price. At the year end, December 31, 2001, a total of $60 should have been collected in addition to the original down payment.

If Hunt makes her January and February payments in 2002 and then defaults, the account balances applicable to Hunt at time of default would be:

Instalment Account Receivable	
($500 − $200 − $20 − $20 − $20 − $20 − $20) =	200 (dr.)
Deferred Gross Profit (Balance Sheet)	
[40% ($500 − $200 − $20 − $20 − $20)] =	96 (cr.)

The deferred gross profit applicable to the Hunt account still has the December 31, 2001 balance ($80) because no entry has yet been made to take up gross profit realized by 2002 cash collections ($40 × 4% = $16). If the repossessed article's estimated fair value is set at $70, the following entry would be required to record the repossession:

Deferred Gross Profit	80	
Repossessed Merchandise	70	
Loss on Repossession	50	
Instalment Account Receivable (Hunt)		200

The loss amount is determined by (1) subtracting the deferred gross profit from the amount of the account receivable, to determine the unrecovered cost (or book value) of the merchandise repossessed, and (2) subtracting the estimated fair value of the merchandise repossessed from the unrecovered cost to get the amount of the loss on repossession.

Financial Statement Presentation of Instalment Sales Transactions

If instalment sales transactions represent a significant part of total sales, full disclosure of **instalment sales**, the **cost of instalment sales**, and any **expenses** allocable to instalment sales is desirable. If, however, instalment sales transactions constitute an insignificant part of total sales, it may be satisfactory to include only the **realized gross profit** in the income statement as a special item following the gross profit on sales, as shown below.

ILLUSTRATION 6-22
Disclosure of Instalment Sales Transactions—Insignificant Amount

HEALTH MACHINE CORP.
Statement of Income
For the Year Ended December 31, 2002

Sales	$620,000
Cost of goods sold	490,000
Gross profit on sales	130,000
Gross profit realized on instalment sales	51,000
Total gross profit on sales	$181,000

If more complete disclosure of instalment sales transactions is desired, a presentation similar to the following may be used:

ILLUSTRATION 6-23
Disclosure of Instalment Sales Transactions—Significant Amount

HEALTH MACHINE CORP.
Statement of Income
For the Year Ended December 31, 2002

	Instalment Sales	Other Sales	Total
Sales	$248,000	$620,000	$868,000
Cost of goods sold	182,000	490,000	672,000
Gross profit on sales	66,000	130,000	196,000
Less: Deferred gross profit on instalment sales of this year	47,000		47,000

Realized gross profit on this year's sales	19,000	130,000	149,000
Add: Gross profit realized on instalment sales of prior years	32,000		32,000
Gross profit realized this year	$51,000	$130,000	$181,000

The apparent awkwardness of this presentation method is difficult to avoid if full disclosure of instalment sales transactions is to be provided in the income statement. One solution, of course, is to prepare a **separate schedule** showing instalment sales transactions with only the final figure carried into the income statement.

In the balance sheet it is generally considered desirable to classify **instalment accounts receivable** by year of collectibility. There is some question as to whether instalment accounts that are not collectible for two or more years should be included in **current assets**. If instalment sales are part of normal operations, they may be considered current assets because they are collectible **within the business operating cycle**. Little confusion should result from this practice if maturity dates are fully disclosed, as illustrated in the following example.

Current assets		
Notes and accounts receivable		
Trade Customers	$78,800	
Less: Allowance for doubtful accounts	3,700	
	75,100	
Instalment accounts collectible in 2002	22,600	
Instalment accounts collectible in 2003	47,200	$144,900

ILLUSTRATION 6-24
Disclosure of Instalment Accounts Receivable, by Year

On the other hand, receivables from an instalment contract, or contracts, resulting from a transaction not related to normal operations should be reported in the **Other Assets** section if due beyond one year.

Repossessed merchandise is a part of inventory and should be included as such in the Current Asset section of the balance sheet. Any gain or loss on repossessions should be included in the income statement in the Other Revenues and Gains or Other Expenses and Losses section.

Deferred gross profit on instalment sales may be treated either as unearned revenue (**current liability**) or a **contra asset account** (as a valuation of instalment accounts receivable).[25]

Cost Recovery Method

Under the **cost recovery method**, no profit is recognized until **cash payments** by the buyer **exceed the seller's cost** of the merchandise sold. After all costs have been recovered, any additional cash collections are included in income. This method is therefore the **most conservative** method of recognizing income under accrual accounting.[26] The income statement for the period of sale reports sales revenue, the cost of goods sold, and the gross profit—both the amount (if any) that is recognized during the period and the amount that is deferred. The deferred gross profit is either presented as unearned revenue or offset against the related receivable—reduced by collections—on the balance sheet. Subsequent income statements report the gross profit as a separate revenue item when it is recognized as earned.

To illustrate the cost recovery method, assume that early in 2001, Fesmire Manufacturing sells inventory with a cost of $25,000 to Higley Limited for $36,000 with

OBJECTIVE 11
....
Explain and apply the cost recovery method of accounting.

---

[25] Statement of Financial Accounting Concepts No. 3,. pars. 156-158.

[26] APB Opinion No. 10 allows a seller to use the cost recovery method to account for sales in which "there is no reasonable basis for estimating collectibility." This method is required under FASB Statements No. 45 (franchises) and No. 66 (real estate) where a high degree of uncertainty exists related to the collection of receivables. In Canada, CICA Accounting Guideline #2 (franchise fee revenue) mentions that either the instalment method or cost recovery method may be used where there is no reasonable basis for estimating collectibility.

payments receivable of $18,000 in 2001, $12,000 in 2002, and $6,000 in 2003. If the cost recovery method applies to this sale transaction and the cash is collected on schedule, cash collections, revenue, cost, and gross profit are recognized as follows:

ILLUSTRATION 6-25
Calculation of Gross Profit—Cost Recovery Method

	2001	2002	2003
Cash collected	$18,000	$12,000	$6,000
Revenue	$36,000	– 0 –	– 0 –
Cost of goods sold	25,000	– 0 –	– 0 –
Deferred gross profit	$11,000	$11,000	$6,000
Recognized gross profit	– 0 –	5,000*	6,000
Deferred gross profit balance (end of period)	$11,000	$ 6,000	$ – 0 –

*$25,000 − $18,000 = $7,000 of unrecovered cost at the end of 2001; $12,000 − $7,000 = $5,000, the excess of cash received in 2002 over unrecovered cost.

Under the cost recovery method, total revenue and cost of goods sold are reported in the **period of sale** similar to the instalment sales method. However, unlike the instalment sales method, which recognizes income as cash is collected, the cost recovery method recognizes profit only when cash **collections exceed the total cost of the goods sold**.

The journal entry to record the deferred gross profit on this transaction (after the sale and the cost of sale were recorded in the normal manner) at the end of 2001 is as follows:

2001		
Deferred (unrealized) Gross Profit (income statement)	11,000	
Deferred Gross Profit (balance sheet)		11,000
(To record deferred gross profit on sales accounted for under the cost recovery method)		

In 2002 and 2003, the deferred gross profit becomes realized gross profit as the cumulative cash collections exceed the total costs by recording the following entries:

2002		
Deferred Gross Profit (balance sheet)	5,000	
Realized Gross Profit (income statement)		5,000
(To recognize gross profit to the extent that cash collections in 2002 exceed costs)		

2003		
Deferred Gross Profit (balance sheet)	6,000	
Realized Gross Profit (income statement)		6,000
(To recognize gross profit to the extent that cash collections in 2003 exceed costs)		

Summary of Learning Objectives

1 Apply the revenue recognition principle. The revenue recognition principle provides that revenue is recognized (1) when it is earned (including measurability) and (2) collection is reasonably assured. Revenues are earned when the entity has substantially accomplished what it must do to be entitled to the benefits represented by the revenues; that is, when the earnings process is complete or virtually complete.

2 Describe accounting issues involved with revenue recognition for sale of goods. The two conditions for recognizing revenue are usually met by the time product or merchandise is delivered (risks and rewards of ownership passed) or services are rendered to customers. Consider earlier or later points.

3 Explain accounting for consignment sales. The risks and rewards remain with the seller in this case and therefore a real sale does not occur until the goods are sold to a third party. Special accounts separate inventory on consignment.

4 Describe accounting issues involved with revenue recognition for services and long-term contracts. The earnings process is more likely a continuous one involving many significant events. Often, the customer is identified upfront. Therefore, revenue is recognized throughout the earnings process.

5 Apply the percentage-of-completion method for long-term contracts. To apply the percentage-of-completion method to long-term contracts, one must have some basis for measuring the progress toward completion at particular interim dates. One of the most popular input measures used to determine the progress toward completion is the cost-to-cost basis. Using this basis, the percentage of completion is measured by comparing costs incurred to date with the most recent estimate of the total costs to complete the contract. The percentage that costs incurred bear to total estimated costs is applied to the total revenue or the estimated total gross profit on the contract in arriving at the revenue or the gross profit amounts to be recognized to date.

6 Apply the completed-contract method for long-term contracts. Under this method, revenue and gross profit are recognized only when the contract is completed. Costs of long-term contracts in process and current billings are accumulated, but there are no interim charges or credits to income statement accounts for revenues, costs, and gross profit. The annual entries to record costs of construction, progress billings, and collections from customers would be identical to those for the percentage-of-completion method with the significant exclusion of the recognition of revenue and gross profit.

7 Account for losses on long-term contracts. Two types of losses can become evident under long-term contracts: (1) Loss in current period on a profitable contract: Under the percentage-of-completion method only, the estimated cost increase requires a current period adjustment of excess gross profit recognized on the project in prior periods. This adjustment is recorded as a loss in the current period because it is a change in accounting estimate. (2) Loss on an unprofitable contract: Under both the percentage-of-completion and the completed-contract methods, the entire expected contract loss must be recognized in the current period.

8 Discuss how to deal with measurement uncertainty. Transactions that involve buy-back or rights of return may require remeasurement. Existence of the practice of trade loading and channel stuffing may also require remeasuring of the transaction.

9 Discuss how to deal with collection uncertainty. Normally, if estimable, a provision for uncollectible amounts is accrued. In certain types of sales arrangements, payment is extended over the longer term. In these cases, the instalments or cost recovery methods may be used. These methods allow revenue recognition upfront but gross profits are deferred.

10 Explain and apply the instalment sales method of accounting. The instalment sales method recognizes income in the periods of collection rather than in the period of sale. The instalment method of accounting is justified on the basis that when there is no reasonable approach for estimating the degree of collectibility, revenue should not be recognized until cash is collected.

11 Explain and apply the cost recovery method of accounting. Under the cost recovery method, no profit is recognized until cash payments by the buyer exceed the seller's cost of the merchandise sold. After all costs have been recovered, any additional cash collections are included in income. The income statement for the period of sale reports sales revenue, the cost of goods sold, and the gross profit—both the amount that is recognized during the period and the amount that is deferred. The deferred gross profit is offset against the related receivable on the balance sheet. Subsequent income statements report the gross profit as a separate revenue item when it is recognized as earned.

KEY TERMS

billings, *257*

collectibility, *253*

completed-contract method, *258*

consignment, *255*

continuous earnings process/continuous sale, *257/258*

cost recovery method, *268*

cost-to-cost basis, *259*

critical event, *254*

discrete earnings process, *254*

earned, *253*

earnings process, *253*

FOB shipping point, *254*

FOB destination, *254*

input measures, *258*

instalment sales method, *268*

legal title, *254*

measurability, *253*

output measures, *258*

percentage-of-completion method, *257*

performance, *253*

point of delivery, *254*

possession, *254*

realized, *253*

revenue recognition principle, *253*

risks and rewards of ownership, *254*

APPENDIX 6A

Revenue Recognition for Special Sales Transactions— Franchises

As indicated throughout this chapter, revenue is recognized on the basis of two criteria: **performance and collectibility**. These criteria are appropriate for most business activities. This appendix looks at how they apply to industries characterized by franchises.

There are many different types of franchise arrangements. Below are listed several of the more well known franchises:

> Soft ice cream/frozen yogurt stores (Baskin Robbins, TCBY, Dairy Queen)
> Food drive-ins (McDonald's, Tim Hortons, Burger King)
> Restaurants (Swiss Chalet, Pizza Hut, Denny's)
> Motels (Holiday Inn, Ramada, Best Western)
> Auto rentals (Avis, Hertz, Tilden)
> Part-time help (Manpower, Kelly)
> Others (H & R Block, Speedy Mufflers, 7-Eleven Stores)

Franchise companies derive their revenue from one or both of two sources: (1) from the sale of initial franchises and related assets or services (**initial franchise fee**), and (2) from **continuing fees** based on franchise operations. The franchisor (the party who grants business rights under the franchise) normally provides the franchisee (the party who operates the franchised business) with the following services:

1. Assistance in site selection:
   (a) analysing location
   (b) negotiating lease
2. Evaluation of potential income
3. Supervision of construction activity
   (a) obtaining financing
   (b) designing building
   (c) supervising contractor while building
4. Assistance in the acquisition of signs, fixtures, and equipment
5. Bookkeeping and advisory services:
   (a) setting up franchisee's records
   (b) advising on income, real estate, and other taxes
   (c) advising on local regulations of the franchisee's business
6. Employee and management training
7. Quality control
8. Advertising and promotion

During the 1960s and early 1970s it was standard practice for franchisors to recognize the entire franchise fee at the date of sale whether the fee was received then or was collectible over a long period of time. Frequently, franchisors recorded the entire amount as revenue in the year of sale even though many of the services were yet to be performed and uncertainty existed regarding the collection of the entire fee.[27]

However, a franchise agreement may provide for refunds to the franchisee if certain conditions are not met, and franchise fee profit can be reduced sharply by future costs of obligations and services to be rendered by the franchisor.[28]

Initial Franchise Fees

The **initial franchise fee** is consideration for establishing the franchise relationship and providing some initial services. Initial franchise fees are to be recorded as revenue only when and as the franchisor has established "**substantial performance;**"[29] i.e., it has substantially completed the services it is obligated to perform **and** collection of the fee is reasonably assured. Substantial performance occurs when the franchisor has no remaining obligation to refund any cash received or excuse any nonpayment of a note and has substantially performed all significant initial services required under the contract. Commencement of operations by the franchisee is normally presumed to be the earliest point at which substantial performance has occurred, unless it can be **demonstrated** that substantial performance has occurred before that time.

Illustration of Entries for Initial Franchise Fee

To illustrate, assume that Tum's Pizza Inc. charges an initial franchise fee of $50,000 for the right to operate as a franchisee of Tum's Pizza. Of this amount, $10,000 is payable when the agreement is signed and the balance is payable in five annual payments of $8,000 each. In return for the initial franchise fee, the franchisor will help locate the site, negotiate the site lease or purchase, supervise the construction activity, and provide the bookkeeping services. The franchisee's credit rating indicates that money can be borrowed at 8%. The present value of an ordinary annuity of five annual receipts of $8,000 each, discounted at 8%, is $31,941.68. The discount of $8,058.32 represents the interest revenue to be accrued by the franchisor over the payment period.

1. If there is reasonable expectation that the down payment may be refunded and if substantial future services remain to be performed by Tum's Pizza Inc., the entry should be:

Cash	10,000	
Notes Receivable	40,000	
Discount on Notes Receivable		8,058 ~ *Financing Charge (Interest)*
Unearned Franchise Fees		41,942

2. If the probability of refunding the initial franchise fee is extremely low, if the amount of future services to be provided to the franchisee is minimal, collectibility of the note is reasonably assured, and if substantial performance has occurred, the entry should be:

---

[27] In 1987 and 1988 the SEC ordered a half-dozen fast-growing startup franchisors, including Jiffy Lube International, Moto Photo, Inc., Swensen's, Inc., and LePeep Restaurants, Inc., to defer their initial franchise fee recognition until earned. See "Claiming Tomorrow's Profits Today," *Forbes*, October 17, 1988, p. 78.

[28] To curb the abuses in revenue recognition that existed and to standardize the accounting and reporting practices in the franchise industry, the CICA issued an Accounting Guideline and the FASB issued Statement No. 45.

[29] *CICA Handbook*, Accounting Guideline #2.

Cash	10,000	
Notes Receivable	40,000	
Discount on Notes Receivable		8,058
Revenue from Franchise Fees		41,942

3. If the initial down payment is not refundable and represents a fair measure of the services already provided, with a significant amount of services still to be performed by the franchisor in future periods, and if collectibility of the note is reasonably assured, the entry should be:

Cash	10,000	
Notes Receivable	40,000	
Discount on Notes Receivable		8,058
Revenue from Franchise Fees		10,000
Unearned Franchise Fees		31,942

4. If the initial down payment is not refundable and no future services are required by the franchisor, but collection of the note is so uncertain that recognition of the note as an asset is unwarranted, the entry should be:

Cash	10,000	
Revenue from Franchise Fees		10,000

5. Under the same conditions as those listed under 4 except that the down payment is refundable or substantial services are yet to be performed, the entry should be:

Cash	10,000	
Unearned Franchise Fees		10,000

In cases 4 and 5—where collection of the note is extremely uncertain—cash collections may be recognized using the instalment method or the cost recovery method.

Continuing Franchise Fees

Continuing franchise fees are received in return for the continuing rights granted by the franchise agreement and for providing such services as management training, advertising and promotion, legal assistance, and other support. Continuing fees should be reported as revenue when they are **earned** and receivable from the franchisee, unless a portion of them has been designated for a particular purpose, such as providing a specified amount for building maintenance or local advertising. In that case, the portion deferred shall be an amount sufficient to cover the estimated cost in excess of continuing franchise fees and provide a reasonable profit on the continuing services.

Bargain Purchases

In addition to paying continuing franchise fees, franchisees frequently purchase some or all of their equipment and supplies from the franchisor. The franchisor would account for these sales as it would for any other product sales. Sometimes, however, the franchise agreement grants the franchisee the right to make **bargain purchases** of equipment or supplies after the initial franchise fee is paid. If the bargain price is lower than the normal selling price of the same product, or if it does not provide the franchisor a reasonable profit, then a portion of the initial franchise fee should be deferred. The deferred portion would be accounted for as an adjustment of the selling price when the franchisee subsequently purchases the equipment or supplies.

Options to Purchase

A franchise agreement may give the franchisor an **option to purchase the franchisee's** business. As a matter of management policy, the franchisor may reserve the right to purchase a profitable franchised outlet, or to purchase one that is in financial difficulty. If it is probable at the time the option is given that the franchisor will ultimately purchase the outlet, then the initial franchise fee should not be recognized as revenue but should be recorded as a liability. When the option is exercised, the liability would reduce the franchisor's investment in the outlet.

Franchisor's Cost

Franchise accounting also involves proper accounting for the **franchisor's cost**. The objective is to match related costs and revenues by reporting them as components of income in the same accounting period. Franchisors should ordinarily defer direct costs (usually incremental costs) relating to specific franchise sales for which revenue has not yet been recognized. Costs should not be deferred, however, without reference to anticipated revenue and its **realizability**. Indirect costs of a regular and recurring nature such as selling and administrative expenses that are incurred irrespective of the level of franchise sales should be expensed as incurred.

Disclosures of Franchisors

Disclosure of all significant commitments and obligations resulting from franchise agreements, including a description of services that have not yet been substantially performed, is required. Any resolution of uncertainties regarding the collectibility of franchise fees should be disclosed. Initial franchise fees should be segregated from other franchise fee revenue if they are significant. Where possible, revenues and costs related to franchisor-owned outlets should be distinguished from those related to franchised outlets.

Summary of Learning Objective for Appendix 6A

· ·

12 Explain revenue recognition for franchises. In a franchise arrangement, the initial franchise fee is recorded as revenue only when and as the franchisor makes substantial performance of the services it is obligated to perform and collection of the fee is reasonably assured. Continuing franchise fees are recognized as revenue when they are earned and receivable from the franchisee.

KEY TERMS – APPENDIX

continuing franchise fees, *276*

initial franchise fee, *276*

substantial performance, *277*

BRIEF EXERCISES

· ·

BE6-1 Scooby Music sold CDs to retailers and recorded sales revenue of $800,000. During 2002, retailers returned CDs to Scooby and were granted credit of $78,000. Past experience indicates that the normal return rate is 15%. Prepare Scooby's entries to record (a) the $78,000 of returns and (b) estimated returns at December 31, 2002.

BE6-2 Wave Inc. began work on a $7 million contract in 2002 to construct an office building. During 2002, Wave, Inc. incurred costs of $1,715,000, billed its customers for $1.2 million, and collected $960,000. At December 31, 2002, the estimated future costs to complete the project total $3,185,000. Prepare Wave's 2002 journal entries using the percentage-of-completion method.

BE6-3 Blasters, Inc. began work on a $7 million contract in 2002 to construct an office building. Blasters uses the percentage-of-completion method. At December 31, 2002, the balances in certain accounts were: construction in process, $2,450,000; accounts receivable, $240,000; and billings on construction in process, $1.2 million. Indicate how these accounts would be reported in Blasters' December 31, 2002 balance sheet.

BE6-4 Use the information from BE6-2, but assume Wave uses the completed-contract method. Prepare the company's 2002 journal entries.

BE6-5 Cordero, Inc. began work on a $7 million contract in 2002 to construct an office building. Cordero uses the completed-contract method. At December 31, 2002, the balances in certain accounts were construction in process, $1,715,000; accounts receivable, $240,000; and billings on construction in process, $1.2 million. Indicate how these accounts would be reported in Cordero's December 31, 2002 balance sheet.

BE6-6 Shaq Fu Construction Corp. began work on a $420,000 construction contract in 2002. During 2002, Shaq Fu incurred costs of $288,000, billed its customer for $215,000, and collected $175,000. At December 31, 2002, the estimated future costs to complete the project total $162,000. Prepare Shaq Fu's journal entry to record profit or loss using (a) the percentage-of-completion method and (b) the completed contract method, if any.

BE6-7 Thunder Paradise Corporation began selling goods on an instalment basis on January 1, 2002. During 2002, Thunder Paradise had instalment sales of $150,000; cash collections of $54,000; and cost of instalment sales of $105,000. Prepare the company's entries to record instalment sales, cash collected, cost of instalment sales, deferral of gross profit, and gross profit recognized, using the instalment sales method.

BE6-8 Shinobi Inc. sells goods on the instalment basis and uses the instalment sales method. Due to a customer default, Shinobi repossessed merchandise, which was originally sold for $800, resulting in a gross profit rate of 40%. At the time of repossession, the uncollected balance is $560, and the fair value of the repossessed merchandise is $275. Prepare Shinobi's entry to record the repossession.

BE6-9 At December 31, 2002, Soul Star Corporation had the following account balances:

Instalment Accounts Receivable, 2001	$ 65,000
Instalment Accounts Receivable, 2002	110,000
Deferred Gross Profit, 2001	23,400
Deferred Gross Profit, 2002	40,700

Most of Soul Star's sales are made on a two-year instalment basis. Indicate how these accounts would be reported in Soul Star's December 31, 2002 balance sheet. The 2001 accounts are collectible in 2003, and the 2002 accounts are collectible in 2004.

BE6-10 Bear Corporation sold equipment to Magellan Limited for $20,000. The equipment is on Bear's books at a net amount of $14,000. Bear collected $10,000 in 2001, $5,000 in 2002, and $5,000 in 2003. If Bear uses the cost recovery method, what amount of gross profit will be recognized in each year?

*BE6-11 Racer Inc. charges an initial franchise fee of $75,000 for the right to operate as a franchisee of Racer. Of this amount, $25,000 is collected immediately. The remainder is collected in four equal annual instalments of $12,500 each. These instalments have a present value of $39,623. There is reasonable expectation that the down payment may be refunded and substantial future services be performed by Racer Inc. Prepare the journal entry required by Racer to record the franchise fee.

BE6-12 TJ Corporation shipped $20,000 of merchandise on consignment to T Company. TJ paid freight costs of $2,000. T Company paid $500 for local advertising, which is reimbursable from TJ. By year end, 60% of the merchandise had been sold for $22,300. T notified TJ, retained a 10% commission, and remitted the cash due to TJ. Prepare TJ's entry when the cash is received.

EXERCISES

E6-1 **(Revenue Recognition on Book Sales with High Returns)** Huish Publishing Inc. publishes college textbooks that are sold to bookstores on the following terms. Each title has a fixed wholesale price, terms f.o.b. shipping point, and payment is due 60 days after shipment. The retailer may return a maximum of 30% of an order at the retailer's expense. Sales are made only to retailers who have good credit ratings. Past experience indicates that the normal return rate is 12% and the average collection period is 72 days.

Instructions

(a) Identify alternative revenue recognition points that Huish could employ concerning textbook sales.
(b) Briefly discuss the reasoning for your answers in (a) above.
(c) In late July, Huish shipped books invoiced at $16 million. Prepare the journal entry to record this event given (a) and (b).
(d) In October, $2 million of the invoiced July sales were returned according to the return policy, and the remaining $14 million was paid; prepare the entry recording the return and payment.

E6-2 (Sales Recorded Both Gross and Net) On June 3, Reid Corp. sold to Kim Rhode merchandise having a sale price of $5,000 with terms of 2/10, n/60, f.o.b. shipping point. An invoice totalling $120, terms n/30, was received by Rhode on June 8 from the Olympic Transport Service for the freight cost. Upon receipt of the goods, June 5, Rhode notified Reid that merchandise costing $400 contained flaws that rendered it worthless; the same day Reid issued a credit memo covering the worthless merchandise and asked that it be returned at company expense. The freight on the returned merchandise was $24, paid by Reid on June 7. On June 12, the company received a cheque for the balance due from Rhode.

Instructions

(a) Prepare journal entries on Reid books to record all the events noted above under each of the following bases:
  1. Sales and receivables are entered at gross selling price.
  2. Sales and receivables are entered net of cash discounts.
(b) Prepare the journal entry under basis 2, assuming that Kim Rhode did not remit payment until August 5.

E6-3 (Revenue Recognition on Marina Sales with Discounts) Brooke Bennett Marina has 300 available slips that rent for $900 per season. Payments must be made in full at the start of the boating season, April 1. Slips for the next season may be reserved if paid for by December 31. Under a new policy, if payment is made by December 31, a 5% discount is allowed. The boating season ends October 31, and the marina has a December 31 year end. To provide cash flow for major dock repairs, the marina operator is also offering a 25% discount to slip renters who pay for the second season following the current December 31.

For the fiscal year ended December 31, 2001, all 300 slips were rented at full price. Two hundred slips were reserved and paid for in advance of the 2002 boating season, and 60 slips were reserved and paid for in advance of the 2003 boating season.

Instructions

Prepare the appropriate journal entries for fiscal 2001.

E6-4 (Recognition of Profit on Long-Term Contracts) During 2001, Pierson started a construction job with a contract price of $1.5 million. The job was completed in 2003. The following information is available:

	2001	2002	2003
Costs incurred to date	$400,000	$935,000	$1,070,000
Estimated costs to complete	600,000	165,000	– 0 –
Billings to date	300,000	900,000	1,500,000
Collections to date	270,000	810,000	1,425,000

Instructions

(a) Calculate the amount of gross profit to be recognized each year assuming the percentage-of-completion method is used.
(b) Prepare all necessary journal entries for 2002.
(c) Calculate the amount of gross profit to be recognized each year assuming the completed-contract method is used.

E6-5 (**Analysis of Percentage-of-Completion Financial Statements**) In 2001, Bin Xia Construction Corp. began construction work under a three-year contract. The contract price was $1 million. Bin Xia uses the percentage-of-completion method for financial accounting purposes. The income to be recognized each year is based on the proportion of cost incurred to total estimated costs for completing the contract. The financial statement presentations relating to this contract at December 31, 2001 follow:

Balance Sheet		
Accounts receivable—construction contract billings		$21,500
Construction in progress	$65,000	
Less contract billings	61,500	
Cost of uncompleted contract in excess of billings		3,500

Income Statement	
Income (before tax) on the contract recognized in 2001	$18,200

Instructions

(a) How much cash was collected in 2001 on this contract?

(b) What was the initial estimated total income before tax on this contract?

(AICPA adapted)

E6-6 (**Gross Profit on Uncompleted Contract**) On April 1, 2001, Bridgewater Inc. entered into a cost-plus-fixed-fee contract to construct an electric generator for Dolan Corporation. At the contract date, Bridgewater estimated that it would take two years to complete the project at a cost of $2 million. The fixed fee stipulated in the contract is $450,000. Bridgewater appropriately accounts for this contract under the percentage-of-completion method. During 2001, Bridgewater incurred costs of $700,000 related to the project. The estimated cost at December 31, 2001 to complete the contract is $1.3 million. Dolan was billed $600,000 under the contract.

Instructions

Prepare a schedule to calculate the amount of gross profit to be recognized by Bridgewater under the contract for the year ended December 31, 2001. Show supporting calculations in good form.

(AICPA adapted)

E6-7 (**Recognition of Profit, Percentage-of-Completion Method**) In 2001, Rouse Construction Inc. Company agreed to construct an apartment building at a price of $1 million. The information relating to the costs and billings for this contract is as follows:

	2001	2002	2003
Costs incurred to date	$280,000	$600,000	$ 785,000
Estimated costs yet to be incurred	520,000	200,000	– 0 –
Customer billings to date	150,000	400,000	1,000,000
Collection of billings to date	120,000	320,000	940,000

Instructions

(a) Assuming that the percentage-of-completion method is used: (1) calculate the amount of gross profit to be recognized in 2001 and 2002, and (2) prepare journal entries for 2002.

(b) For 2002, show how the details related to this construction contract would be disclosed on the balance sheet and on the income statement.

E6-8 (**Recognition of Revenue on Long-Term Contract and Entries**) Van Dyken Construction Corp. uses the percentage-of-completion method of accounting. In 2001, Van Dyken began work under contract #E2-D2, which provided for a contract price of $2.2 million. Other details follow:

	2001	2002
Costs incurred during the year	$ 480,000	$1,425,000
Estimated costs to complete, as of December 31	1,120,000	– 0 –
Billings during the year	420,000	1,680,000
Collections during the year	350,000	1,500,000

Instructions

(a) What portion of the total contract price would be recognized as revenue in 2001? In 2002?

(b) Assuming the same facts as those above except that Van Dyken uses the completed-contract method of accounting, what portion of the total contract price would be recognized as revenue in 2002?

(c) Prepare a complete set of journal entries for 2001 (using percentage of completion).

E6-9 **(Recognition of Profit and Balance Sheet Amounts for Long-Term Contracts)** Agassi Construction Corp. began operations January 1, 2001. During the year, Agassi entered into a contract with Davenport Corp. to construct a manufacturing facility. At that time, Agassi estimated that it would take five years to complete the facility at a total cost of $4.5 million. The total contract price to construct the facility is $6.3 million. During the year, Agassi incurred $1,185,800 in construction costs related to the construction project. The estimated cost to complete the contract is $4,204,200. Davenport was billed and paid 30% of the contract price.

Instructions

Prepare schedules to calculate the amount of gross profit to be recognized for the year ended December 31, 2001, and the amount to be shown as "cost of uncompleted contract in excess of related billings" or "billings on uncompleted contract in excess of related costs" at December 31, 2001, under each of the following methods:

(a) completed-contract method

(b) percentage-of-completion method

Show supporting calculations in good form.

(AICPA adapted)

E6-10 **(Long-Term Contract Reporting)** Adkins Construction Ltd. began operations in 2001. Construction activity for the first year is shown below. All contracts are with different customers, and any work remaining at December 31, 2001 is expected to be completed in 2002.

Project	Total Contract Price	Billings through 12/31/01	Cash Collections through 12/31/01	Contract Costs Incurred through 12/31/01	Estimated Additional Costs to Complete
1	$ 560,000	$ 360,000	$340,000	$450,000	$140,000
2	670,000	220,000	210,000	126,000	504,000
3	500,000	500,000	440,000	330,000	– 0 –
	$1,730,000	$1,080,000	$990,000	$906,000	$644,000

Instructions

Prepare a partial income statement and balance sheet to indicate how the above information would be reported for financial statement purposes. Adkins uses the completed-contract method.

E6-11 **(Instalment Sales Method Calculations, Entries)** Hull Corporation appropriately uses the instalment sales method of accounting to recognize income in its financial statements. The following information is available for 2001 and 2002:

	2001	2002
Instalment sales	$900,000	$1,000,000
Cost of instalment sales	630,000	680,000
Cash collections on 2001 sales	370,000	350,000
Cash collections on 2002 sales	– 0 –	475,000

Instructions

(a) Calculate the amount of realized gross profit recognized in each year.

(b) Prepare all journal entries required in 2002.

E6-12 **(Analysis of Instalment Sales Accounts)** Halifax Ltd. appropriately uses the instalment sales method of accounting. On December 31, 2003, the books show balances as follows:

Instalment Receivables		Deferred Gross Profit (B/S)		Gross Profit on Sales	
2001	$11,000	2001	$ 7,000	2001	35%
2002	40,000	2002	26,000	2002	34%
2003	80,000	2003	95,000	2003	32%

Instructions

(a) Prepare the adjusting entry or entries required on December 31, 2003 to recognize 2003 realized gross profit. (Instalment receivables have already been credited for cash receipts during 2003.)

(b) Calculate the amount of cash collected in 2003 on accounts receivable each year.

E6-13 **(Gross Profit Calculations and Repossessed Merchandise)** Barnes Corporation, which began business on January 1, 2001, appropriately uses the instalment sales method of accounting. The following data were obtained for the years 2001 and 2002:

	2001	2002
Instalment sales	$750,000	$840,000
Cost of instalment sales	525,000	604,800
General & administrative expenses	70,000	84,000
Cash collections on sales of 2001	310,000	300,000
Cash collections on sales of 2002	– 0 –	400,000

Instructions

(a) Calculate the balance in the deferred gross profit balance sheet accounts on December 31, 2001 and on December 31, 2002.

(b) A 2001 sale resulted in default in 2003. At the date of default, the balance on the instalment receivable was $12,000, and the repossessed merchandise had a fair value of $8,000. Prepare the entry to record the repossession. (AICPA adapted)

E6-14 **(Interest Revenue from Instalment Sale)** Devers Corporation sells farm machinery on the instalment plan. On July 1, 2001, Devers entered into an instalment sale contract with Torrence Inc. for a 10-year period. Equal annual payments under the instalment sale are $100,000 and are due on July 1. The first payment was made on July 1, 2001.

Additional information

1. The amount that would be realized on an outright sale of similar farm machinery is $676,000.
2. The cost of the farm machinery sold to Torrence Inc. is $500,000.
3. The finance charges relating to the instalment period are $324,000 based on a stated interest rate of 10%, which is appropriate.
4. Circumstances are such that the collection of the instalments due under the contract is reasonably assured.

Instructions

What income or loss before income taxes should Devers record for the year ended December 31, 2001 as a result of the transaction above? (AICPA adapted)

E6-15 **(Instalment Method and Cost Recovery)** Ho Corp., a capital goods manufacturing business that started on January 4, 2001, and operates on a calendar-year basis, uses the instalment method of profit recognition in accounting for all its sales. The following data were taken from the 2001 and 2002 records:

	2001	2002
Instalment sales	$480,000	$620,000
Gross profit as a percent of sales	25%	28%
Cash collections on sales of 2001	$140,000	$240,000
Cash collections on sales of 2002	– 0 –	$180,000

The amounts given for cash collections exclude amounts collected for interest charges.

Instructions

(a) Calculate the amount of realized gross profit to be recognized on the 2002 income statement, prepared using the instalment method.

(b) State where the balance of Deferred Gross Profit would be reported on the financial statements for 2002.

(c) Calculate the amount of realized gross profit to be recognized on the income statement, prepared using the cost recovery method.

(CIA adapted)

E6-16 **(Instalment Sales Method and Cost Recovery Method)** On January 1, 2001, Tihal Limited sold property for $200,000. The note will be collected as follows: $100,000 in 2001, $60,000 in 2002, and $40,000 in 2003. The property had cost Tihal $150,000 when it was purchased in 1999.

Instructions

(a) Calculate the amount of gross profit realized each year assuming Tihal uses the cost recovery method.

(b) Calculate the amount of gross profit realized each year assuming Tihal uses the instalment sales method.

E6-17 **(Cost Recovery Method)** On January 1, 2002, Johnson Limited sold real estate that cost $110,000 to Karen Lewis for $120,000. Lewis agreed to pay for the purchase over three years by making three end-of-year equal payments of $52,557 that included 15% interest. Shortly after the sale, Johnson learns distressing news about Lewis's financial circumstances and because collection is so uncertain decides to account for the sale using the cost recovery method.

Instructions

Applying the cost recovery method, prepare a schedule showing the amounts of cash collected, the increase (decrease) in deferred interest revenue, the balance of the receivable, the balance of the unrecovered cost, the gross profit realized, and the interest revenue realized for each of the three years assuming the payments are made as agreed.

E6-18 **(Instalment Sales-Default and Repossession)** Johnson Imports Inc. was involved in two default and repossession cases during the year:

1. A refrigerator was sold to Cara Ottey for $1,800, including a 35% gross margin. Ottey made a down payment of 20%, 4 of the remaining 16 equal payments, and then defaulted on further payments. The refrigerator was repossessed, at which time the fair value was determined to be $800.
2. An oven that cost $1,200 was sold to Debbie Bailey for $1,600 on the instalment basis. Bailey made a down payment of $240 and paid $80 a month for six months, after which she defaulted. The oven was repossessed and the estimated value at time of repossession was determined to be $750.

Instructions

Prepare journal entries to record each of these repossessions. (Ignore interest charges.)

E6-19 **(Instalment Sales-Default and Repossession)** Ceplar Inc. uses the instalment sales method in accounting for its instalment sales. On January 1, 2002, Ceplar had an instalment account receivable from Kay Bluhm with a balance of $1,800. During 2002, $400 was collected from Bluhm. When no further collection could be made, the merchandise sold to Bluhm was repossessed. The merchandise had a fair market value of $650 after the company spent $60 for reconditioning the merchandise. The merchandise was originally sold with a gross profit rate of 40%.

Instructions

Prepare the entries on the books of Ceplar to record all transactions related to Bluhm during 2002. (Ignore interest charges.)

E6-20 **(Cost Recovery Method)** On January 1, 2002, Tom Brands sells 200 acres of farmland for $600,000, taking in exchange a 10% interest-bearing note. Tom Brands purchased the farmland in 1987 at a cost of $500,000. The note will be paid in three instalments of $241,269 each on December 31, 2002, 2003, and 2004. Collectibility of the note is uncertain; Tom, therefore, uses the cost recovery method.

Instructions

Prepare for Tom a three-year instalment payment schedule (under the cost recovery method) that shows cash collections, deferred interest revenue, instalment receivable balances, unrecovered cost, realized gross profit, and realized interest revenue by year.

*E6-21 **(Franchise Entries)** Kendall Inc. charges an initial franchise fee of $70,000. Upon the signing of the agreement, a payment of $40,000 is due; thereafter, three annual payments of $10,000 are required. The franchisee's credit rating is such that it would have to pay interest at 10% to borrow money.

Instructions

Prepare the entries to record the initial franchise fee on the franchisor's books under the following assumptions:

(a) The down payment is not refundable, no future services are required by the franchisor, and collection of the note is reasonably assured.

(b) The franchisor has substantial services to perform, the down payment is refundable, and the collection of the note is very uncertain.

(c) The down payment is not refundable, collection of the note is reasonably certain, the franchisor has yet to perform a substantial amount of services, and the down payment represents a fair measure of the services already performed.

*E6-22 **(Franchise Fee, Initial Down Payment)** On January 1, 2001, Svetlana Masterkova signed an agreement to operate as a franchisee of Short-Track Inc. for an initial franchise fee of $50,000. The amount of $20,000 was paid when the agreement was signed, and the balance is payable in five annual payments of $6,000 each, beginning January 1, 2002. The agreement provides that the down payment is not refundable and that no future services are required of the franchisor. Svetlana Masterkova's credit rating indicates that she can borrow money at 11% for a loan of this type.

Instructions

(a) How much should Short-Track record as revenue from franchise fees on January 1, 2001? At what amount should Svetlana record the franchise acquisition cost on January 1, 2001?

(b) What entry would be made by Short-Track on January 1, 2001 if the down payment is refundable and substantial future services remain to be performed by Short-Track?

(c) How much revenue from franchise fees would be recorded by Short-Track on January 1, 2001, if:

1. The initial down payment is not refundable, it represents a fair measure of the services already provided, a significant amount of services is still to be performed by Short-Track in future periods, and collectibility of the note is reasonably assured?

2. The initial down payment is not refundable and no future services are required by the franchisor, but collection of the note is so uncertain that recognition of the note as an asset is unwarranted?

3. The initial down payment has not been earned and collection of the note is so uncertain that recognition of the note as an asset is unwarranted?

E6-23 **(Consignment Calculations)** On May 3, 2001, Branzei Limited consigned 70 freezers, costing $500 each, to Martino Inc. The cost of shipping the freezers amounted to $840 and was paid by Branzei. On December 30, 2001, an account sales report was received from the consignee, reporting that 40 freezers had been sold for $700 each. Remittance was made by the consignee for the amount due, after deducting a commission of 6%, advertising of $200, and total installation costs of $320 on the freezers sold.

Instructions

(a) Calculate the inventory value of the units unsold in the hands of the consignee.

(b) Calculate the profit for the consignor for the units sold.

(c) Calculate the amount of cash that will be remitted by the consignee.

PROBLEMS

P6-1 Amanar Industries has three operating divisions: Gina Construction Division, Gogean Publishing Division, and Chorkina Securities Division. Each division maintains its own accounting system and method of revenue recognition.

Gina Construction Division

During the fiscal year ended November 30, 2001, Gina Construction Division had one construction project in process. A $30 million contract for construction of a civic centre was granted on June 19, 2001, and construction began on August 1, 2001. Estimated costs of completion at the contract date were $25 million over a two-year time period from the date of the contract. On November 30, 2001, construction costs of $7.8 million had been incurred and progress billings of $9.5 million had been made. The construction costs to complete the remainder of the project were reviewed on November 30, 2001, and were estimated to amount to only $16.2 million because of an expected decline in raw materials costs. Revenue recognition is based upon a percentage-of-completion method.

Gogean Publishing Division

The Gogean Publishing Division sells large volumes of novels to a few book distributors, which in turn sell to national bookstore chains. Gogean allows distributors to return up to 30% of sales, and distributors give the same terms to bookstores. While returns from individual titles fluctuate greatly, the returns from distributors have averaged 20% in each of the past five years. A total of $8 million of paperback novel sales were made to distributors during fiscal 2001. On November 30, 2001, $2.5 million of fiscal 2001 sales were still subject to return privileges over the next six months. The remaining $5.5 million of fiscal 2001 sales had actual returns of 21%. Sales from fiscal 2000 totalling $2 million were collected in fiscal 2001 less 18% returns. This division records revenue at the point of sale.

Chorkina Securities Division

Chorkina Securities Division works through manufacturers' agents in various cities. Orders for alarm systems and down payments are forwarded from agents, and the division ships the goods f.o.b. factory directly to customers (usually police departments and security guard companies). Customers are billed directly for the balance due plus actual shipping costs. The company received orders for $6 million of goods during the fiscal year ended November 30, 2001. Down payments of $600,000 were received and $5.2 million of goods were billed and shipped. Actual freight costs of $100,000 were also billed. Commissions of 10% on product price are paid to manufacturing agents after goods are shipped to customers. Such goods are warranted for 90 days after shipment, and warranty returns have been about 1% of sales. Revenue is recognized at the point of sale by this division.

Instructions

(a) There are a variety of methods of revenue recognition. Define and describe each of the following methods of revenue recognition and indicate whether each is in accordance with generally accepted accounting principles.
   1. Point of sale
   2. Completion of production
   3. Percentage of completion
   4. Instalment contract

(b) Calculate the revenue to be recognized in fiscal year 2001 for each of the three operating divisions of Amanar Industries in accordance with generally accepted accounting principles. Discuss your rationale.

(CMA adapted)

P6-2 Diao Construction Ltd. has entered into a contract beginning January 1, 2001 to build a parking complex. It has been estimated that the complex will cost $600,000 and will take three years to construct. The complex will be billed to the purchasing company at $900,000. The following data pertain to the construction period.

	2001	2002	2003
Costs to date	$270,000	$420,000	$600,000
Estimated costs to complete	330,000	180,000	– 0 –
Progress billings to date	270,000	550,000	900,000
Cash collected to date	240,000	500,000	900,000

Instructions

(a) Using the percentage-of-completion method, calculate the estimated gross profit that would be recognized during each year of the construction period.

(b) Using the completed-contract method, calculate the estimated gross profit that would be recognized during each year of the construction period.

P6-3 On March 1, 2001, Stepak Inc. entered into a contract to build an apartment building. It is estimated that the building will cost $2 million and will take three years to complete. The contract price was $3 million. The following information pertains to the construction period:

	2001	2002	2003
Costs to date	$ 600,000	$1,560,000	$2,100,000
Estimated costs to complete	1,400,000	390,000	–0–
Progress billings to date	1,050,000	2,100,000	3,000,000
Cash collected to date	950,000	1,950,000	2,750,000

Instructions

(a) Calculate the amount of gross profit to be recognized each year assuming the percentage-of-completion method is used.

(b) Prepare all necessary journal entries for 2003.

(c) Prepare a partial balance sheet for December 31, 2002, showing the balances in the receivables and inventory accounts.

P6-4 On February 1, 2001, Dandan Inc. obtained a contract to build an athletic stadium. The stadium was to be built at a total cost of $5.4 million and was scheduled for completion by September 1, 2003. One clause of the contract stated that Dandan was to deduct $15,000 from the $6.6 million billing price for each week that completion was delayed. Completion was delayed six weeks, which resulted in a $90,000 penalty. Below are the data pertaining to the construction period.

	2001	2002	2003
Costs to date	$1,782,000	$3,850,000	$5,500,000
Estimated costs to complete	3,618,000	1,650,000	– 0 –
Progress billings to date	1,200,000	3,100,000	6,510,000
Cash collected to date	1,000,000	2,800,000	6,510,000

Instructions

(a) Using the percentage-of-completion method, calculate the estimated gross profit recognized in the years 2001 to 2003.

(b) Prepare a partial balance sheet for December 31, 2002, showing the balances in the receivable and inventory accounts.

P6-5 Zhang Inc. was established in 1972 by Whitney Zhang and initially built high quality customized homes under contract with specific buyers. In the 1980s, Zhang's two sons joined the firm and expanded the company's activities into the high-rise apartment and industrial plant markets. Upon the retirement of the company's long-time financial manager, Zhang's sons recently hired Le Jingyi as controller. Jingyi, a former university friend of Zhang's sons, has been working for a public accounting firm for the last six years.

Upon reviewing the company's accounting practices, Jingyi observed that the company followed the completed-contract method of revenue recognition, a carryover from the years when individual home building was the majority of the company's operations. Several years ago, the predominant portion of the company's activities shifted to the high-rise and industrial building areas. From land acquisition to the completion of construction, most building contracts cover several years. Under the circumstances, Jingyi believes that the company should follow the percentage-of-completion method of accounting. From a typical building contract, Jingyi developed the following data.

Dagmar Haze Tractor Plant

Contract price: $8,000,000

	2000	2001	2002
Estimated costs	$2,010,000	$3,015,000	$1,675,000
Progress billings	1,000,000	2,500,000	4,500,000
Cash collections	800,000	2,300,000	4,900,000

Instructions

(a) Explain the difference between completed-contract revenue recognition and percentage-of-completion revenue recognition.

(b) Using the data provided for the Dagmar Haze Tractor Plant and assuming the percentage-of-completion method of revenue recognition is used, calculate the company's revenue and gross profit for 2000, 2001, and 2002, under each of the following circumstances.

1. Assume that all costs are incurred, all billings to customers are made, and all collections from customers are received within 30 days of billing, as planned.

2. Further assume that, as a result of unforeseen local ordinances and the fact that the building site was in a wetlands area, the company experienced cost overruns of $800,000 in 2000 to bring the site into compliance with the ordinances and to overcome wetlands barriers to construction.

3. Further assume that, in addition to the cost overruns of $800,000 for this contract incurred under Instruction (b)2., inflationary factors over and above those anticipated when developing the original contract cost have caused an additional cost overrun of $540,000 in 2001. It is not anticipated that any cost overruns will occur in 2002.

(CMA adapted)

P6-6 On March 1, 2001, Weksberg Limited contracted to construct a factory building for Xu Manufacturing Inc. for a total contract price of $8.4 million. The building was completed by October 31, 2003. The annual contract costs incurred, estimated costs to complete the contract, and accumulated billings to Xu for 2001, 2002, and 2003 are given below:

	2001	2002	2003
Contract costs incurred during the year	$3,200,000	$2,600,000	$1,450,000
Estimated costs to complete the contract at 12/31	3,200,000	1,450,000	– 0 –
Billings to Xu during the year	3,200,000	3,500,000	1,700,000

Instructions

(a) Using the percentage-of-completion method, prepare schedules to calculate the profit or loss to be recognized as a result of this contract for the years ended December 31, 2001, 2002, and 2003. (Ignore income taxes.)

(b) Using the completed-contract method, prepare schedules to calculate the profit or loss to be recognized as a result of this contract for the years ended December 2001, 2002, and 2003. (Ignore incomes taxes.)

P6-7 On July 1, 2001, Kyung-wook Construction Company Inc. contracted to build an office building for Fu Mingxia Corp. for a total contract price of $1,950,000. On July 1, Kyung-wook estimated that it would take between two and three years to complete the building. On December 31, 2003, the building was deemed substantially completed. Following are accumulated contract costs incurred, estimated costs to complete the contract, and accumulated billings to Mingxia for 2001, 2002, and 2003.

	12/31/01	12/31/02	12/31/03
Contract costs incurred to date	$ 150,000	$1,200,000	$2,100,000
Estimated costs to complete the contract	1,350,000	800,000	– 0 –
Billings to Mingxia	300,000	1,100,000	~~1,850,000~~
			1,950,000

Instructions

(a) Using the percentage-of-completion method, prepare schedules to calculate the profit or loss to be recognized as a result of this contract for the years ended December 31, 2001, 2002, and 2003. (Ignore income taxes.)

(b) Using the completed-contract method, prepare schedules to calculate the profit or loss to be recognized as a result of this contract for the years ended December 2001, 2002, and 2003. (Ignore income taxes.)

P6-8 Presented below is summarized information for Deng Yaping Corp., which sells merchandise on the instalment basis:

	2001	2002	2003
Sales (on instalment plan)	$250,000	$260,000	$280,000
Cost of sales	150,000	163,800	182,000
Gross profit	$100,000	$ 96,200	$ 98,000
Collections from customers on:			
2001 instalment sales	$ 75,000	$100,000	$ 50,000
2002 instalment sales		100,000	120,000
2003 instalment sales			110,000

Instructions

(a) Calculate the realized gross profit for each of the years 2001, 2002, and 2003.

(b) Prepare in journal form all entries required in 2003, applying the instalment sales method of accounting. (Ignore interest charges.)

P6-9 Spearing Inc. sells merchandise on open account as well as on instalment terms.

	2001	2002	2003
Sales on account	$385,000	$426,000	$525,000
Instalment sales	320,000	275,000	380,000
Collections on instalment sales			
Made in 2001	110,000	90,000	40,000
Made in 2002		110,000	140,000
Made in 2003			125,000
Cost of sales			
Sold on account	270,000	277,000	341,000
Sold on instalment	214,400	167,750	224,200
Selling expenses	77,000	87,000	92,000
Administrative expenses	50,000	51,000	52,000

Instructions

From the data above, which cover the three years since Spearing Inc. commenced operations, determine the net income for each year, applying the instalment sales method of accounting. (Ignore interest charges.)

P6-10 Shao Limited sell appliances for cash and also on the instalment plan. Entries to record cost of sales are made monthly.

SHAO LIMITED
Trial Balance
December 31, 2003

	Dr.	Cr.
Cash	$153,000	
Instalment Accounts Receivable, 2002	48,000	
Instalment Accounts Receivable, 2003	91,000	
Inventory—New Merchandise	123,200	
Inventory—Repossessed Merchandise	24,000	
Accounts Payable		$98,500
Deferred Gross Profit, 2002		45,600
Capital Shares		170,000
Retained Earnings		93,900
Sales		343,000
Instalment Sales		200,000
Cost of Sales	255,000	
Cost of Instalment Sales	128,000	
Gain or Loss on Repossessions	800	
Selling and Administrative Expenses	128,000	
	$951,000	$951,000

The accounting department has prepared the following analysis of cash receipts for the year:

Cash sales (including repossessed merchandise)	$424,000
Instalment accounts receivable, 2002	104,000
Instalment accounts receivable, 2003	109,000
Other	36,000
Total	$673,000

Repossessions recorded during the year are summarized as follows:

	2002
Uncollected balance	$8,000
Loss on repossession	800
Repossessed merchandise	4,800

Instructions

From the trial balance and accompanying information:

(a) Calculate the rate of gross profit for 2002 and 2003.

(b) Prepare journal entries as of December 31, 2003 to record any deferred and/or realized profits under the instalment sales method of accounting.

(c) Prepare a statement of income for the year ended December 31, 2003, after booking the journal noted in (b).

P6-11 The following summarized information relates to the instalment sales activity of Greenwood Inc. for the year 2001:

Instalment sales during 2001	$500,000
Costs of goods sold on instalment basis	330,000
Collections from customers	200,000
Unpaid balances on merchandise repossessed	24,000
Estimated value of merchandise repossessed	9,200

Instructions

(a) Prepare journal entries at the end of 2001 to record on the books of Greenwood the summarized data above.

(b) Prepare the entry to record the gross profit realized during 2001.

P6-12 Ruparell Inc. sells merchandise for cash and also on the instalment plan. Entries to record cost of goods sold are made at the end of each year.

Repossessions of merchandise (sold in 2002) were made in 2003 and were recorded correctly as follows:

Deferred Gross Profit, 2002	7,200	
Repossessed Merchandise	8,000	
Loss on Repossessions	2,800	
Instalment Accounts Receivable, 2002		18,000

Part of this repossessed merchandise was sold for cash during 2003, and the sale was recorded by a debit to Cash and a credit to Sales.

The inventory of repossessed merchandise on hand December 31, 2003 is $4,000; of new merchandise, $127,400. There was no repossessed merchandise on hand January 1, 2003.

Collections on accounts receivable during 2003 were:

Instalment Accounts Receivable, 2002	$80,000
Instalment Accounts Receivable, 2003	50,000

The cost of the merchandise sold under the instalment plan during 2003 was $117,000.

The rate of gross profit on 2002 and on 2003 instalment sales can be calculated from the information given above.

RUPARELL INC.
Trial Balance
December 31, 2003

	Dr.	Cr.
Cash	$ 98,400	
Instalment Accounts Receivable, 2002	80,000	
Instalment Accounts Receivable, 2003	130,000	
Inventory, Jan. 1, 2003	120,000	
Repossessed Merchandise	8,000	
Accounts Payable		$ 47,200
Deferred Gross Profit, 2002		64,000
Common Shares		200,000
Retained Earnings		40,000
Sales		400,000
Instalment Sales		180,000
Purchases	380,000	
Loss on Repossessions	2,800	
Operating Expenses	112,000	
	$931,200	$931,200

Instructions

(a) From the trial balance and other information given above, prepare adjusting and closing entries as of December 31, 2003.

(b) Prepare an income statement for the year ended December 31, 2003.

P6-13 Selected transactions of Liping Limited are presented below:

1. A television set costing $560 is sold to Wang Junxia on November 1, 2002 for $800. Junxia makes a down payment of $200 and agrees to pay $30 on the first of each month for 20 months thereafter.
2. Junxia pays the $30 instalment due December 1, 2002.
3. On December 31, 2002, the appropriate entries are made to record profit realized on the instalment sales.
4. The first seven 2003 instalments of $30 each are paid by Junxia. (Make one entry.)
5. In August 2003, the set is repossessed, after Junxia fails to pay the August 1 instalment and indicates that he will be unable to continue the payments. The estimated fair value of the repossessed set is $100.

Instructions
Prepare journal entries to record on the books of Liping Limited the transactions above. Closing entries should not be made.

P6-14 Tian Inc., on January 2, 2001, entered into a contract with a manufacturing company to purchase room-size air conditioners and to sell the units on an instalment plan with collections over approximately 30 months with no carrying charge.

For income tax purposes Tian elected to report income from its sales of air conditioners according to the instalment sales method.

Purchases and sales of new units were as follows:

	Units Purchased			Units Sold	
Year	Quantity	Price Each		Quantity	Price Each
2001	1,400	$130		1,100	$200
2002	1,200	112		1,500	170
2003	900	136		800	182

Collections on instalment sales were as follows:

	Collections Received		
	2001	2002	2003
2001 sales	$42,000	$88,000	$ 80,000
2002 sales		51,000	100,000
2003 sales			34,600

In 2003, 50 units from the 2002 sales were repossessed and sold for $80 each on the instalment plan. At the time of repossession, $1,440 had been collected from the original purchasers and the units had a fair value of $3,000.

General and administrative expenses for 2003 were $60,000. No charge has been made against current income for the applicable insurance expense from a three-year policy expiring June 30, 2004, costing $7,200, and for an advance payment of $12,000 on a new contract to purchase air conditioners beginning January 2, 2004.

Instructions

Assuming that the weighted-average method is used for determining the inventory cost, including repossessed merchandise, prepare schedules calculating for 2001, 2002, and 2003:

- **(a)** **1.** The cost of goods sold on instalments.
  - **2.** The average unit cost of goods sold on instalments for each year.
- **(b)** The gross profit percentages for 2001, 2002, and 2003.
- **(c)** The gain or loss on repossessions in 2003.
- **(d)** The net income from instalment sales for 2003 (ignore income taxes).

(AICPA adapted)

P6-15 Mahoney Inc. entered into a firm fixed-price contract with Ni Clinic on July 1, 1999, to construct a four-storey office building. At that time, Mahoney estimated that it would take between two and three years to complete the project. The total contract price to construct the building is $4.5 million. Mahoney appropriately accounts for this contract under the completed-contract method in its financial statements and for income tax reporting. The building was deemed substantially completed on December 31, 2001. Estimated percentage of completion, accumulated contract costs incurred, estimated costs to complete the contract, and accumulated billings to the Clinic under the contract were as follows:

	December 31, 1999	December 31, 2000	December 31, 2001
Percentage of completion	30%	65%	100%
Contract costs incurred	$1,140,000	$3,055,000	$4,800,000
Estimated costs to complete the contract	$2,660,000	$1,645,000	– 0 –
Billings to Ni Clinic	$1,500,000	$2,500,000	$4,300,000

Instructions

- **(a)** Prepare schedules to calculate the amount to be shown as "cost of uncompleted contract in excess of related billings" or "billings on uncompleted contract in excess of related costs" at December 31, 1999, 2000, and 2001. Ignore income taxes. Show supporting calculations in good form.
- **(b)** Prepare schedules to calculate the profit or loss to be recognized as a result of this contract for the years ended December 31, 1999, 2000, and 2001. Ignore income taxes. Show supporting calculations in good form.

(AICPA adapted)

P6-16 Ye Inc. is in its fourth year of business. Ye performs long-term construction projects and accounts for them using the completed contract method. Ye built an apartment building at a price of $1 million. The costs and billings for this contract for the first three years are as follows:

	2000	2001	2002
Costs incurred to date	$320,000	$600,000	$ 790,000
Estimated costs yet to be incurred	480,000	200,000	– 0 –
Customer billings to date	150,000	410,000	1,000,000
Collection of billings to date	120,000	340,000	950,000

Ye has contacted you, a chartered accountant, about the following concern. She would like to attract some investors, but she believes that in order to recognize revenue she must first "deliver" the product. Therefore, on her balance sheet, she did not recognize any gross profits from the above contract until 2002, when she recognized the entire $210,000. That looked good for 2002, but the preceding years looked grim by comparison. She wants to know about an alternative to this completed-contract revenue recognition.

Instructions

Draft a letter to Ye, telling her about the percentage-of-completion method of recognizing revenue. Compare it with the completed-contract method. Explain the idea behind the percentage-of-completion method. In addition, illustrate how much revenue she could have recognized in 2000, 2001, and 2002 if she had used this method.

P6-17 You have been engaged by Shen Corp. to advise it concerning the proper accounting for a series of long-term contracts. Shen commenced doing business on January 1, 2001. Construction activities for the first year of operations are shown below. All contract costs are with different customers, and any work remaining at December 31, 2001 is expected to be completed in 2002.

Project	Total Contract Price	Billings Through 12/31/01	Cash Collections Through 12/31/01	Contract Costs Incurred Through 12/31/01	Estimated Additional Costs to Complete
A	$ 300,000	$200,000	$180,000	$248,000	$ 67,000
B	350,000	110,000	105,000	67,800	271,200
C	280,000	280,000	255,000	186,000	– 0 –
D	200,000	35,000	25,000	123,000	87,000
E	240,000	205,000	200,000	185,000	15,000
	$1,370,000	$830,000	$765,000	$809,800	$440,200

Instructions

(a) Prepare a schedule to calculate gross profit (loss) to be reported, unbilled contract costs and recognized profit, and billings in excess of costs and recognized profit using the percentage-of-completion method.

(b) Prepare a partial income statement and balance sheet to indicate how the information would be reported for financial statement purposes.

(c) Repeat the requirements for part (a) assuming Shen uses the completed-contract method.

(d) Using the responses above for illustrative purposes, prepare a brief report comparing the conceptual merits (both positive and negative) of the two revenue recognition approaches.

CONCEPTUAL CASES

C6-1 Alexsandra Isosev Industries has three operating divisions—Falilat Mining, Mourning Paperbacks, and Osygus Protection Devices. Each division maintains its own accounting system and method of revenue recognition.

Falilat Mining

Falilat Mining specializes in the extraction of precious metals such as silver, gold, and platinum. During the fiscal year ended November 30, 2001, Falilat entered into contracts worth $2,250,000 and shipped metals worth $2 million. A quarter of the shipments were made from inventories on hand at the beginning of the fiscal year while the remainder were made from metals that were mined during the year. Mining production totals for the year, valued at market prices, were: silver at $750,000, gold at $1.3 million, and platinum at $490,000. Falilat uses the completion-of-production method to recognize revenue, because its operations meet the specified criteria, i.e., reasonably assured sales prices, interchangeable units, and insignificant distribution costs.

Mourning Paperbacks

Mourning Paperbacks sells large quantities of novels to a few book distributors that in turn sell to several national chains of bookstores. Mourning allows distributors to return up to 30% of sales, and distributors give the same terms to bookstores. While returns from individual titles fluctuate greatly, the returns from distributors have averaged 20% in each of the past five years. A total of

$8 million of paperback novel sales were made to distributors during the fiscal year. On November 30, 2001, $3.2 million of fiscal 2001 sales were still subject to return privileges over the next six months. The remaining $4.8 million of fiscal 2001 sales had actual returns of 21%. Sales from fiscal 2001 totalling $2.5 million were collected in fiscal 2001, with less than 18% of sales returned. Mourning records revenue at the point of sale.

Osygus Protection Devices

Osygus Protection Devices works through manufacturers' agents in various cities. Orders for alarm systems and down payments are forwarded from agents, and Osygus ships the goods f.o.b. shipping point. Customers are billed for the balance due plus actual shipping costs. The firm received orders for $6 million of goods during the fiscal year ended November 30, 2001. Down payments of $600,000 were received, and $5 million of goods were billed and shipped. Actual freight costs of $100,000 were also billed. Commissions of 10% on product price were paid to manufacturers' agents after the goods were shipped to customers. Such goods are warranted for 90 days after shipment, and warranty returns have been about 1% of sales. Revenue is recognized at the point of sale by Osygus.

Instructions

Comment on and discuss the revenue recognition policy used by these divisions.

C6-2 Revenue is usually recognized at the point of delivery. Under special circumstances, however, bases other than the point of delivery are used for the timing of revenue recognition.

Instructions

(a) Why is the point of delivery usually used as the basis for the timing of revenue recognition?

(b) Disregarding the special circumstances when bases other than the point of delivery are used, discuss the merits of each of the following objections to using the point of delivery of revenue recognition:

1. It is too conservative because revenue is earned throughout the entire process of production.
2. It is not conservative enough because accounts receivable do not represent disposable funds, sales returns and allowances may be made, and collection and bad debt expenses may be incurred in a later period.

(c) Revenue may also be recognized (1) during production and (2) when cash is received. For each of these two bases of timing revenue recognition, give an example of the circumstances in which it is properly used and discuss the accounting merits of its use in lieu of the sales basis.

(AICPA adapted)

C6-3 The earning of revenue by a business enterprise is recognized for accounting purposes when the transaction is recorded. In some situations, revenue is recognized approximately as it is earned in the economic sense. In other situations, however, accountants have developed guidelines for recognizing revenue by other criteria, such as at the point of delivery.

Instructions (Ignore income taxes)

(a) Explain and justify why revenue is often recognized as it is earned.

(b) Explain in what situations it would be appropriate to recognize revenue as the productive activity takes place.

(c) At what times, other than those included in (a) and (b) above, may it be appropriate to recognize revenue? Explain.

C6-4 Alexei & Nemov Stamps, Inc. was formed early this year to sell trading stamps to retailers who distribute the stamps free to their customers. Books for accumulating the stamps and catalogues illustrating the merchandise for which the stamps may be exchanged are given free to retailers for distribution to stamp recipients. Centres with inventories of merchandise premiums have been established for redemption of the stamps. Retailers may not return unused stamps to Alexei & Nemov.

The following schedule expresses Alexei & Nemov's expectations as to percentages of a normal month's activity that will be attained. For this purpose, a "normal month's activity" is defined as the level of operations expected when expansion of activities ceases or tapers off to a stable rate. The company expects that this level will be attained in the third year and that stamp sales will average $6 million per month throughout the third year.

Month	Actual Stamp Sales Percent	Merchandise Premium Purchases Percent	Stamp Redemptions Percent
6th	30%	40%	10%
12th	60	60	45
18th	80	80	70
24th	90	90	80
30th	100	100	95

Alexei & Nemov plans to adopt an annual closing date at the end of each 12 months of operation.

Instructions

(a) Discuss the factors to be considered in determining when revenue should be recognized in measuring a business enterprise's income.

(b) Discuss the accounting alternatives that should be considered by Alexei & Nemov Stamps, Inc. for the recognition of its revenues and related expenses.

(c) For each accounting alternative discussed in (b), give balance sheet accounts that should be used and indicate how each should be classified.

(AICPA adapted)

C6-5 Cutting Edge is a monthly magazine that has been on the market for 18 months. It currently has a circulation of 1.4 million copies. Currently negotiations are underway to obtain a bank loan in order to update its facilities. It is producing close to capacity and expects to grow at an average of 20% per year over the next three years.

After reviewing the financial statements of Cutting Edge, Gary Hall, the bank loan officer, had indicated that a loan could be offered to Cutting Edge only if it could increase its current ratio and decrease its debt-to-equity ratio to a specified level.

Alexander Popov, the marketing manager of Cutting Edge, has devised a plan to meet these requirements. Popov indicates that an advertising campaign can be initiated to immediately increase circulation. The potential customers would be contacted after the purchase of another magazine's mailing list. The campaign would include:

1. An offer to subscribe to Cutting Edge at ³/₄ the normal price.
2. A special offer to all new subscribers to receive the most current world atlas whenever requested at a guaranteed price of $2.00.
3. An unconditional guarantee that any subscriber will receive a full refund if dissatisfied with the magazine.

Although the offer of a full refund is risky, Popov claims that few people will ask for a refund after receiving half of their subscription issues. Popov notes that other magazine companies have tried this sales promotion technique and experienced great success. Their average cancellation rate was 25%. On average, each company increased its initial circulation threefold and in the long run had increased circulation to twice that before the promotion. In addition, 60% of the new subscribers are expected to take advantage of the atlas premium. Popov feels confident that the increased subscriptions from the advertising campaign will increase the current ratio and decrease the debt-to-equity ratio.

You are Cutting Edge's controller and must give your opinion of the proposed plan.

Instructions

(a) When should revenue from the new subscriptions be recognized? Discuss.

(b) Does the proposed plan achieve the goals of increasing the current ratio and decreasing the debt-to-equity ratio? Discuss.

C6-6 Scherbo Corp. is accounting for a long-term construction contract using the percentage-of-completion method. It is a four-year contract that is currently in its second year. The latest estimates of total contract costs indicate that the contract will be completed at a profit to Scherbo.

Instructions

(a) What theoretical justification is there for Scherbo's use of the percentage-of-completion method?

(b) How would progress billings be accounted for? Include in your discussion the classification of progress billings in Scherbo's financial statements.

(c) How would the income recognized in the second year of the four-year contract be determined using the cost-to-cost method of determining percentage of completion?

(d) What would be the effect on earnings per share in the second year of the four-year contract of using the percentage-of-completion method instead of the completed-contract method? Discuss.

(AICPA adapted)

C6-7 Pankratov Lakes is a new recreational real estate development which consists of 500 lake-front and lakeview lots. As a special incentive to the first 100 buyers of lake-view lots, the developer is offering three years of free financing on 10-year, 12% notes, no down payment, and one week at a nearby established resort—"a $1,200 value." The normal price per lot is $12,000. The cost per lake-view lot to the developer is an estimated average of $2,000. The development costs continue to be incurred; the actual average cost per lot is not known at this time. The resort promotion cost is $700 per lot.

Instructions

(a) Discuss the financial reporting issues.

(b) Assume 50 persons have accepted the offer, signed 10-year notes, and have stayed at the local resort. Prepare the journal entries based on your reasoning in (a) above.

*C6-8 Chou Foods Inc. sells franchises to independent operators. The contract with the franchisee includes the following provisions:

1. The franchisee is charged an initial fee of $80,000. Of this amount, $30,000 is payable when the agreement is signed, and a $10,000 non-interest-bearing note is payable at the end of each of the five subsequent years.

2. All of the initial franchise fee collected by Chou is to be refunded and the remaining obligation cancelled if, for any reason, the franchisee fails to open his or her franchise.

3. In return for the initial franchise fee, Chou agrees to **(a)** assist the franchisee in selecting the business location, **(b)** negotiate the land lease, **(c)** obtain financing and assist with building design, **(d)** supervise construction, **(e)** establish accounting and tax records, and **(f)** provide expert advice over a five-year period relating to such matters as employee and management training, quality control, and promotion.

4. In addition to the initial franchise fee, the franchisee is required to pay to Chou a monthly fee of 2% of sales for menu planning, receipt innovations, and the privilege of purchasing ingredients from Chou. at or below prevailing market prices.

Management of Chou estimates that the value of the services rendered to the franchisee at the time the contract is signed amounts to at least $30,000. All franchisees to date have opened their locations at the scheduled time and none have defaulted on any of the notes receivable.

The credit ratings of all franchisees would entitle them to borrow at the current interest rate of 10%. The present value of an ordinary annuity of five annual receipts of $10,000 each discounted at 10% is $37,908.

Instructions

(a) Discuss the financial reporting issues.

(b) Assume that Chou sells some franchises for $100,000. This amount includes a charge of $20,000 for equipment rental for its useful life of 10 years. $50,000 of the fee is payable immediately and the balance is evidenced by non-interest-bearing notes at $10,000 per year. No portion of the $20,000 rental payment is refundable in case the franchisee goes out of business, and title to the equipment remains with the franchisor. What would be the preferable method of accounting for the rental portion of the initial franchise fee? Explain.

(AICPA adapted)

Using Your Judgement

FINANCIAL REPORTING PROBLEM 1: BARRICK GOLD CORPORATION

Instructions

Refer to the financial statements and accompanying notes in the Digital Tool and answer the following questions.

(a) What were the company's gross revenues for 1998, 1999, and 2000?

(b) What was the percentage of increase in revenues from 1998 to 2000?

(c) Review the notes to the financial statements to determine the company's revenue recognition policy. Discuss, relating to the nature of the business and the industry. (Hint: review the accounting policy for inventory.)

(d) The company uses the U.S.$ to present its Canadian financial statements on the basis that most of the activities take place in the U.S. or in U.S.$. Substantiate this by giving evidence from the financial statements.

FINANCIAL REPORTING PROBLEM 2: SASKATCHEWAN WHEAT POOL

The following is an excerpt from the financial statements of the Saskatchewan Wheat Pool. Amongst other things, the Wheat Pool buys grain from farmers and sells it to the Canadian Wheat Board.

Notes to the Consolidated Financial Statements—July 31, 2000, in thousands

b) Revenue Recognition
Revenue is recognized when goods are shipped or services are performed except for the method of valuing grain inventories. For these inventories a portion of the grain handling revenue is recognized as earned when the grain is received. The balance of the revenue earned is recognized to offset costs when the grain is shipped.

c) Inventories
Grain purchased for sale to the Canadian Wheat Board is valued on the basis of Canadian Wheat Board initial prices less freight and handling costs yet to be incurred. Non-Board grains are valued on the basis of open sales contracts and future contracts, after freight and handling costs yet to be incurred. Grain stocks are hedged through futures commodity contracts in order to protect against market fluctuations. Unrealized gains and losses on the futures commodity contracts are deferred and recognized in income when the hedged inventory is sold. Agri-products and other inventory which consist of raw materials, work in progress and finished goods are valued at the lower of cost and net realizable value.

Instructions

Discuss the financial reporting issues.

FINANCIAL STATEMENT ANALYSIS CASE

Sears, Roebuck and Co.

The 2000 annual report of **Sears, Roebuck and Co.** ("Sears") is included with the Digital Tool. In its "Full line" retail stores, Sears allows independent licensees to set up concession stands and sell products.

According to page 17 of the annual report, Sears changed its accounting policy for accounting for licensee revenues from these concession stands.

Instructions

Discuss the change in accounting policy (read also the note on revenue recognition accounting policies in the financial statements). Is the change material? What key ratios are affected (show calculations).

COMPARATIVE ANALYSIS CASE

Wal-Mart Stores Inc. versus Sears Roebuck and Co.

Wal-Mart Stores Inc. ("Wal-Mart") and Sears, Roebuck and Co. ("Sears") are two major retailers in North America. They both have significant presence in Canada and the U.S. Wal-Mart's business strategy is high volume-low cost. Sears' emphasis is on higher price, higher end products.

Instructions

Using the annual reports on the Digital Tool (Wal-Mart 2001 and Sears 2000) answer the following:

(a) Calculate the gross profit percentage for each company for the most recent two years

(b) Compare the calculations year to year and company to company. Comment. Is Cost of Goods sold calculated the same way for both companies?

(c) Considering the gross profit percentage only, which company would appear to be more successful?

(d) Discuss your findings vis à vis the company strategies. Are the company strategies reflected in the numbers?

ETHICS CASES

Case 1

Nimble Health and Racquet Club (NHRC), which operates eight clubs in the metropolitan area of a large city, offers one-year memberships. The members may use any of the eight facilities but must reserve racquetball court time and pay a separate fee before using the court. As an incentive to new customers, NHRC advertised that any customers not satisfied for any reason could receive a refund of the remaining portion of unused membership fees. Membership fees are due at the beginning of the individual membership period; however, customers are given the option of financing the membership fee over the membership period at a 15% interest rate.

Some customers have expressed a desire to take only the regularly scheduled aerobic classes without paying for a full membership. During the current fiscal year, NHRC began selling coupon books for aerobic classes only to accommodate these customers. Each book is dated and contains 50 coupons that may be redeemed for any regularly scheduled aerobic class over a one-year period. After the one-year period, unused coupons are no longer valid.

During 1995, NHRC expanded into the health equipment market by purchasing a local company that manufactures rowing machines and cross-country ski machines. These machines are used in NHRC's facilities and are sold through the clubs and mail order catalogues. Customers must make a 20% down payment when placing an equipment order; delivery is 60-90 days after order placement. The machines are sold with a two-year unconditional guarantee. Based on past experience, NHRC expects the costs to repair machines under guarantee to be four percent of sales.

NHRC is in the process of preparing financial statements as of May 31, 2001 the end of its fiscal year. James Hogan, corporate controller, expressed concern over the company's performance for the year and decided to review the preliminary financial statements prepared by Barbara Hardy, NHRC's assistant controller. After reviewing the statements, Hogan proposed that the following changes be reflected in the May 31, 2001 published financial statements.

A. Membership revenue should be recognized when the membership fee is collected.

B. Revenue from the coupon books should be recognized when the books are sold.

C. Down payments on equipment purchases and expenses associated with the guarantee on the rowing and cross-country machines should be recognized when paid.

Hardy indicated to Hogan that the proposed changes are not in accordance with generally accepted accounting principles, but Hogan insisted that the changes be made. Hardy believes that Hogan wants to manipulate income to forestall any potential financial problems and increase his year-end bonus. At this point, Hardy is unsure what action to take.

Instructions

(a) Discuss the financial reporting issues.

(b) Discuss why James Hogan's proposed changes and his insistence that the financial statement changes be made is unethical. Structure your answer around or to include the following aspects of ethical conduct: competence, confidentiality, integrity, and/or objectivity.

(c) Identify some specific actions Barbara Hardy could take to resolve this situation.

(CMA adapted)

Case 2

Southwest Health Club offers one-year memberships. Membership fees are due in full at the beginning of the individual membership period. As an incentive to new customers, MHC advertised that any customers not satisfied for any reason could receive a refund of the remaining portion of unused membership fees. As a result of this policy, Stanley Hack, corporate controller, recognized revenue rateably over the life of the membership.

MHC is in the process of preparing its year-end financial statements. Phyllis Cavaretta, MHC's treasurer, is concerned about the company's lacklustre performance this year. She reviews the financial statements Hack prepared and tells Hack to recognize membership revenue when the fees are received.

Instructions

Answer the following questions:

(a) What are the ethical issues involved?

(b) What should Hack do?

CHAPTER 7

Financial Assets: Cash and Receivables

LEARNING OBJECTIVES

··

After studying this chapter, you should be able to:

1. Identify items considered cash.

2. Indicate how cash and related items are reported.

3. Define receivables and identify the different types of receivables.

4. Explain accounting issues related to recognition of accounts receivable.

5. Explain accounting issues related to valuation of accounts receivable.

6. Explain accounting issues related to recognition of notes receivable.

7. Explain accounting issues related to valuation of notes receivable.

8. Explain accounting issues related to disposition of accounts and notes receivable.

9. Explain how receivables are reported and analysed.

Preview of Chapter 7

The purpose of this chapter is to discuss two important assets to companies—cash and receivables. The content and organization of the chapter are as follows:

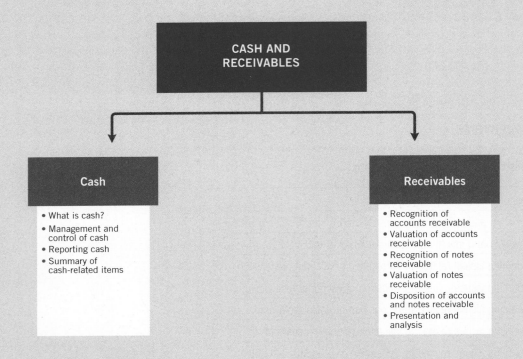

SECTION 1 – Cash

WHAT IS CASH?

OBJECTIVE 1

Identify items considered cash.

Cash, the most liquid of assets, is the standard medium of exchange and the basis for measuring and accounting for all other items. It is generally classified as a current asset. To be reported as **cash**, it must be readily available to pay current obligations, and it must be free from any contractual restriction that limits its use in satisfying debts.

Cash consists of coin, currency, and available funds on deposit at the bank. Negotiable instruments such as money orders, certified cheques, cashier's cheques, personal cheques, and bank drafts are also viewed as cash. Savings accounts are usually classified as cash, although the bank may have a legal right to demand notice before withdrawal. But, because prior notice is rarely demanded by banks, savings accounts are considered cash.

Money market funds, certificates of deposit (CDs), and similar types of deposits and "short-term paper"[1] that provide small investors with an opportunity to earn high rates of interest are more appropriately classified as temporary investments than as cash. The reason is that these securities usually contain restrictions or penalties on their conversion to cash. Money market funds that provide chequing account privileges, however, are usually classified as cash.

Certain items present classification problems: for example, **postdated cheques** and **IOUs** are treated as receivables. **Travel advances** are properly treated as receivables if the advances are to be collected from the employees or deducted from their salaries. Otherwise, classifying the travel advance as a prepaid expense is more appropriate. **Postage stamps** on hand are classified as part of office supplies inventory or as a prepaid expense. **Petty cash funds** and **change funds** are included in current assets as cash because these funds are used to meet current operating expenses and to liquidate current liabilities.

MANAGEMENT AND CONTROL OF CASH

Cash is the asset most susceptible to improper diversion and use. Management must overcome two problems of accounting for cash transactions by (1) establishing proper controls to ensure that no unauthorized transactions are entered into by officers or employees; and (2) providing information necessary to properly manage cash on hand and cash transactions. Yet even with sophisticated control devices, errors can and do happen. *The Wall Street Journal* once ran a story entitled "A $7.8 Million Error Has a Happy Ending for a Horrified Bank," which described how **Manufacturers Hanover Trust Co.** mailed about $7.8 million too much in cash dividends to its shareholders. As implied in the headline, most of the monies were subsequently returned.

To safeguard cash and ensure the accuracy of the accounting records for cash, effective **internal control** over cash is imperative. There are new challenges to maintaining control over liquid assets as more and more transactions are conducted with the swipe of a debit or credit card. For example, it is estimated that over 85% of all banking transactions are now done electronically.[2] In addition, electronic commerce conducted over the Internet continues to grow. Each of these trends contributes to the shift from cold cash to digital cash and poses new challenges for the control of cash. The appendix to this chapter discusses some basic control procedures used to ensure that cash is reported correctly.

REPORTING CASH

Although reporting cash is relatively straightforward, there are a number of issues that merit special attention. These issues relate to the reporting of:

> **OBJECTIVE 2**
> ....
> Indicate how cash and related items are reported.

---

[1] A variety of "short-term paper" is available for investment. For example, **certificates of deposit** (CDs) represent formal evidence of indebtedness, issued by a bank. They must usually be held until maturity, although some CDs in excess of $100,000 are negotiable. **Guaranteed investment certificates (GICs)** are similar time deposits issued by trust companies. The short-term certificates mature in 30 to 360 days and generally pay interest at the short-term rate in effect at the date of issuance. In **money market funds**, a variation of the mutual fund, the yield is determined by the mix of Treasury bills and commercial paper making up the fund's portfolio. **Treasury bills** are Canadian government obligations with 3, 6 and 12 month maturities; they are sold in $1,000, $5,000, $25,000, $100,000 and $1 million denominations at weekly government auctions. **Commercial paper** is short-term unsecured debt notes issued by corporations with good credit ratings, usually in minimum denominations of $50,000.

[2] McKinsey & Company Report, *The Changing Landscape*, 1998, as reported by the Canadian Bankers Association, Fast Facts, October, 2000: www.cba.ca/eng/Statistics/FastFacts/abms.htm.

1. restricted cash
2. cash in foreign currencies
3. bank overdrafts
4. cash equivalents

Restricted Cash

Compensating Balances. Banks and other lending institutions often require customers to whom they lend money to maintain minimum cash balances in chequing or savings accounts. These minimum balances, called compensating balances, are defined as: "that portion of any demand deposit (or any time deposit or certificate of deposit) maintained by a corporation which constitutes support for existing borrowing arrangements of the corporation with a lending institution. Such arrangements would include both outstanding borrowings and the assurance of future credit availability."[3]

Compensating balances may be payment for bank services rendered to the company for which there is no direct fee, for example, cheque processing and lockbox management. By requiring a compensating balance, the bank achieves an effective interest rate on a loan that is higher than the stated rate because it can use the restricted amount that must remain on deposit.

To illustrate, assume that on January 1, 2002, Biddle Co. borrowed $10 million for one year from First Provincial Bank at an interest rate of 10%. In addition, Biddle is required to keep a compensatory balance of $2 million on deposit at First Provincial, which will earn 6%. Normally, Biddle would maintain a balance of $1 million at the bank for transaction purposes. The effective interest that Biddle pays on this loan is 10.4% calculated as follows:

ILLUSTRATION 7-1
Calculation of Interest Cost

$10,000,000 × 10%	$1,000,000
($2,000,000 − $1,000,000) × 4%	40,000
Total interest cost	$1,040,000

$$\frac{\text{Total interest cost}}{\text{Total principal}} = \frac{\$1,040,000}{\$10,000,000} = 10.4\%$$

Biddle pays $1 million interest on the original loan of $10 million and it is required to maintain an additional $1 million cash balance on which it can earn only 6%. If it has to borrow this additional $1,000,000, it will be losing 4% (10% − 6%) on every dollar borrowed.

The need to disclose compensating balances was highlighted in the 1970s when a number of companies were involved in a liquidity crisis. Many investors believed that the cash reported on the balance sheet was fully available to meet recurring obligations, but these funds were actually restricted because these companies needed to maintain compensating cash balances at various lending institutions.

Disclosure of compensating balances depends on the classification of the related loan or borrowing arrangement. If the balances are required for short-term borrowing, then the compensating amount could be separately disclosed under Current Assets. Restricted amounts held as compensating balances against long-term borrowing arrangements should be separately classified as noncurrent assets in either the Investments or Other Assets section using a caption such as "Cash on Deposit Maintained as Compensating Balance." In addition, a note to the financial statements should indicate the nature of the arrangement and cash restriction.

Other Types of Restrictions. Petty cash, payroll, and dividend funds are examples of cash set aside for a particular purpose. In most situations, these fund balances are not material and therefore are not segregated from cash when reported in the financial

---

[3] *Accounting Series Release No. 148*, "Amendments to Regulations S-X and Related Interpretations and Guidelines Regarding the Disclosure of Compensating Balances and Short-Term Borrowing Arrangements," Securities and Exchange Commission (November 13, 1973).

statements. When material in amount, restricted cash is segregated from "regular" cash for reporting purposes. The **restricted cash** is classified either in the Current Assets or in the Long-term Assets section, depending on the date of availability or disbursement. Classification in the current section is appropriate if the cash is to be used (within a year or the operating cycle, whichever is longer) to pay existing or maturing obligations. This is the case for the **Atlantic Lottery Corp. Inc.** as shown in Illustration 7-2. On the other hand, if the cash is to be held for a longer period of time, the restricted cash is shown in the balance sheet's Long-term Assets section.[4] Cash classified in the long-term section is frequently set aside for investment or financing purposes such as plant expansion or long-term debt retirement.

ILLUSTRATION 7-2
Disclosure of Restricted Cash

ATLANTIC LOTTERY CORP. INC.

	2000	1999
Assets		
Cash (note 2)	$33,324	$46,559

Note 2: Cash
Cash is represented by deposits on account less outstanding cheques.

	2000	1999
Deposits on account	$37,941	$48,290
Less outstanding cheques	4,617	1,731
Cash, end of year	$33,324	$46,559

Deposits on account in the amount of $34,296 (1999 – $36,994) are held for the payment of prizes and their use is restricted for that purpose.

Cash in Foreign Currencies

Many companies maintain bank accounts in other countries, especially if they have recurring transactions in that country's currency. The foreign currency is translated into Canadian dollars at the exchange rate on the balance sheet date and, in situations where there is no restriction on the transfer of those funds to the Canadian company, it is included as Cash in current assets. If there are restrictions on the flow of capital out of a country, the cash is reported as restricted. The classification of the cash as current or noncurrent is based on the circumstances and, in extreme cases, the restrictions may be so severe that the foreign balances may not qualify for recognition as assets.

Bank Overdrafts

Bank overdrafts occur when cheques are written for more than the amount in the cash account. They should be reported in the Current Liabilities section and are usually added to the amount reported as accounts payable. If material, these items should be separately disclosed either on the face of the balance sheet or in the related notes.

Bank overdrafts are generally not offset against the Cash account. A major exception is when available cash is present in another account in the same bank on which the overdraft occurred. Offsetting in this case is appropriate.

Cash Equivalents

A current classification that has become popular is "cash and cash equivalents."[5] **Cash equivalents** are short-term, highly liquid investments that are both readily convertible

---

[4] *CICA Handbook*, Section 3000, par. .01.

[5] The increasing popularity of this classification is likely linked to recently revised *CICA Handbook* Section 1540 that now requires the reporting of cash flows defined as "cash and cash equivalents."

to known amounts of cash, and so near their maturity that they present insignificant risk of changes in interest rates. Generally only investments with original maturities of three months or less qualify under these definitions. Examples of cash equivalents are Treasury bills, commercial paper, and money market funds. Some companies combine cash with temporary investments on the balance sheet. In these cases, the amount of the temporary investments is described either parenthetically or in the notes.

For purposes of the Statement of Cash Flows, bank overdrafts may, in some circumstances, be deducted in determining the amount of cash and cash equivalents. If overdrafts are part of the cash management activities of the firm and repayable on demand, and the bank balance fluctuates often between a positive and negative balance, the overdraft may be considered a component of cash and cash equivalents.[6]

SUMMARY OF CASH-RELATED ITEMS

Cash and cash equivalents include the medium of exchange and most negotiable instruments. If the item cannot be converted to coin or currency on short notice, it is separately classified as an investment, as a receivable, or as a prepaid expense. Cash that is not available for payment of currently maturing liabilities is segregated and classified in the long-term assets section. Illustration 7-3 summarizes the classification of cash-related items.

ILLUSTRATION 7-3
Classification of Cash-Related Items

Classification of Cash, Cash Equivalents, and Noncash Items		
Item	**Classification**	**Comment**
Cash	Cash	If unrestricted, report as cash. If restricted, identify and classify as current and noncurrent assets.
Petty cash and change funds	Cash	Report as cash.
Short-term paper	Cash equivalents	Investments with maturity of less than three months, often combined with cash.
Short-term paper	Temporary investments	Investments with maturity of 3 to 12 months.
Postdated cheques and IOUs	Receivables	Assumed to be collectible.
Travel advances	Receivables	Assumed to be collected from employees or deducted from their salaries.
Postage on hand (as stamps or in postage meters)	Prepaid expenses	May also be classified as office supplies inventory.
Bank overdrafts	Current liability	If right of offset exists, reduce cash.
Compensating balances		
1. Legally restricted	Cash separately classified as a deposit maintained as compensating balance	Classify as current or noncurrent in the balance sheet.
2. Arrangement without legal restriction	Cash with note disclosure	Disclose separately in notes details of the arrangement.

Handwritten margin notes:

Postdated cheques it's nothing until that date.

Если мы имеем деньги на счету мы уменьшаем счет на эту сумму если баланс 0 то bank overdrafts это наши liability.

Reduce your мы asset cash

SECTION 2 – Receivables

Receivables are claims held against customers and others for money, goods, or services. When receivables represent contractual rights to receive cash or other financial assets from another party, they are termed **financial assets**. For financial statement purposes, receivables are classified as either **current** (short-term) or **noncurrent** (long-term). **Current receivables** are expected to be collected within a year or during the current operating cycle, whichever is longer. All other receivables are classified as **noncurrent**. Receivables are further classified in the balance sheet as either trade or nontrade receivables.

Trade receivables are amounts owed by customers for goods sold and services rendered as part of normal business operations. Trade receivables, usually the most significant an enterprise possesses, may be subclassified into accounts receivable and notes receivable. **Accounts receivable** are the purchaser's oral promises to pay for goods and services sold. They are normally collectible within 30 to 60 days and represent "open accounts" resulting from short-term extensions of credit. **Notes receivable** are written promises to pay a certain sum of money on a specified future date. They may arise from sales, financing, or other transactions. Notes may be short-term or long-term.

Nontrade receivables arise from a variety of transactions and can be written promises either to pay or to deliver. Some examples of nontrade receivables are:

1. advances to officers and employees
2. advances to subsidiaries
3. deposits to cover potential damages or losses
4. deposits as a guarantee of performance or payment
5. dividends and interest receivable
6. claims against:
   (a) insurance companies for casualties sustained
   (b) defendants under suit
   (c) governmental bodies for tax refunds
   (d) common carriers for damaged or lost goods
   (e) creditors for returned, damaged, or lost goods
   (f) customers for returnable items (crates, containers, etc.)

Because of the peculiar nature of nontrade receivables, they are generally classified and reported as separate items in the balance sheet or in a note cross-referenced to the balance sheet. Illustration 7-4 shows the reporting of trade and nontrade receivables in the financial statements of **Le Groupe Vidéotron**.

> **OBJECTIVE 3**
>
> Define receivables and identify the different types of receivables.

LE GROUPE VIDÉOTRON	as at August 31, 1999
Accounts receivable (note 15)	**211,066**

15. Accounts Receivable	
(in thousands of dollars)	1999
Trade	$145,664
Balance of selling price of cable television operations in Alberta	26,041
Loans to employees for the purchase of shares of the Company	1,162
Amounts receivable from affiliated companies:	
• Wavepath Holdings Inc.	38,129
• Other	70
	$211,066

ILLUSTRATION 7-4
Receivables Reporting

The basic issues in accounting for accounts and notes receivable are the same: **recognition**, **valuation**, and **disposition**. We will discuss these basic issues of accounts and notes receivable in the following sequence:

1. recognition and valuation of accounts receivable
2. recognition and valuation of notes receivable
3. disposition of accounts and notes receivable

RECOGNITION OF ACCOUNTS RECEIVABLE

<table>
<tr><td>

OBJECTIVE 4

Explain accounting issues related to recognition of accounts receivable.

</td></tr>
</table>

In most receivables transactions, the amount to be recognized is the exchange price between the two parties. **The exchange price is the amount due from the debtor** (a customer or a borrower) and is generally evidenced by some type of business document, often an invoice. Two factors that may complicate the measurement of the exchange price are (1) the availability of discounts (trade and cash discounts) and (2) the length of time between the sale and the due date of payments (the interest element).

Trade Discounts

Customers are often quoted prices on the basis of list or catalogue prices that may be subject to a trade or quantity discount. Such **trade discounts** are used to avoid frequent changes in catalogues, to quote different prices for different quantities purchased, or to hide the true invoice price from competitors.

Trade discounts are commonly quoted in percentages. For example, if your textbook has a list price of $80.00 and the publisher sells it to college bookstores for list less a 30% trade discount, the receivable recorded by the publisher is $56.00 per textbook. The normal practice is simply to deduct the trade discount from the list price and bill the customer net.

As another example, the producers of Nabob at one time sold a 285 g jar of its instant coffee that had a list price of $4.65 to supermarkets for $3.90, a trade discount of approximately 16%. The supermarkets in turn sold the instant coffee for $3.99 per jar. Nabob would record the receivable and related sales revenue at $3.90 per jar, not $4.65.

Cash Discounts (Sales Discounts)

Cash discounts (sales discounts) are offered to induce prompt payment. They are communicated in terms that read, for example, 2/10, n/30 (2% if paid within 10 days, gross amount due in 30 days), or 2/10, E.O.M. (2% if paid within 10 days of the end of the month).

Companies buying goods or services that fail to take sales discounts are usually not employing their money advantageously. An enterprise that receives a 1% reduction in the sales price for payment within 10 days, total payment due within 30 days, is effectively earning 18.25% (0.01 divided by 20/365), or at least avoiding that rate of interest cost. For this reason, companies usually take the discount unless their cash is severely limited.

The easiest and most commonly used method of recording sales and related sales discount transactions is to enter the receivable and sale at the gross amount. Under this method, sales discounts are recognized in the accounts only when payment is received within the discount period. Sales discounts would then be shown in the income statement as a deduction from sales to arrive at net sales.

Some accountants contend that sales discounts not taken reflect penalties added to an established price to encourage prompt payment. That is, the seller offers sales on account at a slightly higher price than if selling for cash, and the increase is offset by the cash discount offered. Thus, customers who pay within the discount period purchase at the cash price; those who pay after the discount period expires are penalized because they must pay more than the cash price. If this reasoning is used, sales and receivables are recorded net, and any discounts not taken are subsequently debited to Accounts Receivable and credited to Sales Discounts Forfeited. The following entries illustrate the difference between the gross and net methods.

Gross Method			Net Method		
Sales of $10,000, terms 2/10, n/30:					
Accounts Receivable	10,000		Accounts Receivable	9,800	
Sales		10,000	Sales		9,800
Payment on $4,000 received within discount period:					
Cash	3,920		Cash	3,920	
Sales Discounts	80		Accounts Receivable		3,920
Accounts Receivable		4,000			
Payment on $6,000 received after discount period:					
Cash	6,000		Accounts Receivable	120	
Accounts Receivable		6,000	Sales Discounts		
			Forfeited		120
			Cash	6,000	
			Accounts Receivable		6,000

If the gross method is employed, sales discounts are reported as a deduction from sales in the income statement. Proper matching would dictate that a reasonable estimate of material amounts of expected discounts to be taken also should be charged against sales. An Allowance for Sales Discounts, a contra account to Accounts Receivable, would be credited. If the net method is used, Sales Discounts Forfeited are considered an other revenue item.[7]

Theoretically, recognizing Sales Discounts Forfeited is correct because the receivable is stated closer to its realizable value and the net sale figure measures the revenue earned from the sale. As a practical matter, however, the net method is seldom used because it requires additional analysis and bookkeeping. For one thing, the net method requires adjusting entries to record sales discounts forfeited on accounts receivable that have passed the discount period.

Nonrecognition of Interest Element

Ideally, receivables should be measured in terms of their present value; that is, the discounted value of the cash to be received in the future. When expected cash receipts require a waiting period, the receivable face amount is not a good measure of the amount that is ultimately received.

To illustrate, assume that a company makes a sale on account for $1,000 with payment due in four months. The applicable annual rate of interest is 12%, and payment is made at the end of four months. The receivable's present value is not $1,000 but $961.54 ($1,000 × .96154, Table A-2; $n = 1, i = 4\%$). In other words, $1,000 to be received four months from now is not the same as $1,000 received today.

Theoretically, any revenue after the period of sale is interest revenue. In practice, accountants have generally chosen to ignore this for accounts receivable because the discount amount is not usually material in relation to the net income for the period. Generally, receivables that arise from transactions with customers in the normal course of business, and that are due in customary trade terms not exceeding approximately one year, are excluded from present value considerations.[8]

UNDERLYING CONCEPTS
Materiality means it must make a difference to a decision maker. Standard setters believe that present value concepts can be ignored for short-term notes.

---

[7] To the extent that discounts not taken reflect a short-term financing situation, some argue that an interest revenue account could be used to record these amounts.

[8] *CICA Handbook*, Section 3020, "Accounts and Notes Receivable," is silent on the issue of interest. However, in the U.S., *APB Opinion No. 21*, "Interest on Receivables and Payables," provides that all receivables are subject to present value measurement techniques and interest imputation, if necessary, except for the following specifically excluded types:
(a) normal accounts receivable due within one year
(b) security deposits, retainages, advances, or progress payments
(c) transactions between parent and subsidiary
(d) receivables due at some determinable future date

VALUATION OF ACCOUNTS RECEIVABLE

OBJECTIVE 5

Explain accounting issues related to valuation of accounts receivable.

Having recorded receivables at their face value (the amount due), the problem of financial statement presentation then occurs. Reporting of receivables involves (1) classification and (2) valuation on the balance sheet.

Classification, as already discussed, involves determining the length of time each receivable will be outstanding. Receivables intended to be collected within a year or the operating cycle, whichever is longer, are classified as current; all other receivables are classified as long-term.

The valuation of receivables is more complex. **Short-term receivables are valued and reported at net realizable value—the net amount expected to be received in cash**, which is not necessarily the amount legally receivable. Determining net realizable value requires estimating both uncollectible receivables and any returns or allowances to be granted.

Uncollectible Accounts Receivable

As one accountant so aptly noted, the credit manager's idea of heaven probably would be a place where everyone (eventually) paid his or her debts.[9] The recent experience of **Sears Canada**, as shown in Illustration 7-6, indicates the importance of credit sales for many companies.

ILLUSTRATION 7-6
Sears Canada Customer Method of Payment

	1999	1998
Sears Card	62%	62%
Third Party Credit Cards	13	13
Debit Cards	7	5
Cash	18	20
Total	100%	100%

from: Sears Canada, Annual Report, 1999

Sales on any basis other than for cash make possible the subsequent failure to collect the account. An uncollectible account receivable is a loss of revenue that requires, through proper entry in the accounts, a decrease in the asset accounts receivable and a related decrease in income and shareholders' equity. The loss in revenue and the decrease in income are recognized by recording bad debt expense.

The chief problem in recording uncollectible accounts receivable is establishing the time at which to record the loss. Two general procedures are used:

METHODS FOR RECORDING UNCOLLECTIBLES

1. **Direct Write-Off Method.** No entry is made until a specific account has definitely been established as uncollectible. Then the loss is recorded by crediting Accounts Receivable and debiting Bad Debt Expense.

2. **Allowance Method.** An estimate is made of the expected uncollectible amounts from all sales made on account or from the total of outstanding receivables. This estimate is entered as an expense and an indirect reduction in accounts receivable (via an increase in the allowance account) in the period in which the sale is recorded.

The direct write-off method records bad debt expense in the year it is determined that a specific receivable cannot be collected. The allowance method enters the expense on an estimated basis in the accounting period in which the sales on account are made.

Supporters of the **direct write-off method** contend that facts, not estimates, are recorded. It assumes that a good account receivable resulted from each sale, and that later events proved certain accounts to be uncollectible and worthless. From a practical standpoint this method is simple and convenient to apply, although receivables do not generally become worthless at an identifiable moment of time. The direct write-off

---

[9] William J. Vatter, *Managerial Accounting* (Englewood Cliffs, N.J.: Prentice-Hall, 1950), p. 60.

method is theoretically deficient because it usually does not match the period's costs with revenues, nor does it result in receivables being stated at estimated realizable value on the balance sheet. **As a result, the direct write-off method is not considered appropriate, except when the amount uncollectible is immaterial.**

Advocates of the allowance method believe that bad debt expense should be recorded in the same period as the sale to obtain a proper matching of expenses and revenues and to achieve a proper carrying value for accounts receivable. They support the position that although estimates are involved, the percentage of receivables that will not be collected can be predicted from past experience, present market conditions, and an analysis of the outstanding balances. Many companies set their credit policies to provide for a certain percentage of uncollectible accounts. In fact, many feel that failure to reach that percentage means that sales are being lost by credit policies that are too restrictive.

Because the collectibility of receivables is considered a loss contingency, the allowance method is appropriate in situations where it is probable that an asset has been impaired and that the loss amount can be reasonably estimated.[10] A receivable is a prospective cash inflow, and the probability of its collection must be considered in valuing this inflow. These estimates normally are made either on (1) the basis of percentage of sales or (2) the basis of outstanding receivables.

Percentage-of-Sales (Income Statement) Approach

If there is a fairly stable relationship between previous years' credit sales and bad debts, then that relationship can be turned into a percentage and used to determine this year's bad debt expense.

The percentage-of-sales approach matches costs with revenues because it relates the charge to the period in which the sale is recorded. To illustrate, assume that Dockrill Corp. estimates from past experience that about 2% of credit sales become uncollectible. If Dockrill Corp. has credit sales of $400,000 in 2002, the entry to record bad debt expense using the percentage-of-sales method is as follows:

UNDERLYING CONCEPTS

The percentage-of-sales method is a good illustration of the use of the matching principle, which relates expenses to revenues earned.

| Bad Debt Expense | 8,000 | |
| Allowance for Doubtful Accounts | | 8,000 |

The Allowance for Doubtful Accounts is a valuation account (i.e., a contra asset) and is subtracted from trade receivables on the balance sheet.[11] The amount of bad debt expense and the related credit to the allowance account are unaffected by any balance currently existing in the allowance account. Because the bad debt expense estimate is related to a nominal account (Sales), and any balance in the allowance is ignored, this method is frequently referred to as the income statement approach. A proper matching of cost and revenues is therefore achieved.

Percentage-of-Receivables (Balance Sheet) Approach

Using past experience, a company can estimate the percentage of its outstanding receivables that will become uncollectible, without identifying specific accounts. This procedure provides a reasonably accurate estimate of the receivables' realizable value, but does not fit the concept of matching cost and revenues. Rather, its objective is to report receivables in the balance sheet at net realizable values; hence it is referred to as the percentage-of-receivables (or balance sheet) approach.

The percentage of receivables may be applied using one **composite rate** that reflects an estimate of the uncollectible receivables. Another approach that is more sensitive to the actual status of the accounts receivable sets up an ageing schedule and applies a

INTERNATIONAL INSIGHT

In the People's Republic of China, the rates for providing for bad debts are established by state regulation.

---

[10] *CICA Handbook*, Section 3290, par. .12.

[11] In Canada, few companies actually make reference to or disclose the amount of the Allowance for Doubtful Accounts. The assumption is that an adequate allowance has been made for potentially uncollectible accounts in the absence of a statement to the contrary.

different percentage based on past experience to the various age categories. An ageing schedule is frequently used in practice. It indicates which accounts require special attention by providing the age of such accounts receivable. The schedule of Wilson & Co. in Illustration 7-7 is an example.

ILLUSTRATION 7-7
Accounts Receivable Ageing Schedule

WILSON & CO, Ageing Schedule

Name of Customer	Balance Dec. 31	Under 60 days	61-90 days	91-120 days	Over 120 days
Western Stainless Steel Corp.	$ 98,000	$ 80,000	$18,000		
Brockway Steel Company	320,000	320,000			
Freeport Sheet & Tube Co.	55,000				$55,000
Allegheny Iron Works	74,000	60,000		$14,000	
	$547,000	$460,000	$18,000	$14,000	$55,000

Summary

Age	Amount	Percentage Estimated to be Uncollectible	Required Balance in Allowance
Under 60 days old	$460,000	4%	$18,400
61-90 days old	18,000	15%	2,700
91-120 days old	14,000	20%	2,800
Over 120 days	55,000	25%	13,750
Year-end balance of allowance for doubtful accounts should =			$37,650

Assuming that no balance existed in the allowance account before this adjustment, the bad debt expense to be reported for this year would be $37,650.

To change the illustration slightly, **assume that the allowance account had a credit balance of $800 before adjustment**. In this case, the amount to be added to the allowance account to bring it to the desired balance of $37,650 is $36,850 ($37,650 − $800), and the following entry is made.

Bad Debt Expense	36,850	
Allowance for Doubtful Accounts		36,850

The balance in the Allowance account is therefore stated at $37,650. **If the Allowance balance before adjustment had a debit balance of $200**, then the amount to be recorded for bad debt expense would be $37,850 ($37,650 desired balance + $200 debit balance). In the percentage-of-receivables method, the balance in the allowance account **cannot be ignored**, because it is used to calculate the amount of the adjustment needed.

An ageing schedule is usually not prepared to determine the bad debt expense. Rather, it is prepared as a control device to determine the composition of receivables and to identify delinquent accounts. The estimated loss percentage developed for each category is based on previous loss experience and the advice of credit department personnel. Regardless of whether a composite rate or an aging schedule is employed, the percentage of receivables method's primary objective for financial statement purposes is to report receivables in the balance sheet at net realizable value. However, it is deficient since it may not match bad debt expense to the period in which the sale takes place.

The allowance for doubtful accounts as a percentage of receivables will vary considerably, depending upon the industry and the economic climate.

In summary, the percentage-of-receivables method results in a more accurate valuation of receivables on the balance sheet. From a matching viewpoint, the percentage-of-sales approach provides the better results. Illustration 7-8 relates these methods to the basic theory.

The account title employed for the allowance account is usually Allowance for Doubtful Accounts or simply Allowance.

Regardless of the method chosen, determining the expense associated with uncollectible accounts is an area of accounting that is subject to a large degree of judgement.

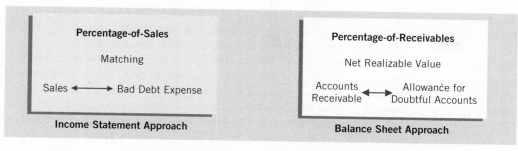

ILLUSTRATION 7-8
Comparison of Methods for
Estimating Uncollectibles

There has been some concern that banks, for instance, use this judgement to manage earnings. By overestimating the amount of uncollectible loans in a good earnings year, the bank can "save for a rainy day" in a future period. In future, less profitable, periods, the overly conservative allowance for its loan loss account can be reduced to increase earnings.[12]

Accounts Receivable Written Off

Under the Allowance method, when a specific account is determined to be uncollectible, its balance is removed from the Accounts Receivable and the Allowance is reduced. For example, assuming the account of Brown Ltd. of $550 is considered uncollectible, the write-off entry is as follows:

Allowance for Doubtful Accounts	550	
Accounts Receivable		550
(To write off the account of Brown Ltd.)		

Note that there is no effect on the income statement from writing off an account because bad debt expense was estimated, recognized and matched with revenue in the period of the sale. There is also no effect on the net amount of the receivables because the Accounts Receivable and its contra account are **both** reduced by equal amounts.

If a collection is made on a receivable that was previously written off, the procedure is first to reestablish the receivable by reversing the write-off entry, and then recognize the cash inflow as a regular receipt on account. To illustrate, assume that Brown Ltd. subsequently remits $300, but indicates that this is all that will be paid. The entries to record this transaction are as follows.

Accounts Receivable	300	
Allowance for Doubtful Accounts		300
(To reinstate the account written off now		
determined to be collectible.)		
Cash	300	
Accounts Receivable		300
(To record the receipt of cash on account from Brown Ltd.)		

If the direct write-off method is employed, no allowance account is used. When an account is determined to be uncollectible, the specific account receivable is written off with the debit recognized as bad debt expense. If amounts are subsequently collected on an account written off, the amount collected is debited to Cash and credited to a revenue account entitled Uncollectible Amounts Recovered, with proper notation in the customer's account.

Sales Returns and Allowances

To properly match expenses to sales revenues, it is sometimes necessary to establish additional allowance accounts. These allowance accounts are reported as contra accounts to accounts receivable, and they establish the receivables at net realizable value. The most common is an Allowance for Sales Returns and Allowances.

---

[12] Recall from the earnings management discussion in Chapter 4 that increasing or decreasing income through management manipulation can reduce the quality of financial reports.

Many question the soundness of recording returns and allowances in the current period when they are derived from sales made in the preceding period. Normally, however, the amount of mismatched returns and allowances is not material if such items are handled consistently from year to year. Yet if a company completes a few special orders involving large amounts near the end of the accounting period, **sales returns and allowances** should be anticipated and recognized in the period of the sale to avoid distorting the current period's income statement. And there are some companies that by their nature have significant returns and customarily establish an allowance for sales returns.

As an example, Astro Corporation recognizes that approximately 5% of its $1 million trade receivables outstanding are returned or some adjustment is made to the sale price. Omission of a $50,000 charge could have a material effect on net income for the period. The entry to reflect anticipated sales returns and allowances is:

Sales Returns and Allowances	50,000	
Allowance for Sales Returns and Allowances		50,000

The account Sales Returns and Allowances is reported as an offset to sales revenue in the income statement. Returns and allowances are accumulated separately instead of debited directly to the Sales account simply to let the business manager and the statement reader know their magnitude. The Allowance is an asset valuation account (contra asset) and is deducted from total Accounts Receivable.

In most cases, reporting all returns and allowances made during the period in the income statement, whether or not they resulted from the current period's sales, is an acceptable accounting procedure justified by practicality and immateriality.[13]

RECOGNITION OF NOTES RECEIVABLE

A note receivable is supported by a formal promissory note, a written promise to pay a certain sum of money at a specific future date. Such a note is a negotiable instrument that is signed by a **maker** in favor of a designated **payee** who may legally and readily sell or otherwise transfer the note to others. Although notes always contain an interest element because of the time value of money, they are classified as interest-bearing or noninterest-bearing. **Interest-bearing notes** have a stated rate of interest, whereas zero-interest-bearing notes (noninterest-bearing) include interest as part of their face amount instead of stating it explicitly. Notes receivable are considered fairly liquid, even if long-term, because they may be easily converted to cash.

Notes receivable are frequently accepted from customers who need to extend the payment period of an outstanding receivable. Notes are also sometimes required of high-risk or new customers. In addition, notes are often used in loans to employees and subsidiaries and in the sales of property, plant, and equipment. In some industries (e.g., the pleasure and sport boat industry) all credit sales are supported by notes. The majority of notes, however, originate from lending transactions. The basic issues in accounting for notes receivable are the same as those for accounts receivable: recognition, valuation, and disposition.

OBJECTIVE 6

Explain accounting issues related to recognition of notes receivable.

Short-term notes are generally recorded at face value (less allowances) because the interest implicit in the maturity value is immaterial. A general rule is that notes treated as cash equivalents (maturities of three months or less) are not subject to premium or discount amortization. Long-term notes receivable, however, should be recorded and reported at the **present value of the cash expected to be collected**. When the interest stated on an interest-bearing note is equal to the effective (market) rate of interest, the note sells at face value.[14] When the stated rate is different from the market rate, the cash

---

[13] An interesting sidelight to the entire problem of returns and allowances is determining when a sale is a sale. In certain circumstances, the seller is exposed to such a high risk of ownership through possible return of the property that the sale is not recognized. Such situations have developed, particularly in sales to related parties. This subject is discussed in more detail in Chapters 6 and 8.

exchanged (present value) is different from the note's face value. The difference between the face value and the cash exchanged, either a discount or a premium, is then recorded and amortized over the note's life so that interest revenue reported approximates the effective (market) rate.

Notes Issued at Face Value

To illustrate the discounting of a note issued at face value, assume that Bigelow Corp. lends Scandinavian Imports $10,000 in exchange for a $10,000, three-year note bearing interest at 10% annually. The market rate of interest for a note of similar risk is also 10%. The time diagram depicting both cash flows is shown below:

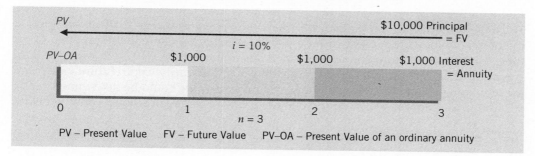

The note's present value or exchange price is calculated as follows:

Face value of the note		$10,000
Present value of the principal:		
$10,000 (PVF*$_{3,10\%}$) = $10,000 (0.75132)	$7,513	
Present value of the interest:		
$1,000 (PVF*–OA$_{3,10\%}$) = $1,000 (2.48685)	2,487	
Present value of the note		10,000
Difference		$ –0–
*Present Value Factor		

ILLUSTRATION 7-9
Present Value of Note-Stated and Market Rates the Same

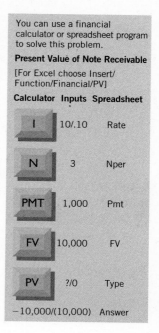

In this case, the note's present value and face value are the same ($10,000) because the effective and stated interest rates are also the same. The note's receipt is recorded by Bigelow Corp. as follows:

Notes Receivable	10,000	
Cash		10,000

Bigelow Corp. recognizes the interest earned each year as follows:

Cash	1,000	
Interest Revenue		1,000

Notes Not Issued at Face Value

Zero-Interest-Bearing Notes. If a zero-interest-bearing note is received in exchange for cash, its present value is the cash paid to the issuer. Because both the note's future amount and present value are known, the interest rate can be calculated, i.e., it is implied. The **implicit interest rate** is the rate that equates the cash paid with the amounts receivable in the future. The difference between the future (face) amount and the present value (cash paid) is recorded as a discount and is amortized to interest revenue over the life of the note.

---

[14] The **stated interest rate**, also referred to as the face rate or the coupon rate, is the rate contracted as part of the note. The **effective interest rate**, also referred to as the market rate or the effective yield, is the rate used in the market to determine the note's value—that is, the discount rate used to determine the present value.

To illustrate, assume Jeremiah Company receives a three-year, $10,000 zero interest-bearing note, the present value of which is known to be $7,721.80. The implied rate of interest of 9% can be determined as follows:

ILLUSTRATION 7-10
Determination of Implicit Interest Rate

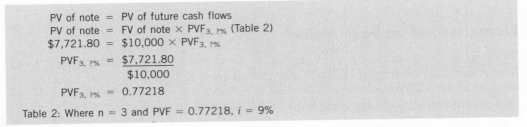

$$
\begin{aligned}
\text{PV of note} &= \text{PV of future cash flows} \\
\text{PV of note} &= \text{FV of note} \times \text{PVF}_{3,\,?\%} \text{ (Table 2)} \\
\$7{,}721.80 &= \$10{,}000 \times \text{PVF}_{3,\,?\%} \\
\text{PVF}_{3,\,?\%} &= \frac{\$7{,}721.80}{\$10{,}000} \\
\text{PVF}_{3,\,?\%} &= 0.77218
\end{aligned}
$$

Table 2: Where n = 3 and PVF = 0.77218, i = 9%

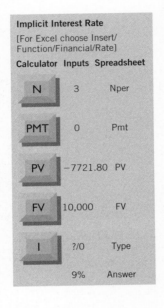

Implicit Interest Rate

[For Excel choose Insert/ Function/Financial/Rate]

Calculator	Inputs	Spreadsheet
N	3	Nper
PMT	0	Pmt
PV	−7721.80	PV
FV	10,000	FV
I	?/0	Type
	9%	Answer

Thus, the implicit rate that equates the total cash to be received ($10,000 at maturity) to the present value of the future cash flows ($7,721.80) is 9%. Note that if any two of the three variables in the equation on the second line of Illustration 7-10 are known, the third variable can be determined. For example, if the note's maturity value (**future value**) and **present value factor** were known, the note's **present value** could be determined.

The time diagram depicting the one cash flow of Jeremiah's note is shown below.

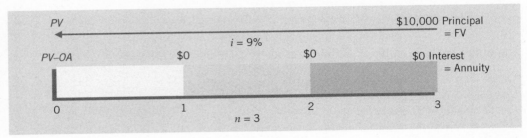

The entry to record the transaction is as follows:

Notes Receivable	10,000.00	
Discount on Notes Receivable ($10,000 − $7,721.80)		2,278.20
Cash		7,721.80

The Discount on Notes Receivable is a valuation account and is reported on the balance sheet as a contra-asset account to Notes Receivable. The discount is then amortized, and interest revenue is recognized annually using the **effective interest method**. The three-year discount amortization and interest revenue schedule is shown in Illustration 7-11.

ILLUSTRATION 7-11
Discount Amortization Schedule- Effective Interest Method

SCHEDULE OF NOTE DISCOUNT AMORTIZATION
Effective Interest Method
0% Note Discounted at 9%

	Cash Received	Interest Revenue	Discount Amortized	Carrying Amount of Note[a]
Date of issue				$ 7,721.80
End of year 1	$ –0–	$ 694.96[b]	$ 694.96[c]	8,416.76[d]
End of year 2	–0–	757.51	757.51	9,174.27
End of year 3	–0–	825.73[e]	825.73	10,000.00
	$ –0–	$2,278.20	$2,278.20	

[a] Note Receivable less Discount on Note Receivable
[b] $7,721.80 × 0.09 = $694.96
[c] $694.96 − 0 = $694.96

[d] $7,721.80 + $694.96 = $8,416.76 or
$10,000 − ($2,278.20 − $694.96)
= $8,416.76
[e] 5¢ adjustment for rounding

Interest revenue at the end of the first year using the effective interest method is recorded as follows:

Discount on Notes Receivable	694.96	
Interest Revenue ($7,721.80 × 9%)		694.96

Note that the amount of the discount, $2,278.20 in this case, represents the interest revenue to be received from the note over the three years. It can be thought of as an Unearned (Interest) Revenue account, except that it is reported netted against the Note Receivable instead of as a liability account.

Interest-Bearing Notes. Often the stated rate and the effective rate are different as in the zero-interest-bearing case above.

To illustrate a more common situation, assume that Morgan Corp. made a loan to Marie Co. and received in exchange a three-year, $10,000 note bearing interest at 10% annually. The market rate of interest for a note of similar risk is 12%. The time diagram depicting both cash flows is shown below. Note that the amount of the interest cash flows is determined by the stated rate (10%). However, all flows must be discounted at the market rate (12%) in determining the note's present value.

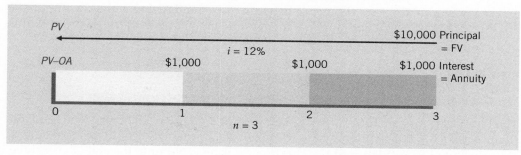

The present value of the two cash flows is calculated as follows:

Face value of the note		$10,000
Present value of the principal:		
$10,000 (PVF*$_{3,12\%}$) = $10,000 (0.71178)	$7,118	
Present value of the interest:		
$1,000 (PVF*–OA$_{3,12\%}$) = $1,000 (2.40183)	2,402	
Present value of the note		9,520
Difference		$ 480
*Present Value Factor		

ILLUSTRATION 7-12
Calculation of Present Value–Effective Rate Different from Stated Rate

In this case, because the effective interest rate (12%) is greater than the stated rate (10%), the note's present value is less than the face value; that is, the note was exchanged at a discount. The receipt of the note at a discount is recorded by Morgan as follows:

Notes Receivable	10,000	
Discount on Notes Receivable		480
Cash		9,520

The discount of $480 represents interest revenue over and above the 10% or $1,000 to be received each year. This account is then amortized and interest revenue is recognized annually using the **effective interest method**. The three-year discount amortization and interest revenue schedule is shown below:

ILLUSTRATION 7-13
Discount Amortization
Schedule—Effective Interest
Method

SCHEDULE OF NOTE DISCOUNT AMORTIZATION
Effective Interest Method
10% Note Discounted at 12%

	Cash Received	Interest Revenue	Discount Amortized	Carrying Amount of Note[a]
Date of issue				$ 9,520
End of year 1	$1,000[b]	$1,142[c]	$142[d]	9,662[e]
End of year 2	1,000	1,159	159	9,821
End of year 3	1,000	1,179	179	10,000
	$3,000	$3,480	$480	

[a] Note Receivable less Discount on Note Receivable
[b] $10,000 × 10% = $1,000
[c] $9,520 × 12% = $1,142
[d] $1,142 − $1,000 = $142 or
$10,000 − ($480 − $142) = $9,662
[e] $9,520 + $142 = $9,662

On the date of issue, the note has a present value of $9,520. Its unamortized discount—additional interest revenue to be spread over the three-year life of the note—is $480.

At the end of year one, Morgan receives $1,000 in cash. But its interest revenue is $1,142 ($9,520 × 12%). The difference between $1,000 and $1,142 is the discount to be amortized, $142. Receipt of the annual interest and amortization of the discount for the first year are recorded by Morgan as follows (amounts per amortization schedule):

Cash	1,000	
Discount on Notes Receivable	142	
Interest Revenue		1,142

The note's carrying amount is now $9,662 ($9,520 + $142), or the balance in the Note Receivable of $10,000 reduced by the adjusted balance of the Discount on Note Receivable account of $338 ($480 − $142). This process is repeated until the end of year three.

When the present value exceeds the face value, the note is exchanged at a premium. The premium on a note receivable is recorded as a debit and amortized using the effective interest method over the life of the note as annual reductions in the amount of interest revenue recognized.

Special Situations

The note transactions just discussed are the common types of situations encountered in practice. Special situations are as follows:

1. notes received for cash and other rights
2. notes received for property, goods, or services
3. imputed interest

Notes Received for Cash and Other Rights.   The lender may also accept a note in exchange for cash and other rights and privileges. For example, Ideal Equipment Co. accepts a five-year, $100,000, zero-interest-bearing note from Outland Steel Corp. plus the right to purchase 10,000 tonnes of steel at a bargain price in exchange for $100,000 in cash. Assume that the rate of interest that would be charged on a note without the right to purchase product at a bargain is 10%. The note's acceptance is recorded and its present value is calculated as follows:

Notes Receivable	100,000	
Prepaid Purchases	37,908	
Discount on Notes Receivable		37,908*
Cash		100,000*

*Present value = $100,000 × (PVF$_{5,10\%}$)= $100,000 × 0.62092 = $62,092;
Discount = $100,000 − $62,092 = $37,908.

The difference between the note's $62,092 present value and its $100,000 maturity value represents implicit interest of $37,908. It is amortized to interest revenue over the note's five-year life using the effective interest method. The excess of the $100,000 over the $62,092 represents an asset, Prepaid Purchases. Prepaid Purchases is allocated to purchases or inventory in proportion to the number of tonnes of steel purchased each year relative to the total 10,000 tonnes for which a bargain price is available. For example, if 3,000 tonnes of steel were purchased during the first year of the five-year bargain period, the following entry would be recorded by Ideal Equipment:

Purchases/Inventory	11,372	
Prepaid Purchases		11,372
(3,000/10,000 × $37,908)		

Note that although prepaid purchases and the discount on notes receivable are both recorded initially at the same amount, $37,908, they are written off differently. Prepaid purchases are amortized in the ratio of tonnes purchased, whereas the discount is amortized using the effective interest method. The value of the right or privilege, in this case the price reduction, helps determine the interest implicit in the transaction.

Notes Received for Property, Goods, or Services.   When property, goods, or services are sold and a note is received as the consideration instead of cash or a short-term receivable, there may be an issue in determining the selling price. It should be the fair value of the property, goods and services given up (if known) or the fair value of the note received, if the latter amount can be more clearly identified. If the fair value of what was given up is known, it also establishes the note's fair value. Otherwise, the fair value of the note must be determined, which in turn establishes the proceeds from the transaction.

The note's fair value is its present value; that is, its future cash flows discounted at the market rate of interest for a note of similar risk. If the note requires payment of interest at the market rate, the note's face value is also its fair value. **If no interest is specified or if the stated rate is not the market rate, the note's face value is not its fair value**. In this case, its present or fair value must be determined and used to account for the note receivable.

To illustrate, Oasis Development Co. sold a corner lot to Rusty Pelican as a restaurant site and accepted in exchange a five-year note having a maturity value of $35,247 and no stated interest rate. The land originally cost Oasis $14,000 and at the date of sale had an appraised fair value of $20,000. What selling price should be used to record this transaction? It should be the fair value of the land sold. If this isn't known, then the note's fair value must be determined and used. Applying this criterion, the land's appraised fair value of $20,000 is appropriate. This also establishes the fair value of the note received in exchange at $20,000.

If the note has a fair value of $20,000, why does it have a face or maturity value of $35,247? The $15,247 difference is interest (or the discount) on the $20,000 "borrowed" from Oasis to pay for the land transaction. The entry to record the sale therefore is:

Notes Receivable	35,247	
Discount on Notes Receivable ($35,247 − $20,000)		15,247
Land		14,000
Gain on Sale of Land ($20,000 − $14,000)		6,000

The discount is amortized to interest revenue over the note's five-year life using the effective interest method.

Imputed Interest.   In note transactions, the effective or real interest rate is either evident or determinable by other factors involved in the exchange, such as the fair market value of what is given or received. But if the fair value of the property, goods, services, or other rights is not determinable and if the note has no ready market, the problem of determining the note's present value is more difficult. To estimate the note's present value under such circumstances, an applicable interest rate that may differ from the stated interest rate must be approximated. This process of interest-rate approximation is called **imputation**, and the resulting interest rate is called an imputed interest rate. The imputed interest rate is used to establish the note's present value by discounting, at that rate, all future receipts (interest and principal) on the note.

> The objective for calculating the appropriate interest rate is to approximate the rate which would have resulted if an independent borrower and an independent lender had negotiated a similar transaction under comparable terms and conditions with the option to pay the cash price upon purchase or to give a note for the amount of the purchase which bears the prevailing rate of interest to maturity. The rate used for valuation purposes will normally be at least equal to the rate at which the debtor can obtain financing of a similar nature from other sources at the date of the transaction.[15]

The choice of a rate is affected by the prevailing rates for similar instruments of issuers with similar credit ratings. It is also affected specifically by restrictive covenants, collateral, payment schedule, the existing prime interest rate, etc. Determination of the imputed interest rate is made when the note is received; any subsequent changes in prevailing interest rates are ignored.

To illustrate, assume that Brown Interiors Company, having rendered architectural services, accepted on December 31, 2002, a long-term promissory note with a face value of $550,000, a due date of December 31, 2007, and a stated interest rate of 2%, interest receivable at the end of each year. The service's fair value is not readily determinable, and the note is not readily marketable. Given the circumstances—the maker's credit rating, the absence of collateral, the prime rate, and the prevailing interest rate on the maker's outstanding debt—an 8% interest rate is determined to be appropriate. The time diagram depicting both cash flows is shown below. **Note again that the cash flows for interest are determined using the stated or nominal rate.**

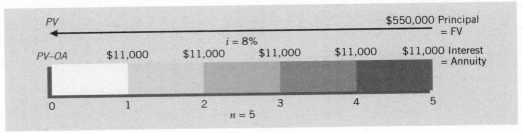

The present value of the note and the imputed fair value of the architectural services are calculated by discounting all cash flows at the (imputed) market rate, as follows:

ILLUSTRATION 7-14

Calculation of Present Value-
Imputed Interest Rate

Face value of the note		$550,000
Present value of $550,000 due in 5 years at 8%—$550,000 (PVF$_{5,8\%}$) = $550,000 × .68058	$374,319	
Present value of $11,000 ($550,000 × .02) payable annually for 5 years at 8% $11,000 (PVF-OA$_{5,8\%}$) = $11,000 × 3.99271	43,920	
Present value of the note		418,239
Discount		$131,761

The value of the services is thus determined to be $418,239, the current value of the note. The note's receipt in exchange for the services is recorded as follows:

December 31, 2002		
Notes Receivable	550,000	
Discount on Notes Receivable ($550,000 − $418,239)		131,761
Revenue from Services		418,239

[15] "Interest on Receivables and Payables," *Opinions of the Accounting Principles Board No. 21,* (New York: AICPA, 1971), par. .13.

An amortization schedule similar to Illustration 7-13 is then prepared to help record transactions in future periods.

VALUATION OF NOTES RECEIVABLE

Like accounts receivable, short-term notes receivable are recorded and reported at their net realizable value; that is, at their face amount less all necessary allowances. The primary notes receivable allowance account is Allowance for Doubtful Accounts. The calculations and estimations involved in valuing short-term notes receivable and in recording bad debt expense and the related allowance are **exactly the same as for trade accounts receivable**. Either a percentage of sales revenue or an analysis of the receivables can be used to estimate the amount of uncollectibles. Long-term notes receivable, however, pose additional estimation problems.

> **OBJECTIVE 7**
> ....
> Explain accounting issues related to valuation of notes receivable.

A note receivable is considered **impaired** when it is probable that the creditor will be unable to collect all amounts due (both principal and interest) according to the loan's contractual terms. In that case, the present value of the expected future cash flows is determined by discounting those flows at the historical effective rate. This present value amount is deducted from the carrying amount of the receivable to measure the loss.[16] Impairments, as well as restructurings, of receivables and debts are discussed and illustrated in considerable detail in Appendix 15A.

DISPOSITION OF ACCOUNTS AND NOTES RECEIVABLE

In the normal course of events, accounts and notes receivable are collected when due and removed from the books. However, as credit sales and receivables have grown in size and significance, this "normal course of events" has evolved. **In order to accelerate the receipt of cash from receivables, the owner may transfer accounts or notes receivable to another company for cash.**

> **OBJECTIVE 8**
> ....
> Explain accounting issues related to disposition of accounts and notes receivable.

There are various reasons for this early transfer. First, for competitive reasons, providing sales financing for customers is virtually mandatory in many industries. In the sale of durable goods, such as automobiles, trucks, industrial and farm equipment, computers, and appliances, a large majority of sales are on an instalment contract basis. Many major companies in these industries have created wholly-owned subsidiaries specializing in receivables financing. **General Motors of Canada Ltd.** has **General Motors Acceptance Corp. of Canada (GMAC)**, and **Sears** has **Sears Acceptance Corp.**

Second, the holder may sell receivables because money is tight and access to normal credit is not available or is prohibitively expensive. Also, a firm may have to sell its receivables, instead of borrowing, to avoid violating existing lending agreements.

Finally, billing and collecting of receivables is often time-consuming and costly. Credit card companies such as **MasterCard**, **VISA**, and others take over the collection process and provide merchants with immediate cash.

Conversely, some **purchasers** of receivables buy them to obtain the legal protection of ownership rights afforded a purchaser of assets versus the lesser rights afforded a secured creditor. In addition, banks and other lending institutions may be forced to purchase receivables because of legal lending limits; that is, they cannot make any additional loans but they can buy receivables and charge a fee for this service.

The transfer of receivables to a third party for cash is accomplished in one of two ways:

1. secured borrowing
2. sales of receivables

---

[16] *CICA Handbook* Section 3025, par. .14 indicates that if the expected future cash flows or their timing cannot be reasonably estimated, the net realizable value to the entity of any underlying security or the loan's market price, if available, could be used.

Secured Borrowing

Receivables are often used as collateral in a borrowing transaction. A creditor often requires that the debtor designate (assign) or pledge receivables as security for the loan. If the loan is not paid when due, the creditor has the right to convert the collateral to cash—that is, to collect the receivables.

To illustrate, on March 1, 2002, Howat Mills Ltd. provides (assigns) $700,000 of its accounts receivable to Provincial Bank as collateral for a $500,000 note. Howat Mills will continue to collect the accounts receivable; the account debtors are not notified of the arrangement. Provincial Bank assesses a finance charge of 1% of the accounts receivable and interest on the note of 12%. Settlement by Howat Mills to the bank is made monthly for all cash collected on the receivables.

ILLUSTRATION 7-15

Entries for Transfer of Receivables—Secured Borrowing

Howat Mills Ltd.			Provincial Bank		
Transfer of accounts receivable and issuance of note on March 1, 2002:					
Cash	493,000		Notes Receivable	500,000	
Finance Charge Expense	7,000*		Finance Revenue		7,000*
Notes Payable		500,000	Cash		493,000
*(1% × $700,000)					
Collection in March of $440,000 of accounts less cash discounts of $6,000. In addition, sales returns of $14,000 were received:					
Cash	434,000				
Sales Discounts	6,000				
Sales Returns	14,000		(No entry)		
Accounts Receivable		454,000			
($440,000 + $14,000 = $454,000)					
Remitted March collections plus accrued interest to the bank on April 1:					
Interest Expense	5,000*		Cash	439,000	
Notes Payable	434,000		Interest Revenue		5,000*
Cash		439,000	Notes Receivable		434,000
*($500,000 × 0.12 × $\frac{1}{12}$)					
Collection in April of the balance of accounts less $2,000 written off as uncollectible:					
Cash	244,000		(No entry)		
Allow for Doubtful Accounts	2,000				
Accounts Receivable		246,000*			
*($700,000 − $454,000)					
Remitted the balance due of $66,000 ($500,000 − $434,000) on the note plus interest on May1:					
Interest Expense	660*		Cash	66,660	
Notes Payable	66,000		Interest Revenue		660*
Cash		66,660	Notes Receivable		66,000
*($66,000 × 0.12 × $\frac{1}{12}$)					

In addition to recording the collection of receivables, all discounts, returns and allowances, and bad debts must be recognized. Each month the proceeds from collecting accounts receivable are used to retire the note obligation. In addition, interest on the note is paid.[17]

Sales of Receivables

Sales of receivables have increased substantially in recent years. A common type is a sale to a factor. **Factors** are finance companies or banks that buy receivables from businesses for a fee and then collect the remittances directly from the customers. **Factoring**

---

[17] What happens if Provincial Bank collected the transferred accounts receivable rather than Howat Mills? In that case, Provincial Bank would simply remit the cash proceeds to Howat Mills, and Howat Mills would make the same entries shown in Illustration 7-15. As a result, the receivables used as collateral continue to be reported as an asset on the transferor's balance sheet.

receivables is traditionally associated with the textile, apparel, footwear, furniture, and home furnishing industries.[18] An illustration of a factoring arrangement is shown below.

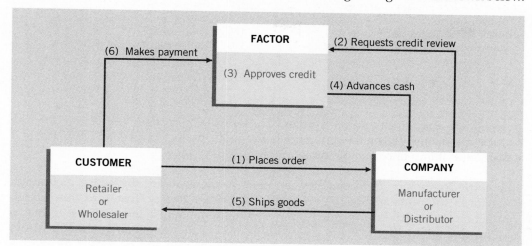

ILLUSTRATION 7-16
Basic Procedures in Factoring

A recent phenomenon in the sale (transfer) of receivables is securitization. **Securitization** takes a pool of assets such as credit card receivables, mortgage receivables, or car loan receivables and sells shares in these pools of interest and principal payments (in effect, creating securities backed by these pools of assets). Virtually every asset with a payment stream and a long-term payment history is a candidate for securitization.

The differences between factoring and securitization are that factoring usually involves sale to only one company, fees are high, the receivables quality is low, and the seller afterward does not service the receivables. In a securitization, many investors are involved, margins are tight, the receivables are of higher quality, and the seller usually continues to service the receivables.

In either a factoring or a securitization transaction, receivables are sold on either a **without recourse** or a **with recourse** basis.[19]

Sale without Recourse. When receivables are sold *without recourse*, the purchaser assumes the risk of collectibility and absorbs any credit losses. The transfer of accounts receivable in a nonrecourse transaction is an outright sale of the receivables both in form (transfer of title) and substance (transfer of control). In nonrecourse transactions, as in any sale of assets, Cash is debited for the proceeds. Accounts Receivable is credited for the receivables' face value. The difference, reduced by any provision for probable adjustments (discounts, returns, allowances, etc.), is recognized as a Loss on the Sale of Receivables. The seller uses a Due from Factor account (reported as a receivable) to account for the proceeds retained by the factor to cover probable sales discounts, sales returns, and sales allowances.

To illustrate, Crest Textiles Ltd. factors $500,000 of accounts receivable with Commercial Factors, Inc., on a **without recourse** basis. The receivable records are transferred to Commercial Factors, Inc., which will receive the collections. Commercial Factors assesses a finance charge of 3% of the amount of accounts receivable and retains an amount equal to 5% of the accounts receivable. The journal entries for both Crest Textiles and Commercial Factors for the receivables transferred without recourse are as follows:

---

[18] Credit cards like MasterCard and VISA are a type of factoring arrangement. Typically the purchaser of the receivable charges a ¾% to 1½% commission of the receivables purchased (the commission is 4–5% for credit card factoring).

[19] According to the 2001 *Accounting Guideline 12* on Transfers of Receivables, the CICA defines recourse as the right of a transferee of receivables to receive payment from the transferor of those receivables for (i) failure of debtors to pay when due, (ii) the effects of prepayments, or (iii) adjustments resulting from defects in the eligibility of the transferred receivables.

ILLUSTRATION 7-17
Entries for Sale of Receivables
Without Recourse

Crest Textiles Ltd.			Commercial Factors, Inc.		
Cash	460,000		Accounts (Notes)		
Due from Factor	25,000*		Receivable	500,000	
Loss on Sale of Receivables	15,000**		Due to Crest Textiles		25,000
Accounts (Notes)			Financing Revenue		15,000
Receivable		500,000	Cash		460,000

*(5% × $500,000)
**(3% × $500,000)

In recognition of the sale of receivables, Crest Textiles records a loss of $15,000. The factor's net income will be the difference between the financing revenue of $15,000 and the amount of any uncollectible receivables.

Sale with Recourse. If receivables are sold **with recourse**, the seller guarantees payment to the purchaser in the event the debtor fails to pay. To record this type of transaction, a **financial components approach** is used, because the seller has a continuing involvement with the receivable.[20] In this approach, each party to the sale recognizes the assets and liabilities that it controls after the sale and no longer recognizes the assets and liabilities that were sold or extinguished.

To illustrate, assume the same information as in Illustration 7-17 for Crest Textiles and for Commercial Factors except that the receivables are sold on a with recourse basis. It is determined that this recourse obligation has a fair value of $6,000. To determine the loss on the sale of the receivables by Crest Textiles, the net proceeds from the sale are calculated:

ILLUSTRATION 7-18
Calculation Net Proceeds

Cash received	$460,000	
Due from factor	25,000	$485,000
Less: Recourse obligation		6,000
Net proceeds		$479,000

Net proceeds are cash or other assets received in a sale less any liabilities incurred. The loss is then calculated as follows:

ILLUSTRATION 7-19
Loss on Sale Calculation

Carrying (book) value	$500,000
Net proceeds	479,000
Loss on sale of receivables	$ 21,000

The journal entries for both Crest Textiles and Commercial Factors for the receivables sold with recourse are as follows:

ILLUSTRATION 7-20
Entries for Sale of Receivables
with Recourse

Crest Textiles Ltd.			Commercial Factors, Inc.		
Cash	460,000		Accounts Receivable	500,000	
Due from Factor	25,000		Due to Crest Textiles		25,000
Loss on Sale of Receivables	21,000		Financing Revenue		15,000
Accounts (Notes)			Cash		460,000
Receivable		500,000			
Recourse Liability		6,000			

[20] Previous accounting guidance generally required that the transferor account for financial assets transferred as an inseparable unit that had been entirely sold or entirely retained. This guidance was difficult to apply and produced inconsistent and arbitrary results. The Accounting Standards Board, through the issue of *Accounting Guideline 12* on Transfers of Receivables in 2001, concluded that an approach that focuses on control should be applied. This approach assigns values to such components as the recourse provision, servicing rights, and agreement to reacquire.

In this case, Crest Textiles recognizes a loss of $21,000. In addition, a liability of $6,000 is recorded to indicate the probable payment to Commercial Factors for uncollectible receivables. If all the receivables are collected, Crest Textiles would eliminate its recourse liability and increase income. Commercial Factors' net income is the financing revenue of $15,000 because it will have no bad debts related to these receivables.

Secured Borrowing Versus Sale

INTERNATIONAL INSIGHT

The IASC has a similar conceptual approach to the sale of receivables, although it provides more flexibility in implementation.

The CICA's Accounting Standards Board concluded that a sale occurs when the seller surrenders control of the receivables to the buyer and receives in exchange consideration other than a beneficial interest in the transferred asset. The following three conditions must be met before a sale can be recorded:

1. The transferred assets have been isolated from the transferor—put beyond the reach of the transferor and its creditors, even in bankruptcy or receivership.

2. Each transferee has the right to pledge or exchange the assets (or beneficial interests) it received, and no condition both constrains the transferee from taking advantage of this right and provides more than a trivial benefit to the transferor.

3. The transferor does not maintain effective control over the transferred assets through either an agreement to repurchase or redeem them before their maturity or through an ability to unilaterally cause the holder to return specific assets.[21]

If the three conditions are met, a sale occurs. Otherwise, the transferor should record the transfer as a secured borrowing. If sale accounting is appropriate, it is still necessary to consider assets obtained and liabilities incurred in the transaction. The general rules of accounting for transfers of receivables are shown in Illustration 7-21.

Applying the accounting and disclosure guidance for transferring of receivables is complicated by specialized contracts among companies that differ in their terms and conditions, the securitization of receivables, and special purpose entities. A discussion of these issues is beyond the purview of an intermediate accounting text.

PRESENTATION AND ANALYSIS

Presentation of Receivables

OBJECTIVE 9

Explain how receivables are reported and analysed.

The general rules in classifying the typical transactions in the receivables section are: (1) segregate the different types of receivables that an enterprise possesses, if material; (2) ensure that the valuation accounts are appropriately offset against the proper receivable accounts; (3) determine that receivables classified in the current assets section will be converted into cash within the next year or the operating cycle, if longer; (4) disclose any loss contingencies that exist on the receivables; (5) disclose any receivables designated or pledged as collateral.

As receivables are financial assets, the general disclosure requirements for financial instruments also apply: (1) disclose information about their terms and conditions; (2) provide information about exposure to interest rate risk and credit risk, including any significant concentrations of credit risk arising from receivables; and (3) disclose their fair value, if practicable.[22]

The asset sections of Colton Corporation's balance sheet shown below illustrate many of the disclosures required for receivables.

---

[21] CICA *Accounting Guideline 12*, par. .9.

[22] Concentrations of credit risk exist when receivables have common characteristics that may affect their collection. These common characteristics might be companies in the same industry or same region of the country. For example, financial statement users want to know if a substantial amount of receivables are with companies in the Middle East, or start-up companies in the "high-tech" sector.

ILLUSTRATION 7-21
Accounting for Transfers of
Receivables

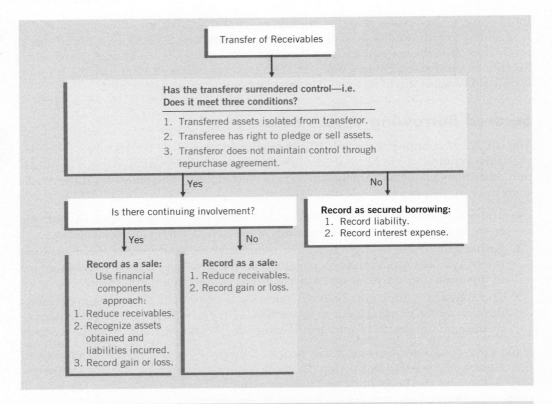

ILLUSTRATION 7-22
Disclosure of Receivables

COLTON CORPORATION
Balance Sheet (partial)
As of December 31, 2002

Current assets		
Cash and cash equivalents		$ 1,870,250
Accounts receivable (Note 2)	$8,977,673	
Less: Allowance for doubtful accounts	500,226	
	8,477,447	
Advances to subsidiaries due 9/30/03	2,090,000	
Notes receivable—trade (Note 2)	1,532,000	
Federal income taxes refundable	146,704	
Dividends and interest receivable	75,500	
Other receivables and claims (including debit balances in accounts payable)	174,620	12,496,271
Total current assets		14,366,521
Noncurrent receivables		
Notes receivable from officers and key employees		376,090
Claims receivable (litigation settlement to be collected over four years)		585,000

Note 2: Accounts and Notes Receivable
In November 2002, the Company arranged with a finance company to refinance a part of its indebtedness. The loan is evidenced by a 12% note payable. The note is payable on demand and is secured by substantially all the accounts receivable.

INTERNATIONAL INSIGHT

Holding receivables that will be paid in a foreign currency represents risk that the exchange rate may move against the company, causing a decrease in the amount collected in terms of Canadian dollars. Companies engaged in cross-border transactions often "hedge" these receivables by buying contracts to exchange currencies at specified amounts at future dates.

Analysis of Receivables

Financial ratios are frequently calculated to evaluate the liquidity of a company's accounts receivable. The ratio used to assess the receivables' liquidity is the **receivables turnover ratio**. This ratio measures the number of times, on average, receivables are collected during the period. The ratio is calculated by dividing net sales by average receivables (net) outstanding during the year. Theoretically, the numerator should include only net credit sales. This information is frequently not available, however, and if the relative amounts of credit and cash sales remain fairly constant, the trend indicated by the ratio will still be valid. Unless seasonal factors are significant, average receivables outstanding can be calculated from the beginning and ending balances of net trade receivables.

To illustrate, **Clearly Canadian Beverage Corporation** reported 1999 sales of $36,605 thousand; its beginning and ending accounts receivable balances were $4,744 thousand and $4,341 thousand, respectively. Its accounts receivable turnover ratio is calculated as follows:

$$\text{Accounts Receivable Turnover} = \frac{\text{Net Sales}}{\text{Average trade receivables (net)}}$$

$$= \frac{\$36,605}{(\$4,744 + \$4,341)/2}$$

$$= 8.06 \text{ times, or every 45 days}$$
$$(365 \text{ days} \div 8.06)^{23}$$

ILLUSTRATION 7-23
Calculation of Accounts Receivable Turnover

This information provides some indication of the receivables' quality, and also an idea of how successful the firm is in collecting its outstanding receivables. If possible, an ageing schedule should also be prepared to determine how long receivables have been outstanding. It is possible that a satisfactory receivables turnover may have resulted because certain receivables were collected quickly though others have been outstanding for a relatively long period. An ageing schedule would reveal such patterns.

UNDERLYING CONCEPTS

Providing information that will help users assess an enterprise's current liquidity and prospective cash flows is a primary objective of accounting.

SUMMARY OF LEARNING OBJECTIVES

1 Identify items considered cash. To be reported as "cash," an asset must be readily available to pay current obligations and free from contractual restrictions that limit its use in satisfying debts. Cash consists of coin, currency, and available funds on deposit at the bank. Negotiable instruments such as money orders, certified cheques, cashier's cheques, personal cheques, and bank drafts are also viewed as cash. Savings accounts are usually classified as cash.

2 Indicate how cash and related items are reported. Cash is reported as a current asset in the balance sheet. The reporting of other related items are: (1) Restricted cash: legally restricted deposits held as compensating balances against short-term borrowing should be stated separately among the "cash and cash equivalent items" in Current Assets. Restricted deposits held against long-term borrowing arrangements should be separately classified as noncurrent assets in either the Investments or Other Assets sections. (2) Bank overdrafts: They should be reported in the current liabilities section and are usually added to the amount reported as accounts payable. If material, these items should be separately disclosed either on the face of the balance sheet or in the related notes. (3) Cash equivalents: This item is often reported together with cash as "cash and cash equivalents."

3 Define receivables and identify the different types of receivables. Receivables are claims held against customers and others for money, goods, or services. Most receivables are financial assets. The receivables are classified into three types: (1) current or noncurrent; (2) trade or nontrade; (3) accounts receivable or notes receivable.

---

[23] Often the receivables turnover is transformed to days to collect accounts receivable or days sales outstanding—an average collection period. In this case, 8.06 is divided into 365 days to obtain 45 days. Several figures other than 365 could be used here; a common alternative is 360 days because it is divisible by 30 (days) and 12 (months). Use 365 days in any homework calculations.

4 Explain accounting issues related to recognition of accounts receivable. Two issues that may complicate the measurement of accounts receivable are: (1) The availability of discounts (trade and cash discounts) and (2) the length of time between the sale and the payment due dates (the interest element).

Ideally, receivables should be measured in terms of their present value; that is, the discounted value of the cash to be received in the future. Receivables arising from normal business transactions that are due in customary trade terms within approximately one year are excluded from present value considerations.

5 Explain accounting issues related to valuation of accounts receivable. Short-term receivables are valued and reported at net realizable value—the net amount expected to be received in cash, which is not necessarily the amount legally receivable. Determining net realizable value requires estimating both uncollectible receivables and any returns or allowances.

6 Explain accounting issues related to recognition of notes receivable. Short-term notes are recorded at face value. Long-term notes receivable are recorded at the present value of the cash expected to be collected. When the interest stated on an interest-bearing note is equal to the effective (market) rate of interest, the note sells at face value. When the stated rate is different from the effective rate, either a discount or premium is recorded.

7 Explain accounting issues related to valuation of notes receivable. Like accounts receivable, short-term notes receivable are recorded and reported at their net realizable value. The same is also true of long-term receivables. Special issues relate to impairments and notes receivable past due.

8 Explain accounting issues related to disposition of accounts and notes receivable. To accelerate the receipt of cash from receivables, the owner may transfer the receivables to another company for cash. The transfer of receivables to a third party for cash may be accomplished in one of two ways: (1) Secured borrowing: A creditor often requires that the debtor designate or pledge receivables as security for the loan. (2) Sales (factoring) of receivables: Factors are finance companies or banks that buy receivables from businesses and then collect the remittances directly from the customers. In many cases, transferors may have some continuing involvement with the receivables sold. A financial components approach is used to record this type of transaction.

9 Explain how receivables are reported and analysed. Disclosure of receivables requires that valuation accounts be appropriately offset against receivables, receivables be appropriately classified as current or noncurrent, pledged or designated receivables be identified, and concentrations of risks arising from receivables be identified. Receivables may be analysed relative to turnover and the number of days outstanding.

APPENDIX 7A

Cash Controls

As indicated in Chapter 7, cash creates many management and control problems. The purpose of this appendix is to discuss some of the basic control issues related to cash.

USING BANK ACCOUNTS

A company can vary the number and location of banks and the types of bank accounts to obtain desired control objectives. For large companies operating in multiple locations, the location of bank accounts can be important. Establishing collection accounts in strategic locations can accelerate the flow of cash into the company by shortening the time between a customer's payment mailing and the company's use of the cash. Multiple collection centres generally are used to reduce the size of a company's **collection float**, which is the difference between the amount on deposit according to the company's records and the amount of collected cash according to the bank record.

The **general chequing account** is the principal bank account in most companies and frequently the only bank account in small businesses. Cash is deposited in and disbursed from this account as all transactions are cycled through it. Deposits from and disbursements to all other bank accounts are made through the general chequing account.

Imprest bank accounts are used to make a specific amount of cash available for a limited purpose. The account acts as a clearing account for a large volume of cheques or for a specific type of cheque. The specific and intended amount to be cleared through the imprest account is deposited by transferring that amount from the general chequing account or other source. Imprest bank accounts are often used for disbursing payroll cheques, dividends, commissions, bonuses, confidential expenses (e.g., officers' salaries), and travel expenses.

Lockbox accounts are frequently used by large, multilocation companies to make collections in cities within areas of heaviest customer billing. The company rents a local post office box and authorizes a local bank to pick up the remittances mailed to that box number. The bank empties the box at least once a day and immediately credits the company's account for collections. The greatest advantage of a lockbox is that it accelerates the availability of collected cash. Generally, in a lockbox arrangement the bank microfilms the cheques for record purposes and provides the company with a deposit slip, a list of collections, and any customer correspondence. If the control over cash is improved and if the income generated from accelerating the receipt of funds exceeds the cost of the lockbox system, then it is considered a worthwhile undertaking.

INTERNATIONAL INSIGHT

Multinational corporations often have cash accounts in more than one currency. For financial statement purposes, these currencies are typically translated into Canadian dollars using the exchange rate in effect at the balance sheet date.

THE IMPREST PETTY CASH SYSTEM

Almost every company finds it necessary to pay small amounts for a great many things such as employee's lunches, taxi fares, minor office supplies, and other miscellaneous expenses. It is frequently impractical to require that such disbursements be made by cheque, yet some control over them is important. A simple method of obtaining reasonable control, while adhering to the rule of disbursement by cheque, is the **imprest system for petty cash** disbursements.

This is how the system works:

1. Someone is designated petty cash custodian and given a small amount of currency from which to make small payments. The transfer of funds to petty cash is recorded as:

Petty Cash	300	
Cash		300

2. As disbursements are made, the petty cash custodian obtains signed receipts from each individual to whom cash is paid. If possible, evidence of the disbursement should be attached to the petty cash receipt. Petty cash transactions are not recorded until the fund is reimbursed, and then such entries are recorded by someone other than the petty cash custodian.

3. When the cash supply runs low, the custodian presents to the general cashier a request for reimbursement supported by the petty cash receipts and other disbursement evidence. The custodian receives a company cheque to replenish the fund. At this point, transactions are recorded based on petty cash receipts:

Office Supplies Expense	42	
Postage Expense	53	
Entertainment Expense	76	
Cash Over and Short	2	
Cash		173

4. If it is decided that the amount of cash in the petty cash fund is excessive, an adjustment may be made as follows (lowering the fund balance from $300 to $250):

Cash	50	
Petty Cash		50

Entries are made to the Petty Cash account only to increase or decrease the size of the fund.

A **Cash Over and Short** account is used when the petty cash fund fails to prove out. When this occurs, it is usually due to an error (failure to provide correct change, overpayment of expense, lost receipt, etc.). If cash proves out **short** (i.e., the sum of the receipts and cash in the fund is less than the imprest amount), the shortage is debited to the Cash Over and Short account. If it proves out **over**, the overage is credited to Cash Over and Short. This account is left open until the end of the year, when it is closed and generally shown on the income statement as an other expense or revenue.

There are usually expense items in the fund except immediately after reimbursement; therefore, if accurate financial statements are desired, the funds must be reimbursed at the end of each accounting period and also when nearly depleted.

Under the imprest system, the petty cash custodian is responsible at all times for the amount of the fund on hand either in the form of cash or signed receipts. These receipts provide the evidence required by the disbursing officer to issue a reimbursement cheque. Two additional procedures are followed to obtain more complete control over the petty cash fund:

1. Surprise counts of the fund are made from time to time by a superior of the petty cash custodian to determine that the fund is being accounted for satisfactorily.

2. Petty cash receipts are cancelled or mutilated after they have been submitted for reimbursement, so that they cannot be used to secure a second reimbursement.

PHYSICAL PROTECTION OF CASH BALANCES

Not only must cash receipts and cash disbursements be safeguarded through internal control measures, but also the cash on hand and in banks must be protected. Because receipts become cash on hand and disbursements are made from cash in banks, adequate control of receipts and disbursements is a part of protecting cash balances. Certain other procedures, however, should be given some consideration.

Physical protection of cash is so elementary a necessity that it requires little discussion. Every effort should be made to minimize the cash on hand in the office. A petty cash fund, the current day's receipts, and perhaps funds for making change should be all that is on hand at any one time. Insofar as possible, these funds should be kept in a vault, safe, or locked cash drawer. Each day's receipts should be transmitted **intact** to the bank as soon as practicable. Accurately stating the amount of available cash both in internal management reports and in external financial statements is also extremely important.

Every company has a record of cash received, disbursed, and the balance. Because of the many cash transactions, however, errors or omissions may be made in keeping this record. Therefore, it is necessary periodically to prove the balance shown in the general ledger. Cash actually present in the office—petty cash, change funds, and undeposited receipts—can be counted, for comparison with the company records. Cash on deposit is not available for count and is proved by preparing a bank reconciliation—a reconciliation of the company's record and the bank's record of the company's cash.

RECONCILIATION OF BANK BALANCES

At the end of each calendar month, the bank supplies each customer with a **bank statement** (a copy of the bank's account with the customer) together with the customer's cheques that have been paid by the bank during the month.[24] If no errors were made by the bank or the customer, if all deposits made and all cheques drawn by the customer reached the bank within the same month, and if no unusual transactions occurred that affected either the company's or the bank's record of cash, the balance of cash reported by the bank to the customer would be the same as that shown in the customer's own records. This condition seldom occurs for one or more of the following reasons:

RECONCILING ITEMS

1. **Deposits in Transit.** End-of-month deposits of cash recorded on the depositor's books in one month are received and recorded by the bank in the following month.

2. **Outstanding Cheques.** Cheques written by the depositor are recorded when written but may not be recorded by (or "clear") the bank until the next month.

3. **Bank Charges.** Charges recorded by the bank against the depositor's balance for such items as bank services, printing cheques, not-sufficient-funds (NSF) cheques, and safe-deposit box rentals. The depositor may not be aware of these charges until the bank statement is received.

4. **Bank Credits.** Collections or deposits by the bank for the depositor's benefit may or may not be known to the depositor until receipt of the bank statement. These are reconciling items to the extent they have not yet been recorded on the company's records. Examples are note collection for the depositor, and interest earned on interest-bearing chequing accounts, direct deposits by customers and others.

5. **Bank or Depositor Errors.** Errors on either the part of the bank or the depositor cause the bank balance to disagree with the depositor's book balance.

Hence, differences between the depositor's record of cash and the bank's record are usual and expected. Therefore, the two must be reconciled to determine the nature of the differences between the two amounts.

A **bank reconciliation** is a schedule explaining any differences between the bank's and the company's records of cash. If the difference results only from transactions not yet recorded by the bank, the company's record of cash is considered correct. But, if

---

[24] As mentioned in Chapter 7, use of paper cheques continues to be a popular means of payment. However, ready availability of desktop publishing software has created new opportunities for cheque fraud in the form of duplicate, altered, and forged cheques. At the same time, new fraud-fighting technologies, such as ultraviolet imaging, high-capacity barcodes, and biometrics are being developed. These technologies convert paper documents into document files that are processed electronically, thereby reducing the risk of fraud.

some part of the difference arises from other items, the bank's records or the company's records must be adjusted.

Two forms of bank reconciliation may be prepared. One form reconciles from the bank statement balance to the book balance or vice versa. The other form reconciles both the bank balance and the book balance to a correct cash balance. This latter form is more widely used. A sample of that form and its common reconciling items are shown in Illustration 7A-1.

ILLUSTRATION 7A-1
Bank Reconciliation Form and Content

Balance per bank statement (end of period)		$$$
Add: Deposits in transit	$$	
Undeposited receipts (cash on hand)	$$	
Bank errors that understate the bank statement balance	$$	$$
		$$$
Deduct: Outstanding cheques	$$	
Bank errors that overstate the bank statement balance	$$	$$
Correct cash balance		$$$
Balance per depositor's books		$$$
Add: Bank credits and collections not yet recorded in the books	$$	
Book errors that understate the book balance	$$	$$
		$$$
Deduct: Bank charges not yet recorded in the books	$$	
Book errors that overstate the book balance	$$	$$
Correct cash balance		$$$

This form of reconciliation consists of two sections: (1) "Balance per bank statement" and (2) "Balance per depositor's books." Both sections end with the same "correct cash balance." The correct cash balance is the amount to which the books must be adjusted and is the amount reported on the balance sheet. **Adjusting journal entries are prepared for all the addition and deduction items appearing in the "Balance per depositor's books" section.** Any errors attributable to the bank should be called to the bank's attention immediately.

To illustrate, Nugget Mining Company's books show a cash balance at the Ottawa National Bank on November 30, 2002, of $20,502. The bank statement covering the month of November shows an ending balance of $22,190. An examination of Nugget's accounting records and November bank statement identified the following reconciling items:

1. A deposit of $3,680 was mailed to the bank on November 30 but does not appear on the bank statement.

2. Cheques written in November but not charged to the November bank statement are:

Cheque	#7327	$ 150
	#7348	4,820
	#7349	31

3. Nugget has not yet recorded the $600 of interest collected by the bank November 20 on Sequoia Co. bonds held by the bank for Nugget.

4. Bank service charges of $18 are not yet recorded on Nugget's books.

5. One of Nugget's customer's cheques for $220 was returned with the bank statement and marked "NSF." The bank treated this bad cheque as a disbursement.

6. Nugget discovered that cheque #7322, written in November for $131 in payment of an account payable, had been incorrectly recorded in its books as $311.

7. A cheque for Nugent Oil Co. in the amount of $175 that had been incorrectly charged to Nugget Mining accompanied the bank statement.

The reconciliation of bank and book balances to the correct cash balance of $21,044 would appear as follows:

NUGGET MINING COMPANY
Bank Reconciliation
Ottawa National Bank, November 30, 2002

Balance per bank statement, November 30/02			$22,190
Add: Deposit in transit	(1)	$3,680	
Bank error—incorrect cheque charged to account by bank	(7)	175	3,855
			26,045
Deduct: Outstanding cheques	(2)		5,001
Correct cash balance, November 30/02			$21,044
Balance per books, November 30/02			$20,502
Add: Interest collected by the bank	(3)	$ 600	
Error in recording cheque #7322	(6)	180	780
			21,282
Deduct: Bank service charges	(4)	18	
NSF cheque returned	(5)	220	238
Correct cash balance, November 30/02			$21,044

The journal entries required to adjust and correct Nugget Mining's books in early December 2002 are taken from the items in the "Balance per books" section and are as follows:

Cash	600	
Interest Revenue		600
(To record interest on Sequoia Co. bonds, collected by bank)		
Cash	180	
Accounts Payable		180
(To correct error in recording amount of cheque #7322)		
Office Expense—Bank Charges	18	
Cash		18
(To record bank service charges for November)		
Accounts Receivable	220	
Cash		220
(To record customer's cheque returned NSF)		

When the entries are posted, Nugget's cash account will have a balance of $21,044. Nugget should return the Nugent Oil Co. cheque to Ottawa National Bank, informing the bank of the error.

SUMMARY OF LEARNING OBJECTIVE FOR APPENDIX 7A

. . . .

10 **Explain common techniques employed to control cash.** The common techniques employed to control cash are: (1) Using bank accounts: a company can vary the number and location of banks and the types of accounts to obtain desired control objectives. (2) The imprest petty cash system: It may be impractical to require small amounts of various expenses be paid by cheque, yet some control over them is important. (3) Physical protection of cash balances: Adequate control of receipts and disbursements is part of protecting of cash balances. Every effort should be made to minimize the cash on hand in the office. (4) Reconciliation of bank balances: Cash on deposit is not available for count and is proved by preparing a bank reconciliation.

KEY TERMS

bank reconciliation, *331*
imprest system for petty cash, *329*
not-sufficient-funds (NSF) cheques, *331*

Note: All asterisked Brief Exercises, Exercises, Problems, and Cases relate to material covered in the appendix to the chapter.

BRIEF EXERCISES

BE7-1 Stowe Enterprises owns the following assets at December 31, 2002:

Cash in bank-savings account	63,000	Chequing account balance	17,000
Cash on hand	9,300	Postdated cheques	750
Cash refund due, overpayment of income taxes	31,400	Certificates of deposit (180-day)	90,000

What amount should be reported as cash?

BE7-2 Hawthorne Corporation on July 1, 2002, obtained a $4 million, six-month loan at an annual rate of 11% from Municipal Bank. As part of the loan agreement, Hawthorne is required to maintain a $500,000 compensating balance in a chequing account at Municipal Bank. Normally Hawthorne would maintain only a balance of $200,000 in this chequing account. The chequing account pays 4% interest. Determine the effective interest rate paid by Hawthorne for this loan.

BE7-3 Saturn Company made sales of $25,000 with terms 1/10, n/30. Within the discount period it received payment from customers owing $15,000; after the discount period it received payment from customers owing $10,000. If Saturn uses the gross method of recording sales, prepare journal entries for the transactions described above.

BE7-4 Use the information presented for Saturn Company in BE7-3. If Saturn uses the net method of recording sales, prepare journal entries for the transactions described.

BE7-5 Battle Tank Limited had net sales in 2002 of $1.2 million. At December 31, 2002, before adjusting entries, the balances in selected accounts were: Accounts Receivable, $250,000 debit, and Allowance for Doubtful Accounts, $2,100 credit. If Battle Tank estimates that 2% of its net sales will prove to be uncollectible, prepare the December 31, 2002, journal entry to record bad debt expense.

BE7-6 Use the information presented for Battle Tank Limited in BE7-5.
  (a) Instead of estimating the uncollectibles at 2% of net sales, assume it is expected that 10% of accounts receivable will prove to be uncollectible. Prepare the entry to record bad debts expense.
  (b) Instead of estimating uncollectibles at 2% of net sales, assume Battle Tank prepares an aging schedule that estimates total uncollectible accounts at $24,600. Prepare the entry to record bad debts expense.

BE7-7 Addams Family Importers sold goods to Acme Decorators for $20,000 on November 1, 2002, accepting Acme's $20,000, six-month, 12% note. Prepare Addams' November 1 entry, December 31 annual adjusting entry, and May 1 entry for the collection of the note and interest.

BE7-8 Aero Acrobats lent $15,944 to Afterburner Limited, accepting Afterburner's two-year, $20,000, zero-interest-bearing note. The implied interest is 12%. Prepare Aero's journal entries for the initial transaction, recognition of interest each year, and the collection of $20,000 at maturity.

BE7-9 On October 1, 2002, Akira, Inc. assigns $1 million of its accounts receivable to Alberta Provincial Bank as collateral for a $700,000 note. The bank assesses a finance charge of 2% of the receivables assigned and interest on the note of 13%. Prepare the October 1 journal entries for both Akira and Alberta.

BE7-10 Landstalker Enterprises sold $400,000 of accounts receivable to Leander Factors, Inc. on a without recourse basis. Leander Factors assesses a finance charge of 4% of the amount of accounts receivable and retains an amount equal to 5% of accounts receivable. Prepare journal entries for both Landstalker and Leander.

BE7-11 Use the information presented for Landstalker Enterprises in BE7-10. Assume the receivables are sold with recourse. Prepare the journal entry for Landstalker to record the sale, assuming the recourse obligation has a fair value of $6,000.

BE7-12 Keyser Woodcrafters sells $200,000 of receivables to Commercial Factors, Inc. on a recourse basis. Commercial assesses a finance charge of 5% and retains an amount equal to 4% of accounts receivable. Keyser estimates the recourse obligation's fair value to be $8,000. Prepare the journal entry for Keyser to record the sale.

BE7-13 Use the information presented for Keyser Woodcrafters in BE7-12 but assume that the recourse obligation has a fair value of $4,000, instead of $8,000. Discuss the effects of this change in the recourse obligation's value on Keyser's balance sheet and income statement.

BE7-14 The financial statements of **Magna International Inc.** report net sales of $9.359 billion. Accounts receivable are $1.452 billion at the beginning of the year and $1.584 billion at the end of the year. Calculate Magna's accounts receivable turnover ratio. Calculate Magna's average collection period for accounts receivable in days.

*BE7-15 Genesis Ltd. designated Alex Kidd as petty cash custodian and established a petty cash fund of $200. The fund is reimbursed when the cash in the fund is at $17. Petty cash receipts indicate funds were disbursed for office supplies, $94, and miscellaneous expense, $87. Prepare journal entries for the establishment of the fund and the reimbursement.

*BE7-16 Jaguar Corporation is preparing a bank reconciliation and has identified the following potential reconciling items. For each item, indicate if it is (1) added to the balance per bank statement, (2) deducted from the balance per bank statement, (3) added to the balance per books, or (4) deducted from the balance per books.

(a)	Deposit in transit	$5,500	**(d)** Outstanding cheques	$7,422
(b)	Interest credited to Jaguar's account	$31	**(e)** NSF cheque returned	$377
(c)	Bank service charges	$25		

*BE7-17 Use the information presented for Jaguar Corporation in BE7-16. Prepare any entries necessary to make Jaguar's accounting records correct and complete.

EXERCISES

E7-1 **(Determining Cash Balance)** The controller for Eastwood Co. is attempting to determine the amount of cash to be reported on its December 31, 2002, balance sheet. The following information is provided:

1. Commercial savings account of $600,000 and a commercial chequing account balance of $900,000 are held at First National Bank.
2. Money market fund account held at Volonte Co. (a mutual fund organization) that permits Eastwood to write cheques on this balance, $5 million.
3. Travel advances of $180,000 for executive travel for the first quarter of next year (employees to complete expense reports after travel completed).
4. A separate cash fund in the amount of $1.5 million is restricted for the retirement of long-term debt.
5. Petty cash fund of $1,000.
6. An IOU from Marianne Koch, a company officer, in the amount of $190,000.
7. A bank overdraft of $110,000 has occurred at one of the banks the company uses to deposit its cash receipts. At the moment, the company has no deposits at this bank.
8. The company has two certificates of deposit, each totalling $500,000. These certificates of deposit have a maturity of 120 days.
9. Eastwood has received a cheque dated January 12, 2003, in the amount of $125,000.
10. Eastwood has agreed to maintain a cash balance of $500,000 at all times at First National Bank to ensure future credit availability.
11. Eastwood has purchased $2.1 million of commercial paper of Sergio Leone Co., which is due in 60 days.
12. Currency and coin on hand amounted to $7,700.

Instructions

(a) Calculate the amount of cash to be reported on Eastwood Co.'s balance sheet at December 31, 2002.

(b) Indicate the proper reporting for items that are not reported as cash on the December 31, 2002, balance sheet.

E7-2 **(Determine Cash Balance)** Presented below are a number of independent situations. For each situation, determine the amount that should be reported as cash. If the item(s) is not reported as cash, explain the rationale.

1. Chequing account balance $925,000; certificate of deposit $1.4 million; cash advance to subsidiary of $980,000; utility deposit paid to gas company $180.
2. Chequing account balance $600,000; an overdraft in special chequing account at same bank as normal chequing account of $17,000; cash held in a bond sinking fund $200,000; petty cash fund $300; coins and currency on hand $1,350.
3. Chequing account balance $590,000; postdated cheque from customer $11,000; cash restricted due to maintaining compensating balance requirement of $100,000; certified cheque from customer $9,800; postage stamps on hand $620.
4. Chequing account balance at bank $37,000; money market balance at mutual fund (has chequing privileges) $48,000; NSF cheque received from customer $800.
5. Chequing account balance $700,000; cash restricted for future plant expansion $500,000; short-term Treasury bills $180,000; cash advance received from customer $900 (not included in chequing account balance); cash advance of $7,000 to company executive, payable on demand; refundable deposit of $26,000 paid to federal government to guarantee performance on construction contract.

E7-3 **(Financial Statement Presentation of Receivables)** Gleason Inc. shows a balance of $181,140 in the Accounts Receivable account on December 31, 2002. The balance consists of the following:

Instalment accounts due in 2003	$23,000
Instalment accounts due after 2003	34,000
Overpayments to creditors	2,640
Due from regular customers, of which $40,000 represents accounts pledged as security for a bank loan	79,000
Advances to employees	1,500
Advance to subsidiary company (made in 1997)	81,000

Instructions

Illustrate how the information above should be shown on the balance sheet of Gleason Inc. on December 31, 2002.

E7-4 **(Determine Ending Accounts Receivable)** Your accounts receivable clerk, Ms. Mitra Adams, to whom you pay a salary of $1,500 per month, has just purchased a new Cadillac. You decided to test the accuracy of the accounts receivable balance of $82,000 as shown in the ledger.

The following information is available for your first year in business:

(1)	Collections from customers	$198,000
(2)	Merchandise purchased	320,000
(3)	Ending merchandise inventory	90,000
(4)	Goods are marked to sell at 40% above cost	

Instructions

Calculate an estimate of the ending balance of accounts receivable from customers that should appear in the ledger and any apparent shortages. Assume that all sales are made on account.

E7-5 **(Record Sales Gross and Net)** On June 3, Arnold Limited sold to Chester Arthur merchandise having a sale price of $3,000 with terms of 2/10, n/60, f.o.b. shipping point. An invoice totalling $90, terms n/30, was received by Chester on June 8 from the John Booth Transport Service for the freight cost. On receipt of the goods, June 5, Chester notified Arnold that merchandise costing $500 contained flaws that rendered it worthless; the same day Arnold Limited issued a credit memo covering the worthless merchandise and asked that it be returned at company expense. The freight on the returned merchandise was $25, paid by Arnold on June 7. On June 12, the company received a cheque for the balance due from Chester Arthur.

Instructions

(a) Prepare journal entries on Arnold Limited's books to record all the events noted above under each of the following bases:

1. Sales and receivables are entered at gross selling price.
2. Sales and receivables are entered at net of cash discounts.

(b) Prepare the journal entry under basis 2, assuming that Chester Arthur did not remit payment until July 29.

E7-6 **(Calculating Bad Debts)**   At January 1, 2003, the credit balance in the Allowance for Doubtful Accounts of the Amos Company was $400,000. For 2003, the provision for doubtful accounts is based on a percentage of net sales. Net sales for 2003 were $70,000,000. On the basis of the latest available facts, the 2003 provision for doubtful accounts is estimated to be 0.8% of net sales. During 2003, uncollectible receivables amounting to $500,000 were written off against the allowance for doubtful accounts.

Instructions

Prepare a schedule calculating the balance in Amos' Allowance for Doubtful Accounts at December 31, 2003.

E7-7 **(Calculating Bad Debts and Preparing Journal Entries)**   The trial balance before adjustment of Cline Inc. shows the following balances:

	Dr.	Cr.
Accounts Receivable	$90,000	
Allowance for Doubtful Accounts	1,750	
Sales (all on credit)		$680,000
Sales Returns and Allowances	30,000	

Instructions

Give the entry for bad debt expense for the current year assuming:
   (a) the allowance should be 4% of gross accounts receivable
   (b) historical records indicate 1% of net sales will not be collected.

E7-8 **(Bad Debt Reporting)**   The chief accountant for Dickinson Corporation provides you with the following list of accounts receivable written off in the current year.

Date	Customer	Amount
March 31	E. L. Masters Ltd.	$7,800
June 30	Stephen Crane Associates	6,700
September 30	Amy Lowell's Dress Shop	7,000
December 31	R. Frost, Inc.	9,830

Dickinson Corporation follows the policy of debiting Bad Debt Expense as accounts are written off. The chief accountant maintains that this procedure is appropriate for financial statement purposes.

All of Dickinson Corporation's sales are on a 30-day credit basis. Sales for the current year total $2.2 million, and research has determined that bad debt losses approximate 2% of sales.

Instructions

   (a) Do you agree or disagree with the Dickinson Corporation policy concerning recognition of bad debt expense? Why or why not?
   (b) By what amount would net income differ if bad debt expense was calculated using the percentage-of-sales approach?

E7-9 **(Bad Debts-Ageing)**   Gerard Manley, Inc. includes the following account among its trade receivables.

Hopkins Co.					
1/1	Balance forward	700	1/28	Cash (#1710)	1,100
1/20	Invoice #1710	1,100	4/2	Cash (#2116)	1,350
3/14	Invoice #2116	1,350	4/10	Cash (1/1 Balance)	155
4/12	Invoice #2412	1,710	4/30	Cash (#2412)	1,000
9/5	Invoice #3614	490	9/20	Cash (#3614 and	
10/17	Invoice #4912	860		part of #2412)	790
11/18	Invoice #5681	2,000	10/31	Cash (#4912)	860
12/20	Invoice #6347	800	12/1	Cash (#5681)	1,250
			12/29	Cash (#6347)	800

Instructions

Age the balance and specify any items that apparently require particular attention at year-end.

E7-10 **(Journalizing Various Receivable Transactions)** Presented below is information related to Garfield Corp.

July 1 Garfield Corp. sold to Harding Ltd. merchandise having a sales price of $8,000 with terms 2/10, net/60. Garfield records its sales and receivables net.

3 Harding Ltd. returned defective merchandise having a sales price of $700.

5 Accounts receivable of $9,000 (gross) are factored with Jackson Credit Corp. without recourse at a financing charge of 9%. Cash is received for the proceeds; collections are handled by the finance company. (These accounts were subject to a 2% discount and were all past the discount period.)

9 Specific accounts receivable of $9,000 (gross) are pledged to Landon Credit Corp. as security for a loan of $6,000 at a finance charge of 6% of the loan amount. The finance company will make the collections. (All the accounts receivable are past the discount period.)

Dec. 29 Harding Ltd. notifies Garfield that it is bankrupt and will pay only 10% of its account. Give the entry to write off the uncollectible balance using the allowance method. (Note: First record the increase in the receivable on July 11 when the discount period passed.)

Instructions

Prepare all necessary entries in general journal form for Garfield Corp.

E7-11 **(Assigned Accounts Receivable)** Presented below is information related to Pearson Co.

1. Customers' accounts in the amount of $40,000 are assigned (designated) to the Yeats Finance Company as security for a loan of $30,000. The finance charge is 4% of the amount borrowed.
2. Cash collections on assigned accounts amount to $18,000.
3. Collections on assigned accounts to date, plus a $300 cheque for interest on the loan, are forwarded to Yeats Finance Company.
4. Additional collections on assigned accounts amount to $16,200.
5. The loan is paid in full plus additional interest of $120.

Instructions

Prepare entries in journal form for Pearson Co.

E7-12 **(Journalizing Various Receivable Transactions)** The trial balance before adjustment for Collins Company shows the following balances:

	Dr.	Cr.
Accounts Receivable	$82,000	
Allowance for Doubtful Accounts	2,120	
Sales		$430,000
Sales Returns and Allowances	7,600	

Instructions

Using the data above, give the journal entries required to record each of the following cases (each situation is independent):

1. To obtain additional cash, Collins factors without recourse $25,000 of accounts receivable with Stills Finance. The finance charge is 10% of the amount factored.
2. To obtain a one-year loan of $55,000, Collins assigns $65,000 of specific receivable accounts to Crosby Financial. The finance charge is 8% of the loan; the cash is received and the accounts turned over to Crosby Financial.
3. The company wants to maintain the Allowance for Doubtful Accounts at 5% of gross accounts receivable.
4. The company wishes to increase the allowance by 1½% of net sales.

E7-13 **(Transfer of Receivables with Recourse)** Quartet Ltd. factors receivables with a carrying amount of $200,000 to Joffrey Company for $160,000 on a with recourse basis.

Instructions

The recourse provision has a fair value of $1,000. Assuming this transaction should be recorded as a sale, prepare the appropriate journal entry to record the transaction on the books of Quartet Ltd.

E7-14 **(Transfer of Receivables with Recourse)** Houseman Corporation factors $175,000 of accounts receivable with Battle Financing, Inc. on a with recourse basis. Battle Financing will collect the receivables. The receivable records are transferred to Battle Financing on August 15, 2002. Battle Financing assesses a finance charge of 2% of the amount of accounts receivable and also reserves an amount equal to 4% of accounts receivable to cover probable adjustments.

Instructions

(a) What conditions must be met for a transfer of receivables with recourse to be accounted for as a sale?

(b) Assume the conditions from part (a) are met. Prepare the journal entry on August 15, 2002, for Houston to record the sale of receivables, assuming the recourse obligation has a fair value of $2,000.

E7-15 **(Transfer of Receivables Without Recourse)** PET Corp. factors $300,000 of accounts receivable with HEC Finance Corporation on a without recourse basis on July 1, 2002. The receivable records are transferred to HEC Finance, which will receive the collections. HEC Finance assesses a finance charge of 1½% of the amount of accounts receivable and retains an amount equal to 4% of accounts receivable to cover sales discounts, returns, and allowances. The transaction is to be recorded as a sale.

Instructions

(a) Prepare the journal entry on July 1, 2002, for PET Corp. to record the sale of receivables without recourse.

(b) Prepare the journal entry on July 1, 2002, for HEC Finance Corporation to record the purchase of receivables without recourse.

E7-16 **(Note Transactions at Unrealistic Interest Rates)** On July 1, 2003, Agincourt Inc. made two sales:

1. It sold land having a fair market value of $700,000 in exchange for a four-year noninterest-bearing promissory note in the face amount of $1,101,460. The land is carried on Agincourt's books at a cost of $590,000.

2. It rendered services in exchange for a 3%, eight-year promissory note having a face value of $400,000 (interest payable annually).

Agincourt Inc. recently had to pay 8% interest for money that it borrowed from British National Bank. The customers in these two transactions have credit ratings that require them to borrow money at 12% interest.

Instructions

Record the two journal entries that should be recorded by Agincourt Inc. for the sales transactions above that took place on July 1, 2003.

E7-17 **(Note Receivable at Unrealistic Interest Rates)** On December 31, 2002, Fenimore Company sold some of its product to Cooper Company, accepting a $340,000 noninterest-bearing note, receivable in full on December 31, 2005. Fenimore Company enjoys a high credit rating and, therefore, borrows funds from its several lines of credit at 9%. Cooper Company, however, pays 12% for its borrowed funds. The product sold is carried on the books of Fenimore Company at a manufactured cost of $180,000. Assume that the effective interest method is used for discount amortization.

Instructions

(a) Prepare journal entries to record the sale on December 31, 2002, by Fenimore Company. Assume that a perpetual inventory system is used.

(b) Prepare the journal entry on the books of Fenimore Company for the year 2003 that are necessitated by the sales transaction of December 31, 2002. Preparing an amortization schedule may help.

(c) Prepare the journal entry on the books of Fenimore Company for the year 2004 that are necessitated by the sale on December 31, 2002.

E7-18 **(Analysis of Receivables)** Presented below is information for Jones Company.

1. Beginning of the year Accounts Receivable balance was $15,000.

2. Net sales for the year were $185,000. (Credit sales were $100,000 of the total sales.) Jones does not offer cash discounts.

3. Collections on accounts receivable during the year were $70,000.

Instructions

(a) Prepare (summary) journal entries to record the items noted above.

(b) Calculate Jones's accounts receivable turnover ratio for the year.

(c) Use the turnover ratio calculated in (b) to analyse Jones's liquidity. The turnover ratio last year was 13.65.

E7-19 **(Transfer of Receivables)** Use the information for Jones Company as presented in E7-18. Jones is planning to factor some accounts receivable at the end of the year. Accounts totalling $25,000 will be transferred to Credit Factors, Inc. with recourse. Credit Factors will retain 5% of the balances and assesses a finance charge of 4%. The recourse obligation's fair value is $1,200.

Instructions

(a) Prepare the journal entry to record the sale of receivables.

(b) Calculate Jones's accounts receivables turnover ratio for the year, assuming the receivables are sold, and discuss how factoring of receivables affects the turnover ratio.

*E7-20 (Petty Cash) Keene, Inc. decided to establish a petty cash fund to help ensure internal control over its small cash expenditures. The following information is available for the month of April.

1. On April 1, it established a petty cash fund in the amount of $200.

2. A summary of the petty cash expenditures made by the petty cash custodian as of April 10 is as follows:

Delivery charges paid on merchandise purchased	$60.00 — *Transportation-in*
Supplies purchased and used	25.00
Postage expense	33.00
IOU from employees	17.00 — *A/R — Debit*
Miscellaneous expense	36.00

The petty cash fund was replenished on April 10. The balance in the fund was $27.

3. The petty cash fund balance was increased $100 to $300 on April 20.

Instructions

Prepare the journal entries to record transactions related to petty cash for the month of April.

*E7-21 (Petty Cash) The petty cash fund of Fonzarelli's Auto Repair Service, a sole proprietorship, contains the following:

1. Coins and currency		$15.20
2. An IOU from Bob Cunningham, an employee, for cash advance		43.00
3. Cheque payable to Fonzarelli's Auto Repair from Pat Webber, an employee, marked NSF		34.00
4. Vouchers for the following:		
Stamps	$ 20.00	
Two NHL play-off tickets for Rick Fonzarelli	170.00	
Printer cartridge	14.35	204.35
		$296.55

The general ledger account Petty Cash has a balance of $300.00.

Instructions

Prepare the journal entry to record the reimbursement of the petty cash fund.

*E7-22 (Bank Reconciliation and Adjusting Entries) Lansbury Company deposits all receipts and makes all payments by cheque. The following information is available from the cash records.

June 30 Bank Reconciliation

Balance per bank	$7,000
Add: Deposits in transit	1,540
Deduct: Outstanding cheques	(2,000)
Balance per books	$6,540

Month of July Results

	Per Bank	Per Books
Balance July 31	$8,650	$9,250
July deposits	5,000	5,810
July cheques	4,000	3,100
July note collected (not included in July deposits)	1,000	—
July bank service charge	15	—
July NSF cheque from a customer, returned by the bank (recorded by bank as a charge)	335	—

Instructions

(a) Prepare a bank reconciliation going from balance per bank and balance per books to correct cash balance.

(b) Prepare the general journal entry or entries to correct the Cash account.

*E7-23 (Bank Reconciliation and Adjusting Entries)   Bruno Corp. has just received the August 31, 2002 bank statement, which is summarized below:

National Bank of Ottawa	Disbursements	Receipts	Balance
Balance, August 1			$ 9,369
Deposits during August		$32,200	41,569
Note collected for depositor, including $40 interest		1,040	42,609
Cheques cleared during August	$34,500		8,109
Bank service charges	20		8,089
Balance, August 31			8,089

The general ledger Cash account contained the following entries for the month of August:

Cash			
Balance, August 1	10,050	Disbursements in August	34,903
Receipts during August	35,000		

Deposits in transit at August 31 are $3,800, and cheques outstanding at August 31 are determined to total $1,050. Cash on hand at August 31 is $310. The bookkeeper improperly entered one cheque in the books at $146.50 that was written for $164.50 for supplies (expense); it cleared the bank during the month of August.

Instructions

(a) Prepare a bank reconciliation dated August 31, 2002, proceeding to a correct balance.
(b) Prepare any entries necessary to make the books correct and complete.
(c) What amount of cash should be reported in the August 31 balance sheet?

PROBLEMS

P7-1   Dumaine Equipment Co. closes its books regularly on December 31, but at the end of 2002 it held its cash book open so that a more favourable balance sheet could be prepared for credit purposes. Cash receipts and disbursements for the first 10 days of January were recorded as December transactions. The following information is given.

1. January cash receipts recorded in the December cash book totalled $39,640, of which $22,000 represents cash sales and $17,640 represents collections on account for which cash discounts of $360 were given.
2. January cash disbursements recorded in the December cheque register liquidated accounts payable of $26,450 on which discounts of $250 were taken.
3. The ledger has not been closed for 2002.
4. The amount shown as inventory was determined by physical count on December 31, 2002.

Instructions

(a) Prepare any entries you consider necessary to correct Dumaine's accounts at December 31.
(b) To what extent was Dumaine Equipment Co. able to show a more favourable balance sheet at December 31 by holding its cash book open? (Use ratio analysis.) Assume that the balance sheet that was prepared by the company showed the following amounts:

	Dr.	Cr.
Cash	$39,000	
Receivables	42,000	
Inventories	67,000	
Accounts payable		$45,000
Other current liabilities		14,200

P7-2   Presented below are a series of unrelated situations.

1. Spock Inc.'s unadjusted trial balance at December 31, 2002, included the following accounts:

	Debit	Credit
Allowance for doubtful accounts	$ 4,000	
Sales		$1,500,000
Sales returns and allowances	70,000	

Spock estimates its bad debt expense to be 1½% of net sales. Determine its bad debt expense for 2002.

2. An analysis and aging of Scotty Corp. accounts receivable at December 31, 2002, disclosed the following:

Amounts estimated to be uncollectible	$ 180,000
Accounts receivable	1,750,000
Allowance for doubtful accounts (per books)	125,000

What is the net realizable value of Scotty's receivables at December 31, 2002?

3. Uhura Co. provides for doubtful accounts based on 3% of credit sales. The following data are available for 2002.

Credit sales during 2002	$2,100,000
Allowance for doubtful accounts 1/1/02	17,000
Collection of accounts written off in prior years (customer credit was reestablished)	8,000
Customer accounts written off as uncollectible during 2002	30,000

What is the balance in the Allowance for Doubtful Accounts at December 31, 2002?

4. At the end of its first year of operations, December 31, 2002, Chekov Inc. reported the following information:

Accounts receivable, net of allowance for doubtful accounts	$950,000
Customer accounts written off as uncollectible during 2002	24,000
Bad debt expense for 2002	84,000

What should be the balance in accounts receivable at December 31, 2002, before subtracting the allowance for doubtful accounts?

5. The following accounts were taken from Chappel Inc.'s balance sheet at December 31, 2002.

	Debit	Credit
Net credit sales		$750,000
Allowance for doubtful accounts	$ 14,000	
Accounts receivable	410,000	

If doubtful accounts are 3% of accounts receivable, determine the bad debt expense to be reported for 2002.

Instructions

Answer the questions relating to each of the five independent situations as requested.

P7-3 Paderewski Corporation operates in an industry that has a high rate of bad debts. Before any year-end adjustments, the balance in Paderewski's Accounts Receivable account was $555,000 and the Allowance for Doubtful Accounts had a credit balance of $35,000. The year-end balance reported in the balance sheet for the Allowance for Doubtful Accounts will be based on the aging schedule shown below.

Days Account Outstanding	Amount	Probability of Collection
Less than 16 days	$300,000	0.98
Between 16 and 30 days	100,000	0.90
Between 31 and 45 days	80,000	0.85
Between 46 and 60 days	40,000	0.75
Between 61 and 75 days	20,000	0.40
Over 75 days	15,000	0.00

Instructions

(a) What is the appropriate balance for the Allowance for Doubtful Accounts at year-end?
(b) Show how accounts receivable would be presented on the balance sheet.
(c) What is the dollar effect of the year-end bad debt adjustment on the before-tax income?

(CMA adapted)

P7-4 From inception of operations to December 31, 2002, Pascal Corporation provided for uncollectible accounts receivable under the allowance method: provisions were made monthly at 2% of credit sales; bad debts written off were charged to the allowance account; recoveries of bad debts previously written off were credited to the allowance account; and no year-end adjustments to the allowance account were made. Pascal's usual credit terms are net 30 days.

The balance in the Allowance for Doubtful Accounts was $154,000 at January 1, 2002. During 2002, credit sales totalled $9 million, interim provisions for doubtful accounts were made at 2% of credit sales, $95,000 of bad debts were written off, and recoveries of accounts previously written off amounted to $15,000. Pascal installed a computer facility in November, 2002 and an aging of accounts receivable was prepared for the first time as of December 31, 2002. A summary of the aging is as follows:

Classification by Month of Sale	Balance in Each Category	Estimated % Uncollectible
November – December 2002	$1,080,000	2%
July – October	650,000	10%
January – June	420,000	25%
Prior to 1/1/02	150,000	70%
	$2,300,000	

Based on the review of collectibility of the account balances in the "prior to 1/1/02" ageing category, additional receivables totalling $60,000 were written off as of December 31, 2002. The 70% uncollectible estimate applies to the remaining $90,000 in the category. Effective with the year ended December 31, 2002, Pascal adopted a new accounting method for estimating the allowance for doubtful accounts at the amount indicated by the year-end aging analysis of accounts receivable.

Instructions

(a) Prepare a schedule analysing the changes in the Allowance for Doubtful Accounts for the year ended December 31, 2002. Show supporting calculations in good form. (Hint: In calculating the 12/31/02 allowance, subtract the $60,000 write-off).

(b) Prepare the journal entry for the year-end adjustment to the Allowance for Doubtful Accounts balance as of December 31, 2002.

(AICPA adapted)

P7-5 Presented below is information related to the Accounts Receivable accounts of Gulistan Inc. during the current year 2002.

1. An ageing schedule of the accounts receivable as of December 31, 2002, is as follows:

Age	Net Debit Balance	% to Be Applied after Correction Is Made
Under 60 days	$172,342	1%
61 – 90 days	136,490	3%
91 – 120 days	39,924*	6%
Over 120 days	23,644	$4,200 definitely uncollectible; estimated remainder uncollectible is 25%
	$372,400	

*The $2,740 write-off of receivables is related to the 91-to-120 day category.

2. The Accounts Receivable control account has a debit balance of $372,400 on December 31, 2002.
3. Two entries were made in the Bad Debt Expense account during the year: (1) a debit on December 31 for the amount credited to Allowance for Doubtful Accounts, and (2) a credit for $2,740 on November 3, 2002, and a debit to Allowance for Doubtful Accounts because of a bankruptcy.
4. The Allowance for Doubtful Accounts is as follows for 2002:

Allowance for Doubtful Accounts			
Nov. 3 Uncollectible accounts written off	2,740	Jan. 1 Beginning balance	8,750
		Dec. 31 5% of $372,400	18,620

5. A credit balance exists in the Accounts Receivable (61 – 90 days) of $4,840, which represents an advance on a sales contract.

Instructions

Assuming that the books have not been closed for 2002, make the necessary correcting entries.

P7-6 The balance sheet of Antonio Company at December 31, 2002, includes the following:

Notes receivable	$36,000	
Accounts receivable	182,100	
Less: Allowance for doubtful accounts	17,300	200,800

Transactions in 2003 include the following:

1. Accounts receivable of $138,000 were collected, including accounts of $40,000, on which 2% sales discounts were allowed.
2. $6,300 was received in payment of an account that was written off the books as worthless in 2001. (Hint: Reestablish the receivable account.)
3. Customer accounts of $17,500 were written off during the year.
4. At year-end the Allowance for Doubtful Accounts was estimated to need a balance of $20,000. This estimate is based on an analysis of aged accounts receivable.

Instructions

Prepare all journal entries necessary to reflect the transactions above.

P7-7 Nikos Company finances some of its current operations by assigning accounts receivable to a finance company. On July 1, 2002, it assigned, under guarantee, specific accounts amounting to $100,000; the finance company advanced to Nikos 80% of the accounts assigned (20% of the total to be withheld until the finance company has made its full recovery), less a finance charge of ½% of the total accounts assigned.

On July 31 Nikos Company received a statement that the finance company had collected $55,000 of these accounts and had made an additional charge of ½% of the total accounts outstanding as of July 31. This charge is to be deducted at the time of the first remittance due Nikos Company from the finance company. (Hint: Make entries at this time.) On August 31, 2002, Nikos Company received a second statement from the finance company, together with a cheque for the amount due. The statement indicated that the finance company had collected an additional $30,000 and had made a further charge of ½% of the balance outstanding as of August 31.

Instructions

Make all entries on the books of Nikos Company that are involved in the transactions above.

(AICPA adapted)

P7-8 Boll Sports Inc. produces soccer, football, and track shoes. The treasurer has recently completed negotiations in which Boll Sports agrees to loan Max Ltd., a leather supplier, $500,000. Max Company will issue a noninterest-bearing note due in five years (a 12% interest rate is appropriate), and has agreed to furnish Boll Sports with leather at prices that are 10% lower than those usually charged.

Instructions

(a) Prepare the accounting entry to record this transaction on Boll Sports's books.
(b) Determine the balances at the end of each year the note is outstanding for the following accounts for Boll Sports: Notes receivable, Unamortized discount, Interest revenue.

P7-9 On December 31, 2002, Mirror Ltd. rendered services to Begin Corporation at an agreed price of $91,844.10, accepting $36,000 down and agreeing to accept the balance in four equal instalments of $18,000 receivable each December 31. An assumed interest rate of 11% is imputed.

Instructions

Prepare the entries that would be recorded by Mirror Ltd. for the sale and for the receipts and interest on the following dates. (Assume that the effective interest method is used for amortization purposes).

(a) December 31, 2002.   (c) December 31, 2004.   (e) December 31, 2006.
(b) December 31, 2003.   (d) December 31, 2005.

P7-10 Lynch Supply produces paints and related products for sale to the construction industry throughout the Atlantic Provinces. While sales have remained relatively stable despite a decline in the amount of new construction, there has been a noticeable change in the timeliness with which Lynch's customers are paying their bills.

Lynch sells its products on payment terms of 2/10, n/30. In the past, over 75% of the credit customers have taken advantage of the discount by paying within 10 days of the invoice date. During the fiscal year ended November 30, 2002, the number of customers taking the full 30 days to pay has increased. Current indications are that less than 60% of the customers are now taking the discount. Uncollectible accounts as a percentage of total credit sales have risen from the 1.5% provided in past years to 4.0% in the current year.

In response to a request for more information on the deterioration of accounts receivable collections, Lynch's controller has prepared the following report.

LYNCH SUPPLY
Accounts Receivable Collections
November 30, 2002

The fact that some credit accounts will prove uncollectible is normal, and annual bad debt write-offs had been 1.5% of total credit sales for many years. However, during the 2001 – 02 fiscal year, this percentage increased to 4.0%. The current accounts receivable balance is $1,500,000, and the condition of this balance in terms of age and probability of collection is shown below.

Proportion of Total	Age Categories	Probability of Collection
64.0%	1 to 10 days	99.0%
18.0	11 to 30 days	97.5
8.0	Past due 31 to 60 days	95.0
5.0	Past due 61 to 120 days	80.0
3.0	Past due 121 to 180 days	65.0
2.0	Past due over 180 days	20.0

At the beginning of the fiscal year, December 1, 2001, the Allowance for Doubtful Accounts had a credit balance of $27,300. Lynch has provided for a monthly bad debt expense accrual during the fiscal year just ended based on the assumption that 4% of total credit sales will be uncollectible. Total credit sales for the 2001-02 fiscal year amounted to $8,000,000, and write-offs of uncollectible accounts during the year totalled $292,500.

Instructions

(a) Prepare an accounts receivable ageing schedule at November 30, 2002, for Lynch Supply using the age categories identified in the controller's report showing:

1. the amount of accounts receivable outstanding for each age category and in total.

2. the estimated amount that is uncollectible for each category and in total.

(b) Calculate the amount of the year-end adjustment necessary to bring Lynch Supply's Allowance for Doubtful Accounts to the balance indicated by the ageing analysis.

(c) Calculate the net realizable value of Lynch Supply's accounts receivable at November 30, 2002. Ignore any discounts that may be applicable to the accounts not yet due.

(d) Describe the accounting to be performed for subsequent collections of previously written-off accounts receivable.

(CMA adapted)

P7-11 Desrosiers Ltd. had the following long-term receivable account balances at December 31, 2002:

Note receivable from sale of division	$1,800,000
Note receivable from officer	400,000

Transactions during 2003 and other information relating to Desrosiers' long-term receivables were as follows:

1. The $1.8 million note receivable is dated May 1, 2002, bears interest at 9%, and represents the balance of the consideration received from the sale of Desrosiers' electronics division to New York Company. Principal payments of $600,000 plus appropriate interest are due on May 1, 2003, 2004, and 2005. The first principal and interest payment was made on May 1, 2003. Collection of the note instalments is reasonably assured.

2. The $400,000 note receivable is dated December 31, 2002, bears interest at 8%, and is due on December 31, 2005. The note is due from Mark Cumby, president of Desrosiers Ltd. and is collateralized by 10,000 Desrosiers' common shares. Interest is payable annually on December 31, and all interest payments were paid on their due dates through December 31, 2003. The quoted market price of Desrosiers' common shares was $45 per share on December 31, 2003.

3. On April 1, 2003, Desrosiers sold a patent to Pinot Company in exchange for a $200,000 noninterest-bearing note due on April 1, 2005. There was no established exchange price for the patent, and the note had no ready market. The prevailing rate of interest for a note of this type at April 1, 2003, was 12%. The present value of $1 for two periods at 12% is 0.797 (use this factor). The patent had a carrying value of $40,000 at January 1, 2003, and the amortization for the year ended December 31, 2003, would have been $8,000. The collection of the note receivable from Pinot is reasonably assured.

4. On July 1, 2003, Desrosiers sold a parcel of land to Harris Inc. for $200,000 under an instalment sale contract. Harris made a $60,000 cash down payment on July 1, 2003, and signed a four-year 11% note for the $140,000 balance. The equal annual payments of principal and interest on the note will be $45,125 payable on July 1, 2004, through July 1, 2007. The land could have been sold at an established cash price of $200,000. The cost of the land to Desrosiers was $150,000. Circumstances are such that the collection of the instalments on the note is reasonably assured.

Instructions

(a) Prepare the long-term receivables section of Desrosiers' balance sheet at December 31, 2003.
(b) Prepare a schedule showing the current portion of the long-term receivables and accrued interest receivable that would appear in Desrosiers' balance sheet at December 31, 2003.
(c) Prepare a schedule showing interest revenue from the long-term receivables that would appear on Desrosiers' income statement for the year ended December 31, 2003.

P7-12 Mike Horn Company manufactures sweatshirts for sale to athletic-wear retailers. The following summary information was available for Horn for the year ended December 31, 2001:

Cash	$20,000
Trade accounts receivable (net)	40,000
Inventories	85,000
Accounts payable	65,000
Other current liabilities	15,000

Part 1

During 2002, Horn had the following transactions:

1. Total sales were $450,000.
2. $200,000 of total sales were made on a credit basis (trade accounts receivable).
3. On June 30, sales of $50,000 to a major customer were settled with Horn accepting a one-year $50,000 note, bearing 11% interest, payable at maturity.
4. Horn collected $160,000 on trade accounts receivable during the year.
5. At December 31, 2002, Cash has a balance of $15,000, Inventories had a balance of $80,000, Accounts Payable were $70,000, and other current liabilities were $16,000.

Instructions

(a) Prepare (summary) journal entries to record the items noted above.
(b) Calculate the current ratio and the receivables turnover ratio for Horn at December 31, 2002. Use these measures to analyse Horn's liquidity. The receivables turnover ratio last year was 10.37.

Part 2

Now assume that at year-end 2002, Horn enters into the following transactions related to the company's receivables:

1. Horn transfers the note receivable to Prairie Bank for $50,000 cash plus accrued interest. Given the creditworthiness of Horn's customer, the bank accepts the note without recourse and assesses a finance charge of 1.5%.
2. Horn factors some accounts receivable at the end of the year. Accounts totalling $40,000 are transferred to First Factors, Inc. with recourse. First Factors will receive the collections from Horn's customers and retains 6% of the balances. Horn is assessed a finance charge of 4% on this transfer. The fair value of the recourse obligation is $4,000.

Instructions

(c) Prepare the journal entry to record the transfer of the note receivable to Prairie Bank.
(d) Prepare the journal entry to record the sale of receivables.
(e) Calculate the current ratio and the receivables turnover ratio for Horn at December 31, 2002. Use these measures to analyse Horn's liquidity. The receivables turnover ratio last year was 10.37.
(f) Discuss how the ratio analysis in (e) would be affected if Horn had transferred the receivables in a secured borrowing transaction.

P7-13 Radisson Company requires additional cash for its business. Radisson has decided to use its accounts receivable to raise the additional cash and has asked you to determine the income statement effects of the following contemplated transactions.

1. On July 1, 2002, Radisson assigned $400,000 of accounts receivable to Stickum Finance Company. Radisson received an advance from Stickum of 85% of the assigned accounts receivable less a commission of 3% on the advance. Prior to December 31, 2002, Radisson collected $220,000 on the assigned accounts receivable, and remitted $232,720 to Stickum, $12,720 of which represented interest on the advance from Stickum.
2. On December 1, 2002, Radisson sold $300,000 of net accounts receivable to Wunsch Company for $250,000. The receivables were sold outright on a without recourse basis.
3. On December 31, 2002, an advance of $120,000 was received from First Bank by pledging $160,000 of Radisson's accounts receivable. Radisson's first payment to First Bank is due on January 30, 2003.

Instructions

Prepare a schedule showing the income statement effects for the year ended December 31, 2002 as a result of the above facts.

*P7-14 Bill Howe is reviewing the cash accounting for Kappeler Company, a local mailing service. Howe's review will focus on the petty cash account and the bank reconciliation for the month ended May 31, 2002. He has collected the following information from Kappeler's bookkeeper for this task.

Petty Cash

1. The petty cash fund was established on May 10, 2002, in the amount of $250.00.
2. Expenditures from the fund by the custodian as of May 31, 2002, were evidenced by approved receipts for the following:

Postage expense	$33.00
Mailing labels and other supplies	75.00
IOU from employees	30.00
Shipping charges	57.45
Newspaper advertising	22.80
Miscellaneous expense	15.35

On May 31, 2002, the petty cash fund was replenished and increased to $300.00; currency and coin in the fund at that time totalled $16.40.

Bank Reconciliation

THIRD NATIONAL BANK
Bank Statement

	Disbursements	Receipts	Balance
Balance, May 1, 2002			$8,769
Deposits		$28,000	
Note payment direct from customer (interest of $30)		930	
Cheques cleared during May	$31,150		
Bank service charges	27		
Balance, May 31, 2002			$6,522

Kappeler's Cash Account

Balance, May 1, 2002	$ 9,150
Deposits during May 2002	31,000
Cheques written during May 2002	(31,835)

Deposits in transit are determined to be $3,000, and cheques outstanding at May 31 total $550. Cash on hand (besides petty cash) at May 31, 2002, is $246.

Instructions

(a) Prepare the journal entries to record the transactions related to the petty cash fund for May.
(b) Prepare a bank reconciliation dated May 31, 2002, proceeding to a correct balance, and prepare the journal entries necessary to make the books correct and complete.
(c) What amount of cash should be reported in the May 31, 2002 balance sheet?

*P7-15 The cash account of Orozco Co. showed a ledger balance of $3,969.85 on June 30, 2002. The bank statement as of that date showed a balance of $4,150. Upon comparing the statement with the cash records, the following facts were determined:

1. There were bank service charges for June of $25.00.
2. A bank memo stated that Bao Dai's note for $900 and interest of $36 had been collected on June 29, and the bank had made a charge of $5.50 on the collection. (No entry had been made on Orozco's books when Bao Dai's note was sent to the bank for collection.)
3. Receipts for June 30 for $2,890 were not deposited until July 2.
4. Cheques outstanding on June 30 totalled $2,136.05.
5. The bank had charged the Orozco Co.'s account for a customer's uncollectible cheque amounting to $453.20 on June 29.
6. A customer's cheque for $90 had been entered as $60 in the cash receipts journal by Orozco on June 15.
7. Cheque no. 742 in the amount of $491 had been entered in the cashbook as $419, and cheque no. 747 in the amount of $58.20 had been entered as $582. Both cheques had been issued to pay for purchases of equipment.

Instructions

(a) Prepare a bank reconciliation dated June 30, 2002, proceeding to a correct cash balance.

(b) Prepare any entries necessary to make the books correct and complete.

*P7-16 Presented below is information related to Tanizaki Ltd.

Balance per books at October 31, $41,847.85; receipts, $173,523.91; disbursements, $166,193.54. Balance per bank statement November 30, $56,274.20.

The following cheques were outstanding at November 30:

1224	$1,635.29
1230	2,468.30
1232	3,625.15
1233	482.17

Included with the November bank statement and not recorded by the company were a bank debit memo for $27.40 covering bank charges for the month, a debit memo for $572.13 for a customer's cheque returned and marked NSF, and a credit memo for $1,400 representing bond interest collected by the bank in the name of Tanizaki Ltd. Cash on hand at November 30 recorded and awaiting deposit amounted to $1,915.40.

Instructions

(a) Prepare a bank reconciliation (to the correct balance) at November 30, 2002, for Tanizaki Ltd. from the information above.

(b) Prepare any journal entries required to adjust the cash account at November 30.

*P7-17 Presented below is information related to Junichiro Industries.

JUNICHIRO INDUSTRIES
Bank Reconciliation
May 31, 2002

Balance per bank statement		$30,928.46
Less: Outstanding cheques		
No. 6124	$2,125.00	
No. 6138	932.65	
No. 6139	960.57	
No. 6140	1,420.00	5,438.22
		25,490.24
Add deposit in transit		4,710.56
Balance per books (correct balance)		$30,200.80

CHEQUE REGISTER-JUNE

Date	Payee	No.	Invoice Amount	Discount	Cash
June 1	Ren Mfg.	6141	$237.50		$237.50
1	Stimpy Mfg.	6142	915.00	$9.15	905.85
8	Rugrats Co., Inc.	6143	122.90	2.45	120.45
9	Ren Mfg.	6144	306.40		306.40
10	Petty Cash	6145	89.93		89.93
17	Muppet Babies Photo	6146	706.00	14.12	691.88 ✓
22	Hey Dude Publishing	6147	447.50		447.50
23	Payroll Account	6148	4,130.00		4,130.00
25	Dragnet Tools, Inc.	6149	390.75	3.91	386.84 ✓
28	Dare Insurance Agency	6150	1,050.00		1,050.00
28	Get Smart Construction	6151	2,250.00		2,250.00
29	MMT, Inc.	6152	750.00		750.00 ✓
30	Lassie Co.	6153	400.00	8.00	392.00 ✓
			$11,795.98	$37.63	$11,758.35

PROVINCIAL BANK
Bank Statement
General Chequing Account of Junichiro Industries – June 2002

Debits			Date	Credits	Balance
					$30,928.46
$2,125.00	$237.50	$905.85	June 1	$4,710.56	32,370.67
932.65	120.45		12	1,507.06	32,824.63
1,420.00	447.50	306.40	23	1,458.55	32,109.28
4,130.00		*11.05	26		27,968.23
89.93	2,250.00	1,050.00	28	4,157.48	28,735.78

*Bank charges

Cash received June 29 and 30 and deposited in the mail for the general chequing account June 30 amounted to $4,607.96. Because the cash account balance at June 30 is not given, it must be calculated from other information in the problem.

Instructions

From the information above, prepare a bank reconciliation (to the correct balance) as of June 30, 2002, for Junichiro Industries.

CONCEPTUAL CASES

C7-1 Ariel Company has significant amounts of trade accounts receivable. Ariel uses the allowance method to estimate bad debts instead of the direct write-off method. During the year, some specific accounts were written off as uncollectible, and some that were previously written off as uncollectible were collected.

Instructions

(a) What are the deficiencies of the direct write-off method?

(b) What are the two basic allowance methods used to estimate bad debts, and what is the theoretical justification for each?

(c) How should Ariel account for the collection of the specific accounts previously written off as uncollectible?

C7-2 Archer Company uses the net method of accounting for sales discounts. Archer also offers trade discounts to various groups of buyers.

On August 1, 2002, Archer sold some accounts receivable on a without recourse basis. Archer incurred a finance charge.

Archer also has some notes receivable bearing an appropriate rate of interest. The principal and total interest are due at maturity. The notes were received on October 1, 2002, and mature on September 30, 2004. Archer's operating cycle is less than one year.

Instructions

(a) Using the net method, how should Archer account for the sales discounts at the date of sale? What is the rationale for the amount recorded as sales under the net method?

(b) Using the net method, what is the effect on Archer's sales revenues and net income when customers do not take the sales discounts?

(c) What is the effect of trade discounts on sales revenues and accounts receivable? Why?

(d) How should Archer account for the accounts receivable factored on August 1, 2002? Why?

(e) How should Archer account for the note receivable and the related interest on December 31, 2002? Why?

C7-3 Ben Gavel conducts a wholesale merchandising business that sells approximately 5,000 items per month with a total monthly average sales value of $250,000. Its annual bad debt ratio has been approximately 1½ % of sales. In recent discussions with his bookkeeper, Mr. Gavel has become confused by all the alternatives apparently available in handling the Allowance for Doubtful Accounts balance. The following information has been shown.

1. An allowance can be set up (a) on the basis of a percentage of sales or (b) on the basis of a valuation of all past due or otherwise questionable accounts receivable-those considered uncollectible being charged to such allowance at the close of the accounting period, or specific items charged off directly against (1) Gross Sales, or to (2) Bad Debt Expense in the year in which they are determined to be uncollectible.

2. Collection agency and legal fees, and so on, incurred in connection with the attempted recovery of bad debts can be charged to (a) Bad Debt Expense, (b) Allowance for Doubtful Accounts, (c) Legal Expense, or (d) General Expense.

3. Debts previously written off in whole or in part but currently recovered can be credited to (a) Other Revenue, (b) Bad Debt Expense, or (c) Allowance for Doubtful Accounts.

Instructions

Which of the foregoing methods would you recommend to Mr. Gavel in regard to (1) allowances and charge-offs, (2) collection expenses, and (3) recoveries? State briefly and clearly the reasons supporting your recommendations.

C7-4 Part 1

On July 1, 2002, Arden Company, a calendar-year company, sold special-order merchandise on credit and received in return an interest-bearing note receivable from the customer. Arden Company will receive interest at the prevailing rate for a note of this type. Both the principal and interest are due in one lump sum on June 30, 2003.

Instructions

When should Arden Company report interest income from the note receivable? Discuss the rationale for your answer.

Part 2

On December 31, 2002, Arden Company had significant amounts of accounts receivable as a result of credit sales to its customers. Arden Company uses the allowance method based on credit sales to estimate bad debts. Past experience indicates that 2% of credit sales normally will not be collected. This pattern is expected to continue.

Instructions

(a) Discuss the rationale for using the allowance method based on credit sales to estimate bad debts. Contrast this method with the allowance method based on the balance in the trade receivables accounts.

(b) How should Arden Company report the allowance for bad debts account on its balance sheet at December 31, 2002? Also, describe the alternatives, if any, for presenting bad debt expense in Arden Company's 2002 income statement.

(AICPA adapted)

C7-5 The Rosita Company sells office equipment and supplies to many organizations in the city and surrounding area on contract terms of 2/10, n/30. In the past, over 75% of the credit customers have taken advantage of the discount by paying within 10 days of the invoice date.

The number of customers taking the full 30 days to pay has increased within the last year. Current indications are that less than 60% of the customers are now taking the discount. Bad debts as a percentage of gross credit sales have risen from the 1.5% provided in past years to about 4% in the current year.

The controller has responded to a request for more information on the deterioration in collections of accounts receivable with the report reproduced below.

THE ROSITA COMPANY
Finance Committee Report-Accounts Receivable Collections
May 31, 2003

The fact that some credit accounts will prove uncollectible is normal. Annual bad debt write-offs have been 1.5% of gross credit sales over the past five years. During the last fiscal year, this percentage increased to slightly less than 4%. The current Accounts Receivable balance is $1.6 million. The condition of this balance in terms of age and probability of collection is as follows:

Proportion of Total	Age Categories	Probability of Collection
68%	not yet due	99%
15%	less than 30 days past due	96½ %
8%	30 to 60 days past due	95%
5%	61 to 120 days past due	91%
2½ %	121 to 180 days past due	70%
1½ %	over 180 days past due	20%

The Allowance for Doubtful Accounts had a credit balance of $43,300 on June 1, 2002. The Rosita Company has provided for a monthly bad debts expense accrual during the current fiscal year based on the assumption that 4% of gross credit sales will be uncollectible. Total gross credit sales for the 2002-03 fiscal year amounted to $4 million. Write-offs of bad accounts during the year totalled $145,000.

Instructions

(a) Prepare an accounts receivable aging schedule for The Rosita Company using the age categories identified in the controller's report to the Finance Committee showing (1) the amount of accounts receivable outstanding for each age category and in total, and (2) the estimated amount that is uncollectible for each category and in total.

(b) Calculate the amount of the year-end adjustment necessary to bring the Allowance for Doubtful Accounts to the balance indicated by the age analysis. Then prepare the necessary journal entry to adjust the accounting records.

(c) In a recessionary environment with tight credit and high interest rates:
   1. Identify steps The Rosita Company might consider to improve the accounts receivable situation.
   2. Then evaluate each step identified in terms of the risks and costs involved.

(CMA adapted)

C7-6 Luzov Wholesalers Co. sells industrial equipment for a standard three-year note receivable. Revenue is recognized at time of sale. Each note is secured by a lien on the equipment and has a face amount equal to the equipment's list price. Each note's stated interest rate is below the customer's market rate at date of sale. All notes are to be collected in three equal annual instalments beginning one year after sale. Some of the notes are subsequently sold to a bank with recourse, some are subsequently sold without recourse, and some are retained by Luzov. At year end, Luzov evaluates all outstanding notes receivable and provides for estimated losses arising from defaults.

Instructions

(a) What is the appropriate valuation basis for Luzov's notes receivable at the date it sells equipment?

(b) How should Luzov account for the sale, without recourse, of a February 1, 2002, note receivable sold on May 1, 2002? Why is it appropriate to account for it in this way?

(c) At December 31, 2002, how should Luzov measure and account for the impact of estimated losses resulting from notes receivable that it
   1. Retained and did not sell?
   2. Sold to the bank with recourse?

(AICPA adapted)

C7-7 On September 30, 2002, Tiger Machinery Co. sold a machine and accepted the customer's nonin-terest-bearing note. Tiger normally makes sales on a cash basis. Since the machine was unique, its sales price was not determinable using Tiger's normal pricing practices.

After receiving the first of two equal annual instalments on September 30, 2003, Tiger immediately sold the note with recourse. On October 9, 2004, Tiger received notice that the note was dishonoured, and it paid all amounts due. At all times prior to default, the note was reasonably expected to be paid in full.

Instructions

(a) How should Tiger determine the machine's sales price?

(b) How should Tiger report the effects of the noninterest-bearing note on its income statement for the year ended December 31, 2002? Why is this accounting presentation appropriate?

(c) What are the effects of the sale of the note receivable with recourse on Tiger's income statement for the year ended December 31, 2003, and its balance sheet at December 31, 2003?

(d) How should Tiger account for the effects of the note being dishonoured?

C7-8 On July 1, 2002, Sondergaard Corp. sold special-order merchandise on credit and received in return an interest-bearing note receivable from the customer. Sondergaard will receive interest at the prevailing rate for a note of this type. Both the principal and interest are due in one lump sum on June 30, 2003.

On September 1, 2002, Sondergaard sold special-order merchandise on credit and received in return a noninterest-bearing note receivable from the customer. The prevailing rate of interest for a note of this type is determinable. The note receivable is due in one lump sum on August 31, 2004.

Sondergaard also has significant amounts of trade accounts receivable as a result of credit sales to its customers. On October 1, 2002, some trade accounts receivable were assigned to Dunne Finance Corp. on a non-notification (Sondergaard handles collections) basis for an advance of 75% of their amount at an interest charge of 12% on the balance outstanding.

On November 1, 2002, other trade accounts receivable were sold on a without recourse basis. The factor withheld 5% of the trade accounts receivable factored as protection against sales returns and allowances and charged a finance charge of 3%.

Instructions

(a) How should Sondergaard determine the interest income for 2002 on (1) the interest-bearing note receivable? Why? (2) on the noninterest-bearing note receivable? Why?

(b) How should Sondergaard report the interest-bearing note receivable and the noninterest-bearing note receivable on its balance sheet at December 31, 2002?

(c) How should Sondergaard account for subsequent collections on the trade accounts receivable assigned on October 1, 2002, and the payments to Dunne Finance? Why?

(d) How should Sondergaard account for the trade accounts receivable factored on November 1, 2002? Why?

(AICPA adapted)

C7-9 Soon after beginning the year-end audit work on March 10 at Arkin Corp., the auditor has the following conversation with the controller.

CONTROLLER: The year ended March 31st should be our most profitable in history and, as a consequence, the Board of Directors has just awarded the officers generous bonuses.

AUDITOR: I thought profits were down this year in the industry, according to your latest interim report.

CONTROLLER: Well, they were down, but 10 days ago we closed a deal that will give us a substantial increase for the year.

AUDITOR: Oh, what was it?

CONTROLLER: Well, you remember a few years ago our former president bought shares of Rocketeer Enterprises Ltd. because he had those grandiose ideas about becoming a conglomerate. For six years we have not been able to sell the shares, which cost us $3 million and has not paid a nickel in dividends. Thursday we sold the shares to Campbell Inc. for $4 million. So, we will have a gain of $700,000 ($1 million pretax) which will increase our net income for the year to $4 million, compared with last year's $3.8 million. As far as I know, we'll be the only company in the industry to register an increase in net income this year. That should help the market value of our stock!

AUDITOR: Do you expect to receive the $4 million in cash by March 31st, your fiscal year-end?

CONTROLLER: No. Although Campbell Inc. is an excellent company, they are a little tight for cash because of their rapid growth. Consequently, they are going to give us a $4 million noninterest-bearing note due $400,000 per year for the next 10 years. The first payment is due on March 31 of next year.

AUDITOR: Why is the note noninterest-bearing?

CONTROLLER: Because that's what everybody agreed to. Since we don't have any interest-bearing debt, the funds invested in the note do not cost us anything and besides, we were not getting any dividends on the Rocketeer Enterprises shares.

Instructions

Do you agree with the way the controller has accounted for the transaction? If not, how should the transaction be accounted for?

C7-10 As the manager of the accounts receivable department for Maher Leather Goods Ltd., you recently noticed that Pete Shelley, your accounts receivable clerk who is paid $1,200 per month, has been wearing unusually tasteful and expensive clothing. (This is Maher's first year in business.) This morning, Shelley drove up to work in a brand new Lexus.

Naturally suspicious, you decide to test the accuracy of the accounts receivable balance of $132,000 as shown in the ledger. The following information is available for your first year (precisely nine months ended September 30, 2002) in business:

(1)	Collections from customers	$198,000
(2)	Merchandise purchased	360,000
(3)	Ending merchandise inventory	90,000
(4)	Goods are marked to sell at 40% above cost.	

Instructions

Assuming all sales were made on account, calculate the ending accounts receivable balance that should appear in the ledger, noting any apparent shortage. Then, draft a memo dated October 3, 2002 to John Castle, the branch manager, explaining the facts in this situation. Remember that this problem is serious, and you do not want to make hasty accusations.

Using Your Judgement

FINANCIAL REPORTING PROBLEM: CANADIAN TIRE CORPORATION, LIMITED

The financial statements of **Canadian Tire Corporation, Limited** appear in Appendix 5B.

Instructions

Refer to these financial statements and the accompanying notes to answer the following questions.

(a) How does Canadian Tire report cash on its latest balance sheet? Of what does this consist?

(b) What criteria does the company use to determine what short-term investments should be included with cash?

(c) What is the breakdown between cash and short-term investments? Is the cash balance positive or negative? Explain how a company could have a negative cash balance.

(d) In recent years, accounting standards have required companies to disclose information about their exposure to credit risk. What is credit risk? What does Canadian Tire report? What is your assessment of its exposure to credit risk?

FINANCIAL STATEMENT ANALYSIS CASE

Saskatchewan Wheat Pool (SWP)

Saskatchewan Wheat Pool reported the information on the following page in its 2000 Annual Report:

Instructions

(a) What is SWP's "cash" balance at July 31, 2000? Explain how a company can have a negative cash balance.

(b) What is an operating line of credit, and how would it affect the financial position of an organization such as SWP?

(c) Do you think that SWP has petty cash funds? If so, why is there no "Petty Cash" reported on the balance sheet?

(d) Explain your understanding of credit risk in general, and in relation to SWP.

(e) How has SWP used its receivables to obtain cash?

Saskatchewan Wheat Pool Annual Report 2000

Excerpts from the Financial Statements

CONSOLIDATED BALANCE SHEETS

As at July 31

(in thousands)

	2000	1999
ASSETS		
Current Assets		
Short-term investments	$ –	$ 10,934
Accounts receivable (Note 5)	239,384	253,196
Inventories (Note 6)	274,159	264,852
Prepaid expenses	16,770	13,375
	530,313	542,357
LIABILITIES AND SHAREHOLDERS' EQUITY		
Current Liabilities		
Bank indebtedness	$ 9,198	$ 8,041
Short-term borrowings (Note 10)	134,000	86,742
Members' demand loans (Note 11)	48,834	71,745
Accounts payable	244,536	280,472
Long-term debt due within one year (Note 12)	16,178	14,077
Dividends payable	–	14,970
	452,746	476,047

Credit Risk

The company is exposed to credit risk from customers in all the business segments. In the grain handling and marketing segment, a significant amount is receivable from the Canadian Wheat Board. The customer base in all other segments is diverse which minimizes significant concentration of credit risk. Credit risk is limited due to the large number of customers in differing industries and geographic areas.

10. Short-Term Borrowings

	2000	1999
Bank operating loans	$ 134,000	$ 79,000
Subsidiaries' and proportionate share of joint ventures' short-term borrowings	–	7,742
	$ 134,000	$ 86,742

At July 31, 2000, bank operating loans bear interest at 6.75% (1999 – 5.32%).

5. Accounts Receivable

Under the terms of an agreement with a financial institution, the company can sell up to $240 million of certain trade accounts receivable. The ability to draw on this facility after October 31, 2000, is dependent on completing the bank financing described in Note 12. In addition, under the terms of an agreement with an independent trust, a joint venture which is owned one-third by the company can sell up to $60 million of certain trade accounts receivable. At July 31, 2000, the trade accounts receivable are reported net of sold amounts of $223 million (1999 - $231 million).

	2000	1999
Canadian Wheat Board	$ 23,911	$ 28,861
Corporate taxes receivable	39,399	12,594
Trade accounts	176,074	211,741
	$ 239,384	$ 253,196

At July 31, 2000, the company has available unsecured demand operating lines of credit totalling $250 million and unsecured committed term bank facilities totalling $340 million. The term bank facilities mature or begin to amortize at various dates from December 2001 to October 2004.

COMPARATIVE ANALYSIS CASE

Sears Canada Inc. versus Hudson's Bay Company

Instructions

Go to the Digital Tool and use the information about **Sears Canada Inc.** and **Hudson's Bay Company** to answer the following questions.

(a) Compare how the two companies report cash and cash equivalents on the statement of financial position at the most recent year end. What is included in the cash and cash equivalents of each? Is there any restricted cash reported by either company? If so, have both companies reported it in a similar manner?

(b) What types of receivables do Sears and Hudson's Bay have? Are they common to both companies?

(c) What amount of "trade" accounts receivable (net) do Sears and Hudson's Bay have? Can you tell which company reports the greater allowance for doubtful accounts (amount and percentage of gross receivable) at the end of the most recent year?

(d) Does either company dispose of receivables prior to the due date to generate cash? Comment.

(e) Calculate, compare, and comment on the Accounts Receivable Turnover ratio for both companies for the most recent year. How does factoring receivables affect this ratio? Be specific.

RESEARCH CASES

Case 1

Financial Reporting in Canada, published annually by the Canadian Institute of Chartered Accountants, is a survey of 200 Canadian company annual reports to shareholders. The survey covers companies from all of the TSE 300 industry groups with the exception of financial institutions.

Instructions

Examine the sections dealing with accounts and notes receivable and answer the following questions:

(a) For the most recent year, how many of the companies surveyed disclosed the existence and amount of an allowance for doubtful accounts?

(b) Although *CICA Handbook* Section 3020 does not cover transfers of receivables, some information is provided about the extent of such disclosures. How common is disclosure of transactions involving the transfer of receivables among the survey companies?

(c) Examine the disclosure provided by a company that sold receivables and a company that used its receivables as collateral. Summarize the major transaction terms.

Case 2

The May 6, 1996, issue of *Forbes* includes an article by Matthew Schifrin and Howard Rudnitsky entitled "Rx for Receivables."

Instructions

Read the article and answer the following questions.

(a) Why has the pharmacy business moved from a cash-based business to a receivables-based business?

(b) What is the economic motivation for pharmacists to sell their receivables?

(c) What is the economic motivation for the Pharmacy Fund to purchase the receivables?

ETHICS CASE

Rudolph Corp. is a subsidiary of Hundley Corp. The controller believes that the yearly allowance for doubtful accounts for Rudolph should be 2% of net credit sales. The president, nervous that the parent company might expect the subsidiary to sustain its 10% growth rate, suggests that the controller increase the allowance for doubtful accounts to 3% yearly. The supervisor thinks that the lower net income, which reflects a 6% growth rate, will be a more sustainable rate for Rudolph.

Instructions

Answer the following questions:

(a) Should the controller be concerned with Rudolph's growth rate in estimating the allowance? Explain your answer.

(b) Does the president's request pose an ethical dilemma for the controller? Give your reasons.

CHAPTER 8

Valuation of Inventories: A Cost Basis Approach

LEARNING OBJECTIVES

After studying this chapter, you should be able to:

1. Identify major classifications of inventory.

2. Distinguish between perpetual and periodic inventory systems.

3. Identify the effects of inventory errors on the financial statements.

4. Identify the items that should be included as inventory cost.

5. Explain the difference between variable costing and absorption costing in assigning manufacturing costs to inventory.

6. Distinguish between the physical flow of inventory and the cost flow assigned to inventory.

7. Identify possible objectives for inventory valuation decisions.

8. Describe and compare the cost flow assumptions used in accounting for inventories.

9. Evaluate LIFO as a basis for understanding the differences between the cost flow methods.

10. Explain the importance of judgement in selecting an inventory cost flow method.

Preview of Chapter 8

Inventories are often a significant portion of a company's total assets. As a result, improper accounting and reporting for this asset can materially affect both the income statement and the balance sheet. Many decisions must be made in determining the final amounts reported for inventory on the balance sheet and for cost of goods sold on the income statement: the quantity of inventory on hand, which costs are to be included in inventory cost, what cost flow assumption is to be used, and whether cost is the appropriate value for the balance sheet.

Some of these topics are covered in other chapters of the text: issues associated with accounting for long-term construction contract inventories were examined in Chapter 6, and balance sheet valuation and methods of estimating inventory are discussed in Chapter 9. The purpose of this chapter is to discuss the basic issues related to accounting and reporting inventory costs. The content and organization of the chapter are as follows:

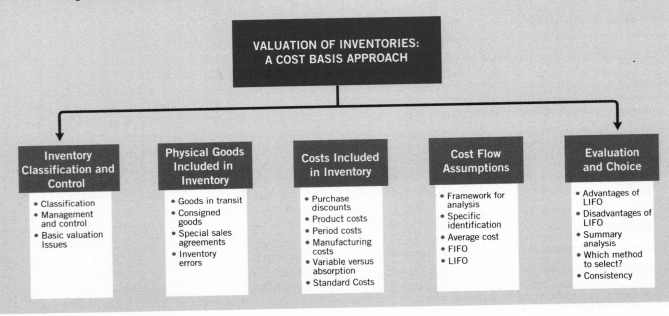

INVENTORY CLASSIFICATION AND CONTROL

Classification

OBJECTIVE 1
....
Identify major classifications of inventory.

Inventories are asset items held for sale in the ordinary course of business or goods that will be used or consumed in the production of goods to be sold. Identification, measurement and disclosure of inventories require careful attention because the investment in inventories is frequently the largest current asset of merchandising (retail) and manufacturing businesses.

A **merchandising concern**, such as **Hudson's Bay Company**, ordinarily purchases its merchandise in a form ready for sale. It reports the cost assigned to unsold units left on hand as merchandise inventory. Only one inventory account, Merchandise Inventories, appears in the financial statements.

Manufacturing concerns, on the other hand, produce goods to be sold to merchandising firms. Many of the largest Canadian businesses—**Bombardier, General Motors of Canada**, and **Magna International Inc.** for example—are manufacturers. Although the products they produce may be quite different, manufacturers normally have three inventory accounts—Raw Materials, Work in Process, and Finished Goods. The cost assigned to goods and materials on hand but not yet placed into production is reported as **raw materials inventory**. Raw materials include the wood to make a baseball bat or the steel to make a car. These materials ultimately can be traced directly to the end product. At any point in a continuous production process, some units are not completely processed. The cost of the raw material on which production has been started but not completed, plus the direct labour cost applied specifically to this material and an applicable share of manufacturing overhead costs, constitute the **work-in-process inventory**. The costs identified with the completed but unsold units on hand at the end of the fiscal period are reported as **finished goods inventory**.

The current assets sections presented in Illustration 8-1 contrast the financial statement presentation of inventories of a merchandising company and those of a manufacturing company. The remainder of the balance sheet is essentially similar for the two types of companies.

IAS NOTE

Unlike Handbook Section 3030, IAS 2 on Inventories specifically excludes specialized inventories such as producers' inventories of livestock, agricultural, and forest products, for example.

MERCHANDISING COMPANY
Hudson's Bay Company
Balance Sheet, January 31, 2000

(thousands of dollars)	Notes 1 t)	
Current assets		
Cash in stores		8,480
Short-term deposits		41,792
Credit card receivables	7	483,940
Other accounts receivable		127,522
Income taxes recoverable		25,445
Merchandise inventories		1,598,695
Prepaid expenses		44,606
Future income taxes	5	38,950
		2,369,430

MANUFACTURING COMPANY
Domtar Inc.
Balance Sheet, December 31, 1999

(In millions of Canadian dollars)	
Assets	
Current assets	
Cash	3
Receivables, net of allowance for doubtful accounts of $13 (1998 – $12)	388
Inventories (Note 5)	436
Prepaid expenses	19
	846

Note 5	
Inventories	
Operating and maintenance supplies	95
Raw materials	118
Work in process and finished goods	223
	436

ILLUSTRATION 8-1
Comparison of Current Assets Presentation for Merchandising and Manufacturing Companies

A manufacturing company also might include a **manufacturing** or **factory supplies inventory** account. In it would be items such as machine oils, nails, cleaning materials, and the like that are used in production but are not the primary materials being processed. The flow of costs through a merchandising company is different from that of a manufacturing company, as shown in Illustration 8-2.

UNDERLYING CONCEPTS

Because inventory provides future economic benefits to the company (revenue from sales), it meets the definition of an asset. Inventory costs will be matched against revenue in the period that sales occur.

Management and Control

Management is vitally interested in inventory planning and control. An accurate accounting system with up-to-date records is essential. If unsaleable items have accumulated in the inventory, a potential loss exists. Sales and customers may be lost if products ordered by customers are not available in the desired style, quality, and quantity. Inefficient purchasing procedures, faulty manufacturing techniques, or inadequate sales efforts may saddle management with excessive and unusable inventories. Businesses must monitor inventory levels carefully to limit the financing and other costs associated with carrying these assets. In recent years, with the introduction and use of "just-in-time" (JIT) inventory order systems and better supplier relationships, inventory levels have become leaner for many enterprises.[1]

---

[1] Technology has played an important role in the development of inventory systems. Radio-frequency data communications warehouse systems, for example, have helped companies such as **Eli Lilly Canada Inc.** and **BC Hot House Foods** increase the accuracy of inventory information and the efficiency and productivity of their inventory management activities. **Toyota** uses bar codes, electronic data interchange, and radio frequency communication terminals to control the shipment of parts throughout North America, much of it through its Ontario parts centre. This has resulted in delivery times and safety stock that are one-third of previous levels.

ILLUSTRATION 8-2
Flow of Costs through
Manufacturing and
Merchandising Companies

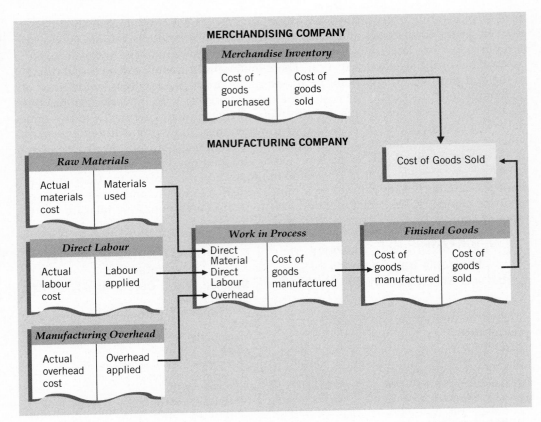

From a perspective of accounting for inventory, management is well aware that determining year-end inventory can significantly affect the amount of net income as well as current assets, total assets, and retained earnings (through the net income amount). These amounts, or totals including them, are used to calculate ratios that, in turn, are used to evaluate management's performance (e.g., payment of bonuses) and adherence to debt restrictions (e.g., to not exceed a specified debt-to-total-asset ratio or dividend payout ratio).

For these and other reasons, management is very interested in having an inventory accounting system that provides accurate, up-to-date information on quantities. As discussed later, the choice of a cost method to value inventories is also of concern.

Perpetual System

OBJECTIVE 2

Distinguish between
perpetual and periodic
inventory systems.

As indicated in Chapter 3, inventory records may be maintained on a perpetual or periodic basis. Under a **perpetual inventory system**, a continuous record of inventory changes is maintained in the Inventory account. That is, all purchases and sales (issues) of goods are recorded directly in the Inventory account **as they occur**. The accounting features of a perpetual inventory system are:

1. Purchases of merchandise for resale or raw materials for production are debited to Inventory rather than to Purchases.
2. Freight-in, purchase returns and allowances, and purchase discounts are recorded in Inventory rather than in separate accounts.
3. Cost of goods sold is recognized for each sale by debiting the account, Cost of Goods Sold, and crediting Inventory.
4. Inventory is a control account that is supported by a subsidiary ledger of individual inventory records. The subsidiary records show the quantity and cost of each type of inventory on hand.

The perpetual inventory system provides a continuous record of the balances in both the Inventory account and the Cost of Goods Sold account.

Under a computerized record keeping system, additions to and issuances from inventory can be recorded nearly instantaneously. The popularity and affordability of computerized accounting software have made the perpetual system cost-effective for many kinds of businesses. Recording sales with optical scanners at the cash register has been incorporated into perpetual inventory systems at many retail stores.

Periodic System

Under a periodic inventory system, the quantity of inventory on hand is determined, as its name implies, only periodically. All inventory acquisitions during the accounting period are recorded by debits to a Purchases account. The total in the Purchases account at the end of the accounting period is added to the cost of the inventory on hand at the beginning of the period to determine the total cost of the goods available for sale during the period. Ending inventory is subtracted from the cost of goods available for sale to calculate the cost of goods sold. Note that under a periodic inventory system, the cost of goods sold is a residual amount that depends upon a physically counted ending inventory.

The **physical inventory count** required by a periodic system is taken once a year at the end of the year.[2] However, most companies need more current information about their inventory levels to protect against stockouts or overpurchasing and to help prepare monthly or quarterly financial data. As a consequence, many companies use a **modified perpetual inventory system** in which increases and decreases in quantities only— not dollar amounts—are kept in a detailed inventory record. It is merely a memorandum device outside the double-entry system that helps determine the level of inventory at any point in time.

Whether a company maintains a perpetual inventory in quantities and dollars, quantities only, or has no perpetual inventory record at all, it probably takes a physical inventory once a year. No matter what type of inventory records are used or how well-organized the procedures for recording purchases and requisitions are, the danger of loss and error is always present. Waste, breakage, theft, improper entry, failure to prepare or record requisitions, and any number of similar possibilities may cause the inventory records to differ from the actual inventory on hand. This requires periodic verification of the inventory records by actual count, weight, or measurement. These counts are compared with the detailed inventory records. The records are corrected to agree with the quantities actually on hand.

Insofar as possible, the physical inventory should be taken near the end of a company's fiscal year so that correct inventory quantities are available for use in preparing annual accounting reports and statements. Because this is not always possible, however, physical inventories taken within two or three months of the year end are satisfactory, if the detailed inventory records are maintained with a fair degree of accuracy.

To illustrate the difference between a perpetual and a periodic system, assume that Fesmire Limited had the following transactions during the current year:

Beginning inventory	100 units at $ 6	=	$600
Purchases	900 units at $ 6	=	$5,400
Sales	600 units at $12	=	$7,200
Ending inventory	400 units at $ 6	=	$2,400

The entries to record these transactions during the current year are shown in Illustration 8-3.

When a perpetual inventory system is used and a difference exists between the perpetual inventory balance and the physical inventory count, a separate entry is needed to adjust the perpetual inventory account. To illustrate, assume that at the end of the reporting period, the perpetual inventory account reported an inventory balance of

---

[2] In recent years, some companies have developed methods of determining inventories, including statistical sampling, that are sufficiently reliable to make an annual physical count of each inventory item unnecessary.

ILLUSTRATION 8-3
Comparative Entries—
Perpetual vs. Periodic

Perpetual Inventory System		Periodic Inventory System	
1. Beginning Inventory, 100 units at $6:			
The inventory account shows the inventory on hand at $600.		The inventory account shows the inventory on hand at $600.	
2. Purchase 900 units at $6:			
Inventory 5,400		Purchases 5,400	
Accounts Payable	5,400	Accounts Payable	5,400
3. Sale of 600 units at $12:			
Accounts Receivable 7,200		Accounts Receivable 7,200	
Sales	7,200	Sales	7,200
Cost of Goods Sold 3,600			
(600 at $6)		(No entry)	
Inventory	3,600		
4. End-of-period entries for inventory accounts, 400 units at $6:			
No entry necessary.			
The account, Inventory, shows the ending balance of $2,400		Inventory (ending, by count) 2,400	
($600 + $5,400 − $3,600).		Cost of Goods Sold 3,600	
		Purchases	5,400
		Inventory (beginning)	600

$4,000, but a physical count indicated $3,800 was actually on hand. The entry to record the necessary writedown is as follows:

Inventory Over and Short	200	
Inventory		200

Perpetual inventory overages and shortages may be recorded as an adjustment of (i.e., closed to) Cost of Goods Sold. This would be appropriate if its cause related to incorrect record keeping. Alternatively, the Inventory Over and Short account may be reported in the Other Revenues and Gains or Other Expenses and Losses section, depending on its balance. If so, an overage or shortage would not be a component of Cost of Goods Sold, and the resulting gross profit percentage would not be distorted because of such things as shrinkage, breakage, and theft. Note that in a periodic inventory system, the account Inventory Over and Short does not arise because there are no accounting records available against which to compare the physical count. Thus, inventory overages and shortages are buried in cost of goods sold.

Basic Valuation Issues

Because the goods sold or used during an accounting period seldom correspond exactly to the goods bought or produced during that period, the physical inventory either increases or decreases. In addition, the cost of the same number of items could be higher or lower than at the beginning of the period. The cost of all the goods available for sale or use should be allocated between the goods that were sold or used and those that are still on hand. The **cost of goods available for sale or use** is the sum of (1) the cost of the goods on hand at the beginning of the period and (2) the cost of the goods acquired or produced during the period. The **cost of goods sold** is the difference between the cost of goods available for sale during the period and the cost of goods on hand at the end of the period, as shown in Illustration 8-4.

ILLUSTRATION 8-4
Calculation of Cost of
Goods Sold

Beginning inventory, Jan. 1	$100,000
Cost of goods acquired or produced during the year	800,000
Total cost of goods available for sale	900,000
Ending inventory, Dec. 31	200,000
Cost of goods sold during the year	$700,000

Determining the cost of inventories can be a complex process that requires decisions about:

1. The physical goods to be included in inventory (whose assets are they?—goods in transit, consigned goods, special sales agreements).
2. The costs to be included in inventory (purchase discounts, product vs. period costs, manufacturing costs, variable costing vs. absorption costing, standard costs).
3. The cost flow assumption to be adopted (specific identification, average cost, FIFO, LIFO).

We will explore these basic issues in the next three sections of the chapter.

PHYSICAL GOODS INCLUDED IN INVENTORY

Technically, purchases should be recorded when legal title to the goods passes to the buyer, as this is usually when the risks and rewards of ownership are transferred. General practice, however, is to record acquisitions when the goods are received, because it is difficult for the buyer to determine the exact time of legal passage of title for every purchase. In addition, no material error is likely to result from such a practice if it is consistently applied. Illustration 8-5 indicates the general guidelines used in evaluating whether the seller or the buyer reports an item as inventory.

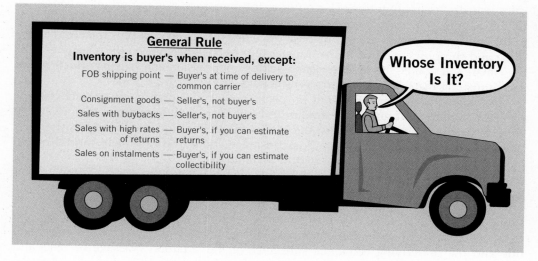

ILLUSTRATION 8-5
Guidelines for Determining Ownership

Goods in Transit

Sometimes purchased merchandise is in transit—not yet received—at the end of a fiscal period. The accounting for these goods depends on who owns them. That can be determined by applying the "transfer of risks and rewards" rule. If the goods are shipped f.o.b. shipping point, the risks and rewards of ownership (i.e., legal title) pass to the buyer when the seller delivers the goods to the common carrier (transporter) who acts as an agent for the buyer. (The abbreviation f.o.b. stands for free on board.) If the goods are shipped f.o.b. destination, risks and rewards do not pass until the goods reach the destination. "Shipping point" and "destination" are often designated by a particular location, for example, f.o.b. Sarnia.[3]

---

[3] Terms other than f.o.b. shipping point or f.o.b. destination (e.g., CIF for cost, insurance, freight) are often used to identify when legal title passes. The f.o.b. terms are used in this text to reflect that an agreement as to when title passes must be reached between the buyer and seller in the purchase-sale contract. In a particular situation, the terms of the sale contract would be examined to determine when the risks and rewards of ownership pass from the seller to the buyer.

Goods in transit at the end of a fiscal period that were sent f.o.b. shipping point should be recorded by the buyer as purchases of the period and should be included in ending inventory. To disregard such purchases would result in understating inventories and accounts payable in the balance sheet, and understating purchases and ending inventories when calculating cost of goods sold for the income statement.

The accountant normally prepares a purchase cut-off schedule for the end of a period to ensure that goods received from suppliers around the end of the year are recorded in the appropriate period. Cut-off procedures can be extensive and include controls such as curtailing and controlling the receipt and shipment of goods around the time of the count, marking freight and shipping documents as "before" and "after" the inventory count, and ensuring that receiving reports covering goods received prior to the count are linked to invoices that also are recorded in the same period. Because goods bought f.o.b. shipping point may have been in transit at the period's end, the cut-off schedule would not be completed until a few days after the period's end (i.e., providing sufficient time for goods shipped at year end to be received). In cases where there is some question as to whether title has passed, the accountant exercises judgement by taking into consideration industry practices, the sales agreement's intent, the policies of the parties involved, and any other available information.

Consigned Goods

In Chapter 6, the nature of consignment shipments and accounting for consignment sales was discussed. In terms of accounting for inventory, it is important to recognize that goods out on consignment remain the consignor's property and must be included in the consignor's inventory at purchase price or production cost plus the cost of handling and shipping involved in the transfer to the consignee. When the consignee sells the **consigned goods**, the revenue less a selling commission and expenses incurred in accomplishing the sale is remitted to the consignor.

Occasionally, the inventory out on consignment is shown as a separate item or reported in notes, but unless the amount is large there is little need for this. No entry is made by the consignee to adjust the Inventory account for goods received because they are the consignor's property. The consignee should be extremely careful not to include any goods consigned as a part of inventory.

Special Sale Agreements

While the transfer of legal title is a general guideline used to determine whether the risks and rewards of ownership have passed from a seller to a buyer, transfer of legal title and the underlying economic substance of the situation (passage of risks and rewards) may not match. For example, it is possible that legal title has passed to the purchaser but the seller of the goods retains the risks of ownership. Conversely, transfer of legal title may not occur, but the economic substance of the transaction is that the seller no longer retains the risks and rewards of ownership. Three special sale situations, discussed in Chapter 6 from a revenue recognition perspective, are considered below in terms of inventory implications. These are:

1. sales with buyback agreement
2. sales with high rates of return
3. sales on instalment

UNDERLYING CONCEPTS

Recognizing revenue at the time the inventory is "parked" violates the revenue recognition principle. This principle requires that the earning process be substantially completed, with the risks and rewards of ownership transferred to the purchaser.

Sales with Buyback Agreement

Sometimes an enterprise finances its inventory without reporting either the liability or the inventory on its balance sheet. Such an approach—often referred to as a **product financing arrangement**—usually involves a "sale" with either an implicit or explicit "buyback" agreement. (These are sometimes referred to as "parking transactions" because the seller simply parks the inventory on another enterprise's balance sheet for a short period of time.)

To illustrate, Hill Enterprises transfers ("sells") inventory to Chase Ltd. and simultaneously agrees to repurchase this merchandise at a specified price over a specified period of time. Chase then uses the inventory as collateral and borrows against it. Chase uses the loan proceeds to pay Hill. Hill repurchases the inventory in the future, and Chase uses the proceeds from repayment to meet its loan obligation.

The essence of this transaction is that Hill Enterprises is financing its inventory—and retaining risk of ownership—even though technical legal title to the merchandise was transferred to Chase Ltd. The advantage to Hill in structuring a transaction in this manner is the removal of the current liability from its balance sheet, and the ability to manipulate income. The advantages to Chase are that the goods purchased may solve a LIFO liquidation problem (discussed later), or that Chase may be interested in a reciprocal agreement at a later date.

The Canadian accounting standards for revenue recognition tend to curtail this practice, at least in terms of enabling a "selling company" to remove the inventory and liability from its balance sheet. This is because the *Handbook* requires the seller to transfer the risks and rewards of ownership before a sale can be recognized.[4] By implication, a "buying company" should not recognize the goods received as its inventory. Canadian practitioners, however, will have to continue to exercise judgement regarding substance over form in such situations.

Sales with High Rates of Return

Formal or informal agreements often exist in industries such as publishing, music, and toys and sporting goods that permit inventory to be returned for a full or partial refund. To illustrate, Quality Publishing Limited sells textbooks to Campus Bookstores Inc. with an agreement that any books not sold may be returned for full credit. In the past, approximately 25% of the textbooks sold to Campus Bookstores were returned. Should Quality Publishing report its deliveries to Campus Bookstores as sales transactions, or should it treat the delivered books as inventory until being notified of how many were sold? An acceptable accounting treatment is that, if a reasonable prediction of the returns can be established, then the goods should be considered sold. Conversely, if returns are unpredictable, removal of these goods from inventory is inappropriate. Essentially, the choice of treatment depends on whether there is reasonable assurance of the measurement of the ultimate consideration to be derived from the sale given that goods may be returned.[5] If not, only the items actually sold by the purchaser are accounted for as revenue, with all remaining items being part of the seller's inventory.

Sales on Instalment

Because the risk of loss from uncollectibles is higher in instalment sale situations than in other sale transactions, the seller often withholds legal title to the merchandise until all payments have been made. Should the inventory be considered sold, even though legal title has not passed? The economic substance of the transaction is that **the goods should be excluded from the seller's inventory if the percentage of bad debts can be reasonably estimated**. Instalment sales are discussed here to show that in some cases, the goods should be removed from inventory, although legal title may not have passed.

Effect of Inventory Errors

Items incorrectly included or excluded in determining ending inventory will result in both income statement and balance sheet errors in the financial statements. Therefore, decisions made using financial statement amounts affected by the errors (e.g., bonus paid to management based on net income) would be in error. Let's look at two cases and the effects on the financial statements.

UNDERLYING CONCEPTS

Revenues should be recognized because they have been substantially earned and are reasonably estimable. The basic risks and rewards of ownership have been transferred. Collection is not the most critical event because bad debts can be reasonably estimated.

OBJECTIVE 3

Identify the effects of inventory errors on the financial statements.

---

[4] *CICA Handbook*, Section 3400, par. .07.

[5] *Ibid.*

Ending Inventory Misstated

What would happen if the beginning inventory and purchases are recorded correctly, but some items are not included in ending inventory (e.g., were on the premises but were missed in the physical count or were out on consignment)? In this situation, the effects on the financial statements at the end of the period would be:

ILLUSTRATION 8-6
Financial Statement Effects of Misstated Ending Inventory

Balance Sheet		Income Statement	
Inventory	Understated	Cost of goods sold	Overstated
Retained earnings	Understated		
Working capital	Understated	Net income	Understated
(current assets less current liabilities)			
Current ratio	Understated		
(Current assets divided by current liabilities)			

Working capital and the current ratio are understated because a portion of the ending inventory is omitted; net income is understated because cost of goods sold is overstated.

UNDERLYING CONCEPTS

When inventory is misstated, its presentation lacks representational faithfulness.

To illustrate the effect on net income over a two-year period, assume that the ending inventory of Weiseman Ltd. is understated by $10,000 and that all other items are correctly stated. **The effect of this error will be an understatement of net income in the current year and an overstatement of net income in the following year relative to the correct net income amounts.** The error will affect the following year because the beginning inventory of that year will be understated, thereby causing net income to be overstated. Both net income figures are misstated, but the total for the two years is correct as the two errors will be counterbalanced (offset), as shown in Illustration 8-7.

ILLUSTRATION 8-7
Effect of Ending Inventory Error on Two Periods

WEISEMAN LTD.
(All figures assumed)

	Incorrect Recording		Correct Recording	
	2002	2003	2002	2003
Revenues	$100,000	$100,000	$100,000	$100,000
Cost of goods sold				
Beginning inventory	25,000	20,000	25,000	30,000
Purchased or produced	45,000	60,000	45,000	60,000
Goods available for sale	70,000	80,000	70,000	90,000
Less: Ending inventory*	20,000	40,000	30,000	40,000
Cost of goods sold	50,000	40,000	40,000	50,000
Gross profit	50,000	60,000	60,000	50,000
Administrative and selling expenses	40,000	40,000	40,000	40,000
Net income	$ 10,000	$ 20,000	$ 20,000	$ 10,000

Total income for two years = $30,000   Total income for two years = $30,000

*Ending inventory understated by $10,000 in 2002.

If the error were discovered in 2002 just before the books were closed, the correcting entry in 2002 is:

Inventory	10,000	
Cost of Goods Sold		10,000

If the error was not discovered until 2003, after the books were closed for 2002, the correcting entry in 2003 is:

Inventory	10,000	
Retained Earnings		10,000

If discovered after the books for 2003 were closed, no entry is required as the error is self-correcting over the two-year period. However, whenever comparative financial statements are prepared for 2002 or 2003, the inventory and net income would be adjusted and reported at the correct figures.

If ending inventory is *overstated*, the reverse effect occurs. Inventory, working capital, current ratio, and net income are overstated and cost of goods sold is understated. The error's effect on net income will be counterbalanced in the next year, but both years' net income figures will be misstated, thus destroying the usefulness of any analysis of trends in earnings and ratios.

Purchases and Inventory Misstated

Suppose that certain goods that the company owns are not recorded as a purchase and are not counted in ending inventory. The effect on the financial statements (assuming this is a purchase on account) is as follows:

Balance Sheet		Income Statement	
Inventory	Understated	Purchases	Understated
Retained earnings	No effect	Inventory (ending)	Understated
Accounts payable	Understated	Cost of goods sold	No effect
Working capital	No effect	Net income	No effect
Current ratio	Overstated		

ILLUSTRATION 8-8
Financial Statement Effects of Misstated Purchases and Inventory

To omit goods from purchases and inventory results in understating of inventory and accounts payable in the balance sheet and understating purchases and ending inventory in the income statement. Net income for the period is not affected by omitting such goods because purchases and ending inventory are both understated by the same amount—the error thereby offsetting itself in cost of goods sold.[6] Total working capital is unchanged, but the current ratio is overstated (assuming it was greater than 1 to 1) because of the omission of equal amounts from inventory and accounts payable.

To determine an error's effect on any particular financial statement amount or ratio, it is helpful to construct a comparison chart based on assumed (if not real) numbers. The chart would include columns based on amounts that include the error(s) and on amounts that would result if there were no error(s). To illustrate the effect on the current ratio, assume that a company understated accounts payable and ending inventory by $40,000. The understated and correct data are shown below.

Purchases and Ending Inventory Understated		Purchases and Ending Inventory Correct	
Current assets	$120,000	Current assets	$160,000
Current liabilities	$ 40,000	Current liabilities	$ 80,000
Current ratio	3 to 1	Current ratio	2 to 1

ILLUSTRATION 8-9
Effects of Purchases and Ending Inventory Errors

---

[6] To correct the error in the year of the error before the books are closed, the following entries are needed:

Periodic Method			**Perpetual Method**		
Purchases	$x		Inventory	$x	
Accounts Payable		$x	Accounts Payable		$x
Inventory	$x				
Cost of Goods Sold		$x			

The correct ratio is 2 to 1 rather than 3 to 1. Thus, understating of accounts payable and ending inventory can lead to a "window dressing" of the current ratio—making it appear better than it is.

If both purchases (on account) and ending inventory are overstated, then the effects on the balance sheet are exactly the reverse. Inventory and accounts payable are overstated and the current ratio is understated; working capital is not affected. Cost of goods sold and net income are not affected because the errors offset one another. While these examples illustrate the nature of some errors that may occur and their consequences, many other types of error are possible: not recording a purchase but counting the acquired inventory; not recording a sale in the current period although the items have been delivered; omitting the adjusting entry to update the Allowance for Future Returns in situations where sales are subject to a high rate of return, etc. The approach illustrated to determine the effect of errors will help in analysing such situations.

The importance of accurately computing purchases and inventory to ensure reliable amounts are presented in the financial statements cannot be overemphasized. One has only to read the financial press to learn how misstating inventory can generate high income numbers.[7] For example, the practice of some Canadian farm equipment manufacturers of treating deliveries to dealers as company sales (with concurrent reductions in inventory) can result in significantly inflating reported income when sales to the ultimate consumer do not keep pace with the deliveries to dealers.

As indicated in Chapter 4, the correction of an error of a prior period is accounted for retroactively as an adjustment to retained earnings. Full disclosure requires a description of the error, and a statement of the effect on the current and prior period financial statements.

<table>
<tr><td>

OBJECTIVE 4

Identify the items that should be included as inventory cost.
</td></tr>
</table>

COSTS INCLUDED IN INVENTORY

One of the most important issues in dealing with inventories concerns the amount at which the inventory should be carried in the accounts. **The acquisition of inventories, like other assets, is generally accounted for on a basis of cost.** (Other bases are discussed in Chapter 9.) But what should be included in "cost?"

Treatment of Purchase Discounts

Purchase discounts are sometimes reported in the income statement as a financial revenue, similar to interest revenue. However, purchase discounts should really be recorded as a reduction in the cost of purchases. Otherwise, to the extent that such purchases are still in inventory at the end of the period, a company is recognizing revenue before the goods have been sold. It is generally held that a business does not realize revenue by buying goods and paying bills; it realizes revenue by selling the goods.

The use of a Purchase Discounts account indicates that the company is reporting its purchases and accounts payable at the gross amount (called the gross method). An alternative approach (called the net method) is to record the purchases and accounts payable at an amount net of the cash discounts. This treatment is considered more theoretically appropriate because it (1) provides a correct reporting of the asset cost and related liability, and (2) presents the opportunity to measure the inefficiency of financial management if the discount is not taken. In the net method, the failure to take a purchase discount within the discount period is recorded in a Purchase Discounts Lost account, for which someone is held responsible. To illustrate the difference between the gross and net methods, assume the following transactions:

---

[7] In 1998, Hamilton, Ontario-based **Philip Services Corp.**—a metal recycler and industrial services company—restated its 1995 to 1997 earnings due, in part, to problems with its inventory management activities. Reporting in U.S. dollars, the company indicated that at least $125 million was due to speculative trading in its copper division plus "costing errors." While not an error with the physical inventory, the trading losses had been improperly recorded through various balance sheet accounts.

Gross Method			Net Method		
Purchase cost of $10,000, terms 2/10, net 30:					
Purchases	10,000		Purchases	9,800	
Accounts Payable		10,000	Accounts Payable		9,800
Invoices of $4,000 are paid within discount period:					
Accounts Payable	4,000		Accounts Payable	3,920	
Purchase Discounts		80	Cash		3,920
Cash		3,920			
Invoices of $6,000 are paid after discount period:					
Accounts Payable	6,000		Accounts Payable	5,880	
Cash		6,000	Purchase Discounts Lost	120	
			Cash		6,000

ILLUSTRATION 8-10
Entries under Gross and Net Methods

If the gross method is employed, purchase discounts should be deducted from purchases in determining cost of goods sold. If the net method is used, purchase discounts lost should be considered a financial expense and reported in the income statement's Other Expenses section. Many believe that the difficulty involved in using the somewhat more complicated net method is not worth the resulting benefits. Also, some contend that management is reluctant to report the amount of purchase discounts lost in the financial statements. These reasons may account for the widespread use of the less logical but simpler gross method.

UNDERLYING CONCEPTS

Not using the net method because of resultant difficulties is an example of the application of the cost-benefit constraint.

Product Costs

Product costs are those costs that "attach" to the inventory and are recorded in the inventory account. These costs are directly connected with bringing goods to the buyer's place of business and converting such goods to a saleable condition. Such charges would include freight charges on goods purchased, other direct costs of acquisition, and labour and other production costs incurred in processing the goods up to the time of sale.

Nonrecoverable taxes (e.g., some provincial sales taxes) paid on goods purchased for resale or manufacturing purposes are a cost of inventory. Since value-added taxes (e.g., the GST) are recoverable by a manufacturer, wholesaler, or retailer, they should not normally be treated as a cost of inventory (see Chapter 14 for a discussion of these types of taxes).

It would be theoretically correct to allocate to inventories a share of any buying costs or expenses of a purchasing department, storage costs, and other costs incurred in storing or handling the goods before they are sold. Because of the practical difficulties involved in allocating such costs and expenses, however, these items are not ordinarily included in valuing inventories.

Period Costs

Selling expenses and, under ordinary circumstances, **general and administrative expenses** are not considered directly related to the acquisition or production of goods and, therefore, are not considered a part of inventories. Such costs are period costs.

Conceptually, these expenses are as much a cost of the product as the initial purchase price and related freight charges attached to the product. Why then are these costs not considered inventoriable items? Selling expenses are generally considered as more directly related to the cost of goods sold than to the unsold inventory. In most cases, though, the costs, especially administrative expenses, are so unrelated or indirectly related to the immediate production process that any allocation is purely arbitrary.

Interest costs associated with getting inventories ready for sale usually are expensed as incurred. A major argument for this approach is that interest costs are really a cost of financing. Additionally, it may be argued that the informational benefit of capitalizing interest costs to inventory does not justify the cost of doing it. Others have argued, however, that interest costs incurred to finance activities associated with bringing

UNDERLYING CONCEPTS

In capitalizing interest, the constraints of materiality and cost/benefit are both applied.

inventories to a condition and place ready for sale are as much a cost of the asset as materials, labour, and overhead and, therefore, should be capitalized.[8] While the FASB has ruled that interest costs related to assets constructed for internal use or assets produced as discrete projects (such as ships or real estate projects) for sale or lease should be capitalized, the *CICA Handbook* requires only that if interest **is** capitalized, this policy and the amount capitalized in the current period be disclosed.[9]

Manufacturing Costs

As previously indicated, a business that manufactures goods uses three inventory accounts—Raw Materials, Work in Process, and Finished Goods. Work in process and finished goods include direct materials, direct labour, and manufacturing overhead costs. Manufacturing overhead costs include indirect material, indirect labour, and such items as amortization, taxes, insurance, heat, and electricity incurred in the manufacturing process. The raw materials and work-in-process inventories are incorporated into a **statement of cost of goods manufactured**, as shown in Illustration 8-11.

ILLUSTRATION 8-11
Statement of Cost of Goods Manufactured

Statement of Cost of Goods Manufactured			
For the Year Ended December 31, 2002			
Raw materials consumed			
Raw materials inventory, Jan 1, 2002			**$14,000**
Add net purchases:			
Purchases		$126,000	
Less: Purchase returns and allowances	$1,800		
Purchase discounts	1,200	3,000	123,000
Raw material available for use			$137,000
Less raw materials inventory, Dec. 31. 2002			17,000
Cost of raw materials consumed			$120,000
Direct labour			200,000
Manufacturing overhead			
Supervisors' salaries		$ 63,000	
Indirect labour		20,000	
Factory supplies used		18,000	
Heat, light, power and water		13,000	
Amortization of building and equipment		27,000	
Tools expense		2,000	
Patent amortization		1,000	
Miscellaneous factory expenses		6,000	150,000
Total manufacturing costs for the period			$470,000
Work-in-process inventory, Jan 1, 2002			**33,000**
Total manufacturing costs			$503,000
Less work-in-process inventory, Dec 31, 2002			**28,000**
Cost of goods manufactured during the year			**$475,000**

Cost of goods manufactured statements are prepared primarily for internal use; such details are rarely disclosed in published financial statements. The cost of goods sold reported in the income statement of a manufacturing firm is determined in a manner similar to that for a merchandising concern except that the cost of goods manufactured during the year is substituted for the cost of goods purchased. For example, if the inventory of finished goods for the company in Illustration 8-11 was $16,000 at the beginning of the year and $10,000 at the end of the year, the calculation of cost of goods sold for the income statement would be as shown in Illustration 8-12.

---

[8] The reporting rules related to interest cost capitalization have their greatest impact in accounting for capital assets and, therefore, are discussed in detail in Chapter 11. This brief overview provides the basic issues when inventories are involved.

[9] *CICA Handbook*, Section 3850, par. .03.

ILLUSTRATION 8-12
Cost of Goods Sold Calculation:
Manufacturing Company

Cost of goods sold	
Finished goods inventory, Jan. 1, 2002	$ 16,000
Cost of goods manufactured during 2002	475,000
Cost of goods available for sale	491,000
Finished goods inventory, Dec. 31, 2002	10,000
Cost of goods sold	$481,000

One issue of importance for costing a manufacturing company's inventory is whether or not fixed manufacturing overhead costs will be included in inventory (absorption costing) or charged to expenses of the period (variable costing).

Variable Costing Versus Absorption Costing

Fixed manufacturing overhead costs present a special problem in costing inventories because two concepts exist relative to the costs that attach to the product as it flows through the manufacturing process. These two concepts are variable costing, frequently called direct costing, and absorption costing, also called full costing. In a **variable costing system**, all costs must be classified as variable or fixed. Variable costs are those that fluctuate in direct proportion to changes in output, and fixed costs are those that remain constant in spite of changes in output. Under variable costing, only costs that vary directly with the production volume are charged to products as manufacturing takes place. Direct material, direct labour, and variable manufacturing overhead are charged to work-in-process and finished goods inventories and subsequently become part of cost of goods sold. Fixed overhead costs such as property taxes, insurance, amortization on plant building, and supervisors' salaries are considered **period costs** and are not viewed as costs of the products being manufactured. Instead, all fixed costs are charged as expenses to the current period.

Under an **absorption costing system**, all manufacturing costs, variable and fixed, direct and indirect, that are incurred in the factory or production process attach to the product. Both fixed and variable overhead are charged to output and are allocated to the cost of inventory, and eventually, cost of goods sold.

Proponents of the variable costing system believe that it provides information on accounting reports that is more useful to management in formulating pricing policies and in controlling costs. Also, because fixed costs are included in inventory under the absorption approach, it may be argued that such a system would result in distorting net income from period to period when production volume fluctuates. If such is the case, variable costing may be a more appropriate basis for reporting income. Absorption costing, however, is the dominant basis for external financial reporting. Its supporters believe it more reasonably represents a firm's investment in inventories.

The Canadian accounting standard for assigning costs to work-in-process and finished goods inventories requires only that the "applicable share of overhead expense properly chargeable to production" be captured in inventory cost.[10] This leaves the decision of treating fixed overhead costs to one's judgement. The *Handbook* also allows for a portion of overhead to be excluded from inventory cost if, by being included, it would distort the income reported due to fluctuating production volume. These statements suggest that while variable costing is acceptable, it would be more the exception than the rule for external reporting.

Standard Costs

A manufacturing company that uses a **standard cost system** predetermines the unit costs for material, labour, and manufacturing overhead. Usually the standard costs are determined based on the costs that should be incurred per unit of finished goods when the plant is operating at normal capacity. Deviations from actual costs are recorded in

OBJECTIVE 5

Explain the difference between variable costing and absorption costing in assigning manufacturing costs to inventory.

IAS NOTE
In contrast to Handbook Section 3030, IAS 2 on Inventories provides very specific guidance on the application of conversion costs (overhead and other costs) to inventory.

INTERNATIONAL INSIGHT
Components of inventory differ internationally. In determining the cost of inventories, U.S. practice requires the inclusion not only of direct material, direct labour and variable overhead, but also fixed manufacturing overhead. In other nations (India and Chile, for example), only direct materials and labour are included.

---

[10] *CICA Handbook*, Section 3030, par. .06.

variance accounts that are examined by management so that appropriate action can be taken to achieve greater control over costs.

For financial statement purposes, reporting inventories at standard costs is acceptable if there is no significant difference between the aggregate actual and standard costs. If there is a significant difference, the inventory amounts should be adjusted to estimated actual cost.[11] Otherwise the net income, assets, and retained earnings would be misstated. A detailed examination of standard costing is available in most managerial and cost accounting texts, but is beyond the scope of this book.

COST FLOW ASSUMPTIONS

A Framework for Analysis

OBJECTIVE 6

Distinguish between the physical flow of inventory and the cost flow assigned to inventory.

During any given fiscal period, it is likely that merchandise will be purchased at several different prices. If inventories are to be priced at cost and numerous purchases have been made at different unit costs, which of the various cost prices should be assigned to Inventory on the balance sheet and which costs should be charged to Cost of Goods Sold on the income statement? Conceptually, to match actual costs with the physical flow of goods, a specific identification of the items sold and unsold seems appropriate, but this is often not only expensive but impossible to achieve. Consequently, the accountant must consistently apply one of several other cost methods that are based on differing but systematic inventory cost flow assumptions. Indeed, the actual physical flow of goods and the cost flow assumption applied are often quite different. **There is no requirement that the cost flow assumption adopted be consistent with the physical movement of goods.**

Issues regarding the various cost flow methods will be illustrated and discussed using the data in Illustration 8-13, which summarizes inventory-related activities of Call-Mart Inc. for the month of March. For illustrative purposes, the beginning inventory's cost per unit is assumed to be the same for all methods. It is important to note that the company experienced **increasing unit costs for its purchases throughout the month**.

The problem is which cost or costs should be assigned to the 6,000 units of ending inventory and which to the 4,000 units sold. The solution depends on what one wishes to accomplish. There are, as previously indicated, several acceptable alternative cost flow methods that may be chosen. These methods are based on different assumptions and accomplish different objectives. A suggested approach to selecting a method is as follows:

1. Identify possible objectives to be accomplished.
2. Know the different acceptable methods, their assumptions, and how they work.
3. Evaluate the advantages and disadvantages of the different methods for achieving the objectives.
4. Choose the method appropriate to the situation and the objective(s) to be accomplished.

Objectives of Inventory Valuation

OBJECTIVE 7

Identify possible objectives for inventory valuation decisions.

The following general objectives are often associated with choosing an inventory cost flow method.

1. to match expenses (cost of goods sold) realistically against revenue
2. to report inventory on the balance sheet at a realistic amount
3. to minimize income taxes

While the first two are legitimate objectives of financial statements, the third should not be relevant to financial statement accounting; however, it sometimes enters into financial accounting decisions for reasons of expediency.

---

[11] *CICA Handbook*, Section 3030, par. .04.

The financial statement objectives of inventory valuation are inherently logical and useful when assessing the various cost flow methods' merits and limitations within the framework of generally accepted accounting principles. They do, however, beg the question of "what is realistic?" The answer will depend on the purpose of preparing financial statements. More will be said about this later in the chapter under the heading "Which Method to Select?"

To illustrate the application of the various cost flow assumptions, assume that Call-Mart Inc. had the following transactions for the month of March.

Call-Mart Inc.

Date	Purchases	Sold or Issued	Balance
March 1	(beginning inventory) 500 @ $3.80		500 units
March 2	1,500 @ $4.00		2,000 units
March 15	6,000 @ $4.40		8,000 units
March 19		4,000 units	4,000 units
March 30	2,000 @ $4.75		6,000 units

ILLUSTRATION 8-13
Data Used to Illustrate Inventory Calculation: Cost Flow Assumptions

From this information, we can calculate the ending inventory of 6,000 units and the cost of goods available for sale (beginning inventory + purchases) of $43,800 [(500 @ $3.80) + (1,500 @ $4.00) + (6,000 @ $4.40) + (2,000 @ $4.75)]. The question is, which price or prices should be assigned to the 6,000 units of ending inventory? The answer depends on which cost flow assumption is chosen.

Specific Identification

Specific identification calls for identifying each item sold and each item in inventory. The costs of the specific items sold are included in the cost of goods sold, and the costs of the specific items on hand are included in the ending inventory. This method may be used only in instances where it is practical to segregate specific items as coming from separate purchases. It can be successfully applied in situations where a relatively small number of costly, easily distinguishable (e.g., by physical characteristics, serial numbers, or special markings) items are handled. In the retail trade this includes some types of jewellery, fur coats, automobiles, and some furniture. In manufacturing it includes special orders and many products manufactured under a job cost system.

> **OBJECTIVE 8**
> ....
> Describe and compare the cost flow assumptions used in accounting for inventories.

To illustrate the specific identification method, assume that Call-Mart Inc.'s 6,000 units of inventory is composed of 100 units from the opening inventory, 900 from the March 2 purchase, 3,000 from the March 15 purchase, and 2,000 from the March 30 purchase. The ending inventory and cost of goods sold would be calculated as shown in Illustration 8-14.

Units from	No. of Units	Unit Cost	Total Cost
Beginning inventory	100	$3.80	$ 380
March 2 purchase	900	4.00	3,600
March 15 purchase	3,000	4.40	13,200
March 30 purchase	2,000	4.75	9,500
Ending inventory	6,000		$26,680
Cost of goods available for sale (beginning inventory + purchases)		$43,800	
Deduct: Ending inventory		26,680	
Cost of goods sold		$17,120	

ILLUSTRATION 8-14
Specific Identification Method

Conceptually, this method appears ideal because actual costs are matched against actual revenue, and ending inventory is reported at actual cost. In other words, under specific identification, the cost flow matches the goods' physical flow. On closer observation, however, this method has certain deficiencies.

One argument against specific identification is that it makes it possible to manipulate net income. For example, assume that a wholesaler purchases otherwise identical plywood early in the year at three different prices. When the plywood is sold, the wholesaler can select either the lowest or the highest price to charge to expense simply by selecting the plywood from a specific lot for delivery to the customer. A business manager, therefore, can manipulate net income simply by delivering to the customer the higher- or lower-priced item, depending on whether lower or higher reported income is desired for the period.

Another problem relates to the arbitrary allocation of costs that sometimes occurs with specific inventory items. In certain circumstances, it is difficult to relate adequately, for example, shipping charges, storage costs, and discounts directly to a given inventory item. The alternative, then, is to allocate these costs somewhat arbitrarily, which leads to a "breakdown" in the precision of the specific identification method.[12]

Average Cost

As the name implies, the average cost method prices inventory items based on the average cost of the goods available for sale during the period. To illustrate, assuming that Call-Mart Inc. used the periodic inventory method (or a perpetual system in units only), the ending inventory and cost of goods sold would be calculated as follows using a weighted-average method:

ILLUSTRATION 8-15
Weighted-Average Method—
Periodic Inventory

	Date	No. Units	Unit Cost	Total Cost
Inventory	Mar. 1	500	$3.80	$ 1,900
Purchases	Mar. 2	1,500	4.00	6,000
Purchases	Mar. 15	6,000	4.40	26,400
Purchases	Mar. 30	2,000	4.75	9,500
Total goods available		10,000		$43,800

Weighted average cost per unit $\dfrac{\$43,800}{10,000} = \$4.38$

Ending inventory in units	6,000
Cost of ending inventory	6,000 × $4.38 = $26,280
Cost of goods available for sale	$43,800
Deduct ending inventory	26,280
Cost of goods sold	**$17,520** (= 4,000 × $4.38)

Note that the beginning inventory is included both in the total units available and in the total cost of goods available in computing the average cost per unit.

Another average cost method is the moving-average method, which is used with perpetual inventory records kept in units and dollars. The application of the average cost method for full perpetual records is shown in Illustration 8-16.

---

[12] A good illustration of the cost allocation problem arises in the motion picture industry. Often actors and actresses receive a percentage of net income for a given movie or television program. Some actors who had these arrangements have alleged that their programs have been extremely profitable to the motion picture studios but they have received little in the way of profit sharing. Actors contend that the studios allocate additional costs to successful projects to ensure that there will be no profits to share. Such contentions illustrate the type of problems that can emerge when contracts are based on accounting numbers that can incorporate arbitrary allocations. One way to help overcome such problems is to establish specific measurement rules regarding how the accounting numbers are to be determined, rather than just stating the numbers to be used. This should be done before the contract is signed so that all parties clearly understand what they are getting into.

ILLUSTRATION 8-16
Moving-Average Method—
Perpetual Inventory

Date	Purchased	Sold or Issued	Balance
Mar. 1	Beginning inventory		(500 @ $3.80) $ 1,900
Mar. 2	(1,500 @ $4.00) $6,000		(2,000 @ $3.95) 7,900
Mar. 15	(6,000 @ $4.40) 26,400		(8,000 @ $4.2875) 34,300
Mar. 19		(4,000 @ $4.2875) $17,150	(4,000 @ $4.2875) 17,150
Mar. 30	(2,000 @ $4.75) 9,500		(6,000 @ $4.4417) 26,650

Calculation of moving-average cost per unit:
After March 2 purchase
   = Cost of units available / Units available
   = [(500 × $3.80) + (1,500 × $4.00)] / (500 + 1,500)
   = ($1,900 + $6,000) / 2,000
   = $7,900 / 2,000
   = $3.95

After March 15 purchase
   = [$7,900 + (6,000 × $4.40)] / (2,000 + 6,000)
   = $34,300 / 8,000
   = $4.2875

After March 30 purchase
   = [(4,000 × $4.2875) + (2,000 × $4.75)] / (4,000 + 2,000)
   = $26,650 / 6,000
   = $4.4417

In this method, a new average unit cost is calculated each time a purchase is made. On March 15, after 6,000 units are purchased for $26,400, 8,000 units costing $34,300 ($7,900 plus $26,400) are on hand. The average unit cost is $34,300 divided by 8,000, or $4.2875. This unit cost is used in costing withdrawals until another purchase is made, when a new average unit cost is calculated. Accordingly, the cost of the 4,000 units withdrawn on March 19 is shown at $4.2875, a total cost of goods sold of $17,150. On March 30, following the purchase of 2,000 units for $9,500, a new unit cost of $4.4417 is determined for an ending inventory of $26,650.

The use of the average cost method is usually justified with practical rather than conceptual reasons. These methods are simple to apply, objective, and not as subject to income manipulation as some other inventory costing methods. In addition, proponents of the average cost method argue that it is often impossible to measure a specific physical flow of inventory and therefore it is better to cost items on an average price basis. This argument is particularly persuasive when the inventory involved is relatively homogeneous in nature.

In terms of achieving financial statement objectives, an average cost method results in an average of costs being employed to determine the cost of goods sold in the income statement and ending inventory in the balance sheet. In comparison to the FIFO method (discussed below), an average cost method results in more recent costs being reflected in the cost of goods sold, but older costs in ending inventory. Relative to the LIFO method (discussed below), an average cost method reflects more recent costs in ending inventory, but older costs in cost of goods sold. Therefore, the average cost method may be viewed as a compromise between the FIFO and LIFO methods. Some would argue that, as a compromise, an average cost method has the advantages of neither and the disadvantages of both of these other methods. For income tax minimization, an average cost method can be used in Canada and it may provide some income tax advantages during periods of rising prices.

First-In, First-Out (FIFO)

The **FIFO method** assigns costs assuming that goods are used in the order in which they are purchased. In other words, it assumes that **the first goods purchased are the first used** (in a manufacturing concern) **or sold** (in a merchandising concern). The inventory remaining must therefore represent the most recent purchases.

To illustrate, assume that Call-Mart Inc. uses the periodic inventory system (or a perpetual system in units only), where the inventory cost is calculated only at the end of the month. The ending inventory's cost is calculated by taking the cost of the most recent purchase and working back until all units in the ending inventory are accounted for. The ending inventory and cost of goods sold are determined as shown in Illustration 8-17.

ILLUSTRATION 8-17
FIFO Method—Periodic Inventory

Date	No. Units	Unit Cost	Total Cost
March 30	2,000	$4.75	$ 9,500
March 15	4,000	4.40	17,600
Ending inventory	6,000		$27,100

Cost of goods available for sale	$43,800	
Deduct: Ending inventory	27,100	
Cost of goods sold	$16,700	

If a perpetual inventory system in quantities and dollars is used, a cost figure is attached to each withdrawal when it is made. In the example, the cost of the 4,000 units removed on March 19 would be made up first from the items in the beginning inventory, then the purchases on March 2, and finally from the March 15 purchases. The inventory record on a FIFO basis perpetual system for Call-Mart Inc. is shown in Illustration 8-18, which discloses the ending inventory of $27,100 and a cost of goods sold of $16,700.

Notice that in these two FIFO examples, the cost of goods sold and ending inventory are the same. **In all cases where FIFO is used, the inventory and cost of goods sold would be the same at the end of the month whether a perpetual or periodic system is used.** This is true because the same costs will always be first in and, therefore, first out whether cost of goods sold is calculated as goods are sold throughout the accounting period (the perpetual system) or as a residual at the end of the accounting period (the periodic system).

ILLUSTRATION 8-18
FIFO Method—
Perpetual Inventory

Date	Purchased	Sold or Issued	Balance	
Mar. 1	Beginning inventory		500 @ $3.80	$ 1,900
Mar. 2	(1,500 @ $4.00) $ 6,000		500 @ 3.80 1,500 @ 4.00	7,900
Mar. 15	(6,000 @ $4.40) 26,400		500 @ 3.80 1,500 @ 4.00 6,000 @ 4.40	34,300
Mar. 19		500 @ $3.80 1,500 @ 4.00 2,000 @ 4.40 **$16,700**	4,000 @ 4.40	17,600
Mar. 30	(2,000 @ $4.75) 9,500		4,000 @ 4.40 2,000 @ 4.75	27,100

One objective of FIFO is to approximate the physical flow of goods. When the physical flow of goods is actually first-in, first-out, the FIFO method very nearly represents specific identification. At the same time, it does not permit manipulation of income because the enterprise is not free to choose a certain cost to be charged to expense.

Another advantage of the FIFO method is that the ending inventory is close to its current cost. Because the cost of the first goods in is in the cost of the first goods out, the ending inventory amount will be composed of the most recent purchases. This approach generally approximates replacement cost for inventory on the balance sheet when the inventory turnover is rapid and/or price changes have not occurred since the most recent purchases.

The FIFO method's basic disadvantage is that current costs are not matched against current revenues on the income statement. The oldest costs are charged against the more current revenue, which can lead to distortions in gross profit and net income.

Last-In, First-Out (LIFO)

The **LIFO method** assigns costs on the assumption that the cost of the most recent purchase is the first cost to be charged to cost of goods sold. The cost assigned to the inventory remaining would therefore come from the earliest acquisitions (i.e., "first-in, still-here").

If a periodic inventory system (or a perpetual system in units only) is used, it would be assumed that **the total quantity sold or issued during the period would have come from the most recent purchases, even though such purchases may have taken place after the actual date of sale.** Conversely, the ending inventory costs would consist first of costs from the beginning inventory and then from purchases early in the period. Using the example for Call-Mart Inc., the assumption would be made that the 4,000 units withdrawn consisted of the 2,000 units purchased on March 30 and 2,000 of the 6,000 units purchased on March 15. Therefore, the cost of the ending inventory of 6,000 units would be assumed to come from the cost of any beginning inventory (500 units) and then the earliest purchases in the period (1,500 units on March 2 and 4,000 units on March 15). The inventory and related cost of goods sold would be calculated as shown in Illustration 8-19.

INTERNATIONAL INSIGHT

Until recently, LIFO was typically used only in the U.S. However, LIFO is acceptable under the Directives of the European Union, and its use is acceptable under international accounting standards. Nonetheless, LIFO is still used primarily in the U.S. and is still prohibited in several nations, including, for example, Australia, Hong Kong, and the U.K.

ILLUSTRATION 8-19
LIFO Method—Periodic Inventory

Date of Invoice	No. Units	Unit Cost	Total Cost
Beginning inventory	500	$3.80	$ 1,900
Mar. 2 purchase	1,500	4.00	6,000
Mar. 15 purchase	4,000	4.40	17,600
Ending inventory	**6,000**		**$25,500**
Cost of goods available for sale	$43,800		
Deduct: Ending inventory	25,500		
Cost of goods sold	**$18,300**		

If a perpetual inventory system is kept in quantities and dollars, applying the last-in, first-out method will result in **different ending inventory and cost of goods sold amounts,** as shown in Illustration 8-20.

ILLUSTRATION 8-20
LIFO Method—
Perpetual Inventory

Date	Purchased	Sold or Issued	Balance	
Mar. 1	Beginning inventory		500 @ $3.80	$ 1,900
Mar. 2	(1,500 @ $4.00) $ 6,000		500 @ 3.80 1,500 @ 4.00	7,900
Mar. 15	(6,000 @ $4.40) 26,400		500 @ 3.80 1,500 @ 4.00 6,000 @ 4.40	34,300
Mar. 19		(4,000 @ $4.40) **$17,600**	500 @ 3.80 1,500 @ 4.00 2,000 @ 4.40	16,700
Mar. 30	(2,000 @ $4.75) 9,500		500 @ 3.80 1,500 @ 4.00 2,000 @ 4.40 2,000 @ 4.75	26,200

The month-end periodic inventory calculation presented in Illustration 8-19 (inventory $25,500 and cost of goods sold $18,300) shows a different amount from the perpetual inventory calculation (inventory $26,200 and cost of goods sold $17,600). This is because the periodic system matches the total withdrawals for the month with the total purchases for the month, whereas the perpetual system matches each withdrawal with the immediately preceding purchases. In effect, the periodic calculation assumed that the goods that were not purchased until March 30 were included in the sale or issue of March 19. While this is not physically possible, remember that it is not necessary to match physical item flows with cost flows when measuring cost of goods sold. The perspective to be taken is that of understanding which costs are matched against the revenues.

EVALUATION AND CHOICE OF A COST FLOW METHOD

Use of the LIFO method is controversial. Some do not believe it is appropriate for conceptual reasons, while others believe it is conceptually superior to other approaches given that financial statements are prepared on an historical cost basis. Arguments for and against the use of LIFO necessarily reflect a perception regarding many fundamental issues about financial accounting: What is relevant? Which is more important, the income statement or the balance sheet? Should income tax requirements dictate methods to be selected for preparing financial statements?

While reaching a conclusion about LIFO's acceptability is a matter of judgement, its major advantages and disadvantages should be considered. Careful reflection on this listing will indicate that, for most points, the advantages of LIFO become the disadvantages of other cost flow methods (FIFO and average cost) and vice versa.

> **OBJECTIVE 9**
>
> Evaluate LIFO as a basis for understanding the differences between the cost flow methods.

Major Advantages of LIFO

Matching. The matching principle requires that we match costs to the same period as related revenues are recognized. **The principle, however, does not say which costs should be matched when alternatives are available.** Therefore, for inventory valuation, the various methods available leave open the choice of matching recent costs (LIFO), average costs (average methods), or older costs (FIFO) against revenues.

In LIFO, the more recent costs are matched against current revenues to provide what may be viewed as a more realistic measure of current earnings in periods of changing prices. For example, in the early 1990s many Canadian oil companies changed to the LIFO method. The explanation given in Petro-Canada's financial report was: "The change was made to more closely match current costs with current revenues in determination of the results of the Company's operations."

During periods of rising prices, many challenge the quality of non-LIFO historical cost-based earnings, noting that by failing to match current costs against current revenues, **transitory "paper" or "inventory profits" are created**. Inventory profits occur because old low inventory costs that are matched against sales are less than the recent, higher costs to replace the inventory. The cost of goods sold therefore is perceived to be understated and profit is overstated. By using LIFO (rather than FIFO or average cost), more recent costs are matched against revenues and inventory profits are thereby reduced.

Future Earnings Hedge. With LIFO, in a period of rising prices, a company's future reported earnings will not be affected substantially by future price declines (due to write-downs under the lower of cost and market rule examined in Chapter 9). LIFO eliminates or substantially minimizes write-downs to market as a result of price decreases. The reason: since the most recent (higher cost) inventory is assumed to be sold first, the ending inventory value ordinarily will be lower than net realizable value. In contrast, inventory costed under FIFO is more vulnerable to price declines, which can reduce net income substantially. When prices are declining, however, this aspect of LIFO becomes a disadvantage.

Major Disadvantages of LIFO

Reduced Earnings. Many corporate managers view the lower profits reported under the LIFO method, relative to other methods, as a distinct disadvantage. They fear that the effect on net income from using LIFO may be misunderstood and that, as a result of the lower profits, the company's share price will fall. In fact, though, there is some evidence to refute this contention. Studies have indicated that users of financial data exhibit a sophistication that enables them to recognize the impact on reported income from using LIFO compared with other methods and, as a consequence, reflect this when assessing a company's share price.

This disadvantage of reduced earnings assumes that prices are increasing; when prices are declining, the opposite effect may occur. For example, oil prices to refineries were declining when many Canadian oil companies switched to LIFO in the early 1990s.

Inventory Distortion.   Under LIFO, the inventory valuation on the balance sheet is normally outdated because the oldest costs remain in inventory. This results in several problems, but manifests itself most directly in evaluating the amounts, ratios, and related trends that include the ending inventory. The magnitude and direction of the variation in the carrying amount of inventory and its current price depend on the degree and direction of the changes in price and the amount of inventory turnover.

Physical Flow.   LIFO does not approximate the items' physical flow except in a few situations. Imagine a coal pile: the last coal bought is the first coal out, since the coal remover will not take coal from inside the pile. However, matching more recent costs against revenues may be viewed as a higher priority objective than reflecting the physical flow of goods when choosing an inventory valuation method.

Inventory Liquidation.   Use of LIFO raises the problem of LIFO liquidation. If the base or layers of old costs in beginning inventory are eliminated (e.g., when units sold exceed the units purchased for a period), strange results can occur. The matching advantage of LIFO would be lost because old, irrelevant costs would be matched against current revenues, resulting in a severe distortion in reported income at least for the given period. For example, **Allied Corporation** reported net earnings of $.09 per share in a year in which its inventory reductions resulted in liquidations of LIFO inventory quantities. The inventory reduction's effect was to increase income by $13 million or $.17 per share.

Poor Buying Habits.   Because of the liquidation problem, LIFO may cause poor buying habits. A company may simply purchase more goods and match the cost of these goods against revenue to ensure that old costs are not charged to expense. Furthermore, the possibility always exists with LIFO that a company will attempt to manage (manipulate) its earnings at year end simply by altering its purchasing pattern.

Not Acceptable for Tax Purposes.   Because of definitions in the Income Tax Act as to how inventory amounts may be determined, LIFO inventory valuation is not accepted by Canada Customs and Revenue Agency for purposes of determining taxable income except in a few special circumstances.

Current Cost Income Not Measured.   LIFO falls short of measuring current cost (replacement cost) income, though not as far short as FIFO. When measuring current cost income, the cost of goods sold should consist not of the most recently incurred costs but rather of the cost that will be incurred to replace the goods that have been sold. Using replacement cost is referred to as the next-in, first-out method, which is not currently acceptable for purposes of inventory valuation.

Summary Analysis of FIFO, Weighted-Average, and LIFO Methods

For review and comparison purposes, a summary of the three major cost flow methods' differing effects on the financial statements is shown in Illustration 8-21. The numbers were derived from the illustrations of each method for Call-Mart Inc. for the month of March, using the periodic system or a perpetual system maintained in units only. The sales revenue reflects that the 4,000 units were sold for $10 each. The difference in gross profit and, therefore, net income (other expenses would be the same) is due to the differing cost flow assumptions associated with each method. Since the example incorporated a period of rising prices, the gross profit (and, therefore, net income) is highest under FIFO and lowest under LIFO.

ILLUSTRATION 8-21
Comparison of FIFO,
Weighted-Average, and
LIFO Methods

	Method		
	FIFO	Weighted-Average	LIFO
Partial Income Statement:			
Sales Revenue	$40,000	$40,000	$40,000
Cost of Goods Sold:			
Beginning inventory	$ 1,900	$ 1,900	$ 1,900
Purchases	41,900	41,900	41,900
Goods Available	$43,800	$43,800	$43,800
Deduct:			
Ending inventory	27,100	26,280	25,500
Cost of Goods Sold	16,700	17,520	18,300
Gross Profit	$23,300	$22,480	$21,700
Balance Sheet:			
Inventory	$27,100	$26,280	$25,500

Objectives:

1. Matching	Old costs against current revenue	Average cost against current revenue	"Current" costs against current revenue*
2. Balance Sheet Valuation	"Current" costs*	Average cost	Old costs
3. Income Tax Minimization	Results in higher taxable income in periods of rising prices.	Best in Canada in periods of rising prices as results in highest cost of goods sold next to LIFO.*	Not allowed in Canada in most situations. If it were, it would be best in periods of rising prices.

*Results in a realistic accomplishment of objective relative to other methods. The * regarding matching for LIFO assumes no liquidation of beginning inventory.

At the bottom of the comparative results is a listing of the three objectives previously identified as being most commonly associated with choosing an inventory method. As developed in the prior discussion, the strongest argument favouring LIFO for financial statement reporting purposes is that it matches more current costs against current revenue. FIFO results in a more current cost for inventory on the balance sheet.

In terms of minimizing income tax or deferring tax payments, the method resulting in the lowest taxable income for the period would be preferred. While LIFO results in the lowest income in periods of rising prices (assuming there is little or no beginning inventory liquidation), it is not permitted for calculating taxable income in Canada for most businesses. Consequently, the average-cost method, which is permitted under income tax legislation, would more effectively accomplish this objective in a period of rising prices.

The fact that LIFO is generally not allowed for determining taxable income in Canada is in direct contrast to the situation in the United States, where it is accepted for tax purposes. While non-LIFO disclosures may be made as supplemental information, the Internal Revenue Service in the U.S. requires that if LIFO is used for income tax purposes, it must also be used for financial reporting purposes (this is known as the LIFO conformity rule). Though one may argue the merits of LIFO for financial reporting purposes on a more conceptual level, the IRS ruling is likely primarily responsible for the much higher use of the LIFO method in financial statements in the U.S. compared with Canada.[13]

INTERNATIONAL INSIGHT

LIFO tends to be found in financial statements in countries where it is allowed for tax purposes, such as Belgium, Germany, Japan, South Korea, Taiwan, and the U.S.

---

[13] *Financial Reporting in Canada—2000* reported that of the 147 inventory cost method disclosures, 48 (33%) used FIFO, 58 (39%) used average cost, 3 (2%) used LIFO, 3 (2%) used other methods, and 35 (24%) used more than one method. For comparison, a similar U.S. study, *Accounting Trends and Techniques—1999*, reported that of 944 inventory method disclosures, 43% used FIFO, 19% used average cost, 34% used LIFO and 4% used other methods. Data from the U.S. indicate that a significant shift from FIFO to LIFO took place in the 1970s and early 1980s. The rate of inflation and tax advantages were, no doubt, at least partially responsible for the shift. Although inflation was also significant in Canada, no shift to LIFO was evident.

Which Method to Select?

The *CICA Handbook* indicates that specific identification, FIFO, average cost, and LIFO are generally acceptable and commonly used methods for determining inventory cost for financial reporting purposes.[14] The *Handbook* also recommends that the method selected should result in the fairest matching of costs against revenues, whether or not the method is consistent with the physical flow of goods.[15]

What method will provide the fairest matching? The answer can be derived only by exercising professional judgement, given knowledge of the particular circumstances and the consequences desired in terms of the financial statements' objectives. As indicated in Chapter 1, a primary objective of financial reporting is to communicate information that is useful to investors, creditors, and others in making their resource allocation decisions and/or assessing management stewardship. Therefore, the inventory valuation method that accomplishes this objective would certainly be the fairest (most relevant) one to choose. Making the appropriate choice, however, depends on awareness of a number of things, such as who the users are, the decisions they are making, and what information fits their decision models. If one method was fairest for all situations, then the accounting profession would certainly not have acceptable alternative methods. Consequently, professional judgement is the basis for determining the method to use.

An important point is that a company can use one method (e.g., FIFO) for financial statement reporting and another method (average cost) for tax purposes. This is legal and reasonable as financial reporting objectives are different from those of income tax determination. Having "two sets of books" may, however, be inefficient—a judgement requiring the accountant to be fully cognizant of the circumstances. If methods used for preparing financial statements differ from those used for determining taxable income, a difference between the book value and the tax value of inventory results. The tax effect on the amount of the temporary difference is accounted for as an interperiod allocation, a topic that is examined in Chapter 19.

Consistency of Inventory Costing

All the inventory costing methods described in this chapter are used to some extent. Indeed, a company may use different methods for different types of inventory.

It can be seen that freedom to shift from one inventory costing method to another at will would permit a wide range of possible net income figures for a given company for any given period. This would affect the comparability of the financial statements. **The variety of methods has been devised to assist appropriate financial reporting rather than to permit manipulation.** Hence, it is necessary that the costing method most suitable to a company be selected and, once selected, be applied consistently thereafter. If conditions indicate that the inventory costing method in use may be unsuitable (e.g., not as relevant as it could be), serious consideration should be given to all possibilities before selecting another method. If a change is made, it should be clearly explained and its effect disclosed in the financial statements.[16]

> **OBJECTIVE 10**
> ....
> Explain the importance of judgement in selecting an inventory cost flow method.

> **IAS NOTE**
> The benchmark treatment is FIFO or weighted average if specific costs cannot be determined. LIFO is permitted as an alternative, but, if used, companies must disclose the lower of net realizable value and cost determined using one of the benchmark methods for inventory at the balance sheet data.

---

[14] *CICA Handbook*, Section 3030, par. .07. Noteworthy about this section is that it does not explicitly identify these methods as the only ones that are acceptable.

[15] *Ibid.*, Section 3030, par. .09.

[16] *Ibid.*, Section 1000, pars. .22 and .23.

SUMMARY OF LEARNING OBJECTIVES

1 Identify major classifications of inventory. Only one inventory account, Merchandise Inventory, appears in the financial statements of a merchandising concern. A manufacturer normally has three inventory accounts: Raw Materials, Work in Process, and Finished Goods. Factory or manufacturing supplies inventory may also exist.

2 Distinguish between perpetual and periodic inventory systems. Under a perpetual inventory system, a continuous record of changes in inventory is maintained in the Inventory account. That is, all purchases and transfers of goods out (issues) are recorded directly in the Inventory account as they occur. No such record is kept under a periodic inventory system. Under the periodic system, year-end inventory must be determined by a physical count upon which the amount of ending inventory and cost of goods sold is based. Even under the perpetual system, an annual count is needed to test the records' accuracy.

3 Identify the effects of inventory errors on the financial statements. If the ending inventory is misstated, (1) the inventory, retained earnings, working capital, and current ratio in the balance sheet will be misstated, and (2) the cost of goods sold and net income in the income statement will be misstated. If purchases and inventory are misstated, (1) the inventory, accounts payable, and current ratio will be misstated, and (2) purchases and ending inventory in the income statement will be misstated.

4 Identify the items that should be included as inventory cost. Product costs are directly connected with the bringing of goods to the buyer's place of business and converting such goods to a saleable condition. Such charges would include freight charges on goods purchased, other direct costs of acquisition, and labour and other production costs incurred in processing the goods up to the time of sale. Manufacturing overhead costs that include indirect material, indirect labour, and such items as amortization, taxes, insurance, heat, and electricity incurred in the manufacturing process are also usually allocated to inventory, although some companies include only the costs of direct or variable overhead.

5 Explain the difference between variable costing and absorption costing in assigning manufacturing costs to inventory. Under variable (direct) costing, direct material, direct labour, and variable manufacturing overhead are charged to inventories and fixed manufacturing overhead is treated as a period cost. In absorption (full) costing, direct material, direct labour, and all manufacturing costs (variable and fixed) are treated as product costs and are included in the cost of inventory.

6 Distinguish between the physical flow of inventory and the cost flow assigned to inventory. If the unit cost is different for various purchases, the question is which costs will be assigned to ending inventory and, as a consequence, to cost of goods sold. In accounting there is no requirement that the costs charged to goods sold be consistent with the goods' physical movement. Consequently, various cost flow methods for assigning costs to cost of goods sold and ending inventory are all generally acceptable. The primary methods are specific identification, average cost, FIFO, and LIFO.

7 Identify possible objectives for inventory valuation decisions. The general objectives are (1) to match expenses realistically against revenues; (2) to report inventory on the balance sheet at a realistic amount; and (3) to minimize income taxes. Inevitably, trade-offs exist between the cost flow methods and the objectives such that no one method will likely satisfy all objectives.

8 Describe and compare the flow assumptions used in accounting for inventories. (1) Average cost prices items in the ending inventory based on the average cost of all similar goods available during the period. (2) First-in, first-out (FIFO) assumes that goods are used in the order in which they are purchased. The inventory remaining must therefore represent the most recent purchases. (3) Last-in, first-out (LIFO) matches the cost of the last goods purchased against revenue.

9 Evaluate LIFO as a basis for understanding the differences between the cost flow methods. In a period of rising prices, LIFO may be viewed as providing a more realistic matching in the income statement (recent costs against revenues) and offering a greater future earnings hedge. Disadvantages include a reduction in net income and old costs for inventory on the balance sheet. In addition, it does not generally reflect physical flow, matching is destroyed when beginning inventory is liquidated, it provides an opportunity to manage (manipulate) earnings, and it is not acceptable for income tax purposes in Canada. To an extent, the advantages and disadvantages of LIFO are the disadvantages and advantages of FIFO. Average cost methods fall between these two extremes.

10 Explain the importance of judgement in selecting an inventory cost flow method. The only guidance provided in the *CICA Handbook* is that the method chosen should result in "the fairest matching of costs against revenues regardless of whether or not the method corresponds to the physical flow of goods." Consequently, exercise of judgement is required when choosing a cost flow method.

BRIEF EXERCISES

BE8-1 Included in the December 31 trial balance of Joel Corp. are the following assets:

Cash	$ 190,000	Work in process	$200,000
Equipment (net)	1,100,000	Receivables (net)	400,000
Prepaid insurance	41,000	Patents	110,000
Raw materials	335,000	Finished goods	150,000

Prepare the current assets section of the December 31 balance sheet.

BE8-2 Alanis Ltd. uses a perpetual inventory system. Its beginning inventory consists of 50 units that cost $30 each. During June, the company purchased 150 units at $30 each, returned 6 units for credit, and sold 125 units at $50 each. Journalize the June transactions.

BE8-3 Mayberry Ltd. took a physical inventory on December 31 and determined that goods costing $200,000 were on hand. Not included in the physical count were $15,000 of goods purchased from Taylor Corporation, f.o.b. shipping point; and $22,000 of goods sold to Mount Pilot Ltd. for $30,000, f.o.b. destination. Both the Taylor purchase and the Mount Pilot sale were in transit at year end. What amount should Mayberry report as its December 31 inventory?

BE8-4 Bryars Enterprises Ltd. reported cost of goods sold for 2002 of $1.4 million and retained earnings of $5.2 million at December 31, 2002. Bryars later discovered that its ending inventories at December 31, 2001 and 2002 were overstated by $110,000 and $45,000, respectively. Determine the corrected amounts for 2002 cost of goods sold and December 31, 2002, retained earnings.

BE8-5 Jose Zorilla Corp. uses a periodic inventory system. For April, when the company sold 700 units, the following information is available:

	Units	Unit Cost	Total Cost
April 1 inventory	250	$10	$ 2,500
April 15 purchase	400	12	4,800
April 23 purchase	350	13	4,550
	1,000		$11,850

Calculate the April 30 inventory and the April cost of goods sold using the average cost method.

BE8-6 Data for Jose Zorilla Corp. are presented in BE8-5. Calculate the April 30 inventory and the April cost of goods sold using the FIFO method.

BE8-7 Data for Jose Zorilla Corp. are presented in BE8-5. Calculate the April 30 inventory and the April cost of goods sold using the LIFO method.

EXERCISES

E8-1 **(Inventoriable Costs)** Presented below is a list of items that may or may not be reported as inventory in a company's December 31 balance sheet.

+ 1. Goods out on consignment at another company's store.
- 2. Goods sold on an instalment basis.
+ 3. Goods purchased f.o.b. shipping point that are in transit at December 31.
- 4. Goods purchased f.o.b. destination that are in transit at December 31.
+ 5. Goods sold to another company, for which our company has signed an agreement to repurchase at a set price that covers all costs related to the inventory.
- 6. Goods sold where large returns are predictable.
- 7. Goods sold f.o.b. shipping point that are in transit at December 31.
+ 8. Freight charges on goods purchased.
+ 9. Factory labour costs incurred on goods still unsold. *Finished Good Inv– Other Expenses on I.S.*
- 10. Interest costs incurred for inventories that are routinely manufactured.
- 11. Costs incurred to advertise goods held for resale. *Advertising Expense*
+ 12. Materials on hand not yet placed into production by a manufacturing firm. *Raw Mat Inv.*
- 13. Office supplies.
+ 14. Raw materials on which a manufacturing firm has started production, but which are not completely processed. *Work in P. Inventory*
+ 15. Factory supplies. *if used in process its WIP inven. If it hasnot Been used ins Current assets*
- 16. Goods held on consignment from another company.
+ 17. Costs identified with units completed by a manufacturing firm, but not yet sold.
+ 18. Goods sold f.o.b. destination that are in transit at December 31.
- 19. Temporary investments in shares and bonds that will be resold in the near future.

Instructions
Indicate which of these items would typically be reported as inventory in the financial statements. If an item should not be reported as inventory, indicate how it should be reported in the financial statements.

E8-2 **(Inventoriable Costs)** In your audit of the Oliva Corp., you find that a physical inventory on December 31, 2002 indicated merchandise with a cost of $441,000 was on hand at that date. You also discover the following items were all excluded from the $441,000.

1. Merchandise of $61,000 that is held by Oliva on consignment. The consignor is Max Company Limited.
2. Merchandise costing $38,000 that was shipped by Oliva f.o.b. destination to a customer on December 31, 2002. The customer was expected to receive the merchandise on January 6, 2003.
3. Merchandise costing $46,000 that was shipped by Oliva f.o.b. shipping point to a customer on December 29, 2002. The customer was scheduled to receive the merchandise on January 2, 2003.
4. Merchandise costing $83,000 shipped by a vendor f.o.b. destination on December 30, 2002, and received by Oliva on January 4, 2003.
5. Merchandise costing $51,000 shipped by a vendor f.o.b. shipping point on December 31, 2002 and received by Oliva on January 5, 2003.

Instructions
Based on the above information, calculate the amount that should appear on Oliva's balance sheet at December 31, 2002 for inventory.

E8-3 **(Inventoriable Costs)** In an annual audit of Matejko Company Limited at December 31, 2002, you find the following transactions near the closing date.

1. A special machine, fabricated to order for a customer, was finished and specifically segregated in the back part of the shipping room on December 31, 2002. The customer was billed on that date and the machine excluded from inventory although it was shipped on January 4, 2003.
2. Merchandise costing $2,800 was received on January 3, 2003, and the related purchase invoice recorded January 5. The invoice showed the shipment was made on December 29, 2002, f.o.b. destination.
3. A packing case containing a product costing $3,400 was standing in the shipping room when the physical inventory was taken. It was not included in the inventory because it was marked "Hold for shipping instructions." Your investigation revealed that the customer's order was dated December 18, 2002, but that the case was shipped and the customer billed on January 10, 2003. The product was a stock item of your client.

4. Merchandise received on January 6, 2003 costing $680 was entered in the purchase journal on January 7, 2003. The invoice showed shipment was made f.o.b. supplier's warehouse on December 31, 2002. Because it was not on hand at December 31, it was not included in inventory.
5. Merchandise costing $720 was received on December 28, 2002, and the invoice was not recorded. You located it in the hands of the purchasing agent; it was marked "on consignment."

Instructions

Assuming that each amount is material, state whether the merchandise should be included in the client's inventory and give your reason for your decision on each item.

E8-4 (Inventoriable Costs-Perpetual) The Davis Machine Corporation maintains a general ledger account for each class of inventory, debiting such accounts for increases during the period and crediting them for decreases. The transactions below relate to the Raw Materials inventory account, which is debited for materials purchased and credited for materials requisitioned for use.

1. An invoice for $8,100, terms f.o.b. destination, was received and entered January 2, 2003. The receiving report shows that the materials were received December 28, 2002.
2. Materials costing $28,000, shipped f.o.b. destination, were not entered by December 31, 2002 "because they were in a railroad car on the company's siding on that date and had not been unloaded."
3. Materials costing $7,300 were returned to the creditor on December 29, 2002, and were shipped f.o.b. shipping point. The return was entered on that date, even though the materials are not expected to reach the creditor's place of business until January 6, 2003.
4. An invoice for $7,500, terms f.o.b. shipping point, was received and entered December 30, 2002. The receiving report shows that the materials were received January 4, 2003, and the bill of lading shows that they were shipped January 2, 2003.
5. Materials costing $19,800 were received December 30, 2002, but no entry was made for them because "they were ordered with a specified delivery of no earlier than January 10, 2003."

Instructions

Prepare correcting general journal entries required at December 31, 2002, assuming that the books have not been closed. Also indicate which entries must be reversed after closing so the next period's accounts will be correct.

E8-5 (Inventoriable Costs-Error Adjustments) Craig Corporation asks you to review its December 31, 2002, inventory values and prepare the necessary adjustments to the books. The following information is given to you.

1. Craig uses the periodic method of recording inventory. A physical count reveals $234,890 of inventory on hand at December 31, 2002, although the books have not yet been adjusted to reflect the ending inventory.
2. Not included in the physical count of inventory is $13,420 of merchandise purchased on December 15 from Browser. This merchandise was shipped f.o.b. shipping point on December 29 and arrived in January. The invoice arrived and was recorded on December 31.
3. Included in inventory is merchandise sold to Champy on December 30, f.o.b. destination. This merchandise was shipped after it was counted. The invoice was prepared and recorded as a sale on account for $12,800 on December 31. The merchandise cost $7,350, and Champy received it on January 3.
4. Included in inventory was merchandise received from Dudley on December 31 with an invoice price of $15,630. The merchandise was shipped f.o.b. destination. The invoice, which has not yet arrived, has not been recorded.
5. Not included in inventory is $8,540 of merchandise purchased from Glowser Industries. This merchandise was received on December 31 after the inventory had been counted. The invoice was received and recorded on December 30.
6. Included in inventory was $10,438 of inventory held by Craig on consignment from Jackel Industries.
7. Included in inventory is merchandise sold to Kemp f.o.b. shipping point. This merchandise was shipped after it was counted on December 31. The invoice was prepared and recorded as a sale for $18,900 on December 31. The cost of this merchandise was $10,520, and Kemp received the merchandise on January 5.
8. Excluded from inventory was a carton labelled "Please accept for credit." This carton contains merchandise costing $1,500, which had been sold to a customer for $2,600. No entry had been made to the books to reflect the return, but none of the returned merchandise seemed damaged.

Instructions

(a) Determine the proper inventory balance for Craig Corporation at December 31, 2002.
(b) Prepare any correcting entries to adjust inventory to its proper amount at December 31, 2002. Assume the books have not been closed.

E8-6 **(Determining Merchandise Amounts-Periodic)**   Two or more items are omitted in each of the following tabulations of income statement data. Fill in the amounts that are missing.

	2002	2003	2004
Sales	$290,000	$ 360,000	$410,000
Sales returns	11,000	13,000	20,000
Net sales	279,000	347,000	390,000
Beginning inventory	20,000	32,000	37,000
Ending inventory	32,000	37,000	44,000
Purchases	242,000	260,000	298,000
Purchase returns and allowances	5,000	8,000	10,000
Transportation-in	8,000	9,000	12,000
Cost of goods sold	233,000	256,000	293,000
Gross profit on sales	46,000	91,000	97,000

E8-7 **(Financial Statement Presentation of Manufacturing Amounts-Periodic)**   Haida Ltd. is a manufacturing firm. Presented below is selected information from its 2002 accounting records.

Raw materials inventory, 1/1/02	$ 30,800	Transportation-out	$8,000
Raw materials inventory, 12/31/02	37,400	Selling expenses	300,000
Work-in-process inventory, 1/1/02	72,600	Administrative expenses	180,000
Work-in-process inventory, 12/31/02	61,600	Purchase discounts	10,640
Finished goods inventory, 1/1/02	35,200	Purchase returns and allowances	6,460
Finished goods inventory, 12/31/02	22,000	Interest expense	15,000
Purchases	278,600	Direct labour	440,000
Transportation-in	6,600	Manufacturing overhead	330,000

Instructions

(a) Calculate the cost of raw materials used.
(b) Calculate the cost of goods manufactured.
(c) Calculate cost of goods sold.
(d) Indicate how inventories would be reported in the December 31, 2002 balance sheet.

E8-8 **(Purchases Recorded Net)**   Presented below are transactions related to Brokaw Limited.

May 10 Purchased goods billed at $15,000 subject to cash discount terms of 2/10, n/60.
     11 Purchased goods billed at $13,200 subject to terms of 1/15, n/30.
     19 Paid invoice of May 10.
     24 Purchased goods billed at $11,500 subject to cash discount terms of 2/10, n/30.

Instructions

(a) Prepare general journal entries for the transactions above, assuming that purchases are to be recorded at net amounts after cash discounts and that discounts lost are to be treated as financial expense. Assume a periodic inventory system.
(b) Assuming no purchase or payment transactions other than those given above, prepare the adjusting entry required on May 31 if financial statements are to be prepared as of that date.

E8-9 **(Purchases Recorded, Gross Method)**   Cruise Industries Ltd. purchased $10,800 of merchandise on February 1, 2002, subject to a trade discount of 10% and with credit terms of 3/15, n/60. It returned $2,500 of goods (gross price before trade or cash discount) on February 4. The invoice was paid on February 13.

Instructions

(a) Assuming that Cruise uses the perpetual method for recording merchandise transactions, record the purchase, return, and payment using the gross method.
(b) Assuming that Cruise uses the periodic method for recording merchandise transactions, record the purchase, return, and payment using the gross method.
(c) At what amount would the purchase on February 1 be recorded if the net method were used?

E8-10 **(Periodic versus Perpetual Entries)**   The Fong Corporation sells one product. Presented below is information for January for the Fong Corporation.

Jan. 1	Inventory	100 units at $5 each
4	Sale	80 units at $8 each
11	Purchase	150 units at $6 each
13	Sale	120 units at $8.75 each
20	Purchase	160 units at $7 each
27	Sale	100 units at $9 each

Fong uses the FIFO cost flow assumption. All purchases and sales are on account.

Instructions

(a) Assume Fong uses a periodic system. Prepare all necessary journal entries, including the end-of-month closing entry to record cost of goods sold. A physical count indicates that the ending inventory for January is 110 units.

(b) Calculate gross profit using the periodic system.

(c) Assume Fong uses a perpetual system. Prepare all necessary journal entries.

(d) Calculate gross profit using the perpetual system.

E8-11 (Inventory Errors-Periodic) Martin Limited makes the following errors during the current year.

1. Ending inventory is overstated, but purchases are recorded correctly.
2. Both ending inventory and purchases on account are understated. (Assume this purchase was recorded in the following year.)
3. Ending inventory is correct, but a purchase on account was not recorded. (Assume this purchase was recorded in the following year.)

Instructions

Indicate the effect of each error on working capital, current ratio (assume that the current ratio is greater than 1), retained earnings, and net income for the current year and the subsequent year.

E8-12 (Inventory Errors) Walker Limited has a calendar-year accounting period. The following errors have been discovered in 2003.

1. The December 31, 2001, merchandise inventory had been understated by $21,000.
2. Merchandise purchased on account during 2002 was recorded on the books for the first time in February 2003, when the original invoice for the correct amount of $5,430 arrived. The merchandise had arrived December 28, 2002, and was included in the December 31, 2002 merchandise inventory. The invoice arrived late because of a mixup by the wholesaler.
3. Accrued interest of $1,300 at December 31, 2002 on notes receivable had not been recorded until the cash for the interest was received in March 2003.

Instructions

(a) Calculate the effect each error had on the 2002 net income.

(b) Calculate the effect, if any, each error had on the related December 31, 2002 balance sheet items.

E8-13 (Inventory Errors) At December 31, 2002, McGill Corporation reported current assets of $370,000 and current liabilities of $200,000. McGill uses a periodic inventory system. The following items may have been recorded incorrectly.

1. Goods purchased costing $22,000 were shipped f.o.b. shipping point by a supplier on December 28. McGill received and recorded the invoice on December 29, but the goods were not included in McGill's physical count of inventory because they were not received until January 4.
2. Goods purchased costing $15,000 were shipped f.o.b. destination by a supplier on December 26. McGill received and recorded the invoice on December 31, but the goods were not included in McGill's physical count of inventory because they were not received until January 2.
3. Goods held on consignment from Kishi Company were included in McGill's physical count of inventory at $13,000.
4. Freight-in of $3,000 was debited to advertising expense on December 28.

Instructions

(a) Calculate the current ratio based on McGill's balance sheet.

(b) Recalculate the current ratio after corrections are made.

(c) By what amount will income (before taxes) be adjusted up or down as a result of the corrections?

E8-14 (Inventory Errors) The net income per books of Patrick Limited was determined without knowledge of the errors indicated.

Year	Net Income per Books	Error in Ending Inventory	
1998	$50,000	Overstated	$ 3,000
1999	52,000	Overstated	9,000
2000	54,000	Understated	11,000
2001	56,000	No error	
2002	58,000	Understated	2,000
2003	60,000	Overstated	8,000

Instructions
Prepare a work sheet to show the adjusted net income figure for each of the six years after taking into account the inventory errors.

E8-15 **(FIFO and LIFO-Periodic and Perpetual)** Inventory information for Part 311 of Monique Limited discloses the following information for the month of June:

June 1	Balance	300 units @ $10		June 10	Sold	200 units @ $24
11	Purchased	800 units @ $12		15	Sold	500 units @ $25
20	Purchased	500 units @ $13		27	Sold	300 units @ $27

Instructions
(a) Assuming that the periodic inventory method is used, calculate the cost of goods sold and ending inventory under (1) LIFO and (2) FIFO.
(b) Assuming that the perpetual inventory record is kept in dollars and costs are computed at the time of each withdrawal, what is the value of the ending inventory at LIFO?
(c) Assuming that the perpetual inventory record is kept in dollars and costs are calculated at the time of each withdrawal, what is the gross profit if the inventory is valued at FIFO?
(d) Why is it stated that LIFO usually produces a lower gross profit than FIFO?

E8-16 **(FIFO, LIFO and Average Cost Determination)** J.A. Corporation record of transactions for the month of April was as follows:

	Purchases				Sales	
April	1 (balance on hand)	600 @ $6.00		April 3	500 @ 10.00	
	4	1,500 @ 6.08		9	1,400 @ 10.00	
	8	800 @ 6.40		11	600 @ 11.00	
	13	1,200 @ 6.50		23	1,200 @ 11.00	
	21	700 @ 6.60		27	900 @ 12.00	
	29	500 @ 6.79			4,600	
		5,300				

Instructions
(a) Assuming that perpetual inventory records are kept in units only, calculate the inventory at April 30 using (1) LIFO and (2) average cost.
(b) Assuming that perpetual inventory records are kept in dollars, determine the inventory using (1) FIFO and (2) LIFO.
(c) Calculate cost of goods sold assuming periodic inventory procedures and inventory priced at FIFO.
(d) In an inflationary period, which inventory method—FIFO, LIFO, average cost—will show the highest net income?

E8-17 **(FIFO, LIFO, Average Cost Inventory)** Mackain Limited was formed on December 1, 2001. The following information is available from Mackain's inventory records for Product BAP:

	Units	Unit Cost
January 1, 2002 (beginning inventory)	600	$ 8.00
Purchases:		
January 5, 2002	1,200	9.00
January 25, 2002	1,300	10.00
February 16, 2002	800	11.00
March 26, 2002	600	12.00

A physical inventory on March 31, 2002, shows 1,600 units on hand. Mackain uses a periodic inventory system.

Instructions
Prepare schedules to calculate the ending inventory at March 31, 2002, under each of the following inventory methods:
(a) FIFO (b) LIFO   (c) Weighted average

E8-18 **(Calculate FIFO, LIFO, Average Cost—Periodic)** Presented below is information related to the inventory of mini radios for Cleartone Company Limited for the month of July:

Date		Units Transaction	Unit In	Cost	Units Total	Selling Sold	Price	Total
July	1	Balance	100	$4.10	$ 410			
	6	Purchase	800	4.20	3,360			
	7	Sale				300	$7.00	$ 2,100
	10	Sale				300	$7.30	2,190
	12	Purchase	400	4.50	1,800			
	15	Sale				200	7.40	1,480
	18	Purchase	300	4.60	1,380			
	22	Sale				400	7.40	2,960
	25	Purchase	500	4.58	2,290			
	30	Sale				200	7.50	1,500
		Totals	2,100		$9,240	1,400		$10,230

Instructions

(a) Assuming that the periodic inventory method is used, calculate the inventory cost at July 31 under each of the following cost flow assumptions:
1. FIFO.
2. LIFO.
3. Weighted-average (Round the weighted-average unit cost to the nearest one-tenth of one cent.)

(b) Answer the following questions:
1. Which of the methods used above will yield the lowest figure for gross profit for the income statement? Explain why.
2. Which of the methods used above will yield the lowest figure for ending inventory for the balance sheet? Explain why.

E8-19 **(FIFO and LIFO—Periodic and Perpetual)** The following is a record of Ellison Corp.'s transactions for ceramic plates for the month of May 2002:

May 1 Balance 400 units @ $20	May 10 Sale 300 units @ $38
12 Purchase 600 units @ $25	20 Sale 540 units @ $38
28 Purchase 400 units @ $30	

Instructions

(a) Assuming that perpetual inventories are not maintained and that a physical count at the end of the month shows 560 units on hand, what is the cost of the ending inventory using (1) FIFO and (2) LIFO?

(b) Assuming that perpetual records are maintained and they tie into the general ledger, calculate the ending inventory using (1) FIFO and (2) LIFO.

E8-20 **(FIFO and LIFO; Income Statement Presentation)** The board of directors of Sanders Limited is considering whether or not it should instruct the accounting department to shift from a first-in, first-out (FIFO) basis of costing inventories to a last-in, first-out (LIFO) basis. The following information is available.

Sales	21,000 units @ $50
Inventory, January 1	6,000 units @ $20
Purchases	6,000 units @ $22
	10,000 units @ $25
	7,000 units @ $30
Inventory, December 31	8,000 units @ ?
Operating expenses	$200,000

Instructions

Prepare a condensed income statement for the year on both bases for comparative purposes, assuming Sanders uses a periodic inventory system.

E8-21 **(FIFO and LIFO Effects)** You are the vice-president of finance of Alomar Corporation, a retail company that prepared two different schedules of gross margin for the first quarter ended March 31, 2003. These schedules appear below.

	Sales ($5 per unit)	Cost of Goods Sold	Gross Margin
Schedule 1	$150,000	$124,900	$25,100
Schedule 2	150,000	129,400	20,600

The calculation of cost of goods sold in each schedule is based on the following data:

	Units	Cost per Unit	Total Cost
Beginning inventory, January 1	10,000	$4.00	$40,000
Purchase, January 10	8,000	4.20	33,600
Purchase, January 30	6,000	4.25	25,500
Purchase, February 11	9,000	4.30	38,700
Purchase, March 17	11,000	4.40	48,400

Jane Torville, the corporation president, cannot understand how two different gross margins can be calculated from the same data set. As the vice-president of finance you have explained to Ms. Torville that the two schedules are based on different assumptions concerning the flow of inventory costs, i.e., first-in, first-out; and last-in, first-out. Schedules 1 and 2 were not necessarily prepared in this sequence of cost flow assumptions.

Instructions

Prepare two separate schedules calculating cost of goods sold and supporting schedules showing the composition of the ending inventory under both cost flow assumptions.

E8-22 **(FIFO, LIFO, weighted average—Periodic)** Long Limited began operations on January 2, 2002. The following stock record card for footballs was taken from the records at the year-end.

Date	Voucher	Terms	Units Received	Unit Invoice Cost	Gross Invoice Amount
1/15	10624	Net 30	50	$20.00	$1,000.00
3/15	11437	1/5, net 30	65	16.00	1,040.00
6/20	21332	1/10, net 30	90	15.00	1,350.00
9/12	27644	1/10, net 30	84	12.00	1,008.00
11/24	31269	1/10, net 30	76	11.00	836.00
	Totals		365		$5,234.00

A physical inventory on December 31, 2002 reveals that 100 footballs were in stock. The bookkeeper informs you that all the discounts were taken. Assume that Long Limited uses a periodic inventory system, and the invoice price less discount for recording purchases.

Instructions
(a) Calculate the December 31, 2002 inventory using the FIFO method.
(b) Calculate the 2002 cost of goods sold using the LIFO method.
(c) Calculate the December 31, 2002 inventory using the weighted-average cost method (round unit cost to nearest cent).
(d) What method would you recommend to minimize income taxes in 2002, using the inventory information for footballs as a guide?

E8-23 **(Alternative Inventory Methods)** Amos Corporation began operations on December 1, 2002. The only inventory transaction in 2002 was the purchase of inventory on December 10, 2002, at a cost of $20 per unit. None of this inventory was sold in 2002. Relevant information is as follows:

Ending inventory units		
December 31, 2002		100
December 31, 2003, by purchase date		
December 2, 2003	100	
July 20, 2003	50	150

During 2003 the following purchases and sales were made:

Purchases		Sales	
March 15	300 units at $24	April 10	200
July 20	300 units at $25	August 20	300
September 4	200 units at $28	November 18	150
December 2	100 units at $30	December 12	200

The company uses the periodic inventory method.

Instructions

Determine ending inventory under (1) specific identification, (2) FIFO, (3) LIFO periodic, and (4) average cost.

PROBLEMS

P8-1 The following independent situations relate to inventory accounting.

1. Jag Co. purchased goods with a list price of $150,000, subject to trade discounts of 20% and 10%, with no cash discounts allowable. How much should Jag Co. record as the cost of these goods?

2. Francis Company's inventory of $1,100,000 at December 31, 2002 was based on a physical count of goods priced at cost and before any year-end adjustments relating to the following items:
   (a) Goods shipped f.o.b. shipping point on December 24, 2002 from a vendor at an invoice cost of $69,000 to Francis Company were received on January 4, 2003.
   (b) The physical count included $29,000 of goods billed to Sakic Corp. f.o.b. shipping point on December 31, 2002. The carrier picked up these goods on January 3, 2003.
   What amount should Francis report as inventory on its balance sheet?

3. Messier Corp. had 1,500 units of part M.O. on hand May 1, 2002, costing $21 each. Purchases of part M.O. during May were as follows:

	Units	Unit Cost
May 9	2,000	$22.00
17	3,500	23.00
26	1,000	24.00

   A physical count on May 31, 2002 shows 2,100 units of part M.O. on hand. Using the FIFO method, what is the cost of part M.O. inventory at May 31, 2002? Using the LIFO method, what is the inventory cost? Using the average cost method, what is the inventory cost?

4. Lindros Ltd., a retail store chain, had the following information in its general ledger for the year 2002:

Merchandise purchased for resale	$909,400
Interest on notes payable to vendors	8,700
Purchase returns	16,500
Freight-in	22,000
Freight-out	17,100
Cash discounts on purchases	6,800

   What is Lindros' inventoriable cost for 2002?

Instructions

Answer each of the questions above about inventories and explain your answers.

P8-2 Kirk Limited, a manufacturer of small tools, provided the following information from its accounting records for the year ended December 31, 2002:

Inventory at December 31, 2002 (based on physical count of goods in Kirk's plant, at cost, on December 31, 2002)	$1,520,000
Accounts payable at December 31, 2002	1,200,000
Net sales (sales less sales returns)	8,150,000

Additional information is as follows:

1. Included in the physical count were tools billed to a customer f.o.b. shipping point on December 31, 2002. These tools had a cost of $31,000 and were billed at $40,000. The shipment was on Kirk's loading dock waiting to be picked up by the common carrier.

2. Goods were in transit from a vendor to Kirk on December 31, 2002. The invoice cost was $71,000, and the goods were shipped f.o.b. shipping point on December 29, 2002.

3. Work-in-process inventory costing $30,000 was sent to an outside processor for plating on December 30, 2002.

4. Tools returned by customers and held pending inspection in the returned goods area on December 31, 2002, were not included in the physical count. On January 8, 2003, tools costing $32,000 were inspected and returned to inventory. Credit memos totalling $47,000 were issued to the customers on the same date.

5. Tools shipped to a customer f.o.b. destination on December 26, 2002, were in transit at December 31, 2002, and had a cost of $21,000. Upon notification of receipt by the customer on January 2, 2003, Kirk issued a sales invoice for $42,000.

6. Goods, with an invoice cost of $27,000, received from a vendor at 5:00 p.m. on December 31, 2002 were recorded on a receiving report dated January 2, 2003. The goods were not included in the physical count, but the invoice was included in accounts payable at December 31, 2002.

7. Goods received from a vendor on December 26, 2002 were included in the physical count. However, the related $56,000 vendor invoice was not included in accounts payable at December 31, 2002, because the accounts payable copy of the receiving report was lost.

8. On January 3, 2003, a monthly freight bill in the amount of $6,000 was received. The bill specifically related to merchandise purchased in December 2002, one-half of which was still in the inventory at December 31, 2002. The freight charges were not included in either the inventory or in accounts payable at December 31, 2002.

Instructions

Using the format shown below, prepare a schedule of adjustments as of December 31, 2002, to the initial amounts per Kirk's accounting records. Show separately the effect, if any, of each of the eight transactions on the December 31, 2002, amounts. If the transactions would have no effect on the initial amount shown, enter NONE.

	Inventory	Accounts Payable	Net Sales
Initial amounts	$1,520,000	$1,200,000	$8,150,000
Adjustments – increase (decrease)			
1			
2			
3			
4			
5			
6			
7			
8			
Total adjustments			
Adjusted amounts	$	$	$

(AICPA adapted)

P8-3 Some of the transactions of Dubois Corp. during August are listed below. Dubois uses the periodic inventory method.

August 10	Purchased merchandise on account, $9,000, terms 2/10, n/30.
13	Returned part of the purchase of August 10, $1,200, and received credit on account.
15	Purchased merchandise on account, $12,000, terms 1/10, n/60.
25	Purchased merchandise on account, $15,000, terms 2/10, n/30.
28	Paid invoice of August 15 in full.

Instructions

(a) Assuming that purchases are recorded at gross amounts and that discounts are to be recorded when taken:
1. Prepare general journal entries to record the transactions.
2. Describe how the various items would be shown in the financial statements.

(b) Assuming that purchases are recorded at net amounts and that discounts lost are treated as financial expenses:
1. Prepare general journal entries to enter the transactions.
2. Prepare the adjusting entry necessary on August 31 if financial statements are to be prepared at that time.
3. Describe how the various items would be shown in the financial statements.

(c) Which of the two methods do you prefer and why?

P8-4 Taos Company's record of transactions concerning part X for the month of April was as follows:

Purchases				Sales	
April 1	(balance on hand)	100 @	$5.00	April 5	300
4		400 @	5.10	12	200
11		300 @	5.30	27	800
18		200 @	5.35	28	100
26		500 @	5.60		
30		200 @	5.80		

Instructions

(a) Calculate the inventory at April 30 on each of the following bases. Assume that perpetual inventory records are kept in units only. Carry unit costs to the nearest cent.

1. First-in, first-out (FIFO)
2. Last-in, first-out (LIFO)
3. Average cost

(b) If the perpetual inventory record is kept in dollars, and costs are calculated at the time of each withdrawal, what amount would be shown as ending inventory in 1, 2, and 3 above? Carry average unit costs to four decimal places.

P8-5 Some of the information found on a detail inventory card for Leif Letter Ltd. for the first month of operations is as follows:

Date	Received No. of Units	Received Unit Cost	Issued, No. of Units	Balance, No. of Units
January 2	1,200	$3.00		1,200
7			700	500
10	600	3.20		1,100
13			500	600
18	1,000	3.30	300	1,300
20			1,100	200
23	1,300	3.40		1,500
26			800	700
28	1,500	3.60		2,200
31			1,300	900

Instructions

(a) From these data, calculate the ending inventory on each of the following bases. Assume that perpetual inventory records are kept in units only. Carry unit costs to the nearest cent and ending inventory to the nearest dollar.

1. First-in, first-out (FIFO)
2. Last-in, first-out (LIFO)
3. Average cost

(b) If the perpetual inventory record is kept in dollars, and costs are calculated at the time of each withdrawal, would the amounts shown as ending inventory in 1, 2, and 3 above be the same? Explain. Recalculate under this revised assumption, carrying average unit costs to four decimal places.

P8-6 B.C. Corporation is a multi-product firm. Presented below is information concerning one of its products, the Hawkeye:

Date	Transaction	Quantity	Price/Cost
1/1	Beginning inventory	1,000	$12
2/4	Purchase	2,000	18
2/20	Sale	2,500	30
4/2	Purchase	3,000	23
11/4	Sale	2,000	33

Instructions

Calculate cost of goods sold, assuming B.C. uses:

(a) Periodic system, FIFO cost flow
(b) Perpetual system, FIFO cost flow
(c) Periodic system, LIFO cost flow
(d) Perpetual system, LIFO cost flow
(e) Periodic system, weighted-average cost flow
(f) Perpetual system, moving-average cost flow

P8-7 The management of Manitoba Ltd. has asked its accounting department to describe the effect on the company's financial position and its income statements of accounting for inventories on the LIFO rather than the FIFO basis during 2002 and 2003. The accounting department is to assume that the change to LIFO would have been effective on January 1, 2002, and that the initial LIFO base would have been the inventory value on December 31, 2001. Presented below are the company's financial statements and other data for the years 2002 and 2003 when the FIFO method was employed.

	Financial Position as of		
	12/31/01	12/31/02	12/31/03
Cash	$ 90,000	$130,000	$141,600
Accounts receivable	80,000	100,000	120,000
Inventory	120,000	140,000	180,000
Other assets	160,000	170,000	200,000
Total assets	$450,000	$540,000	$641,600
Accounts payable	$ 40,000	$ 60,000	$ 80,000
Other liabilities	70,000	80,000	110,000
Common shares	200,000	200,000	200,000
Retained earnings	140,000	200,000	251,600
Total equities	$450,000	$540,000	$641,600

	Income for Years Ended	
	12/31/02	12/31/03
Sales	$900,000	$1,350,000
Less: Cost of goods sold	505,000	770,000
Other expenses	205,000	304,000
	710,000	1,074,000
Net income before income taxes	190,000	276,000
Income taxes (40%)	76,000	110,400
Net income	$114,000	$ 165,600

Other data:

1. Inventory on hand at 12/31/01 consisted of 40,000 units valued at $3.00 each.
2. Sales (all units sold at the same price in a given year):

   2002—150,000 units @ $6.00 each   2003—180,000 units @ $7.50 each

3. Purchases (all units purchased at the same price in given year):

   2002—150,000 units @ $3.50 each   2003—180,000 units @ $4.50 each

4. Income taxes at the effective rate of 40% are paid on December 31 each year.

Instructions

Name the account(s) presented in the financial statements that would have different amounts for 2003 if LIFO rather than FIFO had been used, and state the new amount for each account that is named. Show calculations. Assume both FIFO and LIFO are accepted for income tax purposes.   (CMA adapted)

P8-8   Yama Ltd. sells two products: figure skates and speed skates. At December 31, 2002, Yama used the first-in, first-out (FIFO) inventory method. Effective January 1, 2003, Yama changed to the last-in, first-out (LIFO) inventory method. The cumulative effect of this change is not determinable and, as a result, the ending inventory of 2002 for which the FIFO method was used is also the beginning inventory for 2003 for the LIFO method.

The following information was available from Yama's inventory records for the two most recent years:

	Figure Skates		Speed Skates	
	Units	Unit Cost	Units	Unit Cost
2002 purchases				
January 7	7,000	$40.00	22,000	$20.00
April 16	12,000	45.00		
November 8	17,000	54.00	18,500	34.00
December 13	9,000	62.00		
2003 purchases				
February 11	3,000	66.00	23,000	36.00
May 20	8,000	75.00		
October 15	20,000	81.00		
December 23			15,500	42.00
Units on hand				
December 31, 2002	15,100		15,000	
December 31, 2003	18,000		13,200	

Instructions

Calculate the effect on income before income taxes for the year ended December 31, 2003, resulting from the change from the FIFO to the LIFO inventory method.

(AICPA adapted)

P8-9 Zeda Limited is a wholesale distributor of automotive replacement parts. Initial amounts taken from Zeda's accounting records are as follows:

Inventory at December 31, 2002 (based on physical count of goods in Zeda's warehouse, Dec. 31/02)		$1,520,000

Accounts payable at December 31, 2002:

Vendor	Terms	Amount
Sonny Company Ltd.	2/10, n30	$ 260,000
Avalon Corporation	Net 30	190,000
Bottler Company	Net 30	405,000
Mindle Enterprises	Net 30	20,000
Boot Products	Net 30	—
Cameo Company	Net 30	—
		$ 875,000

Sales in 2002	$9,650,000

Additional information is as follows:

1. Parts received on consignment from Avalon Corporation by Zeda, the consignee, amounting to $150,000 were included in the physical count of goods in Zeda's warehouse on December 31, 2002 and in accounts payable at December 31, 2002.

2. In early January 2003, it was discovered that an invoice from Bottler covering purchases of $17,000 in early December 2002 had been entered twice in the accounting records.

3. Parts costing $20,000 were purchased from Boot and paid for in December, 2002. These parts were sold in the last week of 2002 and appropriately recorded as sales of $38,000. The parts were included in the physical count of goods in the warehouse on December 31, 2002 because the parts were on the loading dock waiting to be picked up by customers who had been informed the parts were ready and had stated they would pick them up as soon as possible.

4. On January 7, 2003, a credit memo for $4,200 was received from Voltz Company, a regular supplier to Zeda for products purchased earlier in 2002. Because Zeda's purchases had exceeded an established minimum in 2002, Voltz issued Zeda the credit memo that allows Zeda to deduct $4,200 from its 2003 purchases from the company. Approximately 10% of the purchases from Voltz remain in Zeda's year-end inventory.

5. Parts in transit to customers on December 31, 2002, shipped f.o.b. shipping point on December 28, 2002, amounted to $43,000. The customers received the parts on January 6, 2003. Invoices for $65,000, including sales taxes of $8,500, were sent to the customers for the parts and were recorded by Zeda on January 2, 2003.

6. Early in January 2003, it was discovered that an invoice had not been sent to one of Zeda's regular customers for a rush order shipped just before the Christmas break. An invoice in the amount of $14,000, including sales taxes of $1,800, was sent immediately.

7. Retailers were holding $233,000 of goods at cost ($310,000 at retail) on consignment from Zeda, the consignor, at their retail stores on December 31, 2002.

8. Goods were in transit from Cameo to Zeda on December 31, 2002. The goods cost $36,000 and were shipped f.o.b. shipping point on December 29.

9. A quarterly freight bill for $4,700 relating specifically to merchandise purchased in December 2002, all of which was still in inventory at December 31, 2002, was received on January 3, 2003. The freight bill was not included in the inventory or accounts payable at December 31, 2002.

10. All of the purchases from Sonny occurred during the last seven days of the year. These items have been recorded in accounts payable and accounted for in the physical inventory at cost before discount. Zeda's policy is to pay invoices in time to take advantage of all cash discounts, adjust inventory accordingly, and record accounts payable, net of cash discounts.

Instructions

Set up a schedule with the amount of Inventory, Accounts Payable, and Sales as reported in the general ledger of Zeda at December 31, 2002 across the top of the page. Analyse each of the 10 situations above. Show the effect, if any, of each situation described, on each of the three general ledger accounts. If the item has no effect on the amount shown, state "N/A" or "no effect." Complete the schedule by determining the correct balance of each of the three accounts.

P8-10 The summary financial statements of DeliMart Ltd. on December 31, 2002 are presented below:

DeliMart Ltd.
Balance Sheet, Dec. 31, 2002

Assets

Cash	$ 2,000
Accounts and notes receivable	36,000
Inventory	60,000
Capital assets (net)	100,000
	$198,000

Liabilities and Shareholders' Equity

Accounts and notes payable	$ 50,000
Long-term debt	50,000
Common shares	50,000
Retained earnings	48,000
	$198,000

The following errors were made by the inexperienced accountant on December 31, 2001 and were not corrected: the inventory was overstated by $15,000, prepaid expense of $2,400 was omitted (was fully expensed in 2001), accrued revenue of $2,500 was omitted (recognized when cash was received in 2002) and a supplier's invoice for $1,700 relating to 2001 purchases was not recorded until 2002. On December 31, 2002, the inventory was understated by $18,000, prepaid expense of $800 was omitted, accrued December 2002 salaries of $1,100 were not recognized, and unearned income of $2,300 was recorded in 2002 revenue. In addition, it was determined that $20,000 of the accounts payable were long-term, and that a $500 dividend was reported as dividend expense and deducted in calculating net income.

The net income reported on the books for 2002 was $55,000.

Instructions
(a) Calculate the working capital, current ratio, and the debt-to-equity ratio for DeliMart Ltd. based on the original balance sheet information provided above.
(b) Calculate the corrected net income for 2002.
(c) Prepare a corrected balance sheet at December 31, 2002.
(d) Re-calculate the ratios identified in part (a). Comment.

P8-11 Count Controllers Corporation (CCC) was incorporated early in January 2002 to manufacture electronic control devices to monitor traffic, of automobiles or people, past specific locations. CCC built a small manufacturing plant and office building in a new industrial park and was in operation by mid-March. General ledger accounts at December 31, 2002 indicated the following:

Sales salaries and expenses	$ 75,000
Supervisory salaries, production	65,000
Executive salaries	100,000
Raw material purchases	123,500
Miscellaneous plant supplies	12,400
Amortization, plant building	26,000
Amortization, office building	8,000
Amortization, plant equipment	10,000
Property taxes on real property (1/5 office building, 4/5 plant building)	6,600
Sales	427,000
Direct labour	62,000
Maintenance labour	27,500
Raw material inventory, December 31, 2002	14,600
Utilities expense (1/10 related to the office)	22,000
General administration expenses	38,800

At December 31, 2002 there was no work in process, but 20% of the units manufactured remained in ending finished goods inventory.

Instructions

(a) Prepare an income statement as far as "income from operations" for CCC for the year ended December 31, 2002, assuming the decision is made to adopt variable costing.

(b) Prepare an income statement as far as "income from operations" for CCC, assuming absorption costing is preferred.

(c) Make a recommendation to the company president on which method CCC should choose, supported with your rationale.

P8-12 John Potter established Dilemma C. as a sole proprietorship on January 5, 2002. The accounts on December 31, 2002, the company's year-end, had balances as follows. The balances are in thousands.

Current assets, excluding inventory		$ 10
Other assets		107
Current liabilities		30
Long-term bank loan		50
Owner's investment (excluding income)		40
Purchases during year		
January 2:	5,000 @ $11	
June 30:	8,000 @ $12	
December 10:	6,000 @ $16	247
Sales		284
Other expenses		40

A count of ending inventory on December 31, 2002 showed there were 4,000 units on hand.

Potter is now preparing financial statements for the year. He is aware that inventory may be costed using the FIFO, LIFO, or weighted-average method. He is unsure of which one to use and requests your assistance. In discussions with Potter, you learn the following.

1. Suppliers to Dilemma provide goods at regular prices as long as the current ratio is at least 2 to 1. If this ratio is lower, the suppliers increase the price charged by 10% in order to compensate for what they consider to be a substantial credit risk.
2. The long-term bank loan terms are that the bank can put Dilemma Co. into a state of bankruptcy if the debt-to-total-asset ratio exceeds 45%.
3. Potter thinks that, for the company to be a success, the rate of return on total assets should be at least 30%.
4. Potter has an agreement with the company's only employee that, for each full percentage point above a 25% rate of return on total assets, she will be given an additional one day off with pay in the following year.

Instructions

(a) Prepare an income statement and a year-end balance sheet assuming the company applies:
   1. the FIFO method
   2. the weighted-average method
   3. the LIFO method
(b) Identify the advantages of each method in (a).
(c) Identify the disadvantages of each method in (a).
(d) What is your recommendation? Explain briefly.

CONCEPTUAL CASES

C8-1 You are asked to travel to Lethbridge to observe and verify the inventory of a client's Lethbridge branch. You arrive on Thursday, December 30, and find that the inventory procedures have just been started. You spot a railway car on the sidetrack at the unloading door and ask the warehouse superintendent Predrag Danilovic how he plans to inventory the car contents. He responds: "We are not going to include the contents in the inventory."

Later in the day, you ask the bookkeeper for the invoice on the carload and the related freight bill. The invoice lists the various items, prices, and extensions of the goods in the car. You note that the carload was shipped December 24 from Windsor, f.o.b. Windsor, and that the total invoice price of the car's goods was $35,300. The freight bill called for a payment of $1,500. Terms were net 30 days. The bookkeeper affirms the fact that this invoice is to be held for recording in January.

Instructions

   (a) Does your client have a liability that should be recorded at December 31? Discuss.

   (b) Prepare a journal entry(ies), if required, to reflect any accounting adjustment required. Assume a perpetual inventory system is used by your client.

   (c) For what possible reason(s) might your client wish to postpone recording the transaction?

C8-2 Alonzo Spellman, an inventory control specialist, is interested in better understanding the accounting for inventories. Although Alonzo understands the more sophisticated computer inventory control systems, he has little knowledge of how inventory cost is determined. In studying the records of Ditka Enterprises Ltd., which sells normal brand-name goods from its own store and on consignment through Wannstedt Inc., he asks you to answer the following questions.

Instructions

   (a) Should Ditka Enterprises include in its inventory normal brand-name goods purchased from its suppliers but not yet received if the terms of purchase are f.o.b. shipping point (manufacturer's plant)? Why?

   (b) Should Ditka Enterprises include freight-in expenditures as an inventory cost? Why?

   (c) If Ditka Enterprises purchases its goods on terms 2/10, net 30, should the purchases be recorded gross or net? Why?

   (d) What are products on consignment? How should they be reported in the financial statements?

(AICPA adapted)

C8-3 Jack McDowell, the controller for McDowell Lumber Corporation, has recently hired you as assistant controller. He wishes to determine your expertise in the area of inventory accounting and therefore asks you to answer the following unrelated questions:

   (a) A company is involved in the wholesaling and retailing of automobile tires for foreign cars. Most of the inventory is imported, and it is valued on the company's records at the actual inventory cost plus freight-in. At year end, the warehousing costs are prorated over cost of goods sold and ending inventory. Are warehousing costs considered a product cost or a period cost?

   (b) A certain portion of a company's "inventory" is composed of obsolete items. Should obsolete items that are not currently consumed in the production of "goods or services to be available for sale" be classified as part of inventory?

   (c) A company purchases airplanes for sale to others. However, until they are sold, the company charters and services the planes. What is the proper way to report these airplanes in the company's financial statements?

   (d) A company wants to buy coal deposits but does not want the financing for the purchase to be reported on its financial statements. The company therefore establishes a trust to acquire the coal deposits. The company agrees to buy the coal over a certain period of time at specified prices. The trust is able to finance the coal purchase and pay off the loan as it is paid by the company for the minerals. How should this transaction be reported?

C8-4 Gretzky Corp., a household appliances dealer, purchases its inventories from various suppliers. Gretzky has consistently stated its inventories at the lower of cost (FIFO) or market.

Instructions

Gretzky is considering alternate methods of accounting for the cash discounts it takes when paying its suppliers promptly. From a theoretical standpoint, discuss the acceptability of each of the following methods:

   (a) Financial income when payments are made

   (b) Reduction of cost of goods sold for period when payments are made

   (c) Direct reduction of purchase cost

(AICPA adapted)

C8-5 In January 2002, Wesley Crusher Inc. requested and secured permission from the Canada Customs and Revenue Agency to calculate inventories under the last-in, first-out (LIFO) method.

Instructions

   (a) Why should inventories be included in (1) a balance sheet and (2) the calculation of net income?

   (b) The Income Tax Act and Regulations allow some accountable events to be considered differently for income tax reporting purposes and financial accounting purposes, while other accountable events must be reported the same for both purposes. Discuss why it might be desirable to report some accountable events differently for financial accounting purposes than for income tax reporting purposes.

(c) Discuss the ways and conditions under which the FIFO and LIFO inventory costing methods produce different inventory valuations. Do not discuss procedures for calculating inventory cost.

C8-6 Akihito Ltd. is a manufacturing business with relatively heavy fixed costs and large inventories of finished goods. These inventories constitute a very material item on the balance sheet. The company has a departmental cost accounting system that assigns all manufacturing costs to the product each period.

Edward Gierek, company controller, has informed you that management is seriously considering adopting variable (direct) costing as a method of accounting for plant operations and inventory valuation. Management wants your opinion of the effect, if any, that such a change would have on: (1) the year-end financial position, and (2) the net income for the year.

Instructions

Draft a reply to the request and the reasons for your conclusions.

(AICPA adapted)

C8-7 Jeanne Honore, president of Fragonard Corp., a Manitoba company, recently read an article that claimed that at least 100 of the largest 500 companies in the United States were either adopting or considering adopting the last-in, first-out (LIFO) method for valuing inventories. The article stated that the firms were switching to LIFO to (1) neutralize the effect of inflation in their financial statements, (2) eliminate inventory profits, and (3) reduce income taxes. Ms. Honore wonders if the switch would benefit her company.

Fragonard currently uses the first-in, first-out (FIFO) method of inventory valuation in its periodic inventory system. The company has a high inventory turnover rate, and inventories represent a significant proportion of the assets.

Ms. Honore has been told that the LIFO system is more costly to operate and will provide little benefit to companies with high turnover. She intends to use the inventory method that is best for the company in the long run rather than selecting a method just because it is the current fad.

Instructions

Write a report to Ms. Honore on the issues she has raised. Ensure you explain how LIFO would neutralize the effects of inflation and what exactly "inventory profits" are.

C8-8 Prepare a memorandum containing responses to the following items.
   (a) Describe the cost flow assumptions used in average cost, FIFO, and LIFO methods of inventory valuation.
   (b) Distinguish between simple average cost, weighted average cost and moving average cost for inventory costing purposes.
   (c) Identify the effects on both the balance sheet and the income statement of using the LIFO method instead of the FIFO method for inventory costing purposes over a substantial time period when purchase prices of inventoriable items are rising. State why these effects take place.

C8-9 The Neshki Corporation is a medium-sized manufacturing company with two divisions and three subsidiaries, all located in southern Ontario. The Metallic Division manufactures metal castings for the automotive industry, and the Plastic Division produces small plastic items for electrical products and other uses. The three subsidiaries manufacture various products for other industrial users.

Neshki's chief financial officer is considering a change in the cost flow method it is now using for assigning costs to inventory and cost of goods sold. The company now uses a weighted average cost method.

Instructions

Prepare a report for the chief financial officer that he will find useful. Lay out the alternatives available, and suggest a process for him to use in coming to a decision.

C8-10 Grass Corp. is considering changing its inventory valuation method from FIFO to weighted average because of the potential tax savings. However, management wishes to consider all of the effects on the company, including its reported performance, before making the final decision.

The inventory account, currently valued on the FIFO basis, consists of 1 million units at $7 per unit on January 1, 2002. There are 1 million common shares outstanding as of January 1, 2002, and the cash balance is $400,000.

The company has made the following forecasts for the period 2002–2004.

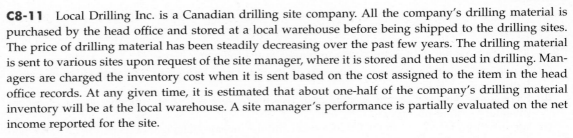

	2002	2003	2004
Unit sales (in millions of units)	1.1	1.0	1.3
Sales price per unit	$10	$10	$12
Unit purchases (in millions of units)	1.0	1.1	1.2
Purchase price per unit	$7	$8	$9
Annual amortization (in thousands of dollars)	$300	$300	$300
Cash dividends per share	.15/sh	.15/sh	.15/sh
Cash payments for additions to and replacement of plant and equipment (in thousands of dollars)	$350	$350	$350
Income tax rate	40%	40%	40%
Operating expense (exclusive of amortization) as a percent of sales	15%	15%	15%
Common shares outstanding (in millions)	1	1	1

Instructions

(a) Prepare a schedule that illustrates and compares the following data for Grass Corp. under the FIFO and the weighted average inventory method for 2002–2004. Assume the company would begin the weighted average method at the beginning of 2002.

1. Year-end inventory balances
2. Annual net income
3. Earnings per share
4. Cash balance

Assume all sales are collected in the year of sale and all purchases, operating expenses, and taxes are paid during the year incurred.

(b) Using the data above, your answer to (a), and any additional issues you believe need to be considered, prepare a report that recommends whether or not Grass Corp. should change from the FIFO inventory method. Support your conclusions with appropriate arguments.

(CMA adapted)

C8-11 Local Drilling Inc. is a Canadian drilling site company. All the company's drilling material is purchased by the head office and stored at a local warehouse before being shipped to the drilling sites. The price of drilling material has been steadily decreasing over the past few years. The drilling material is sent to various sites upon request of the site manager, where it is stored and then used in drilling. Managers are charged the inventory cost when it is sent based on the cost assigned to the item in the head office records. At any given time, it is estimated that about one-half of the company's drilling material inventory will be at the local warehouse. A site manager's performance is partially evaluated on the net income reported for the site.

Instructions

Given the options of choosing the FIFO, moving-average, or LIFO inventory costing methods and use of a perpetual inventory system:

(a) Which costing method would you, as a site manager, want to be used? Why?
(b) As a site manager, what might you do regarding the requesting of inventory if FIFO were used? Why, and what might the implications be for the company as a whole?
(c) As the decision-maker at head office, which method would you recommend if you wanted the results to be "fair" for all site managers? Why?
(d) Which method would you recommend for determining the company's taxable income? Why?
(e) Which method would you recommend for financial statement purposes? Why?

Using Your Judgement

FINANCIAL STATEMENT ANALYSIS CASES

Case 1   Weyerhaeuser Company

Weyerhaeuser Company, based in Seattle, Washington, is one of the world's largest integrated forest product companies with offices or operations in 13 countries. It is engaged primarily in the growing and harvesting of timber, and the manufacture, distribution, and sale of forest products, among other activities. Weyerhaeuser Company Limited, an indirect wholly owned Canadian subsidiary with Exchangeable Shares listed on the Toronto Stock Exchange, acquired the operations of MacMillan Bloedel Limited in 1999.

Excerpts from Weyerhaeuser Company financial statements for its year ending December 26, 1999 are reproduced below.

CONSOLIDATED BALANCE SHEET
Dollar amounts in millions

	December 26, 1999	December 27, 1998
ASSETS		
Weyerhaeuser		
Current assets:		
Cash and short-term investments (Note 1)	$ 1,640	$ 28
Receivables, less allowances of $10 and $5	1,296	886
Inventories (Note 7)	1,329	962
Prepaid expenses	278	294
Total current assets	4,543	2,170

NOTES TO FINANCIAL STATEMENTS
NOTE 1, SUMMARY OF SIGNIFICANT ACCOUNTING POLICIES

INVENTORIES
NOTE 7, INVENTORIES

Inventories are stated at the lower of cost or market. Cost includes labor, materials and production overhead. The last-in, first-out (LIFO) method is used to cost approximately half of domestic raw materials, in process and finished goods inventories. LIFO inventories were $358 million and $253 million at December 26, 1999, and December 27, 1998, respectively. The balance of domestic raw material and product inventories, all materials and supplies inventories, and all foreign inventories is costed at either the first-in, first-out (FIFO) or moving average cost methods. Had the FIFO method been used to cost all inventories, the amounts at which product inventories are stated would have been $227 million and $228 million greater at December 26, 1999, and December 27, 1998, respectively.

Dollar amounts in millions	December 26, 1999	December 27, 1998
Logs and chips	$ 197	$ 108
Lumber, plywood and panels	297	143
Pulp and paper	161	190
Containerboard, paperboard and packaging	160	96
Other products	207	150
Materials and supplies	307	275
	$ 1,329	$ 962

Weyerhaeuser Company reported 1999 net earnings of $527 million and reported an effective rate of tax of approximately 36.5%.

Instructions

(a) How much would income before taxes have been if FIFO costing had been used to value all inventories?

(b) What would income tax have been if FIFO costing had been used to value all inventories? In your opinion, is this difference in net income between the two methods material? Explain.

(c) Does the use of a different costing system for different types of inventory mean that there is a different physical flow of goods among the different types of inventory? Explain.

(d) Why do you think Weyerhaeuser Company uses three different inventory cost flow methods in preparing its financial reports?

Case 2   Biotech Holdings Ltd.

According to its corporate website, "**Biotech Holdings Ltd.** is a Vancouver-based integrated pharmaceutical company engaged in research, development, manufacture and marketing of pharmaceutical, personal care and health products. The focus of the Company is the manufacturing and international marketing of Diab II™, a new drug for the treatment of Type II Diabetes."

Biotech, through a subsidiary in China, has developed and has the rights to market Diab II in China and in a number of Asian countries. In addition, the company has the rights to participate as a 50% partner in the manufacture and marketing of this drug in all non-Asian countries. Biotech has licensees in Brazil, Argentina, Chile, Peru, and Venezuela, with discussions in progress in other Western Hemisphere, European, and Middle East countries.

Through its Biotech Laboratories division, it develops new products and trademarks for products such as sunscreen and other personal care items.

Selected accounts and information from Biotech's financial statements are listed below:

From the balance sheet:	
Inventory – Raw materials	$643,813
– Finished goods	120,462
Capital assets, net book value	3,341,425
Formulations and deferred costs, net book value	1,110,067
From the income statement:	
Sales	$1,273,169
Gross profit	290,851
Amortization expense	1,174,640
Drug research costs, including clinical trials, quality control and testing, and consulting	104,477
General and administrative, interest, professional fees, and rent, utilities, and maintenance	2,279,282
Non-controlling interest share of loss	31,875
Net loss for the year	3,235,673
From the notes to the financial statements:	
Inventory is valued at the lower of FIFO cost and market.	
Capital assets, at net book value	
– Laboratory and production equipment	$835,441
– Production molds	65,788
– Leasehold improvements	811,814
– Patent interests	1,468,219
– Other	160,163
Formulations and deferred costs, at net book value	
– Deferred development costs	$796,553
– Formulations and trademarks	205,602
– Other	107,912

Instructions

(a) What would you expect the physical flow of goods for a pharmaceutical manufacturer to be most like: FIFO, LIFO, or random (flow of goods does not follow a set pattern)? Explain.

(b) What are some factors that Biotech should consider as it selects an inventory measurement method?

(c) What issues are there in determining the cost of developing and manufacturing inventories for biotechnology or pharmaceutical companies? Discuss the type of costs incurred and those that should be treated as product as distinct from period costs.

Case 3 Canadian Tire Corporation Limited

Refer to the financial statements and other documents of Canadian Tire Corporation Limited presented in Appendix 5B. Note that the company provides a 10-year financial review at the end of its Annual Report. This summary provides relevant comparative information useful for determining trends and predicting future results and position.

Instructions (all amounts in $000)

(a) Prepare four graphs covering the 1995 to 1999 period. The first graph is for net earnings over this five-year period, the second for EPS, the third for working capital and the fourth for the current ratio. Based on the graphs, predict the values you might expect for the following fiscal period.

(b) Assume the following errors were discovered after the latest year's financial statements were released:

1. Invoices representing the December 1998 purchases from a major supplier in the amount of $20,000 were not processed through the accounting system until late January 1999 in error, although the ending inventory at year end was correctly stated.

2. At the end of 1999, $10,000 of inventory was excluded from the physical count as it was set aside for delivery to associate dealers. The stock purchase had been appropriately recorded in December. The sales invoice to the associate dealers was issued and accounted for in early January 2000 upon delivery. (You might want to determine what the company's revenue recognition policy is for shipments of merchandise to dealers.)

(c) Assuming an effective income tax rate of 35%, calculate the correct amount of net earnings, EPS, working capital, and current ratio for all years affected by these errors.

(d) In a different colour, redraw the trend lines on the graphs developed in part (a).

(e) Do the revised numbers change your expectations for the following year? Comment.

RESEARCH CASES

Case 1

As indicated in the chapter, the FIFO and LIFO inventory methods can result in significantly different income statement and balance sheet figures. However, it is possible to convert income for a LIFO firm to its FIFO-based equivalent if the inventory cost under both bases is reported.

Although the *CICA Handbook* requires only disclosure of the method of determining cost if the method used results in a cost materially different from recent cost, some companies provide additional information. Imperial Oil Limited and Suncor Energy Inc., for example, both in the oil and gas industry, use LIFO and disclose what the replacement cost of their inventories is. The replacement cost would be close to a FIFO cost. The difference between the inventory shown on the balance sheet and the amount that would have been reported had the firm used a more current cost (such as replacement cost or FIFO) is known as the "LIFO reserve" (LR). The following equation can be used to convert LIFO cost of goods sold (COGS) to FIFO (or replacement) COGS:

$$COGS_{FIFO} = COGS_{LIFO} - LIFO \text{ effect}$$

where

$$LIFO \text{ effect} = [LR_{ending} - LR_{beginning}]$$

The following equation can be used to convert LIFO net income (NI) to FIFO (or replacement cost) net income.

$$NI_{FIFO} = NI_{LIFO} + (LIFO\ effect)\ (1 - tax\ rate)$$

Instructions

Obtain the financial statements of Imperial Oil, Suncor, or another company that uses LIFO and reports more current cost information for its inventories. If replacement cost is provided, assume it approximates FIFO cost.

(a) Identify the LIFO reserve at the two most recent balance sheet dates.

(b) Determine the LIFO effect during the most recent year.

(c) By how much would cost of goods sold during the most recent year change if the firm used FIFO?

(d) By how much would net income during the most recent year change if the firm used FIFO? (Hint: To estimate the tax rate, divide income tax expense by income before taxes.)

Case 2

The Globe and Mail's "Report on Business" magazine produces an issue on "The Top 1000 Corporations," which can serve as a useful reference about publicly traded Canadian companies. This annual issue, generally appearing in July, also contains a great deal of information regarding the top private companies, large Crown corporations and co-operatives.

Instructions

Examine the most recent edition and answer the following questions.

(a) Identify the three largest Canadian corporations in terms of revenue, profit, assets, and employees. How do they compare in terms of return on common equity?

(b) Which industries tend to report the largest revenues?

(c) Revenue and profit growth is of interest to most investors. Which industries appear to be most highly represented as having growth potential?

ETHICS CASE

Gamble Corporation uses the LIFO method for inventory costing. In an effort to lower net income, company president Oscar Gamble tells the plant accountant to take the unusual step of recommending to the purchasing department a large purchase of inventory at year end. The price of the item to be purchased has nearly doubled during the year, and the item represents a major portion of inventory value.

Instructions

Answer the following questions:

(a) Identify the major stakeholders. If the plant accountant recommends the purchase, what are the consequences?

(b) If Gamble Coroporation were using the FIFO method of inventory costing, would Oscar Gamble give the same order? Why or why not?

CHAPTER 9

Inventories: Additional Valuation Issues

LEARNING OBJECTIVES

....

After studying this chapter, you should be able to:

1. Recognize that the lower of cost and market basis is a departure from the historical cost principle, and understand why this is appropriate.

2. Explain various definitions of possible market amounts that may be used when applying lower of cost and market.

3. Explain how LCM (lower of cost and market) works and how it is applied.

4. Know how to account for inventory on the lower of cost and market basis.

5. Identify when inventories are carried regularly at net realizable value.

6. Explain when the relative sales value method is used to value inventories.

7. Explain accounting issues related to purchase commitments.

8. Estimate ending inventory by applying the gross profit method.

9. Explain the limitations of the gross profit method.

10. Estimate ending inventory by applying the retail inventory method.

11. Explain how inventory is reported and analysed.

PREVIEW OF CHAPTER 9

Information on inventories and changes in inventory is relevant to predicting profits. The purpose of this chapter is to discuss and illustrate some valuation and estimation concepts used to develop relevant inventory information. For example, what happens if the inventory value increases or decreases after the initial purchase date? Does the financial reporting system recognize these increases and decreases in inventory valuation? The answers, in terms of financial statement preparation, lie in the lower of cost and market rule.

A variety of other valuation issues are identified. The relative sales value method (used when "basket" purchases are made of more than one type of inventory item) is discussed, as is the valuation of inventory at net realizable value instead of historic cost. In addition, the accounting for outstanding purchase commitments is explained.

What happens if there is a fire and a physical count of lost inventory cannot be made? How is the amount of the destroyed inventory determined so that an insurance claim can be justified? What happens in large department stores where monthly inventory figures are needed, but monthly counts are not feasible? These questions involve the development and use of estimation techniques to value the ending inventory without a physical count. The gross profit method and the retail inventory method are widely used estimation methods and are discussed in this chapter.

The chapter ends with inventory disclosure requirements and ratios used to analyse inventories and related accounts to help users assess performance. The content and organization of the chapter are as follows:

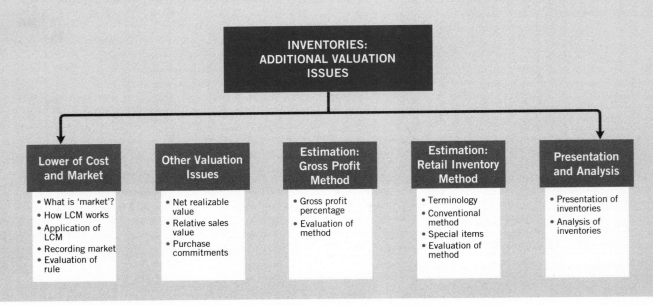

LOWER OF COST AND MARKET

OBJECTIVE 1

Recognize that the lower of cost and market basis is a departure from the historical cost principle, and understand why this is appropriate.

As noted in Chapter 8, inventories are recorded at their original cost. However, a major departure from the historical cost principle occurs with inventory valuation if inventory declines in value below its original cost. Whatever the reason for a decline (e.g., obsolescence, price-level changes, damaged goods), the inventory should be written down to reflect this loss. **The general rule is that the historical cost principle is abandoned when the asset's future utility (revenue-producing ability) is no longer as great as its original cost.** Inventories that experience a decline in utility are valued therefore on the basis of the lower of cost and market, instead of on the original cost.

A departure from cost is justified for two primary reasons. First, readers presume that **current assets can be converted into at least as much cash as the value reported for them on the balance sheet**; and second, matching requires that **a loss of utility be charged against revenues in the period in which the loss occurs**, not in the period in which the inventory is sold. In addition, the lower of cost and market method is **a conservative approach to inventory valuation**. That is, when doubt exists about an asset's value, it is preferable to undervalue rather than to overvalue it.

What is "Market?"

As we learned in Chapter 8, **cost** is the acquisition price of inventory calculated using one of the historical cost-based methods—specific identification, average cost, FIFO, or LIFO. The term **market** in the phrase "the lower of cost and market" (LCM) requires a specific definition as it has a number of different meanings. The *CICA Handbook*, recognizing this, states that it is desirable to use a more specific description in lieu of the term "market."[1] Other, more descriptive terms include replacement cost, net realizable value, and net realizable value less a normal profit margin.

Replacement cost generally means the amount that would be needed to acquire an equivalent item, by purchase or production, as would be incurred in the normal course of business operations (i.e., buying from usual sources or manufacturing in normal quantities). **Net realizable value (NRV)** is the item's estimated selling price in the ordinary course of business, less reasonably predictable future costs to complete and dispose of the item. **Net realizable value (NRV) less a normal profit margin** is determined by deducting a normal profit margin from the previously defined net realizable value amount. For example, a retailer may have some calculator wristwatches on hand that cost $30.00 each when purchased. If their purchase cost is presently $28.00, that would be their replacement cost. If their selling price today is $50.00, and there were no additional costs to sell them, then this amount would be their net realizable value. If a normal profit margin is 35% of selling price, the net realizable value less a normal profit margin would be $32.50 (i.e., $50 − [.35 × $50]). Consequently, in this example, the inventory would be valued at $30.00 per unit (its historical cost) under the lower of cost and market rule if market were either net realizable value or net realizable value less a normal profit margin, but would be valued at $28.00 per unit if market were replacement cost.

Given different interpretations as to what market can be, the question becomes: What definition of market should be used when applying the lower of cost and market rule? The *CICA Handbook* recognizes several possibilities, all of which are generally accepted, but is silent on which is appropriate in particular circumstances. (Some of these considerations are identified later under the heading "Evaluation of Lower of Cost and Market Rule.") However, **net realizable value is the most commonly used method of determining "market" in Canada**.[2] Why is there such support for this method?

The use of replacement cost as "market" is based on the assumption that a decline in an item's replacement cost usually results in a decline in selling price. If selling prices fall, a company holding units of that inventory will report an eventual loss, or at least a lower profit margin. It is true that products in a very competitive market are likely to experience declines in selling price if production costs decline. However, it is not reasonable to assume that prices will fall in the same proportion as input costs, nor below inventory cost, nor that such market conditions exist for all products. Replacement cost may be appropriate in limited specific circumstances.

---

[1] *CICA Handbook*, Section 3030, par. .11.

[2] *Financial Reporting in Canada, 2000* (Toronto: CICA, 2000) reports that, of the interpretations of market disclosed in 1999 financial statements of 161 of the surveyed companies, 82 used only net realizable value or estimated net realizable value, 9 used only replacement cost, 2 used only net realizable value less a normal profit margin, and 65 companies used more than one method. Only 3 companies did not disclose how they defined "market."

UNDERLYING CONCEPTS

The use of the lower of cost and market method is an excellent example of the conservatism constraint and the matching principle.

OBJECTIVE 2

Explain various definitions of possible market amounts that may be used when applying lower of cost and market.

IAS NOTE

IAS 2 requires that inventory be valued at the lower of cost and net realizable value.

This leaves net realizable value and net realizable value less a normal profit margin to consider. To illustrate the effects of reducing the carrying value of inventory under these two methods, assume that a company has unfinished inventory at December 31, 2002 with a cost of $760, a completed sales value of $1,000, estimated cost of completion of $275, and a normal profit margin of 10% of sales. The determination of both "market" calculations follows:

ILLUSTRATION 9-1
Calculation of Net Realizable Value

Inventory — sales value	$1,000
Less: Estimated cost of completion and disposal	275
Net realizable value	**725**
Less: Allowance for normal profit margin (10% of sales)	100
Net realizable value less a normal profit margin	**$ 625**

To understand the arguments related to the use of these terms, it is important to understand what the effects are on the financial statements of the current and subsequent periods. Illustration 9-2 first summarizes the effects of using net realizable value as the definition of market, and then the effects of using the more conservative net realizable value less a normal profit margin.

ILLUSTRATION 9-2
Income Statement Effects of Using Net Realizable Value

	Inventory Value December 31, 2002 Balance Sheet	Profit (loss) recognized in 2002	Profit (loss) recognized in 2003
If Market = NRV			
Cost = $760			
Market = $725			
LCM =	$725		
Effect on 2002 Income Statement:			
$760 − $725		($ 35)	
Effect on 2003 Income Statement:			
Revenue			$1,000
Expenses: Carrying value, Dec. 31/02			(725)
2003 costs to complete			
and sell			(275)
			$0
If Market = NRV less a normal profit margin			
Cost = $760			
Market = $625			
LCM =	$625		
Effect on 2002 Income Statement:			
$760 − $625		($135)	
Effect on 2003 Income Statement:			
Revenue			$1,000
Expenses: Carrying value, Dec. 31/02			(625)
2003 costs to complete			
and sell			(275)
			$ 100

Those who support the idea that any loss to be recognized should not exceed the estimated costs that will not be recovered would argue for the first definition of market as net realizable value. In this situation, the total expected costs are $760 + $275, or $1,035. With a selling price of $1,000, there is $35 of expected unrecoverable cost, and this is the amount recognized in 2002 in the inventory writedown. In 2003 when the inventory is sold, the result is a break even because the unrecoverable costs were recognized in 2002 when the actual reduction in value took place.

   Others support a higher inventory writedown. They believe the inventory should be reduced sufficiently in the **current** period so that a normal profit will be reported when the inventory is subsequently sold. This results when market is defined as net realizable value less a normal profit margin, and is illustrated in the bottom part of Illustration 9-2. In this example, a loss of $135 is reported in 2002 and a normal profit of $100 is recognized in 2003 when the inventory is sold.

Because the normal process of matching deducts cost from revenue when determining income, any downward adjustment of the inventory carrying amount to "market" shifts income from one period to the next. In the first example above using NRV, the loss of $35 was shifted from 2003 to 2002, leaving $0 income in 2003. In the second example using NRV less a normal profit margin, a loss of $135 was shifted into 2002 so that a normal profit of $100 could be recognized in 2003. Many consider this latter approach to be too arbitrary in shifting profits between periods, and too far removed from an appropriate application of the matching principle. For this reason, net realizable value remains the most commonly used definition of "market" in Canada.

The accounting profession in the United States has adopted a different approach for determining "market" when applying the lower of cost and market rule.[3] Generally, market is the item's replacement cost. When applying the lower of cost and market rule, however, "market" cannot exceed net realizable value (a ceiling or upper limit value) or be less than net realizable value less a normal profit margin (a floor or lower limit value).[4] Therefore, the value designated as "market" is the middle value of these three possibilities. Once the designated market has been determined, it is compared with the cost and the lower amount is used for inventory valuation. These guidelines are shown in Illustration 9-3.

UNDERLYING CONCEPTS

Regardless of the definition of "market" used, the intent is the same: current assets should not be reported at more than their realizable value to the company.

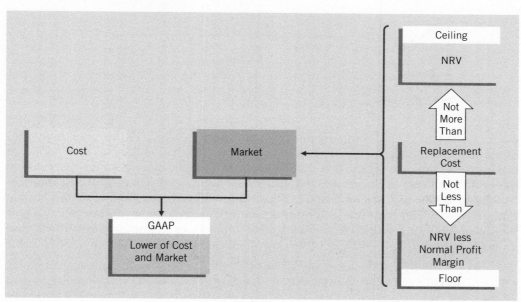

ILLUSTRATION 9-3
U.S. Inventory Valuation—Lower of Cost and Market

---

[3] Generally, we do not identify U.S. financial reporting standards in this Canadian text, particularly when a specific Canadian position exists. We do so in this particular case because awareness of the U.S. standard may help to better understand the rationale of Canadian practice. Also, the comparison serves to illustrate that different countries can come to different conclusions when trying to account for the same phenomenon—a problem that is faced head-on by the International Accounting Standards Committee when it is trying to develop international accounting standards, or by international finance professionals when they are assessing financial statements of companies from different countries.

[4] "Restatement and Revision of Accounting Research Bulletins," *Accounting Research Bulletin No. 43* (New York: AICPA, 1953), Ch. 4, par. 8. It should be noted that a literal interpretation of the U.S. rules is frequently not applied in practice. Rather, ARB No. 43 is considered a guide, and professional judgement is often exercised. Indeed, *Accounting Research Study No. 13 "The Accounting Basis of Inventories"* (New York: AICPA, 1973) recommends that net realizable value be adopted.

The U.S. approach is based on the premise that declines in replacement cost are reflective of or predict a decline in selling price (realizable value). The ceiling and floor limits are introduced to protect against situations where this premise is in serious error. Consequently, while the underlying objective of reflecting a decline in utility of inventory is common in both Canada and the United States, each has reached a different conclusion as to how this is best accomplished.

How Lower of Cost and Market Works

OBJECTIVE 3

Explain how LCM (lower of cost and market) works and how it is applied.

The **lower of cost and market (LCM)** rule requires that the inventory be valued at cost unless market is lower than cost, in which case the inventory is valued at market. To apply this rule (regardless of whether a Canadian or U.S. definition of market is used):

1. Determine the cost using an acceptable historical cost flow method.
2. Determine the market value to be used.
3. Compare the cost with the market.

The lower of the cost and market figures is then used for inventory valuation on the financial statements.

To demonstrate, consider the following information relative to the inventory of Regner Foods Limited.

ILLUSTRATION 9-4

Possible Market Values

Food	Replacement Cost	Net Realizable Value	Net Realizable Value Less a Normal Profit Margin
Spinach	$ 88,000	$120,000	$104,000
Carrots	90,000	100,000	70,000
Cut beans	45,000	40,000	27,500
Peas	36,000	72,000	48,000
Mixed vegetables	105,000	92,000	80,000

Under Canadian GAAP, company management specifies which of the three definitions of market it will adopt. If net realizable value is designated as the "market" value, as is commonly the case for Canadian companies, the Net Realizable Values provided in the middle column of Illustration 9-4 will be the values compared with cost in establishing the lower of cost and market. Illustration 9-5 completes the inventory valuation process by choosing the lower of the two values for each inventory item. Cost is the lower amount for spinach, net realizable value is lower for cut beans, peas, and mixed vegetables, and cost and NRV are identical for carrots. The inventory value reported on Regner Foods' balance sheet is $384,000.

ILLUSTRATION 9-5

Determining Final Inventory Value Using NRV

Food	Cost	Net Realizable Value	LCM
Spinach	$ 80,000	$120,000	$ 80,000
Carrots	100,000	100,000	100,000
Cut beans	50,000	40,000	40,000
Peas	90,000	72,000	72,000
Mixed vegetables	95,000	92,000	92,000
Final inventory value			$384,000

If management uses NRV less a normal profit margin as its definition of market, a lower market value in each case is compared with cost, and the final balance sheet valuation for inventory would be significantly lower.

To determine market under U.S. rules, the first step is to determine amounts for all three possible market values, as indicated in Illustration 9-4. Given this, the next step is to determine which of these is the **designated market value**. The designated market value is always the middle value of three amounts: replacement cost, net realizable value (the ceiling), and net realizable value less a normal profit margin (the floor).

The designated market value is then compared with cost to determine the lower of cost and market. The choice of designated market value and the application of LCM in determining the final inventory value for Regner Foods is illustrated below:

Food	Cost	Replacement Cost	Net Realizable Value (Ceiling)	Net Realizable Value Less a Normal Profit Margin (Floor)	Designated Market Value	Final Inventory Value
Spinach	$ 80,000	$ 88,000	$120,000	$104,000	$104,000	$ 80,000
Carrots	100,000	90,000	100,000	70,000	90,000	90,000
Cut beans	50,000	45,000	40,000	27,500	40,000	40,000
Peas	90,000	36,000	72,000	48,000	48,000	48,000
Mixed vegetables	95,000	105,000	92,000	80,000	92,000	92,000
						$350,000

Final Inventory Value:

Spinach	Cost ($80,000) is selected because it is lower than designated market value (net realizable value less a normal profit margin).
Carrots	Designated market value (replacement cost, $90,000) is selected because it is lower than cost.
Cut beans	Designated market value (net realizable value, $40,000) is selected because it is lower than cost.
Peas	Designated market value (net realizable value less a normal profit margin, $48,000) is selected because it is lower than cost.
Mixed vegetables	Designated market value (net realizable value, $92,000) is selected because it is lower than cost.

ILLUSTRATION 9-6
Determining Final Inventory Value—U.S. Approach

For spinach and peas, the "floor" value of NRV less a normal profit margin is chosen as the designated market value because it is the middle value. For carrots, replacement cost is designated as market because it is the middle value. For the cut beans and mixed vegetables, net realizable value is designated as market because it is the middle value. In Illustration 9-6, the Designated Market Value column contains the values that are compared with "Cost" in determining the lower of cost and market.

Under both Canadian and U.S. standards, applying the lower of cost and market rule incorporates only losses in value that occur in the normal course of business from such causes as style changes, shift in demand, or regular shop wear. Damaged or deteriorated goods are reduced directly to net realizable value. If the amount is significant, such goods may be carried in separate inventory accounts.

Methods of Applying Lower of Cost and Market

In the previous illustration for Regner Foods, we assumed that the lower of cost and market rule was applied to each type of food. However, the lower of cost and market rule may be applied on an **item-by-item basis**, a **category basis**, or a **total inventory basis**. Increases in market prices of some goods tend to offset decreases in market prices of others if a major category or total inventory approach is followed. To illustrate, assume that Regner Foods separates its food products into frozen and canned to designate major categories. Note that market is defined as net realizable value in this illustration.

As indicated in Illustration 9-7, if the lower of cost and market rule is applied to individual items, the LCM valuation of inventory is $384,000; if applied to major categories, it is $394,000; if applied to the total inventory, it is $415,000. The reason for the difference is that market values higher than cost are offset against market values lower than cost when the major categories or total inventory approach is adopted. For Regner Foods, the high market value for spinach is partially offset when the major categories approach is adopted, and is almost totally offset when the total inventory approach is used. Therefore, the item-by-item approach is more conservative than the others because the likelihood of having to reduce cost to market is greater and the amount of any reduction is larger.

OBJECTIVE 4

Know how to account for inventory on the lower of cost and market basis.

ILLUSTRATION 9-7
Alternative Applications of Lower of Cost and Market (Market is Net Realizable Value)

	Cost	Market (NRV)	Lower of Cost and Market By: Individual Items	Major Categories	Total Inventory
Frozen					
Spinach	$ 80,000	$120,000	$ 80,000		
Carrots	100,000	100,000	100,000		
Cut beans	50,000	40,000	40,000		
Total frozen	230,000	260,000		$230,000	
Canned					
Peas	90,000	72,000	72,000		
Mixed vegetables	95,000	92,000	92,000		
Total canned	185,000	164,000		164,000	
Total	$415,000	$424,000	$384,000	$394,000	$415,000

INTERNATIONAL INSIGHT

In Japan, companies typically value their inventories at cost, rather than at lower of cost and market.

The Canada Customs and Revenue Agency dictates that "in comparing 'cost' and 'fair market value' in order to determine which is the lower, the comparison should be made separately and individually in respect of each item (or each usual class of items if specific items are not readily distinguishable) in the inventory." A comparison of total cost and total market is permitted on an exception basis where the cost of the specific items (using specific identification, FIFO or average cost) is not known and only an average cost is available.[5] The tax rules in the U.S., require that an individual item basis be used unless it involves practical difficulties. **Whichever method is selected, it should be applied consistently from one period to another.**

Recording "Market" Instead of Cost

Two methods are used for recording inventory at market. One method, referred to as the **direct method**, simply records the ending inventory at the market figure at the year end, substituting the market value figure for cost when valuing the inventory. As a result, no loss is reported in the income statement because the loss is buried in cost of goods sold. The second method, referred to as the **indirect method** or **allowance method**, does not change the cost amount, but establishes a separate contra asset account and a loss account to record the write-off.

The following illustrations of entries under both methods are based on the following inventory data:

Inventory	At Cost	At Market
Beginning of the period	$65,000	$65,000
End of the period	82,000	70,000

The following entries assume the use of a **periodic** inventory system.

ILLUSTRATION 9-8
Accounting for the Reduction of Inventory to Market— Periodic Inventory System

Ending Inventory Recorded at Market (Direct Method)		Ending Inventory Recorded at Cost and Reduced to Market (Indirect or Allowance Method)	
To close beginning inventory:			
Cost of Goods Sold (or Income Summary)	65,000	Cost of Goods Sold (or Income Summary)	65,000
Inventory	65,000	Inventory	65,000
To record ending inventory:			
Inventory	70,000	Inventory	82,000
Cost of Goods Sold (or Income Summary)	70,000	Cost of Goods Sold (or Income Summary)	82,000
To write down inventory to market:			
No entry		Loss Due to Market Decline of Inventory	12,000
		Allowance to Reduce Inventory to Market	12,000

Allowance for Market Decline

---

[5] *CCRA Interpretation Bulletin–473R*, December 21, 1998 on "Inventory Valuation," par. .3.

If the company used a **perpetual** inventory system, the entries would be as follows:

ILLUSTRATION 9-9
Accounting for the Reduction of Inventory to Market—Perpetual Inventory System

(No inventory closing entries are necessary under the perpetual method; only the reduction to market is recorded.)

Direct Method		Indirect or Allowance Method	
To reduce inventory from cost to market:			
Cost of Goods Sold	12,000	Loss Due to Market	
Inventory	12,000	Decline of Inventory	12,000
		Allowance to Reduce	
		Inventory to Market	12,000

The advantage of identifying the loss due to market decline is that it is shown separately from cost of goods sold in the income statement, and the cost of goods sold for the year is not distorted. The data from the preceding illustration are used to contrast the differing amounts reported in the income statements below.

ILLUSTRATION 9-10
Income Statement Presentation—Direct and Indirect Methods of Reducing Inventory to Market

	Direct Method		
Sales			$200,000
Cost of goods sold			
Inventory, Jan. 1		$ 65,000	
Purchases		125,000	
Goods available		190,000	
Inventory, Dec. 31 (at market which is lower than cost)		70,000	
Cost of goods sold			120,000
Gross profit on sales			$ 80,000

	Indirect or Allowance Method		
Sales			$200,000
Cost of goods sold			
Inventory, Jan. 1		$ 65,000	
Purchases		125,000	
Goods available		190,000	
Inventory, Dec. 31 (at cost)		82,000	
Cost of goods sold			108,000
Gross profit on sales			92,000
Loss due to market decline of inventory (reported in other expenses and losses)			12,000
			$ 80,000

The second presentation is preferable. It clearly discloses the loss resulting from the market decline of inventory prices instead of burying the loss in the cost of goods sold. This method permits both the income statement and the balance sheet to show the ending inventory of $82,000 with the Allowance to Reduce Inventory to Market reported on the balance sheet as a $12,000 deduction from the inventory cost. It also keeps subsidiary inventory ledgers and records in correspondence with the control account without changing unit costs.

Although using an allowance account permits balance sheet disclosure of the inventory at cost and at the lower of cost and market, it raises the problem of how to dispose of the new account balance in the following period. If the merchandise in question is still on hand, the allowance account should be retained. Otherwise, beginning inventory and cost of goods are overstated. But if the goods have been sold, then the account should be closed. A new allowance account balance is then established for any decline in inventory value that has taken place in the current year.

Some accountants leave this account on the books and merely adjust the balance at the next balance sheet date to agree with the discrepancy between cost and the lower of cost and market at that time. Thus, if prices are falling, a loss is recorded. If prices are rising, a loss recorded in prior years is recovered and a "gain" (which is not

UNDERLYING CONCEPTS

The income statement under the first presentation lacks representational faithfulness. The cost of goods sold does not represent what it purports to represent. However, allowing the first presentation illustrates the concept of materiality. The presentation does not affect net income and would not "change the judgement of a reasonable person."

really a gain, but a recovery of a previously recognized loss) is recorded, as illustrated in the example below.

Date	Inventory at Cost	Inventory at Market	Amount Required in Allowance Account	Adjustment of Allowance Account Balance	Effect on Net Income
Dec. 31, 2001	$188,000	$176,000	$12,000 cr.	$12,000 inc.	Loss
Dec. 31, 2002	194,000	187,000	7,000 cr.	5,000 dec.	Gain
Dec. 31, 2003	173,000	174,000	0	7,000 dec.	Gain
Dec. 31, 2004	182,000	180,000	2,000 cr.	2,000 inc.	Loss

UNDERLYING CONCEPTS

The inconsistency in the presentation of inventory is an example of the trade-off between relevance and reliability. Market is more relevant than cost, and cost is more reliable than market. Apparently, relevance takes precedence in a down market, and reliability is more important in an up market.

This net "gain" can be thought of as the excess of the credit effect of closing the beginning allowance balance over the debit effect of setting up the current year-end allowance account. Recognizing a separate gain or loss has the same effect on net income as would closing the allowance balance to beginning inventory or to cost of goods sold. Recovering the loss up to the original cost is permitted, **but it may not exceed original cost**.

Evaluation of the Lower of Cost and Market Rule

The lower of cost and market rule suffers some conceptual deficiencies:

1. Decreases in the asset's value and the charge to expense are recognized in the period in which the loss in utility occurs—not in the period of sale. On the other hand, increases in the asset's value are recognized only at the point of sale. This treatment is inconsistent and can lead to distortions in income data.
2. Applying the rule results in inconsistency because a company's inventory may be valued at cost in one year and at market in the next year.
3. Lower of cost and market values the balance sheet inventory conservatively, but its effect on the income statement may or may not be conservative. Net income for the year in which the loss is taken is definitely lower; net income of the subsequent period may be higher than normal if the expected reduction in sales price does not materialize.
4. Applying the lower of cost and market rule uses a "normal" profit in determining inventory values. Since "normal" profit is an estimated figure based upon past experience and one that might not be attained in the future, it is not objective and presents an opportunity for income manipulation.

Many financial statement users appreciate the lower of cost and market rule because they at least know that the inventory is not overstated. In addition, recognizing all losses but anticipating no gains always results in a lower, more conservative measure of income.

OTHER VALUATION ISSUES

Valuation at Net Realizable Value

OBJECTIVE 5

Identify when inventories are carried regularly at net realizable value.

For most companies and in most situations, inventory is recorded at cost or the lower of cost and market. Some believe that inventory should always be valued at market defined as net realizable value, since that is the net amount that will be collected in cash from the inventory in the future. Under limited circumstances, support exists for **recording inventory at net realizable value (selling price less estimated costs to complete and sell)** even if that amount is **above** cost. This exception to the normal recognition rule is permitted where (1) there is a controlled market with a quoted price applicable to all quantities and (2) no significant costs of disposal are involved. Inventories of certain minerals (rare metals especially) are ordinarily reported at selling prices because there is often a controlled market without significant costs of disposal. A similar treatment is given agricultural products that are immediately marketable at quoted prices. This is consistent with recognition of revenue on completion of production as discussed in Chapter 6.

Another reason for allowing this method of valuation is that sometimes the cost figures are too difficult to obtain. In a manufacturing plant, various raw materials and purchased parts are put together to create a finished product. The various items in inventory, whether completely or partially finished, can be accounted for on a basis of cost because the cost of each individual component part is known. In a meat-packing house, however, a different situation prevails. The "raw material" consists of cattle, hogs, or sheep, each unit of which is purchased as a whole and then divided into parts that are the products. Instead of one product out of many raw materials or parts, many products are made from one "unit" of raw material. To allocate the cost of the animal "on the hoof" into the cost of ribs, chucks, and shoulders, for instance, is a practical impossibility. It is much easier and more useful to determine the various products' market price and value them in the inventory at selling price less the various future costs, such as shipping and handling, necessary to get them to market. Hence, because of a peculiarity of the meat-packing industry, for example, **inventories are sometimes carried at sales price less distribution costs; i.e., at NRV.**

Valuation Using Relative Sales Value

A special problem arises when a group of varying units is purchased at a single **lump sum price**, a so-called basket purchase. Assume that Woodland Developers purchases land for $1 million that can be subdivided into 400 lots. These lots are of different sizes and shapes but can be roughly sorted into three groups graded A, B, and C. As lots are sold, the purchase cost of $1 million must be apportioned among the lots sold (for cost of goods sold) and those remaining on hand (for ending inventory).

It is inappropriate to divide 400 lots into the total cost of $1 million to get a cost of $2,500 for each lot, because they vary in size, shape, and attractiveness. When such a situation is encountered—and it is not at all unusual—the common and most logical practice is to allocate the total cost among the various units on the basis of their relative sales value. For the example given, the allocation works out as follows:

INTERNATIONAL INSIGHT

The U.S. is the only country that defines market as something other than net realizable value.

OBJECTIVE 6

Explain when the relative sales value method is used to value inventories.

Lots	Number of Lots	Sales Price Per Lot	Total Sales Value	Relative Sales Value	Total Cost	Cost Allocated to Lots	Cost Per Lot
A	100	$10,000	$1,000,000	100/250	$1,000,000	$ 400,000	$4,000
B	100	6,000	600,000	60/250	1,000,000	240,000	2,400
C	200	4,500	900,000	90/250	1,000,000	360,000	1,800
			$2,500,000			$1,000,000	

ILLUSTRATION 9-12
Allocation of Costs, Using Relative Sales Value

The cost of lots sold can be calculated by using the amounts given in the column for "Cost Per Lot," and the gross profit is determined as follows:

Lots	Number of Lots Sold	Cost Per Lot	Cost of Lots Sold	Sales	Gross Profit
A	77	$4,000	$308,000	$ 770,000	$ 462,000
B	80	2,400	192,000	480,000	288,000
C	100	1,800	180,000	450,000	270,000
			$680,000	$1,700,000	$1,020,000

ILLUSTRATION 9-13
Determination of Gross Profit, Using Relative Sales Value

The ending inventory is, therefore, $320,000 ($1,000,000 − $680,000). The cost of lots sold can also be calculated in another manner. The ratio of cost to selling price for all the lots is $1 million divided by $2,500,000, or 40%. Accordingly, if the total sales price of lots sold is, say $1,700,000, then the cost of the lots sold is 40% of $1,700,000, or $680,000. The inventory of lots on hand is then $1 million less $680,000, or $320,000.

The relative sales value method is used throughout the petroleum industry to value (at cost) the many products and by-products obtained from a barrel of crude oil.

OBJECTIVE 7

Explain accounting issues related to purchase commitments.

Purchase Commitments—A Special Problem

In many lines of business, a firm's survival and continued profitability depends on having a sufficient stock of merchandise to meet all customer demands. Consequently, it is quite common for a company to agree to buy inventory weeks, months, or even years in advance. Such arrangements may be made based on estimated or firm sales commitments by the company's customers. Generally, title to the merchandise or materials described in these purchase commitments has not passed to the buyer. Indeed, the goods may exist only as natural resources or, in the case of commodities, as unplanted seed, or in the case of a product, as work in process.

Usually it is neither necessary nor proper for the buyer to make any entries to reflect commitments for purchases of goods that have not been shipped by the seller. Ordinary orders, for which the prices are determined at the time of shipment and **are subject to cancellation** by the buyer or seller, do not represent either an asset or a liability to the buyer. Therefore, they need not be recorded in the books or reported in the financial statements.

Even with formal, **noncancellable purchase contracts**, no asset or liability is recognized at the date of inception, **because the contract is "executory" in nature**: neither party has fulfilled its part of the contract. However, if material, such contract details should be disclosed in the buyer's balance sheet in a note, such as in the following examples.

ILLUSTRATION 9-14
Disclosure of Purchase Commitments—Emera Inc.

16. **COMMITMENTS (in part)**
Emera had the following significant commitments at December 31, 2000:

- A requirement to purchase the coal output of the Cape Breton Development Corporation's (CBDC) Prince Mine, which is not expected to exceed 1.1 million tonnes of coal.

- Purchases from CBDC may be reduced to the extent that the company purchases coal from alternative sources in the event of production problems at CBDC, as was the case in 2000.

- Annual requirement to purchase approximately $15 million of electricity from independent power producers for each of the next five years.

ILLUSTRATION 9-15
Disclosure of Purchase Commitment

Note 1: Contracts for the purchase of raw materials in 2003 have been executed in the amount of $600,000. The market price of such raw materials on December 31, 2002, is $640,000.

In Illustration 9-15, the contracted price was less than the market price at the balance sheet date. **If the contracted price exceeds the market price and losses are reasonably determinable and likely to occur at the time of purchase, losses should be recognized in the period during which such declines in prices take place.**[6] For example, if purchase contracts for delivery in 2003 have been executed at a firm price of $640,000 and the materials' market price on the company's year end of December 31, 2002 is $600,000, the following entry is made on December 31, 2002:

UNDERLYING CONCEPTS

Reporting the loss is conservative. However, reporting the decline in market price is debatable because no asset is recorded. This area demonstrates the need for good definitions of assets and liabilities.

Loss on Purchase Contracts	40,000	
Accrued Liability on Purchase Contracts		40,000

This loss is shown on the income statement under Other Expenses and Losses. The Accrued Liability on Purchase Contracts is reported in the balance sheet's liability section. When the goods are delivered in 2003, the entry (periodic system) is:

Purchases	600,000	
Accrued Liability on Purchase Contracts	40,000	
Accounts Payable		640,000

If the price has partially or fully recovered before the inventory is received, the Accrued Liability on Purchase Contracts would be reduced. A resulting gain (Recovery of Loss) is then reported in the period of the price increase for the amount of the partial or full recovery.

The purchasers in purchase commitments can protect themselves against the possibility of market price declines of goods under contract by hedging. **Hedging** is accom-

---

[6] *CICA Handbook*, Section 3290, par. .12.

plished through a futures contract in which the purchaser in the purchase commitment simultaneously contracts to a future sale of the same quantity of the same or similar goods at a fixed price. When a company holds a buy position in a purchase commitment and a sell position in a futures contract in the same commodity, it will be better off under one contract by approximately (maybe exactly) the same amount by which it is worse off under the other contract. That is, a loss on one will be offset by a gain on the other.[7]

Accounting for purchase commitments (and, for that matter, all commitments) is unsettled and controversial. Some argue that these contracts should be reported as assets and liabilities when the contract is signed; others believe that recognition at the delivery date is more appropriate.[8] Clearly, the treatment of such contracts in particular situations rests on judgement being exercised within the context of generally accepted accounting principles and experience.

THE GROSS PROFIT METHOD OF ESTIMATING INVENTORY

Recall that the basic purpose of taking a physical inventory is to verify the accuracy of the perpetual inventory records' accuracy or, if no perpetual records exist, to arrive at an inventory amount. Sometimes, taking a physical inventory is impractical or impossible. Then, estimation methods are used to approximate inventory on hand. One such method is called the gross profit (or gross margin) method. This method is used in situations where only an estimate of inventory is needed (e.g., preparing interim reports or testing the reasonableness of the cost derived by some other method) or where inventory has been destroyed by fire or other catastrophe. It may also be used to provide a rough check on the accuracy of a physical inventory count (e.g., compare the estimated amount with physical count amount to see if they are reasonably close; if not, a reason should be found).

The gross profit method is based on three assumptions: (1) the beginning inventory plus purchases equal total goods to be accounted for; (2) goods not sold must be on hand; and (3) when the net sales, reduced to cost, are deducted from the total goods to be accounted for, the result is the ending inventory.

To illustrate, assume that a company has a beginning inventory of $60,000 and purchases of $200,000, both at cost. Sales at selling price amount to $280,000. The gross profit on selling price is 30%. The gross margin method is applied as follows:

Beginning inventory (at cost)		$ 60,000
Purchases (at cost)		200,000
Goods available (at cost)		260,000
Sales (at selling price)	$280,000	
Less: Gross profit (30% of $280,000)	84,000	
Estimated cost of goods sold		196,000
Estimated inventory (at cost)		$ 64,000

> **OBJECTIVE 8**
>
> Estimate ending inventory by applying the gross profit method.

ILLUSTRATION 9-16
Application of Gross Profit Method

Note that the estimated cost of goods sold could also have been calculated directly as 70% of sales. The cost of goods sold percentage **is always** the complement of the gross profit percentage.

All the information needed to calculate the inventory at cost, except for the gross profit percentage, is available in the current period's records. The gross profit percent-

---

[7] A discussion of hedging and the use of derivatives such as futures is provided in the Appendix to Chapter 15.

[8] *FASB Concepts Statement No. 6*, "Elements of Financial Statements," (Stamford, Conn.: FASB, 1985) states in paragraphs 251 to 253 that "a purchase commitment involves both an item that might be recorded as an asset and an item that might be recorded as a liability. That is, it involves both a right to receive assets and an obligation to pay. . . . If both the right to receive assets and the obligation to pay were recorded at the time of the purchase commitment, the nature of the loss and the valuation account that records it when the price falls would be clearly seen." Although the discussion in *Concepts Statement No. 6* does not exclude the possibility of recording assets and liabilities for purchase commitments, it contains no conclusions or implications about whether they should be recorded.

age is determined by reviewing company policies and prior period records. In some cases, this percentage must be adjusted if prior periods are not considered representative of the current period.[9]

Calculation of Gross Profit Percentage

In most situations, the **gross profit percentage** is used and it is the gross profit as a percentage of selling price. The previous illustration, for example, used a 30% gross profit on sales. Gross profit on selling price is the common method for quoting the profit for several reasons: (1) Most goods are stated on a retail basis, not a cost basis. (2) A profit quoted on selling price is lower than one based on cost, and this lower rate gives a favourable impression to the consumer. (3) The gross profit based on selling price can never exceed 100%.[10]

In the previous example, the gross profit was a given. But how was that figure derived? To see how a gross profit percentage is calculated, assume that an article cost $15.00 and sells for $20.00, a gross profit of $5.00. This markup of $5.00 is ¼ or 25% of retail (i.e., the selling price) but is only ⅓ or 33⅓% of cost (see Illustration 9-17).

ILLUSTRATION 9-17
Gross Profit Percent versus
Percent of Markup on Cost

$$\frac{\text{Gross profit}}{\text{Selling price}} = \frac{\$\ 5.00}{\$20.00} = 25\% \text{ of selling price} \qquad \frac{\text{Gross profit}}{\text{Cost}} = \frac{\$\ 5.00}{\$15.00} = 33\tfrac{1}{3}\% \text{ of cost}$$

Although it is normal to calculate the gross profit on the basis of selling price, you should understand the basic relationship between this ratio and the percent of **markup on cost**.

For example, assume that you were told that the **markup on cost** for a given item is 25%. What, then, is the **gross profit on selling price**? To find the answer, assume that the item's selling price is $1.00. In this case, the following formula applies:

$$
\begin{aligned}
\text{Cost} + \text{Gross profit} &= \text{Selling price} \\
C + .25C &= \$1.00 \\
1.25C &= \$1.00 \\
C &= \$0.80
\end{aligned}
$$

The gross profit equals $0.20 ($1.00 − $0.80), and the rate of gross profit on selling price is therefore 20% ($0.20/$1.00).

Conversely, assume that you were told that the gross profit on selling price is 20%. What is the **markup on cost**? To find the answer, again assume that the selling price is $1.00. Again, the same formula holds:

---

[9] An alternative method of estimating inventory using the gross profit percentage, considered by some to be less complicated than the traditional method illustrated above, uses the standard income statement format as follows (assume the same data as in the illustration above):

Sales		$280,000		$280,000
Cost of sales				
Beginning inventory	$ 60,000		$ 60,000	
Purchases	200,000		200,000	
Goods available for sale	260,000		260,000	
Ending inventory	(3) ?		(3) 64,000 Est.	
Cost of goods sold		(2) ?		(2)196,000 Est.
Gross profit on sales (30%)		(1) ?		(1) 84,000 Est.

Calculate the unknowns as follows: first the gross profit amount, then cost of goods sold, and then the ending inventory.

(1) $280,000 × 30% = $84,000 (gross profit on sales)

(2) $280,000 − $84,000 = $196,000 (cost of goods sold)

(3) $260,000 − $196,000 = $64,000 (ending inventory)

[10] The terms "gross profit percentage," "gross margin percentage," "rate of gross profit," and "rate of gross margin" are synonymous, reflecting the relationship of gross profit to selling price. The terms "percentage markup" or "rate of markup" are used to describe the relationship of markup (equals gross margin) to cost, although some continue to refer to this as a gross profit percentage.

$$
\begin{aligned}
\text{Cost} + \text{Gross profit} &= \text{Selling price} \\
\text{C} + .20\text{SP} &= \text{SP} \\
\text{C} &= .80\text{SP} \\
\text{C} &= .80(\$1.00) \\
\text{C} &= \$0.80
\end{aligned}
$$

Here, as in the example above, the markup equals $0.20 ($1.00 − $0.80), and the markup on cost is 25% ($0.20/$0.80).

Retailers use the following formulas to express these relationships:

1. Percent gross profit on selling price $= \dfrac{\text{Percent markup on cost}}{100\% + \text{Percent markup on cost}}$

2. Percent markup on cost $= \dfrac{\text{Percent gross profit on selling price}}{100\% - \text{Percent gross profit on selling price}}$

ILLUSTRATION 9-18
Formulas Relating to Gross Profit

Gross profits are closely followed by management and analysts. A small change in the gross profit rate can significantly affect the bottom line. In 1993, **Apple Computer** suffered a textbook case of shrinking gross profits. In response to pricing wars in the personal computer market, Apple was forced to quickly reduce the price of its signature Macintosh computers—reducing prices more quickly than it could reduce its costs. As a result, its gross profit rate fell from 44% in 1992 to 40% in 1993. While the drop of 4 percentage points may appear small, its impact on the bottom line caused Apple's share price to drop from $57 per share on June 1, 1993, to $27.50 by mid-July 1993.

Evaluation of Gross Profit Method

What are the major disadvantages of the gross profit method? One is that it provides an **estimate**; as a result, a physical inventory must be taken once a year to verify that the inventory is actually on hand. Second, the gross profit method uses **past percentages** in determining the markup. Although the past can often provide predictions about the future, a current rate is more appropriate. It is important to emphasize that whenever significant fluctuations occur, the percentage should be adjusted appropriately. Third, care must be taken in applying a **blanket gross profit rate**. Frequently, a store or department handles merchandise with widely varying rates of gross profit. In these situations, the gross profit method may have to be applied by subsections, lines of merchandise, or a similar basis that classifies merchandise according to their respective rates of gross profit.

The gross profit method is not normally acceptable for financial reporting purposes because it provides only an estimate. A physical inventory is needed as additional verification that the inventory indicated in the records is actually on hand. Nevertheless, the gross profit method is used to estimate ending inventory for insurance purposes (e.g., fire losses) and interim (monthly and quarterly) reporting purposes. Note that the gross profit method will follow closely the inventory method used (FIFO, LIFO, average cost) because it is based on historical records.

OBJECTIVE 9

Explain the limitations of the gross profit method.

THE RETAIL INVENTORY METHOD OF ESTIMATING INVENTORY

Accounting for inventory in a retail operation presents several challenges. Retailers with certain types of inventory may use the specific identification method to value their inventories. Such an approach makes sense when individual inventory units are significant, such as automobiles, pianos, or fur coats. However, imagine attempting to use such an approach at **Canadian Tire, Zellers**, or **Sears**—high-volume retailers that have many different types of merchandise at relatively low unit costs.

Many retailers have installed computers and point-of-sale terminals that enable them to keep excellent perpetual inventory records for the multitude of items they stock and sell. From these inventory systems, information regarding units on hand and their cost may be readily available.

OBJECTIVE 10

Estimate ending inventory by applying the retail inventory method.

Many retailers, however, do not have such systems, or their computer systems may not be sophisticated enough to provide all the necessary information. For these retailers, any type of unit cost inventory method will be unsatisfactory. Consequently, they may use what is called the retail inventory method. This method enables the retailer to estimate inventory when necessary and take a physical inventory at retail prices. Because an observable pattern between cost and selling price usually exists, an inventory taken at retail (i.e., at selling prices) can be converted to inventory at cost by applying a cost-to-retail (i.e., a cost to selling price) formula. **The retail inventory method requires that a record be kept of (1) the total cost and retail value of goods purchased, (2) the total cost and retail value of the goods available for sale, and (3) the sales for the period.**

Here is how it works: The sales for the period are deducted from the retail value of the goods available for sale, to produce an estimate of the inventory at retail or selling prices. The ratio of cost-to-retail for all goods passing through a department or company is determined by dividing the total goods available for sale **at cost** by the total goods available for sale **at retail**. The inventory valued at retail is converted to ending inventory at cost by applying the cost-to-retail ratio. Use of the retail inventory method is very common. For example, **Hart Stores Inc., Reitmans (Canada) Ltd., Suzy Shier Ltd.,** and **Hudson's Bay Company** all report using the retail inventory method in determining their inventory cost. The retail inventory method is illustrated below.

ILLUSTRATION 9-19
Retail Inventory Method

	Cost	Retail
Beginning inventory	$14,000	$ 20,000
Purchases	63,000	90,000
Goods available for sale	$77,000	110,000
Deduct: Sales		85,000
Ending inventory, at retail		$ 25,000
Ratio of cost to retail ($77,000 ÷ $110,000)		70%
Ending inventory at cost (70% of $25,000)		$ 17,500

To avoid a potential misstatement of the inventory, periodic inventory counts are made, especially in retail operations where loss due to shoplifting and breakage is common. When a physical count at retail is taken, the inventory cost is determined by multiplying the resulting amount at retail by the cost-to-retail ratio. Discrepancies between the records and the physical count will require an adjustment to make the records agree with the count.

The retail method is sanctioned by various retail associations and the accounting profession, and is allowed (except for methods approximating a LIFO valuation) by the CCRA (Canada Customs and Revenue Agency). One advantage of the retail inventory method is that the inventory balance **can be approximated without a physical count.** This makes the method particularly useful when preparing interim reports. Insurance adjusters use this approach to estimate losses from fire, flood, or other type of casualty. This method also acts as a **control device** because any deviations from a physical count at year end have to be explained. In addition, the retail method **expedites the physical inventory count** at the year end. The crew taking the inventory need record only the retail price of each item. There is no need to determine each item's invoice cost, thus saving time and expense.

Retail Method Terminology

The amounts shown in the Retail column of Illustration 9-19 represent the original retail or selling prices (cost plus an original markup or markon), assuming no price changes. Sales prices, however, are frequently marked up or down. For retailers, the term markup means an additional markup on the original selling price (i.e., an increase in the price above the original sales price). Markup cancellations are decreases in merchandise prices that had been marked up above the original retail price. Markup cancellations cannot be greater than markups. Net markups refer to markups less markup cancellations.

Markdowns are decreases in price below the original selling price. They are a common phenomenon and occur because of a decline in general price levels, special sales, soiled or damaged goods, overstocking, and competition. **Markdown cancellations** occur when the markdowns are later offset by increases in the prices of goods that had been marked down—such as after a one-day sale. A markdown cancellation cannot exceed the original markdown. Markdowns less markdown cancellations are known as **net markdowns**.

To illustrate these different concepts, assume that the Designer Clothing Store recently purchased 100 dress shirts from a supplier. The cost for these shirts was $1,500, or $15 a shirt. Designer Clothing established the selling price on these shirts at $30 each. The manager noted that the shirts were selling quickly, so she added $5 to the price of each shirt. This markup made the price too high for customers and sales lagged. Consequently, the manager reduced the price to $32. To this point there has been a markup of $5 and a markup cancellation of $3 on the original selling price of a shirt. When the major marketing season ended, the manager set the price of the remaining shirts at $23. This price change constitutes a markup cancellation of $2 and a $7 markdown. If the shirts are later priced at $24, a markdown cancellation of $1 occurs.

Retail Inventory Method with Markups and Markdowns—Conventional Method

To determine the ending inventory figures using the retail inventory method, a decision must be made on the treatment of markups, markup cancellations, markdowns, and markdown cancellations when calculating the ratio of cost-to-retail.

To illustrate the different possibilities, consider the data for In-Fashion Stores Inc., shown in Illustration 9-20. In-Fashion's ending inventory at cost can be calculated under two different cost-to-retail ratios. **(A)** reflects a cost percentage after net markups but

ILLUSTRATION 9-20
Retail Inventory Method with Markups and Markdowns: In-Fashion Stores Inc.

Information in Records

	Cost	Retail
Beginning inventory	$ 500	$ 1,000
Purchases (net)	20,000	35,000
Markups		3,000
Markup cancellations		1,000
Markdowns		2,500
Markdown cancellations		2,000
Sales (net)		25,000

Retail Inventory Method

	Cost		Retail
Beginning inventory	$ 500		$ 1,000
Purchases (net)	20,000		35,000
Merchandise available for sale	20,500		36,000
Add:			
Markups		$3,000	
Less: Markup cancellations		(1,000)	
Net markups			2,000
	20,500		38,000
Cost-to-retail ratio $\frac{\$20,500}{\$38,000} = 53.9\%$			**(A)**
Deduct:			
Markdowns		2,500	
Less: Markdown cancellations		(2,000)	
Net markdowns			500
	$20,500		37,500
Cost-to-retail ratio $\frac{\$20,500}{\$37,500} = 54.7\%$			**(B)**
Deduct: Sales (net)			25,000
Ending inventory at retail			$12,500

before net markdowns. The second percentage, **(B)**, is determined after both the net markups and markdowns are taken into account.

The calculations to determine the cost of ending inventory for In-Fashion Stores are:

Ending inventory at retail × Cost ratio = Ending inventory, at cost

Under **(A)**:	$12,500 × 53.9%	= $6,737.50
Under **(B)**:	$12,500 × 54.7%	= $6,837.50

Which percentage should be used to calculate the ending inventory? The answer depends on what the ending inventory amount is expected to reflect.

The conventional retail inventory method **uses the cost-to-retail ratio incorporating net markups (markups less markup cancellations) but excluding net markdowns (markdowns less markdown cancellations)** as shown in the calculation of ratio **(A)**. **It is designed to approximate the lower of average cost and market**, with market being net realizable value less normal profit margin. To understand why net markups but not net markdowns are included in the cost-to-retail ratio, we must understand how a retail outlet operates. When a company has a net markup on an item, it normally indicates that the item's market value has increased. On the other hand, if the item has a net markdown, it means that the item's utility has declined. Therefore, to approximate the lower of cost and market, net markdowns are considered a current loss and are not involved in calculating the cost-to-retail ratio. Thus, the cost-to-retail ratio is lower, which leads to an approximate lower of cost and market amount.

To help clarify, assume two different items were purchased for $5 each, and the original sales price was established at $10 each. One item was subsequently marked down to a selling price of $2. Assuming no sales for the period, **if markdowns are included** in the cost-to-retail ratio (ratio **(B)** above), the ending inventory is calculated as shown in Illustration 9-21.

ILLUSTRATION 9-21

Retail Inventory Method Including Markdowns—Cost Method

Markdowns Included in Cost-to-Retail Ratio

	Cost	Retail
Purchases	$10.00	$20.00
Deduct: Markdowns		8.00
Ending inventory, at retail		$12.00

Cost-to-retail ratio $\dfrac{\$10.00}{\$12.00} = 83.3\%$

Ending inventory at average cost ($12.00 × .833) = $10.00

This approach is the **cost method**. It results in ending inventory at the average cost of the two items on hand without considering the loss on the one item.

If markdowns are excluded from the ratio (ratio **(A)** above), the result is ending inventory at the lower of average cost and market. The calculation is shown in Illustration 9-22.

ILLUSTRATION 9-22

Retail Inventory Method Excluding Markdowns— Conventional Method (LCM)

Markdowns Not Included in Cost-to-Retail Ratio

	Cost	Retail
Purchases	$10.00	$20.00

Cost-to-retail ratio $\dfrac{\$10.00}{\$20.00} = 50\%$

	Cost	Retail
Deduct: Markdowns		8.00
Ending inventory, at retail		$12.00

Ending inventory at lower of average cost and market ($12 × .50) = $6.00

The $6 inventory valuation includes two inventory items, one inventoried at $5 and the other at $1. Basically, for the item with the market decline, the sales price was reduced from $10 to $2 and the cost reduced from $5 to $1.[11] Therefore, to approximate the lower of average cost and market, the cost-to-retail ratio must be established by dividing the cost of goods available by the sum of the original retail price of these goods plus the net markups; the net markdowns are excluded from the ratio.

In-Fashion Stores Inc.

	Cost		Retail
Beginning inventory	$ 500		$ 1,000
Purchases (net)	20,000		35,000
Totals	20,500		36,000
Add: Net markups			
Markups		$3,000	
Markup cancellations		(1,000)	2,000
Totals	$20,500 ⟷		38,000
Deduct: Net markdowns			
Markdowns		2,500	
Markdown cancellations		(2,000)	500
Goods available, at retail			37,500
Deduct: Sales (net)			25,000
Ending inventory, at retail			$12,500

$$\text{Cost-to-retail ratio} = \frac{\text{Cost of goods available}}{\text{Original retail price of goods available, plus net markups}}$$

$$= \frac{\$20,500}{\$38,000} = 53.9\%$$

Ending inventory at lower of average cost and market (53.9% × $12,500) $ 6,737.50

ILLUSTRATION 9-23
Comprehensive Conventional Retail Inventory Method Example

The basic format for the retail inventory method using the conventional approach and the In-Fashion Stores Inc. information is shown in Illustration 9-23.

Many possible cost-to-retail ratios could be calculated, depending upon whether or not the beginning inventory, net markups, and net markdowns are included. The schedule below summarizes some inventory valuation methods approximated by the inclusion or exclusion of various items in the cost-to-retail ratio, given that net purchases are always included in the ratio.

Beginning Inventory	Net Markups	Net Markdowns	Inventory Valuation Method Approximated
Include	Include	Include	Average cost
Include	Include	Exclude	Lower of average cost and market (conventional method)
Exclude	Include	Include	FIFO cost
Exclude	Include	Exclude	Lower of FIFO cost and market

Using the FIFO method, the estimated ending inventory (and its cost) will, by definition, come from the purchases of the current period. Therefore, the opening inventory, at cost and retail, is excluded in determining the cost ratio. The retail price of the opening inventory is added subsequently to determine the total selling price of goods available for the period.

Special Items Relating to Retail Method

The retail inventory method becomes more complicated when such items as freight-in, purchase returns and allowances, and purchase discounts are involved. **Freight costs**

[11] The conventional method defines market as net realizable value less the normal profit margin. In other words, the sale price of the item marked down is $2, but after subtracting a normal profit of 50% of selling price, the inventoriable amount becomes $1.

are treated as a part of the purchase cost. **Purchase returns and allowances** are ordinarily considered a reduction of the cost price and retail price and **purchase discounts** usually are considered a reduction of the purchases' cost. In short, the treatment for the items affecting the cost column of the retail inventory approach follows the calculation of cost of goods available for sale.

Note also that **sales returns and allowances** are considered proper adjustments to gross sales; **sales discounts to customers**, however, are not recognized when sales are recorded gross. To adjust for the Sales Discount account in such a situation would provide an ending inventory figure at retail that would be overvalued.

In addition, a number of special items require careful analysis. **Transfers-in** from another department, for example, should be reported in the same way as purchases from an outside enterprise. **Normal shortages** (breakage, damage, theft, shrinkage) should reduce the retail column because these goods are no longer available for sale. Such costs are reflected in the selling price because a certain amount of shortage is considered normal in a retail enterprise. As a result, this amount is not considered in computing the cost-to-retail percentage. Rather, it is shown as a deduction similar to sales to arrive at ending inventory at retail. **Abnormal shortages** should be deducted from both the cost and retail columns prior to calculating the cost-to-retail ratio and reported as a special inventory amount or as a loss. To do otherwise distorts the cost-to-retail ratio and overstates ending inventory. Finally, companies often provide their employees with special discounts to encourage loyalty, better performance, and so on. **Employee discounts** should be deducted from the retail column in the same way as sales. These discounts should not be considered in the cost-to-retail percentage because they do not reflect an overall change in the selling price.

Illustration 9-24 shows some of these treatments in more detail, using the conventional retail inventory method to determine the ending inventory.

ILLUSTRATION 9-24
Conventional Retail Inventory
Method—Special Items Included

	Cost	Retail
Beginning inventory	$ 1,000	$ 1,800
Purchases	30,000	60,000
Freight-in	600	—
Purchase returns	(1,500)	(3,000)
Totals	30,100	58,800
Net markups		9,000
Abnormal shrinkage	(1,200)	(2,000)
Totals	$28,900	65,800
Deduct:		
Net markdowns		1,400
Sales	$36,000	
Sales returns	(900)	35,100
Employee discounts		800
Normal shrinkage		1,300
		$27,200

Cost-to-retail ratio $\dfrac{\$28,900}{\$65,800} = 43.9\%$

Ending inventory at lower of average cost and market (43.9% × $27,200) = $11,940.80

Evaluation of Retail Inventory Method

The retail inventory method of calculating inventory is used (1) to permit the calculation of net income without a physical count of inventory, (2) as a control measure in determining inventory shortages, (3) in controlling quantities of merchandise on hand, and (4) as a source of information for insurance and tax purposes.

One characteristic of the retail inventory method is that it **has an averaging effect for varying rates of gross profit**. When applied to an entire business where rates of gross profit vary among departments, no allowance is made for possible distortion of results because of these differences. Many companies refine the retail method under such conditions by calculating inventory separately by departments or by classes of merchandise with similar rates of gross profit. In addition, this method's reliability rests on the assumption that the distribution of inventory items is similar to the "mix" in the total goods available for sale.

PRESENTATION AND ANALYSIS

Presentation of Inventories

Inventories are one of the most significant assets of manufacturing and merchandising enterprises. The *CICA Handbook* requires disclosure of the basis of inventory valuation and a description of the method used to determine cost if it is materially different from recent cost. The standards also require that the basis of inventory valuation be consistently applied. Any change in the basis from that used in the previous period must be reported along with the change's effect on the period's results. It is also desirable that the amounts of the major categories making up the total inventory be disclosed; e.g., finished goods, work in process, and raw materials.

The following excerpts from the financial statements of **Canadian Pacific Limited** and **Sobeys Inc.** illustrate the presentation of the company's disclosure of the basis for inventory valuation, the cost flow method, and the definition of market used for the major categories making up the total inventory. It is quite acceptable, as shown in the illustrations, for a company to use different methods for different inventory components. The use of notes is the basic means of disclosing such information.

Canadian Pacific Limited

CONSOLIDATED BALANCE SHEET
December 31
(in millions)

	1999	1998
Assets		
CURRENT ASSETS		
Cash and temporary investments	$ 561.2	$ 612.8
Accounts receivable	1,711.0	1,545.4
Inventories (Note 9)	473.1	478.2
	2,745.3	2,636.4

NOTES TO CONSOLIDATED FINANCIAL STATEMENTS

Note 1.
SIGNIFICANT ACCOUNTING POLICIES

INVENTORIES
Rail materials and supplies are valued at the lower of average cost and replacement cost. Raw materials and finished goods are valued at the lower of average cost and net realizable value. Stores and materials are valued at cost, less an allowance for obsolescence.

Note 9
INVENTORIES
(in millions)

	1999	1998
Rail materials and supplies	$ 176.1	$ 194.6
Raw materials and work in progress	39.0	41.0
Finished goods	176.2	170.2
Stores and materials	81.8	72.4
	$ 473.1	$ 478.2

Analysis of Inventories

Because the amount of inventory that a company carries can have significant economic consequences, it is crucial that inventories be managed effectively. Inventory management, however, is a double-edged sword. On the one hand, management wants to have a great variety and quantity on hand so customers have the greatest selection and

ILLUSTRATION 9-26
Disclosure of Inventory Methods
—Sobeys Inc.

Go to the Digital Tool for
additional inventory disclosures.

CONSOLIDATED BALANCE SHEET			SOBEYS INC.
(in thousands) May 6, 2000	**2000**	1999	1998
ASSETS			
Current			
Cash	$ **53,138**	$ 71,133	$ 27,176
Short term investments, at cost			
(quoted market value $2,807; 1999 $5,445; 1998 $316,095)	**1,689**	4,546	315,205
Receivables	**420,050**	380,313	76,524
Current portion mortgages and loans receivable	**59,264**	14,010	765
Income taxes recoverable	**8,322**	9,623	—
Inventories	**485,464**	462,122	190,289
Prepaid expenses	**40,963**	31,284	8,446
Due from parent company	**—**	—	9,950
	1,068,890	973,031	628,355

NOTES TO CONSOLIDATED FINANCIAL STATEMENTS

(in thousands except share capital) May 6, 2000

1. ACCOUNTING POLICIES
Inventories
Warehouse inventories are valued at the lower of cost and net realizable value with cost being substantially determined on a first-in, first-out basis. Retail inventories are valued at the lower of cost and net realizable value less normal profit margins as determined by the retail method of inventory valuation.

always find what they want in stock. On the other hand, such an inventory policy may result in excessive carrying costs (e.g., investment, storage, insurance, taxes, obsolescence, and damage). Low inventory levels, which incur minimum carrying costs, lead to stockouts, lost sales, and disgruntled customers. Financial ratios can be used to help management chart a middle course between these two dangers. Common ratios used to evaluate inventory levels are inventory turnover and a related measure—average days to sell the inventory.

The **inventory turnover ratio** measures the number of times on average the inventory was sold during the period. Its purpose is to measure the liquidity of the investment in inventory. A manager may use past turnover experience to determine how long the inventory now in stock will take to be sold. The inventory turnover is calculated by dividing the cost of goods sold by the average inventory on hand during the period. Unless seasonal factors are significant, average inventory can be calculated from the beginning and ending inventory balances.[12] For example, in its 1999 annual report, **General Fasteners Inc.** reported a beginning inventory of $6,218,840, an ending inventory of $6,131,174, and cost of goods sold of $36,219,657 for the year. The calculation of the 1999 inventory turnover of General Fasteners is shown below.

ILLUSTRATION 9-27
Inventory Turnover Ratio

$$\text{Inventory Turnover} = \frac{\text{Cost of Goods Sold}}{\text{Average Inventory}}$$

$$= \frac{\$36,219,657}{\dfrac{\$6,218,840 + \$6,131,174}{2}} = 5.9 \text{ times}$$

A variant of the inventory turnover ratio is the **average days to sell inventory**, which represents the average age of the inventory on hand or the number of days it takes to sell inventory once purchased. For example, if General Fasteners' inventory turns over 5.9 times per year, that means it takes, on average, 365 days divided by 5.9 or approximately 62 days to sell the average investment in inventory.

---

[12] Some seasonality is common in most companies. The fiscal year end is usually chosen at a low activity point in the year's operations, so that inventories in the annual financial statements are usually at one of the lowest levels in the year. Internally, management has access to additional information and can adjust to use the average monthly inventory level. External users, without access to monthly financial reports, are limited to using the average between the opening and closing annual inventory balances. Public companies are required to report to shareholders on a quarterly basis. In this case, the average can be based on four data points.

Is this a good ratio? If General Fasteners sells fruit and vegetables, you would know that this is not a good number. However, for other products, it is not as easy to come to a firm conclusion. Each industry has its norms, so the industry average is one standard against which you could compare the company's ratio. Internally, company management would compare these numbers with what they had forecast and set as objectives for the year. There is no absolute standard of comparison for most ratios, but generally speaking, companies that are able to keep their inventory at lower levels with higher turnovers than those of their competitors, and still satisfy customer needs, are the most successful.

SUMMARY OF LEARNING OBJECTIVES

1 Recognize that the lower of cost and market basis is a departure from the historical cost principle, and understand why this is appropriate. The lower of cost and market approach is a departure from historical cost. It is justified on the basis that assets in general, and current assets in particular, should not be reported at an amount greater than the cash expected to be realized from their use, sale, or conversion. It is also justified based on the matching principle. Any decline in an asset's utility (represented by a reduction in the future cash flows expected) should be recognized in the accounting period when the loss in utility occurs.

2 Explain various definitions of possible market amounts that may be used when applying lower of cost and market. Replacement cost is the amount needed to acquire an equivalent item in the normal course of business. Net realizable value is an item's estimated selling price in the ordinary course of business less reasonably predictable future costs to complete and dispose of it. Net realizable value less a normal profit margin is determined by deducting a normal profit margin from an item's net realizable value. All three are acceptable definitions of market, although net realizable value is the one used by a large majority of Canadian companies. The U.S. rules are more prescriptive and require that the middle value be chosen. Some Canadian companies follow this latter approach.

3 Explain how LCM (lower of cost and market) works and how it is applied. Under the lower of cost and market approach, the cost (specific identification, FIFO, average cost, or LIFO) and market (replacement cost, net realizable value, or net realizable value less a normal profit margin) of inventory are separately determined. The inventory value for the balance sheet is then the lower of the two amounts. The lower of cost and market may be determined on an item-by-item basis, major category basis, or total inventory basis.

4 Know how to account for inventory on the lower of cost and market basis. If it is determined that market is less than cost, inventory may be directly written down to market (direct method) or the difference may be accounted for in a contra inventory allowance account (indirect or allowance method).

5 Identify when inventories are carried regularly at net realizable value. Inventories are valued at net realizable value when (1) there is a controlled market with a quoted price applicable to all quantities, (2) no significant costs of disposal are involved, and (3) the cost figures are too difficult or not possible to obtain.

6 Explain when the relative sales value method is used to value inventories. When a group of varying units is purchased at a single lump sum price—a so-called basket purchase—the total purchase price may be allocated to the individual items based on their relative sales value. Such an allocation results in appropriately assigning a relevant cost to each item or type of inventory. This facilitates the subsequent matching of costs against revenues when an item is sold, and the reporting of an amount in the balance sheet as inventory before the item is sold.

KEY TERMS

average days to sell inventory, *428*

basket purchase, *417*

conventional retail inventory method, *424*

cost-to-retail ratio, *422*

designated market value, *412*

gross profit method, *419*

gross profit percentage, *420*

hedging, *418*

inventory turnover ratio, *428*

lower of cost and market (LCM), *412*

markdown cancellations, *423*

markdowns, *423*

market (for LCM), *409*

markup, *422*

markup on cost, *420*

markup cancellations, *422*

net markdowns, *423*

net markups, *422*

net realizable value (NRV), *409*

net realizable value less a normal profit margin, *409*

purchase commitments, *418*

replacement cost, *409*

retail inventory method, *422*

7 Explain accounting issues related to purchase commitments. Accounting for purchase commitments is controversial. Some argue that these contracts should be reported as assets and liabilities when the contract is signed; others believe that recognition at the delivery date is more appropriate. Generally, if purchase commitments are significant relative to the company's financial position and operations, they should be disclosed in a note to the financial statements. If a contract requires future payment of a price in excess of market value at the balance sheet date, the contingent loss should be recognized.

8 Estimate ending inventory by applying the gross profit method. The steps in estimating ending inventory by applying the gross profit method are as follows: (1) calculate the gross profit percentage on selling price; (2) calculate gross profit by multiplying net sales by the gross profit percentage; (3) calculate cost of goods sold by subtracting gross profit from net sales; (4) calculate ending inventory by subtracting cost of goods sold from total cost of goods available for sale.

9 Explain the limitations of the gross profit method. Care must be taken in applying the gross profit method. The resulting estimate of ending inventory is only as good as the gross profit percent is appropriate to the current period's mix of sales and operations.

10 Estimate ending inventory by applying the retail inventory method. The retail inventory method is based on multiplying the retail price of ending inventory (determined by a count or from the accounting records) by a cost-to-retail percentage (derived from information in the accounting records). To apply the retail inventory method, records must be kept of the costs and retail prices for beginning inventory, net purchases, and abnormal spoilage, as well as the retail amount of net markups, net markdowns, and net sales. Determination of the items going into the numerator and denominator of the cost-to-retail ratio depend on the type of inventory valuation estimate desired.

11 Explain how inventory is reported and analysed. Disclosure of the basis of inventory valuation and any change in the basis are required by the *CICA Handbook*. Also, it is desirable to disclose major categories of inventory, the method used to determine cost, and the definition of market applied under the lower of cost and market method. Common ratios used in the management and evaluation of inventory levels are inventory turnover and a related measure—average days to sell the inventory, often called the average age of inventory.

BRIEF EXERCISES

BE9-1 Presented below is information related to Alstott Inc.'s inventory.

(per unit)	Skis	Boots	Parkas
Historical cost	$190.00	$106.00	$53.00
Selling price	217.00	145.00	73.75
Cost to distribute	19.00	8.00	2.50
Current replacement cost	203.00	105.00	51.00
Normal profit margin	32.00	29.00	21.25

Using a U.S. definition of market, determine the following: (a) the two limits to market value (i.e., the ceiling and the floor) that should be used in the lower of cost and market calculation for skis; (b) the cost amount that should be used in the lower of cost and market comparison of boots; and (c) the market amount that should be used to value parkas on the basis of the lower of cost and market.

BE9-2 Robin Corporation has the following four items in its ending inventory:

Item	Cost	Replacement Cost	Net Realizable Value (NRV)	NRV Less Normal Profit Margin
Jokers	$2,000	$1,900	$2,100	$1,600
Penguins	5,000	5,100	4,950	4,100
Riddlers	4,400	4,550	4,625	3,700
Scarecrows	3,200	2,990	3,830	3,070

Determine the total lower of cost and market inventory value for the ending inventory using the most widely used Canadian approach applied on a total inventory basis.

BE9-3 Battle Inc. uses a perpetual inventory system. At January 1, 2002, inventory was $214,000 at both cost and market value. At December 31, 2002, the inventory was $286,000 at cost and $269,000 at market value. Prepare the necessary December 31 entry under (a) the direct method and (b) the indirect method.

BE9-4 PC Plus buys 1,000 computer game CDs from a distributor that is discontinuing those games. The purchase price for the lot is $6,000. PC Plus will group the CDs into three price categories for resale, as indicated below:

Group	No. of CDs	Price per CD
1	100	$ 5.00
2	800	10.00
3	100	15.00

Determine the cost per CD for each group, using the relative sales value method.

BE9-5 Beaver Corp. signed a long-term noncancellable purchase commitment with a major supplier to purchase raw materials in 2003 at a cost of $1 million. At December 31, 2002, the raw materials to be purchased have a market value of $930,000. Prepare any necessary December 31 entry.

BE9-6 Use the information for Beaver Corp. from BE9-5. In 2003, Beaver paid $1 million to obtain the raw materials, which were worth $930,000. Prepare the entry to record the purchase.

BE9-7 Big Hunt Corporation's April 30 inventory was destroyed by fire. January 1 inventory was $150,000, and purchases for January through April totalled $500,000. Sales for the same period were $700,000. Big Hunt's normal gross profit percentage is 31%. Using the gross profit method, estimate Big Hunt's April 30 inventory that was destroyed by fire.

BE9-8 Bikini Inc. had beginning inventory of $12,000 at cost and $20,000 at retail. Net purchases were $120,000 at cost and $170,000 at retail. Net markups were $10,000; net markdowns were $7,000; and sales were $157,000. Calculate ending inventory at cost using the conventional retail method.

BE9-9 In its 1999 Annual Report, **Domtar Inc.** reported inventory of $436 million on December 31, 1999, and $453 million on December 31, 1998, cost of goods sold of $2,313 million for fiscal year 1999, and net sales of $3,083 million. Calculate Domtar's inventory turnover and the average days to sell inventory for the fiscal year 1999.

EXERCISES

E9-1 **(Lower of Cost and Market)** The inventory of 3T Corporation on December 31, 2002, consists of these items:

Part No.	Quantity	Cost per Unit	Net Realizable Value per Unit
110	600	$ 90	$100
111	1,000	60	52
112	500	80	76
113	200	170	180
120	400	205	208
121a	1,600	16	?
122	300	240	235

aPart No. 121 is obsolete and has a realizable value of $0.20 each as scrap.

Instructions

(a) Determine the inventory as of December 31, 2002, by the lower of cost and market method, applying this method directly to each item.

(b) Determine the inventory by the lower of cost and market method, applying the method to the inventory total.

E9-2 **(Lower of Cost and Market)** Singing Pump Corp. uses the lower of cost and market method on an individual item basis in pricing its inventory items. The inventory at December 31, 2002 consists of products D, E, F, G, H, and I. Relevant per-unit data for these products appear below:

	Item D	Item E	Item F	Item G	Item H	Item I
Estimated selling price	$120	$110	$95	$90	$110	$90
Cost	75	80	80	80	50	36
Replacement cost	120	72	70	30	70	30
Estimated selling expense	30	30	30	25	30	30
Normal profit	20	20	20	20	20	20

Instructions

Using the lower of cost and market rule, determine the proper unit value for balance sheet reporting purposes at December 31, 2002 for each inventory item above using (1) the most commonly used Canadian definition of market and (2) the U.S. rules to determine market.

E9-3 **(Lower of Cost and Market)** Bolton Ltd. follows the practice of pricing its inventory at the lower of cost and market, on an individual item basis.

Item No.	Quantity	Cost per Unit	Cost to Replace	Estimated Selling Price	Cost of Completion and Disposal	Normal Profit
1320	1,200	$3.20	$3.00	$4.50	$.35	$1.25
1333	900	2.70	2.30	3.50	.50	.50
1426	800	4.50	3.70	5.00	.40	1.00
1437	1,000	3.60	3.10	3.20	.25	.90
1510	700	2.25	2.00	3.25	.80	.60
1522	500	3.00	2.70	3.80	.40	.50
1573	3,000	1.80	1.60	2.50	.75	.50
1626	1,000	4.70	5.20	6.00	.50	1.00

Instructions

From the information above, determine the amount of Bolton's inventory assuming use of (1) the most commonly used definition of market in Canadian practice and (2) U.S. rules to determine market.

E9-4 **(Lower of Cost and Market—Journal Entries)** Corrs Corp. determined its ending inventory at cost and at lower of cost and market at December 31, 2001, and December 31, 2002. This information is presented below:

	Cost	Lower of Cost and Market
12/31/01	$346,000	$327,000
12/31/02	410,000	395,000

Instructions

(a) Prepare the journal entries required at 12/31/01 and 12/31/02, assuming that the inventory is recorded directly at market, and a periodic inventory system is used.

(b) Prepare journal entries required at 12/31/01 and 12/31/02, assuming that the inventory is recorded at cost and an allowance account is adjusted at each year end under a periodic system.

(c) Which of the two methods above provides the higher net income in each year?

E9-5 **(Lower of Cost and Market—Valuation Account)** Presented below is information related to Candlebox Enterprises:

	Jan. 31	Feb. 28	Mar. 31	Apr. 30
Inventory at cost	$15,000	$15,100	$17,000	$13,000
Inventory at the lower of cost and market	14,500	12,600	15,600	12,300
Purchases for the month		20,000	24,000	26,500
Sales for the month		29,000	35,000	40,000

Instructions

(a) From the information, prepare (as far as the data permit) monthly income statements in columnar form for February, March, and April. Show the inventory in the statement at cost, show the gain or loss due to market fluctuations separately, and set up a valuation account for the difference between cost and the lower of cost and market.

(b) Prepare the journal entry required to establish the valuation account at January 31 and entries to adjust it monthly thereafter.

E9-6 **(Lower of Cost and Market—Error Effect)** Oickle Corporation uses the lower of FIFO cost and net realizable value method, on an individual item basis, applying the direct method. The inventory at December 31, 2002 included product MX. Relevant per-unit data for product MX appear below:

Estimated selling price	$45
Cost	40
Replacement cost	35
Estimated selling expense	14
Normal profit	9

There were 1,000 units of product MX on hand at December 31, 2002. Product MX was incorrectly valued at $35 per unit for reporting purposes. All 1,000 units were sold in 2003.

Instructions

(a) Was net income for 2002 over or understated? By how much (ignore income tax aspects)?

(b) Was net income for 2003 over or understated? By how much?

(c) Indicate whether the current ratio, inventory turnover ratio, and debt-to-total assets ratio would be overstated, understated, or not affected for the years ended December 31, 2002 and December 31, 2003.

E9-7 **(Relative Sales Value Method)** Yuri Realty Corporation purchased a tract of unimproved land for $55,000. This land was improved and subdivided into building lots at an additional cost of $34,460. These building lots were all the same size but owing to differences in location were offered for sale at different prices as follows:

Group	No. of Lots	Price per Lot
1	9	$3,000
2	15	4,000
3	17	2,400

Operating expenses for the year allocated to this project totalled $18,200. Lots unsold at year end were as follows:

Group 1	5 lots
Group 2	7 lots
Group 3	2 lots

Instructions

Determine the year-end inventory and net income of Yuri Realty Corporation.

E9-8 **(Relative Sales Value Method)** During 2002, Trainor Furniture Limited purchased a carload of wicker chairs. The manufacturer sold the chairs to Trainor for a lump sum of $59,850, because it was discontinuing manufacturing operations and wished to dispose of its entire stock. Three types of chairs are included in the carload. The three types and the estimated selling price for each are listed below.

Type	No. of Chairs	Estimated Selling Price Each
Lounge chairs	400	$90
Armchairs	300	80
Straight chairs	700	50

During 2002, Trainor sells 200 lounge chairs, 100 armchairs, and 120 straight chairs, all at the same prices as estimated.

Instructions
What is the amount of gross profit earned during 2002? What is the amount of inventory of unsold lounge chairs on December 31, 2002?

E9-9 (Purchase Commitments) Han Chen Corp. has been having difficulty obtaining key raw materials for its manufacturing process. The company therefore signed a long-term noncancellable purchase commitment with its largest supplier of this raw material on November 30, 2002, at an agreed price of $400,000. At December 31, 2002, the raw material had declined in price to $365,000. It was further anticipated that the price will drop another $15,000 so that, at the date of delivery, the inventory value will be $350,000.

Instructions
(a) What entry would you make on December 31, 2002 to recognize these facts? Explain.
(b) What entry would you make if the price was expected to recover $15,000 before the date of delivery, so that the inventory value will be $380,000? Explain.

E9-10 (Purchase Commitments) At December 31, 2002, Indigo Ltd. has outstanding noncancellable purchase commitments for 36,000 litres, at $3.00 per litre, of raw material to be used in its manufacturing process. The company prices its raw material inventory at cost or market, whichever is lower.

Instructions
(a) Assuming that the market price as of December 31, 2002 is $3.30 per litre, how would this commitment be treated in the accounts and statements? Explain.
(b) Assuming that the market price as of December 31, 2002 is $2.70 per litre instead of $3.30, how would you treat this commitment in the accounts and statements?
(c) Provide the entry in January 2003, when the 36,000 litre shipment is received, assuming that the situation given in (b) existed at December 31, 2002, and that the market price in January 2003 is $2.70 per litre. Give an explanation of your treatment.

E9-11 (Gross Profit Method) Each of the following percentages is expressed in terms of markup on cost.

1. 20%	**3.** 33⅓%
2. 25%	**4.** 50%

Instructions
Indicate the gross profit percentage of sales for each of the above.

E9-12 (Gross Profit Method) Terry Arthur Company uses the gross profit method to estimate inventory for monthly reporting purposes. Presented below is information for the month of May:

Inventory, May 1	$160,000
Purchases (gross)	640,000
Freight-in	30,000
Sales	1,000,000
Sales returns	70,000
Purchase discounts	12,000

Instructions
(a) Calculate the estimated inventory at May 31, assuming that the gross profit is 30% of sales.
(b) Calculate the estimated inventory at May 31, assuming that the markup on cost is 30%.

E9-13 (Gross Profit Method) Tim Cheng requires an estimate of the cost of goods lost by fire on March 9. Merchandise on hand on January 1 was $38,000. Purchases since January 1 were $72,000; freight-in, $3,400; purchase returns and allowances, $2,400. Sales are made at a markup of 33⅓% on cost and totalled $100,000 to March 9. Goods costing $10,900 were left undamaged by the fire; the remaining goods were destroyed.

Instructions
(a) Calculate the cost of goods destroyed.
(b) Calculate the cost of goods destroyed, assuming that the gross profit is 33⅓% of sales.

E9-14 **(Gross Profit Method)** Rashid Corp. lost most of its inventory in a fire in December just before the year-end physical inventory was taken. The corporation's books disclosed the following:

Beginning inventory	$170,000	Sales	$650,000
Purchases for the year	390,000	Sales returns	24,000
Purchase returns	30,000	Gross margin on sales	40%

Merchandise with a selling price of $21,000 remained undamaged after the fire. Damaged merchandise with an original selling price of $15,000 had a net realizable value of $5,300.

Instructions

Calculate the amount lost due to the fire, assuming that the corporation had no insurance coverage.

E9-15 **(Gross Profit Method)** You are called by Brenda Scott of Wizard Corp. on July 16 and asked to prepare an insurance claim resulting from a theft that took place the night before. You suggest that an inventory be taken immediately. The following data are available:

Inventory, July 1	$ 38,000
Purchases—goods placed in stock July 1–15	85,000
Sales—goods delivered to customers (gross)	116,000
Sales returns—goods returned to stock	4,000

Your client reports that the goods on hand on July 16 cost $30,500, but you determine that this figure includes goods of $6,000 received on a consignment basis. Your past records show that sales are made at approximately 40% over cost.

Instructions

Calculate the claim against the insurance company.

E9-16 **(Gross Profit Method)** Chernin Lumber Ltd. handles three principal lines of merchandise with these varying rates of markup on cost:

Lumber	25%
Millwork	30%
Hardware and fittings	40%

On August 18, a fire destroyed the office, lumber shed, and a considerable portion of the lumber stacked in the yard. To file a report of loss for insurance purposes, the company must know what the inventories were immediately preceding the fire. No detail or perpetual inventory records of any kind were maintained. The only pertinent information you are able to obtain is the following facts from the general ledger, which was kept in a fireproof vault and thus escaped destruction.

	Lumber	Millwork	Hardware
Inventory, Jan. 1, 2002	$ 250,000	$ 90,000	$ 45,000
Purchases to Aug. 18, 2002	1,500,000	375,000	160,000
Sales to Aug. 18, 2002	2,080,000	533,000	210,000

Instructions

Submit your estimate of the inventory amounts immediately preceding the fire.

E9-17 **(Gross Profit Method)** Presented below is information related to Warren Smith Corporation for the current year:

Beginning inventory	$ 600,000	
Purchases	1,500,000	
Total goods available for sale		$2,100,000
Sales		2,500,000

Instructions

Calculate the ending inventory, assuming that **(a)** gross profit is 45% of sales; **(b)** markup on cost is 60%; **(c)** gross margin is 35% of sales; and **(d)** markup on cost is 25%.

E9-18 **(Retail Inventory Method)** Presented below is information related to Bobby Stoddart Corporation:

	Cost	Retail
Beginning inventory	$ 58,000	$100,000
Purchases (net)	122,000	200,000
Net markups		10,345
Net markdowns		26,135
Sales		186,000

Instructions

(a) Calculate the ending inventory at retail.
(b) Calculate a cost-to-retail percentage (round to two decimals):
  1. excluding both markups and markdowns
  2. excluding markups but including markdowns
  3. excluding markdowns but including markups
  4. including both markdowns and markups
(c) Which of the methods in (b) above (1, 2, 3, or 4):
  1. provides the most conservative estimate of ending inventory?
  2. provides an approximation of lower of cost and market?
  3. is used in the conventional retail method?
(d) Calculate ending inventory at lower of cost and market (round to nearest dollar).
(e) Calculate cost of goods sold based on (d).
(f) Calculate gross margin based on (d).

E9-19 **(Retail Inventory Method)** Presented below is information related to Elsie Henderson Limited.

	Cost	Retail
Beginning inventory	$ 200,000	$ 280,000
Purchases	1,375,000	2,140,000
Markups		95,000
Markup cancellations		15,000
Markdowns		35,000
Markdown cancellations		5,000
Sales		2,200,000

Instructions

Calculate the inventory by the conventional retail inventory method.

E9-20 **(Retail Inventory Method)** The records of Ellen's Boutique report the following data for the month of April:

Sales	$99,000	Purchases (at cost)	$48,000
Sales returns	2,000	Purchases (at sales price)	88,000
Additional markups	10,000	Purchase returns (at cost)	2,000
Markup cancellations	1,500	Purchase returns (at sales price)	3,000
Markdowns	9,300	Beginning inventory (at cost)	30,000
Markdown cancellations	2,800	Beginning inventory (at sales price)	46,500
Freight on purchases	2,400		

Instructions

Calculate the ending inventory by the conventional retail inventory method.

E9-21 **(Analysis of Inventories)** The financial statements of High Liner Foods Incorporated for the 52 weeks ended January 1, 2000, January 2, 1999, and January 3, 1998 disclose the following information:

(in $000)	January 1, 2000	January 2, 1999	January 3, 1998
Inventories of finished goods and retail stores	$31,359	$37,657	$26,778

	52 weeks ended	
	1/1/2000	1/2/1999
Sales	$302,392	$291,655
Cost of goods sold	225,235	209,024
Net income (loss)	(4,067)	6,487

Instructions

Calculate High Liner Foods' (a) inventory turnover and (b) the average days to sell inventory for the two years ending in 1999 and 2000.

E9-22 (**Retail Inventory Method—Conventional and Average Cost**)   A. Randall Smith Limited began operations on January 1, 2002, adopting the conventional retail inventory system. None of its merchandise was marked down in 2002 and, because there was no beginning inventory, its ending inventory for 2002 of $38,100 would have been the same under either the conventional retail system or the average cost system. All pertinent data regarding purchases, sales, markups, and markdowns are shown below.

	Cost	Retail
Inventory, Jan. 1, 2003	$ 38,100	$ 60,000
Markdowns (net)		13,000
Markups (net)		22,000
Purchases (net)	130,900	178,000
Sales (net)		167,000

Instructions

Determine the cost of the 2003 ending inventory under (a) the conventional retail method and (b) the average cost retail method.

E9-23 (**Retail Inventory Method—Conventional and Lower of FIFO Cost and Market**)   Clilverd Corp. began operations late in 2001 and adopted the conventional retail inventory method. Because there was no beginning inventory for 2001 and no markdowns during 2001, the ending inventory for 2001 was $14,000 under both the conventional retail method and the lower of FIFO cost and market retail method. At the end of 2002, management wants to compare the results of applying the conventional method, which assumes the lower of average cost and market with a lower of FIFO cost and market method. The following data are available for calculations:

	Cost	Retail
Inventory, January 1, 2002	$14,000	$20,000
Sales		80,000
Net markups		9,000
Net markdowns		1,600
Purchases	58,800	81,000
Freight-in	7,500	
Estimated theft		2,000

Instructions

Calculate the valuation of the 2002 ending inventory under both (a) the conventional retail method and (b) the lower of FIFO cost and market retail method.

PROBLEMS

P9-1   The Pendse Wood Corporation manufactures desks. Most of the company's desks are standard models sold at catalogue prices. At December 31, 2002, the following finished desks appear in the company's inventory:

Finished Desks	A	B	C	D
2002 catalogue selling price	$450	$480	$900	$1,050
FIFO cost per inventory list 12/31/02	470	450	830	960

Finished Desks (cont'd)	A	B	C	D
Estimated current cost to manufacture (at December 31, 2002, and early 2003)	460	440	610	1,000
Sales commissions and estimated other costs of disposal	45	60	90	130
2003 catalogue selling price	500	540	900	1,200

The 2002 catalogue was in effect through November 2002, and the 2003 catalogue is effective as of December 1, 2002. All catalogue prices are net of the usual discounts. Generally, the company attempts to obtain a 20% gross margin on selling price and has usually been successful in doing so.

Instructions

(a) At what total inventory value will the desks appear on the company's December 31, 2002 balance sheet, assuming that the company has adopted a lower of FIFO cost and market approach for the valuation of inventories, applied on a total inventory basis? Use net realizable value as the definition of market.

(b) Assume control of Pendse Wood was acquired during 2002 and that it is now a 60% owned subsidiary of Shripad Inc., a U.S. wood products company. The controller of Shripad advises that, for consolidation purposes, Pendse's inventory valuation methods should be consistent with those of the parent company. Shripad uses the U.S. rules for determining the lower of cost and market, and applies it on an individual item basis. What inventory value should Pendse's controller report to the parent company?

(c) As controller of Pendse, report to its president what the accounting and reporting implications are of using the valuation determined in (b) for reporting under Canadian GAAP.

P9-2 Secord Home Improvement Limited installs replacement siding, windows, and louvered glass doors for single family homes and condominium complexes in southern Ontario. The company is in the process of preparing its annual financial statements for the fiscal year ended May 31, 2002, and Tim Taylor, controller for Secord, has gathered the following data concerning inventory.

At May 31, 2002, the balance in Secord's Raw Material Inventory account was $408,000, and the Allowance to Reduce Inventory to Market had a credit balance of $29,500. Taylor summarized the relevant inventory cost and market data at May 31, 2002 in the schedule below.

Taylor assigned Patricia Richardson, an intern from a local college, the task of calculating the amount that should appear on Secord's May 31, 2002, financial statements for inventory under the lower of cost and market rule as applied to total inventory. Market is defined by Secord to be net realizable value. Richardson expressed concern over departing from the cost principle.

	Cost	Replacement Cost	Sales Price	Net Realizable Value	Normal Profit
Aluminum siding	$ 70,000	$ 62,500	$ 64,000	$ 56,000	$ 5,100
Cedar shake siding	86,000	79,400	94,000	84,800	7,400
Louvered glass doors	112,000	124,000	186,400	168,300	18,500
Thermal windows	140,000	122,000	154,800	140,000	15,400
Total	$408,000	$387,900	$499,200	$449,100	$46,400

Instructions

(a) Determine the proper balance in the Allowance to Reduce Inventory to LCM account at May 31, 2002 and make the necessary entry to adjust the accounts.

(b) Explain the rationale for using the lower of cost and market rule as it applies to inventories.

(c) Peter Secord, the company president, takes great care in analysing his company's financial statements, and he often compares notes with his cousin, who operates a similar company in northern New York. The use of different accounting methods makes their financial statements less comparable than they otherwise would be. For example, his cousin uses the standard U.S. approach to the valuation of inventory, and applies it on an item-by-item basis. Determine the impact on Secord Home Improvement's reported income before tax of the two approaches. (Assume a zero balance in the opening Allowance account.)

(d) What other ratios or relationships would also be affected by the different approaches? Explain.

P9-3 Wicks Corporation is a food wholesaler that supplies independent grocery stores in the immediate region. The company has a perpetual inventory system for all of its food products. The first-in, first-out (FIFO) method of inventory valuation is used to determine the inventory cost at the end of each month.

Transactions and other related information regarding two of the items (instant coffee and sugar) carried by Wicks are given below for October 2002, the last month of Wicks' fiscal year.

	Instant Coffee	Sugar
Standard unit of packaging:	Case containing 24, 1 kg jars	Baler containing 12, 5 kg bags
Inventory, 10/1/02:	1,000 cases @ $60.20 per case	500 balers @$6.50 per baler
Purchases:	**1.** 10/10/02—1,600 cases @ $62.10 per case plus freight of $480. **2.** 10/20/02—2,400 cases @ $64.00 per case plus freight of $480	**1.** 10/5/02—850 balers @ $5.76 per baler plus freight of $320. **2.** 10/16/02—640 balers @ $6.00 per baler plus freight of $320. **3.** 10/24/02—600 balers @ $6.20 per baler plus freight of $360.
Purchase terms:	2/10, n/30, f.o.b. shipping point	Net 30 days, f.o.b. shipping point
October sales:	3,600 cases @ $76.00 per case	1,950 balers @ $8.00 per baler
Returns and allowances:	A customer returned 50 cases that had been shipped in error. The customer's account was credited for $3,800.	As the October 16 purchase was unloaded, 20 balers were discovered damaged. A trucking firm representative confirmed the damage and the balers were discarded. A credit of $120 for the merchandise and $10 for the freight was received by Wicks.
Inventory values 10/31/02:		
• Net realizable value	$66.00 per case	$6.60 per baler
• Net realizable value less a normal profit of 15%	$56.10 per case	$5.61 per baler

Wicks' sales terms are 1/10, n/30, f.o.b. shipping point. Wicks records all purchases net of purchase discounts and takes all purchase discounts. The most recent quoted supplier price for coffee is $60 per case and for sugar $6.10 per baler before freight and purchase discounts.

Instructions

(a) Calculate the number of units in inventory and the FIFO unit cost for instant coffee and sugar as of October 31, 2002.
(b) Wicks applies the lower of cost and market (net realizable value) rule in valuing its year-end inventory. Calculate the total dollar amount of the instant coffee and sugar inventory applying the lower of cost and market rule on an individual product basis.
(c) Can Wicks apply the lower of cost and market rule to groups of products or the inventory, as a whole rather than on an individual product basis? Explain your answer.
(d) Can Wicks, a Canadian company, apply lower of cost and market according to the U.S. rule?

(CMA adapted)

P9-4 The Bateman Company determined its ending inventory at cost and at lower of cost and market at December 31, 2001, December 31, 2002, and December 31, 2003, as shown below:

	Cost	Lower of Cost and Market
12/31/01	$650,000	$650,000
12/31/02	780,000	722,000
12/31/03	900,000	830,000

Instructions

(a) Prepare the journal entries required at 12/31/02 and 12/31/03, assuming that a periodic inventory system and the direct method of adjusting to market is used.
(b) Prepare the journal entries required at 12/31/02 and 12/31/03, assuming that a periodic inventory is recorded at cost and reduced to market through the use of an allowance account.

P9-5 Hasselholf Ltd. lost most of its inventory in a fire in December just before the year-end physical inventory was taken. Corporate records disclose the following:

Inventory (beginning)	$ 80,000	Sales	$415,000
Purchases	280,000	Sales returns	21,000
Purchase returns	28,000	Gross profit on sales	34%

Purchases includes an in-transit shipment from a supplier, shipped f.o.b. shipping point, with an invoice cost of $535. Merchandise on hand with a selling price of $30,000 remained undamaged after the fire, and damaged merchandise has a salvage value of $7,150. The company does not carry fire insurance on its inventory.

Instructions

Prepare a schedule calculating the fire loss incurred by Hasselholf. (Do not use the retail inventory method.)

P9-6 On April 15, 2003, fire damaged the office and warehouse of John Kimmel Corporation. The only accounting record saved was the general ledger, from which the trial balance below was prepared.

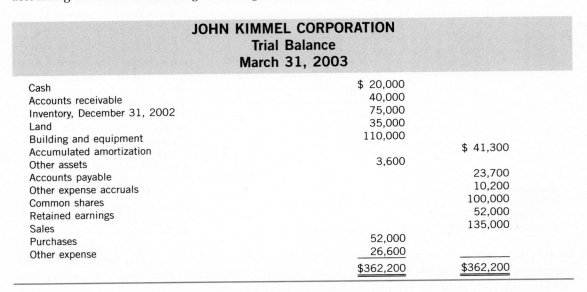

JOHN KIMMEL CORPORATION Trial Balance March 31, 2003		
Cash	$ 20,000	
Accounts receivable	40,000	
Inventory, December 31, 2002	75,000	
Land	35,000	
Building and equipment	110,000	
Accumulated amortization		$ 41,300
Other assets	3,600	
Accounts payable		23,700
Other expense accruals		10,200
Common shares		100,000
Retained earnings		52,000
Sales		135,000
Purchases	52,000	
Other expense	26,600	
	$362,200	$362,200

The following data and information have been gathered:

1. The corporation's fiscal year ends on December 31.
2. An examination of the April bank statement and cancelled cheques revealed that cheques written during the period April 1–15 totalled $13,000: $5,700 paid on accounts payable as of March 31, $3,400 for April merchandise shipments, and $3,900 paid for other expenses. Deposits during the same period amounted to $12,950, which consisted of receipts on account from customers with the exception of a $950 refund from a vendor for merchandise returned in April.
3. Correspondence with suppliers revealed unrecorded obligations at April 15 of $10,600 for April merchandise shipments, including $2,300 for shipments in transit (f.o.b. shipping point) on that date.
4. Customers acknowledged indebtedness of $36,000 at April 15, 2003. It was also estimated that customers owed another $8,000 that will never be acknowledged or recovered. Of the acknowledged indebtedness, $600 will probably be uncollectible.
5. The companies insuring the inventory agreed that the corporation's fire-loss claim should be based on the assumption that the overall gross profit ratio for the past two years was in effect during the current year. The corporation's audited financial statements disclosed this information:

	Year Ended December 31	
	2002	2001
Net sales	$530,000	$390,000
Net purchases	280,000	235,000
Beginning inventory	50,000	75,200
Ending inventory	75,000	50,000

6. Inventory with a cost of $7,000 was salvaged and sold for $3,500. The balance of the inventory was a total loss.

Instructions

Prepare a schedule calculating the amount of inventory fire loss. The supporting schedule to calculate the gross profit should be in good form. (AICPA adapted)

P9-7 The records for the Clothing Department of Dar's Discount Store are summarized below for the month of January.

Inventory; January 1: at retail, $25,000; at cost, $17,000
Purchases in January: at retail, $137,000; at cost, $86,500
Freight-in: $7,000
Purchase returns: at retail, $3,000; at cost, $2,300
Purchase allowances: $2,200
Transfers in from suburb branch: at retail, $13,000; at cost, $9,200
Net markups: $8,000
Net markdowns: $4,000
Inventory losses due to normal breakage, etc.: at retail, $400
Sales at retail: $85,000
Sales returns: $2,400

Instructions

Calculate the inventory for this department as of January 31, at (a) retail and (b) lower of average cost and market.

P9-8 Presented below is information related to S. Babcock Inc.

	Cost	Retail
Inventory, 12/31/01	$250,000	$ 390,000
Purchases	914,500	1,460,000
Purchase returns	60,000	80,000
Purchase discounts	18,000	—
Gross sales (after employee discounts)	—	1,460,000
Sales returns	—	97,500
Markups	—	120,000
Markup cancellations	—	40,000
Markdowns	—	45,000
Markdown cancellations	—	20,000
Freight-in	79,000	—
Employee discounts granted	—	8,000
Loss from breakage (normal)	—	2,500

Instructions

Assuming that S. Babcock Inc. uses the conventional retail inventory method, calculate the cost of its ending inventory at December 31, 2002.

P9-9 Chesley Jones Inc. uses the retail inventory method to estimate ending inventory for its monthly financial statements. The following data pertain to a single company department for the month of October 2003.

Inventory, October 1, 2003	
At cost	$ 52,000
At retail	78,000
Purchases (exclusive of freight and returns)	
At cost	262,000
At retail	423,000
Freight-in	16,600
Purchase returns	
At cost	5,600
At retail	8,000
Additional markups	9,000
Markup cancellations	2,000
Markdowns (net)	3,600
Normal spoilage and breakage	10,000
Sales	380,000

Instructions

(a) Using the conventional retail method, prepare a schedule calculating estimated lower of average cost and market inventory for October 31, 2003.

(b) A department store using the conventional retail inventory method estimates the ending inventory as $60,000. An accurate physical count reveals only $47,000 of inventory at lower of average cost and market. List the factors that may have caused the difference between the estimated inventory and the physical count.

P9-10 Brooks Specialty Corp., a division of FH Inc., manufactures three models of gear shift components for bicycles that are sold to bicycle manufacturers, retailers, and catalogue outlets. Since beginning operations in 1969, Brooks has used normal absorption costing and has assumed a first-in, first-out cost flow in its perpetual inventory system. Except for overhead, manufacturing costs are accumulated using actual costs. Overhead is applied to production using predetermined overhead rates. The balances of the inventory accounts at the end of Brooks' fiscal year, November 30, 2002, are shown below. The inventories are stated at cost before any year-end adjustments.

Finished goods	$647,000
Work in process	112,500
Raw materials	240,000
Factory supplies	69,000

The following information relates to Brooks' inventory and operations.

1. The finished goods inventory consists of the items analysed below.

	Cost	Market
Down tube shifter		
Standard model	$ 67,500	$ 67,000
Click adjustment model	94,500	87,000
Deluxe model	108,000	110,000
Total down tube shifters	270,000	264,000
Bar end shifter		
Standard model	83,000	90,050
Click adjustment model	99,000	97,550
Total bar end shifters	182,000	187,600
Head tube shifter		
Standard model	78,000	77,650
Click adjustment model	117,000	119,300
Total head tube shifters	195,000	196,950
Total finished goods	$647,000	$648,550

2. One-half of the head tube shifter finished goods inventory is held by catalogue outlets on consignment.
3. Three-quarters of the bar end shifter finished goods inventory has been pledged as collateral for a bank loan.
4. One-half of the raw materials balance represents derailleurs acquired at a contracted price 20% above the current market price. The market value of the rest of the raw materials is $127,400.
5. The total market value of the work-in-process inventory is $108,700.
6. Included in the cost of factory supplies are obsolete items with an historical cost of $4,200. The remaining factory supplies' market value is $65,900.
7. Brooks applies the lower of cost and market method to each of the three types of shifters in finished goods inventory. For each of the other three inventory accounts, Brooks applies the lower of cost and market method to the total of each inventory account.
8. Consider all amounts presented above to be material in relation to Brooks' financial statements taken as a whole.

Instructions

(a) Prepare the inventory section of Brooks' statement of financial position as of November 30, 2002, including any required note(s).

(b) Without prejudice to your answer to requirement (a), assume that the market value of Brooks' inventories is less than cost. Explain how this decline would be presented in Brooks' income statement for the fiscal year ended November 30, 2002.

(c) Assume that Brooks has a firm purchase commitment for the same type of derailleur included in the raw materials inventory as of November 30, 2002, and that the purchase commitment is at a contracted price 15% greater than the current market price. These derailleurs are to be delivered to Brooks after November 30, 2002. Discuss the impact, if any, that this purchase commitment would have on Brooks' financial statements prepared for the fiscal year ended November 30, 2002.

(CMA adapted)

P9-11 Fournier Corp. follows the practice of valuing its inventory at the lower of cost and market. The following information is available from the company's inventory records as of December 31, 2002:

Item	Quantity	Unit Cost	Replacement Cost/Unit	Estimated Selling Price/Unit	Completion & Disposal Cost/Unit	Normal Profit Margin/Unit
A	1,100	$7.50	$8.40	$10.50	$1.50	$1.80
B	800	8.20	8.00	9.40	.90	1.20
C	1,000	5.60	5.40	7.20	1.10	.60
D	1,000	3.80	4.20	6.30	.80	1.50
E	1,400	6.40	6.30	6.80	.70	1.00

Instructions

(a) Indicate the inventory amount that should be used for each item under the lower of cost and market rule assuming (1) the definition of market used most commonly in Canada and (2) U.S. rules.

(b) Fournier applies the lower of cost and market rule directly to each item in the inventory but maintains its inventory account at cost to account for the items above. Give the adjusting entry, if one is necessary, to write down the ending inventory from cost to market assuming (1) the definition of market used most commonly in Canada and (2) U.S. rules.

(c) Fournier applies the lower of cost and market rule to the inventory total. What is the dollar amount for inventory as of December 31, 2002, assuming (1) the definition of market used most commonly in Canada and (2) U.S. rules?

P9-12 As of January 1, 2002, Ather Inc. began to use the retail method of accounting for its merchandise inventory.

To prepare the store's financial statements at June 30, 2002, you obtain these data.

	Cost	Selling Price
Inventory, January 1	$ 30,000	$ 43,000
Markdowns		10,500
Markups		9,200
Markdown cancellations		6,500
Markup cancellations		3,200
Purchases	108,800	155,000
Sales		159,000
Purchase returns and allowances	2,800	4,000
Sales returns and allowances		8,000

Instructions

(a) Prepare a schedule to calculate Ather's June 30, 2002, inventory under the conventional retail method of accounting for inventories.

(b) Prepare as much of the income statement for Ather Inc. for the six months ended June 30, 2002 as possible from the data given.

(c) Determine the inventory turnover for the six month period, and the average age of the inventory. Comment on the relationships you calculated and what additional information you need before evaluating the company's inventory management performance.

P9-13 Late in 1999, Sara Teasdale and four other investors took the chain of Sprint Department Stores Ltd. private, and the company has just completed its third year of operations under the investment group's ownership. Elinor Wylie, controller of Sprint Department Stores, is in the process of preparing the year-end financial statements. Based on the preliminary statements, Teasdale has expressed concern over inventory shortages, and she has asked Wylie to determine whether an abnormal amount of theft and breakage has occurred. The accounting records of Sprint Department Stores Ltd. contain the following amounts on November 30, 2002—the fiscal year end.

	Cost	Retail
Beginning inventory	$ 68,000	$100,000
Purchases	248,200	400,000
Net markups		50,000
Net markdowns		110,000
Sales		330,000

According to the November 30, 2002 physical inventory, the actual inventory at retail is $107,000.

Instructions

(a) Describe the circumstances under which the retail inventory method would be applied, and the advantages of using the retail inventory method.

(b) Assuming that prices have been stable, calculate the lower of cost and market value of Sprint Department Stores' ending inventory using the conventional retail method. Furnish supporting calculations.

(c) Estimate the amount of shortage, at retail, that has occurred at Sprint Department Stores during the year ended November 30, 2002.

(d) Complications in the retail method can be caused by such items as (1) freight-in expense, (2) purchase returns and allowances, (3) sales returns and allowances, and (4) employee discounts. Explain how each of these four special items is handled in the retail inventory method.

(CMA adapted)

P9-14 Ulysses Inc. is an office supply and stationery wholesaler and retailer. Its merchandise is purchased from many suppliers and is warehoused until sold or shipped to the retail outlets.

In conducting the audit for the year ended June 30, 2002, the corporation's auditor determined that the internal control system was good. Accordingly, she observed the physical inventory at an interim date, May 31, 2002, instead of at year end. The following information was available from the general ledger:

Inventory, July 1, 2001	$ 120,000
Physical inventory, May 31, 2002	98,500
Sales for 11 months ended May 31, 2002	970,000
Sales for year ended June 30, 2002	1,060,000
Purchases for 11 months ended May 31, 2002, before audit adjustments	650,000
Purchases for year ended June 30, 2002, before audit adjustments	755,000

The audit disclosed the following information:

Shipments received in May and included in the physical inventory but recorded as June purchases	11,000
Shipments received in unsaleable condition and excluded from physical inventory; credit memos had not been received nor had chargebacks to vendors been recorded	
—Total at May 31, 2002	2,500
—Total at June 30, 2002 (including the May unrecorded chargebacks)	3,000
Deposit made with vendor and charged to purchases in April 2002, product was shipped in July 2002	3,100
Deposit made with vendor and charged to purchases in May 2002; product was shipped f.o.b. destination on May 29, 2002 and was included in May 31 physical inventory as goods in transit	6,500
Through the carelessness of the receiving department, a June shipment was damaged by rain. These goods were later sold in June at their cost of $8,000.	

Instructions

(a) In audit engagements in which interim physical inventories are observed, a frequently used auditing procedure is to test the reasonableness of the year-end inventory by applying gross profit ratios. Given this, you are asked to prepare schedules that show the determination of:

1. the gross profit ratio for the 11 months ended May 31, 2002
2. the cost of goods sold during June, 2002
3. the June 30, 2002 inventory

(b) Are there any reasons why the gross profit ratio calculated above may not be appropriate to use in assessing the June 30 inventory? Explain.

CONCEPTUAL CASES

C9-1 You have been asked by the financial vice-president to develop a short presentation on the lower of cost and market method for inventory purposes. The financial VP needs to explain this method to the president, because it appears that a portion of the company's inventory has declined in value.

Instructions

The financial VP asks you to answer the following questions.
  (a) What is the purpose of the lower of cost and market method?
  (b) How is the term "market" generally interpreted?
  (c) What is the effect of choosing one method over another?
  (d) Do you apply the lower of cost and market method to each individual item, to a category, or to the inventory total? Explain.
  (e) Is the valuation of inventory in this manner consistent with the treatment of other current assets?
  (f) What are the potential disadvantages of the lower of cost and market method?

C9-2 YoYoMa Inc. manufactures and sells four products, the inventories of which are carried at the lower of cost and market. A normal profit margin of 30% is usually maintained on each product.
  The following information was compiled as of December 31, 2002.

Product	Original Cost	Cost to Replace	Estimated Cost to Dispose	Expected Selling Price
A	$17.50	$14.00	$ 6.00	$ 30.00
B	48.00	78.00	26.00	100.00
C	35.00	42.00	15.00	80.00
D	47.50	45.00	20.50	95.00

Instructions

  (a) Why are expected selling prices important in the valuation of inventory at the lower of cost and market?
  (b) Prepare a schedule identifying three possible acceptable definitions of "market" for each product.
  (c) Determine the range of acceptable inventory valuations for the December 31, 2002 balance sheet.
  (d) Comment on how a company should choose which combination of alternatives is best for its particular circumstances.

C9-3 Horne Corporation purchased a significant amount of raw materials inventory for a new product it is manufacturing. Horne uses the lower of cost and market rule for these raw materials and applies it using the direct method. The replacement cost of the raw materials is above the net realizable value, and both are below the original cost.
  Horne uses the average cost inventory method for these raw materials. In the last two years, each purchase has been at a lower price than the previous purchase, and the ending inventory quantity for each period has been higher than the beginning inventory quantity for that period.

Instructions

  (a) At which amount should Horne's raw materials inventory be reported on the balance sheet? Why?
  (b) In general, why is the lower of cost and market rule used to report inventory?
  (c) What would have been the effect on ending inventory and cost of goods sold had Horne used the LIFO inventory method instead of the average cost inventory method for the raw materials? Why?
  (d) Part of the criteria for evaluating management's performance is the inventory turnover ratio and the number of days sales in inventory. The company's chief accountant has suggested to management that it may wish to switch from the direct method to the allowance method in applying the lower of cost and market rule. If this were done, the net carrying value of inventory would be used to calculate the inventory turnover. As a member of management, would you agree with the suggestion? Explain.

C9-4 Harvey Corporation, your client, manufactures paint. The company's president, Andy Harvey, has decided to open a retail store to sell his specialty paint products as well as wallpaper and other supplies that would be purchased from other suppliers. He has asked you for information about the conventional retail method of determining the cost of inventories at the retail store.

Instructions

Prepare a report to the president explaining the retail method of valuing inventories. Your report should include these points:

(a) description and accounting features of the method
(b) the conditions that may distort the results under the method
(c) a comparison of the advantages of using the retail method with those of using cost methods of inventory pricing
(d) the accounting theory underlying the treatment of net markdowns and net markups under the method

C9-5 A. Pox Corporation, a retailer and wholesaler of national brand-name household lighting fixtures, purchases its inventories from various suppliers.

Instructions

(a) 1. What criteria should be used to determine which of Pox's costs are inventoriable?
   2. Are Pox's administrative costs inventoriable? Defend your answer.
(b) 1. Pox uses the lower of cost and market rule for its wholesale inventories. What are the theoretical arguments for that rule?
   2. The inventories' replacement cost is below the net realizable value less a normal profit margin, which, in turn, is below the original cost. Net realizable value, however, is greater than cost. What amount should be used to value the inventories? Why?
(c) Pox calculates the estimated cost of its ending inventories held for sale at retail using the conventional retail inventory method. How would Pox treat the beginning inventories and net markdowns in calculating the cost ratio used to determine its ending inventories? Why?

(AICPA adapted)

C9-6 Presented below are a number of items that may be encountered in calculating the cost-to-retail percentage when using the conventional retail method or the FIFO retail method.

1. markdowns
2. markdown cancellations
3. cost of items transferred in from other departments
4. retail value of items transferred in from other departments
5. sales discounts
6. purchases discounts (purchases recorded gross)
7. estimated retail value of goods broken or stolen
8. cost of beginning inventory
9. retail value of beginning inventory
10. cost of purchases
11. retail value of purchases
12. markups
13. markup cancellations
14. employee discounts (sales recorded net)

Instructions

Prepare a skeleton schedule (i.e., without any numbers) for determining the inventory cost under the retail inventory method using all 14 of the above items, as necessary, under (1) the conventional retail method and (2) under the FIFO cost retail method. For each item that is handled in a different way, provide a brief explanation.

C9-7 You have just been hired by a heavy equipment dealer outside Winnipeg. The company's major business activities involve the purchase and resale of used heavy mining and construction equipment, including trucks, cranes, shovels, conveyors, crushers, etc. The company was incorporated in 1983, and in its early years, it purchased individual items of heavy equipment and resold them to customers throughout Canada.

In the early 1990s, the company began negotiating the "package" purchase of all the existing equipment at mine sites, concurrent with the closing down of several of the large iron mines in Ontario and exhausted coal mines in Saskatchewan. The mine operators preferred to liquidate their mine assets on that basis rather than hold auctions or leave the mine site open until all the equipment could be liquidated.

As there were numerous pieces of equipment in these package purchases, the client found it difficult to assign costs to each item individually. As a result, the company followed the policy of valuing these "package" purchases by the cost recovery method. Under this method, the company recognized no income until the entire cost had been recovered through sales revenues. This produced the effect of deferring income to later periods and represented, for financial reporting purposes, a conservative valuation of inventories in what was essentially a new field for the company where its level of experience had not been demonstrated.

Instructions

Comment on the propriety of this approach.

Using Your Judgement

···

FINANCIAL STATEMENT ANALYSIS CASES

Case 1   Domtar Inc.

Domtar Inc. is a well known Canadian company that manufactures and distributes communication and specialty papers (as well as pulp), produces lumber and veneer from its forest resources, sawmill operations and remanufacturing facilities, and has a major interest in a company that manufactures and distributes containerboard and corrugated products. Domtar reports the following information for its fiscal years ending December 31, 1998, 1999, and 2000.

Domtar Inc.
(in millions of Canadian dollars)

	2000	1999	1998
Current assets			
Cash	29	3	9
Receivables	404	388	322
Inventories	546	436	453
Prepaid expenses	19	19	13
Future income taxes	30	–	—
	1,028	846	797
Net sales	3,598	3,067	2,348
Cost of sales	2,703	2,297	1,835
Inventories			
Work-in-process and finished goods	311	223	224
Raw materials	131	118	137
Operating and maintenance supplies	104	95	92
	546	436	453

Significant accounting policy

Inventories of operating and maintenance supplies and raw materials are valued at the lower of average cost and replacement cost. Work-in-process and finished goods are valued at the lower of average cost and net realizable value and include the cost of raw materials, direct labour, and manufacturing overhead expenses.

Instructions

(a) Suggest reasons why Domtar uses two different definitions of "market" in valuing its inventory.

(b) Calculate the inventory turnover for Domtar's 1999 and 2000 fiscal years. Also determine the average number of days to sell the inventory. What inventory numbers did you use in these ratios? Justify your choices.

(c) Determine Domtar's percentage gross profit on sales and its markup on cost.

(d) Suggest possible reasons why the gross profit percentage has varied over the three-year period. What would have been the effect on Domtar's income before taxes in 2000 if the company generated the same gross profit in 2000 that it did in 1998?

Case 2   Magnotta Winery Corporation

Access the financial statements of **Magnotta Winery Corporation** on the Digital Tool.

Instructions

Refer to these financial statements and the accompanying notes to answer the following questions.

(a) What categories of inventory does Magnotta Winery report?

(b) How does Magnotta value its inventories? Which inventory costing method does the company use as a basis for reporting its inventories?

(c) Identify the types of costs included in each inventory category.

(d) What was Magnotta's inventory turnover ratio for the most recent year? What is the average age of the inventory? What is its gross profit percentage?

(e) Comment on the results of your calculations in part (d).

(f) How would you evaluate this company's inventory management activities?

Case 3   Barrick Gold Corporation

Barrick Gold Corporation, with headquarters in Toronto, is one of the largest gold mining companies in the world, and the most profitable gold mining company outside South Africa. It boasts the lowest costs and highest margins in the industry. Part of the key to Barrick's success has been its ability to maintain cash flow while improving production and increasing its reserves of gold-containing property. Barrick continues to achieve record growth in cash flow, production, and reserves.

The company maintains an aggressive policy of exploring on and around existing producing properties and pursuing the disciplined acquisition of other companies with significant portfolios of mineral properties. Barrick limits the riskiness of this development by choosing only properties that are located in politically stable regions, and by using internally generated funds, rather than debt, to finance growth. Barrick's inventories are as follows:

Inventories (in millions, U.S. dollars)	1999
Current	
Gold in process	$56
Mine operating supplies	32
Non-current (included in property, plant, and equipment)	
Ore in stockpiles	$172

The notes to the financial statements for the year ended December 31, 1999 indicate that "gold in process and mine operating supplies are valued at the lower of average cost and net realizable value." Another note on revenue recognition states "Gold poured, in transit and at refineries, is recorded at net realizable value and included in bullion settlements and other receivables and gold sales. Revenue from the sale of by-products such as silver and copper is credited against operating costs."

Instructions

(a) Why are there are no finished goods inventories? What is the revenue recognition point for Barrick's primary product? Prepare skeleton journal entries that would be made to recognize revenue and cost of sales.

(b) Why do you think the raw material—ore in stockpiles—is considered a non-current asset?

(c) Briefly describe how you think Barrick keeps track of and accounts for any mineral by-products, including its inventory valuation.

(d) Would the inventory turnover and average days to sell inventory be relevant ratios for a gold producer? What is critical to success in this type of industry? What information would be relevant?

COMPARATIVE ANALYSIS CASE

Sears Canada Inc. versus Hudson's Bay Company

Instructions
Go to the Digital Tool and, using **Sears Canada Inc.** and **Hudson's Bay Company** annual report information, answer the following questions.

(a) What is the amount of inventory reported by Sears Canada at December 31, 2000, and by Hudson's Bay at January 31, 2001? What percent of total assets is invested in inventory by each company?

(b) What inventory costing methods are used by Sears Canada and Hudson's Bay? How does each company value its inventories?

(c) Calculate and compare the inventory turnover ratios and days to sell inventory for the most current period for the two companies. If COGS is not reported, use a surrogate. What choices are there? Identify the limitations of the surrogate you chose.

(d) Comment on the results of your calculations in (c) above. Would any differences identified in (b) above help explain variations in the ratios?

(e) Is COGS required to be reported by GAAP? Why do you think many companies do not report COGS?

RESEARCH CASES

Case 1

Most public companies have established home pages on the Internet; for example, **Phillips Petroleum Company** (http://www.phillips66.com), **Transalta Corporation** (http://www.transalta.com), **Canadian Pacific Limited** (http://www.cp.ca), and **Loblaw Companies Limited** (http://www.loblaw.com). You undoubtedly have noticed company Internet addresses in television commercials or magazine advertisements.

Instructions
Examine the home pages of any two companies of interest to you and answer the following questions.

(a) What type of information is available?

(b) Is any accounting-related information presented?

(c) Would you describe the home page as informative, promotional, or both? Why?

Case 2

Derlan Industries Limited's 1999 Annual Report states that it is "a Toronto Stock Exchange listed corporation manufacturing products for the aerospace and pump industries," with operations in Canada, the United States, Mexico, and Germany. Find the latest annual financial statements for this company (try the company's website at http://www.derlan.com, access the company's information at http://www.sedar.com), or find their financial statements on the Digital Tool.

Instructions

(a) Identify the types of inventory reported by Derlan.

(b) What accounting policies has the company chosen in relation to inventory valuation?

(c) For each category of inventory, explain how the company would likely generate the information needed to determine "market." Be specific.

(d) Briefly discuss the application of "market" to long-term construction contract inventories.

ETHICS CASES

Case 1

The market value of Lake Corporation's inventory has declined below its cost. Vickie Maher, the controller, wants to use the allowance method to write down inventory because it more clearly discloses the decline in market value, and it does not distort the cost of goods sold. Her supervisor, financial vice-president Doug Bruce, prefers the direct method to write down inventory because it does not call attention to the decline in market value.

Instructions

Answer the following questions:

(a) What, if any, is the ethical issue involved?

(b) Is any stakeholder harmed if Bruce's preference is used?

(c) What should Vickie Maher do?

Case 2

Vineland Limited signed a long-term purchase contract to buy timber from the British Columbia Forest Service at $300 per thousand board feet. Under this contract, Vineland must cut and pay $6 million for this timber during the next year. Currently the market value is $250 per thousand board feet. Ruben Walker, the controller, wants to recognize the loss in value in the year-end financial statements, but the financial vice-president, Billie Hands, argues that the loss is temporary and should be ignored. Walker notes that market value has remained near $250 for many months, and he sees no sign of significant change.

Instructions

Answer the following questions:

(a) What are the ethical issues, if any?

(b) Is any particular stakeholder harmed by the financial vice-president's decision?

(c) What should the controller do?

Investments

LEARNING OBJECTIVES

After studying this chapter, you should be able to:

1. Identify the different types of categories of investments and describe how investments are classified.

2. Explain the nature of temporary investments and describe the accounting and reporting treatment for temporary investments.

3. Explain the nature of long-term investments and describe the accounting and financial reporting for these investments.

4. Explain the equity method of accounting and compare it with the cost method for equity securities.

5. Describe the disclosure requirements for long-term investments in debt and equity securities.

Preview of Chapter 10

Investments may include common shares, preference shares, bonds, commodities, and other types of instruments[1]—both temporary and long-term. This chapter deals with accounting for these items, which are for the most part considered financial instruments.[2] The more complex types of investments such as stock options, rights and warrants will be dealt with in the appendices to Chapters 10 and 18.

In the U.S., many investments are carried at fair value with the realized and unrealized gains included either in net income (realized) or comprehensive income (unrealized). In Canada, investments are still largely governed by the historical cost principle, although there is a move toward fair value accounting.[3] Certain specialized industries in Canada already use fair value for valuing some or all of their investments (such as life insurance companies, pensions, and mutual fund companies).[4]

The content and organization of this chapter are as follows:

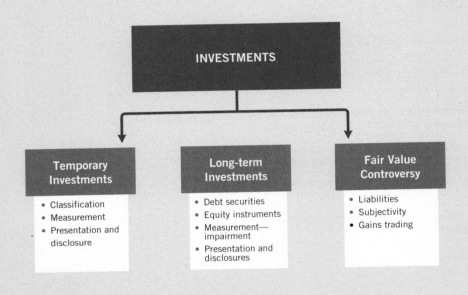

---

[1] As per *CICA Handbook*, Section 3010, par. .01.

[2] Commodities futures however are not considered to be financial instruments as they do not involve transfer of a financial asset (*CICA Handbook*, Section 3860, par. .14).

[3] As of 2001, the AcSB issued an invitation to comment on the Joint Working Group Standard entitled "Financial Instruments and Similar Items" (issued December 2000). By becoming involved with this standard at an early stage, harmonization between the accounting standards supported by the different countries will be enhanced. The draft standard supports measurement of virtually all financial instruments at fair value. The CICA AcSB plans to issue an exposure draft in this area once all comments have been received.

[4] *CICA Handbook*, Sections 4100 and 4210.

Companies have **different motivations for investing** in securities[5] issued by other companies. One motivation relates to the **returns** provided by investments, i.e., through interest, dividends, or capital gains (an increase in underlying value of the investment). Note that some types of investments provide guaranteed returns (such as term deposits), while others are more risky (such as investments in shares of other companies). Managers may intend to invest for **short-term returns** or **longer-term returns** depending on their business and whether they need the excess cash for another purpose.

Aside from returns, another motivation deals more with **strategic choice**. Companies may invest in common shares of other companies (which allow the holder to vote on key company decisions) in order to have some **influence or control over the operations** of that company. For instance, a strategic investment may give the investing company access to distribution channels or a guaranteed supply of raw materials.

Consider **Franco-Nevada Mining Corp.**, a gold mining company whose shares trade on the TSE. The company's business model is to earn revenues from royalty streams and investments in the precious metals industry. Strategically, it is attempting to expand geographically. In April 2001, the company sold its interest in a major mine in Nevada to **Normandy Mining Ltd.** (Normandy), the world's seventh-largest gold mining company, and took back royalty rights to gold produced and sold from the mine. This means that the company gets a 5-10% royalty on all revenues. As part of the deal, the company purchased an interest in Normandy.

The deal allows the company to focus on its **core business**; royalties and investments. By taking back a minority interest in Normandy, it frees the company from operating cash calls made by the mine if it owned it directly and also from potential environmental issues related to the mine. The deal also allows the company to diversify its "geopolitical" risk, resulting in its earnings being sourced in the U.S., Canada, and Australia.

Accounting for investments reflects both the **type of security** or instrument (debt or equity) and management's **intent**, which, as noted above, may be quite different from security to security.

UNDERLYING CONCEPTS

Knowledge of management intent allows the financial reporting treatment to reflect the investment's economic substance.

TEMPORARY INVESTMENTS

Often, companies will invest excess cash in temporary investments[6] that are highly liquid. This allows the company to **maximize returns** on its assets and yet affords it the **flexibility to liquidate** the investments should the cash be needed. Usually, these investments take the form of short-term paper (certificates of deposit, treasury bills, and commercial paper), debt securities (government and corporate bonds), and equity securities/instruments (preferred, common shares, options, warrants).[7]

OBJECTIVE 1

Identify the different types of categories of investments and describe how investments are classified.

---

[5] A security is a share, participation, or other interest in property or in an enterprise of the issuer or an obligation of the issuer that: (a) either is represented by an instrument issued in bearer or registered form or, if not represented by an instrument, is registered in books maintained to record transfers by or on behalf of the issuer; (b) is of a type commonly dealt in on securities exchanges or markets or, when represented by an instrument, is commonly recognized in any area in which it is issued or dealt in as a medium for investment; and (c) either is one of a class or series or by its terms is divisible into a class or series of shares, participations, interests, or obligations. From "Accounting for Certain Investments in Debt and Equity Securities," *Statement of Financial Accounting Standards No. 115* (Norwalk, Conn.: FASB, 1993), p. 48, par. 137.

[6] *CICA Handbook*, Section 3010 identifies temporary investments as those that are "transitional or current in nature...made to obtain a return on a temporary basis."

[7] An equity instrument is defined as "any contract that evidences a residual interest in the assets of an entity after deducting all of its liabilities" per *CICA Handbook*, Section 3860, par. .05(d).

Classification

To be classified as a **temporary investment** and included in **current assets**, investments must meet two criteria:

1. They must be **capable of reasonably prompt liquidation**[8] and,
2. There must be management intent to convert them to cash as needed, within one year or the operating cycle—whichever is longer.

Investments are normally considered **capable of reasonably prompt liquidation** when a ready market exists for the instruments, such as stock exchanges or money markets (banks). Readily marketable means that the security can be sold quite easily, with minimal transaction costs and without undue delay. If the shares are closely held (not publicly traded) there may be limited or no market for the security and its classification as a long-term investment may be more appropriate.

Intent to convert is extremely difficult to substantiate in practice. Intent may be established when the invested cash is seen by management as a contingency fund to be used whenever the need arises or perhaps when the investment was made out of cash that is temporarily idle due to the seasonality of the business. Management's expressed intent should be **supported by evidence**, such as the history of investment activities, events subsequent to the balance sheet date, and the investment's nature and purpose.

Temporary investments generally meet the definition of financial instruments, which are defined as "contracts that give rise to financial assets of one party and financial liabilities or equity instruments of another party."[9]

Financial assets are defined as

(a) **cash**; or
(b) contractual right to receive **cash** or another **financial asset** from another party; or
(c) a contractual right to **exchange financial instruments** with another party under conditions that are potentially **favourable**; or
(d) an **equity instrument** of another entity.[10]

Financial instruments will be dealt with in various chapters as they often represent much of a company's balance sheet. In terms of financial assets, Chapter 7 deals with cash and receivables (included in the definition under (b) above). For purposes of this chapter, most temporary investments fall under (b) i.e., debt instruments (investments in financial liabilities of another party) or (d) i.e., equity instruments. The instruments referred to in (c) will be dealt with in Chapter 18 (Appendix A) as they are more complex. **Financial liabilities** will be covered in Chapters 14 and 15.

Measurement

IAS NOTE

IAS 39 requires that financial assets be initially recorded at cost and then remeasured to market (with certain exceptions).

When acquired, temporary investments are recorded at cost under the **historical cost principle**. Cost includes both the purchase price and incidental direct costs such as brokerage commissions,[11] legal fees, and taxes. Shares may be acquired on margin. This means that the investor only pays part of the purchase price to acquire the shares. The rest is funded/financed by the broker. Since the shares **legally belong to the investor**, the full amount of the share price should be recorded with a corresponding liability to the broker.

---

8 *CICA Handbook*, Section 3010, par. .02.

9 *CICA Handbook*, Section 3860, par. .05(a).

10 *Ibid*, par. .05(b).

11 Brokerage commissions are usually incurred when buying and selling most securities. Commissions vary with the share value and the number of shares/units purchased and are often between 1% and 3% of the trade value for smaller trades. For larger trades, the commissions are often substantially lower in terms of percentage. Discount brokerages offer significant discounts even on smaller trades. Transactions involving mutual funds may have no commission attached to them (no load funds) but some sort of commission may be charged upon redemption (back end commission).

In some cases, **cost** is difficult to determine. For example, equity securities acquired in exchange for noncash consideration (property or services) should be recorded at (1) the fair value of the consideration given or (2) the **fair value** of the security received, whichever is more clearly determinable. The absence of clearly determinable values for the property or services or a market price for the security acquired may require the use of appraisals or estimates to arrive at a cost.[12]

Consistent with valuation of other current assets (such as inventories), temporary investments are subsequently valued using the lower of cost and market rule. When the current market value declines below the carrying value, the assets are written down to market value.[13]

Portfolio versus Individual Investments

The lower of cost and market rule may be applied to the **portfolio as a whole** or to **individual securities**. This is a matter of professional judgement, although once decided, **consistency** would dictate that the practice be continued.[14] In either case, a valuation account is set up and thereafter adjusted at each reporting date depending on the portfolio's value at the reporting date.

To illustrate, assume that on December 31, 2002, Western Publishing Corporation determined its temporary investment securities portfolio to be as shown in Illustration 10-1 (assume that 2002 is the first year that Western Publishing held temporary investments). At the date of acquisition, these securities were recorded at cost, including brokerage commissions and taxes. This is the first valuation of this recently purchased portfolio.

UNDERLYING CONCEPTS

Temporary investments (which generally are marketable) are reported at the lower of cost and market, not only because the information is relevant, but also because it is reliable.

INTERNATIONAL INSIGHT

In Germany, marketable securities are presented at lower of cost and market value. In the U.S., "trading" securities and securities that are available for sale are carried at market.

SECURITY PORTFOLIO
December 31, 2002

Investments	Cost	Fair Value	Unrealized Gain (Loss)
Air Canada shares	$ 43,860	$ 51,500	$7,640
CIBC shares	184,230	175,200	(9,030)
Magna shares	86,360	91,500	5,140
Total of portfolio	$314,450	$318,200	$3,750

ILLUSTRATION 10-1

Measurements of Portfolio Using LCM-Valuation Based on Individual Securities

Note that if only the **individual** securities are considered, only the CIBC shares will be revalued as their **market value is lower than cost**. The journal entry would be as follows:

Loss on Investment (I/S)	9,030	
Investment Allowance (B/S)		9,030

This allowance would be **eliminated and factored into the gain or loss** once the bonds were **sold**.

Looking at the **total** portfolio, the **total** cost of Western's portfolio is $314,450 and **total** market is $318,200—**greater than historical cost**. Therefore, there would be **no allowance**. If the total fair value is less than the cost, an **allowance account** would be set up using the same journal entry as above and at each reporting date, the allowance would be reassessed to determine if more allowance or less was needed, similar to allowance for doubtful accounts. To illustrate, assume that the portfolio remains the

---

[12] If the consideration given up involves shares—either of the company or of another company not only is there a measurement issue, but also an issue as to whether **in substance** a purchase and sale have occurred. *CICA Handbook*, EIC Abstracts #67 and #81 consider whether the investments exchanged are similar. Factors such as **line of business** of the companies whose shares are exchanged and the **nature of the investment**, i.e. portfolio, significant influence, or control (as discussed in the next section on long-term investments) are looked at.

[13] *CICA Handbook*, Section 3010, par. .06.

[14] The **whole portfolio** approach might appear to make more sense given the nature of temporary investment; for most companies, temporary investments represent a **pool** of excess cash that has been invested until needed in order to maximize return on assets.

same in 2003 except that the **Air Canada** shares are sold for the fair value noted above.[15] A gain would be realized. The journal entry to record the sale would be as follows:

Cash	51,500	
Temporary Investments		43,860
Investment Income—Gain		7,640

Any brokerage fees would reduce the cash received as well as the gain. Note that if there were a valuation allowance set up, it would not affect the gain calculation. Assume that the Air Canada shares are replaced with shares of **Nortel**. The remaining portfolio is shown in Illustration 10-2.

ILLUSTRATION 10-2
Measurement of Portfolio Using LCM—Valuation Based on Whole Portfolio—2003

SECURITY PORTFOLIO
December 31, 2003

Investments	Cost	Fair Value	Unrealized Gain (Loss)
CIBC shares	$184,230	$190,300	$6,070
Magna shares	86,360	81,500	(4,860)
Nortel shares	50,998	45,876	(5,122)
Total of portfolio	$321,588	$317,676	$(3,912)

Measuring based on the whole portfolio basis, the fair value is less than cost and a valuation allowance is required for $3,912. If the fair value **subsequently recovers** such that it is greater than the cost, the whole allowance would be eliminated, with the credit being booked to investment income.

Investment Allowance (B/S)	3,912	
Investment Income—Gain		3,912

Management intent should be reassessed in this case since the CIBC and **Magna** shares are still in the portfolio. Is management intent to continue to hold the shares as a temporary investment? If not, the shares should be reclassified to **long-term investments**.

Bonds

Debt securities, such as bonds, have added complexities. Bonds arise from a contract known as an indenture and represent a **promise by the issuing company to pay** a sum of money at maturity (**principal**) and periodic interest payments (fixed or variable), which are based on the bond's **face value**. The bonds are evidenced by a certificate, which states the bond's face or maturity value, interest rate (known as the **stated interest rate**), term, and date of interest payments. Bond prices are quoted as a percentage of the instrument's face value.

For instance, the purchase price of a $5,000 Government of Canada bond selling at 97½% is not $5,000. The price is $5,000 (face value) × 0.975 or $4,875. Why would the bond sell for less than the face value, i.e., at a discount? Assume the bond pays interest at 10% (stated rate). Subsequently, interest rates may change. If the interest rate on similar term, newer bonds is now 11%, the $5,000 bond will now be less attractive and therefore worth less than the face value. Thus the **market price of bonds changes all the time**. The investment community values the bond at the **present value of the remaining future cash flows (principal and interest)** discounted at the current market rate of interest (known as the **effective rate of interest** or **bond yield** when valuing bonds).

Junk bonds are bonds that carry a higher risk of default. Because of this higher risk, they also pay more interest. The higher risk may stem from the **riskiness of the industry** that the issuing company does business in or perhaps due to the company's **cash**

---

[15] If only part of the investment in the Air Canada shares were sold, the shares' average cost would be used to measure a gain or loss on sale. *CICA Handbook*, Section 3050, par. .27 supports this for long-term investments and it is not unreasonable to apply this recommendation to temporary investments as the situation is similar.

flow position. Who buys junk bonds? **American Express Company** (**Amex**) held 11% of its investment portfolio in these "high yield" bonds in 2001. Publicly traded life insurance companies also invest in these bonds along with many other investors of various size and in different industries. In the first quarter of 2001, Amex reported first quarter results that were 18% lower than market expectations (a material amount) due to losses on these bonds, writing off 5% of its junk-bond portfolio.[16] Investors invest in these bonds due to the high returns (keeping in mind the large potential for losses).

Bonds normally **pay interest at certain fixed dates** during the year, e.g., interest may be payable to holders as of June 30 and December 31 each year. This poses an interesting issue if the investment in bonds is made **between interest dates**, say September 30. In this case, the acquirer is not only purchasing the instrument itself but also rights to the interest accrued from July 1 to September 30.

Assume Sparkling Corporation buys a $1,000 10% bond at 86% on September 30, 2001. Interest dates on the bond are June 30 and December 31. Because the bondholder will be entitled to interest accumulating from July 1 on the next interest date, the purchase price is higher. Sparkling Corporation would pay the following for the bond:

$1,000 × 0.86	=	$860
$1,000 × 10% × 6/12 × 50%	=	25
		$885

When purchased, the following entry would be recorded:

Temporary Investment	860	
Interest Income	25	
Cash		885

When the interest is paid on December 31, the following entry would be recorded:

Cash	50	
Interest Income		50
($1,000 × 10% × 6/12)		

As discussed later in this chapter under **long-term investments**, any **discount or premium** is normally amortized over the period to maturity. For **temporary investments in bonds**, this practice is not followed, as the bonds will not be carried to maturity.

Presentation and Disclosure

The following basic presentation and disclosure requirements are set out in the *CICA Handbook* (Section 3010):

- separate presentation of investments in **affiliated companies**
- **basis of valuation** should be disclosed
- **market and carrying value** for all marketable securities should be disclosed

Note that information relating to **terms and conditions, interest rate risk, and credit risk concentrations** are also required disclosures for financial instruments.

UNDERLYING CONCEPTS

Providing supplemental information on the fair values of financial instruments illustrates application of the full disclosure principle.

LONG-TERM INVESTMENTS

Long-term investments are investments that are not considered temporary. As previously mentioned, **management intent** with respect to these investments is to hold onto them for a period beyond a year, either for **long-term returns or for strategic reasons**. **Long-term investments in bonds and most preferred shares** are considered **financial instruments** and therefore governed by *CICA Handbook* Section 3860. However, **long-term investments in common shares**, although meeting the definition of financial instruments and equity instruments, are not governed by *CICA Handbook* Section 3860 on Financial Instruments. These investments in common shares present some unique

OBJECTIVE 3

Explain the nature of long-term investments and describe the accounting and financial reporting for these investments.

---

[16] "Amex junk-bond losses take bite out of earnings," *The Globe and Mail* April 5, 2001.

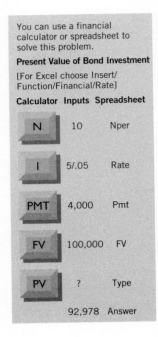

You can use a financial calculator or spreadsheet to solve this problem.

Present Value of Bond Investment

[For Excel choose Insert/ Function/Financial/Rate]

Calculator	Inputs	Spreadsheet
N	10	Nper
I	5/.05	Rate
PMT	4,000	Pmt
FV	100,000	FV
PV	?	Type
	92,978	Answer

challenges for accountants, because the shares have voting rights attached to them. They are therefore dealt with separately under *CICA Handbook* Sections 3050 and 1590. The existence of voting rights results in the nature of the investment changing with the number of shares held. This will be discussed in further depth in this chapter.

Debt Securities

Temporary investments in **debt securities** such as bonds are recorded at **historical cost** as noted under temporary investments. For **long-term** bond holdings, however, the **intent** is to hold the bond until maturity and therefore, **bond discounts or premiums are recorded and amortized** such that the bond's carrying value reflects its face value upon maturity. (A discount occurs when the bond is issued at less than face value. A premium occurs when the bond is issued at greater than face value.) Thus the bonds are carried at amortized cost. Amortized cost is defined as the acquisition cost, adjusted for the **amortization of discount or premium**, if appropriate.

Acquisition

To illustrate the accounting for long-term debt securities, assume that Robinson Limited purchased $100,000 of 8% bonds of Chan Corporation on January 1, 2001, paying $92,278.[17] The bonds mature January 1, 2006; interest is payable each July 1 and January 1. The discount of $7,722 ($100,000 − $92,278) provides an effective interest yield of 10%. The entry to record the investment is:

January 1, 2001		
Long-term Investments	92,278	
Cash		92,278

Discounts and premiums on long-term investments in bonds are amortized in a manner similar to discounts and premiums on bonds payable, discussed in Chapter 15. Illustration 10-3 shows the effect of the discount amortization on the interest income recorded each period for the investment in Chan Corporation bonds.

ILLUSTRATION 10-3

Schedule of Interest Income and Bond Discount Amortization— Effective Interest Method

	8% Bonds Purchased to Yield 10%			
Date	Cash Received	Interest Revenue	Bond Discount Amortization	Carrying Amount of Bonds
1/1/01				$92,278
7/1/01	$4,000a	$4,614b	$614c	92,892d
1/1/02	4,000	4,645	645	93,537
7/1/02	4,000	4,677	677	94,214
1/1/03	4,000	4,711	711	94,925
7/1/03	4,000	4,746	746	95,671
1/1/04	4,000	4,783	783	96,454
7/1/04	4,000	4,823	823	97,277
1/1/05	4,000	4,864	864	98,141
7/1/05	4,000	4,907	907	99,048
1/1/06	4,000	4,952	952	100,000
	$40,000	$47,722	$7,722	

a$4,000 = $100,000 × .08 × 6/12
b$4,614 = $92,278 × .10 × 6/12
c$614 = $4,614 − $4,000
d$92,892 = $92,278 + $614

---

[17] As previously mentioned, the value would be determined by the investment community and be roughly equal to the present value of the stream of principal and interest payments on the bond, discounted at the market rate.

The effective interest method is often used to amortize premiums and discounts[18] and is applied to bond investments in a fashion similar to that described for bonds payable. The effective interest rate or yield is calculated at the time of investment and is applied to its beginning carrying amount (book value) for each interest period in order to calculate interest revenue. The investment carrying amount is increased by the amortized discount or decreased by the amortized premium in each period. Thus the carrying value is always equal to the present value of the bond's cash flows (principal and interest payments) discounted at the market rate.

The journal entry to record receipt of the first semiannual interest payment on July 1, 2001 (using the data in Illustration 10-3), is:

July 1, 2001		
Cash	4,000	
Long-term Investments	614	
Interest Income		4,614

Because Robinson Corporation is on a calendar-year basis, it accrues interest and amortizes the discount at December 31, 2001 as follows:

December 31, 2001		
Interest Receivable	4,000	
Long-term Investments	645	
Interest Income		4,645

Again, the interest and amortization amounts are provided in Illustration 10-3.

Robinson Corporation would report the following items related to its investment in Chan bonds in its December 31, 2001 financial statements:

Balance Sheet	
Current assets	
Interest receivable	$ 4,000
Long-term investments	
Bonds, at amortized cost	$93,537
Income Statement	
Other income	
Interest income	$ 9,259

ILLUSTRATION 10-4
Reporting of Long-term investments

Disposition

Assuming Robinson Corporation sells its investment in Chan bonds on November 1, 2005, (close to its maturity date) at 99 ¾ plus accrued interest, the following calculations and entries would be made. The discount amortization from July 1, 2005 to November 1, 2005 is $635 (4/6 × $952). The entry to record this discount amortization is as follows:

November 1, 2005		
Long-term Investments	635	
Interest Income		635

The calculation of the realized gain on the sale is shown in Illustration 10-5.

Selling price of bonds (exclusive of accrued interest)		$99,750
Less: Book value of bonds on November 1, 2005:		
Amortized cost, July 1, 2005	$99,048	
Add: Discount amortized for the period		
July 1, 2005, to November 1, 2005	635	
		99,683
Gain on sale of bonds		$ 67

ILLUSTRATION 10-5
Calculation of Gain on Sale of Bonds

---

[18] *CICA Handbook*, Section 3050, par. .19 calls for a systematic method of allocating the premium or discount. This would encompass methods such as the **effective interest method** and the **straight-line method**.

The entry to record the sale of the bonds is:

November 1, 2005

Cash	102,417	
Interest Income (4/6 × $4,000)		2,667
Long-term Investments		99,683
Other Income—Gain		67

The credit to Interest Income represents accrued interest for four months, for which the purchaser pays cash. The debit to Cash represents the selling price of the bonds, $99,750, plus accrued interest of $2,667. The credit to the Long-term Investments account represents the bonds' book value on the sale date and the credit to Other Income represents the excess of the selling price over the bonds' book value.

Equity Instruments

Common Shares

Common or residual shares carry **voting rights**—the more shares held, the more votes and therefore the more say the investor has in the decisions made by the company invested in.

The degree to which one corporation (**investor**) acquires an interest in the common shares of another corporation (**investee**) generally determines the accounting treatment for the investment subsequent to acquisition. Investments by one corporation in the common shares of another can be **classified according to the percentage of the investee's voting shares held by the investor**. These **levels of interest or influence** and the corresponding **accounting method** that must be applied to the investment are displayed in Illustration 10-6.

ILLUSTRATION 10-6
Levels of Influence Determine Accounting Methods

Percentage Ownership	0% ◄─► 20% ◄────	50% ◄──────►	100%
Level of Influence	Little or None	Significant	Control
Type of Investment	Portfolio	Significant Influence	Subsidiary
Accounting Method	Cost Method	Equity Method	Consolidation

The accounting and reporting for investment in common shares therefore depends upon the **level of influence**, as shown in Illustration 10-6.[19]

Each of these types of investments is discussed in detail below.

Portfolio Investments **Portfolio investments** are securities where there is no **significant influence** or **control**. When an investor has an interest of less than 20%, it is presumed that the investor has little or no influence over the investee and thus the **cost method** is used to reflect this relationship.

Cost Method Portfolio investments are recorded at cost and the **cost method** is used to determine when income is recognized. Under the cost method, income is not recognized until a dividend is declared or received, whichever is earlier.

To illustrate, assume that on November 3, 2002, Canada Corporation purchased common shares of three companies, each investment representing a 15% interest:

UNDERLYING CONCEPTS

Revenue to be recognized should be earned and realized or realizable. A low level of ownership indicates that the income from an investee should be deferred until cash is received, or imminently receivable (i.e., when dividend declared).

---

[19] Joint ventures may take the form of incorporated companies and therefore issue shares. Joint ventures are characterized by **joint control** (versus **control**). The accounting method used for joint ventures is the **proportionate consolidation** method (*CICA Handbook*, Section 3055, par. .17). The key to determining whether the investment is a joint venture or not is determining whether there is **joint control**. This could be evidenced by percentage ownership or through a contractual agreement that states that the venturers (investors) must **share** key decision-making.

	Cost
Northwest Industries, Inc.	$259,700
Campbell Can Corp.	317,500
St. John's Pulp Corp.	141,350
Total cost	$718,550

These investments would be recorded as follows:

November 3, 2002		
Long-term Investments	718,550	
Cash		718,550

On December 6, 2002, Canada Corp. receives a cash dividend of $4,200 on its investment in the common shares of Campbell Can Corp. The cash dividend is recorded as follows:

December 6, 2002		
Cash	4,200	
Investment Income		4,200

All three of the investee companies reported net income for the year but only Campbell declared and paid a dividend to Canada Corp. As indicated, when an investor owns less than 20% of the common shares of another corporation, it is presumed that the investor has relatively **little influence** on the investee. As a result, net income earned by the investee is not considered an appropriate basis for recognizing income from the investment by the investor. The reason is that the investee may choose to retain (for use in the business) increased net assets resulting from profitable operations. Investment income is not considered **earned** by the investor until cash dividends are declared by the investee (**the critical event**).

The amount of investment income that may be recognized under the cost method is capped at the investor's **proportionate share of post-acquisition earnings of the investee**; that is, earnings since the date of acquisition. If the dividend received exceeds this amount, the excess is credited to the Long-term Investment account and treated as though it is a "liquidating dividend," i.e., a return of capital.[20]

In the example noted above, assume further that Campbell had NI of $20,000 for the period November 3–December 31, 2002 (the **post acquisition period**). Canada Corp's share of the post acquisition earnings would be as follows:

$$\$20,000 \times .15 = \$3,000$$

Therefore the dividends received are in excess of Canada Corp's share of post acquisition earnings by $1200 ($4,200–3,000). In this case, the journal entry to record the cash dividend would be as follows

December 6, 2002		
Cash	4,200	
Investment Income		4,200
December 31, 2002		
Investment Income	1,200	
Long-term Investment		1,200

For practical purposes, the "excess" is determined as at year-end and the calculation is **cumulative,** i.e., the calculation includes the investor's share of all **post acquisition earnings** since the acquisition date as well as all dividends received since the acquisition date.

---

[20] Note that it is not legally a **liquidating dividend**. The accounting treatment afforded to it is similar because from the investor's perspective (only) the excess dividend is like a return of capital as it is paid out of pre-acquisition earnings. *CICA Handbook* Section 3050, par. .02(c).

Significant Influence Investments An investor corporation may hold an interest of less than 50% in an investee corporation and thus not possess **legal control**. However, an investment in voting shares of less than 50% can still give the investor the ability to exercise **significant influence** over the investee's operating and financial policies. To provide a guide for accounting for investors when 50% or less of the common voting shares is held and to develop an operational definition of "significant influence," accountants have developed the following guidelines as noted in Illustration 10-7.[21]

ILLUSTRATION 10-7
Indications of the Existence of
Significant Influence

Quantitative factor:

1. percentage ownership—roughly 20% to approximately 50%,

Qualitative factor:

1. representation on the board of directors,

2. participation in policy-making processes,

3. material intercompany transactions,

4. interchange of managerial personnel, or

5. provision of technical information.

Another important consideration is the extent of ownership by an investor in relation to the concentration of other shareholdings. However, substantial or majority ownership of the voting shares of an investee by another investor does not necessarily preclude the ability to exercise significant influence by the investor.

Judgement is frequently required in determining whether an investment of 20% or more results in "significant influence" over investee's policies. The basic presumption is that **investments of less than 20% are presumed to be portfolio investments unless significant influence is clearly demonstrated**. Note further that **investments of 20% or more are not necessarily significant influence investments** unless significant influence is clearly demonstrated.

Sometimes the level of influence is difficult to determine. For instance, in the earlier mentioned Franco-Nevada Mining Corp. transaction, the company purchased a 19.9% interest in Normandy. This is almost right on the threshold. Other factors would have to be considered in order to determine the existence of significant influence. For instance, as part of the deal, the company was able to place one of its own management team members of the six-member Board of Directors of Normandy. The company accounts for the investment using the equity method.

In instances of "significant influence" (generally an investment of 20% or more), the investor is required to account for the investment using the **equity method**.

Equity Method Under the equity method, a substantive economic relationship is acknowledged between the investor and the investee. The investment is originally recorded at the **cost** of the shares acquired but is **subsequently adjusted each period for changes in the investee's net assets**. That is, the investment's carrying amount is periodically increased (decreased) by the investor's **proportionate share of the investee's post-acquisition earnings (losses)** and decreased by all **dividends received** by the investor from the investee. The equity method recognizes that the investee's earnings increase its net assets, and that the investee's losses and dividends decrease these net assets.

To illustrate the equity method and compare it with the cost method, assume that Maxi Limited purchases a 20% interest in Mini Limited. To apply the cost method in this example, assume that Maxi does not have the ability to exercise significant influence and the securities are classified as portfolio investments. Where the equity method is applied in this example, assume that the 20% interest permits Maxi to exercise significant influence. The entries are shown in Illustration 10-8.

INTERNATIONAL INSIGHT

In the European Community, the Seventh Directive requires the use of the equity method of accounting for investments in affiliates. However, there is still strong disagreement internationally concerning accounting for such investments. Currently, some nations (U.S., UK, Japan) require the use of the equity method; others (Sweden, Switzerland) do not.

OBJECTIVE 4

Explain the equity method of accounting and compare it with the cost method for equity securities.

---

[21] *CICA Handbook*, Section 3050, par. .04.

ILLUSTRATION 10-8
Comparison of Cost Method and Equity Method

Entries by Maxi

Cost Method	Equity Method

On January 2, 2002, Maxi acquired 48,000 shares (20% of Mini common shares) at a cost of $10 a share.

Cost Method		Equity Method	
Long-term Investments 480,000		Long-term Investments 480,000	
Cash	480,000	Cash	480,000

For the year 2002, Mini reported net income of $200,000; Maxi's share is 20% or $40,000.

Cost Method	Equity Method	
No entry	Long-term Investments 40,000	
	Investment Income*	40,000

At December 31, 2002, the 48,000 shares of Mini have a fair value (market price) of $12 a share, or $576,000.

Cost Method	Equity Method
No entry	No entry

On January 28, 2003, Mini announced and paid a cash dividend of $100,000; Maxi received 20% or $20,000.

Cost Method		Equity Method	
Cash 20,000		Cash 20,000	
Investment Income	20,000	Long-term Investments	20,000

For the year 2003, Mini reported a net loss of $50,000; Maxi's share is 20% or $10,000.

Cost Method	Equity Method	
No entry	Investment Income (Loss) 10,000	
	Long-term Investments	10,000

* sometimes referred to as "equity pickup" on the financial statements. This refers to the fact that the investor is picking up its share of income under the equity method.

Note that under the cost method, **only the cash dividends received** from Mini are reported as income by Maxi. Under the equity method, Maxi reports as income **its share of the net income reported by Mini**; the cash dividends received from Mini are recorded as a decrease in the **investment carrying value**. As a result, the investor records its share of the investee's net income in the year when it is earned. In this case, the investor can ensure that any net asset increases of the investee resulting from net income will be paid in dividends if desired. To wait until a dividend is received ignores the fact that the investor is better off if the investee has earned income. The **critical event in the earnings process** for the investment income for significant influence investments is when the investee earns the income.

If the acquisition of common shares results in a significant influence investment or subsidiary, a purchase equation must be calculated to determine the **excess of the purchase price over the asset's book value.**

Why would an investor pay more than book value for a company? Two main reasons are as follows:

1. The recorded assets may have fair values in excess of carrying values, e.g., land is very often undervalued on financial statements
2. Unrecorded goodwill and intangible assets.

The purchase equation first **identifies the excess paid** by the investor over book value and then identifies whether the excess paid is due to the **recorded assets or the unrecorded assets (e.g., goodwill, intangibles)**. This excess must be amortized against the investor's share of the investee's earnings unless it relates to an underlying asset that would not normally be amortized (e.g., land). Under the equity method, the investor's net income includes its proportionate share of investee earnings (adjusted to eliminate intercompany gains and losses) and amortization of the difference between the investor's initial cost and the investor's proportionate share of the investee's underlying book value at date of acquisition.[22]

---

[22] *CICA Handbook*, Section 3050, par. .02(a).

If the investee's net income includes **discontinued operations or extraordinary items**, the investor treats a proportionate share of the extraordinary items as an extraordinary item, rather than as ordinary investment revenue before extraordinary items.[23]

Assume that on January 1, 2002, Investor Limited purchased 250,000 shares of Investee Limited's 1 million shares of outstanding common shares for $8.5 million. Investee's total net worth or book value was $30 million at the date of Investor's 25% investment. Investor thereby paid $1 million [$8,500,000 − 0.25 ($30,000,000)] in excess of book value. It was determined that $600,000 of this is attributable to its share of undervalued depreciable assets of Investee and $400,000 to unrecorded intangibles. Investor estimated the average remaining life of the undervalued assets to be 10 years and decided upon a 10-year amortization period for the intangibles.

For the year 2002, Investee reported net income of $2.8 million including an extraordinary loss of $400,000, and paid dividends at June 30, 2002 of $500,000 and at December 31, 2002 of $900,000. The following entries would be recorded on Investor's books to report its long-term investment using the equity method.

January 1, 2002

Long-term Investment	8,500,000	
Cash		8,500,000
(To record the acquisition of 250,000 shares of Investee common share)		

June 30, 2002

Cash	125,000	
Long-term Investment		125,000
(To record dividend received ($500,000 × 0.25) from Investee)		

The entries on December 31, however, are more complex. In addition to the dividend received, Investor must **recognize its share of Investee's income**. Both an **ordinary and extraordinary component** must be recorded by Investor, because Investee's income includes both. Furthermore, Investor paid more than the book value for an interest in Investee's net assets. As a result, this **additional cost must be allocated to the proper accounting periods**. Assume no intercompany transactions.

December 31, 2002

Long-term Investments	700,000	
Extraordinary Item	100,000	
Investment Income		800,000
(To record share of Investee ordinary income ($3,200,000 × 0.25) and extraordinary loss ($400,000 × 0.25))		

December 31, 2002

Cash	225,000	
Long-term Investments		225,000
(To record dividend received ($900,000 × 0.25) from Investee)		

December 31, 2002

Investment Income	100,000	
Long-term Investment		100,000
(To record amortization of investment cost in excess of book value represented by:		
Undervalued depreciable assets—$600,000 / 10	=	$60,000
Unrecorded intangibles—$400,000 / 10	=	$40,000
Total		$100,000)

---

[23] *Ibid*, par. .09.

The investment in Investee is presented in the balance sheet of Investor at a carrying amount of $8,780,000, calculated as shown below.

Investment in Investee Company		
Acquisition cost, 1/1/02	$8,500,000	
Plus: Share of 2002 income before extraordinary item	800,000	$9,300,000
Less: Share of extraordinary loss	100,000	
Dividends received 6/30 and 12/31	350,000	
Amortization of undervalued depreciable assets	60,000	
Amortization of unrecorded intangibles	40,000	550,000
Carrying amount, 12/31/02		$8,750,000

ILLUSTRATION 10-9
Calculation of Investment Carrying Amount

In the preceding illustration, the investment cost exceeded the underlying book value. In some cases, an investor may acquire an investment at a cost less than the underlying book value (known as **negative goodwill**). In such cases, specific assets are assumed to be overvalued and, if depreciable, the excess of the investee's book value over the investor's acquisition cost is amortized into investment income over the remaining lives of the assets.[24] Investment income is increased under the presumption that the investee's net income as reported is actually understated because the investee is charging amortization on overstated asset values.

In cases where the acquisition is part of a **series of acquisitions** that lead to a **significant influence investment**, the **purchase equation** is completed on a cumulative basis, i.e., compare **total** cost paid for the **total** investment with **cumulative** percentage of book value of the investee's net assets.[25]

If an investor's share of the investee's losses exceeds the investment's carrying amount should the investor recognize additional losses? Ordinarily the investor should **discontinue applying the equity method and not recognize additional losses, once the investment account balance has reached a nil balance.**

However, if the investor's potential loss is not limited to the amount of its original investment (by guarantee of the investee's obligations or other commitment to provide further financial support), or if imminent return to profitable operations by the investee appears to be assured, it is appropriate for the investor to recognize additional losses.[26]

If the investor level of ownership influence falls below that necessary for continued use of the equity method, a change must be made to the cost method. Similarly, an investment in common share of an investee that has been accounted for by other than the equity method may become qualified for use of the equity method by an increase in the ownership level. Both these situations are discussed and illustrated in Chapter 22.

Subsidiary Investments   When one corporation acquires a voting interest of more than 50%—**controlling interest**—in another corporation, the investor corporation is referred to as the **parent** and the investee corporation as the **subsidiary**. The investment in the common shares of the subsidiary is presented as a long-term investment on the parent's separate financial statements.

When the parent treats the subsidiary as an investment, **consolidated financial statements** are generally prepared instead of separate financial statements for the parent and the subsidiary. Consolidated financial statements disregard the distinction between separate **legal entities** and treat the parent and subsidiary corporations as a single **economic entity**. The subject of when and how to prepare consolidated financial statements is discussed extensively in advanced accounting courses. Whether or not consolidated financial statements are prepared, the investment in the subsidiary is generally accounted for on the parent's legal entity books **using either the cost or equity method** as explained in this chapter. Subsequently, at any reporting date, the **consolidated statements** are prepared.

INTERNATIONAL INSIGHT

Historically, consolidation practices in Europe differ in terms of how the group of companies is determined. The UK approach focuses on ownership and the legal right to control; in contrast, the German approach focuses on management control.

---

[24] *CICA Handbook*, Section 1580, par. .44.

[25] This is referred to as a **step-by-step acquisition**. (*CICA Handbook*, Section 1600, par. .11).

[26] *CICA Handbook*, EIC Abstract #8.

Preferred shares

Investments in senior or preferred shares are carried at cost and are treated as **portfolio investments** as the shares do not carry voting rights. Therefore, there is no significant influence or control exercised by the company holding the shares.

Measurement—Impairment

Every investment should be evaluated at each reporting date to determine if it has suffered a **loss in value**. As previously mentioned, **temporary investments** are revalued to market under the **lower of cost and market rule** where the market is less than cost. Since **long-term investments** are held for longer time periods, a **longer time frame** is used to determine whether there has been a **decline in value that is other than temporary**. A bankruptcy or a significant liquidity crisis being experienced by an investee are examples of situations in which a loss in value to the investor may be permanent. If the decline is judged to be **other than temporary**, the cost basis of the individual security is written down to a new cost basis. The amount of the writedown is included in net income.

For debt securities that are held as long-term investments, there is generally no writedown as a result of general market price decline as the instruments are meant to be **held to maturity**. The exception to this is if the market price is low because it reflects cash flow difficulties of the issuing company (as opposed to interest rate differentials). A write down would only exist if it were felt that the principal or interest owed on the bond was no longer collectible.[27]

For equity securities, there are several factors to consider. Factors involved are as follows as noted in Illustration 10-10:

ILLUSTRATION 10-10
Impairment in Value—Long-term Equity Investments

> In determining whether impairment exists, the following factors may be considered:[28]
>
> 1. prolonged period during which **market is less than carrying value**
> 2. **severe investee losses**
> 3. **continued investee losses**
> 4. **suspension of trading** of investee shares
> 5. **investee liquidity or going concern** problems
> 6. appraised **fair value of shares** is less than carrying value

As can be seen by the above, the time frame is a longer one than used for temporary investments.[29] Once the investment has been written down, **this becomes the new cost base**.

Presentation and Disclosures

OBJECTIVE 5

Describe the disclosure requirements for long-term investments in debt and equity securities.

Basic required presentation and disclosures for long-term investments include the following:[30]

- The **basis of valuation** should be shown.
- **Investments** in companies subject to significant influence, other affiliated companies, and other long-term investment should be **shown separately**,
- **Income** from the items mentioned above should also be **shown separately**,

---

[27] In this case, the impairment may be assessed using the same principles as for impaired loans (as identified in *CICA Handbook*, Section 3025). Alternatively, if there is an active market, market prices may be used.

[28] *CICA Handbook*, Section 3050, par. .24.

[29] A time frame of three to four years is generally used to determine impairment.

[30] *CICA Handbook*, Section 3050, pars. .29–.38.

- Where the equity method is used, disclosure should be made of the **difference** between the investment cost and the underlying net book value of the investee's net assets at the date of purchase as well as the treatment of the components of the difference.
- **Fair value** as well as **carrying value** for all marketable securities classified as portfolio investments must be disclosed.

Similar to temporary investments, for those long-term investments categorized as financial instruments, the following must be disclosed: **terms and conditions**, **interest rate risk**, and **credit risk concentrations**.

FAIR VALUE CONTROVERSY

Currently, Canadian standards consider valuing investment at market only if it is less than carrying value.

The U.S. standard setters have moved one step beyond that, allowing fair value accounting for any investments that are **trading investments** or that are **held for sale**. Even this approach is subject to criticism, as noted below.

Liabilities Not Fairly Valued

Many argue that if investment securities are going to be reported at fair value, so also should liabilities. They note that by recognizing changes in value on only one side (the asset side), a high degree of volatility can occur in the income and shareholders' equity amounts. It is further argued that financial institutions are involved in asset and liability management (not just asset management) and that viewing only one side may lead managers to make uneconomic decisions as a result of the accounting.

Subjectivity of Fair Values

Often fair values or market values are not readily available and therefore any **benefits** derived from introducing fair value would be outweighed by the **costs** of determining fair value in certain situations and by the subjectivity of the resulting numbers.[31] Where markets exist for the instruments, this is not an issue. But does it make sense to value only marketable securities at fair value, leaving others at cost?

Gains Trading

At present, where most investments are held at cost, some feel that management may be induced to sell winner investments in order to generate quick gains on the income statements. This may be detrimental to the companies in the longer term as they will tend to sell the "winners" and hold on to the "losers."

Summary of Learning Objectives

1 Identify the different types of categories of investments and describe how investments are classified. Investments are classified based primarily on management intent and to a lesser extent whether there is a ready market. They are either classified as temporary or long-term and may be debt or equity securities/instruments.

---

[31] Members of the French delegation of the Joint Working Group project on Financial Instruments and Similar Items expressed this view and felt that this would reduce comparability.

2 Explain the nature of temporary investments and describe the accounting and reporting treatment for temporary investments. Temporary investments are held for a short time and are generally liquidated within the year. They are valued using the lower of cost and market rule, which may be applied to the portfolio as a whole or to individual securities. Investments in affiliated companies, basis of valuation, market and carrying value, terms and conditions as well as interest rate and credit risks should be disclosed.

3 Explain the nature of long-term investments and describe the accounting and financial reporting for these investments. Long-term investments are normally held for a longer time and often reflect management's strategic business plan. They are recorded at cost and then the accounting treatment is a function of whether they are debt or equity securities. Debt securities are carried at amortized cost and are not written down unless there are collectibility issues. Equity investments are also recorded at cost and if the securities carry voting privileges, either the cost, equity, or consolidation methods are used to account for them. Long-term equity investments are assessed for non temporary impairment of value.

4 Explain the equity method of accounting and compare it with the cost method for equity securities. Under the equity method, a substantive economic relationship is acknowledged between the investor and the investee. The investment is originally recorded at cost but is subsequently adjusted each period for changes in the investee's net assets. That is, the investment's carrying amount is periodically increased (decreased) by the investor's proportionate share of the investee's earnings (losses) and decreased by all dividends received by the investor from the investee. Under the cost method, the equity investment is reported by the investor at cost and investment income is recognized when dividends are declared or paid to the investor. The equity method is applied to investment holdings between 20% and 50% of ownership where significant influence exists, whereas the cost method is applied to holdings below 20% where no significant influence exists.

5 Describe the disclosure requirements for long-term investments in debt and equity securities. The following are required: (a) basis of valuation must be disclosed, (b) investments in companies subject to significant influence, other affiliated companies and other long-term investment should be shown separately, (c) income from the items mentioned above should also be shown separately (d) where the equity method is used, disclosure should be made of the difference between the investment cost investment and the underlying net book value of the investee's net assets at the date of purchase as well as the treatment of the components of the difference, and (e) fair value as well as carrying value for all marketable securities classified as portfolio investments. Similar to temporary investments, for those long-term investments categorized as financial instruments, the following must be disclosed: terms and conditions, interest rate risk, and credit risk concentrations.

APPENDIX 10A

Special Issues Related to Investments

Special issues relate to accounting for investments:

1. dividends received in shares,
2. stock rights,
3. cash surrender value of life insurance, and
4. accounting for funds.

OBJECTIVE 6

After studying Appendix 10A, you should be able to: Discuss the special issues that relate to accounting for investments.

DIVIDENDS RECEIVED IN SHARES

If the investee corporation declares a dividend distributable in its own shares of the same class, instead of in cash, each shareholder owns a larger number of shares but retains the same proportionate interest in the firm as before. The issuing corporation has distributed no assets; it has merely transferred a specified amount of retained earnings to paid-in capital, thus indicating that this amount will not provide a basis in the future for cash dividends.

Therefore, shares received as a result of a share (or stock) dividend or share (stock) split do not constitute revenue to the recipients. The reason they do not is that the recipients' interest in the issuing corporation is unchanged and the issuing corporation has not distributed any of its assets. The recipient of such additional shares would make no formal entry, but should make a memorandum entry and record a notation in the investments account to show that additional shares have been received.

Although no dollar amount is entered at the time of the receipt of stock dividends, the fact that additional shares have been received must be considered in calculating the carrying amount of any shares sold. The cost of the original shares purchased (plus the effect of any adjustments under the equity method) now constitutes the total carrying amount of both those shares plus the additional shares received, because no price was paid for the additional shares. The carrying amount per share is calculated by dividing the total shares into the carrying amount of the original shares purchased.

To illustrate, assume that 100 common shares of Shanmuganathan Limited are purchased for $9,600, and that two years later the company issues to shareholders one additional share for every two shares held; 150 shares that cost a total of $9,600 are then held. Therefore, if 60 shares are sold for $4,300, the carrying amount of the 60 shares would be calculated as shown below, assuming that the investment has been accounted for under the cost method.

Cost of 100 shares originally purchased	$9,600
Cost of 50 shares received as share dividend	0
Carrying amount of 150 shares held	$9,600
Carrying amount per share is $9,600/150, or $64	
Carrying amount of 60 shares sold is 60 × $64, or	$3,840

ILLUSTRATION 10A-1
Calculation of the Carrying Amount of Shares Received in a Share Dividend

The entry to record the sale is:

Cash	4,300	
Long-term Investments		3,840
Other Income		460

A total of 90 shares is still retained, and they are carried in the Long-term Investment account at $9,600 − $3,840, or $5,760. Thus the carrying amount for those shares remaining is also $64 per share, or a total of $5,760 for the 90 shares.

STOCK RIGHTS

When a corporation is about to offer for sale additional shares of an issue already outstanding, it may forward to present holders of that issue certificates permitting them to purchase additional shares in proportion to their present holdings. These certificates represent **rights to purchase additional shares** and are called stock rights. In rights offerings, rights generally are issued on the basis of one right per share, but it may take many rights to purchase one new share.

The certificate representing the stock rights, called a warrant, states the number of shares that the rights holder may purchase and also the price at which they may be purchased. If this price is less than these shares' current market value the rights have value, and from the time they are issued until they expire, they may be purchased and sold like any other security.

Stock rights have three important dates:

1. The date the rights offering is **announced**.
2. The date as of which the certificates or rights are **issued**.
3. The date the rights **expire**.

From the date the right is announced until it is issued, the share and the right are not separable, and the share is described as rights-on. After the certificate or right is received and up to the time it expires, the share and right can be sold separately. A share sold separately from an effective share right is sold ex-rights.

When a right is received, the shareholders have actually received nothing that they did not have before, because the shares already owned brought them the right; they have received no distribution of the corporation assets. The **carrying amount of the original shares held is now the carrying amount of those shares plus the rights, and it should be allocated between the two** on the basis of their total market values at the time the rights are received.

Disposition of Rights

The investor who receives rights to purchase additional shares has three alternatives:

1. Exercise the rights by purchasing additional shares.
2. Sell the rights.
3. Permit them to expire without selling or using them.

If the investor buys additional shares, the carrying amount of the original shares allocated to the rights becomes a part of the carrying amount of the new shares purchased. If the investor sells the rights, the allocated carrying amount compared with the selling price determines the gain or loss on sale. If the investor permits the rights to expire, a loss is suffered, and the investment should be reduced accordingly. The following example illustrates the problem involved.

Shares owned before issuance of rights—100
Cost of shares owned—$50 a share for a total cost of $5,000
Rights received—one right for every share owned, or 100 rights; two rights are required to purchase one new share at $50
Market value at date rights issued: Shares $60 a share, Rights $3 a right

Total market value of shares (100 × $60)		$6,000
Total market value of rights (100 × $3)		300
Combined market value		$6,300
Cost allocated to shares: $6,000/$6,300 × $5,000	=	$4,762
Cost allocated to rights: $3,00/$6,300 × $5,000	=	238
		$5,000
Cost allocated to each share: $4,762/100	=	$47.62
Cost allocated to each right: $238/100	=	$2.38

ILLUSTRATION 10A-2
Cost Allocations to Shares and to Rights

If some of the original shares are later sold, their cost for purposes of determining gain or loss on sale is $47.62 per share, as calculated above. If 10 of the original shares are sold at $58 per share, the entry would be:

Cash	580	
Long-term Investments		476
Other Income		104

CASH SURRENDER VALUE OF LIFE INSURANCE

There are many different kinds of insurance. The kinds usually carried by businesses include (1) casualty insurance, (2) liability insurance, and (3) life insurance. Certain types of life insurance constitute an investment, whereas casualty insurance and liability insurance do not. The three common types of life insurance policies that companies often carry on the lives of their principal officers are (a) ordinary life, (b) limited payment, and (c) term insurance. During the period that ordinary life and limited payment policies are in force, there is a cash surrender value and a loan value. Term insurance ordinarily has no cash surrender value or loan value.

If the insured officers or their heirs are the policy beneficiaries, the premiums paid by the company represent expense to the company, in the nature of salary expense (benefits). In this case, the policy's cash surrender value does not represent an asset to the company.

If the company, however, is the beneficiary and has the right to cancel the policy at its own option, the cash surrender value of the policy or policies is an asset of the company.

Accordingly, part of the premiums paid is not an expense, because the cash surrender value increases each year. Only the difference between the premium paid and the increase in cash surrender value represents expense to the company.

For example, if Suzi Corporation pays an insurance premium of $2,300 on a $100,000 policy covering its president and, as a result, the policy's cash surrender value increases from $15,000 to $16,400 during the period, the entry to record the premium payment is:

UNDERLYING CONCEPTS
The cash surrender value represents an asset since the future benefit is the potential payout and the company has access to this benefit as it is the beneficiary.

Expense	900	
Other Assets	1,400	
Cash		2,300

If the insured officer were to die halfway through the most recent period of coverage for which the $2,300 premium payment was made, the following entry would be made (assuming cash surrender value of $15,700 and refund of a pro rata share of the premium paid):

Cash [$100,000 + (1/2 of $2,300)]	101,150	
Other Asset		16,400
Expense (1/2 × $900)		450
Other Income ($100,000 − $15,700)		84,300

The gain on life insurance coverage is not generally reported as an extraordinary item because it is considered a "normal" business transaction. The cash surrender value of such life insurance policies should be reported in the balance sheet as a long-term investment or Other Asset, inasmuch as it is unlikely that the policies will be surrendered and cancelled in the immediate future.

FUNDS

Assets may be set aside in special **funds** for specific purposes and, therefore, become unavailable for ordinary business operations. Assets segregated in the special funds are then available when needed for the intended purposes.

There are two general types of funds: **(1) those in which cash is set aside to meet specific current obligations, and (2) those that are not directly related to current operations and are therefore in the nature of long-term investments**.

Several funds of the first type, discussed in preceding chapters, include the following:

Fund	Purpose
Petty Cash Fund	Payment of small expenditures, in currency
Payroll Cash Account	Payment of salaries and wages
Dividend Cash Account	Payment of dividends
Interest Fund	Payment of interest on long-term debt

In general, these funds are used to handle more expeditiously the payments of certain current obligations, to maintain better control over such expenditures, and to divide adequately the responsibility for cash disbursements. They are ordinarily shown as current assets (as part of Cash if immaterial), because the obligations to which they relate are ordinarily current liabilities.

Funds of the second type are similar to long-term investments, as they do not relate directly to current operations. They are ordinarily shown in the balance sheet's long-term investments section or in a separate section if relatively large in amount. The more common funds of this type and the purpose of each are listed below:

Fund	Purpose
Sinking Fund	Payment of long-term debt
Plant Expansion Fund	Purchase or construction of additional plant
Share Redemption Fund	Retirement of capital shares (usually preferred shares)
Contingency Fund	Payment of unforeseen obligations

Because the cash set aside will not be needed until some time in the future, it is usually invested in securities so that revenue may be earned on the fund assets. The assets of a fund may or may not be placed in the hands of a trustee. If appointed, the trustee becomes the assets' custodian, accounts to the company for them, and reports fund revenues and expenses.

To keep track of fund assets, revenues, and expenses, it is desirable to maintain separate accounts. For example, if a fund is kept to redeem a preferred shares issue that was issued with a redemption provision after a certain date, the following accounts relating to that fund might be kept:

Share Redemption Fund Cash

Share Redemption Fund Investments

Share Redemption Fund Revenue

Share Redemption Fund Expenses

Gain on Sale of Share Redemption Fund Investments

Loss on Sale of Share Redemption Fund Investments

Alternately, the assets might be held with Long-term Investments and any income or losses booked through the Other Income account. If securities purchased for the fund are to be held temporarily, they would be treated in the accounts in the same manner as temporary investments, described earlier in this chapter. If they are to be held for a long time, they are treated in accordance with the entries described for long-term investments.

In some cases, a company purchases its own shares or bonds when it is using a share redemption fund or sinking fund. In these situations, these **treasury shares** should be deducted from common shares (or the Shareholders' Equity section), and treasury bonds should be deducted from bonds payable. Dividend or interest income should not be recorded for these securities.

Distinction between Funds and Reserves

Although funds and reserves (appropriations) are not similar, they are sometimes confused because they may be related and often have similar titles. A simple distinction may be drawn: A fund is always an asset and always has a debit balance; a reserve (if used only in the limited sense recommended) is an appropriation of retained earnings, always has a credit balance, and is never an asset.

Summary of Learning Objective for Appendix 10A

6 Discuss the special issues that relate to accounting for investments. The special issues that relate to investments are: recognizing dividends received in shares (stock dividends and stock splits); allocating cost between shares and share rights; accounting for changes in the cash surrender value of life insurance; and accounting for assets set aside in special funds.

KEY TERMS – APPENDIX

cash surrender value, 473

ex-rights, 472

funds, 474

reserves (appropriations), 475

rights-on, 472

stock rights, 472

warrant, 472

BRIEF EXERCISES

BE10-1 Montreal Limited purchased as a long-term investment $50,000 of the 9%, five-year bonds of Parry Sound Corporation for $46,304, which provides an 11% return. Prepare Montreal's journal entries for **(a)** the investment purchase and **(b)** the receipt of annual interest and discount amortization. Assume effective interest amortization is used.

BE10-2 Mu Corporation purchased, as a long-term investment, $40,000 of the 8%, 5-year bonds of Phang Inc. for $43,412, which provides a 6% return. The bonds pay interest semiannually. Prepare Mu's journal entries for **(a)** the investment purchase and **(b)** the receipt of semiannual interest and premium amortization. Assume effective interest amortization is used.

BE10-3 Use the information from BE10-1, but assume the bonds are purchased as a temporary investment. Prepare Montreal's journal entries for **(a)** the investment purchase and **(b)** the receipt of annual interest. The bonds have a year-end fair value of $47,200.

BE10-4 Use the information from BE10-2, but assume the bonds are purchased as a temporary investment. Prepare Mu's journal entries for **(a)** the investment purchase and **(b)** the receipt of semi-annual interest. Assume the first interest payment is received on December 31, when the bonds' fair value is $42,900.

BE10-5 Singh Corporation purchased for $22,500 (as temporary investments) bonds with a face value of $20,000. At December 31, Singh received annual interest of $2,000 and the bonds' fair value was $20,900. Prepare Singh's journal entries for **(a)** the investment purchase and **(b)** the interest received.

BE10-6 Pacioli Corporation purchased 300 shares of Galetti Inc. common shares as a temporary investment for $9,900. During the year, Galetti paid a cash dividend of $3.25 per share. At year end, Galetti shares were selling for $34.50 per share. Prepare Pacioli's journal entries to record **(a)** the investment purchase and **(b)** the dividends received.

BE10-7 Penn Corporation purchased for $300,000 a 25% interest in Teller, Inc. This investment enables Penn to exert significant influence over Teller. During the year, Teller earned net income of $180,000 and paid dividends of $60,000. Prepare Penn's journal entries related to this investment.

BE10-8 Muhammad Corporation purchased for $630,000 a 30% interest in Mahmood Corporation on January 2, 2002. At that time, the book value of Mahmood's net assets was $1.9 million. Any excess of cost over book value is attributable to unrecorded intangibles with a useful life of 20 years. Prepare Muhammad's December 31, 2002 entry to amortize the excess of cost over book value.

*BE10-9 Rocky Corporation owns 200 shares of Boulder, Inc., which cost $11,000 and are held as a long-term investment. Rocky receives 20 shares of Boulder as a stock dividend and later sells 60 shares for $3,340. Prepare Rocky's entry to record receipt of the stock dividend and the sale of 60 shares.

*BE10-10 In 2001, Rolling Thunder Corporation purchased 200 shares of Twin Cobra common shares for $8,000. In July, Rolling Thunder received rights to purchase 50 shares (one right received for every four shares held) for $35 each. When the rights are received, the fair values are $42 per share and $12 per right. In August, the rights are sold for $625. Prepare Rolling Thunder's journal entries to record the rights' receipt and sale.

*BE10-11 Three Kingdoms Corporation paid an insurance premium of $3,150 on a life insurance policy covering its president. As a result, the policy's cash surrender value increased from $20,550 to $22,468. Prepare Three Kingdoms' journal entry to record the premium payment.

*BE10-12 Seaquest Corporation established a sinking fund by transferring $100,000 from the regular cash account. At the same time, the corporation established a $100,000 retained earnings appropriation for bond retirement. Prepare Seaquest's journal entries to record these transactions.

EXERCISES

E10-1 **(Entries for Debt Securities)** On July 1, 2001, Barone Corporation purchased $200,000 of the 9%, 10-year bonds of Wayne Inc. for $185,216. This investment will provide Barone an effective yield of 11%. Interest is received semiannually on June 30 and December 31. The bonds have a fair value of $188,500 on December 31, 2001.

Instructions

Prepare journal entries for Barone to record (1) the purchase of these securities and (2) any entries required at December 31, 2001, assuming:

    (a) Barone intends, and has the ability, to hold these securities to maturity.

    (b) Barone plans to liquidate these assets within the year.

E10-2 **(Entries for Long-term Investments)** On January 1, 2001, Halal Ltd. purchased 12% bonds, having a maturity value of $300,000, for $322,744. The bonds provide the bondholders with a 10% yield. They are dated January 1, 2001 and mature January 1, 2006, with interest receivable December 31 of each year. Halal uses the effective interest method to allocate unamortized discount or premium. The bonds are considered long-term investments.

Instructions

    (a) Prepare the journal entry at the date of the bond purchase.

    (b) Prepare a bond amortization schedule.

    (c) Prepare the journal entry to record the interest received and the amortization for 2001.

    (d) Prepare the journal entry to record the interest received and the amortization for 2002.

E10-3 **(Entries for Temporary Investments)** Assume the same information as in E10-2 except that the securities are classified as temporary investments. The fair value of the bonds at December 31 of each year end is as follows:

2001	$320,500		2004	$310,000
2002	$309,000		2005	$300,000
2003	$308,000			

Instructions

(a) Prepare the journal entry at the date of the bond purchase.
(b) Prepare the journal entries for 2001.
(c) Prepare the journal entries for 2002.

E10-4 **(Effective Interest Amortization)** On January 1, 2001, Phantom Inc. acquires $200,000 of Sy Inc., 9% bonds at a price of $185,589. The interest is payable each December 31, and the bonds mature December 31, 2003. The investment will provide Phantom a 12% yield. The bonds are classified as long-term investments.

Instructions

(a) Prepare a three-year schedule of interest income and bond discount amortization, applying the effective interest method.
(b) Prepare the journal entry for the interest receipt of December 31, 2002 and the discount amortization under the effective interest method.

E10-5 **(Entries for Temporary Investments)** The following information is available for Benaducci Inc. at December 31, 2001, regarding its investments:

Securities	Cost	Fair Value
3,000 shares of Mia Corporation Common Shares	$40,000	$48,000
1,000 shares of Calente Incorporated Preferred Shares	$25,000	$22,000
	$65,000	$70,000

Instructions

(a) Prepare the adjusting entry (if any) for 2001, assuming the securities are classified as temporary and the company assesses value based on individual shares.
(b) Prepare the adjusting entry (if any) for 2001, assuming the securities are classified as temporary and the company assesses value based on the whole portfolio.
(c) Discuss how the amounts reported in the financial statements are affected by the entries in (a) and (b).

E10-6 **(Entries for Temporary Investments)** On December 31, 2001, Tiger Limited provided you with the following information regarding its trading securities.

December 31, 2001

Investments	Cost	Fair Value	Unrealized Gain (Loss)
Kelowna Corp. shares	$20,000	$19,000	$(1,000)
Pembroke Corp. shares	10,000	9,000	(1,000)
Barrie Corp. shares	20,000	20,600	600
Total of portfolio	$50,000	$48,600	$(1,400)

During 2002, Pembroke Company shares were sold for $9,400. The shares' fair value on December 31, 2002 was: Kelowna Corp. shares—$19,100; Barrie Co. shares—$20,500.

Instructions

(a) Prepare the adjusting journal entry needed on December 31, 2001, assuming Tiger applies the LCM rule based on the whole portfolio.
(b) Prepare the journal entry to record the sale of the Pembroke shares during 2002.
(c) Prepare the adjusting journal entry needed on December 31, 2002, assuming Tiger applies the LCM rule based on the whole portfolio.

E10-7 **(Temporary Investment Entries and Reporting)** Rams Corporation purchases equity securities costing $73,000 and classifies them as temporary investments. At December 31, the portfolio's fair value is $65,000.

Instructions

Prepare the adjusting entry to report the securities properly. Indicate the statement presentation of the accounts in your entry.

E10-8 **(Temporary Investment Entries and Financial Statement Presentation)**   At December 31, 2000, the investment portfolio for Steffi Inc. is as follows:

Security	Cost	Fair Value	Unrealized Gain (Loss)
A	$17,500	$15,000	($2,500)
B	12,500	14,000	1,500
C	23,000	25,500	2,500
Total	$53,000	$54,500	$1,500

On January 20, 2001, Steffi Inc. sold security A for $15,100. The sale proceeds are net of brokerage fees.

Instructions

(a) Prepare the adjusting entry at December 31, 2000 to report the portfolio under the LCM rule. Look at individual securities.

(b) Show the balance sheet presentation of the investment, related accounts at December 31, 2000. (Ignore notes presentation.)

(c) Prepare the journal entry for the 2001 sale of security A.

E10-9 **(Equity Securities Entries)**   Arantxa Corporation made the following cash purchases of securities during 2001, which is the first year in which Arantxa invested in securities:

1. On January 15, purchased 10,000 shares of Sanchez Corp's common shares at $33.50 per share plus commission $1,980.

2. On April 1, purchased 5,000 shares of Vicario Corp's common shares at $52.00 per share plus commission $3,370.

3. On September 10, purchased 7,000 shares of WTA Corp's preferred shares at $26.50 per share plus commission $4,910.

On May 20, 2001, Arantxa sold 4,000 shares of Sanchez common shares at a market price of $35 per share less brokerage commissions, taxes, and fees of $3,850. The year-end fair values per share were: Sanchez $30, Vicario $55, and WTA $28. In addition, the chief accountant of Arantxa told you that Arantxa Corporation holds these securities with the intention of selling them in order to earn profits from appreciation in prices.

Instructions

(a) Prepare the journal entries to record the above three security purchases.

(b) Prepare the journal entry for the security sale on May 20.

(c) Calculate the unrealized gains or losses and prepare the adjusting entries for Arantxa on December 31, 2001, assuming the LCM rule is applied on individual securities.

E10-10 **(Journal Entries for Cost and Equity Methods)**   Presented below are two independent situations.

Situation 1

Conchita Cosmetics acquired 10% of the 200,000 common shares of Martinez Fashion at a total cost of $13 per share on March 18, 2001. On June 30, Martinez declared and paid a $75,000 cash dividend. On December 31, Martinez reported net income of $122,000 for the year. At December 31, the market price of Martinez Fashion was $15 per share. The securities are classified as portfolio investments.

Situation 2

Monica, Inc. obtained significant influence over Gurion Corporation by buying 30% of Gurion's 30,000 outstanding common shares at a total cost of $9 per share on January 1, 2001. On June 15, Gurion declared and paid a cash dividend of $36,000. On December 31, Gurion reported a net income of $85,000 for the year.

Instructions

Prepare all necessary journal entries in 2001 for both situations.

E10-11 **(Equity Method with Revalued Assets)**   On January 1, 2002, Jana Limited purchased 2,500 shares (25%) of the common shares of Novotna Corp. for $355,000. Additional information related to the identifiable assets and liabilities of Novotna at the date of acquisition is as follows:

	Cost	Fair Value
Assets not subject to amortization	$ 500,000	$ 500,000
Assets subject to amortization (10 years remaining)	800,000	860,000
Total identifiable assets	$1,300,000	$1,360,000
Liabilities	$100,000	$100,000

During 2002, Novotna reported the following information on its income statement:

Income before extraordinary item	$200,000
Extraordinary gain (net of tax)	70,000
Net income	$270,000
Dividends declared and paid by Novotna during 2002 were	$120,000

Instructions

(a) Prepare the journal entry to record the purchase by Jana of Novotna on January 1, 2002.

(b) Prepare the journal entries to record Jana's equity in the net income and dividends of Novotna for 2002. Depreciable assets are depreciated on a straight-line basis.

E10-12   (Securities Entries-Buy and Sell)   Lazier Corporation has the following securities in its temporary investments on December 31, 2001.

Investments	Cost	Fair Value
1,500 shares of DJ, Inc., Common	$ 73,500	$ 69,000
5,000 shares of RH Corp., Common	180,000	175,000
400 shares of AZ, Inc., Preferred	60,000	61,600
	$313,500	$305,600

All the securities were purchased in 2001. The company applies the LCM rule based on the total portfolio.

In 2002, Lazier completed the following securities transactions:

March 1   Sold the 1,500 shares of DJ, Inc., @ $45 less fees of $1,200.
April 1   Bought 700 shares of RG Corp., @ $75 plus fees of $1,300.
Lazier Company's portfolio of securities appeared as follows on December 31, 2002.

Investments	Cost	Fair Value
5,000 shares of RH Corp., Common	$180,000	$175,000
700 shares of RG Corp., Common	53,800	50,400
400 shares of AZ Inc. Preferred	60,000	58,000
	$293,800	$283,400

Instructions

Prepare the general journal entries for Lazier for:

(a) The 2001 adjusting entry

(b) The sale of the D J shares

(c) The purchase of the RG shares

(d) The 2002 valuation adjusting entry (including the AZ preferred)

E10-13   (Cost and Equity Method Compared)   Jaycie Inc. acquired 20% of the outstanding common shares of Kulikowski Inc. on December 31, 2000. The purchase price was $1.2 million for 50,000 shares. Kulikowski declared and paid an $0.85 per share cash dividend on June 30 and on December 31, 2001. Kulikowski reported net income of $730,000 for 2001. The fair value of Kulikowski's shares was $27 per share at December 31, 2001.

Instructions

(a) Prepare the journal entries for Jaycie for 2001, assuming that Jaycie cannot exercise significant influence over Kulikowski. The securities should be classified as long-term.

(b) Prepare the journal entries for Jaycie for 2001, assuming that Jaycie can exercise significant influence over Kulikowski.

(c) At what amount is the investment in securities reported on the balance sheet under each of these methods at December 31, 2001? What is the total net income reported in 2001 under each of these methods?

E10-14 **(Equity Method with Revalued Assets)** On January 1, 2002, Strug Inc. purchased 40% of the common shares of Chow Corp. for $400,000. The balance sheet reported the following information related to Chow at the date of acquisition.

Assets not subject to amortization	$200,000
Assets subjects to amortization (8-year life remaining)	600,000
Liabilities	100,000

Additional information:
1. Both book value and fair value are the same for assets not subject to amortization and the liabilities.
2. The fair market value of the assets subject to amortization is $680,000.
3. The company depreciates its assets on a straight-line basis; intangible assets are amortized over 10 years.
4. Chow reports net income of $160,000 and declares and pays dividends of $125,000 in 2002.

Instructions
(a) Prepare the journal entry to record Strug's purchase of Chow.
(b) Prepare the journal entries to record Strug's equity in the net income and dividends of Chow for 2002.
(c) Assume the same facts as above, except that Chow's net income included an extraordinary loss (net of tax) of $30,000. Prepare the journal entries to record Strug's equity in the net income of Chow for 2002.

E10-15 **(Equity Method with Revalued Assets)** On January 1, 2001, Warner Corporation purchased 30% of the common shares of Vermeil Company for $180,000. The book value of Vermeil's net assets was $500,000 on that date. During the year, Vermeil earned net income of $80,000 and paid dividends of $20,000. Any excess of cost over book value is attributable to unrecorded intangibles and is amortized over 20 years.

Instructions
(a) Prepare the entries for Warner to record the purchase and any additional entries related to this investment in Vermeil in 2001.
(b) Repeat the requirements in part (a), assuming the same facts as above, except that Vermeil's net income included an extraordinary loss (net of tax) of $10,000.

*E10-16 **(Determine Proper Income Reporting)** Presented below are three independent situations that you are to solve:
1. Bacall Inc. received dividends from its common share investments during the year ended December 31, 2002 as follows:
   (a) A cash dividend of $12,000 is received from Sleep Corporation. (Bacall owns a 2% interest in Sleep.)
   (b) A cash dividend of $60,000 is received from Largo Corporation. (Bacall owns a 30% interest in Largo.) A majority of Bacall's directors are also directors of Largo Corporation.
   (c) A share dividend of 300 shares from Orient Inc. was received on December 10, 2002, on which date the quoted market value of Orient's shares was $10 per share. Bacall owns less than 1% of Orient's common shares.
   Determine how much dividend income Bacall should report in its 2002 income statement.

2. On January 3, 2002, Bach Co. purchased as a long-term investment 5,000 common shares of Starr Co. for $79 per share, which represents a 2% interest. On December 31, 2002, the shares' market price was $83 per share. On March 3, 2003, it sold all 5,000 shares of Starr for $102 per share. The company regularly sells securities of this type. The income tax rate is 35%. Determine the amount of gain or loss on disposal that should be reported on the income statement in 2003.

3. Kinski Inc. owns a 5% common share interest in Magdalene Corporation, which declared a cash dividend of $620,000 on November 27, 2002 to shareholders of record on December 16, 2002, payable on January 6, 2003. In addition, on October 15, 2002, Kinski received a liquidating dividend of $10,200 from Velocity Corp. Kinski owns 6% of the common shares of Velocity. Determine the amount of dividend income Kinski should report in its financial statements for 2002.

*E10-17 **(Entries for Share Rights)** On January 10, 2001, Bacon Inc. purchased 240 common shares (a 3% interest) of Diner Corporation for $24,000 as a long-term investment. On July 12, 2001, Diner announced that one right would be issued for every two shares held.

July 30, 2001	Rights to purchase 120 shares at $100 per share are received. The shares' market value is $120 per share and the rights' market value is $30 per right.
Aug. 10	The rights to purchase 50 shares are sold at $29 per right.
Aug. 11	The additional 70 rights are exercised, and 70 shares are purchased at $100 per share.
Nov. 15	50 shares of those purchased on January 10, 2001 are sold at $128 per share.

Instructions

Prepare general journal entries on the books of Bacon for each of the foregoing transactions.

*E10-18 **(Entries for Share Rights)** Bailey Ltd. purchases 240 common shares of Jones Inc. on February 17. The investment, costing $27,300, is to be a long-term investment for Bailey.

1. On June 30, Jones announces that rights are to be issued. One right will be received for every two shares owned.
2. The rights mentioned in (1) are received on July 15; 120 shares may be purchased with these rights at $100. The shares are currently selling for $120 per share. Market value of the share rights is $20 per right.
3. On August 5, 70 rights are exercised and 70 shares are purchased .
4. On August 12, the remaining share rights are sold at $23 per right.
5. On September 28, Bailey sells 50 shares of those purchased February 17, at $124 a share.

Instructions

Prepare necessary journal entries for the five items above.

*E10-19 **(Investment in Life Insurance Policy)** Bain Limited pays the premiums on two insurance policies on the life of its president, Bain. Information concerning premiums paid in 2002 is given below.

Beneficiary	Face	Prem.	Dividends Cr. to Prem.	Net Prem.	Cash Surrender Value 1/1/02	Cash Surrender Value 12/31/02
1. Bain Limited	$250,000	$8,500	$2,940	$5,560	$35,000	$37,900
2. President's spouse	75,000	3,000		3,000	9,000	9,750

Instructions

(a) Prepare entries in journal form to record the payment of premiums in 2002.
(b) If the president died in January 2003, and the beneficiaries are paid the policies' face amounts, what entry would Bain Limited make?

*E10-20 **(Entries and Disclosure for Bond Sinking Fund)** The general ledger of Joe Limited shows an account for Bonds Payable with a balance of $2 million. Interest is payable on these bonds semiannually. Of the $2 million, bonds in the amount of $400,000 were recently purchased at par by the sinking fund trustee and are held in the sinking fund as an investment of the fund. The annual rate of interest is 10%.

Instructions

(a) What entry or entries should be made by Joe Limited to record payment of the semiannual interest? (The company makes interest payments directly to bondholders.)
(b) Illustrate how the bonds payable and the sinking fund accounts should be shown in the balance sheet. Assume that the sinking fund investments other than Joe Limited's bonds amount to $511,000 and that the sinking fund cash amounts to $16,000.

*E10-21 **(Entries for Plant Expansion Fund, Numbers Omitted)** The transactions given below relate to a fund being accumulated by Brooks Electrical Limited over a period of 20 years to construct additional buildings.

1. Cash is transferred from the general cash account to the fund.
2. Preferred shares of Moranis Inc. are purchased as an investment of the fund.
3. Bonds of Candy Corporation are purchased between interest dates at a discount as an investment of the fund.
4. Expenses of the fund are paid from the fund cash.
5. Interest is collected on Candy Corporation bonds.

6. Bonds held in the fund are sold at a gain between interest dates.
7. Dividends are received on Moranis preferred shares.
8. Common shares held in the fund are sold at a loss.
9. Cash is paid from the fund for building construction.
10. The cash balance remaining in the fund is transferred to general cash.

Instructions

Prepare journal entries to record the miscellaneous transactions listed above with amounts omitted.

PROBLEMS

P10-1 Presented below is an amortization schedule related to Baker Corp.'s five-year, $100,000 bond with a 7% interest rate and a 5% yield, purchased on December 31, 1999, for $108,660.

Date	Cash Received	Interest Revenue	Bond Premium Amortization	Carry Amount of Bonds
12/31/99				$108,660
12/31/00	$7,000	$5,433	$1,567	107,093
12/31/01	7,000	5,354	1,646	105,447
12/31/02	7,000	5,272	1,728	103,719
12/31/03	7,000	5,186	1,814	101,905
12/31/04	7,000	5,095	1,905	100,000

The following schedule presents a comparison of the bonds' amortized cost and fair value at year end:

	12/31/00	12/31/01	12/31/02	12/31/03	12/31/04
Amortized cost	$107,093	$105,447	$103,719	$101,905	$100,000
Fair value	$106,500	$107,500	$105,650	$103,000	$100,000

Instructions

(a) Prepare the journal entry to record the purchase of these bonds on December 31, 1999, assuming the bonds are classified as long-term investments.
(b) Prepare the journal entry(ies) related to the bonds for 2000.
(c) Prepare the journal entry(ies) related to the bonds for 2002.
(d) Prepare the journal entry(ies) to record the purchase of these bonds, assuming they are classified as temporary investments.
(e) Prepare the journal entry(ies) related to the temporary investment bonds for 2000.
(f) Prepare the journal entry(ies) related to the temporary investment bonds for 2002.

P10-2 On January 1, 2002, Jovi Inc. purchased $200,000, 8% bonds of Mercury Ltd. for $184,557. The bonds were purchased to yield 10% interest. Interest is payable semiannually on July 1 and January 1. The bonds mature on January 1, 2007. Jovi uses the effective interest method to amortize discount or premium. On January 1, 2004, Jovi sold the bonds for $185,363 after receiving interest.

Instructions

(a) Prepare the journal entry to record the purchase of bonds on January 1. Assume that the bonds are classified as long-term.
(b) Prepare the bonds' amortization schedule.
(c) Prepare the journal entries to record the semiannual interest on July 1, 2002 and December 31, 2002.
(d) Prepare the journal entry to record the sale of the bonds on January 1, 2004.

P10-3 Presented below is information taken from a bond investment amortization schedule with related fair values provided. These bonds are classified as long-term.

	12/31/01	12/31/02	12/31/03
Amortized cost	$491,150	$519,442	$550,000
Fair value	$499,000	$506,000	$550,000

Instructions

(a) Indicate whether the bonds were purchased at a discount or at a premium.
(b) Indicate whether the amortization schedule is based on the effective interest method and how you can determine this.

P10-4 Incognito Limited has the following securities in its investment portfolio on December 31, 2001 (all securities were purchased in 2001): **(1)** 3,000 shares of Bush Inc. common shares, which cost $58,500, **(2)** 10,000 shares of Sanborn Ltd. common shares, which cost $580,000, and **(3)** 6,000 shares of Abba Inc. preferred shares, which cost $255,000. The investment allowance account shows a credit of $10,100 at the end of 2001.

In 2002, Incognito completed the following securities transactions:

1. On January 15, sold 3,000 shares of Bush's common shares at $23 per share less fees of $2,150.
2. On April 17, purchased 1,000 shares of Tractor Limited's common shares at $31.50 per share plus fees of $1,980.

On December 31, 2002, the market values per share of these securities were: Bush $20, Sanborn $62, Abba $40, and Tractors $29. In addition, the accounting supervisor of Incognito told you that even though all these securities have readily determinable fair values, Incognito will not actively trade these securities because the top management intends to hold them for more than one year. The LCM rule is applied based on the total portfolio.

Instructions

(a) Prepare the entry for the security sale on January 15, 2002.
(b) Prepare the journal entry to record the security purchase on April 17, 2002.
(c) Determine whether there is an adjustment needed in the investment allowance account.
(d) How should the unrealized gains or losses be reported on Incognito's balance sheet?

P10-5 Kings Limited has the following portfolio of investment securities at September 30, 2001, its last reporting date.

Temporary Securities	Cost	Fair Value
Fogelberg, Inc. common (5,000 shares)	$225,000	$200,000
Petra, Inc. preferred (3,500 shares)	133,000	140,000
Weisberg Corp. common (1,000 shares)	180,000	179,000

On October 10, 2001, the Fogelberg shares were sold at a price of $54 per share. In addition, 3,000 shares of Los Tigres Inc. common shares were acquired at $59.50 per share on November 2, 2001. The December 31, 2001 fair values were: Petra $96,000, Los Tigres $132,000, and Weisberg $193,000. All the securities are classified as temporary. The LCM rule is applied based on individual securities.

Instructions

(a) Prepare the journal entries to record the sale, purchase, and adjusting entries related to the securities in the last quarter of 2001.
(b) How would the entries in part (a) change if the securities were classified as long-term?

P10-6 The following information relates to the debt securities investments of Yellowjackets Ltd.

1. On February 1, the company purchased 12% bonds of Williams Inc. having a par value of $500,000 at 100 plus accrued interest. Interest is payable April 1 and October 1.
2. On April 1, semiannual interest is received.
3. On July 1, 9% bonds of Chieftains, Inc. were purchased. These bonds with a par value of $200,000 were purchased at 100 plus accrued interest. Interest dates are June 1 and December 1.
4. On September 1, bonds of a par value of $100,000, purchased on February 1, are sold at 99 plus accrued interest.
5. On October 1, semiannual interest is received.
6. On December 1, semiannual interest is received.
7. On December 31, the fair value of the bonds purchased February 1 and July 1 are 95 and 93, respectively.

Instructions

(a) Prepare any journal entries you consider necessary, including year-end entries (December 31), assuming these are long-term investments.
(b) If Yellowjackets classified these as temporary investments, explain how the journal entries would differ from those in part (a).

P10-7 Pacers Corp. is a medium-sized corporation specializing in quarrying stone for building construction. The company has long dominated the market, at one time achieving a 70% market penetration. During prosperous years, the company's profits, coupled with a conservative dividend policy, resulted in funds available for outside investment. Over the years, Pacers has had a policy of investing idle cash in equity securities. In particular, Pacers has made periodic investments in the company's principal supplier, Pierce Industries. Although the firm currently owns 12% of the outstanding common shares of Pierce Industries, Pacers does not have significant influence over Pierce Industries' operations.

Cheryl Miller has recently joined Pacers as Assistant Controller, and her first assignment is to prepare the 2002 year-end adjusting entries for the investments for financial reporting purposes. Miller has gathered the following information about Pacers' pertinent accounts.

1. Pacers has temporary investments related to Davis Motors and Smits Electric. During this fiscal year, Pacers purchased 100,000 shares of Davis Motors for $1.4 million; these shares currently have a market value of $1.6 million. Pacers' investment in Smits Electric has not been profitable; the company acquired 50,000 shares of Smits Electric in April 2002 at $20 per share, a purchase that currently has a value of $620,000.
2. Prior to 2002, Pacers invested $22.5 million in Pierce Industries and has not changed its holdings this year. This investment in Pierce Industries was valued at $21.5 million on December 31, 2001. Pacers' 12% ownership of Pierce Industries has a current market value of $22,275,000.

Instructions

(a) Prepare the appropriate adjusting entries for Pacers as of December 31, 2002. (Assume the company values its temporary investments based on the total portfolio).

(b) For both classes of securities presented above, describe how the results of the valuation adjustments made in Instruction (a) would be reflected in the body of and/or notes to Pacers' 2002 financial statements.

P10-8 Woolford Inc. has the following portfolio of long-term investments at December 31, 2002.

Security	Quantity	Percent Interest	Per Share Cost	Per Share Market
Favre, Inc.	2,000 shares	8%	$11	$16
Walsh Corp.	5,000 shares	14%	23	17
Dilfer Ltd.	4,000 shares	2%	31	24

Instructions

(a) What should be reported on Woolford's December 31, 2002 balance sheet relative to these long-term investments? Assume the LCM rule is applied based on the total portfolio.

On December 31, 2003, Woolford's portfolio of lomg-term investments consisted of the following common shares.

Security	Quantity	Percent Interest	Per Share Cost	Per Share Market
Walsh Corp.	5,000 shares	14%	$23	$30
Dilfer Ltd.	4,000 shares	2%	31	23
Dilfer Ltd.	2,000 shares	1%	25	23

At the end of year 2003, Woolford changed its intent relative to its investment in Favre, Inc. and reclassified the shares to temporary investments status when the shares were selling for $9 per share.

(b) What should be reported on the face of Woolford's December 31, 2003 balance sheet relative to long-term investments? What should be reported to reflect the transactions above in Woolford's 2003 income statement?

(c) Assuming that comparative financial statements for 2002 and 2003 are presented, draft the footnote necessary for full disclosure of Woolford's transactions and position in equity securities.

P10-9 Octavio Paz Corp. carries an account in its general ledger called "Long-term Investments," which contained the following debits for investment purchases, and no credits.

Feb. 1, 2001	Kai-Shek Ltd. common shares, 200 shares	$37,400
April 1	Government of Canada bonds, 11%, due April 1, 2011, interest payable April 1 and October 1, 100 bonds of $1,000 par each	100,000
July 1	Monet Corp. 12% bonds, par $50,000, dated March 1, 2001 purchased at 104 plus accrued interest, interest payable annually on March 1, due March 1, 2021	54,000

Instructions

(a) Prepare the entry to record the accrued interest and amortization of premium on December 31, 2001, using the effective interest method.

(b) The securities' fair values on December 31, 2001 were:

Kai-shek common shares (1% interest)	$ 33,800
Government of Canada bonds	124,700
Monet bonds	58,600

What entry or entries, if any, would you recommend be made?

(c) The government bonds were sold on July 1, 2002 for $119,200 plus accrued interest. Give the proper entry.

P10-10 Fuentes Incorporated is a publicly traded company that manufactures products to clean and demagnetize video and audio tape recorders and players. The company grew rapidly during its first 10 years and made three public offerings during this period. During its rapid growth period, Fuentes acquired common shares in Yukasato Inc. and Dimna Importers. In 1991, Fuentes acquired 25% of Yukasato's common shares for $588,000 and properly accounts for this investment using the equity method. For its fiscal year ended November 30, 2002, Yukasato Inc. reported net income of $250,000 and paid dividends of $100,000. In 1993, Fuentes acquired 10% of Dimna Importers' common shares for $204,000 and properly accounts for this investment using the cost method. Fuentes has a policy of investing idle cash in equity securities. The following data pertain to the securities in Fuentes' temporary investment portfolio.

Investments at November 30, 2001

Security	Cost	Fair Value
Craxi Electric	$326,000	$314,000
Renoir Inc.	184,000	181,000
Seferis Inc.	95,000	98,500
	$605,000	593,500
Dimna Importers	204,000	198,000
	$809,000	$791,500

Investments at November 30, 2002

Security	Cost	Fair Value
Craxi Electric	$326,000	$323,000
Renoir Inc.	184,000	180,000
Mer Limited	105,000	108,000
	$615,000	611,000
Dimna Importers	204,000	205,000
	$819,000	$816,000

On November 14, 2002, Tasha Yan was hired by Fuentes as assistant controller. Her first assignment was to propose the entries to record the November activity and the November 30, 2002 year-end adjusting entries for the investments in the temporary securities and the long-term investment in common shares. Using Fuentes' ledger of investment transactions and the data given above, Yan proposed the following entries and submitted them to Miles O'Brien, controller, for review.

Entry 1 (November 8, 2002)		
Cash	99,500	
Temporary Investments		98,500
Investment Income		1,000
To record the sale of Seferis Inc. shares for $99,500.		

Entry 2 (November 26, 2002)

Temporary Investments	105,000	
Cash		105,000

To record the purchase of Mer common shares for $102,200 plus brokerage fees of $2,800.

Entry 3 (November 30, 2002)

Investment Income	3,000	
Investment Allowance		3,000

To recognize a loss equal to the excess of cost over market value of equity securities.

Entry 4 (November 30, 2002)

Cash	38,500	
Investment Income		38,500

To record dividends received from securities.

Yukasato Inc.	$25,000
Dimna Importers	9,000
Craxi Electric	4,500

Entry 5 (November 30, 2002)

Investment in Yukasato Inc.	62,500	
Investment Income		62,500

To record share of Yukasato Inc. income under the equity method, $250,000 × 0.25

Instructions

(a) Distinguish between the characteristics of temporary and long-term investments.

(b) The journal entries proposed by Tasha Yan will establish the value of Fuentes equity investments to be reported on the company's external financial statements. Review each journal entry proposed by Yan and indicate whether or not it is in accordance with the applicable reporting standards. If an entry is incorrect, prepare the correct entry or entries that should have been made.

(c) Because Fuentes owns more than 20% of Yukasato Inc., Miles O'Brien has adopted the equity method to account for the investment in Yukasato Inc. Under what circumstances would it be inappropriate to use the equity method to account for a 25% interest in the common shares of Yukasato Inc.?

P10-11 On January 1, 2001, Howard Corporation acquired 10,000 of the 50,000 outstanding common shares of Kline Corp. for $25 per share. The balance sheet of Kline reported the following information at the date of the acquisition:

Assets not subject to amortization	$290,000
Assets subject to amortization	860,000
Liabilities	150,000

Additional information:

1. Kline reported net income of $100,000 and paid dividends of $30,000 in 2001.
2. On the acquisition date, the fair value is the same as the book value for both the assets not subject to amortization and the liabilities.
3. On the acquisition date, the fair value of the assets subject to amortization is $960,000.
4. Kline's share had a fair value of $24 per share on December 31, 2001.
5. Intangibles are amortized over 20 years and assets subject to amortization have a remaining useful life of 8 years.

Instructions

(a) Prepare the journal entries for Howard Corporation for 2001, assuming that Howard cannot exercise significant influence over Kline.

(b) Prepare the journal entries for Howard Corporation for 2001, assuming that Howard can exercise significant influence over Kline.

P10-12 Alvarez Corp. invested its excess cash in securities during 2002. As of December 31, 2002, the securities portfolio consisted of the following common shares:

Security	Quantity	Cost	Fair Value
Jones, Inc.	1,000 shares	$15,000	$21,000
Eola Corp.	2,000 shares	50,000	42,000
Yevette Aircraft	2,000 shares	72,000	60,000
Totals		$137,000	$123,000

Instructions

(a) What should be reported on Alvarez's December 31, 2002 balance sheet relative to these securities? What should be reported on Alvarez' 2002 income statement?

On December 31, 2003, Alvarez's securities portfolio consisted of the following common shares:

Security	Quantity	Cost	Fair Value
Jones, Inc.	1,000 shares	$15,000	$20,000
Jones, Inc.	2,000 shares	38,000	40,000
King Corp.	1,000 shares	16,000	12,000
Yevette Aircraft	2,000 shares	72,000	22,000
Totals		$141,000	$94,000

During the year 2003, Alvarez sold 2,000 shares of Eola Corp. for $38,200 and purchased 2,000 more shares of Jones, Inc. and 1,000 shares of King Corp.

(b) What should be reported on Alvarez's December 31, 2003, balance sheet? What should be reported on Alvarez's 2003 income statement?

On December 31, 2004, Alvarez's portfolio of securities consisted of the following common shares:

Security	Quantity	Cost	Fair Value
Yevette Aircraft	2,000 shares	$72,000	$82,000
King Corp.	500 shares	8,000	6,000
Totals		$80,000	$88,000

During 2004, Alvarez sold 3,000 shares of Jones, Inc. for $39,900 and 500 shares of King Corp. at a loss of $2,700.

(c) What should be reported on the face of Alvarez's December 31, 2004 balance sheet? What should be reported on Alvarez's 2004 income statement?

*P10-13 Millard Corp. holds 300 common shares of Fillmore's Decorating Inc. that it purchased for $31,629 as a long-term investment. On January 15, 2002, it is announced that one right will be issued for every four shares of Fillmore's Decorating Inc. shares held.

Instructions

(a) Prepare entries on Millard's books for the transactions below that occurred after the date of this announcement. Show all calculations in good form.
1. 100 shares are sold rights-on for $11,500.
2. Rights to purchase 50 additional shares at $100 per share are received. The shares' market value on this date is $105 per share and the rights' market value of the rights is $6 per right.
3. The rights are exercised, and 50 additional shares are purchased at $100 per share.
4. 100 of the shares originally held are sold at $106 per share.

(b) If the rights had not been exercised but instead had been sold at $6 per right, what would have been the amount of the gain or loss on the sale of the rights?

(c) If the shares purchased through the exercise of the rights are later sold at $107 per share, what is the amount of the gain or loss on the sale?

(d) If the rights had not been exercised, but had been allowed to expire, what would be the proper entry?

*P10-14 The transactions given below relate to a sinking fund for retirement of long-term bonds of Fremont Roofing:

1. In accordance with the terms of the bond indenture, cash in the amount of $150,000 is transferred at the end of the first year, from the regular cash account to the sinking fund.
2. Hull Siding Inc. 10% bonds of a par value of $50,000, maturing in five years, are purchased for $47,000.
3. 500 shares of Lee Limited 8% preferred share are purchased at $54 per share.
4. Annual interest of $5,000 is received on Hull Siding bonds. (Amortize a full year of discount using effective interest method of amortization.)
5. Sinking fund expenses of $480 are paid from sinking fund cash.
6. Hutchinson Glass Inc. 9% bonds with interest payable February 1 and August 1 are purchased on April 15 at $60,000 plus accrued interest.
7. Dividends of $2,000 are received on Lee preferred shares.
8. All the Hutchinson Glass Inc. bonds are sold on September 1 at 101 plus accrued interest. Assume interest collected August 1 was properly recorded.
9. Investments carried in the fund at $1,583,000 are sold for $1,538,000.
10. The fund contains cash of $1,627,000 after disposing of all investments and paying all expenses. $1.6 million of this amount is used to retire the bonds payable at maturity date.
11. The remaining cash balance is returned to the general account.

Instructions
Prepare the journal entries required by Fremont Roofing for the transactions above.

CONCEPTUAL CASES

C10-1 You have just started work for Villeneuve Ltd. as part of the controller's group involved in current financial reporting problems. Jackie Franklin, controller, is interested in your accounting background because the company has experienced a series of financial reporting surprises over the last few years. She asks how the following situations should be reported in the financial statements.

Situation 1
Temporary investments in the current asset section have a fair value of $4,200 lower than cost.

Situation 2
A temporary investment whose market value is currently less than cost is transferred to the long-term investment category.

Situation 3
A long-term investment, whose market value is currently less than cost, is to be reclassified as current.

Situation 4
A company's portfolio of long-term investments consists of the common shares of one company. At the end of the prior year, the security's fair value was 50% of original cost. The year prior to that, the market value had exceeded cost.

Situation 5
The company has purchased some convertible debentures that it plans to hold for less than a year. The convertible debentures' fair value is $7,700 below cost.

Instructions
What is the effect upon carrying value and earnings for each situation above? Assume that these situations are unrelated.

C10-2 Presented below are three unrelated situations involving equity securities:

Situation 1
An equity security, whose market value is currently less than cost, is classified as long-term but is to be reclassified as temporary.

Situation 2

A noncurrent portfolio with an aggregate market value in excess of cost includes one particular security whose market value has declined to less than one-half of the original cost. The decline in value is considered to be other than temporary.

Situation 3

The portfolio of temporary securities has a cost in excess of fair value of $13,500. One of the securities in this portfolio has a market value less than cost.

Instructions

What is the effect upon carrying value and earnings for each situation above? Complete your response to each situation before proceeding to the next situation.

C10-3 Companies generally hold investments on a temporary and long-term basis.

Instructions

(a) Why does a company maintain an investment portfolio of temporary versus long-term investment?
(b) What factors should be considered in determining whether investments in securities should be classified as temporary and long-term and how do these factors affect the accounting treatment for unrealized losses?

C10-4 On July 1, 2002, Warner Inc. purchased for cash 40% of the outstanding common shares of Graves Ltd. Both Warner and Graves have a December 31 year end. Graves, whose common shares are actively traded in the over-the-counter market, reported its total net income for the year to Warner and also paid cash dividends on November 15, 2002 to Warner and its other shareholders.

Instructions

How should Warner report the above facts in its December 31, 2002 balance sheet and its income statement for the year then ended? Discuss the rationale for your answer.

(AICPA adapted)

C10-5 On July 1, 2001, Munns Inc. purchased for cash 40% of the outstanding common shares of Huber Corporation. Both Munns and Huber have a December 31 year end. Huber, whose common shares are actively traded on the CDNX, paid a cash dividend on November 15, 2001 to Munns and its other shareholders. It also reported its total net income for the year of $920,000 to Munns.

Instructions

Prepare a one-page memorandum of instructions on how Munns should report the above facts in its December 31, 2001 balance sheet and its 2001 income statement. In your memo, identify and describe the method of valuation you recommend. Provide rationale where you can. Address your memo to the chief accountant at Munns.

*C10-6 In the course of your examination of the financial statements of Ax Corporation as of December 31, 2002, the following entry came to your attention.

January 4, 2002		
Receivable from Insurance Company	1,000,000	
Cash Surrender Value of Life Insurance Policies		132,000
Retained Earnings		163,000
Donated Capital from Life Insurance Proceeds		705,000
(Disposition of the proceeds of the life insurance policy on		
Mr. Cliburn's life. Mr. Cliburn died on January 1, 2002.)		

You are aware that Mr. Cliburn, an officer-shareholder in the small manufacturing firm, insisted that the corporation's board of directors authorize the purchase of an insurance policy to compensate for any loss of earning potential upon his death. The corporation paid $295,000 in premiums prior to Mr. Cliburn's death, and was the policy's sole beneficiary. At the date of death, there had been no premium prepayment and no rebate was due. In prior years, cash surrender value in the amount of $132,000 had been recorded in the accounts.

Instructions

(a) What is the cash surrender value of a life insurance policy?

(b) How should the cash surrender value of a life insurance policy be classified in the financial statements while the policy is in force? Why?

(c) Comment on the propriety of the entry recording the insurance receivable.

*C10-7   Part A   To manufacture and sell its products, a company must invest in inventories, plant and equipment, and other operating assets. In addition, a manufacturing company often finds it desirable or necessary to invest a portion of its available resources, either directly or through the operation of special funds, in shares, bonds, and other securities.

Instructions

(a) List the reasons why a manufacturing company might invest funds in shares, bonds, and other securities.

(b) What are the criteria for classifying investments as current or noncurrent assets?

Part B   Because of favourable market prices, the trustee of Saint Hubert Limited's bond sinking fund invested the current year's contribution to the fund in the company's own bonds. The bonds are being held in the fund without cancellation. The fund also includes cash and securities of other companies.

Instructions

Describe three methods of classifying the bond sinking fund on the balance sheet of Saint Hubert. Include a discussion of the propriety of using each method.

*C10-8   Souriere Inc. administers the sinking fund applicable to its own outstanding long-term bonds. The following four proposals relate to the accounting treatment of sinking fund cash and securities.

1. Mingle sinking fund cash with general cash and sinking fund securities with other securities, and show both as current assets on the balance sheet.

2. Keep sinking fund cash in a separate bank account and sinking fund securities separate from other securities, but on the balance sheet treat cash as a part of the general cash and the securities as part of general investments, both being shown as current assets.

3. Keep sinking fund cash in a separate bank account and sinking fund securities separate from other securities, but combine the two accounts on the balance sheet under one caption, such as "Sinking Fund Cash and Investments," to be listed as a noncurrent asset.

4. Keep sinking fund cash in a separate bank account and sinking fund securities separate from other securities, and identify each separately on the balance sheet among the current assets.

Instructions

Identify the proposal that is most appropriate. Give the reasons for your selection.

Using Your Judgement

FINANCIAL REPORTING PROBLEM:
FRANCO-NEVADA MINING CORPORATION LIMITED

Refer to the 2001 Annual Report for **Franco-Nevada** included in the Digital Tool.

Instructions

(a) Franco-Nevada is in the precious metals industry. Its core business as described in its 2001 Annual Report is in "royalties and strategic interests in precious metals." It also has interests in the oil and gas sector. How does the company present these investments in the balance sheet? Discuss. How are the investments valued?

(b) Discuss the different types of royalty income arrangements (NSR, NPI, WI). What is the major type of royalty arrangement that the company has?

(c) What is the impact on riskiness of earnings and cash flows of these different royalty streams? (Hint: consider metal/oil and gas prices, gross versus net cash flows etc.)

(d) Review the segmented information provided in the financial statements and compare segmented earnings before tax with segment revenues for each segment (as a percentage of segment revenues). Reviewing other information in the Annual Report and considering the nature of the earnings (e.g., royalty streams, investment income, operating income), comment on the percentage calculated above. Why are some higher and some lower?

FINANCIAL STATEMENT ANALYSIS CASE

CIBC

Refer to the 2000 financial statements and accompanying notes of **Canadian Imperial Bank of Commerce** included in the Digital Tool.

Instructions

(a) What percentage of total assets is held in securities (2000 versus 1999)? Note that CIBC holds a significant loan portfolio also. What is the business reason for holding loans versus securities? Comment on how the investments are classified/presented in the balance sheet.

(b) What percentage of total "interest income" comes from securities (2000 versus 1999)? Are there any other lines on the income statement relating to securities? What percentage of net income relates to securities (2000 versus 1999)? Calculate a rough return on the investments in securities. Comment looking at the nature of the securities invested in.

(c) Read the notes to the financial statements relating to securities and note the valuation method. Is this consistent with GAAP as noted in *CICA Handbook* Sections 3010 and 3050 (temporary and long-term investments)?

(d) Given your answer to (c) above, discuss possible reasons for any differences.

COMPARATIVE ANALYSIS CASE

Altamira Family of Mutual Funds

The 2000 Annual Report for the **Altamira** family of mutual funds is included in the Digital Tool.

Instructions

The mutual fund industry follows industry specific accounting policies for its investments. Altamira Mutual Fund Company develops various funds, markets, and sells units/shares in these funds. It also manages the assets/investments, deciding which assets to invest in and which to sell. The funds present their own financial statements that are separate from the financial statements of Altamira Mutual Fund Company. The fund financial statements are presented in the Annual Report included in the Digital Tool. Please refer to the fund financial statements when answering the following:

(a) List the types of funds that Altamira has and note the types of investments in each. How are these investments valued?

(b) List the types of income streams that these different funds generate. Which funds are more risky and why?

(c) Who are the auditors of these funds and what type of audit report was issued for the year ended December 31, 2000? Is this appropriate given the accounting policies relating to investments? Discuss.

(d) Where assets are revalued to reflect market prices, where are the resulting gains/losses booked? Explain the difference between realized and unrealized gains/losses.

(e) Discuss the predictability of cash flow and earnings for the various funds. Does the choice of accounting policies assist in assessing predictability?

RESEARCH CASES

Case 1

Last year, your company invested in the common shares of **Nortel Networks** when they were trading at a share price in excess of $100. The share value has been declining steadily over the past year and John Roth, the company CEO, has recently announced his retirement. You are presently putting together your year-end draft financial statements and have presented the securities as long-term investments although you may sell these shares in the near term if they decline in value much further.

Instructions

(a) Discuss the financial reporting issues including presentation, measurement, and disclosure.

(b) If the shares are presented as long-term investments, discuss the specific information that you might consider in measuring/valuing the shares. Research the issue on the Internet and select specific quotes and sources of information to support your analysis, or the value of the Nortel investment.

Case 2

As mentioned in the chapter, there is much controversy surrounding investment accounting.

Instructions

Write an essay assessing the issues. Consider the following:

- the conceptual framework and the overall objective of providing useful information to users
- international standards
- why differences exist between countries
- accounting for financial instruments that are investments
- any other relevant points

INTERNATIONAL CASE

Addison Manufacturing holds a large portfolio of debt and equity securities as an investment. The portfolio's fair value is greater than its original cost, even though some securities have decreased in value. Ted Abernathy, the financial vice-president, and Donna Nottebart, the controller, are near year end in the process of classifying for the first time this securities portfolio in accordance with FASB Statement No. 115. Abernathy wants to classify those securities that have increased in value during the period as trading securities in order to increase net income this year. He wants to classify all the securities that have decreased in value as available-for-sale (the equity securities) and as held-to-maturity (the debt securities).

Nottebart disagrees and wants to classify those securities that have decreased in value as trading securities and those that have increased in value as available-for-sale (equity) and held-to-maturity (debt). She contends that the company is having a good earnings year and that recognizing the losses will help to smooth the income this year. As a result, the company will have built-in gains for future periods when the company may not be as profitable.

Instructions

Answer the following questions:

(a) Research and explain the separate classifications proposed, i.e., trading, available for sale, and held to maturity. These are the classifications as required under U.S. accounting standards.

(b) Compare briefly with Canadian accounting policies.

(c) Will classifying the portfolio as each proposes actually have the effect on earnings that each says it will?

(d) Is there anything unethical in what each of them proposes? Who are the stakeholders affected by their proposals?

(e) Assume that Abernathy and Nottebart properly classify the entire portfolio into trading, available-for-sale, and held-to-maturity categories, but then each proposes to sell just before year end the securities with gains or with losses, as the case may be, to accomplish their effect on earnings. Is this unethical?

CHAPTER 11

Acquisition and Disposition of Tangible Capital Assets

LEARNING OBJECTIVES

After studying this chapter, you should be able to:

1.	Describe the major characteristics of tangible capital assets.
2.	Identify the costs included in the initial valuation of land, buildings, and equipment.
3.	Describe the accounting problems associated with self-constructed assets.
4.	Describe the accounting problems associated with interest capitalization.
5.	Understand accounting issues related to acquiring and valuing plant assets.
6.	Describe the accounting treatment for costs subsequent to acquisition.
7.	Describe the accounting treatment for the disposal of property, plant, and equipment.

Preview of Chapter 11

The purpose of this chapter is to discuss (1) the proper accounting for costs related to tangible capital assets, and (2) the accounting methods used to record the retirement or disposal of these assets. Amortization—allocating capital asset costs to accounting periods—is presented in Chapter 12 as are the disclosure requirements and analysis issues related to capital assets. The content and organization of this chapter are as follows.

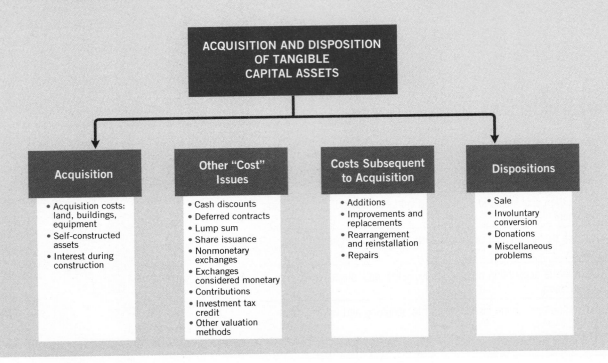

Almost every business enterprise of any size or activity uses assets of a durable nature. Such "capital assets" include both those that have physical substance, tangible capital assets, and those without physical substance, **intangible assets**. (The accounting for intangible assets is the subject of Chapter 13.) Tangible capital assets, also commonly referred to as property, plant, and equipment; plant assets; or fixed assets, include land, building structures (offices, factories, warehouses), and equipment (machinery, furniture, tools). These terms are used interchangeably by organizations and throughout this textbook. In the past, the term "depreciation" was used to denote the amortization of tangible capital assets and "amortization" was used for intangibles. While these terms are still in common usage, "amortization" is used throughout this text to refer to the allocation of capital asset costs to accounting periods.

The major characteristics of tangible capital assets are:

OBJECTIVE 1

Describe the major characteristics of tangible capital assets.

1. *They are acquired for use in operations and not for resale.* Only assets used in normal business operations should be classified as property, plant, and equipment.[1] An idle building is more appropriately classified separately as an investment; land held by land developers or subdividers is classified as inventory.

2. *They are long-term in nature and usually subject to amortization.* Tangible capital assets yield services over a number of years. The investment in these assets is

---

[1] Use in normal business operations includes the production or supply of goods and services, administrative purposes, and the development and maintenance of other capital assets.

assigned to the periods benefiting from their use through periodic amortization charges. The exception is land, which is not depreciated unless a material decline in value occurs; for example, due to a loss of agricultural land fertility because of poor crop rotation, drought, or soil erosion.

3. *They possess physical substance.* Tangible capital assets are characterized by physical existence or substance and thus are differentiated from intangible assets, such as patents or goodwill.

ACQUISITION OF TANGIBLE CAPITAL ASSETS

Historical cost is the usual basis for valuing property, plant, and equipment. **Historical cost is measured by the cash or cash equivalent price of obtaining the asset and bringing it to the location and condition necessary for its intended use.** The purchase price, freight costs, most provincial sales taxes, and a productive asset's installation costs are considered part of the asset's cost. These costs are allocated to future periods through the amortization process. Any related costs incurred **after the asset's acquisition,** such as additions, improvements, or replacements, are **added to the asset's cost if they provide future service potential.** Otherwise they are expensed immediately.

Cost should be the basis used at the acquisition date because the cash or cash equivalent price best measures the asset's value at that time. Disagreement does exist about what to do with changes in value after acquisition. Should the asset value be adjusted to recognize changes in its replacement cost or its fair market value? Writing up fixed asset values is not considered appropriate in ordinary circumstances. Although minor exceptions are noted (during financial reorganizations, for example), current standards indicate that departures from historical cost are rare.

The main reasons for this position are (1) at the acquisition date, cost reflects fair value; (2) historical cost involves actual, not hypothetical transactions, and as a result is more reliable; and (3) gains should not be anticipated and recognized before they are realized; that is, before the asset is sold.

Several other valuation methods have been considered, such as (1) constant dollar accounting (adjustments for general price-level changes), (2) current cost accounting (adjustments for specific price-level changes), (3) net realizable value, or (4) a combination of constant dollar accounting and current cost or net realizable value.

Cost of Land

All expenditures made to acquire land and to ready it for use should be considered as part of the land cost. Land costs typically include (1) the purchase price; (2) closing costs, such as title to the land, legal fees, and recording fees; (3) costs incurred to condition the land for its intended use (e.g., grading, filling, draining, and clearing); (4) assumption of any liens, such as taxes in arrears or mortgages or encumbrances on the property; and (5) any additional land improvements that have an indefinite life.

When land has been purchased to construct a building, all costs incurred up to the excavation for the new building are considered land costs. **Removal of old buildings, clearing, grading, and filling are considered land costs because these costs are necessary to get the land in condition for its intended purpose.** Any proceeds obtained in the process of getting the land ready for its intended use, such as salvage receipts on the demolition of an old building or the sale of timber that has been cleared, are treated as **reductions in the land cost.**

In some cases, the land purchaser has to assume certain obligations on the land such as back taxes or liens. In such situations, the cost of the land is the cash paid for it, plus the encumbrances. In other words, if the land purchase price is $50,000 cash, but accrued property taxes of $5,000 and liens of $10,000 are assumed by the purchaser, the land cost is $65,000.

Special assessments for local improvements, such as pavements, street lights, sewers, and drainage systems, are usually charged to the Land account because they

UNDERLYING CONCEPTS

Market value is relevant to inventory but less so for property, plant, and equipment which, consistent with the going concern assumption, are held for use in the business, not for sale like inventory.

Go to the Digital Tool for a discussion of accounting for changing price levels.

OBJECTIVE 2

Identify the costs included in the initial valuation of land, buildings, and equipment.

INTERNATIONAL INSIGHT

In many nations, such as Great Britain and Brazil, companies are allowed to revalue their fixed assets at amounts above historical cost. These revaluations may be at appraisal values or at amounts linked to a specified index. Other nations, such as Japan and Germany, do not allow such revaluations.

are relatively permanent in nature and are maintained and replaced by the local government body. In addition, permanent improvements made by the owner, such as landscaping, are properly chargeable to the Land account. **Improvements with limited lives**, such as private driveways, walks, fences, and parking lots, are recorded separately as Land Improvements so they can be amortized over their estimated lives.

Generally, land is considered part of property, plant, and equipment. If the major purpose of acquiring and holding land is speculative, however, it is more appropriately classified as an investment. If the land is held by a real estate concern for resale, it should be classified as inventory.

In cases where land is held as an investment, what accounting treatment should be given taxes, insurance, and other direct costs incurred while holding the land? Many believe these costs should be capitalized because the investment revenue has not been received. This approach is reasonable as long as the total amount capitalized does not exceed the property's fair value, and seems justified except in cases where the asset is currently producing revenue (such as rental property).

Cost of Buildings

The cost of buildings should include all expenditures related directly to their acquisition or construction. These costs include (1) materials, labour, and overhead costs incurred during construction and (2) professional fees and building permits. Generally, companies contract to have their buildings constructed. All costs incurred, from excavation to completion, are considered part of the building costs.

One accounting issue relates to the cost of an old building that is on the site of a newly proposed building. Is the cost to remove the old building a cost of the land, or of the new building? The answer is that if land is purchased with an old building on it, then the demolition cost less its salvage value is a cost of getting the land ready for its intended use and relates to the land rather than to the new building. As indicated earlier, all costs of getting an asset ready for its intended use are costs of that asset.

IAS NOTE

Under IAS 16, historical cost is the benchmark (preferred) treatment for property, plant, and equipment. However, it is also allowable to use revalued amounts. If revaluation is used, companies are required to revalue the class of assets regularly.

Cost of Equipment

The term "equipment" in accounting includes delivery equipment, office equipment, machinery, furniture and fixtures, furnishings, factory equipment, and similar tangible capital assets. The cost of such assets includes the purchase price, freight and handling charges incurred, insurance on the equipment while in transit, cost of special foundations if required, assembling and installation costs, and costs of conducting trial runs. Costs thus include all reasonable and necessary expenditures incurred in acquiring the equipment and preparing it for use. The Goods and Services Tax (GST) or Harmonized Sales Tax (HST) paid on assets acquired is treated as an Input Tax Credit used to reduce the amount of GST or HST payable—it does not increase the acquisition cost of the assets.

OBJECTIVE 3

Describe the accounting problems associated with self-constructed assets.

Self-Constructed Assets

Occasionally companies (particularly those with significant in-house maintenance and construction facilities, such as railroads and utilities) construct their own assets. Determining the cost of such machinery and other capital assets can be a problem. Without a purchase price or contract price, the company must allocate costs and expenses to arrive at the cost of the self-constructed asset. Materials and direct labour used in construction pose no problem; these costs can be traced directly to work and material orders related to the assets constructed.

However, assigning indirect costs of manufacturing creates special problems. These indirect costs, called **overhead** or burden, include power, heat, light, insurance, property taxes on factory buildings and equipment, factory supervisory labour, amortization of fixed assets, and supplies.

These costs may be handled in one of three ways:

1. *Assign no fixed overhead to the cost of the constructed asset.* The major argument for this treatment is that indirect overhead is generally fixed in nature and does not increase as a result of constructing one's own plant or equipment. This approach assumes that the company will have the same costs regardless of whether the company constructs the asset or not, so to charge a portion of the overhead costs to the equipment will normally relieve current expenses and consequently overstate the current period's income. In contrast, variable overhead costs that increase as a result of the construction are assigned to the asset cost.

2. *Assign a portion of all overhead to the construction process.* This approach, a full costing concept, is appropriate if one believes that costs attach to all products and assets manufactured or constructed. This procedure assigns overhead costs to construction as it would to normal production. Advocates say that failure to allocate overhead costs understates the initial cost of the asset and results in an inaccurate future allocation.

3. *Allocate on the basis of lost production.* A third alternative is to allocate to the construction project the cost of any curtailed production that occurs because the asset is built instead of purchased. This method is conceptually appealing, but is based on "what might have occurred"—an opportunity cost concept—which is difficult to measure.

A pro rata portion of the fixed overhead should be assigned to the asset to obtain its cost. This treatment is employed extensively because many believe a better matching of costs with revenues is obtained. If the allocated overhead results in recording construction costs exceeding the costs that would be charged by an outside independent producer, the excess overhead should be recorded as a period loss rather than be capitalized. This avoids capitalizing the asset at more than the expected cash flows to be generated from its use and eventual salvage—its **net recoverable amount**.

Interest Costs During Construction

The proper accounting for interest costs has been a long-standing controversy. Three approaches have been suggested to account for the interest incurred in financing the construction or acquisition of property, plant, and equipment:

1. *Capitalize no interest charges during construction.* Under this approach, interest is considered a cost of financing, not construction. It is contended that if the company had used equity financing rather than debt financing, this expense would not have been incurred. The major argument against this approach is that an implicit interest cost is associated with using cash regardless of its source; if equity financing is employed, a real cost exists to the shareholders, although a contractual claim does not develop.

2. *Charge construction with all costs of funds employed, whether identifiable or not.* This method maintains that one part of construction cost is the cost of financing, whether by debt, equity, or internal financing. An asset should be charged with all costs necessary to get it ready for its intended use. Interest, whether actual or imputed, is a cost of building, just as labour, materials, and overhead are costs. A major criticism of this approach is that imputing a cost of equity capital is subjective and outside the framework of a historical cost system.

3. *Capitalize only the actual interest costs incurred during construction.* This approach relies on the historical cost concept that only actual transactions are recorded. It is argued that interest incurred is as much a cost of acquiring the asset as the cost of the materials, labour, and other resources used. As a result, a company that uses debt financing will have an asset of higher cost than an enterprise that uses equity financing. The results achieved by this approach are considered unsatisfactory by some because an asset's cost should be the same whether internal financing, debt financing, or equity financing is employed.

<aside>

OBJECTIVE 4

Describe the accounting problems associated with interest capitalization.

IAS NOTE

Under international accounting standards, capitalization of interest is allowed, but it is not the preferred treatment. The benchmark treatment is to expense interest in the period incurred.

</aside>

The profession generally supports the third approach: actual interest may be capitalized in accordance with the concept that the historical cost of acquiring an asset includes all costs (including interest costs) incurred to bring the asset to the condition and location necessary for its intended use. As a result, capitalization of interest is permitted in Canada and disclosure of the amount of any interest capitalized is required.[2]

The amount of interest to be capitalized, however, is subject to professional judgement. *CICA Handbook*, par. 1000.60(b), indicates that professional judgement may be based on such factors as analogous situations in the *Handbook, Accounting Guidelines, Abstracts of Issues Discussed* by the CICA Emerging Issues Committee, International Accounting Standards, accounting standards established in other jurisdictions, and CICA research studies. Since the CICA does not provide any guidelines for the measurement of interest to be capitalized, the discussion below is based on FASB Statement 34. There may be other appropriate methods of measuring capitalizable interest.

Implementing FASB's approach requires considering three items:

1. qualifying assets
2. capitalization period
3. amount to capitalize

INTERNATIONAL INSIGHT

In the U.S., capitalization of interest is required for qualifying assets that require a period of time to get them ready for their intended use.

Qualifying Assets

To qualify for interest capitalization, assets must require a time period to get them ready for their intended use. Interest costs may be capitalized starting with the first expenditure related to the asset, and continuing until the asset is substantially completed and ready for its intended use.

Assets that qualify for interest cost capitalization include assets under construction for an enterprise's own use (including buildings, plants, and large machinery) and assets intended for sale or lease that are constructed or otherwise produced as discrete projects (e.g., ships or real estate developments).

Examples of assets that do not qualify for interest capitalization are (1) assets that are in use or ready for their intended use and (2) assets that are not being used in the enterprise's earnings activities and that are not undergoing the activities necessary to get them ready for use (such as land that is not being developed and assets not being used because of obsolescence, excess capacity, or need for repair).

Capitalization Period

The capitalization period is the time period during which interest may be capitalized. It begins when three conditions are present:

1. Expenditures for the asset have been made.
2. Activities that are necessary to get the asset ready for its intended use are in progress.
3. Interest cost is being incurred.

Interest capitalization **continues as long as these three conditions are present**. The capitalization period ends when the asset is substantially complete and ready for its intended use.

Amount to Capitalize

To be capitalized, interest must be directly attributable to the project, and is limited to the lower of actual interest cost incurred during the period and avoidable interest. Avoidable interest is the amount of interest cost during the period that theoretically could have been avoided if expenditures for the asset had not been made. If the actual

---

[2] *CICA Handbook*, Section 3061, par. .23 permits interest capitalization and Section 3850, par. .03 requires disclosure.

interest cost for the period is $90,000 and the avoidable interest is $80,000, only $80,000 may be capitalized. Or, if the actual interest cost is $80,000 and the avoidable interest is $90,000, a maximum of $80,000 would be capitalized. In no situation should interest cost include a cost of capital charge for shareholders' equity.

To apply the avoidable interest concept, the potential amount of interest to be capitalized during an accounting period is determined by multiplying the weighted-average accumulated expenditures for qualifying assets during the period by the interest rate(s).

Weighted-Average Accumulated Expenditures In calculating the weighted-average accumulated expenditures, the construction expenditures are weighted by the amount of time (fraction of a year or accounting period) that interest cost could be incurred on the expenditure. To illustrate, assume a 17-month bridge construction project with current-year payments to the contractor of $240,000 on March 1, $480,000 on July 1, and $360,000 on November 1. The weighted-average accumulated expenditure for the year ended December 31 is calculated as follows:

| Expenditures | | | Capitalization | | Weighted-Average Accumulated |
Date	Amount	×	Period*	=	Expenditures
March 1	$ 240,000		10/12		$200,000
July 1	480,000		6/12		240,000
November 1	360,000		2/12		60,000
	$1,080,000				$500,000

*Months between the date of expenditure and the date interest capitalization stops or end of year, whichever comes first (in this case December 31).

ILLUSTRATION 11-1
Calculation of Weighted-Average Accumulated Expenditures

To calculate the weighted-average accumulated expenditures, we weight the expenditures by the amount of time that interest cost could be incurred on each one. For the March 1 expenditure, 10 months' interest cost can be associated with the expenditure, whereas for the expenditure on July 1, only 6 months' interest costs can be incurred. For the expenditure made on November 1, only 2 months of interest cost can be incurred.

Interest Rates The principles used to select the appropriate interest rates to be applied to the weighted-average accumulated expenditures are:

1. For the portion of weighted-average accumulated expenditures that is less than or equal to any amounts borrowed specifically to finance construction of the assets, **use the interest rate incurred on the specific borrowings**.

2. For the portion of weighted-average accumulated expenditures that is greater than any debt incurred specifically to finance construction of the assets, **use a weighted average of interest rates incurred on all other outstanding debt during the period**.[3]

---

[3] The interest rate to be used may be based exclusively on an average rate of all the borrowings, if desired. For our purposes, we will use the specific borrowing rate followed by the average interest rate because we believe it to be more conceptually consistent. Either method can be used; FASB Statement 34 does not provide explicit guidance on this measurement. For a discussion of this issue and others related to interest capitalization, see Kathryn M. Means and Paul M. Kazenski, "SFAS 34: Recipe for Diversity," *Accounting Horizons*, September 1988; and Wendy A. Duffy, "A Graphical Analysis of Interest Capitalization," *Journal of Accounting Education*, Fall 1990.

An illustration of the calculation of a weighted-average interest rate for debt greater than the amount incurred specifically to finance construction of the assets is shown below. It assumes that the principal amounts were outstanding for the full year.

ILLUSTRATION 11-2
Calculation of Weighted-Average
Interest Rate

	Principal	Interest
12%, 2-year note	$ 600,000	$ 72,000
9%, 10-year bonds	2,000,000	180,000
7.5%, 20-year bonds	5,000,000	375,000
	$7,600,000	$627,000

$$\text{Weighted-average interest rate} = \frac{\text{Total interest}}{\text{Total principal}} = \frac{\$627,000}{\$7,600,000} = 8.25\%$$

The avoidable interest in this example, assuming there were no specific borrowings, is the weighted-average amount of accumulated expenditures multiplied by the weighted-average interest rate, or $500,000 × 8.25% = $41,250.

Special Issues Related to Interest Capitalization

Three issues related to interest capitalization merit special attention:

1. expenditures for land
2. interest revenue
3. significance of interest capitalization

Expenditures for Land   When land is purchased with the intention of developing it for a particular use, interest costs associated with those expenditures may be capitalized. If the land is purchased as a site for a structure (such as a plant site), interest costs capitalized during the construction period are part of the cost of the plant, not of the land. Conversely, if land is being developed for lot sales, any capitalized interest cost should be part of the developed land's acquisition cost. However, interest costs involved in purchasing land held **for speculation** should **not** be capitalized because the asset is ready for its intended use.

Interest Revenue   Companies frequently borrow money to finance construction of assets and temporarily invest any excess borrowed funds in interest-bearing securities until the funds are needed to pay for construction. During the early stages of construction, interest revenue earned may exceed the interest cost incurred on the borrowed funds. The question is whether it is appropriate to offset interest revenue against interest cost when determining the amount of interest to be capitalized as part of the assets' construction cost. If it is assumed that short-term investment decisions are not related to the interest incurred as part of the acquisition cost of assets, then interest revenue should not be netted with capitalized interest. Some are critical of this accounting because a company may defer the interest cost but report the interest revenue in the current period.

Significance of Interest Capitalization   Interest capitalization can have a substantial impact on the financial statements of business enterprises. When Jim Walter Corporation's earnings dropped from $1.51 to $1.17 per share, the building manufacturer, looking for ways to regain its profitability, was able to pick up an additional 11 cents per share by capitalizing the interest on coal mining projects and several plants under construction. The **Saskatchewan Wheat Pool** reported interest expense of $25.1 million for its year ended July 31, 1999 and $13.4 million of interest capitalized.

Many Canadian companies have adopted this method of capitalizing interest, while others use different methods of determining the amount to be capitalized. Some refuse to capitalize interest.[4] Many believe that "interest should be capitalized on all pre-earning assets"[5] while others argue that no interest cost should be capitalized.[6] An example showing the calculation, recording, and reporting of capitalized interest is presented in Appendix 11A.

OTHER "COST" ISSUES

OBJECTIVE 5

Understand accounting issues related to acquiring and valuing plant assets.

We have seen that assets should be recorded at cost, i.e., the amount of cash or cash equivalents paid to acquire the asset. For non-monetary transactions, cost is the fair market value of what is given up or the fair value of the asset received, whichever is more clearly evident. Cost and fair market value, however, are sometimes obscured by the process through which an asset is acquired. As an example, assume that land and buildings are bought together for one price. How are separate costs for the land and buildings determined? A number of accounting issues of this nature are examined in the following sections.

Cash Discounts

When plant assets are purchased subject to cash discounts for prompt payment, how should the discount be reported? If the discount is taken, it should be considered a reduction in the asset's purchase price. What is not clear, however, is whether a reduction in the asset cost should occur even if the discount is not taken.

Two points of view exist on this matter. Under one approach, the net-of-discount amount, regardless of whether the discount is taken or not, is considered the asset's cost. The rationale for this approach is that the asset's cost should be its cash or cash equivalent price. In addition, some argue that the terms of cash discounts are so attractive that failure to take them indicates management error or inefficiency. Proponents of the other approach argue that the discount should not always be considered a loss because the terms may be unfavourable or because it might not be prudent for the company to take the discount. At present, both methods are employed in practice. The former method is generally preferred.

Deferred Payment Contracts

Often, plant assets are purchased on long-term credit contracts through the use of notes, mortgages, bonds, or equipment obligations. **To properly reflect cost, assets purchased on long-term credit contracts should be accounted for at the present value of the consideration exchanged between the contracting parties at the transaction date.** For example, an asset purchased today in exchange for a $10,000 noninterest-bearing note payable four years from now should not be recorded at $10,000. The $10,000 note's present value establishes the transaction's exchange price (the asset's cash cost). Assuming an appropriate interest rate of 12% at which to discount this single payment of $10,000 due four years from now, this asset's cost should be recognized at $6,355.20 [$10,000 × 0.63552; see Table A-2 for the present value of a single sum, PV = $10,000 ($i=12$, $n=4$)].

---

[4] See John M. Boersema and Mark van Helden, "The Case Against Interest Capitalization," *CAMagazine*, December, 1986, pp. 58–60.

[5] J. Alex Milburn, *Incorporating the Time Value of Money Within Financial Accounting*, (Toronto: CICA, 1988).

[6] Clarence Byrd, Ida Chen, and Heather Chapman, in *Financial Reporting in Canada, 2000*, [CICA] report that of 200 Canadian companies surveyed, 79 companies reported having capitalized interest in 1999.

When no interest rate is stated, or if the specified rate is unreasonable, an appropriate interest rate must be imputed. The objective is to approximate the interest rate that the buyer and seller would negotiate at arm's length in a similar borrowing transaction. Factors to be considered in imputing an interest rate are the borrower's credit rating, the note's amount and maturity date, and prevailing interest rates. If determinable, the acquired asset's cash exchange price should be used as the basis for recording the asset and measuring the interest element.

To illustrate, Sutter Corporation purchases a specially built robot spray painter for its production line. The company issues a $100,000, 5-year, noninterest-bearing note to Wrigley Robotics Ltd. for the new equipment when the prevailing market interest rate for obligations of this nature is 10%. Sutter is to pay off the note in five $20,000 installments made at the end of each year. The fair market value of this specially built robot is not readily determinable and must therefore be approximated by establishing the note's fair value (present value). Calculation of the note's present value and the entries at the purchase date and payment dates are as follows:

At date of purchase

Equipment	75,816	
Discount on Notes Payable	24,184	
Notes Payable		100,000

Present value of note = $20,000$ (PVF $-$ OA$_{5, 10\%}$)
= $20,000$ (3.79079) (Table A-4)
= $75,816$

At end of first year

Interest Expense	7,582	
Discount on Notes Payable		7,582
Notes Payable	20,000	
Cash		20,000

Interest expense under the effective interest approach is $7,582 [($100,000 − $24,184) × 10%]. The entries at the end of the second year to record interest and to pay off a portion of the note's principal are as follows:

At end of second year

Interest Expense	6,340	
Discount on Notes Payable		6,340
Notes Payable	20,000	
Cash		20,000

Interest expense in the second year is determined by applying the 10% interest rate to the net book value of the outstanding Note Payable, that is, the Note Payable less its contra account, Discount on Notes Payable. At the end of the first year, the Note Payable account was reduced to $80,000 ($100,000 − $20,000) and the Discount account was reduced to $16,602 ($24,184 − $7,582). The note's net book value, therefore, has been $63,398 throughout the second year. The second year's interest expense is thus $63,398 × 10% or $6,340.

If an interest rate is not imputed in such deferred payment contracts, the asset will be recorded at an amount greater than its fair value. In addition, interest expense reported in the income statement will be understated for all periods involved.

Lump Sum Purchase

A special problem of determining the cost of capital assets arises when a group of such assets is purchased at a single lump sum price. When such a situation occurs, and it is not at all unusual, the practice is to allocate the total cost among the various assets based on their relative fair market values. The assumption is that costs will vary in direct proportion to their relative values. This is the same principle that is applied to allocate a lump sum cost in a "basket purchase" of different inventory items.

To determine fair market value, any of the following might be used: an appraisal for insurance purposes, the assessed valuation for property taxes, or simply an independent appraisal by an engineer or other appraiser.

To illustrate, assume that a company decides to purchase several assets of a smaller company in the same business for a total price of $80,000. The assets purchased are as follows:

	Seller's Book Value	Fair Market Value
Inventory	$30,000	$ 25,000
Land	20,000	25,000
Building	35,000	50,000
	$85,000	$100,000

The $80,000 purchase price would be allocated based on the relative fair market values as shown in Illustration 11-3. Note that the assets' carrying values on the seller's books are not representative of the assets' fair values. They are irrelevant.

				Asset Cost
Inventory	$\dfrac{\$25,000}{\$100,000}$	× $80,000	=	$20,000
Land	$\dfrac{\$25,000}{\$100,000}$	× $80,000	=	$20,000
Building	$\dfrac{\$50,000}{\$100,000}$	× $80,000	=	$40,000

ILLUSTRATION 11-3
Allocation of Purchase Price—Relative Fair Market Value Basis

Issuance of Shares

When property is acquired by issuing securities, such as common shares, the property's cost is not properly measured by the par, stated, or book value of such shares. If the shares are actively traded, **the issued shares' market value is a good indication of the fair value of the property acquired because the shares are a good measure of the current cash equivalent price.**

For example, a hardware enterprise decides to purchase some adjacent land to expand its carpeting and cabinet operation. In lieu of paying cash for the land, it issues to the other company 5,000 no par value common shares that have a fair market value of $12 per share. The purchasing company would make the following entry.

Land (5,000 × $12)	60,000	
Common Shares		60,000

If the market value of the shares given up is not determinable, the market value of the property should be established and used as the basis for determining the asset's cost and the amount credited to the common shares.[7]

---

[7] When the shares' fair market value is used as the basis of valuation, careful consideration must be given to the effect that the issuance of additional shares will have on the existing market price. Where the effect on market price appears significant, an independent appraisal of the asset received should be made. This valuation should be employed as the basis for determining the cost of the asset as well as for the shares issued. In the unusual case where the fair market value of the shares or asset cannot be determined objectively, the corporation's board of directors may set the value.

Nonmonetary Exchanges of Assets

Nonmonetary exchanges of assets involve transactions where nonmonetary assets are exchanged for other nonmonetary assets with little or no cash or other monetary assets changing hands.[8] The *CICA Handbook* specifies that the exchange is deemed to be **nonmonetary only where monetary consideration makes up 10% or less of the total fair value of the consideration given up or received in the transaction**.[9] If this isn't the case, different standards apply.

The proper accounting for exchanges of nonmonetary assets (such as inventories and property, plant, and equipment) has been controversial. Some argue that the acquired asset's cost should be determined by the fair value of the asset given up or received, with a gain or loss recognized on the disposal of the asset given up. Others believe that the cost of the acquired asset should be determined by the book value of the asset given up, with no gain or loss recognized. Still others favour an approach that would recognize losses in all cases, but defer gains in special situations.

The main issue underlying any discussion of this topic is that ordinarily, gains are not recognized until realized; that is, until an asset is exchanged for cash or a claim to cash. This point is chosen because the proceeds can be measured reliably, and it is a critical point in the earnings process where we can state that the earnings process is substantially complete.[10] When nonmonetary assets are received instead of cash or other monetary assets, questions arise about whether the earnings process is complete and the gain can be considered realized.

The general standard for determining cost in a nonmonetary transaction or exchange of nonmonetary assets is that the asset acquired should be measured at the **fair value of the asset given up, unless the fair value of the asset received is more clearly evident**, with the resulting gain or loss recognized in income.[11] The rationale for such immediate recognition is that the earnings process related to the assets given up is completed (or culminated) and, therefore, it is appropriate to recognize a gain or loss. Although cash or claims to cash have not been received, the earnings process is considered substantially complete if the assets exchanged are **dissimilar** in nature, such as the exchange of computers for a truck, or the exchange of equipment for inventory. In these situations, the dissimilarity of the assets assumes the end of one earnings process (for the asset given up) and the beginning of another (for the asset acquired).

Nonmonetary Exchange of Dissimilar Assets

Assume that Cathay Computers needs a new delivery van, and it contracts with Porter Motors, which is in the market for new computer hardware, to exchange computers for a van. Cathay orders in the required equipment at a cost of $20,000 (retail value of $24,000) and installs it at Porter Motors. The automobile dealership has a suitable van on the lot with a cost of $18,000 and a fair value of $25,000. They agree to exchange the assets, with Cathay also paying $1,000 cash to Porter Motors.

This transaction is considered a nonmonetary exchange **because the monetary component is less than 10% of the fair value of the total consideration**. Because it involves the exchange of dissimilar assets, the general standard for determining the acquired assets' cost applies, i.e., the fair market value of what is given up, or what is acquired, the clearer. The gain or loss will also be recognized. The accounting entries to record the exchange by both Cathay Computers and Porter Motors follow.

---

[8] Nonmonetary assets are items whose price in terms of the monetary unit may change over time, whereas monetary assets are fixed in terms of units of currency by contract or otherwise; for example, cash and short or long-term accounts and notes receivable.

[9] *CICA Handbook*, Section 3830.04(e).

[10] **The earnings process** is basically the cash-to-cash cycle. Goods and services are purchased, and when they are sold and converted to cash, or a claim to cash, again, the earnings process is said to be substantially complete.

[11] *CICA Handbook*, Section 3830.05 and .06.

ILLUSTRATION 11-4
Nonmonetary Exchange of
Dissimilar Assets

Cathay Computers		
Delivery Van	25,000	
Cash		1,000
Sales		24,000
Cost of Goods Sold	20,000	
Inventory of Computers		20,000
Fair value of consideration given:		
Computer hardware		$24,000
Cash		1,000
		$25,000

Porter Motors		
Computers	24,000	
Cash	1,000	
Sales		25,000
Cost of Goods Sold	18,000	
New Van Inventory		18,000
Van		$25,000

In both cases, the acquired assets are recognized at the fair value of what was given up, and a gross profit on sale is recognized in income. Because the assets exchanged are inventory items, the exchange represents sales for both companies. Companies could also exchange non-inventory assets and report gains or losses on the disposal of those assets.

Nonmonetary Exchanges of Similar Assets

In a nonmonetary transaction where **similar** assets are exchanged, it is assumed that the earnings process has not been completed. Similar nonmonetary assets are those that are of the same general type, or that perform the same function, or that are employed in the same line of business. In substance, the company's circumstances have not changed and there is no basis on which to recognize the asset acquired at fair value and a gain or loss on the asset given up. For example, when a company exchanges its inventory items with similar inventory of another company because of colour, size, etc. to facilitate sale to an outside customer, the earnings process is not considered completed and a gain should not be recognized. Likewise if a company trades **productive assets** such as land for similar land or equipment for similar equipment, the earnings process is not considered complete and, therefore, **a gain should not be recognized**.

The real estate industry provides a good example of why the accounting profession decided not to recognize gains on exchanges of similar nonmonetary assets. In this industry, it is common practice for companies to "swap" real estate holdings. Assume that Landmark Corp. and Hillfarm, Inc. each had undeveloped land on which they intended to build shopping centres. Appraisals indicated that both companies' land had increased significantly in value. The companies decided to exchange (swap) their undeveloped land, record a gain, and report their new land parcels at current fair values. Should gains be recognized at this point? No: the earnings process is not completed because the companies remain in the same economic position after the swap as before. Therefore, the asset acquired should be recorded at the book value of the asset given up with no gain recognized.

In contrast, if the book value of the asset given up exceeds the fair value of the asset acquired, a loss is indicated. **When similar nonmonetary assets are exchanged and a loss results, the loss should be recognized immediately.**

To illustrate the nonmonetary exchange of similar assets, assume Davis Rent-A-Car has an automobile rental fleet consisting primarily of Ford Motor Company products. Davis' management is interested in increasing the variety of automobiles in its rental fleet by adding numerous General Motors models. Davis arranges with Ned's Rent-A-Car to exchange a group of Ford automobiles with a fair value of $160,000 and a book value of $135,000 (cost $150,000 less accumulated depreciation $15,000) for a number of Chevy and Pontiac models with a fair value of $170,000; Davis pays $10,000 in cash in addition to the Ford automobiles exchanged.

The total gain to Davis Rent-A-Car is calculated as shown in Illustration 11-5. The gain does not get recognized in this situation, however, as the cost assigned to the GM automobiles received is equal to the net book value of the Ford automobiles and cash given up.

ILLUSTRATION 11-5
Calculation of Gain
(Unrecognized)

Fair value of Ford automobiles exchanged	$160,000
Book value of Ford automobiles exchanged	135,000
Total gain (unrecognized)	$ 25,000

The earnings process is not considered completed in this transaction because the company still has a fleet of cars, although different models. While the gain is not recognized, it could be considered deferred. The cost of the General Motors automobiles can be determined via two different but acceptable calculations as shown below:

ILLUSTRATION 11-6
Cost of New Automobiles—Fair Value vs. Book Value

Fair value of GM automobiles	$170,000		Book value of Ford automobiles	$135,000
Less: Gain deferred	(25,000)	OR	Cash paid	10,000
Cost of GM automobiles	$145,000		Cost of GM automobiles	$145,000

The entry by Davis to record this transaction is as follows:

Automobiles (GM)	145,000	
Accumulated Amortization (Ford)	15,000	
Automobiles (Ford)		150,000
Cash		10,000

The gain that reduced the new automobiles' cost basis will be recognized as the automobiles are used to generate rental income. That is, while these automobiles are held and used to earn income, the amortization charges will be lower and net income will be higher over their remaining useful life because of the reduced cost basis.

An enterprise that engages in nonmonetary exchanges during a period should disclose the nature, the basis of measurement, and the amount of any resulting gains or losses in its financial statements.[12]

Exchanges with Significant Monetary Component

Often when assets are exchanged or traded in, the transaction includes the payment or receipt of a significant amount of cash or other monetary asset, sometimes called boot. Where the monetary component exceeds 10% of the fair value of the consideration given up or received, **the transaction is not considered a nonmonetary exchange**. In this situation, the general standard for determining cost applies, and the resulting gain or loss is recognized in income in the period.

To illustrate the accounting for an asset exchange along with a significant monetary component, assume Interprovincial Transportation Company Ltd. exchanged a number of used trucks plus cash for vacant land that might be used for a future plant site. The trucks have a combined book value of $42,000 (cost $64,000 less $22,000 accumulated amortization). Interprovincial's purchasing agent, who has had previous dealings in the second-hand market, indicates that the trucks have a fair market value of $49,000. In addition to the trucks, Interprovincial must pay $17,000 cash for the land. In this case, the $17,000 monetary asset is in excess of 10% of the fair value of the consideration given up. Therefore, this transaction is not considered a nonmonetary exchange. It does not matter whether the assets exchanged are similar or dissimilar. The cost of the land to Interprovincial is $66,000 calculated as follows:

ILLUSTRATION 11-7
Calculation of Land Cost

Fair value of assets given up:	
Fair value of trucks exchanged	$49,000
Cash paid	17,000
Cost of land	$66,000

The journal entry to record the exchange transaction must (1) take the assets given up off the books at their book value, (2) record the new asset at its "cost," and

---

[12] *CICA Handbook*, Section 3830, par. .13.

(3) recognize the difference between the book value of the assets given up and the fair value of the assets given up as a gain or loss:

Land (2)	66,000	
Accumulated Amortization—Trucks (1)	22,000	
Trucks (1)		64,000
Cash (1)		17,000
Gain on Disposal of Trucks (3)		7,000

The gain—the difference between the fair value of the trucks and their book value—is verified as follows:

Fair value of trucks		$49,000	**ILLUSTRATION 11-8**
Cost of trucks	$64,000		Calculation of Gain on Disposal
Less: Accumulated amortization	22,000		of Used Trucks
Book value of trucks		42,000	
Gain on disposal of used trucks		$ 7,000	

It follows that if the trucks' fair value was $39,000 instead of $49,000, a loss on the exchange of $3,000 ($42,000 − $39,000) would be reported. In either case, as a result of the exchange of assets including a significant cash component, the earnings process on the used trucks is considered complete and **a gain or loss is recognized**.

Trade-ins

Often companies will trade in existing assets for newer assets of a similar type. For example, Information Processing, Inc. trades its used machine for a new model. The machine given up has a book value of $8,000 (original cost $12,000 less $4,000 accumulated amortization) and a fair value of $6,000. It is traded for a new model that has a list price of $16,000. In negotiations with the seller, a trade-in allowance of $9,000 is finally agreed on for the used machine. The cash payment that must be made for the new asset and the cost of the new machine are calculated as follows:

List price of new machine	$16,000	**ILLUSTRATION 11-9**
Less: Trade-in allowance for used machine	9,000	Calculation of Cost of
Cash payment due	7,000	New Machine
Fair value of used machine	6,000	
Cost of new machine—fair value of consideration given up	$13,000	

Note that the cash component again exceeds 10% of the fair value of the total consideration. The journal entry to record this transaction is:

Equipment (new)	13,000	
Accumulated Amortization—Equipment (old)	4,000	
Loss on Disposal of Equipment	2,000	
Equipment (old)		12,000
Cash		7,000

The loss on the disposal of the used machine can be verified as follows:

Fair value of used machine	$6,000	**ILLUSTRATION 11-10**
Book value of used machine	8,000	Calculation of Loss on Disposal
Loss on disposal of used machine	$2,000	of Used Machine

Why was the trade-in allowance or the old asset's book value not used as a basis for the new equipment? The trade-in allowance is not used because it included a price concession (similar to a price discount) to the purchaser. Few individuals pay list price for a new car, for example. Trade-in allowances on the used car are often inflated so that actual selling prices are below list prices. To record the car at list price would state it at an amount exceeding its cash equivalent price because the new car's list price is usually inflated. Use of book value in this situation would overstate the new machine's value by $2,000. Because **assets should not be valued at more than their cash equivalent price or fair value**, the loss should be recognized immediately rather than added to the cost of the newly acquired asset.

Accounting for Contributions of Assets

Companies sometimes receive contributions of assets as a donation, gift, or government grant. Such contributions are referred to as nonreciprocal transfers because they are transfers of assets in one direction only—nothing is given in exchange. Contributions are usually assets (such as cash, securities, land, buildings, or use of facilities), but they also could be the forgiveness of a debt.

When assets are acquired as a donation, a strict cost concept dictates that the asset's valuation should be zero. A departure from the cost principle seems justified, however, because the only costs incurred (legal fees and other relatively minor expenditures) do not constitute a reasonable basis of accounting for the assets acquired. To record nothing is to ignore the economic realities of an increase in wealth and resources. Therefore, **the asset's fair value should be used to establish its value on the books**.

Two general approaches have been used to record the credit for the asset received. Some believe the credit should be to Donated Capital, a contributed surplus account. This is termed a capital approach. The increase in assets is viewed more as contributed capital than as earned revenue. To illustrate, assume a company has recently accepted the donation of a land parcel with a fair value of $150,000 from the City of Winnipeg. The company, which has promised to build a manufacturing plant on this site, makes the following entry.

Land	150,000	
Donated Capital		150,000

Others argue that capital is contributed only by the business owners and that all inflows of assets from non-owner sources are income components. That is, donations are benefits to the enterprise that should be reported as revenues. Whether the revenue should be reported immediately or over the period that the asset is employed is another consideration. To attract new industry, a municipality may offer land, but the receiving enterprise may incur additional costs in the future (transportation, higher taxes, etc.) because the location is not the most desirable. As a consequence, some argue that the revenue should be deferred and recognized as these costs are incurred.

INTERNATIONAL INSIGHT

There is no U.S. standard on accounting for government assistance, although SFAS No. 116 takes the position that, in general, contributions received should be recognized as revenues in the period received.

Regardless of whether assets or funds to acquire assets are received from federal, provincial, or municipal governments, Section 3800 of the *Handbook* requires that recipients follow prescribed accounting methods. These methods are based on an income approach that requires the amount received to be deferred and recognized over the period that the related assets are employed. This is accomplished by either reducing the asset cost and future amortization by the amount of government assistance received, or recording the amount of assistance received as a deferred credit, amortizing it to revenue over the life of the related asset. To illustrate, assume a company receives a grant of $225,000 from the federal government to upgrade its sewage treatment facility. The entry to record the receipt of the grant if the **cost reduction method** is used is as follows:

Cash	225,000	
Equipment		225,000

This results in the equipment being carried on the books at cost less the related government assistance. As a result, the annual amortization charge for the equipment will be reduced over its useful life and net income will be increased.

Alternatively, a deferred revenue account can be credited with the grant amount. This amount will then be recognized in income on the same basis as the underlying asset is amortized. The entries to record receipt of the grant and its amortization for the first year under the **deferral method**, assuming straight-line amortization of the capital asset and a 10-year life, is as follows:

Cash	225,000	
Deferred Revenue—Government Grants		225,000
Deferred Revenue—Government Grants	22,500	
Revenue—Government Grants		22,500

It should be noted that the donation of land by a government unit cannot be deferred and taken into income over the period it is used, as it has an infinite life. Two choices are available: either recognize land with a zero cost, or recognize the full cost of the land, offset by an equal credit to a Contributed Capital account—Donated Capital.

Government grants awarded to a company for incurring current expenditures, such as for research and development or for payroll, are recognized in income in the same period as the related expenses.

If grants or donations received are contingent upon the occurrence of a future event, such as being required to construct a plant or maintain a specified number of employees on the payroll, the contingency should be reported in the notes to the financial statements.

IAS NOTE
Under IAS 20, the requirements for accounting for government assistance are similar to the Canadian standard.

The Investment Tax Credit

From time to time, federal and provincial governments have attempted to stimulate the economy, particularly in areas of high unemployment, by permitting special tax advantages to enterprises that invest in qualifying capital assets. The **investment tax credit** or **ITC** is one such incentive where tax legislation permits enterprises to deduct a specified percentage of the cost of eligible new capital assets directly from their income tax liability.

To illustrate, suppose that in 2002, an enterprise purchases an asset for $100,000 that qualifies for a 10% investment tax credit. If the company has a tax liability of $30,000 before the credit, its final tax liability is determined as follows:

Taxes payable for 2002 prior to ITC	$30,000
Less Investment tax credit ($100,000 × 10%)	10,000
Final tax liability	$20,000

ILLUSTRATION 11-11
Determination of Tax Liability after an Investment Tax Credit

There has been much debate within the accounting profession about the appropriate way to account for the benefit provided by an investment tax credit. Many believe the ITC is a reduction in the cost of qualified property similar to a purchase discount, and that it should be accounted for over the same period as that of the related asset; that is, by the cost reduction or deferral approach. Others believe the ITC is a selective reduction in income tax expense in the purchase year. This approach—called the **flowthrough approach**—takes the full benefit into income in the year of the asset acquisition by recognizing the full reduction in income tax expense. The justification for this treatment is that the tax credit is earned by the act of investment, not by the asset's use or nonuse, retention, or nonretention.

The Accounting Standards Board concluded that investment tax credits are a form of government assistance that should be accounted for on a basis consistent with government grants as described above.[13] That is, the benefit should be taken into income on the same basis as the underlying asset, using either the cost reduction or deferral method.

To illustrate the accounting for investment tax credits, assume that Shikkiah Corporation purchases machinery in early January 2002 for $100,000. The machinery qualifies for a 10% investment tax credit, has a useful life of 10 years with no residual value, and Shikkiah uses the straight-line method of amortizing similar capital assets. For income tax purposes, the asset's capital cost is deemed to be $90,000 (the $100,000 acqui-

---

[13] *CICA Handbook*, Section 3805.

sition cost less the investment tax credit of $10,000), as is required by tax legislation. (Assume $9,000 is deductible each year when determining taxable income.) Furthermore, assume the company's net income before amortization and income taxes is $35,000, and that the tax rate is 50%. The entries under the income approach using the cost reduction and the deferral method follow.

ILLUSTRATION 11-12
Accounting for Investment Tax Credit Benefits

Investment Tax Credit Treated as a Reduction of Asset's Cost		Investment Tax Credit Deferred and Amortized		
At time of purchase, 1/1/02:				
Machinery	100,000	Machinery	100,000	
Cash	100,000	Cash		100,000
Recognition of taxes in 2002:				
Income Tax Expense	13,000*	Income Tax Expense	13,000*	
Cash/Income Taxes Payable	3,000	Cash/Income Taxes Payable		3,000
Machinery	10,000	Deferred Investment Tax Credit		10,000
		Deferred Investment Tax Credit	1,000	
		Income Tax Expense**		1,000
Recognition of amortization in 2002:				
Amortization Expense	9,000	Amortization Expense	10,000	
Accumulated Amortization	9,000	Accumulated Amortization		10,000
Annual entries in subsequent periods assuming income before amortization and income taxes of $35,000:				
Income Tax Expense	13,000*	Income Tax Expense	13,000*	
Cash/Income Taxes Payable	13,000	Cash/Income Taxes Payable		13,000
		Deferred Investment Tax Credit	1,000	
		Income Tax Expense**		1,000
Amortization Expense	9,000	Amortization Expense	10,000	
Accumulated Amortization	9,000	Accumulated Amortization		10,000

*($35,000 − 9,000) × 50% = $13,000
**Other acceptable accounts to credit are Amortization Expense, Other Income, etc.

Note 15 from **Canadian Pacific Limited**'s financial statements for the company's year ended December 31, 1999 provides a good illustration of the disclosures required in relation to government assistance. The Deferred Income Credits referred to in Note 15 were reported on the Balance Sheet as a non-current Liability.

ILLUSTRATION 11-13
Note Disclosure of Government Assistance—Canadian Pacific Limited

Note 15 DEFERRED INCOME CREDITS *(in millions)*	1999	1998
Federal government	$ 140.1	$ 151.9
Other bodies	151.1	182.5
Investment tax credits	56.9	59.7
Surplus accumulated depreciation	37.9	46.1
Other	48.3	22.9
	$ 434.3	$ 463.1

Federal government funds were primarily for the rehabilitation of certain western branch lines. Funds received from other bodies were mainly for the relocation of railway lines. Deferred income credits are being amortized to income on the same basis as the related properties are being depreciated.

Other Asset Valuation Methods

As indicated above, an exception to the historical cost principle arises in the acquisition of plant assets through donation, which is based on fair value. Another approach that is sometimes allowed and not considered a violation of historical cost is a concept often referred to as prudent cost. This concept states that if for some reason you were ignorant about a certain price and paid too much for the asset originally, it is theoretically preferable, once known, to write down the asset and recognize a loss immediately.

As an example, assume that a company constructs an asset at a cost substantially in excess of its present economic usefulness. In this case, it would be appropriate to charge these excess costs as a loss to the current period, rather than capitalize them as part of the asset cost. This problem seldom develops because at the outset, individuals either use good reasoning in paying a given price or fail to recognize any such errors.

On the other hand, a purchase that is obtained at a bargain, or a piece of equipment internally constructed at a cost savings, should not result in immediate recognition of a gain under any circumstances. Although reporting the asset at an amount closer to its fair value and immediate recognition of a gain are conceptually appealing, the implications of such a treatment would be to change completely the entire historical cost basis of accounting.

COSTS SUBSEQUENT TO ACQUISITION

After plant assets are installed and ready for use, additional costs are incurred that range from ordinary repair to significant additions. The major problem is allocating these costs to the proper time periods. **In general, costs incurred to achieve greater future benefits should be capitalized, whereas expenditures that simply maintain a given level of services should be expensed.** In order for costs to be capitalized, one of three conditions must be present:

1. The asset's useful life must be increased.
2. The quantity of units produced from the asset must be increased.
3. The quality of the units produced must be enhanced.

Expenditures that do not increase an asset's future benefits should be expensed. Ordinary repairs are expenditures that maintain the asset's existing condition or restore it to normal operating efficiency and should be expensed immediately.

Most expenditures below an established arbitrary minimum amount are expensed rather than capitalized. Many enterprises have adopted the rule that expenditures below, say, $100 or $500, should always be expensed. Although conceptually this treatment may not be correct, expediency demands it. Otherwise, amortization schedules would have to be set up for such items as wastepaper baskets and staplers.

The distinction between a capital expenditure (an asset) and a revenue expenditure (an expense) is not always clear-cut. Determining the **property unit** with which costs should be associated is critical. If a fully equipped steamship is considered a property unit, then replacing the engine might be considered an expense. On the other hand, if the ship's engine is considered a property unit, then its replacement would be capitalized. In most cases, **consistent application of a capital/expense policy** is more important than attempting to provide general theoretical guidelines for each transaction.

Generally, four major types of expenditures are incurred relative to existing assets.

UNDERLYING CONCEPTS

Expensing long-lived staplers, pencil sharpeners, and wastebaskets is an application of the materiality constraint.

MAJOR TYPES OF EXPENDITURES

Additions.   Increase or extension of existing assets.

Improvements and replacements.   Substitution of an improved asset for an existing one.

Rearrangement and reinstallation.   Movement of assets from one location to another.

Repairs.   Expenditures that maintain assets in condition for operation.

Additions

Additions should present no major accounting problems. By definition, **any addition to plant assets is capitalized** because a new asset has been created. Adding a wing to a hospital or an air conditioning system to an office, for example, increases the service potential of that facility. Such expenditures should be capitalized and matched against the revenues that will result in future periods.

The most difficult problem that develops in this area is how to account for any changes related to the existing structure as a result of the addition. Is the cost that is incurred to tear down an old wall to make room for an addition a cost of the addition or an expense or loss of the period? The answer is that it depends on the original intent. If the company had anticipated that an addition was going to be added later, then this removal cost is a proper cost of the addition. But if the company had not anticipated this development, it should properly be reported as a loss in the current period on the basis that the company was inefficient in its planning. Normally, because of practical difficulties in determining the wall's cost, its carrying amount remains in the accounts, although theoretically it should be removed.

Improvements and Replacements

Improvements (often referred to as betterments) and replacements are substitutions of one asset for another. What is the difference between an improvement and a replacement? An improvement is the substitution of a **better asset** for the one currently used (say, a concrete floor for a wooden floor). A replacement, on the other hand, is the substitution of a **similar asset** (a wooden floor for a wooden floor).

Many times improvements and replacements result from a general policy to modernize or rehabilitate an older building or piece of equipment. The problem is differentiating these types of expenditure from normal repairs. Does the expenditure increase the asset's **future service potential**, or does it merely **maintain the existing service level**? Frequently, the answer is not clear-cut, and good judgement must be used in order to classify these expenditures properly.

If it is determined that the expenditure increases the asset's future service potential and, therefore, should be capitalized, the accounting is handled in one of three ways, depending on the circumstances.

1. **Substitution approach.** Conceptually, the substitution approach is the correct procedure if the old asset's carrying amount is available. If that amount can be determined, it is a simple matter to remove the cost of the old asset and replace it with the cost of the new asset.

   To illustrate, Instinct Enterprises Ltd. decides to replace its plumbing pipes. A plumber suggests that in place of the cast iron pipes and copper tubing, a newly developed plastic tubing be used. The old pipe and tubing have a book value of $15,000 (cost of $150,000 less accumulated amortization of $135,000), and a scrap value of $1,000. The plastic tubing system has a cost of $125,000. Assuming that Instinct has to pay $124,000 for the new tubing after exchanging the old tubing, the entry is:

Plumbing System	125,000	
Accumulated Amortization	135,000	
Loss on Disposal of Plant Assets	14,000	
Plumbing System		150,000
Cash ($125,000 − $1,000)		124,000

   The problem with this approach is determining the old asset's book value. Generally, the components of a given asset depreciate at different rates, but no separate accounting is made. As an example, a truck's tires, motor, and body depreciate at different rates, but most companies use only one amortization rate for the entire truck. Separate amortization rates could be set for each component, but it would be impractical. If the old asset's carrying amount cannot be determined, one of two other approaches is adopted.

2. **Capitalizing the new cost.** The justification for capitalizing the improvement or replacement cost is that even though the old asset's carrying amount is not

removed from the accounts, sufficient amortization was taken on the item to reduce the carrying amount almost to zero. Although this assumption may not be true in every case, the differences are not often significant. Improvements are usually handled in this manner.

3. **Charging to accumulated amortization.** There are times when the production quantity or quality of the asset itself has not been improved, but its useful life has been extended. Replacements, particularly, may extend the asset's useful life, yet may not improve the quality or quantity of its output. In these circumstances, the expenditure may be debited to Accumulated Amortization rather than to an asset account. The theory behind this approach is that the replacement extends the asset's useful life and thereby recaptures some or all of the past amortization. The net carrying amount of the asset is the same whether the asset is debited or the accumulated amortization is debited.

Rearrangement and Reinstallation

Rearrangement and reinstallation costs, which are expenditures intended to benefit future periods, are different from additions, replacements, and improvements. An example is the rearrangement and reinstallation of a group of machines to facilitate future production. If the original installation cost and the accumulated amortization taken to date can be determined or estimated, the rearrangement and reinstallation cost is handled as a replacement. If not, the new costs, if material in amount, should be capitalized as an asset to be amortized over those future periods expected to benefit. This is generally the situation that exists. If these costs are not material, if they cannot be separated from other operating expenses, or if their future benefit is questionable, they should be expensed immediately.

Repairs

Ordinary repairs are expenditures made to maintain plant assets in operating condition; they are charged to an expense account in the period in which they are incurred on the basis that **it is the primary period benefited**. Replacing minor parts, lubricating and adjusting equipment, repainting, and cleaning are examples of maintenance charges that occur regularly and are treated as ordinary operating expenses.

It is often difficult to distinguish a repair from an improvement or replacement. The major consideration is whether the expenditure benefits more than one year or one operating cycle, whichever is longer. If a major repair, such as an overhaul, occurs, several periods will benefit and the cost should be handled as an addition, improvement, or replacement.

If income statements are prepared for short time periods, say, monthly or quarterly, the same principles apply. Ordinary repairs and other regular maintenance charges for an annual period may benefit several quarters, and allocation of the cost among the periods concerned might be required. A company will often find it advantageous to concentrate its repair program at a certain time of the year, perhaps during the period of least activity or when the plant is shut down for vacation. Short-term comparative statements might be misleading if such expenditures were shown as expenses of the quarter in which they were incurred. To give comparability to monthly or quarterly income statements, some companies use an account such as Allowance for Repairs so that repair costs are better assigned to the periods benefiting.[14]

To illustrate, Tractor Corp. estimates that the total cost of the plant's semi-annual closedown for maintenance in the second and fourth quarters will be $720,000. The

---

[14] See *CICA Handbook* Section 1751 on Interim Financial Statements. Paragraph B2 indicates that the expectation of a major annual maintenance expenditure is not sufficient to accrue the expense over interim periods. Rather, the decision to accrue is made based on whether a legal or constructive obligation—a liability—exists. Section 1000.34 defines a constructive obligation as "one that can be inferred from the facts in a particular situation as opposed to a contractually based obligation."

company has no choice but to undertake this activity. It decides to charge each quarter for a portion of the repair cost even though the costs for the year would be incurred in two quarters only.

End of first quarter (zero repair costs incurred)

Repair Expense	180,000	
Accrued Liability for Repairs (¼ × $720,000)		180,000

End of second quarter ($344,000 repair costs incurred)

Accrued Liability for Repairs	344,000	
Cash, Wages Payable, Inventory, etc.		344,000
Repair Expense	180,000	
Accrued Liability for Repairs (¼ × $720,000)		180,000

End of third quarter (zero repair costs incurred)

Repair Expense	180,000	
Accrued Liability for Repairs (¼ × $720,000)		180,000

End of fourth quarter ($380,800 repair costs incurred)

Accrued Liability for Repairs	380,800	
Cash, Wages Payable, Inventory, etc.		380,800
Repair Expense	184,800	
Accrued Liability for Repairs		184,800
($344,000 + $380,800 − $180,000 − $180,000 − $180,000)		

Ordinarily, no balance in the Accrued Liability for Repairs account would be carried over to the following year. The fourth quarter would normally absorb the variation from estimates as illustrated above. When balance sheets are prepared during the year, the Accrued Liability account is reported as a current liability. A debit balance is treated as a prepaid expense.

Some advocate accruing estimated repair costs beyond one year on the assumption that amortization does not take into consideration the incurrence of repair costs. For example, in aircraft overhaul and open hearth furnace rebuilding, an allowance for repairs is sometimes established because it is felt there is an obligation to close down the asset for known and required periodic maintenance, and the amount of repairs can be estimated with a high degree of certainty. In general, expenses should not be anticipated nor liabilities accrued based merely on intention or necessity to incur expenditures in the future.

Summary of Costs Subsequent to Acquisition

The following schedule summarizes the accounting treatment for various costs incurred subsequent to the acquisition of capitalized assets.

ILLUSTRATION 11-14
Summary of Costs Subsequent to Acquisition of Tangible Capital Assets

Type of Expenditure	Normal Accounting Treatment
Additions	Capitalize cost of addition to asset account.

Improvements and replacements	(a) **Carrying value known:** Remove cost of and accumulated amortization on old asset, recognizing any gain or loss. Capitalize cost of improvement/replacement.
	(b) **Carrying value unknown:**
	  1. If the asset's useful life is extended, debit accumulated amortization for cost of improvement/replacement.
	  2. If the quantity or quality of the asset's productivity is increased, capitalize cost of improvement/replacement to asset account.

Rearrangement and reinstallation	(a) If original installation cost is **known**, account for cost of rearrangement/reinstallation as a replacement (carrying value known). (b) If original installation cost is unknown and rearrangement/reinstallation cost is **material** in amount and benefits future periods, capitalize as an asset.

(c) If original installation cost is **unknown** and rearrangement/
reinstallation cost is **not material or future benefit is
questionable**, expense the cost when incurred.

Repairs

(a) **Ordinary:** Expense cost of repairs when incurred.
(b) **Major:** As appropriate, treat as an addition, improvement, or
replacement.

DISPOSITIONS OF TANGIBLE CAPITAL ASSETS

OBJECTIVE 7

Describe the accounting
treatment for the disposal of
property, plant, and
equipment.

Tangible capital assets may be retired voluntarily or disposed of by sale, exchange, involuntary conversion, or abandonment. Regardless of the time of disposal, amortization must be taken up to the date of disposition, and then all accounts related to the retired asset should be removed. Ideally, the specific asset's book value would be equal to its disposal value, but this is rarely the case. As a result, a gain or loss is usually reported.

The reason: the amortization amount is an estimate of the cost to be allocated, and not a process of valuation. **The gain or loss is really a correction of net income** for the years during which the capital asset was used. If it had been possible at the time of acquisition to forecast the exact date of disposal and the amount to be realized at disposition, then a more accurate estimate of amortization would have been recorded and no gain or loss would result.

Gains or losses on the retirement of plant assets are shown in the income statement along with other items that arise from customary business activities. If, however, the operations of a business segment are sold, abandoned, spun off, or otherwise disposed of, then the results of "continuing operations" should be reported separately from "discontinued operations." Any gain or loss from disposing of the tangible capital assets of a discontinued business segment should be reported with the related results of discontinued operations. These reporting requirements were discussed in Chapter 4.

Sale of Tangible Capital Assets

Amortization must be recorded for the time period between the date of the last amortization entry and the date of sale. To illustrate, assume that amortization on a machine costing $18,000 has been recorded for nine years at the rate of $1,200 per year. If the machine is sold in the middle of the tenth year for $7,000, the entry to record amortization to the sale date is:

Amortization Expense	600	
Accumulated Amortization—Machinery		600

This separate entry may not be made because many companies enter all amortization, including this amount, in one entry at the year end. In either case the entry for the asset's sale is:

Cash	7,000	
Accumulated Amortization—Machinery	11,400	
[($1,200 × 9) + $600]		
Machinery		18,000
Gain on Disposal of Machinery		400

With the machinery's book value at the time of the sale of $6,600 ($18,000 − $11,400) and proceeds on disposal of $7,000, the amount of the gain on the sale is $400.

Involuntary Conversion

Sometimes, an asset's service is terminated through some type of *involuntary conversion* such as fire, flood, theft, or expropriation. The gains or losses are calculated no differently from those in any other type of disposition except that **they are often reported as Extraordinary Items in the income statement**.

To illustrate, assume a company was forced to sell a plant located on company property that stood directly in the path of a planned major highway. For a number of years the provincial government had sought to purchase the land on which the plant stood, but the company resisted. The government ultimately exercised its right of eminent domain and its actions were upheld by the courts. In settlement, the company received $500,000, which substantially exceeded the $100,000 book value of the plant (cost of $300,000 less accumulated amortization of $200,000) and the $100,000 book value of the land. The following entry was made:

Cash	500,000	
Accumulated Amortization—Plant Assets	200,000	
Plant Assets		300,000
Land		100,000
Gain on Expropriation of Land and Plant Assets		300,000

The gain or loss that develops on this type of unusual, nonrecurring transaction that is not a result of management actions is normally shown as an extraordinary item. Similar treatment is given to other types of involuntary conversions such as those resulting from a major nonrecurring casualty (such as an earthquake or flood) or theft, assuming that it meets other conditions for extraordinary item treatment. The difference between the amount recovered (such as an insurance recovery), if any, and the asset's carrying value is reported as a gain or loss.

Donations of Capital Assets

In a situation **where a company donates or contributes a nonmonetary asset**, the donation amount should be recorded as an expense at the donated asset's fair value. If a difference exists between the asset's fair value and its book value, a gain or loss should be recognized. To illustrate, assume that Kline Industries donates land that cost $30,000 and a small building located on the property that cost $95,000 with accumulated amortization to the contribution date of $45,000 to the City of Sydney for a city park. The land and building together have a fair market value of $110,000. The entry to record the donation is:

Contribution (or Donations) Expense	110,000	
Accumulated Amortization—Building	45,000	
Building		95,000
Land		30,000
Gain on Disposal of Land and Building		30,000

Miscellaneous Problems

If an asset is scrapped or abandoned without any cash recovery, a loss should be recognized equal to the asset's net carrying amount or book value. If scrap value exists, the gain or loss that results is the difference between the asset's scrap value and its book value. If an asset still can be used even though it is fully amortized, it may be kept on the books at historical cost less its related amortization, or the asset may be carried at scrap value.

SUMMARY OF LEARNING OBJECTIVES

1 Describe the major characteristics of tangible capital assets. The major characteristics of tangible capital assets are: (1) they are acquired for use in operations and not for resale; (2) they are long-term in nature and usually subject to amortization; and (3) they possess physical substance.

2 Identify the costs included in the initial valuation of land, buildings, and equipment. Cost of land: Includes all expenditures made to acquire land and to ready it for use. Land costs typically include (1) the purchase price; (2) closing costs, such as title to the land, legal fees, and registration fees; (3) costs incurred to condition the land for its intended use, such as grading, filling, draining, and clearing; (4) assumption of any liens, mortgages, or encumbrances on the property; and (5) any additional land improvements that have an indefinite life. **Cost of buildings:** Includes all expenditures related directly to their acquisition or construction. These costs include (1) materials, labour, and overhead costs incurred during construction and (2) professional fees and building permits. **Cost of equipment:** Includes the purchase price, freight, and handling charges incurred, insurance on the equipment while in transit, cost of special foundations if required, assembling and installation costs, and costs of conducting trial runs.

3 Describe the accounting problems associated with self-constructed assets. The assignment of indirect costs of manufacturing creates special problems because these costs cannot be traced directly to work and material orders related to the fixed assets constructed. These costs might be handled in one of three ways: (1) assign no fixed overhead to the cost of the constructed asset, (2) assign a portion of all overhead to the construction process, or (3) allocate on the basis of lost production. The second method is used extensively in practice.

4 Describe the accounting problems associated with interest capitalization. Companies may choose whether to expense or capitalize interest during the construction of tangible capital assets. However, only actual interest (with modifications) may be capitalized. The rationale for capitalization is that during construction, interest incurred is a cost necessary to acquire the asset, put it in place, and ready for use. Once construction is completed, the asset is ready for its intended use. Also, if the asset had been purchased fully constructed, the manufacturer's costs, such as interest, would make up part of the costs recovered in the selling price to the buyer. Any interest cost incurred in financing the purchase of an asset that is ready for its intended use should be expensed.

5 Understand accounting issues related to acquiring and valuing plant assets. The following issues relate to acquiring and valuing plant assets: (1) *Cash discounts:* Whether taken or not, they are generally considered a reduction in the asset's cost; its real cost is its cash or cash equivalent price. (2) *Assets purchased on long-term credit contracts:* Account for these at the present value of the consideration exchanged between the contracting parties. (3) *Lump sum or basket purchase:* Allocate the total cost among the various assets based on their relative fair market values. (4) *Issuance of shares:* If the shares are actively traded, the issued shares' market value is a fair indication of the acquired property's cost. If the exchanged shares' market value is not determinable, the acquired property's fair value should be determined and used as the basis for recording the asset's cost and amount credited to the common shares. (5) *Nonmonetary exchanges:* When assets are acquired with little or no cash or other monetary assets as part of the consideration, the new asset's cost depends on whether the assets exchanged are similar or dissimilar. If the assets are similar, it is assumed that the earnings process has not been completed, so no gain can be recognized on the disposal of

KEY TERMS

additions, *513*

avoidable interest, *500*

betterments, *514*

boot, *508*

capital approach, *510*

capital expenditure, *513*

capitalization period, *500*

earnings process, *506*

fixed assets, *496*

flowthrough approach,*511*

improvements, *514*

income approach, *510*

investment tax credit (ITC), *511*

involuntary conversion, *517*

lump sum price, *504*

major repair, *515*

net recoverable amount, *499*

nonmonetary assets, *506*

nonmonetary exchanges, *506*

nonreciprocal transfers, *510*

ordinary repairs, *515*

plant assets, *496*

property, plant, and equipment, *496*

prudent cost, *512*

rearrangement and reinstallation costs, *515*

replacements, *514*

revenue expenditure, *513*

self-constructed asset, *498*

similar nonmonetary assets, *507*

tangible capital assets, *496*

weighted-average accumulated expenditures, *501*

the asset given up. The acquired asset's cost in this case is the carrying amount of the asset(s) given up. If the assets exchanged are not similar, the earnings process is considered completed and a gain or loss on disposal can be recognized. In this case, the acquired asset's cost is recognized as the fair value of the assets given up or those acquired, if clearer. (6) *Exchanges with a significant monetary component:* The cost of the asset acquired is determined by the fair value of the consideration given up, or the fair value of the asset acquired, if clearer, with the resulting gain or loss recognized in income. (7) *Contributions:* Contributed assets, other than from shareholders, should be recorded at the received asset's fair value with a related credit that will be taken to income over the same period as the asset contributed is used. (8) *Investment tax credits:* An immediate tax reduction benefit should be accounted for in the same manner as a government contribution.

6 Describe the accounting treatment for costs subsequent to acquisition. The accounting treatment of costs incurred subsequent to acquisition depends on whether the cost is a capital expenditure or a revenue expenditure. In general, a capital expenditure—one that results in an increase in the asset's useful life, or in the efficiency of the output obtained from that asset—is charged to the asset account. A revenue expenditure, one that does not increase the asset's future benefits, should be expensed immediately. The specific accounting treatment depends on the circumstances.

7 Describe the accounting treatment for the disposal of property, plant, and equipment. Regardless of the time of disposal, amortization must be taken up to the date of disposition, and then all accounts related to the retired asset should be removed. Gains or losses on the retirement of plant assets should be shown in the income statement along with other items that arise from customary business activities. Gains or losses on involuntary conversions may meet the definition of an extraordinary item. If an asset is scrapped or abandoned without any cash recovery, a loss should be recognized equal to the asset's carrying amount. If scrap value exists, the gain or loss recognized is the difference between the asset's scrap value and its book value. If a tangible capital asset is donated to an organization outside the reporting entity, the donation should be reported at its fair value with a gain or loss reported.

APPENDIX 11A

Illustration of Interest Capitalization

LEARNING OBJECTIVE 8

After studying Appendix 11A, you should be able to: Calculate the amount of capitalizable interest on projects involving expenditures over a period of time and borrowings from different sources at varying rates.

To illustrate the issues related to interest capitalization, assume that on November 1, 2001, Shalla Corporation contracted with Pfeifer Construction Co. Ltd. to have a building constructed for $1.4 million on land costing $100,000. The land is acquired from the contractor and its purchase price is included in the first payment. Shalla made the following payments to the construction company during 2002:

January 1	March 1	May 1	December 31	Total
$210,000	$300,000	$540,000	$450,000	$1,500,000

Construction was completed and the building was ready for occupancy on December 31, 2002. Shalla had the following debt outstanding at December 31, 2002:

Specific Construction Debt	
1.	15%, three-year note to finance construction of the building, dated December 31, 2001, with interest payable annually on December 31	$750,000

Other Debt	
2.	10%, five-year note payable, dated December 31, 1998, with interest payable annually on December 31	$550,000
3.	12%, 10-year bonds issued December 31, 1997, with interest payable annually on December 31	$600,000

The weighted-average accumulated expenditures during 2002 are calculated as follows:

Expenditures			Current Year Capitalization		Weighted-Average Accumulated
Date	Amount	×	Period	=	Expenditures
January 1	$ 210,000		12/12		$210,000
March 1	300,000		10/12		250,000
May 1	540,000		8/12		360,000
December 31	450,000		0		0
	$1,500,000				$820,000

ILLUSTRATION 11-15
Calculation of Weighted-Average Accumulated Expenditures

Note that the expenditure made on December 31, the last day of the year, gets a zero-weighting in the calculation, and thus will have no interest cost assigned to it.

The avoidable interest is calculated as follows:

Weighted-Average Accumulated Expenditures	×	Interest Rate	=	Avoidable Interest
$750,000		0.15 (construction note)		$112,500
70,000[a]		0.1104 (weighted average of		7,728
$820,000		other debt)[b]		$120,228

ILLUSTRATION 11-16
Calculation of Avoidable Interest

[a]The amount by which the weighted-average accumulated expenditures exceeds the specific construction loan.

[b]Weighted-average interest rate calculation:

	Principal	Interest
10%, 5-year note	$ 550,000	$ 55,000
12%, 10-year bonds	600,000	72,000
	$1,150,000	$127,000

$$\text{Weighted-average interest rate} = \frac{\text{Total interest}}{\text{Total principal}} = \frac{\$127,000}{\$1,150,000} = 11.04\%$$

The actual interest cost, which represents the maximum amount of interest that may be capitalized during 2002, is calculated as shown below.

Construction note	$750,000 × 0.15	=	$112,500
5-year note	$550,000 × 0.10	=	55,000
10-year bonds	$600,000 × 0.12	=	72,000
Actual interest			$239,500

ILLUSTRATION 11-17
Calculation of Actual Interest Cost

The interest cost to be capitalized is the lesser of $120,228 (avoidable interest) and $239,500 (actual interest), which is $120,228.

The journal entries to be made by Shalla Company during 2002 are as follows:

January 1

Land	100,000	
Building (or Construction in Process)	110,000	
Cash		210,000

March 1

Building	300,000	
Cash		300,000

May 1

Building	540,000	
Cash		540,000

December 31

Building	450,000	
Cash		450,000
Building (Capitalized Interest)	120,228	
Interest Expense		120,228

The capitalized interest cost will be written off as part of the asset's cost amortization. It is thus recognized in expense over the useful life of the asset and not over the term of the debt. The total interest cost incurred during the period should be disclosed, with the portion charged to expense and the portion capitalized indicated.

At December 31, 2002, Shalla should report the amount of interest capitalized either as part of the income statement's nonoperating section or in the notes accompanying the financial statements. Both forms of disclosure are illustrated below.

ILLUSTRATION 11-18
Capitalized Interest Reported in the Income Statement

Income from operations		XXXX
Other expenses and losses:		
Interest expense	$239,500	
Less: Capitalized interest	120,228	119,272
Income before taxes on income		XXXX
Income taxes		XXX
Net income		XXXX

ILLUSTRATION 11-19
Capitalized Interest Disclosed in a Note

Note X: Capitalized Interest. During 2002 total interest cost was $239,500, of which $120,228 was capitalized and $119,272 was charged to expense.

Summary of Learning Objective for Appendix 11A

8 Calculate the amount of capitalizable interest on projects involving expenditures over a period of time and borrowings from different sources at varying rates. The amount of interest capitalized must be disclosed in the notes to the financial statements. The amount capitalized is usually based on the amount of avoidable interest during the construction period.

Note: All asterisked Brief Exercises, Exercises, Problems, and Cases relate to material in the appendix to the chapter.

BRIEF EXERCISES

BE11-1 Bonanza Brothers Inc. purchased land at a price of $27,000. Closing costs were $1,400. An old building was removed at a cost of $12,200. What amount should be recorded as the land cost?

*BE11-2 Brent Hill Company is constructing a building. Construction began on February 1 and was completed on December 31. Expenditures were $1.5 million on March 1, $1.2 million on June 1, and $3 million on December 31. Calculate Hill's weighted-average accumulated expenditures for interest capitalization purposes.

*BE11-3 Brent Hill Company (see BE11-2) borrowed $1 million on March 1 on a 5-year, 12% note to help finance the building construction. In addition, the company had outstanding all year a 13%, 5-year, $2 million note payable and a 15%, 4-year, $3.5 million note payable. Calculate the weighted-average interest rate used for interest capitalization purposes.

*BE11-4 Use the information for Brent Hill Company from BE11-2 and BE11-3. Calculate avoidable interest for Brent Hill Company.

BE11-5 Chavez Corporation purchased a truck by issuing an $80,000, 4-year, noninterest-bearing note to Equinox Inc. The market interest rate for obligations of this nature is 12%. Prepare the journal entry to record the truck purchase.

BE11-6 Cool Spot Inc. purchased land, building, and equipment from Pinball Wizard Corporation for a cash payment of $306,000. The assets' estimated fair values are land $60,000; building $220,000; and equipment $80,000. At what amounts should each of the three assets be recorded?

BE11-7 Wizard Corp. obtained land by issuing 2,000 of its par value common shares. The land was recently appraised at $85,000. The common shares are actively traded at $41 per share. Prepare the journal entry to record the land acquisition.

BE11-8 Strider Corporation traded a used truck (cost $20,000, accumulated amortization $18,000) for another used truck worth $3,700. Strider also paid $300 in the transaction. Prepare the journal entry to record the exchange.

BE11-9 Sloan Ltd. traded a used welding machine (cost $9,000, accumulated amortization $3,000) for office equipment with an estimated fair value of $5,000. Sloan also paid $2,000 cash in the transaction. Prepare the journal entry to record the exchange.

BE11-10 Bulb Ltd. traded a used truck for a new truck. The used truck cost $30,000 and has accumulated amortization of $27,000. The new truck is worth $35,000. Bulb also made a cash payment of $33,000. Prepare Bulb's entry to record the exchange.

BE11-11 Rogers Corporation traded a used truck for a new truck. The used truck cost $20,000 and has accumulated amortization of $17,000. The new truck is worth $35,000. Rogers also made a cash payment of $33,000. Prepare Rogers' entry to record the exchange.

BE11-12 Indicate which of the following costs should be expensed when incurred.
(a) $13,000 paid to rearrange and reinstall machinery
(b) $200 paid for tune-up and oil change on delivery truck
(c) $200,000 paid for addition to building
(d) $7,000 paid to replace a wooden floor with a concrete floor
(e) $2,000 paid for a major overhaul on a truck, which extends useful life
(f) $700,000 paid for relocation of company headquarters

BE11-13 Simcoe City Corporation owns machinery that cost $20,000 when purchased on January 1, 1999. Amortization has been recorded at a rate of $3,000 per year, resulting in a balance in accumulated amortization of $9,000 at December 31, 2001. The machinery is sold on September 1, 2002 for $10,500. Prepare journal entries to (a) update amortization for 2002 and (b) record the sale.

BE11-14 Use the information presented for Simcoe City Corporation in BE11-13, but assume the machinery is sold for $5,200 instead of $10,500. Prepare journal entries to (a) update amortization for 2002 and (b) record the sale.

BE11-15 Use the information presented for Simcoe City Corporation in BE11-13. Assume that the company was entitled to a 15% investment tax credit on the purchase of the machinery which was credited to a deferred credit account. Prepare all entries required on September 1, 2002 to (a) update amortization for 2002, (b) adjust the deferred credit account, and (c) record the sale.

EXERCISES

E11-1 (Acquisition Costs of Realty) The following expenditures and receipts are related to land, land improvements, and buildings acquired for use in a business enterprise. The receipts are enclosed in parentheses.

(a)	Money borrowed to pay building contractor (signed a note)	$(275,000)
(b)	Payment for construction from note proceeds	275,000
(c)	Cost of land fill and clearing	8,000
(d)	Delinquent real estate taxes on property assumed by purchaser	7,000
(e)	Premium on six-month insurance policy during construction	6,000
(f)	Refund of one-month insurance premium because construction was completed early	(1,000)
(g)	Architect's fee on building	22,000
(h)	Cost of real estate purchased as a plant site (land $200,000 and building $50,000)	250,000
(i)	Commission fee paid to real estate agency	9,000
(j)	Installation of fences around property	4,000
(k)	Cost of razing and removing building	11,000
(l)	Proceeds from salvage of demolished building	(5,000)
(m)	Interest paid during construction on money borrowed for construction	13,000
(n)	Cost of parking lots and driveways	19,000
(o)	Cost of trees and shrubbery planted (permanent in nature)	14,000
(p)	Excavation costs for new building	3,000
(q)	GST on excavation cost	210

Instructions

Identify each item by letter and list the items in columnar form, as shown below. All receipt amounts should be reported in parentheses. For any amounts entered in the Other Accounts column, also indicate the account title.

Item	Land	Land Improvements	Building	Other Accounts

E11-2 (Acquisition Costs of Realty) Martin Buer Co. purchased land as a factory site for $400,000. The process of tearing down two old buildings on the site and constructing the factory required six months.

The company paid $42,000 to raze the old buildings and sold salvaged lumber and brick for $6,300. Legal fees of $1,850 were paid for title investigation and drawing the purchase contract. Payment to an engineering firm was made for a land survey, $2,200, and for drawing the factory plans, $68,000. The land survey had to be made before definitive plans could be drawn. The liability insurance premium paid during construction was $900. The contractor's charge for construction was $2,740,000. The company paid the contractor in two instalments: $1.2 million at the end of three months and $1,540,000 upon completion. Interest costs of $170,000 were incurred to finance the construction.

Instructions

Determine the land and building costs as they should be recorded on the books of Martin Buer Corp. Assume that the land survey was for the building.

E11-3 (Acquisition Costs of Trucks)   Alexei Corporation operates a retail computer store. To improve delivery services to customers, the company purchases four new trucks on April 1, 2002. The terms of acquisition for each truck are described below:

1. Truck #1 has a list price of $15,000 and is acquired for a cash payment of $13,900.
2. Truck #2 has a list price of $16,000 and is acquired for a down payment of $2,000 cash and a non-interest-bearing note with a face amount of $14,000. The note is due April 1, 2003. Alexei would normally have to pay interest at a rate of 10% for such a borrowing, and the dealership has an incremental borrowing rate of 8%.
3. Truck #3 has a list price of $16,000. It is acquired in exchange for a computer system that Alexei carries in inventory. The computer system cost $12,000 and is normally sold by Alexei for $15,200. Alexei uses a perpetual inventory system.
4. Truck #4 has a list price of $14,000. It is acquired in exchange for 1,000 common shares of Alexei Corporation. The common shares are no par value shares with a market value of $13 per share.

Instructions

Prepare the appropriate journal entries for the foregoing transactions for Alexei Corporation.

E11-4   (Purchase and Self-Constructed Cost of Assets)   Wen Corp. both purchases and constructs various equipment it uses in its operations. The following items for two different types of equipment were recorded in random order during the calendar year 2003.

Purchase

Cash paid for equipment, including sales tax of $8,000 and GST of $7,000	$115,000 — 7000 GST
Freight and insurance cost while in transit	2,000 +
Cost of moving equipment into place at factory	3,100 +
Wage cost for technicians to test equipment	4,000 +
Insurance premium paid during first year of operation on the equipment	1,500 —
Special plumbing fixtures required for new equipment	8,000 +
Repair cost incurred in first year of operations related to the equipment	1,300 —

Construction

It's not Real Pretanded Calculation

Material and purchased parts (gross cost $200,000; failed to take 2% cash discount)	$200,000 — 4000
Imputed interest on funds used during construction (share financing)	14,000 —
Labour costs	190,000 +
Overhead costs (fixed—$20,000; variable—$30,000)	50,000 +
Profit on self-construction	30,000 —
Cost of installing equipment	4,400 +

Save or

by issuing shares company avoid interest которую был получил на взял loan

Instructions

Calculate the total cost for each of these two pieces of equipment. If an item is not capitalized as an equipment cost, indicate how it should be reported.

E11-5   (Treatment of Various Costs)   Siska Supply Ltd., a newly formed corporation, incurred the following expenditures related to Land, to Buildings, and to Machinery and Equipment.

Land Legal fees for title search		$ 520
Building Architect's fees		2,800
Land Cash paid for land and dilapidated building thereon		87,000
Land Removal of old building >14,500	$20,000	
Less: Salvage	5,500	14,500
Building Surveying before construction — because before cons-on		370
Building Interest on short-term loans during construction		7,400
Building Excavation before construction for basement		19,000
Machinery Machinery purchased (subject to 2% cash discount, which was not taken)		53,900 55,000 должны быть 53,900
Machinery Freight on machinery purchased		1,340
Expenses or others Storage charges on machinery, necessitated by noncompletion of building when machinery was delivered — because it's not normal and reasonable cost of machinery		2,180
Building New building constructed (building construction took six months from date of purchase of land and old building)		485,000
Land Assessment by city for drainage project		1,600
Expense Hauling charges for delivery of machinery from storage to new building — because storage was expense		620
Machinery Installation of machinery		2,000
Land Trees, shrubs, and other landscaping after completion of building (permanent in nature)		5,400

Instructions

Determine the amounts that should be debited to Land, to Buildings, and to Machinery and Equipment. Assume Siska follows a policy of capitalizing interest on self-constructed assets. Indicate how any costs not debited to these accounts should be recorded.

E11-6 **(Correction of Improper Cost Entries)** Plant acquisitions for selected companies are as follows:

1. Bella Industries Inc. acquired land, buildings, and equipment from a bankrupt company, Torres Co., for a lump sum price of $700,000. At the time of purchase, Torres' assets had the following book and appraisal values: *↑ LCM*

	Book Values	Appraisal Values	
Land	$200,000	$150,000	*18.75 %*
Buildings	250,000	350,000	*43.75 %*
Equipment	300,000	300,000	*37.5 %*
	750,000	*800,000*	

To be conservative, the company decided to take the lower of the two values for each asset acquired. The following entry was made:

Land	150,000 *131,250*	
Buildings	250,000 *306,250*	
Equipment	300,000 *262,500*	
Cash		700,000

2. Hari Enterprises purchased store equipment by making a $2,000 cash down payment and signing a one-year, $23,000, 10% note payable. The purchase was recorded as follows:

Store Equipment	~~27,300~~ *25,000*	
Cash		2,000
Note Payable		23,000
~~Interest Payable~~		~~2,300~~

3. Kim Company purchased office equipment for $20,000, terms 2/10, n/30. Because the company intended to take the discount, it made no entry until it paid for the acquisition. The entry was:

Office Equipment	~~20,000~~ *19,600*	
Cash		19,600
Purchase Discounts		400

4. Kaiser Inc. recently received, at zero cost, land from the Village of Chester as an inducement to locate its business in the village. The appraised value of the land is $27,000. The company made no entry to record the land because it had no cost basis.

5. Zimmerman Company built a warehouse for $600,000. It could have contracted out and purchased the building for $740,000. The controller made the following entry:

Warehouse	740,000	
Cash		600,000
Profit on Construction		140,000

Instructions

(a) Prepare the entry that should have been made at the date of each acquisition.

(b) Prepare the correcting entry required in each case to correct the accounts. That is, do not reverse the incorrect entry and replace it with the entry in part (a).

*E11-7 **(Capitalization of Interest)** Harrisburg Furniture Corporation started construction of a combination office and warehouse building for its own use at an estimated cost of $5 million on January 1, 2002. Harrisburg expected to complete the building by December 31, 2002. Harrisburg has the following debt obligations outstanding during the construction period.

Construction loan—12% interest, payable semiannually, issued December 31, 2001	$2,000,000
Short-term loan—10% interest, payable monthly, and principal payable at maturity on May 30, 2003	1,400,000
Long-term loan—11% interest, payable on January 1 of each year. Principal payable on January 1, 2006	1,000,000

Instructions (Carry all calculations to two decimal places.)

(a) Assume that Harrisburg completed the office and warehouse building on December 31, 2002 as planned, at a total cost of $5.2 million, and the weighted average of accumulated expenditures was $3.6 million. Calculate the avoidable interest on this project.

(b) Calculate the amortization expense for the year ended December 31, 2003. Harrisburg elected to capitalize interest during construction and to amortize the building on a straight-line basis. The company determined that the asset has a useful life of 30 years and a residual value of $300,000.

*E11-8 (**Capitalization of Interest**) On December 31, 2001, Omega Inc. borrowed $3 million at 12% payable annually to finance the construction of a new building. In 2002, the company made the following expenditures related to this building: March 1, $360,000; June 1, $600,000; July 1, $1.5 million; December 1, $1.5 million. Additional information is provided as follows:

1. Other debt outstanding
   10-year, 13% bond, December 31, 1995, interest payable
   annually $4,000,000
   6-year, 10% note, dated December 31, 1999, interest payable
   annually $1,600,000
2. March 1, 2002 expenditure included land costs of $150,000
3. Interest revenue earned in 2002 $49,000

Instructions

(a) Determine the interest amount that could be capitalized in 2002 in relation to the building construction.

(b) Prepare the journal entry to record the capitalization of interest and the recognition of interest expense, if any, at December 31, 2002.

E11-9 (**Capitalization of Interest**) On July 31, 2002, Amsterdam Corporation engaged Minsk Tooling Company to construct a special-purpose piece of factory machinery. Construction was begun immediately and was completed on November 1, 2002. To help finance construction, on July 31 Amsterdam issued a $300,000, 3-year, 12% note payable at Netherlands National Bank, on which interest is payable each July 31. $200,000 of the note's proceeds was paid to Minsk on July 31. The remainder of the proceeds was temporarily invested in short-term marketable securities at 10% until November 1. On November 1, Amsterdam made a final $100,000 payment to Minsk. Other than the note to Netherlands, Amsterdam's only outstanding liability at December 31, 2002 is a $30,000, 8%, 6-year note payable, dated January 1, 1999, on which interest is payable each December 31.

Instructions

(a) Calculate the interest revenue, weighted-average accumulated expenditures, avoidable interest, and total interest cost that could be capitalized during 2002. Round all calculations to the nearest dollar.

(b) Prepare the journal entries needed on the books of Amsterdam Corporation at each of the following dates, assuming the company follows a policy of capitalizing interest.
   1. July 31, 2002
   2. November 1, 2002
   3. December 31, 2002

*E11-10 (**Capitalization of Interest**) The following three situations involve the capitalization of interest:

Situation I

On January 1, 2002, Oksana Inc. signed a fixed-price contract to have Builder Associates construct a major head office facility at a cost of $4 million. It was estimated that it would take three years to complete the project. Also on January 1, 2002, to finance the construction cost, Oksana borrowed $4 million payable in 10 annual instalments of $400,000, plus interest at the rate of 10%. During 2002, Oksana made deposit and progress payments totalling $1.5 million under the contract; the weighted-average amount of accumulated expenditures was $800,000 for the year. The excess borrowed funds were invested in short-term securities, from which Oksana realized investment income of $250,000.

Instructions

What amount should Oksana report as capitalized interest at December 31, 2002?

Situation II

During 2002, Midori Ito Corporation constructed and manufactured certain assets and incurred the following interest cost in connection with those activities:

	Interest costs Incurred
Warehouse constructed for Ito's own use	$30,000
Special-order machine for sale to unrelated customer, produced according to customer's specifications	9,000
Inventories routinely manufactured, produced on a repetitive basis	8,000

All of these assets required an extended time period for completion.

Instructions

Assuming the effect of interest capitalization is material, what is the total amount of interest costs to be capitalized?

Situation III

Fleming, Inc. has a fiscal year ending April 30. On May 1, 2002, Fleming borrowed $10 million at 11% to finance construction of its own building. Repayments of the loan are to commence the month following the building's completion. During the year ended April 30, 2003, expenditures for the partially completed structure totalled $7 million. These expenditures were incurred evenly throughout the year. Interest earned on the loan's unexpended portion amounted to $650,000 for the year.

Instructions

How much should be shown as capitalized interest on Fleming's financial statements at April 30, 2003?

(CPA adapted)

E11-11 (Entries for Equipment Acquisitions)   Geddes Engineering Corporation purchased conveyor equipment with a list price of $50,000. The vendor's credit terms were 1/10, n/30. Presented below are three independent cases related to the equipment. Assume that the equipment purchases are recorded gross. (Round to nearest dollar.)

(a) Geddes paid cash for the equipment 15 days after the purchase, along with 7% GST and provincial sales tax of $3,210.

(b) Geddes traded in equipment with a book value of $2,000 (initial cost $40,000), and paid $40,500 in cash one month after the purchase. The old equipment could have been sold for $8,000 at the date of trade, but was accepted for a trade-in allowance of $9,500 on the new equipment.

(c) Geddes gave the vendor a $10,000 cash down payment and a 9% note payable with blended principal and interest payments of $20,000 each, due at the end of each of the next two years.

Instructions

Prepare the general journal entries required to record the acquisition and payment in each of the independent cases above. Round to the nearest dollar.

E11-12 (Entries for Asset Acquisition, Including Self-Construction)   Below are transactions related to Frede Corporation.

(a) The City of Piedmont gives the company five hectares of land as a plant site. This land's market value is determined to be $81,000.

(b) 13,000 no-par common shares are issued in exchange for land and buildings. The property has been appraised at a fair market value of $810,000, of which $180,000 has been allocated to land and $630,000 to buildings. The Frede shares are not listed on any exchange, but a block of 100 shares was sold by a shareholder 12 months ago at $65 per share, and a block of 200 shares was sold by another shareholder 18 months ago at $58 per share.

(c) No entry has been made to remove from the accounts for Materials, Direct Labour, and Overhead the amounts properly chargeable to plant asset accounts for machinery constructed during the year. The following information is given relative to costs of the machinery constructed.

Materials used	$12,500
Factory supplies used	900
Direct labour incurred	15,000
Additional overhead (over regular) caused by construction of machinery, excluding factory supplies used	2,700

Fixed overhead rate applied to regular manufacturing operations   60% of direct labour cost
Cost of similar machinery if it had been purchased from outside suppliers   44,000

Instructions

Prepare journal entries on the books of Frede Corporation to record these transactions.

E11-13 (Entries for Acquisition of Assets) Presented below is information related to Zoe Limited.

1. On July 6, Zoe acquired the plant assets of Desbury Company, which had discontinued operations. The property's appraised value is:

Land	$ 400,000
Building	1,200,000
Machinery and equipment	800,000
Total	$2,400,000

Zoe gave 12,500 of its no par value common shares in exchange. The shares had a market value of $168 per share on the date of the property purchase.

2. Zoe Ltd. expended the following amounts in cash between July 6 and December 15, the date when it first occupied the building:

Repairs to building	$105,000
Construction of bases for machinery to be installed later	135,000
Driveways and parking lots	122,000
Remodelling of office space in building, including new partitions and walls	161,000
Special assessment by city on land	18,000

3. On December 20, the company paid cash for machinery, $260,000, subject to a 2% cash discount, and freight on machinery of $10,500.

Instructions

Prepare entries on the books of Zoe Ltd. for these transactions.

E11-14 (Purchase of Equipment with Noninterest-Bearing Debt) Mohawk Inc. decided to purchase equipment from Central Ontario Industries on January 2, 2002 to expand its production capacity to meet customers' demand for its product. Mohawk issues an $800,000, 5-year, noninterest-bearing note to Central Ontario for the new equipment when the prevailing market interest rate for obligations of this nature is 12%. The company will pay off the note in five $160,000 instalments due at the end of each year over the life of the note.

Instructions

(a) Prepare the journal entry(ies) at the date of purchase. (Round to nearest dollar in all calculations.)
(b) Prepare the journal entry(ies) at the end of the first year to record the payment and interest, assuming that the company employs the effective interest method.
(c) Prepare the journal entry(ies) at the end of the second year to record the payment and interest.
(d) Assuming that the equipment had a 10-year life and no residual value, prepare the journal entry necessary to record amortization in the first year. (Straight-line amortization is employed.)

E11-15 (Purchase of Computer with Noninterest-Bearing Debt) Cardinals Corporation purchased a computer on December 31, 2001 for $105,000, paying $30,000 down and agreeing to pay the balance in five equal instalments of $15,000 payable each December 31 beginning in 2002. An assumed interest rate of 10% is implicit in the purchase price.

Instructions

(a) Prepare the journal entry(ies) at the purchase date. (Round to two decimal places.)
(b) Prepare the journal entry(ies) at December 31, 2002 to record the payment and interest (effective interest method employed).
(c) Prepare the journal entry(ies) at December 31, 2003 to record the payment and interest (effective interest method employed).

E11-16 (Asset Acquisition)   Hayes Industries purchased the following assets and constructed a building as well. All this was done during the current year.

Assets 1 and 2

These assets were purchased as a lump sum for $100,000 cash. The following information was gathered.

Description	Initial Cost on Seller's Books	Amortization to Date on Seller's Books	Book Value on Seller's Books	Appraised Value
Machinery	$100,000	$50,000	$50,000	$85,000
Office equipment	60,000	10,000	50,000	45,000

Asset 3

This machine was acquired by making a $10,000 down payment and issuing a $30,000, 2-year, zero-interest-bearing note. The note is to be paid off in two $15,000 instalments made at the end of the first and second years. It was estimated that the asset could have been purchased outright for $35,900.

Asset 4

This machinery was acquired by trading in similar used machinery. Facts concerning the trade-in are as follows:

Cost of machinery traded	$100,000
Accumulated amortization to date of sale	40,000
Fair market value of machinery traded	75,000
Cash received	5,000
Fair market value of machinery acquired	70,000

Asset 5

Office equipment was acquired by issuing 100 no par value common shares with a market value of $11 per share.

Construction of Building

A building was constructed on land purchased last year at a cost of $150,000. Construction began on February 1 and was completed on November 1. The payments to the contractor were as follows:

Date	Payment
2/1	$120,000
6/1	360,000
9/1	480,000
11/1	100,000

To finance the building construction, a $600,000, 12% construction loan was taken out on June 1. The loan was repaid on November 1. The firm had $200,000 of other outstanding debt during the year at a borrowing rate of 8%.

Instructions

Record the acquisition of each asset.

E11-17 (Asset Exchange with Boot)   Busytown Corporation, which manufactures shoes, hired a recent university graduate to work in its accounting department. On the first day of work, the accountant was assigned to total a batch of invoices using an adding machine. Before long, the accountant, who had never before seen such a machine, managed to break it. Busytown Corporation gave the machine plus $340 to Business Machine Company (a dealer) in exchange for a new machine. Assume the following information about the machines:

	Busytown Corp. (Old Machine)	Business Machine Co. (New Machine)
Machine cost	$290	$270
Accumulated amortization	140	- 0 -
Fair value	85	425

Instructions

For each company, prepare the necessary journal entry to record the exchange.

E11-18 (Asset Exchange with Boot) Cannondale Company purchased an electric wax melter on April 30, 2003 by trading in its old gas model and paying the balance in cash. The following data relate to the purchase:

List price of new melter	$15,800
Cash paid	10,000
Cost of old melter (5-year life, $700 residual value)	11,200
Accumulated amortization—old melter (straight-line)	6,300
Second-hand market value of old melter	5,200

Instructions

Prepare the journal entry(ies) necessary to record this exchange, assuming that the melters exchanged are (a) similar in nature, and (b) dissimilar in nature. Cannondale's fiscal year ends on December 31, and amortization has been recorded through December 31, 2002.

E11-19 (Nonmonetary Exchange) Carlos Company exchanged equipment used in its manufacturing operations plus $1,500 in cash for similar equipment used in the operations of LoBianco Company. The following information pertains to the exchange:

	Carlos Co.	LoBianco Co.
Equipment (cost)	$28,000	$28,000
Accumulated amortization	19,000	10,000
Fair value of equipment	15,500	17,000
Cash given up	1,500	

< 10% or 17,000
we are not recording Gains.

Instructions

Prepare the journal entries to record the exchange on the books of both companies.

E11-20 (Nonmonetary Exchanges) Ashbrook Inc. has negotiated the purchase of a new piece of automatic equipment at a price of $4,000 plus trade-in, f.o.b. factory. Ashbrook Inc. paid $4,000 cash and traded in used equipment. The used equipment had originally cost $62,000; it had a book value of $42,000 and a secondhand market value of $47,800, as indicated by recent transactions involving similar equipment. Freight and installation charges for the new equipment required a cash payment of $1,100.

Instructions

(a) Prepare the general journal entry to record this transaction, assuming that the assets Ashbrook Inc. exchanged are similar in nature.
(b) Assuming the same facts as in (a) except that the assets exchanged are dissimilar in nature, prepare the general journal entry to record this transaction.

E11-21 (Analysis of Subsequent Expenditures) Donovan Resources Group has been in its plant facility for 15 years. Although the plant is quite functional, numerous repair costs are incurred to maintain it in sound working order. The company's plant asset book value is currently $800,000, as indicated below:

Original cost	$1,200,000
Accumulated amortization	400,000
	$ 800,000

During the current year, the following expenditures were made to the plant facility:

(a) Because of increased demands for its product, the company increased its plant capacity by building a new addition at a cost of $270,000.
(b) The entire plant was repainted at a cost of $23,000.
(c) The roof was an asbestos cement slate; for safety purposes it was removed and replaced with a wood shingle roof at a cost of $61,000. The carrying amount of the old roof was $41,000.
(d) The electrical system was completely updated at a cost of $22,000. The cost of the old electrical system was not known. It is estimated that the building's useful life will not change as a result of this updating.

(e) A series of major repairs were made at a cost of $47,000, because parts of the wood structure were rotting. The cost of the old wood structure was not known. These extensive repairs are estimated to increase the building's useful life.

Instructions

Indicate how each of these transactions would be recorded in the accounting records.

E11-22 **(Analysis of Subsequent Expenditures)** The following transactions occurred during 2002. Assume that amortization of 10% per year is charged on all machinery and 5% per year on buildings, on a straight-line basis, with no estimated residual value. Amortization is charged for a full year on all fixed assets acquired during the year, and no amortization is charged on fixed assets disposed of during the year.

Jan. 30 A building that cost $132,000 in 1985 is torn down to make room for a new building. The wrecking contractor was paid $5,100 and was permitted to keep all materials salvaged.

Mar. 10 Machinery that was purchased in 1995 for $16,000 is sold for $2,900 cash, f.o.b. purchaser's plant. Freight of $300 is paid on this machinery.

Mar. 20 A gear breaks on a machine that cost $9,000 in 1997, and is replaced at a cost of $385. The replacement does not extend the machine's useful life.

May 18 A special base installed for a machine in 1996 when it was purchased has to be replaced at a cost of $5,500 because of defective workmanship on the original base. The cost of the machinery was $14,200 in 1996; the cost of the base was $3,500, and this amount was charged to the Machinery account in 1996.

June 23 One of the buildings is repainted at a cost of $6,900. It had not been painted since it was constructed in 1998.

Instructions

Prepare general journal entries for the transactions. (Round to nearest dollar.)

E11-23 **(Analysis of Subsequent Expenditures)** Plant assets often require expenditures subsequent to acquisition. It is important that they be accounted for properly. Any errors will affect both the balance sheets and income statements for a number of years.

Instructions

For each of the following items, indicate whether the expenditure should be capitalized (C) or expensed (E) in the period incurred.

1. _____ Betterment

2. _____ Replacement of a minor broken part on a machine

3. _____ Expenditure that increases an existing asset's useful life.

4. _____ Expenditure that increases the efficiency and effectiveness of a productive asset but does not increase its residual value

5. _____ Expenditure that increases the efficiency and effectiveness of a productive asset and its residual value

6. _____ Expenditure that increases the productive asset's output quality

7. _____ Improvement to a machine that increased its fair market value and its production capacity by 30% without extending the machine's useful life

8. _____ Ordinary repairs

9. _____ Improvement

10. _____ Interest on borrowing necessary to finance a major overhaul of machinery that extended its life.

E11-24 **(Entries for Disposition of Assets)** On December 31, 2002, Travis Inc. has a machine with a carrying amount of $940,000. The original cost and related accumulated amortization at this date are as follows:

Machine	$1,300,000
Accumulated amortization	360,000
	$ 940,000

Amortization is calculated at $60,000 per year on a straight-line basis.

Instructions

Presented below is a set of independent situations. For each independent situation, indicate the journal entry to be made to record the transaction. Make sure that amortization entries are made to update the machine's book value prior to its disposal.

(a) A fire completely destroys the machine on August 31, 2003. An insurance settlement of $430,000 was received for this casualty. Assume the settlement was received immediately.

(b) On April 1, 2003, Travis sold the machine for $1,040,000 to Yoakam Company.

(c) On July 31, 2003, the company donated this machine to the Mountain City Council. The machine's fair market value at the time of the donation was estimated to be $1.1 million.

E11-25 **(Disposition of Assets)** On April 1, 2002, Estefan Corp. received an award of $430,000 cash as compensation for the forced sale of the company's land and building, which stood in the path of a new highway. The land and building cost $60,000 and $280,000, respectively, when they were acquired. At April 1, 2002, the accumulated amortization relating to the building amounted to $160,000. On August 1, 2002, Estefan purchased a piece of replacement property for cash. The new land cost $90,000 and the new building cost $400,000.

Instructions

Prepare the journal entries to record the transactions on April 1 and August 1, 2002.

E11-26 **(Investment Tax Credit: Cost Reduction Method, Alternative Approaches)** Spiropolous Corporation invested in additional machinery in 2002, partially motivated by the 12% investment tax credit available for new equipment purchases. The machinery, delivered in early January, cost $394,000 plus delivery charges of $6,000. Spiropolous amortizes such equipment on a straight-line basis over its estimated five-year life, with no residual value expected. Assume that the same amortization policy is permitted for tax purposes, based on the asset cost less the investment tax credit. Spiropolous reported income before amortization and income taxes of $985,000 for its year ending December 31, 3002. The tax rate is 40%.

Instructions

(a) Prepare the entries for 2002 to account for the purchase of the equipment, income taxes, the investment tax credit, and amortization. Assume the investment tax credit is treated as a reduction of the asset's cost under the cost reduction method.

(b) Assume the investment tax credit is recognized as a deferred credit and amortized under the cost reduction method. Prepare the entries requested in part (a).

E11-27 **(Investment Tax Credit: Cost Reduction Method, Alternative Approaches)** Denning Limited decided to follow a policy of expansion into an area of the province with relatively high unemployment and a work force that could be trained for the work required. Machinery and equipment needed for the expansion were purchased on October 2, 2002 at a total cost of $296,000. All capital purchases qualified for a 10% investment tax credit. Denning expected to use the machinery and equipment evenly over an eight-year period and no residual value was expected. Assume that amortization for tax purposes is based on the straight-line method applied to the equipment cost net of the investment tax credit. The company pays income tax at a rate of 35% and reported income before amortization and taxes of $749,000 for its fiscal year ended September 30, 2003.

Instructions

(a) Prepare the entries required at September 30, 2003 to account for the income tax expense, investment tax credit, and amortization expense, assuming that the investment tax credit is treated as a reduction of the assets' cost.

(b) Prepare the entries required at September 30, 2003 to account for the income tax expense, investment tax credit, and amortization expense, assuming that the investment tax credit is deferred and amortized.

(c) Calculate and compare the net income under these two approaches. Comment.

PROBLEMS

P11-1 At December 31, 2001, certain accounts included in the property, plant, and equipment section of Cilantro Corporation's balance sheet had the following balances:

Land	$230,000
Buildings	890,000
Leasehold improvements	660,000
Machinery and equipment	875,000

During 2002, the following transactions occurred:

Land site number 621 was acquired for $850,000. In addition, to acquire the land, Cilantro paid a $51,000 commission to a real estate agent. Costs of $35,000 were incurred to clear the land. During the course of clearing the land, timber and gravel were recovered and sold for $13,000.

A second tract of land (site number 622) with a building was acquired for $420,000. The closing statement indicated that the land value was $300,000 and the building value was $120,000. Shortly after acquisition, the building was demolished at a cost of $41,000. A new building was constructed for $330,000 plus the following costs:

Excavation fees	$38,000
Architectural design fees	11,000
Building permit fee	2,500
Imputed interest on funds used during construction (share financing)	8,500

The building was completed and occupied on September 30, 2002.

A third tract of land (site number 623) was acquired for $650,000 and was put on the market for resale.

During December 2002, costs of $89,000 were incurred to improve leased office space. The related lease will terminate on December 31, 2004, and is not expected to be renewed. (Hint: Leasehold improvements should be handled in the same manner as land improvements.)

A group of new machines was purchased under a royalty agreement that provides for payment of royalties based on units of production for the machines. The machines' invoice price was $87,000, freight costs were $3,300, installation costs were $2,400, and royalty payments for 2002 were $17,500.

Instructions

(a) Prepare a detailed analysis of the changes in each of the following balance sheet accounts for 2002: Land, Leasehold Improvements, Buildings, and Machinery and Equipment. Disregard the related accumulated amortization accounts.

(b) List the items in the situation that were not used to determine the answer to (a) above, and indicate where, or if, these items should be included in Cilantro's financial statements.

(AICPA adapted)

P11-2 Selected accounts included in the property, plant, and equipment section of Webb Corporation's balance sheet at December 31, 2001 had the following balances:

Land	$ 300,000
Land improvements	140,000
Buildings	1,100,000
Machinery and equipment	960,000

During 2002, the following transactions occurred:

1. A tract of land was acquired for $150,000 as a potential future building site.

2. A plant facility consisting of land and building was acquired from Knorman Company in exchange for 20,000 of Webb's common shares. On the acquisition date, Webb's shares had a closing market price of $37 per share on the Toronto Stock Exchange. The plant facility was carried on Knorman's books at $110,000 for land and $320,000 for the building at the exchange date. Current appraised values for the land and building, respectively, are $230,000 and $690,000.

3. Items of machinery and equipment were purchased at a total cost of $400,000. Additional costs were incurred as follows:

Freight and unloading	$13,000
Sales taxes	20,000
GST	28,000
Installation	26,000

4. Expenditures totalling $95,000 were made for new parking lots, streets, and sidewalks at the corporation's various plant locations. These expenditures had an estimated useful life of 15 years.
5. A machine costing $80,000 on January 1, 1994 was scrapped on June 30, 2002. Double-declining-balance amortization has been recorded on the basis of a 10-year life.
6. A machine was sold for $20,000 on July 1, 2002. Its original cost was $44,000 on January 1, 1999 and it was amortized on the straight-line basis over an estimated useful life of seven years and a residual value of $2,000.

Instructions

(a) Prepare a detailed analysis of the changes in each of the following balance sheet accounts for 2002: Land, Land Improvements, Buildings, Machinery and Equipment. (Hint: Disregard the related accumulated amortization accounts.)

(b) List the items in the fact situation that were not used to determine the answer to (a), showing the pertinent amounts and supporting calculations in good form for each item. In addition, indicate where, or if, these items should be included in Webb's financial statements.

(AICPA adapted)

P11-3 Kiev Corp. was incorporated on January 2, 2002, but was unable to begin manufacturing activities until July 1, 2002 because new factory facilities were not completed until that date.

The Land and Building account at December 31, 2002, was as follows:

January 31, 2002	Land and building	$160,000
February 28, 2002	Cost of removal of building	9,800
May 1, 2002	Partial payment of new construction	60,000
May 1, 2002	Legal fees paid	3,770
June 1, 2002	Second payment on new construction	40,000
June 1, 2002	Insurance premium	2,280
June 1, 2002	Special tax assessment	4,000
June 30, 2002	General expenses	36,300
July 1, 2002	Final payment on new construction	40,000
December 31, 2002	Asset write-up	43,800
		399,950
December 31, 2002	Amortization—2002 at 1%	4,000
	Account balance	$395,950

The following additional information is to be considered:

1. To acquire land and building, the company paid $80,000 cash and 800 of its no par value 8% cumulative preferred shares. Fair market value is $107 per share.
2. Cost of removal of old buildings amounted to $9,800, and the demolition company retained all the building materials.
3. Legal fees covered the following:

Cost of organization	$ 610
Examination of title covering purchase of land	1,300
Legal work in connection with construction contract	1,860
	$3,770

4. The insurance premium covered the building for a 2-year term beginning May 1, 2002.
5. The special tax assessment covered street improvements that are permanent in nature.
6. General expenses covered the following for the period from January 2, 2002 to June 30, 2002.

President's salary	$32,100
Plant superintendent covering supervision of new building	4,200
	$36,300

7. Because of a general increase in construction costs after entering into the building contract, the board of directors increased the building's value by $43,800, believing that such an increase was

justified to reflect the current market at the time the building was completed. Retained earnings were credited for this amount.

8. Estimated life of building—50 years.
Write-off for 2002—1% of asset value (1% of $400,000, or $4,000).

Instructions

(a) Prepare entries to reflect correct land, building, and accumulated amortization accounts at December 31, 2002.

(b) Show the proper presentation of land, building, and accumulated amortization accounts on the balance sheet at December 31, 2002.

(AICPA adapted)

P11-4 Presented below is a schedule of property dispositions for Tomasino Corp.

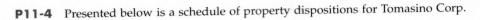

SCHEDULE OF PROPERTY DISPOSITIONS

	Cost	Accumulated Amortization	Cash Proceeds	Fair Market Value	Nature of Disposition
Land	$40,000	—	$31,000	$31,000	Condemnation
Building	15,000	—	3,600	—	Demolition
Warehouse	70,000	$11,000	74,000	74,000	Destruction by fire
Machine	8,000	3,200	900	7,200	Trade-in
Furniture	10,000	7,850	—	3,100	Contribution
Automobile	8,000	3,460	2,960	2,960	Sale

The following additional information is available:

Land
On February 15, land held primarily as an investment was expropriated by the city, and on March 31, another parcel of unimproved land to be held as an investment was purchased at a cost of $35,000.

Building
On April 2, land and building were purchased at a total cost of $75,000, of which 20% was allocated to the building on the corporate books. The real estate was acquired with the intention of demolishing the building, and this was accomplished during November. Cash proceeds received in November represent the net proceeds from the building demolition.

Warehouse
On June 30, the warehouse was destroyed by fire. The warehouse was purchased January 2, 1988 and accumulated amortization of $11,000 had been reported. On December 27, the insurance proceeds and other funds were used to purchase a replacement warehouse at a cost of $90,000.

Machine
On December 26, the machine was exchanged for another machine having a fair market value of $6,300 and cash of $900 was received.

Furniture
On August 15, furniture was contributed to a registered charitable organization. No other contributions were made or pledged during the year.

Automobile
On November 3, the automobile was sold to Una Guillen, a shareholder.

Instructions
Indicate how these items would be reported on the income statement of Tomasino Corp.

(AICPA adapted)

P11-5 On January 1, 2002, Solti Corporation purchased for $600,000 a tract of land (site number 101) with a building. Solti paid a real estate broker's commission of $36,000 and legal fees of $6,000. The closing statement indicated that the land value was $500,000 and the building value was $100,000. Shortly after acquisition, the building was razed at a cost of $54,000.

Solti entered into a $3 million fixed-price contract with Slatkin Builders, Inc. on March 1, 2002 for the construction of an office building on land site number 101. The building was completed and occupied on September 30, 2003. Additional construction costs were incurred as follows:

Plans, specifications, and blueprints	$21,000
Architects' fees for design and supervision	82,000

The building is estimated to have a 40-year life from date of completion and will be amortized using the straight-line method.

To finance construction costs, Solti borrowed $3 million on March 1, 2002. The loan is payable in 10 annual instalments of $300,000 plus interest at the rate of 10%. Solti's weighted-average amounts of accumulated building construction expenditures were as follows:

For the period March 1 to December 31, 2002	$1,200,000
For the period January 1 to September 30, 2003	1,900,000

Assume Solti follows a policy of interest capitalization.

Instructions

(a) Prepare a schedule that discloses the individual costs making up the balance in the land account in respect of land site number 101 as of September 30, 2003.

(b) Prepare a schedule that discloses the individual costs that should be capitalized in the office building account as of September 30, 2003. Show supporting calculations in good form.

(c) Identify the effects on Solti's financial statements for its years ending December 31, 2003 and 2004 if the company followed a policy of expensing all interest as incurred.

(AICPA adapted)

*P11-6 Jehri Landscaping began constructing a new plant on December 1, 2002. On this date the company purchased a parcel of land for $142,000 in cash. In addition, it paid $2,000 in surveying costs and $4,000 for title transfer fees. An old dwelling on the premises was demolished at a cost of $3,000, with $1,000 being received from the sale of materials.

Architectural plans were also formalized on December 1, 2002, when the architect was paid $30,000. The necessary building permits costing $3,000 were obtained from the city and paid for on December 1 as well. The excavation work began during the first week in December with payments made to the contractor as follows:

Date of Payment	Amount of Payment
March 1	$240,000
May 1	360,000
July 1	60,000

The building was completed on July 1, 2003.

To finance the plant construction, Jehri borrowed $600,000 from the bank on December 1, 2002. Jehri had no other borrowings. The $600,000 was a 10-year loan bearing interest at 8%.

Instructions

(a) Calculate the balance in each of the following accounts at December 31, 2002 and December 31, 2003. Assume Jehri follows a policy of capitalizing interest on self-constructed assets.
   1. Land
   2. Buildings
   3. Interest Expense

(b) Identify the effects on Jehri's financial statements for the years ending December 31, 2002 and 2003 if its policy was to expense all interest costs as incurred.

*P11-7 Wordcrafters Inc. is a book distributor that had been operating in its original facility since 1976. The increase in certification programs and continuing education requirements in several professions has contributed to an annual growth rate of 15% for Wordcrafters since 1996. Wordcrafters' original facility became obsolete by early 2002 because of the increased sales volume and the fact that Wordcrafters now carries tapes and disks in addition to books.

On June 1, 2002, Wordcrafters contracted with Favre Construction to have a new building constructed for $5 million on land owned by Wordcrafters. The payments made by Wordcrafters to Favre Construction are shown in the schedule below.

Date	Amount
July 30, 2002	$1,200,000
January 30, 2003	1,500,000
May 30, 2003	1,300,000
Total payments	$4,000,000

Construction was completed and the building was ready for occupancy on May 27, 2003. Wordcrafters had no new borrowings directly associated with the new building but had the following debt outstanding at May 31, 2003, the end of its fiscal year:

14½%, 5-year note payable of $2 million, dated April 1, 1999, with interest payable annually on April 1.

12%, 10-year bond issue of $3 million sold at par on June 30, 1995, with interest payable annually on June 30.

The company follows a policy of capitalizing interest during construction of major assets.

Instructions

(a) Calculate the weighted average accumulated expenditures on Wordcrafters' new building during the capitalization period.

(b) Calculate the avoidable interest on Wordcrafters' new building.

(c) Some interest cost of Wordcrafters Inc. is capitalized for the year ended May 31, 2003.

1. Identify the item(s) relating to interest costs that must be disclosed in Wordcrafters' financial statements.

2. Calculate the amount of the item(s) that must be disclosed.

(CMA adapted)

P11-8   Chesley Corporation wishes to exchange a machine used in its operations. Chesley has received the following offers from other companies in the industry:

1. Secord Company offered to exchange a similar machine plus $23,000.
2. Bateman Company offered to exchange a similar machine.
3. Shripad Company offered to exchange a similar machine, but wanted $8,000 in addition to Chesley's machine.

In addition, Chesley contacted Ansong Corporation, a dealer in machines. To obtain a new machine, Chesley must pay $93,000 in addition to trading in its old machine.

	Chesley	Secord	Bateman	Shripad	Ansong
Machine cost	$160,000	$120,000	$147,000	$160,000	$130,000
Accumulated amortization	50,000	45,000	71,000	75,000	- 0 -
Fair value	92,000	69,000	92,000	100,000	185,000

Instructions

For each of the four independent situations, prepare the journal entries to record the exchange on the books of each company. (Round to nearest dollar.)

P11-9   On August 1, 2002, Arna, Inc. exchanged productive assets with Bontemps, Inc. Arna's asset is referred to below as "Asset A" and Bontemps' is referred to as "Asset B." The following facts pertain to these assets:

	Asset A	Asset B
Original cost	$96,000	$110,000
Accumulated amortization (to date of exchange)	45,000	52,000
Fair market value at date of exchange	70,000	75,000
Cash paid by Arna, Inc.	5,000	
Cash received by Bontemps, Inc.		5,000

Instructions

(a) Assume that Assets A and B are dissimilar. Record the exchange for both Arna, Inc. and Bontemps, Inc. in accordance with generally accepted accounting principles.

(b) Assume that Assets A and B are similar in nature and use. Record the exchange for both Arna, Inc. and Bontemps, Inc. in accordance with generally accepted accounting principles.

P11-10 During the current year, Garrison Construction trades in two relatively new small cranes (crane # 6RT and #S79) for a larger crane that Garrison expects to be more useful given the contracts the company has committed itself to over the next couple of years. The new crane is acquired from Keillor Manufacturing Co., which has agreed to take the smaller equipment as trade-ins and pay $17,500 cash to Garrison as well. The new crane cost Keillor $165,000 to manufacture and is classified as inventory. The following information is available.

	Garrison Const.	Keillor Mfg. Co.
Cost of crane #6RT	$130,000	
Cost of crane #S79	120,000	
Accumulated amortization, #6RT	15,000	
Accumulated amortization, #S79	18,000	
Fair value, #6RT	120,000	
Fair value, #S79	87,500	
Fair market value of new crane		$190,000
Cash paid		17,500
Cash received	17,500	

Instructions

(a) Assume that this exchange is considered to involve dissimilar assets. Prepare the journal entries on the books of (1) Garrison Construction and (2) Keillor Manufacturing.

(b) Assume that this exchange is considered to involve similar assets and one where the earnings process has not been culminated. Prepare the journal entries on the books of (1) Garrison Construction and (2) Keillor Manufacturing.

(c) Assume you have been asked to recommend which accounting method is appropriate in this circumstance. Develop separate arguments for presentation to the controllers of both Garrison Construction and Keillor Manufacturing to justify both methods. Which arguments are more persuasive?

P11-11 Fayne Mining Corp. received a $760,000 low bid from a reputable manufacturer for the construction of special production equipment needed by Fayne in an expansion program. Because the company's own plant was not operating at capacity, Fayne decided to construct the equipment there and recorded the following production costs related to the construction:

Services of consulting engineer	$ 40,000
Work subcontracted	31,000
Materials	300,000
Plant labour normally assigned to production	114,000
Plant labour normally assigned to maintenance	160,000
Total	$645,000

Management prefers to record the equipment cost under the incremental cost method. Approximately 40% of the company's production is devoted to government supply contracts which are all based in some way on cost. The contracts require that any self-constructed equipment be allocated its full share of all costs related to the construction.

The following information is also available:

1. The production labour was for partial fabrication of the plant equipment. Skilled personnel were required and were assigned from other projects. The maintenance labour represents idle time of nonproduction plant employees who would have been retained on the payroll whether or not their services were used.

2. Payroll taxes and employee fringe benefits are approximately 35% of labour cost and are included in manufacturing overhead cost. Total manufacturing overhead for the year was $6,084,000, including the $160,000 maintenance labour used to construct the equipment.

3. Manufacturing overhead is approximately 60% variable and is applied based on production labour cost. Production labour cost for the year for the corporation's normal products totalled $8,286,000.

4. General and administrative expenses include $27,000 of allocated executive salary cost and $13,750 of postage, telephone, supplies, and miscellaneous expenses identifiable with this equipment construction.

Instructions

(a) Prepare a schedule calculating the amount that should be reported as the full cost of the constructed equipment to meet the government contract requirements. Any supporting calculations should be in good form.

(b) Prepare a schedule calculating the incremental cost of the constructed equipment.

(c) What is the greatest amount that should be capitalized as the equipment cost? Why?

(AICPA adapted)

P11-12 Adamski Corporation manufactures ballet shoes and is experiencing a period of sustained growth. In an effort to expand its production capacity to meet the increased demand for its product, the company recently made several acquisitions of plant and equipment. Tim Mullinger, newly hired in the position of Capital Asset Accountant, requested that Walter Kaster, Adamski's controller, review the following transactions.

Transaction 1

On June 1, 2002, Adamski Corporation purchased equipment from Venghaus Corporation. Adamski issued a $20,000, 4-year, noninterest-bearing note to Venghaus for the new equipment. Adamski will pay off the note in four equal instalments due at the end of each of the next four years. At the transaction date, the prevailing market interest rate for obligations of this nature was 10%. Freight costs of $425 and installation costs of $500 were incurred in completing this transaction. The new equipment qualifies for a 5% investment tax credit. The appropriate factors for the time value of money at a 10% interest rate are given below.

Future value of $1 for 4 periods	1.46
Future value of an ordinary annuity for 4 periods	4.64
Present value of $1 for 4 periods	0.68
Present value of an ordinary annuity for 4 periods	3.17

Transaction 2

On December 1, 2002, Adamski purchased several assets of Haukap Shoes Inc., a small shoe manufacturer whose owner was retiring. The purchase amounted to $210,000 and included the assets listed below. Adamski engaged the services of Tennyson Appraisal Inc., an independent appraiser, to determine the assets' fair market values, which are also presented below.

	Haukap Book Value	Fair Market Value
Inventory	$ 60,000	$ 50,000
Land	40,000	80,000
Building	70,000	120,000
	$170,000	$250,000

During its fiscal year ended May 31, 2003, Adamski incurred $8,000 for interest expense in connection with the financing of these assets.

Transaction 3

On March 1, 2003, Adamski traded in four units of specialized equipment plus $25,000 cash for a technologically up-to-date machine that should do the same job as the other machines, but much more efficiently. The equipment traded in had a combined carrying value of $35,000, as Adamski had recorded $45,000 of accumulated amortization against these assets. It was agreed between Adamski's controller and the supplier company's sales manager that the new equipment had a fair value of $64,000.

Instructions

(a) Tangible capital assets such as land, buildings, and equipment receive special accounting treatment. Describe the major characteristics of these assets that differentiate them from other types of assets.

(b) For each of the three transactions described above, determine the value at which Adamski Corporation should record the acquired assets. Support your calculations with an explanation of the underlying rationale.

(c) The books of Adamski Corporation show the following additional transactions for the fiscal year ended May 31, 2003.

1. acquisition of a building for speculative purposes
2. purchase of a two-year insurance policy covering plant equipment
3. purchase of the rights for the exclusive use of a process used in the manufacture of ballet shoes

For each of these transactions, indicate whether the asset should be classified as a tangible capital asset. If it is, explain why. If it is not, explain why not, and identify the proper classification.

(CMA adapted)

P11-13 Vidi Corporation made the following purchases related to its tangible capital assets during its fiscal year ended December 31, 2002. The company uses the straight-line method of amortization for all its capital assets.

1. In early January, Vidi issued 140,000 common shares with a market value of $6 per share (based on a recent sale of 1,000 shares on the Toronto Stock Exchange) in exchange for property consisting of land and a warehouse. The company's property management division estimated the market value of the land ($600,000) and the warehouse ($300,000). The seller advertised in a commercial retail magazine a price of "$860,000 for the land and warehouse, or best offer." The company paid a local real estate broker a finder's fee of $35,000.

2. On March 31, the company acquired equipment on credit. Terms were $7,000 cash down payment plus payments of $5,000 at the end of each of the next two years. The seller's implicit interest rate was 12%. The equipment's list price was $17,000. Additional costs incurred to install the equipment included $1,000 to tear down and replace a wall, and $1,500 to rearrange existing equipment to make room for the new equipment. $500 was spent repairing the equipment after it was dropped during installation.

During the year, the following events also occurred:

3. A new motor was purchased for $50,000 for a large grinding machine (original cost of the machine, $350,000; accumulated amortization at the replacement date, $100,000). The motor will not improve the quality or quantity of production; however, it will extend the grinding machine's useful life from 8 to 10 years.

4. On September 30, the company purchased a small building in a nearby town for $125,000 to use as a display and sales location. The municipal tax assessment indicated that the property was assessed for $95,000; $68,000 for the building and $27,000 for the land. The building had been empty for six months and required considerable maintenance work before it could be used. The following costs were incurred in 2002: previous owner's unpaid property taxes on the property for the previous year—$900; current year's (2002) taxes—$1,000; reshingling of roof—$2,200; cost of hauling refuse out of the basement—$230; cost of spray cleaning the outside walls and washing windows—$750; cost of painting inside walls—$3,170; and incremental fire and liability insurance of $940 for 15 months.

5. The company completely overhauled the plumbing system in its factory for $55,000. The original plumbing costs were not known.

6. On June 30, the company replaced a freezer with a new one that cost $20,000 cash (market value of the new freezer of $21,000 less trade-in value of old freezer). The cost of the old freezer was $15,000. At the beginning of the year, the company had amortized 60% of the asset, that is, 10% per year of use.

7. The company had the factory exterior painted at a cost of $12,000.

Instructions

(a) Prepare the journal entries required to record the acquisitions and/or costs incurred in the above transactions.

(b) In any case where there are alternative methods to account for the transactions, indicate what the alternatives are and the reason why you chose the method you did.

CONCEPTUAL CASES

C11-1 Your client, Salvador Plastics Corp., found three suitable sites, each having certain unique advantages, for a new plant facility. In order to thoroughly investigate the advantages and disadvantages of each site, one-year options were purchased for an amount equal to 6% of the contract price of each site. The costs of the options cannot be applied against the contracts. Before the options expired, one of the sites was purchased at the contract price of $400,000. The option on this site had cost $24,000. The two options not exercised had cost $16,000 each.

Instructions

Present arguments in support of recording the land cost at each of the following amounts.

(a) $400,000   (b) $424,000   (c) $456,000

(AICPA adapted)

C11-2 Bradford Company Ltd. purchased land for its corporate headquarters. A small factory that was on the land when it was purchased was torn down before the office building construction began. Furthermore, a substantial amount of rock blasting and removal had to be done to the site before construction of the building foundation began. Because the office building was set back on the land far from the public road, Bradford Company had the contractor construct a paved road that led from the public road to the office building parking lot.

Three years after the office building was occupied, Bradford Company added four storeys to the office building. The four storeys had an estimated useful life of five years more than the remaining estimated useful life of the original office building.

Ten years later, the land and building were sold at an amount more than their net book value, and Bradford Company had a new office building constructed in another province for its new corporate headquarters.

Instructions

(a) Which of the expenditures above should be capitalized? How should each be amortized? Discuss the rationale for your answers.

(b) How would the land and building sale be accounted for? Include in your answer an explanation of how to determine the net carrying amount at the sale date. Discuss the rationale for your answer.

C11-3 Gomi Medical Labs, Inc., began operations five years ago producing stetrics, a new type of instrument it hoped to sell to doctors, dentists, and hospitals. The demand for stetrics far exceeded initial expectations, and the company was unable to produce enough stetrics to meet demand.

The company was manufacturing its product on equipment that had been built at the start of its operations. To meet demand, more efficient equipment was needed. The company decided to design and build the equipment, because the equipment currently available on the market was unsuitable for producing this product.

In 2002, a section of the plant was devoted to developing the new equipment and a special staff was hired. Within six months a machine, developed at a cost of $714,000, increased production dramatically and reduced labour costs substantially. Elated by the new machine's success, the company built three more machines of the same type at a cost of $441,000 each.

Instructions

(a) In general, what costs should be capitalized for self-constructed equipment?

(b) Discuss the propriety of including in the capitalized cost of self-constructed assets:
   1. the increase in overhead caused by the self-construction of fixed assets
   2. a proportionate share of overhead on the same basis as that applied to goods manufactured for sale

(c) Discuss the proper accounting treatment of the $273,000 ($714,000 − $441,000) by which the cost of the first machine exceeded the cost of the subsequent machines. This additional cost should not be considered research and development costs.

C11-4 Zucker Airline is converting from piston-type planes to jets. Delivery time for the jets is three years, during which substantial progress payments must be made. The planes' multimillion-dollar cost cannot be financed from working capital; Zucker must borrow funds for the payments.

Because of high interest rates and the large sum to be borrowed, management estimates that interest costs in the second year of the period will be equal to one-third of income before interest and taxes, and one-half of such income in the third year.

After conversion, Zucker's passenger-carrying capacity will be doubled with no increase in the number of planes, although the investment in planes will be substantially increased. The jets have a seven-year service life.

Instructions

Give your recommendation concerning the proper accounting for interest during the conversion period. Support your recommendation with reasons and suggested accounting treatment. (Disregard income tax implications.)

(AICPA adapted)

C11-5 Petri Magazine Company Ltd. started constructing a warehouse building for its own use at an estimated cost of $6 million on January 1, 2001 and completed the building on December 31, 2001. During the construction period, Petri has the following debt obligations outstanding:

Construction loan—12% interest, payable semiannually, issued December 31, 2000	$2,000,000
Short-term loan—10% interest, payable monthly, and principal payable at maturity, on May 30, 2002	1,400,000
Long-term loan—11% interest, payable on January 1 of each year. Principal payable on January 1, 2004	2,000,000

Total cost amounted to $6.2 million, and the weighted average accumulated expenditures was $4 million.

Dee Pettigrew, the company president, has been shown the costs associated with this construction project and capitalized on the balance sheet. She is bothered by the "avoidable interest" included in the cost. She argues that, first, all the interest is unavoidable—no one lends money without expecting to be compensated for it. Second, why can't the company use all the interest on all the loans when calculating this avoidable interest? Finally, why can't her company capitalize all the annual interest that accrued over the construction period?

Instructions

You are the company's accounting manager. In a memo, explain what avoidable interest is, how you calculated it (being especially careful to explain why you used the interest rates that you did), and why the company cannot capitalize all its interest for the year. Attach a schedule supporting any calculations that you use.

C11-6 You have two clients that are considering trading machinery with each other. Although the machines are different, you believe that they have many features that make them similar in nature. The facts are as follows:

	Client A	Client B
Original cost	$100,000	$150,000
Accumulated amortization	40,000	80,000
Market value	90,000	120,000
Cash received (paid)	(30,000)	30,000

Instructions

(a) Write a memo to the accountant of Client A explaining how this transaction should be recorded on A's books.

(b) You receive a voice mail message from the accountant at Client B. She doesn't remember the accounting standard for asset exchanges, but recalls that if the assets are similar, she may not be able to recognize a gain on the transaction. She asks that you identify the standard and the rationale for it. She also asks you to respond to her idea of recognizing a portion of the gain equal to the proportion of the fair value received in cash, an alternative she thinks makes sense.

C11-7 You have been engaged to examine the financial statements of Richard Corporation for the year ending December 31, 2002. Richard was organized in January 2002 by Messrs. Duff and Henderson, original owners of options to acquire oil leases on 5,000 hectares of land for $1.2 million. They expected that (1) the oil leases would be acquired by the corporation and (2) subsequently 180,000 common shares of the corporation would be sold to the public at $20 per share. In February 2002, they exchanged their options, $400,000 cash, and $200,000 of other assets for 75,000 common shares of the corporation. The corporation's board of directors appraised the leases at $2.1 million, basing its appraisal on the price of other parcels recently leased in the same area. The options were, therefore, recorded at $900,000 ($2.1 million minus the $1.2 million option price).

The options were exercised by the corporation in March 2002, prior to the sale of the common shares to the public in April 2002. Leases on approximately 500 hectares of land were abandoned as worthless during the year.

Instructions

(a) Why is the valuation of assets acquired by a corporation in exchange for its own common shares sometimes difficult?

(b) 1. What reasoning might Richard Corporation use to support valuing the leases at $2.1 million—the amount of the appraisal by the board of directors?

2. Assuming that the board's appraisal was sincere, what steps might Richard Corporation have taken to strengthen its position to use the $2.1 million value and to provide additional information if questions were raised about possible overvaluation of the leases?

(c) Discuss the propriety of charging one-tenth of the leases' recorded value to expense at December 31, 2002, because leases on 500 hectares of land were abandoned during the year.

(AICPA adapted)

C11-8 A machine's invoice price is $40,000. Various other costs relating to the acquisition and installation of the machine, including transportation, electrical wiring, special base, and so on, amount to $7,500. The machine has an estimated life of 10 years, with no residual value at the end of that period.

The business owner suggests that the incidental costs of $7,500 be charged to expense immediately for the following reasons.

1. If the machine should be sold, these costs cannot be recovered in the sales price.
2. The inclusion of the $7,500 in the machinery account on the books will not necessarily result in a closer approximation of this asset's market price over the years, because demand and supply levels could change.
3. Charging the $7,500 to expense immediately will reduce income taxes.

Instructions
Discuss each point raised by the business owner.

(AICPA adapted)

Using Your Judgement

FINANCIAL STATEMENT ANALYSIS CASES

Case 1 Canadian Tire Corporation

Refer to the financial statements of Canadian Tire Corporation presented in Appendix 5B. Note that the company provides a 10-year financial review at the end of its Annual Report. This summary provides relevant comparative information for determining trends and predicting future results and position.

One way to analyse the results of a company's investments in tangible capital assets is to look at its tangible capital asset turnover ratio. This ratio reflects how many dollars of sales are generated for every dollar invested in plant and equipment. As you might expect, the more sales dollars generated per dollar of fixed investment, the more efficient the use is of those assets.

Instructions

(a) Review the financial statements for information relating to the company's tangible capital assets. What information is contained in each major financial statement and in the notes to the financial statements?

(b) Does the company construct any of its own plant and equipment? If so, what is its policy on the capitalization of costs? Is this a conservative policy? Comment.

(c) Prepare a computer spreadsheet of the following amounts covering Canadian Tire's 1991 to 2000 fiscal years:

  1. gross operating revenue for the year

  2. property and equipment, end of year

  3. total assets, end of year

(d) Using the spreadsheet program capabilities, determine the year-over-year compound growth rate in each of (c) 1. to 3.

(e) Graph all three growth rates on one graph for comparison purposes.

(f) Using the spreadsheet program capabilities, calculate the tangible capital asset turnover ratio for each year. You will be able to do this for nine years only as the calculation should use the average investment in tangible capital assets for each year, not the year-end balance.

(g) Graph the turnover ratios.

(h) Analyse the results of the graphs in (e) and (g) above. Write a brief explanation about the company's growth over the past 10 years and the efficiency in its use of its investment in plant and equipment.

Case 2 Canadian Imperial Bank of Commerce (CIBC), Royal Bank of Canada (Royal), The Toronto-Dominion Bank (TD)

Over the past few years, some Canadian banks have stated that they would follow a strategy of divesting themselves of their real estate holdings such as the office towers that house their operations, in order to allow themselves to concentrate on the banking industry, their core business.

Instructions

Access the financial statements of the CIBC, Royal, and TD banks for their fiscal years ended in 2000 on the Digital Tool. Review the financial statements for information about their tangible capital assets, and answer the following questions:

(a) On a comparative basis for 2000 and 1999, identify the net book values (net carrying amounts) of each bank's tangible capital assets at the end of each year, the amount of new investment in such assets during each year, and the cash proceeds received from the sale of such assets during each year. Does it appear that the banks are following the strategy indicated? Comment on the results of your findings.

(b) How significant are the banks' holdings of tangible capital assets to their total assets? Comment.

RESEARCH CASE

In groups, identify eight different companies, taking one from each of the following industry groups: Consumer products—autos and parts; Consumer products—biotechnology/pharmaceuticals; Film production; Financial services—investment companies and funds; Industrial products—steel; Merchandising—specialty stores; Metals and minerals—integrated mines; and Utilities—telephone utilities. An excellent source is the SEDAR website at www.sedar.com. If you search the database by industry group for financial statements for the most recent 12-month period, you will be able to choose from the large number of public companies on the site.

Instructions

(a) Determine for each company the relative importance of tangible capital assets to total assets invested, and the percentage that depreciation or amortization expense is of total expenses.

(b) For each company, determine the percentage of total assets that is financed by long-term debt.

(c) What industries require the highest relative investment in tangible capital assets?

(d) Is there any relationship between the investment in tangible capital property and financing by long-term debt? Comment.

(e) How would the strategies of companies with significant investment in fixed assets or property, plant, and equipment differ from those with little investment in such assets?

ETHICS CASE 1

Field Corporation purchased a warehouse in a downtown district where land values are rapidly increasing. Adolph Phillips, controller, and Wilma Smith, financial vice-president, are trying to allocate the purchase cost between the land and the building. Phillips, noting that amortization can be taken only on the building, favours placing a very high proportion of the cost on the warehouse itself, thus reducing taxable income and income taxes. Smith, his supervisor, argues that the allocation should recognize the land's increasing value, regardless of the depreciation potential. Besides, she says, net income is negatively impacted by additional amortization and will cause the company's share price to go down.

Instructions

(a) What stakeholder interests are in conflict?

(b) What ethical issues does Phillips face?

(c) How should these costs be allocated?

ETHICS CASE 2

You have been working as a professional accounting trainee for about two months when the audit manager introduces you to one of the firm's clients, Angus Dickson, to whom you have been assigned. Mr. Dickson owns a couple of businesses including a very successful automobile dealership. He greets you warmly and indicates a file of material he would like you to deal with in preparation for his current year's income tax return.

"I've just purchased a rental property for $200,000," he says. "The municipal assessment indicates that the land itself is worth about half that amount, but I want you to allocate no more than 10% of the purchase price to the land. We all know that land isn't deductible for tax purposes! The building was in terrible shape, so I had a new roof put on, installed a new furnace, completely rewired the structure, and had the whole place painted. These are just maintenance expenses, aren't they?"

You know that the more expenses your client can recognize, the better tax position he'll be in. The property is held in your client's name and will affect only his personal income tax.

Instructions

(a) Who are the stakeholders in this situation?

(b) What are the ethical issues, if any?

(c) What should you do?

CHAPTER 12

Amortization, Impairments, and Depletion

LEARNING OBJECTIVES

....

After studying this chapter, you should be able to:

1.	Explain the concept of amortization.
2.	Identify and describe the factors that must be considered when determining amortization charges.
3.	Determine amortization charges using the activity, straight-line, and decreasing charge methods and compare the methods.
4.	Explain special amortization methods.
5.	Identify and understand reasons why amortization methods are selected.
6.	Explain the accounting issues related to asset impairment.
7.	Explain the accounting procedures for depletion of natural resources.
8.	Explain how tangible capital assets, including natural resources, are reported and analysed.

Preview of Chapter 12

The purpose of this chapter is to examine the amortization process and the methods of writing off the cost of tangible capital assets such as plant, equipment, and natural resources. An appendix outlines key aspects of capital cost allowance required for income tax purposes. The content and organization of the chapter are as follows:

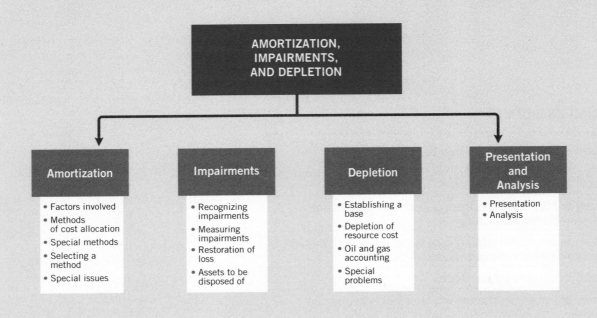

```
                    AMORTIZATION,
                    IMPAIRMENTS,
                    AND DEPLETION


    Amortization        Impairments          Depletion        Presentation
                                                                  and
                                                               Analysis

 • Factors involved   • Recognizing       • Establishing a    • Presentation
 • Methods              impairments         base              • Analysis
   of cost allocation • Measuring          • Depletion of
 • Special methods      impairments          resource cost
 • Selecting a        • Restoration of     • Oil and gas
   method               loss                 accounting
 • Special issues     • Assets to be       • Special
                        disposed of          problems
```

AMORTIZATION—A METHOD OF COST ALLOCATION

OBJECTIVE 1

Explain the concept of amortization.

Many individuals at one time or another purchase and trade in an automobile. In discussions with the automobile dealer, depreciation is a consideration on two points. First, how much has the old car "depreciated"? That is, what is the trade-in value? Second, how fast will the new car depreciate? That is, what will its trade-in value be? In both cases depreciation is thought of as a loss in value.

To accountants, however, **depreciation—or amortization—is not a matter of valuation but a means of cost allocation**. Assets are not amortized based on a decline in their fair market value, but on the basis of a systematic allocation of their cost to expense.

It is undeniably true that an asset's value will fluctuate between the time it is purchased and the time it is sold or scrapped. An allocation rather than a valuation approach is employed, however, because measuring the interim value changes in an objective manner is often difficult and costly to determine. Therefore, the asset's cost is charged to amortization expense over its estimated life, making no attempt to value the asset at fair market value between acquisition and disposition. The cost allocation approach results in a matching of costs with benefits (revenues). Further, because of the going concern assumption and the fact that a capital asset is generally expected to be held until the end of its useful life, interim market value changes are not considered relevant to the determination of income or financial position.

The CICA defines the term amortization as the charge to income which recognizes that life is finite and that the cost less salvage or residual value of a capital

IAS NOTE

IAS 16 requires companies with capital assets that are remeasured to fair value to base the amortization on the revalued amount.

asset is allocated to the periods of service provided by the asset.[1] The *CICA Handbook* continues on to say that "amortization may also be termed depreciation or depletion." In the past, the term depreciation was used to denote the amortization of tangible capital assets such as buildings, plant, and equipment. Depletion referred to the amortization of natural resources (a subset of tangible capital assets such as timber, oil, or mineral deposits), and **amortization** was reserved for intangible assets such as patents and goodwill.[2] These terms are still in common usage. Amortization is used throughout this text to refer to the general process of allocating the cost of capital assets to the accounting periods benefiting from their use, although depletion has been retained when referring specifically to natural resource assets.

Factors Involved in the Amortization Process

Before the dollar charges to revenue can be established, three basic questions must be answered:

1. What amount of the asset's cost is to be amortized?
2. What is the asset's useful life?
3. What pattern and method of cost apportionment is best for this asset?

The answers to these questions distill several estimates into the resulting amortization charge. A perfect measure of amortization for each period is not attainable because, except for the asset's acquisition cost, all other variables involved in the calculations are estimates. Knowledge of the future is never attainable. Ultimately, the difference between the net book value of the asset—a function of the amortization taken—and the asset's proceeds at disposition, results in the recognition of a gain or loss on disposal.

> **OBJECTIVE 2**
> ....
> Identify and describe the factors that must be considered when determining amortization charges.

Amount to Be Amortized

The base established for amortization is a function of two factors: the asset's acquisition cost and residual value of the asset. While historical cost was discussed in Chapter 11, little attention was given to residual value. Residual value is defined as the estimated net realizable value of an item of property, plant, and equipment at the end of its useful life to an enterprise.[3] It is the amount to which the asset must be amortized or written down during its useful life. Illustration 12-1 shows that if an asset has a cost of $10,000 and a residual value of $1,000, the accounting process should amortize only $9,000 of its cost.

Original cost	$10,000
Less: residual value	1,000
Amortizable amount	$ 9,000

ILLUSTRATION 12-1
Calculation of Amount to Be Amortized

From a practical standpoint, residual value is often considered to be zero because the amount is immaterial. Some long-lived assets, however, have substantial net realizable values at the end of their useful lives to a specific enterprise. Companies with similar

---

[1] *CICA Handbook*, Section 3061, par. .29.

[2] The Accounting Standards Board of the CICA and FASB worked together to develop revised standards for business combinations and the attendant issue of accounting for goodwill. In mid-2001, new accounting standards were released that specified goodwill will no longer be amortized, but instead will be reviewed for impairment and written down when circumstances indicate a write-down is needed.

[3] *CICA Handbook*, Section 3061, par. .12. Technically, the amortization charge should be based on the greater of the cost less *salvage* value over the *life* of the asset and the cost less *residual* value over its *useful life*. (par. .28) Salvage value is the asset's estimated net realizable value at the end of its life and is normally negligible. (par. .13) The effect is to ensure that the charges to the income statement as the asset is used are adequate. For purposes of this text, the discussions and illustrations will consider cost less residual value as the amortizable amount.

assets may calculate different amortizable amounts and amortization expense because of differences in estimates of these final values. Examples presented in this chapter include residual values to illustrate how they affect the calculation of amortization expense under various methods.

Estimation of Useful Life

A capital asset's useful life is the period over which the asset is expected to contribute economic benefits to the organization. Useful life can also be stated in terms of the number of units of product or service the asset is expected to produce or provide to the enterprise.

Useful life and physical life are often not the same. A piece of machinery may be physically capable of producing a given product for many years beyond its service life, but the equipment may not be used for all of those years because the cost of producing the product in later years may be too high.[4] For example, many tractors in the Saskatchewan Western Development Museum at Saskatoon are preserved in remarkable physical condition and could be used, although their service lives were terminated many years ago. The reasons for scrapping an asset before its physical life expires are varied. New processes or techniques or improved machines may provide the same service at lower cost and with higher quality. Changes in the product may shorten an asset's service life. Environmental factors can also influence a decision to retire a given asset.

Assets are retired for two major reasons: **physical factors** (e.g., casualty or expiration of physical life) and **economic factors** (e.g., technological or commercial obsolescence). Physical factors relate to such things as decay or wear and tear that result from use and the passage of time. Physical factors set the outside limit for an asset's service life.

Economic or functional factors can be classified into three categories: inadequacy, supersession, and obsolescence. Inadequacy results when an asset ceases to be useful to a given enterprise because the firm's demands have changed. For example, a company may require a larger building to handle increased production. Although the old building may still be sound, it may have become inadequate for the enterprise's purposes. Supersession is the replacement of one asset with a more efficient and economical asset. Examples include the replacement of a mainframe computer with a PC network, or the replacement of a Boeing 767 with a Boeing 777. Obsolescence is the catchall for situations not involving inadequacy and supersession. Because the distinctions among these categories is fuzzy, it is probably best to consider economic factors totally instead of trying to make distinctions that are not clear-cut.

To illustrate these concepts, consider a new nuclear power plant. Which do you think are the more important factors that determine its useful life: physical factors or economic factors? The limiting factors seem to be (1) ecological considerations, (2) competition from other power sources (non-nuclear), and (3) safety concerns. Physical life does not appear to be the primary factor affecting useful life. Although the plant's physical life may be far from over, the plant may become obsolete in 10 years.

For a house, physical factors undoubtedly are more important than the economic or functional factors relative to useful life. Whenever the asset's physical nature is the primary determinant of useful life, maintenance plays a vital role. The better the maintenance, the longer the life of the asset.[5]

The problem of estimating service life is difficult; experience and judgement are the primary means of determining service lives. In some cases, arbitrary lives are

---

[4] *Ibid.*, par. .27 indicates that the life of any capital asset, other than land, is finite and is normally the shortest of the physical, technological, commercial, and legal life. Par. .32 specifies that when the life "is extended into the future, it becomes increasingly difficult to identify a reasonable basis for estimating the life."

[5] The airline industry also illustrates the type of problem involved in estimation. In the past, aircraft were assumed not to wear out—they just became obsolete. However, some jets have been in service as long as 20 years, and maintenance of these aircraft has become increasingly expensive. In addition, the public's concern about worn-out aircraft has been heightened by some recent air disasters. As a result, some airlines are finding it necessary to replace aircraft, not because of obsolescence, but because of physical deterioration.

selected; in others, sophisticated statistical methods are employed to establish a useful life for accounting purposes. In many cases, the primary basis for estimating an asset's useful life is the enterprise's past experience with the same or similar assets. In a highly industrial economy such as Canada's, where research and innovation are so prominent, economic and technological factors have as much effect, if not more, on service lives of tangible assets as do physical factors.

Methods of Cost Allocation (Amortization)

The third factor involved in the amortization decision is the **pattern and method** of cost allocation. The accounting profession requires that the amortization method employed be "rational and systematic" and consistent with the capital asset's nature and its use by the enterprise.[6]

A number of amortization methods may be used, classified as follows:

1. Activity methods (units of use or production)
2. Straight-line method
3. Decreasing charge (or accelerated) methods:
   (a) Declining-balance
   (b) Sum-of-the-years'-digits
4. Increasing charge methods
5. Special depreciation methods:
   (a) Group and composite methods
   (b) Hybrid or combination methods[7]

UNDERLYING CONCEPTS

Amortization is an attempt to match an asset's cost to the periods that benefit from its use.

To illustrate, assume that a company recently purchased a crane for heavy construction purposes. Pertinent data concerning the crane's purchase are:

Cost of crane	$500,000
Estimated useful life in years	5 years
Productive life in hours	30,000 hours
Estimated residual value	$ 50,000

ILLUSTRATION 12-2
Data Used to Illustrate Amortization Methods

Activity Methods

The **activity method**, sometimes called a variable charge approach, determines amortization as **a function of use or productivity instead of the passage of time**. The asset's life is defined in terms of either the output it provides (units it produces), or the input required (the number of hours it works) to produce the output. Conceptually, a better cost association is established by using an **output measure** rather than the hours put in, but often the output is not homogeneous or is difficult to measure. In such cases, an **input measure** such as machine hours is an appropriate basis for determining the amount of the amortization charge for the accounting period.

OBJECTIVE 3

Determine amortization charges using the activity, straight-line, and decreasing charge methods and compare the methods.

The crane poses no particular problem because the usage (hours) is relatively easy to measure. If the crane is used 4,000 hours the first year, the amortization charge is:

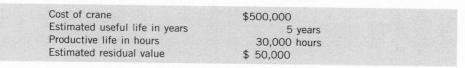

$$\frac{\text{Cost less residual value}}{\text{Total estimated hours}} = \text{Amortization expense per hour}$$

$$\frac{\$500,000 - \$50,000}{30,000 \text{ hours}} = \$15 \text{ per hour}$$

First year amortization expense: 4,000 hours × $15 = $60,000

ILLUSTRATION 12-3
Amortization Calculation, Activity Method-Crane Example

---

[6] *CICA Handbook*, Section 3061, par. .28.

[7] Clarence Byrd, Ida Chen, Heather Chapman, *Financial Reporting in Canada, 2000*, (CICA, Toronto, 2000) reports that, of the companies surveyed in 1999 that used only one method of amortization, 90% used straight-line, 6% used units of production, 2% used diminishing balance and 2% used an increasing charge method. A small majority of the surveyed companies, however, reported using more than one method, with a combination of straight-line and units of production or diminishing balance (i.e., decreasing charge) being the most popular.

Where reduction in utility is a result of use, activity, or productivity, the activity method will best match costs and revenues. Companies that adopt this approach will have low amortization during periods of low productivity and high charges during high productivity.

This method's major limitation is that it is not appropriate in situations where depreciation is a function of time instead of activity. For example, a building is subject to a great deal of steady deterioration from the elements (a function of time) regardless of its use. In addition, where an asset's useful life is subject to economic or functional factors independent of its use, the activity method loses much of its appeal. For example, if a company is expanding rapidly, a particular building may soon become obsolete for its intended purposes, without the extent of use playing any role in its loss of utility. Another limitation in using an activity method is that the total units of output or service hours to be received over the useful life are often difficult to determine.

UNDERLYING CONCEPTS

If the benefits flow on a "straight-line" basis, then justification exists for matching the asset's cost on a straight-line basis with the benefits.

ILLUSTRATION 12-4

Amortization Calculation, Straight-Line Method —Crane Example

Straight-Line Method

Under the straight-line method, depreciation is considered **a function of the passage of time**. This method is widely employed in practice because of its simplicity. The straight-line procedure is often the most conceptually appropriate, as well. When creeping obsolescence is the primary reason for a limited service life, the decline in usefulness may be constant from period to period. The amortization charge for the crane is calculated as follows.

$$\frac{\text{Cost less residual}}{\text{Estimated service life}} = \text{Amortization charge}$$

$$\frac{\$500,000 - \$50,000}{5} = \$90,000$$

The major objection to the straight-line method is that it rests on two tenuous assumptions: (1) the asset's economic usefulness is the same each year, and (2) maintenance expense is about the same each period (given constant revenue flows). If such is not the case, a rational matching of expense with revenues will not result from applying this method.

Another problem stems from distortions in the rate of return analysis (income ÷ assets) that can develop. Illustration 12-5 indicates how the rate of return increases, given constant revenue flows, because the asset's book value decreases. Relying on the increasing trend of the rate of return in such circumstances can be very misleading as a basis for evaluating the success of operations. The increase in the rate of return is the result of an accounting method and does not reflect significant improvement in underlying economic performance. With the exception of the compound interest methods, the rate of return trend can be similarly distorted by other amortization methods.

ILLUSTRATION 12-5

Amortization and Rate of Return Analysis—Crane Example

Year	Amortization Expense	Unamortized Asset Balance (net book value)	Income (after amortization expense)	Rate of Return (income ÷ assets)
0		$500,000		
1	$90,000	410,000	$100,000	24.4%
2	90,000	320,000	100,000	31.2%
3	90,000	230,000	100,000	43.5%
4	90,000	140,000	100,000	71.4%
5	90,000	50,000	100,000	200.0%

UNDERLYING CONCEPTS

The matching concept does not justify a constant charge to income. If the asset's benefits decline as it gets older, then a decreasing charge to income would better match cost to benefits.

Decreasing Charge Methods

The decreasing charge methods, often called accelerated amortization or diminishing balance methods, provide for a higher amortization expense in the earlier years and lower charges in later periods. The main justification for this approach is that more amortization should be charged in earlier years when the asset offers the greatest benefits. Another argument is that repair and maintenance costs are often higher in the later periods, and the accelerated methods thus provide a fairly constant total cost (for amortization plus repairs and maintenance) because the amortization charge is lower in the later periods. When a decreasing charge approach is used by Canadian companies, it is usually a version of what is called the declining-balance method.[8]

Declining-Balance Method. The declining-balance method uses an amortization rate (expressed as a percentage and called the declining-balance rate) that remains constant throughout the asset's life (assuming no change in estimates occurs). This rate is applied to the reducing book value (cost less accumulated amortization) each year to determine the amortization expense. The declining-balance rate may be determined in a variety of ways, but we will use a multiple of the straight-line rate.[9] For example, the double-declining-balance rate for a 10-year life asset is 20% (the straight-line rate, which is 100% ÷ 10 or 10% multiplied by 2). For an asset with a 20-year life, the triple-declining-balance rate is 15% (the straight-line rate of 100% ÷ 20 or 5% multiplied by 3), while the double-declining-balance rate is 10% (100% ÷ 20 or 5% multiplied by 2).

Unlike other methods, **the declining-balance method does not apply the rate to the amortizable amount. Instead, this method applies the appropriate rate to the asset's net book value or net carrying amount.** The asset's book value at the beginning of each period is multiplied by the declining-balance rate. Since the asset's book value is reduced each period by the amortization charge, the rate is applied to a successively lower book value. The result is a lower amortization charge each year. This process continues until the asset's book value is reduced to its estimated residual value, at which time amortization ceases.

Application of the double-declining-balance method using the crane example is illustrated below.

Year	Book Value of Asset First of Year	Rate on Declining Balance[a]	Amortization Expense	Balance of Accumulated Amortization	Net Book Value, End of Year
1	$500,000	40%	$200,000	$200,000	$300,000
2	300,000	40%	120,000	320,000	180,000
3	180,000	40%	72,000	392,000	108,000
4	108,000	40%	43,200	435,200	64,800
5	64,800	40%	14,800[b]	450,000	50,000

[a](100% ÷ 5) × 2.
[b]Limited to $14,800 because book value should not be less than residual value.

ILLUSTRATION 12-6
Amortization Calculation, Double-Declining-Balance Method—Crane Example

Enterprises sometimes switch from the declining-balance to the straight-line method near the end of an asset's useful life to ensure that the asset is amortized only to its residual value. This may be done on practical grounds and, because amounts involved are not material, a retroactive adjustment for a change in accounting policy is not made.

---

[8] Another decreasing charge approach called the sum-of-the-years'-digits method exists but is used infrequently in Canada. Under this method, the amortizable amount (i.e., cost less residual value) is multiplied each year by a decreasing fraction. For example, the sum of the years' digits of an asset with a five-year life is 1 + 2 + 3 + 4 + 5 = 15. Because this is a decreasing charge approach, amortization expense is 5/15 of the amortizable amount in the first year, 4/15 of the amortizable amount in the second year, etc.

[9] The straight-line rate (%) is equal to 100% divided by the estimated useful life of the asset being amortized. A pure form of the declining-balance method (sometimes called the "fixed percentage of book value method") has also been suggested as a possibility, but is not used extensively in practice. This approach finds a rate that amortizes the asset exactly to residual value at the end of its expected useful (n years) life. The formula for determining this rate is as follows:

Amortization rate = 1 − the nth root of (the Residual value ÷ Acquisition cost)

Once the rate is calculated, it is applied on the asset's declining book value from period to period, which means that amortization expense will be successively lower.

Increasing Charge Methods

Increasing charge methods, such as compound interest and sinking fund approaches, provide for lower amortization charges in the early years and higher amounts in the later years of an asset's life. This method is not widely used except by companies with significant real estate holdings. Real estate tends to be financed heavily by debt, making interest expense one of the most significant expenses. Over time, as the debt is paid down, the interest charges become smaller and smaller. Companies with this pattern of interest expense want an amortization policy with the opposite effect on expense; that is, one with low charges in the early years and higher expense in later years. The result is a fairly stable level of total expenses over time.

The most common application of this pattern of amortization is called the **sinking fund method**. In general, the amount of amortization expense is the annual increase in a "virtual" sinking fund designed to accumulate the amortizable amount over the asset's useful life.[10] As the "sinking fund" increases in size, so too does the amount of the annual increase representing principal plus interest. Because its use tends to be industry-specific, this text does not provide further details of its application.

Special Methods of Amortization

Sometimes an enterprise does not select one of the more popular amortization methods because the assets involved have unique characteristics, or the nature of the industry dictates that a special amortization method be adopted. Alternatively, a company may develop its own special or tailor-made amortization method. GAAP requires only that the method result in an allocation of the asset's cost over its life in a rational and systematic manner.

Group and Composite Methods

Amortization methods are usually applied to a single asset. In some circumstances, however, a company may place all of its computers (regardless of type, use, or life) into a single multiple-asset account. Multiple-asset accounts are often amortized using one rate. A telecommunications company, for example, might amortize telephone poles, microwave systems, or switchboards by groups.

Two methods of amortizing multiple-asset accounts can be employed: the group method and the composite method. **The two methods are not different in the calculations involved;** both find an average and amortize on that basis. The different names for the methods reflect the degree of similarity of the assets subject to the calculations: the term "group" refers to a collection of assets that are similar in nature; "composite" refers to a collection of assets that are dissimilar in nature.

The **group method** is frequently used when the assets are fairly homogeneous and have approximately the same useful lives. The **composite method** is used when the assets are heterogeneous and have different lives. The group method more closely approximates a single-unit cost procedure because the dispersion from the average is not as great. The method of calculation for group or composite is essentially the same: find an average and amortize on that basis.

To illustrate, a vehicle leasing company amortizes its fleet of cars, trucks, and campers on a composite basis. The amortization rate is established as shown in Illustration 12-7.

ILLUSTRATION 12-7
Amortization Calculation, Composite Basis

Asset	Original Cost	Residual Value	Amortizable Amount	Estimated Life (yrs.)	Amortization per Year (straight-line)
Cars	$145,000	$25,000	$120,000	3	$40,000
Trucks	44,000	4,000	40,000	4	10,000
Campers	35,000	5,000	30,000	5	6,000
	$224,000	$34,000	$190,000		$56,000

---

[10] This is termed a "virtual" sinking fund because no amounts are set aside in an actual sinking fund.

$$\text{Composite amortization rate on original cost} = \frac{\$56,000}{\$224,000} = 25\%$$

$$\text{Composite life} = 3.39 \text{ years } (\$190,000 \div \$56,000)$$

The **composite amortization rate** is determined by dividing the total amortization per year for the collection of assets by their total original cost. If there are no changes in the assets, they will be amortized to the residual value in the amount of $56,000 per year (the original cost of $224,000 × the composite rate of 25%). As a result, it will take the company 3.39 years (composite life as indicated in the exhibit) to amortize these assets.

The differences between the group or composite method and the single-unit amortization method become accentuated when examining asset retirements. If an asset is retired before or after the average service life of the group is reached, the resulting gain or loss is buried in the Accumulated Amortization account. This practice is justified because some assets will be retired before the average service life, while others will be retired after the average life. For this reason, **the debit to Accumulated Amortization is the difference between original cost and cash received**. **No gain or loss on disposition is recorded.**

To illustrate, suppose that one of the campers with a cost of $5,000 is sold for $2,600 at the end of the third year. The entry is:

Accumulated Amortization	2,400	
Cash	2,600	
Cars, Trucks, and Campers		5,000

If a new type of asset is purchased (mopeds, for example), a new amortization rate must be calculated and applied in subsequent periods.

A typical financial statement disclosure of the group amortization method is shown for **Canadian National Railway Company** as follows:

Canadian National Railway Company

Notes to Consolidated Financial Statements
Year Ended December 31, 2000

1 Summary of Significant accounting policies

G. Properties
Railroad properties are carried at cost less accumulated depreciation including asset impairment write-downs. All costs of materials associated with the installation of rail, ties, ballast and other track improvements are capitalized to the extent they meet the Company's definition of "unit of property." The related labor and overhead costs are also capitalized for the installation of new, non-replacement track. All other labor and overhead costs and maintenance costs are expensed as incurred.

The cost of railroad properties, less salvage value, retired or disposed of in the normal course of business is charged to accumulated depreciation, in accordance with the group method of depreciation. The Company reviews the carrying amounts of properties whenever events or changes in circumstances indicate that such carrying amounts may not be recoverable based on future undiscounted cash flows or estimated net realizable value. Assets that are deemed impaired as a result of such review are recorded at the lower of carrying amount or fair value.

ILLUSTRATION 12-8
Disclosure of Group Amortization Method

The group or composite method simplifies the bookkeeping process and tends to average out errors caused by over- or under-amortization. As a result, periodic income is not distorted by gains or losses on asset disposals.

On the other hand, the single-asset approach (1) simplifies the calculation mathematically; (2) identifies gains and losses on disposal; (3) isolates amortization on idle assets; and (4) represents the best estimate of the amortization of each asset, not the result of averaging the cost over a longer period of time. As a consequence, it is generally used in practice.

Go to the Digital Tool for a discussion of other special amortization methods.

Hybrid or Combination Methods

In addition to the amortization methods described above, companies are free to develop their own special or tailor-made methods. A hybrid amortization method used by some companies in the steel industry is referred to as the production variable method. One example is a modified units of production approach used for equipment whose depreciation is a function of physical wear and tear as well as time. The annual charge for amortization is a straight-line amount adjusted by the level of raw steel production. Therefore, in some periods the amortization expense is larger than the straight-line amount and in others it is less.

Selecting an Amortization Method

OBJECTIVE 5

Identify and understand reasons why amortization methods are selected.

Which amortization method should be selected, and why? Conceptually, an amortization method should be selected based on which method best meets the objectives of financial reporting in the particular circumstances. To achieve these objectives, many believe that **expenses should be rationally matched against benefits (revenues)**.

If the method to be chosen is the one that rationally matches amortization expense against the benefits received from the asset, it is first necessary to identify the pattern of benefits to be received. Possible benefit patterns are indicated in Illustration 12-9.

ILLUSTRATION 12-9
Possible Benefit Patterns for Assets

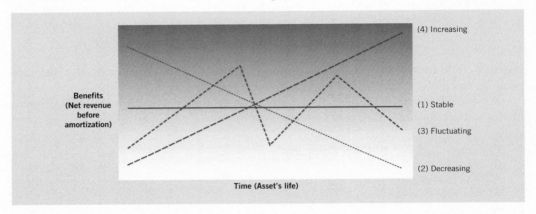

Pattern (1) represents an asset providing roughly the same level of benefits in each year of its life. A warehouse could be an example. For such assets, the straight-line method would be rational because it gives a constant amortization expense each period. An airplane may be an example of an asset with a decreasing benefit pattern (2). When it is new, it is constantly in service on major routes but, as it gets older, it may be repaired more often and used for more peripheral routes. Therefore, amortization expense should decline each year. The use of a truck, in terms of kilometres driven, may fluctuate considerably from period to period, yielding a benefit pattern that varies (3). An activity method would rationally match amortization expense against such a benefit pattern. An increasing benefit pattern (4) may result from ownership of a hotel. Over time, the net revenues may increase as occupancy rates increase. As such, a compound interest or sinking fund method may be most appropriate for matching.

While appropriate matching is important, it may be difficult in many cases to develop projections of future revenues. **Simplicity** may therefore govern. In such cases, it might be argued that the straight-line method of amortization should be used. However, others might argue that whatever is used for tax purposes should be used for book purposes because it **eliminates some record-keeping costs**. Because Canadian companies must use the capital cost allowance approach for income tax purposes (discussed in Appendix 12A to this chapter), they may be tempted to use the same for financial reporting purposes. The objectives of financial reporting differ, however, from those of income tax determination. Therefore, it is not uncommon for companies to have two sets of records when accounting for amortization. While this is legal and acceptable given the differences in objectives, a consequence is that financial statement amounts for capital assets and for income before taxes will differ from the tax basis of the capital assets and taxable income. The financial accounting consequences of such differences are examined in Chapter 19.

The **perceived economic consequences** of the financial reporting may also be a factor that influences the selection of an amortization method. For example, at one time, **U.S. Steel** (now USX) changed its method of amortization from an accelerated to a straight-line method for financial reporting purposes. Many observers noted that the reason for the change was to report higher income so that the company would be less susceptible to takeover by another enterprise. In effect, the company wanted to report higher income so that the market value of its shares would rise.[11] In 1995 the giant chemical company **Du Pont** switched from accelerated amortization to straight-line for a $250 million U.S. drop in depreciation expense and a warning that the eventual impact on net income would depend "on the level of future capital spending" (averaging $3.5 billion annually from 1993 to 1995).

The real estate industry in the U.S. is frustrated with amortization accounting because it argues that real estate often does not decline in value. In addition, because real estate is highly debt financed, most U.S. real estate concerns report losses in earlier years when the sum of amortization and interest charges exceeds the revenues from the real estate project. The industry argues for some form of increasing charge method of amortization (lower amortization at the beginning and higher amortization at the end), so that higher total assets and net income are reported in the earlier years of the project.[12] Some even use an economic consequences argument that Canadian real estate companies (which could and do use increasing charge methods) have a competitive edge over American ones. In support of this view, they have pointed to the increasing number of acquisitions by Canadian real estate companies of U.S. real estate companies and properties.

Choice of an amortization method will affect both the balance sheet (i.e., carrying value of capital assets) and the income statement (i.e., amortization expense). Therefore, various ratios will be affected. These include the rate of return on total assets, debt to total assets, and the total asset turnover. Consequently, contractual commitments (e.g., agreements related to management compensation plans and bond indentures) are potentially important aspects that should be considered in selecting an amortization method.

Special Amortization Issues

Several special issues related to amortization remain to be discussed. These are:

1. How should amortization be calculated for partial periods?
2. Does amortization provide for the replacement of assets?
3. How are revisions in amortization rates handled?

UNDERLYING CONCEPTS

Failure to consider the economic consequences of accounting principles is a frequent criticism of the profession. However, the neutrality concept requires that the statements be free from bias. Freedom from bias requires that the statements reflect economic reality, even if undesirable effects occur.

INTERNATIONAL INSIGHT

In most non-Anglo-Saxon nations, companies are not permitted to use one amortization method for financial statements and a different method for tax returns. The financial statements must conform to the tax return.

---

[11] This assumption is highly tenuous. It is based on the belief that stock market analysts will not be able to recognize that the change in amortization methods is purely cosmetic and therefore will give more value to the shares after the change. In fact, research in this area reports just the opposite. One study showed that companies that switched from accelerated to straight-line (which increased income) methods experienced declines in share value after the change; see Robert J. Kaplan and Richard Roll, "Investor Evaluation of Accounting Information: Some Empirical Evidence," *The Journal of Business*, April 1972, pp. 225–257. Others have noted that switches to more liberal accounting policies (generating higher income numbers) have resulted in lower stock market performance. One rationale is that such changes signal that the company is in trouble and also leads to skepticism about management's attitudes and behaviour.

[12] In this regard, real estate investment trusts (REITs) often report (in addition to net income) an earnings measure, funds from operations (FFO), that adjusts income for amortization expense and other noncash expenses. This method is not GAAP, and there is mixed empirical evidence about whether FFO or GAAP income is more useful to real estate investment trust investors. See, for example, Richard Gore and David Stott, "Toward a More Informative Measure of Operating Performance in the REIT Industry: Net Income vs. FFO," *Accounting Horizons*, December 1998; and Linda Vincent, "The Information Content of FFO for REITs," *Journal of Accounting and Economics*, January 1999.

Amortization and Partial Periods

Plant assets are seldom purchased on the first day of a fiscal period or disposed of on the last day of a fiscal period. A practical question is: How much amortization should be charged for the partial periods involved?

Assume, for example, that an automated drill machine with a five-year life is purchased for $45,000 (no residual value) on June 10, 2001. The company's fiscal year ends December 31, and amortization is charged for 6 2/3 months during that year. The total amortization for a full year (assuming the straight-line method) is $9,000 ($45,000 ÷ 5), and the amortization for the partial year is $5,000 ($9,000 × [6⅔ ÷ 12]).

Rather than making a precise allocation of cost for a partial period, many companies establish a policy to simplify the calculations. For example, amortization may be calculated for the full period on the opening balance in the asset account and no depreciation charged on acquisitions during the year. Other variations charge a full year's amortization on assets used for a full year and charge one-half year's amortization in the years of acquisition and disposal. Alternatively, they may charge a full year's amortization in the year of acquisition and none in the year of disposal.

A company is at liberty to adopt any one of these fractional-year policies in allocating cost to the first and last years of an asset's life, provided the method is applied consistently. **For purposes of the illustrations and problem material in this text, amortization is calculated on the basis of the nearest full month, unless otherwise directed.** Illustration 12-10 shows amortization allocated under five different fractional-year policies using the straight-line method on the automated drill machine purchased above for $45,000 on June 10, 2001.

ILLUSTRATION 12-10

Fractional-Year Amortization Policies

Machine Cost = $45,000 Fractional-Year Policy	Amortization Allocated per Period Over 5-Year Life*					
	2001	2002	2003	2004	2005	2006
1. Nearest fraction of a year.	$5,000ᵃ	$9,000	$9,000	$9,000	$9,000	$4,000ᵇ
2. Nearest full month.	5,250ᶜ	9,000	9,000	9,000	9,000	3,750ᵈ
3. Half year in period of acquisition and disposal.	4,500	9,000	9,000	9,000	9,000	4,500
4. Full year in period of acquisition, none in period of disposal.	9,000	9,000	9,000	9,000	9,000	– 0 –
5. None in period of acquisition, full year in period of disposal.	– 0 –	9,000	9,000	9,000	9,000	9,000

ᵃ6.667/12 ($9,000)   ᵇ5.333/12 ($9,000)   ᶜ7/12 ($9,000)   ᵈ5/12 ($9,000)
*Rounded to nearest dollar.

The partial period calculation is relatively simple when the straight-line method is used. But how is partial period amortization handled when an accelerated method is used? To illustrate, assume that an asset was purchased for $10,000 on July 1, 2001, with an estimated useful life of five years. The amortization expense for 2001, 2002, and 2003 using the double-declining-balance method is shown in Illustration 12-11.

ILLUSTRATION 12-11

Calculation of Partial Period Amortization, Double-Declining-Balance Method

1st full year	(40% × $10,000) =	$4,000
2nd full year	(40% × 6,000) =	2,400
3rd full year	(40% × 3,600) =	1,440

Amortization July 1, 2001, to December 31, 2001:

$$6/12 × \$4,000 = \underline{\$2,000}$$

Amortization for 2002:

6/12 × $4,000 =	$2,000
6/12 × $2,400 =	1,200
	$3,200
or ($10,000 − $2,000) × 40% =	$3,200

Amortization for 2003:

6/12 × $2,400 =	$1,200
6/12 × $1,440 =	720
	$1,920
or ($10,000 − $2,000 − $3,200) × 40% =	$1,920

In calculating amortization expense for partial periods in this example, the amortization charge for a full year was determined first. This amount was then prorated on a straight-line basis to amortization expense between the two accounting periods involved. A simpler approach when using the declining-balance method is to calculate the partial year amortization expense for the acquisition year (e.g., $2,000 for 2001 as shown in the example) and then apply the amortization rate (40%) to the book value at the beginning of each successive year. This is shown in the illustration as the "or" calculations. The charge for each year is the same regardless of the alternative arithmetic employed.

Amortization and Replacement of Assets

A common misconception about amortization is that it provides funds to replace capital assets. Amortization is similar to any other expense in that it reduces net income, but it differs in that **it does not involve a current cash outflow**.

To illustrate why amortization does not provide funds for replacing plant assets, assume that a business starts operating with plant assets of $500,000, with a useful life of five years. The company's balance sheet at the beginning of the period is:

Plant assets	$500,000	Owners' equity	$500,000

Now if we assume that the enterprise earned no revenue over the five years, the income statements are:

	Year 1	Year 2	Year 3	Year 4	Year 5
Revenue	$ -0-	$ -0-	$ -0-	$ -0-	$ -0-
Amortization	(100,000)	(100,000)	(100,000)	(100,000)	(100,000)
Loss	$(100,000)	$(100,000)	$(100,000)	$(100,000)	$(100,000)

The balance sheet at the end of the five years is:

Plant assets	-0-	Owners' equity	-0-

This extreme example illustrates that amortization in no way provides funds to replace assets. **The funds for the replacement of the assets come from the revenues** (generated through use of the asset); without the revenues, no income is earned and no cash inflow results. A separate decision must be made by management to set aside cash to accumulate asset replacement funds.

Revision of Amortization Rates

When a plant asset is purchased, amortization rates are carefully determined based on past experience with similar assets and other pertinent information. Amortization is only an estimate, however, and it may be necessary to revise the calculations during the life of the asset.[13] Unexpected physical deterioration or unforeseen obsolescence may make the asset's useful life less than originally estimated. Improved maintenance procedures, revision of operating policies, or similar developments may prolong the asset's life beyond the expected period.[14]

---

[13] *CICA Handbook*, Section 3061, par. .33 states that the amortization method and estimates of the life and useful life of property, plant, and equipment should be reviewed on a regular basis.

[14] As an example of a change in operating procedures, General Motors (GM) used to write off its tools—such as dies and equipment used to manufacture car bodies—over the life of the body type. Through this procedure, it expensed tools twice as fast as Ford and three times as fast as Chrysler (now DaimlerChrysler). However, it slowed the depreciation process on these tools and lengthened the lives on its plant and equipment. These revisions had the effect of reducing depreciation and amortization charges by approximately $1.23 billion, or $2.55 per share, in the year of the change.

For example, assume that machinery that cost $90,000 is estimated to have a 20-year life with no residual value and has already been amortized for 10 years. In year 11 it is estimated that the machine will be used an additional 20 years. Its total life, therefore, is now expected to be 30 years. Amortization has been recorded at the rate of 1/20 of $90,000, or $4,500 per year, by the straight-line method. On the basis of a 30-year life, amortization should have been 1/30 of $90,000, or $3,000 per year. Amortization, therefore, has been overestimated, and net income understated by $1,500 for each of the past 10 years, or a total amount of $15,000. The amount of the difference can be calculated as shown below.

ILLUSTRATION 12-12
Calculation of Accumulated Difference Due to Revision of Estimate

	Per Year	For Ten Years
Amortization charged per books (1/20 × $90,000)	$4,500	$45,000
Amortization based on a 30-year life (1/30 × $90,000)	3,000	30,000
Excess amortization charged	$1,500	$15,000

Canadian accounting standards do not permit companies to go back and "correct" the records when a change in an estimate is made, nor to make a "catch up" adjustment for the $15,000 accumulated difference in the year of the change. Section 1506 of the *CICA Handbook* requires instead that the effects of any changes in estimates **be accounted for in the period of change and applicable future periods**. The reason is that changes in estimates are a continual and inherent part of any estimation process. As new information becomes available, it is incorporated into current and future reports.

Therefore, when a change in estimate occurs, no entry is made to change previously recorded amounts. Instead, a new amortization schedule is prepared for the asset using the revised information: the unamortized costs remaining on the books, and the most recent estimates of residual value and remaining useful life. Charges for amortization in the current and subsequent periods are based on the revised calculations as illustrated below.

ILLUSTRATION 12-13
Calculating Amortization after Revision of Estimated Life

Machinery	$90,000
Less: Accumulated amortization to date	45,000
Book value of machinery at end of tenth year	$45,000

Revised amortization = $45,000 book value ÷ 20 years remaining life = $2,250

The entry to record amortization for each of the remaining 20 years is:

Amortization Expense	2,250	
Accumulated Amortization—Machinery		2,250

If the machinery now has an estimated residual value of $5,000 at the end of its revised useful life, the revised amortization rate is $2,000 ([$45,000 − $5,000] ÷ 20) each year.

If the double-declining-balance method were used, the change in estimated life would result in a new amortization rate to be applied to the book value in the current (11th) and subsequent years.[15] In this example, a revised remaining life of 20 years results in a revised 5% straight-line and a 10% double-declining rate, coincidentally the same as the rate used for the first 10 years. As this method ignores residual value in determining amortization expense, a change in residual value is ignored in the revised calculation.

---

[15] To determine the unamortized book value to date when using the double-declining-balance method, the following formula can be used:

Book value = $C(1 − r)^n$ where C = cost of asset; r = amortization rate; and n = number of full years from the asset's acquisition date. For example, if the machinery in the illustration had been amortized using the double-declining-balance method instead of the straight-line method, C = $90,000; r = 2 × (100% ÷ 20) = 10%; and n = 10.

The asset's book value at the end of year 10, therefore, is $90,000(1 − .10)^{10}$ or $31,381.

IMPAIRMENTS

Unlike current assets such as inventories, the general valuation rule of the **lower of cost and market does not apply to property, plant, and equipment**. Because current assets are expected to be converted into cash within the operating cycle, it is important to report them on the balance sheet at no more than the net cash you expect to obtain. Tangible capital assets, however, ordinarily are used in operations over the long term, not converted to cash. Therefore, the lower of cost and market is not an appropriate valuation for this asset type.

Even when long-lived capital assets suffer partial obsolescence, accountants have been reluctant to reduce the assets' carrying amount. This reluctance occurs because, unlike inventories, it is difficult to arrive at a fair value for property, plant, and equipment that is not subjective and arbitrary. For example, **Falconbridge Ltd. Nickel Mines** had to decide whether all or a part of its property, plant, and equipment in a nickel-mining operation in the Dominican Republic should be written off. The project had been incurring losses because nickel prices were low and operating costs were high. Only if nickel prices increased by approximately 33% would the project be reasonably profitable. Whether a write-off was appropriate depended on the future price of nickel. Even if the decision were made to write off the asset, another important question was: How much should be written off?[16]

Recognizing Impairments

An *impairment* occurs when the carrying amount of an asset is not recoverable and, therefore, a write-off is needed. Various events and changes in circumstances might lead to an impairment. Examples include:

(a) A significant decrease in an asset's market value.

(b) A significant change in the extent or manner in which an asset is used.

(c) A significant adverse change in legal factors or in the business climate that affects an asset's value.

(d) An accumulation of costs significantly in excess of the amount originally expected to acquire or construct an asset.

(e) A projection or forecast that demonstrates continuing losses associated with an asset.

If these events or changes in circumstances indicate that the asset's carrying amount may not be recoverable, a *recoverability test* is used to determine whether an impairment has occurred. This entails estimating the future net cash flows expected from the **use of the asset and its eventual disposition**. If this sum (*undiscounted*) is **less than the asset's carrying amount**, the asset is considered impaired. Conversely, if the sum of the expected future net cash flows (*undiscounted*) is **equal to or greater than the asset's carrying amount**, no impairment has occurred.

The recoverability test is a screening device to determine whether an impairment has occurred. For example, if the expected future net cash flows from an asset are $400,000 and its carrying amount is $350,000, no impairment has occurred. However, if the expected future net cash flows are $300,000, an impairment has occurred.

UNDERLYING CONCEPTS

The going concern concept assumes that the firm can recover the cost of the investment in its assets. Under GAAP, the fair value of long-lived assets is not reported because a going concern does not plan to sell such assets. However, if the assumption of being able to recover the investment cost is not valid, then a reduction in value should be reported.

IAS NOTE

An asset's recoverable amount under IAS 36 is the greater of its net selling price and the discounted present value of its estimated future cash flows.

Measuring Impairments

As this text went to print, the Canadian accounting standard for the impairment of property, plant, and equipment required that when the net carrying amount of an item

---

(less any related accumulated provision for future site removal and restoration costs and future income taxes), exceeds the net recoverable amount, the excess should be charged to income.[17] The **net recoverable amount** is the estimated *undiscounted* future net cash flow from the use of an asset during its remaining useful life, together with its residual value.[18] The entry to record an impairment recognizes the loss and increases the accumulated amortization account as follows:

Loss on Impairment	$xxx	
Accumulated Amortization		$xxx

While crediting the asset account directly would accomplish the objective of reducing the asset's carrying value, crediting the Accumulated Amortization account has the benefit of preserving the asset's original cost. Once an asset's carrying value has been written down, **it is not reversed for any subsequent increases in the net recoverable amount**. The amount of any writedown of a capital asset is required to be charged to expense, and disclosed in the period the impairment is recognized.

The Accounting Standards Board has approved a proposal to harmonize the Canadian standard on impairment of capital assets with a revised U.S. standard on asset impairment and disposal issues with the fundamental recognition and measurement provisions described below.[19]

Under the FASB standard, **the impairment loss is the amount by which the asset's carrying amount exceeds its fair value.** An asset's fair value is measured by its market value if an active market for it exists. If no active market exists, the **present value of expected future net cash flows** should be used, discounted at the company's market interest rate. Thus, although the impairment test itself requires the use of **undiscounted** cash flows, the determination of fair value is usually directly related to **discounted** cash flows.

The process of determining an impairment loss under FASB is summarized as follows:

1. Review events or changes in circumstances for possible impairment.
2. If a possible impairment, apply the recoverability test. If the sum of the expected future net cash flows from the long-lived asset is less than the asset's carrying amount, an impairment has occurred.
3. The impairment loss is the amount by which the asset's carrying amount exceeds its fair value.

To illustrate, assume a company has a capital asset that, due to changes in its use, is reviewed for possible impairment. The asset's carrying amount is $600,000 ($800,000 cost less $200,000 accumulated amortization). The expected future net cash flows (undiscounted) from the asset's use and eventual disposition are determined to be $650,000. The recoverability test indicates that the $650,000 of expected future net cash flows from the asset's use and disposal exceed its carrying amount of $600,000. No impairment is assumed to have occurred and the company will not recognize an impairment loss.

---

[17] *CICA Handbook*, Section 3061, par. .38. Provisions for future removal and site restoration costs are considered later in this chapter and accounting for income taxes is considered in Chapter 19.

[18] *Ibid.*, par. .08. The future cash flow is not discounted because the purpose of the calculation is to determine recovery, not valuation (par. .49). Projecting the net recoverable amount is based on assumptions that reflect the enterprise's planned course of action and management's judgement of the most probable set of circumstances.

[19] In July 2000, the FASB issued an Exposure Draft of a proposed Statement, *Accounting for the Impairment or Disposal of Long-Lived Assets and for Obligations Associated with Disposal Activities*, which would supersede Statement 121 (impairment) and APB Opinion No. 30 (reporting the effects of disposing of a business segment). FASB expected a final statement on the impairment or disposal of long-lived assets before the end of 2001. It is expected to retain the fundamental recognition and measurement provisions of Statement 121 for assets to be held and used, and the fundamental measurement provisions for assets to be disposed of by sale described above. Once resolved, the AcSB proposes to harmonize its impairment standard with the FASB requirements.

In contrast, assume the same facts as above except that the expected future net cash flow from the equipment's use and disposal is $580,000. The recoverability test indicates that the expected future net cash flows are less than the equipment's carrying amount of $600,000. Therefore an impairment has occurred. The impairment loss is calculated as the difference between the asset's carrying amount and fair value. If the asset has a market value of $525,000, the loss to be recognized is $75,000.

Carrying amount of the equipment	$600,000
Fair value of equipment	525,000 _580,000_
Loss on impairment	$ 75,000 _20,000_

ILLUSTRATION 12-14
Calculation of Impairment Loss

The entry to record the impairment loss is:

Loss on Impairment	75,000 _20,000_	
Accumulated Amortization		75,000 _20,000_

IAS NOTE
For assets carried at cost, impairment losses are recognized in the income statement. If carried at revalued amounts, the asset's impairment is treated as a decrease of the revaluation surplus in equity.

The impairment loss is not an extraordinary item but, because it occurs infrequently and if material in amount, it could be reported as a separate item in the income statement.

A company that recognizes an impairment loss should disclose the asset(s) impaired, the events leading to the impairment, the loss amount, how fair value was determined (disclosing the interest rate used, if appropriate), and where the loss was reported in the income statement.

Rio Algom Limited, a mining, exploration and development company, reported the following information related to asset writedowns in its financial statements for the year ended December 31, 1999.

ILLUSTRATION 12-15
Disclosure of Impairment Loss

Excerpts from **Rio Algom Limited**
Notes to the Consolidated Financial Statements

1. ACCOUNTING POLICIES

Mining, Exploration and Development Properties

The company reviews and evaluates the recoverability of mining properties on a periodic basis. Estimated future net cash flows, on an undiscounted basis, from each property are calculated using estimated recoverable quantities; estimated future price realizations (considering contracts in place, historical and current prices, price trends and related factors); and operating, capital and reclamation costs. Reductions in the carrying value of mining properties with a corresponding charge to earnings, are recorded to the extent that the estimated future net cash flows are less than the carrying value.

Estimates of future cash flows are subject to risks and uncertainties. It is possible that changes could occur which may affect the recoverability of the carrying value of mining properties.

Consolidated Statements of Earnings and Retained Earnings
Years ended December 31, 1999 and 1998

(in millions of Canadian dollars except per share data)	1999	1998
EXPENSES		
Cost of mine production and metal sales	1,582	1,609
Selling, general and administration	238	232
Depreciation and amortization (note 22)	103	85
Interest (note 23)	23	23
Exploration	19	15
Receivables securitization expense (note 6)	6	—
Asset valuation writedowns (note 24)	293	—
	2,264	1,964

24. ASSET VALUATION WRITEDOWNS

The company performs evalutions to assess the recoverability of the carrying value of its mining properties and investment. In August 1999, based on the evaluations, a writedown of the carrying value of certain assets was required as follows:

ILLUSTRATION 12-15
Disclosure of Impairment Loss
(continued)

(in millions of Canadian dollars)	1999	1998
Minera Alumbrera Limited	$ 125	$ —
Nicolet Minerals Company (the Crandon project)	76	—
Rio Algom Mining Corp.	70	—
Bullmoose Coal	22	—
	293	—
Deferred tax recovery	(79)	—
Writedowns, net of deferred taxes	$ 214	$ —

IAS NOTE

IAS 36 permits write-ups for subsequent recoveries of impairment when there has been a change in the estimates used to determine the recoverable amount.

Restoration of Impairment Loss

Once an impairment loss is recorded, the reduced carrying amount of an asset held for use becomes its new cost basis. As a result, the new cost basis is not changed except for amortization in future periods or for additional impairments. To illustrate, assume that at December 31, 2001, equipment with a carrying amount of $500,000 is considered impaired and is written down to its fair value of $400,000. At the end of 2002, the fair value of this asset has increased to $480,000. The asset's carrying amount should not change in 2002 except for the amortization recorded in 2002. The **impairment loss may not be restored for an asset held for use**.

Assets to Be Disposed of

The impairment recognition and measurement standards described assume that the impaired capital assets will continue to be held and used by the enterprise. In this case, new amortization schedules are likely to be required, taking into account the reduction in costs remaining to be amortized, and perhaps new estimates of useful life and residual value. When the impaired tangible capital assets are expected to be held for sale, different standards apply.

In general, an impaired asset that is held for sale is reported separately in the balance sheet and is accounted for at the lower of cost and net realizable value. Because the asset is intended for disposal in a short period of time, net realizable value is used in order to provide a better measure of the net cash flows that will be received from the asset. Such assets are not amortized. Amortization is inconsistent with the notion of assets not in use and with lower of cost and net realizable value valuation. The assets, however, will be continually revalued to the lower of cost and net realizable value, written up or down in future periods, as long as the write-up is never greater than the asset's carrying amount or book value before the impairment.

When the impaired tangible capital assets are expected to be abandoned, exchanged, or sold as a fundamental part of an asset group associated with discontinued operations, different standards apply. These are beyond the scope of an intermediate text.

DEPLETION

OBJECTIVE 7

Explain the accounting procedures for depletion of natural resources.

Natural resources, sometimes called wasting assets, include petroleum, minerals, and timber. They are characterized by two main features: (1) complete removal (consumption) of the asset, and (2) replacement of the asset only by an act of nature. Unlike buildings and machinery, natural resources are consumed physically over the period of use and do not retain their physical characteristics. Still, the accounting problems associated with natural resources are similar to those encountered with other tangible capital assets. The questions to be answered are:

1. How is the depletion base (amortizable amount) established?
2. What pattern of depletion (amortization) should be employed?

Establishing a Depletion Base

How is the depletion base for an oil well determined? Sizeable expenditures are needed to find the natural resource, and for every successful discovery there are many "dry holes." Furthermore, long delays are encountered between the time the costs are incurred and benefits are obtained from the extracted resources. As a result, a conservative policy frequently is adopted in accounting for the expenditures incurred in finding and extracting natural resources.

The costs of natural resources can be divided into three categories: (1) property acquisition costs, (2) exploration costs, and (3) development costs.

Acquisition Costs

Acquisition cost is the price paid to obtain the property right to search and find an undiscovered natural resource, or the price paid for an already discovered resource. In some cases, property is leased and special royalty payments are paid to the lessor if a productive natural resource is found and is commercially profitable. Generally, the acquisition cost is placed in an account titled Undeveloped or Unproved Property and held in that account pending the results of exploration efforts.

Exploration Costs

As soon as the enterprise has the right to use the property, exploration costs are likely to be incurred to find the resource. The accounting treatment for these costs varies: some firms expense all exploration costs; others capitalize only those costs that are directly related to successful projects (successful efforts approach); and still others capitalize all these costs whether or not they are related to successful or unsuccessful projects (full-cost approach).

The debate between the use of the successful efforts and the full-cost approach is particularly prevalent in the oil and gas industry. Proponents of the full-cost approach believe that unsuccessful ventures are a cost of those that are successful, because the cost of drilling a dry hole is a cost that is needed to find the commercially profitable wells. Those who believe that only the costs of successful projects should be capitalized contend that unsuccessful companies will otherwise end up capitalizing many costs that will enable them, over a short period of time, to show an income that will be similar to a successful company. In addition, it is contended that to appropriately measure cost and effort for a single property unit, the only relevant measure is the cost directly related to that unit. The remainder of the costs should be absorbed as period charges, like advertising costs.

Under the successful efforts and full-cost approaches, exploration costs are initially capitalized to an Undeveloped or Unproved Property account. Only when it is determined whether or not the result is successful and extraction will be commercially viable do the accounting methods begin to differ in their determination of costs to be included in the depletion base. Under successful efforts, the costs for unsuccessful exploration activities are charged to earnings, whereas under the full-cost method, they remain capitalized as part of the cost of the natural resource.[20]

Canadian practice is mixed in terms of these two approaches. Larger companies such as **Imperial Oil** and **Petro-Canada** use the successful efforts approach. Small to medium-

---

[20] In 1978, the Securities and Exchange Commission (SEC) in the U.S. argued in favour of a yet-to-be developed method, reserve recognition accounting (RRA), which it believed would provide more relevant information. Under RRA, as soon as a company discovers oil, the value of the oil is reported on the balance sheet and in the income statement—a current value approach. By 1981, the SEC renounced this method for use in the primary financial statements because of the inherent uncertainty of determining and valuing recoverable quantities of proved oil and gas reserves. In 1982, the FASB issued *Statement No. 69*, which requires current value disclosures. The use of RRA would make a substantial difference in the balance sheets and income statements of oil companies. For example, Atlantic Richfield Co. at one time reported net producing property of $2.6 billion (U.S.). If RRA were adopted, the same properties would be valued at $11.8 billion.

sized companies favour the full-cost approach. Exceptions to this generality regarding size include **Canadian Natural Resources Ltd.** and **PanCanadian Petroleum Ltd.**, which are fairly large companies that use the full-cost method; others, like **Paramount Resources Ltd.**, although relatively small, use the successful efforts method. The difference in net income under the two methods can be staggering.

Development Costs

Development costs are costs incurred to obtain access to proven reserves and to provide facilities for extracting, treating, gathering, and storing the resource. Such costs include amortization and operating costs of support equipment (e.g., moveable heavy machinery) used in the development activities. Because equipment can be moved from one drilling or mining site to another, **tangible equipment costs are normally not considered in the depletion base**. Instead, the amortization of tangible capital assets is calculated using an appropriate method and, instead of charging the amount to Amortization Expense as a period cost, it is capitalized to the natural resource asset account. It becomes part of the depletion base by being recognized as a development cost. **Intangible development costs, on the other hand, are directly considered part of the depletion base.** These costs include such items as drilling costs, tunnels, shafts, and wells, which have no tangible characteristics but are needed to produce the natural resource.

The preproduction costs that become components of the depletion base, therefore, are based on the approach used. Under the full-cost approach, the depletion base consists of all acquisition, exploration, and development costs regardless of whether they are incurred for successful or unsuccessful efforts. Under the successful efforts approach, only the acquisition, exploration, and development costs associated with successful finds that are commercially viable are included in the depletion base.

Depletion of Resource Cost

Once the depletion base is established, the next decision is determining how the cost of the natural resource will be allocated to accounting periods. Normally, depletion is calculated using an activity approach such as the units of production method. Using this method, the natural resource's total cost less any residual value is divided by the number of units estimated to be in the resource deposit to obtain a cost per unit of product. The cost per unit is multiplied by the number of units extracted to determine the period's depletion.

For example, assume a mining company has acquired the right to use 1,000 ha of land in the Northwest Territories to mine for gold. The lease cost is $50,000; the related exploration costs on the property are $100,000; and intangible development costs incurred in opening the mine are $850,000. Total costs related to the mine before the first ounce of gold is extracted are, therefore, $1 million. The company estimates that the mine will provide approximately 100,000 ounces of gold. The depletion rate established is calculated in the following manner:

ILLUSTRATION 12-16
Calculation of Depletion Rate

$$\frac{\text{Total cost} - \text{Residual value}}{\text{Total estimated units available}} = \text{Depletion cost per unit}$$

$$\frac{\$1,000,000}{100,000} = \$10 \text{ per ounce}$$

If 25,000 ounces are extracted in the first year, the depletion for the year is $250,000 (25,000 ounces at $10). The entry to record the depletion is:

Inventory	250,000	
Accumulated Depletion		250,000

The depletion charge for the resource extracted (in addition to labour and other direct costs) is initially charged (debited) to inventory, which is later credited for the cost of the resource sold during the year. This cost flow is similar to that of amortization of factory buildings in a manufacturing company. The amortization is charged initially to inventory through the cost of goods manufactured. The amortization is charged to the income statement only in the period in which the related goods are sold. The amount not sold remains in inventory and is reported in the current asset section.

The natural resource is reported as part of property, plant, and equipment. The balance sheet presents the property cost and the amount of accumulated depletion entered to date as follows:

Gold mine (at cost)	$1,000,000	
Less: Accumulated depletion	250,000	$750,000

ILLUSTRATION 12-17
Balance Sheet Presentation of Natural Resource

In some instances an Accumulated Depletion account is not used, and the credit goes directly to the natural resources asset account.

The tangible equipment used in extracting the gold may also be amortized on a units of production basis, especially if the equipment's useful life can be directly assigned to one specific resource deposit. If the equipment is used on more than one job, other cost allocation methods such as the straight-line or an accelerated depreciation method may be more appropriate.

Oil and Gas Accounting

As indicated, either the successful efforts or the full-cost method is acceptable in accounting for costs in the oil and gas industry. The actual application of either method is complex and constitutes a significant amount of detailed study, which is beyond the scope of this book. As there is a multitude of judgemental and definitional factors associated with each method, one major accounting problem concerns the wide range of interpretations that may be employed. Consequently, even though a company states it is following one particular method, assuming comparability of financial statements with other companies using the same method can be misleading.

The problem is overcome, to some extent, because companies using the full cost method follow a fairly common set of accounting policies reflected in a guideline (not a recommendation) issued by the Accounting Standards Board in 1986 and revised in 1990.[21] Additionally, some basic aspects of accounting for oil and gas properties are addressed in Section 3061 of the *CICA Handbook* on property, plant, and equipment.

Special Problems in Accounting for Natural Resources

Accounting for natural resources has some interesting issues that do not usually arise with other types of assets. These issues are divided into three categories:

1. Difficulty in estimating recoverable reserves.
2. Future removal and site restoration costs.
3. Accounting for liquidating dividends.

Estimating Recoverable Reserves

Not infrequently, the estimate of recoverable (proven) reserves has to be changed either because new information becomes available or because production processes become more sophisticated. Natural resources such as oil and gas deposits and some rare metals have provided the greatest challenges. Estimates of these reserves are in large measure "knowledgeable guesses."

This problem is the **same as that faced in accounting for changes in estimates of the useful lives of plant and equipment**. The procedure is to revise the depletion rate on a prospective basis by dividing the remaining cost by the estimate of the new recoverable reserves. This approach has much merit because the required estimates are so tenuous.

---

[21] "Full Cost Accounting in the Oil and Gas Industry," *Accounting Guideline 5* (Toronto: CICA, 1990).

IAS NOTE

Similar to the effect of the Canadian standard, IAS 16 specifies that costs to be incurred at the end of an asset's life should be either accrued and charged to expense over its useful life, or treated as a reduction in its residual value.

Future Removal and Site Restoration Costs

Companies sometimes incur substantial costs to dismantle structures and equipment, abandon the site and restore property to its natural state after extraction activities have been completed. Such future removal and site restoration costs may be incurred because of environmental laws, contracts, or established company policies and are not unique to natural resource businesses. The costs, measured net of any expected recoveries, can be substantial. Since these costs are likely to be made far into the future, issues include whether they should and can be recognized, measured, and disclosed in financial statements of periods when extraction of the property's resources is taking place.

Accounting standards require recognition of these net costs during periods of extraction, provided they can be reasonably measured. If it is not possible to determine a reasonable estimate, a contingent liability should be disclosed in the notes to the financial statements, consistent with standards for contingent liabilities. Essentially, the accounting is similar to recording any accrued expense—an expense account is debited and a liability account is credited. For future removal and site restoration costs, however, the debit may be charged to the Inventory account initially and then through cost of goods sold when the inventory of resource is sold. Some companies, on the other hand, simply recognize the charge as a period cost. Regardless of the treatment of the entry's debit side, the credit goes to increase a liability account such as Liability for Future Site Restoration. This account grows each year as a systematic and rational portion of the total estimated cost is recognized.[22] When the actual costs are incurred to restore the property, the liability account is charged with the expenditures made.

To illustrate, assume in the mining company described earlier that future site restoration costs are estimated to be $360,000, to be incurred six years after production begins. Given that 100,000 ounces of gold are expected over the life of the mine and that 25,000 ounces are extracted in the current year, the entry to recognize the future costs in the current year is:

Inventory (or Site Restoration Expense)	90,000*	
Liability for Future Site Restoration		90,000
*($360,000 ÷ 100,000) × 25,000 ounces		

Although not required, the *CICA Handbook* suggests that disclosure of the balance in the liability account, the charge for the period, and the major assumptions underlying its calculation are desirable.[23]

Liquidating Dividends

A company may own a property from which it intends to extract natural resources as its only major asset. If the company does not expect to purchase additional properties, it may distribute gradually to shareholders their capital investment by paying dividends equal to the accumulated amount of net income (after depletion) plus the amount of depletion charged. The major accounting issue is to distinguish between dividends that are a return of capital and those that are not. A company issuing a liquidating dividend should reduce the appropriate Share Capital account for that portion related to the original investment instead of Retained Earnings, because the dividend is a return of part of the investor's original contribution. Shareholders must be informed that the total dividend consists of the liquidation of capital as well as a distribution of income.

To illustrate, a mining company has a retained earnings balance of $1,650,000, accumulated depletion on mineral properties of $2.1 million, and common share capital of $5,435,493. The board of directors declares a dividend of $3 per share on the 1 million shares outstanding. The entry to record the $3 million dividend is as follows:

---

[22] Most companies allocate this cost based on a units-of-production basis, but some use other acceptable methods.

[23] *Financial Reporting in Canada, 2000* (CICA; Toronto, 2000) indicates that 66 of the 200 companies surveyed in 1999 provided disclosures related to future site removal and restoration costs. This high proportion tends to support the contention that this is an issue in a variety of industries, not just natural resources.

Retained Earnings	1,650,000	
Common Shares	*1,350,000	
Dividends Payable/Cash		3,000,000
*($3,000,000 − $1,650,000)		

The $3 dividend represents a $1.65 ($1,650,000 ÷ 1,000,000) per share **return on investment** and a $1.35 ($1,350,000 ÷ 1,000,000) per share liquidating dividend, or **return of capital**.

PRESENTATION AND ANALYSIS

Presentation of Property, Plant, and Equipment

General standards of financial statement presentation require that the basis of valuation—usually historical cost—for tangible capital assets be disclosed along with the carrying value of any assets pledged as collateral against company liabilities. Section 3061 of the *CICA Handbook* requires disclosure of the cost, accumulated amortization, and the method and rate of amortization. The net book value of property, plant, and equipment (including natural resources) not currently being amortized because it is under construction or development or because it has been removed from service for an extended period of time should be separately disclosed. The charge for amortization expense and any writedowns in the accounting period should be reported.[24]

The requirement for separate disclosure of both the cost and accumulated amortization provides financial statement readers with more information than if only the carrying amount or net book value is disclosed. As an example, consider two companies, both having capital assets with a carrying value of $100,000. You determine that the first company's assets cost $1 million and have had accumulated amortization of $900,000 charged against them. The second company, on the other hand, has assets with a cost of $105,000, and accumulated amortization of $5,000. With the additional data, information is provided about the size of the original investment in the capital assets and their relative age. Information about amortization amounts and rates are important disclosures as this is generally the largest non-cash expense recognized by most enterprises.

Whenever a company has a choice among alternative accounting policies, general reporting standards require that the method chosen be reported. Therefore, companies in the oil and gas industry must disclose whether they follow the full-cost or successful efforts method for their development costs. Additional guidance on financial reporting in this industry is provided by the CICA's *Accounting Guideline 5* "Full Cost Accounting in the Oil and Gas Industry" and U.S. standards. In summary, these latter documents require disclosure about the manner of determining and disposing of costs related to development activities. Some of the most relevant information about natural resource companies is information about their estimated reserves, and whether they are proved or unproved in nature. This information is generally reported as supplementary disclosures outside the summary financial statements.

Excerpts from the 2000 financial statements of Canfor Corporation in Illustration 12-18 illustrate the disclosures underlying their property, plant, equipment, and timber of $1,518,444 on the December 31, 2000 balance sheet, and depreciation, depletion, and amortization of $112,691 reported on the 2000 income statement (all amounts in thousands).

OBJECTIVE 8

Explain how tangible capital assets, including natural resources, are reported and analysed.

IAS NOTE

IAS 16 requires a reconciliation of the opening and closing balances in the capital asset accounts, disclosure of their historical cost, and the change in any revaluation surplus.

Go to the Digital Tool for additional property, plant, equipment, and natural resources disclosures.

Canfor Corporation
SUMMARY OF PRINCIPAL ACCOUNTING POLICIES
Property, Plant, Equipment and Timber   **December 31, 2000**

Canfor capitalizes the costs of major replacements, extensions and improvements to plant and equipment, together with related interest incurred during the construction period on major projects.

The rates of depreciation are based upon depreciating the assets over the following estimated productive lives:

Buildings	10 to 50 years
Mobile equipment	3 to 20 years
Pulp and kraft paper machinery and equipment	20 years

ILLUSTRATION 12-18
Disclosures for Tangible Capital Assets

---

[24] *CICA Handbook*, Section 3061, pars. .54 to .57.

ILLUSTRATION 12-18
Disclosures for Tangible Capital
Assets (continued)

Sawmill machinery and equipment	8 to 10 years
Logging machinery and equipment	4 to 20 years
Logging roads and bridges	5 to 20 years
Other machinery and equipment	4 to 20 years

Depreciation of logging and manufacturing assets is calculated on a unit of production basis.

Depreciation of plant and equipment not employed in logging and manufacturing is calculated on a straight-line basis.

Amortization of logging roads and depletion of timber are calculated on a basis related to the volume of timber harvested.

Deferred Reforestation
Canfor accrues the cost of the reforestation required under its timber harvest agreements at the time the timber is harvested.

5. Property, Plant, Equipment and Timber

December 31, 2000 (thousands of dollars)	Cost	Accumulated Depreciation and Depletion	Net Book Value
Land	$ 14,633	$ —	$ 14,633
Pulp and kraft paper mills	1,089,047	411,845	677,202
Wood products mills	510,056	265,855	244,201
Logging buildings and equipment	67,105	51,177	15,928
Logging roads and bridges	214,791	151,676	63,115
Other equipment and facilities	108,635	52,464	56,171
Timber	481,542	34,348	447,194
	$ 2,485,809	$ 967,365	$ 1,518,444

Included in the above are assets under construction in the amount of $24,298,000 (1999—$25,137,000) which are not being depreciated.

Analysis of Property, Plant, and Equipment

Assets may be analysed relative to activity (turnover) and profitability. How efficiently a company uses its assets to generate revenue is measured by the asset turnover ratio. This ratio is determined by dividing net revenue or sales by average total assets for the period. The resulting number is the dollars of revenue or sales produced by each dollar invested in assets. For a given level of investment in assets, a company that generates more revenue is likely to be more profitable. While this may not hold true if the profit margin on each dollar of revenue is lower than another company's, the asset turnover ratio is one of the key components of return on investment. To illustrate, the following data from **WestJet Airlines Ltd.** financial statements for its year ended December 31, 2000 is provided.

ILLUSTRATION 12-19
Asset Turnover Ratio

WESTJET AIRLINES LTD. (in thousands)	
Net revenue	$332,519
Total assets, Dec.31/00	337,172
Total assets, Dec.31/99	186,598
Net income	30,254

$$\text{Asset turnover} = \frac{\text{Net revenue}}{\text{Average total assets}}$$

$$= \frac{\$332,519}{\dfrac{\$337,172 + \$186,598}{2}}$$

$$= 1.27$$

The asset turnover ratio shows that WestJet Airlines generated $1.27 revenue for each dollar of assets in the year ended December 31, 2000.

Asset turnover ratios vary considerably among industries. For example, a utility company like **Nova Scotia Power Incorporated** has a ratio of 0.29 times, and a grocery chain like **Loblaw Companies Limited** has a ratio of 2.46 times.

Use of the **profit margin ratio** in conjunction with the asset turnover ratio offers an interplay that leads to a **rate of return on total assets**. By using the WestJet data shown above, the profit margin ratio and the rate of return on total assets are calculated as follows:

$$\text{Profit margin} = \frac{\text{Net income}}{\text{Net revenue}}$$

$$= \frac{\$30,254}{\$332,519}$$

$$= 9.1\%$$

$$\text{Rate of return on assets} = \text{Profit margin} \times \text{Asset turnover}$$

$$= 9.1\% \times 1.27$$

$$= 11.6\%$$

ILLUSTRATION 12-20
Profit Margin

The profit margin indicates how much is left over from each sales dollar after all expenses are covered. In the WestJet example, a profit margin of 9.1% indicates that 9.1 cents of profit remained from each dollar of revenue generated. By combining the profit margin with the asset turnover, it is possible to determine the rate of return on assets for the period. It makes intuitive sense. All else being equal, the more revenue generated per dollar invested in assets, the better off the company. The more of each sales dollar that is profit, the better off the company should be. Combined, the ratio provides a measure of the profitability of the investment in assets.

The **rate of return on assets (ROA)** can be directly calculated by dividing net income by average total assets.[25] By using WestJet Airlines' data, the ratio is calculated as follows:

$$\text{Rate of return on assets} = \frac{\text{Net income}}{\text{Average total assets}}$$

$$= \frac{\$30,254}{\dfrac{\$337,172 + \$186.598}{2}}$$

$$= 11.6\%$$

ILLUSTRATION 12-21
Rate of Return on Assets

The 11.6% rate of return calculated in this manner is identical to the 11.6% rate calculated by multiplying the profit margin by the asset turnover. The rate of return on assets is a good measure of profitability because it combines the effects of cost control (profit margin) and asset management (asset turnover).

Care must be taken in interpreting the numbers, however. A manager who is interested in reporting a high return on asset ratio can achieve this in the short run by not investing in new plant and equipment and by holding back on expenditures such as those for research and development and employee training, decisions that will result in lower long term corporate value. In the short run, the result is a higher return on investment because the net income number (the numerator) will be higher and the total asset number (the denominator) lower.

SUMMARY OF LEARNING OBJECTIVES

1 Explain the concept of amortization. Amortization is the accounting process of allocating the cost of capital assets to expense in a systematic and rational manner to those periods expected to benefit from the use of the asset. The objective is matching, not the valuation of assets at their fair values. Amortization is a generic term. The allocation of the cost of intangible capital assets is termed amortization as well, while that of property, plant, and equipment is usually referred to as depreciation. The allocation of cap-

KEY TERMS

accelerated amortization, *554*

activity method, *553*

amortization, *550*

asset turnover ratio, *572*

composite amortization rate, *557*

composite method, *556*

declining-balance method, *555*

---

[25] A more sophisticated calculation adds back the after-tax interest expense to net income so that the results aren't skewed by how the assets are financed. The ratio can then be used more legitimately for inter-company comparisons.

italized costs of natural resources is termed depletion.

2 Identify and describe the factors that must be considered when determining amortization charges. Three factors involved in determining amortization expense are: (1) the amount to be amortized (amortizable amount), (2) the estimated useful life, and (3) the pattern and method of cost allocation to be used.

3 Determine amortization charges using the activity, straight-line, and decreasing charge methods and compare the methods. The *activity method* assumes that the benefits provided by the asset are a function of use or productivity instead of the passage of time. The asset's life is considered in terms of either the output it provides, or an input measure such as the number of hours it works. The amortization charge per unit of activity (cost less residual value divided by estimated total units of output or input) is determined and multiplied by the units of activity produced or consumed in a period to derive amortization expense for the period. The *straight-line method* assumes that the provision of asset benefits is a function of time. As such, cost less residual value is divided by the useful economic life to determine amortization expense per period. This method is widely employed in practice because of its simplicity. The straight-line procedure is often the most conceptually appropriate when the decline in usefulness is constant from period to period. The *decreasing charge method* provides for a higher amortization charge in the early years and lower charges in later periods. For this method, a constant rate (e.g., double the straight-line rate) is multiplied by the net book value (cost less accumulated amortization) at the start of the period to determine each period's amortization expense. The main justification for this approach is that the asset provides more benefits in the earlier periods.

4 Explain special amortization methods. Two special depreciation methods are the group and composite methods, and hybrid or combination methods. The term "group" refers to a collection of assets that are similar in nature, while "composite" refers to a collection of assets that are dissimilar in nature. The group and composite methods develop one average rate of amortization for all the assets involved and apply this rate as if they were a single asset. The hybrid or combination methods develop an amortization expense that is based on two or more approaches and that suits the specific circumstances of the assets involved.

5 Identify and understand reasons why amortization methods are selected. Various amortization methods are generally acceptable. The accountant must exercise judgement when selecting and implementing the method that is most appropriate for the circumstances. Rational matching, tax reporting, simplicity, perceived economic consequences, and impact on ratios are factors that influence such judgements.

6 Explain the accounting issues related to asset impairment. The Canadian standards for asset impairments are in process (in 2001) of being harmonized with those of the FASB. The process to determine an impairment loss is as follows: (1) Review events and changes in circumstances for possible impairment. (2) If events or changes suggest impairment, determine if the sum of the undiscounted expected future net cash flows from the long-lived asset is less than the asset's carrying amount. If less, measure the impairment loss. (3) Under 2001 Canadian Standards, the impairment loss is the amount by which the asset's carrying amount exceeds its net recoverable amount. Under the FASB standards, the impairment loss is the amount by which the asset's carrying amount is greater than its fair value. After an impairment loss is recorded, the reduced carrying amount of the long-lived asset is considered its new cost basis. Impairment losses may not be restored for assets held for use. If the asset is not in use but instead is held for sale, the impaired asset should be reported at the lower of cost or net realizable value. It is not amortized. It can be continuously revalued, as long as the write-up is never greater than the carrying amount before impairment.

7 Explain the accounting procedures for depletion of natural resources. The accounting procedures for the amortization of natural resources are (1) establishment of the depletion base, and (2) write-off of resource cost. Three factors are involved in establishing the depletion base: (a) acquisition costs, (b) exploration costs, and (c) development costs. In the oil and gas industry, both the full cost and successful efforts methods are acceptable in determining the costs to be capitalized. Amortization of the resource cost, or depletion, is normally calculated on the units of production method, which means that depletion is a function of the number of units withdrawn during the period. In this approach, the natural resource's total cost less residual value is divided by the number of units estimated to be in the resource deposit, to obtain a cost per unit of product. The cost per unit is multiplied by the number of units withdrawn in the period to calculate depletion expense. Future removal and site restoration costs are accrued and charged either to the cost of inventory or to income each period.

8 Explain how tangible capital assets, including natural resources, are reported and analysed. The basis of valuation for property, plant, equipment, and natural resources should be disclosed along with pledges, liens, and other commitments related to these assets. Any liability secured by property, plant, equipment, and natural resources should be disclosed. When assets are amortized, an accumulated amortization account is credited. Companies engaged in significant oil and gas producing activities must provide special additional disclosures about these activities. Analysis may be performed to evaluate the efficiency of use of a company's investment in assets through the calculation and interpretation of the asset turnover rate, the profit margin, and the rate of return on assets.

APPENDIX **12A**

Amortization and Income Tax– The Capital Cost Allowance Method

THE CAPITAL COST ALLOWANCE METHOD

For the most part, issues related to the calculation of income taxes are not discussed in a financial accounting course. However, because the concepts of "tax amortization" or "tax depreciation" are similar to those of amortization for financial reporting purposes and because the tax method is sometimes adopted for book purposes, an overview of this subject is presented.

The capital cost allowance method is **used to determine "amortization" in calculating taxable income and the tax value of assets by Canadian businesses regardless of the method used for financial reporting purposes.** Because companies use this method for tax purposes, some (particularly small businesses) also use it for financial reporting, judging that the benefits of keeping two sets of records, one for financial reporting and one for tax purposes, are less than the costs involved.[26] Such an action,

> **OBJECTIVE 9**
>
> After studying Appendix 12A, you should be able to: Describe the income tax method of determining capital cost allowance.

---

[26] The widespread availability of accounting software, capable of maintaining detailed records for capital assets, the related amortization expense, and accumulated amortization under a variety of methods has significantly reduced the cost of record keeping and the possibility for errors.

while expedient, may not provide a rational allocation of costs in the financial reports. Therefore, many companies keep a record of capital cost allowance for tax purposes and use another method to determine amortization for their financial statements.

The mechanics of this method are similar to the declining-balance method covered in the chapter except that:

1. Instead of being labelled amortization or depreciation expense, it is called capital cost allowance (CCA) in tax returns.

2. The *Income Tax Act* (Income Tax Regulations, Schedule II) specifies the rate to be used for an asset class. This rate is called the capital cost allowance (CCA) rate. The *Income Tax Act* identifies several different classes of assets and the maximum CCA rate for each class. Examination of the definition of each asset class and the examples given in the *Income Tax Act* is necessary to determine the class into which a particular asset falls. Illustration 12A-1 provides examples of various CCA classes, the maximum rate attached to the class and the type of assets included in each.

3. CCA is determined separately for each asset class and can be claimed only on year end amounts in each class. Assuming no net additions (purchases less disposals, if any) to a class during a year, the maximum CCA allowed is the undepreciated capital cost (UCC) at year end multiplied by the CCA rate for the class. In a year when there is a net addition (regardless of when it occurs), the maximum CCA on the net addition is one-half of the allowed CCA rate multiplied by the amount of the net addition. The CCA for the net addition plus the CCA on the remaining UCC is the total CCA for the asset class. If there is only one asset in a class, the maximum CCA allowed in the acquisition year is the acquisition cost multiplied by one-half of the CCA rate, even if the asset was purchased one week before year end. No CCA is allowed in the year of disposal for this single asset, even if it is sold just before year end.

4. The government, through the *Income Tax Act*, requires that the benefits received by a company from government grants and investment tax credits on the acquisition of a capital asset reduce the cost basis of the capital asset acquired for tax purposes. For investment tax credits, the capital cost of the asset and the undepreciated capital cost (UCC) of the class of asset are reduced **in the taxation year following the year of acquisition**.

5. CCA can be taken even if it results in an undepreciated capital cost (UCC) that is less than the estimated residual value.

6. It is not required that the maximum rate, or that any CCA, be taken in a given year, although that would be the normal case as long as a company had taxable income after taking the maximum. If less than the maximum CCA is taken in one year, the remainder cannot be added to the amount claimed in a subsequent year. In every year, the maximum that can be claimed is limited to the UCC times the specified capital cost allowance rate.

ILLUSTRATION 12A-1
Examples of CCA Classes

Class	Rate	Examples of assets included in the class
3	5%	–buildings not included in another class
4	6%	–railway, tramway, or trolley bus system
6	10%	–frame, log, stucco on frame, galvanized iron or corrugated metal building; greenhouse; oil or water storage tank
8	20%	–manufacturing or processing machinery or equipment not included in other specified classes
10	30%	–automotive equipment, general purpose electronic data processing equipment
16	40%	–taxicab, coin-operated video game
33	15%	–timber resource property
42	12%	–fibre optic cable

Source: Stikeman, *Income Tax Act* (Annotated), 29th edition, Carswell, 2000

To illustrate amortization calculations under the CCA system, assume the following facts for a company's March 28, 2001 acquisition of a crane for construction purposes, the only asset in the CCA class:

Cost of crane	$500,000	CCA class	Class 8
Estimated useful life	10 years	CCA rate for Class 8	20%
Estimated residual value	$30,000		

Illustration 12A-2 shows the calculations necessary to determine the CCA for the first three years and the UCC at the end of each of the three years.[27]

Class 8-20%	CCA	UCC
January 1, 2001		0
Additions during 2001		
Cost of new asset acquisition		$500,000
Disposals during 2001		0
CCA 2001: $500,000 × 1/2 × 20%	$50,000	(50,000)
December 31, 2001		**$450,000**
Additions less disposals, 2002		0
		$450,000
CCA, 2002: $450,000 × 20%	$90,000	(90,000)
December 31, 2002		**$360,000**
Additions less disposals, 2003		0
		$360,000
CCA, 2003: $360,000 × 20%	$72,000	(72,000)
December 31, 2003		**$288,000**

ILLUSTRATION 12A-2
CCA Schedule for Crane

The **undepreciated capital cost (UCC)** at any point in time is known as the capital asset's **tax value**. Note that the capital asset's carrying value (or net book value) on the balance sheet will differ from its tax value for any method of amortization for financial reporting other than the tax method. The significance of this difference is explained in Chapter 19.

Illustration 12A-3 is a continuation of Illustration 12A-2. It incorporates the following complexities:

1. In 2004, the company bought another crane (or any other Class 8 asset) for $700,000.
2. In 2005, the company sold the first crane for $300,000.
3. In 2006, the company sold the second crane for $500,000. This resulted in no assets remaining in Class 8.

INTERNATIONAL INSIGHT

German companies amortize their capital assets at a much faster rate than Canadian companies because German tax laws permit accelerated amortization of up to triple the straight-line rate. Canadian tax rates, for the most part, are designed to be double the straight-line rate.

ILLUSTRATION 12A-3
CCA Schedule for Class 8

Class 8-20%		CCA	UCC
December 31, 2003			$288,000
Additions less disposals, 2004			
−Crane No. 2			700,000
			$988,000
CCA, 2004			
$288,000 × 20% =	$57,600		
$700,000 × 1/2 × 20% =	70,000	$127,600	(127,600)
December 31, 2004			**$860,400**
Additions less disposals, 2005			
−Crane No. 1 (lesser of original			
cost of $500,000 and proceeds			
of disposal of $300,000)			(300,000)
			$560,400
CCA,2005: $560,400 × 20% =		$112,080	(112,080)
December 31, 2005			**$448,320**

---

[27] CCA is subject to rules set by government legislation and, as such, is subject to change from time to time. Furthermore, various provincial governments can have different rules with regard to determining CCA for purposes of calculating the income on which provincial taxes are based. The examples in this chapter are based on the *Federal Income Tax Act* for 2000.

ILLUSTRATION 12A-3
CCA Schedule for Class 8
Continued

Additions less disposals, 2006		
–Crane No. 2 (lesser of original cost of $700,000 and proceeds of disposal of $500,000)		(500,000)
		($51,680)
Recaptured CCA, 2006	($51,680)	51,680
December 31, 2006		**0**

Additions to Asset Class

The purchase of another crane (No. 2) in 2004 resulted in a **net addition** of $700,000 to the undepreciated capital cost at the end of 2004. Consequently, the balance of the UCC at the end of 2004 prior to determining CCA for the year is made up of this $700,000 plus the $288,000 UCC of crane No. 1. The capital cost allowance for 2004 is, therefore, 20% of $288,000 ($57,600) plus one-half of 20% of the net addition of $700,000 ($70,000) for a total of $127,600.

If a government grant of $35,000 was received in 2004 to help finance the acquisition of this asset, the addition in 2004 is reported net of the government grant, i.e. at $700,000 – $35,000 = $665,000. If the 2004 acquisition was eligible instead for an investment tax credit of $35,000, the tax legislation specifies that the ITC should reduce the asset's capital cost and the UCC of the class of assets in the year following the year of acquisition. Assuming crane No. 2 in Illustration 12A-3 was eligible for a $35,000 ITC, the $700,000 addition is recognized in 2004, and the UCC is reduced by the $35,000 ITC in 2005 along with the $300,000 proceeds from crane No. 1. The CCA claimed in 2005 is reduced accordingly.

Retirements from an Asset Class, Continuation of Class

While the CCA class is increased by the cost of additions, it is usually reduced **by the proceeds on the asset's disposal**, not its cost. However, if the proceeds on disposal exceed the asset's capital cost, the class is reduced by the cost only. There is a good reason for this. If the proceeds on disposal are greater than the original cost, there has been a capital gain on the disposal. Capital gains are taxed separately from ordinary business income in the tax system, thus the portion that is capital gain must be identified as such. This leaves only the cost to be deducted from the CCA class. It is not common for depreciable assets to be sold at amounts in excess of their cost, but when this does occur, it is important to separate out the portion that is a capital gain.

In 2005, crane No. 1 is sold for $300,000. Since this is less than its $500,000 capital cost, there is no capital gain on disposal. Therefore, Class 8 is reduced by the proceeds on disposal of $300,000, and the CCA for the year is calculated on the remaining balance in the class.

Retirements from an Asset Class, Elimination of Class

When disposing of an asset eliminates an asset class, either because there are no more assets remaining in the class or because the disposal results in the elimination of the UCC balance of the class, the following may result.

1. A recapture of capital cost allowance, with or without a capital gain.
2. A terminal loss, with or without a capital gain. This occurs only when the last asset in the class is disposed of and an undepreciated capital cost balance still exists in the class after deducting the appropriate amount on the asset disposal.

The amount of proceeds, the asset's original cost, and the balance of the undepreciated capital cost for the class must be examined to determine which of these results occurs.

A **recapture** of capital cost allowance occurs when, after deducting the appropriate amount from the class on disposal of the last asset, a negative amount is left as the

UCC balance. The negative balance is the recaptured amount, and it must be included in the calculation of taxable income in the year, subject to income tax at the normal rates. In effect, events have shown that "too much" CCA was deducted throughout the lives of the assets, and the taxing of the recaptured capital cost allowance adjusts for this. This is what occurred in 2006. When the proceeds of disposal (being less than the original cost of the asset) on the last asset in the class were deducted from the UCC, the UCC became negative. The excess of $51,680 is included in taxable income in 2006.

As indicated above, if an asset is sold for more than its cost, a **capital gain** results. This may occur whether or not the class is eliminated. For tax purposes, a capital gain is treated differently from a recapture of capital cost allowance. Essentially, the *taxable* capital gain (i.e., the amount subject to tax) is a specified percentage of the capital gain as defined above.[28] The *taxable* capital gain is included with other taxable income.

If crane No. 2 had been sold in 2006 for $750,000, a capital gain and a recapture of capital cost allowance would have resulted. The capital gain would be $50,000, but only 50% or $25,000 would be the taxable capital gain. In this case, Class 8 would have been reduced by $700,000 and the recapture would be $251,680 ($700,000 less the $448,320 UCC).

A **terminal loss** occurs when the appropriate reduction made to the CCA class from the disposal of the last asset results in a positive balance remaining in the class. This remaining balance is a terminal loss that is deductible in full when calculating taxable income for the period. If crane No. 2 had been sold in 2006 for $300,000, a terminal loss of $148,320 would have resulted (the UCC of $448,320 less the $300,000 proceeds).

This example illustrating the basic calculations of capital gains, taxable capital gains, recaptured capital cost allowance and terminal losses has necessarily been oversimplified. In essence, the tax rate on taxable capital gains is specified by tax law, which may change from time to time and have implications in terms of other considerations (e.g., refundable dividend tax on hand). Similarly, the tax rate applicable to recaptured CCA is subject to the particular circumstances of the nature of taxable income being reported, of which the recaptured amount is a component. These and other technical and definitional aspects are beyond the scope of this text. The reader is warned that specialist knowledge regarding tax laws is often required to determine income taxes payable.

INTERNATIONAL INSIGHT

In Switzerland, amortization in the financial statements conforms to that on the tax returns. As a consequence, companies may amortize as much as 80% of the cost of assets in the first year.

SUMMARY OF LEARNING OBJECTIVE FOR APPENDIX 12A

9 Describe the income tax method of determining capital cost allowance. Capital cost allowance is the term used for amortization when calculating taxable income in income tax returns. The CCA method mechanics are similar to those of the declining-balance method except that rates are specified for asset classes and the amount claimed is based on year end balances. The half-year rule is applied to net additions in the year whereby only 50% of the normal rate is permitted. For an asset class, retirements are accounted for under specific rules that govern the determination of taxable income. Capital gains will occur if the proceeds on disposal exceed the asset's original cost. When an asset class is eliminated, a terminal loss or recapture of capital cost allowance can occur.

KEY TERMS

capital cost allowance (CCA), *575*

capital cost allowance method, *575*

capital gain, *578*

net addition, *578*

recapture, *578*

tax value, *577*

terminal loss, *579*

undepreciated capital cost (UCC), *577*

---

[28] In recent years, only 75% of a capital gain was considered taxable. In 2000, the inclusion rate was reduced twice—the first time to 66⅔% and then to 50%.

Note: All asterisked Brief Exercises, Exercises, Problems, and Cases relate to material in the appendix to the chapter.

BRIEF EXERCISES

BE12-1 Castlevania Corporation purchased a truck at the beginning of 2002 for $42,000. The truck is estimated to have a residual value of $2,000 and a useful life of 250,000 km. It was driven 38,000 km in 2002 and 52,000 km in 2003. Calculate amortization expense for 2002 and 2003.

BE12-2 Cheetah Ltd. purchased machinery on January 1, 2002 for $60,000. The machinery is estimated to have a residual value of $6,000 after a useful life of eight years. **(a)** Calculate 2002 amortization expense using the straight-line method. **(b)** Calculate 2002 amortization expense using the straight-line method assuming the machinery was purchased on September 1, 2002.

BE12-3 Use the information for Cheetah Ltd. given in BE12-2. **(a)** Calculate 2002 amortization expense using the sum-of-the-years'-digits method. **(b)** Calculate 2002 amortization expense using the sum-of-the-years'-digits method assuming the machinery was purchased on April 1, 2002.

BE12-4 Use the information for Cheetah Ltd given in BE12-2. **(a)** Calculate 2002 amortization expense using the double-declining-balance method. **(b)** Calculate 2002 amortization expense using the double-declining-balance method assuming the machinery was purchased on October 1, 2002.

BE12-5 Garfield Corp. purchased a machine on July 1, 2001 for $25,000. Garfield paid $200 in title fees and a legal fee of $125 related to the machine. In addition, Garfield paid $500 shipping charges for delivery, and $475 was paid to a local contractor to build and wire a platform for the machine on the plant floor. The machine has an estimated useful life of six years with a residual value of $3,000. Determine the amortization base of Garfield's new machine. Garfield uses straight-line amortization.

BE12-6 Battlesport Inc. owns the following assets:

Asset	Cost	Residual	Estimated Useful Life
A	$70,000	$17,000	10 years
B	50,000	10,000	15 years
C	82,000	14,000	12 years

Calculate the composite amortization rate and the composite life of Battlesport's assets.

BE12-7 Myst Limited purchased a computer for $7,000 on January 1, 2001. Straight-line amortization is used, based on a five-year life and a $1,000 residual value. In 2003, the estimates are revised. Myst now feels the computer will be used until December 31, 2004, when it can be sold for $500. Calculate the 2003 amortization.

BE12-8 Dinoland Corp. owns machinery that cost $900,000 and has accumulated amortization of $360,000. The expected future net cash flows from the use of the asset are expected to be $500,000. The equipment fair value is $400,000. Prepare the journal entry, if any, to record the impairment loss.

BE12-9 Khan Corporation acquires a coal mine at a cost of $400,000. Intangible development costs total $100,000. After the mine is exhausted, $75,000 will be spent to restore the property, after which it can be sold for $160,000. Khan estimates that 4,000 tonnes of coal can be extracted. If 700 tonnes are extracted the first year, prepare the journal entry to record depletion.

BE12-10 In its 2000 Annual , **Danier Leather Inc.** reports beginning-of-the-year total assets of $41,655 thousand, end-of-the-year total assets of $59,007 thousand, total revenue of $143,011 thousand, and net income of $10,710 thousand. **(a)** Calculate Danier's asset turnover ratio. **(b)** Calculate Danier's profit margin. **(c)** Calculate Danier's rate of return on assets **(1)** using asset turnover and profit margin, and **(2)** using net income.

*BE12-11 Timecap Limited purchased an asset at a cost of $40,000 on March 1, 2002. The asset has a useful life of eight years and an estimated residual value of $4,000. For tax purposes, the asset belongs in CCA Class 8, with a rate of 20%. Calculate the CCA for each year 2002 to 2005.

EXERCISES

E12-1 **(Amortization Calculations—SL, DDB)** Deluxe Company Ltd. purchases equipment on January 1, 2002 at a cost of $469,000. The asset is expected to have a service life of 12 years and a residual value of $40,000.

Instructions

(a) Calculate the amount of amortization for each of 2002, 2003, and 2004 using the straight-line amortization method.

(b) Calculate the amount of amortization for each of 2002, 2003, and 2004 using the double-declining-balance method. (In performing your calculations, round constant percentage to the nearest one-hundredth and round answers to the nearest dollar.)

E12-2 **(Amortization—Conceptual Understanding)** Chesley Company Ltd. acquired a plant asset at the beginning of Year 1. The asset has an estimated service life of five years. An employee has prepared amortization schedules for this asset using two different methods to compare the results of using one method with the results of using the other. You are to assume that the following schedules have been correctly prepared for this asset using (1) the straight-line method and (2) the double-declining-balance method.

Year	Straight-line	Double-declining Balance
1	$9,000	$20,000
2	9,000	12,000
3	9,000	7,200
4	9,000	4,320
5	9,000	1,480
Total	$45,000	$45,000

Instructions

Answer the following questions:

(a) What is the cost of the asset being amortized?

(b) What amount, if any, was used in the amortization calculations for the residual value for this asset?

(c) Which method will produce the higher net income in Year 1?

(d) Which method will produce the higher charge to income in Year 4?

(e) Which method will produce the higher book value for the asset at the end of Year 3?

(f) Which method will produce the higher cash flow in Year 1? In Year 4?

(g) If the asset is sold at the end of Year 3, which method would yield the higher gain (or lower loss) on disposal of the asset?

E12-3 **(Amortization Calculations—SL, DDB-Partial Periods)** Judds Corporation purchased a new plant asset on April 1, 2002 at a cost of $711,000. It was estimated to have a service life of 20 years and a residual value of $60,000. Judds' accounting period is the calendar year.

Instructions

(a) Calculate the amortization for this asset for 2002 and 2003 using the straight-line method.

(b) Calculate the amortization for this asset for 2002 and 2003 using the double-declining-balance method.

E12-4 **(Amortization for Partial Periods—Four methods)** On January 1, 1999, a machine was purchased for $77,000. The machine has an estimated residual value of $5,000 and an estimated useful life of five years. The machine can operate for 100,000 hours before it needs to be replaced. The company operates the machine as follows: 1999, 20,000 hrs; 2000, 25,000 hrs; 2001, 15,000 hrs; 2002, 30,000 hrs; 2003, 10,000 hrs.

Instructions

(a) Calculate the annual amortization charges over the machine's life assuming a December 31 year end for each of the following amortization methods:

1. Straight-line method

2. Activity method

3. Double-declining-balance method

4. CCA, Class 8—20%

(b) Assume a fiscal year end of September 30. Calculate the annual amortization charges over the asset's life applying
1. Straight-line method
2. Double-declining-balance method

(c) Assuming a September 30 fiscal year end, what is the carrying value of the machine on the September 30, 2002 balance sheet under the straight-line method? Under the double-declining-balance method? How do these compare with its tax value at the same date?

E12-5 **(Amortization Calculations—Four Methods, Partial Periods)**   Parish Corporation purchased a new machine for its assembly process on August 1, 2002. The cost of this machine was $117,900. The company estimated that the machine would have a trade-in value of $12,900 at the end of its service life. Its useful life was estimated to be five years and its working hours were estimated to be 21,000 hours. Parish's year end is December 31.

Instructions
Calculate the amortization expense under the following methods: **(1)** straight-line amortization for 2002, **(2)** activity method for 2002, assuming that machine usage was 800 hours, **(3)** double-declining-balance for 2003, and **(4)** capital cost allowance for 2002 and 2003 using a CCA rate of 25%.

E12-6   **(Amortization Calculations—Four Methods, Partial Periods)**   Rogues Limited purchased equipment for $212,000 on October 1, 2002. It is estimated that the equipment will have a useful life of eight years and a residual value of $12,000. Estimated production is 40,000 units with an estimated working life of 20,000 hours. During 2002, Rogues uses the equipment for 525 hours and the equipment produces 1,000 units.

Instructions
Calculate amortization expense under each of the following methods assuming Rogues has a December 31 year end.
(a) Straight-line method for 2002
(b) Activity method (units of output) for 2002
(c) Activity method (working hours) for 2002
(d) Double-declining-balance method for 2003

E12-7   **(Different Methods of Amortization)**   Jackson Industries Ltd. presents you with the following information:

Description	Date Purchased	Cost	Residual Value	Life in Years	Amortization Method	Accumulated Amortization to 12/31/01	Amortization for 2002
Machine A	2/12/00	$142,500	$16,000	10	(a)	$39,900	(b)
Machine B	8/15/99	(c)	21,000	5	SL	29,000	(d)
Machine C	7/21/98	75,400	23,500	8	DDB	(e)	(f)

Instructions
Complete the table for the year ended December 31, 2002. The company amortizes all assets using the half-year convention.

E12-8   **(Amortization Calculation—Replacement, Trade-in)**   Zidek Corporation bought a machine on June 1, 1999 for $31,000, f.o.b. the place of manufacture. Freight costs were $200, and $500 was expended to install it. The machine's useful life was estimated at 10 years, with a residual value of $2,500. On June 1, 2000, an essential part of the machine was replaced at a cost of $1,980, with a part designed to reduce the machine's operating costs.

On June 1, 2003, the company bought a new machine with a larger capacity for $35,000 delivered. A trade-in value was received on the old machine equal to its fair market value of $20,000. Removing the old machine from the plant cost $75, and installing the new one cost $1,500. It was estimated that the new machine would have a useful life of 10 years, with a residual value of $4,000.

Instructions
Assuming that amortization is calculated on the straight-line basis, determine the amount of gain or loss on the disposal of the first machine on June 1, 2003, and the amount of amortization that should be provided during the company's fiscal year, which begins on June 1, 2003.

E12-9 **(Composite Amortization)** Presented below is information related to Curry Manufacturing Corporation:

Asset	Cost	Estimated Residual	Estimated Life (in years)
A	$40,500	$5,500	10
B	33,600	4,800	9
C	36,000	3,600	9
D	19,000	1,500	7
E	23,500	2,500	6

Instructions

(a) Calculate the rate of amortization per year to be applied to the plant assets under the composite method.
(b) Prepare the adjusting entry necessary at year end to record amortization for a year.
(c) Prepare the entry to record the sale of asset D for cash of $4,800. It was used for six years, and amortization was entered under the composite method.

E12-10 **(Amortization Calculations, Sinking Fund Method)** The Five Towers Company Limited purchased a rental property for $600,000 at the beginning of 1999, with $170,000 of the property cost allocated to land. The building itself has an estimated useful life of 30 years with an expected residual value of $70,000. Five Towers uses the sinking fund method of amortization and an interest factor of 8%.

Instructions

Prepare an amortization table for the rental building that identifies the amount of amortization for each year from 1999 to 2003.

E12-11 **(Amortization—Change in Estimate)** Machinery purchased for $60,000 by Shawinigan Corp. in 1998 was originally estimated to have a life of eight years with a residual value of $4,000. Amortization has been entered for five years on this basis. In 2003, it is determined that the total estimated life (including 2003) should have been 10 years with a residual value of $4,500 at the end of that time. Assume straight-line amortization.

Instructions

(a) Prepare the entry required to correct the prior years' amortization.
(b) Prepare the entry to record amortization for 2003.

E12-12 **(Amortization Calculation—Addition, Change in Estimate)** In 1974, Applied Science Limited completed the construction of a building at a cost of $2 million and occupied it in January 1975. It was estimated that the building would have a useful life of 40 years and a residual value of $60,000.

Early in 1985, an addition to the building was constructed at a cost of $500,000. At that time it was estimated that the remaining life of the building would be, as originally estimated, an additional 30 years, and that the addition would have a life of 30 years and increase the building's residual value by $20,000.

In 2003, it is determined that the probable life of the building and addition will extend to the end of 2034 or 20 years beyond the original estimate, with no change expected in the residual value.

Instructions

(a) Using the straight-line method, calculate the annual amortization that would have been charged from 1975 through 1984.
(b) Calculate the annual amortization that would have been charged from 1985 through 2002.
(c) Prepare the entry, if necessary, to adjust the account balances because of the revision of the estimated life in 2003.
(d) Calculate the annual amortization to be charged beginning with 2003.

E12-13 **(Amortization—Replacement, Change in Estimate)** Orel Limited constructed a building at a cost of $2.2 million and has occupied it since January 1982. It was estimated at that time that its life would be 40 years, with no residual value.

In January 2002, a new roof was installed at a cost of $300,000, and it was estimated then that the building would have a useful life of 25 years from that date. The cost of the old roof was $160,000.

Instructions

(a) What amount of amortization was charged annually from the years 1982 through 2001? (Assume straight-line amortization.)

(b) What entry should be made in 2002 to record the roof replacement?

(c) Prepare the entry in January 2002 to record the revision in the building's estimated life, if necessary.

(d) What amount of amortization should be charged for the year 2002?

E12-14 **(Error Analysis and Amortization)**   The Devereaux Company Ltd. shows the following entries in its Equipment account for 2002; all amounts are based on historical cost.

	Equipment				
Jan. 1	Balance	134,750	June 30	Cost of equipment sold	
Aug.10	Purchases	32,000		(purchased prior	
12	Freight on equipment			to 2002)	23,000
	purchased	700			
25	Installation costs	2,700			
Nov. 10	Repairs	500			

Instructions

(a) Prepare any correcting entries necessary.

(b) Assuming that amortization is to be charged for a full year on the ending balance in the asset account, calculate the proper amortization charge for 2002 under both methods listed below. Assume an estimated life of 10 years, with no residual value. The machinery included in the January 1, 2002 balance was purchased in 2000.

  1. Straight-line
  2. Declining-balance (assume twice the straight-line rate)

E12-15 **(Amortization for Fractional Periods)**   On March 10, 2003, Lotus Limited sold equipment that it purchased for $192,000 on August 20, 1996. It was originally estimated that the equipment would have a life of 12 years and a residual value of $16,800 at the end of that time, and amortization has been calculated on that basis. The company uses the straight-line method of amortization.

Instructions

(a) Calculate the amortization charge on this equipment for 1996, for 2003, and the total charge for the period from 1997 to 2002, inclusive, under each of the six following assumptions with respect to partial periods.

  1. Amortization is calculated for the exact period of time during which the asset is owned. (Use 365 days for base.)
  2. Amortization is calculated for the full year on the January 1 balance in the asset account.
  3. Amortization is calculated for the full year on the December 31 balance in the asset account.
  4. Amortization for one-half year is charged on plant assets acquired or disposed of during the year.
  5. Amortization is calculated on additions from the beginning of the month following acquisition and on disposals to the beginning of the month following disposal.
  6. Amortization is calculated for a full period on all assets in use for over one-half year, and no amortization is charged on assets in use for less than one-half year. (Use 365 days for base.)

(b) Briefly evaluate the methods above, considering them from the point of view of basic accounting theory as well as simplicity of application.

E12-16 **(Impairment)**   Presented below is information related to equipment owned by Gobi Limited at December 31, 2002.

Cost	$9,000,000
Accumulated amortization to date	1,000,000
Expected future net cash flows	7,000,000
Fair value	4,800,000

Assume that Gobi will continue to use this asset in the future. As of December 31, 2002, the equipment has a remaining useful life of four years.

Instructions

(a) Prepare the journal entry (if any) to record the impairment of the asset at December 31, 2002.

(b) Prepare the journal entry (if any) to record amortization expense for 2003.

(c) The equipment's fair value at December 31, 2003 is $5.1 million. Prepare the journal entry (if any) necessary to record this increase in fair value.

E12-17 (Impairment) Assume the same information as E12-16, except that Gobi intends to dispose of the equipment in the coming year. It is expected that the disposal cost will be $20,000.

Instructions

(a) Prepare the journal entry (if any) to record the impairment of the asset at December 31, 2002.
(b) Prepare the journal entry (if any) to record amortization expense for 2003.
(c) The asset was not sold by December 31, 2003. The equipment's fair value on that date is $5.3 million. Prepare the journal entry (if any) necessary to record this increase in fair value. It is expected that the cost of disposal is still $20,000.

E12-18 (Impairment) The management of Luis Inc. was discussing whether certain equipment should be written down as a charge to current operations because of obsolescence. The assets in question had a cost of $900,000 with amortization taken to December 31, 2002 of $400,000. On December 31, 2002, management projected the future net cash flows from this equipment to be $300,000 and its fair value to be $230,000. The company intends to use this equipment in the future.

Instructions

(a) Prepare the journal entry (if any) to record the impairment at December 31, 2002.
(b) Where should the gain or loss (if any) on the writedown be reported in the income statement?
(c) At December 31, 2003, the equipment's fair value increased to $260,000. Prepare the journal entry (if any) to record this increase in fair value.
(d) What accounting issues did management face in accounting for this impairment?

E12-19 (Depletion Calculations—Timber) Stanislaw Timber Inc. owns 9,000 ha of timberland purchased in 1990 at a cost of $1,400 per hectare. At the time of purchase the land without the timber was valued at $400 per hectare. In 1991, Stanislaw built fire lanes and roads, with a life of 30 years, at a cost of $84,000. Every year Stanislaw sprays to prevent disease at a cost of $3,000 per year and spends $7,000 to maintain the fire lanes and roads. During 1992, Stanislaw selectively logged and sold 700,000 m^3 of the estimated 3.5 million m^3 of timber. In 1993, Stanislaw planted new seedlings to replace the trees cut at a cost of $100,000.

Instructions

(a) Determine the depletion charge and the cost of timber sold related to depletion for 1992.
(b) Stanislaw has not logged since 1992. If Stanislaw logged and sold 900,000 m^3 of timber in 2003, when the timber cruise (appraiser) estimated a total resource of 5 million m^3, determine the cost of timber sold related to depletion for 2003.

E12-20 (Depletion Calculations—Oil) Diderot Drilling Limited leases property on which oil has been discovered. Wells on this property produced 18,000 barrels of oil during the past year that sold at an average $15 per barrel. Total oil resources of this property are estimated to be 250,000 barrels.

The lease provides for an outright payment of $500,000 to the lessor before drilling is commenced and an annual rental of $31,500. A premium of 5% of the sales price of every barrel of oil removed is to be paid annually to the lessor. In addition, the lessee is to clean up all the waste and debris from drilling and to bear the costs of reconditioning the land for farming when the wells are abandoned. It is estimated that this clean-up and reconditioning will cost $30,000.

Instructions

From the provisions of the lease agreement, you are to calculate the cost per barrel for the past year, exclusive of operating costs, to Diderot Drilling Limited.

E12-21 (Depletion Calculations—Timber) Forda Lumber Inc. owns a 7,000 ha timber tract purchased in 1995 at a cost of $1,300 per hectare. At the time of purchase the land was estimated to have a value of $300 per hectare without the timber. Forda Lumber Inc. has not logged this tract since it was purchased. In 2002, Forda had the timber cruised. The cruise (appraiser) estimated that each hectare contained 8,000 m^3 of timber. In 2002, Forda built 10 km of roads at a cost of $7,840 per km. After the roads were completed, Forda logged and sold 3,500 trees containing 850,000 m^3.

Instructions

(a) Determine the cost of timber sold related to depletion for 2002.
(b) If Forda amortizes the logging roads based on timber cut, determine the amortization expense for 2002.
(c) If Forda plants five seedlings at a cost of $4 per seedling for each tree cut, how should Forda treat the reforestation?

E12-22 **(Depletion Calculations—Mining)** Beronja Mining Corp. purchased land on February 1, 2002 at a cost of $1,190,000. The company estimated that a total of 60,000 tonnes of mineral was available for mining. After the natural resource has all been removed, the company is required to restore the property to its previous state because of strict environmental protection laws, and it estimates the cost of this restoration at $90,000. Beronja believes it will be able to sell the property afterwards for $100,000. Developmental costs of $200,000 were incurred before Beronja was able to do any mining. In 2002, 30,000 tonnes were removed, and 22,000 tonnes were sold.

Instructions
Calculate the following information for 2002 (Round to two decimals): **(1)** per unit material cost; **(2)** total material cost of 12/31/02 inventory; and **(3)** total material cost in cost of goods sold at 12/31/02.

E12-23 **(Depletion Calculations—Minerals)** At the beginning of 2002, Aristotle Corporation acquired a mine for $970,000. Of this amount, $100,000 was ascribed to the land value and the remaining portion to the minerals in the mine. Surveys conducted by geologists have indicated that approximately 12 million units of the ore appear to be in the mine. Aristotle incurred $170,000 of development costs prior to any extraction of minerals and estimates that it will require $40,000 to prepare the land for an alternative use when all of the mineral has been removed. During 2002, 2.5 million units of ore were extracted and 2.1 million of these units were sold.

Instructions
Calculate (1) the total depletion for 2002, and (2) the cost of the minerals sold during 2002.

E12-24 **(Ratio Analysis)** The 2000 Annual Report of **Four Seasons Hotels Inc.** contains the following information:

(in thousands)	December 31, 2000	December 31, 1999
Total assets	$984,397	$832,139
Total liabilities	276,233	244,442
Consolidated revenues	347,507	277,548
Net earnings	103,074	86,479

Instructions
Calculate the following ratios for Four Seasons Hotels for 2000:
  (a) Asset turnover ratio
  (b) Rate of return on assets
  (c) Profit margin on sales
  (d) How can the asset turnover ratio be used to calculate the rate of return on assets?

*E12-25 **(CCA)** During 2002, Futabatei Limited sold its only Class 3 asset. At the time of sale, the balance of the undepreciated capital cost for this class was $37,450. The asset originally cost $129,500. Indicate what the resulting amounts would be for any recapture of CCA, capital gain, and terminal loss, if any, assuming the asset was sold for proceeds of **(a)** $132,700, **(b)** $ 51,000, **(c)** $22,000.

*E12-26 **(Book vs. Tax Amortization)** Shimei Inc. purchased computer equipment on March 1, 2001 for $31,000. The computer equipment has a useful life of five years and a residual value of $1,000. Shimei uses a double-declining-balance method of amortization for this type of capital asset. For tax purposes, the computer is assigned to Class 10 with a 30% rate.

Instructions
  (a) Prepare a schedule of amortization for financial reporting purposes for the new asset purchase covering 2001, 2002, and 2003. The company follows a policy of taking a full year's amortization in the year of purchase and none in the year of disposal.
  (b) Prepare a schedule of CCA and UCC for this asset covering 2001, 2002, and 2003 assuming it is the only Class 10 asset owned by Shimei.
  (c) How much amortization is deducted over the three-year period on the financial statements? In determining taxable income? What is the carrying value of the computer equipment on the December 31, 2003 balance sheet? What is the tax value of the computer equipment at December 31, 2003?

E12-27 **(Government Assistance)** Quadros Limited was attracted to the Town of LePage by its municipal industry commission. The Town donated a plant site to Quadros, and the provincial government provided $100,000 toward the cost of the new manufacturing facility. The total cost of plant construction came to $335,000 and it was ready for use in early October, 2002. Quadros expects the plant to have a useful life of 15 years before it becomes obsolete and is demolished. The company uses the straight-line method of amortization for buildings, and is required to include the plant in Class 6 (10% rate) for tax purposes.

Instructions

(a) Prepare the entry(ies) required in 2002 to record the payment to the contractor for the building, and the receipt of the provincial government assistance. Assume the company treats the assistance as a reduction of the asset's cost. Also prepare any adjusting entries needed at the company's year end, December 31, 2002 and 2003.

(b) Prepare the entry(ies) required in 2002 to record the payment to the contractor for the building, and the receipt of the provincial government assistance. Assume the company treats the assistance as a deferred credit. Also prepare any adjusting entries needed at the company's year end, December 31, 2002 and 2003.

(c) If Quadros reports 2003 income of $79,000 before amortization related to the plant and government assistance, what income before tax will the company report assuming **(a)** above? Assuming **(b)** above?

(d) What is the building's tax value at December 31, 2003?

PROBLEMS

P12-1 Onassis Corp. purchased Machine #201 on May 1, 2002. The following information relating to Machine #201 was gathered at the end of May.

Price	$73,500
Credit terms	2/10, n/30
Freight-in costs	$ 970
Preparation and installation costs	$ 3,800
Labour costs during regular production operations	$10,500

It was expected that the machine could be used for 10 years, after which the residual value would be zero. Onassis intends to use the machine for only eight years, however, after which it expects to be able to sell it for $1,200. The invoice for Machine #201 was paid May 5, 2002. Onassis uses the calendar year as the basis for the preparation of financial statements.

Instructions

(a) Calculate the amortization expense for the years indicated using the following methods. (Round to the nearest dollar.)
  1. Straight-line method for 2002 and 2003.
  2. Double-declining-balance method for 2002 and 2003.

(b) Calculate the capital cost allowance for 2002 and 2003, assuming a CCA rate of 25%.

(c) The president of Onassis tells you that because the company is a new organization, she expects it will be several years before production and sales reach optimum levels. She asks you to recommend an amortization method that will allocate less of the company's amortization expense to the early years and more to later years of the assets' lives. What method would you recommend? Explain.

P12-2 The cost of second hand equipment purchased by Becker Limited on June 1, 2002 is $67,000. Before being put into service, the equipment was repaired at a cost of $4,800. Further, direct material of $220 and direct labour of $400 were used in adjusting and fine-tuning the controls. It is estimated that the machine will have a $4,000 residual value at the end of its seven-year service life. Its total working hours are estimated at 42,000 and total production is estimated at 525,000 units. During 2002 the machine was operated 6,000 hours and produced 55,000 units. During 2003 the machine was operated 5,500 hours and produced 48,000 units.

Instructions

Calculate amortization expense on the machine for the year ending December 31, 2002 and the year ending December 31, 2003 using the following methods:

(a) Straight-line
(b) Activity based: Units-of-output

(c) Activity based: Working hours
(d) Declining-balance (twice the straight-line rate)

P12-3 Goran Tool Corp. records amortization annually at the end of the year. Its policy is to take a full year's amortization on all assets used throughout the year and amortization for one-half a year on all machines acquired or disposed of during the year. The amortization rate for the machinery is 10% applied on a straight-line basis, with no estimated scrap value.

The balance of the Machinery account at the beginning of 2002 was $172,300; the Accumulated Amortization on Machinery account had a balance of $72,900. The following transactions affecting the machinery accounts took place during 2002.

Jan. 15   Machine No. 38, which cost $9,600 when acquired June 3, 1995, was retired and sold as scrap metal for $600.

Feb. 27   Machine No. 81 was purchased. The fair market value of this machine was $12,500. It replaced Machines No. 12 and No. 27, which were traded in on the new machine. Machine No.12 was acquired Feb. 4, 1990, at a cost of $5,500 and was still carried in the accounts although fully depreciated and not in use; Machine No. 27 was acquired June 11, 1995, at a cost of $8,200. In addition to these two used machines, $9,000 was paid in cash.

Apr. 7   Machine No. 54 was equipped with electric control equipment at a cost of $940. This machine, originally equipped with simple hand controls, was purchased Dec. 11, 1998, for $1,800. The new electric controls can be attached to any one of several machines in the shop.

12   Machine No. 24 was repaired at a cost of $720 after a fire caused by a short circuit in the wiring burned out the motor and damaged certain essential parts.

July 22   Machines No. 25, 26, and 41 were sold for $3,100 cash. The purchase dates and cost of these machines were:

No. 25	$4,000	May 8, 1994
No. 26	3,200	May 8, 1994
No. 41	2,800	June 1, 1996

Instructions

(a) Record each transaction in general journal form.

(b) Calculate and record amortization for the year. No machines now included in the balance of the account were acquired before January 1, 1993.

P12-4 The following data relate to the Plant Assets account of Fiedler Inc. at December 31, 2001:

Plant Assets

	A	B	C	D
Original cost	$35,000	$51,000	$80,000	$80,000
Year purchased	1996	1997	1998	2000
Useful life	10 years	15,000 hours	15 years	10 years
Residual value	$3,100	$3,000	$5,000	$5,000
Amortization method	Straight-line	Activity	Straight-line	Dbl. decl.
Accum. Amort'n through 2001[a]	$15,950	$35,200	$15,000	$16,000

[a] In the year an asset is purchased, Fiedler does not record any amortization expense on the asset. In the year an asset is retired or traded in, Fiedler takes a full year's amortization on the asset.

The following transactions occurred during 2002:

(a) On May 5, Asset A was sold for $13,000 cash. The company's bookkeeper recorded this retirement in the following manner:

| Cash | 13,000 | |
| Asset A | | 13,000 |

(b) On December 31, it was determined that Asset B had been used 2,100 hours during 2002.

(c) On December 31, before calculating amortization expense on Asset C, the management of Fiedler decided the useful life remaining as of year end was nine years.

(d) On December 31, it was discovered that a plant asset purchased in 2001 had been expensed completely in that year. The asset cost $22,000 and had a useful life of 10 years when it was acquired and had no residual value. Management has decided to use the double-declining-balance method for this asset, which can be referred to as "Asset E."

Instructions

Prepare the necessary correcting entries for the year 2002 and any additional entries necessary to record the appropriate amortization expense on the above-mentioned assets.

P12-5 Soon after December 31, 2002, Qu Manufacturing Corp. was requested by its auditor to prepare an amortization schedule for semitrucks that showed the additions, retirements, amortization, and other data affecting the income of the company in the four-year period 1999 to 2002, inclusive. The following data were obtained:

Balance of Semitrucks account, Jan. 1, 1999:

Truck No. 1 purchased Jan. 1, 1996, cost	$18,000
Truck No. 2 purchased July 1, 1996, cost	22,000
Truck No. 3 purchased Jan. 1, 1998, cost	30,000
Truck No. 4 purchased July 1, 1998, cost	24,000
Balance, Jan. 1, 1999	$94,000

The Semitrucks-Accumulated Amortization account had a correct balance of $30,200 on January 1, 1999 (amortization on the four trucks from the respective dates of purchase, based on a five-year life, no residual value). No charges had been made against the account before January 1, 1999.

Transactions between January 1, 1999 and December 31, 2002 and their record in the ledger were as follows:

July 1, 1999   Truck No. 3 was traded for a larger one (No. 5), the agreed purchase price (fair market value) being $34,000. Qu Manufacturing paid the automobile dealer $15,000 cash on the transaction. The entry was a debit to Semitrucks and a credit to Cash, $15,000.

Jan. 1, 2000   Truck No. 1 was sold for $3,500 cash; the entry was a debit to Cash and a credit to Semitrucks, $3,500.

July 1, 2001   A new truck (No. 6) was acquired for $36,000 cash and was charged at that amount to the Semitrucks account. (Assume truck No. 2 was not retired.)

July 1, 2001   Truck No. 4 was damaged in an accident to such an extent that it was sold for scrap for $700 cash. Qu Manufacturing received $2,500 from the insurance company. The entry made by the bookkeeper was a debit to Cash, $3,200, and credits to Miscellaneous Income, $700, and Semitrucks, $2,500.

Entries for amortization had been made at the close of each year as follows: 1999, $20,300; 2000, $21,100; 2001, $24,450; 2002, $27,800.

Instructions

(a) For each of the four years calculate separately the increase or decrease in net income arising from the company's errors in determining or entering amortization or in recording transactions affecting trucks. Ignore income tax considerations.

(b) Prepare one compound journal entry as of December 31, 2002 for adjustment of the Semitrucks account to reflect the correct balances as revealed by your schedule, assuming that the books have not been closed for 2002.

P12-6   Wright Mining Ltd. purchased a tract of land for $600,000. The company estimated that this tract will yield 120,000 tonnes of ore with sufficient mineral content to make mining and processing profitable. It is further estimated that 6,000 tonnes of ore will be mined the first and last year and 12,000 tonnes every year in between. The land is expected to have a residual value of $30,000.

The company built necessary structures and sheds on the site at a cost of $36,000. It estimated that these structures would have a physical life of 15 years but, because they must be dismantled if they are to be moved, they have no residual value. The company does not intend to use the buildings elsewhere. Mining machinery installed at the mine was purchased second-hand at a cost of $48,000. This machinery cost the former owner $100,000 and was 50% depreciated when purchased. Wright Mining estimated that about half of this machinery will still be useful when the present mineral resources are exhausted but that dismantling and removal costs would just about offset their value at that time. The company does not intend to use the machinery elsewhere. The remaining machinery is expected to last until about one-half the present estimated mineral ore has been removed and will then be worthless. Cost is to be allocated equally between these two classes of machinery.

Instructions

(a) As chief accountant for the company, you are to prepare a schedule showing estimated depletion and amortization costs for each year of the expected life of the mine.

(b) Draft entries in general journal form to record amortization and depletion for the first year. Assume actual production of 7,000 tonnes. Nothing occurred during the year to cause the company engineers to change their estimates of either the mineral resources or the life of the structures and equipment.

P12-7   Koppel Logging and Lumber Inc. owns 3,000 ha of timberland on the north side of Mount St. Helens, purchased in 1968 at a cost of $550 per hectare. In 1980, Koppel began selectively logging this timber tract. In May of 1980, Mount St. Helens erupted, burying the timberland under a foot of ash. All of the timber on the Koppel tract was downed. In addition, the logging roads, built at a cost of $150,000, were destroyed, as was logging equipment that had a net book value of $300,000.

At the time of the eruption, Koppel had logged 20% of the estimated 500,000 m³ of timber. Prior to the eruption, Koppel estimated the land to have a value of $200 per hectare after the timber was harvested. Koppel includes the logging roads in the depletion base.

Koppel estimates it will take three years to salvage the downed timber at a cost of $700,000. The timber can be sold for pulp wood at an estimated price of $3 per cubic metre. The land value is unknown, but until it will grow vegetation again, which scientists say may be as long as 50 to 100 years, the value is nominal.

Instructions

(a) Determine the depletion cost per cubic metre for the timber harvested prior to the eruption of Mount St. Helens.
(b) Prepare the journal entry to record the depletion prior to the eruption.
(c) If this tract represents approximately half of Koppel's timber holdings, determine the amount of the estimated loss before income taxes and show how the losses of roads, machinery, and timber and the timber salvage value should be reported in the financial statements of Koppel for the year ended December 31, 1980.

P12-8 Western Paper Products Ltd. purchased 10,000 ha of forested timberland in March 2002. The company paid $1,700 per hectare for this land, which was above the $800 per hectare most farmers were paying for cleared land. During April, May, June, and July 2002, Western cut enough timber to build roads using moveable equipment purchased on April 1, 2002. The cost of the roads was $195,000, and the cost of the equipment was $189,000; the equipment was expected to have a $9,000 residual value and would be used for the next 15 years. Western selected the straight-line method of amortization for the moveable equipment. The company began actively harvesting timber in August and by December had harvested and sold 472,500 m³ of timber of the estimated 6,750,000 m³ available for cutting.

In March 2003, Western planted new seedlings in the area harvested during the winter. Cost of planting these seedlings was $120,000. In addition, Western spent $8,000 in road maintenance and $6,000 for pest spraying during 2003. The road maintenance and spraying are annual costs. During 2003, Western harvested and sold 774,000 m³ of timber of the estimated 6,450,000 m³ available for cutting.

In March 2004, Western again planted new seedlings at a cost of $150,000, and also spent $15,000 on road maintenance and pest spraying. During 2004, the company harvested and sold 650,000 m³ of timber of the estimated 6.5 million m³ available for cutting.

Instructions

Calculate the amount of amortization and depletion expense for each of the three years. Assume that the roads are usable only for logging and therefore are included in the depletion base.

P12-9 Selig Sporting Goods Inc. has been experiencing growth in product demand over the last several years. The last two Olympic Games greatly increased the popularity of basketball around the world. As a result, a European sports retailing consortium entered into an agreement with Selig's Roundball Division to purchase basketballs and other accessories on an increasing basis over the next five years.

To be able to meet the quantity commitments of this agreement, Selig had to obtain additional manufacturing capacity. A real estate firm located an available factory in close proximity to Selig's Roundball manufacturing facility, and Selig agreed to purchase the factory and used machinery from Sparks Athletic Equipment Company on October 1, 2000. Renovations were necessary to convert the factory for Selig's manufacturing use.

The terms of the agreement required Selig to pay Sparks $50,000 when renovations started on January 1, 2001, with the balance to be paid as renovations were completed. The overall purchase price for the factory and machinery was $400,000. The building renovations were contracted to Malone Construction at $100,000. The payments made, as renovations progressed during 2001, are shown below. The factory was placed in service on January 1, 2002.

	1/1	4/1	10/1	12/31
Sparks	$50,000	$100,000	$100,000	$150,000
Malone		30,000	30,000	40,000

On January 1, 2001, Selig secured a $500,000 line of credit with a 12% interest rate to finance the factory and machinery purchase and the renovation costs. Selig drew down on the line of credit to meet the payment schedule shown above; this was Selig's only outstanding loan during 2001.

Rob Stewart, Selig's controller, capitalized the interest costs for this project. Selig's policy regarding purchases of this nature is to use the land's appraisal value for book purposes and prorate the balance of the purchase price over the remaining items. The building had originally cost Sparks $300,000 and had a net book value of $50,000, while the machinery originally cost $125,000 and had a net book value of $40,000 on the date of sale. The land was recorded on Sparks' books at $40,000. An appraisal, conducted by independent appraisers at the time of acquisition, valued the land at $280,000, the building at $105,000, and the machinery at $45,000.

Linda Safford, chief engineer, estimated that the renovated plant would be used for 15 years, with an estimated residual value of $30,000. Safford estimated that the production machinery would have a remaining useful life of five years and a residual value of $3,000. Selig's amortization policy specifies the 200% declining-balance method for machinery and the 150% declining-balance method for the plant. One-half year's amortization is taken in the year assets are placed in service and one-half year is allowed when the assets are disposed of or retired.

Instructions

(a) Determine the amounts to be recorded on the books of Selig Sporting Goods Inc. as of December 31, 2001 for each of the following properties acquired from Sparks Athletic Equipment Company.

    1. Land   **2.** Building   **3.** Machinery

(b) Calculate Selig Sporting Goods Inc.'s 2002 amortization expense, for book purposes, for each of the properties acquired from Sparks Athletic Equipment Company.

(c) Discuss the arguments for and against the capitalization of interest costs.

(CMA adapted)

P12-10 Olsson Corporation uses special strapping equipment in its packaging business. The equipment was purchased in January 2001 for $8 million and had an estimated useful life of eight years with no residual value. At December 31, 2002, new technology was introduced that would accelerate the obsolescence of Olsson's equipment. Olsson's controller estimates that expected future net cash flows on the equipment will be $5.3 million and that the fair value of the equipment is $4.4 million. Olsson intends to continue using the equipment, but estimates that its remaining useful life is four years. Olsson uses straight-line amortization.

Instructions

(a) Prepare the journal entry (if any) to record the impairment at December 31, 2002.

(b) Prepare any journal entries for the equipment at December 31, 2003. The fair value of the equipment at December 31, 2003, is estimated to be $4.6 million.

(c) Repeat the requirements for (a) and (b), assuming that Olsson intends to dispose of the equipment and that it has not been disposed of as of December 31, 2003.

P12-11 Huston Corporation, a manufacturer of steel products, began operations on October 1, 2000. Huston's accounting department has started the capital asset and amortization schedule presented below. You have been asked to assist in completing this schedule. In addition to determining that the data already on the schedule are correct, you have obtained the following information from the company's records and personnel:

1. Amortization is calculated from the first of the month of acquisition to the first of the month of disposition.

2. Land A and Building A were acquired from a predecessor corporation. Huston paid $820,000 for the land and building together. At the time of acquisition, the land had an appraised value of $90,000, and the building had an appraised value of $810,000.

3. Land B was acquired on October 2, 2000, in exchange for 2,500 newly issued common shares. At the date of acquisition, the shares had a fair value of $30 each. During October 2000, Huston paid $16,000 to demolish an existing building on this land so it could construct a new building.

4. Construction of Building B on the newly acquired land began on October 1, 2001. By September 30, 2002, Huston had paid $320,000 of the estimated total construction costs of $450,000. It is estimated that the building will be completed and occupied by July 2003.

5. Certain equipment was donated to the corporation by a local university. An independent appraisal of the equipment when donated placed the fair market value at $30,000 and the residual value at $3,000.

6. Machinery A's total cost of $164,900 includes installation expense of $600 and normal repairs and maintenance of $14,900. Residual value is estimated at $6,000. Machinery A was sold on February 1, 2002.

7. On October 1, 2001, Machinery B was acquired with a down payment of $5,740 and the remaining payments to be made in 11 annual instalments of $6,000 each beginning October 1, 2001. The prevailing interest rate was 8%. The following data were abstracted from present-value tables (rounded):

PV of $1 at 8%		PV of an ordinary annuity of $1 at 8%	
10 years	0.463	10 years	6.710
11 years	0.429	11 years	7.139
15 years	0.315	15 years	8.559

HUSTON CORPORATION
Capital Asset and Amortization Schedule
For Fiscal Years Ended September 30, 2001, and September 30, 2002

Assets	Acquisition Date	Cost	Residual	Amortization Method	Estimated Life in Years	Amortization Expense Year Ended September 30 2001	2002
Land A	Oct. 1, 2000	$ (1)	N/A	N/A	N/A	N/A	N/A
Building A	Oct. 1, 2000	(2)	$40,000	Straight-line	(3)	$17,450	(4)
Land B	Oct. 2, 2000	(5)	N/A	N/A	N/A	N/A	N/A
Building B	Under	$320,000	—	Straight-line	30	—	(6)
		Construction to date					
Donated Equipment	Oct. 2, 2000	(7)	3,000	150% declining balance	10	(8)	(9)
Machinery A	Oct. 2, 2000	(10)	6,000	Double-declining-balance	8	(11)	(12)
Machinery B	Oct. 1, 2001	(13)	—	Straight-line	20	—	(14)

N/A – Not applicable

Instructions

For each numbered item on the foregoing schedule, supply the correct amount. Round each answer to the nearest dollar.

P12-12 Situation 1 Zitar Corporation purchased electrical equipment at a cost of $12,400 on June 2, 1998. From 1998 through 2001, the equipment was amortized on a straight-line basis, under the assumption that it would have a 10-year useful life and a $2,400 residual value. After more experience and before recording 2002's amortization, Zitar revised its estimate of the machine's useful life downward from a total of 10 years to 8 years, and revised the estimated residual value to $2,000.

On April 29, 2003, after recording part of a year's amortization for 2003, the company traded in the equipment on a newer model, receiving a $4,000 trade-in allowance, although its fair value was only $2,800. The new asset had a list price of $15,300 and the supplier accepted $11,300 cash for the balance. The new equipment was amortized on a straight-line basis under the assumption of a seven-year useful life and a $1,300 salvage value.

Instructions

Determine the amount of amortization expense reported by Zitar for each fiscal year ending on December 31, 1998 through to December 31, 2003.

Situation 2 Boda Limited acquired a truck to deliver and install its specialized products at the customer's site. The vehicle's list price was $45,000, but customization added another $10,000 of costs. Boda took delivery of the truck on September 30, 2002 with a downpayment of $5,000, signing a four-year 8% note for the remainder, payable in equal payments of $14,496 beginning September 30, 2003.

Boda expects the truck to be usable for 500 deliveries and installations by which time the product's technology will have changed so as to make the vehicle obsolete. In late July 2005, the truck was destroyed when a concrete garage collapsed. Boda used the truck for 45 deliveries in 2002, 125 in 2003, 134 in 2004, and 79 in 2005. The company received a cheque for $12,000 from the insurance company and paid what remained on the note.

Instructions

Prepare all entries to record the events and activities related to the truck, including the amortization expense on the truck each year. Assume Boda uses an activity approach to amortize the truck, based on deliveries.

Situation 3 A group of new machines was purchased on February 17, 2002 under a royalty agreement that provides for Townsand Corp. to pay a royalty of $1 to the machinery supplier for each unit of product produced by the machines each year. The machines are expected to produce 200,000 units over their useful lives. The invoice price of the machines was $75,000, freight costs were $2,000, unloading charges were $1,500, and royalty payments for 2002 were $13,000. Townsand uses the units of production method to amortize its machinery.

Instructions

Prepare journal entries to record the purchase of the new machines, the related amortization for 2002, and the royalty payment.

*P12-13 Taber Limited reports the following information in its tax files covering the five-year period from 1999 to 2003. All assets relate to Class 10 with a 30% maximum CCA rate.

1999	Purchased assets A, B, and C for $20,000, $8,000, and $1,200 respectively.
2000	Sold asset B for $7,000; bought asset D for $4,800.
2001	Purchased asset E for $5,000; received an investment tax credit of $1,000.
2002	Sold asset A for $9,900 and asset C for $1,800.
2003	Uninsured asset D was destroyed by fire; asset E was sold to an employee for $500.

Instructions

(a) Prepare a capital cost allowance schedule for Class 10 assets covering the 1999 to 2003 period.
(b) Identify any capital gains, terminal losses, or recapture of CCA and indicate how each would be taxed.

CONCEPTUAL CASES

C12-1 Prophet Manufacturing Limited was organized January 1, 2002. During 2002, it used the straight-line method of amortizing its plant assets in its reports to management.

On November 8 you are having a conference with Prophet's officers to discuss the amortization method to be used for income tax and for reporting to shareholders. Fred Peretti, president of Prophet, has suggested the use of a new method, which he feels is more suitable than the straight-line method for the company's needs during the period of rapid expansion of production and capacity that he foresees. Following is an example in which the proposed method is applied to a capital asset with an original cost of $248,000, an estimated useful life of five years, and a residual value of approximately $8,000.

Year	Years of Life Used	Fraction Rate	Amortization Expense	Accumulated Amortization at End of Year	Book Value at End of Year
1	1	1/15	$16,000	$ 16,000	$232,000
2	2	2/15	32,000	48,000	200,000
3	3	3/15	48,000	96,000	152,000
4	4	4/15	64,000	160,000	88,000
5	5	5/15	80,000	240,000	8,000

The president favours the new method because he has heard that:

1. It will increase the funds recovered during the years near the end of the assets' useful lives when maintenance and replacement disbursements are high.
2. It will result in increased write-offs in later years when the company is likely to be in a better operating position.

Instructions

(a) What is the purpose of accounting for amortization?

(b) Is the president's proposal within the scope of generally accepted accounting principles? In making your decision, discuss the circumstances, if any, under which using the method would be reasonable and those, if any, under which it would not be reasonable.

(c) Do amortization charges recover or create funds? Explain.

C12-2 The independent public accountant is frequently called upon by management for advice regarding methods of calculating amortization. Of comparable importance, although it arises less often, is the question of whether the amortization method should be based on consideration of the assets as a unit, or as part of a group of assets.

Instructions

(a) Briefly describe the amortization methods based on treating assets as (1) units and (2) part of a group or as having a composite life.

(b) Present the arguments for and against the use of each of the two methods.

(c) Describe how retirements are recorded under each of the two methods.

(AICPA adapted)

C12-3 Presented below are three different and unrelated situations involving amortization accounting. Answer the question(s) at the end of each case situation.

Situation I

Recently, Brunet Company Ltd. experienced a strike that affected a number of its operating plants. The company president indicated that it was not appropriate to report amortization expense during this period because the equipment did not depreciate and an improper matching of costs and revenues would result. She based her position on the following points:

1. It is inappropriate to charge the period with costs for which there are no related revenues arising from production.

2. The basic factor of amortization in this instance is wear and tear, and because equipment was idle, no wear and tear occurred.

Instructions

Comment on the appropriateness of the president's comments.

Situation II

Carnago Corporation manufactures home electrical appliances. Company engineers have designed a new type of blender that, through the use of a few attachments, will perform more functions than any other blender currently on the market. Demand for the new blender can be projected with reasonable probability. In order to manufacture the blenders, Carnago needs a specialized machine that is not available from outside sources. It has been decided to make such a machine in Carnago's own plant.

Instructions

(a) Discuss the effect of projected demand in units for the new blenders (which may be steady, decreasing, or increasing) on the determination of an amortization method for the machine.

(b) What other matters should be considered in determining the amortization method? Ignore income tax considerations.

Situation III

Puma Paper Company Ltd. operates a 300-tonnes-per-day kraft pulp mill and four sawmills in New Brunswick. The company is expanding its pulp mill facilities to a capacity of 1,000 tonnes per day and plans to replace three of its older, less efficient sawmills with an expanded facility. One of the mills to be replaced did not operate for most of 2002 (current year), and there are no plans to reopen it before the new sawmill facility becomes operational.

In reviewing the amortization rates and in discussing the residual values of the sawmills that were to be replaced, it was noted that if present amortization rates were not adjusted, substantial amounts of plant costs on these three mills would not be depreciated by the time the new mill comes on stream.

Instructions

What is the proper accounting for the four sawmills at the end of 2002?

C12-4 As a cost accountant for Digby Cannery Inc., you have been approached by Merle Morash, canning room supervisor, about the 2000 costs charged to his department. In particular, he is concerned about the line item "amortization." Morash is very proud of the excellent condition of his canning room equipment. He has always been vigilant about keeping all equipment serviced and well oiled. He is sure that the huge charge to amortization is a mistake; it does not at all reflect the cost of minimal wear and tear that the machines have experienced over the last year. He believes that the charge should be considerably lower.

The machines being amortized are six automatic canning machines. All were put into use on January 1, 2000. Each cost $469,000, having a residual value of $40,000 and a useful life of 12 years. Digby depreciates this and similar assets using the double-declining-balance method. Morash has also pointed out that if you used straight-line amortization the charge to his department would not be so great.

Instructions

Write a memo to Merle Morash to clear up his misunderstanding of the term "amortization." Also, calculate the first year amortization on all machines using both methods. Explain the theoretical justification for double-declining-balance and why, in the long run, the aggregate charge to amortization will be the same under both methods.

C12-5 Linda Monkland established Monkland Ltd. as the sole shareholder in mid-2001. The accounts on June 30, 2002, the company's year end, just prior to preparing required adjusting entries, indicated the following amounts:

Current assets		$100,000
Capital assets		
Land	$40,000	
Building	90,000	
Equipment	50,000	180,000
Current liabilities		40,000
Long-term bank loan		120,000
Share capital		90,000
Net income prior to amortization		30,000

All the capital assets were acquired and put into operation in early July 2001. Estimates regarding these assets include:

Building: 25-year life, $15,000 residual value

Equipment: Five-year life, 15,000 hours of use, $5,000 residual value.

The equipment was used for 1,000 hours in 2001 and 1,400 hours in 2002 up to June 30.

Linda Monkland is now considering which amortization method or methods would be appropriate. She has narrowed the choices down for the building to the straight-line or double-declining methods, and for the equipment to the straight-line, double-declining-balance, or activity methods. She has requested your advice and recommendation. In discussions with her, the following concerns were raised.

1. The company presently acquires goods from suppliers with terms of 2/10,n/30. The suppliers have indicated that these terms will continue as long as the current ratio does not fall below 2 to 1. If the ratio were less, then no purchase discounts would be given.
2. The bank will continue the loan from year to year as long as the ratio of long-term debt to total assets does not exceed 46%.
3. Linda Monkland has contracted with the company's manager to pay him a bonus equal to 50% of any net income in excess of $14,000. She prefers to minimize or pay no bonus as long as conditions of agreements with suppliers and the bank can be met.
4. In order to provide a strong signal to attract potential investors to join her in the company, Ms. Monkland believes that a rate of return on total assets of at least 5% must be achieved.

Instructions

Prepare a report for Linda Monkland that analyses the situation, provides a recommendation on which method or methods should be used, and justifies your recommendation in light of her concerns and the requirement that the method(s) used be systematic and rational.

Using Your Judgement

FINANCIAL REPORTING PROBLEM: CANADIAN TIRE CORPORATION (A)

The financial statements of **Canadian Tire Corporation** appear in Appendix 5B. Refer to these financial statements and the accompanying notes to answer the following questions.

Instructions

(a) What descriptions are used by Canadian Tire in its balance sheet to classify its tangible capital assets?

(b) What method or methods of amortization does Canadian Tire use to amortize its property and equipment?

(c) Does the company disclose the useful lives of these assets or the rates at which they are amortized? Comment.

(d) What amount of amortization expense did Canadian Tire charge to its income statement in 2000 and 1999?

(e) What amounts of interest expense were capitalized by Canadian Tire as part of construction costs in 2000 and 1999?

(f) What was the cost of the additions to property and equipment made by Canadian Tire in 2000 and 1999?

(g) Does "Property and Equipment" include only tangible capital assets being used to generate income for the company?

CANADIAN TIRE CORPORATION (B)

Refer to the financial statements of **Canadian Tire Corporation** that appear in Appendix 5B, including the Ten Year Financial Review if necessary, as a basis for answering the following questions.

Instructions

(a) How significant is Canadian Tire's investment in Property and Equipment relative to its investment in other assets? Compare this with sample companies in other industries, such as financial services, utilities, and technology. Comment.

(b) Calculate the company's total asset turnover for 1998, 1999, and 2000.

(c) Calculate the company's profit margin for the same three years.

(d) Calculate the company's return on assets for the same three years by using the ratios calculated in (c) and (d) above.

(e) Based on your calculations in (d), suggest ways in which Canadian Tire might increase the return it earns on its investment in assets.

FINANCIAL STATEMENT ANALYSIS CASES

Case 1   Chapters versus Barnes and Noble

Chapters and **Barnes & Noble** are two of the largest book sellers in Canada and the U.S., respectively. This has been an interesting and challenging industry over the past decade with Amazon.com making huge inroads into the market on the one hand and small independent bookstores not being able to compete on the other. Both Chapters and Barnes & Noble operate large bookstores as well as having a significant on-line presence. Provided below are figures taken from the financial statements of the two companies.

(in thousands)	Chapters year ended April 1, 2000	Barnes & Noble year ended January 29, 2000
Total revenue	$660,309	$3,486,043
Net income	17,195	124,498
Total assets	495,310	2,413,791
Land	nil	3,247
Buildings, leasehold improvements, before accumulated amortization	85,076	417,535
Fixtures and equipment, before accumulated amortization	143,117	565,345
Total property and equipment (at cost)	228,193	986,127
Accumulated amortization	85,955	418,078
Amortization expense	22,887	112,304

Instructions

(a) Based on the asset turnover ratio, which company used its assets more effectively to generate sales? Assume that total assets reported are a reasonable average of beginning and ending balances.

(b) Which company had a better profit margin on sales?

(c) Which company had the higher rate of return on total assets?

(d) What proportion of each company's total assets are invested in tangible capital assets?

(e) If both companies followed a strategy of marketing a higher proportion of total sales on-line, what effect do you think this would have on their return on assets ratio? Explain.

Case 2   McDonald's Corporation

McDonald's is the largest and best-known global food service retailer, with more than 28,000 restaurants in 120 countries. The company's system-wide sales in 2000 exceeded $40 billion. Presented below is information related to property and equipment.

McDONALD'S CORPORATION
Significant Accounting Policies Section

Property and Equipment. Property and equipment are stated at cost, with depreciation and amortization provided using the straight-line method over the following estimated useful lives: buildings—up to 40 years; leasehold improvements—the lesser of useful lives of assets or lease terms including option periods; and equipment—3 to 12 years.

Property and Equipment (in millions of $U.S.)	Dec. 31, 2000	1999
Land	$3,932.7	$3,838.6
Buildings and improvements on owned land	8,250.0	7,953.6
Buildings and improvements on leased land	7,513.3	7,076.6
Equipment, signs, and seating	3,172.2	2,906.6
Other	700.8	675.4
	23,569.0	22,450.8
Accumulated depreciation and amortization	(6,521.4)	(6,126.3)
Net property and equipment	$17,047.6	$16,324.5

Depreciation and amortization expense was (in millions):
2000—$900.9; 1999—$858.1; 1998—$808.0.

Other information

(in millions)	2000	1999	1998
Cash provided by operations	$2,751	$3,009	$2,766
Capital expenditures	$1,945	$1,868	$1,879
Free cash flow	$ 806	$1,141	$ 887
Cash provided by operations as a percent of capital expenditures	141%	161%	147%
Cash provided by operations as a percent of average total debt	35%	42%	41%

Instructions

(a) What method of amortization is used by McDonald's? Does this method seem appropriate given the type of assets McDonald's has? Comment.

(b) Does depreciation and amortization expense cause cash flow from operations to increase? Explain.

(c) What is "free cash flow"? What is its significance?

(d) Comment on the level of McDonald's cash flow from operations.

COMPARATIVE ANALYSIS CASES

Loblaw Companies Limited versus Sobeys Inc.

Instructions

Go to the Digital Tool and use information about **Loblaw Companies Limited** and **Sobeys Inc.** found there to answer the following questions.

(a) What amount is reported in the balance sheets as tangible capital assets (net) of Loblaw Companies at December 30, 2000 and of Sobeys Inc. at May 6, 2000? What percentage of total assets is invested in this type of asset by each company?

(b) What amortization methods are used by Loblaw and Sobeys? What types of tangible capital assets do both companies report? Are they similar? Are their amortization policies and rates similar? How much amortization was reported by each company in 2000 and 1999?

(c) Calculate, compare, and comment on the following ratios for Loblaw and Sobeys for 2000:

1. Asset turnover.

2. Profit margin on sales.

3. Return on assets.

(d) What amount was spent in 2000 for capital expenditures by Loblaw? By Sobeys? Where do you find this information in the financial statements? What amount of interest was capitalized in 2000?

(e) Do Loblaw or Sobeys make any reference to impairments of long-lived assets?

Paper and Forest Products Industry

Instructions

Canfor Corporation, Bowater Canada Inc., Cascades Inc., Doman Industries Limited, and **Tembec Industries Inc.** are all large companies in the paper and forest products industry in Canada. Their latest annual financial statements can be accessed through their company websites or through the www.sedar.com website.

A. Because these companies are all in the same industry, it is likely that they have similar types of assets, including tangible capital assets. Because of the similarity of their operations, the expectation might be that their capitalization policies, amortization policies, and amortization rates are similar. Is this the case? Prepare a report on your findings.

B. It is unlikely that major companies in a single industry earn the same return on the assets employed. Determine, for each of the companies identified above, the total asset turnover, the profit margin, and the return on assets calculated in two ways. Which companies perform the best measured by the return on assets? Do they do this by virtue of generating more revenue with the assets they have at work, or through good cost control? Review the companies' income statements to determine if any anomalies exist. Write a report on your findings.

RESEARCH CASES

Case 1

A wealth of accounting-related information is available via the Internet. For example, the Rutgers Accounting Web (http://www.rutgers.edu/accounting/raw) offers access to a great variety of sources. Although a U.S. site, it has links to many international sites, including accounting associations in Canada.

Instructions

Once in the Rutgers Accounting Web, click on "Accounting Resources."

(a) List the categories of information available through the "Accounting Resources" link.

(b) Select any one of these categories and briefly describe the types of information available.

Case 2

A topic of significance to not-for-profit organizations that is related to tangible capital assets is that of "deferred maintenance." Canadian schools and universities are particularly concerned about this issue.

Instructions

(a) Research the topic of deferred maintenance sufficiently that you understand the term. Explain the concept in 50 words or less.

(b) Interview the chief financial officer of your school, university, or other not-for-profit or government organization to discuss the issue. Can you determine from an organization's financial statements that it has a deferred maintenance problem? Should you be able to? Discuss.

ETHICS CASE

Billy Williams, HK Corporation's controller, is concerned that net income may be lower this year. He is afraid upper-level management might recommend cost reductions by laying off accounting staff, himself included.

Williams knows that amortization is a major expense for HK. The company currently uses the double-declining-balance method for financial reporting, similar to the method required for tax purposes, and he's thinking of a change to the straight-line method. A change in an accounting method such as this is required to be disclosed in the financial statements along with the effect on the current year's income, and a retroactive adjustment made to opening retained earnings. Williams does not want to highlight the increasing of income in this manner. He thinks, "Why don't I increase the estimated useful lives and the residual values of the tangible capital assets? They are only estimates anyway. The effect will be to decrease amortization expense and since the changes are accounted for prospectively, this will not be disclosed in the income statement. I may be able to save my job and those of my staff."

Instructions

Answer the following questions:

(a) Who are the stakeholders in this situation?

(b) What are the ethical issues involved?

(c) What should Williams do?

CHAPTER 13

Intangible Assets

LEARNING OBJECTIVES

After studying this chapter, you should be able to:

1. Describe the characteristics of intangible assets.

2. Discuss the recognition and measurement issues of acquiring intangibles.

3. Explain how specifically identifiable intangibles are valued subsequent to acquisition.

4. Identify the types of specifically identifiable intangible assets.

5. Explain the conceptual issues related to goodwill.

6. Describe the accounting procedures for recording goodwill at acquisition and subsequently.

7. Differentiate between research and development expenditures and describe and explain the rationale for the accounting for each.

8. Identify other examples of deferred charges and the accounting requirements for them.

9. Identify the disclosure requirements for intangibles, including deferred charges.

Preview of Chapter 13

The accounting and reporting of intangibles is taking on increasing importance in this information age. The purpose of this chapter is to explain the basic conceptual and reporting issues related to intangible assets. The content and organization of the chapter are as follows:

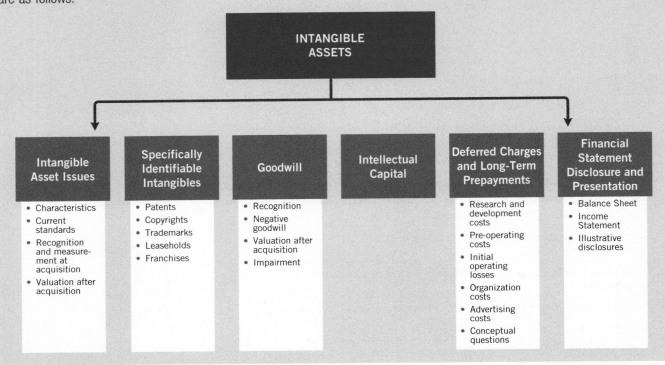

INTANGIBLE ASSET ISSUES

Characteristics

Roots Canada's most important asset is not store fixtures—it's the brand image. The major asset of **Coca-Cola** is not its plant facilities—it's the secret formula for making Coke. **Sympatico**'s most important asset is not its Internet connection equipment—it's the subscriber base. As these examples show, we have an economy increasingly dominated by information and service providers, and their major assets are often intangible in nature. Accounting for these intangibles is difficult, and as a result many intangibles have not been captured on companies' balance sheets.

What are intangible assets? Broadly defined, intangible assets are assets that lack physical substance and are not financial assets.[1] Examples of intangibles under this definition include widely diverse assets such as patents, broadcast licences, secret formulas, licensing agreements, customer lists, trademarks, computer software, goodwill, technological know-how, superior management, deferred charges, prepayments, and research and development. The *CICA Handbook*, however, deals with some of these items in separate sections of the *Handbook*, leaving the more traditional specifically identifiable intangibles to be covered by new Section 3062 on "Goodwill and Other Intangible Assets."

---

[1] *CICA Handbook*, Section 3062, par. .05(c).

Assets such as bank deposits, accounts receivable, and long-term investments in bonds and shares lack physical substance, but are not classified as intangible assets. These assets are financial instruments that derive their value from the right (claim) to receive cash or cash equivalents in the future.

Unlike tangible capital assets such as property, plant, and equipment, most intangible assets derive their value from the rights and privileges granted to the company using them. Companies acquire intangible assets in a variety of ways. They can purchase or otherwise acquire intangibles singly, in a basket purchase, as part of a merger or business combination, or they can be developed internally. As explained below, accounting standards for the recognition, measurement, and subsequent valuation of intangible assets differ according to their characteristics. *APB Opinion No. 17* identified the following characteristics of intangible assets that are useful in determining the most appropriate methods of accounting for them.

1. **Identifiability.** Some intangibles and their values are separately identifiable, while others, such as goodwill, cannot be specifically identified.

2. **Manner of acquisition.** Intangibles can be acquired singly, in groups, in business combinations, or developed internally.

3. **Expected period of benefit.** The useful lives of some intangibles are limited by law or contract, others are related to human or economic factors, and others have useful lives of indefinite or indeterminate duration.

4. **Separability from an entire enterprise.** Many intangible assets are saleable, some are rights transferable without title, and some cannot be purchased or sold on a stand-alone basis.[2]

These characteristics differentiate intangible assets and may provide a basis for differing accounting and reporting requirements for them.

Current Standards

As this text went to print in August 2001, new accounting and reporting standards had just been released for business combinations (new Section 1581) and goodwill and other intangible assets (new Section 3062). The Accounting Standards Board's goal is to harmonize standards on business combinations, goodwill, and intangibles with those of FASB and the release of the Handbook standards is a significant accomplishment. The material in this chapter is based on these new sections.

The standards discussed in this chapter on research and development costs and deferred charges are those in existing Sections 3450 and 3070, respectively. The Accounting Standards Board has identified these topics as possible projects for its future agenda.

Recognition and Measurement Issues at Acquisition

Purchased Intangibles

Consistent with the valuation of most assets, **purchased intangible assets are measured at cost—their fair value at acquisition.** Cost includes the acquisition cost and all expenditures necessary to make the intangible asset ready for its intended use; for example, the purchase price, legal fees, and other incidental expenses. Cost, as we've seen in earlier chapters, is the "cash cost." If there are delayed payment terms, any portion of the payments representing interest must be recognized as financing expenses rather than part of the capitalized asset cost.

When several intangibles, or a combination of intangibles and tangibles, are bought in a "basket purchase," the cost should be allocated based on their relative fair values. Essentially, application of the cost principle for purchased intangibles parallels that for

---

[2] "Intangible Assets," *Opinions of the Accounting Principles Board No. 17*, (New York: AICPA, 1970), par. .10.

OBJECTIVE 2

....

Discuss the recognition and measurement issues of acquiring intangibles.

 UNDERLYING CONCEPTS

The basic attributes of intangibles, their uncertainty as to future benefits, and their uniqueness have discouraged valuation in excess of cost.

IAS NOTE

IAS 38 allows intangibles that
have an active market to be
revalued periodically to fair
value.

purchased tangible capital assets. The profession has resisted using other bases of valuation, such as current replacement cost or appraisal value for intangible assets.[3]

When an enterprise purchases intangible assets as single assets, the accounting is straightforward. When acquired as part of a group of assets, however, such as in a business combination, the extent to which intangible assets should be given separate recognition and the extent to which they should be considered a part of goodwill must be determined. A **business combination** occurs when one entity acquires control over the net assets of another business either by acquiring the net assets directly or the equity interests representing control over the net assets. In both cases, the purchase price must be allocated among the identifiable assets and liabilities, with any unidentified excess recognized as goodwill.[4]

Identifiable intangibles generate identifiable cash flow streams, singly or in combination with other assets. For example, the right to lease space at favourable rates has future cash flow implications and the value of this right can be determined. The entitlement to the benefits is granted through a contractual agreement (the lease) and the right may or may not be transferable to others. A subscription list of a newspaper or successful magazine has value in contributing to future revenue streams and is saleable, resulting in future cash flows. These are examples of identifiable intangibles that should be given separate recognition.

Goodwill and other intangibles, on the other hand, do not generate identifiable cash flow streams on their own, are not separable from the rest of the entity, and control over the future benefits does not result from contractual or legal rights. For example, the synergies of a combined sales force or a superior management team can be identified as intangibles, but the inability to separately hive off these benefits to exchange them with others or the inability to control the benefits through contractual or other legal rights means that they cannot be granted recognition as separate identifiable intangibles. They, therefore, are considered part of goodwill.[5] Illustration 13-1 lists a number of intangible assets that might be acquired in a business combination. From this, you can understand some of the difficulties in identifying those that should be recognized separately from goodwill!

ILLUSTRATION 13-1

Examples of Intangibles Acquired
in a Business Combination

Intangible assets that relate to customer structure or market factors of the business:
  a. Lists (advertising, customer, dealer, mailing, subscription, and so forth)
  b. Customer base
  c. Customer routes
  d. Delivery system, distribution channels
  e. Customer service capability, product or service support
  f. Effective advertising programs
  g. Trademarked brand names
  h. Presence in geographic locations or markets
  i. Production backlog.

Intangible assets that have a fixed or definite term:
  a. Agreements (consulting, income, licensing, manufacturing, royalty, standstill)
  b. Contracts (advertising, construction, consulting, customer, employment, insurance, maintenance, management, marketing, mortgage, presold, purchase, service, supply)
  c. Covenants (not to compete)
  d. Leases (valuable or favourable terms)
  e. Rights (broadcasting, development, gas allocation, landing, lease, mineral, mortgage servicing, reacquired franchise, servicing, timber cutting, use, water).

---

[3] Even Sprouse and Moonitz, who advocated abandonment of historical cost in favour of replacement cost for most asset items in *AICPA Accounting Research Study No. 3*, "A Tentative Set of Broad Accounting Principles for a Business Enterprise," suggested that intangibles should normally be carried at acquisition cost less amortization because valuation problems are so difficult.

[4] If net assets are acquired directly, the purchase price must be allocated directly to the individual assets and liabilities acquired. If control over the assets is acquired by the acquisition of voting shares, the purchase price must be allocated to the identifiable assets and liabilities as part of the consolidation process.

[5] *CICA Handbook*, Section 1581, par. .48.

Intangible assets that relate to innovations or technological advances within the business:
a. Computer software and licence, computer programs, information systems, program formats, Internet domain names and portals
b. Secret formulas and processes, recipes
c. Technical drawings, technical and procedural manuals, blueprints
d. Manufacturing processes, procedures, production line.

Intangible assets with statutorily established useful lives:
a. Patents
b. Copyrights (manuscripts, literary works, musical compositions)
c. Franchises (cable, radio, television)
d. Trademarks, trade names.

Intangible assets that relate to the value of the established employees or workforce of a company:
a. Assembled workforce, trained staff
b. Non-union status, strong labour relations, favourable wage rates
c. Superior management or other key employees
d. Technical expertise

Intangible assets relating to the organizational structure of an entity:
a. Favourable financial arrangements, outstanding credit rating
b. Fundraising capabilities, access to capital markets
c. Favourable government relations

Source: Adapted from "Business Combinations" *Exposure Draft*, September, 1999, CICA.

For accounting purposes, **intangible assets should be recognized separately from goodwill** if the asset results from contractual or other legal rights, or if the asset can be separated or divided from the acquired enterprise and sold, transferred, licensed, rented, or exchanged.[6] Intangibles acquired in a business combination that do not meet either of these two conditions, or that cannot meet general recognition criteria, become part of the residual goodwill.

It is also **important to distinguish one identifiable intangible from another**. Financial reporting objectives are not well met if each and every identifiable intangible is recognized separately. At a minimum, those with similar characteristics (such as continuity, stability, and risk) should be grouped and recognized together. Because knowledge-based and high-technology companies with large investments in "soft" intangible assets are an important component of our modern economy, the accounting treatment accorded them is a substantive issue.

Lastly, similar to tangible capital assets, subsequent costs incurred to enhance the service potential of the intangibles should be accounted for as a betterment and be capitalized.

Internally Created Intangibles

Costs incurred internally to create intangible assets are generally expensed as incurred. For example, even though a company incurs substantial research and development costs that result in eventually being granted a patent, these costs generally are expensed as incurred, except for the direct cost of obtaining the intangible asset, such as legal costs. Various reasons are given for this approach. The primary argument relates to the uncertainty of the future benefits to be derived from the specific expenditure. Some argue that the costs incurred internally to create intangibles such as patents and brand names bear no relationship to their real value; therefore, expensing these costs is appropriate. In any case, the underlying subjectivity related to intangibles dictates a conservative approach. When future benefits are reasonably assured, however, both the direct development costs and overhead costs directly attributable to the development activity are capitalized.[7]

INTERNATIONAL INSIGHT

In Japan, the cost of intangibles can be capitalized whether they are externally purchased or internally developed.

---

[6] *CICA Handbook,* Section 1581, par. .48.

[7] *CICA Handbook,* Section 3062, par. .07.

Deferred Charges

Some costs incurred currently may be deemed to provide the enterprise with future benefits in excess of the costs incurred. In this situation, a case can be made to defer the costs' recognition until the future benefits are received. Over the last 25 years or so, with the shift toward an accounting model focused on asset and liability definition and away from a revenue and expense approach, it has become less acceptable to recognize deferred charges as assets.[8] As a consequence, accounting standards have been tightened to permit the capitalization of deferred costs only where specific requirements are met.

For subsequent discussion, intangibles are classified into intangible assets that are specifically identifiable, goodwill-type intangible assets, and those that represent deferred charges. The accounting treatment accorded these three types of intangible is shown in Illustration 13-2.

ILLUSTRATION 13-2
Accounting for the Acquisition
Costs of Intangibles

| | Manner Acquired | |
Type of Intangible	Purchased	Internally Created
Identifiable intangibles	Capitalize	Expense, except certain costs
Goodwill-type intangibles	Capitalize	Expense
Deferred charges	Capitalize restricted amounts	Capitalize restricted amounts

Valuation after Acquisition

OBJECTIVE 3

Explain how specifically identifiable intangibles are valued subsequent to acquisition.

As indicated above, intangibles are a diverse mix of assets. Goodwill, an unidentifiable intangible, is not separable from the enterprise and may have an indefinite life; that is, a life that extends beyond the foreseeable horizon. Some intangibles have values based on rights that are conveyed legally by contract, statute, or similar means. Examples include the granting of a **Tim Hortons** franchise or licences granted by government to cable companies. Some of these rights have finite lives that can be easily renewed; others have lives that are not renewable, or are renewable at a significant cost. Some may be granted into perpetuity and be saleable, or they may not be exchangeable. Internally developed intangibles such as customer lists and databases have a variety of useful lives, which may even be indefinite if the asset is maintained.

IAS NOTE

IAS 38 specifies that intangibles should be amortized over a maximum period of 20 years, except in rare circumstances where a longer period can be justified.

The accounting standards prior to mid-2001 required that all intangibles be amortized over their useful lives, not exceeding 40 years. While this simplified the accounting, the reality is that intangibles are diverse, and the approach to their valuation subsequent to acquisition should be based on their specific characteristics. If an intangible has a finite useful life, it is amortized over that useful life, using a best estimate if it is not know with certainty. If the intangible has an indefinite infinite life and gives no indication of impairment, financial reporting is better served by retaining the asset in the accounts unless the asset is determined to be impaired or its life becomes finite. This reasoning is very persuasive, especially if the asset rights have an observable exchange value above their carrying value.

Illustration 13-3 summarizes the conclusions reached by the CICA Accounting Standards Board in 2001. It replaces the "one size fits all" approach previously applied to intangibles with an approach that takes into account the differing nature of the particular intangibles.

Identifiable Intangibles

Finite life: Many identifiable intangible assets have determinable or finite useful lives, and thus their cost less residual value should be amortized over the period the asset is

---

[8] The *CICA Handbook*, Section 1000, par. .29 defines assets as "economic resources controlled by an entity as a result of past transactions or events and from which future economic benefits may be obtained." Many accountants contend that because deferred charges cannot be considered economic resources, they should not be accorded asset status.

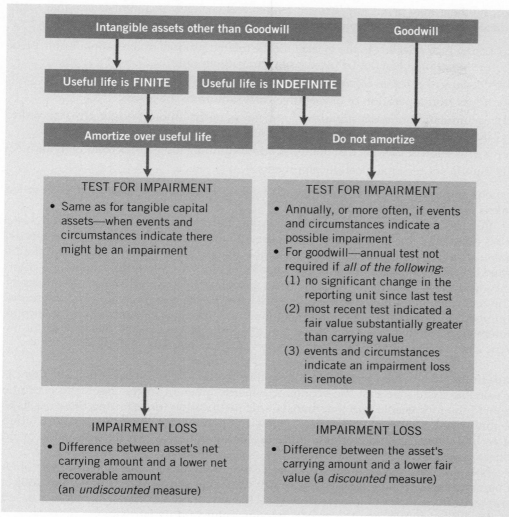

ILLUSTRATION 13-3
Valuation of Intangible Assets
after Acquisition

expected to generate future economic benefits. Uncertainties about **residual values** for intangibles are greater than those for tangible capital assets. Because of this, an intangible asset's residual value is assumed to be zero unless there is a commitment from a third party to purchase the asset in the future, or there is an observable market for the asset and it is expected to exist at the end of its useful life to the enterprise.[9]

Factors to consider in determining useful economic life are similar to those for tangible capital assets:

1. expected future usage of the asset or related asset or other economic factors
2. effects of technological or commercial obsolescence
3. level of maintenance expenditures required to obtain the future benefits

In addition, legal, regulatory, or contractual provisions may either limit an asset's useful life or may provide opportunities to extend its legal or contractual life beyond current provisions. Whether it will be cost-effective to extend the life of the asset must also be considered.[10]

Similar to capital assets, the pattern of recognizing amortization expense should be consistent with the way in which the enterprise benefits from the asset's use. If no specific pattern is reliably discernible, the straight-line method is used.

Also consistent with tangible capital assets that are amortized, intangible assets that are amortized on a regular basis need to be reviewed when events and circumstances

---

[9] *CICA Handbook,* Section 3062, par. .13.

[10] *CICA Handbook,* Section 3062, par. .15.

indicate there may be an impairment. Events and changes in circumstances that might indicate that the asset's carrying amount may not be recoverable include:

(a) a significant decline in the market for the related product or the net realizable value of the intangible asset below the net carrying amount

(b) changes in external legal or economic conditions

(c) a loss from operation of or negative cash flow from the asset

(d) accumulation of costs significantly in excess of the amount originally expected to acquire the asset, or inability to complete the acquisition

(e) a projection or forecast that demonstrates continuing losses associated with the asset

(f) significant technological developments.[11]

If such conditions continue over a period of years, the need for a writedown is assumed unless there is evidence to the contrary.

In performing the review for recoverability, the company estimates the future cash flows expected to result from the asset's use and eventual disposition. If the net recoverable amount (undiscounted) is less than the asset's carrying value, an impairment in value is indicated. The amount of the impairment loss for intangibles subject to amortization is calculated in the same way as described in Chapter 12 for capital assets. Under current standards, it is the difference between the carrying value and the undiscounted net recoverable amount.[12] The impairment loss, is recognized on the income statement before extraordinary items and discontinued operations. No reversal of the write-down is permitted if the recoverable value subsequently increases.

Indefinite life: Some identifiable intangibles have indefinite useful lives. If there is reasonable assurance that the economic benefits inherent in the asset will continue beyond the foreseeable horizon, there is little justification for requiring these assets to be amortized. Therefore, the revised standards require that there be no amortization of an intangible asset with an indefinite useful life until its life is determined to be no longer indefinite.[13]

Non-amortized intangibles should be tested for impairment annually, or more often if circumstances dictate. Unlike the current Canadian standard for intangibles subject to amortization, the test for impairment and the amount of the impairment loss is based on the difference between the asset's carrying value and its fair value.

Goodwill

Accounting for goodwill has been a contentious issue for many years, with support for positions including no recognition as an asset at all, recognition and amortization, and recognition but no amortization.

As indicated in Illustration 13-3, the "maintain asset at cost until impaired" approach to accounting for goodwill is the new Canadian accounting standard. The revised requirements for separating out the specifically identifiable intangibles from goodwill result in a goodwill asset that incorporates few wasting types of intangibles. That is, goodwill is restricted mainly to asset values that are maintainable or renewable on a continuing basis. Consistent with this approach is the need for goodwill to be tested regularly for impairment. When the implied fair value of a reporting unit's goodwill is less than the carrying amount, an impairment loss is recognized. This topic is covered in more detail later in this chapter.

---

[11] *CICA Handbook*, Section 3061, par. .42.

[12] As explained in Chapter 12, the accounting for impairment of such assets is on the agenda of the CICA who are hoping to harmonize the Canadian standard with that of the FASB in 2002. The FASB standard, described in Chapter 12, dictates that although the **test for impairment** is the same comparison of the **undiscounted** net recoverable amount and carrying value, the **write-down** is calculated as the difference between the carrying amount and the asset's fair value, i.e., a **discounted** value.

[13] *CICA Handbook*, Section 3062, par. .10.

SPECIFICALLY IDENTIFIABLE INTANGIBLES

Patents

Patents are granted by the federal government. The two principal kinds of patents are **product patents**, which cover actual physical products, and **process patents**, which govern the process by which products are made. A patent gives the holder exclusive right to use, manufacture, and sell a product or process **for a period of 20 years** from the date of application without interference or infringement by others. Companies such as **Bombardier, IMAX, Polaroid,** and **Xerox** were founded on patents.[14]

OBJECTIVE 4

Identify the types of specifically identifiable intangible assets.

If a patent is purchased from an inventor or other owner, the purchase price represents its cost. Other costs incurred in connection with securing a patent, legal fees, and other unrecovered costs of a successful legal suit to protect the patent can be capitalized as part of the patent cost. Legal fees and other costs associated with a successful defence of a patent are capitalized as part of the asset's cost because such a suit establishes the legal rights of the patent holder. Research and development costs related to **developing** the product, process, or idea that is subsequently patented **are usually expensed as incurred**, however. A more complete presentation of accounting for research and development costs is found later in this chapter.

The cost of a patent should be amortized over its legal life or its useful life (the period during which benefits from the product or process are expected to be received), whichever is shorter. Its residual value is usually assumed to be zero. Assuming that, on average, it requires three years to process a patent application, the life of a patent after the date of grant is only 17 years. If it is owned from the date it is granted and is expected to be useful during its entire remaining legal life, it should be amortized over 17 years. If it appears the patent will be useful for a shorter period of time, say, for five years, its cost should be amortized to expense over five years. A change in demand, new inventions that supersede old ones, inadequacy, and other factors often limit a patent's useful life to less than its legal life.[15]

Ideally, patent amortization should follow a pattern consistent with the benefits received. This could be based on time or on units produced. To illustrate, assume that on January 1, 2002, Harcott Ltd. either pays $180,000 to acquire a patent, or incurs $180,000 in legal costs to successfully defend an internally developed patent. Further, assume the patent has a remaining useful life of 12 years, and is amortized on a straight-line basis. The entries to record the $180,000 expenditure and the amortization at the end of each year are as follows:

January 1, 2002		
Patents	180,000	
Cash		180,000
(To record expenditure related to patent)		

December 31, 2002		
Patent Amortization Expense	15,000	
Accumulated Amortization, Patents		15,000
(To record amortization of patent)		

[14] Consider the opposite result: Sir Alexander Fleming, who discovered penicillin, decided not to use a patent to protect his discovery. He hoped that companies would produce it more quickly to help save sufferers. Companies, however, refused to develop it because they did not have the protection of a patent shield and, therefore, were afraid to make the investment.

[15] For example, the useful life of patents in the pharmaceutical industry is frequently less than the legal life because of the testing and approval period that follows their issuance. A typical drug patent has 5 to 11 years knocked off its 20-year legal life because 1 to 4 years must be spent on animal tests, 4 to 6 years on human tests, and 2 to 3 years for government agencies to review the tests—all after the patent is issued but before the product goes on a pharmacist's shelves.

Amortization on a units-of-production basis is calculated in the same manner as the activity method described for amortization of property, plant, and equipment in Chapter 12.

Although a patent's useful life may be limited by its legal life, small modifications or additions may lead to a new patent. The effect may be to extend the life of the old patent. In that case it is permissible to apply the unamortized costs of the old patent to the new patent if the new patent provides essentially the same benefits. Alternatively, if a patent's value is reduced because demand drops for the product produced, for example, the asset should be tested for impairment. If the patent's net recoverable amount is less than its carrying value, an impairment loss should be recognized. Under 2001 standards, the loss is the difference between the patent's net recoverable amount and its carrying amount.

To illustrate, assume an enterprise has a patent on a process to extract oil from shale rock. Unfortunately, reduced oil prices have made the shale oil technology somewhat unprofitable, and the patent has provided little income to date. As a result, a recoverability test is performed, and it is found that the expected net future cash flows from this patent are $35 million. The patent has a carrying amount of $60 million. Because the net recoverable amount of $35 million is less than the carrying amount of $60 million, an impairment loss must be measured. The impairment loss calculation is shown in Illustration 13-4.[16]

ILLUSTRATION 13-4
Calculation of Loss on Impairment of Patent

Carrying amount of patent	$ 60,000,000
Net recoverable amount	35,000,000
Loss on impairment	$ 25,000,000

The journal entry to record this loss is:

Loss on Impairment	25,000,000	
Accumulated Amortization, Patents		25,000,000

After the impairment is recognized, the patent's reduced carrying amount is its new cost basis. The patent's revised net book value should be amortized over its useful life or legal life, whichever is shorter. If oil prices increase in subsequent periods and the patent's net recoverable amount recovers, **restoration of the previously recognized impairment loss is not permitted**.

Copyrights

A **copyright** is a federally granted right that all authors, painters, musicians, sculptors, and other artists have in their creations and expressions. A copyright is granted for the **life of the creator plus 50 years**, and gives the owner, or heirs, the exclusive right to reproduce and sell an artistic or published work. Copyrights are not renewable. Like patents, they may be assigned or sold to other individuals. The costs of acquiring and defending a copyright may be capitalized, but the research costs involved must be expensed as incurred.

Generally, the copyright's useful life is less than its legal life. Determination of its useful life is unique to the facts and circumstances in each case. Consumer habits, market trends and prior experience all play a part. The difficulty in determining the periods benefiting normally encourages companies to write these costs off over a fairly short period of time. Amortization of the copyright should be charged to the years in which the benefits are expected to be received. If circumstances indicate a carrying amount in excess of the asset's recoverable value, an impairment loss is recognized, and the asset's carrying amount is reduced.

---

[16] As indicated earlier, harmonization of the impairment standard with that of FASB is on the agenda of the CICA. Harmonization would require the loss to be measured as the difference between the asset's fair value (a discounted amount) and its carrying value.

Trademarks and Trade Names

A **trademark** or **trade name** is one or more words, or a series of letters or numbers, or a design or shape that distinguishes or identifies a particular enterprise or product. The right to use a trademark or trade name in Canada is granted by the federal government. In order to obtain and maintain a protected trademark or trade name, the owner must have made prior and continuing use of it. Trade names like Kleenex, Pepsi-Cola, Oldsmobile, Excedrin, Shreddies, and Sunkist create immediate product recognition in our minds, thereby enhancing their marketability. **Company names** themselves identify qualities and characteristics that the companies have worked hard and spent much to develop.[17]

The value of a trademark or trade name can be substantial. Consider Internet domain names as an example. The name **Drugs.com** recently sold for US$800,000, and bidding for the name **Loans.com** approached US$500,000.

If a trademark or trade name is purchased, its capitalizable cost is the purchase price and other direct costs of acquisition. If a trademark or trade name is developed by the enterprise itself and its future benefits to the company are reasonably assured, the capitalizable cost includes lawyers' fees, registration fees, design costs, consulting fees, successful legal defence costs, expenditures related to securing it, direct development costs, and overhead costs directly related to its development. When a trademark or trade name's total cost is insignificant or if future benefits are uncertain, it is expensed rather than capitalized.

Trademark registrations in Canada last for 15 years, and are renewable at a reasonable cost. Although the legal life of a trademark, trade name, or company name in substance may be unlimited, the period over which they provide benefits to the enterprise may be **finite**. In most cases, therefore, the cost is amortized over the estimated useful life.

Trademarks could be determined to provide benefits to an enterprise indefinitely. A trade name such as Coca-Cola may reasonably be determined to have an **indefinite** useful life. In this case, the trade name is not amortized.

Whether amortized or not, the asset's carrying value must be tested for impairment and a loss recognized if appropriate.

INTERNATIONAL INSIGHT

Traditionally, when brand names are included in the acquisition of another company, the value of the brand name has been included in goodwill. In recent years, however, a number of firms in Great Britain and Australia have begun to value brand names separately in their balance sheets. This practice is highly controversial.

Leaseholds

A **leasehold** is a contractual understanding between a lessor (property owner) and a lessee (property renter) that grants the lessee **the right to use specific property, owned by the lessor, for a specific period of time in return for stipulated, and generally periodic, cash payments**. In most cases, the rent is included as an expense on the lessee's books. Special problems, however, develop in the following situations.

Lease Prepayments

If the rent for the lease period is paid in advance, or if a lump sum payment is made in advance in addition to periodic rental payments, it is necessary to allocate this rent to the proper periods. The lessee has purchased the exclusive right to use the property for an extended period of time. These prepayments should be reported as a prepaid expense or deferred charge rather than an identifiable intangible asset.

Leasehold Improvements

Long-term leases ordinarily provide that any **leasehold improvements**—improvements made to the leased property by the lessee—revert to the lessor at the end of the lease.

---

[17] To illustrate how various intangibles might arise from a given product, consider what the creators of the highly successful game, Trivial Pursuit, did to protect their creation. First, they copyrighted the 6,000 questions that are at the heart of the game. Then they shielded the Trivial Pursuit name by applying for a registered trademark. As a third mode of protection, the creators obtained a design patent on the playing board's design because it represents a unique graphic creation.

If the lessee constructs new buildings on leased land or reconstructs and improves existing buildings, **the lessee has the right to use such facilities during the life of the lease, but they become the property of the lessor when the lease expires**.

The lessee should charge the facilities' cost to the Leasehold Improvements account and **amortize the cost as an operating expense over the remaining life of the lease, or the useful life of the improvements, whichever is shorter**. If a building with an estimated useful life of 25 years is constructed on land leased for 35 years, the cost of the building should be amortized over 25 years. On the other hand, if the building has an estimated life of 50 years, the costs should be recognized as expense over 35 years, the life of the lease.

If the lease contains an option to renew for a period of additional years and the likelihood of renewal is too uncertain to warrant apportioning the cost over the longer time period, the leasehold improvements are generally written off over the original term of the lease (assuming that the life of the lease is shorter than the useful life of the improvements). **Leasehold improvements are generally shown in the tangible capital assets section**, although some accountants classify them as intangible assets. The rationale for intangible asset treatment is that the improvements revert to the lessor at the end of the lease and are therefore more of a right than a tangible asset.

Capital Leases

UNDERLYING CONCEPTS

The treatment of leases is an example of the importance of the definition of an asset. The definition does not require ownership but it does require that an asset's benefits flow to and be under the control of the entity.

In some cases, the lease agreement transfers substantially all of the benefits and risks incident to property ownership so that the economic effect on both parties is similar to that of an instalment purchase. As a result, the asset value recognized when a lease is capitalized is classified as a tangible rather than an intangible asset. Such a lease is referred to as a capital lease. Accounting for leases is covered in more detail in Chapter 21.

Franchises and Licences

When you drive down the street in an automobile purchased from a **Toyota** dealer, fill your tank at the corner **Petro-Canada** station, grab a coffee at **Tim Horton's**, eat lunch at **McDonald's**, cool off with a **Baskin-Robbins** cone, work at a **Coca-Cola** bottling plant, live in a home purchased through a **Century 21** real estate broker, or vacation at a **Holiday Inn** resort, you are dealing with franchises. A **franchise** is a contractual arrangement under which the franchisor grants the franchisee the right to sell certain products or services, to use certain trademarks or trade names, or to perform certain functions, usually within a designated geographical area.

The franchisor, having developed a unique concept or product, protects its concept or product through a patent, copyright, trademark, or trade name. The franchisee acquires the right to exploit the franchisor's idea or product by signing a franchise agreement.

Another type of franchise is the arrangement commonly entered into by a municipality (or other governmental body) and a business enterprise that uses public property. In such cases, a privately owned enterprise is permitted to use public property in performing its services. Examples are the use of public waterways for a ferry service, the use of public land for telephone or electric lines, the use of city streets for a bus line, or the use of the airwaves for radio or TV broadcasting. Such operating rights, obtained through agreements with governmental units or agencies, are frequently referred to as licences or **permits**.

Franchises and licences may be granted for a definite period of time, for an indefinite period of time, or in perpetuity. The enterprise securing the franchise or licence recognizes an intangible asset account entitled Franchise or Licence on its books only when there are costs (such as a lump sum payment in advance or legal fees and other expenditures) that are identified with the acquisition of the operating right.

Accounting for the intangible after acquisition depends on the nature of the asset. The cost of a franchise or licence with a limited life should be amortized over the lesser of its legal or useful life. A franchise with an indefinite life, or a perpetual franchise, should be amortized if its useful life to the enterprise is deemed to be limited. Otherwise, it should not be amortized. It should continue to be carried at cost.

Franchises and licences subject to amortization must be reviewed for impairment as events and circumstances warrant. Those not subject to amortization must be reviewed at least annually. If written down, no subsequent recovery in value is permitted to be recognized.

Annual payments made under a franchise agreement should be entered as operating expenses in the period in which they are incurred. They do not represent an asset to the enterprise since they do not relate to future rights.

GOODWILL

Although companies are permitted to capitalize certain costs to develop specifically identifiable assets such as patents and copyrights, the amounts capitalized are generally not significant. Material amounts of intangible assets, however, are recorded when companies purchase intangible assets from others, particularly in situations involving the purchase of another business, referred to for accounting purposes as a business combination. For example, **Nortel Networks Corporation** reported goodwill with a cost of US$3.728 billion on its December 31, 1999 balance sheet. One year later, it reported goodwill of US$22.3 billion!

In a business combination, the cost (purchase price) of the business acquired is assigned or allocated to the identifiable tangible and intangible net assets, and the remainder is recorded in an intangible asset account called goodwill. Goodwill is recorded only when an entire business is purchased as it cannot be separated from the business as a whole. It is defined as the excess of the cost of the acquired entity over the net of the amounts assigned to identifiable assets acquired and liabilities assumed.[18] The only way it can be sold is to sell the business.

> **OBJECTIVE 5**
>
> Explain the conceptual issues related to goodwill.

Recognition of Goodwill

Internally Created Goodwill

Goodwill generated internally should not be capitalized in the accounts, because measuring the components of goodwill is simply too complex and associating any costs with future benefits too difficult. The future benefits of goodwill may have no relationship to the costs incurred in developing that goodwill. To add to the mystery, goodwill may even exist in the absence of specific costs to develop it. In addition, because no objective transaction with outside parties has taken place, a great deal of subjectivity—even misrepresentation—might be involved in trying to measure it.

UNDERLYING CONCEPTS

Capitalizing goodwill only when it is purchased in an arm's-length transaction and not capitalizing any goodwill generated internally is another example of reliability winning out over relevance.

Purchased Goodwill

Goodwill is recognized for accounting purposes only in a business combination. The problem of determining the proper cost to allocate to **identifiable** intangible assets in a business combination is complex because of the many different types of intangibles that might be acquired. Because goodwill is a residual amount, every dollar that is allocated to an identifiable intangible is one less dollar assigned to goodwill. As discussed earlier in the chapter, many intangibles can be identified as providing future economic benefits to an enterprise, but the only intangibles that are separately recognized in the accounts are those where control over the benefits is accomplished through contractual or other legal rights, or the asset can be separated and sold, transferred, licensed, rented or exchanged. All others are recognized as part of goodwill.

To determine the amount of goodwill, the purchase price paid for the acquired business is compared with the fair value of the identifiable net assets acquired. The differ-

---

[18] *CICA Handbook*, Section 1581, par. .06(c).

ence is considered goodwill, which is why goodwill is sometimes referred to as a "plug" or "gap filler" or "master valuation" account. **Goodwill is the residual: the excess of cost over fair value of the identifiable net assets acquired.**

OBJECTIVE 6

Describe the accounting procedures for recording goodwill at acquisition and subsequently.

To illustrate, Multi-Diversified, Inc. decides that it needs a parts division to supplement its existing tractor distributorship. The president of Multi-Diversified is interested in buying a small concern near Toronto (Tractorling Corporation) that has an established reputation and is seeking a merger candidate. The balance sheet of Tractorling Corporation is presented in Illustration 13-5.

ILLUSTRATION 13-5
Tractorling Balance Sheet

TRACTORLING CORPORATION
Balance Sheet
as of December 31, 2000

Assets		Equities	
Cash	$ 25,000	Current liabilities	$ 55,000
Receivables	35,000	Share capital	100,000
Inventories	42,000	Retained earnings	100,000
Property, plant, and equipment, net	153,000		
Total assets	$255,000	Total equities	$255,000

After considerable negotiation, Tractorling Corporation shareholders decide to accept Multi-Diversified's offer of $400,000. What is the value of the goodwill, if any?

The answer is not obvious. The fair values of Tractorling's identifiable assets are not disclosed in its cost-based balance sheet. Suppose, though, that as the negotiations progressed, Multi-Diversified conducted an investigation of Tractorling's underlying assets to determine their fair values. Such an investigation may be accomplished either through a purchase audit undertaken by Multi-Diversified's auditors in order to estimate the values of the seller's assets, or an independent appraisal from some other source. The following valuations are determined.

ILLUSTRATION 13-6
Fair Values of Tractorling's Indentifiable Net Assets

Fair Values	
Cash	$ 25,000
Receivables	35,000
Inventories	122,000
Property, plant, and equipment, net	205,000
Patents	18,000
Liabilities	(55,000)
Fair value of identifiable net assets	$350,000

Normally, differences between current fair value and book value are more common among long-term assets, although significant differences can also develop in the current asset category. Cash obviously poses no problems, and receivables normally are fairly close to current valuation, although at times certain adjustments need to be made because of inadequate bad debt provisions. The fair values of liabilities usually are relatively close to recorded book values. However, if interest rates have changed since long-term liabilities were incurred, their current value, determined using current interest rates, may differ substantially from book value. Careful analysis must be made to determine that no unrecorded liabilities are present.

The $80,000 difference between the cost and fair value of inventories ($122,000 − $42,000) could result from a number of factors. One explanation might be that Tractorling uses a LIFO cost valuation. Recall that during periods of inflation, LIFO better matches expenses against revenues, but in doing so creates a balance sheet distortion. Ending inventory is composed of older layers at lower costs.

In many cases, the values of long-lived assets such as property, plant, and equipment, and intangibles may have increased substantially over the years. This difference could be due to inaccurate estimates of useful lives, a policy of continual expensing of small expenditures (say, less than $1,000), inaccurate estimates of residual values, the recognition of some unrecorded assets, or substantial increases in replacement costs. In Tractorling's case, internally developed patents had not been recognized in the accounts, yet they have a fair value of $18,000.

Since the fair value of net assets is determined to be $350,000, why would Multi-Diversified pay $400,000? Undoubtedly, the seller points to an established reputation, good credit rating, top management team, well-trained employees, and so on, as factors that make the business value greater than $350,000. At the same time, Multi-Diversified places a premium on the future earning power of these attributes as well as the enterprise's basic asset structure today. At this point in the negotiations, price can be a function of many factors; the most important is probably sheer skill at the bargaining table.[19]

The difference between the purchase price of $400,000 and the fair value of the identifiable net assets of $350,000 is labelled goodwill. Goodwill is viewed as one or a group of unidentifiable values plus the value of the identifiable intangibles that don't meet the criteria for separate recognition. The cost assigned to goodwill is the difference between the cost to the purchaser of the business as a whole and the costs assigned to the identifiable net assets acquired. This procedure for valuation, shown in Illustration 13-7, is referred to as a **master valuation approach**, because goodwill is assumed to cover all the values that cannot be specifically identified with any identifiable tangible or intangible asset.

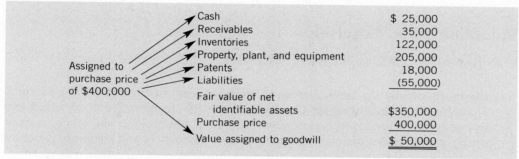

	Cash	$ 25,000
	Receivables	35,000
	Inventories	122,000
Assigned to	Property, plant, and equipment	205,000
purchase price	Patents	18,000
of $400,000	Liabilities	(55,000)
	Fair value of net	
	identifiable assets	$350,000
	Purchase price	400,000
	Value assigned to goodwill	$ 50,000

ILLUSTRATION 13-7
Determination of Goodwill-Master Valuation Approach

The entry to record the purchase of the net assets of Tractorling is as follows:[20]

Cash	25,000	
Receivables	35,000	
Inventories	122,000	
Property, plant, and equipment	205,000	
Patents	18,000	
Goodwill	50,000	
Liabilities		55,000
Cash		400,000

Goodwill is sometimes identified on the balance sheet as the **excess of cost over the fair value** of the net assets acquired.

---

[19] Sometimes the excess paid is a function of the purchaser's stubborness or ego; i.e. wanting the business at any price. In this situation, the price paid in excess of the business' fair value should be recognized as a loss.

[20] If Multi-Diversified purchased all of Tractorling's shares instead of the net assets directly, the entry would be:

Investment in Shares of Tractorling	400,000	
Cash		400,000

When Multi-Diversified prepares consolidated financial statements, the Investment account is removed from the balance sheet and is replaced with the underlying assets and liabilities it represents. Regardless of the transaction's legal form, the goodwill appears on its balance sheet.

IAS NOTE

Under IAS 22, negative goodwill due to expected future losses or expenses is deferred and recognized in income when the losses or expenses are recognized; amounts up to the fair value of the identifiable assets are recognized over the life of those assets; any excess is recognized in income immediately.

Negative Goodwill—Badwill

Negative goodwill, often appropriately dubbed badwill, or bargain purchase, **arises when the fair value of the net identifiable assets acquired is higher than the purchase price of the acquired entity**. This situation is a result of market imperfection because the seller would be better off to sell the assets individually than in total. Situations do occur in which the purchase price is less than the value of the net identifiable assets and therefore a credit develops; this credit is referred to as negative goodwill or **excess of acquired net assets over cost**.

How should this resulting credit be handled in the accounts? Should it be taken to retained earnings directly, to the income statement in the year of purchase, or amortized to income over a reasonable future period? New *CICA Handbook* Section 1581 recommends that the excess be used to reduce the amounts assigned to other acquired assets. If their values are reduced to zero and some of the excess still remains, the excess amount should be treated as an extraordinary gain.

The accounting standard specifies which of the acquired assets should have their fair values adjusted. Because it is not reasonable to arbitrarily reduce assets valued at their realizable values, the recommendation is to reduce, on a pro rata basis, amounts that would otherwise be assigned to all non-current assets acquired **except** financial assets other than equity method investments, assets to be disposed of by sale, future tax assets, and prepaid assets relating to employee future benefit plans.[21]

Valuation after Acquisition

Once goodwill has been recognized in the accounts, how should it be treated in subsequent periods? Three basic approaches have been suggested.

INTERNATIONAL INSIGHT

Until recently, companies in the UK were allowed to write off goodwill immediately against equity. In 1998, UK companies were required to capitalize and amortize goodwill. This change in goodwill accounting is an example of international accounting harmonization.

1. **Charge goodwill off immediately to shareholders' equity.** *Accounting Research Study No. 10,* "Accounting for Goodwill," takes the position that goodwill differs from other types of assets and demands special attention.[22] Unlike other assets, it is not separable and distinct from the business as a whole and therefore is not an asset in the same sense as cash, receivables, or plant assets. In other words, goodwill cannot be sold without selling the business.

   Furthermore, say proponents of this approach, the accounting treatment for purchased goodwill and goodwill internally created should be consistent. Goodwill created internally is immediately expensed and does not appear as an asset: the same treatment should be accorded purchased goodwill. Amortization of purchased goodwill leads to double counting, because net income is reduced by amortization of the purchased goodwill as well as by the internal expenditure made to maintain or enhance the value of assets.

   Perhaps the best rationale for direct write-off is that determining the periods over which the future benefits are to be received is so difficult that immediate charging to shareholders' equity is justified.

2. **Amortize goodwill over its useful life.** Others believe that goodwill has value when acquired, but that its value eventually disappears and it is proper that the asset be charged to expense over the periods affected. Supporters of this view contend that to the extent goodwill represents wasting assets, this method provides a better matching of costs and revenues than other methods, even though the useful life may be difficult to determine.

3. **Retain goodwill indefinitely unless reduction in value occurs.** Many believe that goodwill can have an indefinite life and should be retained as an asset until a

IAS NOTE

The international standard is to amortize goodwill over its useful life to a maximum of 20 years, unless a longer period can be justified. The straight-line method is recommended unless there is persuasive evidence of a more suitable method.

---

21 *CICA Handbook*, Section 1581, par. .50.

22 George R. Catlett and Norman O. Olsen, "Accounting for Goodwill," *Accounting Research Study No. 10*, (New York: AICPA, 1968), pp. 89-95.

decline in value occurs. They contend that some form of goodwill should always be an asset inasmuch as internal goodwill is being expensed to maintain or enhance the purchased goodwill. In addition, without sufficient evidence that a decline in value has occurred, a write-off of goodwill is both arbitrary and capricious and leads to distortions in net income.

This is an issue that has been difficult to resolve. Immediate write-off is not considered proper, because it leads to the untenable conclusion that goodwill has no future service potential. The established standard for many years in Canada and the United States was to amortize goodwill over its useful life, not exceeding 40 years. Because goodwill amortization directly affects the amount of income reported, many companies either spread the often significant goodwill cost over very long periods of time, or alternatively, wrote it off very quickly in order to eliminate the recurring effect on reported results. When the accounting standard for business combinations came up for revision in 1999, both the CICA and FASB began with a position of requiring amortization of the resulting goodwill over a period not exceeding 20 years, consistent with the international standard.

Both the CICA and FASB 1999 *Exposure Drafts*, however, also introduced the requirement for non-amortization of an identifiable intangible asset with an indefinite useful life. *Exposure Draft* respondents saw the similarities between identifiable intangibles with indefinite lives and goodwill, especially goodwill whose value is maintained. After due process, the standard setters in both countries ultimately agreed on a policy of not amortizing goodwill under any circumstance. Instead, the carrying amount of goodwill is reduced only if it is found to be impaired, or is associated with assets to be sold or otherwise disposed of. Further justification for this position was provided by the requirement that identifiable intangibles be separately recorded, leaving the non-wasting type of intangibles making up most of recognized goodwill.

Impairment of Goodwill

With no amortization of goodwill, the onus is on management to ensure the carrying value of this intangible asset is tested for impairment. When should goodwill be tested for impairment, what might indicate that recognized goodwill is impaired, and how do you determine the amount of the impairment loss?

When to Test for Impairment

Because of the significance of purchased goodwill, it is important to stipulate when impairment tests should be carried out. If circumstances indicate that an impairment loss is remote, the reporting unit's assets and liabilities have not changed considerably over the period, and the estimated value of goodwill in the last assessment was substantial relative to its carrying value, full impairment tests are not required. Otherwise, the accounting standard requires an assessment on an annual basis (although this need not be at the end of the fiscal period) and on an interim basis if events or circumstances occur between the annual reviews that indicate it is more likely than not that there has been an impairment.

A variety of events or circumstances might indicate that goodwill should be tested for impairment between regular annual reviews. Such factors generally flag the potential for a decline in the fair value of a reporting unit and, therefore, to a reduction in the residual that is goodwill. Examples include either continuing past or projected operating or cash flow losses, adverse changes in variables supporting past determinations of fair value, and an other-than-temporary decline in the market capitalization of the reporting unit, to the extent this information is available.

Impairment Test and Determination of Loss

Testing the goodwill of each reporting unit making up an enterprise for impairment is a more complex process than testing an identifiable asset, because goodwill can only be valued in connection with a business as a whole. One issue is the need to identify the business unit that should be used for this test. If a company merges with or acquires other businesses, the groups of net assets acquired often lose their identities as separate entities. How, then, do you calculate a current value for the business, its net identifiable assets, and therefore goodwill?

This question has been resolved by requiring all purchased goodwill to be assigned to a specific **reporting unit** at the date of acquisition.[23] If the reporting unit's fair value is less than its carrying value including the goodwill, an impairment of goodwill is indicated. This is the first step. The second step requires a calculation of the impairment loss. The amount of the impairment loss is determined by comparing the current implied value of goodwill with its carrying value on the books.

The current implied value of the reporting unit's goodwill is calculated the same way as the original calculation of goodwill: its implied fair value is the excess of the fair value of the reporting unit over and above the fair value of the unit's net identifiable assets. The residual is the implied fair value of the goodwill.

A goodwill impairment loss is recognized when the implied fair value as calculated is less than the carrying amount of goodwill. The adjusted carrying amount becomes the new cost basis and no subsequent increase in value is recognized. The impairment loss is reported separately on the income statement before extraordinary items and discontinued operations.[24]

To illustrate the calculation of an impairment loss, assume that Koberg Corporation has three divisions in its company. One division, Pritt Products, was purchased two years ago for $2 million and has been identified as a reporting unit. Unfortunately, it has experienced operating losses over the last three quarters and management is reviewing the reporting unit to determine whether there has been an impairment of goodwill. The **carrying amounts** of Pritt Division's net assets including the associated goodwill of $800,000 are listed in Illustration 13-8.

ILLUSTRATION 13-8
Pritt Reporting Unit-Net Assets

Cash	$ 200,000
Receivables	300,000
Inventory	400,000
Property, plant, and equipment (net)	1,200,000
Goodwill	800,000
Less: Accounts and notes payable	(500,000)
Net assets, at carrying amounts	$2,400,000

The **fair value** of the reporting unit as a whole is estimated to be $2,150,000, the present value of the expected future net cash flows. The test for impairment indicates that an impairment exists because the unit's fair value is less than its carrying value including goodwill.

The impairment loss, assuming the net identifiable assets' current fair value is $1,650,000, is calculated as follows:

ILLUSTRATION 13-9
Calculation of Impairment Loss on Pritt Division

Fair value of Pritt Division	$2,150,000
Fair value of Pritt Division's recognized net Identifiable assets (assumed)	1,650,000
Implied fair value of goodwill	500,000
Carrying amount of goodwill	800,000
Impairment loss, goodwill	$(300,000)

---

[23] Section 3062 defines a reporting unit as the same level or one level below an operating segment as defined in *CICA Handbook* Section 1701 on "Segment Disclosures."

[24] *CICA Handbook*, Section 3062, par. .49. However, if the impairment loss is associated with a discontinued operation, it should be reported net-of-tax within the discontinued operation section.

The entry to record the impairment is:

Loss on Impairment of Goodwill	300,000	
Goodwill		300,000

Note that there does not appear to be any impairment of the identifiable net assets. The carrying amount of the net assets without reported goodwill is $1.6 million (that is, $2.4 million net assets less the $800,000 carrying value of goodwill). The fair value of the same net assets without goodwill is $1,650,000. Management must also be alert for the impairment of other intangible and tangible capital assets.

INTELLECTUAL CAPITAL

During the 1990s, there was increased criticism about the inability of the conventional financial accounting model to capture many of the aspects that give a business value. In November 1997, for example, **Microsoft** had a total book value of US$10.8 billion, but its market capitalization (i.e., the market value of its outstanding shares) was US$166.5 billion! Why such a significant difference?

The answer is that financial accounting is not able to capture and report many of the assets that contribute to future cash flows, and this is seen by some as the greatest challenge facing the accounting profession today. Many of the missing values belong to unrecognized, internally developed intangible assets known as knowledge assets or intellectual capital. These include the value of key personnel—not only Bill Gates, but the many creative and technologically proficient personnel in general, investment in and the potential for products from research and development, organizational adaptability, customer retention, strategic direction, flexible and innovative management, customer service capability, and effective advertising programs, to name some.

Our conventional financial accounting model, for the most part, captures the results of past transactions. This has been considered a very significant benefit in the past as it is responsible for the verifiability of the reported measures and hence the reliability of the financial statements. In most cases, the intellectual capital and knowledge assets identified above are not measurable in financial terms with sufficient reliability to give them accounting recognition. Some cannot be included as assets because of the enterprise's inability to control access to the benefits. Investments made in employee education and development, for example, walk out the door when employees leave the company to work elsewhere.

These indicators of longer term value that has been created in an organization will ultimately result in realized values through future transactions and, therefore, is relevant information for financial statement readers. Companies increasingly disclose more of this "soft" information in annual reports outside of the financial statements, in news releases and interviews with market analysts. While some believe that standard setters should work to ensure more of these intangibles are captured on the balance sheet, others believe that new performance reporting frameworks need to be developed in conjunction with, or even to displace, the existing financial reporting model. Much research is being carried out in the search for solutions to the discrepancies between what gets reported as having value on the financial statements and what the capital markets perceive as value in share prices.[25]

---

[25] The decline in market value of technology shares in particular, from summer 2000 to summer 2001 when Nortel lost 90% of its value, supports the arguments of many that the historical cost model still has much to recommend it!

DEFERRED CHARGES AND LONG-TERM PREPAYMENTS

Deferred charges is a classification often used to describe a number of different items that have debit balances, including certain types of intangibles. Intangibles sometimes classified as deferred charges include deferred development costs, pre-operating and start-up costs, and organization costs.

Deferred charges also includes such items as debt discount and issue costs as well as long-term prepayments for insurance, rent, taxes, and other down payments. The deferred charge classification probably should be abolished because it cannot be clearly differentiated from other amortizable assets (which are also deferred costs), and a more informative disclosure could be made of the smaller items often found in this section of the balance sheet. Such a classification has even less relevance today because the conceptual framework in *Handbook* Section 1000 establishes a definition for assets that seems to exclude deferred charges.

Although there are far fewer deferred charges recognized on the balance sheet than in the past, *Handbook* Section 3070 still requires separate disclosure of deferred charges as well as the amount charged for amortization of this asset type.[26]

Research and Development Costs

OBJECTIVE 7

Differentiate between research and development expenditures and describe and explain the rationale for the accounting for each.

Research and development (R & D) costs are not in themselves intangible assets. The accounting for R & D costs is presented here, however, for two reasons. The first is because research and development activities are often significant and they frequently result in the development of something that is eventually patented or copyrighted. Examples include a new product, process, idea, formula, composition, or literary work. In addition, some development costs are capitalized as deferred charges, a type of intangible asset.

Many businesses spend considerable sums of money on research and development to create new products or processes, to improve present products, and to discover new knowledge that may be valuable at some future date. The following schedule shows the outlays for R & D reported by selected Canadian companies in 2000:

ILLUSTRATION 13-10
R & D Expenditures, as a Percentage of Revenue and Net Income

Company	R&D Expenditures	% of Revenue	% of Net Income
Nortel Networks Corp.	U.S. $3,839 million	12.7	(129.8)
Mitel Corporation	$152.9 million	10.9	273.0
Research in Motion Ltd.	U.S. $7,738 thousands	9.1	73.7
Alcan Inc.	U.S. $81 million	0.9	13.1
Bombardier Inc.	$123.4 million	0.8	12.7
MOSAID Technologies Inc.	$18,450 thousand	39.2	969.0
Ridley Inc.	$2,670 thousand	0.5	41.7

INTERNATIONAL INSIGHT

Contrary to practice in Canada and most other nations (The Netherlands and Japan, for example), in the U.S., all research and development costs are required to be expensed.

The difficulties in accounting for these research and development expenditures are (1) identifying the costs associated with particular activities, projects, or achievements and (2) determining the magnitude of the future benefits and length of time over which such benefits may be realized. Because of these latter uncertainties, the accounting profession, through *CICA Handbook* Section 3450, has standardized and simplified accounting practice in this area by requiring that **all research costs be charged to expense when incurred. Development costs should also be expensed when incurred except in certain narrowly defined circumstances**.

---

[26] *Financial Reporting in Canada, 2000*, Clarence Byrd, Ida Chen and Heather Chapman, CICA, 2000 reported that 54.5% of the companies surveyed in 1999 made reference to a Deferred Charges category on their balance sheets.

Identifying R & D Activities

To differentiate research and development costs from each other and from similar costs, the CICA adopted the following definitions.

> **Research** is planned investigation undertaken with the hope of gaining new scientific or technical knowledge and understanding. Such investigation may or may not be directed toward a specific practical aim or application.
>
> **Development** is the translation of research findings or other knowledge into a plan or design for new or substantially improved materials, devices, products, processes, systems, or services prior to the commencement of commercial production or use.[27]

Examples of each are provided in Illustration 13-11.[28]

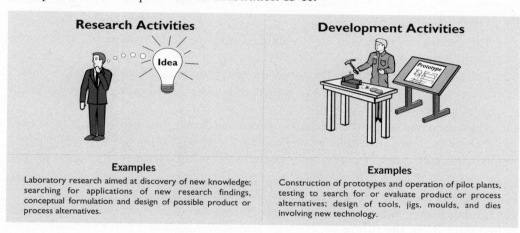

Research Activities

Idea

Development Activities

Prototype

Examples

Laboratory research aimed at discovery of new knowledge; searching for applications of new research findings, conceptual formulation and design of possible product or process alternatives.

Examples

Construction of prototypes and operation of pilot plants, testing to search for or evaluate product or process alternatives; design of tools, jigs, moulds, and dies involving new technology.

ILLUSTRATION 13-11
Examples of Research and Development Activities

It should be emphasized that R & D activities do not include routine or periodic alterations to existing products, production lines, manufacturing processes, and other ongoing operations, even though these alterations may represent improvements. Routine ongoing efforts to refine, enrich, or improve the qualities of an existing product are not considered R & D activities. They also do not include expenditures related to engineering follow-through, quality control, or trouble-shooting during any part of the commercial production phase, nor routine or promotional market research activities.

A special problem arises in distinguishing R & D costs from selling and administrative activities. Research and development costs may include expenditures associated with any product or process regardless of whether they are related to production, marketing, or administrative activities. For example, the costs of software incurred by an airline in acquiring, developing, or improving its computerized reservation system or for development of a general management information system would be considered development costs.

Accounting for R & D Activities

The costs associated with R & D activities are as follows:[29]

1. materials and services consumed
2. direct costs of personnel such as salaries, wages, payroll taxes, and other related costs
3. amortization of equipment and facilities used in R & D activities
4. amortization of intangibles related to R & D activities
5. a reasonable allocation of overhead

---

[27] *CICA Handbook*, Section 3450, par. .02.

[28] *Ibid.*, pars. .04–.05.

[29] *Ibid.*, par. .13.

Consistent with (3) above, if an enterprise conducts R & D activities using its own research facility consisting of buildings, laboratories, and equipment that has alternative future uses (in other R & D projects or otherwise), the facility should be accounted for as a capitalized operational asset. The amortization and other costs related to such research facilities are accounted for as R & D expenses.

Sometimes enterprises conduct R & D activities for other entities **under a contractual arrangement**. In this case, the contract usually specifies that all direct costs, certain specific indirect costs, plus a profit element should be reimbursed to the enterprise performing the R & D work. Because reimbursement is expected, such R & D costs should be recorded as a receivable. It is the company for whom the work has been performed that reports these costs as R & D activities.

As previously emphasized, Canadian firms must write off *research costs* incurred as expenses of the period. *Development costs* must be expensed as well, except when **all of the following criteria** are met.

1. The product or process is clearly defined and the costs attributable to it can be identified.
2. The technical feasibility of the product or process has been established.
3. The enterprise management has indicated its intention to produce and market or use the product or process.
4. The future market for the product or process is clearly defined or, if it is to be used internally rather than sold, its usefulness to the enterprise has been established.
5. Adequate resources exist or are expected to be available to complete the project.

Furthermore, the total amount of development costs deferred must be limited to the extent that their recovery can reasonably be regarded as assured.[30]

Having to meet all five criteria indicates that deferral of development costs is permitted **only when the future benefits are reasonably certain**. Costs expensed in previous periods before the criteria were met should not be restated as assets, nor should amounts be deferred that are greater than the amount expected to be recovered from the sale or use of the product or process. The deferred development costs are subsequently amortized to expense, preferably on a basis related to the sale or use of the underlying product or process. Consistent with other intangibles, the unamortized development costs must be reviewed for impairment.

To illustrate the identification of R & D activities and the accounting treatment of related costs, assume an enterprise develops, produces, and markets laser machines for medical, industrial, and defence uses. The types of expenditures related to its laser machine activities, along with the recommended accounting treatment, are listed in Illustration 13-12.

IAS NOTE

International accounting standards also identify certain circumstances that justify the capitalization and deferral of appropriate development costs.

UNDERLYING CONCEPTS

The requirement that all research and most development costs be expensed as incurred is an example of the conflict between relevance and reliability, with this requirement leaning strongly in support of reliability and comparability. The matching of costs with revenues is not as important as ensuring assets are not overstated.

ILLUSTRATION 13-12
Sample R & D Expenditures and their Accounting Treatment

Type of Expenditure	Accounting Treatment
1. Construction of long-range research facility (three-storey, 100,000 m² building) for use in current and future projects.	Capitalize and amortize as R & D expense. *DR: Building (the amortization of R & D)*
2. Acquisition of R & D equipment for use on current project only.	Capitalize and amortize as R & D expense. *DR: Equipment*
3. Purchase of materials to be used on current and future R & D projects.	Inventory and allocate to R & D projects as consumed.
4. Salaries of research staff designing new laser bone scanner.	Expense immediately as research.
5. Research costs incurred under contract for customer and billable monthly.	Expense as operating expense in period of related revenue recognition.
6. Material, labour, and overhead costs of prototype laser scanner.	Capitalize as development cost if all criteria are met, otherwise expense.
7. Costs of testing prototype and design modifications.	Capitalize as development cost if all criteria are met, otherwise expense.

---

[30] *Ibid.*, pars. .21 and .23.

8. Legal fees to obtain patent on new laser scanner.	Capitalize as patent and amortize to cost of goods manufactured as used.
9. Executive salaries.	Expense as operating expense (general and administrative).
10. Cost of marketing research related to promotion of new laser scanner.	Expense as operating expense (selling).
11. Engineering costs incurred to advance the laser scanner to full production stage.	Capitalize as development cost if all criteria are met, otherwise expense.
12. Costs of successfully defending patent on laser scanner.	Capitalize as patent and amortize to cost of goods manufactured as used.
13. Commissions to sales staff marketing new laser scanner.	Expense as operating expense (selling).

Acceptable accounting practice requires that disclosure be made in the financial statements of the total R & D costs charged to expense in each period for which an income statement is presented. Because income tax incentives are associated with this type of activity, it is common for companies to disclose their R & D expenses net of tax recoveries, either on the face of the income statement or in the notes to the financial statements. The following excerpts from the financial statements of **MOSAID Technologies Incorporated** for the year ended April 28, 2000 provide a good example of such disclosures.

ILLUSTRATION 13-13
R & D Disclosures

MOSAID Technologies Incorporated

NOTES TO THE CONSOLIDATED FINANCIAL STATEMENTS
year ended April 28, 2000 (tabular dollar amounts in thousands, except per share amounts)

I. ACCOUNTING POLICIES

Research and development

Research costs are expensed as incurred. Development costs are deferred once technical feasibility has been established and all criteria for deferral under general accepted accounting principles have been met. Such costs are amortized commencing when the product is released over the expected life of the product. To date, no development costs have met the criteria for deferral.

Government assistance and investment tax credits

Government assistance and investment tax credits are recorded as a reduction of the related expense or cost of the asset acquired. The benefits are recognized when the Company has complied with the terms and conditions of the approved grant program or applicable tax legislation.

9. RESEARCH AND DEVELOPMENT

Investment tax credits and government grants were applied to reduce current research and development expenses in the statements of earnings and retained earnings as summarized below.

	2000	1999
Total current research and development	$ 23,517	$ 14,819
Less: Investment tax credits	(928)	(726)
Government grants	(4,139)	(1,181)
Net research and development	$ 18,450	$ 12,912

As part of a Research and Development Contribution Agreement between the Company and the Government of Canada, the Government agreed to contribute up to $6.2 million toward research and development work. The terms of the agreement call for repayment of the contributed amounts through royalties based on the eventual commercial use of the technology.

Go to the Digital Tool for additional disclosures of R & D costs.

Costs of research and development activities unique to companies in the **extractive industries** (prospecting, acquisition of mineral rights, exploration, drilling, mining, and related mineral development) and those costs discussed above that are similar to, but not classified as, R & D may be (1) expensed as incurred; (2) capitalized and amortized over an appropriate period of time; or (3) accumulated as part of inventoriable costs. Choice of the appropriate accounting treatment for such costs should be guided by the degree of certainty of future benefits and the principle of matching expenses with revenue.

An example of reported explorati.on and development costs for an extractive industry company is shown below as excerpted from the 2000 annual report of **Noranda Inc.**

ILLUSTRATION 13-14
Exploration and Development
Cost Disclosures

Noranda Inc.
Notes to the Consolidated Financial Statements

($millions except as otherwise indicated) December 31, 2000

ACCOUNTING POLICIES
Preproduction Costs
Preproduction costs related to major projects are deferred until the facilities achieve commercial
production or are deemed to be uneconomic. These deferred costs are amortized on a unit-of-
production method over the estimated useful life of the project or are written off when the project
is determined to be uneconomic.

Exploration
Mining exploration expenditures are charged against current earnings unless they relate to
properties from which a productive result is reasonably certain. Gains on sales of mining
exploration properties or recoveries of costs previously written off are credited against exploration
expense.

3. CAPITAL ASSETS
As at December 31

						2000	
	Aluminum	Copper and Recycling	Falconbridge Copper	Falconbridge Nickel	Zinc	Corporate and Other	Total
Property, plant and equipment at cost	$1,580	1,350	2,643	2,303	1,557	758	$10,191
Accumulated depreciation	(995)	(665)	(1,106)	(1,180)	(800)	(456)	(5,202)
	585	685	1,537	1,123	757	302	4,989
Deferred preproduction, development and exploration (net)	–	4	585	445	119	132	1,285
Projects under development	295	29	–	–	8	1,578	1,910
	$880	718	2,122	1,568	884	2,012	$8,184

OBJECTIVE 8

Identify other examples of
deferred charges and the
accounting requirements
for them.

Pre-operating Costs

Companies that are in the development stage face numerous questions about what costs
should be expensed and which should be capitalized. The general principle is that the
type of expenditure not the **enterprise's stage of development**, dictates the accounting treatment. Standards exist for tangible capital assets, intangible assets, and research
and development activities, and these standards should be followed regardless of the
maturity of the business. Revenues and expenditures in the pre-operating period,
however, are a separate issue.

Pre-operating costs are costs incurred by an entity during the pre-operating period
of a new facility or business for such purposes as employee training and relocation,
promotional activities, and the use of materials and supplies. A company may realize
small amounts of revenue during this period as well. To what extent should such costs
that are not part of the cost of a capital asset be deferred?

The Emerging Issues Committee of the CICA, in *EIC-27*, agreed that an expenditure incurred during the pre-operating period could be deferred if the following three
criteria are all met.

1. It relates directly to placing the new business into service.
2. It is incremental in nature, and would not have been incurred in the absence of
the new business.
3. It is probable that the expenditure is recoverable from the future operations of the
new business.[31]

The pre-operating period is the period prior to when the new business is ready to commence commercial operations (i.e., is capable of consistently providing its intended

---

[31] EIC-27, "Revenues and Expenditures During the Pre-Operating Period," CICA.

product or service.) This period will differ depending on circumstances and the industry involved, and should be predefined by management in terms of the activity level attained or the time period passed.

When the pre-operating period is over, the deferral of expenditures and any offsetting revenues should cease, and the amortization of the deferred charges should begin. The amortization should be based on the pattern of benefits received and the expected period of benefit. A five-year period is assumed to be the likely maximum period for amortization.[32]

To illustrate the type of costs that are permitted to be deferred as pre-operating costs, assume that Canadian-based Hilo Beverage Inc. decides to construct a new plant in Brazil. This represents Hilo's first entry into the Brazilian market. As part of its overall strategy, Hilo plans to introduce the company's major Canadian brands into Brazil, on a locally produced basis. Following are some of the pre-operating costs that might be involved with these start-up activities.

1. Travel-related costs, costs related to employee salaries, and costs related to feasibility studies, accounting, tax, and government affairs.
2. Training of local employees related to product, maintenance, computer systems, finance, and operations.
3. Recruiting, organizing, and training related to establishing a distribution network.

All of these costs meet the three criteria imposed and are incurred during the predetermined pre-operating period. They therefore qualify for deferral.

It is not uncommon for development activities to occur at the same time as other activities, such as the acquisition or development of assets. For example, property, plant, and equipment for Hilo's new plant should be capitalized and a careful analysis of costs during the pre-operating is needed to ensure all capital asset costs are appropriately accounted for. The capital assets as well as the deferred charges are reported on the balance sheet and charged to operations as appropriate under GAAP.

Initial Operating Losses

Some contend that initial operating losses incurred in a business start-up should be capitalized, since they are unavoidable and are a cost of starting a business. For example, assume that Hilo lost money in its first year of operations and wished to capitalize this loss arguing that as the company becomes profitable, it will offset these losses in future periods. What do you think? Deferring losses after commercial operations have begun is unsound. Losses have no future service potential and therefore cannot be considered an asset.

This position is supported by the CICA's *Accounting Guideline*—11, "Enterprises in the Development Stage," that clarifies the accounting and reporting practices for **development stage enterprises**. The *Guideline* concludes that the accounting practices and reporting standards should not be a function of an entity's maturity, but rather they should be a function of the type of transaction.

Organization Costs

Deferred costs include organization costs. These are costs incurred in the formation of a corporation, such as fees to underwriters (investment bankers) for handling issues of shares or bonds, legal fees, provincial or federal fees of various sorts, and promotional expenditures involving the organization of a business.

These items are usually charged to an account called Organization Costs and may be carried as an asset on the balance sheet as expenditures that will benefit the company over its life. If recognized as a deferred charge, the costs are amortized over an arbitrary period of time, since the corporation's life is indeterminable. However, the amortization period is frequently short (perhaps 5 to 10 years) because the amounts tend

---

[32] *Ibid.*

not to be significant or because it is assumed that the early years benefit most from these expenditures.

Advertising Costs

Recently, **PepsiCo** hired supermodel Cindy Crawford to advertise some of its products. How should these advertising costs related to Cindy Crawford be reported? These costs could be expensed at a variety of times:

1. When she has completed her acting assignment.
2. The first time the advertising takes place.
3. Over the estimated useful life of the advertising.
4. In an appropriate fashion to each of the three periods identified above.
5. Over the period revenues are expected to result.

Because there is no specific Canadian standard on advertising costs, the U.S. standard tends to be applied. This holds that future benefits from advertising generally are not sufficiently defined or measurable with a degree of reliability that is required to recognize these costs as an asset. **As a result, for the most part, advertising costs must be expensed as incurred or the first time the advertising takes place.** These two alternatives are permitted because whichever approach is followed, the results are essentially the same. Tangible assets used in advertising, such as billboards or blimps, are recorded as assets because they do have alternative future uses. Again, the profession has taken a conservative approach to recording advertising costs because identifying and measuring the future benefits is so difficult.[33]

Conceptual Questions

The requirement that most costs mentioned above should be expensed immediately is a conservative, practical solution that ensures consistency in practice and uniformity among companies. But the practice of immediately writing off expenditures made in the expectation of benefiting future periods cannot be justified on the grounds that it is good accounting theory.

Defendants of immediate expensing contend that from an income statement standpoint, long-run application of these standards usually makes little difference. They contend, for example, that the amount of R & D cost charged to expense each accounting period would be about the same whether there is immediate expensing or capitalization and subsequent amortization because of the ongoing nature of most companies' R & D activities. Critics argue that the balance sheet should report an intangible asset related to expenditures that have future benefit. To preclude capitalization of all R & D and similar expenditures removes from the balance sheet what may be a company's most valuable assets. These decisions represent some of the many trade-offs made between relevance and reliability, and cost-benefit considerations.[34]

---

[33] "Reporting on Advertising Costs," *Statement of Position 93-7*, (New York: AICPA, 1993). Note that there are some exceptions for immediate expensing of advertising costs when they relate to direct-response advertising, but this subject is beyond the scope of this text.

[34] Recent research suggests that capitalizing research and development costs may be helpful to investors. For example, one study showed that a significant relationship exists between R & D outlays and subsequent benefits in the form of increased productivity, earnings, and shareholder value for R & D-intensive companies. Baruch Lev and Theodore Sougiannis, "The Capitalization, Amortization, and Value-Relevance of R & D," *Journal of Accounting and Economics*, February 1996. In another study, it was found that there was a significant decline in earnings usefulness for companies that were forced to switch from capitalizing to expensing R & D costs and that the decline appears to persist over time. Martha L. Loudder and Bruce K. Behn, "Alternative Income Determination Rules and Earnings Usefulness: The Case of R & D Costs," *Contemporary Accounting Research*, Fall 1995.

FINANCIAL STATEMENT DISCLOSURE AND PRESENTATION

A recent survey indicates a trend toward more disclosure of intangibles other than goodwill, with the following typically being disclosed: broadcast rights, publishing rights, trademarks, patents, licences, customer lists, non-competition agreements, franchise and purchased R & D.[35]

OBJECTIVE 9
••••••••••••••••••••••••••

Identify the disclosure requirements for intangibles, including deferred charges.

Balance Sheet

On the balance sheet, goodwill is the only intangible requiring separate, single line item disclosure. Details of the changes in the carrying amount of goodwill on the balance sheet are also required. This includes goodwill acquired, writedowns due to impairment, and goodwill included in the disposition of any part of a reporting unit. All other intangible assets other than goodwill should be aggregated and reported as a separate line item on the balance sheet. For intangibles subject to amortization, the amount of such assets acquired during the period should be disclosed along with the cost and accumulated amortization for major intangible asset classes and in total. For intangibles not subject to amortization, similar disclosures are required with the exception of the amount of accumulated amortization.

Major items included in deferred charges should be reported separately, along with disclosure of the fact, where applicable, that they are reported net of amortization.

Income Statement

For intangibles subject to amortization, disclosure is required of the amortization methods and rates used, as well as the amount of amortization expense charged to income for the period. Each goodwill impairment loss is required to be reported separately in the income statement before extraordinary items and discontinued operations, unless the impairment loss is associated with a discontinued operation. In addition, the enterprise must describe the facts and circumstances leading to the impairment; identify the loss amount and the adjusted carrying amount of goodwill along with the associated reporting unit (and segment, if applicable); and provide explanatory information if the loss is an estimate only.[36]

Impairment losses associated with other intangibles do not require separate line disclosure on the face of the income statement, but a description of each impaired asset, the amount of the loss, where it is reported, and the business segment affected must be identified.[37]

In addition, amounts recognized for amortization of deferred charges should be separately reported along with the basis of amortization.[38]

Illustrative Disclosures

Excerpts from the financial statements of **Alliance Atlantis Communications Inc.** for its year ended March 31, 2000 are provided in Illustration 13-15. The company is a leading Canadian broadcaster, creator, and international distributor of filmed entertainment content, with interests in specialty television networks. Business activities are organized into Broadcast, Motion Picture, and Television operating groups. Note that the accounting policies are those in effect in 2000, and that some of the policies differ from those described in this chapter that were finalized in 2001.

Go to the Digital Tool for additional disclosures of intangible assets.

---

[35] *Financial Reporting in Canada, 2000*, Clarence Byrd, Ida Chen, and Heather Chapman; CICA, 2000, pp. 284–285.

[36] *CICA Handbook*, Section 3062, pars. .48–.54.

[37] *Ibid*.

[38] *CICA Handbook*, Section 3070, par. .04.

ILLUSTRATION 13-15
Balance Sheet Presentation and
Related Notes on Intangible
Assets

Alliance Atlantis Communications Inc.
AS AT MARCH 31, 2000 AND 1999
(IN MILLIONS OF CANADIAN DOLLARS)

Consolidated Balance Sheets	2000	1999
Assets		
Cash and cash equivalents	**1.0**	56.9
Accounts receivable	**476.8**	470.1
Loans receivable	**27.2**	39.9
Income taxes (note 13)	**7.3**	32.0
Investment in film and television programs (note 2)	**591.6**	542.7
Development costs	**30.7**	23.4
Property and equipment (note 3)	**53.7**	38.7
Broadcasting licences	**76.4**	78.3
Goodwill	**80.0**	81.5
Other assets (note 4)	**65.4**	21.9
	1,410.1	1,385.4

Note to Consolidated Financial Statements
(In millions of Canadian dollars – except per share amounts)

Broadcast rights Broadcast rights included within investment in film and television programs represent long-term contracts acquired from third parties to broadcast film and television programs. Broadcast rights and corresponding liabilities are recorded when the licence period begins and the program is available for telecast.

The cost of the broadcast rights is amortized over the contracted exhibition period beginning in the month the film or television program is premiered based on the estimated useful life of the program to the Company.

Development costs Development costs represent expenditures made and interest capitalized on projects prior to production, including investment in scripts. Advances or contributions received from third parties to assist in development are deducted from these costs. Upon commencement of production, development costs are added to the investment in film and television programs. Development costs are amortized on a straight-line basis over three years commencing in the year following the year such costs are incurred. Development costs are written off when determined not to be recoverable.

Broadcasting licences In business acquisitions involving broadcasting, fair value is assigned to the broadcasting licences acquired. Broadcasting licences are carried at assigned value less accumulated amortization. Amortization is provided on a straight-line basis over a period of forty years. Broadcasting licences are written down to the net recoverable amount if there is an expectation that the net carrying amount of the licence will not be recovered. Accumulated amortization at March 31, 2000 was $3.2 (1999 – $1.3).

Goodwill Goodwill represents the cost of acquired businesses in excess of the fair value of net identifiable assets acquired. Goodwill is amortized on a straight-line basis over periods up to forty years. Periodically, management reviews the carrying value of goodwill by considering the expected undiscounted future cash flows of the related businesses. Goodwill is written down to the net recoverable amount if this review indicates that the net carrying amount of the goodwill will not be recovered. Accumulated amortization of goodwill at March 31, 2000 was $5.2 (1999 – $3.0).

Other assets Other assets include long-term investments which are accounted for at cost when the conditions for equity accounting are not present. Other assets also include deferred financing charges which are being amortized on a straight-line basis over the life of the loan.

Note: 4. Other Assets

	2000	1999
Prepaid and other deferred charges	**27.3**	16.4
Long-term investments	**38.1**	5.5
	65.4	21.9

SUMMARY OF LEARNING OBJECTIVES

1 Describe the characteristics of intangible assets. Intangible assets have two main characteristics: (1) they lack physical existence and (2) they are not financial assets. Intangibles may be subdivided on the basis of the following characteristics: (1) Identifiability: separately identifiable or lacking specific identification. (2) Manner of acquisition: acquired singly, in groups, in business combinations, or developed internally. (3) Expected period of benefit: limited by law or contract, related to human or economic factors, or of indefinite or indeterminate duration. (4) Separability from the enterprise: rights transferable without title, saleable, or inseparable from the enterprise.

2 Discuss the recognition and measurement issues of acquiring intangibles. Intangibles, like other assets, are recorded at cost. When several intangibles, or a combination of intangibles and tangibles, are bought in a "basket purchase," the cost is allocated on the basis of relative fair values. Costs incurred to develop an intangible internally are generally expensed immediately because of the uncertainty of the future benefits, and the inability to relate the costs with specific intangible assets. Deferred charges are permitted in restricted circumstances where the future benefits associated with the costs incurred can be identified. When acquired in a business combination, it is necessary that any identifiable intangibles be recognized separately from the goodwill component. Only those that can be exchanged or whose future benefits can be controlled through contractual or other legal means should be recognized separately as identifiable intangibles.

3 Explain how specifically identifiable intangibles are valued subsequent to acquisition. An intangible with a finite useful life should be amortized over its useful life to the entity. Except in unusual and specific circumstances, the residual value is assumed to be zero. An intangible with an indefinite life should not be amortized until its life is determined to be no longer indefinite. The carrying values of the intangibles are subsequently tested for impairment. The test for intangibles that are amortized is against the net recoverable amount, while the test for those not amortized is against their fair value.

4 Identify the types of specifically identifiable intangible assets. The major identifiable assets are: (1) Patents: the exclusive right to use, manufacture, and sell a product or process for a period of 20 years without interference or infringement by others. (2) Copyrights: a federally granted right that all authors, painters, musicians, sculptors, and other artists have in their creations and expressions. (3) Trademarks and trade names: a word, phrase, or symbol that distinguishes or identifies a particular enterprise or product. (4) Leaseholds: a contractual understanding between a lessor (owner of property) and a lessee (renter of property) that grants the lessee the right to use specific property, owned by the lessor, for a specific time period in return for stipulated, and generally periodic, cash payments. (5) Franchises and licences: a contractual arrangement under which the franchisor grants the franchisee the right to sell certain products or services, to use certain trademarks or trade names, or to perform certain functions, usually within a designated geographical area.

5 Explain the conceptual issues related to goodwill. Goodwill is unique because unlike receivables, inventories, and patents that can be sold or exchanged individually in the marketplace, goodwill can be identified only with the business as a whole. Goodwill is a "going concern" valuation and is recorded only when an entire business is purchased. Goodwill generated internally is not capitalized in the accounts, because measuring the components of goodwill is simply too complex and associating any costs with future benefits too difficult. The future benefits of goodwill may have no relationship to the costs incurred in developing that goodwill. Also, goodwill may exist even in the absence of specific costs to develop it.

KEY TERMS

business combination, *604*

capital lease, *612*

copyright, *610*

deferred charges, *620*

development, *621*

franchise, *612*

goodwill, *613*

identifiable intangibles, *604*

indefinite life, *606*

intangible assets, *602*

intellectual capital, *619*

knowledge assets, *619*

leasehold, *611*

leasehold improvements, *611*

licences, *612*

master valuation approach, *615*

negative goodwill, *616*

organization costs, *625*

patents, *609*

pre-operating costs, *624*

pre-operating period, *624*

research, *621*

research and development (R & D) costs, *620*

trademark, *611*

trade name, *611*

6 Describe the accounting procedures for recording goodwill at acquisition and subsequently. To calculate goodwill, the fair value of the identifiable assets acquired and liabilities assumed is compared with the purchase price of the acquired business. The residual is goodwill—the excess of cost over fair value of the net identifiable assets acquired. Goodwill is sometimes identified on the balance sheet as the excess of cost over the fair value of the net assets acquired. Subsequent to acquisition, goodwill is tested annually for impairment, and, at other times, is tested on an events and circumstances basis. When the implied fair value of goodwill is less than its carrying value, an impairment loss is recognized.

7 Differentiate between research and development expenditures and describe and explain the rationale for the accounting for each. R & D costs are not in themselves intangible assets, but research and development activities frequently result in the development of something that is patented or copyrighted. Research is planned investigation undertaken with the hope of gaining new scientific or technical knowledge and understanding. Development is the translation of research findings or other knowledge into a plan or design for new or substantially improved products or processes prior to commercial production or use. The difficulties in accounting for R & D expenditures are (1) identifying the costs associated with particular activities, projects, or achievements and (2) determining the magnitude of the future benefits and length of time over which such benefits may be realized. Accounting practice requires that all research expenditures be expensed, and that all development costs be expensed except in prescribed circumstances. The circumstances require reasonable assurance of realization of future benefits.

8 Identify other examples of deferred charges and the accounting requirements for them. Other deferred charges include long-term prepayments, debt discount and issue costs, pre-operating costs, organization costs, and advertising costs. In general, only costs determined to have specific future benefits may be deferred. They are charged to income on the same basis that the future benefits are recognized.

9 Identify the disclosure requirements for intangibles, including deferred charges. Similar to tangible capital assets, the cost and any accumulated amortization must be reported on the balance sheet, with separate disclosure of the amortization expense on the income statement. For intangibles that are not amortized, companies must indicate the amount of any impairment losses recognized as well as information about the circumstances requiring the writedown. Goodwill is required to be separately reported, as are the major classes of intangible assets.

APPENDIX 13A

VALUING GOODWILL

In this chapter we discussed the generally accepted method of measuring and recording goodwill as the excess of cost over fair value of the net identifiable assets acquired in a business acquisition. Accountants are frequently asked to participate in the valuation of businesses as part of a planned business acquisition.

> **OBJECTIVE 10**
>
> After studying Appendix 13A, you should be able to: Explain various approaches to valuing goodwill.

To determine the purchase price for a business and the resulting goodwill is a difficult and inexact process. As indicated, it is usually possible to determine the fair value of identifiable assets. But how does a buyer value intangible factors such as superior management, good credit rating, and so on?

EXCESS EARNING APPROACH

One method is called the excess earnings approach. Using this approach, the total earning power that the company commands (i.e., the annual earnings that the business is likely to generate) is calculated. The next step is to calculate the annual average or "normal" earnings generated by firms in the same industry. The average or normal earnings are determined by assuming the company earned the same return on capital invested as the average industry firm. The rate of return is the percentage that income is of the net assets, or shareholders' equity, employed. Only if the business earns a higher rate of return than the industry average is there likely to be any excess value, or goodwill.

The difference between what the firm earns and what the industry earns is referred to as the excess earnings. The ability to generate a higher income level indicates that the business has an unidentifiable value (intangible asset) that provides this incremental earning power. Calculating this value—the value of goodwill—is a matter of discounting the excess future earnings to their present value.

This approach appears to be a systematic and logical way to determine goodwill. However, each factor needed to calculate a value under this approach is subject to question. Answers are needed to the following questions:

1. What is the normal rate of return?
2. How does one determine the expected future earnings?
3. What discount rate should be applied to the excess earnings?
4. Over what period should the excess earnings be discounted?

Finding a Normal Rate of Return

Determining the normal rate of return earned on net assets employed by a company requires analysis of companies similar to the enterprise in question. An industry average may be determined by examining annual reports or data from statistical services. Assume that a rate of 15% is determined to be normal for a concern such as Tractorling (see pages 614–615). In this case, the estimate of Tractorling's earnings considered normal for the industry is calculated in the following manner.[39]

ILLUSTRATION 13A-1
Calculation of Normal Earnings

Fair value of Tractorling's net identifiable assets	$350,000
Normal rate of return	15%
Normal earnings	$ 52,500

Determining Future Earnings

The starting point for determining future earnings is normally the enterprise's past earnings. The past often provides useful information concerning the enterprise's future earnings potential. Past earnings—generally three to six years—are also useful because future estimates are often overly optimistic; the hard facts of previous periods bring a sobering reality to the negotiations.

Tractorling's net incomes for the last five years and the calculation of the company's average earnings over this period are as follows:

ILLUSTRATION 13A-2
Calculation of Average Past Earnings

Earnings History – Tractorling		
1997	$ 60,000	**Average Earnings**
1998	55,000	
1999	110,000[a]	$\dfrac{\$375,000}{5 \text{ years}} = \$75,000$
2000	70,000	
2001	80,000	
	$375,000	

[a]Includes extraordinary gain of $25,000

The average earnings for the last five years is $75,000. This is a rate of return of approximately 21.4% on the current value of the assets excluding goodwill ($75,000 ÷ $350,000). Before we go further, however, we need to know whether $75,000 is representative of this enterprise's future earnings.

The past earnings of a company to be acquired need to be analysed to determine whether any adjustments are needed in estimating expected future earnings. This process is often termed normalizing earnings. First, the accounting policies applied should be consistent with those of the purchaser. For example, assume that in determining earnings power, the purchasing company measures earnings in relation to a FIFO inventory valuation figure rather than LIFO, which Tractorling employs. Further assume that the use of LIFO had the effect of reducing Tractorling's net income by $2,000 each year below a FIFO-based net income. In addition, Tractorling uses accelerated depreciation while the purchaser uses straight-line. As a result, the reported earnings were $3,000 lower each year than they would have been under a straight-line basis.

Also, differences between the carrying amounts and fair values of the assets may affect reported earnings in the future. For example, internally developed patent costs not previously recognized as an asset will be recognized on the purchase of Tractorling. This asset will need to be amortized, say, at the rate of $1,000 per period. Finally, because we are attempting to estimate future earnings, amounts not expected to recur should be adjusted out of our calculations. The extraordinary gain of $25,000 is an example of such an item. An analysis can now be made of what the purchaser expects the annual future earnings of Tractorling to be.

---

[39] The **fair value** of Tractorling's net assets, rather than **historical cost**, is used to compute the normal income, because fair value is closer to the true value of the company's assets exclusive of goodwill. If a company is interested in purchasing Tractorling, the cost to it of the net identifiable assets will be their fair value when purchased. Therefore, their fair value is the relevant measure.

Average past earnings per Tractorling calculation		$75,000
Add		
Adjustment for switch from LIFO to FIFO	$2,000	
Adjustment for change from accelerated to straight-line approach	3,000	5,000
		80,000
Deduct		
Extraordinary gain ($25,000 ÷ 5)	5,000	
Patent amortization on straight-line basis	1,000	6,000
Expected future earnings of Tractorling		$74,000

ILLUSTRATION 13A-3
Calculation of Expected Future Earnings

Note that it was necessary to divide the extraordinary gain of $25,000 by five years to adjust it correctly. The whole $25,000 was included in the total income earned over the five-year history, but only one-fifth of it, or $5,000, is included in the average earnings.

The next step is to determine the excess earnings, if any. This is the extent to which Tractorling's normalized future earnings exceed the industry average rate of earnings. **The excess earnings, therefore, are $21,500 ($74,000 minus $52,500).**

Choosing a Discount Rate to Apply to Excess Earnings

Because the purchaser is buying the expected future earnings, the earnings must be discounted back to their present value. The choice of discount rate is fairly subjective.[40] **The lower the discount rate, the higher the goodwill value and vice versa.** To illustrate, assume that the excess earnings of $21,500 are expected to continue indefinitely. If the excess earnings are capitalized at a rate of 25% in perpetuity, for example, the results are:

Capitalization at 25%

$$\frac{\text{Excess earnings}}{\text{Capitalization rate}} = \frac{\$21,500}{0.25} = \$86,000$$

ILLUSTRATION 13A-4
Capitalization of Excess Earnings at 25% in Perpetuity

If the excess earnings are capitalized in perpetuity at a somewhat lower rate, say 15%, a much higher goodwill figure results.[41]

Capitalization at 15%

$$\frac{\text{Excess earnings}}{\text{Capitalization rate}} = \frac{\$21,500}{0.15} = \$143,333$$

ILLUSTRATION 13A-5
Capitalization of Excess Earnings at 15% in Perpetuity

---

[40] The following illustration shows how the capitalization or discount rate might be calculated for a small business:

A Method of Selecting a Capitalization Rate

	%
Long-term Canadian government bond rate	10
Add: Average premium return on small company shares over government bonds	10
Expected total rate of return on small publicly held shares	20
Add: Premium for greater risk and illiquidity	6
Total required expected rate of return, including inflation component	26
Deduct: Consensus long-term inflation expectation	6
Capitalization rate to apply to current earnings	20

From Warren Kissin and Ronald Zulli, "Valuation of a Closely Held Business," *The Journal of Accountancy*, June 1988, p. 42.

[41] Why do we divide by the capitalization or discount rate to arrive at the goodwill amount? Recall that the present value of an ordinary annuity is equal to:

$$P\overline{n}|\,i = \frac{1 - \frac{1}{(1 + i)^n}}{i}$$

When a number is capitalized into perpetuity, $(1 + i)^n$ becomes so large that $1/(1 + i)^n$ essentially equals zero, which leaves $1/i$ or, as in the case above, $21,500/0.25$, or $21,500/0.15$.

What do these numbers mean? In effect, if a company pays $86,000 over and above the fair value of Tractorling's identifiable net assets because the company generates earnings above the industry norm, and Tractorling actually does generate these excess profits into perpetuity, the $21,500 of extra earnings per year represents a 25% return on the amount invested: a $21,500 return relative to the $86,000 invested.

If the purchaser invests $143,333 for the goodwill, the extra $21,500 represents a 15% return on investment: $21,500 relative to the $143,333 invested.

Because the continuance of excess profits is uncertain, a conservative rate (higher than the normal rate) is usually employed. Factors that are considered in determining the rate are the stability of past earnings, the speculative nature of the business, and general economic conditions.

Choosing a Discounting Period

Determining the period over which excess earnings will continue is perhaps the most difficult problem associated with estimating goodwill. The perpetuity examples above assume the excess earnings will last indefinitely. Often, however, the excess earnings are assumed to last a limited number of years and then these earnings are discounted over that period only.

Assume that the company interested in purchasing Tractorling's business believes that the excess earnings will last only 10 years and, because of general economic uncertainty, chooses 25% as an appropriate rate of return. The present value of a 10-year annuity of excess earnings of $21,500 discounted at 25% is $76,766.[42] That is the amount that a purchaser should be willing to pay above the fair value of net identifiable assets (that is, for goodwill) given the assumptions stated.

There is another way to estimate goodwill that is similar and that should enhance your understanding of the process and the resulting numbers. Under this approach, the value **of the company as a whole** is determined, based on the **total expected earnings**, not just the excess earnings. The fair value of the net identifiable assets is then deducted from the value of the company as a whole. **The difference is goodwill.** The calculations under both approaches are provided in Illustration 13A-6, assuming the purchaser is looking for a 15% return on amounts invested in Tractorling, and the earnings are expected to continue into perpetuity.

ILLUSTRATION 13A-6
Alternative Approaches to the Calculation of Goodwill

Assumptions:	Expected future earnings	$74,000
	Normal earnings	$52,500
	Expected excess future earnings	$21,500
	Discount rate	15%
	Discount period	perpetuity, ∞

Direct Approach: Goodwill = present value of the annuity of excess future earnings
= present value of annuity of $21,500 ($n = ∞$, $i = 0.15$)

$$= \frac{\$21,500}{0.15} = \underline{\$143,333}$$

Indirect Approach: Goodwill = difference between the fair value of the company and the fair value of its net identifiable assets

Fair value of company = present value of the annuity of future earnings
= present value of annuity of $74,000 ($n = ∞$, $i = 0.15$)

$$= \frac{\$74,000}{0.15} = \underline{\$493,333}$$

---

[42] The present value of an annuity of $1 received in a steady stream for 10 years in the future discounted at 25% is 3.57050. The present value of an annuity of $21,500, therefore, is $21,500 × 3.57050 = $76,765.75.

Fair value of net identifiable assets	=	present value of the annuity of normal earnings		
	=	present value of annuity of $52,500 ($n = \infty$, $i = 0.15$)		
	=	$\dfrac{\$52,500}{0.15}$	=	350,000
Goodwill	=			$\$143,333$

OTHER METHODS OF VALUATION

A number of methods of valuing goodwill exist, some "quick and dirty" and some fairly sophisticated.[43] Simply multiplying the excess earnings by the number of years the excess earnings are expected to continue is one of the least complex approaches. Often referred to as the **number of years method**, it is used to provide a rough measure of the goodwill factor. The approach has only the advantage of simplicity; it fails to discount the future flows and consider the time value of money.

An even simpler method is one that relies on multiples of average yearly earnings that are paid for other companies in the same industry. If Skyward Airlines was recently acquired for five times its average yearly earnings of $50 million, or $250 million, then Worldwide Airways, a close competitor, with $80 million in average yearly earnings would be worth $400 million.

Another method (similar to discounting excess earnings) is the **discounted free cash flow method**, which involves a projection of the company's free cash flow over a long period, typically 10 or 20 years. The method first projects into the future a dozen or so important financial variables, including production, prices, noncash expenses such as amortization, taxes, and capital outlays—all adjusted for inflation. The objective is to determine the amount of operating cash flow that will be generated over and above the amount needed to maintain existing capacity. The present value of the free cash flows is then calculated. This amount represents the value of the business.

For example, if Magnaputer Ltd. is expected to generate $1 million a year of free cash flow for 20 years, and the buyer's rate-of-return objective is 15%, the buyer would be willing to pay about $6.26 million for Magnaputer. (The present value of $1 million to be received for 20 years discounted at 15% is $6,259,330.) The goodwill, then, is the difference between the $6.26 million and the fair value of the company's net identifiable assets.

In practice, prospective buyers use a variety of methods to produce a "valuation curve" or range of prices. But the actual price paid may be more a factor of the buyer's or seller's ego and horse-trading acumen.

Valuation of a business and its inherent goodwill is at best a highly uncertain process.[44] The estimated value of goodwill depends on a number of factors, all of which are tenuous and subject to bargaining.

---

[43] One article lists three "asset-based approaches" (tangible net worth, adjusted book value, and price-book value ratio methods) and three "earnings-based approaches" (capitalization of earnings, capitalization of excess earnings, and discounted cash flow methods) as the popular methods for valuing closely held businesses. See Warren Rissin and Ronald Zulli, "Valuation of a Closely Held Business," *The Journal of Accountancy*, June 1988, pp. 38–44.

[44] Business valuation is a specialist field. The Canadian Institute of Chartered Business Valuators (CICBV) oversees the granting of the specialist designation, Chartered Business Valuator (CBV), to professionals who meet the education, experience, and examination requirements.

SUMMARY OF LEARNING OBJECTIVE FOR APPENDIX 13A

10 **Explain various approaches to valuing goodwill.** One method of valuing goodwill is the excess earnings approach. Using this approach, the total expected future earnings the company is expected to generate is calculated. The next step is to calculate "normal earnings" by determining and applying the normal rate of return on net assets in that industry. The difference between what the firm earns and what the industry earns is referred to as the excess earnings. This excess earning power indicates that there are unidentifiable underlying asset values that result in the higher than average earnings. Finding the value of goodwill is a matter of discounting these excess future earnings to their present value. The number of years method of valuing goodwill, which simply multiplies the excess earnings by the number of years of expected excess earnings, is used to provide a rough measure of goodwill. Another method of valuing goodwill is the discounted free cash flow method, which projects the future operating cash that will be generated over and above the amount needed to maintain current operating levels. The present value of the free cash flows is today's value of the firm.

Note: All asterisked Brief Exercises, Exercises, Problems, and Cases relate to material in the appendix to the chapter.

BRIEF EXERCISES

BE13-1   Troopers Corporation purchases a patent from MacAskill Corp. on January 1, 2002, for $64,000. The patent has a remaining legal life of 16 years. Troopers feels the patent will be useful for 10 years. Prepare Troopers' journal entries to record the patent purchase and 2002 amortization.

BE13-2   Use the information provided in BE13-1. Assume that at January 1, 2004, the carrying amount of the patent on Troopers' books is $51,200. In January, Troopers spends $24,000 successfully defending a patent suit. Troopers still feels the patent will be useful until the end of 2011. Prepare the journal entries to record the $24,000 expenditure and 2004 amortization.

BE13-3   Stauder, Inc. spent $60,000 in legal fees while developing the trade name of its new product, the Mean Bean Machine. Prepare the journal entries to record the $60,000 expenditure and the first year's amortization, using an eight-year life.

BE13-4   Haysom Corporation commenced operations in early 2002. The corporation incurred $70,000 of costs such as fees to underwriters, legal fees, provincial incorporation fees, and promotional expenditures during its formation. Prepare journal entries to record the $70,000 expenditure and 2002 amortization. If applicable, assume a full year's amortization based on a five-year life.

BE13-5   Cyborg Corp. leased a building on July 1, 2002, for eight years ending June 30, 2010. The building has an estimated remaining useful life of 20 years. Cyborg immediately made improvements to the building. The improvements, which cost $89,120, have a useful life of 10 years. Prepare journal entries to record the $89,120 expenditure and 2002 amortization.

BE13-6   Knickle Corporation obtained a franchise from Sonic Products Inc. for a cash payment of $100,000 on April 1. The franchise grants Knickle the right to sell certain products and services for a period of eight years. Prepare Knickle's April 1 journal entry and December 31 adjusting entry.

BE13-7   On September 1, 2002, Dunvegan Corporation acquired Edinburgh Enterprises for a cash payment of $750,000. At the time of purchase, Edinburgh's balance sheet showed assets of $620,000, liabilities of $200,000, and owners' equity of $420,000. The fair value of Edinburgh's assets is estimated to be $800,000. **(a)** Calculate the amount of goodwill acquired by Dunvegan. **(b)** Prepare the December 31 entry to record amortization, if any, based on a 10-year life.

BE13-8 Nobunaga Corporation owns a patent that has a carrying amount net of accumulated amortization of $330,000. Nobunaga expects future net cash flows from this patent to total $190,000. The patent's fair value is $110,000. Prepare Nobunaga's journal entry, if necessary, to record the loss on impairment.

BE13-9 Evans Corporation purchased Hofield Company three years ago and at that time recorded goodwill of $400,000. The carrying amount of the goodwill today is $340,000. The Hofield Division's net assets, including the goodwill, have a carrying amount of $800,000. Evans expects net future cash flows of $700,000 from the Hofield Division. The division's fair value is estimated to be $525,000. Prepare Evans' journal entry, if necessary, to record impairment of the goodwill.

BE13-10 Dorsett Corporation incurred the following costs in 2002:

Cost of laboratory research aimed at discovery of new knowledge	$140,000
Cost of testing in search for product alternatives	100,000
Cost of engineering activity required to advance the design of a product to the manufacturing stage	210,000
	$450,000

Prepare the necessary 2002 journal entry for Dorsett.

BE2-11 Indicate whether the following items are capitalized or expensed in the current year:
  (a) purchase cost of a patent from a competitor;
  (b) product development costs;
  (c) organization costs; and
  (d) costs incurred internally to create goodwill.

BE13-12 Lager Industries Ltd. had one patent recorded on its books as of January 1, 2002. This patent had a book value of $240,000 and a remaining useful life of eight years. During 2002, Lager incurred research costs of $96,000 and brought a patent infringement suit against a competitor. On December 1, 2002, Lager received the good news that its patent was valid and that its competitor could not use the process Lager had patented. The company incurred $85,000 to defend this patent. At what amount should patent(s) be reported on the December 31, 2002 balance sheet, assuming monthly amortization of patents?

BE13-13 Wiggens Industries Ltd. acquired two copyrights during 2002. One copyright related to a textbook that was developed internally at a cost of $9,900. This textbook is estimated to have a useful life of three years from September 1, 2002, the date it was published. The second copyright, for a history research textbook, was purchased from University Press on December 1, 2002, for $19,200. This textbook has an indefinite useful life. How should these two copyrights be reported on Wiggens' balance sheet as of December 31, 2002? Assume that Wiggens will use the maximum period of amortization for intangibles, whenever possible.

***BE13-14** Nigel Corporation is interested in purchasing Lau Car Company Ltd. The total of Lau's net incomes over the last five years is $600,000. During one of those years, Lau reported an extraordinary gain of $80,000. The fair value of Lau's net identifiable assets is $560,000. A normal rate of return is 15%, and Nigel wishes to capitalize excess earnings at 20%. Calculate the estimated value of Lau's goodwill.

EXERCISES

E13-1 **(Classification Issues—Intangibles)** Presented below is a list of items that could be included in the intangible assets section of the balance sheet.
  1. investment in a subsidiary company *Long-Term Investment*
  2. timberland *Natural Resources*
  3. cost of engineering activity required to advance a product's design to the manufacturing stage *Intangable Asset — if 5 criteria are met.*
  4. lease prepayment (six months' rent paid in advance) *Prepaid asset - CA*
  5. cost of equipment obtained under a capital lease *CA, Equip - Land, Plant and Equipment*
  6. cost of searching for applications of new research findings *Expense or capitalize if consept was not fers. Dev. if 5 crit. me*
  7. costs incurred in forming a corporation *Intangables → Organization Costs*
  8. operating losses incurred in the start-up of a business *Loss on the Income Statment*
  9. training costs incurred in start-up of new operation *Intangable → Capitalize → Organizational Cost*
  10. purchase cost of a franchise *Intangable*

11. goodwill generated internally — *Nothing*
12. cost of testing in search for product alternatives — *Research Expense*
13. goodwill acquired in the purchase of a business — *Intangible→Goodwill*
14. cost of developing a patent — *Capitalize into Research and Dev. if it meets all criteria*
15. cost of purchasing a patent from an inventor *Intangible → Patent*
16. legal costs incurred in securing a patent *Capitalize into Patent*
17. unrecovered costs of a successful legal suit to protect the patent *Patent*
18. cost of conceptual formulation of possible product alternatives *Expense*
19. cost of purchasing a copyright *Intangible Copyright*
20. product development costs *Cap. to Research and Develop. or Expense*
21. long-term receivables *Long-term Investment*
22. cost of developing a trademark *Intangible → Research and Develop. if all criteria*
23. cost of purchasing a trademark

Instructions

(a) Indicate which items on the list above would be reported as intangible assets on the balance sheet.
(b) Indicate how, if at all, the items not reportable as intangible assets would be reported in the financial statements.

E13-2 (Classification Issues—Intangibles) Presented below is selected account information related to Martinez Inc. as of December 21, 2002. All these accounts have debit balances.

Cable television franchises	Film contract rights
Music copyrights	Customer lists
Research costs	Prepaid expenses
Goodwill	Covenants not to compete
Cash	Brand names
Discount on notes payable	Notes receivable
Accounts receivable	Investments in affiliated companies
Property, plant, and equipment	Organization cost
Leasehold improvements	Land

Instructions

Identify which items should be classified as an intangible asset. For those items not classified as an intangible asset, indicate where they would be reported in the financial statements.

E13-3 (Classification Issues—Intangible Asset) Hyde Inc. has the following amounts included in its general ledger at December 31, 2002:

Organization costs	$24,000
Trademarks	15,000
Discount on bonds payable	35,000
Deposits with advertising agency for ads to promote goodwill of company	10,000
Excess of cost over fair value of net identifiable assets of acquired subsidiary	75,000
Cost of equipment acquired for research and development projects; the equipment has an alternative future use	90,000
Costs of developing a secret formula for a product that is expected to be marketed for at least 20 years	80,000

Instructions

(a) Based on the information above, calculate the total amount to be reported by Hyde for intangible assets on its balance sheet at December 31, 2002.
(b) If an item is not to be included in intangible assets, explain its proper treatment for reporting purposes.

E13-4 (Intangible Amortization) Presented below is selected information for Torrens Corporation. Answer each of the factual situations.

1. Torrens purchased a patent from Vania Co. for $1 million on January 1, 2000. The patent is being amortized over its remaining legal life of 10 years, expiring on January 1, 2010. During 2002, Torrens determined that the patent's economic benefits would not last longer than six years from the date of acquisition. What amount should be reported in the balance sheet for the patent, net of accumulated amortization, at December 31, 2002?

2. Torrens bought a perpetual franchise from Alexander Inc. on January 1, 2001 for $400,000. Its carrying amount on Alexander's books at January 1, 2001 was $500,000. Torrens has decided to amortize the franchise over the maximum period permitted. Assume that Torrens can substantiate clearly identifiable cash flows only for 25 years, but thinks it could have value for up to 60 years. What amount of amortization expense should be reported for the year ended December 31, 2002?

3. On January 1, 1998, Torrens incurred organization costs of $275,000. Torrens is amortizing these costs over five years. What amount, if any, should be reported as unamortized organization costs as of December 31, 2002?

E13-5 (Correct Intangible Asset Account) As the recently appointed auditor for Briffett Corporation, you have been asked to examine selected accounts before the six-month financial statements of June 30, 2002 are prepared. The controller for Briffett Corporation mentions that only one account (shown below) is kept for Intangible Assets.

Intangible Assets

		Debit	Credit	Balance
January 4	Research costs	940,000		940,000
January 5	Legal costs to obtain patent	75,000		1,015,000
January 31	Payment of seven months' rent on property leased by Briffett (Feb. to Aug.)	91,000		1,106,000
February 11	Proceeds from issue of common shares		250,000	856,000
March 31	Unamortized bond discount on bonds due March 31, 2022	84,000		940,000
April 30	Promotional expenses related to start-up of business	207,000		1,147,000
June 30	Operating losses for first six months	241,000		1,388,000

[handwritten: Orig Ent: DR: Cash 416,0000 / DR: Disc. on Bond 84,000 / CR: Bond Pay 500,000]

Instructions

Prepare the entry or entries necessary to correct this account. Assume that the patent has a useful life of 10 years.

E13-6 (Recording and Amortization of Intangibles) Bateman Limited, organized late in 2001, has set up a single account for all intangible assets. The following summary discloses the entries (all debits) that have been recorded since then:

1/2/02	Purchased patent (8-year life)	$ 350,000
4/1/02	Purchased goodwill (indefinite life)	360,000
7/1/02	Purchased franchise with 10-year life; expiration date 7/1/12	450,000
8/1/02	Payment for copyright (5-year life)	156,000
9/1/02	Research and development costs	215,000
		$1,531,000

Instructions

Prepare the necessary entries to clear the Intangible Assets account and to set up separate accounts for distinct types of intangibles. Make the entries as of December 31, 2002, recording any necessary amortization and reflecting all balances accurately as of that date.

E13-7 (Accounting for Trade Name) In early January of 2002, Crystal Corporation applied for and received a trade name, incurring legal costs of $16,000. In January of 2003, Crystal incurred $7,800 of legal fees in a successful defence of its trade name.

Instructions

(a) Identify the variables that must be considered in determining the appropriate amortization period for this trade name.

(b) Calculate 2002 amortization, 12/31/02 book value, 2003 amortization, and 12/31/03 book value if the company amortizes the trade name over its 15-year legal life.

(c) Repeat part (b), assuming a useful life of five years.

E13-8 (Accounting for Lease Transaction) Benet Inc. leases an old building that it intends to improve and use as a warehouse. To obtain the lease, the company pays a bonus of $72,000. Annual rental for the six-year lease period is $120,000. No option to renew the lease or right to purchase the property is given.

After the lease is obtained, improvements costing $144,000 are made. The building has an estimated remaining useful life of 17 years.

Instructions

(a) What is the annual cost of this lease to Benet Inc.?

(b) What amount of annual amortization, if any, on a straight-line basis should Benet record?

E13-9 **(Accounting for Organization Costs)** Greeley Corporation was organized in 2001 and began operations at the beginning of 2002. The company is involved in interior design consulting services. The following costs were incurred prior to the start of operations:

Legal fees in connection with organization of the company	$15,000
Improvements to leased offices prior to occupancy	25,000
Costs of meetings of incorporators to discuss	
organizational activities	7,000
Provincial filing fees to incorporate	1,000
	$48,000

Instructions

(a) Calculate the total amount of organization costs incurred by Greeley.

(b) Prepare a summary journal entry to record the $48,000 of expenditures in 2002.

E13-10 **(Accounting for Patents, Franchises, and R & D)** Carter Corp. has provided information on intangible assets as follows:

A patent was purchased from Gerald Inc. for $2 million on January 1, 2002. Carter estimated the patent's remaining useful life to be 10 years. The patent was carried in Gerald's accounting records at a net book value of $2.3 million when Gerald sold it to Carter.

During 2003, a franchise was purchased from Reagan Ltd. for $480,000. In addition, 5% of revenue from the franchise must be paid to Reagan. Revenue from the franchise for 2003 was $2.5 million. Carter estimates the franchise's useful life to be 10 years and takes a full year's amortization in the year of purchase.

Carter incurred research and development costs in 2003 as follows:

Materials and equipment	$142,000
Personnel	189,000
Indirect costs	102,000
	$433,000

Carter estimates that these costs will be recouped by December 31, 2006.

On January 1, 2003, Carter, because of recent events in the field, estimates that the remaining life of the patent purchased on January 1, 2002 is only five years from January 1, 2003.

Instructions

(a) Prepare a schedule showing the intangibles section of Carter's balance sheet at December 31, 2003. Show supporting calculations in good form.

(b) Prepare a schedule showing the income statement effect for the year ended December 31, 2003, as a result of the facts above. Show supporting calculations in good form.

(AICPA adapted)

E13-11 **(Accounting for Patents)** During 1998, Weinstein Corporation spent $170,000 in research and development costs. As a result, a new product called the New Age Piano was patented at additional legal and other costs of $18,000. The patent obtained on October 1, 1998 had a legal life of 20 years and a useful life of 10 years.

Instructions

(a) Prepare all journal entries required in 1998 and 1999 as a result of the transactions above.

(b) On June 1, 2000, Weinstein spent $9,480 to successfully prosecute a patent infringement. As a result, the estimate of useful life was extended to 12 years from June 1, 2000. Prepare all journal entries required in 2000 and 2001.

(c) In 2002, Weinstein determined that a competitor's product would make the New Age Piano obsolete and the patent worthless by December 31, 2003. Prepare all journal entries required in 2002 and 2003.

E13-12 **(Accounting for Patents)** Tones Industries Ltd. has the following patents on its December 31, 2003, balance sheet:

Patent Item	Initial Cost	Date Acquired	Useful Life at Date Acquired
Patent A	$30,600	3/1/00	17 years
Patent B	$15,000	7/1/01	10 years
Patent C	$14,400	9/1/02	4 years

The following events occurred during the year ended December 31, 2004:

1. Research and development costs of $245,700 were incurred during the year.
2. Patent D was purchased on July 1 for $36,480. This patent has a useful life of 9½ years.
3. As a result of reduced demands for certain products protected by Patent B, a possible impairment of Patent B's value may have occurred at December 31, 2004. The controller for Tones estimates the future cash flows from Patent B will be as follows:

For the Year Ended	Future Cash Flows
December 31, 2005	$2,000
December 31, 2006	2,000
December 31, 2007	2,000

The proper discount rate to be used for these flows is 8%. (Assume that the cash flows occur at the end of the year.)

Instructions

(a) Calculate the total carrying amount of Tones' patents on its December 31, 2003 balance sheet.
(b) Calculate the total carrying amount of Tones' patents on its December 31, 2004 balance sheet.

E13-13 **(Accounting for Goodwill)** Fred Moss, owner of Moss Interiors Inc., is negotiating for the purchase of Zweifel Galleries Ltd. The condensed balance sheet of Zweifel is given in an abbreviated form below:

ZWEIFEL GALLERIES LTD.
Balance Sheet
As of December 31, 2002

Assets		Liabilities and Shareholders' Equity		
Cash	$100,000	Accounts payable		$ 50,000
Land	70,000	Long-term notes payable		300,000
Building (net)	200,000	Total liabilities		350,000
Equipment (net)	175,000	Common shares	$200,000	
Copyright (net)	30,000	Retained earnings	25,000	225,000
Total assets	$575,000	Total liabilities and shareholders' equity		$575,000

(handwritten annotations: Land "30,000 + 70,000"; Building (net) "−5,000 ↗ 200,000"; Total assets "600,000"; Assets "600,000")

Moss and Zweifel agree that:

1. Land is undervalued by $30,000.
2. Equipment is overvalued by $5,000.

Zweifel agrees to sell the gallery to Moss for $350,000.

(handwritten: DR: assets 600,000 / DR: Goodwill 100,000 / CR: Cash 550,000 / CR: Liabil 350,000)

Instructions

Prepare the entry to record the purchase of the gallery's net assets on Moss' books.

E13-14 **(Accounting for Goodwill)** On July 1, 2002, Brigham Corporation purchased the net assets of Young Company by paying $250,000 cash and issuing a $100,000 note payable to Young Company. At July 1, 2002, the balance sheet of Young Company was as follows:

Cash	$ 50,000	Accounts payable	$200,000
Receivables	90,000	Young, capital	235,000
Inventory	100,000		$435,000
Land	40,000		
Buildings (net)	75,000		
Equipment (net)	70,000		
Trademarks (net)	10,000		
	$435,000		

The recorded amounts all approximate current values except for land (worth $60,000), inventory (worth $125,000), and trademarks (worthless).

Instructions

(a) Prepare the July 1, 2002 entry for Brigham Corporation to record the purchase.
(b) Assume that Brigham tested Goodwill for impairment on December 31, 2003 and determined that it had an implied value of $55,000. Prepare the entry, if any, on December 31, 2003.

E13-15   (Intangible Impairment) Presented below is information related to copyrights owned by La Mare Corp. at December 31, 2002.

Cost	$8,600,000
Carrying amount	4,300,000
Expected future net cash flows	4,000,000
Fair value	3,200,000

Assume that La Mare Corp. will continue to use this copyright in the future. As of December 31, 2002, the copyright is estimated to have a remaining useful life of 10 years.

Instructions

(a) Prepare the journal entry, if any, to record the asset's impairment at December 31, 2002.
(b) Prepare the journal entry to record amortization expense for 2003 related to the copyrights.
(c) The copyright's fair value at December 31, 2003 is $3.4 million. Prepare the journal entry, if any, necessary to record the increase in fair value.

E13-16   (Goodwill Impairment) Presented below is net asset information (including associated goodwill of $200 million) related to the Carlos Division of Santana, Inc.

CARLOS DIVISION
Net Assets
as of December 31, 2002

(in millions)

Cash	$ 50
Receivables	200
Property, plant, and equipment (net)	2,600
Goodwill	200
Less: Notes payable	(2,700)
Net assets	$ 350

The purpose of this division (also identified as a reporting unit) is to develop a nuclear-powered aircraft. If successful, travelling delays associated with refuelling could be substantially reduced. Many other benefits would also occur. To date, management has not had much success and is deciding whether a write-down at this time is appropriate. Management estimated its future net cash flows from the project to be $300 million. Management has also received an offer to purchase the division for $220 million.

Instructions

(a) Prepare the journal entry, if any, to record the impairment at December 31, 2002.
(b) At December 31, 2003, it is estimated that the division's fair value increased to $240 million. Prepare the journal entry, if any, to record this increase in fair value.

E13-17   (Accounting for R & D Costs) Leontyne Corp. from time to time embarks on a research program when a special project seems to offer possibilities. In 2002, the company expends $325,000 on a research project, but by the end of 2002, it is impossible to determine whether any benefit will be derived from it.

Instructions

(a) What account should be charged for the $325,000, and how should it be shown in the financial statements?
(b) The project is completed in 2003, and a successful patent is obtained. The R & D costs to complete the project are $110,000. The administrative and legal expenses incurred in obtaining patent number 472-1001-84 in 2003 total $16,000. The patent has an expected useful life of five years. Record these costs in journal entry form. Also, record patent amortization (full year) in 2003.

(c) In 2004, the company successfully defends the patent in extended litigation at a cost of $47,200, thereby extending the patent life to 12/31/11. What is the proper way to account for this cost? Also, record patent amortization (full year) in 2004.

(d) Additional engineering and consulting costs incurred in 2004 required to advance a product design to the manufacturing stage total $60,000. These costs enhance the product design considerably. Discuss the proper accounting treatment for this cost.

E13-18 (Accounting for R & D Costs) Heifitz Ltd. incurred the following costs during 2002:

Quality control during commercial production, including routine product testing	$58,000
Laboratory research aimed at discovery of new knowledge	68,000
Testing for new product evaluation	23,000
Modification of the formulation of a plastics product	4,500
Engineering follow-through in an early phase of commercial production	15,000
Adaptation of an existing capability to a particular requirement or customer's need as a part of continuing commercial activity	13,000
Trouble-shooting in connection with breakdowns during commercial production	29,000
Searching for applications of new research findings	19,000

Instructions

Calculate the total amount Heifitz should classify and expense as research and development costs for 2002.

E13-19 (Accounting for R & D Costs) Timothy Corp. incurred the following costs during 2002 in connection with its research and development activities:

Cost of equipment acquired that will have alternative uses in future research and development projects over the next five years (uses straight-line depreciation)	$280,000
Materials consumed in research projects	59,000
Materials consumed in the development of a product committed for manufacturing in 1st quarter 2003	27,000
Consulting fees paid to outsiders for research and development projects, including $4,500 for advice related to the $27,000 of materials usage above	100,000
Personnel costs of persons involved in research and development projects	128,000
Indirect costs reasonably allocable to research and development projects	50,000
Materials purchased for future research and development projects	34,000

Instructions

Calculate the amount to be reported as research and development expense by Timothy on its income statement for 2002. Assume equipment is purchased at beginning of year.

E13-20 (Accounting for R & D Costs) Listed below are four independent situations involving research and development costs:

1. During 2002, Sisco Corp. incurred the following costs:

Research and development services performed by Miles Company for Sisco	$350,000
Testing for evaluation of new products	300,000
Laboratory research aimed at discovery of new knowledge	425,000

For the year ended December 31, 2002, how much research and development expense should Sisco Corp. report?

2. Odo Corp. incurred the following costs during the year ended December 31, 2002:

Design, construction, and testing of preproduction prototypes and models	$290,000
Routine, ongoing efforts to refine, enrich, or otherwise improve upon the qualities of an existing product	250,000

Quality control during commercial production including routine
    product testing   300,000
Laboratory research aimed at discovery of new knowledge   420,000

What is the total amount to be classified and expensed as research and development for 2002?

3.   Quark Ltd. incurred costs in 2002 as follows:

Equipment acquired for use in various research and development projects	$900,000
Amortization on the equipment above	210,000
Materials used in R & D	300,000
Compensation costs of personnel in R & D	400,000
Outside consulting fees for R & D work	220,000
Indirect costs appropriately allocated to R & D	260,000

What is the total amount of research and development that should be reported in Quark's 2002 income statement?

4.   Julian Inc. incurred the following costs during the year ended December 31, 2002:

Laboratory research aimed at discovery of new knowledge	$200,000
Radical modification to the formulation of a chemical product	145,000
Research and development costs reimbursable under a contract to perform research and development for Bashir Inc.	350,000
Testing for evaluation of new products	225,000

What is the total amount to be classified and expensed as research and development for 2002?

Instructions

Provide the correct answer to each of the four situations.

*E13-21   **(Calculate Goodwill)**   The fair value of Yunnan Corp.'s net assets excluding goodwill totals $800,000 and earnings for the last five years total $890,000. Included in the latter figure are extraordinary gains of $75,000, nonrecurring losses of $40,000, and sales commissions of $15,000. In developing a sales price for the business, a 14% return on net worth is considered normal for the industry, and annual excess earnings, if any, are capitalized at 20% in arriving at goodwill.

Instructions

Calculate estimated goodwill.

*E13-22   **(Calculate Normal Earnings)**   Beronja Corporation's pretax accounting income for the year 2002 was $850,000 and included the following items:

Amortization of identifiable intangibles	$87,000
Amortization of building	110,000
Extraordinary losses	44,000
Extraordinary gains	150,000
Profit-sharing payments to employees	65,000

Ewing Industries Ltd. is seeking to purchase Beronja Corporation. In attempting to measure Beronja's normal earnings for 2002, Ewing determines that the building's fair value is triple the book value and that the remaining economic life is double that used by Beronja. Ewing would continue the profit-sharing payments to employees; such payments are based on income before amortization.

Instructions

Calculate the normal earnings (for purposes of computing goodwill) of Beronja Corporation for the year 2002.

*E13-23   **(Calculate Goodwill)**   Newfoundland Inc. is considering acquiring Alberta Company in total as a going concern. Newfoundland makes the following calculations and conclusions:

1.   The fair value of the identifiable assets of Alberta Company is $720,000.
2.   Alberta Company's liabilities are $380,000.
3.   A fair estimate of annual earnings for the indefinite future is $120,000 per year.
4.   Considering the risk and potential of Alberta Company, Newfoundland feels that it must earn a 25% return on its investment.

Instructions

(a) How much should Newfoundland be willing to pay for Alberta Company?

(b) How much of the purchase price would be goodwill?

*E13-24 (Calculate Goodwill) As the president of Manitoba Recording Corp., you are considering purchasing Moose Jaw CD Corp., whose balance sheet is summarized as follows:

Current assets	$ 300,000	Current liabilities	$ 300,000
Fixed assets (net of amortization)	700,000	Long-term liabilities	500,000
Other assets	300,000	Common shares	400,000
		Retained earnings	100,000
Total	$1,300,000	Total	$1,300,000

The current assets' fair value is $550,000 because of inventory undervaluation . The normal rate of return on net assets for the industry is 15%. The expected annual earnings projected for Moose Jaw CD Corp. is $140,000.

Instructions

Assuming that the excess earnings continue for five years, how much would you be willing to pay for goodwill? (Estimate goodwill by the present-value method.)

*E13-25 (Calculate Goodwill) Net income figures for Ontario Ltd. are as follows:

1998 – $64,000	2001 – $80,000
1999 – $50,000	2002 – $75,000
2000 – $81,000	

Identifiable net assets of this company are appraised at $400,000 on December 31, 2002. This business is to be acquired by Annapolis Corp. early in 2003.

Instructions

What amount should be paid for goodwill if:

(a) 14% is assumed to be a normal rate of return on net identifiable assets, and average excess earnings for the last five years are to be capitalized at 25%?

(b) 12% is assumed to be a normal rate of return on net identifiable assets, and payment is to be made for excess earnings for the last four years?

*E13-26 (Calculate Goodwill) Xiaofei Corporation is interested in acquiring Richmond Plastics Limited. It has determined that Richmond's excess earnings have averaged approximately $150,000 annually over the last six years. Richmond shareholders agree with the calculation of $150,000 as the approximate excess earnings and feel that such an amount should be capitalized over an unlimited period at a 20% rate. Xiaofei Corporation feels that because of increased competition, the excess earnings of Richmond Plastics will continue for seven years at best and that a 15% discount rate is appropriate.

Instructions

(a) How far apart are the positions of these two parties?

(b) Is there really any difference in the two approaches used by the two parties in evaluating Richmond Plastics' goodwill? Explain.

*E13-27 (Calculate Goodwill) Venus Corporation is contemplating the purchase of Mars Industries and evaluating the amount of goodwill to be recognized in the purchase.

Mars reported the following net incomes:

1997	$170,000
1998	200,000
1999	240,000
2000	250,000
2001	380,000

Mars has indicated that 2001 net income included the sale of one of its warehouses at a gain of $115,000 (net of tax). Net identifiable assets of Mars have a total fair value of $900,000.

Instructions

Calculate goodwill in the following cases, assuming that future expected income is a simple average of normalized income for the past five years.

(a) Goodwill is determined by capitalizing average earnings at 16%.

(b) Goodwill is determined by presuming a 16% return on identifiable net assets and capitalizing excess earnings at 25%.

*E13-28 (Calculate Fair Value of Identifiable Assets) Hartley Inc. bought a business that would yield exactly a 20% annual rate of return on its investment. Of the total amount paid for the business, $80,000 was deemed to be goodwill, and the remaining was attributable to the identifiable net assets.

Hartley Inc. projected that the estimated annual future earnings of the new business would be equal to its average annual ordinary earnings over the past four years. The total of the net incomes over the past four years was $380,000, which included an extraordinary loss of $35,000 in one year and an extraordinary gain of $115,000 in one of the other three years.

Instructions

Calculate the fair value of the identifiable net assets that Hartley Inc. purchased in this transaction.

PROLEMS
PROBLEMS

P13-1 Esplanade Corp., organized in 2001, has set up a single account for all intangible assets. The following summary discloses the debit entries that have been recorded during 2001 and 2002:

Intangible Assets

7/1/01	8-year franchise; expiration date 6/30/09	$ 42,000
10/1/01	Advance payment on leasehold (2-year lease)	28,000
12/31/01	Net loss for 2001 including incorporation fee, $1,000, and related legal fees of organizing, $5,000 (all fees incurred in 2001)	16,000
1/2/02	Patent purchased (10-year life)	74,000
3/1/02	Cost of developing a secret formula (indefinite life)	75,000
4/1/02	Goodwill purchased (indefinite life)	278,400
6/1/02	Legal fee for successful defence of patent (see above)	12,650
9/1/02	Research and development costs	160,000

Instructions

Prepare the necessary entries to clear the Intangible Assets account and to set up separate accounts for distinct types of intangibles. Make the entries as of December 31, 2002, recording any necessary amortization and reflecting all balances accurately as of that date. State any assumptions you need to make to support your entries.

P13-2 Ankara Laboratories holds a valuable patent (No. 758-6002-1A) on a precipitator that prevents certain types of air pollution. Ankara does not manufacture or sell the products and processes it develops; it conducts research and develops products and processes which it patents, and then assigns the patents to manufacturers on a royalty basis. Occasionally it sells a patent. The history of Ankara patent number 758-6002-1A is as follows:

Date	Activity	Cost
1992–1993	Research conducted to develop precipitator	$384,000
Jan. 1994	Design and construction of a prototype	87,600
March 1994	Testing of models	42,000
Jan. 1995	Fees paid engineers and lawyers to prepare patent application; patent granted July 1, 1995	62,050
Nov. 1996	Engineering activity necessary to advance the precipitator design to the manufacturing stage	81,500
Dec. 1997	Legal fees paid to successfully defend precipitator patent	35,700
April 1998	Research aimed at modifying the patented precipitator design	43,000
July 2002	Legal fees paid in unsuccessful patent infringement suit against a competitor	34,000

Ankara assumed a useful life of 17 years when it received the initial precipitator patent. On January 1, 2000, it revised its useful life estimate downward to five remaining years. Amortization is calculated for a full year if the cost is incurred prior to July 1, and no amortization for the year if the cost is incurred after June 30. The company's year end is December 31.

Instructions

Calculate the carrying value of patent No. 758-6002-1A on each of the following dates:

(a) December 31, 1995

(b) December 31, 1999

(c) December 31, 2002

P13-3 Information concerning Haerhpin Corporation's intangible assets is as follows:

1. On January 1, 2002, Haerhpin signed an agreement to operate as a franchisee of Hsian Copy Service, Inc. for an initial franchise fee of $75,000. Of this amount, $15,000 was paid when the agreement was signed and the balance is payable in four annual payments of $15,000 each, beginning January 1, 2003. The agreement provides that the down payment is not refundable and no future services are required of the franchisor. The present value at January 1, 2002 of the four annual payments discounted at 14% (the implicit rate for a loan of this type) is $43,700. The agreement also provides that 5% of the franchise's revenue must be paid to the franchisor annually. Haerhpin's revenue from the franchise for 2002 was $950,000. Haerhpin estimates the franchise's useful life to be 10 years. (Hint: Refer to Appendix 6A to determine the proper accounting treatment for the franchise fee and payments.)

2. Haerhpin incurred $65,000 of experimental costs in its laboratory to develop a patent which was granted on January 2, 2002. Legal fees and other costs associated with patent registration totalled $13,600. Haerhpin estimates that the useful life of the patent will be eight years.

3. A trademark was purchased from Shanghai Company for $32,000 on July 1, 1999. Expenditures for successful litigation in defense of the trademark totalling $8,160 were paid on July 1, 2002. Haerhpin estimates that the trademark's useful life will be 20 years from the acquisition date.

Instructions

(a) Prepare a schedule showing the intangible section of Haerhpin's balance sheet at December 31, 2002. Show supporting calculations in good form.

(b) Prepare a schedule showing all expenses resulting from the transactions that would appear on Haerhpin's income statement for the year ended December 31, 2002. Show supporting calculations in good form.

(AICPA adapted)

P13-4 The following information relates to the intangible assets of Goldberg Products Limited:

	Goodwill	Purchased Patent Costs
Original cost at 1/1/2002	$280,000	$48,000
Useful life at 1/1/2002 (estimated)		6 years
Implied fair value 12/31/2002	200,000	
Implied fair value 12/31/2004	250,000	

Instructions

(a) Assuming straight-line amortization, calculate the amortization amount for 2002 in accordance with generally accepted accounting principles.

(b) Prepare required journal entry(ies), if any, related to goodwill for 2002.

(c) Assume that at January 1, 2003, Goldberg Products Limited incurred $6,000 of legal fees in successfully defending the rights to the patents. Prepare the entry for the year 2003 to amortize the patents.

(d) The company decided at the beginning of 2004 that the patent costs would benefit only 2004 and 2005. (A competitor has developed a product that will eventually make Goldberg Products' patent obsolete.) Record the patent amortization at the end of 2004.

(e) Prepare required journal entry(ies), if any, related to goodwill for 2004.

P13-5 During 2000, Nightingale Tool Ltd. purchased a building site for its proposed product development laboratory at a cost of $60,000. Construction of the building was started in 2000. The building was completed on December 31, 2001 at a cost of $280,000 and was placed in service on January 2, 2002. The building's estimated useful life for amortization purposes was 20 years; the straight-line method of amortization is used and there was no estimated residual value.

Management estimates that about 50% of the development projects will result in long-term benefits (i.e., at least 10 years) to the corporation. The remaining projects either benefited the current period or were abandoned before completion. A summary of the number of projects and the direct costs incurred in conjunction with the development activities for 2002 appears below.

Upon recommendation of the research and development group, Nightingale Tool Ltd. acquired a patent for manufacturing rights at a cost of $80,000. The patent was acquired on April 1, 2001 and has an economic life of 10 years.

	Number of Projects	Salaries and Employee Benefits	Other Expenses (excluding Building Amortization Charges)
Development of viable products (management intent and capability criteria are met)	15	$ 90,000	$50,000
Abandoned projects or projects that benefit the current period	10	65,000	15,000
Projects in process—results indeterminate	5	40,000	12,000
Total	30	$195,000	$77,000

Instructions

If generally accepted accounting principles are followed, how should the items above relating to product development activities be reported on the company's:

(a) income statement for 2002?

(b) balance sheet as of December 31, 2002?

Be sure to give account titles and amounts, and briefly justify your presentation.

(CMA adapted)

*P13-6 Anshan Inc. has recently become interested in acquiring a South American plant to handle many of its production functions in that market. One possible candidate is La Paz Inc., a closely held corporation, whose owners have decided to sell their business if a proper settlement can be obtained. La Paz's balance sheet appears as follows:

Current assets	$150,000
Investments	50,000
Plant assets (net)	400,000
Total assets	$600,000
Current liabilities	$ 80,000
Long-term debt	100,000
Share capital	220,000
Retained earnings	200,000
Total equities	$600,000

Anshan has hired Palermo Appraisal Corporation to determine the proper price to pay for La Paz Inc. The appraisal firm finds that the investments have a fair market value of $150,000 and that inventory is understated by $80,000. All other assets and liabilities have book values that approximate their fair values. An examination of the company's income for the last four years indicates that the net income has steadily increased. In 2002, the company had a net operating income of $100,000, and this income should increase 20% each year over the next four years. Anshan believes that a normal return in this type of business is 18% on net assets. The asset investment in the South American plant is expected to stay the same for the next four years.

Instructions

(a) Palermo Appraisal Corporation has indicated that the company's fair value can be estimated in a number of ways. Prepare an estimate of the value of La Paz Inc., assuming that any goodwill will be calculated as:

1. The capitalization of the average excess earnings of La Paz Inc. at 18%.

2. The purchase of average excess earnings over the next four years.

3. The capitalization of average excess earnings of La Paz Inc. at 24%.

4. The present value of the average excess earnings over the next four years discounted at 15%.

(b) La Paz Inc. is willing to sell the business for $1 million. How do you believe Palermo Appraisal should advise Anshan?

(c) If Anshan were to pay $770,000 to purchase the assets and assume the liabilities of La Paz Inc., how would this transaction be reflected on Anshan's books?

P13-7 Sato Corporation was incorporated on January 3, 2001. The corporation's financial statements for its first year's operations were not examined by a public accountant. You have been engaged to audit the financial statements for the year ended December 31, 2002, and your audit is substantially completed. The corporation's trial balance appears below.

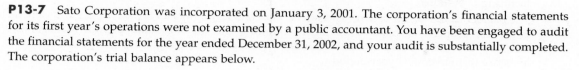

	Debit	Credit
Cash	$ 47,000	
Accounts Receivable	73,000	
Allowance for Doubtful Accounts		$ 1,460
Inventories	50,200	
Machinery	82,000	
Equipment	37,000	
Accumulated Amortization		26,200
Patents	128,200	
Leasehold Improvements	36,100	
Prepaid Expenses	13,000	
Goodwill	30,000	
Licensing Agreement No. 1	60,000	
Licensing Agreement No. 2	56,000	
Accounts Payable		73,000
Unearned Revenue		17,280
Share Capital		300,000
Retained Earnings, January 1, 2002		159,060
Sales		720,000
Cost of Goods Sold	475,000	
Selling and General Expenses	180,000	
Interest Expense	9,500	
Extraordinary Losses	20,000	
Totals	$1,297,000	$1,297,000

The following information relates to accounts that may yet require adjustment.

1. Patents for Sato's manufacturing process were acquired January 2, 2002, at a cost of $93,500. An additional $34,700 was spent in December 2002 to improve machinery covered by the patents and was charged to the Patents account. Amortization on fixed assets was properly recorded for 2002 in accordance with Sato's practice, which provides a full year's amortization for property on hand June 30 and no amortization otherwise. Sato uses the straight-line method for all amortization and amortizes its patents over their legal life, which was 17 years when granted.

2. On January 3, 2001, Sato purchased licensing agreement No. 1, which management believed had an unlimited useful life. Licences similar to this are frequently bought and sold. Sato could only clearly identify cash flows from agreement No. 1 for 18 years, after which further cash flows are likely, but somewhat uncertain. The balance in the Licensing Agreement No. 1 account includes its purchase price of $57,000 and expenses of $3,000 related to the acquisition. On January 1, 2002, Sato purchases licensing agreement No. 2, which has a life expectancy of 10 years. The balance in the Licensing Agreement No. 2 account includes its $54,000 purchase price and $6,000 in acquisition expenses, but it has been reduced by a credit of $4,000 for the advance collection of 2003 revenue from the agreement.

   In late December 2001, an explosion caused a permanent 70% reduction in the expected revenue-producing value of licensing agreement No. 1, and in January 2003, a flood caused additional damage that rendered the agreement worthless.

3. The balance in the Goodwill account results from legal expenses of $30,000 incurred for Sato's incorporation on January 3, 2001.

4. The Leasehold Improvements account includes **(a)** the $15,000 cost of improvements with a total estimated useful life of 12 years, which Sato, as tenant, made to leased premises in January 2001,

(b) movable assembly line equipment costing $15,000 that was installed in the leased premises in December 2002, and (c) real estate taxes of $6,100 paid by Sato in 2002, which under the terms of the lease should have been paid by the landlord. Sato paid its rent in full during 2002. A 10-year nonrenewable lease was signed January 3, 2001, for the leased building that Sato used in manufacturing operations.

5. The balance in the Organization Expenses account of $32,000 (included with Selling and General Expenses) properly includes costs incurred during the organizational period. Management assumed these costs would benefit the company for the entire life of the company, but decided to amortize them over a 30-year period.

Instructions

Prepare an 8-column work sheet to adjust accounts that require adjustment and include columns for an income statement and a balance sheet.

A separate account should be used for the accumulation of each type of amortization. Formal adjusting journal entries and financial statements are not required.

(AICPA adapted)

P13-8 Presented below are six examples of purchased intangible assets reported on the balance sheet of HTM Enterprises Limited, including information about their useful and legal lives.

Intangible #1(a): The trade name for one of the company's subsidiaries. The trade name has a remaining legal life of 16 years, but it can be renewed indefinitely at a very low cost. The subsidiary has grown quickly, has been very successful and its name is well known to Canadian consumers. HTM management has concluded that it can identify positive cash flows from the use of the trade name for another 25 years, and assumes they will continue beyond this as well.

Intangible #1(b): The trade name is as identified above, but assume instead that HTM Enterprises expects to sell this subsidiary in three years' time as the subsidiary operates in a non-core area.

Intangible #2: A licence granted by the federal government to HTM to permit it to provide essential services to a key military installation overseas. The licence expires in five years, but is renewable indefinitely at little cost. Because of the profitability associated with this licence, HTM expects to renew it indefinitely. The licence is very marketable, and will generate cash flows indefinitely.

Intangible #3: Magazine subscription list. HTM expects to use this subscriber list to generate revenues and cash flows for at least 25 years. It has determined the cash flow potential of this intangible by analysing past renewal history, the behaviour of the group, and its responses to questionnaires.

Intangible #4: Non-competition covenant. HTM acquired this intangible asset when the company bought out a major owner-managed competitor. The seller signed an agreement contracting not to set up or work for another business that was in direct or indirect competition with HTM. The projected cash flows resulting from this agreement are expected to continue for at least 25 years.

Intangible #5: Medical files. One of HTM's subsidiary companies owns a number of medical clinics. A recent purchase of a retiring doctor's practice required a significant payment for the praactice's medical files and clients. HTM considers that this base will benefit the business throughout its organizational existence, providing cash flows indefinitely.

Intangible #6: Favourable lease. HTM acquired a sub-lease on a large warehouse property that requires annual rentals that are 50% below competitive rates in the area. The lease extends for 35 years.

Instructions

For each intangible asset and situation described above, identify the appropriate method of accounting for the asset subsequent to acquisition. Justify your response. For each of the six, provide an example of a specific situation that would prompt you to test the intangible asset for impairment.

*P13-9 Presented below are financial forecasts related to Bushnell Inc. for the next 10 years.

Forecasted average earnings (per year)	$ 70,000
Forecasted market value of net assets, exclusive of goodwill (average over 10 years)	340,000

Instructions

You have been asked to calculate goodwill and determine the company's total value under the following methods. The normal rate of return on net assets for the industry is 15%.

(a) Goodwill is equal to five years' excess earnings.
(b) Goodwill is equal to the present value of five years' excess earnings discounted at 12%.
(c) Goodwill is equal to the average excess earnings capitalized at 16%.
(d) The company's total value is equal to its expected earnings capitalized at the normal rate of return for the industry of 15%.

*P13-10   Foster Corporation, a high-flying conglomerate, has recently been involved in discussions with McLaren Inc. As its accountant, you have been instructed by Foster to conduct a purchase audit of McLaren's books to determine a possible purchase price for McLaren's net assets. The following information is found.

Total identifiable assets (fair value)	$250,000
Liabilities (fair value)	60,000
Average rate of return on net assets for McLaren's industry	15%
Forecasted earnings per year based on past earnings figures	35,000

Instructions

(a) Foster asks you to determine the purchase price and the amount of implied goodwill based on the following assumptions:
1. Goodwill is equal to three years' excess earnings.
2. Goodwill is equal to the present value of excess earnings discounted at 15% for four years.
3. The company's total value is equal to its expected earnings capitalized at 15%.
4. Goodwill is equal to the capitalization of excess earnings at 25%.

(b) Foster asks you which of the methods above is the most theoretically sound. Justify your answer. Any assumptions made should be clearly indicated.

*P13-11   (Calculation of Goodwill—Various Methods)   The president of Birch Corp., Joyce Pollachek, is considering purchasing Balloon Bunch Company. She thinks that the offer sounds pretty good, but she wants to consult a professional accountant to be sure. Balloon Bunch Company is asking $78,000 over the fair value of the net identifiable assets. Balloon Bunch's net income figures for the last five years are as follows:

1998 – $64,000	2001 – $80,000
1999 – $50,000	2002 – $70,000
2000 – $81,000	

The company's net identifiable assets were appraised at $400,000 on December 31, 2002.

You have done some initial research on the balloon industry and discovered that the normal rate of return on net identifiable assets is 13%. After analysing variables such as stability of past earnings, the nature of the business, and general economic conditions, you have decided that the average excess earnings for the last five years should be capitalized at 25% and that the excess earnings will continue for about five more years. Further research led you to discover that the Happy Balloon Company, a competitor of similar size and profitability, was recently sold for $540,000, six times its average yearly earnings of $90,000.

Instructions

(a) Prepare a schedule that includes the calculation of Balloon Bunch Company's goodwill and purchase price under at least three methods.
(b) Write a letter to Joyce Pollachek that includes:
1. An explanation of the nature of goodwill.
2. An explanation of the different acceptable methods of determining its fair value. (Include with your explanation of the different methods the rationale of how each method arrives at a goodwill value.)
3. Advice for Joyce Pollachek on how to determine her purchase price.

CONCEPTUAL CASES

C13-1   In examining the books of Sorenstam Manufacturing Limited, you find on the December 31, 2002 balance sheet the item "Costs of patents, $922,000."

Referring to the ledger accounts, you note the following items regarding one patent acquired in 1999:

1999	Legal costs incurred in defending the patent's validity	$ 55,000
2001	Legal costs in prosecuting an infringement suit	94,000
2002	Legal costs (additional expenses) in the infringement suit	44,500
2002	Cost of improvements (unpatented) on the patented device	151,200

There are no credits in the account, and no accumulated amortization account has been set up on the books for any of the patents. Three other patents issued in 1996, 1998, and 1999 were developed by the client's staff. The patented articles are currently very marketable, but it is estimated that they will be in demand only for the next few years.

Instructions

Discuss the items included in the Patent account from an accounting standpoint.

(AICPA adapted)

C13-2 MMG Inc. is a large, publicly held corporation. Listed below are six selected expenditures made by the company during the current fiscal year ended April 30, 2002. The proper accounting treatment of these transactions must be determined in order to ensure MMG's annual financial statements are prepared in accordance with generally accepted accounting principles.

1. MMG Inc. spent $3 million on a program designed to improve relations with its dealers. This project was favourably received by the dealers and MMG's management believes that significant future benefits will be received from this program. The program was conducted during the fourth quarter of the current fiscal year.

2. A pilot plant was constructed during 2001-02 at a cost of $5.5 million to test a new production process. The plant will be operated for approximately five years. At that time, the company will make a decision regarding the economic value of the process. The pilot plant is too small for commercial production, so it will be dismantled when the test is over.

3. During the year, MMG began a new manufacturing operation in Newfoundland, its first plant east of Montreal. To get the plant into operation, the following costs were incurred: (a) $100,000 to make the building fully wheelchair accessible; (b) $41,600 to outfit the new employees with MMG uniforms; (c) $12,700 for the reception to introduce the company to others in the industrial mall where the plant was located; and (d) $64,400 payroll costs covering the new employees while being trained.

4. MMG Inc. purchased Eagle Company for $6 million in cash in early August 2001. The fair value of Eagle's net identifiable assets was $5.2 million.

5. The company spent $14 million on advertising during the year: $2.5 million was spent in April 2002 to introduce a new product to be released during the first quarter of the 2003 fiscal year; $200,000 was dedicated to advertising the opening of the new plant in Newfoundland; $5 million was spent on the company product catelogue for the 2002 calendar year. The remaining expenditures were for recurring advertising and promotion coverage.

6. During the first six months of the 2001-02 fiscal year, $400,000 was expended for legal work in connection with a successful patent application. The patent became effective November 2001. The patent's legal life is 20 years and its economic life is expected to be approximately 10 years.

Instructions

For each of the six items presented, determine and justify:

(a) The amount, if any, that should be capitalized and included on MMG's statement of financial position prepared as of April 30, 2002.

(b) The amount that should be included in MMG's statement of income for the year ended April 30, 2002.

(CMA adapted)

C13-3 Pickelson Company operates several plants at which limestone is processed into quicklime and hydrated lime. The Harbour Ridge plant, where most of the equipment was installed many years ago, continually deposits a dusty white substance over the surrounding countryside. Citing the unsanitary condition of the neighbouring community of Eastern Passage, the pollution of the Bedford River, and the high incidence of lung disease among workers at Harbour Ridge, the province's Pollution Control Agency has ordered the installation of air pollution control equipment. Also, the agency has assessed a substantial penalty, which will be used to clean up Eastern Passage. After considering the costs involved (which could not have been reasonably estimated prior to the agency's action), Pickelson Company decides to comply with the agency's orders, the alternative being to cease operations at Harbour Ridge at the end of the current fiscal year. The company officers agree that the air pollution control equipment should be capitalized and amortized over its useful life, but they disagree over the period(s) to which the penalty should be charged.

Instructions

Discuss the conceptual merits and reporting requirements of accounting for the penalty as a:

(a) charge to the current period

(b) correction of prior periods

(c) capitalizable item to be amortized over future periods

(AICPA adapted)

C13-4 After securing lease commitments from several major stores, Kolber Shopping Centres Ltd. was organized and built a shopping centre in a growing suburb.

The shopping centre would have opened on schedule on January 1, 2002, if it had not been struck by a severe tornado in December; it opened for business on October 1, 2002. All of the additional construction costs that were incurred as a result of the tornado were covered by insurance.

In July 2001, in anticipation of the scheduled January opening, a permanent staff had been hired to promote the shopping centre, obtain tenants for the uncommitted space, and manage the property.

A summary of some of the costs incurred in 2001 and the first nine months of 2002 follows.

	2001	January 1, 2002 through September 30, 2002
Interest on mortgage bonds	$720,000	$540,000
Cost of obtaining tenants	300,000	360,000
Promotional advertising	540,000	557,000

The promotional advertising campaign was designed to familiarize shoppers with the centre. Had it been known in time that the centre would not open until October 2002, the 2001 expenditure for promotional advertising would not have been made. The advertising had to be repeated in 2002.

All of the tenants who had leased space in the shopping centre at the time of the tornado accepted the October occupancy date on condition that the monthly rental charges for the first nine months of 2002 be cancelled.

Instructions

Explain how each of the costs for 2001 and the first nine months of 2002 should be treated in the accounts of the shopping centre corporation. Give the reasons for each treatment.

(AICPA adapted)

C13-5 On June 30, 2002, your client, Bearcat Limited, was granted two patents covering plastic cartons that it had been producing and marketing profitably for the past three years. One patent covers the manufacturing process and the other covers related products.

Bearcat executives tell you that these patents represent the most significant breakthrough in the industry in the past 30 years. The products have been marketed under the registered trademarks Evertight, Duratainer, and Sealrite. Licences under the patents have already been granted by your client to other manufacturers in Canada and abroad and are producing substantial royalties.

On July 1, Bearcat commenced patent infringement actions against several companies whose names you recognize as those of substantial and prominent competitors. Bearcat's management is optimistic that these suits will result in a permanent injunction against the manufacture and sale of the infringing products and collection of damages for loss of profits caused by the alleged infringement.

The financial vice-president has suggested that the patents be recorded at the discounted value of expected net royalty receipts.

Instructions

(a) What is the meaning of "discounted value of expected net receipts"? Explain.

(b) How would such a value be calculated for net royalty receipts?

(c) What basis of valuation for Bearcat's patents would be generally accepted in accounting? Give supporting reasons for this basis.

(d) Assuming no practical problems of implementation and ignoring generally accepted accounting principles, what is the preferable basis of valuation for patents? Explain.

(e) What would be the preferred theoretical basis of amortization? Explain.

(f) What recognition, if any, should be made of the infringement litigation in the financial statements for the year ending September 30, 2002? Discuss.

(AICPA adapted)

C13-6 Echo Corp., a retail propane gas distributor, has increased its annual sales volume to a level three times greater than the annual sales of a dealer it purchased in 2000 in order to begin operations.

The board of directors of Echo Corp. recently received an offer to negotiate the sale of Echo to a large competitor. As a result, the majority of the board wants to increase the stated value of goodwill on the balance sheet to reflect the larger sales volume developed through intensive promotion and the product's current market price. A few of the board members, however, would prefer to eliminate goodwill altogether from the balance sheet in order to prevent "possible misinterpretations." Goodwill was recorded properly in 2000.

Instructions

(a) Discuss the meaning of the term "goodwill."

(b) List the techniques used to calculate the tentative value of goodwill in negotiations to purchase a going concern.

(c) Why are the book and fair values of Echo Corp.'s goodwill different?

(d) Discuss the propriety of

1. Increasing the stated value of goodwill prior to the negotiations.
2. Eliminating goodwill completely from the balance sheet.

(AICPA adapted)

C13-7 Nova Jones Ltd. is developing a revolutionary new product. A new division of the company was formed to develop, manufacture, and market this new product. As of year end (December 31, 2002), the new product had not been manufactured for resale; however, a prototype unit was built and is in operation.

Throughout 2002, the new division incurred costs. These costs include design and engineering studies, prototype manufacturing costs, administrative expenses (including salaries of administrative personnel), and market research costs. In addition, approximately $900,000 in equipment (estimated useful life of 10 years) was purchased to develop and manufacture the new product. Approximately $315,000 of this equipment was built specifically for the design development of the new product; the remaining $585,000 of equipment was used to manufacture the pre-production prototype and will be used to manufacture the new product once it is in commercial production.

Instructions

(a) How are "research" and "development" defined in *CICA Handbook*, Section 3450?

(b) Briefly indicate the practical and conceptual reasons for the conclusions reached by the Accounting Standards Board on accounting and reporting practices for research and development costs.

(c) In accordance with Section 3450, how should the various costs of Nova Jones described above be recorded on its financial statements for the year ended December 31, 2002? Provide support for your conclusions.

(AICPA adapted)

Using Your Judgement

FINANCIAL REPORTING PROBLEM: CANADIAN TIRE CORPORATION

Refer to the financial statements and accompanying notes and discussion of **Canadian Tire Corporation** presented in Appendix 5B and answer the following questions:

Instructions

(a) Does Canadian Tire report any non-goodwill intangible assets (broadly defined) in its 2000 financial statements and accompanying notes? Identify all intangibles and the accounting for these assets.

(b) What accounting policy does Canadian Tire apply in accounting for goodwill? Reconcile the opening and closing balances of goodwill reported by the company. In what respect would the accounting for goodwill differ, if at all, as a result of the revised accounting standards approved in 2001?

(c) The notes to the financial statements indicate that the company entered into two business combinations in 2000. Indicate how the amount of goodwill purchased as a result of these transactions was determined. Draft a journal entry for each of the purchase transactions that captures what happened in each combination.

FINANCIAL STATEMENT ANALYSIS CASE

Nortel Networks Corporation

Nortel Networks announced on June 15, 2001 a predicted $19.2 billion loss for its second quarter ending June 30. Nortel had been the darling of the telecommmunications industry with its share price reaching a high of $124.50 a year earlier. On June 15, 2001, it closed at $15.17, although it traded as low as $13.75 earlier that day.

As usual, there is considerable information in the components of the (expected) earnings and in the news announcement itself. The following details were provided:

— plans to slash 10,000 more jobs and 8.8 million square feet of office and manufacturing space

— discontinuation of further common share dividends

— $950 million writedown of excess and obsolete inventory, bad debts, and investments

— $830 million for severance packages and downsizing costs

— $2.6 billion for closing of non-core businesses, including $750 million writedown of goodwill

— $12.3 billion writedown of intangibles (goodwill) from recent large acquisitions where shares of Nortel had been given as the consideration to the other company shareholders in return for their ownership interests in the net assets acquired

— $2 billion of intangibles amortization from continuing operations

Instructions

1. Explain why Nortel probably recognized the $12.3 billion writedown of intangibles from the recent acquisitions. As part of your explanation, prepare skeleton journal entries to record the original purchases. Assume they had been made when the Nortel share price was at its highest.

2. Obtain access to the actual financial statements of Nortel subsequent to the release of the 2001 second quarter results. Explain how these various writedowns and allowances were reported by the company in 2001.

3. What is the effect on future reported earnings of recognizing these writedowns in the current period? Comment.

FINANCIAL STATEMENT ANALYSIS CASE

Merck and Johnson & Johnson

Merck & Co., Inc. and Johnson & Johnson are two leading producers of health care products. Each has considerable assets, and each expends considerable funds each year toward the development of new products. The development of a new health care product is often very expensive, and risky. New products frequently must undergo considerable testing before approval for distribution to the public. For example, it took Johnson & Johnson four years and $200 million to develop its 1-DAY ACUVUE contact lenses. Below are some basic data compiled from the financial statements of these two companies.

(in US$ millions)	Johnson & Johnson	Merck
Total assets	$31,321	$39,910
Total revenue	29,139	40,363
Net income	4,800	6,822
Research and development expense	2,926	2,344
Intangible assets	7,256	7,374

Instructions

(a) What kinds of intangible assets might a health care products company have? Does the composition of these intangibles matter to investors; that is, would it be perceived differently if all of Merck's intangibles were goodwill, than if all of its intangibles were patents?

(b) Suppose the president of Merck has come to you for advice. He has noted that by eliminating research and development expenditures, the company could have reported $2.3 billion more in net income. He is frustrated because much of the research never results in a product, or the products take years to develop. He says shareholders are eager for higher returns, so he is considering eliminating research and development expenditures for at least a couple of years. What would you advise?

(c) The notes to Merck's financial statements note that Merck has goodwill of $3.8 billion. Where does recorded goodwill come from? Is it necessarily a good thing to have a lot of goodwill on your books?

COMPARATIVE ANALYSIS CASE

Instructions

Go to the http://www.sedar.com website and choose two companies from each of four different industry classifications. Choose from a variety of industries such as real estate and construction, foodstores (under merchandising), biotechnology and pharmaceuticals (under consumer products), publishing (under communications and media), etc. From the companies' most recent financial statements, identify the intangibles and deferred charges, the total assets, and the accounting policies for each type of intangible and deferred charge reported.

(a) 1. What amounts were reported for intangible assets and deferred charges by each company?

2. What percentage of total assets does each company have invested in intangible assets and deferred charges?

3. Does the type of intangible and deferred charge differ depending on the type of industry? Does the relative investment in this category of asset differ among industries? Comment.

(b) 1. List all the intangible assets you identified and the policies used by these companies in amortizing them, if applicable. Do the policies differ by type of intangible? by type of industry?

2. Are the amounts of accumulated amortization reported by these companies? Have any impairments been reported in the current period? If so, what disclosure was made about the impairment?

RESEARCH CASES

Case 1

Instructions

Examine the financial statements and related footnotes for three companies of your choice, and answer the following questions with respect to each company.

(a) Identify any intangible assets included on the balance sheet.

(b) What is the useful life over which the intangibles are being amortized? If an intangible is not being amortized, explain the basis for the non-amortization.

(c) Does the company report an Accumulated Amortization account?

(d) What were the company's research and development expenses in the most recent two years? Did the company receive any external funding to help finance the R & D expenditures?

Case 2

The February 19, 1996 issue of *Fortune* magazine includes an article by Thomas A. Stewart entitled "The Coins in the Knowledge Bank."

Instructions

Read the article and answer the following questions.

(a) What is the rationale for estimating the "knowledge bank" and reporting it on the balance sheet?

(b) What is the purpose of income measurement under the proposed approach?

(c) Why should capital spending be treated as an expense?

(d) What items treated as expenses under GAAP should be capitalized on the balance sheet?

(e) While the article admits that the method is subjective, why might it still be appropriate for financial reporting?

INTERNATIONAL REPORTING CASE

Presented below are 1998 data and accounting policy notes for the goodwill of three international drug companies. **Bayer**, a German company, prepared its statements in accordance with International Accounting Standards (IAS); **Smithkline Beecham** followed United Kingdom (UK) rules; and **Merck**, a U.S. company, prepared its financial statements in accordance with U.S. GAAP.

Related Information for 1998	Bayer (DM millions)	Smithkline Beecham (£ millions)	Merck (U.S. $ millions)
Amortization expense	136	69	264
Net income	3,157	606	5,248
Accumulated goodwill amortization	306	313	1,124
Shareholders' equity	24,991	1,747	31,853

The following accounting policy notes related to goodwill appeared with the companies' financial statements.

Bayer

Intangible assets that have been acquired are recognized at cost and amortized over their estimated useful lives. Goodwill, including that resulting from capital consolidation, is capitalized in accordance with IAS 22 (Business Combinations) and normally is amortized over a period of 5 or at most 20 years.

Smithkline Beecham

Goodwill, representing the excess of the purchase consideration over the fair value of the net separable assets acquired, is capitalised and amortised over an appropriate period not exceeding 20 years. Prior to 1998, all goodwill, except for diversified goodwill, was eliminated in the Group balance sheet against reserves in the year of acquisition.

Merck

Goodwill represents the excess of acquisition costs over the fair value of net assets of businesses purchased and is amortized on a straight-line basis over periods up to 40 years.

Instructions

(a) Calculate the return on equity for each of these companies, and use this analysis to briefly discuss the relative profitability of the three companies.

(b) Assume that each company used the maximum amortization period indicated in its notes for goodwill. Discuss how these companies' goodwill amortization policies affect your ability to compare their amortization expense and income.

(c) Some analysts believe that the only valid way to compare companies that follow different goodwill accounting practices is to treat all goodwill as an asset and record expense only if the goodwill is impaired.[45] This policy, as Chapter 13 indicates, has been approved as GAAP by both the Accounting Standards Board and FASB in 2001. Using the data above, make these adjustments, and compare the profitability of the three drug companies, comparing this information with your analysis in (a).

ETHICS CASE

Waveland Corporation's research and development department has an idea for a project it believes will culminate in a new product that would be very profitable for the company. Because the project will be very expensive, the department requests approval from Waveland Corporation's controller, Ron Santo.

Santo recognizes that corporate profits have been down lately and is hesitant to approve a project that will incur significant expenses that cannot be capitalized under *Handbook*, Section 3450 on Research and Development Costs. He knows that if they hire an outside firm that does the work and obtains a patent for the process, Waveland Corporation can purchase the patent from the outside firm and record the expenditure as an asset. Santo knows that the company's own R&D department is first-rate, and he is confident they can do the work well.

Instructions

Answer the following questions:

(a) Who are the stakeholders in this situation?

(b) What are the ethical issues involved?

(c) What should Santo do?

---

[45] Trevor Harris, *Apples to Apples: Accounting for Value in World Markets*, (New York: Morgan Stanley Dean Witter, February 1998).

Appendix

Accounting and the Time Value of Money

LEARNING OBJECTIVES

After studying this appendix, you should be able to:

1. Identify accounting topics where time value of money is relevant.
2. Distinguish between simple and compound interest.
3. Know how to use appropriate compound interest tables.
4. Identify variables fundamental to solving interest problems.
5. Solve future and present value of single sum problems.
6. Solve future value of ordinary and annuity due problems.
7. Solve present value of ordinary and annuity due problems.
8. Use spreadsheet functions to solve time value of money problems.

PREVIEW FOR APPENDIX

The timing of the returns on investments has an important effect on the worth of the investment (asset), and the timing of debt repayments has a similarly important effect on the value of the debt commitment (liability). As a business person, you will be expected to make present and future value measurements and to understand their implications. The purpose of this appendix is to present the tools and techniques that will help you measure the present value of future cash inflows and outflows. The content and organization of the appendix are as follows:

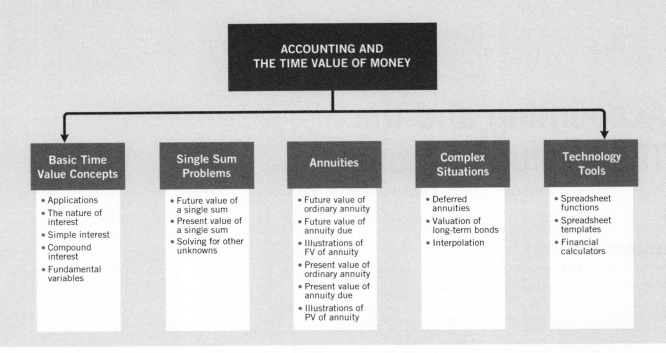

BASIC TIME VALUE CONCEPTS

In accounting (and finance), the term **time value of money** is used to indicate a relationship between time and money—that a dollar received today is worth more than a dollar promised at some time in the future. Why? Because of the opportunity to invest today's dollar and receive interest on the investment. Yet, when you have to decide among various investment or borrowing alternatives, it is essential to be able to compare today's dollar and tomorrow's dollar on the same footing—to "compare apples to apples." We do that by using the concept of **present value**, which has many applications in accounting.

Applications of Time Value Concepts

OBJECTIVE 1

Identify accounting topics where time value of money is relevant.

Compound interest, annuities, and application of present value concepts are relevant to making measurements and disclosures when accounting for various financial statement elements.[1] The following are some examples examined in this book and the chapters in which they appear:

1. **Notes.** Valuing receivables and payables that carry no stated interest rate or a different than market interest rate (Chapters 7 and 15).

2. **Leases.** Valuing assets and obligations to be capitalized under long-term leases, and measuring the amount of the lease payments and annual leasehold amortization (Chapter 21).

3. **Amortization of Premiums and Discounts.** Measuring amortization of premium or discount on both bond investments and bonds payable (Chapters 10 and 15).

4. **Pensions and Other Post-Retirement Benefits.** Measuring service cost components of employers' post-retirement benefits expense and benefit obligations (Chapter 20).

5. **Capital Assets.** Determining the value of assets acquired under deferred-payment contracts (Chapter 11).

6. **Sinking Funds.** Determining the contributions necessary to accumulate a fund for debt retirement (Chapter 15).

7. **Business Combinations.** Determining the value of receivables, payables, liabilities, accruals, goodwill, and commitments acquired or assumed in a "purchase" (Chapters 10 and 13).

8. **Amortization.** Measuring amortization charges under the sinking fund and the annuity methods (Chapter 12).

9. **Instalment Contracts.** Measuring periodic payments on long-term sales or purchase contracts (Chapters 6 and 15).

In addition to their accounting and business applications, compound interest, annuity, and present value concepts are applicable to personal finance and investment decisions. In purchasing a home, planning for retirement, and evaluating alternative investments, you must understand time value of money concepts.

Nature of Interest

Interest **is payment for the use of money.** It is the excess cash received or paid over and above the amount lent or borrowed (principal). For example, if the Toronto Dominion Bank lends you $1,000 with the understanding that you will repay $1,150, the $150 excess over $1,000 represents interest expense to you and interest revenue to the bank.

The amount of interest to be paid is generally stated as a rate over a specific period of time. For example, if you use the $1,000 for one year before repaying $1,150, the rate of interest is 15% per year ($150/$1,000). The custom of expressing interest as a rate is an established business practice.[2]

The interest rate is commonly expressed as it is applied to a one-year time period. Interest of 12% represents a rate of 12% per year, unless otherwise stipulated. The state-

---

[1] J. Alex Milburn, *Incorporating the Time Value of Money Within Financial Accounting* (Toronto: Canadian Institute of Chartered Accountants, 1988), p. 1. This is an excellent study regarding financial accounting and present value measurements. Its objective is to "develop proposals for reflecting the time value of money more fully within the existing financial accounting framework so as to enable a substantive improvement in the usefulness and credibility of financial statements" (p. 1). While we, the authors, accept the basic premise of this study, it is not our intention to examine the model and suggested changes to current financial accounting that are presented. The purpose of this appendix is more basic—to examine the time value of money and show how it can be incorporated in making measurements.

[2] Federal and provincial legislation requires the disclosure of the effective interest rate on an *annual basis* in contracts. That is, instead of, or in addition to, stating the rate as "1% per month," it must be stated as "12% per year" if it is simple interest or "12.68% per year" if it is compounded monthly.

ment that a corporation will pay bond interest of 12%, payable semiannually, means a rate of 6% every six months, not 12% every six months.

How is the *rate* of interest determined? One of the most important factors is the level of **credit risk** (risk of nonpayment). Other factors being equal, the higher the credit risk, the higher the interest rate. Every borrower's risk is evaluated by the lender. A low-risk borrower like Canadian Pacific Ltd. may obtain a loan at or slightly below the going market "prime" rate of interest. You or the neighbourhood delicatessen, however, will probably be charged several percentage points above the prime rate.

Another important factor is **inflation** (change in the general purchasing power of the dollar). Lenders want to protect the purchasing power of the future cash flows to be received (interest payments and return of the principal). If inflation is expected to be significant in the future, lenders will require a higher number of dollars (i.e., a higher interest rate) in order to offset their anticipation that the purchasing power of these dollars will be reduced.

In addition to receiving compensation for risk and expected inflation, lenders also desire a **pure** or **real return** for letting someone else use their money. This real return reflects the amount the lender would charge if there were no possibility of default or expectation of inflation.

The *amount* of interest related to any financing transaction is a function of three variables:

1. **Principal**—the amount borrowed or invested.
2. **Interest Rate**—a percentage of the outstanding principal.
3. **Time**—the number of years or portion of a year that the principal is outstanding.

Simple Interest

OBJECTIVE 2

Distinguish between simple and compound interest.

Simple interest is calculated on the amount of the principal only. It is the return on (or growth of) the principal for one time period. Simple interest[3] is commonly expressed as:

$$\text{Interest} = p \times i \times n$$

where

p = principal
i = rate of interest for a single period
n = number of periods

To illustrate, if you borrowed $1,000 for a three-year period, with a simple interest rate of 15% per year, the total interest to be paid would be $450, calculated as follows:

$$\begin{aligned}\text{Interest} &= (p)(i)(n)\\ &= (\$1,000)(0.15)(3)\\ &= \$450\end{aligned}$$

Compound Interest

John Maynard Keynes, the legendary English economist, supposedly called it magic. Mayer Rothschild, the founder of the famous European banking firm, is said to have proclaimed it the eighth wonder of the world. Today people continue to extol its wonder and its power.[4] The object of their affection is compound interest.

Compound interest *is calculated on the principal and any interest earned that has not been paid.* To illustrate the difference between simple interest and compound inter-

---

[3] Simple interest is also expressed as i (interest) = P(principal) $\times$ R(rate) $\times$ T(time).

[4] Here is an illustration of the power of time and compounding interest on money. In 1626, Peter Minuit bought Manhatten Island from the Manhattoe Indians for $24 worth of trinkets and beads. If the Indians had taken a boat to Holland, invested the $24 in Dutch securities returning just 6% per year, and kept the money and interest invested at 6%, by 1971 they would have had $13 billion, enough to buy back all the land on the island and still have a couple of billion dollars left (*Forbes*, June 1, 1971). By 1998, 372 years after the trade, the $24 would have grown to approximately $63 billion—$62 trillion had the interest rate been 8%.

est, assume that you deposit $1,000 in the Last Canadian Bank, where it earns simple interest of 9% per year. Assume that you deposit another $1,000 in the First Canadian Bank, where it earns annually compounded interest of 9%. Finally, assume that in both cases you do not withdraw any interest until three years from the date of deposit. The calculation of interest to be received is shown in Illustration A-1.

ILLUSTRATION A-1
Simple vs. Compound Interest

| | Last Canadian Bank | | | First Canadian Bank | | |
	Simple Interest Calculation	Simple Interest	Accumulated Year-End Balance	Compound Interest Calculation	Compound Interest	Accumulated Year-End Balance
Year 1	$1,000.00 × 9%	$ 90.00	$1,090.00	$1,000.00 × 9%	$ 90.00	$1,090.00
Year 2	1,000.00 × 9%	90.00	1,180.00	1,090.00 × 9%	98.10	1,188.10
Year 3	1,000.00 × 9%	90.00	1,270.00	1,188.10 × 9%	106.93	1,295.03
		$270.00	◀— $25.03 Difference —▶			$295.03

Note that simple interest uses the initial principal of $1,000 to calculate the interest in all three years, while compound interest uses the accumulated balance (principal plus interest to date) at each year end to calculate interest in the succeeding year. Obviously, if you had a choice between investing at simple interest or at compound interest, you would choose compound interest, all other things—especially risk—being equal. In the example, compounding provides $25.03 of additional interest income.

Compound interest is generally applied in business situations. Financial managers view and evaluate their investment opportunities in terms of a series of periodic returns, each of which can be reinvested to yield additional returns. Simple interest is generally applicable only to short-term investments and debts that are due within one year.

Compound Interest Tables

Five different compound interest tables are presented at the end of this appendix (see pages A-27–A-31). These tables are the source for various "interest factors" used to solve problems that involve interest in this appendix and throughout the book. The titles of these five tables and their contents are:

OBJECTIVE 3

Know how to use appropriate compound interest tables.

1. **Future Value of 1.** Contains the amounts to which $1.00 will accumulate if deposited now at a specified rate and left for a specified number of periods (Table A-1).
2. **Present Value of 1.** Contains the amounts that must be deposited now at a specified rate of interest to equal $1.00 at the end of a specified number of periods (Table A-2).
3. **Future Value of an Ordinary Annuity of 1.** Contains the amounts to which periodic rents of $1.00 will accumulate if the rents are invested at the end of each period at a specified rate of interest for a specified number of periods (Table A-3).
4. **Present Value of an Ordinary Annuity of 1.** Contains the amounts that must be deposited now at a specified rate of interest to permit withdrawals of $1.00 at the end of regular periodic intervals for the specified number of periods (Table A-4).
5. **Present Value of an Annuity Due of 1.** Contains the amounts that must be deposited now at a specified rate of interest to permit withdrawals of $1.00 at the beginning of regular periodic intervals for the specified number of periods (Table A-5).

Illustration A-2 shows the general format and content of these tables. It is from Table A-1, "Future Value of 1," which indicates the amount to which a dollar accumulates at the end of each of five periods at three different rates of compound interest.

ILLUSTRATION A-2
Excerpt from Table A-1

	Future Value of 1 at Compounding Interest		
Period	9%	10%	11%
1	1.09000	1.10000	1.11000
2	1.18810	1.21000	1.23210
3	1.29503	1.33100	1.36763
4	1.41158	1.46410	1.51807
5	1.53862	1.61051	1.68506

Interpreting the table, if $1.00 is invested for three periods at a compound interest rate of 9% per period, it will amount to $1.30 (1.29503 × $1.00), the compound future avalue. If $1.00 is invested at 11%, at the end of four periods it amounts to $1.52. If the investment is $1,000 instead of $1.00, it will amount to $1,295.03 ($1,000 × 1.29503) if invested at 9% for three periods, or $1,518.07 if invested at 11% for four periods.

Throughout the foregoing discussion and the discussion that follows, the use of the term *periods* instead of *years* is intentional. While interest is generally expressed as an annual rate, the compounding period is often shorter. Therefore, the annual interest rate must be converted to correspond to the length of the period. To convert the "annual interest rate" into the "compounding period interest rate," *divide the annual rate by the number of compounding periods per year.* In addition, the number of periods is determined by *multiplying the number of years involved by the number of compounding periods per year.*

To illustrate, assume that $1.00 is invested for six years at 8% annual interest compounded quarterly. Using Table A-1, the amount to which this $1.00 will accumulate is determined by reading the factor that appears in the 2% column (8% ÷ 4) on the 24th row (6 years × 4), namely 1.60844, or approximately $1.61.

Because interest is theoretically earned every second of every day, it is possible to calculate continuously compounded interest. As a practical matter, however, most business transactions assume interest is compounded no more frequently than daily.

How often interest is compounded can make a substantial difference to the rate of return achieved. For example, 9% interest compounded daily provides a 9.42% annual yield, or a difference of 0.42%. The 9.42% is referred to as the effective yield or rate,[5] whereas the 9% annual interest rate is called the stated, nominal, coupon, or face rate. When the compounding frequency is greater than once a year, the effective interest rate is higher than the stated rate.

Fundamental Variables

The following four variables are fundamental to all compound interest problems:

OBJECTIVE 4
. . . .
Identify variables fundamental to solving interest problems.

1. **Rate of Interest.** This rate, unless otherwise stated, is an annual rate that must be adjusted to reflect the length of the compounding period if it is less than a year.
2. **Number of Time Periods.** This is the number of compounding periods for which interest is to be computed.
3. **Future Value.** The value at a future date of a given sum or sums invested, assuming compound interest.
4. **Present Value.** The value now (present time) of a future sum or sums discounted, assuming compound interest.

The relationship of these four variables is depicted in the **time diagram** in Illustration A-3.

---

[5] The formula for calculating the effective annual rate in situations where the compounding frequency (n) is more than once a year is as follows:

$$\text{Effective rate} = (1 + i)^n - 1$$

where i = the interest rate per compounding period, and
n = the number of compounding periods per year

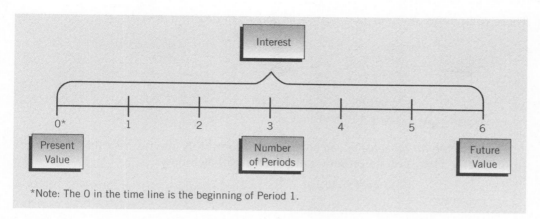

In some cases all four of these variables are known, but in many business situations at least one is unknown. Frequently, the accountant is expected to determine the unknown amount or amounts. To do this, a time diagram can be very helpful in understanding the nature of the problem and finding a solution.

The remainder of the appendix covers the following six major time value of money concepts. Both formula and interest table approaches are used to illustrate how problems may be solved:

1. Future value of a single sum.
2. Present value of a single sum.
3. Future value of an ordinary annuity.
4. Future value of an annuity due.
5. Present value of an ordinary annuity.
6. Present value of an annuity due.

SINGLE SUM PROBLEMS

Many business and investment decisions involve a single amount of money that either exists now or will exist in the future. Single sum problems can generally be classified into one of the following two categories:

1. Determining the *unknown future value* of a known single sum of money that is invested for a specified number of periods at a specified interest rate.
2. Determining the *unknown present value* of a known single sum of money that is discounted for a specified number of periods at a specified interest rate.

OBJECTIVE 5

Solve future and present value of single sum problems.

Future Value of a Single Sum

The **future value** of a sum of money is the future value of that sum when left to accumulate for a certain number of periods at a specified rate of interest per period.

The amount to which 1 (one) will accumulate may be expressed as a formula:

$$FVF_{n,\,i} = (1 + i)^n$$

where

$FVF_{n,\,i}$ = future value factor for n periods at i interest
i = rate of interest for a single period
n = number of periods

To illustrate, assume that $1.00 is invested at 9% interest compounded annually for three years. The amounts to which the $1.00 will accumulate at the end of each year are:

$FVF_{1,\,9\%} = (1 + 0.09)^1$ for the end of the first year.
$FVF_{2,\,9\%} = (1 + 0.09)^2$ for the end of the second year.
$FVF_{3,\,9\%} = (1 + 0.09)^3$ for the end of the third year.

These compound amounts accumulate as shown in Illustration A-4.

ILLUSTRATION A-4
Accumulation of Compounding Amounts

Period	Beginning-of-Period Amount	×	Multiplier $(1 + i)$	=	End-of-Period Amount*	Formula $(1+i)^n$
1	1.00000		1.09		1.09000	$(1.09)^1$
2	1.09000		1.09		1.18810	$(1.09)^2$
3	1.18810		1.09		1.29503	$(1.09)^3$

*These amounts appear in Table A-1 in the 9% column.

To calculate the *future value of any single amount*, multiply the future value of 1 factor (future value factor) by its present value (principal) as follows:

$$FV = PV(FVF_{n, i})$$

where

FV = future value
PV = present value (principal or single sum)
$FVF_{n, i}$ = future value factor for n periods at i interest

For example, what is the future value of $50,000 invested for five years at 11% compounded annually? In time-diagram form, this investment situation is indicated in Illustration A-5.

ILLUSTRATION A-5
Time Diagram for Future Value Calculation

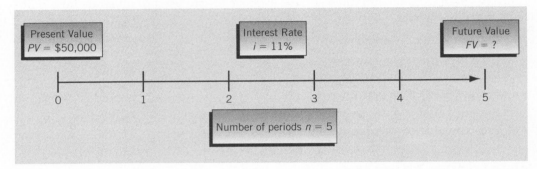

This investment problem is solved as follows.

$$FV = PV(FVF_{n, i})$$
$$= \$50{,}000(FVF_{5,\ 11\%})$$
$$= \$50{,}000\ (1.68506)$$
$$= \$84{,}253.$$

The future value factor of 1.68506 appears in Table A-1 in the 11% column and 5-period row.

To illustrate a more complex business situation, assume that at the beginning of 2001 Ontario Hydro deposits $250 million in an escrow account with the Royal Bank as a commitment toward a small nuclear power plant to be completed December 31, 2004. How much will be on deposit at the end of four years if interest is compounded semiannually at 10%?

With a known present value of $250 million, a total of eight compounding periods (4 × 2), and an interest rate of 5% per compounding period (10% ÷ 2), this problem can be time-diagrammed and the future value determined as indicated in Illustration A-6.

ILLUSTRATION A-6
Time Diagram for Future Value Calculation

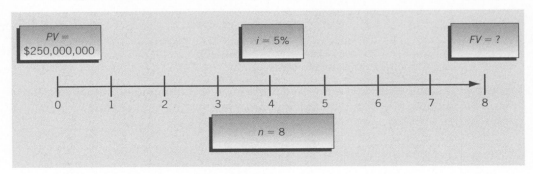

$$FV = \$250,000,000(FVF_{8,\ 5\%})$$
$$= \$250,000,000(1.47746)$$
$$= \$369,365,000.$$

The deposit of $250 million will accumulate to $369,365,000 by December 31, 2004. The future value factor is found in Table A-1 (5% column and the 8-period row).

Present Value of a Single Sum

A previous example showed that $50,000 invested at an annually compounded interest rate of 11% will be worth $84,253 at the end of five years. It follows that $84,253 to be received five years from now is presently worth $50,000, given an 11% interest rate (i.e., $50,000 is the present value of this $84,253). The present value is the amount that must be invested now to produce a known future value. The *present value is always a smaller amount than the known future value because interest is earned and accumulated on the present value to the future date.* In determining the future value we move forward in time using a process of accumulation, while in determining present value we move backward in time using the process of discounting.

The present value of 1 (one) (present value factor) may be expressed as a formula:

where
$$PVF_{n,\ i} = \frac{1}{(1+i)^n}$$

$PVF_{n,\ i}$ = present value factor for n periods at i interest

To illustrate, assume that $1.00 is discounted for three periods at 9%. The present value of the $1.00 is discounted each period as follows.

$$PVF_{1,\ 9\%} = 1/(1+0.09)^1 \text{ for the first period}$$
$$PVF_{2,\ 9\%} = 1/(1+0.09)^2 \text{ for the second period}$$
$$PVF_{3,\ 9\%} = 1/(1+0.09)^3 \text{ for the third period}$$

Therefore, the $1.00 is discounted as shown in Illustration A-7.

Discount Periods	Future Value	÷	Divisor $(1+i)^n$	=	Present Value*	Formula $1/(1+i)^n$
1	1.00000		1.09		0.91743	$1/(1.09)^1$
2	1.00000		$(1.09)^2$		0.84168	$1/(1.09)^2$
3	1.00000		$(1.09)^3$		0.77218	$1/(1.09)^3$

*These amounts appear in Table A-2 in the 9% column.

ILLUSTRATION A-7
Present Value of $1 Discounted at 9% for Three Periods

Table A-2, "Present Value of 1," shows how much must be invested now at various interest rates to equal 1 at the end of various periods of time.

The present value of *any single future value* is as follows:

where
$$PV = FV(PVF_{n,\ i})$$

PV = present value
FV = future value

$PVF_{n,\ i}$ = present value of 1 for n periods at i interest

To illustrate, assume that your favourite uncle proposes to give you $4,000 for a trip to Europe when you graduate three years from now. He will finance the trip by investing a sum of money now at 8% compound interest that will accumulate to $4,000 upon your graduation. The only conditions are that you graduate and that you tell him how much to invest now.

To impress your uncle, you might set up a time diagram as shown in Illustration A-8 and solve the problem as follows.

ILLUSTRATION A-8
Time Diagram for Present Value
Calculation

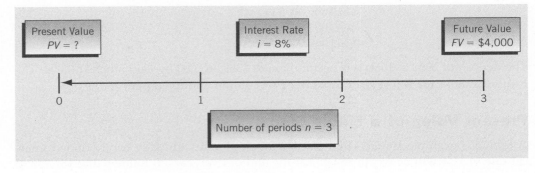

$$PV = \$4,000(PVF_{3,\ 8\%})$$
$$= \$4,000(0.79383)$$
$$= \$3,175.32.$$

Advise your uncle to invest $3,175.32 now to provide you with $4,000 upon graduation. To satisfy your uncle's other condition, you must simply pass this course and many more. Note that the present value factor of 0.79383 is found in Table A-2 (8% column, 3-period row).

Solving for Other Unknowns

In calculating either the future value or the present value in the previous single sum illustrations, both the number of periods and the interest rate were known. In business situations, both the future value and the present value may be known, and either the number of periods or the interest rate may be unknown. The following two illustrations demonstrate how to solve single sum problems when there is either an unknown number of periods (n) or an unknown interest rate (i). These illustrations show that if any three of the four values (future value, FV; present value, PV; number of periods, n; interest rate, i) are known, the one unknown can be derived.

Illustration: Calculation of the Number of Periods. A local charity in Regina wants to accumulate $70,000 for the construction of a day-care centre. If at the beginning of the current year the association is able to deposit $47,811 in a building fund that earns 10% interest compounded annually, how many years will it take for the fund to accumulate to $70,000?

In this situation, the present value ($47,811), future value ($70,000), and interest rate (10%) are known. A time diagram of this investment is shown in Illustration A-9.

ILLUSTRATION A-9
Time Diagram for Number of
Periods Calculation

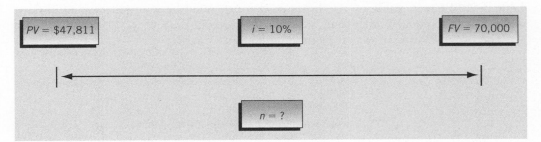

The unknown number of periods can be determined using either the future value or present value approaches, as shown below.

Future Value Approach	Present Value Approach
$FV = PV(FVF_{n,\ 10\%})$	$PV = FV(PVF_{n,\ 10\%})$
$\$70,000 = \$47,811(FVF_{n,\ 10\%})$	$\$47,811 = \$70,000(PVF_{n,\ 10\%})$
$FVF_{n,\ 10\%} = \dfrac{\$70,000}{\$47,811} = 1.46410$	$PVF_{n,\ 10\%} = \dfrac{\$47,811}{\$70,000} = 0.68301$

Using the future value factor of 1.46410, refer to Table A-1 and read down the 10% column to find that factor in the 4-period row. Thus, it will take four years for the $47,811 to accumulate to $70,000. Using the present value factor of 0.68301, refer to Table A-2 and read down the 10% column to also find that factor is in the 4-period row.

Illustration: Calculation of the Interest Rate. The Canadian Academic Accounting Association wants to have $141,000 available five years from now to provide scholarships to individuals who undertake a PhD program. At present, the executive of the CAAA has determined that $80,000 may be invested for this purpose. What rate of interest must be earned on the investments in order to accumulate the $141,000 five years from now?

Illustration A-10 provides a time diagram of this problem.

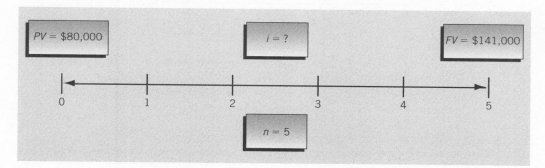

ILLUSTRATION A-10
Time Diagram for Rate of Interest Calculation

Given that the present value, future value, and number of periods are known, the unknown interest rate can be determined using either the future value or present value approaches, as shown below.

Future Value Approach	Present Value Approach
$FV = PV(FVF_{5, i})$	$PV = FV(PVF_{5, i})$
$141{,}000 = 80{,}000(FVF_{5, i})$	$80{,}000 = 141{,}000(PVF_{5, i})$
$FVF_{5, i} = \dfrac{141{,}000}{80{,}000} = 1.7625$	$PVF_{5, i} = \dfrac{80{,}000}{141{,}000} = 0.5674$

Using the future value factor of 1.7625, refer to Table A-1 and read across the 5-period row to find a close match of this future value factor in the 12% column. Thus, the $80,000 must be invested at 12% to accumulate to $141,000 at the end of five years. Using the present value factor of 0.5674 and Table A-2, reading across the 5-period row shows this factor in the 12% column.

ANNUITIES

The preceding discussion involved only the accumulation or discounting of a single principal sum. Accountants frequently encounter situations in which a series of amounts are to be paid or received over time (e.g., when loans or sales are paid in instalments, invested funds are partially recovered at regular intervals, and cost savings are realized repeatedly). When a commitment involves a series of equal payments made at equal intervals of time, it is called an **annuity**. By definition, an annuity requires that (1) *the periodic payments or receipts* (called *rents*) *always be the same amount*; (2) the *interval between such rents always be the same*; and (3) the *interest be compounded once each interval*.

The **future value of an annuity** *is the sum of all the rents plus the accumulated compound interest on them*. Rents may, however, occur at either the beginning or the end of the periods. To distinguish annuities under these two alternatives, an annuity is classified as an **ordinary annuity** *if the rents occur at the end of each period, and as an annuity due if the rents occur at the beginning of each period*.

Future Value of an Ordinary Annuity

OBJECTIVE 6

Solve future value of ordinary and annuity due problems.

One approach to calculating the future value of an annuity is to determine the future value of each rent in the series and then aggregate these individual future values. For example, assume that $1 is deposited at the **end** of each of five years (an ordinary annuity) and earns 12% interest compounded annually. The future value can be calculated as indicated in Illustration A-11 using the "Future Value of 1" for each of the five $1 rents.

ILLUSTRATION A-11
Solving for the Future Value of an Ordinary Annuity

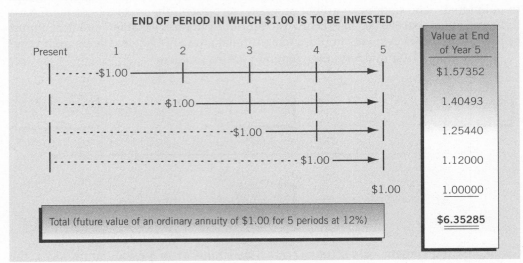

Although the foregoing procedure for computing the future value of an ordinary annuity produces the correct answer, it is cumbersome if the number of rents is large. A more efficient way of determining the future value of an ordinary annuity of 1 is to apply the following formula:

$$FVF - OA_{n,i} = \frac{(1+i)^n - 1}{i}$$

where

$FVF - OA_{n,i}$ = future value factor of an ordinary annuity
n = number of compounding periods
i = rate of interest per period

Using this formula, Table A-3 has been developed to show the "Future Value of an Ordinary Annuity of 1" for various interest rates and investment periods. Illustration A-12 is an excerpt from this table.

ILLUSTRATION A-12
Excerpt from Table A-3

	Future value of an ordinary annuity of 1		
Period	10%	11%	12%
1	1.00000	1.00000	1.00000
2	2.10000	2.11000	2.12000
3	3.31000	3.34210	3.37440
4	4.64100	4.70973	4.77933
5	6.10510	6.22780	6.35285*

*Note that this factor is the same as the sum of the future values of 1 factors shown in Illustration A-11.

Interpreting the table, if $1.00 is invested at the end of each year for four years at 11% interest compounded annually, the value of the annuity at the end of the fourth year will be $4.71 (4.70973 × $1.00). The $4.71 is made up of $4 of rent payments ($1 at the end of each of the 4 years) and compound interest of $0.71.

The future value of an ordinary annuity is calculated as follows.

$$\text{Future value of an ordinary annuity} = R(FVF - OA_{n,i})$$

where

$FVF - OA_{n,i}$ = future value factor of an ordinary annuity for n periods at i interest
R = periodic rent

To illustrate, what is the future value of five $5,000 deposits made at the end of each of the next five years, earning interest at 12%? The time diagram is shown in Illustration A-13 and the derivation of the solution for this problem follows.

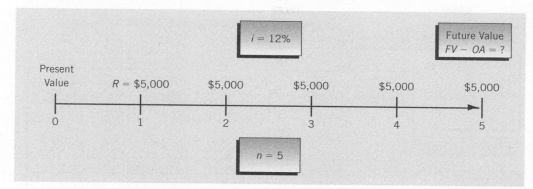

ILLUSTRATION A-13
Time Diagram for Future Value Calculation of an Ordinary Annuity

$$\text{Future value of an ordinary annuity} = R(FVF - OA_{n,\,i})$$
$$= \$5,000(FVF - OA_{5,\,12\%})$$
$$= \$5,000\left(\frac{(1 + 0.12)^5 - 1}{0.12}\right)$$
$$= \$5,000(6.35285)$$
$$= \$31,764.25$$

The future value factor of an ordinary annuity of 6.35285 is found in Table A-3 (12% column, 5-period row).

To illustrate these calculations in a business situation, assume that Lightning Electronics Limited's management decides to deposit $75,000 at the end of each six-month period for the next three years for the purpose of accumulating enough money to meet debts that mature in three years. What is the future value that will be on deposit at the end of three years if the annual interest rate is 10%?

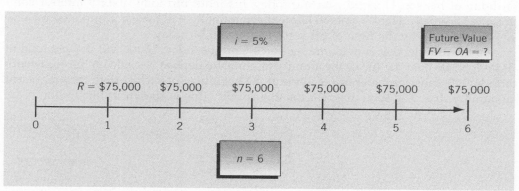

ILLUSTRATION A-14
Time Diagram for Future Value Calculation of an Ordinary Annuity

$$\text{Future value of an ordinary annuity} = R(FVF - OA_{n,\,i})$$
$$= \$75,000(FVF - OA_{6,\,5\%})$$
$$= \$75,000\left(\frac{(1 + 0.05)^6 - 1}{0.05}\right)$$
$$= \$75,000(6.80191)$$
$$= \$510,143.25$$

Thus, six deposits of $75,000 made at the end of every six months and earning 5% per period will grow to $510,143.25 at the time of the last deposit.

Future Value of an Annuity Due

The preceding analysis of an **ordinary annuity** was based on the fact that the periodic rents occur at the **end** of each period. An *annuity due* is based on the fact that the periodic rents occur at the **beginning** of each period. This means an annuity due will accumulate interest during the first period whereas an ordinary annuity will not. Therefore, the significant difference between the two types of annuities is in the number of interest accumulation periods involved. The distinction is shown graphically in Illustration A-15.

ILLUSTRATION A-15
Comparison of the Future Value of an Ordinary Annuity With that of an Annuity Due

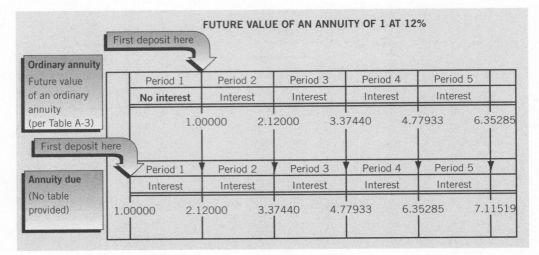

Because the cash flows from the annuity due come exactly one period earlier than for an ordinary annuity, the future value of the annuity due factor is exactly 12% higher than the ordinary annuity factor. Therefore, *to determine the future value of an annuity due factor, multiply the corresponding future value of the ordinary annuity factor by one plus the interest rate*. For example, to determine the future value of an annuity due factor for five periods at 12% compound interest, simply multiply the future value of an ordinary annuity factor for five periods (6.35285) by one plus the interest rate (1 + 0.12) to arrive at the future value of an annuity due, 7.11519 (6.35285 × 1.12).

To illustrate, assume that Hank Lotadough plans to deposit $800 a year on each birthday of his son Howard, starting today, his tenth birthday, at 12% interest compounded annually. Hank wants to know the amount he will have accumulated for university expenses by the time of his son's eighteenth birthday.

As the first deposit is made on his son's tenth birthday, Hank will make a total of eight deposits over the life of the annuity (assume no deposit is made on the eighteenth birthday). Because each deposit is made at the beginning of each period, they represent an annuity due. The time diagram for this annuity due is shown in Illustration A-16.

ILLUSTRATION A-16
Time Diagram for Future Value Calculation of an Annuity Due

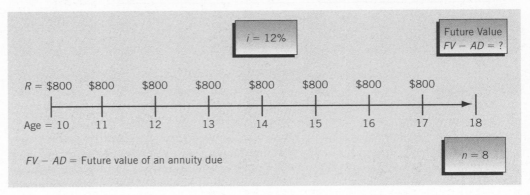

Referring to Table A-3, "Future Value of an Ordinary Annuity of 1," for eight periods at 12%, a factor of 12.29969 is found. This factor is then multiplied by (1 + 0.12) to arrive at the future value of an annuity due factor. As a result, the accumulated amount on his son's eighteenth birthday is calculated as shown in Illustration A-17.

1. Future value of an ordinary annuity of 1 for 8 periods at 12% (Table A-3)	12.29969
2. Factor (1 + 0.12)	× 1.12
3. Future value of an annuity due of 1 for 8 periods at 12%	13.77565
4. Periodic deposit (rent)	× $800
5. Accumulated value on son's eighteenth birthday	$11,020.52

Because expenses to go to university for four years are considerably in excess of $11,000, Howard will likely have to develop his own plan to save additional funds.

Illustrations of Future Value of Annuity Problems

In the previous annuity examples, three values were known (amount of each rent, interest rate, and number of periods) and were used to determine the unknown fourth value (future value). The following illustrations demonstrate how to solve problems when the unknown is (1) the amount of the rents; or (2) the number of rents in ordinary annuity situations.

Illustration: Calculating the Amount of Each Rent. Assume that you wish to accumulate $14,000 for a down payment on a condominium five years from now and that you can earn an annual return of 8% compounded semiannually during the next five years. How much should you deposit at the end of each six-month period?

The $14,000 is the future value of 10 (5 × 2) semiannual end-of-period payments of an unknown amount at an interest rate of 4% (8% ÷ 2). This problem is time-diagrammed in Illustration A-18.

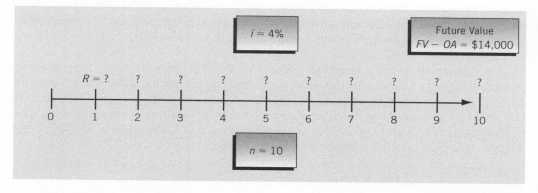

Using the formula for the future value of an ordinary annuity, the amount of each rent is determined as follows.

$$\text{Future value of an ordinary annuity} = R(FVF - OA_{n,\,i})$$
$$\$14,000 = R(FVF - OA_{10,\,4\%})$$
$$\$14,000 = R(12.00611)$$
$$\frac{\$14,000}{12.00611} = R$$
$$R = \$1,166.07$$

Thus, you must make 10 semiannual deposits of $1,166.07 each in order to accumulate $14,000 for your down payment. The future value of an ordinary annuity of 1 factor of 12.00611 is provided in Table A-3 (4% column, 10-period row).

Illustration: Calculating the Number of Periodic Rents. Suppose that your company wants to accumulate $117,332 by making periodic deposits of $20,000 at the end of each year that will earn 8% compounded annually. How many deposits must be made?

The $117,332 represents the future value of $n(?)$ $20,000 deposits at an 8% annual rate of interest. Illustration A-19 provides a time diagram for this problem.

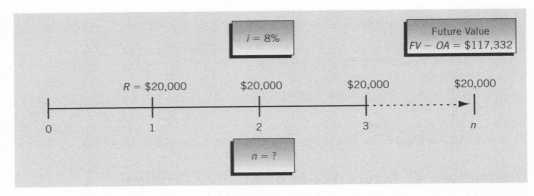

Using the future value of an ordinary annuity formula, the factor is determined as follows.

$$\text{Future value of an ordinary annuity} = R(FVF - OA_{n,\,i})$$
$$\$117,332 = \$20,000(FVF - OA_{n,\,8\%})$$
$$(FVF - OA_{n,\,8\%}) = \frac{\$117,332}{\$20,000} = 5.86660$$

Using Table A-3 and reading down the 8% column, 5.86660 is in the 5-period row. Thus, five deposits of $20,000 each must be made.

Present Value of an Ordinary Annuity

The **present value of an annuity** *may be viewed as the single amount that, if invested now at compound interest, would provide for a series of withdrawals of a certain amount per period for a specific number of future periods*. In other words, the present value of an ordinary annuity is the present value of a series of rents to be withdrawn at the end of each equal interval.

One approach to calculating the present value of an annuity is to determine the present value of each rent in the series and then aggregate these individual present values. For example, assume that $1.00 is to be received at the *end* of each of five periods (an ordinary annuity) and that the interest rate is 12% compounded annually. The present value of this annuity can be calculated as shown in Illustration A-20 using Table A-2, "Present Value of 1," for each of the five $1 rents.

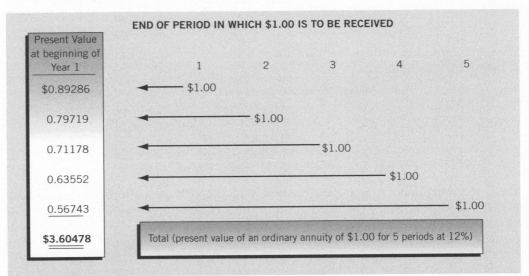

This calculation indicates that if the single sum of $3.60 is invested today at 12% interest, $1.00 can be withdrawn at the end of each period for five periods. This procedure is cumbersome. Using the following formula is a more efficient way to determine the present value of an ordinary annuity of 1:

$$PVF - OA_{n,\,i} = \frac{1 - \dfrac{1}{(1+i)^n}}{i}$$

Table A-4, "Present Value of an Ordinary Annuity of 1," is based on this formula. Illustration A-21 is an excerpt from this table.

Period	Present Value of an Ordinary Annuity of 1		
	10%	11%	12%
1	0.90909	0.90090	0.89286
2	1.73554	1.71252	1.69005
3	2.48685	2.44371	2.40183
4	3.16986	3.10245	3.03735
5	3.79079	3.69590	3.60478*

*Note that this factor is equal to the sum of the present value of 1 factors shown in the previous schedule.

ILLUSTRATION A-21
Excerpt from Table A-4

The general formula for the present value of any ordinary annuity is as follows.

Present value of an ordinary annuity $= R(PVF - OA_{n,\,i})$

where

$PVF - OA_{n,\,i}$ = present value of an ordinary annuity of 1 factor
R = periodic rent (ordinary annuity)

To illustrate, what is the present value of rental receipts of $6,000, each to be received at the end of each of the next five years when discounted at 12%? This problem is time-diagrammed in Illustration A-22 and the solution follows.

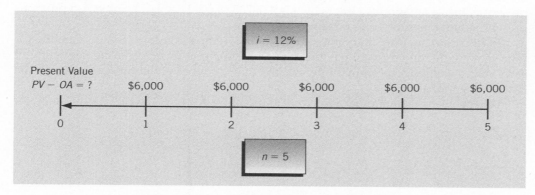

ILLUSTRATION A-22
Time Diagram for Present Value Calculation of an Ordinary Annuity

Present value of an ordinary annuity $= R(PVF - OA_{n,\,i})$
$= \$6,000(PVF - OA_{5,\,12\%})$
$= \$6,000(3.60478)$
$= \$21,628.68$

The present value of the five ordinary annuity rental receipts of $6,000 each is $21,628.68. The present value of the ordinary annuity factor, 3.60478, is from Table A-4 (12% column, 5-period row).

Present Value of An Annuity Due

In the discussion of the present value of an ordinary annuity, the final rent was discounted back the same number of periods as there were rents. In determining the present value of an annuity due, there is one fewer discount periods. This distinction is shown graphically in Illustration A-23.

ILLUSTRATION A-23

Comparison of the Present Value of an Ordinary Annuity with that of an Annuity Due

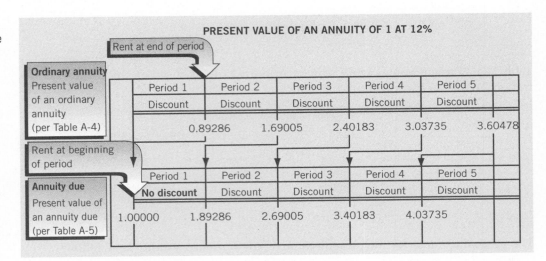

Because each cash flow (rent) comes exactly one period sooner in the present value of an annuity due, the present value of the cash flows is exactly 12% higher than the present value of an ordinary annuity. Thus, *the present value of an annuity due factor can be found by multiplying the present value of an ordinary annuity factor by one plus the interest rate.* For example, to determine the present value of an annuity due factor for five periods at 12% interest, take the present value of an ordinary annuity factor for five periods at 12% interest (3.60478) and multiply it by 1.12 to arrive at the present value of an annuity due, which is 4.03735 (3.60478 × 1.12). Table A-5 provides present value of annuity due factors.

To illustrate, assume that Space Odyssey Inc. rents a communications satellite for four years with annual rental payments of $4.8 million to be made at the beginning of each year. Assuming an annual interest rate of 11%, what is the present value of the rental obligations?

This problem is time-diagrammed in Illustration A-24.

ILLUSTRATION A-24

Time Diagram for Present Value Calculation of an Annuity Due

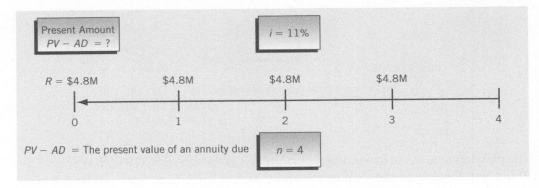

This problem can be solved as shown in Illustration A-25.

ILLUSTRATION A-25

Calculations of Present Value of an Annuity Due

1. Present value factor of an ordinary annuity of 1 for 4 periods at 11% (Table A-4)	3.10245
2. Factor (1 + 0.11)	× 1.11
3. Present value factor of an annuity due of 1 for 4 periods at 11%	3.44371
4. Periodic deposit (rent)	× $4,800,000
5. Present value of payments	$16,529.808

Since Table A-5 gives present value of an annuity due factors, it can be used to obtain the required factor 3.44371 (in the 11% column, 4-period row).

Illustrations of Present Value of Annuity Problems

The following illustrations show how to solve problems when the unknown is (1) the present value; (2) the interest rate; or (3) the amount of each rent for present value of annuity problems.

Illustration: Calculation of the Present Value of an Ordinary Annuity. You have just won Lotto B.C. totalling $4,000,000. You will be paid the amount of $200,000 at the end of each of the next 20 years. What amount have you really won? That is, what is the present value of the $200,000 cheques you will receive over the next 20 years? A time diagram of this enviable situation is shown in Illustration A-26 (assuming an interest rate of 10%).

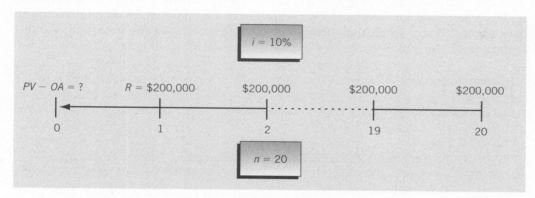

ILLUSTRATION A-26
Time Diagram for Present Value
Calculation of an Annuity Due

The present value is determined as follows:

$$\text{Present value of an ordinary annuity} = R(PVF - OA_{n,\,i})$$
$$= \$200,000(PVF - OA_{20,\,10\%})$$
$$= \$200,000(8.51356)$$
$$= \$1,702,712$$

As a result, if Lotto B.C. deposits $1,702,712 now and earns 10% interest, it can draw $200,000 a year for 20 years to pay you the $4,000,000.

Illustration: Calculation of the Interest Rate. Many shoppers make purchases by using a credit card. When you receive an invoice for payment, you may pay the total amount due or pay the balance in a certain number of payments. For example, if you receive an invoice from VISA with a balance due of $528.77 and are invited to pay it off in 12 equal monthly payments of $50.00 each with the first payment due one month from now, what rate of interest are you paying?

The $528.77 represents the present value of the twelve $50 payments at an unknown rate of interest. This situation is time-diagrammed in Illustration A-27, which is followed by the determination of the interest rate.

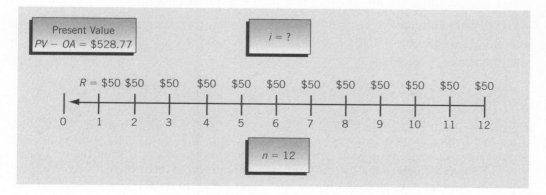

ILLUSTRATION A-27
Time Diagram for Rate of
Interest Calculation of an
Ordinary Annuity

$$\text{Present value of an ordinary annuity} = R(PVF - OA_{n,\,i})$$
$$\$528.77 = \$50(PVF - OA_{12,\,i})$$
$$PVF - OA_{12,\,i} = \frac{\$528.77}{\$50} = 10.57540$$

Referring to Table A-4 and reading across the 12-period row, the 10.57534 factor is in the 2% column. Since 2% is a monthly rate, the nominal annual rate of interest is 24% $(12 \times 2\%)$ and the effective annual rate is 26.82413% $[(1 + 0.02)^{12} - 1]$. At such a high rate of interest, you are better off paying the entire bill now if possible.

Illustration: Calculation of a Periodic Rent. Vern and Marilyn have saved $18,000 to finance their daughter Dawn's university education. The money has been deposited with the National Trust Company and is earning 10% interest compounded semiannually. What equal amounts can Dawn withdraw at the end of every six months during the next four years while she attends university and exhaust the fund with the last withdrawal? This problem is time-diagrammed as shown in Illustration A-28.

ILLUSTRATION A-28
Time Diagram for Calculation of the Withdrawal Amount of an Ordinary Annuity

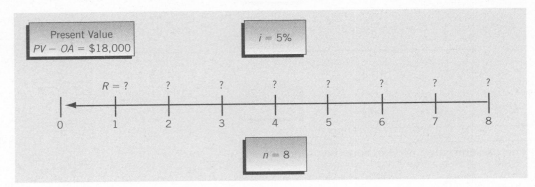

The answer is not determined simply by dividing $18,000 by 8 withdrawals because that ignores the interest earned on the money remaining on deposit. Given that interest is compounded semiannually at 5% $(10\% \div 2)$ for eight periods (4 years $\times$ 2) and using the present value of an ordinary annuity formula, the amount of each withdrawal is determined as follows:

$$\text{Present value of an ordinary annuity} = R(PVF - OA_{n,\,i})$$
$$\$18,000 = R(PVF - OA_{8,\,5\%})$$
$$\$18,000 = R(6.46321)$$
$$R = \$2,784.99$$

COMPLEX SITUATIONS

It is often necessary to use more than one table to solve time value of money problems. Two common situations are illustrated to demonstrate this point:

1. Deferred annuities.
2. Bond problems.
3. Interpolation of tables

Deferred Annuities

A deferred annuity *is an annuity in which the rents begin a specified number of periods after the arrangement or contract is made*. For example, "an ordinary annuity of six annual rents deferred four years" means that no rents will occur during the first four years and that the first of the six rents will occur at the end of the fifth year. "An annuity due of six annual rents deferred four years" means that no rents will occur during the first four years, and that the first of six rents will occur at the beginning of the fifth year.

Future Value of a Deferred Annuity. Determining the future value of a deferred annuity is relatively straightforward. Because there is no accumulation or investment on which interest accrues during the deferred periods, the future value of a deferred annuity is the same as the future value of an annuity not deferred.

To illustrate, assume that Sutton Co. Ltd. plans to purchase a land site in six years for the construction of its new corporate headquarters. Because of cash flow problems, Sutton is able to budget deposits of $80,000 only at the end of the fourth, fifth, and sixth years, which are expected to earn 12% annually. What future value will Sutton have accumulated at the end of the sixth year?

Illustration A-29 gives a time diagram of this situation.

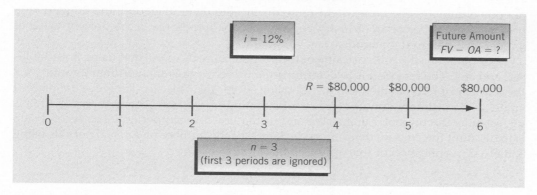

ILLUSTRATION A-29
Time Diagram for Calculation of the Future Value of a Deferred Annuity

The amount accumulated is determined by using the standard formula for the future value of an ordinary annuity:

$$FV - OA = R(FVF - OA_{n, i})$$
$$= \$80,000(FVF - OA_{3, 12\%})$$
$$= \$80,000(3.37440)$$
$$= \$269,952$$

Present Value of a Deferred Annuity. In determining the present value of a deferred annuity, recognition must be given to the facts that no rents occur during the deferral period, and that the future actual rents must be discounted for the entire period.

For example, Shelly Desrosiers has developed and copyrighted a software computer program that is a tutorial for students in introductory accounting. She agrees to sell the copyright to Campus Micro Systems for six annual payments of $5,000 each, the payments to begin five years from today. The annual interest rate is 8%. What is the present value of the six payments?

This situation is an ordinary annuity of six payments deferred four periods as is time-diagrammed in Illustration A-30.

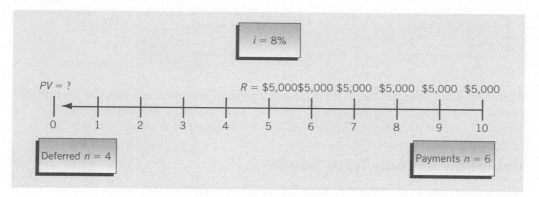

ILLUSTRATION A-30
Time Diagram for Calculation of the Present Value of a Deferred Annuity

Two options are available to solve this problem. The first is by using only Table A-4 and making the calculations shown in Illustration A-31.

ILLUSTRATION A-31
Calculation of the Present Value
of a Deferred Annuity

1. Each periodic rent		$ 5,000
2. Present value factor of an ordinary annuity of 1 for total periods (10) [(number of rents (6) plus number of deferred periods (4)] at 8%	6.71008	
3. Less: Present value factor of an ordinary annuity of 1 for the number of deferred periods (4) at 8%	3.31213	
4. Difference		× 3.39795
5. Present value of 6 rents of $5,000 deferred 4 periods		$16,989.75

The subtraction of the present value factor of an ordinary annuity of 1 for the deferred periods eliminates the nonexistent rents during the deferral period and converts the present value factor of an ordinary annuity of 1 for 10 periods to the present value of 6 rents of 1, deferred 4 periods.

Alternatively, the present value of the six rents may be calculated using both Tables A-2 and A-4. The first step is to determine the present value of an ordinary annuity for the number of rent payments involved using Table A-4. This step provides the present value of the ordinary annuity as at the beginning of the first payment period (this is the same as the present value at the end of the last deferral period). The second step is to discount the amount determined in Step 1 for the number of deferral periods using Table A-2. Application of this approach is as follows.

Step 1:
$$PV - OA = R(PVF - OA_{n, i})$$
$$= \$5,000(PVF - OA_{6, 8\%})$$
$$= \$5,000(4.62288) \text{ Table A-4 (Present Value of an Ordinary Annuity)}$$
$$= \$23,114.40$$

Step 2:
$$PV = FV(PVF_{n, i})$$
$$= \$23,114.40(PVF_{4, 8\%})$$
$$= \$23,114.40 (0.73503) \text{ Table A-2 (Present Value of a Single Sum)}$$
$$= \$16,989.75$$

A time diagram reflecting the completion of this two-step approach is shown in Illustration A-32.

ILLUSTRATION A-32
Time Diagram Reflecting
the Two-step Approach for
Present Value Calculation of
a Deferred Annuity

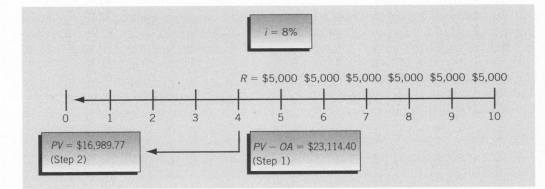

Applying the present value of an ordinary annuity formula discounts the annuity six periods, but because the annuity is deferred four periods, the present value of the annuity must be treated as a future value to be discounted another four periods.

Valuation of Long-Term Bonds

A long-term bond provides two cash flows: (1) periodic interest payments during the life of the bond; and (2) the principal (face value) paid at maturity. At the date of issue, bond buyers determine the present value of these two cash flows using the market rate of interest.

The periodic interest payments represent an annuity while the principal represents a single sum. The current market value of the bonds is the combined present values of the interest annuity and the principal amount.

To illustrate, Servicemaster Inc. issues $100,000 of 9% bonds due in five years with interest payable annually at year end. The current market rate of interest for bonds of similar risk is 11%. What will the buyers pay for this bond issue?

The time diagram depicting both cash flows is shown in Illustration A-33.

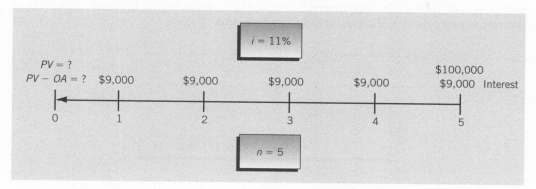

ILLUSTRATION A-33
Time Diagram for Valuation of Long-term Bonds

Illustration A-34 shows how the present value of the two cash flows is calculated.

1. Present value of the principal: $FV(PVF_{5,\ 11\%}) = \$100,000(.59345) =$ $59,345.00
2. Present value of interest payments: $R(PVF - OA_{5,\ 11\%}) = \$9,000(3.69590)$ 33,263.10
3. Combined present value (market price) $92,608.10

ILLUSTRATION A-34
Calculation of the Present Value of an Interest Bearing Bond

By paying $92,608.10 at date of issue, the buyers of the bonds will earn an effective yield of 11% over the 5-year term of the bonds.

Interpolation of Tables to Derive Interest Rates

Throughout the previous discussion, the illustrations were designed to produce interest rates and factors that could be found in the tables. Frequently it is necessary to interpolate to derive the exact or required interest rate. **Interpolation** is used to calculate a particular unknown value that lies between two values given in a table. The following examples illustrate interpolation using Tables A-1 and A-4.

Example 1. If $2,000 accumulates to $5,900 after being invested for 20 years, what is the annual interest rate on the investment?

Dividing the future value of $5,900 by the investment of $2,000 gives 2.95, which is the amount to which $1.00 will grow if invested for 20 years at the unknown interest rate. Using Table A-1 and reading across the 20-period line, the value 2.65330 is found in the 5% column and the value 3.20714 is in the 6% column. The factor 2.95 is between 5% and 6%, which means that the interest rate is also between 5% and 6%. By interpolation, the rate is determined to be 5.536%, as shown in Illustration A-35 ($i =$ unknown rate and $d =$ difference between 5% and i).

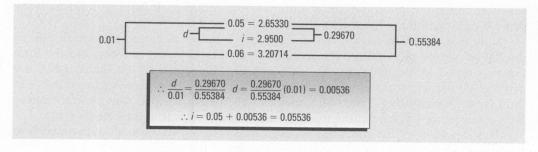

ILLUSTRATION A-35
Interpolating to Derive the Rate of Interest for an Amount

Example 2. You are offered an annuity of $1,000 a year, beginning one year from now for 25 years, for investing $7,000 cash today. What rate of interest is your investment earning?

Dividing the investment of $7,000 by the annuity of $1,000 gives a factor of 7, which is the present value of an ordinary annuity of 1 for 25 years at an unknown interest rate. Using Table A-4 and reading across the 25-period line, the value 7.84314 in the 12% column and the value 6.46415 is in the 15% column. The factor 7 is between 12% and 15%, which means that the unknown interest rate is between 12% and 15%. By interpolation, the rate is determined to be 13.834%, as shown in Illustration A-36 ($i =$ unknown rate and $d =$ difference between 12% and i):

ILLUSTRATION A-36
Interpolating to Derive the Rate of Interest for an Ordinary Annuity

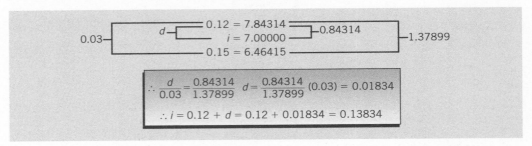

$$\therefore \frac{d}{0.03} = \frac{0.84314}{1.37899} \quad d = \frac{0.84314}{1.37899}(0.03) = 0.01834$$

$$\therefore i = 0.12 + d = 0.12 + 0.01834 = 0.13834$$

Interpolation assumes that the difference between any two values in a table is linear. Although such an assumption is incorrect, the margin of error is generally insignificant if the table value ranges are not too wide.

TECHNOLOGY TOOLS FOR TIME VALUE PROBLEMS

OBJECTIVE 8

Use spreadsheet functions to solve time value of money problems.

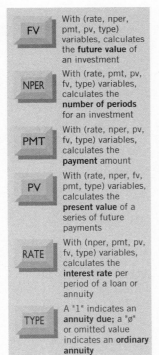

FV	With (rate, nper, pmt, pv, type) variables, calculates the **future value** of an investment
NPER	With (rate, pmt, pv, fv, type) variables, calculates the **number of periods** for an investment
PMT	With (rate, nper, pv, fv, type) variables, calculates the **payment** amount
PV	With (rate, nper, fv, pmt, type) variables, calculates the **present value** of a series of future payments
RATE	With (nper, pmt, pv, fv, type) variables, calculates the **interest rate** per period of a loan or annuity
TYPE	A "1" indicates an **annuity due**; a "ø" or omitted value indicates an **ordinary annuity**

Business professionals, once they have mastered the underlying concepts of present and future values, will often use a spreadsheet program or financial calculator to solve time value of money problems instead of using compound interest tables.

Using Spreadsheet Functions

Spreadsheet software programs, such as Excel and Lotus, are commonly used to help formulate and solve business problems. As they become more sophisticated, more functions that are commonly used are built into the options available to the user. Excel, for example, has a variety of functions available to "INSERT" into the spreadsheet. These include such function categories as Financial, Math & Trig, Statistical, Logical, and Database, among others.

Assuming the "Financial" option is chosen, many common functions are available. Function names associated with this appendix and the time value of money are described in the margin note.

To use this capability in Excel, choose the spreadsheet cell where you want the result of the time value calculation to be displayed. Then, from the Menu bar, click on "Insert," and choose the "Financial" function from the drop-down list. The next step depends on which variable you are trying to determine. Refer to the margin note to determine which "Function name" is appropriate. When a "Function name" is chosen, the program provides you with a list of variables needed to determine the value of the function. Insert the amounts, one at a time. The program itself helps you through the process by describing what each term means.

Note that the **FV** is recognized as a positive number as it is a future cash inflow, the **PV** should be preceded with a minus sign as it is a current outflow, and the **Rate** must be typed in decimal form, i.e., 10% is 0.10. "Type" can be left blank if you are dealing with single sums only or with an ordinary annuity, otherwise, insert a "1" to indicate an annuity due. When all variables have been provided, the program calculates and provides you with the missing value, and inserts it in the cell chosen.

This capability of the spreadsheet program is very useful, especially if you wish to prepare an amortization table using the outcomes of the calculations.

Spreadsheet Applications Using Templates

Quite apart from using the built-in functions available, spreadsheets can be used by programming the future and present value formulas discussed in the appendix into the spreadsheet cells. Once programmed, the spreadsheet "template" can then be used to solve time value of money problems repeatedly. Refer to the Digital Tool for an explanation of how this can be done.

Financial Calculators

Financial calculators allow you to solve present and future value problems by entering the time value of money variables into the calculator. Instructions on how to use a financial calculator are provided on the Digital Tool that accompanies this text.

Summary of Learning Objectives

1 Identify accounting topics where the time value of money is relevant. Some of the applications of time value of money measurements to accounting topics are: (1) notes; (2) leases; (3) amortization of premiums and discounts; (4) pensions and other post-retirement benefits; (5) capital assets; (6) sinking funds; (7) business combinations; (8) amortization; and (9) instalment contracts.

2 Distinguish between simple and compound interest. See Fundamental Concepts following this Summary.

3 Know how to use appropriate compound interest tables. In order to identify the appropriate compound interest table to use of the five given, you must identify whether you are solving for (1) the future value of a single sum; (2) the present value of a single sum; (3) the future value of an annuity; or (4) the present value of an annuity. In addition, when an annuity is involved, you must identify whether these amounts are received or paid (1) at the beginning of each period (ordinary annuity); or (2) at the end of each period (annuity due).

4 Identify variables fundamental to solving interest problems. The following four variables are fundamental to all compound interest problems: (1) *Rate of interest:* unless otherwise stated, an annual rate that must be adjusted to reflect the length of the compounding period if less than a year. (2) *Number of time periods:* the number of compounding periods (a period may be equal to or less than a year). (3) *Future value:* the amount at a future date of a given sum or sums invested assuming compound interest. (4) *Present value:* the value now (present time) of a future sum or sums discounted assuming compound interest.

5 Solve future and present value of single sum problems. See Fundamental Concepts following this Summary, items 5(a) and 6(a).

6 Solve future value of ordinary and annuity due problems. See Fundamental Concepts following this Summary, item 5(b).

7 Solve present values of ordinary and annuity due problems. See Fundamental Concepts following this Summary, item 6(b).

8 Use spreadsheet functions to solve time value of money problems. Using spreadsheet functions is only one way of using technology to help with the calculations. Instructions on the use of spreadsheet templates and financial calculators are located on the Digital Tool.

KEY TERMS

accumulation, *A-9*

annuity, *A-11*

annuity due, *A-13*

compound interest, *A-4*

deferred annuity, *A-20*

discounting, *A-9*

effective yield or rate, *A-6*

future value, *A-7*

future value of an annuity, *A-11*

interest, *A-3*

interpolation, *A-23*

ordinary annuity, *A-11*

present value, *A-9*

present value of an annuity, *A-16*

principal, *A-3*

simple interest, *A-4*

stated, nominal, coupon, or face rate, *A-16*

FUNDAMENTAL CONCEPTS

1. **Simple Interest.** Interest is calculated only on the principal, regardless of interest that may have accrued in the past.

2. **Compound Interest.** Interest is calculated on the unpaid interest of past periods, as well as on the principal.

3. **Rate of Interest.** Interest is usually expressed as an annual rate, but when the interest period is shorter than one year, the interest rate for the shorter period must be determined.

4. **Annuity.** A series of payments or receipts (called rents) that occur at equal intervals of time. The types of annuities are:

   (a) **Ordinary Annuity.** Each rent is payable (receivable) at the end of a period.

   (b) **Annuity Due.** Each rent is payable (receivable) at the beginning of a period.

5. **Future Value.** Value at a later date of a given sum that is invested at compound interest.

   (a) **Future Value of 1** (or amount of a given sum). The future value of $1.00 (or a single given sum), a, at the end of n periods at i compound interest rate (Table A-1).

   (b) **Future Value of an Annuity.** The future value of a series of rents invested at compound interest; it is the accumulated total that results from a series of equal deposits at regular intervals invested at compound interest. Both deposits and interest increase the accumulation.

      1. **Future Value of an Ordinary Annuity.** The future value on the date of the last rent (Table A-3).

      2. **Future Value of an Annuity Due.** The future value one period after the date of the last rent. When an annuity due table is not available, use Table A-3 with the following formula:

$$\frac{\text{Amount of annuity due}}{\text{of 1 for } n \text{ rents}} = \frac{\text{Amount of ordinary annuity of}}{\text{1 for } n \text{ rents} \times (1 + \text{interest rate}).}$$

6. **Present Value.** The value at an earlier date (usually now) of a given sum discounted at compound interest.

   (a) **Present Value of 1** (or present value of a single sum). The present value (worth) of $1.00 (or a given sum), p, due n periods hence, discounted at i compound interest (Table A-2).

   (b) **Present Value of an Annuity.** The present value (worth) of a series of rents discounted at compound interest; it is the present sum when invested at compound interest that will permit a series of equal withdrawals at regular intervals.

      1. **Present Value of an Ordinary Annuity.** The value now of $1.00 to be received or paid each period (rents) for n periods, discounted at i compound interest (Table A-4).

      2. **Present Value of an Annuity Due.** The value now of $1.00 to be received or paid at the beginning of each period (rents) for n periods, discounted at i compound interest (Table A-5). To use Table A-4 for an annuity due, apply this formula:

$$\frac{\text{Present value of an annuity}}{\text{due of 1 for } n \text{ rents}} = \frac{\text{Present value of ordinary annuity}}{\text{of 1 for } n \text{ rents} \times (1 + \text{interest rate}).}$$

TABLE A-1

FUTURE VALUE OF 1
(FUTURE VALUE OF A SINGLE SUM)

$$FVF_{n,i} = (1 + i)^n$$

(n) periods	2%	2½%	3%	4%	5%	6%	8%	9%	10%	11%	12%	15%
1	1.02000	1.02500	1.03000	1.04000	1.05000	1.06000	1.08000	1.09000	1.10000	1.11000	1.12000	1.15000
2	1.04040	1.05063	1.06090	1.08160	1.10250	1.12360	1.16640	1.18810	1.21000	1.23210	1.25440	1.32250
3	1.06121	1.07689	1.09273	1.12486	1.15763	1.19102	1.25971	1.29503	1.33100	1.36763	1.40493	1.52088
4	1.08243	1.10381	1.12551	1.16986	1.21551	1.26248	1.36049	1.41158	1.46410	1.51807	1.57352	1.74901
5	1.10408	1.13141	1.15927	1.21665	1.27628	1.33823	1.46933	1.53862	1.61051	1.68506	1.76234	2.01136
6	1.12616	1.15969	1.19405	1.26532	1.34010	1.41852	1.58687	1.67710	1.77156	1.87041	1.97382	2.31306
7	1.14869	1.18869	1.22987	1.31593	1.40710	1.50363	1.71382	1.82804	1.94872	2.07616	2.21068	2.66002
8	1.17166	1.21840	1.26677	1.36857	1.47746	1.59385	1.85093	1.99256	2.14359	2.30454	2.47596	3.05902
9	1.19509	1.24886	1.30477	1.42331	1.55133	1.68948	1.99900	2.17189	2.35795	2.55803	2.77308	3.51788
10	1.21899	1.28008	1.34392	1.48024	1.62889	1.79085	2.15892	2.36736	2.59374	2.83942	3.10585	4.04556
11	1.24337	1.31209	1.38423	1.53945	1.71034	1.89830	2.33164	2.58043	2.85312	3.15176	3.47855	4.65239
12	1.26824	1.34489	1.42576	1.60103	1.79586	2.01220	2.51817	2.81267	3.13843	3.49845	3.89598	5.35025
13	1.29361	1.37851	1.46853	1.66507	1.88565	2.13293	2.71962	3.06581	3.45227	3.88328	4.36349	6.15279
14	1.31948	1.41297	1.51259	1.73168	1.97993	2.26090	2.93719	3.34173	3.79750	4.31044	4.88711	7.07571
15	1.34587	1.44830	1.55797	1.80094	2.07893	2.39656	3.17217	3.64248	4.17725	4.78459	5.47357	8.13706
16	1.37279	1.48451	1.60471	1.87298	2.18287	2.54035	3.42594	3.97031	4.59497	5.31089	6.13039	9.35762
17	1.40024	1.52162	1.65285	1.94790	2.29202	2.69277	3.70002	4.32763	5.05447	5.89509	6.86604	10.76126
18	1.42825	1.55966	1.70243	2.02582	2.40662	2.85434	3.99602	4.71712	5.55992	6.54355	7.68997	12.37545
19	1.45681	1.59865	1.75351	2.10685	2.52695	3.02560	4.31570	5.14166	6.11591	7.26334	8.61276	14.23177
20	1.48595	1.63862	1.80611	2.19112	2.65330	3.20714	4.66096	5.60441	6.72750	8.06231	9.64629	16.36654
21	1.51567	1.67958	1.86029	2.27877	2.78596	3.39956	5.03383	6.10881	7.40025	8.94917	10.80385	18.82152
22	1.54598	1.72157	1.91610	2.36992	2.92526	3.60354	5.43654	6.65860	8.14028	9.93357	12.10031	21.64475
23	1.57690	1.76461	1.97359	2.46472	3.07152	3.81975	5.87146	7.25787	8.95430	11.02627	13.55235	24.89146
24	1.60844	1.80873	2.03279	2.56330	3.22510	4.04893	6.34118	7.91108	9.84973	12.23916	15.17863	28.62518
25	1.64061	1.85394	2.09378	2.66584	3.38635	4.29187	6.84847	8.62308	10.83471	13.58546	17.00000	32.91895
26	1.67342	1.90029	2.15659	2.77247	3.55567	4.54938	7.39635	9.39916	11.91818	15.07986	19.04007	37.85680
27	1.70689	1.94780	2.22129	2.88337	3.73346	4.82235	7.98806	10.24508	13.10999	16.73865	21.32488	43.53532
28	1.74102	1.99650	2.28793	2.99870	3.92013	5.11169	8.62711	11.16714	14.42099	18.57990	23.88387	50.06561
29	1.77584	2.04641	2.35657	3.11865	4.11614	5.41839	9.31727	12.17218	15.86309	20.62369	26.74993	57.57545
30	1.81136	2.09757	2.42726	3.24340	4.32194	5.74349	10.06266	13.26768	17.44940	22.89230	29.95992	66.21177
31	1.84759	2.15001	2.50008	3.37313	4.53804	6.08810	10.86767	14.46177	19.19434	25.41045	33.55511	76.14354
32	1.88454	2.20376	2.57508	3.50806	4.76494	6.45339	11.73708	15.76333	21.11378	28.20560	37.58173	87.56507
33	1.92223	2.25885	2.65234	3.64838	5.00319	6.84059	12.67605	17.18203	23.22515	31.30821	42.09153	100.69983
34	1.96068	2.31532	2.73191	3.79432	5.25335	7.25103	13.69013	18.72841	25.54767	34.75212	47.14252	115.80480
35	1.99989	2.37321	2.81386	3.94609	5.51602	7.68609	14.78534	20.41397	28.10244	38.57485	52.79962	133.17552
36	2.03989	2.43254	2.88928	4.10393	5.79182	8.14725	15.96817	22.25123	30.91268	42.81808	59.13557	153.15185
37	2.08069	2.49335	2.98523	4.26809	6.08141	8.63609	17.24563	24.25384	34.00395	47.52807	66.23184	176.12463
38	2.12230	2.55568	3.07478	4.43881	6.38548	9.15425	18.62528	26.43668	37.40434	52.75616	74.17966	202.54332
39	2.16474	2.61957	3.16703	4.61637	6.70475	9.70351	20.11530	28.81598	41.14479	58.55934	83.08122	232.92482
40	2.20804	2.68506	3.26204	4.80102	7.03999	10.28572	21.72452	31.40942	45.25926	65.00087	93.05097	267.86355

TABLE A-2

PRESENT VALUE OF 1
(PRESENT VALUE OF A SINGLE SUM)

$$PVF_{n,\,i} = \frac{1}{(1+i)^n} = (1+i)^{-n}$$

(n) periods	2%	2½%	3%	4%	5%	6%	8%	9%	10%	11%	12%	15%
1	.98039	.97561	.97087	.96156	.95238	.94340	.92593	.91743	.90909	.90090	.89286	.86957
2	.96117	.95181	.94260	.92456	.90703	.89000	.85734	.84168	.82645	.81162	.79719	.75614
3	.94232	.92860	.91514	.88900	.86384	.83962	.79383	.77218	.75132	.73119	.71178	.65752
4	.92385	.90595	.88849	.85480	.82270	.79209	.73503	.70843	.68301	.65873	.63552	.57175
5	.90583	.88385	.86261	.82193	.78353	.74726	.68058	.64993	.62092	.59345	.56743	.49718
6	.88797	.86230	.83748	.79031	.74622	.70496	.63017	.59627	.56447	.53464	.50663	.43233
7	.87056	.84127	.81309	.75992	.71068	.66506	.58349	.54703	.51316	.48166	.45235	.37594
8	.85349	.82075	.78941	.73069	.67684	.62741	.54027	.50187	.46651	.43393	.40388	.32690
9	.83676	.80073	.76642	.70259	.64461	.59190	.50025	.46043	.42410	.39092	.36061	.28426
10	.82035	.78120	.74409	.67556	.61391	.55839	.46319	.42241	.38554	.35218	.32197	.24719
11	.80426	.76214	.72242	.64958	.58468	.52679	.42888	.38753	.35049	.31728	.28748	.21494
12	.78849	.74356	.70138	.62460	.55684	.49697	.39711	.35554	.31863	.28584	.25668	.18691
13	.77303	.72542	.68095	.60057	.53032	.46884	.36770	.32618	.28966	.25751	.22917	.16253
14	.75788	.70773	.66112	.57748	.50507	.44230	.34046	.29925	.26333	.23199	.20462	.14133
15	.74301	.69047	.64186	.55526	.48102	.41727	.31524	.27454	.23939	.20900	.18270	.12289
16	.72845	.67362	.62317	.53391	.45811	.39365	.29189	.25187	.21763	.18829	.16312	.10687
17	.71416	.65720	.60502	.51337	.43630	.37136	.27027	.23107	.19785	.16963	.14564	.09293
18	.70016	.64117	.58739	.49363	.41552	.35034	.25025	.21199	.17986	.15282	.13004	.08081
19	.68643	.62553	.57029	.47464	.39573	.33051	.23171	.19449	.16351	.13768	.11611	.07027
20	.67297	.61027	.55368	.45639	.37689	.31180	.21455	.17843	.14864	.12403	.10367	.06110
21	.65978	.59539	.53755	.43883	.35894	.29416	.19866	.16370	.13513	.11174	.09256	.05313
22	.64684	.58086	.52189	.42196	.34185	.27751	.18394	.15018	.12285	.10067	.08264	.04620
23	.63416	.56670	.50669	.40573	.32557	.26180	.17032	.13778	.11168	.09069	.07379	.04017
24	.62172	.55288	.49193	.39012	.31007	.24698	.15770	.12641	.10153	.08170	.06588	.03493
25	.60953	.53939	.47761	.37512	.29530	.23300	.14602	.11597	.09230	.07361	.05882	.03038
26	.59758	.52623	.46369	.36069	.28124	.21981	.13520	.10639	.08391	.06631	.05252	.02642
27	.58586	.51340	.45019	.34682	.26785	.20737	.12519	.09761	.07628	.05974	.04689	.02297
28	.57437	.50088	.43708	.33348	.25509	.19563	.11591	.08955	.06934	.05382	.04187	.01997
29	.56311	.48866	.42435	.32065	.24295	.18456	.10733	.08216	.06304	.04849	.03738	.01737
30	.55207	.47674	.41199	.30832	.23138	.17411	.09938	.07537	.05731	.04368	.03338	.01510
31	.54125	.46511	.39999	.29646	.22036	.16425	.09202	.06915	.05210	.03935	.02980	.01313
32	.53063	.45377	.38834	.28506	.20987	.15496	.08520	.06344	.04736	.03545	.02661	.01142
33	.52023	.44270	.37703	.27409	.19987	.14619	.07889	.05820	.04306	.03194	.02376	.00993
34	.51003	.43191	.36604	.26355	.19035	.13791	.07305	.05340	.03914	.02878	.02121	.00864
35	.50003	.42137	.35538	.25342	.18129	.13011	.06763	.04899	.03558	.02592	.01894	.00751
36	.49022	.41109	.34503	.24367	.17266	.12274	.06262	.04494	.03235	.02335	.01691	.00653
37	.48061	.40107	.33498	.23430	.16444	.11579	.05799	.04123	.02941	.02104	.01510	.00568
38	.47119	.39128	.32523	.22529	.15661	.10924	.05369	.03783	.02674	.01896	.01348	.00494
39	.46195	.38174	.31575	.21662	.14915	.10306	.04971	.03470	.02430	.01708	.01204	.00429
40	.45289	.37243	.30656	.20829	.14205	.09722	.04603	.03184	.02210	.01538	.01075	.00373

TABLE A-3

FUTURE VALUE OF AN ORDINARY ANNUITY OF 1

$$FVF - OA_{n,\,i} = \frac{(1 + i)^n - 1}{i}$$

(n) periods	2%	2½%	3%	4%	5%	6%	8%	9%	10%	11%	12%	15%
1	1.00000	1.00000	1.00000	1.00000	1.00000	1.00000	1.00000	1.00000	1.00000	1.00000	1.00000	1.00000
2	2.02000	2.02500	2.03000	2.04000	2.05000	2.06000	2.08000	2.09000	2.10000	2.11000	2.12000	2.15000
3	3.06040	3.07563	3.09090	3.12160	3.15250	3.18360	3.24640	3.27810	3.31000	3.34210	3.37440	3.47250
4	4.12161	4.15252	4.18363	4.24646	4.31013	4.37462	4.50611	4.57313	4.64100	4.70973	4.77933	4.99338
5	5.20404	5.25633	5.30914	5.41632	5.52563	5.63709	5.86660	5.98471	6.10510	6.22780	6.35285	6.74238
6	6.30812	6.38774	6.46841	6.63298	6.80191	6.97532	7.33592	7.52334	7.71561	7.91286	8.11519	8.75374
7	7.43428	7.54743	7.66246	7.89829	8.14201	8.39384	8.92280	9.20044	9.48717	9.78327	10.08901	11.06680
8	8.58297	8.73612	8.89234	9.21423	9.54911	9.89747	10.63663	11.02847	11.43589	11.85943	12.29969	13.72682
9	9.75463	9.95452	10.15911	10.58280	11.02656	11.49132	12.48756	13.02104	13.57948	14.16397	14.77566	16.78584
10	10.94972	11.20338	11.46338	12.00611	12.57789	13.18079	14.48656	15.19293	15.93743	16.72201	17.54874	20.30372
11	12.16872	12.48347	12.80780	13.48635	14.20679	14.97164	16.64549	17.56029	18.53117	19.56143	20.65458	24.34928
12	13.41209	13.79555	14.19203	15.02581	15.91713	16.86994	18.97713	20.14072	21.38428	22.71319	24.13313	29.00167
13	14.68033	15.14044	15.61779	16.62684	17.71298	18.88214	21.49530	22.95339	24.52271	26.21164	28.02911	34.35192
14	15.97394	16.51895	17.08632	18.29191	19.59863	21.01507	24.21492	26.01919	27.97498	30.09492	32.39260	40.50471
15	17.29342	17.93193	18.59891	20.02359	21.57856	23.27597	27.15211	29.36092	31.77248	34.40536	37.27972	47.58041
16	18.63929	19.38022	20.15688	21.82453	23.65749	25.67253	30.32428	33.00340	35.94973	39.18995	42.75328	55.71747
17	20.01207	20.86473	21.76159	23.69751	25.84037	28.21288	33.75023	36.97371	40.54470	44.50084	48.88367	65.07509
18	21.41231	22.38635	23.41444	25.64541	28.13238	30.90565	37.45024	41.30134	45.59917	50.39593	55.74972	75.83636
19	22.84056	23.94601	25.11687	27.67123	30.53900	33.75999	41.44626	46.01846	51.15909	56.93949	63.43968	88.21181
20	24.29737	25.54466	26.87037	29.77808	33.06595	36.78559	45.76196	51.16012	57.27500	64.20283	72.05244	102.44358
21	25.78332	27.18327	28.67649	31.96920	35.71925	39.99273	50.42292	56.76453	64.00250	72.26514	81.69874	118.81012
22	27.29898	28.86286	30.53678	34.24797	38.50521	43.39229	55.45676	62.87334	71.40275	81.21431	92.50258	137.63164
23	28.84496	30.58443	32.45288	36.61789	41.43048	46.99583	60.89330	69.53194	79.54302	91.14788	104.60289	159.27638
24	30.42186	32.34904	34.42647	39.08260	44.50200	50.81558	66.76476	76.78981	88.49733	102.17415	118.15524	184.16784
25	32.03030	34.15776	36.45926	41.64591	47.72710	54.86451	73.10594	84.70090	98.34706	114.41331	133.33387	212.79302
26	33.67091	36.01171	38.55304	44.31174	51.11345	59.15638	79.95442	93.32398	109.18177	127.99877	150.33393	245.71197
27	35.34432	37.91200	40.70963	47.08421	54.66913	63.70577	87.35077	102.72314	121.09994	143.07864	169.37401	283.56877
28	37.05121	39.85990	42.93092	49.96758	58.40258	68.52811	95.33883	112.96822	134.20994	159.81729	190.69889	327.10408
29	38.79223	41.85630	45.21885	52.96629	62.32271	73.63980	103.96594	124.13536	148.63093	178.39719	214.58275	377.16969
30	40.56808	43.90270	47.57542	56.08494	66.43885	79.05819	113.28321	136.30754	164.49402	199.02088	241.33268	434.74515
31	42.37944	46.00027	50.00268	59.32834	70.76079	84.80168	123.34587	149.57522	181.94343	221.91317	271.29261	500.95692
32	44.22703	48.15028	52.50276	62.70147	75.29883	90.88978	134.21354	164.03699	201.13777	247.32362	304.84772	577.10046
33	46.11157	50.35403	55.07784	66.20953	80.06377	97.34316	145.95062	179.80032	222.25154	275.52922	342.42945	644.66553
34	48.03380	52.61289	57.73018	69.85791	85.06696	104.18376	158.62667	196.98234	245.47670	306.83744	384.52098	765.36535
35	49.99448	54.92821	60.46208	73.65222	90.32031	111.43478	172.31680	215.71076	271.02437	341.58955	431.66350	881.17016
36	51.99437	57.30141	63.27594	77.59831	95.83632	119.12087	187.10215	236.12472	299.12681	380.16441	484.46312	1014.34568
37	54.03425	59.73395	66.17422	81.70225	101.62814	127.26812	203.07032	258.37595	330.03949	422.98249	543.59869	1167.49753
38	56.11494	62.22730	69.15945	85.97034	107.70955	135.90421	220.31595	282.62978	364.04343	470.51056	609.83053	1343.62216
39	58.23724	64.78298	72.23423	90.40915	114.09502	145.05846	238.94122	309.06646	401.44778	523.26673	684.01020	1546.16549
40	60.40198	67.40255	75.40126	95.02552	120.79977	154.76197	259.05652	337.88245	442.59256	581.82607	767.09142	1779.09031

TABLE A-4

PRESENT VALUE OF AN ORDINARY ANNUITY OF 1

$$PVF - OA_{n,\,i} = \dfrac{1 - \dfrac{1}{(1+i)^n}}{i}$$

(n) periods	2%	2½%	3%	4%	5%	6%	8%	9%	10%	11%	12%	15%
1	.98039	.97561	.97087	.96154	.95238	.94340	.92593	.91743	.90909	.90090	.89286	.86957
2	1.94156	1.92742	1.91347	1.88609	1.85941	1.83339	1.78326	1.75911	1.73554	1.71252	1.69005	1.62571
3	2.88388	2.85602	2.82861	2.77509	2.72325	2.67301	2.57710	2.53130	2.48685	2.44371	2.40183	2.28323
4	3.80773	3.76197	3.71710	3.62990	3.54595	3.46511	3.31213	3.23972	3.16986	3.10245	3.03735	2.85498
5	4.71346	4.64583	4.57971	4.45182	4.32948	4.21236	3.99271	3.88965	3.79079	3.69590	3.60478	3.35216
6	5.60143	5.50813	5.41719	5.24214	5.07569	4.91732	4.62288	4.48592	4.35526	4.23054	4.11141	3.78448
7	6.47199	6.34939	6.23028	6.00205	5.78637	5.58238	5.20637	5.03295	4.86842	4.71220	4.56376	4.16042
8	7.32548	7.17014	7.01969	6.73274	6.46321	6.20979	5.74664	5.53482	5.33493	5.14612	4.96764	4.48732
9	8.16224	7.97087	7.78611	7.43533	7.10782	6.80169	6.24689	5.99525	5.75902	5.53705	5.32825	4.77158
10	8.98259	8.75206	8.53020	8.11090	7.72173	7.36009	6.71008	6.41766	6.14457	5.88923	5.65022	5.01877
11	9.78685	9.51421	9.25262	8.76048	8.30641	7.88687	7.13896	6.80519	6.49506	6.20652	5.93770	5.23371
12	10.57534	10.25776	9.95400	9.38507	8.86325	8.38384	7.53608	7.16073	6.81369	6.49236	6.19437	5.42062
13	11.34837	10.98319	10.63496	9.98565	9.39357	8.85268	7.90378	7.48690	7.10336	6.74987	6.42355	5.58315
14	12.10625	11.69091	11.29607	10.56312	9.89864	9.29498	8.24424	7.78615	7.36669	6.98187	6.62817	5.72448
15	12.84926	12.38138	11.93794	11.11839	10.37966	9.71225	8.55948	8.06069	7.60608	7.19087	6.81086	5.84737
16	13.57771	13.05500	12.56110	11.65230	10.83777	10.10590	8.85137	8.31256	7.82371	7.37916	6.97399	5.95424
17	14.29187	13.71220	13.16612	12.16567	11.27407	10.47726	9.12164	8.54363	8.02155	7.54879	7.11963	6.04716
18	14.99203	14.35336	13.75351	12.65930	11.68959	10.82760	9.37189	8.75563	8.20141	7.70162	7.24967	6.12797
19	15.67846	14.97889	14.32380	13.13394	12.08532	11.15812	9.60360	8.95012	8.36492	7.83929	7.36578	6.19823
20	16.35143	15.58916	14.87747	13.59033	12.46221	11.46992	9.81815	9.12855	8.51356	7.96333	7.46944	6.25933
21	17.01121	16.18455	15.41502	14.02916	12.82115	11.76408	10.01680	9.29224	8.64869	8.07507	7.56200	6.31246
22	17.65805	16.76541	15.93692	14.45112	13.16800	12.04158	10.20074	9.44243	8.77154	8.17574	7.64465	6.35866
23	18.29220	17.33211	16.44361	14.85684	13.48857	12.30338	10.37106	9.58021	8.88322	8.26643	7.71843	6.39884
24	18.91393	17.88499	16.93554	15.24696	13.79864	12.55036	10.52876	9.70661	8.98474	8.34814	7.78432	6.43377
25	19.52346	18.42438	17.41315	15.62208	14.09394	12.78336	10.67478	9.82258	9.07704	8.42174	7.84314	6.46415
26	20.12104	18.95061	17.87684	15.98277	14.37519	13.00317	10.80998	9.92897	9.16095	8.48806	7.89566	6.49056
27	20.70690	19.46401	18.32703	16.32959	14.64303	13.21053	10.93516	10.02658	9.23722	8.45780	7.94255	6.51353
28	21.28127	19.96489	18.76411	16.66306	14.89813	13.40616	11.05108	10.11613	9.30657	8.60162	7.98442	6.53351
29	21.84438	20.45355	19.18845	16.98371	15.14107	13.59072	11.15841	10.19828	9.36961	8.65011	8.02181	6.55088
30	22.39646	20.93029	19.60044	17.29203	15.37245	13.76483	11.25778	10.27365	9.42691	8.69379	8.05518	6.56598
31	22.93770	21.39541	20.00043	17.58849	15.59281	13.92909	11.34980	10.34280	9.47901	8.73315	8.08499	6.57911
32	23.46833	21.84918	20.38877	17.87355	15.80268	14.08404	11.43500	10.40624	9.52638	8.76860	8.11159	6.59053
33	23.98856	22.29188	20.76579	18.14765	16.00255	14.23023	11.51389	10.46444	9.56943	8.80054	8.13535	6.60046
34	24.49859	22.72379	21.13184	18.41120	16.19290	14.36814	11.58693	10.51784	9.60858	8.82932	8.15656	6.60910
35	24.99862	23.14516	21.48722	18.66461	16.37419	14.49825	11.65457	10.56682	9.64416	8.85524	8.17550	6.61661
36	25.48884	23.55625	21.83225	18.90828	16.54685	14.62099	11.71719	10.61176	9.67651	8.87859	8.19241	6.62314
37	25.96945	23.95732	22.16724	19.14258	16.71129	14.73678	11.77518	10.65299	9.70592	8.89963	8.20751	6.62882
38	26.44064	24.34860	22.49246	19.36786	16.86789	14.84602	11.82887	10.69082	9.73265	8.91859	8.22099	6.63375
39	26.90259	24.73034	22.80822	19.58448	17.01704	14.94907	11.87858	10.72552	9.75697	8.93567	8.23303	6.63805
40	27.35548	25.10278	23.11477	19.79277	17.15909	15.04630	11.92461	10.75736	9.77905	8.95105	8.24378	6.64178

TABLE A-5

PRESENT VALUE OF AN ANNUITY DUE OF 1

$$PVF - AD_{n,\,i} = 1 + \frac{1 - \dfrac{1}{(1+i)^{n-1}}}{i}$$

(n) periods	2%	2½%	3%	4%	5%	6%	8%	9%	10%	11%	12%	15%
1	1.00000	1.00000	1.00000	1.00000	1.00000	1.00000	1.00000	1.00000	1.00000	1.00000	1.00000	1.00000
2	1.98039	1.97561	1.97087	1.96154	1.95238	1.94340	1.92593	1.91743	1.90909	1.90090	1.89286	1.86957
3	2.94156	2.92742	2.91347	2.88609	2.85941	2.83339	2.78326	2.75911	2.73554	2.71252	2.69005	2.62571
4	3.88388	3.85602	3.82861	3.77509	3.72325	3.67301	3.57710	3.53130	3.48685	3.44371	3.40183	3.28323
5	4.80773	4.76197	4.71710	4.62990	4.54595	4.46511	4.31213	4.23972	4.16986	4.10245	4.03735	3.85498
6	5.71346	5.64583	5.57971	5.45182	5.32948	5.21236	4.99271	4.88965	4.79079	4.69590	4.60478	4.35216
7	6.60143	6.50813	6.41719	6.24214	6.07569	5.91732	5.62288	5.48592	5.35526	5.23054	5.11141	4.78448
8	7.47199	7.34939	7.23028	7.00205	6.78637	6.58238	6.20637	6.03295	5.86842	5.71220	5.56376	5.16042
9	8.32548	8.17014	8.01969	7.73274	7.46321	7.20979	6.74664	6.53482	6.33493	6.14612	5.96764	5.48732
10	9.16224	8.97087	8.78611	8.43533	8.10782	7.80169	7.24689	6.99525	6.75902	6.53705	6.32825	5.77158
11	9.98259	9.75206	9.53020	9.11090	8.72173	8.36009	7.71008	7.41766	7.14457	6.88923	6.65022	6.01877
12	10.78685	10.51421	10.25262	9.76048	9.30641	8.88687	8.13896	7.80519	7.49506	7.20652	6.93770	6.23371
13	11.57534	11.25776	10.95400	10.38507	9.86325	9.38384	8.53608	8.16073	7.81369	7.49236	7.19437	6.42062
14	12.34837	11.98319	11.63496	10.98565	10.39357	9.85268	8.90378	8.48690	8.10336	7.74987	7.42355	6.58315
15	13.10625	12.69091	12.29607	11.56312	10.89864	10.29498	9.24424	8.78615	9.36669	7.98187	7.62817	6.72448
16	13.84926	13.38138	12.93794	12.11839	11.37966	10.71225	9.55948	9.06069	8.60608	8.19087	7.81086	6.84737
17	14.57771	14.05500	13.56110	12.65230	11.83777	11.10590	9.85137	9.31256	8.82371	8.37916	7.97399	6.95424
18	15.29187	14.71220	14.16612	13.16567	12.27407	11.47726	10.12164	9.54363	9.02155	8.54879	8.11963	7.04716
19	15.99203	15.35336	14.75351	13.65930	12.68959	11.82760	10.37189	9.75563	9.20141	8.70162	8.24967	7.12797
20	16.67846	15.97889	15.32380	14.13394	13.08532	12.15812	10.60360	9.95012	9.36492	8.83929	8.36578	7.19823
21	17.35143	16.58916	15.87747	14.59033	13.46221	12.46992	10.81815	10.12855	9.51356	8.96333	8.46944	7.25933
22	18.01121	17.18455	16.41502	15.02916	13.82115	12.76408	11.01680	10.29224	9.64869	9.07507	8.56200	7.31246
23	18.65805	17.76541	16.93692	15.45112	14.16300	13.04158	11.20074	10.44243	9.77154	9.17574	8.64465	7.35866
24	19.29220	18.33211	17.44361	15.85684	14.48857	13.30338	11.37106	10.58021	9.88322	9.26643	8.71843	7.39884
25	19.91393	18.88499	17.93554	16.24696	14.79864	13.55036	11.52876	10.70661	9.98474	9.34814	8.78432	7.43377
26	20.52346	19.42438	18.41315	16.62208	15.09394	13.78336	11.67478	10.82258	10.07704	9.42174	8.84314	7.46415
27	21.12104	19.95061	18.87684	16.98277	15.37519	14.00317	11.80998	10.92897	10.16095	9.48806	8.89566	7.49056
28	21.70690	20.46401	19.32703	17.32959	15.64303	14.21053	11.93518	11.02658	10.23722	9.54780	8.94255	7.51353
29	22.28127	20.96489	19.76411	17.66306	15.89813	14.40616	12.05108	11.11613	10.30657	9.60162	8.98442	7.53351
30	22.84438	21.45355	20.18845	17.98371	16.14107	14.59072	12.15841	11.19828	10.36961	9.65011	9.02181	7.55088
31	23.39646	21.93029	20.60044	18.29203	16.37245	14.76483	12.25778	11.27365	10.42691	9.69379	9.05518	7.56598
32	23.93770	22.39541	21.00043	18.58849	16.59281	14.92909	12.34980	11.34280	10.47901	9.73315	9.08499	7.57911
33	24.46833	22.84918	21.38877	18.87355	16.80268	15.08404	12.43500	11.40624	10.52638	9.76860	9.11159	7.59053
34	24.98856	23.29188	21.76579	19.14765	17.00255	15.23023	12.51389	11.46444	10.56943	9.80054	9.13535	7.60046
35	25.49859	23.72379	22.13184	19.41120	17.19290	15.36814	12.58693	11.51784	10.60858	9.82932	9.15656	7.60910
36	25.99862	24.14516	22.48722	19.66461	17.37419	15.49825	12.65457	11.56682	10.64416	9.85524	9.17550	7.61661
37	26.48884	24.55625	22.83225	19.90828	17.54685	15.62099	12.71719	11.61176	10.67651	9.87859	9.19241	7.62314
38	26.96945	24.95732	23.16724	20.14258	17.71129	15.73678	12.77518	11.65299	10.70592	9.89963	9.20751	7.62882
39	27.44064	25.34860	23.49246	20.36786	17.86789	15.84602	12.82887	11.69082	10.73265	9.91859	9.22099	7.63375
40	27.90259	25.73034	23.80822	20.58448	18.01704	15.94907	12.87858	11.72552	10.75697	9.93567	9.23303	7.63805

BRIEF EXERCISES

(Interest rates are per annum unless otherwise indicated.)

BEA-1   Prof. Cheng invested $10,000 today in a fund that earns 8% compounded annually. To what amount will the investment grow in 3 years? To what amount would the investment grow in 3 years if the fund earns 8% annual interest compounded semiannually?

BEA-2   Itzak Lo needs $20,000 in 4 years. What amount must he invest today if his investment earns 12% compounded annually? What amount must he invest if his investment earns 12% annual interest compounded quarterly?

BEA-3   Janet Jack will invest $30,000 today. She needs $222,000 in 21 years. What annual interest rate must she earn?

BEA-4   Webster Corp. will invest $10,000 today in a fund that earns 5% annual interest. How many years will it take for the fund to grow to $13,400?

BEA-5   Boleyn Ltd. will invest $5,000 a year for 20 years in a fund that will earn 12% annual interest. If the first payment into the fund occurs today, what amount will be in the fund in 20 years? If the first payment occurs at year-end, what amount will be in the fund in 20 years?

BEA-6   Williams needs $200,000 in 10 years. How much must he invest at the end of each year, at 11% interest, to meet his needs?

BEA-7   Jack Thompson's lifelong dream is to own his own fishing boat to use in his retirement. Jack has recently come into an inheritance of $400,000. He estimates that the boat he wants will cost $350,000 when he retires in 5 years. How much of his inheritance must he invest at an annual rate of 12% (compounded annually) to buy the boat at retirement?

BEA-8   Refer to the data in BEA-7. Assuming quarterly compounding of amounts invested at 12%, how much of Jack Thompson's inheritance must be invested to have enough at retirement to buy the boat?

BEA-9   Linda Van Esch is investing $12,961 at the end of each year in a fund that earns 10% interest. In how many years will the fund be at $100,000?

BEA-10   Aaron Rana wants to withdraw $20,000 each year for 10 years from a fund that earns 8% interest. How much must he invest today if the first withdrawal is at year-end? How much must he invest today if the first withdrawal takes place immediately?

BEA-11   Mark Link's VISA balance is $1,124.40. He may pay if off in 18 equal end-of-month payments of $75 each. What interest rate is Mark paying?

BEA-12   Corinne Donne is investing $200,000 in a fund that earns 8% interest compounded annually. What equal amounts can Corinne withdraw at the end of each of the next 20 years?

BEA-13   Bayou Inc. will deposit $20,000 in a 12% fund at the end of each year for 8 years beginning December 31, 2002. What amount will be in the fund immediately after the last deposit?

BEA-14   Hollis Sho wants to create a fund today that will enable her to withdraw $20,000 per year for 8 years, with the first withdrawal to take place 5 years from today. If the fund earns 8% interest, how much must Hollis invest today?

BEA-15   Acadian Inc. issues $1,000,000 of 7% bonds due in 10 years with interest payable at year-end. The current market rate of interest for bonds of similar risk is 8%. What amount will Acadian receive when it issues the bonds?

BEA-16   Walt Frazier is settling a $20,000 loan due today by making 6 equal annual payments of $4,864.51. Determine the interest rate on this loan, if the payments begin one year after the loan is signed.

BEA-17   Consider the loan in BEA-16. What payments must Walt Frazier make to settle the loan at the same interest rate but with the 6 payments beginning on the day the loan is signed?

EXERCISES

(Interest rates are per annum unless otherwise indicated.)

EA-1 (Present Value Problem) A hockey player was reported to have received an $11 million contract. The terms were a signing bonus of $500,000 in 2000 plus $500,000 in 2010 through the year 2013. In addition, he was to receive a base salary of $300,000 in 2000 that was to increase $100,000 a year to the year 2004; in 2005 he was to receive $1 million a year that would increase $100,000 per year to the year 2009. Assuming that the appropriate interest rate was 9% and that each payment occurred on December 31 of the respective year, calculate the present value of this contract as of December 31, 2000.

EA-2 (Future Value and Present Value Problems) Presented below are three unrelated situations:
1. Fishbone Ltd. recently signed a 10-year lease for a new office building. Under the lease agreement, a security deposit of $12,000 was made that would be returned at the expiration of the lease with interest compounded at 10% per year. What amount will the company receive when the lease expires?
2. Stevenson Corporation, having recently issued a $20 million, 15-year bond, is committed to make annual sinking fund deposits of $600,000. The deposits are made on the last day of each year and yield a return of 10%. Will the fund at the end of 15 years be sufficient to retire the bonds? If not, what will the excess or deficiency be?
3. Under the terms of her salary agreement, President Joanie McKaig has an option of receiving either an immediate bonus of $40,000 or a deferred bonus of $70,000, payable in 10 years. Ignoring tax considerations and assuming a relevant interest rate of 8%, which form of settlement should President McKaig accept?

EA-3 (Calculations for a Retirement Fund) Greg Parent, a super salesman who is contemplating retirement on his fifty-fifth birthday, plans to create a fund that will earn 8% and enable him to withdraw $20,000 per year on June 30, beginning in 2007 and continuing through 2010. Greg intends to make equal contributions to this fund on June 30 of each of the years 2003–2006.

Instructions
(a) How much must the balance of the fund equal on June 30, 2006 in order for Greg Parent to satisfy his objective?
(b) What is the required amount of each of Greg's contributions to the fund?

EA-4 (Unknown Rate) LEW Corporation purchased a machine at a price of $100,000 by signing a note payable, which requires a single payment of $123,210 in 2 years. Assuming annual compounding of interest, what rate of interest is being paid on the loan?

EA-5 (Unknown Periods and Unknown Interest Rate)
1. Curtis Joseph wishes to become a millionaire. His money market fund has a balance of $92,296 and has a guaranteed interest rate of 10%.

Instructions
How many years must Curtis leave the balance in the fund in order to get his desired $1,000,000?
2. Oleta Firestone desires to accumulate $1 million in 15 years using her money market fund balance of $182,696.

Instructions
At what interest rate must her investment compound annually?

EA-6 (Calculation of Bond Prices) What will you pay for a $50,000 debenture bond that matures in 15 years and pays $5,000 interest at the end of each year if you want to earn a yield of **(a)** 8%? **(b)** 10%? **(c)** 12%?

EA-7 (Evaluation of Purchase Options) Hsang Excavating Inc. is purchasing a bulldozer. The equipment has a price of $100,000. The manufacturer has offered a payment plan that would allow Hsang to make 10 equal annual payments of $16,274.53, with the first payment due one year after the purchase.

Instructions

(a) How much interest will Hsang pay on this payment plan?

(b) Hsang could borrow $100,000 from its bank to finance the purchase at an annual rate of 9%. Should Hsang borrow from the bank or use the manufacturer's payment plan to pay for the equipment?

EA-8 (Calculation of Pension Liability) Erasure Inc. is a furniture manufacturing company with 50 employees. Recently, after a long negotiation with the local union, the company decided to initiate a pension plan as part of its compensation package. The plan will start on January 1, 2002. Each employee covered by the plan is entitled to a pension payment each year after retirement. As required by accounting standards, the controller of the company needs to report the projected pension obligation (liability). On the basis of a discussion with the supervisor of the Personnel Department and an actuary from an insurance company, the controller develops the following information related to the pension plan:

Average length of time to retirement	15 years
Expected life duration after retirement	10 years
Total pension payment expected each year for all retired employees.	
Payment made at the end of the year.	$700,000/year
The interest rate is 8%.	

Instructions

On the basis of the information given, determine the projected pension obligation.

EA-9 (Amount Needed to Retire Shares) Debugit Inc. is a computer software development company. In recent years, it has experienced significant growth in sales. As a result, the Board of Directors has decided to raise funds by issuing redeemable preferred shares to meet cash needs for expansion. On January 1, 2002 the company issued 100,000 redeemable preferred shares with the intent to redeem them on January 1, 2012. The redemption price per share is $25.

As the controller of the company, Kriss Krass is asked to set up a plan to accumulate the funds that will be needed to retire the redeemable preferred shares in 2012. She expects the company to have a surplus of funds of $125,000 each year for the next 10 years, and decides to put these amounts into a sinking fund. Beginning January 1, 2003 the company will deposit $125,000 into the sinking fund annually for 10 years. The sinking fund is expected to earn 10% interest compounded annually. However, the sinking fund will not be sufficient for the redemption of the preferred shares. Therefore, Kriss plans to deposit on January 1, 2007 a single amount into a savings account that is expected to earn 9% interest.

Instructions

What is the amount that must be deposited on January 1, 2007?

EA-10 (Analysis of Alternatives) S.O. Simple Ltd., a manufacturer of low-sodium, low-cholesterol T.V. dinners, would like to increase its market share in Atlantic Canada. In order to do so, S.O. Simple has decided to locate a new factory in the Halifax area. S.O. Simple will either buy or lease a building, depending upon which is more advantageous. The site location committee has narrowed down the options to the following three buildings:

Building A: Purchase for a cash price of $600,000, useful life 25 years.

Building B: Lease for 25 years, making annual payments of $69,000 at the beginning of each year.

Building C: Purchase for $650,000 cash. This building is larger than needed; however, the excess space can be sublet for 25 years at a net annual rental of $7,000. Rental payments will be received at the end of each year. S.O. Simple has no aversion to being a landlord.

Instructions

In which building would you recommend that S.O. Simple locate, assuming a 12% interest rate?

EA-11 (Calculation of Bond Liability) Wittar Ltd. manufactures skating equipment. Recently the vice president of operations of the company has requested construction of a new plant to meet the increasing needs for the company skates. After a careful evaluation of the request, the board of directors has decided to raise funds for the new plant by issuing $2 million of 11% corporate bonds on March 1, 2002, due on March 1, 2017, with interest payable each March 1 and September 1. At the time of issuance, the market rate of interest for similar financial instruments is 10%.

Instructions

As the controller of the company, determine the selling price of the bonds.

EA-12   (Future Value and Changing Interest Rates)   Melanie Doane intends to invest $10,000 in a trust on January 10 of every year, 2002 to 2016, inclusive. She anticipates that interest rates will change during that period of time as follows:

1/10/02–1/09/05	10%
1/10/05–1/09/12	11%
1/10/12–1/09/16	12%

How much will Melanie have in trust on January 10, 2016?

EA-13   (Retirement of Debt)   Glen Chan borrowed $70,000 on March 1, 2002. This amount plus accrued interest at 12% compounded semiannually is to be repaid on March 1, 2012. To retire this debt, Glen plans to contribute five equal amounts to a debt retirement fund starting on March 1, 2007 and continuing for the next four years. The fund is expected to earn 10% per annum.

Instructions

How much must Glen Chan contribute each year to provide a fund sufficient to retire the debt on March 1, 2012?

EA-14   (Unknown Rate)   On July 17, 2002 Bruce Lendrum borrowed $42,000 from his grandfather to open a clothing store. Starting July 17, 2003 Bruce has to make 10 equal annual payments of $6,500 each to repay the loan.

Instructions

What interest rate is Bruce Lendrum paying? (Interpolation is required.)

EA-15   (Unknown Rate)   As the purchaser of a new house, Sandra Pederson signed a mortgage note to pay the Canadian Bank $14,000 every six months for 20 years, at the end of which time she will own the house. At the date the mortgage was signed, the purchase price was $198,000 and Sandra made a down payment of $20,000. The first mortgage payment is to be made six months after the date the mortgage was signed.

Instructions

Calculate the exact rate of interest earned by the bank on the mortgage. (Interpolate if necessary.)

PROBLEMS

PA-1   Answer each of these unrelated questions:

1. On January 1, 2002 Gadget Corporation sold a building that cost $250,000 and had accumulated amortization of $100,000 on the date of sale. Gadget received as consideration a $275,000 noninterest-bearing note due on January 1, 2005. There was no established exchange price for the building and the note had no ready market. The prevailing rate of interest for a note of this type on January 1, 2002 was 9%. At what amount should the gain from the sale of the building be reported?

2. On January 1, 2002 Gadget Corporation purchased 200 of the $1,000 face value, 9%, 10-year bonds of Fox Inc. The bonds mature on January 1, 2012, and pay interest annually beginning January 1, 2003. Gadget Corporation purchased the bonds to yield 11%. How much did Gadget pay for the bonds?

3. Gadget Corporation bought a new machine and agreed to pay for it in equal annual instalments of $4,000 at the end of each of the next 10 years. Assuming an interest rate of 8% applies to this contract, how much should Gadget record as the cost of the machine?

4. Gadget Corporation purchased a tractor on December 31, 2002, paying $20,000 cash on that date and agreeing to pay $5,000 at the end of each of the next eight years. At what amount should the tractor be valued on December 31, 2002, assuming an interest rate of 12%?

5. Gadget Corporation wants to withdraw $100,000 (including principal) from an investment fund at the end of each year for nine years. What is the required initial investment at the beginning of the first year if the fund earns 11%?

PA-2 When Norman Peterson died, he left his wife Vera an insurance policy contract that permitted her to choose any one of the following four options:

1. $55,000 immediate cash.
2. $3,700 every three months, payable at the end of each quarter for five years.
3. $18,000 immediate cash and $1,600 every three months for 10 years, payable at the beginning of each three-month period.
4. $4,000 every three months for three years and $1,200 each quarter for the following 25 quarters, all payments payable at the end of each quarter.

Instructions

If money is worth 2½% per quarter, compounded quarterly, which option will you recommend that Vera choose?

PA-3 Pennywise Inc. has decided to surface and maintain for 10 years a vacant lot next to one of its discount retail outlets to serve as a parking lot for customers. Management is considering the following bids that involve two different qualities of surfacing for a parking area of 12,000 m².

Bid A. A surface that costs $5.25 per square metre. This surface will have to be replaced at the end of five years. The annual maintenance cost on this surface is estimated at 20 cents per square metre for each year except the last of its service. The replacement surface will be similar to the initial surface.

Bid B. A surface that costs $9.50 per square metre. This surface has a probable useful life of 10 years and will require annual maintenance in each year except the last year, at an estimated cost of 9 cents per square metre.

Instructions

Prepare calculations that show which bid should be accepted by Pennywise Inc. You may assume that the cost of capital is 9%, that the annual maintenance expenditures are incurred at the end of each year, and that prices are not expected to change during the next 10 years.

PA-4 Robyn Hood, a bank robber, is worried about her retirement. She decides to start a savings account. Robyn deposits annually her net share of the "loot," which consists of $75,000 per year, for three years beginning January 1, 2002. Robyn is arrested on January 4, 2004 (after making the third deposit) and spends the rest of 2004 and most of 2005 in jail. She escapes in September of 2005 and resumes her savings plan with semiannual deposits of $30,000 each, beginning January 1, 2006. Assume that the bank's interest rate is 9% compounded annually from January 1, 2002 through January 1, 2005, and 12% compounded semiannually thereafter.

Instructions

When Robyn retires on January 1, 2009 (six months after her last deposit), what will be the balance in her savings account?

PA-5 Provide a solution to each of the following situations by calculating the unknowns (use the interest tables):

1. Leslie Rooke invests in a $180,000 annuity insurance policy at 9% compounded annually on February 8, 2002. The first of 20 receipts from the annuity is payable to Leslie 10 years after the annuity is purchased (February 8, 2012). What will be the amount of each of the 20 equal annual receipts?
2. Kevin Tait owes a debt of $30,000 from the purchase of his new sports car. The debt bears interest of 8% payable annually. Kevin wishes to pay the debt and interest in eight annual instalments, beginning one year hence. What equal annual instalments will pay the debt and interest?
3. On January 1, 2002 Mike Myers offers to buy Dan Carbey's used combine for $45,000, payable in 10 equal instalments that include 9% interest on the unpaid balance and a portion of the principal, with the first payment to be made on January 1, 2002. How much will each payment be?

PA-6 During the past year, Leanne Cundall planted a new vineyard on 150 ha of land that she leases for $27,000 a year. She has asked you to assist in determining the value of her vineyard operation.

The vineyard will bear no grapes for the first five years (Years 1–5). In the next five years (Years 6–10), Leanne estimates that the vines will bear grapes that can be sold for $60,000 each year. For the next 20 years (Years 11–30), she expects the harvest to provide annual revenues of $100,000. During the last 10 years (Years 31–40) of the vineyard's life, she estimates that revenues will decline to $80,000 per year.

During the first five years the annual cost of pruning, fertilizing, and caring for the vineyard is estimated at $9,000; during the years of production, Years 6–40, these costs will rise to $10,000 per year. The relevant market rate of interest for the entire period is 12%. Assume that all receipts and payments are made at the end of each year.

Instructions

Tanya McIvor has offered to buy Leanne's vineyard business. On the basis of the present value of the business, what is the minimum price Leanne should accept?

PA-7 Handyman Inc. owns and operates a number of hardware stores on the Prairies. Recently the company has decided to locate another store in a rapidly growing area of Manitoba; the company is trying to decide whether to purchase or lease the building and related facilities.

Purchase. The company can purchase the site, construct the building, and purchase all store fixtures. The cost would be $1,650,000. An immediate down payment of $400,000 is required, and the remaining $1,250,000 would be paid off over five years at $300,000 per year (including interest). The property is expected to have a useful life of 12 years and then it will be sold for $500,000. As the owner of the property, the company will have the following out-of-pocket expenses each period:

Property taxes (to be paid at the end of each year)	$40,000
Insurance (to be paid at the beginning of each year)	$27,000
Other (primarily maintenance, which occurs at the end of each year)	$16,000
	$83,000

Lease. Jensen Corp. Ltd. has agreed to purchase the site, construct the building, and install the appropriate fixtures for Handyman Inc. if Handyman will lease the completed facility for 12 years. The annual costs for the lease will be $240,000. The lease would be a triple-net lease, which means that Handyman will have no responsibility related to the facility over the 12 years. The terms of the lease are that Handyman would be required to make 12 annual payments (the first payment to be made at the time the store opens and then each following year). In addition, a deposit of $100,000 is required when the store is opened that will be returned at the end of the twelfth year, assuming no unusual damage to the building structure or fixtures.

Currently the cost of funds for Handyman Inc. is 10%.

Instructions

Which of the two approaches should Handyman Inc. follow?

PA-8 Presented below are a series of time value of money problems for you to solve.

1. Your client, Kate Greenaway, wishes to provide for the payment of an obligation of $250,000 that is due on July 1, 2008. Kate plans to deposit $20,000 in a special fund each July 1 for eight years, starting July 1, 2001. She also wishes to make a deposit on July 1, 2000 of an amount that, with its accumulated interest, will bring the fund up to $250,000 at the maturity of the obligation. She expects the fund to earn interest at the rate of 4% compounded annually. Calculate the amount to be deposited on July 1, 2000.

2. On January 1, 2000 Keeley Inc. initiated a pension plan under which each of its employees will receive a pension annuity of $10,000 per year beginning one year after retirement and continuing until death. Employee A will retire at the end of 2006 and, according to mortality tables, is expected to live long enough to receive eight pension payments. What is the present value of Keeley Inc.'s pension obligation for employee A at the beginning of 2000 if the interest rate is 10%?

3. McLachlan Ltd. purchases bonds from Rankin Inc. in the amount of $500,000. The bonds are 10-year, 12% bonds that pay interest semiannually. After three years (and receipt of interest for three years), McLachlan needs money and, therefore, sells the bonds to Doyle Corp., which demands interest at 16% compounded semiannually. What is the amount that McLachlan will receive on the sale of the bonds?

PA-9 Answer the following questions related to Gervais Inc.

1. Gervais Inc. has $572,000 to invest. The company is trying to decide between two alternative uses of the funds. One alternative provides $80,000 at the end of each year for 12 years; the other pays a single lump sum of $1,900,000 at the end of 12 years. Which alternative should Gervais select? Assume the interest rate is constant over the entire investment.

2. Gervais Inc. has just purchased a new computer system. The fair market value of the equipment is $824,150. The purchase agreement specified an immediate down payment of $200,000 and semiannual payments of $76,952 that begin at the end of six months for five years. What interest rate, to the nearest percent, was used in discounting this purchase transaction?

3. Gervais Inc. loaned $600,000 to Whistler Corporation. Gervais accepted a note due in seven years at 8% compounded semiannually. After two years (and receipt of interest for two years), Gervais needed money and therefore sold the note to Royal Canadian Bank, which required interest on the note of 10% compounded semi-annually. What amount did Gervais receive from the sale of the note?

4. Gervais Inc. wishes to accumulate $1,300,000 by December 31, 2012 to retire outstanding bonds. The company deposits $300,000 on December 31, 2002, which will earn interest at 10% per year compounded quarterly, to help in the debt retirement. The company wants to know what additional equal amounts should be deposited at the end of each quarter for 10 years to ensure that $1,300,000 is available at the end of 2012. (The quarterly deposits will also earn interest at a rate of 10%, compounded quarterly.) Round to even dollars.

PA-10 Laird Wightman is a financial executive with Marsh Corporation. Although Laird has not had any formal training in finance or accounting, he has a "good sense" for numbers and has helped the company grow from a very small ($500,000 sales) to a large operation ($45 million sales). With the business growing steadily, however, the company needs to make a number of difficult financial decisions that Laird feels are a little "over his head." He has therefore decided to hire a new employee with facility in "numbers" to help him. As a basis for determining whom to employ, he asked each prospective employee to prepare answers to questions relating to the following situations he has encountered recently. Here are the questions that you are asked to answer:

1. In 2000 Marsh Corporation negotiated and closed a long-term lease contract for newly constructed truck terminals and freight storage facilities. The buildings were constructed on land owned by the company. On January 1, 2001 Marsh took possession of the leased property. The 20-year lease is effective for the period January 1, 2001 through December 31, 2020. Rental payments of $800,000 are payable to the lessor (owner of facilities) on January 1 of each of the first 10 years of the lease term. Payments of $300,000 are due on January 1 for each of the last 10 years of the lease term. Marsh has an option to purchase all the leased facilities for $1.00 on December 31, 2020. At the time the lease was negotiated, the fair market value of the truck terminals and freight storage facilities was approximately $7.2 million. If the company had borrowed the money to purchase the facilities, it would have had to pay 10% interest. Should the company have purchased rather than leased the facilities?

2. Last year the company exchanged some land for a noninterest-bearing note. The note was to be paid at the rate of $12,000 per year for nine years, beginning one year from the date of the exchange. The interest rate for the note was 11%. At the time the land was originally purchased, it cost $90,000. What is the fair value of the note?

3. The company has always followed the policy to take any cash discounts offered on goods purchased. Recently the company purchased a large amount of raw materials at a price of $800,000 with terms 2/10, n/30 on which it took the discount. If Marsh's cost of funds was 10%, should the policy of always taking cash discounts be continued?

Company Index

A company index for both volumes appears at the end of Volume 2.

Subject Index

A subject index for both volumes appears at the end of Volume 2.